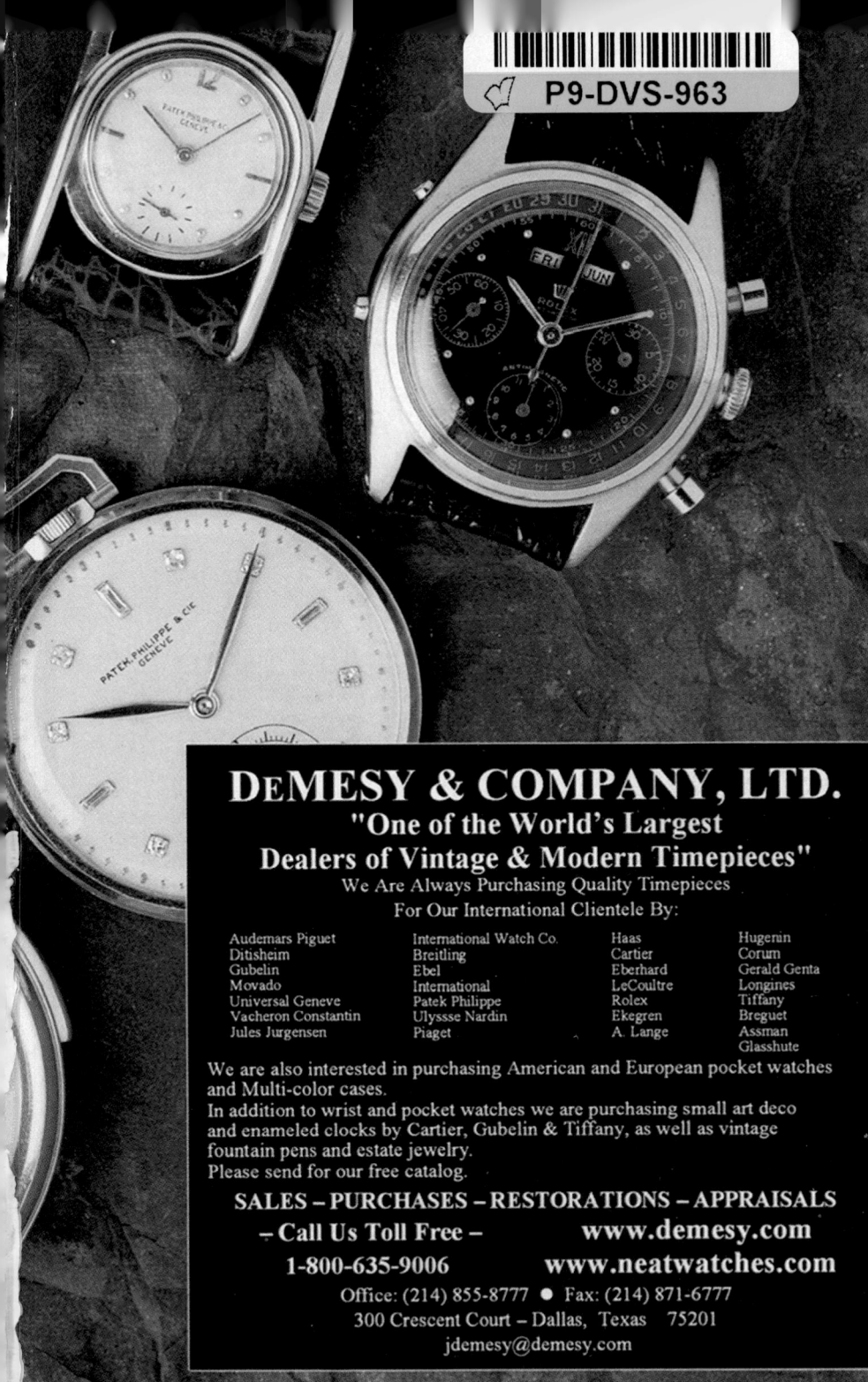

RICHARD E. GILBERT   TOM ENGLE

COOKSEY SHUGART

The Complete Price Guide To Watches, published by TinderBox Press, is authored by Tom Engle, Richard E. Gilbert and Cooksey Shugart. All three have been active horologists since the early 1960's and members of the National Association of Watch and Clock Collectors since the early 1970's. They have searched for fine timepieces all over the world and are the foremost experts in the field of antique horology.

They each have traveled extensively to auctions throughout the United States and Europe, to regional and national conventions, meets and shows, and keep an up-to-date pulse of the watch market. They continually expand their horological reference library and their extensive selection of watch photographs. Because of the unique knowledge of the market these co-authors possess, this volume should be considered one of the most authoritative watch references on the market today. Each edition contains updated and revised information and prices, and has become the accepted standard reference work of the watch market. "We see this book as an extension of the information we have been gathering for years and take great pride in sharing it with other collectors who have a deep and abiding interest in watches," the authors stated.

Mr. Gilbert resides in Sarasota, FL, Mr. Engle resides in Louisville, KY and Mr. Shugart resides in Cleveland, TN.

COMPLETE
PRICE GUIDE TO
WATCHES

RICHARD E. GILBERT ✶ TOM ENGLE ✶ COOKSEY SHUGART

Disclaimers: All of the information, including valuations, in this book have been compiled from the most reliable sources, and every effort has been made to eliminate errors and questionable data. Nevertheless, the possibility of error, in a work of such immense scope, always exists. The publisher or authors will not be held responsible for losses which may occur in the purchase, sale, statements of its advertisers or other transaction of items, because of information contained herein. Readers who feel they have discovered errors are invited to write and inform us, so they may be corrected in subsequent editions.

The Complete Price Guide To Watches is published
independently and is not associatedwith any watch manufacturer

This book endeavors to be a Guide or helpful manual and offers a wealth of material and information to be used as a tool not as an absolute document. The Complete Price Guide To Watches is like some watches, the worst may be better than none at all, but at best cannot be expected to be 100% accurate. We will respect & appreciate positive sound reliable comments, corrections, improvements or remarks but reserve the right to accept or reject any suggestions offered.

Published by:

TINDERBOX PRESS
1150 Hungryneck Blvd., Suite C-310
Mount Pleasant, SC 29464
www.tinderboxpress.com
843-856-4280

Distributed by:

COLLECTOR BOOKS
P.O. BOX 3009
5801 KENTUCKY DAM ROAD
PADUCAH, KY. 42002-3009
TEL. 1 - 800 - 626 - 5420

Copyright 2008 by TinderBox Press

TWENTY EIGHTH EDITION: JANUARY 2008

Manufactured in the United States of America

TABLE OF CONTENTS

LIST OF ESCAPEMENTS

1,156 Rack & Pinion, Straight Hairspring, various fork action - 1,157 Potter & MacDowall One Tooth.

1,158 One Jewel Lever by E. Bourquin, Inverted Lever - 1,159 Woerd Pat. escap., Jeunet seconds beating.

1,160 Detent and Pivoted escapement - 1,161 G.P. Reed Detent escap, Patent union Chronometer.

1,162 Fleurier, English & Chinese Duplex - 1,163 Breguets Naturel & Hanging Ruby Cylinder.

1,164 Breguet Lateral, Arnold Chron. Detent - 1,165 Robins Anti-overbanking, Duplex & two lever styles.

1,166 Typical Glashutte Escap. and balance - 1,167 Constant Force, M.B. Pray, Peto's Chron., & Savage.

4

ACKNOWLEDGMENTS

A special thanks to Henry B. Fried and Dr. George Daniels for their assistance in the creation of this book and for their establishment of and their contribution to the watch collecting industry.

To Antiquoram, the NAWCC Museum, Hamilton Watch Co., Bowman Technical School, and Christie's for allowing us to photograph their watches

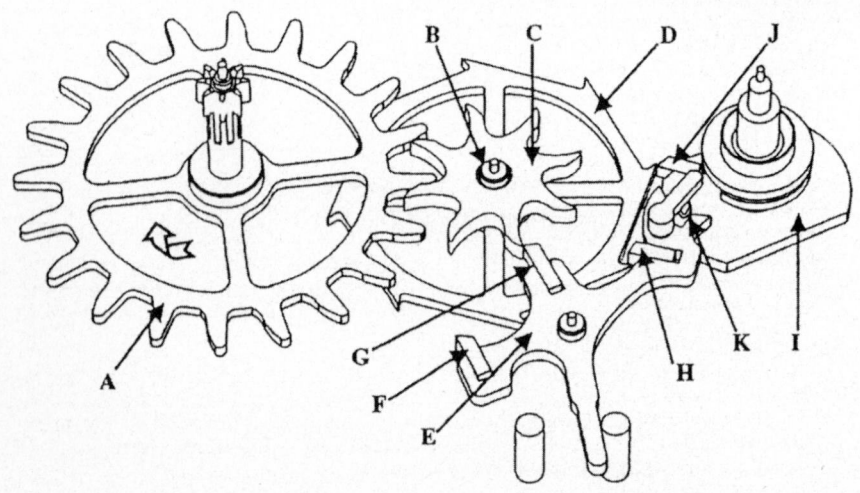

Please send all corrections, additions, deletions
and comments in writing to:

TINDERBOX PRESS
STE. C-310 1150 HUNGRYNECK BLVD.
MT. PLEASANT, SC 29464
843.856.4280
WATCHES@TINDERBOXPRESS.COM

When corresponding, please send a 🖂 self-addressed, stamped envelope.

Cover Photo: ***C.H. Meylan, Brassus (Switz)***, minute repeater with perpetual calendar, moonphase and split second chronograph, 50mm, 18k case, 40 jewel superior grade nickel movement, c. 1910
American Waltham, "Dominion Railway" rare locomotive dial, model 83, 18 size, c. 1887
Patek Philippe, gents early Tonneau wristwatch, 18k, 30mm x 38mm, c. 1930

Spine Photo: ***Ball***, "Official Railroad Standard" Trainmaster wristwatch, gold filled, 35mm, 25 jewel automatic, c. 1965

INTRODUCTION

This book is dedicated to all watch collectors who, we hope, will find it an enjoyable and valuable reference to carry on buying trips or to trace the lost history of that priceless family heirloom.

Understand the value of watches. Studying this book should repay its cost to you many times over. Be informed - "buy the book before the watch." You can't have too much knowledge. Collecting without regards to cost and value can be expensive. This price guide will be helpful for several reasons; it will teach you about market value, identification, desirability, how to determine the age and much more. We strongly recommend you read the first 100 pages and study to gain insight into, understand and master the subject of watch collecting. Be an informed buyer and seller. Please remember your job is to determine the many factors that will define the watches true value. This book is designed to help you.

Watches are unique collectibles and since the beginning of civilization man has held a fascination for time. When man first scooped up a handful of sand and created the hourglass, portable timepieces have been in demand for the wealthy and poor alike. Man has sought constantly to improve his time-measuring instruments and has made them with the finest metals and jewels. The pocket watch, in particular, became ornamentation and a source of pride, and this accounts for its value among families for generation after generation.

The watch has become precious and sentimental to so many because it is one of the true personal companions of the individual, night and day. Mahatma Gandhi, the father of India and one of the rare people in history who was able to renounce worldly possessions, was obsessed with the proper use of his time. Each minute, he held, was to be used in the service of his fellow man. His own days were ordered by one of his few personal possessions, a sixteen-year-old, eight-shilling Ingersoll pocket watch that was always tied to his waist with a piece of string.

Another factor that has made watches unique collectibles is the intricate artisanship with which they are put together. Many of the watches of yesteryear, which were assembled with extreme accuracy and fine workmanship, continue to be reliable timepieces today. They stand out as unique because that type of watch is no longer hand made. In today's world of mass production, the watch, with individual craftsmanship, containing precious jewels and metals, can rarely be found—and, if found, it is rarely affordable.

The well-made watch is a tribute to man's skills, artisanship and craftsmanship at their finest level. That is why the watch holds a special place in the collectible field. In America, there are more than 240,000 avid watch collectors and millions own several watches. An untold number possess at least one or more of these precious heirlooms. The word "complete" is in the title of this book. Any watch listed in this guide is complete, *with case and movement, with out any of the parts missing.*

The Complete Price Guide to Watches does not attempt to establish or fix values or selling prices in the watch trade market. It does, however, reflect the trends of buying and selling in the collector market. Prices listed in this volume are based on data collected and analyzed from auctions, internet sales and dealers price lists throughout the world. These prices should serve the collector as a guide only. The price you pay for any watch will be determined by the value it has to you. The intrinsic value of any particular watch can be measured only by you, the collector, and a fair price can be derived only after mutual agreement between both the buyer and the seller.

Keep in mind the fair market values at the trade show level (as outlined in this price guide) and buy wisely, but don't hesitate, as the better and scarce pieces are quickly sold.

It is our hope that this volume can help make your watch collecting venture both pleasurable and profitable. Hopefully, everyone interested in horology will research the watch and add to his library on the subject. *Information contained herein may not necessarily apply to every situation. Data is still being found, which may alter statements made in this book. These changes, however, will be reflected in future editions.*

COLLECTAMANIA

Hobby — Business — Pastime — Entertainment

Just name it. More than likely someone will want to buy or sell it: books, coins, stamps, bottles, beer cans, gold, glassware, baseball cards, guns, clocks, watches, comics, art, cars - the list goes on and on.

Most Americans seem to be caught up in "collectamania." More and more Americans are spending hour after hour searching though antique shops, auctions, flea markets and yard sales for those rare treasures of delight that have been lying tucked away for generations just waiting to be found.

This sudden boom in the field of collecting may have been influenced by fears of inflation or disenchantment with other types of investments. However, more people are coming into the field because they gain some degree of nostalgic satisfaction from these "new" tangible ties with yesteryear. Collecting provides great fun and excitement. The tales of collecting and the resultant "fabulous finds" could fill volumes and inspire even the non-collector to embark upon a treasure hunt.

Collecting for the primary purpose of investment may prove to have many pitfalls for the amateur. Lack of sufficient knowledge and the inability to spot fakes or flawed merchandise are the main causes of disappointment. In many fields, high class forgers are at work, doing good and faithful reproductions in large quantities, that can sometimes fool even the experts the first time they see them. Collecting for fun and profit can be just that if you observe a fair amount of caution. Always remember, amidst your enthusiasm, that an object may not be what it would first appear. On the following pages are a few guidelines that may be helpful.

LEARN - FOCUS - CONDITION – TRUST

"LOOK UNDER THE HOOD"
"If it is worth faking it will be."

1. **Gain all the knowledge you can** and learn all about the objects you collect. The more knowledge you have, the more successful you will be in finding valuable, quality pieces. The best way to predict the future is to study the past. Amassing the knowledge required to be a good collector is easier if you have narrowed your scope of interest. Otherwise, it may take years to become an "expert." Don't try to learn everything there is to know about a variety of fields. This will end in frustration and disappointment. Specialize and learn NAWCC trade show fair market values.

2. **Make up your mind and focus** on what you want to collect and concentrate in this area. Your field of collecting should be one that you are genuinely passionate about. It may also help to narrow your field even further. For instance, in collecting watches, choose only one company or one type or style and have a method of collecting that specific category.

3. **Buy the best condition you can afford**, assuming the prices are fair. The advanced collector may want only mint articles; but the novice collector may be willing to accept something far less than mint condition, due to caution and economics. Collectible items in better condition continue to rise in value at a steady rate.

4. **Deal with reputable dealers** whom you can trust . Talk with the dealer and get to know the seller. Ask for a business card. Know where you can contact the dealer if you have problems or if you want the dealer to help you find something else you may be looking for.

Fair Market Price: Fair price may be defined as a fair, reasonable range of prices usually paid for a watch or a watch of good value as used in this book. This market level includes a particular time frame, desirability, condition and quality.

A guide to fair purchase prices is subject to sales and transactions between a large number of buyers and sellers who are informed and up to date on all normal market influences (while keeping in mind the difference between compulsiveness and acceptable buying), and buy and sell on a large scale from coast to coast.

A willing buyer and a willing seller acting carefully and judiciously, in their own best interest, should amicably be able to conduct business in a normal and fair manner (preferably with payment immediately).

HOW TO USE THIS BOOK

The Complete Price Guide to Watches is a simple reference, with clear and carefully selected information. The first part of the book is devoted to history, general information, and a how-to section. The second part consists mainly of a listing of watch manufacturers, identification guides, and prices. This is a unique book because it is designed to be taken along as a handy reference for identifying and pricing watches. With the aid of this book, the collector should be able to make on-the-spot judgments as to identification, age, quality, and value. This book, money, a folding pocket knife case opener, and pocket magnifying glass or watchmaker's loupe will be good to take on your buying trips.

Right: Folding pocket case opener. Middle: A Magnification glass. Left: Watchmakers Loupe.

Watch collecting is fast growing as a hobby and business. Many people collect for enjoyment and profit. The popularity of watches continues to rise because watches are a part of history. The watch is collected for its beauty, quality in movement and case, and the value of metal content. Solid gold and platinum are the top of the line; silver is also very desirable. Consider that some watches in the early 1900's sold between $700 and $1,000. This is equal to or greater than the price of a good car of the same period. As with limited edition prints, a watch of supreme excellence is also limited and will increase in value. There is universal appeal and excitement in owning a piece of history, and your heirloom is just that. At one time pocket watches were a status symbol. Everyone competed for beauty and quality in the movement and case. Solid gold cases were adorned with elaborate engravings, diamonds, and other precious jewels. The movements were beautiful and of high quality. Manufacturers went to great lengths to provide movements that were both accurate and lovely. Fancy damaskeening on the back plates of nickel with gold lettering, 26 jewels in gold settings, and a solid gold train (gears) were features of some of the more elaborate timepieces. The jewels were red rubies or diamond-end stones or sapphires for the pallet stones. There were gold timing screws, and more. The enamel double-sunk dials were made by the best artisans of the day, hand-painted and with fancy hands.

The American railroad brought about the greatest watch of that time, the railroad pocket watch. Since that time America has produced some of the best quality pocket watches that money could buy. The gold-filled cases made in America have never been surpassed in quality or price in the foreign market. With the quality of movement and cases being made with guaranteed high standards as well as beauty, the American pocket watch became very desirable. Because they are no longer being made in the U.S.A., pocket watches continue to rise in value.

HOW TO DETERMINE MANUFACTURER

When identifying a watch, look on the face or dial for the name of the company and then refer to the alphabetical list of watch companies in this book. If the face or dial does not reveal the company name, you will have to seek information from the movement's back plate. First, determine from what country the watch originated. The company name or the town where it was manufactured will likely be inscribed there. The name engraved on the back plate is referred to as the "signature." After locating the place of manufacture, see what companies manufactured in that town. This may require reading the histories of several companies to find the exact one. Use the process of elimination to narrow the list. *Note: Some of the hard-to-identify watches are extremely collectible and valuable. Therefore, it is important to learn to identify them.*

In order to establish the true manufacturer of the movement, one must study the construction, taking note of the size, number and location of jewels, shape, location of parts, plate layout (is it full or 3/4), shape of the balance cock and regulator, location of screws, etc. Compare and match your watch movement with every photograph or drawing from each watch company in this volume until the manufacturer is located.

Important Note: Generic or Nameless = Unmarked grades, for watch movements are listed under the company name or initials of the company, etc. by size, jewel count and description, such as: American Watch Co. or Amn Watch Co. or A.W.W.Co., Elgin W. Co. or Elgin National W. Co., Hampden W.Co. or Duber W.Co., Illinois W. Co.or I.W.Co., Rockford or R.W.Co., South Bend, etc.

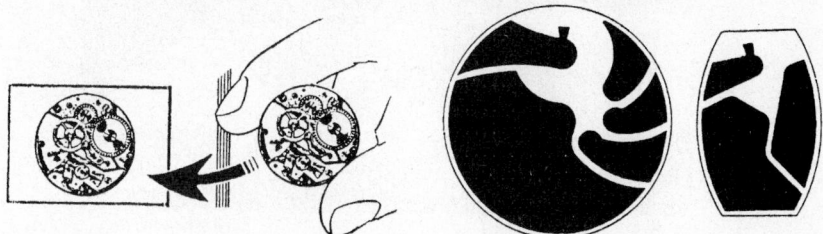

Compare & match your watch to a illustration in this book.

HOW TO DETERMINE AGE

After establishing the name of the manufacturer, you may be interested in the age of the watch. This information can be obtained by using the serial number inscribed on the back movement plate and referring to the production table. It is often difficult to establish the exact age, but this method will put you within a two or three year period of the date of the manufacture.

To establish the age of a pre-1850 watch there are many points to be considered. The dial, hands, pillars, balance cock and pendant, for example, contain important clues in determining the age of your watch. However, no one part alone should be considered sufficient evidence to draw a definite conclusion as to age. The watch as a whole must be considered. First, determine from what country the case originated and from what country did the movement originate. For example, an English made silver cased watch will have a hallmark inside the case. It is quite simple to refer to the London Hallmark Table for hallmarks after 1697. The hallmark will reveal the age of the case only. This does not fix the age of the movement. Many movements are housed in cases made years before or after the movement was produced.

The case that houses the movement is not necessarily a good clue to the origin of the movement and the case serial number is of no help. It was a common practice for manufacturers to ship the movements to the jewelers and watchmakers uncased.

The customer then married the movement and case. That explains why an expensive movement can be found in a cheaper case or vice versa.

If the manufacturer's name and location are no help, the inscription could possibly be that of a jeweler and his location. In an instance such as this, it becomes obvious there is no quick and easy way to identify the watch. However, the following steps may be helpful. Some watches can be identified by comparing the models of each company until the correct model is found. Start by sizing the watch and then compare the varied plate shapes and styles. The cock or bridge for the balance may also be a clue. The general arrangement of the movement as to jeweling, whether it is an open face or hunting case, and style of regulators may help to correctly identify the manufacturer of the movement.

Numbers on a watch case should not be considered as clues to the age of the movement because cases were both American and foreign made, and many of the good watches were re-cased through the years.

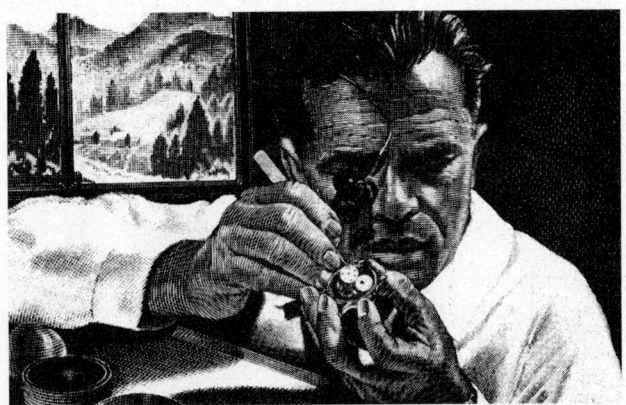

APPRAISING WATCHES

Watch collecting is still young when compared to the standard collectible fields of coins and stamps. The watch collecting field is growing but information is still scarce, fragmented, and sometimes unreliable. To be knowledgeable in any field, one must spend the time required to study it.

The value of any collectible is determined first by demand. Without demand there is no market. In the watch trade, the law of supply and demand is also true. The supply of the American watches has stopped and the demand among collectors continues to rise. There are many factors that make a watch desired or in demand. Only time and study will tell a collector just which pieces are most collectible. After the collector or investor finds out what is desirable, a value must be placed on it before it is sold. If it is priced too high, the watch will not sell; however, if it is priced too low, it will be hard to replace at the selling price. The dealer must arrive at a fair market price that will move the watch. As with limited edition prints, a watch of supreme excellence is also limited and will increase in value. There is universal appeal and excitement in owning a piece of history and your heirloom is just that.

There are no two watches alike. This makes the appraising more difficult and often times, arbitrary. However, there are certain guidelines one can follow to arrive at a fair market price. As previously mentioned, when watches were manufactured, most companies sold the movements to a jeweler, and the buyer had a choice of dials and cases. Some high-grade movements were placed in a low-grade case and vice versa.

Some had hand-painted, multi-colored dials; some were plain. The list of contrasts goes on. Conditions of watches will vary greatly and this is a big factor in the value. The best movement in the best original case will bring the top price for any type of watch.

Prices are constantly changing in the watch field. Gold and silver markets affect the price of cases. Scarcity and age also affect the value. These prices will fluctuate regularly.

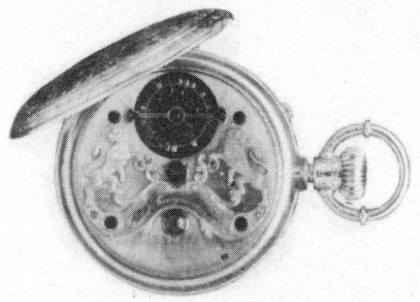 

APPRAISING GUIDELINES

Demand, supply, desirability, condition, and value must be the prime factors in appraising a watch. Demand maybe the most important element. Demand can be determined by the number of buyers for that particular item. The watch may be rare (only one or a few produced or still in existence) but the number of collectors may be even more rare and those collectors just as hard to find. A simple but true axiom is that value is determined by the price someone is willing to pay. What is it worth to you? In order to obtain a better knowledge in appraising and judging watches, the following guidelines are most useful. Consider all these factors before placing a value on the watch. There is no rank or priority to the considerations listed.

1. Demand: interest-high or low, desirability is very important. How many collectors want your rare watch?
2. Supply and Availability: How rare or scarce is the watch? How many of the total production remain? Survival rate is key.
3. Condition: the case, dial and movement are all extremely important.
4. Low Serial Numbers: the first one made would be more valuable than later models.
5. Type of Escapement: also technical design of movement and uniqueness.
6. Historical Value.
7. Age: How old is the watch?
8. Case: Is it in its original case? Original dial? Very important.
9. Is it an early handmade watch?
10. Complications: Repeaters, for example.
11. Value: Metal content, style or type of case, beauty and eye appeal.
12. Parts: Size, number of jewels, type of plates(3/4, full and bridge), type of balance, type of winding(key-wind, lever-set, etc.), number of adjustments, gold jeweled settings, damaskeening, gold train.
13. Grade: What grade of condition is it? Pristine, Mint, Extra Fine, Average, Fair, or Scrap? You must determine condition and value or price.
14. Identification: Easy or difficult?
15. Future: Potential as an investment.
16. Quality: High of Low gr ade or low cost production watches(dollar watch). How much will this watch scrap for?

GRADING WATCHES
Pricing in this book is based on the following grading system:

PRISTINE MINT(G-1O)-100%: New old stock. Absolutely factory new; unused in factory box with wax paper still intact & all tags & papers etc. The pristine mint grade is not listed in this book & commands significant premiums. (A select group of watches maybe assigned to a "rarity grade" which are also historical or technically important, often as early horological examples.)

MINT PLUS(G-9)-99%: Still in factory box. Exceptional, perfect

MINT(G-8)-97%: Same as factory new but with very little use; no faint scratches & no trace of a screwdriver mark; is original in every way - crystal, hands, dial, case, movement; used briefly & stored away, may still be in box. Dealers "trade show" price after overhaul.

NEAR MINT(G-7)-93%: Completely original in every way; faint marks may be seen with a loupe only; expertly repaired; movement may have been cleaned and oiled. (Excellent)

EXTRA FINE(G-6)-87%: May or may not be in factory box; looks as though watch was used very little; original case, hands, dial, and movement. If watch has been repaired, all original replacement parts have been used. Faint case scratches are evident but hard to detect with the eye. No dents or hairline on dial are detectable.

FINE(G-5)-80%: May have new hands and new crystal, but original case, dial and movement; faint hairline & no chips on dial; no large scratches & no brass seen on case; slight stain on movement, movement must be sharp with only minor scratches.

AVERAGE(G-4)-75%: Original case, dial & movement, movement may have had a part replaced, but part was near to original; no brass showing through on gold-filled case; no rust or chips in dial; may have hairlines in dial that are hard to see. Marks are hard to detect, but may be seen without a loupe. (What some dealer "may" pay = wholesale price.)

FAIR(G-3)-60% : Hairlines in dial and small chips; slight amount of brass can be seen through worn spots on gold-filled case; rust marks in movement; a small dent in case; wear in case, dial, and movement; well used; may not have original dial or case.

POOR(G-2)-30%: Watch not working; needs new dial; case well worn, many dents; hands may be gone; replacement crystal may be needed.

SCRAP(G-1)-15%: Movement not working; bad dial; rusty movement; brass showing badly; may not have case; some parts not original; no crystal or hands. Good for parts only.

Hamilton 992B

	MINT	
	G-8 = (Trade Show)	
	AVERAGE	
	G-4=(Dealers May Pay)	
100%	G-10	$800
99%	G-9	$650
97%	G-8	$575
93%	G-7	$425
87%	G-6	$335
80%	G-5	$290
75%	G-4	$275
60%	G-3	$185
30%	G-2	$95
15%	G-1	$65

Above is an example of how the price is affected by the different grades of the same watch.

Note: The value of a watch may be $5,000.00 today, $1,000.00 or $50,000.00 five years from now.

The value of a watch can only be assessed after the watch has been carefully inspected and graded. It may be difficult to evaluate a watch honestly and objectively, especially in the rare or scarce models. If the watch has any defects, such as a small scratch on it, it can not be Pristine. It is important to realize that older watches in grades of Extra Fine or above are extremely rare and may never be found.

COLLECTING ON A LIMITED BUDGET

Most collectors are always looking for that sleeper, which is out there waiting to be found. One story goes that a collector went into a pawn shop and asked the owner if he had any gold pocket watches for sale. The pawn broker replied, "No, but I have a 23J, silver cased pocket watch at a good price." Even though the pocket watch was in a cheaper case, the collector decided to further explore the movement. When he opened the back to look at the movement, there he saw engraved on the plates 24J Bunn Special and knew immediately he wanted to buy the pocket watch. The movement was running, and looked to be in first grade shape. The collector asked the price. The broker said he has been trying to get rid of the pocket watch, but had no luck and if he wanted it, he would sell it for $35. The collector took the pocket watch and replaced the bent-up silver case for a gold-filled J. Boss case, and sold it a month later for $400. He had a total of $100 invested when he sold it, netting a cool $300 profit.

Most collectors want a pocket watch that is in mint or near-mint condition and original in every way. But consider the railroad pocket watches such as the Bunn Special in a cheaper case. The railroad man was compelled to buy a watch with a quality movement, even though he may have only been able to afford a cheap case. The railroad man had to have a pocket watch that met certain standards set by the railroad company. A watch should always be judged on quality and performance and not just on its appearance. The American railroad pocket watch was unsurpassed in reliability. It was durable and accurate for its time, and that accounts for its continuing value today.

If you are a limited-budget collector, you would be well advised not to go beyond your means. Even on a budget, watch collecting can be an interesting, adventurous, and profitable hobby. If you are to be successful in quadrupling your purchases that you believe to be sleepers, you must first be a hard worker, have perseverance and let shrewdness and skill of knowledge take the place of money. A good starting place is to get a working knowledge of how a pocket watch works. Learn the basic skills such as cleaning, mainspring and staff replacement. One does not have to be a watchmaker, but should learn the names of parts and what they do. If a watch that you are considering buying does not work, you should know how and what it takes to get it in good running order or pass it by. Stay away from pocket watches that do not wind and set. Also avoid "odd" movements that you hope to be able to find a case for.

Old watches with broken or missing parts are expensive and all but impossible to have repaired. Some parts must be made by hand. The odd and low-cost production watches are fun to get but hard to repair. Start out with the more common basic jeweled lever pocket watches. The older the watch, the harder it is to get parts. Buy an inexpensive pocket watch movement that runs and play with it. Get one that is newer and for which parts can be bought; and get a book on watch repairing. You will need to know the pricing history and demand of a watch. Know what collectors are looking for in your area. If you cannot find a buyer, then, of course, someone else's unwanted stock has become yours.

JOIN THE NAWCC ® - See their ad on Pg. 1209

The authors of this book, Mr. Richard Gilbert, Mr. Tom Engle & Mr. Shugart, recommend you join the NAWCC today and share a fascination for watches with other members. The National Association of Watch and Clock Collectors is a non-profit, scientific and educational corporation founded in 1943 and now serving the horological needs and interests of tens of thousands of members (professional horologists and amateurs) in the United States and 40 others countries. Help to its members is only a telephone call away. Participation in National & Regional Conventions also Local Activities and Seminars.

The NAWCC prints special publications for its members: The NAWCC Bulletin and the NAWCC Mart are both released 6 times per year. The Bulletin is an absorbing publications, with abundantly illustrated articles on historic, artistic and technical aspects of time keeping, answers from the experts, book reviews, members' opinions and comments, research findings and extensive news about local chapters, regional and national activities. The Mart is an informal medium of exchange in which, for a nominal fee, you can list any horological item you may wish to buy, sell or trade. It is an absorbing and entertaining way to find items to fill out your collection or dispose of pieces you no longer want. It also contains announcements of regional and national conventions & seminars.

THE GREAT AMERICAN
RAILROAD POCKET WATCH

It was the late nineteenth century in America. The automobile had not yet been discovered. The personal Kodak camera was still not on the market. Women wore long dresses, and the rub board was still the most common way to wash clothes. Few homes had electricity, and certainly the radio had not yet invaded their lives. Benjamin Harrison was president. To be sure, those days of yesteryear were not quite as nostalgically simple as most reminiscing would have them be. They were slower, yes, because it took longer to get things done and longer to get from one place to another. The U.S. mail was the chief form of communication linking this country together, as America was inching toward the Twentieth Century.

The tremendous impact of the railroad on the country during this era should not be under estimated. Most of the progress since the 1830s had chugged along on the back of the black giant locomotives that belched steam and fire, up and down the countryside. In fact, the trains brought much life and hope to the people all across the country, delivering their goods and food, bringing people from one city to another, carrying the U.S. mail, and bringing the democratic process to the people by enabling candidates for the U.S. Presidency to meet and talk with people in every state. Truly the train station held memories for most everyone and had a link with every family.

Taking effect June 15, 1892, the Illinois Central Railroad inaugurated a watch inspection. Employees are now required to summit their watches for a quarterly examination & weekly comparison with standard time to the various local inspectors who have been appointed for the purpose. The minimum standard of excellence adopted by this company for watches is of a grade equal to what is known among American movements as 15 jewels, patent regulator, adjusted to temperature, the variation of which must not exceed 30 seconds per week.

Note: A railroad watch is a watch that satisfies the requirements in effect at the time the watch was made. (Railroad rules evolved and changed from year to year.)

Left: Allen A. Shugart (my father) was photographed in the summer of 1981 at the Chattanooga Tenn. train station also called Chattanooga Choo-Choo Station.

16

16

DATE COMPARED	SECONDS FAST	SECONDS SLOW	R-REG S-SET	
4 9-6			0 K	Bowers

Above part of a Watch inspection card.
Carried by a Fireman on Erie
Lackawanna R. R. Co.

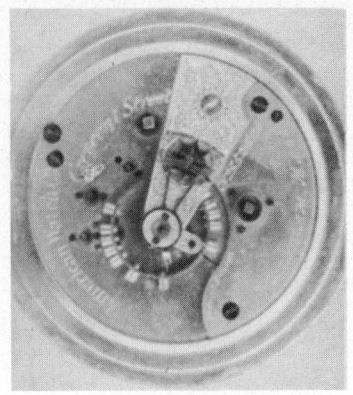

The first watch constructed especially
for railroad service was this Crescent St.,
made in 1870, see pg. 115 and 137

The Great American Railroad Pocket Watch, unrivaled in quality and reliability. "What is a railroad watch"? There is not an easy answer to this question. With 500 to 1,000 American Railroads & each one used many different rules and specifications. Some railroads used requirements only and some listed only watch company grades that were acceptable. Also Railroad rules & watches evolved and changed from year to year. In the late 1860's a movement was commissioned by Pennsylvania Railroad Co. & had "Pennsylvania Railroad Co." on the dial and "B.W. Raymond" on the movement. The movement made by Elgin was a 18 size, 15 jewels, key wind and set. In 1887 the American Railroad Companies had a meeting to interpret and specify requirements of standard time and watch inspection. In the spring of 1894, a American Waltham Watch Co ad states "Systematic railroad watch inspection was first adopted during recent years". The ad also says "Waltham watch movements expressly designed for railroad use". The ad shows a 1892 model Vanguard grade with 17 jewels and double roller. In Feb. of 1894, The United States Watch Co. of Waltham introduced a watch & their ad states "Fellow Engineers & Railroad Men: The President, is a first quality nickel, 18 size, full plate, stem winding & lever setting, double roller escapement and adjusted to heat cold, isochronism & all positions. The Company guarantees the movement will-vary less than six seconds in a calendar month."

Prior to 1893, the definition of a railroad watch was optional with individual railroads. About 1893 the General Railroad Timepiece Standards Commission presented these new guidelines (below). After 1893, American watch manufacturers set out to meet these guidelines, later railroad lines used these standards as a guideline for new railway watches, but not all. Some Railroad Companies were vague about their regulations and some had none at all. Note: With over 500 American Railroad Companies and each one (No nation-wide rules) used similar but different rules and specifications. NOTE: 15 jewel watches were accepted by some Railroad Watch Inspectors as late as early 1900's.

Be open faced, size 18 or 16, have a minimum of 17 jewels, adjusted to at least five positions, keep time accurately to within a gain or loss of only 30 seconds a week, adjusted to temperatures of 34 to 100 degrees Fahrenheit, have a double roller, steel escape wheel, lever set, micro metric regulator, winding stem at 12 o'clock, grade on back plate, use plain Arabic numbers printed bold and black on a white dial, and have bold black hands.

NOTE: By about 1900 the above guidelines were used by many Railroad Companies Inspectors.

1916 Waltham Ad

The first watch constructed especially for railroad service was the
Crescent St., made in 1870

The American watch industry was compelled to produce just such an instrument which it did. The railroad watch was a phenomenal timekeeper and durable in long life and service. It had the most minute adjustments, no small feat because watchmaking was rendered far more difficult than clock making, due to the fact that a clock is always in one position and powered by a constant force-it's weights, while watches must be accurate in several positions with a variable power source. After 1875-80 a RR employee had to buy his own watch.

After 1893 railroad pocket watch standards guidelines were adopted by some railroad lines for new watches. While each company had its individual standards guideline, many included the basic recommendations of the commission.

One of the figures in developing the railroad watch standards was Webb C. Ball of Cleveland, Ohio, the general time inspector for over 125,000 miles of railroad in the U.S., Mexico, and Canada. Ball was authorized by railroad officials to help to establish the timepiece inspection system. After Ball presented his guidelines, most American manufacturers set out to meet those standards and a list of the different manufacturers producing watches of the grade that would pass inspection, was soon available. These standards changed from year to year.

According to the regulations, if a watch fell behind or gained 30 seconds in 7 to 14 days, it must be sent in for adjustment or repair. Small cards were given to the engineers and conductors the railroad timekeepers and a complete record of the watch's performance was written in ink. All repairs and adjustments were conducted by experienced and approved watchmakers; inspections were conducted by authorized inspectors.

Because this system was adopted the American watch manufacturers produced a superior railroad watch, the traveling public was assured of increased safety and indeed the number of railroad accidents occurring as a result of faulty timepieces was minimized.

Prior to the 1890s, some railroad companies had already initiated standards and were issuing lists of those watches approved for railroad use. Included were the Waltham 18s, 1883 model, Crescent Street Grade, and the B.W. Raymond, 18s, both in open & hunter cases with lever or pendant set.

By the mid 1890s hunter cases were being turned down as well as pendant set. Watches meeting approval then included Waltham, 18s, 1892 model; Elgin, 7th model; and Hamilton, 17J, open face, lever set.

Hamilton Grade 992, 16 size, 21 jewels, nickel 3/4 plate movement, lever set only, gold jewel settings, gold center wheel, steel escape wheel, micro metric regulator, double roller, compensating balance. Adjusted to temperature, isochronism and 5 positions. Marked Elinvar under balance wheel, Serial number 2584307 & listed as 992E under the "Hamilton serial numbers and grades" section.

By 1900 the double roller, sapphire pallets and steel escape wheels with a minimum of five positions were required.

The early Ball Watch Co. movements, made by Howard, used initials of railroad labor organizations such as "B. of L.E. Standard" and "B. of L.F. Standard." Ball also used the trademark "999" and "Official Railroad Standard." Some watches may turn up that are marked as "loaners." These were issued by the railroad inspectors when a watch had to be kept for repairs.

By 1920 the 18 size watch had lost popularity with the railroad men and by 1950 most railroad companies were turning them down all together. In 1936 duty on Swiss watches were lowered by 50 percent, and by 1950 the Swiss imports had reached a level of five million a year. In 1969 the last American railroad pocket watch was sold by Hamilton Watch Co. a Grade 992B.

RAILROAD GRADE WATCH ADJUSTMENTS

The railroad watch, as well as other fine timepieces, had to compensate for several factors in order to be reliable and accurate at all times. These compensations, called adjustments, were for heat and cold, isochronism, and five to six different positions. These adjustments were perfected only after experimentation and a great deal of careful hand labor on each individual movement. All railroad grade watches were adjusted to a closer rate to compensate for heat and cold. The compensation balance has screws in the rim of the balance wheel which can be regulated by the watchmaker. The movement was tested in an ice box and in an oven, and if it did not keep the same time in both temperature extremes, as well as under average conditions, the screws in the balance wheel was shifted or adjusted until accuracy was achieved.

The isochronism adjustment maintained accuracy of the watch both when the mainspring was fully wound up and when it was nearly run down. This was achieved by selecting a hairspring of exact proportions to cause the balance wheel to give the same length of arc of rotation regardless of the amount of the mainspring that had been spent.

Railroad Standards, Approved and Grade Terminolory as used in this book:

Railroad Standards: A set of requirements to be accepted or approved by each railroad line outlined by a commission or board appointed by railroad companies.

Railroad Approved: From around 1875 on, a RR employee had to buy their own watch. "RR Approved" refers to a list of watches each railroad line would approve if purchased by their employees. This list changed over thr years.

Railroad Grade: A watch made by manufacturers to meet or exceed railroad standards. Grades such as 992, Vanguard, B.W. Raymond, etc.

NOTE: Some GRADES exceeded the R.R. standards or requirements, such as watches with 23 jewels, diamond end stone, gold train, raised gold jewel settings, double sunk dial and the list goes on. Examples: such as Veritas, Sangamo, 950 & Riverside Maximus and many others.

Railroad watches were adjusted to be accurate whether they were laying on their face or back, or being carried on their edges with pendants up or down, or with the three up or the nine up. These adjustments were accomplished by having the jewels, in which the balance pivots rest, of proper thickness in proportion to the diameter of the pivot and, at the same time, equal to the surface on the end of the pivot which rests on the cap jewel. To be fully adjusted for positions, the balance wheel and the pallet and escape wheel must be perfectly poised. Perfect poise is achieved when the pivots can be supported on two knife-edged surfaces, perfectly smooth and polished and when the wheel is placed in any edge, it will remain exactly as it is placed. If it is not perfectly poised, the heaviest part of the wheel will always turn to the point immediately under the lines of support.

The micro metric regulator or the patent regulator is a device used on all railroad grade and higher grade watches for the purpose of assisting in the finer manipulation of the regulator. It is arranged so that the regulator can be moved the shortest possible distance without fear of moving it too far. There is always a fine graduated index attached which makes it possible to determine just how much the regulator has been moved.

The hairspring used on the so-called ordinary and medium-grade watches is known as the flat hairspring. The Breguet hairspring was an improvement over the flat hairspring and was used on railroad and high-grade watches. The inside coil of any hairspring is attached to a collet on the balance staff and the end of the outside coil of the hairspring is attached to a stud which is held firmly by a screw in the balance wheel bridge. Two small regulator pins are fastened to the regulator. These pins clasp the outer side of the hairspring a short distance from the hairspring stud. If the regulator index is moved toward the "S," the regulator pins will move, allowing the hairspring to lengthen and the balance wheel to make a longer arc of rotation. This causes the watch to run slower because it requires a longer time for the wheel to perform the longer arc. When the regulator is moved toward the "F" these regulator pins are moved from the stud which shortens the hairspring and makes shorter arcs of the balance wheel, thus causing the movement to run faster.

Example Of a Bunn 16 size, 17 jewels, nickel 3/4 plate movement, lever set gold jewel settings, gold center wheel, double roller, steel escape wheel, micro metric regulator, compensating balance. Adjusted to temperature, isochronism and 5 positions artistically damaskeened.

NOTE: Railroad grade watches had a compensation balance made of brass and steel. Brass was used on the outside rim and steel on the inside. Brass is twice as sensitive to temperature changes and twice as thick as the steel balance (one-piece is welded to the steel balance wheel) and after finishing, the rim is cut at one end near the arm of the balance and at the same spot 180 across. In higher temperature, the dominant brass would "grow" longer but welded to the steel rim, it would curve inward, thus, in effect, placing the mass of the balance closer to the center of the balance wheel. This would cause the balance to go faster. However, the steel hairspring in rising temperature would also grow longer but more important would also lose some of its resilience. This would cause the watch to lose time. The balance, remember under the same condition, in effect became smaller and this action by the balance compensated for the loss of the hairsprings elasticity and lengthening. In cold temperatures, the opposite effect took place. This is why the balance is called a "compensation" balance. (It compensates for the temperature errors in the hairspring.) NOTE: Movements marked Adjusted have a diversity or combination, of features. The best way to know for sure is to check the factory grade lists for specific adjustments. After about 1905 the movements were marked with the number of adjustments.

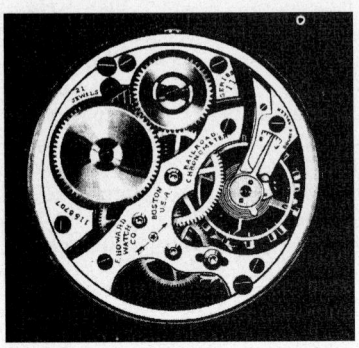

E. Howard Watch Co. Railroad Chronometer, Series 11, 16 size, 21 jewels, designed for the railroad trade.

Uncommon RADIAL, note the Arabic numbers slant to the center of dial. Seen on many dials with Roman numerals.

Sometimes, after a heavy jolt, the coil next to the outside one will catch between these regulator pins and this will shorten the length of the hairspring just one round, causing a gaining rate of one hour per day. When this occurs, the hairspring can be easily released and will resume its former rate.

The Breguet <u>overcoil</u> hairspring, which is used on railroad grade movements, prevented the hairspring from catching on the regulator pins and protected against any lateral or side motion of the balance wheel ensuring equal expansion of the outside coil.

Railroad grade watches also used the patent or safety pinion which was developed to protect the train of gears from damage in the event of breakage of the mainspring. These pinions unscrewed in event of mainspring breakage, allowing the force to be harmlessly spent by the spinning barrel.

Some earlier railroad grade watches had non-magnetic movements. This was achieved by the use of non-magnetic metals for the balance wheel, hairspring, roller table and pallet. Two of the metals used were iridium and palladium, both very expensive.

RAILROAD WATCH DIALS

Railroad watch dials are distinguished by their simplicity. A true railroad watch dial contained no fancy lettering or beautiful backgrounds. The watches were designed to be functional and in order to achieve that, the dials contained bold black Arabic numbers against a white background. This facilitated ease of reading the time under even the most adverse conditions.

𝔅unn 𝔖pecial

1924 AD
Jewelers listed cost for
Movement only = $24.00
&
Jewelers selling price for
Movement only = $45.00

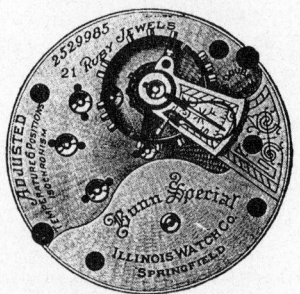

18 Size, 21 Jewels, Adjusted 6 Positions

21 ruby and sapphire jewels; gold settings; adjusted to temperature, SIX positions and isochronism; compensating balance; gold screws including timing screws; double roller; steel escape wheel; Breguet hairspring, patent micrometric screw regulator, safety screw center pinion, beautifully damaskeened with black enamel lettering, double sunk dial.

Waltham, 18 size, unusual Railroad double sunk white porcelain dial is marked with uniquely placed minute numbers on the outer chapter and the hour chapter is in the center, the dial is also marked "Waltham Pat. Appl'd. For". This watch is a 1892 model & Appleton Tracy & co. grade.

Ball Watch Co. Motto: "Carry a Ball and Time Them All." This case is made of base metal with a Ball's patented Stirrup Bow. With the simple easy to read dial, this watch was a favorite among railroad men. WWII Ball and cased for Railroad watches.

True railroad watches had the winding stem at the 12 o'clock position. The so-called side winder, that winds at the 3 o'clock position, was not approved for railroad use. (The side winder is a watch movement designed for a hunter case but one that has been placed in an open-faced case.)

One railroad watch dial design was patented by a Mr. Ferguson. On this dial, the five minute numbers were much larger than the hour numbers which were on the inside. This dial never became very popular. About 1904 the Montgomery dials began to appear on some RR watches. The distinguishing feature of the Montgomery dial is that each minute is numbered around the hour chapter. The five-minute divisions were in red, and the true Montgomery dial has the number "6" inside the minute register. These dials were favored by the railroad men. The so-called Canadian dial had a 24-hour division inside the hour chapter.

The double time hands are also found on some railroad grade watches. One hour hand was in blue or black and the other was in red or gold, one hour apart, to compensate for passing from one time zone to another. About 1900 "Double Time Hands" began to appear on 18 & 16 size watches.

RAILROAD WATCH CASES

Open face cases were the only ones approved for railroad use. Railroad men sought a case that was tough and durable; one that would provide a dust-free environment for the movement.

The swing-out case offered the best protection against dust, but the screw-on back and bezel were the most popular open-face cases.

The lever-set was a must for railroad-approved watches and some of the case manufacturers patented their own styles of cases, most with a heavy bow. One example is the Stirrup Bow by the Ball Watch Co. Hamilton used a bar above the crown to prevent the stem from being pulled out. Glass was most commonly used for the crystal because it was not as likely to scratch.

Note: Not all railroad GRADE watches were railroad <u>APPROVED</u>. Not all watches listed here are railroad approved, even though all are railroad grade. Below are some watches that were railroad grade but may not have been railroad APPROVED. (below not a complete list)

BALL All official R.R. standard with 19, 21, & 23J, Adj.5p, 18 &16S, open face.

COLUMBUS WATCH CO.
    Columbus King, 21,23, 25J; Railway King, 17-25J; Time King, 21-25J, 18S; Ruby Model, 16S.

ELGIN
1. "Pennsylvania Railroad Co." on dial, 18S, 15J & 17J, KW-KS, first model "B. W. Raymond."
2. "No. 349," 18S, seventh model, 17-213.
3. Veritas, B. W. Raymond, or Father Time, 18S, 21-233.
4. Grades 162, 270, 280, or 342 marked on back plate, 16S, 17-213.
5. Veritas, Father Time, or Paillard Non-Magnetic, 16S, 19-233.
6. 571, 21J or 572, 16S, 19J., also All wind indicator models.

HAMILTON
1. 18S Grade 946= 23J, & 940, 942= 21J, & 944 19J, & 924, 926, 934, 936, 938, 948 = 17J.
2. 16S = Grades 950, 950B, 950E=23J, & 992, 992B, 992E, 954, 960, 970, 994, 990= 21J.
3. 16S = Grade 996= 19J & 972, 968, 964= 17J.

HAMPDEN
1. Special Railway, 17J, 21J, 23J; New Railway, 23J & 17J; North Am. Railroad, 21J; Win. McKinley, 21J; John Hancock, 21J & 23J; John C. Duber, 21J, 18S.
2. 105, 21J; 104, 23J; John C. Duber, 21J; Win. McKinley, 17, 21; New Railway, 21J; Railway, 19J; Special Railway, 23J, 16S.

E. HOWARD & CO.
1. All Howard models marked "Adjusted" or deer symbol.
2. Split plate models, 18S or N size; 16S or L size.

HOWARD WATCH CO.
    All 16S with 19, 21, & 23J.

Above: Double Hour Time Zone Hands, available in, RED & BLUE or GOLD & BLACK.

ILLINOIS
1. Bunn 15J "Adjusted," & Stuart, 15J "Adjusted," 18S; Burlington,19J.DR.Adj. 16S;
2. Benjamin Franklin,17-26J; Bunn 17- 24J; Bunn Special,21-26J; Chesapeake & Ohio Sp.,21-24J; Interstate Chronometer, 23J;Lafayette, 24J; A. Lincoln, 21J; Paillard W. Co., 17-24J; Trainsmen, 23J; Pennsylvania Special 17-26J; The Railroader & Railroad King, 18S.
3. Benjamin Franklin,17-25J; Bunn,17-19J; Bunn Special,21 -23J; Diamond Ruby Sapphire,21-233; Interstate Chronometer,23J; Lafayette,23J; A.Lincoln,21J; Paillard Non-Magnetic W.Co.,17-21J; Pennsylvania Special, 17, 21, & 23J; Santa Fe Special, 21J; Sangamo, 21-26J; Sangamo Special, 19-23J; grades 161, 161A=21J;163, 163A=23J & 187, and 189, 17J, 16S.

PEORIA WATCH CO.
    15 & 17J with a patented regulator, 18S.

ROCKFORD
1. All 21 or more jewels, 16-18S, All and wind indicators.
2. Grades 900, 905, 910, 912, 918, 945, 200, 205, 18S.
3. Winnebago, 17-213, 505, 515, 525, 535, 545, 555, 16S.

SETH THOMAS
    Maiden Lane, 21-28J; Henry Molineux, 20J; G#260,185.

SOUTH BEND
1. The Studebaker 329, 323, Grade Nos. 327, 21J, 18S.
2. The Studebaker 229, 223, G# 227, 293, 295, 21J, also Polaris,21J;16 size

UNITED STATES WATCH CO., MARION
    United States, 18 size, 17-19J, gold train.

U. S. WATCH CO., WALTHAM
    The President, 17-21J, 18 size, double roller.

WALTHAM
1. 1857 KW with Pennsylvania R.R. on dial, Appleton Tracy & Co. on movement.
2. Crescent Street, 17-233; 1883 & 1892 Models; Appleton Tracy & Co., 1892 Model; Railroader, 1892 Model; Pennsylvania Railroad; Special RR, Special RR King, Vanguard, 17 -23J, 1892 Model; Grade 845, All wind indicators 18S.
3. American Watch Co., 17-21J, 1872 Models; American Watch Co., All wind indicators, ALL 17-23J Bridge Models; Crescent Street, 17-21J, 1899 & 1908 Models; Premier Maximus; Railroader; Riverside Maximus, 21-23J; Vanguard, 19-23J; 645 16S.

Note: A railroad watch is a watch that satisfies the requirements in effect at the time the watch was made. There were no rules or guidelines used NATION-WIDE, each railroad used their own rules and list of approved watches.

CANADIAN PACIFIC SERVICE
RAILROAD APPROVED WATCHES 1899 to 1910

WALTHAM
Vanguard, 18-16S, 19-21-23 jewels
Crescent St., 18S, 19J; 18-16S,21J
Appleton-Tracy 17J; also No. 845, 21J
Riverside 16S, 19J; Riverside Maximus, 16S, 23J;
No.645,16S,21J,C.P.R. 18-16S, 173; C.T.S. 18-16S, 17J

ELGIN
Veritas, 18-16S,21-23J
B. W. R. 18-16S, 17-19-21J
Father Time 18-16S,21J
Grade 349, 18S, 21J

HAMILTON
18S, 946, 23J; 940-942, 21J; 944, 19J; 936-938, 17J
16S, 950, 23J; 960-990-992, 21J; 952, 19J; 972, 17J
SOUTH BEND
18S, 327-329, 21J; 323, 17J
16S, 227-229, 21J; 223, 17J

BALL
All Balls 18S, 16S, 17-19-21-23J

ILLINOIS
Bunn Special, 18-16S, 21-23J; also Bunn 18-16S, 17-19J
A. Lincoln, 13-16S, 21J; Sangamo Special, 16S, 19-21-23J

SETH THOMAS
Maiden Lane, 18S, 25J; No. 260, 2W; No. 382, 17J

E. HOWARD WATCH CO.
16S Series, 0-23J, 5-19J, 2-17J, 10-21J; also No. 1,21J

ROCKFORD
18S, Grade 918-905, 21J; Winnebago, 17J; also Grade 900, 24J
16S, Grades 545, 525, 515, 505, 21J; 655 WI., 21J; and Grade 405, 17J

LONGINES
18S, Express Monarch, 17-19-21-23J
16S, Express Monarch, 17-19-21-23J

BRANDT-OMEGA
18S& 16S, D.D.R., 23J = very best, 18 gold settings; DR., 19J = extra fine, 15 gold settings;
C.C.C.R., 23J = fine quality; 15 gold settings; C.C.R., 19J = quality, 10 gold settings.

(This list changed from year to year.)

Rockford Watch Co., Enamel Railroad double sunk dial, with two hour hands for a second time zone the hour hand at 2 O'clock is BLUE, the hour hand at 3 O'clock is RED or GOLD

This style Illinois railroad watch cases were fitted with movements, re-rated and timed in their specially designed case at the factory as complete watches in a gold filled case with a hinged bezel .Note: This Illinois 60 hour single sunk dial, 17 size & referred to as a 16 size by the trade.

RAILROAD
MODEL
NO. 2

American Waltham Watch Co. Vanguard,16 size, 19-23 jewels, winding indicator which alerts user to how far up or down the mainspring is wound. This watch was made to promote new sales in the railway industry.

Hamilton Watch Co., This was a favorite railroad style case by Hamilton model NO. 2 supplied in 10K or 14K gold filled. Note the Railroad style dial with red marginal figures as well as the bar-over-crown with "Hamilton Railroad" on crown.

AMERICAN RAILROAD APPROVED WATCHES 1930

The following requirements for railroad approved watches are outlined by Mr. R. D. Montgomery, General Watch Inspector of the Santa Fe Railway System:

"Regulation for new watches designated as of 1930 to be standard is described as follows: 16 size, American, lever-setting, 19 jewels or more, open face, winding at '12", double-roller escapement, steel escape wheel, adjusted to 5 positions, temperature and isochronism, which will rate within a variation not exceeding 6 seconds in 72 hour tests, pendant up, dial up and dial down, and be regulated to run within a variation not exceeding 30 seconds per week. The following listed makes and grades meet the requirements and comprise a complete list of watches acceptable. Watches bearing the name of jewelers or other names not standard trade marks or trade numbers will not be accepted:" This list changed from year to year.

AMERICAN WALTHAM W. Co. (16 Size)		ELGIN WATCH CO.(16 Size)		HOWARD WATCH CO.(16 Size)	
23J	Premier Maximus	23J	Veritas	All	23J
23J	Riverside Maximus	21J	Veritas	All	21J
23J	Vanguard	21J	B. W. Raymond	All	19J
	6 position	21J	Father Time		
	winding indicator	21J	No.270	ILLINOIS WATCH CO. (16 Size)	
23J	vanguard			23J	Sangamo Special
	6 position	HAMILTON WATCH CO. (16 Size)		23J	Sangamo
21J	Crescent Street	23J	No.950	23J	Bunn Special
21J	No.645	21J	No.990	21J	Bunn Special
19J	vanguard	21J	No.992	21J	Sangamo
19J	Riverside	19J	No. 952	21J	A. Lincoln
		19J	No.996	19J	Bunn
BALL WATCH CO.(16 Size)		HAMPDEN WATCH CO. (16 Size)		SOUTH BEND WATCH CO. (16 Size)	
23J	Official R.R. Standard	23J	Special Railway	21J	No.227
21J	Official R.R. Standard	21J	New Railway	21J	No.229
19J	Official R.R. Standard	19J	Railway	21J	No.295
				19J	No.293

Union Pacific Railroad Time Inspectors, June 1936

All new WATCHES must be 16 size with double roller adjust to 5 positions & so stamped on plates, lever set, plain Arabic numbers open-faced & wind at 12, maintain a rate of 30 seconds. The following will govern the NEW RAILROAD STANDARDS. BALL=21&23 jeweled "Official Railroad Standard"; ELGIN=21&23 jeweled "B. W. Raymond"; HAMILTON="950 & 992"; ILLINOIS 21&23 jeweled "Buns Special"; WALTHAM=23 jeweled "Vanguard".

CP RAIL SERVICE AS OF FEBRUARY 1,1957

WALTHAM (16 SIZE)		HAMILTON (16 SIZE)		ZENITH(16Size)	
23J	Vanguard S. # 29, 634, 001 and up	23J	No. 950B	21J	Extra RR56
		21J	No. 992B		
ELGIN(16 Size)					
21J	B.W.R.	BALL W. Co.(16 Size)			
21J	No.571	21J	(Hamilton) No. 992B		
		21J	No.435C		

APPROVED WRIST WATCHES IN CP RAIL SERVICE

CYMA		GIRARD PERREGAUX		LONGINES		UNIVERSAL		ZENITH	
17J	RR2852M			17J	RR280	19J	RR1205	18J	RR12OT
25J	RR2872A	17J	CP3O7 H.F						

APPROVED WRIST WATCHES IN
CP RAIL SERVICE 1965 - BATTERY POWERED

BULOVA ACCUTRON	RODANIA	WITTNAUER
17J 214	13J RR 2760 Calendar	13J RR 12 WT Calendar
17J 216 Calendar		

APPROVED WRIST WATCHES SEMI-MECHANICAL
Q = QUARTZ ANALOG BATTERY POWERED IN CP RAIL SERVICE AS OF 1978

CYMA	RODANIA	WYLER
7J Calendar RR 9361 Q	6J Calendar 9952.111 RR	7J Calendar RR 9361 Q
6J Calendar RR 960 Q	7J Calendar RR 9361 Q	

BULOVA	ROTARY	WITTNAUER
7J Calendar RR 9362 Q	7J Calendar RR 9366 Q	7J Calendar RR2 Q 115 C
6J Calendar RR 960.111Q		

ADJUSTMENTS

There are **nine** basic adjustments for watch movements.
They are: **heat 1, cold 1, isochronism 1, positions 6 = TOTAL 9**
THE SIX POSITION ADJUSTMENTS ARE:

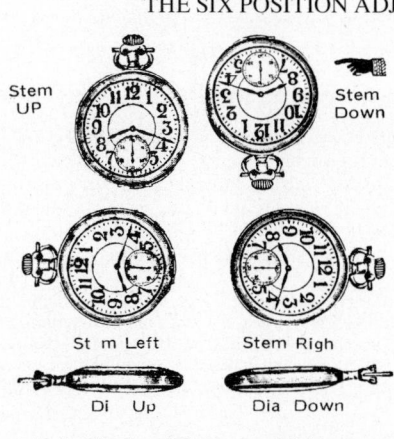
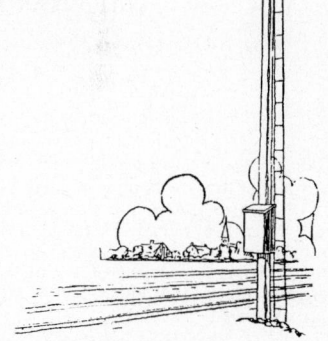

This position adjust-
required
railroad watches

Stem
UP

Stem
Down

St m Left   Stem Righ

Di Up   Dia Down

A watch marked as 5 positions is <u>equivalent</u> to one marked eight adjustments (the most common found on RR watches) and will be listed in this book as: "Adj.5P" (adjusted to heat, cold, isochronism and 5 positions). A watch marked as nine adjustments is <u>equivalent</u> to one marked 6 positions & listed as "Adj.6P" (adjusted to heat, cold, isochronism and <u>6 positions</u>). A watch that is marked as ADJUSTED only is adjusted to isochronism & in poise in all temperatures & is listed as "Adj.". * Later some manufactures used a variations of 8 adjustments, six to position, 1-isochronism, 1-temperature or as in the Elgin grade 571 two to temperature in about 1950.

WRIST WATCHES POSITION ADJUSTMENTS

CROWN UP	CROWN DOWN	CROWN LEFT	CROWN RIGHT	DIAL DOWN	DIAL UP

Main vertical position: Wrist Watches = CROWN DOWN & Pocket Watches = PENDANT UP.

FERGUSON Patented RR Dial: Patent numbers on back. Hr.1-12 in red, Min. 5-60 in black, hr. hand red, min. hand black. Valued at: BALL = $1,000-$1,500, A.W.W.Co. Elgin, Hamilton. Illinois, etc. = $700-$1000, Ball (Illinois) = $1500-$2500 and Rockford & S. Bend = $600-$1000 for MINT dials.

ELGIN WATCH CO., Classic Montgomery RR Dial (note 6 inside seconds bit) with red marginal numbers at 5,10,15, 20, 25, 30,35, 40, 45, 50, 55, & 60. Valued at $75 to $1 35. Montgomery RR Dials first used <u>about</u> 1904.

The total number of pocket watches made for the railroad industry was small in comparison to the total pocket watches produced. Generally, watches defined as "Railroad Watches" fall into five categories:

1. **Railroad Approved**- A list of grades and Models approved by the railway companies.
   Note: Only RR employees who were responsible for schedules were required to purchase or use approved watches. Many employees, regardless of position, bought approved watches because they were the standard of reliability.
2. **Railroad Grade**- Those advertised as being able to pass or exceed railroad inspection. These were used primarily by those railroaders who were not required to submit their watches for inspection.
3. **Pre-Commission Watches**- Those used by the railroads before 1893. There were many watches made for the railroad use prior to 1893. Some of the key wind ones of good quality are highly collectible.
4. **Company Watches**- Those with railroad logo or company name on the dial.
5. **Train Watches**- Those with a locomotive painted on the dial or inscribed on the case.
   Note: Some manufacturers inscribed logos and terms such as railroader, special railroad, dispatcher, etc., on the dials and back plate of the movements.

12 Size Prestige Gentleman's Superior Pocket Watches

Some American made 12 size watches are equal or superior to many railroad grade 18 or 16 size watches and are also a higher grade than European made pocket watches. The marvel is how any micro mechanism so exquisite in design, highly finished throughout in every detail, so thin and graceful, can combine in such a high degree the rigorous qualities of accuracy and durability. Waltham first sold a 12 size pocket watch around 1895 and by 1897, Elgin began to sell their version of the 12 size prestige gentleman's superior pocket watch. These pocket watches are remarkable examples of the American watchmakers' craft.

1. 23 extra-fine jewels, motor barrel pivots running in jewels, solid nickel plates, full gold train and polished, raised gold jewel settings held by 2 or 3 screws, exposed poised sapphire pallets and fork, straight line double roller escapement with steel escape wheel, micro metric regulator, compensating balance with gold balance screws, including 1 or 2 mean time screws, over coil hairspring, adjusted to temperature, isochronism and 5 to 6 positions, superior quality, carefully timed and all parts highly finished throughout.

American Waltham: 23J. Riverside Maximus 1894 model, *earlier examples have 6 diamond cap jewels, 2 at the balance wheel, 2 on pallet arbor and 2 for the escape wheel.*

Elgin: grade 190, 23J. HC, grade 194, 23J. OF, *early examples have a counterpoised "Moustache" lever.*

Hamilton: 23J, grades 920, 922 and 922 marked Masterpiece. Also note 920 and 922 grades have white gold finish bridges. *Grade 900, 19J also has a white gold finish with fish-scale damaskeening.*

Illinois: 23J, grades 299 and 410 are adjusted to 6 positions and some are marked **jeweled barrel**, advertised as "the best 12 size watch on the market".

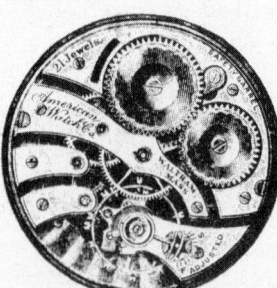

American Waltham 12 size, 23J, OF, Riverside Maximus 1894 Model, polished gold train, raised gold jewel settings, diamond endstones onto the balance and escape wheel, total diamonds=4, c. 1911, S#18,102,833

Elgin W. Co., 23J grade 194, OF, counterpoised "Moustache" lever, polished gold train, raised gold jewel settings. Special note: the regulator adjustable nut screw is gold, c. 1897 S#7, 425, 394

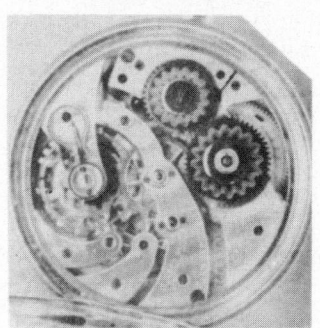

Hamilton, 23J, OF, grade 920, polished gold train, raised gold jewel settings, 4 mean time screws, sapphire pallets. Special note: white gold damaskeening finish bridges, c. 1920, S#1,782,349.

Illinois, 23J, OF, grade 410, polished gold train, raised gold jewel settings, marked 6 positions & motor barrel, crosshatched damaskeening, c. 1926, S# 4, 863, 173

A very interesting frame of reference of these 12 size watches is that the Hamilton grade 920 (23J) sells for much less than a 16 size grade 950 (23J) in today's collector market but it was more expensive when new and is clearly a better movement. In 1919, a Hamilton grade 950, 16 size. gold filled case sold for $77.00 while a 12 size, grade 920 in a gold filled case sold for $85.00. In a 1915 ad, the Hamilton grade 920 was referred to as "the masterpiece of masterpieces".

  2. 19, 21 or 23 Jewels - Most have extra-fine jewels, solid nickel plates, full gold train and polished, raised gold jewel settins held by 2 or 3 screws, exposed poised sapphire pallets and fork, straight line double roller escapement with steel escape wheel, micro metric regulator, compensating balance with gold balance screws including 1 or 2 pairs timing screws, over coil hairspring, adjusted to temperature, isochronism abd 5 to 6 positions, superior quality, carefully timed and all parts highly finished throughout.

> **American Waltham**: American Watch Co. Bridge model 21J, equivalent to any size but more scarce, Riverside Maximus 21J
> **Ball Watch Co.**: 19J, Illinois, M#3, G#417, raised jewel settings, gold polished center wheel, sapphire pallets, 2 mean time screws, 1927-1935.
> **Elgin**: grades 189=19J, HC, 193+ 19J, OF, C.H.Hulburd 19J, unique size and design, also 21J, grade 236 or 237. 19J B. W. Raymond form grade 193.
> **Dudley**: 12-14 size, 19J, Masonic symbols designed movement.
> **Gruen**: 50th Anniversary model, not American made but a prestige superior gentlemen's 10 size pocket watch with 23J, 12K solid gold
> **Hamilton**: 21J, grade 400 inherited from Illinois with 5 tooth click designed by C.E. DeLong and a slender wafer thin watch, also note the motor barrel pivots running in jewels. Note: G#400, S#H1001 to H1800, the original Illinois S# can be found under the dial on pillar plate. Also G#904, 21J has a jeweled barrel. Grades 900-19J, 902-19J. 900 has fish-scale damaskeening.
> **Hampden**: John Hancock 21J, gold center wheel
> **E. Howard & Co.**: "J", 15J, Deer grade, historically important, first sold in 1892, in original case

Ball W. Co., 19J, OF, Illinois, M#3, G#417, raised jewel settings, gold polished center wheel, sapphire pallets, 2 mean time screws, S# B405035, c. 1927-1935

Hamilton, 21J, OF, grade 400, gold train, 5 tooth click, note the motor barrel pivots running in jewels, S#H1513, c. 1930.
Note:original Illinois S#3,869,348 is found under the dial on pillar plate, c. 1921

28

Gruen, 50th Anniversary model, not American made but a prestige superior gentleman's 10 size pocket watch with 23J, 12K solid gold movement.

Illinois, A. Lincoln, open face, 21J, beveled and polished gold center wheel, S# 3,300,705. A. Lincoln was the only grade Illinois made in 3 sizes: 18, 16 and 12.

Howard Keystone: 19-23J, by Waltham
Illinois: Illini 23J, high level of finish or 21J, grades 528, 538 & 539 marke extra
Rockford: 23J, grade 300 or 305, gold train, gold jewel settings, the third wheel has two extra jewels, barrel not jeweled.
South Bend: 21J, grade 431
The above list are just some of the 12 size high grade examples and most are very affordable when compared to many high grade railroad pocket watches.

COLONIAL WATCHMAKERS (PRE-1850)

Early American Colonial watchmakers came from Europe and most all the movements were made near Prescot Lancashire, England. These hand-fabricated watches were made largely from imported parts. It was common practice for a watchmaker to use rough castings made by several craftsmen. 99% of English watches were made by numerous tradesmen and each person made a separate portion of the watch before completion. These were referred to as ebauche or "movements in the gray". The watchmaker finished the ebauche movements & parts, then assembled them to make a complete watch. He would then engrave his name on the finished timepiece. Some of the early American watchmakers designed the cases and other parts, but most imported what they needed. The Colonial watchmakers were also clock makers. The Colonial clock/watchmakers made the cases for the tall clocks and imported the clock movement. The demand was low and most made both clocks and watches. These early hand-made watches are hard to find; therefore, only the name of the watchmaker will be listed. This compilation comes from old ads in newspapers and journals and other sources. It is not considered to be complete. Because of the shortage and condition of these early Colonial watches, prices may vary widely from $400 to $1,200 to $12,000.

As early as 1775, the first Swiss made watches, and made in the London style, came into the U.S.A. In 1830, Vacheron & Constantin established a connection in New York through Jean Magnin. Later in the mid 1830's, they extended their trade to Philadelphia and New Orleans and by 1838, Agassiz and later to Jurgensen. Early in the 1860's the Swiss Firms of Cortebert, E. Borel and Courvoisier made and designed watches to closely resemble the style of American watch case and movement. For example, the Ohio Watch Co. was distributed by Leon Lesquereaux and son (Junior) of Columbus, Ohio. E. Borel & Co. produced American style watches and shipped them to Lucien Morel & Ed Droz in New York. These were followed later by the entire, original designs of the Swiss watch manufactures.

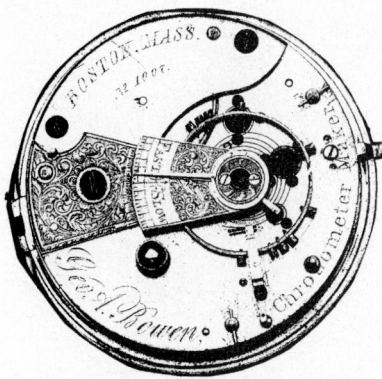

George Bowen, Boston Mass., engraved on movement "chronometer Maker, KW KS, Spring Detent., ca. 1850.

Davis Watson & Co. Boston, Fusee with right angle escapement lever, serial No. 8028 ca. 1850.

Example of watch paper placed inside a pair-cased watch by a watchmaker. This was a form of advertisement placed in the watch after repair was made.

Ephraim Clark, 18 size, non-jeweled, made between 1780-1800; a good example of a colonial watch, These early watches usually included chain driven fusees, verge type escapements, hand pierced balance cock, key wind & set: note the circular shaped regulator above the balance Cock

Effingham Clark, New York, on dial & movement, the inner with Roman hour chapter and a sweep second outer dial diamond stone, serial No. 720, Ca. 1800.

E. EMBREE, NEW YORK engraved on movement, serial # 790, chain driven fusee, silver pair cased watch, ca. early 1800's.

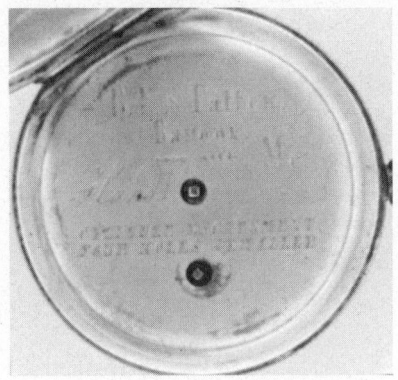

B.F.S Patten, Bangor, Maine, LEFT & RIGHT; left a 48mm, 6J, <u>Cylinder</u> escapement bar style Ebauche movement which may have been manufactured by Japy Freres with branches in France, Switzerland & England. Right; showing the movement cover that reads four holes jeweled but 6 jewels exits Ca 1855 to 1865. ("Continental Watch")

GREENLEUF & OAKES, Hartford Ca. 1805, Greenleuf & Oakes formed a partnership in 1804, verge, pierced cock.

MARQUAND & CO., New York, 1850s, gold case, right angle lever escapement, fusee, gold dial.

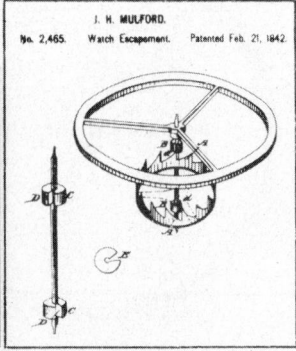

J.H.MULFORD Albany, N. Y., produced watches from about 1835 to 1875, the two watch movements (A & B) are illustrated, A is about size 18, KWKS, gold jewel settings, compensated balance with gold screws. Movement B is 3 arm balance, diamond end stone. Note the J. H. Mulford patented verge style escapement patented # 2465, dated Feb. 21,1842. illustrated to the far right.

EARLY AMERICAN WATCHMAKERS
(With Location and Approximate Date)

Adams, Nathan (Boston, MA, 1800)
Adams, William (Boston, MA, 1810)
Alden, & Eldridge (Bristol, Conn., 1820)
Aldrich, Jacob (Wilmington, DE, 1802)
Alrichs, Jonas (Wilmington, DE, 1880)
Allebach, Jacob (Phila., PA, 1825-1840)
Amant, Fester (Phila., PA, 1793)
Atherton, Nathan (Phila., PA, 1825)
Atkins & Allen (Bristol, Ct., 1820)
Atkinson, James (Boston, MA, 1745)
Austin, Isaac (Phila., PA, 1785)
Backhouse, John (Lancaster, PA, 1725)
Bagnall, Benjamin (Phila., PA, 1750)
Bailey, John (Boston, MA, 1810)
Bailey & Kitchen:(Phila, PA, 1832-46) name
changed to Bailey, Banks & Biddle
Bailey, William (Phila., PA, 1820)
Baker, Benjamin (Phila., PA, 1825)
Banks, Joseph (Phila., PA, 1790)
Banstein, John (Phila., PA, 1790)
Barnes, Timothy (Litchfield, Conn. 1790)
Barnhill, Robert (Phila., PA, 1775)
Barrow, Samuel (Phila., PA, 177t)
Barry, Standish (Baltimore, MD, 1785)
Basset, John F. (Phila., PA, 1798)
Batterson, James (New York 1705-30)
Bayley, Simeon C., (Phila., PA 1795)
Beard, Duncan (Appoquinemonk, Del.1765)
Belk, William (Phila., PA 1796)
Belknap, William (Boston, MA, 1815)
Bell, William (Phila., PA, 1805)
Benedict, S. W. (New York, NY, 1835)
Bigger & Clarke (Baltimore, MD, 1783)
Billion, C. (Phila., PA, 1775-1800)
Billow, Charles & Co. (Phila., PA 1796
Bingham & Bricerly (Phila., PA, 1778-1799)
Birge, Mallory & Co. (Bristol, Conn. 1830)
Birge, Peck & Co. (Bristol, Conn. 1830)
Birnie, Laurence (Phila., PA, 1774)
Blundy, Charles (Charleston, SC, 1750)
Blunt & Nichols (New York, NY, 1850)
Boardman, Chauncey (Bristol, Conn.1815)
Boardman, & Dunbar (Bristol, Conn. 1811)
Boardman, & Wells (Bristol, Conn. 1815)
Bode, William (Phila., Pa 1796)
Bogardus, Evarardus (New York, 1698)
Bond, William (Boston, MA, 1800-1810)
Bonnaud (Phila., PA, 1799)
Bower, Michael (Phila., PA, 1790-1800)
Bowman, Joseph (Lancaster, PA, 1821-44)
Boyd & Richards (Phila., PA, 1808)
Boyter, Daniel (Lancaster, PA, 1805)
Brands & Matthey (Phila., PA, 1799)
Brandt, Aime (Phila., PA, 1820)
Brant, Brown & Lewis (Phila., PA, 1795)
Brazier, Amable (Phila., PA, 1795)
Brearley, James (Phila., PA, 1790-1800)
Brewer, William (Phila., PA, 1785-1791)
Brewster, Abel (Norwich, CT) 1802
Brewster &Ingraham (Bristol,CT,1 827-39)
Brown, Davis (Boston, 1800)
Brown, Garven (Boston, MA, 1767)
Brown, John (Lancaster, PA, 1840)
Brown, Samuel (New York, 1820-1850)
Brownell, A. P. (New Bedford, MA.1840-60)
Burkelow, Samuel (Phila., PA, 1791-1799)

Burnop, Daniei (E. Windsor, Conn., 1793)
Bush, George (Easton, PA, 1790-1 800)
Cairns, John (Providence, 1785-1809)
Campbell, Charles (Phila., PA, 1796)
Campbell, William (Carlisle, PA, 1765)
Canby, Charles (Wilmington, Del., 1825)
Capper, Michael (Phila., PA, 1799)
Carey, James (Brunswick, ME, 1830)
Carrell, John (Phila., PA, 1791-1793)
Carter, Jacob (Phila., PA, 1805)
Carter, Thomas (Phila., PA, 1823)
Carver, Jacob (Phila., PA, 1790)
Carvill, James (New York, NY, 1803)
Chandlee, John (Wilmington,DE,1795-1810)
Chaudron, Co., (Phila., PA, 1799- 1815)
Chauncey & Joseph Ives (Bristol, CT, 1825)
Cheney, Martin (Windsor, VT, 1800)
Chick, M. M. (Concord, NH, 1845)
Clark, Benjamin(Wilmington,DE,1737-1750)
Clark, Charles (Phila., PA 1810)
Clark, Ephraim (Phila., PA, 1780-1820)
Clark, J. H. & Co. (Memphis Tenn, 1835)
Clark, John (New York, NY, 1770-1790)
Clark, John (Phila., PA, 1799)
Clark, Thomas (Boston, MA, 1764)
Claudon, John-George (Charleston SC,1773)
Cook, William (Boston, MA, 1810)
Crow, George (Wilmington, DE, 1740-1770)
Crow, John (Wilmington, DE, 1770-1798)
Crow, Thomas (Wilmington, DE, 1770-98)
Currier & Trott (Boston, MA, 1800)
Curtis, Solomon (Phila., PA, 1793-1795)
Dakin, James (Boston, MA, 1795)
Davis, Samuel (Boston, MA, 1820)
Davis, Watson & Co.(Boston, 1840-1850)
Delaplaine, James K.(New York, 1786-1800)
DeVacht, Joseph & Frances (Gallipolis, OH, 1792)
Dickinson, Thos. (Boston, 1810)
Dix, Joseph (Phila., PA, 1770)
Downes, Anson (Bristol, CT, 1830)
Downes, Arthur (Charleston, SC, 1765)
Downes, Ephriam (Bristol, CT, 1830)
Droz, Hannah (Phila., PA, 1840)
Droz, Humbert(Phila., PA, 1793-1799)
Duffield, Edward W. (Whiteland, PA, 1775)
Dunheim, Andrew (New York, NY, 1775)
Dupuy, John (Phila., PA, 1770)
Dupuy, Odran (Phila., PA, 1735)
Dutch, Stephen, Jr. (Boston, MA.1800-l0)
Eberman, George (Lancaster, PA, 1800)
Eberman, John (Lancaster, PA, 1780-1820)
Ellicott, Joseph (Buckingham, PA, 1763)
Elsworth, David (Baltimore, MD.1 780-1800)
Embree, Effingham (New York, NY, 1785)
Evans, David (Baltimore, MD, 1770-1773)
Fales, James (New Bedford, MA.1 810-20)
Ferris, Tiba (Wilmington, DE, 1812-1850)
Fessler, John (Phila., PA, 1785-1820)
Feton, J. (Phila., PA, 1825-1840)
Filber, John (Lancaster, PA, 1810-1825)
Fister, Amon (Phila., PA, 1794)
Fix, Joseph (Reading, PA, 1820-1840)
Fowell, J & N (Boston, MA, 1800-1810)
Frances, Basil & Alexander Vuille(Baltimore,1766)
Galbraith, Patrick (Phila., PA, 1795)
Gibbons, Thomas (Phila., PA, 1750)

EARLY AMERICAN WATCHMAKERS (Continued)

Goodfellow, William (Phila., PA,1793-1795)
Goodfellow & Son, William (Phila., PA,1796)
Gooding, Henry (Boston, MA, 1810-1820)
Green, John (Phila., PA, 1794)
Griffen, Henry (New York, 1790)
Groppengeiser, I. L. (Phila., PA, 1840)
Grotz, Issac (Easton, PA, 1810-1835)
Hall, Jonas (Boston, MA, 1848-1858)
Harland, Theodore (Norwich, CT, 1750-90)
Harland, Thomas (New York, 1805)
Harland, Thomas (Norwich, CT, 1802)
Harrison, James (Shrewbury, MA, 1805)
Hawxhurst & Demilt (New York, 1800)
Hawxhurst, Nath. (New York, NY, 1784)
Heilig, Jacob (Phila., PA, 1770-1824)
Heilig, John (Germantown, PA, 1824-1830)
Hepton, Frederick (Phila., PA, 1785)
Hequembourg, C. (Paterson N.J. 1815-1830)
Heron, Isaac (New York, NY, 1770-1780)
Hill, D. (Reading, PA 1830)
Hodgson, William (Phila., PA, 1785)
Hoff, John (Lancaster, PA, 1800)
Hoffner, Henry (Phila., PA, 1791)
Howard, Thomas (Phila., PA, 1789-1791)
Howe, Jubal (Shrewbury, MA, 1800)
Huguenail, Charles (Phila., PA, 1799)
Hunt, Hiram (Robbinston, ME, 1800)
Hutchins, Abel (Concord, MA, 1785-1818)
Hutchins, Levi (Concord, MA, 1785-1815)
Hyde, John E. (New York, NY, 1805)
Hyde & Goodrich (New Orleans, LA, 1850)
Ingersoll, Daniel B. (Boston, MA, 1800-10)
Ingold, Pierre Frederick (NY, NY,1845-50)
Ives, Chauncy & Joseph (Bristol, CT, 1825)
Jacob, Charles & Claude (Annapolis, 1775)
Jackson, Joseph H. (Phila., PA, 1802-1810)
Jessop, Jonathan (Park Town, PA, 1790)
Jeunit, Joseph (Meadville, PA, 1763)
Johnson, Chauncy (Albany N.Y., (1825-1840)
Johnson, David (Boston, MA, 1690)
Johnson, John (Charleston, SC, 1763)
Jones, George (Wilmington, DE, 1815-35)
Jones, Low & Ball (Boston, MA, 1830)
Keith, William (Shrewbury, MA, 1810)
Kennedy, Patrick (Phila., PA, 1795-1799)
Kincaid, Thomas (Christiana Bridge, DE, Ca 1775)
Kirkwood, John (Charleston, SC, 1761)
Kumble, Wm. (New York- 1776)
Launy, David F. (Boston & N. Y., 1800)
Leavenworth, Mark (Waterbury, CT, 1820)
Leavenworth, Win. (Waterbury, CT, 1810)
Leslie & Co., Baltimore, MD, 1795)
Leslie & Price (Phila., PA, 1793-1799)
Leslie, Robert (Baltimore, MD, 1788-1791)
Levely, George (Phila., PA, 1774)
Levi, Michael & Issac (Baltimore,MD,1785)
Limeburner, John (Phila., PA, 1790)
Lind, John (Phila., PA, 1791-1799)
Lowens, David (Phila., PA, 1785)
Ludwig, John (Phila., PA, 1791)
Lufkins & Johnson (Boston, MA, 1800-10)
Lukins, Isaac (Phila., PA, 1825)
Macdowell, Robert (Phila., PA, 1798)
MacFarlane, John (Boston, MA, 1800-1810)
Mahve, Matthew (Phila., PA, 1761)
Manross, Elisha (Bristol, CT, 1827)
Martin, Patrick (Phila., PA, 1830)
Mathey, Louis (Phia., PA, 1800)

Maunroe & Whitney (Concord,MA,1800's)
Maus, Frederick (Phila., PA, 1785- 1793)
Maynard, George(New York, NY, 1702-1730)
McCabe, John (Baltimore, MD, 1774)
McDowell, James (Phila., PA, 1795)
McGraw, Donald (Annapolis, MD, 1767)
Medley, Josia (Boston, 1732)
Mends, James (Phila., PA, 1795)
Merriman, Titus (Bristol, CT, 1830)
Merry, Charles F. (Phila., PA, 1799)
Meters, John(Fredricktown, MD,1795-1 825)
Miller, Abraham (Easton, PA, 1810-1830)
Mitchell & Atkins (Bristol, CT, 1830)
Mitchell, Henry (N. Y., NY, 1787-1800)
Mohler, Jacob (Baltimore, MD, 1773)
Moir, J & W (Waterbury, CT, 1790)
Montandon, Julien (Shrewbury, CT, 1812)
Moollinger, Henry (Phila., PA, 1794)
Morgan, Thomas (Phila. & Balti., 1774-93)
Moris, William (Grafton, MA, 1765-1775)
Mulford, J. H. (Albany, NY, 1845)
Mulliken, Nathaniel (Boston, MA, 1765)
Munroe & Whitney (Concord, MA, 1820)
Narney, Joseph (Charleston, SC, 1753)
Neiser, Augustine (Phila., PA, 1739-1780)
Nicholls, George (New York, NY, 1728-50)
Nicollette, Mary (Phila., PA, 1793-1799)
O'Hara, Charles (Phila., PA, 1799)
Oliver, Griffith (Phila., PA, 1785-1793)
Ormsby, James (Baltimore, MD, 1771)
Palmer, John (Phila., PA, 1795)
Palmer, John Peter (Phila., PA, 1795)
Park, Seth (Parktown, PA, 1790)
Parke, Solomon (Phila., PA, 179 1-1795)
Parke, Solomon & Co. (Phila., PA, 1799)
Parker, James (Cambridge, OH, 1790)
Parker, Thomas (Phila., PA, 1783)
Parry, John J. (Phila., PA, 1795-1800)
Patton, Abraham (Phila., PA, 1799)
Patton, David (Phila., PA, 1800)
Payne, Lawrence (New York, NY,1732-55)
Pearman, W. (Richmond, VA, 1834)
Perkins, Thomas (Phila., PA. 1785-1800)
Perry, Marvin (New York, NY, 1770-1780)
Perry, Thomas (New York, NY, 1750-1775)
Phillips, Joseph (New York, NY, 1713-35)
Pierret, Mathew (Phila., PA, 1795)
Pope, Joseph (Boston, MA, 1790)
Price, Philip (Phila., PA, 1825)
Proctor, Cardan (New York, NY.1747-75)
Proctor, William (New York,NY.1737-1760)
Proud, R. (Newport, RI, 1775)
Potter, J.O.&J.R. (Providence, R.I. 1849-59)
Purse, Thomas (Baltimore, MD, 1805)
Quimby, Phineas & William (Belfast, ME, 1825)
Reily, John (Phila., PA, 1785-1795)
Rich, John (Bristol, CT, 1800)
Richardson, Francis (Phila., PA, 1736)
Ritchie, George (Phila., PA, 1785-1790)
Roberts, John (Phila., PA, 1799)
Roberts, S & E (Trenton, NJ, 1830)
Rode, William (Phila., PA, 1785)
Rodger, James (New York, NY, 1822-1878)
Rodgers, Samuel (Plymouth, MA, 1800's)
Russell, George (Phila., PA, 1840)
Saxton & Lukens (Phila., PA, 1828)
Schriner, Martin (Lancaster, PA.1790-1830)
Schriner, M & P (Lancaster, PA, 1830-40)

EARLY AMERICAN WATCHMAKERS (Continued)

Seddinger, Margaret (Phila., PA, 1846)
Severberg, Christian (NY, NY, 1755-1775)
Sherman, Robert(Wilmington, DE. 1760-70)
Sibley, 0. E. (New York, NY, 1820)
Simpson, Saml. (Clarksville, Tenn - 1855)
Smith, J. L. (Middletown, CT, 1830)
Smith & Goodrich (Bristol, CT, 1827-1840)
Soloman, Henry (Boston, MA, 1820)
Souza, Sammuel (Phila., PA, 1820)
Sprogell, John (Phila., PA, 1791)
Spurck, Peter (Phila., PA, 1795-1799)
Stanton, Job (New York, NY, 1810)
Stein, Abraham (Phila., PA, 1799)
Stevens, E. (Boston, 1730)
Stever & Bryant (Wigville, CT, 1830)
Stillas, John (Phila., PA, 1785-1793)
Stinnett, John (Phila., PA, 1769)
Stokel, John (New York, NY, 1820-1840)
Store, Marmaduke (Phila., PA, 1742)
Strech, Thomas (Phila., PA, 1782)
Syderman, Philip (Phila., PA, 1785)
Taf, John James (Phila., PA, 1794)

Taylor, Samuel (Phila, PA, 1799)
Tonchure, Francis (Baltimore, MD, 1805)
Townsend, Charles (Phila., PA, 1799)
Townsend, David (Boston, MA, 1800)
Trott, Andrew (Boston, MA, 1800-18 10)
Turrell, Samuel (Boston, MA, 1790)
Voight, Henry (Phila., PA, 1775-1793)
Voight, Sebastian (Phila., PA, 1775-1799)
Voight, Thomas (Henry's son) (Phila., PA, 1811-1835)
Vuille, Alexander (Baltimore, MD, 1766)
Warner, George T. (New York, NY, 1795)
Watson, Davis (Boston, 1840-50)
Weller, Francis (Phila., PA, 1780)
Wells, George & Co. (Boston, MA, 1825)
Wells, J.S. (Boston, MA, 1800)
Wetherell, Nathan (Phila., PA, 1830-1840)
Wheaton, Caleb (Providence, RI, 1800)
White, Sebastian (Phila., PA, 1795)
Whittaker, William (NY, NY, 173 1-1755)
Wood, John (Phila., PA, 1770-1793)
Wright, John (New York, NY, 1712-1735)
Zahm, G.M. (Lancaster, PA, 1865)

Watch made by Andrew, Dunheim of New York in about 1775. Note the hand pierced case.

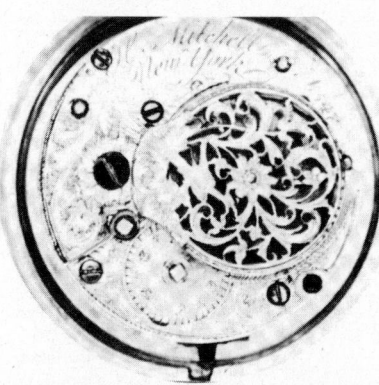

Louis Mathey, Philadelphia engraved on movement, about 18 size, very thin movement, Virgule escapement key wind & set from back, Ca.1 795-1805.

H. Mitchell, New York, 18 size, verge chain driven fusee; note the regulator below hand-pierced cock, Ca. 1790.

HOW TO DETERMINE SIZE

AMERICAN MOVEMENT SIZES
LANCASHIRE GAUGE

Size	Inches	Inches	mm	Lignes	Size	Inches	Inches	mm	Lignes
18/0	18/30	.600	15.24	6 3/4	2	1 7/30	1.233	31.32	13 7/8
17/0	19/30	.633	16.08	7 1/8	3	1 8/30	1.266	32.16	14 1/4
16/0	20/30	.666	16.92	7 1/2	4	1 9/30	1.300	33.02	14 7/8
15/0	21/30	.700	17.78	7 7/8	5	1 10/30	1.333	33.86	15 1/8
14/0	22/30	.733	18.62	8 1/4	6	1 11/30	1.366	34.70	15 3/8
13/0	23/30	.766	19.46	8 5/8	7	1 12/30	1.400	35.56	15 3/4
12/0	24/30	.800	20.32	9 1/8	8	1 13/30	1.433	36.40	16 1/8
11/0	25/30	.833	21.16	9 3/8	9	1 14/30	1.466	37.24	16 1/2
10/0	26/30	.866	22.00	9 3/4	10	1 15/30	1.500	38.10	16 7/8
9/0	27/30	.900	22.86	10 1/8	11	1 16/30	1.533	38.94	17 1/4
8/0	28/30	.933	23.70	10 1/2	12	1 17/30	1.566	39.78	17 5/8
7/0	29/30	.966	24.54	10 7/8	13	1 18/30	1.600	40.64	18 1/8
6/0	1	1.000	25.40	11 1/4	14	1 19/30	1.633	41.48	18 3/8
5/0	1 1/30	1.033	26.24	11 5/8	15	1 20/30	1.666	42.32	18 3/4
4/0	1 2/30	1.066	27.08	12 1/8	16	1 21/30	1.700	43.18	19 1/8
3/0	1 3/30	1.100	27.94	12 3/8	17	1 22/30	1.733	44.02	19 1/2
2/0	1 4/30	1.133	28.78	12 3/4	18	1 23/30	1.766	44.86	19 7/8
0	1 5/30	1.166	29.62	13 1/8	19	1 24/30	1.800	45.72	20 1/4
1	1 6/30	1.200	30.48	13 1/2	20	1 25/30	1.833	46.56	20 3/4

NOTE: There are many movements styles wit many different sizes in thickness and diameter, making it very difficult trying to find a case to fit a movement. This it true in ALL sizes.

SWISS MOVEMENT SIZES
Lignes With Their Equivalents in Millimeters and Decimal Parts of an Inch

Lignes	Inches Decimals	Millimeters
7	.622	15.79
8	.710	18.05
9	.799	20.30
10	.888	22.56
11	.977	24.81
12	1.066	27.07
13	1.154	29.32
14	1.243	31.58
15	1.332	33.84
16	1.421	36.09
17	1.5 10	38.35
18	1.599	40.60
19	1.687	42.86
20	1.776	45.11
21	1.865	47.37
22	1.954	49.63

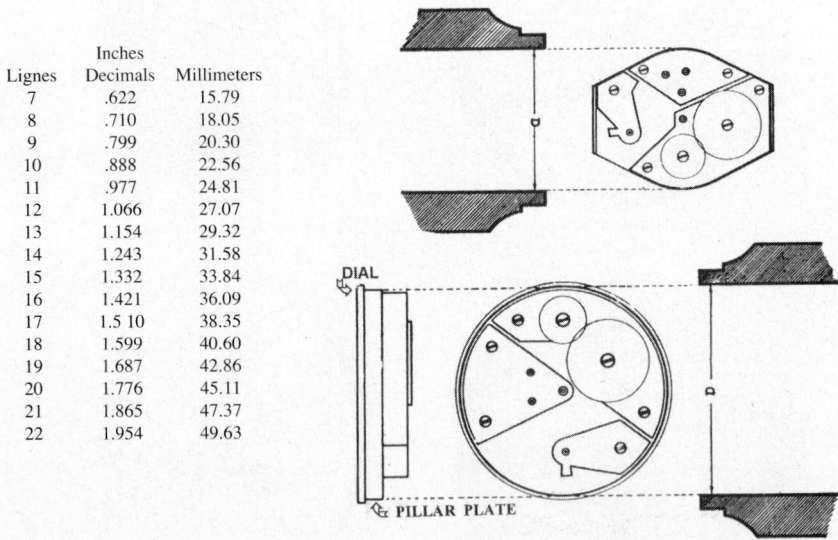

DIAL

PILLAR PLATE

GAUGES FOR MEASURING YOUR WATCH SIZE

The size of a watch is determined by measuring the outside diameter of the dial side of the lower pillar plate.
The gauges below may be placed across the face of your watch to calculate its approximate size.

AMER. MOVEMENT SIZES

26/0 21/0 20/0 16/0 18/0 12/0 10/0 8/0 5/0 4/0 3/0 0 6 8 10 12 14 16 18

SWISS MOVEMENT SIZES
LIGNES

2 4 6 8 10 12 14 16 18 20
3 5 7 9 11 13 15 17 19

SOLID GOLD MARKS

IMPORTANT NOTE: Have your watch case TESTED to make sure of gold quality or Karat.

The term KARAT is a word of definition in regards to the quality of gold, one 24th part (of pure gold). For example: Pure or fine gold is 24 karats; 18 Karat (abbreviated 18 K)consist of 18 parts of pure gold and mixed with 6 parts of other metal. The term CARAT is a unit of weight for gemstones, 200 milligrams equal 1 Carat. Karat = gold content & Carat = weight of GEMS.

GOLD-FILLED CASES

The first patent for gold-filled cases was given to J. Boss on May 3, 1859. Gold-filled cases are far more common than solid gold cases. Only about 5 percent of the cases were solid gold. In making the gold-filled case, the following process was used: two bars of 10k or 14k gold, 12" long, 2" wide, and 1/2" thick were placed on either side of a bar of base metal. The bar of base metal was 3/4" thick and the same length and width as the gold bars. These three bars were soldered together under pressure at high temperature. The bars were sent through rolling mills under tremendous pressure; this rolling was repeated until the desired thickness was reached. The new sandwich-type gold was now in a sheet. Discs were punched out of the sheet and pressed in a die to form a dish-shaped cover. Finally the lip, or ridge, was added. The bezel, snap, and dust caps were added in the finishing room. Gold-filled cases are usually 10k or 14k gold. The cases were marked ten-year, fifteen-year, twenty-year, twenty-five-year, or thirty-year. The number of years indicated the duration of guarantee that the gold on the case would not wear through to the base metal. The higher the number of years indicates that more gold used and that a higher original price was paid.

In 1924 the government prohibited any further use of the guarantee terms of 5, 10, 15, 20, 25, or 30 years. After that, manufacturers marked their cases 10k or 14k Gold-Filled and 10k Rolled Gold Plate. Anytime you see the terms "5, 10, 15, 20, 25 and 30-year," this immediately identifies the case as being gold-filled. The word "guaranteed" on the case also denotes gold-filled.

Rolled Gold

Rolled gold involved rolling gold into a micro thinness and, under extreme pressure, bonding it to each sheet of base metal. Rolled gold carried a five-year guarantee. The thickness of the gold sheet varied and had a direct bearing on value, as did the richness of the engraving.

Gold Gilding

Brass plates, wheels and cases are often gilded with gold. To do this, the parts are hung by a copper wire in a vessel or porous cell of a galvanic battery filled with a solution of ferro-cyanide of potassium, carbonate of soda, chloride of gold, and distilled water. An electric current deposits the gold evenly over the surface in about a six-minute period. One ounce of gold is enough for heavy gilding of six hundred watches. After gilding, the plates are polished with a soft buff using powdered rouge mixed with water and alcohol. The older method is fire-gilt which uses a gold and mercury solution. The metal is subjected to a high temperature so the mercury will evaporate and leave the gold plating. This is a very dangerous method, however, due to the harmful mercury vapor.

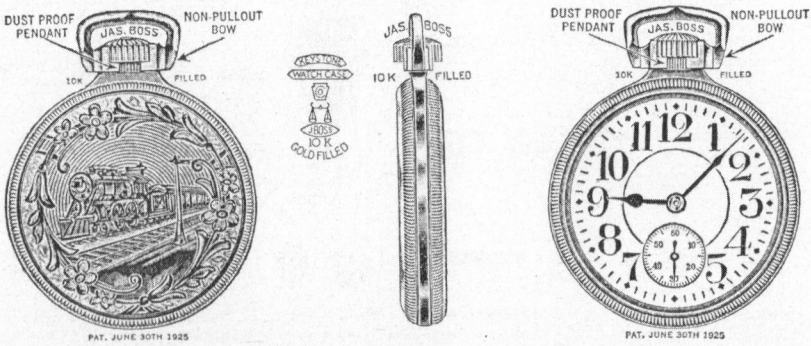

JAS. BOSS Railroad Model 10K Gold Filled cases sold for $14.00 in 1927

GOLD-FILLED MARKS

The following gold-filled and rolled gold plate marks are not complete, but if you have any doubt that the case is solid gold, pay only the *gold-filled* price.

GOLD FILLED MARKS

☆ 10K ROLLED GOLD PLATE

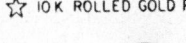 

BEE HIVE

(14K. Filled.)

(Jas. Boss 10K. Filled. 20 Years.)

(Keystone Extra, Substitute for All-Gold Case.)

CROWN 14K. FILLED
(25 Years.)

CROWN 10K. FILLED
(20 Years.)

(Rolled Gold.)

(Jas. Boss 14K. Filled. 25 Years.)

EMPRESS
(Gold Filled, 10 Years.)

FORTUNE
(Gold Filled, 20 Years.)

(10 Years.)

PREMIER
(Gold Filled, 25 Years.)

ELGIN COMMANDER

(14K. Filled.)

XV.

THE BELL 14K.
(25 Years.)

XX.

CASHIER
(Gold Filled, 25 Years.)

(10K. Gold Filled.)

V.

(5 Years.)

(15 Years.)

(20 Years.)

(25 Years.)

THE COMET
(10 Years.)

SILVER CASE MARKS

IMPORTANT NOTE: Have your watch case TESTED to make sure of gold quality or Karat.
NICKEL SILVER is 66% Copper, 24% Zinc and 10% Nickel (also known as Silveroid etc.)

SILVER CASE MARKS

(*Sterling Silver.*)   STERLING SILVER UNITED STATES ASSAY 925./1000 FINE.   ILLINOIS W.C.CO, ELGIN STERLING

HUNTING CASES

A hunting case is identified by a cover over the face (concealed dial) of the watch. The case is opened by pressing the stem or the crown of the watch. The hunter style watch was used for protection of the watch and carried by men of status and used as a dress watch.

HOW TO HANDLE A HUNTING CASE WATCH

Hold the watch in your right hand with the bow or swing ring between the index finger and thumb. Press on the pendant-crown with the right thumb to release the cover exposing the face.

When closing, do not SNAP the cover. Press the crown to move the catch in, close the cover, then release the crown. This will prevent wear to the soft gold on the rim and catch.

Above: Example of a hunting case

Right: Example of a swing-out case

SWING-OUT MOVEMENT

On some pocket watches the movement swings out from the front. On these type watches the movement can be swung out by unscrewing the bezel and pulling the stem out to release the movement. **SEE EXAMPLE ABOVE.**

40

Above: Engine - Turned
Demi-Hunting Case

Example of a 14 Karat gold TRUE Box Hinged case, selling for $94.00 in 1890. Note to be a TRUE Box Hinged case the top will match the bottom.

Left: Example of a screw bezel and screw back case.

Note: The screw on bezel was invented by E. C. Fitch in 1886.

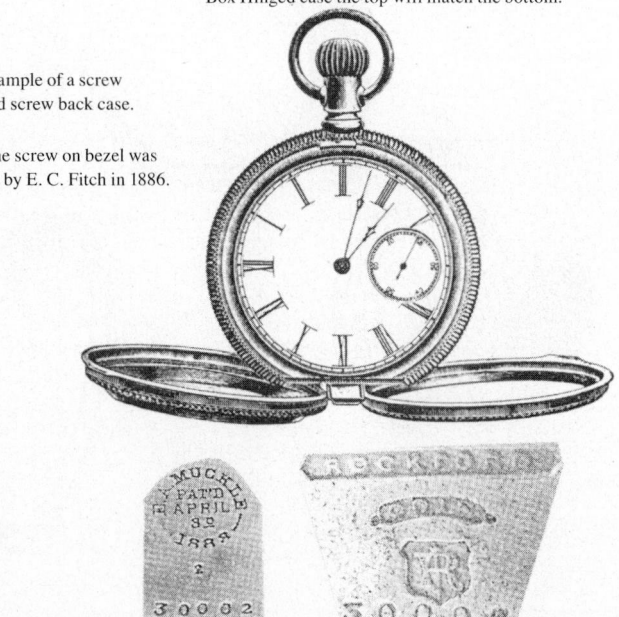

Above Right: Example of a reversible case to either hunting case or open face.

Also 2 illustrations of a Muckle reversible case markings stamped or engraved inside the case. (1.) Engraved on movement cover - E. A. Muckle, Pat'd April 3, 1883 + 2 & case serial It 30002. (2.) Marked on the lid or cover of same case - ROCKFORD COIN + a shield with R and I interwoven also case serial # 30002 (E. A. Muckle case, patent dates, Aug. 3, 1883 also April 3, 1883).

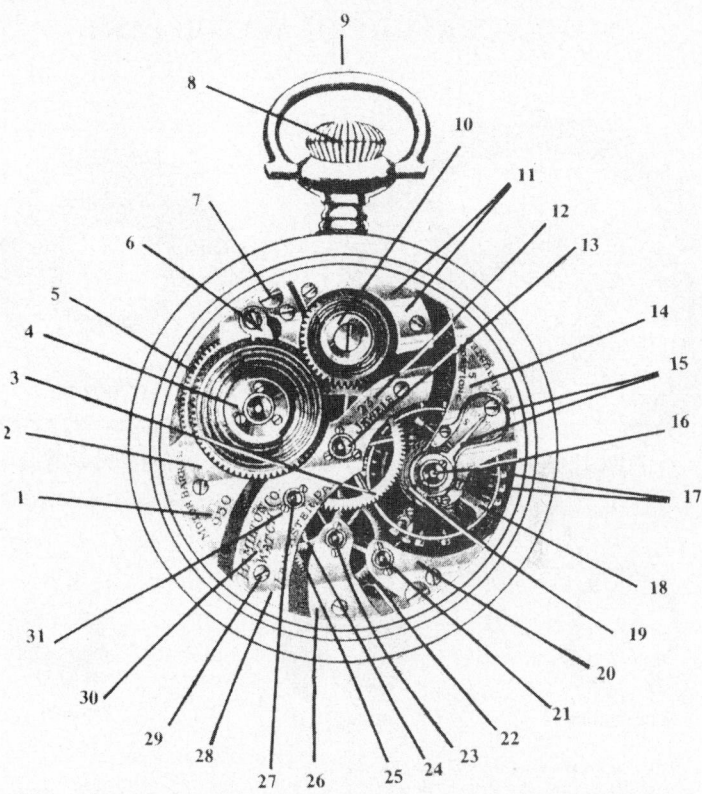

MOVEMENT IDENTIFICATION

1.Grade Number. 2. Nickel Motor Barrel Bridge. 3. Center Wheel (2nd Wheel). 4. Winding Wheel with Jewel Setting. 5. First Barrel Wheel, 6. Winding Click. 7. Case Screw. 8. Pendant Crown. 9. Pendant Bow or Swing Ring. 10. Crown Wheel with Screw. 11. Damaskeening-horizontal pattern. 12. Number of Jewels. 13. Center Wheel Jewel with Setting. 14. Adjusted to Heat, Cold, Isochronism & 5 Positions. 15. Patented Regulator with Index & Spring. 16. Balance End Stones (Diamonds, Rubies, & Sapphires were used). 17. Balance Screws. 18. Compensating Balance Wheel. 19. Hairspring. 20. Escapement Bridge. 21. Escapement Wheel Jewel with Setting (Diamonds, Rubies, & Sapphires were used). 22. Escapement Wheel. 23. Fourth Wheel Jewel with Setting. 24. Third Wheel. 25. Fourth Wheel. 26. Fourth Wheel Bridge. 27. Third Wheel Jewel with Setting. 28. Center & Third Wheel Bridge. 29. Bridge Screw. 30. Manufacturers Name & Location. 31. Jewel Setting Screw.

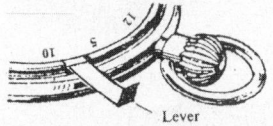

Lever

Many railroad company's required a watch to be lever set. Lever set means moving a lever allowing the crown (winding button) to engage with the hands to set them, to correct time. This was used to prevent accidentally changing the time while winding. The lever is located under the bezel that hold the crystal. On a open face watch, the lever is usually located between 6 minutes to 11 minutes, note the lever has a tab extending up. Remove the bezel to expose the lever, the bezel may be hinged, snap or screw off. Now that the bezel is off, with your thumbnail against the tab on lever move the lever outward, in the outward position turning the crown the hands may be set to the correct time.

NOMENCLATURE OF WATCH PARTS

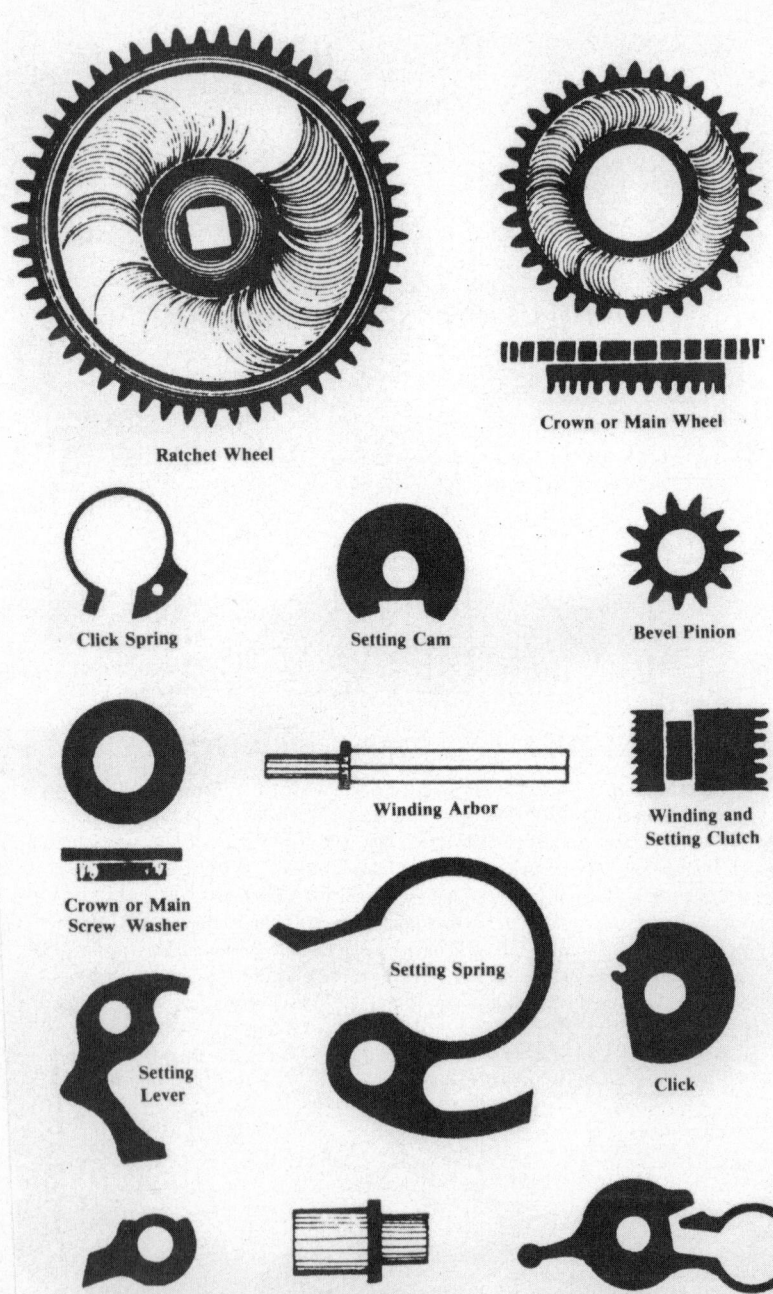

Ratchet Wheel

Crown or Main Wheel

Click Spring

Setting Cam

Bevel Pinion

Winding Arbor

Winding and Setting Clutch

Crown or Main Screw Washer

Setting Spring

Setting Lever

Click

Setting Spring Cam

Winding Sleeve

Clutch Lever

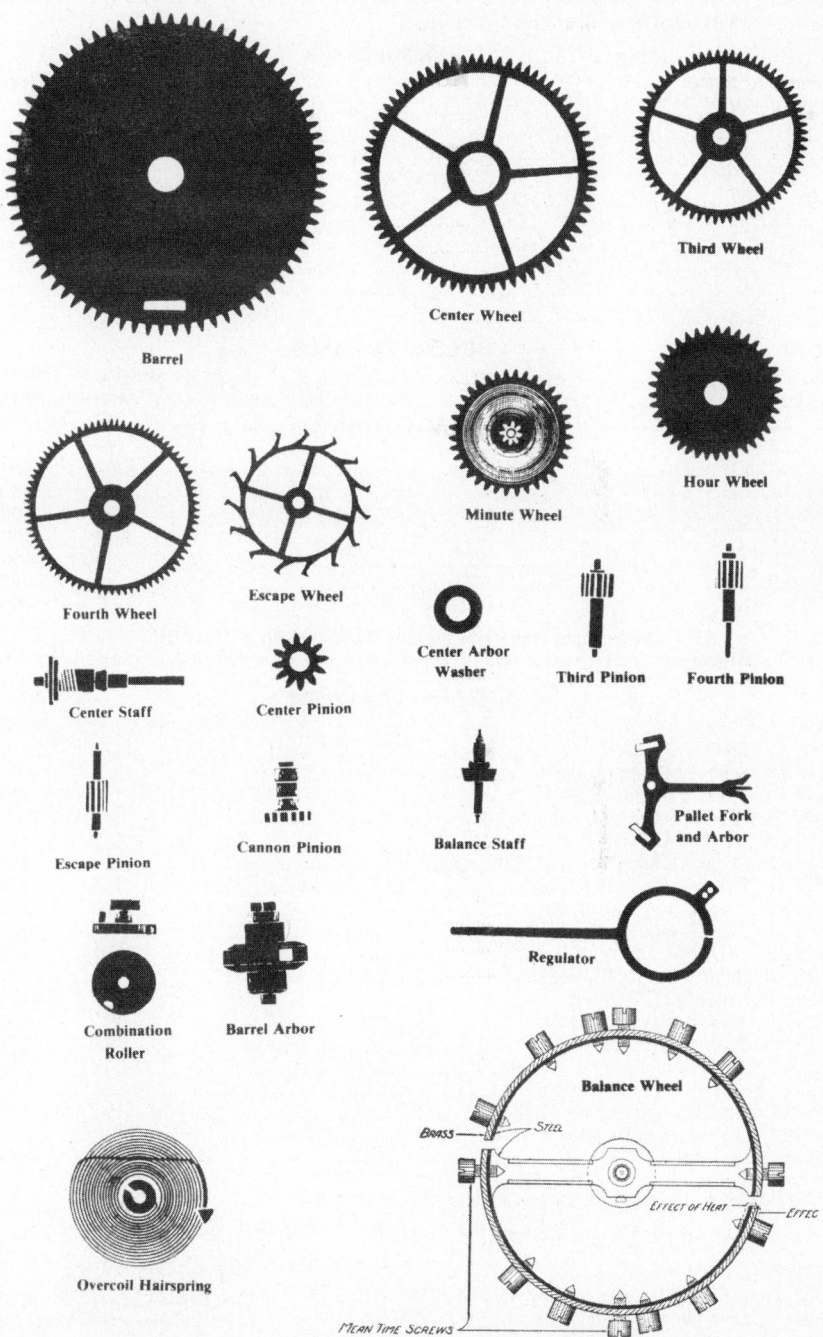

NOMENCLATURE OF WATCH PARTS

43

CASE PRICES

Case prices are for complete cases with bezel, crystal, stem, crown and bow. Hunting case style watches must have workable lift spring.

SILVEROID CASES

Size and Style	Avg	Ex-Fn	Mint
18S,OF,SW	$25	$35	$85
18S,OF,KW	45	50	100
18S,HC,SW	50	60	105
18S,HC,KW	60	70	135
16S,OF,SW	25	35	85
16S,HC	50	55	95
12S, OF	20	25	70
12S,HC	45	55	95
6S-0S, OF	15	20	65
6S-0S,HC	40	45	95

COIN-SILVER CASES

Size and Style	Avg	Ex-Fn	Mint
18S, OF, SW	$50	$100	$175
18S OF,KW	60	125	225
18S,HC,SW	70	100	200
18S,HC,KW	80	150	250
16S,OF	40	75	150
16S,HC	55	125	200
12S,OF	20	45	100
12S,HC	35	75	150
6S & 0S,OF	15	40	85
6S & 0S,HC	35	65	100

Note: Fancy engraved Cases are Worth 20% to 50% MORE.
Mint or near mint silver cases hard to find & 4 oz 18-16 size add 50% to 100% more.

GOLD-FILLED CASES

Size and Style	Avg	Ex-Fn	Mint
18S, OF, Plain or Engine-Turned	$75	$110	$225
18S, OF, Fancy or RR or Ex-Heavy	125	200	300
18S, HC, Plain or Engine-Turned	100	175	300
18S, HC, BOX & Fancy or Ex-Heavy	200	285	500
18S, HC, MULTI-COLOR BOX & Fancy	350	425	750
16S, OF, Plain or Engine-Turned (DISPLAY CASES)	75	100	175
16S, OF, Fancy or RR or Ex-Heavy	100	175	275
16S, HC, Plain or Engine-Turned	100	175	225
16S, HC, BOX & Fancy or Ex-Heavy	225	300	500
16S, HC, MULTI-COLOR BOX & Fancy	250	400	700
12S, OF, Plain or Engine-Turned	30	55	95
12S, OF, Fancy or Ex-Heavy	35	65	125
12S, HC, Plain or Engine-Turned	55	100	200
12S, HC, Fancy or Ex-Heavy	60	100	225
6S & OS, OF, Plain or Engine-Turned	25	45	100
6S & OS, OF, Fancy or Ex-Heavy	30	50	125
6S & OS, HC, Plain or Engine-Turned	35	50	125
6S & OS, HC, BOX or Ex-Heavy	75	130	250
6S & OS, HC, MULTI-color BOX	150	245	400

Note: Ladies size watches are used for jewelry, thus decorative quality effects their value.

Note: Plain enamel single sunk dial bring $30 to $60.

Clue to a recased watch.
The screw mark indicates a recased watch.
Not original to the movement.

—movement
—case

The screw on left is a case screw, extra screw mark (⟲) on case indicates a recased watch.

14K SOLID GOLD CASES
(Gold at $650/oz)

Size and Style	Avg	Ex-Fn	Mint
18S, OF, Plain or Engine-Turned	$325	$500	$700
18S, OF, Fancy or RR or Ex-Heavy	375	500	700
18S, HC, Plain or Engine-Turned	400	600	900
18S, HC, Fancy or Ex-Heavy	450	700	1,000
18S, HC, BOX & Fancy	650	1,500	2,000
16S, OF, Plain or Engine-Turned	225	325	450
16S, OF, Fancy or RR or Ex-Heavy	325	400	575
16S, HC, Plain or Engine-Turned	375	450	725
16S, HC, Fancy or Ex-Heavy	375	500	800
16S, HC, BOX & Fancy	525	700	1,200
12S, OF, Plain or Engine-Turned	175	225	350
12S, OF, Fancy or Ex-Heavy	225	275	450
12S, HC, Plain or Engine-Turned	250	325	475
12S, HC, Fancy or Ex-Heavy	275	400	500
6S & OS, OF	135	200	285
6S & OS, HC, Plain or Engine-Turned	165	225	335
6S & OS, HG, BOX or Heavy	200	300	485

18K SOLID GOLD CASES

Size and Style	Avg	Ex-Fn	Mint
18S, OF, Plain or Engine-Turned	$500	$600	$900
18S, OF, Fancy or RR or Ex-Heavy	650	700	1,100
18S, HG, Plain or Engine-Turned	685	900	1,200
18S, HC, Fancy or Ex-Heavy	1000	1,500	2,100
18S, HG, BOX & Heavy & Fancy	1200	2,000	2,600
16S, OF, Plain or Engine-Turned	425	500	700
16S, OF, Fancy or RR or Ex-Heavy	475	700	1,000
16S, HC, Plain or Engine-Turned	525	750	1,100
16S, HC, Fancy or Ex-Heavy	550	800	1,250
16S, HC, BOX & Fancy	750	1,200	1,650
12S, OF, Plain or Engine-Turned	275	325	450
12S, OF, Fancy or Ex-Heavy	275	325	550
12S, HG, Plain or Engine-Turned	350	385	550
12S, HG, Fancy or Ex-Heavy	400	450	675
6S & OS,OF	175	225	350
6S & OS, HC, Plain or Engine-Turned	225	300	500
6S & OS, HC, BOX or Heavy	300	400	675

14K MULTI-COLOR SOLID GOLD CASES

Size and Style	Avg	Ex-Fn	Mint
18S, OF, Plain or Engine-Turned	$800	$1,100	$1,500
18S, OF, BOX or Ex-Heavy	1,100	1,500	2,000
18S, HC, Plain or Engine-Turned	1,000	1,300	1,800
18S, HG, BOX	1,600	2,500	3,500
18S, HG, BOX & Fancy or Ex-Heavy	2,500	3,800	5,000
16S, OF, Plain or Engine-Turned	600	750	1,000
16S, OF, BOX or Ex-Heavy	850	1,000	1,500
16S, HC, Plain or Engine-Turned	800	1,150	1,600
16S, HC, BOX	800	1,200	1,750
16S, HG, BOX & Fancy or Ex-Heavy	1,500	2,000	3,000
6S & OS, OF	350	425	525
6S & OS, HC, Plain or Engine-Turned	425	500	625
6S & OS, HC, BOX & Fancy or Ex-Heavy	450	600	785

* Note: ADD 25-35% for 18K Multi & Multi with box cases.

Note: Most 18 & 16 size movements were not cased by the factory. Between 1910 and 1925 marked the start of advertised factory cased movements. Most high grade 12 & 10 after 1915 were factory cased. 12 & 10 size Hamilton & Howard were all cased by the factory. All Hampden 12 size (thin) & most South Bend 12 & 10 size were factory cased. Some Illinois and Waltham were cased at factory. Brand names as Ariston, Santa Fe, Burlington and others using Illinois movements used their name. Dollar watches were factory cased. Early Walthams made their own cases, so were cased at factory. Most or many European movements were cased by the watchmaker.

INSPECTING OPEN-FACED WATCHES

For watches with a screw-on front and back, as in railroad models, hold the watch in the left hand and, with the right hand, turn the bezel counter clockwise. While removing the bezel, hold onto the stem and swing ring in order to not drop the watch. Lay the bezel down, check the dial for cracks and crazing, nicks, chips, etc. Look for lever and check to see that it will allow hands to be set. After close examination, replace the bezel and turn the watch over. Again, while holding the stem between the left thumb and index finger, remove the back cover. If it is a screw-on back cover, turn it counter clockwise. If it is a snap on cover, look for the lip on the back and use a watch opener to pry the back off.

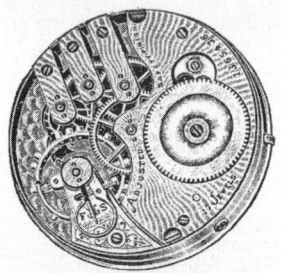

Left: Example of OPEN FACE case.

16 Size, Bridge, Lever Set, New Thin Model, Hunting or Open Face.

Nickel, 17 ex'ra fine, high colored ruby jewels, gold settings; accurately adjusted to temperature, six positions and isochronism, very carefully timed; compensation balance, gold screws, including four timing screws; gold beveled polished train; highly finished, hardened, beveled steel escape wheel, chamfered teeth; hand finished conical pivots on balance staff; counterpoised fork and pallet; best quality Swiss Breguet hairspring, Phillippe coil; patent micrometric screw regulator; all steel parts highly polished; visible concaved winding wheel; best quality Swiss mainspring; double sunk glass enameled dial; damaskeened in new style bright rayed pattern, black enamel lettering. A strictly high-grade watch for exacting requirements.

No. 187 Bridge................**$40 00**

1905 Illinois AD

"damaskeened in new style bright rayed pattern"

DAMASKEENING

A special, American factory term used in all their advertisements, damaskeening is a technique of embellishing movement plates by using small polishing wheels of ivory or boxwood with abrasive paste (pronounced dam-a-skeen-ing). Mr. F. Wilmot came from St. Imier Switzerland to help develop and teach this process first to U.S. Watch Co. of Marion, then to other USA factories. Damaskeening was first used in USA by the U.S. Watch Co. of Marion in about 1868-69. Am. Waltham Watch Co. first used Damaskeening in about 1871 on the 16 size model 1872 & Elgin started Damaskeening about mid 1870's. Damaskeening on watch plates became popular in the late 1870s by most manufactures. Howard, Illinois, Rockford, Seth Thomas and others competed fiercely for the beauty of Damaskeening. Damaskeening can be in two colors (2 tone) of metal such as copper or gold on nickel or gilt, not the gold, red or black lettering.

In Europe this decoration on watches, the terminology or expression is, Fausse Cotes, Cotes de Geneve or Geneva Stripes.

DISPLAY CASE WATCHES

Display case watches were used by salesmen and in jewelry stores to show the customer the movement. Both front and back had a glass crystal. These are not rare, but they are nice to have in a collection to show off a watch movement.

SALESMAN OR DISPLAY CASE with a bezel & glass crystal to view movement.

WATCH CASE PRODUCTION

Before the Civil War, watchmaking was being done on a very small scale, and most of the companies in business were making their own movements as well as their own cases. After the War, tradesmen set up shops specializing exclusively in cases, while other artisans were making the movements. The case factories, because of mass production, could supply watch manufacturers with cases more economically than the manufacturers could produce their own.

A patent granted to James Boss on May 3, 1859, were not the first gold-filled cases made from sandwich-type sheets of metal, but Boss did invent a new process that proved to be very successful, resulting in a more durable case that he sold with a 20-year money-back guarantee.

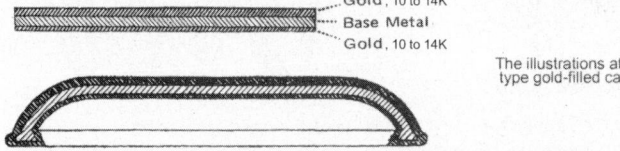

Gold, 10 to 14K
Base Metal
Gold, 10 to 14K

The illustrations at left is a sandwiched type gold-filled case.

GOLD CASE WEIGHTS BY SIZE

Size & Style of Case	Pennyweights (DWT)				
	Ex. Heavy	Heavy	Medium	Light	Ex. Light
18 size Hunting Case	60 to 65	50 to 55	45 to 50	40 to 45	35
16 size Hunting Case	55 to 60	45 to 50	40 to 45	35 to 40	32
18 size Open Face Case	40 to 45	38	35		
16 size Open Face Case	40	36	30		
12 size Open Face Case			14 to 16		
6 size Hunting Case	24	22	20	18	
0 size Hunting Case			14 to 16		

An 18 size movement with a full plate weighs 50 DWT; a 16 size movement with a ¾ plate weighs 35 DWT. These weights do not include the case.

TROY WEIGHT = 24 grains=1dwt., 1 Grain= 0.0648 grams, 20dwt = 1 OZ., 12oz = 1 LB.
NOTE: Gold & Silver Standards Vary from County to County. U.S.A. Coin Gold =.900 or 21 3/5K, Silver Coin=.900.
Gold Standards: 24K=1,000%or 1.0, 23K=.958 1/3, 22K=.91 6 2/3, 21K=.875, 20K=.833 1/3, 19K=.791 2/3, 18K=.750, 17K=.708 1/3, 16K=.666 2/3, 15K=.625, 14K=.583 1/3, 13K=.541 2/3, 12K=.500, 11=458 1/3, 10K=.416 2/3, 9K. 375.
8K=.333 1/3, 7K=.291 2/3, 6K=.250, 5K=.206 1/3, 4K=.166 2/3, 3K=.125, 2K=.63 1/3, 1K=41 2/3.

OPENING WATCH CASES

Most American watch factories made movements and not the cases; with only a few exceptions the watch factory movements were made to fit a standard size case. To buy a watch, the buyer would go to a jeweler or a watchmaker, decide on the maker of watch, model, size, and grade of a movement and next, select a case style to fit the movement. Some time after the mid 1920's this changed and factories started to provide assembly for complete watches (case & movement). Complete factory cased watches could also be found with different models, size, and grade of a movement, as well as, choose from a variety of cases. Which brings us to how to open the case to see the movement. It is important to open a case to see the works for inspection and to identify make, model, grade, quality & size of the movement. So first and foremost take care and do not force it open but open with normal amounts of effort or force.

A hunting case (HC) is identified by a front lid or cover over the face (concealed dial) of the watch. The front case lid is opened by pressing the stem or the crown of the watch. The hunter style watch was used for protection of the watch and carried by men of status and used as a dress watch. Hold the watch in your right hand with the bow or swing ring between the index finger and thumb. Press on the pendant-crown with the right thumb to release the cover also at the same time hold your left hand over the cover which will ease the lid without letting it snap open hard which may spring the lid. When closing, do not Snap the cover. Press the crown to move the catch in, close the cover, then release the crown. This will prevent wear to the soft gold on the nm and catch. A hunting cased watch may have a hinged front lid, back lid & hinged Cuvetté (dust cover) for a total of 3 hinges (front ,back lid & cuvette). To open the back (to see movement) check to see if there is a slightly raised opening or lip on the back, next it is best to use your thumb-nail in the slot or slit and slide your nail around the edge of the case and with pressure it should open. Snap back use the same method as before insert the fingernail and with a circular motion snap the back open. Do not try to pry with your nail, it just may break your nail. For lifting or prying the front snap bezel or hinge back or bezel use a case opener. A dull knife for safety may be used with a cloth or mouse pad. Set the watch face down on your pad and with the edge of opener use moderate force by rotating the opener with the movement of your wrist in each direction till it snaps open. Warning: If your watch case does not want to open with a normal applied effort, do NOT force it open.

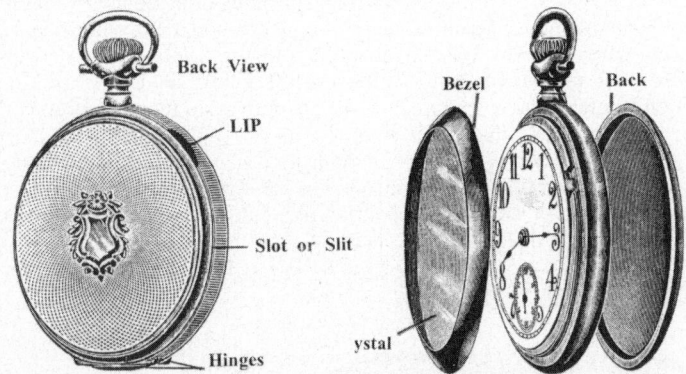

LEFT: Hunting Case (HC), note Up, also Slot or Slit and Hinges. Right: Screw Bezel, (Watch in center) & Screw Back.

Screw Backs & Bezels (that holds glass crystal) watches have no hinges but can be recognized by a fine line or slit between the back or bezel and the center of the watch case (the part that the winding stem is attached). For watches with a screw-on front and back, as in railroad models, hold the watch in the left hand, and with the right hand, turn the bezel counter clockwise. While removing the bezel, hold onto the stem and swing ring in order not to drop the watch. After close examination, replace the bezel and turn the watch over. Again, while holding the stem between the left thumb and index finger, remove the back cover. To unscrew the back turn it counter clockwise.

Slit or fine line  Center View

There are some screw back cases, English style, that may screw or turn clockwise. You may also use a rubber jar opener or a rubber sheet type household pad to assist you in opening the case. If it is hard to unscrew the back or bezel, check again to see that it is not a hinged style case. Try asking a watch collector friend or dealer for help. There is a useful WEB site: the National Association of Watch & Clock Collectors (NAWCC), www.nawcc.org/home.htm, click on Message Board. You may post a message on their board. Describe your problem and hopefully you will get your difficulty solved. This Board will NOT help with VALUES of timepieces, or accept Sale Ads.

Swing out cases there is only one fine line or slit visible, which is for the screw off bezel. Screw off the bezel pull up on the crown as if to set the hands, the stem is now in a outer position. Note the grove opening just under the dial at 6 O'clock put your finger nail into the grove and lift up swing-ring and the movement upward away from the case. You may also have to rotate the crown.

Many railroad company's required a watch to be lever set. Lever set means moving a lever allowing the crown (winding button) to engage with the hands to set them, to correct time. This was used to prevent accidentally changing the time while winding. The lever is located under the bezel that hold the crystal. On a open face watch, the lever is usually located between 6 minutes to 11 minutes, note the lever has a tab extending up. Remove the bezel to expose the lever, the bezel may be hinged, snap or screw off Now that the bezel is off, with your thumbnail against the tab on lever move the lever outward, in the outward position turning the crown the hands may be set to correct time.

Early American Colonial and European watches may have double, triple or as many as four cases. Most of these watches have a button on the rim or side of the case, also note that the case is hinged. Push the button and the cover or bezel will swing up and open the case. For the last case check to see if there is a slightly raised opening or lip on this bezel or back, also note this case is hinged, it is best to use your thumb-nail in the slot and slide your nail around the edge of the case and with pressure it should open to expose the dial. Now that you have it opened check at the bottom of the dial (at the 6 o'clock position) for a pin on top of the dial or a latch just under the dial, push the pin or latch toward the center of the dial and swing the dial and movement open. If the movement is not exposed it will have a dust cover over the movement. The dust cover has a crescent shaped slide spring catch, in the center find a pin and with your thumbnail slide the catch to the right or left. After you have moved the slide you can now lift the dust cover up to expose the movement.

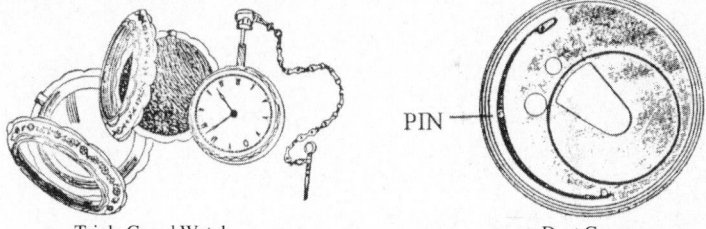

Triple Cased Watch   Dust Cover

Wrist watches usually have snap on back or bezel or a screw on back. For the snap on back or bezel use a case opener or your thumbnail. Check to see if there is a slit and slightly raised opening or lip on the back, next in the slit type slot or lip apply pressure and the back or bezel should open. Some wrist watches are also hinged so you may use the same method to open the case as the snap on back case. The water tight style screw on back, wrist watches will have <u>slots or notches</u> on the back and require a case wrench.

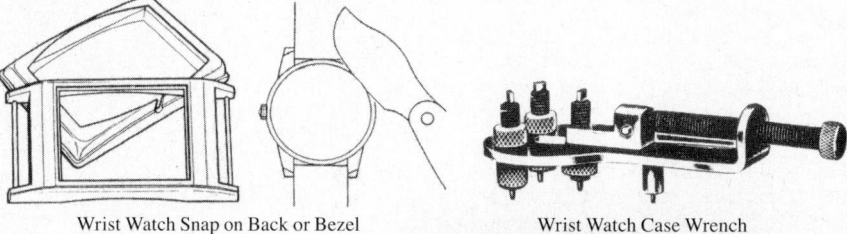

Wrist Watch Snap on Back or Bezel   Wrist Watch Case Wrench

Fold Up Pocket Knife style Case opener

CARE OF WATCHES

To some people a watch is just a device that keeps time. They do not know the history of its development nor how it operates. They have no appreciation for improvements made over the years. That the watch is a true miracle of mechanical genius and skill, is seldom more than a fleeting thought. The average person will know it must be wound to run, that it has a mainspring and possibly a hairspring. Some even realize there are wheels and gears and, by some strange method, these work in harmony to keep time. If for some reason the watch should stop, the owner will merely take it to a watch repair shop and await the verdict on damage and cost.

To be a good collector, one must have some knowledge of the components of a watch and how they work and the history of the development of the watch. To buy a watch on blind faith is indeed risky, but many collectors do it every day because they have limited knowledge.

How does a watch measure time and perform so well? Within the case one can find the fulcrum, lever, gear, bearing, axle, wheel, screw, and the spring which overcomes nature's law of gravity. All these parts harmonize to provide an accurate reading, minute by minute. A good collector will be able to identify all of them.

After acquiring a watch, you will want to take good care of it. A watch should be cleaned inside and out. Dirt will wear it out much faster, and gummy oil will restrict it and keep it from running all together. After the watch has been cleaned, it should be stored in a dry place. Rust is a watch's No. 1 enemy. A watch is a delicate instrument but, if it is given proper care, it will provide many years of quality service. A pocket watch should be wound at regular intervals about once every 24 hours, early each morning so the mainspring has its full power to withstand the abuse of daily use. Do not carry a watch in the same pocket with articles that will scratch or tarnish the case. A fully wound watch can withstand a jar easier than a watch that has been allowed to run down. Always wind a watch and leave it running when you ship it. If you are one who enjoys carrying a watch, be sure to have it cleaned at least once every two years.

EXAMINATION AND INSPECTION OF A WATCH BEFORE PURCHASING

The examination & inspection of a watch before purchasing is of paramount importance. This is by no means a simple task, for there are many steps involved in a complete inspection.

The first thing you should do is to listen to a watch and see how it sounds. Many times the trained ear can pick up problems in the escapement and balance. The discriminating buyer will know that sounds cannot be relied on entirely because each watch sounds different, but the sound test is worthwhile and is comparable to the doctor putting a stethoscope to a patient's heart as his first source of data.

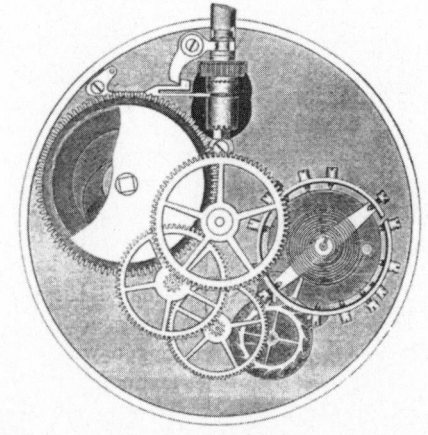

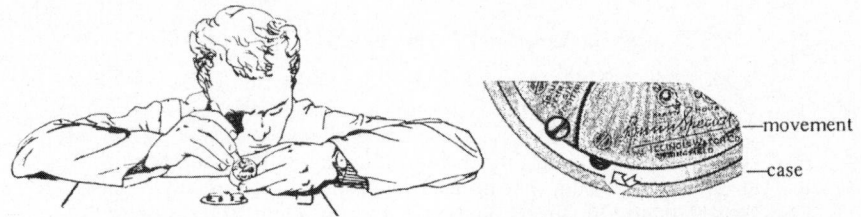

The screw on left is a case screw, extra screw mark (⟨ᴁᴏ⟩) on case indicates a recased watch.

Check the bow to see if it is securely fastened to the case and look at the case to see if correction is necessary at the joints. The case should close firmly at both the back and front. (If the case closes too firmly, rub the rim with beeswax which will ease the condition and prolong the life of the rim.) Take note of the dents, scratches, wear and other evidence of misuse. Does the watch have a generally good appearance? Check the bezel for proper fit and the crystal to see if it is free of chips. Remove the bezel and check the dial for chips and hairline cracks. Look for stains and discoloration and check to see if the dial is loose. It is important to note that a simple dial with only a single sunk dial is by nature a stronger unit due to the fact that a double sunk dial is constructed of three separate pieces. If it is a stem-winder, try winding and setting. Problems in this area can be hard to correct. Parts are hard to locate and may possibly have to be handmade. If it is a lever set, pull the lever out to see if it sets properly into gear. Also check to see that the hands have proper clearance.

Now that the external parts have been inspected, open the case to view the movement. Check to see that the screws hold the movement in place securely. Note any repair marks and any missing screws. Check for extra case screw marks on case, this indicates a recased watch. Check all the components for discoloration and similarity in color this will tell you if a part has been recently replaced. Make a visual check for rust and discoloration, dust, dirt and general appearance. If the movement needs cleaning and oiling, this should be deducted from the price of the watch, as well as any repair that will have to be made. Note the quality of the movement. Does it have raised gold jewel settings or a gold train (center wheel or all gears)? Are the jewels set in or pressed in? Does it have gold screws in the balance wheel? Diamond end stones? Jeweled motor barrel? How many adjustments does it have? Does it have overall beauty and eye appeal?

Examine the balance for truth. First look directly down upon the balance to detect error truth in the roundness. Then look at it from the side to detect error in the flat swing or rotation. It should be smooth in appearance. Examine the hairspring in the same manner to detect errors in truth. When a spring is true in the round, there will be no appearance of jumping when it is viewed from the upper side. The coils will appear to uniformly dilate and contract in perfect rhythm when the balance is in motion. Check the exposed portion of the train wheels for burred, bent, or broken teeth. Inspect pinions and pivots for wear. If a watch has complicated features such as a repeater, push the slides, plungers, and buttons to see that they are in good working order.

After the movement and case have been examined to your satisfaction and all the errors and faults are found, talk to the owner as to the history and his personal thoughts about the watch. Is the movement in the original case? Is the dial the original one? Just what has been replaced?

Has the watch been cleaned? Does it need any repairs? If so, can the seller recommend anyone to repair the watch? Finally, see if the seller makes any type of guarantee, and get an address and phone number. It may be valuable if problems arise, or if you want to buy another watch in the future.

HOW A WATCH WORKS

There are five basic components of a watch:

1. The mainspring, and its winding mechanism, which provides power.
2. The train which consists of gears, wheels & pinions that turn the hands.
3. The escapement consisting of the escape wheel and balance that regulates or controls.
4. The dial and hands that tell the time & setting mechanism.
5. The housing consisting of the case and plates that protect.

A watch is a machine with a power source that drives the escapement through a train of gears, and it has a subsidiary train to drive a hand. The motion of the balance serves the watch the same as a pendulum serves a clock. The balance wheel and roller oscillate in each direction moving the fork and lever by means of a roller jewel or pin. As the lever moves back and forth it allows the escape wheel to unlock at even intervals to insure equal time through the 24 hours and causes the train of gears to move in one direction under the power of the mainspring. Thus, the mainspring is allowed to be let down or unwind one pulse at a time. (The escape wheel moves in one direction similar to a turnstile.)

WATCH MOVEMENT PARTS

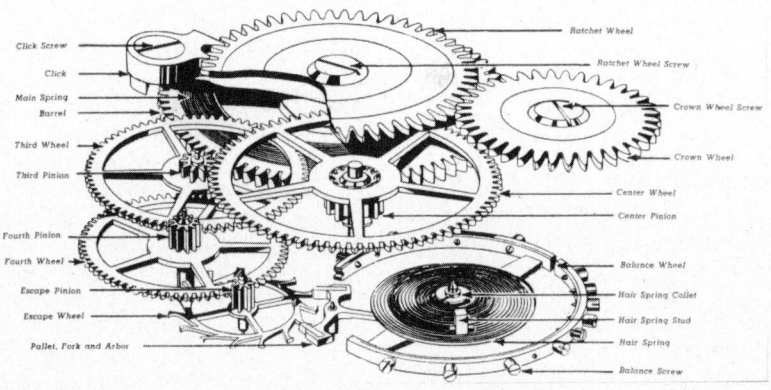

Mechanical watches are small engines powered by a main spring, which keeps the balance in motion. The uniformity of this motion relies on the balance and escapement the durability rests on the quality of material and construction of the complete movement.

JOIN THE AWI

For those interested in Horology as a profession or a vocation the authors of this book recommend the American Watchmakers-Clockmakers Institute. This international non-profit corporation is dedicated to the advancement of the art and science of horology. The AWI publishes the "Horological Times" a monthly magazine. The AWI offers watch & clock repair programs of one-week and two-week classes in various phases of watch & clock repair techniques. See their ad in the back of this book. For a brochure & sample copy of "Horological Times" phone (513) 367-9800 or write to: American Watchmakers-Clockmakers Institute
701 Enterprise Drive
Harrison, OH 45030

TRAIN OF A ELGIN VERITAS
(18 size 23 jewel) MOVEMENT & EACH PART NAMED

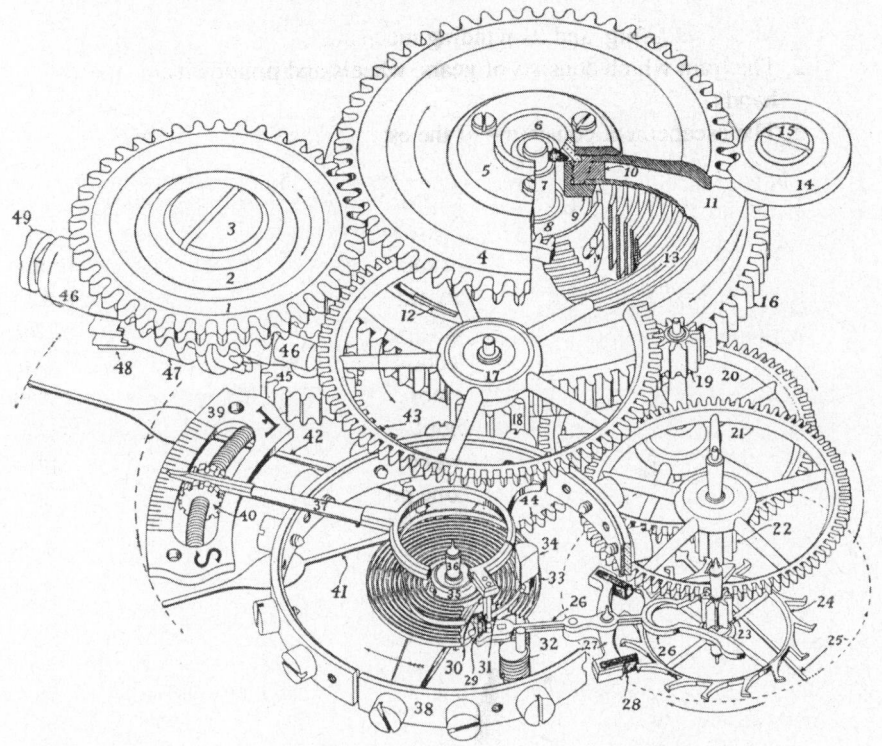

1 Main Wheel.
2 Main Wheel Washer.
3 Main Screw.
4 Ratchet Wheel.
5 Ratchet Wheel Washer.
6 Jewel Setting.
7 Barrel Arbor.
8 Barrel Arbor Hub.
9 Barrel Hub Screw.
10 Barrel Hub.
11 Barrel.
12 Main Spring Hooked.
13 Main Spring.
14 Recoiling Click.
15 Click Screw.
16 First Wheel.
17 Center Wheel.
18 Center Pinion.
19 Third Pinion.
20 Third Wheel.
21 Fourth Wheel.
22 Fourth Pinion.
23 Escape Pinion
24 Escape Wheel.
25 Second Hand

26 Fork or (Counter-poised lever)
27 Pallet
28 Pallet Stones.
29 Roller Jewel Pin.
30 Safety Roller.
31 Table Roller.
32 Banking Screws.
33 Dreg. Hair Spring.
34 Hair Spring Stud.
35 Hair Spring Collet
36 Balance Staff.
37 Regulator.
38 Balance.
39 Index.
40 Reg. Adj. Nut.
41 Hour Hand.
42 Minute Hand.
43 Minute Wheel.
44 Hour Wheel.
45 Setting Wheel.
46 Winding Arbor.
47 Wind. & Set Clutch.
48 Bevel Pinion.
49 Pendant Bar.

First Wheel 78 Teeth, 1 Rev. In 6 Hours, 30 Minutes.
Center Pinion 12 Teeth, 1 Rev, in 1 Hour.
Center Wheel 80 Teeth, 1 Rev. In 1 Hour.
3rd Pinion 10 Teeth, 1 Rev, in 7 1/2 Minutes.
3rd Wheel 75 Teeth, 1 Rev, in 7 1/2 Minutes.
4th Pinion 10 Teeth, 1 Rev, in 1 Minute.
4th Wheel 80 Teeth, 1 Rev, in 1 Minute.
Escape Pinion 8 Teeth, 1 Rev. In 6 Seconds.
Escape Wheel 15 teeth, 1 Rev, in 6 Seconds.
Balance Vibrates 30 times in 6 Seconds.
300 times in 1 Minute.
18,000 times in 1 Hour.
432,000 times in 1 Day.
157,680,000 times in 1 Year.

Note: Model is not the same definition as grade. A model may exist in many different grades & grade names (as Bunn, Riverside, Veritas) may be used in many different models (as model 1 18 size, model 1 in 16 size).

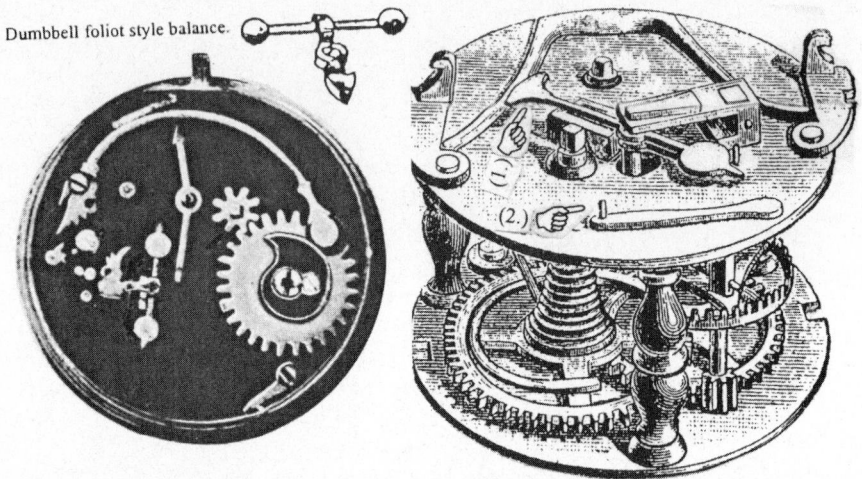

Dumbbell foliot style balance.

Early style watch with a stackfreed (tear shaped cam). Note the dumbbell shaped foliot balance & hog-bristle regulator.

Early Drum shaped portable tine-piece, (1.) note the foliot balance with T-shaped end, iron plates, 3 or 4 wheel train brass gut fusee on a steel great wheel, steel contrate wheel with brass teeth, (2.) hog-bristle regulator, about 34mm high. Examples of ball-shaped case with a loop on top allows the watch to be worn on a chain. Ca. 1530- 1550

TILE MAINSPRING

Watches were developed from the early portable clocks. The coiled spring or mainspring provided the drive power. The first coiled springs were applied to clocks about 1450. For the small portable watch, coiled springs were first used about 1470. The power from a mainspring is not consistent and this irregular power was disastrous to the first watches.

The Germans' answer to irregular power was a device called a stackfreed. Another apparatus employed was the fusee. The fusee proved to be the best choice. At first catgut was used between the spring barrel and fusee. By around 1660 the catgut was replaced by a chain. Today, the fusee is still used in naval chronometers. One drawback to the fusee is the amount of space it takes up in the watch. Generally, the simplest devices are best.

The mainspring is made of a piece of hardened and tempered steel about 20 inches long and coiled in a closed barrel between the upper and lower plates of the movement. It is matched in degree of strength, width, and thickness most suitable for the watch's need or design. It is subject to differing conditions of temperature and tensions (the wound-up position having the greatest tension). The lack of uniformity in the mainspring affects the time keeping qualities.

The power assembly in a watch consists of the mainspring, mainspring barrel, arbor, and cap. The mainspring furnishes the power to run the watch. It is coiled around the arbor and is contained in the mainspring barrel, which is cylindrical and has a gear on it which serves as the first wheel of the train. The arbor is a cylindrical shaft with a hook for the mainspring in the center of the body. The cap is a flat disk which snaps into a recess in the barrel. A hook on the inside of the mainspring barrel is for attaching the mainspring to the barrel.

The mainspring is made of a long thin strip of steel, hardened to give the desired resiliency. Mainsprings vary in size but are similar in design; they have a hook on the outer end to attach to the mainspring barrel, and a hole in the inner end to fasten to the mainspring barrel arbor.

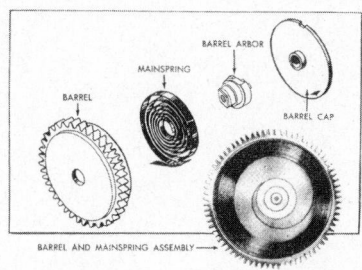

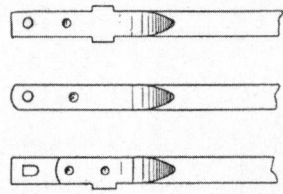

Power unit for modern watch showing the various parts.   Mainspring Bridles showing a few different designs.

By turning the crown clockwise, the barrel arbor is rotated and the mainspring is wound around it. The mainspring barrel arbor is held stationary after winding by means of the ratchet wheel and click. As the mainspring uncoils, it causes the mainspring barrel to revolve. The barrel is meshed with the pinion on the center wheel, and as it revolves it sets the train wheels in motion. Pocket and wrist watches, in most cases, will run up to 40 hours on one winding.

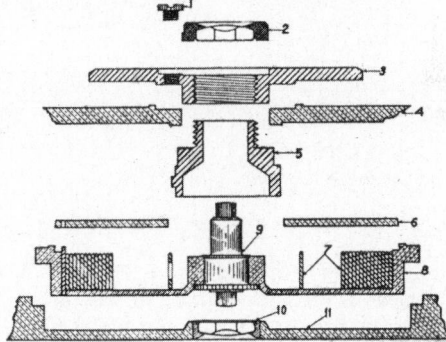

Jeweled Motor Barrel Unit: 1. Bane! top jewel screw. 2. Barrel top jewel and setting. 3. Ratchet wheel. 4. Barrel bridge. 5. Barrel hub. 6. Band head. 7. Mainspring (in barrel). 8. Barrel. 9. Barrel arbor (riveted to barrel). 10. Barrel lower jewel and setting. 11. Pillar plate.

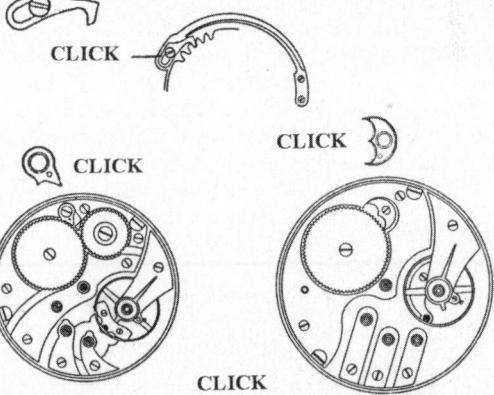

A click acts on the teeth of the ratchet wheel, so that the barrel-arbor can turn in one direction only, that of the winding. The click is made to mesh constantly with the ratchet teeth by the click spring. In older watches a device known as stop-work which restricted the two extremes of the mainspring was used. A modem watch uses the click-work which prevents the mainspring from being over wound by a certain amount of recoil.

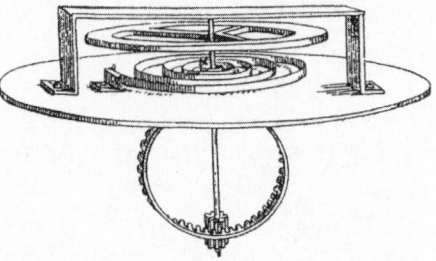

Above a sketch of Huygen's spiral balance spring. Also note the balance staff with a pinion driven by a wheel on the arbor carrying the balance spring is called a pirouette.

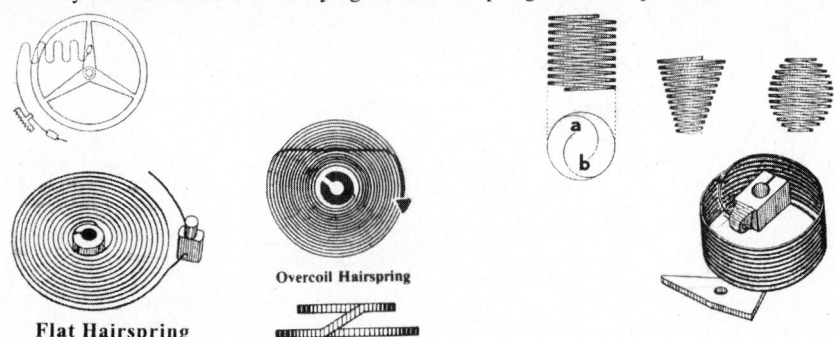

Overcoil Hairspring

Flat Hairspring

BALANCE - SPRING or HAIRSPRING

In about 1675 a contest between Huygens and Hooke for priority in inventing the spiral balance spring. The balance-spring or hairspring is the brain of the watch and is kept in motion by the mainspring. The hairspring is the most delicate tension spring made. It is a piece of flat wire about 12 inches long, 1/100th of an inch wide, 0.05mm or 0.0019685 inches thick, and weighs only about 1/9,000th of a pound. Thousands of these hairsprings can be made from one pound of steel. The hairspring controls the action of the balance wheel. The hairspring steel is drawn through the diamond surfaces to a third the size of a human hair. There are two kinds of hairsprings in the watches of later times, the flat one and the Breguet. The Breguet (named for its French inventor) is an overcoil given to the spring. There are two methods for overcoil, the oldest is the way the spring is bent by hand; and with the other method the overcoil is bent or completed in a form at one end and at the same time is hardened and tempered in the form. The hairspring contracts and expands 432,000 times a day.

A (Am. Waltham Co.) PATENTED regulator. Note the triangular shaped hairspring stud which is located on the balance bridge between the screw and curb pin.

REGULATORS
Identification

Overcoil
concentric to
travel of
regulator
pins

Regulator pins

Curve of Hairspring
overcoil

Hairspring
stud

Hairspring
stud screw

Regulator

Balance Cock

E. Howard & Co.

South Bend

AM. Waltham

Breguet

Ball
Howard
18S

Ball
Hamilton
18s

Ball
Elgin
18s

Ball
Hamilton
16s

Ball
Illinois
16s

Ball
Waltham
16s

Hampden

Marion

E. Howard & Co.

J.P. Stevens

F S

Agassiz

Waltham

Petek
Philippe

swiss- 2 piece

Fasoldt

Hampden

U.S. Waltham

U.S. Waltham

AM. Waltham

Early Columbus

REGULATORS
Identification

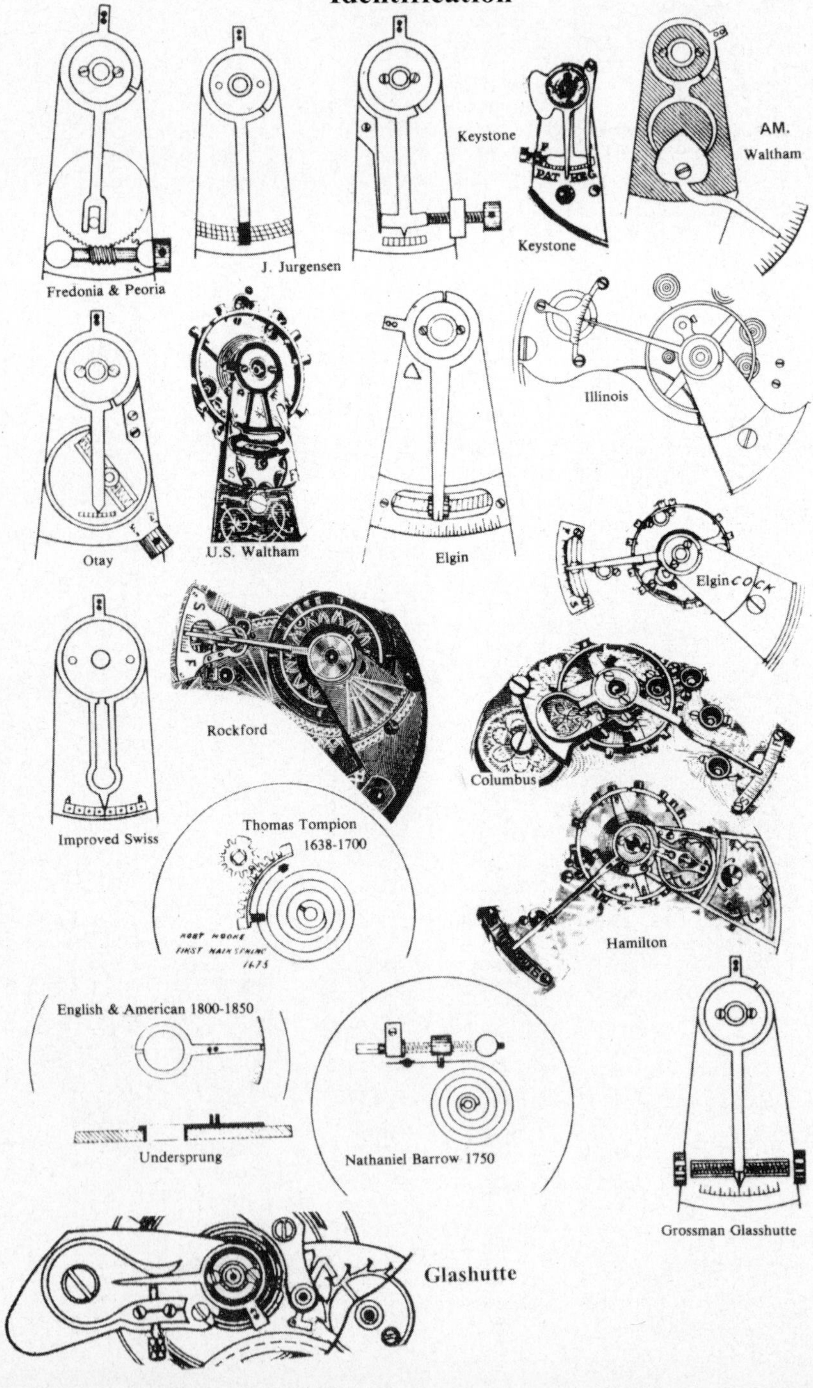

Keystone

AM.
Waltham

Keystone

Fredonia & Peoria

J. Jurgensen

Illinois

Otay

U.S. Waltham

Elgin

Elgin COCK

Rockford

Columbus

Improved Swiss

Thomas Tompion
1638-1700

ROBT HOOKE
FIRST MAINSPRING
1675

Hamilton

English & American 1800-1850

Undersprung

Nathaniel Barrow 1750

Grossman Glasshutte

Glashutte

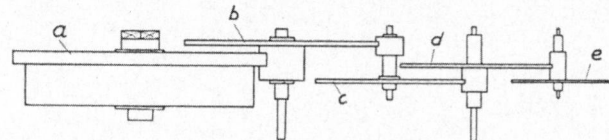

Elevation of a GEAR-TRAIN
(a) mainspring barrel. (b.) center wheel (carries minute hand), (c.) third wheel,
(d.) fourth wheel (carries seconds hand), (e.) escape wheel, 5 day watches use a
intermediate (8 day wheel) placed between the barrel and the center wheel.

THE TRAIN

The gear-train which, transmits mainspring-barrel torque to the escape-wheel consists of a four-wheel multiplying train. The time train consists of the mainspring barrel, center wheel and pinion, third wheel and pinion, fourth wheel and pinion, and escape wheel which is part of the escapement. The function of the time train is to reduce the power of the mainspring and extend its time to 36 hours or more. The mainspring supplies energy in small units to the escapement, and the escapement delays the power from being spent too quickly. The Escapement is the turnstile of the watch, metering out a tiny unit of power for each tick and tock.

The long center wheel arbor projects through the pillar plate and above the dial to receive the cannon pinion and hour wheel. The cannon pinion receives the minute hand and the hour wheel the hour hand. As the mainspring drives the barrel, the center wheel is rotated once each hour.

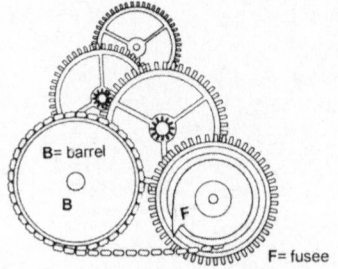

Alignment of chain driven fusee with train. Fusee at right and main-spring barrel at left. Note chain between fusee and main-spring barrel. F= fusee B= barrel

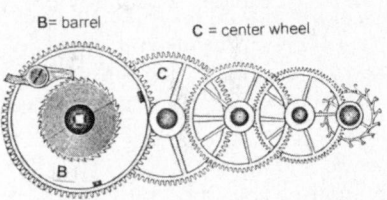

The gear-train which "transmits" mainspring-barrel torque to the escape wheel consists of a four-wheel multiplying train. B = barrel, C = center wheel

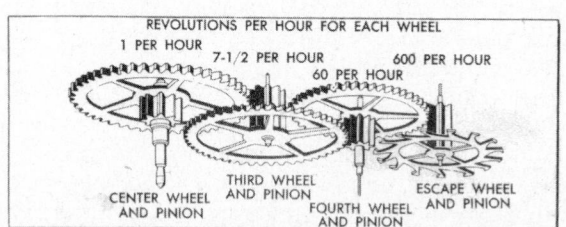

Actual alignment of **Train Unit**

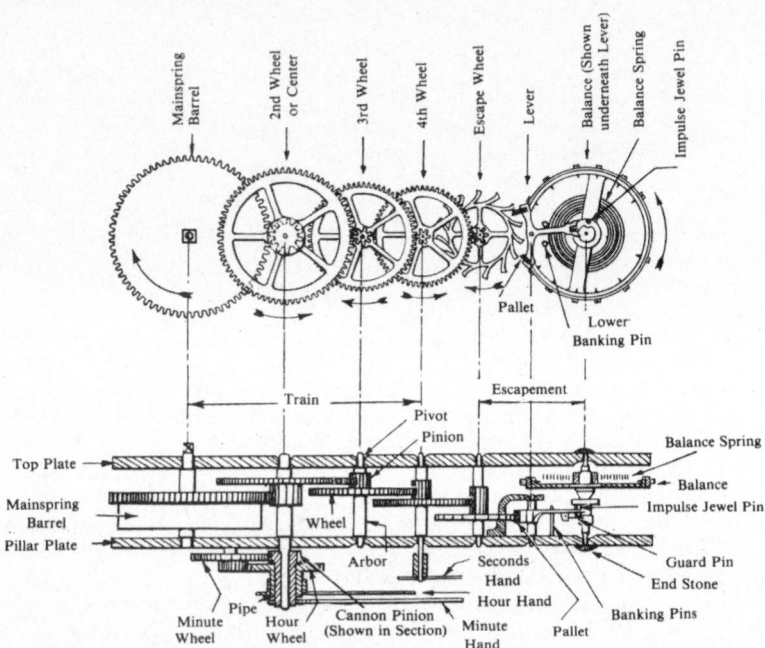

The second or center wheel of the watch turns once every hour. It is the second largest wheel in the watch, and the arbor or post of the center wheel carries the minute hand. The center wheel pinion is in mesh with the mainspring barrel (pinions follow and the wheel supplies the power). The center wheel is in mesh with the third wheel pinion (the third wheel makes eight turns to each of the center wheel). The third wheel is in mesh with the fourth wheel pinion and the fourth wheel pinion is in mesh with the escape wheel pinion. The fourth wheel post carries the second hand and is in a 1:60 ratio to the center wheel (the center wheel turns once every hour and the fourth wheel turns 60 turns every hour). The escape wheel has 15 teeth (shaped like a flat foot) and works with two pallets on the lever. The two pallet jewels lock and unlock the escape wheel at intervals(1/5 sec.) allowing the train of gears to move in one direction under the influence of the mainspring. The lever (quick train) vibrates 18,000 times to one turn of the center wheel (every hour). The hour hand works from a motion train. The mainspring barrel generally makes about five turns every 36 hours.

SOLID GOLD TRAIN

Some watches have a gold train instead of brass wheels. These watches are more desirable. To identify gold wheels within the train, look at a Hamilton 992; in most of these watches, the center wheel is made of gold and the other wheels are made of brass. Why a gold train? Pure gold is soft, but it has a smooth surface and it molds easily. Therefore, the wheels have less friction and properly alloyed, it is sturdy. These wheels do not move fast, and a smooth action is more important than a hard metal. Gold does not tarnish or rust and is non-magnetic. The arbors and pinions in these watches will be steel. Many watches have some gold in them and the collector should learn to distinguish it. Special note: Some wheels or gears are gold gilded on brass and not solid gold, the appearance is rough and not, as smooth as, solid gold gears or wheels.

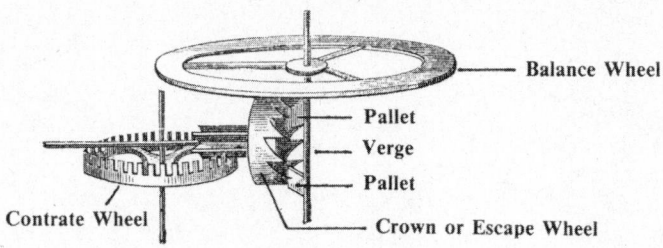

Balance Wheel

Pallet

Verge

Pallet

Contrate Wheel

Crown or Escape Wheel

ABOVE: **Verge Escapement**

TYPES OF ESCAPEMENTS

The purpose of the escapement is to control or maintain the rate of speed which causes the train to move in tiny increments in one direction (a governor). The verge escapement is the earliest form of escapement. It was first used in clocks as far back as the early 1300s. The verge escapement consists of a crown escape wheel, a verge which has two flags called pallets, and a balance. Early German watches had a balance shaped like a dumbbell, called a "foliot." Later most other watches used a balance shaped like a wheel. The crude weights of the foliot could be adjusted closer to or farther from the center of the balance for better time keeping. In about 1675 a contest between Huygens and Hooke for priority in inventing the spiral balance spring.

The verge escapement was used by Luther Goddard in America as well as most of the Colonial watchmakers.

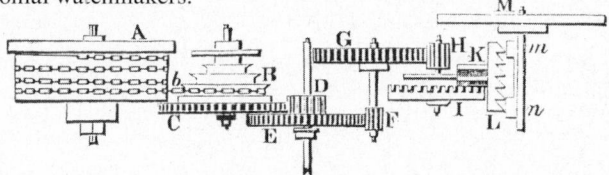

Movement of the common chain driven fusee & verge escapement.

A- is the barrel containing the mainspring. B.- is the fusee, to which the key is applied in winding, and which is connected with the barrel by the chain b. C.- is the fusee wheel, called also the first or great wheel, which turns with the fusee, and works into the pinion D, called the center-wheel pinion. This pinion, with the center-wheel, or second wheel, E, turns once in an hour. The center-wheel E works into the third-wheel pinion F; and on the same arbor is G, the third wheel, which drives the fourth or contrate-wheel pinion H, and along with it the contrate wheel I. The teeth of this wheel are placed at right angles to its plane, and act in the pinion K, called the balance-wheel pinion, L being the balance-wheel, escape-wheel, or crown-wheel. The escape-wheel acts on the two pallets, m and n attached to the verge, or arbor, of the balance M, which regulates the movement.

Note: Escapements may be classified into 2 categories Frictional & Detached. (1.) Frictional Escapements example: Verge, Virgule, Duplex and Cylinder. (2.) Detached or Free Escapements example Lever Escapements, Detent Escapements also combination of lever, detent and Rotating Escapement as Karrusel and Tourbillon. Frictional Escapements the escape wheel is in contact with the balance staff or a part of it during the whole oscillation of the balance. Detached or Free Escapements have an arrangement where the escape teeth wheel are arrested for unlocking & impulse & then made free. Thus the Balance can rotate an arc of an oscillation with complete freedom.

☞ The isochronism test consists of reading your watch every two hours until the watch has run down. This will show how much the rate varies according to the time elapsed since winding.

Escape Wheel
Cylinder

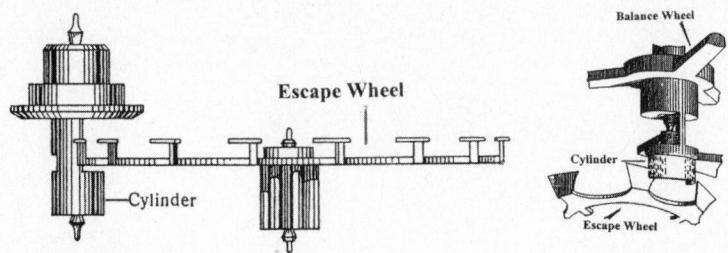

Right: Cylinder Escapement

Balance Wheel
Cylinder
Escape Wheel

Left: Breguet's Hanging Ruby Cylinder Escapement

About 1695 the cylinder escapement was invented by Tompion & improved by George Graham, both Englishman. The cylinder escapement was a great improvement over the verge. Even so, the cylinder escapement was not popular until Abraham Louis Breguet adopted the idea in the late 1790s. Thomas Mudge's invention of the detached lever escapement in about 1759. (Below)

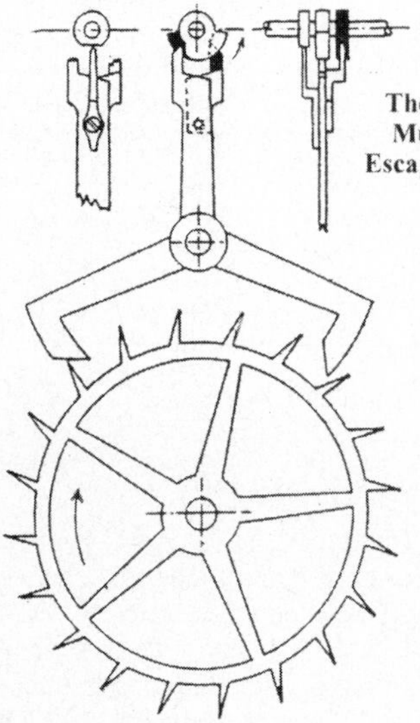

Thomas Mudge Escapement

Thomas Mudge Escapement

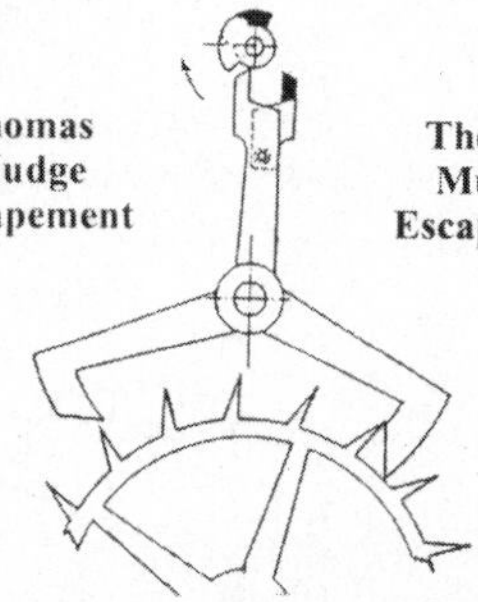

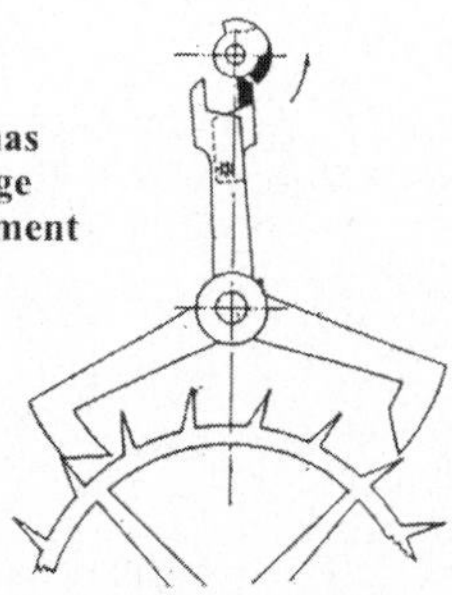

Below: Duplex Escapement

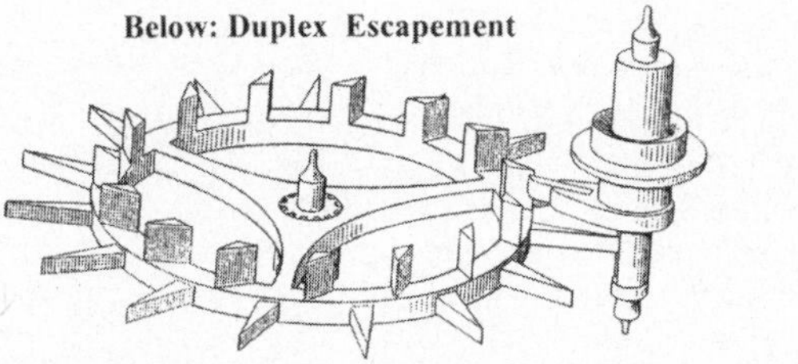

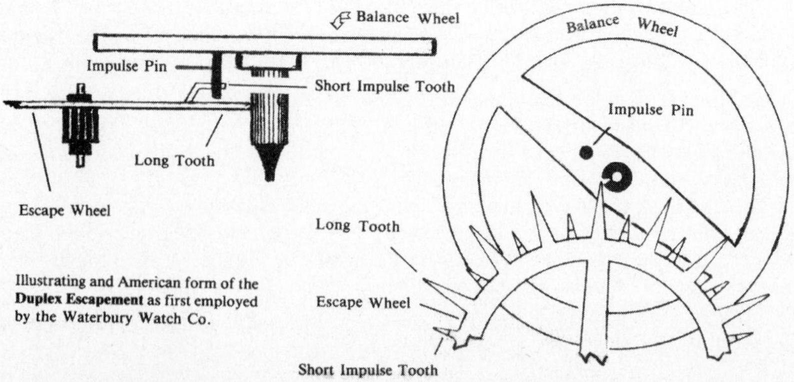

Balance Wheel
Impulse Pin
Short Impulse Tooth
Long Tooth
Escape Wheel
Balance Wheel
Impulse Pin
Long Tooth
Escape Wheel
Short Impulse Tooth

Illustrating and American form of the **Duplex Escapement** as first employed by the Waterbury Watch Co.

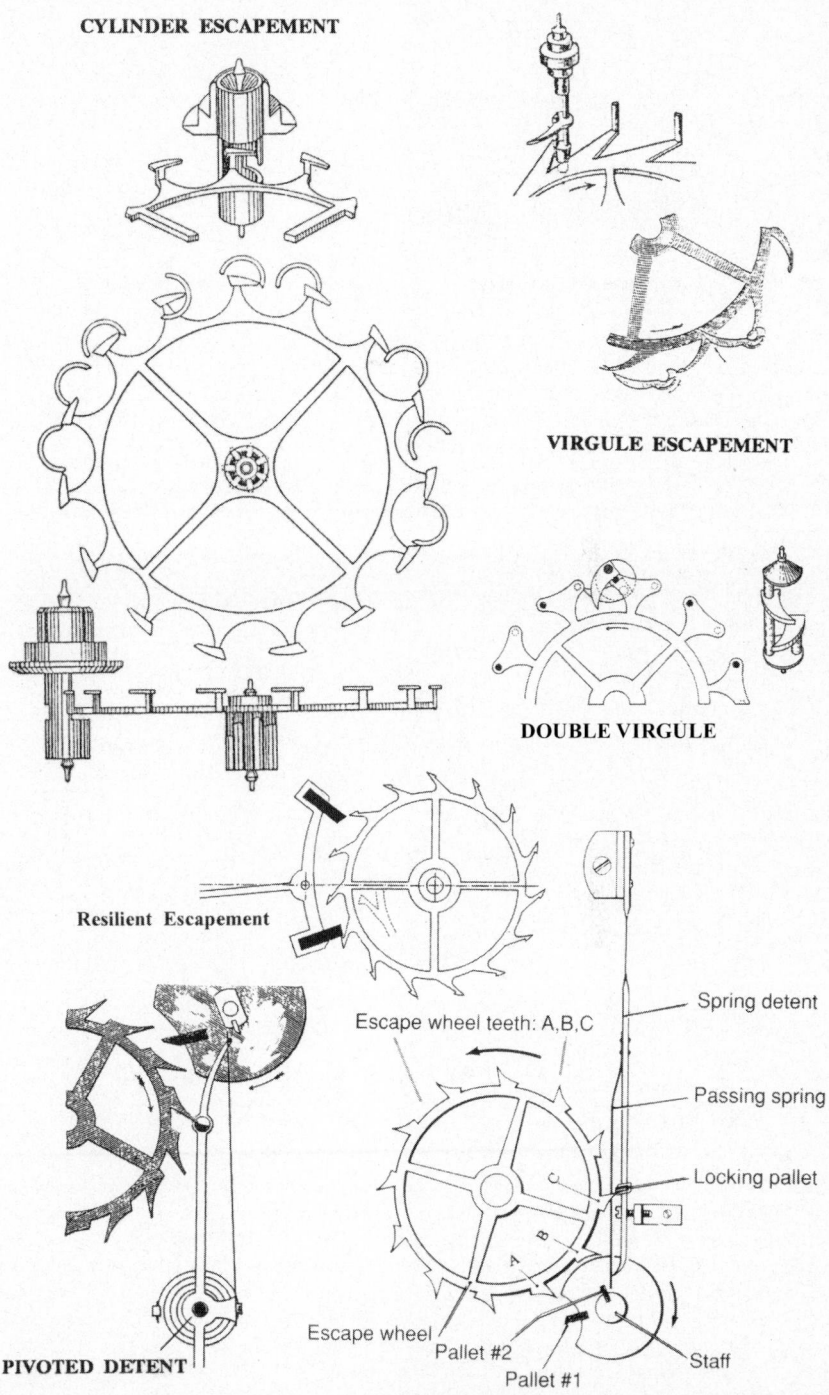

CYLINDER ESCAPEMENT

VIRGULE ESCAPEMENT

DOUBLE VIRGULE

Resilient Escapement

Escape wheel teeth: A,B,C

Spring detent

Passing spring

Locking pallet

Escape wheel

Pallet #2

Pallet #1

Staff

PIVOTED DETENT

SPRING DETENT (chronometer escapement)

64

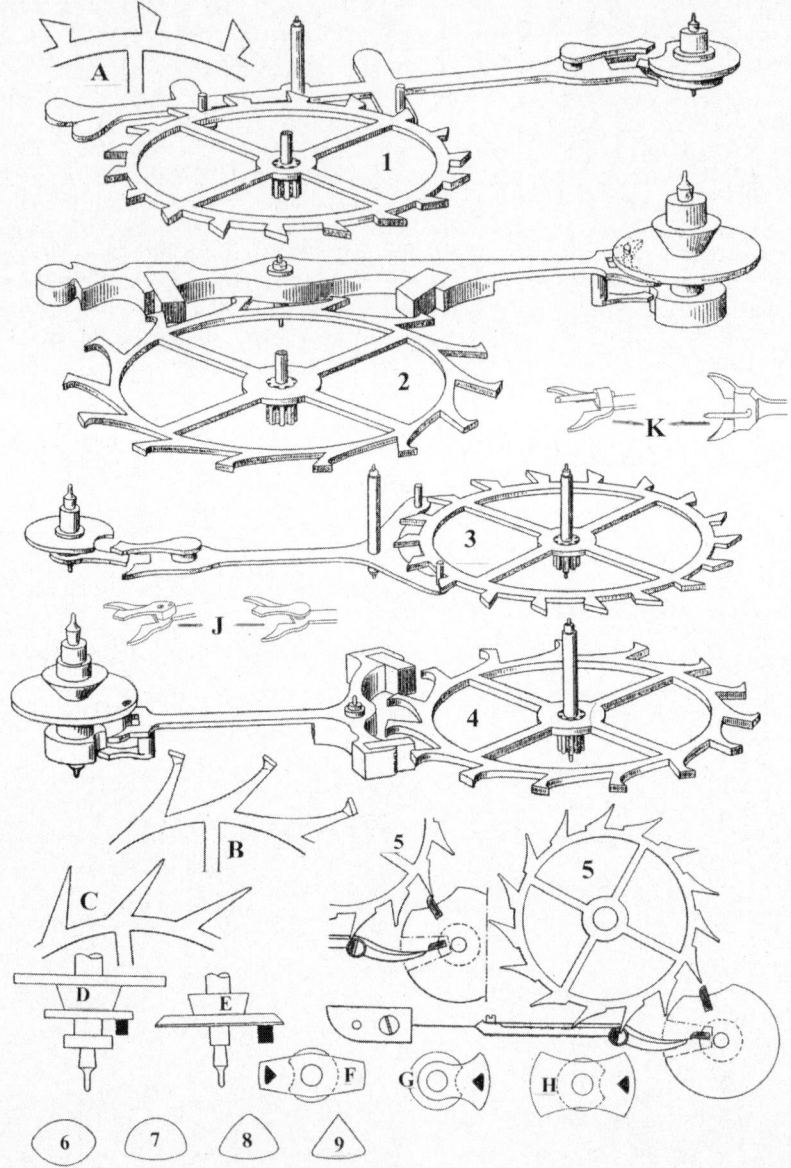

The Escapement has many modifications, long and short lever, single and two roller table, right angle and straight line lever, pointed teeth and club-teeth escape wheel. Escapements (1) & (2) right angle lever and (3) & (4) straight line lever. (5) Chronometer Spring Detent Escapement. (A) Club-Tooth escape wheel, (B) Club-tooth escape wheel, (C) Pointed tooth escape wheel. (D) Double Roller made of 2 discs, upper disc with the impulse jewel is called the impulse roller and the lower disc is the safety roller. (E) Single Roller made of 1 disc with impulse jewel. (F)-(G)-(H) different style of table & safety rollers. (J)-(K) different style horns, safety fingers or guard pins. (6-7-8-9-) different style impulse jewels. (6) nearly elliptic. (7) semi-circular with convex base. (8) triangular with convex sides and radius corners. (9) triangular with one convex side.

Escape wheel is fixed on the last pinion of the train.

DeLONG Escapement

The Charles E. DeLong upright D shaped pallet escapement is similar to a Brocot escapement and may be seen in front of the dial in some French clocks. The Delong pallets are slightly over half-cylinder shaped and are staked into a steel lever having holes with spring action and require no cement. The DeLong escapement can be found and listed in the Ball, Hamilton and Illinois pricing sections under the heading 16 size as DeLong upright D shaped pallet escapement. Manhattan used their own version of upright D shaped pallet type of escapement as early 1883-84. Delong had patents No. 1,192,812 in July, 1916 and No. 1,327,226 in 1920. He claimed a watch to have strong draw and the recoil was extremely low and his escapement system was not interchangeable (different in many respects). Some of his escapement depthing could be adjusted by rotating the arbor which used a eccentric style pivot on the pallet arbor. In 1908 he was employed by McIntyre W. Co. and 1912 to 1919 by Illinois W. Co..

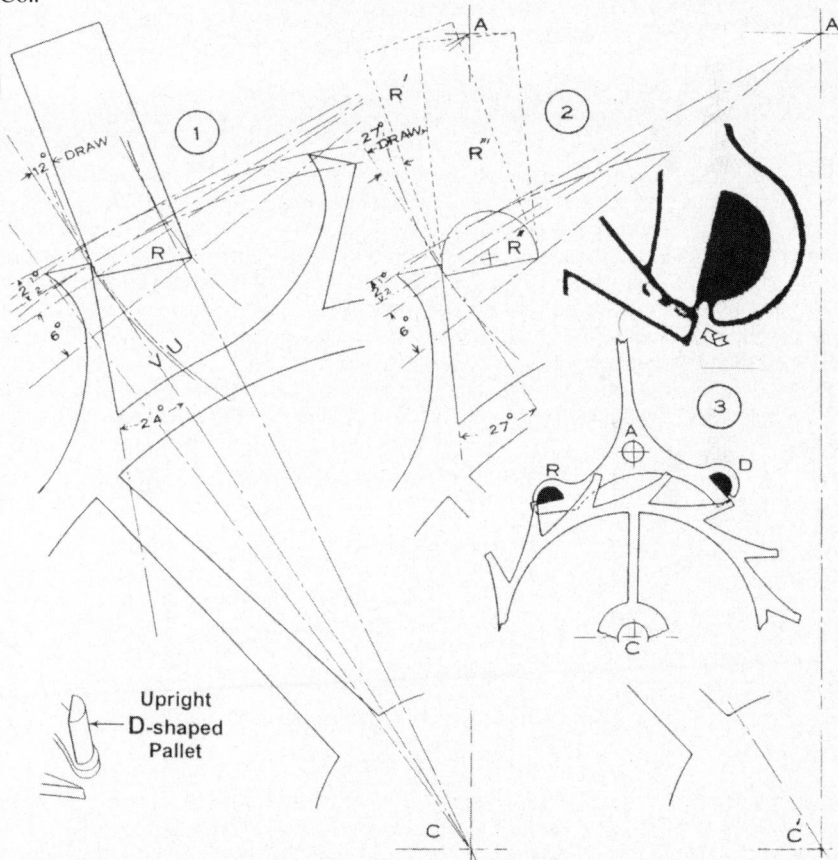

Above comparison of the standard lever escapement and the DeLong escapement.
(1.)- Receiving pallet action in standard escapement. The distance between arcs V & U show the distance the escape wheel must be turned back by stored energy in the balance during unlocking.
(2.)- With same center distance and same lift and lock the arrangement of the Delong D shaped pallet giving 27 degree lock instead of 12 degree as in Fig 1. The pallet R''' with rounded locking corner is a possible substitution of R''.
(3.)- Note: The R and D pallets are staked into spring friction holes in the lever.

The duplex escapement is accredited generally to Pierre LeRoy, a Frenchman, around 1750, but was never popular in France. This type of escapement was favored in England up to the mid 1850s. The New England Watch Co. of Waterbury, Conn., used the duplex from 1898 until 1910. The Waterbury Watch Company used it from 1880 to 1898. The roller and lever escapement was invented by Thomas Mudge in about 1750.

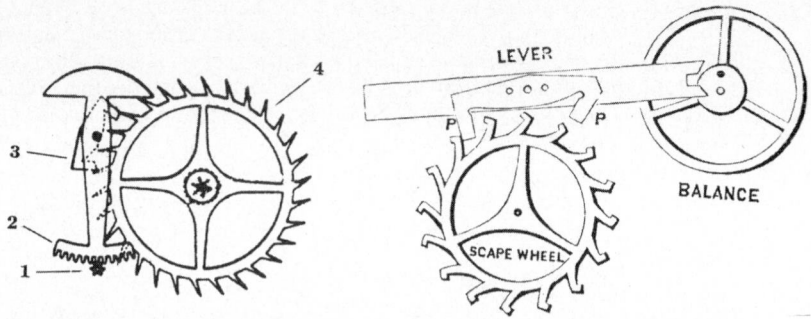

Rack and pinion lever escapement. 1. Balance wheel pinion. 2. Rack. 3. Lever. 4. Ratchet escape wheel

Right Angle Lever Used in earlier American made watches & the Detached Escapement which was used extensively in England. note: P = pallet.

The rack and pinion lever escapement was invented by Hautefeuille in 1722. The famous Breguet used the detached lever escapement early in the 1800s. By 1830 the English watchmakers had established the superiority of the lever escapement. In France and Switzerland the teeth of the lever escapement wheel were boot-shaped to provide a wider impulse plane. In England, pointed or ratchet teeth were preferred, and the right-angle lever was preferred over the straight line lever, also referred to as the Swiss lever. Pitkins and Custer both used the lever escapements. The right-angle lever was used in the early Am. Walthams, Elgin, Newark, Tremont, New York, Hampden, Illinois, Cornell, and other early American watches. The American factories settled on a Swiss style escapement (straight line lever & club tooth escape wheel) by the 1870s.

The escape wheel turns in one direction much as a turnstile.

Purpose of Escape Wheel

The purpose of the escapement is to control or maintain the rate of speed which causes the train to move in tiny increments in one direction (a governor). If a movement consisted only of the mainspring and a train of wheels, and the mainspring were wound up, the train would run at full speed resulting in the power being spent in a few moments. For this reason, the escapement has been arranged to check it (the brakes). The duty of the escapement is to allow each tooth of the escape wheel to pass at a regulated interval. The escapement is of no service alone and, therefore, must have some other arrangement to measure and regulate these intervals. This is accomplished by the balance assembly.

The escape wheel is in most cases made of steel and is staked on a pinion and arbor. It is the last wheel of the train and connects the train with the escapement. It is constructed so that the pallet jewels move in and out between its teeth, allowing but one tooth to escape at a time, turnstile fashion. The teeth are club-foot-shaped for additional impulse.

The pallet jewels are set at an angle to make their inside corners reach over three teeth and two spaces of the escape wheel. The outside corners of the jewels will reach over two teeth and three spaces of the escape wheel with a small amount of clearance. At the opposite end of the pallet, directly under the center of the fork slot, is a steel or brass pin called the guard pin. The fork is the connecting link to the balance assembly.

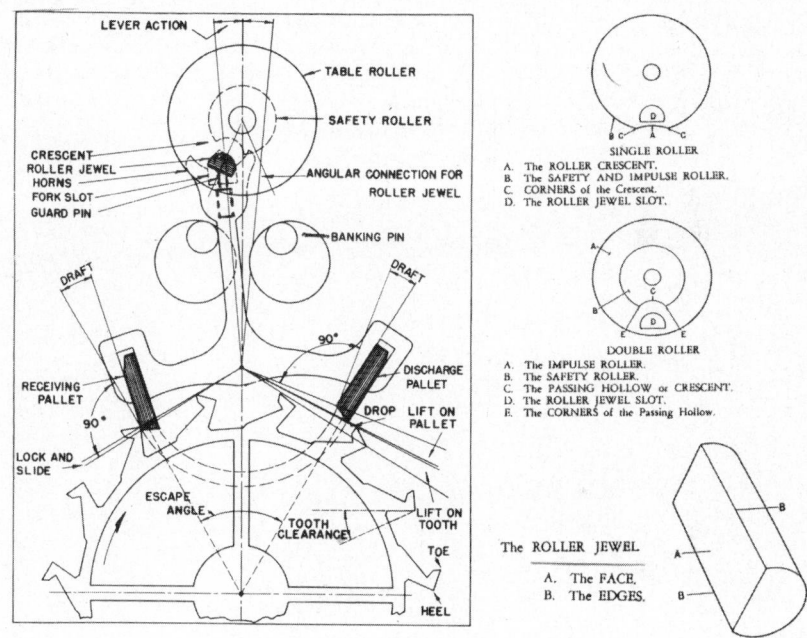

BALANCE AND HAIRSPRING

In earlier watches the hairspring was just that. Bristles from a wild boar was used to control the balance wheel. The spiral hair-spring was invented in about 1675. The rotation of the balance wheel is controlled by the hairspring. The inner end of the hairspring is pinned to the collet, and the collet is held friction-tight on the staff above the balance wheel.

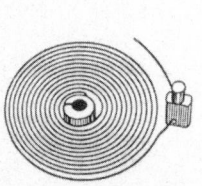

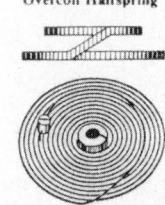

Left: example of flat hairspring.　　　Center: Balance & Hairspring.　　　Right: example of Breguet or overcoil hairspring.

68

The outer end of the hairspring is pinned to a stud which is held stationary on the balance cock by the stud screw. The roller jewel is cemented in the large roller assembly, which is mounted on the staff directly under the balance wheel. Under the first roller is a smaller one which acts as a safety roller. This is necessary because of the crescent cut out in the roller table which allows the guard pin of the escapement assembly to pass through.

The balance wheel rotates clockwise and counterclockwise on its axis by means of the impulse it receives from the escapement. The motion of the balance wheel is constant due to the coiling and uncoiling of the hairspring. The impulse, transmitted to the roller jewel by the swinging of the pallet fork to the left, causes the balance to rotate in a counterclockwise direction. The position of the fork allows the roller jewel to move out of the slot of the fork freely and in the same direction. The fork continues on until it reaches the banking pin. Meanwhile the balance continues in the same direction until the tension of the hairspring overcomes the momentum of the balance wheel. When this occurs the balance returns to its original position, which causes the roller jewel to again enter the slot of the fork.

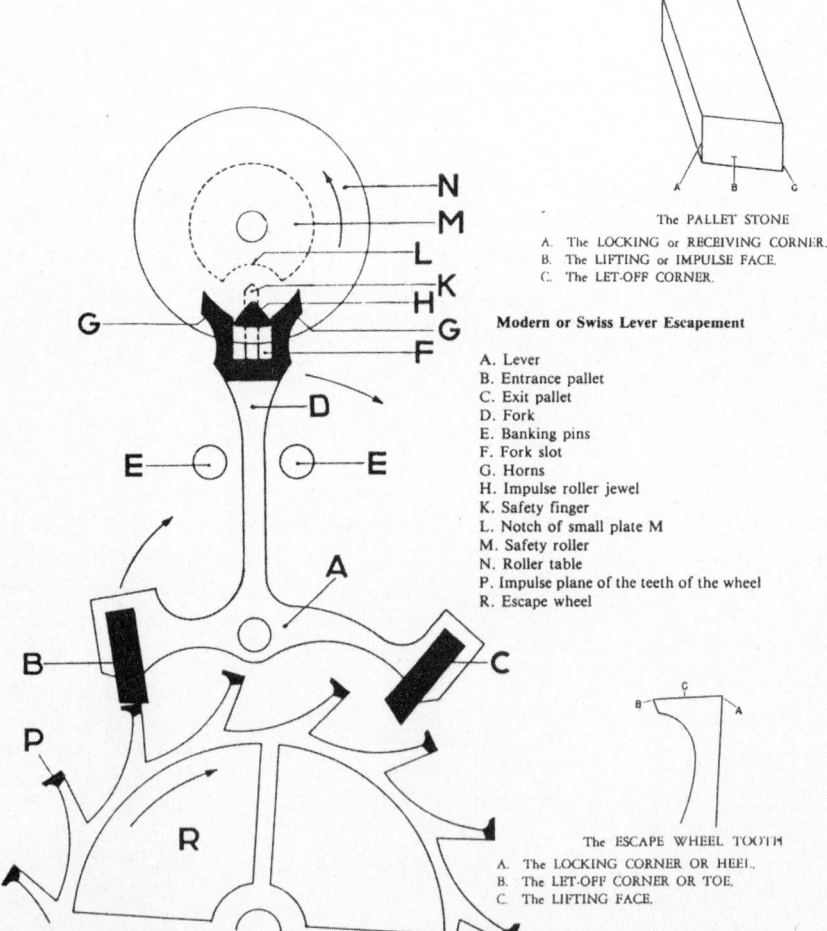

The PALLET STONE

A. The LOCKING or RECEIVING CORNER.
B. The LIFTING or IMPULSE FACE.
C. The LET-OFF CORNER.

Modern or Swiss Lever Escapement

A. Lever
B. Entrance pallet
C. Exit pallet
D. Fork
E. Banking pins
F. Fork slot
G. Horns
H. Impulse roller jewel
K. Safety finger
L. Notch of small plate M
M. Safety roller
N. Roller table
P. Impulse plane of the teeth of the wheel
R. Escape wheel

The ESCAPE WHEEL TOOTH

A. The LOCKING CORNER OR HEEL.
B. The LET-OFF CORNER OR TOE.
C. The LIFTING FACE.

Pallet and Escape Tooth Action. The momentum that has been built up during the return of the balance, causes the roller pin to impart an impulse on the inside of the fork slot. This impulse is great enough to push the fork away from its position against the banking pin. As the fork is pushed away, it causes the pallet stone to slide on the toe of the escape wheel tooth. When the pallet stone has slid down to its edge, it frees the escape wheel tooth, thereby unlocking the escape wheel. The escape wheel, being impelled by the force of the mainspring, starts to rotate. As the escape wheel turns, the tooth glides along the impulse face of the pallet jewel, forcing it to move out of the way. The moving pallet carries the fork with it and imparts the impulse to the roller jewel. The right pallet stone intercepts a tooth of the escape wheel to lock it, as the fork moves toward the banking pin. Having a short "run" left to the banking pin, the pressure of the escape wheel tooth against the locking face of the pallet jewel draws the stone deeper into the escape wheel and, therefore, causes the fork to complete its run and holds it against the banking pin. Meanwhile the balance continues in a clockwise direction until the tension of the hairspring overcomes the momentum of the balance and returns it to its original position.

Rate of Escape Tooth Release. Through the motion of the escapement, the mainspring keeps the balance vibrating, and the balance regulates the train. The escape wheel has 15 teeth and is allowed to revolve 10 turns per minute. Thus, 150 teeth glide over each pallet stone in 1 minute. The gliding of the escape wheel teeth over the impulse faces of the pallet stones will cause the balance to vibrate 300 vibrations or beats per minute. These vibrations will continue until the force of the mainspring is spent.

SCREWS

Screws used in watches are very small and precise. These screws measure 254 threads to the inch and 47,000 of them can be put into a thimble. The screws were hardened and tempered and polished to a cold hard brilliance. By looking at these screws through a magnifying glass one can see the uniformity.

EQUIDISTANT ESCAPEMENT

The term Equidistant Escapement is a form of lever escapement. The locking of each pallet takes place at the same distance from the pallet arbor. A similar form of escapement is the circular pallet with the circular form of escapement. The impulses are given at equal distance from the center line. The Swiss preferred the equidistant while the Americans preferred the circular. There is little difference in performance between these two types of escapement.

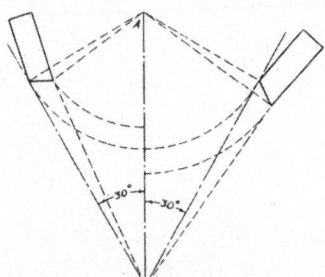

Equidistant form of Escapement

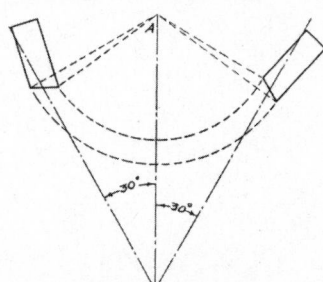

Circular form of Escapement

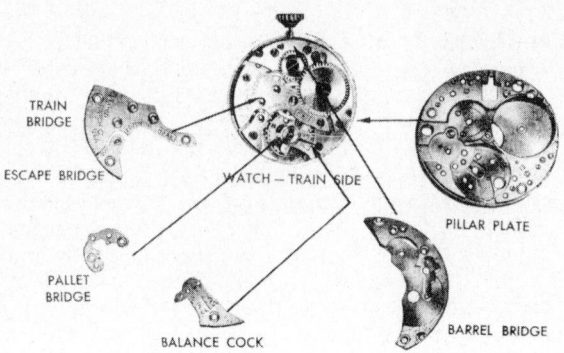

TRAIN
BRIDGE

ESCAPE BRIDGE

WATCH — TRAIN SIDE

PILLAR PLATE

PALLET
BRIDGE

BALANCE COCK

BARREL BRIDGE

The plates and bridges which hold all the parts in proper relation to each other.

THE PLATES

The movement of a watch has two plates and the works are sandwiched in between. The plates are called the top plate and the pillar plate. The top plate fully covers the movement. The 3/4 plate watch and the balance cock are flush and about 1/4 of a full plate is cut out to allow for the balance, thus the 3/4 plate. The bridge style watch has two or three fingers to hold the wheels in place and together are called a bridge. The term bridge (horologically) is one that is anchored at both ends. A cock is a wheel support that is attached at one end only. English balance cock for verge watches and lever watches have but one screw. French and Dutch verge watches have their balance bridges secured at both ends. The metal is generally brass, but on better grade watches, nickel is used. The full plate is held apart by four pillars. In older watches the pillars were very fancy, and the plates were pinned, not screwed, together. The plates can be gilded or engraved when using brass. Some of the nickel plates have damaskeening. There are a few watches with plates made of gold. The plates are also used to hold the jewels, settings, etc. Over 30 holes are drilled in each plate for pillars, pivots, and screws.

The pinion is the smaller of the two wheels that exist on the shaft or arbor. They are small steel gears and usually have six teeth called leaves. Steel is used wherever there is great strain, but where there is much friction, steel and brass are used together; one gear of brass, and a pinion of steel. After the leaves have been cut, the pinions are hardened, tempered, and polished.

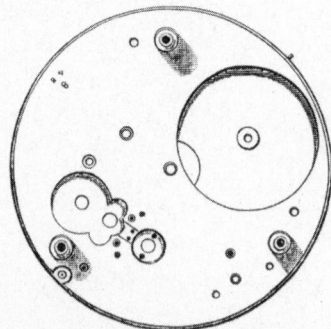

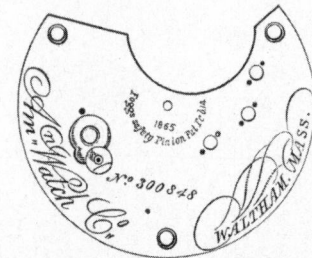

LEFT = PILLAR PLATE

RIGHT = TOP PLATE -(3/4 plate)

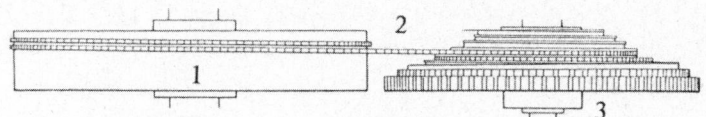

THE FUSEE FIRST UTILIZED IN 1525
1. MAINSPRING BARREL   2. FUSEE CHAIN   3. FUSEE WHEEL

THE FUSEE

A mainspring gives less and less power as it lets down. To equalize the power a fusee was first used. Fusee leverage increases as the main spring lets down. A fusee is smaller at the top for a full mainspring. When the chain is at the bottom, the mainspring is almost spent, and the fusee has more leverage. Leonardo da Vinci is said to have invented the fusee.

When the mainspring is fully wound, it also pulls the hardest. At that time the chain is at the small end of the fusee. As the spring grows weaker, the chain descends to the larger part of the fusee. In shifting the tension, it equalizes the power.

On the American watch, the fusee was abandoned for the most part in 1850 and an adjustment is used on the hairspring and balance wheel to equalize the power through the 24 hours. When a watch is first wound the mainspring has more power than it does when it is nearly run down. With or without the fusee, the number of parts in a watch are about the same: close to 300.

NOTE: Most fusee style watches wind to left or counter-clock wise. Most non-fusse watches wind clock-wise.

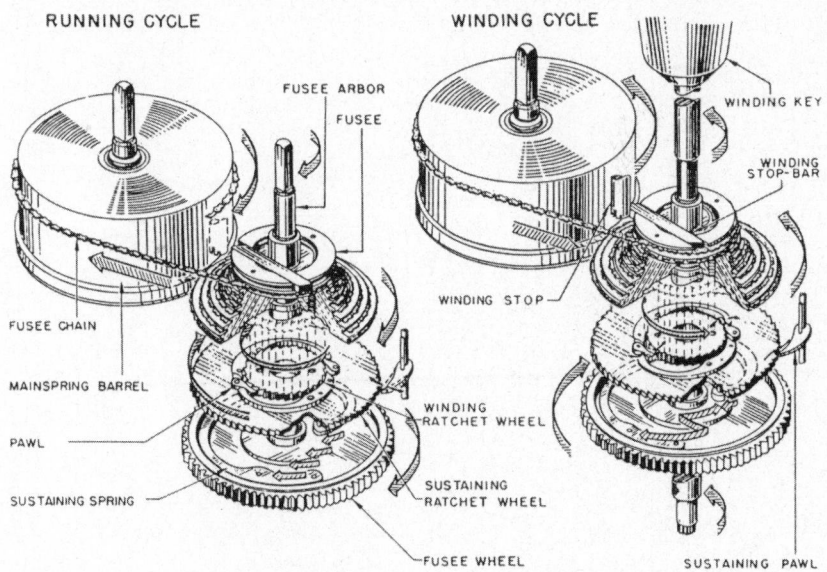

The above is a HAMILTON MODEL 21 FUSEE used in a Ships Chronometer.

Note the sustaining spring which is also called maintaining spring, to avoid a watch from trying to stop while being wound, therefore maintaining the power to the escapement, this device was introduced by Harrison.

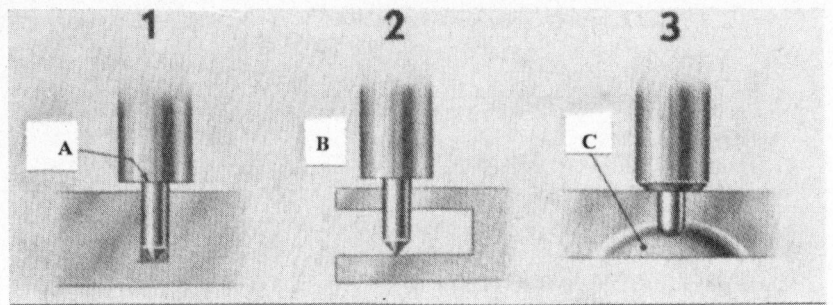

1. Illustration of pivot before 1700. 2. Pivot used in early 1700s. 3. Pivot used in late 1700s.

JEWELS AND PIVOTS

Before 1700, holes were drilled only part way into the plates and the pivot rested directly on the bottom of the hole, as in Illustration No. 1. The shoulder of the pivot was above the plate, however, reducing part of the function, as in Illustration No. 1A. In the early 1700s, a French watchmaker, Sully, improved the pivot friction as seen in Illustration No. 2B. Illustration No. 3 shows a later improvement, perfected by Julien Le Roy.

N. F. de Duiller of Geneva, in conjunction with Peter and Jacob Debaufre, French immigrants living in London, developed a method of piercing jewels. This method was patented in 1704; however, it was not until around 1800 that holed jewels started to appear in watch movements and then only in high grade watches.

In the mid-1800s experiments were already being made for artificial rubies. In 1891 Fremy solved the problem and by the early 1900s the reconstructed ruby was popular.

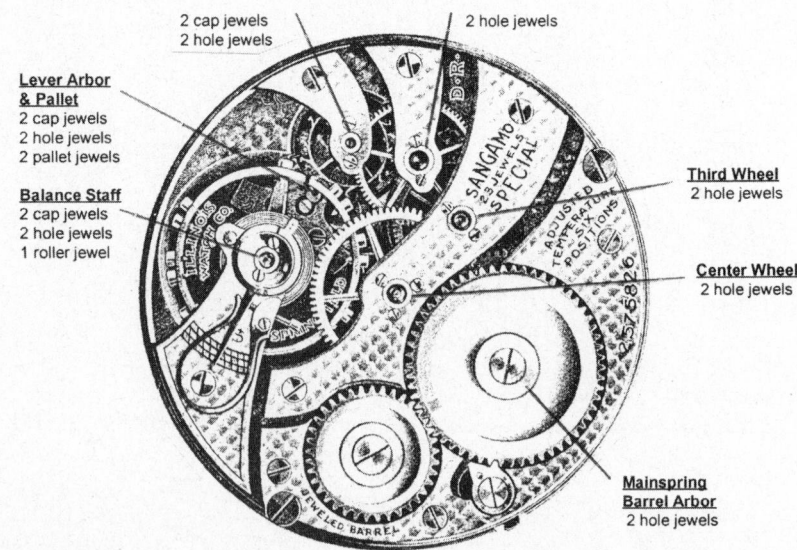

Jewel Count and location for a 23 Jewel, 16 Size, Samago Special. (Ca.1913)

SHOCK ABSORBERS

When a watch is dropped or subjected to a hard shock, the balance and pivots usually suffer the most. A shock-resisting device was invented by Breguet in 1789; he called it a parachute; This device was a spring steel arm supporting the endstone. The parachute gives a cushioning effect to the balance staff. The American watch industry tried to find a device to protect pocket watch pivots, but it was the Swiss who perfected the device for wrist watches around 1933.

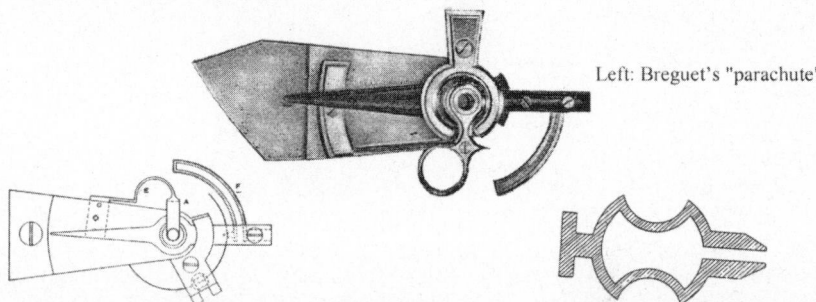

Left: Breguet's "parachute"

Above: A & E = **Parachute,** popular after 1800. (**F** for temperature)   Above **Right**: Incabloc 1st used about 1933.

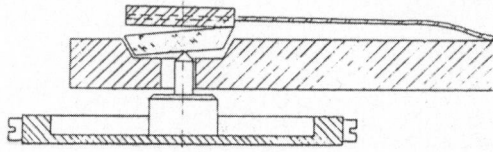

Above: Illustrates Parachute shock absorbing system. Note end stone and spring in raised position giving a cushioning effect to the balance staff.

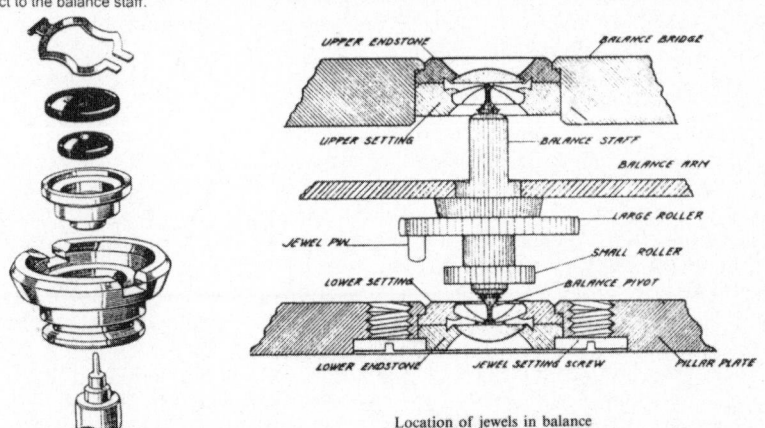

Location of jewels in balance

Above LEFT : Incabloc spring, cap-jewel, hole jewel, bearing block & balance-staff.

NOTE: Collectable watches with a higher jewel count usually demand a greater price, when watches were produced the higher the jewel count the higher the cost, however, lower production of some models this collectable rule does not apply. Example 7, 11 and 15 jewel Hamiltons will bring higher prices than a 17 jewel Hamilton, also a 19 jeweled "Sangamo Special" will bring a higher price than 21 jeweled "Sangamo Special". Most American made watches with 15 jewels and up are marked. Generally speaking it is accepted that good to medium quality watches have 15 to 17 jewels and are said to be "fully jeweled".

When counting visible jewels beware that some manufactures added non-functional jewels for eye appeal, disassembling the watch is the only way to get a true accurate count.

COUNTERPOISED LEVER

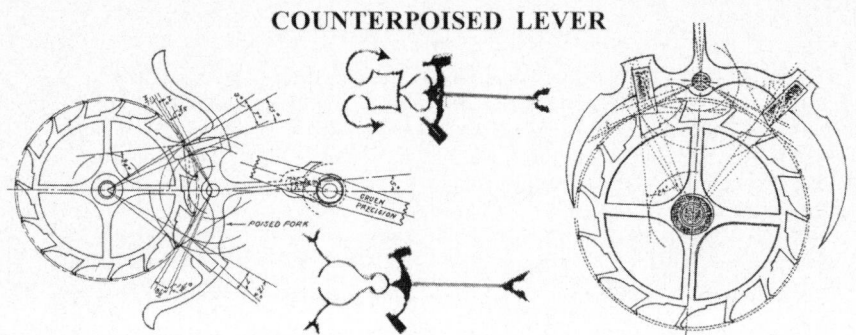

Left:Example of counterpoised Lever used in some of D. Gruen Extra Precision watches. This style counterbalance lever is referred to as a "Moustache" lever. (may be GOLD)

Right: Example of Counterpoised Lever used in Elgin found in some early 12 size, grade 190. This style counterbalance lever is referred to as a "Moustache" lever.

TYPES OF JEWELS

Watch jewels are of four distinct types, each type having a particular function. (1) HOLE JEWELS. Hole jewels are used to form the bearing surface for wheel arbors and balance staff pivots. (2) CAP JEWELS. Cap jewels (also called end stones) are flat jewels. They are positioned at the ends of wheel staffs, outside the hole jewels, and limit the end thrust of the staff (3) ROLLER JEWELS. The roller jewel (pin) is positioned on the roller table to receive the impulse for the balance from the fork. (4) PALLET JEWELS. The pallet jewels (stones) are the angular shaped jewels positioned in the pallet to engage the teeth of the escape wheel.

JEWEL COUNT (American)

Jewels are used as bearings to reduce metal-to-metal contacts which produce friction and wear. They improve the performance and accuracy of the watch, and materially prolong its usefulness. The materials used for making watch jewels are diamonds, sapphires, rubies, and garnets. The diamond is the hardest but is seldom used except for cap jewels. The sapphire is the next in hardness and is the most commonly used because of its fine texture. Garnets are softer than sapphires and rubies.

Number and Location of Jewels. Most American watches have either 7, 9, 11, 15, 17, 19, 21, or 23 jewels. The problem in jewel counting is that you can not see the jewels in the pillar plate. In most American watches, 9,11 and 13 jewel watches the extra jewels (the other half) are in the top plate not in the pillar plate. So do not assume all jewels are in pairs. The location of the jewels vary somewhat in different makes & grades, but the general practice is as follows:

7 JEWEL WATCHES. Seven-jewel watches have: two hole jewels-one at each end of the balance staff; two cap jewels-one at each end of the balance staff one roller jewel; and two pallet jewels.

9-11-13 JEWEL WATCHES. These have the 7 jewels mentioned in 7 jewel watches. In most American watches, 9,11 and 13 jewel watches the extra jewels (the other half) are in the top plate not in the pillar plate. So 11 jewel watches look like 15 jewel watches.

*Do not assume all jewels are in pairs.

15 JEWEL WATCHES. These watches have the 11 jewels found in

11 jewel watches, with the addition of the following: two hole jewels-one at each end of the third-wheel; and two hole jewels-one at each end of the fourth-wheel staff Note: There are some 16 jewel watches.

17 JEWEL WATCHES. The 15 jewels in 15-jewel watches are used with the addition of two hole jewels- one at each end of the center wheel staff

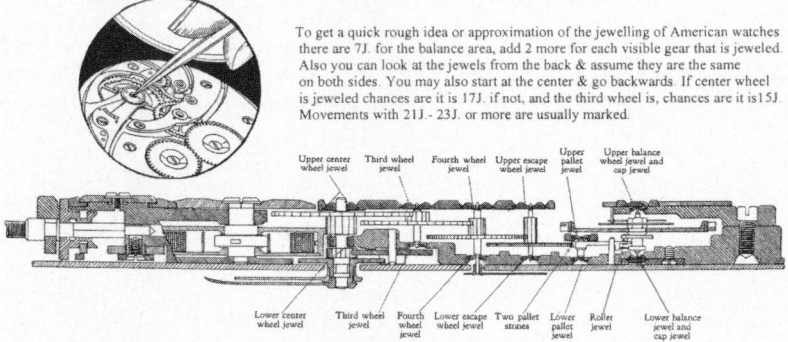

To get a quick rough idea or approximation of the jewelling of American watches there are 7J. for the balance area, add 2 more for each visible gear that is jeweled. Also you can look at the jewels from the back & assume they are the same on both sides. You may also start at the center & go backwards. If center wheel is jeweled chances are it is 17J. if not, and the third wheel is, chances are it is 15J. Movements with 21J.- 23J. or more are usually marked.

Above: Cross section of a 17 jewel pocket watch showing upper and lower jewel location.

19 JEWEL WATCHES. In these watches, the jewels are distributed as in the 17-jewel watch, with the addition of two hole jewels-one for each pivot of the barrel mainspring.

21 JEWEL WATCHES. The jewels in these are distributed as in the 17-jeweled grade, with the addition of two cap jewels (USUALLY 2 at pallet arbor and 2 at escape wheel) a few have 2 jewels for the barrel.

Center Wheel —	2	Center Wheel—	2	Center Wheel—	2	Center Wheel—	2
Third Wheel —	2	Third Wheel —	2	Third Wheel —	2	Third Wheel —	2
Fourth Wheel —	2	Fourth Wheel —	2	Fourth Wheel —	2	Fourth Wheel —	2
Escape Wheel—	2	Escape Wheel—	2	Escape Wheel—	2+2	Escape Wheel—	2+2
Pallet & Arbor —	4	Barrel Arbor —	2	Pallet & Arbor—	4+2	Barrel Arbor —	2
Balance Staff —	4	Pallet & Arbor—	4	Balance Staff —	4	Pallet & Arbor—	4+2
Roller jewel —	1	Balance Staff —	4	Roller jewel —	1	Balance Staff —	4
TOTAL —	17J	Roller jewel —	1	TOTAL —	21J	Roller jewel —	1
		TOTAL —	19J			TOTAL —	23J

23 JEWEL WATCHES. The jewels are distributed as in the 21-jewel watch, with the addition of one for each pivot of the barrel & mainspring.

24J,25J, and 26 JEWEL WATCHES. In all of these watches, the additional jewels were distributed as cap jewels. These were not very functional but were offered as prestige movements for the person who wanted more.

In many cases, these jewel arrangements varied according to manufacturer. All jeweled watches may not fit these descriptions.

Collectable watches with a higher jewel count usually demand a greater price, when watches were produced the higher the jewel count the higher the cost, however, lower production of some models this collectable rule does not apply. Example 7, 11 and 15 jewel Hamiltons will bring higher prices than a 17 jewel Hamilton, also a 19 jeweled "Sangamo Special" will bring a higher price than 21 jeweled "Sangamo Special". Most American made watches with 15 jewels and up are marked. Generally speaking it is accepted that good to medium quality watches have 15 to 17 jewels and are said to be "fully jeweled".

When counting visible jewels beware that some manufactures added non-functional jewels for eye appeal, disassembling the watch is the only way to get a true accurate count.

Note: When counting jewels from the movement back plate (with dial on) at the visible jewels a 11J. could appear to be a 15J. watch. A jewel which has a scribed circle around it plus two screws is a mock setting and usually have one jewel for top jewel only & no lower jewel.

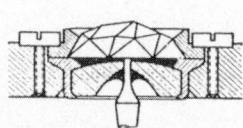

Left: Diamond faceted end stone.

Center: Cylindrical pivot.

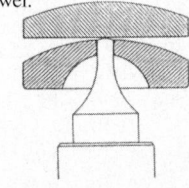

Right: Conical pivot & Cap jewel.

WINDING AND SETTING

The simplest, but not the most practical method for winding up the mainspring of a pocket watch was to wind the barrel staff by means of a key, but then it is necessary to open up the watch case. The key method of winding proved unpopular, as oftentimes the key became lost.

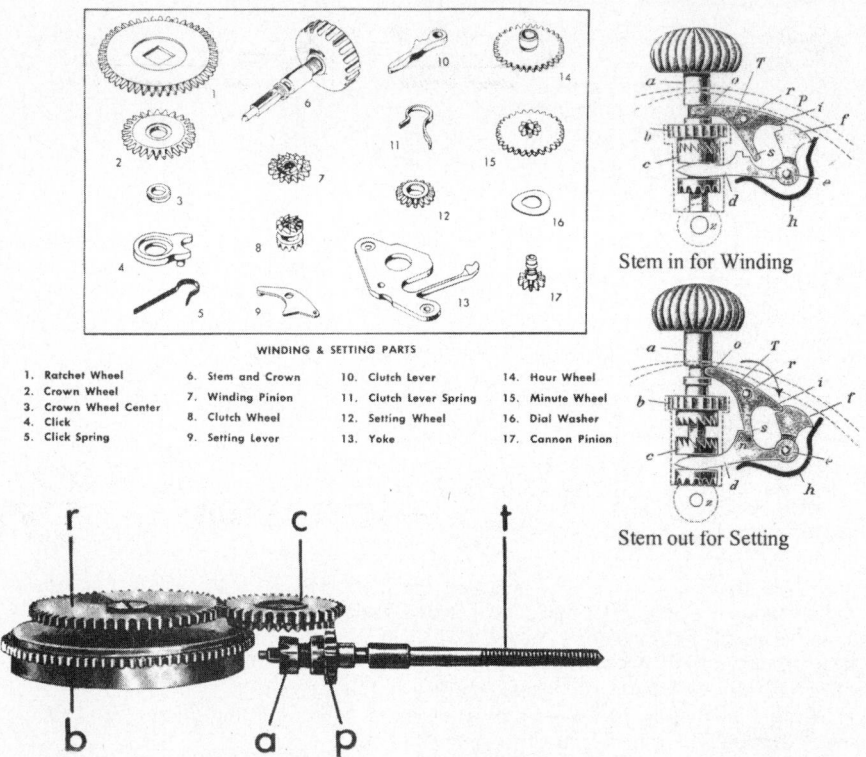

WINDING & SETTING PARTS

1. Ratchet Wheel	6. Stem and Crown	10. Clutch Lever	14. Hour Wheel
2. Crown Wheel	7. Winding Pinion	11. Clutch Lever Spring	15. Minute Wheel
3. Crown Wheel Center	8. Clutch Wheel	12. Setting Wheel	16. Dial Washer
4. Click	9. Setting Lever	13. Yoke	17. Cannon Pinion
5. Click Spring			

Stem in for Winding

Stem out for Setting

WINDING MECHANISM. a-Winding and setting clutch. p-Winding pinion. b-Barrel. r-Ratchet wheel. c-Crown or main wheel. t- Winding arbor.

The modern principle of the winding of the mainspring and hand setting by pulling on the crown, dates back to 1842. We owe this combination to Adrian Philippe, associate of Patek, of Geneva.

The winding and setting mechanism consists of the stem, crown, winding pinion, clutch wheel, setting wheel, setting lever, clutch lever, clutch spring, crown wheel, and ratchet wheel. When the stem is pushed in, the clutch lever throws the clutch wheel to winding position. Then, when the stem is turned clockwise, it causes the winding pinion to turn the crown and ratchet wheels. The ratchet wheel is fitted on the square of the mainspring arbor and is held in place with a screw. When the stem and crown are turned, the ratchet wheel turns and revolves the arbor which winds the mainspring, thereby giving motive power to the train. Pulling the stem and crown outward pushes the setting lever against the clutch lever, engaging the clutch wheel with the setting wheel. The setting wheel is in constant mesh with the minute wheel; therefore, turning the stem and crown permits setting the hands to any desired time.

SETTING MECHANISM. Clutch a. meshes with m. and the minute works wheel b. The minute works wheel meshes with the cannon pinion h. The hour cannon d. bears the hour hand H. C. center wheel M. Minute hand.

The dial train consists of the cannon pinion, minute, and hour wheels. The cannon pinion is a hollow steel pinion which is mounted on the center wheel arbor. A stud which is secured in the pillar plate holds the minute wheel in mesh with the cannon pinion. A small pinion is attached to the minute wheel which is meshed with the hour wheel.

The center arbor revolves once per hour. A hand affixed to the cannon pinion on the center arbor would travel around the dial once per hour. This hand is used to denote minutes. The hour wheel has a pipe that allows the hour wheel to telescope over the cannon pinion. The hour wheel meshes with the minute wheel pinion. This completes the train of the cannon pinion, minute wheel, and hour wheel. The ratio between the cannon pinion and the hour wheel is 12 to 1; therefore, the hand affixed to the hour wheel is to denote the hours. With this arrangement, time is recorded and read.

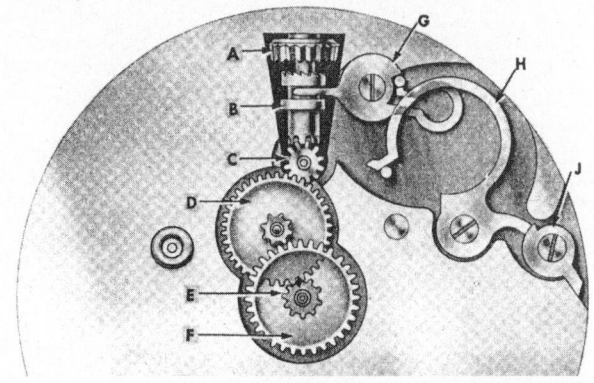

A—PINION
B—CLUTCH WHEEL
C—SETTING WHEEL
D—MINUTE WHEEL
E—CANNON PINION
F—HOUR WHEEL
G—CLUTCH LEVER
H—SETTING SPRING
J—SETTING SPRING CAM

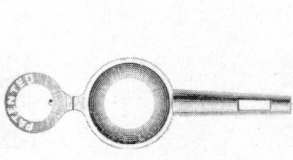

KENDRICK & DAVIS, WATCH KEY FACTORY was founded in 1876. They produced a dust-proof key which was looked upon as quite a wonderful patented watch key & sold world wide & also found with different foreign trade marks.

AUTOMATIC WINDING

The self-winding watch uses the movements of the body in order to wind up the mainspring slowly and nearly continuously. The first pocket self-winding watches were executed by a watchmaker from Le Lode, Abraham-Louis Perrelet, around 1770. They were improved soon after by Abraham-Louis Breguet. In the case of the pocket watch, the movements causing the winding of the watch were essentially the result of walking. This system of winding was never widely adopted. The watch was a fancy model and not a really useful one. Herman von der Heydt was the only maker in America to work with the self-winding pocket watch. However, inventors always kept the idea of the self-winding watch in mind.

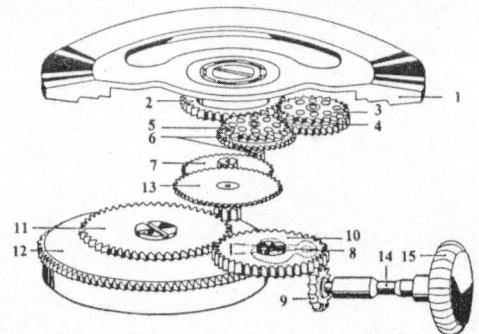

Early self wind pocket watch by Breguet.

ETERNA-MATIC AUTOMATIC WINDING MECHANISM. 1-Oscillating Weight. 2-Oscillating gear. 3—Upper wheel of auxiliary pawl-wheel. 4—Lower wheel of auxiliary pawl-wheel. 5—Pawl-wheel with pinion. 6—Lower wheel of pawl-wheel with pinion. 7—Transmission-wheel with pinion. 8—Crown-wheel yoke. 9—Winding pinion. 10—Crown-wheel. 11—Ratchet-wheel. 12—Barrel. 13—Driving runner for ratchet-wheel. 14—Winding stem. 15—Winding button.

In 1923, the British firm Harwood took up once again the solution of the problem of automatic winding, for wrist watches. This was the spark which rapidly resulted in research to improve and simplify this type of mechanism. A company was formed in London to manufacture Harwood's watch, and before long over 500 jewelers in the United Kingdom were selling his automatic watch. A second company was formed in France, and a third in the United States. The business flourished about two and one-half years. Then, in 1931, these companies were liquidated.

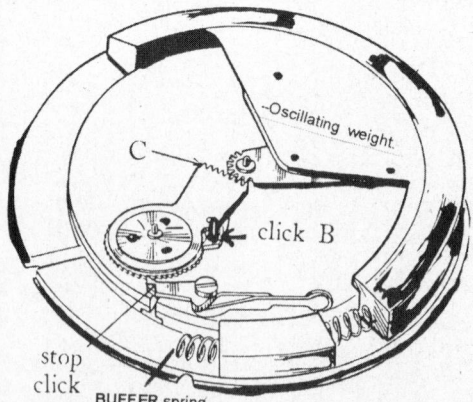
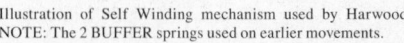
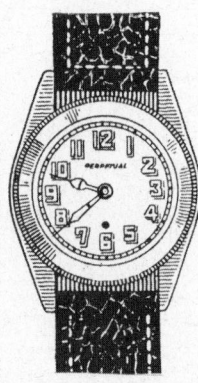

Illustration of Self Winding mechanism used by Harwood NOTE: The 2 BUFFER springs used on earlier movements.

This 1931 wrist watch made by Perpetual Self-Winding Watch Co. of America originally sold for $29.75.

THE BALANCE ARC OF VIBRATION

If the watch is to function with any degree of satisfaction, the proper arc of motion of a balance should be no less than 180 degrees in a single vibration direction. Wind up the watch, stop the balance; upon releasing the balance, carefully observe the extent of the swing or vibration. After 30 seconds it should have reached its maximum. If it takes longer, the full power of the mainspring is not being communicated strongly enough. With the watch fully wound, the balance should vibrate between 180 degrees and 315 degrees in a single vibration direction. 220 degrees is said to be perfect.

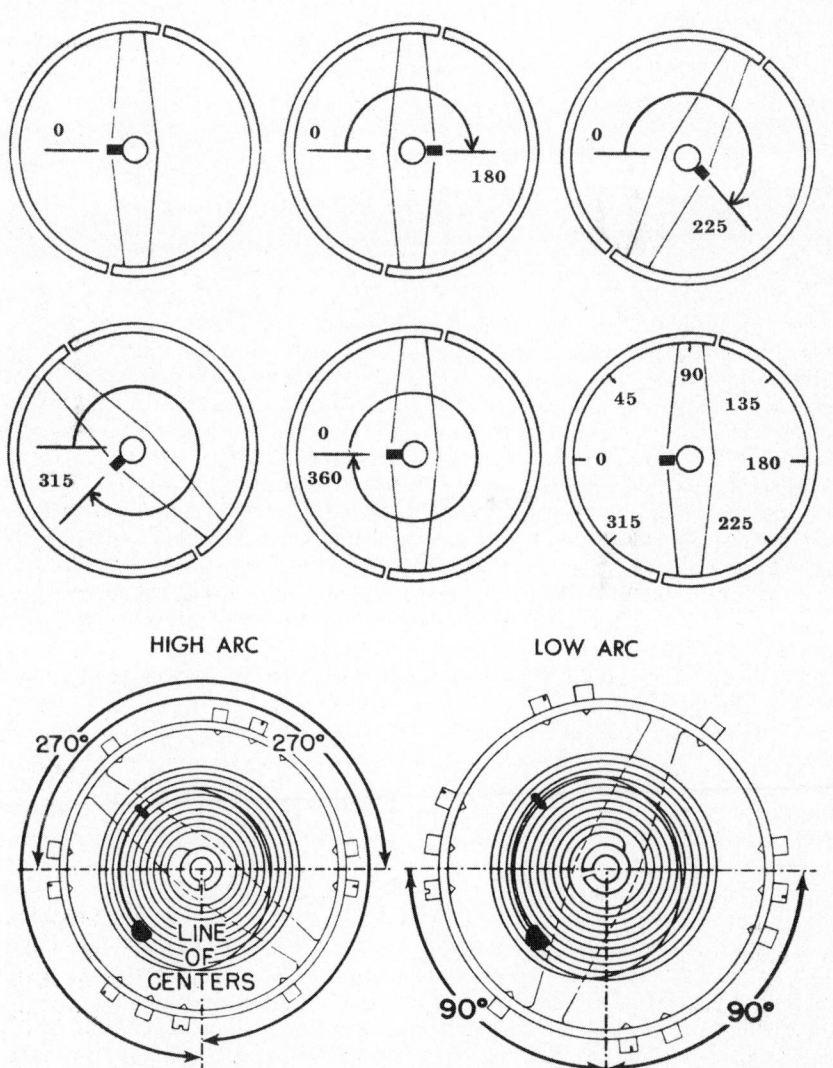

HIGH ARC   LOW ARC

JUDGING QUALITY

Judging the quality of a watch need not be difficult. While observing a watch movement there are two major determining factors to keep in mind. One, The quality or precious material, and two, the amount of workmanship and time it takes to produce the parts for the movement. About 85% of the cost of a high-grade watch movement is labor. The precious materials such as 18k or 14k gold, diamond or rubies, gold jewel settings or brass jewel settings. The amount of labor may be measured by the finished parts of the movement such as polishing, chamfered parts (removing sharp edges), & bluing of screws, also complications require more labor. The collector must learn to compare watches from the same time period because changes were made to improve the time keeping. To assist you the partial list below may be helpful in judging the quality of a watch.

LARGE CROWN for EASY WINDING
EXTRA HEAVY PENDANT
SAFETY RECOILING CLICK
CONCAVED AND POLISHED WINDING WHEELS
SAFETY CENTER PINION
JEWELED MOTOR BARREL
19 TO 23 SELECTED RUBY AND SAPPHIRE JEWELS
GOLD TRAIN WHEELS
BREGUET OVER COILED HAIRSPRING

NON PULL-OUT BOW
DUST PROOF CASE
RAISED SOLID GOLD JEWEL SETTINGS
9 ADJUSTMENTS = 6 POSITIONS - 1 HEAT 1 COLD AND 1 ISOCHRONISM
POSITIVE MICROMETRIC REGULATOR
SPRING TEMPERED COMPENSATING BALANCE WITH SOLID GOLD SCREWS
DOUBLE ROLLER & ENTIRE ESCAPEMENT IS CAP JEWELED
STEEL ESCAPE WHEEL

Escapement: detent, lever (with banking pins) or cylinder; gold, steel, gilded or brass escape wheel. Balance Wheel; number of platinum, gold or brass screws, mean-time screws are used in higher grade watches and two pair (4) of mean-time screws is higher than one pair (2), expansion full cut, 1/2 cut or uncut. In older movements gold or brass balance wheel. Balance cock;diamond or ruby end stone, amount of engraving or hand pierced workmanship. Regulator; free sprung, precision or simple. Hair spring; helical, elinvar, overcoil or flat. Adjustments; Isochronism, temperature, 6 to 3 positions, adjusted or unadjusted.
Note polished and quality finish under dial also under side of wheels and all parts.

The train of gears: Wolf tooth gearing, highly polished, gold train, gilded or brass gears; chamfered above & below, rounded, beveled or flat spokes.

Finish to the plates: Engraved, carved, skeletonized, damaskeened with lavished or conservative finish, highly finished or polished, solid or plated, nickel, brass, gold inlaid, gilt or frosted plates. Hardening of various parts.

Screws: Highly finished or polished, chamfered or beveled, oval or flat heads, blued or plain, also chamfered screw holes.

Jewels and settings: Number of jewels; diamond, sapphire, ruby, other semi-precious jewels as garnet, aquamarine. Size of raised gold jewel settings held by 3 or 2 screws, flush gold jewel settings held by 3 or 2 screws, composition or gilded settings, fake engraved settings or jewels pressed directly into plates. Roller with jeweled impulse pin. Entire escapement with capped jewels as lever, balance & escape wheel. Sapphire pallet jewels. Jeweled mainspring barrel.

Dials: Enamel dial; enamel on gold or copper, triple sunk, double sunk, single sunk or unsunk. Metal dial; gold or silver, hand carved or engraved, etched or plated; applied, raised, inlaid or hand painted numbers.

Cases: Platinum or white gold, 18k or 14k gold, multi-color gold, "Pinchbeck gold", silver or silveroid. Hand pierced, Repousse, porcelain or enamel, engraved or engine turned. Boxed hinged or reversible, Hunting & Demi-hunter, open face, unusual shape, heavy or light weight, thick, thin. Raised applied ornamentation, diamonds or semi-precious jewels. Inter-dust cover, bow & crown made of gold or brass. Beware of Pinchbeck gold which is fake gold.

Metals used in watches: Bell metal or bronze, Beryllium white colored alloyed with iron, cobalt, copper, etc.; Bi-metallic (brass fused to steel), Nickel, Brass, Carbon steel, Chromium, Chrome steel, Copper; Elinvar, German metal, gilding metal, Glucinum, Gold, Gold-filled, Gunmetal, Invar, Iron, Palladium, Platinum, White gold, Silver, Silver plated, Stainless steel, Steel, Tin and Zinc.

NOTE: Top first quality watches are fully chamfered, polished and finished, above and below on all the pads, as lever, escape wheel and train wheels, etc. The next down from Top First quality only the top or visible side are camfered, polished and finished. Extra flat watches the thinner the watch - the higher the production cost and Extra flat watches was considered the Highest or Top of the line.

1903 AD

1907 AD
PRICE
$2.25

"Locomotice Special" $7 00
Guaranteed Good Timekeeper.
American manufacture, 18 size, elaborately damaskeened nickel and gilt movement, ruby jewels in raised settings, quick train, straight line escapement, exposed pallets, compensation balance, stem wind and set, hard enameled dial, locomotive on movement and dial and movement stamped "17 Jewels Adjusted." Has the appearance of $25.00 railroad movement. Hunting or open face.

Right: Min. Repeater with perpetual calendar.
(Complications + Extra Flat + Quality finish.)

Left: (1903 AD) **Cheap Imitation** Watch made by Trenton W. Co. also made in 23 jewels (GLASS jewels)

OFFER VERSUS APPRAISALS

When you want to sell your watches you need an offer, not an appraisal. An offer is the actual price someone will pay for your item at a given point in time. The price will be determined by several factors. Demand or collect-ability, rarity, condition, quality, grade, complications, appeal, size, age, metal content, style and the timing may be very critical in determining the price.

Jewelers and most appraisers use the insurance replacement cost, (an estimate of the retail replacement price). This type of appraisal is fine for contemporary watches and jewelry, but not for collectable watches and antique jewelry items. The fair market value at the NAWCC trade show level is a more realistic estimate of price. If done by an appraiser with "current market" knowledge, then a fair market appraisal will be the correct evaluation of the dollar level at that time for your items.

Selling your watches may be a new experience. The task requires experience in the sale of watches. There is a market for watches, but as in any area of sales, knowledge of your BUYER is important. Collectors may not advertise that they are willing buyers; they may not have enough ready cash at the time. Sending watches to a prospective buyer is a judgment call-- is the buyer trustworthy? Will it be worth the time involved? As a seller, you must guarantee the watch to work, offer return privileges and refunds. The task of selling requires a knowledge of repair, shipping, the cost of advertising, time to market the watch, and someone standing by to talk to the collector. This is a short list and almost imperative that the seller be in the business of selling watches to be successful at selling. The collector may pay a higher price than a dealer, but the collectors are hard to find and may not have the ready cash at that time.

Selling to dealers may be more pleasant. Dealers will have a qualified staff, including buyers and seller, ready to respond to ads, as well as a cash reserve for purchases. One of the benefits of dealing with an established business is that they can provide you with good references and they have a trustworthy record. Each customer is handled in a professional manner by a competent staff member. A dealer understands that selling maybe a new experience and will take you though the process one step at a time. In summary, considering the cost, time and effort required in attempting to find a willing collector, you may be ahead to sell your watches to a qualified dealer.

Selling your watches to collectors or dealers may involve sending the watch from one place to another. To receive the best price it will be vital to see the watch before an offer is made, this is a common practice in the watch market. Some of the following are good suggestions for mailing your package to the buyer. Make a detailed list of the items you are sending. Keep a copy and send a copy. List your name, address and daytime phone number. The jewelry industry sends millions of dollars worth of jewelry by REGISTERED MAIL. The Post Office service has close control of the registered mail. Each person who handles the package must sign for it and be responsible for it's safety. Your package will be kept in a secure area much like a bank vault. Your package may be insured up to $25,000.00. Your package must also be able to withstand the shipping stress. Before sealing the box make sure to add one or two inches of padding between your watch and the sides, bottom and top of the box. Cushion these spaces with newspaper, tissue, cotton, bubble or foam padding. Seal the box securely, then wrap the outside with gummed PAPER tape that can be written on.

When your package arrives at the dealer, the mail staff will open and inspect your package and log each item. One of the experts in charge will examine each item and call as soon as possible with the offer. If you accept the offer, a check will be delivered to you. If the offer is turned down, the items will be returned.

When buying watches for resale, know what the buyer will pay. How many buyers are there for prices above $1,000.00, $2,000.00, $5,000.00, $10,000.00 or as high as $50,000.00 to $100,000.00 and do they have ready cash? Can you find the collector that will pay more or pay your asking price? The collector may be just as rare as your rare watch! Supply and demand.

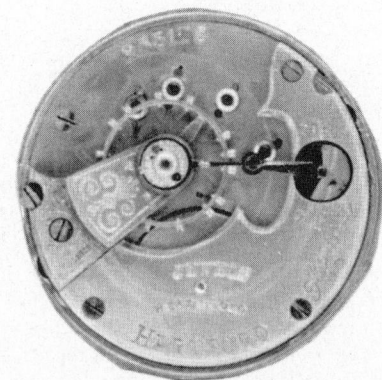

"George Washington, New York', engraved on movement, patterned after the 1857 model by Waltham, (SWISS)

"The Nassau" on dial, "Hartford adjusted, jewels, heat & cold" on the movement. (SWISS FAKE)

COTTAGE INDUSTRY WATCHMAING
IN COLONIAL AMERICA

The cottage industry (pre-1700s to 1800s) consisted of organized, skilled craftsmen having separate divisions for the purpose of producing watches. The movements were handmade using man powered tools. The parts generally were not given a final finish. The cottage industries were in most countries including France, England, Switzerland, Germany, and others, but not in America. Each skilled parts maker specialized in a specific part of the watch. There were fusee makers, wheel makers, plate and cock makers, spring makers, case makers and enamelers, to name a few. In the cottage industry each maker became an expert in his field. Expenses and overhead were less because fewer tools and less labor were required. Because all components were produced separately, a larger volume of watches resulted.

The enterprising colonial watchmaker in America would order all the parts and assemble them to complete a finished movement. This finisher or watchmaker, would detail the parts, such as filing them to fit, polishing and gilding the parts, fining the movement to a case, installing a dial, and adjusting the movement to perform. The finisher would then engrave his name and town of manufacture to the movement or dial. The finisher determined the time keeping quality of the completed watch, thus gaining a good reputation.

Most watchmakers used this system during this period, even, to some extent, Abraham L. Breguet. A colonial watchmaker or finisher could produce about 50 watches a year. There were few colonial watchmakers because only the wealthy could afford such a prized possession as a watch. Most colonial watchmakers struggled financially, and supplemented their businesses with repair work on European-made watches. Since most of them understood the verge escapement, and imported this type of part from England to produce watches, many colonial watches have the verge escapement. Few colonial watches survive today.

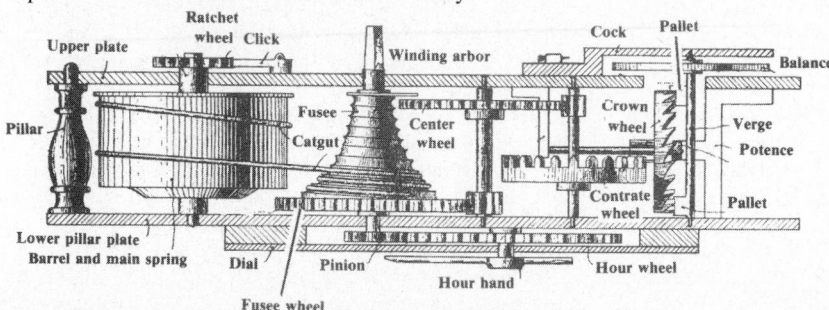

Side-view of 17th century single-hand movement with fusee and catgut line to barrel. This three-wheel movement normally ran from 15 to 16 hours between windings. Also note the balance has no hairspring. Watch movements changed from 3 wheel to 4 wheels after about 1700.

84

English style 1/4 Hr. Repeater Ebauche. thought to be from Nicole, Nielsen for the Charles Frodsham work shop in London, no escape wheel, right angle lever, 30J., wolfs tooth winding, highly finished repeater steel works, Ca.1850-60.

Dial side of English style 1/4 Hr. Repeater Ebauche thought to be from Nicole, Nielsen for the Charles Frodsham work shop in London, no escape wheel, right angle lever, 30J., wolfs tooth winding, highly finished repeater steel works.

EBAUCHES

The stamping out of plates and bridges began with Frederic Japy of Beaucourt, France, around 1770. First Ebauche in 1771-72 and by 1795, 400 workers and 40,000 movements; in 1813, 300,000 movements and in 1851, 500,000. At first, ebauches consisted of two plates with barrel and train bridges, the cock and fusee, pillars, and the clicks and assembly screws. The ebauches were stamped-out or rough movements. Japy invented machinery a common laborer could operate, including a circular saw to cut brass sheets into strips, a machine for cutting teeth in a wheel, a machine for making pillars, a press for the balance, and more. These machines were semi-automatic and hard to keep in alignment or register. But, with the aid of these new machines, the principal parts of the movement could be produced in a short period of time with some precision. However, the parts of watches at this time were not interchangeable. These movements in the rough or "gray" were purchased by finishers. The finisher was responsible for fitting and polishing all parts and seeing to the freedom and depth of these wheels and working parts. He had to drill the holes to fit the dial and hands. The plates, cock and wheel, after being fitted and polished, were gilded. After the parts were gilded, the movement would be reassembled, regulated for good time keeping, and placed in a case. The finisher had to be a master watchmaker.

In England, during the early 1700s to late 1800s, Lancashire became the center of the ebauche movement trade. One of the better known English ebauche makers was Joseph Preston & Sons of Prescot. The movements were stamped J.P. Some Swiss ebauches would imitate or stylize the movement for the country in which they were to be sold, making it even harder to identify the origin.

As the watch industry progressed, the transformation of the ebauche to a more completed movement occurred. Automation eventually made possible the watch with interchangeable parts, standard sizing, and precision movements that did not need retouching. This automation began about 1850 (in America) with such talented mechanics as Pierre Fredric Ingold, the Pitkins Brothers, A. L. Dennison, G. A. Leschot with Vacheron and Constantin, Patek, Philippe, and Frederic Japy of Beaucourt. The pioneers in the 1850s who set the standards for modern watchmaking included the American Pitkin Brothers, Dennison, Howard, and Jacob Custer. By 1880 most other countries had begun to follow the lead of America in the manufacturing of the complete pocket watch with interchangeable parts.

In Switzerland there are four major categories of watch producers:
1. Complete   2. Ebauche   3. Parts or Specialized   4. Finishers.
Complete watch producers manufacture 75% to 100% on their own premises as Le Coultre. Ebauche produce rough movements or movements in the gray called ebauche or blank movements such as ETA in Grenchen. These are made in the valley of Joux and Val-de-Ruz regions, in and around the towns of Granges, Grenchen, La Chaux-de-Fonds, Le Lode and Solothurn in the Bernese Jura, the valley of St. Imier, Val-de-Travers, at Preseux, in the Ticino, and elsewhere. Parts or Specialized watch producers are more or less all over the Swiss region. Balances more so in Valley of Sagne and at Les Ponts Lever assortments as the escape wheel, fork, & roller in Jour Valley, at Bienne, in Bernese Jura and especially, at Le Lode. Hairsprings as "Nivarox" are made near La Chaux-de-Fonds, Geneva, Bienne and St. Imier. Mainsprings, dials, hands, cases, jewels, pendants, bows, crowns, crystals, screws and pins, generally speaking, are made throughout Switzerland. Finishers buy blank movements, parts, cases, etc. and finish the watch as a complete watch with their own name engraved on the watch as Tiffany & Co., Ball UK Co. and many more.

By the mid 1950s the high quality watches made under "one roof" by Am. Waltham, Elgin, Hamilton and Illinois could not compete with the Swiss division of manufacturing. This Swiss system of manufacturing encourages improvement within its own field. Each specialist company has experience and can improve quality while speeding up large production at a competitive price. This specialized system is still used today with most Swiss watch companies.

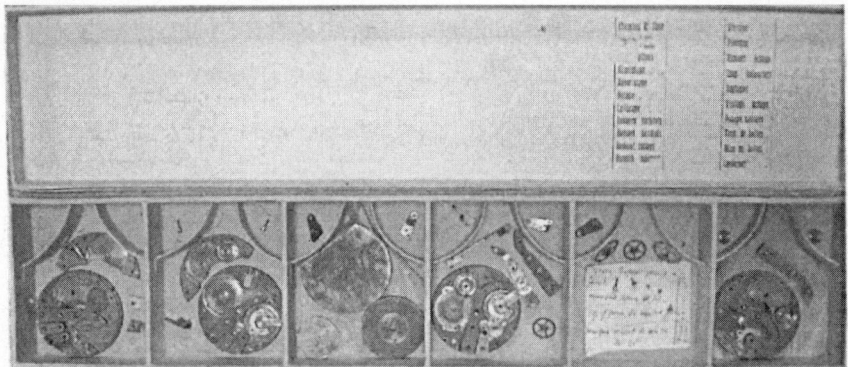

Swiss Ebauche Assembly Tray, cardboard production tray has 6 compartments with 4 raw movements and extra parts. Upper right of lid is a operation card and printed on the 1st line is Ebauches No. Serie = ebauches number series, 4th line Demontagt = dismantling, 5th line Adoucissage = smoothing, 7th line Dorage = gilding, also hand written notes. On cover of box St. Imier & a Coat of Arms.

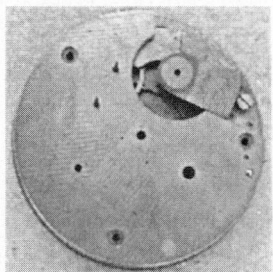 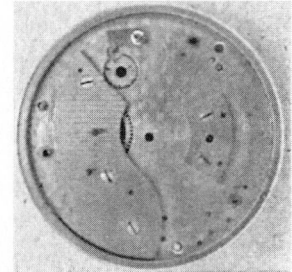

English Ebauche by J. Wycherly of Prescot, Left 8 size, 3/4 plate movement, Right dial side & engraved on plate 8*04 JW. Mr. Wycherly started making raw movements in early 1867.

86

Ebauches S.A.

Ebauches S.A. had its main office in Neuchatel, Switzerland. At one time the following 17 affiliated firms were part of Ebauche S.A. and in the year of 1968 they had produced ABOUT 40,000,000 WATCHES. In 1932 Eterna divided into two companies, Eterna and ETA.

A. Schild S.A., Grenchen

Fabrique d'Horlogerie de Fontainemelon, fontainemelon

Eta S.A., Fabrique d'Ebauches, Grenchen

Fabrique d'Horlogerie de Fontainemelon, Succursale du Landeron, Le Landeron

A. Michel S.A., Grenchen

Felsa S.A., Grenchen

Fabriques d'Ebauches Bernoises S.A., Etablissement Aurore, Villeret

Fabrique d'Ebauches Venus S.A., Moutier

Fabrique d'Ebauches Unitas S.A., Tramelan

Fabrique d'Ebauches de Fleurier S.A., Fleurier

Fabrique d' Ebauches de Peseux S.A., Peseux

Fabriques d'Ebauches Reunies Arogno S.A., Arogno

Fabriques d'Ebauches de bettlach, Bettlach

Fabrique d'Ebauches de Chezard S.A., Chezard

Derby S.A., La Chaux-de-Fonds

Nouvelle Fabrique S.A., Tavannes

Valjoux S.A., Les Bioux

FRENCH EBAUCHE

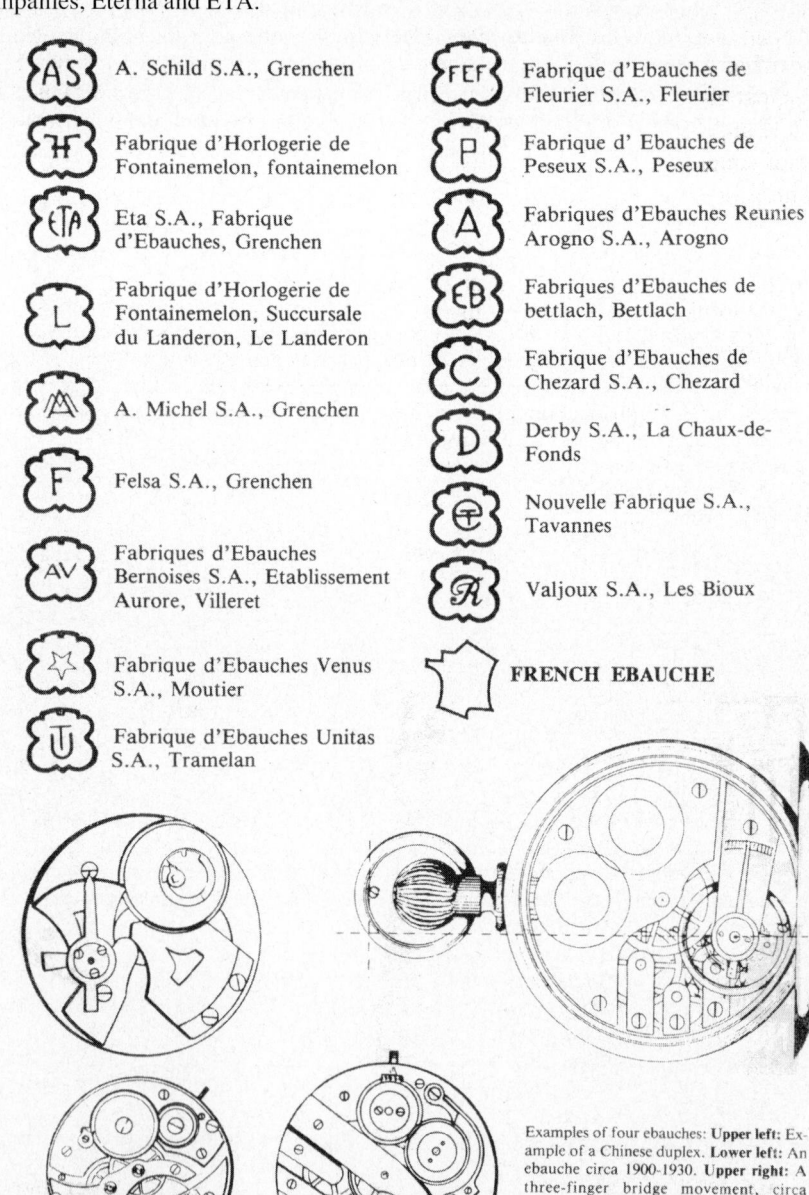

Examples of four ebauches: **Upper left:** Example of a Chinese duplex. **Lower left:** An ebauche circa 1900-1930. **Upper right:** A three-finger bridge movement, circa 1890-1910. **Lower right:** Bridge movement, circa 1885-1900.

WORM GEAR ESCAPEMENT

This oddity was advertised as "The Watch With a Worm in It". Robert J. Clay of Jersey City was given a patent on October 16, 1886. Mr. Clay said, "The principal object of my invention is to provide a watch movement that is very simple and has but few parts." The worm gear or continuous screw was by no means simple. Mr. Clay and William Hanson of Brooklyn revamped the original worm gear and obtained another patent on January 18, 1887.

The first watch containing a worm gear escapement reached the market in 1887. However, the New York Standard Watch Co. soon converted to a more conventional lever escapement. About 12,000 watches with the worm gear were made, but few survived.

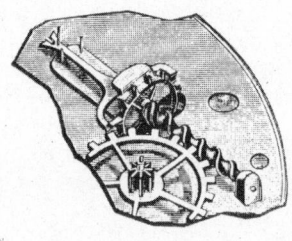

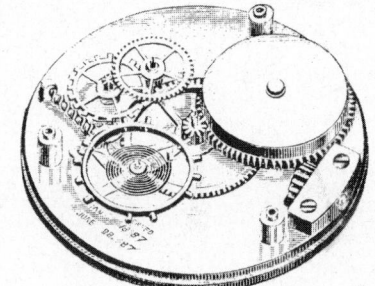

Enlarged worm gear escapement. Note endless screw was referred to by the New York Watch Co. as "A watch with a worm In It'

Movement with top plate removed.

ENAMEL WATCH DIAL MAKING

In ALL American watch ads the words "glass enamel dial" were always used and never referred to as porcelain dials. Enamel may be described as the art of fusing melted glass on metal. Enamel should not be confused with paint or baking enamels. Enamel is made of silica (quartz) and also may contain borax, lead, and potash. The more lead and potash used, the softer and more brilliant the enamel becomes. Enamel watch dials are basically hand produced. The base for enamel dials is a metal disc whose edge has been turned up to hold the enamel in place. Next, temporary feet are soldered on the disc. Enamel is ground to a very fine powder and sifted through a sieve upon the copper disc. It is then fired in a furnace at a high heat (about 1400 to 1800 degrees Fahrenheit) which fuses the enamel and causes it to flow evenly over the copper disc. This process may be repeated 2 or 3 times. Next, a steel plate with numbers engraved on it, these depressions are filled with a black enamel. A soft gelatin pad then comes in contact with the steel plate, the black enamel adhering to the rubber pad, is then transferred to the enameled dial. This operation is repeated in order to insure a good impression.

Note: Enamel dials can be glass enamel or hard enamel. Glass type uses a clear coat over the dial also called under glaze. Hard type has no clear seal on top of the dial. Glass enamel dials have a higher gloss. Hard dial enamel does not shine as much. In hard enamel dials, the numbers are raised or standing proud.

Note: American hand-painted dials were declining by 1880s.

Next the dial with the new applied numbers is placed in a furnace at a lower heat than the original process. Then the dial is laid on a template for drilling the center hole, the turned-up edge that held the enamel in place is now ground off and at the same time is reduced to the required diameter. Subdials or double-sunk dials are formed by stamping these parts out separately, treating them the same as the main part of the dial already described and then soldering these dial pieces carefully together. So, a double sunk dial is really a combination of three separate dials.

Note: Due to numbers being fired at a lower heat, a enamel dial can not be fired again at a higher heat (such as for repair purposes).

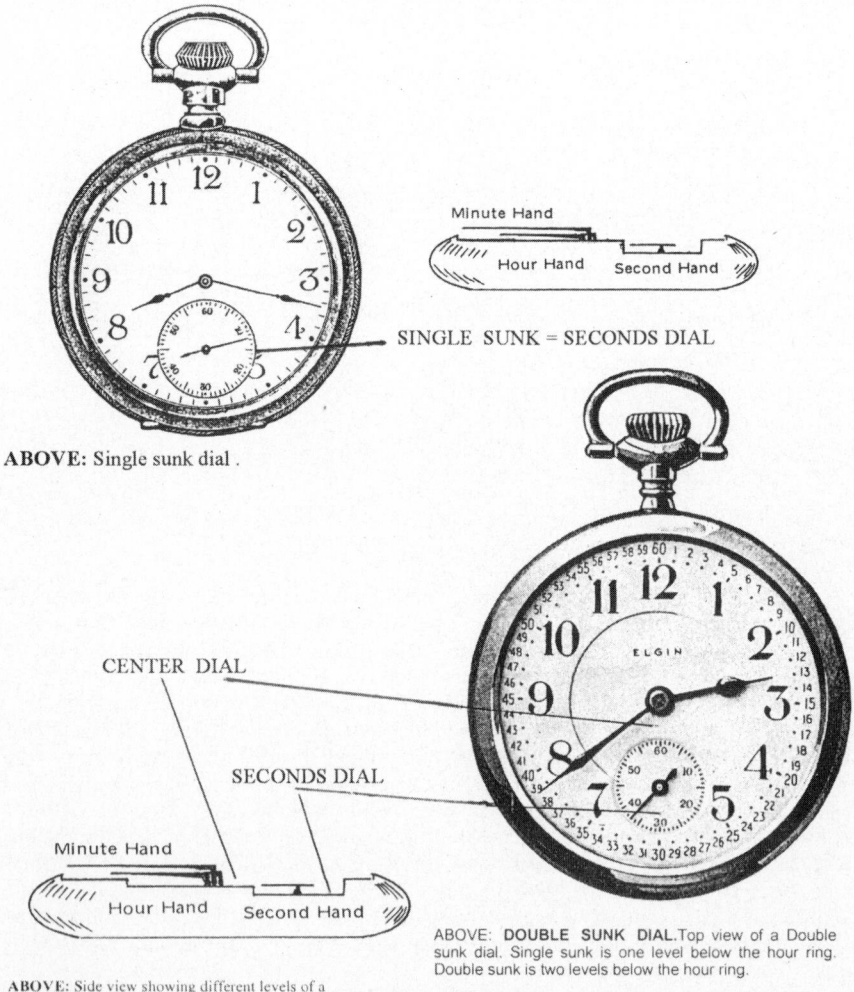

SINGLE SUNK = SECONDS DIAL

ABOVE: Single sunk dial .

CENTER DIAL

SECONDS DIAL

ABOVE: Side view showing different levels of a **double sunk dial.**

ABOVE: **DOUBLE SUNK DIAL.** Top view of a Double sunk dial. Single sunk is one level below the hour ring. Double sunk is two levels below the hour ring.

Note: Some single sunk dials have inner marked circle made to look like double sunk dial.
Note: Due to numbers being fired at a lower heat, a enamel dial can not be fired again at a higher heat (such as for repair purposes).

CRAZING

The word "craze" means a minute crack in the glaze of the enamel. This is not a crack in the dial because the dial has a backing of copper. Crazing does little damage to the structure of the enamel, even though it may go all the way through to the copper.

FIRST DIALS

Thomas Gold was the first to make enamel dials in America in about 1838 in New York City. Thomas had a partner from 1846-51 named Thomas Reeves of Brooklyn. American Watch Co. (Waltham) made their own dials from the beginning by dial-makers John Todd & John T. Gold. Henry Foucy found employment in 1856 with the American Watch Co. He was from Geneva.

PIN LEVER ESCAPEMENT (DOLLAR WATCHES)

The pin lever escapement is sometimes erroneously referred to as "Roskopf escapement" and watches with pin lever escapements are sometimes referred to as "Roskopf watches."

The original Roskopf watch, which was first exhibited at the Paris Exposition in 1867, was a rugged "poor man's watch." The chief Roskopf patent, decreases the number of wheels by creating a large barrel whose diameter encroached upon the center of the watch. The loose cannon pinion and hour wheel were driven by a friction-clutch minute wheel mounted to the barrel cover and enmeshed with the loose cannon pinion and hour wheel. The cannon pinion rode loosely on a steel pin threaded to the center of the main plate. The true term "Roskopf" applies to the barrel with its clutch fitted minute wheel driving the dial train. The Roskopf ebauches watch was made by Cortebert factory in La Chaux-de-Fonds, Switzerland. The first Roskopf watch was sold for 25 francs in January of 1870.

NOTE: Some fakes use the name "Rosskopf."

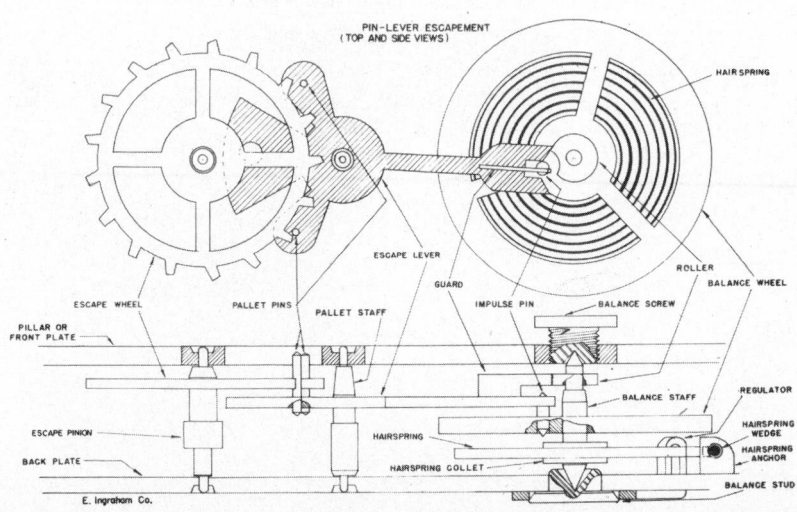

LOW COST PRODUCTION WATCHES
(DOLLAR WATCHES)

Jason R. Hopkins hoped to produce a watch that would sell for no more than 50 cents as early as the 1870s. He had a plan for which he received a patent (No. 161513) on July 20, 1875. It was a noble idea even though it was never fully realized. In 1876, Mr. Hopkins met a Mr. Fowle who bought an interest in the Hopkins watch. The movement was developed by the Auburndale Watch Co., and the Auburndale Rotary Watch was marketed in 1877. It cost $10, and 1,000 were made. The 20 size had two jewels and was open-face, pendant wind, lever set, and detent escapement. The 18 size had no jewels and was open-face.

In December, 1878, D.A.A. Buck introduced a new watch, at a record low price of $3.50, under the name of Benedict and Burnham Manufacturing Co. It was a rotary watch, open-face, with a skeleton dial which was covered with paper and celluloid. The movement turned around in the case, once every hour, and carried the minute hand with it. There were 58 parts and all of them were interchangeable. They had no jewels but did have a duplex style escapement. The teeth on the brass escape wheel were alternately long and short, and the short teeth were bent down to give the impulse. The long main spring is laid on a plate on the bed of the case. The click was also fastened to the case. The extremely long mainspring took 120 to 140 full turns of the stem to be fully wound. It came to be known as the "long wind" Waterbury and was the source of many jokes, "Here, wind my Waterbury for awhile; when you get tired, I'll finish winding it."

"Trail Blazer" by E. Ingraham Co. TOP view is the original Box, bottom. LEFT is Fob "Wings Over The Pole".
RIGHT: Watch has original green crystal. Note: engraving on the back of watch is same scene as depicted on box.

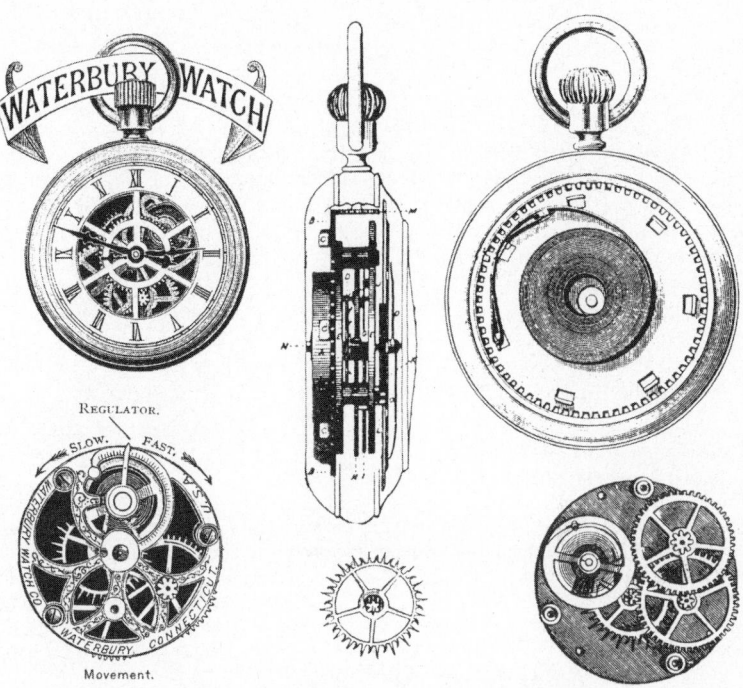

Waterbury long wind with duplex escapement & long mainspring.
Right: 2 wheel train rather than the standard 4 wheel train.

The Waterbury Clock Co., Jumbo and the New Haven Clock Co. line of watches first appeared in about 1889. They were large backwind and set watches about 2 inches in size. In 1892, Ingersoll ordered 10,000 watches from Waterbury and offered them for sale for $12.00/dozen, they were sold retail at $1.50 per watch. In 1896, Ingersoll sold the first watch at $1.00, the Yankee. "The Watch that made the Dollar Famous" slogan was used by Ingersoll later. Typical wages in 1892 was about 8 cents an hour.

The E.N. Welch Manufacturing Co. sold a very large watch with a embossed commemorative back at the 1893 Columbia Exposition, but dropped production soon after. In 1895 the New York City Watch Co. introduced a watch with a unique pendant crank to wind the watch ("Lever Winder"). The Ansonia Watch Co. produced a large number of watches from 1896 to 1929. In 1899 came the Western Clock Mfg. Co., and later became the Westclox Corporation.

Also, among the low cost production watches were the "comic character" watches. They have become prime collectibles in recent years.

About 70 percent of the watches sold in the U.S. were Dollar type. These watches were characterized by the pin lever, non-jeweled (for the most part), and with a paper dial or other inexpensive material. These watches were difficult to repair and the repairs cost more than the price of a new one. Thus, they were thrown away and today it is hard to find one in good condition.

DOLLAR WATCH CHARACTERISTICS:

1.Sold at a price that everyone could afford. 2. Used pin lever or duplex escapement.
3.Stamped or pressed out fewer parts. 4. Were non-jeweled but rugged and practical.
5.Dial made of paper or inexpensive material. 6. Case and movement were sold as one unit.

PRODUCTION LEDGER FOR MOVEMENTS

The superintendent decided on what model and grade to produce and how many to each lot or batch. This lot of unassembled movement frames (100 to 1,000) were numbered, but were not all completed in one lot Typically ten finished frames were stored in a wooden assembly tray.

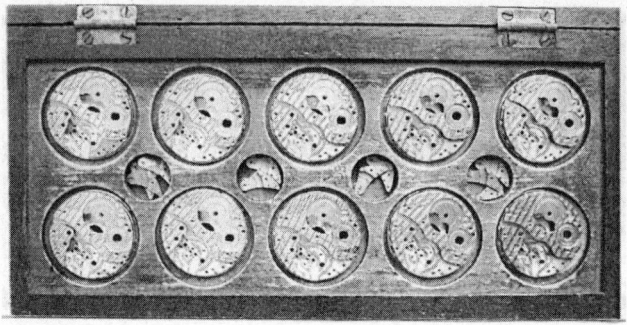

Above: Ten numbered movement frames ready for the works. (All Hamilton plates & S# = 4CI44XXX.)

The ten-compartment tray served many purposes. 1. Inventory control kept each numbered movement and it parts together during the manufacturing process. 2. Each lot of ten unassembled movements could be produced as demand required. 3. They were carried from one sub-assembly department to a another, such as balance wheel, hairspring and timing (16 or more). 4. Storage of movements, it required several months for parts & material to emerge as a finished movement. All the while the factory is producing all sizes, models & grades. (Watches not shipped in numeric order.)

Model is not the same definition as grade. A model may exist in many different grade names or number (as Bunn, 992, Riverside, Veritas) and grade names may be used in many different models (as model 1, 18 size, model I in 16 size and model 1 in 12 size, etc.). The model # is to identify the size, movement layout (full plate or 3/4 plate), location of jewels screws and gears (as model # 1892, or model 5, 18 size). The grade of a movement was to identify the quality of the finished movement such as gold jewel settings, 23 jewels and 5 to 6 adjustments high grade (Riverside Maximus) or as a low grade with 7 jewels (Sterling). The company assigned a grade name or number to a movement. However, they also may have changed with the quality upgraded or downgraded as the years passed on. Unassembled movements could be produced as demand required, a batch of movements could be side tracked, thus allowing a different grade for the same model to be made. For example, a finished Rockford grade, marked 915 on movement (18 size, OF, 17J, same model 7) is listed in Rockford Company Production Ledger as a 920 grade (18 size, OF, 17J, same model 7) and in the Sales Ledger as 915. The greater cost of a finished movement was the labor factor. About 85% of the cost of a high-grade watch movement is labor. Some unfinished movements were destroyed. The destroyed movements were listed in production ledger but not in the sales ledger. This occurred in most American Watch Factories. The average production cost of a Waltham movement in 1913 was $3.75.

SALES LEDGER for FINISHED MOVEMENTS

The Sales Ledger reflects movements that were finished and sold. The sales ledger lists the serial number, date sold, price, buyers name and how many movements purchased. Example: The production ledger listed date Oct. 5th, 1924 + serial numbers 4,540,001 to 4,541,000 16 size, model 9, grade Bunn Special and description. Later (months or years) when a order came in, the movements were completed and an entry in the sales ledger was made with date shipped March 8th 1926, serial numbers of watches 4,540,075 to 4,541,080, grade Bunn, price $43.25 per movement, along with the buyers name (Smiths Jewelry). Smiths Jewelry later sells a customer a gold filled Boss 16 size case & 16 size, grade Bunn Special with serial 4,540,079 on movement as a complete watch for $75.50 on June, 10th 1929.(Watches not shipped in numeric order.)

LEFT: Factories shipped some movements in a selling case. Note hang tag "BUNN Special 21 jewels 4540079 Open Face 16 size" Thus a customer could view the movement, then was sold a new case of his choice to fit the movement. Jobber retained the selling case.

SPECIAL NAMED or PRIVATE LABEL MOVEMENTS

It was common practice for watch manufacturers to personalize watches for wholesalers, distributors, jobbers, firms, jewelers & individuals.

This was done either by engraving a name on the movement or painting on the dial, such as Ball Watch Co., Sears, Montgomery Ward, and Burlington Watch Co..

Each manufacturer used its own serial number system even though there may have been a variety of names on the movement and/or dial. Knowledge of this will aid the collector in identifying watches as well as determining age.

Decorated Dials and Louis XIV Hands on all grades of Movements, $1.00 (list) extra.

Orders will be accepted for special named Elgin Movements in all grades. Full Plate requiring about one month and Three-quarter Plate about three months for Delivery.

A charge of 80 cents (list) each will be made for naming all 7 Jeweled Movements, and Orders for less than five, either Hunting or Open Face, of these will not be accepted. Other grades of Movements named Free of Charge. Special named Dials, no charge on any grade.

Orders accepted subject to prices ruling on date of delivery.

Note Above: A 1903 Elgin AD for wholesale dealers only. "Special named' all 7 jewel movements 80 cents charge. Other "Special named" grades "5. or more no extra charge.

To establish the true manufacturer of the "Special Named" movement, study the construction, taking note of the shape & plate layout (is it full or 3/4), shape of the balance cock and the regulator, location of jewels, location of screws, etc. Compare and match your watch movement with every photograph or drawing from each watch company until the manufacturer is located.

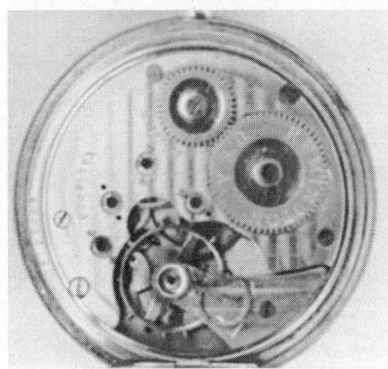

"Remington Watch co-marked on movement and case, made by N.Y. Standard Watch co., NOTE: The CROWN wheel and RATCHET without a CLICK, these visible wheels are for show only, 16 size, 11 jewels.

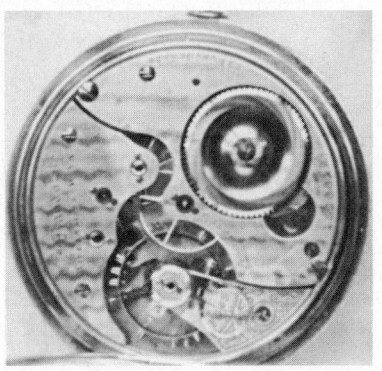

"EF. Randolph'-marked on movement, made by Illinois Watch co., 23j, hunting, model No. 4. NOTE: The wavy ribbon damaskeening pattern

16 size, No. 390, made by New York Standard Watch Co. Same model as above,

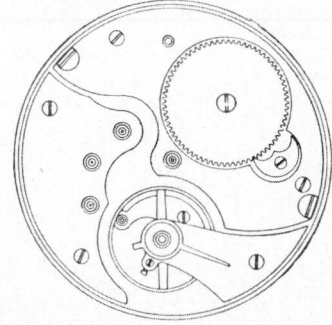

Model 4, 16 size, made by Illinois Watch Co. Same model as above.

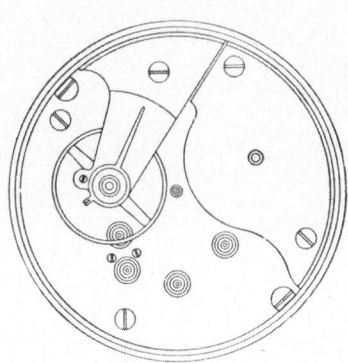

PRIVATE LABEL watch movement by ILLINOIS, engraved on movement & on dial B.A. BELL Chattanooga, Tenn., 18 size, adjusted, 15 jewels, OF.

MODEL 4, 18 size, open face, fine train, this matches the watch on the LEFT

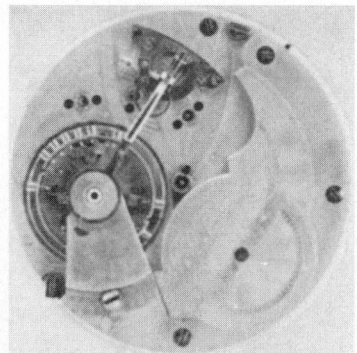

PRIVATE LABEL watch movement by ROCKFORD. Engraved on movement. 'W.G. Gane, Special Railway, 17J, Adj, serial No. 344551.' To identify, see the Identification of Movement section of all watch companies, noting plate design & screw locations to determine that it is a ROCKFORD Model No. 8.

PRIVATE LABEL watch movement by HAMILTON. Engraved on movement, "Mayer, Chattanooga, Tenn., Adjusted, 21J., Grade 940, serial No. 254507." To identify, see the Identification of Movement section of all watch companies, noting plate design & screw locations to determine that   i   t is an 18 size, open face HAMILTON model. Then by using the serial number, the grade can be determined.

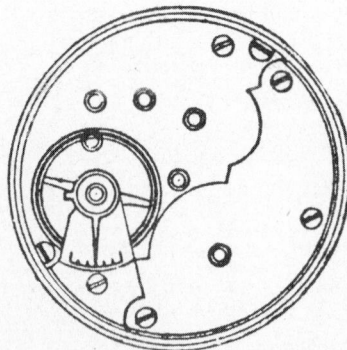

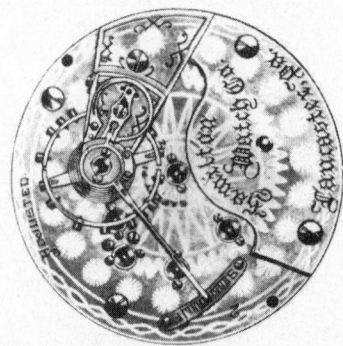

Model 8,18 size, Rockford, full plate, hunting, lever set. This illustration from the identification section matches the model above.

Grade 936, 18 size, Hamilton, open face. This matches the model above.

The basic model will have the key mechanical features and construction. The decoration, damaskeening and jewel count determine the grade. Basic models will have such things as, size, hunting or open face, key or stem wind, lever or stem set, and basic layout design. The 18 size may be Transition models and note the location of the cock to the barrel bridge. The 16 size consider the winding parts may not be seen or they could be exposed (crown & ratchet wheel).

Example: Washington Watch Co. 16 size, 17 jewel, Senate grade. Illinois Watch Co. made a custom watch for (Montgomery Ward) using the name Washington Watch Co. and altered the appearance of the movement, however, the basic model was not significantly changed. The mechanical function remain the same to allow the parts to fit the altered model.

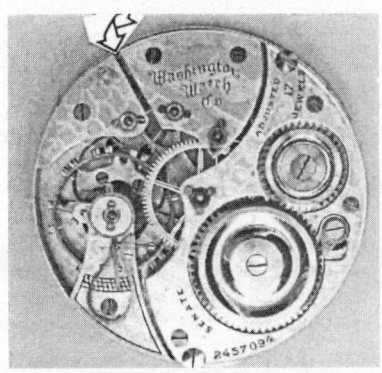

Washington Watch Co. SENATE, 16 size, 17 J Adj.3 P HC polished jewel settings, damaskeen finish, double sunk enamel dial, pendant set, serial # 2457094.

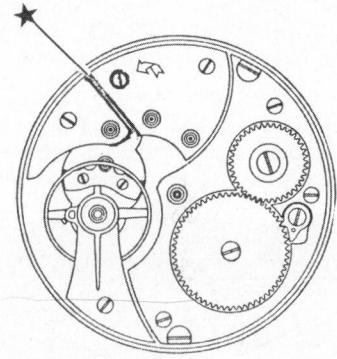

ALTERED drawing of Illinois w. Co., this matches the watch to the left. NOTE: The extra screw & cut out. This also is the same model as below (MODEL # 6).

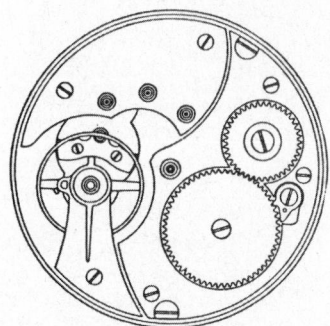

BASIC Illinois Watch co. MODEL 6 as shown in the Illinois W. co. section. note this drawing is NOT altered.

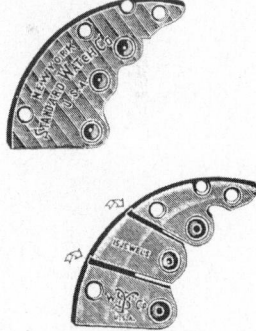

Upper drawing is Example of a BASIC train bridge not cut out. Lower drawing is the same train bridge and cut out to give It a different appearance only. The lower train bridge is cut out to look like three separate bridges.

Generic, nameless, custom or private label watches or unmarked grades for watch movements are listed under the company name or initials of the company, etc. by size, jewel count and description.

After the correct manufacturer has been determined, the serial number can be used to determine the age. Taking the age, grade, size, and manufacturer into consideration, the approximate value can be determined by comparing similar watches from the parent company. If a jeweler's name and location are on the watch, this particular watch will command a higher price in that area.

The custom or Special Named watches are really just variations of a type or style of a grade and may show the serial number production dates. The production run may have called for 1,000 movements of a basic model and grade that may contain 700 with the Watch Co; name on movement and 300 of the custom or personalized watches with customers name on the watch. Therefore its difficult to determine how many of this type of custom made watches were produced. Usually the differences between the custom and basic grades can be seen with out a tear down of the movement. Unfortunately it may require a disassembling of the watch and you may want to have a watchmaker to help to make positive identification.

Compare and match the following list, it may aid you in the identification of your watches: first determine SIZE, then hunting or open face model, key or lever or pendant set, location of balance cock to winding barrel, location of jewels, location of screws, full, 3/4, 1/2, plate or bridge model. Grade differences may include: number of jewels (7-23J.), unadjusted - Adjusted to 3-5 positions, style of regulator & click, (some regulators and click were patented), style of decoration as damaskeening, no name or grade name. The grade without a name were the generic type or style of grade. Generic, nameless, private label, Jobber watches or unmarked grades for watch movements are listed under the company name or initials of the company, etc. by size, jewel count and description.

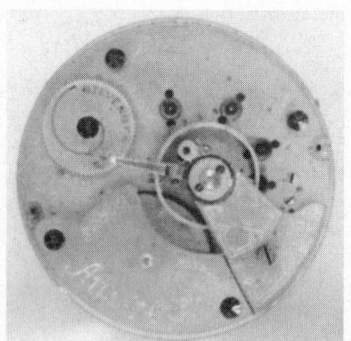 

(A): ON MOVEMENT: J. P. STEVENS & BRO. 15 jewels, ON DIAL J.P. STEVENS & BRO. ATLANTA, GA. the size is 18 Size, hunting case model = a Aurora new model.

(B): ON DIAL EAGLE, On movement illustration of a EAGLE and serial number 512929, hunting case model, and is 16 size made by Seth Thomas model #7.

Special Note on fake watches: Be a knowledgeable wise buyer. Do your homework before you buy. If it is worth faking it will be. If you are not sure of the difference between a fake and a true original and non-original case, dial and movement, find a expert that will know. If you can not determine a fake from a real one, no matter how bad or good the fake is, do not buy it. Investing in watches is not "risk free".

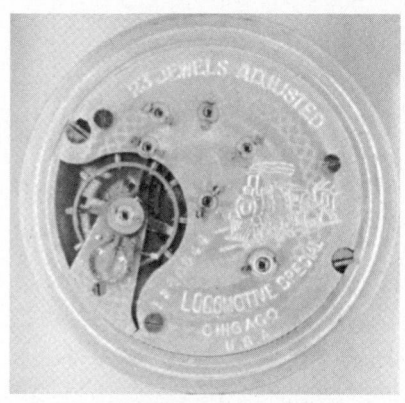

MARKED: adjusted, R. R. SPECIAL on movement, the watch has 21 fake Jewels and is not adjusted also the R. R. SPECIAL implies it is a railroad watch. Also a Locomotive is depicted on movement. (Swiss movement)

Marked: "23 jewels adjusted, Locomotive Special Chicago U.S.A." on 2-tone movement, 23 glass jewels & is not fully adjusted, Locomotive on dial which implies it is a railroad watch. Made by Trenton W. Co. M#6, 18 size, OF, Ca.1903.

SWISS IMPORTED FAKES

Before 1871 a flood of pocket watches were made with names strikingly similar to many well-known American watches. These were made in foreign countries as well as in America and looked and sounded like high quality watches. But they were fakes, inferior in quality.

These key-wind imitations of American pocket watches are a fascinating and inexpensive watch type that would make a good collection. The watches closely resembled the ones they were intended to emulate. Names such as "Hampton Watch Company" might fool the casual buyer into thinking he had purchased a watch from Hampden. "Rockville Watch Co." could easily be mistaken for the American Rockford Watch Co. Initials were also used such as H. W. Co., R. W. Co., and W. W. Co., making it even harder to determine the true identity.

In 1871 Congress passed a law requiring all watches to be marked with the country of origin. The Swiss tried to get around this by printing "Swiss" so small on the movement that it was almost impossible to see. Also the word "Swiss" was printed on the top of the scroll or on a highly engraved area of the movement, making it difficult to spot.

By 1885 these Swiss imitations were of better quality and resembled even more closely what was popular in America. But the Swiss fakes did not succeed, and by 1900-10 they were no longer being sold here.

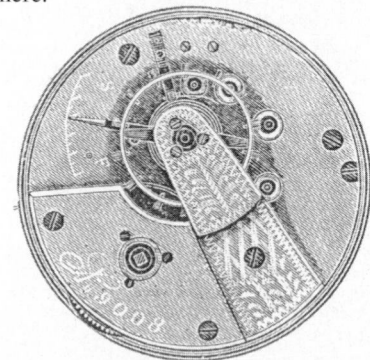

Boston.

98

Note: Right example similar to the authentic American Waltham W. Co. model 1857, many Swiss fake are similar to this.

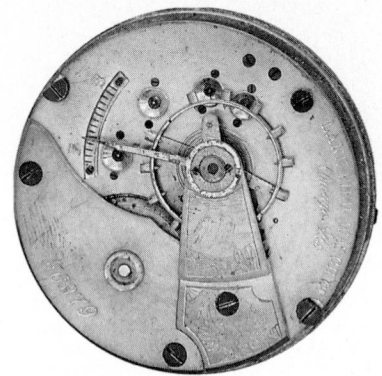

Example of a Swiss imported fake. Note misspelled signature "P.S. Barrett." The authentic American Waltham watch is spelled "P.S. Bartlett.'

Lakeview Watch Co. Chicago, Illinois, Swiss fake, full plate, c. 1885

HOW TO IDENTIFY A SWISS FAKE

1. At first they were keywind and keyset; then they became stem wind, full plate, about 18 size, large jewels on the plate side, and used Roman numerals.

2. Most had American-sounding names so close to the original that it looks merely like a misspelling.

3. The material was often crudely finished with very light gilding.

4. The dial used two feet; American watches used thee.

5. The balance wheel was made to look like a compensated balance, but it did not have the cut in the balance wheel.

6. The large flat capped jewels were blue in color.

These characteristics are not present with all imported fakes. Some or none of these factors may be present. The later the date, the more closely the fake resembled the American watch.

Ohio Watch co. imported Swiss fake distributed by Leon Lesquereaux of Columbus Ohio. This style watch may have been made by E. Borel & co. (Swiss) about 1860-75.

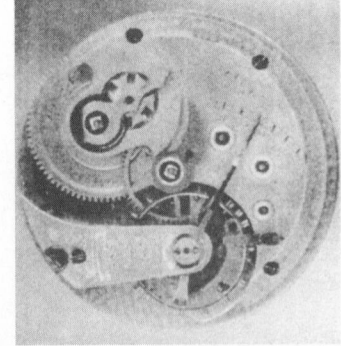

Brooklyn Watch co. New York serial # 6423, note the similarity to E. Howard & co. Boston watch movement.

CONDENSED PRICE LIST
High Grade Movements.
MANUFACTURED BY THE
HAMPDEN WATCH COMPANY.

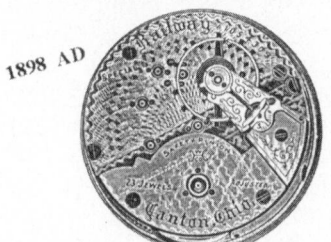

1898 AD

18 Size Movements. O. F. and Htg.

Special Railway	23 Jewels, Nickel Adj.			$35.00
New Railway	23	"	"	28.00
John Hancock	21	"	"	23.00
Special Railway	17	"	"	30.00
New Railway	17	"	"	20.00
Anchor	17	"	"	16.00
No. 48 or 68	17	"	"	16.00
John C. Dueber Special	17	"	"	15.00
No. 47 or 67	17	"	"	15.00
John C. Dueber	17	"	"	12.00
No. 43 or 63	17	"	"	12.00
No. 80 or 81	17	"	"	10.00
No. 49 or 69	17	"	Gilt	9.50
Dueber	17	"	Nickel	8.00
The Dueber Watch Co.	15	"	"	6.50
No. 45 or 65	11	"	"	5.00
No. 46 or 66	11	"	Gilt	4.75
Champion	7	"	"	3.00

John C. Dueber, No. 43 and 63, damaskeened in two
colors when specially ordered.

1906 AD

18 Size

No. 800 Hunting }
No. 900 Open Face } $60.00

24 extra fine ruby and sapphire jewels in gold
settings, sapphire jewel pin, double roller escapement, steel escape wheel, sapphire exposed
pallets, compensating balance in recess, adjusted
to temperature, isochronism and five positions,
mean time screws, Breguet hair spring, patent
micrometric regulator, safety pinion, poised
pallet and fork, handsomely damaskeened nickel
plates, gold lettering, champfered steel parts,
double sunk glass, enamel dial with red marginal
figures, Roman or Arabic, elegantly finished
throughout.   Certificate of rating furnished upon
application.

1926 AD

BUNN SPECIAL
9 Adjustments   21 Jewels
$45.00

SUGGESTED PRICES: Complete in any plain screw—
10K Filled Case, $55.00   14K Filled Case, $65.00
Fancy Cases and Fancy Dials Proportionately More.

21 ruby and sapphire jewels; gold settings; adjusted to SIX positions,
heat, cold and isochronism; compensating balance; gold screws including
timing screws; double roller; steel escape wheel; Breguet hairspring; patent
micrometric screw regulator; safety screw center pinion; beautifully damaskeened with black enamel lettering; double sunk dial.

—

No. 89
17 Jewels, Adjusted to Temperature
$22.50

SUGGESTED PRICES: Complete in any plain screw—
10K Filled Case, $32.50   14K Filled Case, $40.00
Fancy Cases and Fancy Dials Proportionately More.

17 jewels; polished settings; adjusted to temperature; compensating
balance with timing screws; Breguet hairspring; patent regulator; safety screw
center pinion; polished steel work; damaskeened in attractive pattern; double
sunk dial.

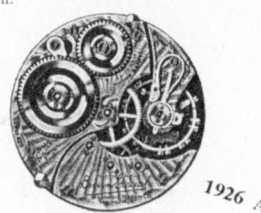

1926 AD

THE 60 HOUR 6 POSITION
BUNN SPECIAL
23 Jewels, $58.00 ⁘ 21 Jewels, $50.00
9 ADJUSTMENTS

SUGGESTED PRICES: Complete in any plain screw cases.
23J., 10K Filled Case, $65.00   14K Filled Case, $72.50
21J., 10K Filled Case, $57.50   14K Filled Case, $65.00
Special or Fancy Cases and Fancy Dials Proportionately More.

Ruby and sapphire jewels; raised gold settings; adjusted to SIX positions,
heat, cold and isochronism; spring tempered compensating balance with
gold screws including timing screws; double roller; steel escape wheel; gold
train wheels; safety screw center pinion; Illinois superior motor barrel; patent
micrometric screw regulator; recoiling safety click; concaved and polished
winding wheels; double sunk dial.

The 23 jewel grade contains the Illinois Superior Jeweled
Motor Barrel and two jewels in which barrel staff pivots operate.

THE 60 HOUR
BUNN
8 Adjustments   19 Jewels
$43.50

SUGGESTED PRICES: Complete in any plain screw—
10K Filled Case, $50.00   14K Filled Case, $57.50
Fancy Cases and Fancy Dials Proportionately More.

19 ruby and sapphire jewels; raised gold settings; adjusted to five
positions, heat, cold and isochronism; special quality hardened and tempered
compensating balance with gold screws, including mean time screws; gold
train wheels; double roller escapement; steel escape wheel; Breguet hairspring; safety screw center pinion; Illinois superior mainspring; patent micrometric screw regulator; recoiling click; Illinois superior jeweled motor barrel;
concaved and polished winding wheels; double sunk dial.

The average Manufactured cost of a Waltham movement in 1913 was $3.75 (case not included).

MARKET REPORT 2007

The 2007 watch market followed many of the trends which were established in the prior year. High grade vintage wristwatches (Patek Philippe, Vacheron Constantin and Rolex) continued to rise and thematic auctions like Antiquorum's "Omegamania" set records and influenced the values on secondary level names such as Omega, Longines, International Watch Co. etc. Vintage chronograph wristwatches were up sharply and condition continued to be a prime factor relative to value.

The strong showing by wristwatches were matched by substantial increases in value for high end pocket watches such as perpetuals, repeaters and chronometers. The rare American pocket watch sector held its values well but the number of rare pieces on the market tended to drop off dramatically from past years. Railroad watches slowed and prices softened a little, which is most likely a reflection of the economic uncertainty felt by most Americans in 2007.

Early 17th century watches showed tremendous gains in price and demand as the availability is dwindling faster than ever. More "common" verge fusees are still a super value. These sleepers are long overdue for an increase in price. Gold pocket watch prices remained steady thanks to a stronger bullion market yet demand for this segment is still soft. Multi colors in gold were also quiet this year.

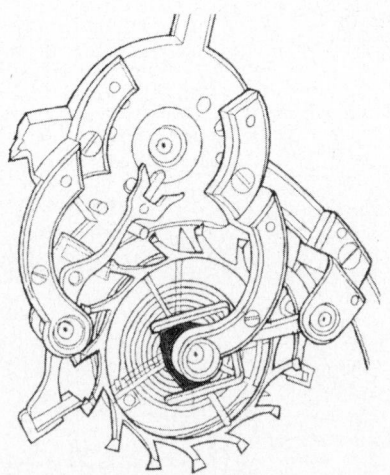

Derek Pratt's one-second remontoire incorporated
into the one-minute tourbillon escapement

AMERICAN POCKET WATCH LISTINGS

(As Complete Watches With Case & Movement)

The prices shown in this book are averaged from dealers listings, catalog sales, auction results, trade shows and internet transactions. Each entry is followed by three prices: A, B and C. The three levels represent watches as follows:

A   B   C

A - An approximate dealer buying price, ABP, for a watch which is running and complete. (ABP)

B - A dealer selling price for a watch, fully restored, good case and dial. (Ex-Fn)

C - A dealer selling price for a mint condition watch, all original. (Mint)

Variations can take place in the pricing structure due to several factors. The cost of restoration, for example, can be quite high and some lower level watches may not warrant the restoration cost. Also, complicated watches such as repeaters, chronographs, etc., as well as early watches, especially verge and other early escapements, can also be very costly to restore. Therefore, the variations in the A level price and the C level price can vary widely if the restoration costs are excessive. The availability of parts for certain vintage and antique watches is becoming more endangered as every year passes. Some watches are simply not restorable do to this parts dilemma. The ease of sale for certain type of watches will aslo have an effect on pricing at a dealers or wholesale level. Certain watches are simply more in demand and can be sold at a quicker rate to eager collectors. Watches which are slow to sell must be held in inventory; therefore, the A level prices will be lower to offset the inventory holding cost. All watches can bring significantly higher prices when the condition is outstanding. Watches which are in virtually new condition with pristine original dials, original boxes, certificates or bills of sale (especially rare wrist watches) will often bring record price levels above the top indicator listed in this publication.

Many of the watch manufacturers were commissioned to put jewelers' or jobbers' names on their movements in place of their own. Due to this practice, the true manufacturers of these movements are difficult to identify. These watch models are listed under the original manufacturer and can be identified by comparison with the model sections under each manufacturer. See "Personalized & Custom Watches" for more detailed information.

The watch manufacturers who personalized & custom made watches for jobbers or jewelry firms, with exclusive private signed or marked movements must first be found by using a illustration & matched to the manufacture shown in this book. After you identify the movement now the value can be determined. The valuable collectable watches are listed under the signed or marked movement. Other exclusive private signed or marked movements will have equivalent value are only slightly higher value & should be compared to Generic or Nameless movements. Railroad signed or marked (dials & movements) are usually more collectable & higher in value.

Important Notice. All of the information, including valuations, in this book has been compiled from the most reliable sources, and every effort has been made to eliminate errors and questionable data. Nevertheless, the possibility of error, in a work of such immense scope, always exists. The publisher or authors will not be held responsible for losses which may occur in the purchase, sale, statements of its advertisers, or other transaction of items, because of information contained herein. Readers who feel they have discovered errors are invited to write and inform the publisher, so that they may be corrected in subsequent editions.

Descriptions and serial number ranges listed for early watches cannot be considered 100 percent accurate due to the manner in which records were kept by these companies.

ABBREVIATIONS USED IN
THE COMPLETE PRICE GUIDE TO WATCHES

  Below a rating scale for rarity.
(★ Star Rating) & 5 Stars = Rarest
★★★★★ ....RARE - 1-25
★★★★ ....SCARCE -100
★★★ ....VERY FEW -350
★★ SPARSE-1,OOO
★ .... UNCOMMON - 2,500
▱ .... In Demand, technical or
                            historical interest.
ABP .... Approximate Dealer Buying Price
ADJ .... Adjusted (to temperature or or
            heat & cold, also isochronism).
            Adj.5P = Adjusted to 5 positions,
            3 positions or 4 positions etc
aux. sec .... auxiliary seconds
BASE .... Base metal used in cases; e.g., silveroid
BB .... Bubble Back (Rolex style case)
BRG .... Bridge plate design movement
Ca. .... Circa (about or approximate date)
Cal. .... Calendar also Calibre (model)
C&B ....Case and Band
Chrono .... Chronograph
Co .... Company
COIN.. Coin silver
DES .... Diamond end stones
DMK .... Damaskeened
DSD... Double sunk dial
DR .... Double roller
DWT...................... Penny weight: 1/20 Troy ounce
ETP .... Estimated total production
ESC. .... Escapement
EX .... Extra nice; far above average
FULL .... Full plate design movement
3/4................................... 3,4 plate design movement
1 F brg .... One finger bridge design and a
            3/4 plate (see Illinois 16s M#5)
2F brg .... Two finger bridge design
3F brg .... Three finger bridge design
GF.. Gold filled
GJS .... Gold jewel settings
G#.. Grade number
GT .... Gold train (gold gears)
GCW .... Gold center wheel
GRO .... Good running order
HC .... Hunter case
id. .... identification

(illo.) .... Illustration of watches etc.
J .... jewel (as 21J)
K .... Karat (14k solid gold not gold filled)
K(w) .... WHITE GOLD as in 14k(w)
K(y) .... YELLOW GOLD as in 14k(y)
KS... Key set
KW .... Key wind
KW/SW............... transition (Key wind/stem wind)
LS .... Lever set
MCC.. Multi-color case
MCD .... Multi-color dial
M#.. Model number
mm .... Millimeter (over all case size)
mvt. .... movement or movment only no case
NI .... Nickel plates or frames
OF... Open face
P..................... as Adj.5P = Adjusted to 5 positions,
            3 positions or 4 positions etc.
PORC .... Porcelain (pow. dial)
PS .... Pendant set
PW .... Pocket Watch
RF# .... Reference Factory number
Reg .... Register on a chronograph
REP .... Repeater
RGJS .... Raised gold jewel setting
RGP .... Rolled gold plate
RR .... Railroad
S.. Size as 16S = 16 size
SBB .... Screw back and bezel
SR .... Single Roller
SRC .... Swing ring case
SS .... Stainless steel
SSD .... Single Sunk Dial
SW.. Stem wind
Sit .... Serial number
TEMP.. Temperature
TP .... Total production
2T .... Two-tone (damaskeened in 2 colors)
WGF.. White gold filled
W.I. also W. Ind.   Wind indicator
            or (up and down indicator)
/ = ... **WITH** as KW/SW or SW/LS
/ = ... Also as OF/HC
WW .... Wrist watch
YGF.. Yellow gold filled
@=.. AT or About

MODEL = Size, open face or hunter, full or 3/4 plate, key or stem wind, design & layout of parts.
GRADE 1st., 2nd., & 3rd., Quality etc. some manufactures used names or numbers (Bunn , 992).
Note: Model is not the same defination as grade. A model may exist in many different grades or grade names (as 992, Bunn, Riverside, Veritas) and may be used in many different models (as model 1, 18 size, open or hunting case, model 1, in 16 size open or hunting case, model 1 in 12 size) etc..

1. **Ebauche** = Manufacture movements in the rough.
2. **Manufacture** = 75% to 100% of movements Manufacture on premises.
3. **Watchmaker & Finisher** = Finished movement in the rough or used Special named movement.
4. **Jobber**, Distributor, Firms, Special named, Customized or Personalized movement = Retail only.

Railroad Standards, Railroad Approved & Railroad Grade TERMINOLOGY

1. **RAILROAD STANDARDS** = A commission or board appointed by the railroad companies outlined a set of guidelines to be accepted or approved by each railroad line.

2. **RAILROAD APPROVED** = A list of watches each railroad line would approve if purchased by their employee's. (this list changed through the years).

3. **RAILROAD GRADE** = A watch made by manufactures to meet or exceed the guidelines set by the railroad standards. Grades such as 992, Vanguard and B.W. Raymond, etc.

    Some grades exceeded the R.R. standards such as 23 jewels, diamond end stone, gold train, raised gold jewel settings, double sunk dial and the list goes on. Examples: such as Veritas, Sangamo, 950 & Riverside Maximus and many others.

ABOVE: **GENERIC, NAMELESS OR UNMARKED MOVEMENTS**

Generic, nameless or unmarked grades for watch movements are listed under the Company name or initials of the company, etc. by size, jewel count and description. Such as American Watch Co. or Ann Watch Co. or A.W.W.Co., Elgin W. Co. or Elgin National W. Co., Hampden W.Co. or Duber W.Co., Illinois W. Co. or I.W.Co., Rockford or R.W.Co., South Bend. Example name on movement Illinois Watch Co. and the watch is 18 size, 17 jewels, stem wind, adjusted, nickel, and damaskeened this watch can be found and will be listed under Illinois Watch Co. next look under the correct size (18 size) unmarked grade section as Illinois Watch Co. or I.W.C., 15J, SW, ADJ, NI, DMK these are generic or unmarked grades. Movements with a grade name such as Bunn can be found and listed under size, then name (Bunn), then jewels, etc.

MODEL = Size, open face or hunter, full or 3/4 plate, key or stem wind, design & layout of parts.

GRADE = 1st., 2nd., & 3rd., Quality etc. some manufactures used names or numbers (Bunn , 992).

ABBOTT'S STEM WIND

Henry Abbott first patented his stem wind attachment on June 30, 1876. The complete Abbott's stem wind mechanism is arranged in such a way as to convert key wind to stem wind. He also made a repeater-type slide mechanism for winding. On January 18, 1881, he received a patent for an improved stem wind attachment. Abbott sold over 50,000 wind attachments, and were fitted to Cornell, Elgin, Hampden, Illinois, N.Y. W. Co., Rockford, Tremont, U.S. Marion, Waltham 16-18-20 size and Howard above S# 30,000.

Abbott Stem Wind Attachment. LEFT: normal view of an Elgin watch movement with hidden Abbot stem wind attachment (pat. Jan, 18 1881). RIGHT: Same watch with dial removed exposing the Abbott Stem Wind Attachment.
**NOTE: Most Abbott's stem wind levers move up and down, while most standard
levers move up & out. Some watches this may increase in value.**

ABBOTT WATCH CO.
(MADE BY HOWARD WATCH CO.) 1908 - 1912

Abbott Sure Time Watches were made by the E. Howard Watch Co.(Keystone), and are similar to Howard Watch Co. 1905 model. These watches sold for $8.75 and had 17 jewels. Some of the open face watches are actually hunting case models without the second bits register.

Description		ABP	Ex-Fn	Mint
Abbott Sure Time, 16S, 17J, OF, GF Case . . . . ★		$100	$200	$350
Abbott Sure Time, 16S, 17J, HC, GF Case.		125	275	375
Abbott Sure Time, 16S. 17J, **14K Abbott HC** . . . . ◁		400	600	900

Abbott Watch Co., 16 size, 17 jewels, gold jeweled settings, hunting case. Note similarity to the Howard Watch Co. model 1905. Serial number 993932

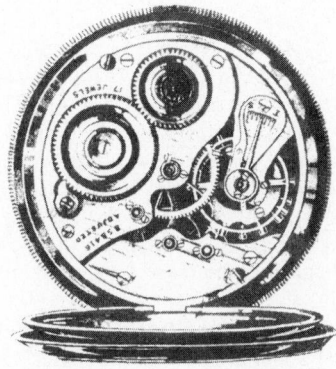

Abbott Watch Co., 16 size, 17 jewels, gold jeweled settings, open face, Note similarity to the Howard Watch Co. series 9

ADAMS PERRY WATCH MANUFACTURING CO.

Lancaster, Pennsylvania (1874-1877)

This company, like so many others, did not have sufficient capital to stay in business for long. The first year was spent in setting up and becoming incorporated. The building was completed in mid-1875, and watches were being produced by September. The first watches were limited to three grades, and the escapement and balance were bought from other sources. The first movement was finished April 7, 1876, but in May of 1876, they closed. *(very few watches were sold from this factory)* The next year the company remained idle. In August 1877, the company was sold to the Lancaster Watch Company. In 1892 Hamilton acquired the assets. Seen: Serial # 1, movement marked "Adams Perry & Co. Lancaster Pa., Perrys Patents, No.1, (also next to the click marked with a Z").

Description		ABP	Ex-Fn	Mint
19S, 20J, GJS, PS, SW, 2 GJS, **18K** original case . . . . ★★★		$2,500	$3,500	$6,600
19S, 20J, GJS, PS, SW, 2 GJS, gilt mvt, gold filled case . . . . . . ★★		1,200	2,000	3,500
19S, 20J, GJS, PS, SW, 2 GJS, DMK, **nickel mvt.,** GF case . . ★★★		2,000	2,800	4,500
19S, 20J, GJS, PS, SW, 2 GJS, DMK, **nickel mvt.,** 18K orig case, Signed by Adams and Perry, 1st watch they produced. ★★★★★		20,000	30,000	50,000

Marked on movement **"Lancaster Watch Penna. 1681"**. This basic model about 19 size, consists of 20 jewels, 2 gold jeweled settings screwed in place, stem wind and pendant set, Geneva stop-works, serial number 1681. The above is the so called **Adams Perry & Co.**, model.

J. H. ALLISON movement 16 jewels, gold train and escape wheel with a pivoted detent key wind and key set, serial number 19.

J. H. ALLISON

Detroit, Michigan
1853-1890

The first watch J. H. Allison made was in 1853; it was a chronometer with full plate and a fusee with chain drive. The balance had time screws and sliding weights. In 1864, he made a 3/4 plate chronometer with gold wheels. He also damaskeened the nickel movement. He produced only about 25 watches, of which 20 were chronometers. By 1883 he was making 3/4 plate movements with a stem wind of his own design. Allison made most of his own parts and designed his own tools. He also altered some key wind watches to stem wind. Allison died in 1890.

Description	ABP	Ex-Fn	Mint
Full Plate & 3\4 Plate, GT, NI, DMK . . . . ★★★★ . $10,000		$15,000	$20,000
Detent Chronometer Escapement, 16J, KW/KS, GT . . . ★★★★ . . 15,000		20,000	25,000

AMERICAN REPEATING WATCH CO.

Elizabeth, New Jersey

1885-1892

Around 1675, a repeating mechanism was attached to a clock for the first time. The first repeating watch was made about 1687 by Thomas Tompion or Daniel Quare. Five-minute, quarter-hour and half-hour repeaters were popular by 1730. The minute repeater became common about 1830.

Fred Terstegen applied for a patent on August 21, 1882, for a repeating attachment that would work with any American key-wind or stem-wind watch. He was granted three patents: No. 311,270 on January 27, 1885; No. 421,844 on February 18, 1890; and No. 436,162 in September 1890. It is not known how many repeaters were made, but it is estimated to be about **500** to **1,000**. This repeating attachment fits most American **18 & 16** size movements. The Terstegen repeating attachments were made and sold as a **KIT** to fit different models of American watches.

18 SIZE, with REPEATER ATTACHMENT

Name —Description		ABP	Ex-Fn	Mint
HOWARD, w/ 5 min. repeater attachment, COIN	★★	$4,400	$5,500	$11,000
GOLD CASE	★★	7,700	9,000	16,500
Keystone, or Lancaster, w/ 5 min rep. attachment, COIN	★★	3,850	5,000	9,000
GOLD CASE	★★	4,400	5,500	11,000
SETH THOMAS, w/ 5 min. repeater attachment, COIN	★★	3,850	5,000	9,000
GOLD CASE	★★	5,500	7,000	11,000

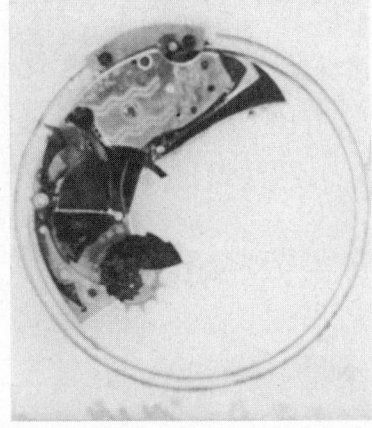 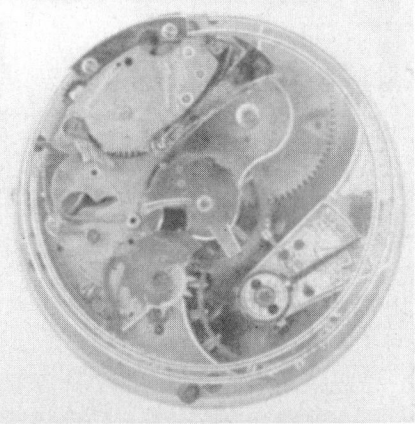

ABOVE: **American Repeating Attachment**. illustration at **LEFT** shows Terstegen's patented repeating attachment only. Illustration at **RIGHT** shows attachment as normally found on movement The two outside circles on left illustration are wire gongs. The hammer can be seen at upper **LEFT** Illustration in the shape of a boot.

&ᴑ Watches listed in this book are priced at the collectable fair market value at the Trade Show level, as complete watches having an original 14k gold filled case, KEY WIND with silver, an original white enamel single sunk dial, and with the entire original movement in good working order with no repairs needed, unless otherwise noted.

&ᴑ Some grades are not included. Their values can be determined by comparing with similar age, size, metal content, style, models and grades listed.

16 SIZE, with REPEATER ATTACHMENT

Name — Description		ABP	Ex-Fn	Mint
COLUMBUS, w/ 5 min. rep. attachment, GF or COIN	★★	$3,850	$5,000	$9,000
GOLD CASE	★★	4,620	5,500	11,000
ELGIN, w/ 5 min. rep. attachment, GF or COIN	★★	3,850	5,000	9,000
GOLD CASE	★★	4,620	5,500	11,000
HAMPDEN, w/5 min. rep. attachment, GE or COIN	★★	3,300	5,000	9,000
GOLD CASE	★★	3,850	5,000	11,000
HOWARD, w/5 min. rep. attachment, GF or COIN	★★	6,050	7,000	10,000
GOLD CASE	★★	7,700	9,000	15,400
ILLINOIS, w/5 min. rep. attachment, GF or COIN	★★	3,850	5,000	9,000
GOLD CASE	★★	6,600	8,800	14,300
Non-magnetic (Paillard),w/5 min. rep. attachment, gold-filled	★★	2,420	4,000	7,000
GOLD CASE	★★	3,430	5,000	8,000

NOVEL STRIKING ATTACHMENTS

Five-Minute Repeaters.

(Manufactured under Terstegen's Patents.)

They are made to fit the following American Watch Movements:

16 SIZE	18 SIZE
ILLINOIS	ONLY TO
COLUMBUS	
HOWARD	LANCASTER
HAMPDEN	or
NON-MAGNETIC	KEYSTONE
PAILLARD	SETH THOMAS
WALTHAM and	and
ELGIN	HOWARD

HUNTING OR OPEN-FACE.

Handsome, Simple and Durable.

**American
Repeating Watch Factory**
of Elizabeth, N. J.

&✓ A collector should expect to pay modestly higher prices at local shops.

&✓ Watches listed in this book are priced at the collectable fair market value at the Trade Show level, as complete watches having an original 14k gold filled case, key wind with silver, an original white enamel single sunk dial, and with the entire original movement in good working order with no repairs needed.

&✓ Some grades are not included. Their values can be determined by comparing with similar age, size, metal content, style, models and grades listed.

&✓ The Complete Price Guide to Watches goal is to stimulate the orderly exchange of Watches between "buyers"and "sellers".

THE AMERICAN WALTHAM WATCH CO.

1851 - 1957 (Waltham Watch Co.)

To trace the roots of the Waltham family one must start with the year 1850 in Roxbury, Massachusetts, No. 34 Water Street. That fall David Davis, a Mr. Dennison, and Mr. Howard together formed a watch company. Howard and Dennison had a dream of producing watches with interchangeable parts that were less expensive and did not result in less quality.

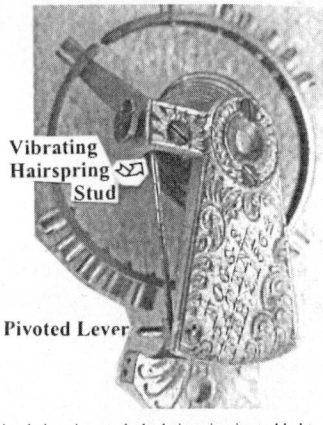

American Watch Co., 18-20 size, serial #50, 100, thought to be a prototype model.

Vibrating hairspring stud, the hairspring is studded to a pivoted lever and movement is restricted by a regulating screw. Thus, the length of the hairspring remains constant.

Howard served an apprenticeship to Aaron Willard Jr. in about 1829. Several years later, in 1842, Howard formed a clock and balance scale manufacturing company with Davis. Howard and Dennison combined their ideas and, with financing provided by Samuel Curtis, the first of their watches was made in 1850. But they had problems. They were trying out ideas such as using jewels, making dials, and producing steel with mirror finishes. This required all new machinery and resulted in a great financial burden. They discovered, too, that although all watches were produced on the same machines and of the same style, each watch was individual with its own set of errors to be corrected. This they had not anticipated. It took months to adjust the watches to the point they were any better than any other timepieces on the market. The first watch was sold in 1853 the **Warren** model.

Example of a Warren model, about 18S, 15J., engraved on the movement ***Warren NO 44 BOSTON***, plain dial, under sprung, steel balance, right angle lever, escape wheel has pointed teeth, KW & KS from front, Ca.1853. Note: This movement was made to fit an English size case and will not fit a standard 18S American case. (No.44 may be highest # known)

But Howard had perfected and patented many automatic watchmaking machines that produced precision watch parts. In 1851 the factory building was completed and the name Warren Manufacturing Co. andnot American Horologe Co. The first 17 watches were not placed on the market but went to officials of the company. It was not until late 1853 that the first watches were sold to the public, signed "Warren Boston", after a famed Revolutionary War hero. Watches numbered 18 through 110 were marked "Warren Boston" the next 800 were marked "Samuel Curtis" a few were marked "Fellows & Schell" and sold for $40. Note: The first watches were marketed in 1853.

The name was changed to the Boston Watch Company in September 1853, and a factory was built in Waltham, Massachusetts, in October 1854. The movements that were produced here carried serial numbers 1,001 to 5,000 and were marked "Dennison, Howard & Davis," "C. T. Parker," and "P. S. Bartlett." Boston Watch Company failed in 1857 and was sold at a sheriff's auction to Royal E. Robbins. In May 1857, it was reorganized as the Appleton, Tracy & Co., and the watches produced carried serial numbers 5,001 to 14,000, model 1857. The first movements were marked Appleton, Tracy & Co. The C. T. Parker was introduced as model 1857 and sold for $12.00, 399 of these models were made. In 1855 brass clocks were selling just over $1.00. Also 598 chronodrometers were produced and in January 1858 the P. S. Bartlett grade. In August of 1865 prices for movement only: Ellery-$13, P.S. Bartlett-$16, Bartlett Ladies-$30, Appleton Tracy & Co.-$38, A. T. & Co. Ladies-$40, and the American Watch Co. grade was $175

Engraved on movement **SAMUEL CURTIS ROXBURY. NO 112**. 18 size. 15 jewels, under sprung, steel balance, This movement was made to fit in the typical English size case. (112 may be lowest # known)

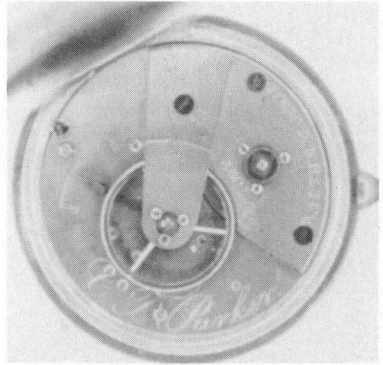

Engraved on movement "*C.T. PARKER WALTHAM MASS. NO 1099*", 7 jewels, under sprung, steel balance. Ca. 1853. Ca. November 1857. Note: Balance cock not engraved.

In January 1859, the Waltham Improvement Co. and the Appleton, Tracy & Co. merged to form the American Watch Company. In 1860, as Lincoln was elected president and the country was in Civil War, the American Watch Co. was faced with serious problems. The next year, business came to a standstill. There seemed to be little hope of finding a market for watches, and bankruptcy again seemed close at hand. At this point it was decided to cut expenditures to the lowest possible figure and keep the factory in operation.

American horology owes much to members of the Waltham Watch group such as Bacon, Church, Dennison, Fogg, Howard, Marsh, Webster, and Woerd, who contributed much to its development and success. In early 1861, the name "J. Watson" appeared on model 1857 (first run: Nos. 23,601 to 24,300 total production 1,200).

The next model 1857 was the "R. E. Robbins" of which 2,800 were made. The William Ellery, marked "Wm. Ellery," (model 1857) was then introduced with the first serial number of 46,201. It was key wind and key set and had 7 to 15 jewels.

A size 10 woman's watch was made in July of 1861 with first serial numbers of 44,201. It was marked "Appleton, Tracy & Co." gold balance, key wind and key set, 3/4 plate, 13 to 15 jewels. Some were marked "P. S. Bartlett" and a 15 jewel was marked "Appleton, Tracy & Co." A special model, 10 size, serial numbers of 45,801 to 46,200, is extremely rare. The first stem wind, beginning with serial number 410,698, was produced in 1868. By 1880 all watches were quick train. The last key wind was serial No. 22,577,000, about 1919, 18 size, 1883 model, 7J, sterling, produced for export.

Abraham Lincoln owned & carried a "William Ellery" model, silver-cased, key wind, 11 jewels, so stated Carl Sandburg in his biography of Lincoln. The watch was produced by American Watch Co. in Jan., of 1863 & was a 18 size, hunting case.

WALTHAM ESTIMATED SERIAL NUMBERS AND PRODUCTION DATES

DATE	SERIAL NO.	DATE	SERIAL NO.	DATE	SERIAL NO.
1852 –	50	1888 –	3,800,000	1924 –	24,550,000
1853 –	400	1889 –	4,200,000	1925 –	24,800,000
1854 –	1,000	1890 –	4,700,000	1926 –	25,200,000
1855 –	2,500	1891 –	5,200,000	1927 –	26,100,000
1856 –	4,000	1892 –	5,800,000	1928 –	26,400,000
1857 –	6,000	1893 –	6,300,000	1929 –	26,900,000
1858 –	10,000	1894 –	6,700,000	1930 –	27,100,000
1859 –	15,000	1895 –	7,100,000	1931 –	27,300,000
1860 –	20,000	1896 –	7,450,000	1932 –	27,550,000
1861 –	30,000	1897 –	8,100,000	1933 –	27,750,000
1862 –	45,000	1898 –	8,400,000	1934 –	28,100,000
1863 –	65,000	1899 –	9,000,000	1935 –	28,600,000
1864 –	110,000	1900 –	9,500,000	1936 –	29,100,000
1865 –	180,000	1901 –	10,200,000	1937 –	29,400,000
1866 –	260,000	1902 –	11,100,000	1938 –	29,750,000
1867 –	330,000	1903 –	12,100,000	1939 –	30,050,000
1868 –	410,000	1904 –	13,500,000	1940 –	30,250,000
1869 –	460,000	1905 –	14,300,000	1941 –	30,750,000
1870 –	500,000	1906 –	14,700,000	1942 –	31,050,000
1871 –	540,000	1907 –	15,500,000	1943 –	31,400,000
1872 –	590,000	1908 –	16,400,000	1944 –	31,700,000
1873 –	680,000	1909 –	17,600,000	1945 –	32,100,000
1874 –	730,000	1910 –	17,900,000	1946 –	32,350,000
1875 –	810,000	1911 –	18,100,000	1947 –	32,750,000
1876 –	910,000	1912 –	18,200,000	1948 –	33,100,000
1877 –	1,000,000	1913 –	18,900,000	1949 –	33,500,000
1878 –	1,150,000	1914 –	19,500,000	1950 –	33,560,000
1879 –	1,350,000	1915 –	20,000,000	1951 –	33,600,000
1880 –	1,500.000	1916 –	20,500,000	1952 –	33,700,000
1881 –	1,670,000	1917 –	20,900,000	1953 –	33,800,000
1882 –	1,835,000	1918 –	21,800,000	1954 –	34,100,000
1883 –	2,000,000	1919 –	22,500,000	1955 –	34,450,000
1884 –	2,350,000	1920 –	23,400,000	1956 –	34,700,000
1885 –	2,650,000	1921 –	23,900,000	1957 –	35,000,000
1886 –	3,000,000	1922 –	24,100,000		
1887 –	3,400,000	1923 –	24,300,000		

D.S. Marsh, No. 1852 engraved on
movement. (8 day watch)

★ The above list is provided for determining the APPROXIMATE age of your watch. Match serial number with date. Watches were not necessarily **SOLD** and **DELIVERED** in the exact order of manufactured or production dates.

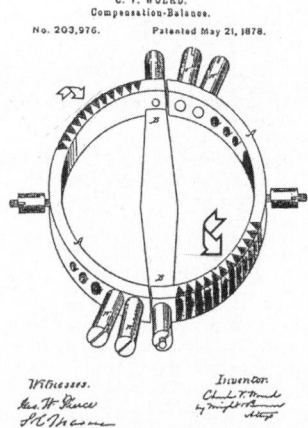

HOWARD, DAVIS & DENNISON: 20 Size, 15 Jewels, 8 day, two mainsprings and gilt movement. Serial#1 -17 were made for the officials of the company, Ca. 1852.

Woerd's patented compensating balance the above illustration is a copy of the blue print of Mr. Woerd's patented **SAW TOOTH BALANCE** The Serrated Tooth Balance may be found on some 16 size 1872 models. **(VERY RARE)**

☞ A collector should expect to pay modestly higher prices at local shops.

☞ Generic, nameless or unmarked grades for watch movements are listed under the Company name or initials of the Company, etc. by size, jewel count and description.

20 SIZE
MODEL 1862 = 20 KW - (T. P.3,500)

Grade or Name—Description		ABP	Ex-Fn	Mint
American Watch Co., 19J, KW, **18K, HC**, all original	★★★	$6,600	$11,000	$16,500
American Watch Co., 15 to 19J, KW, KS,3/4, vibrating hair-spring stud, silver case	★★	2,200	4,500	9,000
American Watch Co., 15 to 19J, KW, KS, 3/4, vibrating hair-spring stud, **18K HC**, all original	★★★	5,500	7,700	13,000
American Watch Co., 15 & 17J, 3/4, KW, ADJ	★	550	800	1,500
American Watch Co., 19J, 3/4, KW, ADJ	★★	3,500	5,000	7,700
American Watch Co., 19J, 3/4, KW, ADJ, with Maltese cross stopwork, all original silver case.	★★	4,500	6,000	9,000
American W. Co., Nashua S# under dial, (below 51,000)	★★★	7,000	11,000	18,000
Am'n W. Co., 7-11J, 3/4, KW	★	550	900	1,600
Am'n W. Co., 15J, KW,3/4, coin case.	★	650	1,000	1,700
Appleton, Tracy & Co., 15J, 3/4, KW, with Maltese cross stopwork, all original	★	800	1,100	2,200
Appleton, Tracy & Co., 15-17J, 3/4, KW	★	700	1,100	1,700
Appleton, Tracy & Co., 15 & 17J, 3/4, KW, vibrating hair spring stud, silver case	★★	2,200	4,000	5,500
Appleton, Tracy & Co., 15 & 17J, 3/4, KW, vibrating hair spring stud, **18K HC**	★★★	4,500	8,300	11,000
Appleton Tracy & Co., 15J, KW, vibrating hairspring stud Straton barrel, Foggs Pat.	★★	1,100	2,200	3,900
Appleton Tracy & Co., 15J, KW, 3/4, **Mvt. only no case**		275	350	650
Appleton Tracy & Co., 19J, KW, 3/4	★★	550	1,100	1,700
Howard, Davis & Dennison, S#1-17, 8 day, Ca.1852	★★★★★	110,000	165,000	300,000

NOTE: **RARE in original gold cases add ($1,500.00 in 14K) & ($2,000.00 in 18K).**

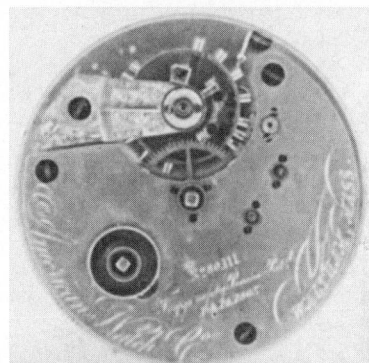

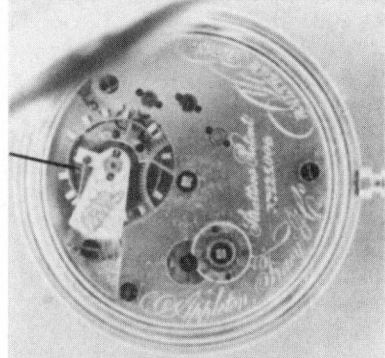

American Watch Co., Model 1862, 20 size, 17-19 jewels, gold balance and escape wheel, gold jeweled settings, key wind, key set from back, serial number 80111.

Appleton Tracy & Co., Model 20KW, 20 size, 15 jewels, serial number 125004. Note vibrating hairspring stud.

Escape Wheel for the 'Chronodrometer". Note: 8 tooth, solid brass, escape wheel. Also it has a sweep second hand which makes one circuit in 4 minutes. In the lower part of the dial there is a second hand in the usual place, and it makes one round in 4 seconds in beats of 1/4 second each as it is mounted on the escape wheel arbor. In the upper portion of the dial is the usual hour & minute hands in a small 12 hour circle.

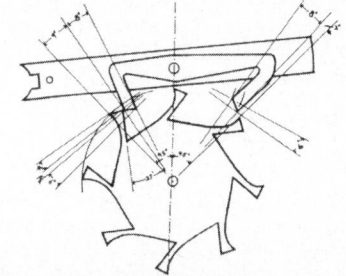

American Watch Co., Model 18KW, 18 size, 15 jewels, serial number 36369. Reversible clutch center pinion, patented Nov. 30th, 1858. Note: Thin disk at the center of the center wheel.

Model 1857,18 size, 15-18 jewels, 'Chronodrometer" on dial, "Appleton Tracy & Co." or "P.S. Bartlett, key wind & set, 1/4 jump seconds, S.# 14,752. Listed under **"Appleton Tracy & Co. Chronodrometer",** 1st serial #13,701. Note: Stop - start botton at 4 o'clock.

18 SIZE
MODELS 1857, (18KW =1859), 1870, 1877,1879, 1883, 1892

Grade or Name — Description		ABP	Ex-Fn	Mint
American Watch Co., 17J,3/4, M#1859 or M#**I8KW**	★★★★	$3,300	$7,200	$13,200
American Watch Co., 19J, 3/4, M#1859	★★★★	6,000	9,300	16,500
American Watch Co., 15J, M#1859,3/4, Pat. Nov. 30, 1858,				
Reversible center pinion, original silver case	★★★	4,700	7,700	13,200
American Watch Co., 17J, M#1859,3/4, KW, Fitts Pat.				
Reversible center pinion, Originial 18K case	★★★★	5,500	8,800	15,500
American Watch Co., 21J, M#1883, Special, ADJ, GJS	★★★★	1,100	2,200	4,400

&⌒ Generic, nameless or unmarked grades for watch movements are listed under the Company name or initials of the Company, etc. by size, jewel count and description.

		ABP	Ex-Fn	Mint
AM'n. Watch Co., 15J, M#1857, (*Waltham W. Co.*), KW, KS		$250	$350	$600
AM'n. Watch Co., 15J, M#1857, (*Waltham W. Co.*), SW/ KS	★	275	400	700
AM'n. Watch Co., 15J, M#1857, (Waltham W. Co.), SW /KW	★	300	400	700
AM'n. Watch Co., 15-17J, M#1857, (*Waltham W Co.,*), SW, LS		175	300	500
AM'n. Watch Co., 17J, M#1857, KW, KS	★	200	325	550
AM'n. Watch Co., **14K, HC, heavy box hinged, multi - 4 colors.**		2,500	4,000	6,500
AM'n. Watch Co., 11J, thin model, KW, 3/4 plate	★	200	300	700
AM'n Watch Co., 15J, M#1870, KW		125	250	550
AM'n. Watch Co., 17J, M#1870, KW, ADJ		150	300	600
AM'n. Watch Co., 17J, M#1892		125	200	400
AM'n. Watch Co., 21J, M#1892		200	325	650
AM'n. Watch Co., 7J, M#1877		100	150	250
AM'n. Watch Co., 11J, M#1877		100	150	250
AM'n. Watch Co., 7J, M#1883, SW/ KW.		100	150	250
AM'n. Watch Co., 11-13J, M#1883, SW, KW		100	175	300
AM'n. Watch Co., 15J, M#1883, SW/ KW.		100	175	300
AM'n Watch Co., 16-17J,M#1883		125	175	300
Appleton, Tracy & Co., 15J, M#1857, SW/ LS.		200	300	400
Appleton, Tracy & Co., 7-11J, KW, M#1857		200	300	450
Appleton, Tracy & Co., 11J, **thin model**, KW,3/4	★	225	400	700
Appleton, Tracy & Co., 15J, M#1857, KW.		200	300	450
Appleton, Tracy & Co., 15-16J, M#1 857, KW,				
serial # below 10,000	★	1,200	1,800	3,000

&⌒ Some watch manufacturers personalize watches for jobbers or jewelry firms, with exclusive private signed or marked movements. The valuable collectable watches are listed under the signed or marked movement. Other exclusive private signed or marked movements will have equivalent value or only slightly higher value and should be compared to Generic or Nameless movements. Railroad signed or marked (dials & movements) are usually more collectable & higher in value.

Grade or Name—Description	ABP	Ex-Fn	Mint
Appleton, Tracy & Co., 15J, M#1859, 3/4, reverse pinion,			
Pat Nov. 30, 1858, orig. silver case .... ★★★	$2,000	$3,000	$5,500
Appleton, Tracy & Co., 11-15-16-17J, KW, 3/4, M# 1859 .... ★	200	350	700
Appleton, Tracy & Co., 16J, M# 1857, **1st run** (5,001-5,100)			
Am. W. Co. (Eagle) silver HC .... ★★★★	2,000	3,500	6,000
Appleton, Tracy & Co., 15J, M#1857, KW, **18K HC**..............	1,500	2,500	4,000
Appleton, Tracy & Co., 16J, M#1857, KW.....................	250	350	700
Appleton, Tracy & Co., 15J, 3/4, KW, with vibrating hairspring stud,			
Stratton's Pat., Foggs Pat., orig. coin case .... ★★★	2,000	3,200	5,500
Appleton, Tracy & Co., 15J, 3/4, KW, with vibrating hairspring stud,			
Stratton's Pat., Foggs Pat., orig. **18K** case .... ★★★	3,000	4,500	7,500
Appleton, Tracy & Co., **Sporting, (Chronodrometer)**,M#1 857,			
15-16J, KW, KS, orig. case, with stop feature .... ★★★	3,000	5,000	7,500
Appleton, Tracy & Co., 15J, 3/4, M# 1859, KW .... ★	225	325	600
Appleton, Tracy & Co., 11-15J, M#s 1877, 1879, SW	100	150	300
Appleton, Tracy & Co., 15J, M#1877, KW	100	150	300
Appleton, Tracy & Co., 15J, M#s 1877-1879, SW, OF...........	100	150	300
Appleton, Tracy & Co., 15J, M#s 1877-1879, SW, HC	125	200	350
Appleton, Tracy & Co., 15J, M#1883,SW,OF...................	100	150	300
Appleton, Tracy & Co., 15J, M#1883, SW, **non- magnet,** OF	200	300	500
Appleton, Tracy & Co., 15-17J, M#1883, gold plate -Mvt.........	250	400	650
Appleton, Tracy & Co., 15J, M#1883, SW, HC	100	175	300
Appleton, Tracy & Co., 15J, M#1892,SW,OF ....★★	250	375	675
Appleton, Tracy & Co., 17J, M#1883, SW, HC	125	175	300
Appleton, Tracy & Co., 17J, M#1892, SW, Premiere	100	150	300
Appleton, Tracy & Co., 17J, M#1892, NI, SW, OF	100	150	300
Appleton, Tracy & Co., 17J, M#1883,OF......................	100	150	300
Appleton, Tracy & Co., 17J, M#1892, SW, HC	125	175	400
Appleton, Tracy & Co., 19J, M#1892, SW, OF	200	350	550
Appleton, Tracy & Co., 19J, M#1892,SW,HC...................	250	400	600
Appleton, Tracy & Co., 21J, M#1 892, SW, OF.................	225	325	500
Appleton, Tracy & Co., 21J, M#1892,SW,HC .... ★	300	500	700

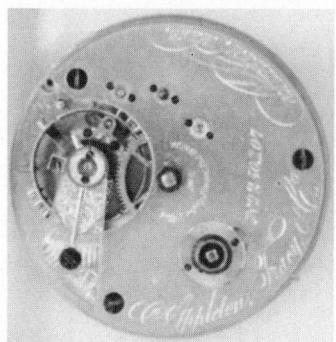

Appleton, Tracy & Co. (20 size), 15-17 jewels, Foggs safety pinion pat. Feb. 14,1865, key wind & set from back, serial number 250107,

P.S. Bartlett, Model 18KW or 1859, 18 size, 11 jewels, key wind & set from back, serial number 41597.

☞ A collector should expect to pay modestly higher prices at local shops.

☞ The Complete Price Guide to Watches goal is to stimulate the orderly exchange of watches between "buyers" and "sellers".

▢ Generic, nameless or unmarked grades for watch movements are listed under the Company name or initials of the Company, etc. by size, jewel count and description.

Grade or Name — Description		ABP	Ex-Fn	Mint
A.W.W.Co.,7-9J, M#1883, **KW**, ... ★		$200	$300	$650
A. W. W. Co., 7-9J, M#1883, SW		100	125	250
A. W. W. Co., 11-13J, LS, HC		100	175	300
A. W. W. Co., 11-13J, M#1879, OF		100	125	225
A. W. W. Co., 11-13J, M#1883, SW, OF		100	125	225
A. W. W. Co., 15J, OF		100	125	240
A. W. W. Co., 15J, HC		125	175	325
A. W. W. Co., 15J, **14K (5) multi-colors TRUE boxcase HC**		2,700	3,800	7,000
A. W. W. Co., 15J, **14K (4) multi-colors TRUE boxcase HC**		2,500	3,300	6,000
A. W. W. Co., 15J, **14K (3) multi-colors boxcase HC**		2,000	2,600	4,400
A. W. W. Co., 15J, M#1879, OF		100	125	200
A. W. W. Co., 15J, M#1883		100	125	200
A. W. W. Co., 16 or 18J, OF		100	125	300
A. W. W. Co., 16 or 18J, HC		125	175	300
A. W. W. Co., 17J, M#1857, gold bal, wheel, GJS .... ★		250	450	800
A. W. W. Co., 17J, "for R.R. Service" on dial ....★★		600	1,100	1,800
A. W. W. Co., 17J, M# 1883, OF		125	175	250
A. W. W. Co., 17J, M# 1883, HC		150	200	300
A. W. W. Co., 17J, M# 1892, LS, OF		125	150	200
A. W. W. Co., 17J, M# 1892, PS, OF		150	175	200
A. W. W. Co., 17J, M# 1892, HC		100	175	300
A. W. W. Co., 19J, M# 1892, OF		200	250	600
A. W. W. Co., 21J, M# 1892, OF		250	395	750
A. W. W. Co., 23J, M# 1892, OF		325	500	950

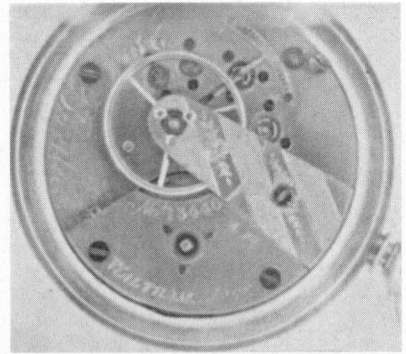 

P.S. Bartlett, 18 size, 15 jewels, Model 1857, Engraved on back "4 PR. Jewels." Serial number 13446.

Appleton, Tracy & Co. 18S, 15J, M #1877, stem wind, quick train, S # 1,389,078. Note the TRUE Box Hinged Case.

Grade or Name —Description		ABP	Ex-Fn	Mint
P. S. Bartlett, 7J, M# 1857, KW, **1st Run** (1,401-1,500)				
Am. W. Co. (Eagle) silver HC................... ★★★★		$2,000	$3,500	$7,000
P. S. Bartlett, 15J, M# 1857, KW, **2nd Run** (1,551-1,650)				
Am. W. Co. (Eagle) silver HC...................... ★★★		1,500	2,500	4,000
P. S. Bartlett, 11J, M# 1857, KW, **3rd Run** ....★★		800	1,200	2,000
P. S. Bartlett, 15J, M# 1857, KW, **3rd Run** ....★★		900	1,400	2,300
P. S. Bartlett, 7J, M# 1857, KW		150	200	300
P. S. Bartlett, 11J, M# 1857, KW		165	200	335
P. S. Bartlett, 15J, M# 1857, KW		150	200	300
P. S. Bartlett, 15J, M# 1857, KW , S# below <u>180,000</u> (Pre Civil War).		365	500	800
P. S. Bartlett, 11-15J, M# 1857, KW, Eagle inside case lid..........		400	675	1,000
P. S. Bartlett, 15J, M# 1857, SW / LS **(note let down screw)**		275	375	650
P. S. Bartlett, 7-11J, M# 1859, KW/KS.......................		165	225	350
P. S. Bartlett, 11-15J, M# 1877, KW-SW, HC.................		125	165	300

Grade or Name —Description	ABP	Ex-Fn	Mint
P. S. Bartlett, 15J, M# 1877, SW, marked special, HC.............	$150	$200	$400
P. S. Bartlett, 11-15J, M# 1879, KW-SW, OF....................	100	175	250
P. S. Bartlett, 11J, M# 1883, SW.........................	100	125	200
P. S. Bartlett, 15J, M# 1883, KW .... ★	200	350	575
P. S. Bartlett, 15J, M# 1883, SW.........................	100	125	200
P. S. Bartlett, 17J, M# 1883, SW.........................	100	125	200
P. S. Bartlett, 11J, M# 1859, 3/4, thin model, KS from back........	400	600	1,000
P. S. Bartlett, 15J, M# 1859, 3/4, thin model, KS from back........	500	700	1,100
P. S. Bartlett, 15J, **pinned plates,** M# 1857, KW .... ★	700	1,200	1,600
P. S. Bartlett, 15J, M# 1892, SW	125	250	400
P. S. Bartlett, 17J, M# 1892, SW, OF, LS	125	175	300
P. S. Bartlett, 17J, M# 1892, SW, HC....................	125	200	350
P. S. Bartlett, 17J, M# 1892, SW, OF, PS	100	150	300
P. S. Bartlett, 17J, M# 1892, SW, 2-Tone	175	300	450
P. S. Bartlett, 19J, M# 1892, SW	150	275	450
P. S. Bartlett, 21J, M# 1892, SW	225	300	525
P. S. Bartlett, 21J, M# 1892, SW, 2-Tone	300	400	650
Broadway, 7J, M# 1857, KW, HC........................	125	175	350
Broadway, 11J, M# 1857, KW, HC.......................	125	175	375
Broadway, 7-11J, M# 1877, KW, SW, NI, HC	125	175	350
Broadway, 7J, M# 1883, KW, HC........................	125	175	350
Broadway, 11J, M# 1883, KW, HC.......................	125	175	350
Broadway, 11J, M# 1883, SW, HC	125	175	300
Canadian Pacific R.R., 17J, M# 1883 ....★★	500	900	1,500
Canadian Pacific R.R., 17J, M# 1892 ....★★	600	1,000	1,800
Canadian Pacific R.R., 21J, M# 1892, OF ....★★	800	1,100	2,200
Canadian Pacific R.R., 21J, M# 1892, HC ....★★★	1,000	1,800	3,000
Canadian Railway Time Service, 17J, M# 1883-1892, Adj. SP...★★	500	700	1,000
Central Park, 15J, M# 1857, KW	200	275	400
Champion, 15J, M# 1877, OF	100	125	175
Conklins Railroad Special, 21J, G# 1892 ....★★	500	700	1,000

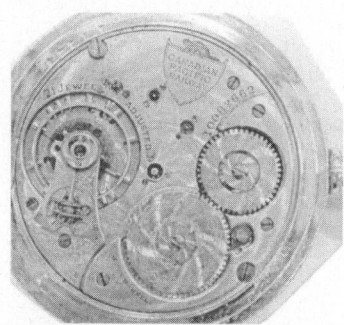

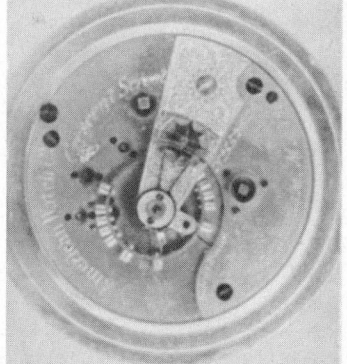

Marked **Canadian Pacific Railway**, Model 1892 HC,18 size, 21 jewels. S# 10,082,662. Note beaver on shield.

Crescent Street. Model 1870, 18 size, 15 J., Key wind & set from back, serial number 552,528. This grade was the **first** American watch to be advertised as a railroad watch

IMPORTANT NOTE: Railroad Standards, Railroad Approved & Railroad Grade terminology, as defined and used in this book.

1. **RAILROAD STANDARDS** = A commission or board appointed ,by the railroad companies outlined a set of guidelines to be accepted or approved by each railroad line.

2. **RAILROAD APPROVED** = A list of watches each railroad line would approve if purchased by their employee's. (this list changed through the years).

3. **RAILROAD GRADE** = A watch made by manufactures to meet or exceed the guidelines set by the railroad standards. Grades such as 992, van Guard and B. W. Raymond, etc.

Some GRADES **exceeded** the R.R. standards such as 23 jewels, diamond end stone, gold train, raised gold jewel settings, double sunk dial and the list goes on.

Grade or Name—Description	ABP	Ex-Fn	Mint
Crescent Street, 15J, M# 1870, KW	$150	$250	$600
Crescent Street, 15J, M# 1870, **pin or nail set**	185	275	700
Crescent Street, 17J, M# 1870, KW/SW . . . . ★	200	350	600
Crescent Street, 15J, M# 1870, SW	100	145	300
Crescent Street, 15J, M# 1883, SW, non-magnetic, OF	125	200	325
Crescent Street, 15J, M# 1883, SW, non-magnetic, HC	150	250	425
Crescent Street, 15J, M# 1883, SW, 2-Tone	175	250	450
Crescent Street, 17J, M# 1883, SW, OF	100	150	300
Crescent Street, 17J, M# 1883, SW, HC	100	175	300
Crescent Street, 19J, M# 1883 . . . . ★	250	400	600
Crescent Street, 17J, M# 1892, SW, **GJS**	100	185	275
Crescent Street, 17J, M# 1892, SW, OF	100	165	265
Crescent Street, 17J, M# 1892, SW, HC	125	200	300
Crescent Street, 19J, M# 1892, SW, Adj.5P, GJS, OF	150	250	375
Crescent Street, 19J, M# 1892, SW, Adj.5P, GJS, HC	200	300	450
Crescent Street, 21J, M# 1892, 5W Adj.5P, GJS, OF	200	325	550
Crescent Street, 21J, M# 1892, SW, Adj.5P, GJS, 2 tone, OF	300	400	650
Crescent Street, 21J, M# 1892, SW, Adj.5P, GJS, HC	250	400	550
Crescent Street, 21J, M# 1892, **Wind Indicator** . . . . ★	1,400	1,800	2,600
Cronometro Supremo, 21J, M# 1892, Adj., GJS, OF . . . . ★★★	600	700	1,000
Cronometro Victoria, 17J, dial & mvt. marked Adjusted . . . . . ★★★	600	700	1,000
Samuel Curtis, 11-15J, M# 1857, KW, S# less than **200,**			
original 17S silver case . . . . ★★	3,000	5,000	7,500
Samuel Curtis, 11-15J, M# 1857, KW, S# less than **400,**			
original 17S silver case . . . . ★★	2,500	4,500	7,500
Samuel Curtis, 11-15J, M# 1857, KW, S# less than **600,**			
original 17S silver case . . . . ★★	2,200	3,000	4,500
Samuel Curtis, 11-1 53, M# 1857, KW, S# less than **1,000,**			
original 17S silver case . . . . ★★	2,000	3,000	4,500
(Samuel Curtis **"not"** in original silver case, deduct $800to $1,000 from value)			
Dennison, Howard, Davis, 7J, M# 1857, KW, W/**original case**	1,000	2,000	3,000
Dennison, Howard, Davis, 11-13J, M# 1857, KW, W/**original case** . .	1,200	2,200	3,400
Dennison, Howard, Davis, 15J, M# 1857, KW, W/**original case**	1,400	2,400	3,600
Dennison, Howard, Davis, 15J, M# 1857, KW, 1st. run (**1,002-1,100**			
W/**original** case Am. W. Co. (**Eagle**)silver HC . . . . ★★★	2,000	3,000	5,000
Dennison, Howard, Davis, 15J, M# 1857, KW, S# less than **2,000**			
W/**original** case Am. W. Co. (**Eagle**)silver HC . . . . ★	1,500	2,500	4,500

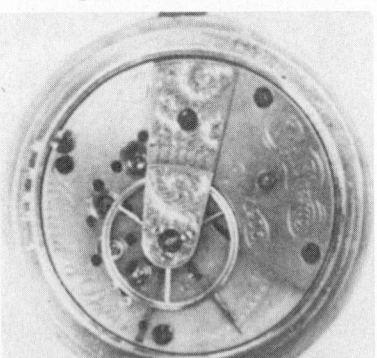

Dennison, Howard, Davis, Model 1857. 18 size, 16 jewels, under sprung, key wind, serial number 1205.

Howard & Rice, Model 1857, 18 size, 15 jewels, under sprung, serial number 6003.

🖛 Watches listed in this book are priced at the collectable Trade Show level, as complete watches having an original 14k gold-filled case and Key Wind with silver, an original white enamel single sunk dial, and with the entire original movement in good working order with no repairs needed.

Grade or Name -Description	ABP	Ex-Fn	Mint
D.& R. G. Special (Denver & Rio Grande), 17J, M# 1892, GJS, Adj.5P ....★★★	$2,500	$3,500	$6,000
D.& R. G. Special (Denver & Rio Grande), 21J, M# 1892, GJS, Adj.5P ....★★★	3,000	4,000	7,500
Dominion Railways, 15-17J, M# 1883, OF, SW, train on dial ....★★★	2,500	4,500	7,500
Wm. Ellery, 7-11J, M# 1857, Boston, Mass. all original silver HC case with Am. Watch Co.& eagle, serial # below **46,600** ....★★	400	600	1,000
Wm. Ellery, 7-11J, M# 1857, Boston, Mass	100	150	300
Wm. Ellery, 7-11J, M# KW, 3/4, M# 1859	100	150	300
Wm. Ellery, 15J, KW, 3/4, M# 1859 ....★	200	300	500
Wm. Ellery, 7-11J, M# 1859, KW-KS from back, **18K, HC**	1,600	2,500	3,500
Wm. Ellery, 7J, M# 1857, KW, KS from back	200	300	550
Wm. Ellery, 15J, M# 1857, **SW** / LS, (with let down screw) ......★	225	350	650
Wm. Ellery, 7-15J, M# 1877, M# 1879, KW....................	100	185	300
Wm. Ellery, 11-15J, M# 1877 & 1879, SW....................	100	185	300
Wm. Ellery, 7-13J, M# 1883	100	185	300
Excelsior, 1-15J, M# 1857, engraved on bal. cock (made only for Howard & Co. Fifth Avenue New York)	100	185	300
Excelsior, 11-15J, M# 1877, KW..............................	100	185	300
Export, 7-11J, M# 1877.....................................	100	185	300
Export,7-11J,M# 1883,KW...................................	100	185	300
Express Train, 15-17J, M# 1883, LS, OF ....★★	400	600	1,000
Favorite, 15J, M# 1877	100	175	300
Fellows & Schell, 15J, KW, KS, 1857 model ....★★★	2,000	4,000	7,000
Franklin, 7J, M# 1877, SW.................................	125	200	350
Home Watch Co., 7-15J, M# 1857-1883, KW....................	100	175	300
Home Watch Co., 7J, M# 1877, KW..........................	100	175	300
Home Watch Co., 7-11J, M# 1879, SW........................	100	175	300
Howard & Rice, 15J, M# 1857, KW, KS, **mvt. by Waltham,** (serial numbers range from 6,000 to 6,500) ....★★★	2,500	4,000	6,000
E. Howard & Co., Boston (on dial & mvt.), English style escape wheel, upright pallets, 15J, M# 1857, KW, KS, mvt. by Waltham, S#s about 6,400 to 6,500 ....★★★★	3,000	5,000	8,000
Lehigh Valley Railroad 17J, M# 1883, SW, Appleton, Tracy & Co. grade ....★★	1,000	1,500	2,500
Lehigh Valley Railroad 17J, M# 1883, SW, **2 tone mvt.** Appleton, Tracy & Co. grade ....★★	1,200	2,000	3,000
Martyn Square, 7-15J, M# 1857-77-79, KW, SW (exported) .....★	200	275	400
Mermod, Jaccard & King Paragon Timekeeper, 23J, M# 1892, Vanguard, LS, GJS, HC...........................★★	400	650	1,000

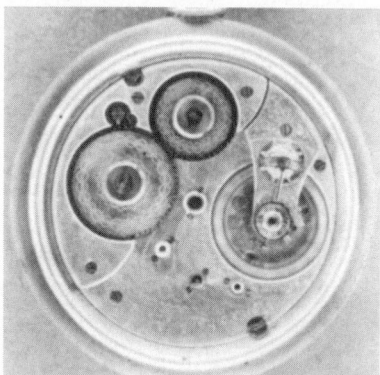

Pennsylvania Special, Model 1892, 18 size, 21 jewels, serial number 14,000,015.

American Waltham Watch Co., Model 1883, 18 size, 15 jewels, serial number 3,093,425.

Grade or Name -Description	ABP	Ex-Fn	Mint
Non-Magnetic, 15J, M# 1892, SW, LS.........................	$100	$175	$300
Non-Magnetic, 17J, M# 1892, SW, LS.........................	125	200	325
Paragon, 15J, M# 1883, HC .... ★	300	400	650
"Chas. T. Parker" marked, 11-15J, M# 1857, KW, HC..........★★	1,500	2,500	4,000
C. T. Parker, 7-11J, M# 1857, KW, Am. W. Co. (Eagle) silver HC serial # below **1,200**...............................★★	2,000	3,000	4,600
C. T. Parker, 7-11J, M# 1857, KW, Am. W. Co. 18K, HC serial # below **1,200**...............................★★	3,000	4,500	7,500
Pennsylvania R.R. on dial, **Appleton, Tracy & Co**. on Mvt., KW, KS, M# 1857 ....★★★★★	4,000	7,000	12,500
Pennsylvania Special, 21J, M# 1892, HC................★★★	2,500	3,600	5,500
Pennsylvania Special, 21J, M# 1892, OF................★★★	3,000	4,000	6,000
Pennsylvania Special, 21J, M# 1892, HC GOLD DAMASKEENED, gold train.............★★★★★	7,000	12,000	18,000
Pennsylvania Special, 23J, M# 1892, OF............... ★★★★	4,000	5,000	7,500
Pioneer, 7J, M# 1883	100	125	200
Premier, 17J, M# 1892, LS, OF	125	150	250
Railroader, 17J, M# 1892, LS..........................★★★	1,500	2,500	4,000
Railroader, 21J, M# 1892, LS..........................★★★	2,000	3,000	4,500
Railroad Inspector, 21J, M# 1892, LS, (loaner with # on case)..........................★★	500	800	1,800
Railroad King, 15J, M# 1883, LS.....................★★	350	500	700
Railroad King, 15J, M# 1883, **2-Tone** ....★★	450	600	1,000
Railroad King, 17J, **Special**, M# 1883, LS ....★★	550	750	1,000
Railroad Standard, 19J, G#1892, OF ....★★★	1,500	2,500	3,500
Railway Time Keeper 15J, 1892.........................★★	200	300	550
Riverside, 17J, M# 1892 .... ★	175	275	525
Roadmaster, 17J, M# 1892, LS.......................★★	600	800	1,200
R. E. Robbins, 11-15J, M# 1857, KW S# (25,101-25,200) ....★★	1,500	2,500	3,500
R. E. Robbins, 13-15J, M# 1877, KW.....................	225	325	575
R. E. Robbins, 13J, M# 1883	125	175	300
Royal, 17J, M# 1892, OF	100	150	275
Royal, 17J, M# 1892, HC	150	200	325

Sidereal, model #1892, 17j. 24 hour dial used by astronomers. (marked **Sidereal** on dial above sub. seconds dial)

Vanguard, model 1892, 18S, 23J, diamond end stone, gold jewel settings, exposed winding gears. S# 10,533,465.

 A collector should expect to pay modestly higher prices at local shops.

Grade or Name —Description	ABP	Ex-Fn	Mint
Santa Fe Route, 17J, M# 1883, HC-OF.....................★★	$550	$800	$1,400
Santa Fe Route, 21J, M# 1892, OF........................★★	850	1,200	2,200
Santa Fe Route, 21J, M# 1892, HC ....★★★	1,000	1,700	2,500
Sidereal, M# 1892, 19J, (marked **Sidereal** on dial) OF ......★★★	1,500	2,200	3,500
M# 1892, 17J, Astronomical (marked **Sidereal** on dial) OF ...★★★	1,500	2,200	3,500
Sol, 7-11J, M# 1883, (with sun on dial), OF..................★	150	300	500
Sol, 17J, OF...	100	135	200
Special Railroad, 17J, M# 1883, LS, OF ....★★	400	600	1,000
Special R. R. King, 15-17J, M# 1883 ....★★	500	700	1,100
Special R. R. King, 15-17J, M# 1883, HC ....★★	600	800	1,300
Sterling, 7J, M# 1857, KW, **Silver** case	125	175	300
Sterling, 7-11J, M# 1877, M# 1879.........................	100	125	250
Sterling, 7-11J, M# 1883, **KW** ....★	200	300	450
Sterling, 11-15J, M# 1883, SW.............................	100	150	250
Tourist, 11J, M# 1877....................................	100	150	250
Tourist, 7J, M# 1877.....................................	100	150	250
Tracy, Baker & Co., 15J, **18K original A. W. W. Co.**			
case ....★★★★★	10,000	20,000	35,000
Vanguard, 17J, M# 1892, GJS, HC........................★★	450	700	1,100
Vanguard, 17J, M# 1892, LS, Adj.5P, DR, GJS, OF ....★★	400	650	1,000
Vanguard, 17J, M# 1892, **Wind Indicator,** Adj.5P, DR, GJS.....★	1,500	2,500	4,000
Vanguard, 19J, M# 1892, LS, Adj.5P, Diamond end stones	250	400	700
Vanguard, 19J, M# 1892, LS, Adj.5P, DR, GJS, OF	200	350	650
Vanguard, 19J, M# 1892, **Wind Ind.,** LS, Adj.5P, DR, GJS .....★★	1,800	3,000	4,500
Vanguard, 19J, M# 1892, Adj.5P, GJS, HC ....★	325	500	750
Vanguard, 21J, M# 1892, Adj.5P, PS	250	350	550
Vanguard, 21J, M# 1892, GJS, Adj.5P, HC	325	425	650
Vanguard, 21J, M# 1892, LS, Adj.5P, DR, GJS, OF	250	350	550
Vanguard, 21J, M# 1892, LS, Adj.5P, Diamond end stone	300	400	550
Vanguard, 21J, M# 1892, **Wind Indicator,** Adj.5P, GJS, OF ....★★	2,000	3,200	4,700
Vanguard, 23J, M# 1892, LS, Adj.5P, DR, GJS, OF	300	400	600
Vanguard, 23J, M# 1892, LS, Adj.5P, DR, GJS, HC ....★	400	550	850
Vanguard, 23J, M# 1892, LS, Adj.5P, DR, GJS, Diamond end. stone	300	425	650
Vanguard, 23J, M# 1892, PS, Adj.5P, DR, GJS, OF	300	400	600
Vanguard, 23J, M# 1892, **Wind Indicator,** Adj.5P, OF ....★★	2,200	3,400	5,000
Vanguard, 23J, M# 1892, **Wind Indicator,** Adj.5P, HC .... ★★★★	4,000	6,000	8,500
Waltham,17J, Adj., G#1892, **(non magnetic),** OF...............	200	300	500
Waltham Standard,17J, Adj., G#1892, (locomotive), OF .....★★★	1,000	1,700	2,700
Waltham Standard,19J, Adj., G#1892, (locomotive), OF .....★★★	1,200	2,100	3,200
Waltham Watch Co., 15J, **M# 1857,** SW / LS, (W/let down screw)...	225	400	600

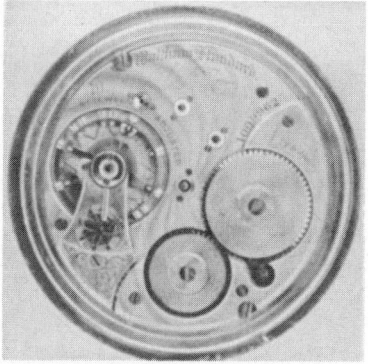

Waltham Standard, Grade 1892, 18size, 19jewels, Adj5P, open face. note engine & coal car (locomotive) engraved on movement, serial number 10,099,625.

Marked **845**, Model 1892, 18 size, 21 jewels, railroad grade, Adj.5P, serial number 15,097,475

 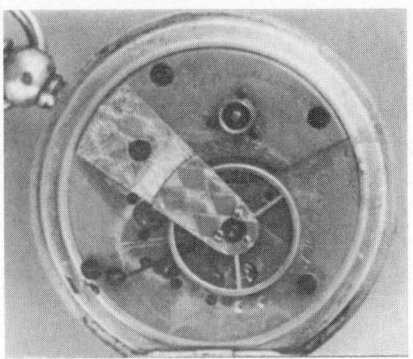

Waltham Watch Co., 1857 model with factory stem wind, 18S, 15J, Fogg's Patent. This is not a Abbott's stem wind conversion. Most Abbott's stem wind with lever set, the levers move up and down, while most stem winds the levers move up & out.

J. WATSON, Boston Mass engraved on movement, 18size, 11 jewels, hunting case, key wind key set, serial number 28,635, Ca. April 1863.

Grade or Name — Description		ABP	Ex-Fn	Mint
Warren, 15J, M# 1857, KW, KS, **S#18-29**, original 17S silver case.	★★★★★	$25,000	$40,000	$70,000
Warren, 15J, M# 1857, KW, KS, **S#30-60**, original 17S silver case.	★★★★	20,000	30,000	50,000
Warren, 15J, M# 1857, KW, KS, **S#61-90**, original 17S silver case.	★★★★	15,000	25,000	45,000
Warren, 15J, M# 1857, KW, KS, **S#91-110**, original 17S silver case.	★★★★	13,000	20,000	40,000
(Warren not in original silver case, deduct $6,000 to $12,000)				
George Washington, M# 1857, KW	★★	700	1,000	1,800
George Washington, M# 1879, SW		300	500	800
J. Watson, 7J, M# 1857, KW, marked "Boston" ★ S#(**28,201-28,270**)	★★★	1,200	1,800	3,500
J. Watson, 7-11J, M# 1857, KW, marked "London" S# (**23,700-23,800**)	★★★	1,200	2,000	3,500
454, 21J, GT, 3/4	★	200	300	550
820, 15J,OF		100	125	175
845, 21J, M# 1892, OF		200	300	550
845, 21J, M# 1892,HC		300	500	800
836, 17J, DR, Adj.4P, LS, OF		100	150	300

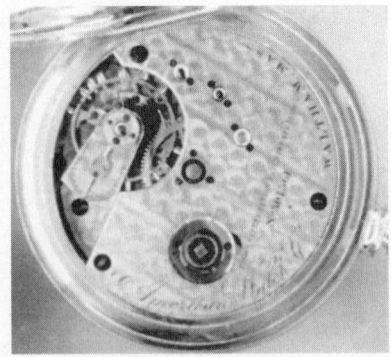 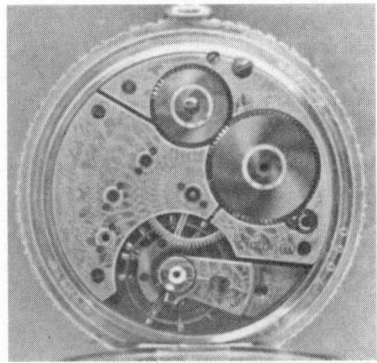

American Watch Co., Model 16KW or Model 1868, 16 size, key wind and set from back, Gold Train, serial number 501,561.

American Watch Co., Model 1888,16 size, 19jewels, gold jewel settings, gold train, high grade movement, serial number 5,000,297.

16 SIZE
MODELS 16KW =1860,1868,1872,1888, 1899,1908, BRIDGE MODEL

Grade or Name — Description		ABP	Ex-Fn	Mint
AM'n. Watch Co., 7-15J, M#1872, KW KS,				
sweep sec. with a **slide stop** button................★★★		$700	$1,200	$2,000
AM'n. Watch Co., 7-11J, M#1888, 3/4,SW		100	150	225
AM'n. Watch Co., 7-11J, M#1888-1899........................		100	150	225
AM'n. Watch Co., 11J, M#16KW or 1868, KW & KS from back,				
original silver case .... ★★		1,000	1,500	3,000
AM'n. Watch Co., 11J,M#1868,3/4,KW		700	1,000	1,700
AM'n. Watch Co., 13J,M#1888-1899.........................		100	150	250
AM'n. Watch Co., 15-17J, M#1868, 3/4, KW .... ★		700	1,000	1,700
AM'n. Watch Co., 15J, M#1868-1872, 3/4,SW		300	500	1,000
AM'n. Watch Co., 15J, M#16KW, KW & KS from back....... ★★		500	700	1,500
AM'n. Watch Co., 15-16J, M#1888-1899, HC		100	150	325
AM'n. Watch Co., 15J, M#1888-1899, SW, HC.................		100	150	325
AM'n. Watch Co., 15J, M#1888-1899, SW,		100	150	325
AM'n. Watch Co., 16-17J, M#1872, 3/4, SW		200	400	650
AM'n. Watch Co., 17J, M#1888-1899		100	175	300
AM'n. Watch Co., 19J, M#1872, 3/4,SW.................★★★		1,200	2,200	3400
AM'n. Watch Co., 19J, M#1899............................		125	300	500

☞ Generic, nameless or unmarked grades for watch movements are listed under the Company name or initials of the Company, etc. by size, jewel count and description.

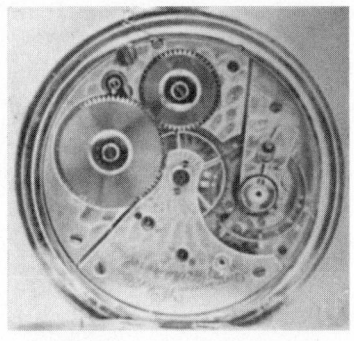

American Watch Co., Model 1888, 16 size,19 jewels, gold train note tadpole regulator

American Watch Co.. Bridge Model, 16 size, 23 jewels gold train, Adj.5P.

Grade or Name —Description		ABP	Ex-Fn	Mint
American Watch Co., 19J Maltese cross stopwork, gilt mvt.				
all original 1860 Model, **18K** case ....★★		$2,000	$3,500	$5,500
American Watch Co., 17-19J, 3/4, KW & KS from back,				
vibrating hairspring stud, 1860 Model, **18Kcase** ...... ★★★		2,500	3,600	5,200
American Watch Co., 19J, 3/4 , KW & KS from back, nickel mvt.				
1860 Model, original case, **18K** case .... ★★★★		4,500	7,500	12,000
American Watch Co., 15J, M#1868, 3/4, KW, Silver.......★★★		1,000	1,500	3,000
American Watch Co., 17-18J, M#1872,3/4,SW,**HC,14K**......... ★		1,500	2,200	3,800
American Watch Co., 17J M#1868, 3/4, KW, ADJ, Silver ......★★		1,000	1,500	2,600
American Watch Co., 17J M#1899, Adj. 5P, ... ★		395	500	750
American Watch Co., 18J M#1868, SW, nickel mvt .... ★		500	650	1,050
American Watch Co., 19J M#1868, SW, nickel mvt.				
Silver case .... ★★★		4,500	6,000	8,500
American Watch Co., 19J, M#1888, SW, nickel mvt......... ★★★		1,500	2,000	3,500
American Watch Co., 19J, M#1899, SW, nickel mvt ....★★		550	800	1,300

Grade or Name — Description		ABP	Ex-Fn	Mint
American Watch Co., 19-21J, M#**1872**, 3/4, SW .... ★★★		$2,500	$3,500	$6,000
American Watch Co., 19-21J, M#**1872**, 3/4, SW, 18k .... ★★★		3,500	5,000	8,000
American Watch Co., 19-21J, M# **1872**, GJS, **With sawtooth bal.(see illus. below)**				
marked *"Woerd's pat. compensating balance"* .... ★★★★★		5,000	8,000	12,000
American Watch Co., 15-21J, M#1868-1872, 3/4, GJS,"NO" sawtooth bal.				
'Woerd's patents" under balance, **square roller jewel** ..... ★		1,500	2,000	4,000
American Watch Co., 19J, M#1888, **14K**................. ★★★		2,000	2,500	4,500
American Watch Co., 19J, M#1888 .... ★★★		800	1,200	2,200
American Watch Co., 21J, M#1888,NI, 3/4 .... ★★★		1,000	1,400	2,500
American Watch Co., 23J, M# 1899, Adj.5P, GT, GJS ....★★		650	1,000	2,000
American Watch Co., 23J, BRG, Adj.5P, GT, GJS, **14K**				
original case.................................★★		1,500	2,200	3,500
American Watch Co., 23J, BRG, Adj.5P, GT, GJS, **18K**				
original case.................................★★		2,000	3,000	4,000
American Watch Co., 23J, BRG, Adj.5P, GT, GJS............★★		800	1,200	1,900
American Watch Co., 21J, BRG, Adj.5P, GT, GJS............. ★		450	700	1,100
American Watch Co., 19J, BRG, Adj.5P, GT, GJS............. ★		350	550	900
American Watch Co., 17J, BRG, Adj.5P, GT, GJS...............		250	350	650
Appleton, Tracy & Co., 15J, M#1860, 3/4, KW & KS from				
back, all original silver case		500	800	1,500
Appleton, Tracy & Co., 15-19J, M#1868, 3/4, KW		500	800	1,500
Appleton, Tracy & Co., 15-19J, 3/4, KW, with vibrating				
hairspring stud, all original, silver case ....★★		1,100	1,800	3,000
Appleton, Tracy & Co., 15-19J, 3/4, KW, with vibrating				
hairspring stud, **18K**, original case.................. ★★★		1,800	2,500	4,000

▢Generic, nameless or unmarked grades for watch movements are listed under the Company name or initials of the Company, etc. by size, jewel count and description.

A.W.Co.,7J,M#1872,SW,HC.		$125	$175	$325
A.W.W.Co.,7J,SW,M#1888.............................		100	150	250
A. W. Co., 7J, SW, DMK		100	150	250
A. W. Co., 9J, SW		100	150	250
A.W.W.Co.,11-13J,SW.............................		100	150	250
A.W.Co., 11J,M#1899,SW		100	150	250
A.W.Co., 11-15J,M#1872,SW,HC.............................		125	225	350
A.W.W.Co., 13J,M#1888-99,OF		100	150	250

RIGHT: **Woerd's pat compensating balance,** is engraved on movement, from a blue print of Mr. Woerd's patented **Saw Tooth Balance**. This balance **must** be in watch for **top prices**.

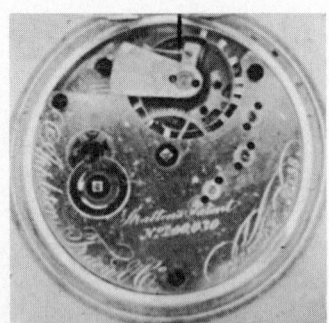

Appleton, Tracy & Co. (16 size), 15J, KW & KS from back, S# 140,030 Ca. 1864. **Stratton's Patent** engraved on movement = safety maintaining barrel. **Fogg's Pat.**

Crescent Street, Model 16-S(CENTER SECONDS),16 size, movement, 22J, Adj6p, lever set, Wind indicator. Top Right Fogg's Patented, vibrating hairspring stud **Feb.2,1864, engraved on cock = vibrating hairspring stud.**

Grade or Name—Descripion	ABP	Ex-Fn	Mint
A. W. W. Co., 15J, M#1899, OF	$100	$175	$250
A. W. W. Co., 15J, M#1888, SW, HC	125	200	325
A. W. W. Co., 16-17J, M#1888, SW, OF	100	175	275
A. W. W. Co., 16J, M#1899, SW, DMK, HC	125	200	325
A. W. W. Co., 17J, M#1872, SW, DMK, GJS, DES, HC .... ★	300	500	850
A. W. W. Co., 17J, SW, OF	100	175	250
A. W. W. Co., 19J, Adj.5P, LS, OF	150	200	300
A. W. W. Co., 19J, Adj.5P, LS, HC	200	300	425
A. W. W. Co., 21J, Adj.5P, PS, OF	200	300	550
A. W. W. Co., 21J, Adj.5P, PS, HC	300	450	650
A. W. W. Co., 23J, Adj.5P, PS, OF	300	450	650
A. W. W. Co., 23J, Adj.5P, PS, HC	400	600	800
P. S. Bartlett, 17J, M#1899, OF	100	150	200
P. S. Bartlett, 17J, M#1899, HC	125	200	300
P. S. Bartlett, 17J, M#1908, OF	100	175	250
Bond St., 7J, M#1888, OF	100	175	250
Bond St, 11J, M#1888, OF	100	175	250
Bond St., 15J, M#1888, OF	100	175	250
Bond St., 7J, M#1899, OF	100	175	250
Canadian Pacific RR, M#s 1888, 1899, 1908 .... ★★★	700	1,000	1,500
Canadian Railway Time Service, M#1908 .... ★★	500	800	1,300
CHRONOGRAPH are listed as 14 size, see Chronograph under 14 size			
Crescent St., 19J, M#1899, Adj.5P, LS, OF	125	200	325
Crescent St., 19J, M#1899, Adj.5P, PS, OF	125	200	325
Crescent St., 19J, M#1899, AcIJ.5P,LS, HC	200	350	500
Crescent St., 21J, M#1899, Adj.5P, PS, OF	150	250	350
Crescent St., 21J, M#1899, Adj.5P, LS, OF	150	250	350
Crescent St., 21J, M#1899, Adj.5P, PS, **HC**	200	450	550
Crescent St., 19J, M#1908, Adj.5P, LS, OF	125	200	325
Crescent St., 19J, M#1908, Adj.5P, PS, OF	125	200	325
Crescent St., 21J, M#1908, Adj.5P, LS, OF	150	325	425
Crescent St., 21J, M#1908, Adj.5P, PS, OF	175	325	425
Crescent St., 21J, M#1908, Adj.6P, LS, OF	175	325	425
Crescent St., 21J, M#1908, Adj.5P, PS, HC	250	450	550
Crescent St., 21J, M#1908, Adj.5P, LS, **Wind Indicator** .... ★	800	1,300	1,700
Crescent St., 21J, M#1912, Adj.5P, LS, **Wind Indicator** .... ★	800	1,300	1,700
Crescent St., 22J, M#16—S, Adj.6P, **DECK WATCH**			
LS, center sec., **Wind Indicator** .... ★★★	900	1,400	2,200
|Cronometro Supremo & Victoria, may have a Sun logo, ("EXPORT") to Spanish Countries.			
Cronometro Victoria, 15J, M#1899, OF.................... ★★	250	350	650
Cronometro Victoria, 15J, M#1899, HC .... ★★	300	400	700
Cronometro Supremo, 21J, M#1899, LS, OF............... ★★	350	500	950
Cronometro Supremo, 21J, M#1899, LS, HC............... ★★	400	550	1,000
Cronometro Victoria, 21J, M#1899, HC .... ★★	350	500	950
Diamond Express, 17J, M#1888, PS, OF,			
Diamond End Stones........................... ★★	750	1,200	2,000
Electric Railway, 17J, OF, LS, Adj.3P	150	250	450
Equity, 7-11J, PS, OF, 16 1/2Size	100	150	200
Equity, 7-11J, PS, HC, 16 1/2Size	100	150	200
Equity, 15-17J, PS, OF, 16 1/2 Size	100	150	200
Equity, 15-17J, PS, HC, 16 1/2 Size	100	150	200
Giant, 7-11J, PS, OF, 16 1/2Size	100	150	200
Giant, 7-11J, PS, HC, 16 1/2 Size	100	150	200
Hillside, 7J, M#1868, ADJ	125	175	300
Hillside, 7J, M#1868-1872, **sweep sec. & STOP** .... ★★★	1,200	2,000	3,700
Marquis, 15J, M#1899, LS	100	150	200
Marquis, 15J, M#1908, LS	100	150	200
Non-Magnetic, 15J, NI, HC	125	175	285
Park Road, 11-13-15J, M#1872, PS	175	225	400
Park Road, 16J, M#1872,PS	175	225	400

Note: A true O'Hara dial is signed O'Hara Dial Company in a logo on back of the dial.

Premier Maximus, 'Premier' on movement. "Maximus' on dial, 16 size, 23 jewels (two diamond end stones), open face, pendant set, serial number 17,000,014.

American Waltham Watch Co., 5 minute repeater, 16 size, 16 jewels, 3/4 plate, adj, 2 gongs, Note: The slide on side of case to activate repeater, Pat. June 1888, S# 3,793,502.

Grade or Name — Description	ABP	Ex-Fn	Mint
Premier, 9J, M#1908, PS, OF	$75	$125	$175
Premier, 11J, M#1908	75	125	185
Premier, 15J, M#1908, LS, OF	75	125	185
Premier, 17J, M#1908, PS, OF	75	125	185
Premier, 17J, M#1908, PS, OF, Silveroid	75	125	185
Premier, 21J, M#1908	175	275	400
Premier, 22J, M#1908, LS, Adj.6P, **Stainless steel case**, OF	200	400	600
Premier, 23J, M#1908, LS, OF	200	400	600
Premier Maximus, 23J, GT, gold case, LS, GJS, Adj.6P, original WI, DR, **18K** Maximus case, **box & papers** ★★★	9,000	14,000	20,000
Premier Maximus, 23J, GT, gold case, LS, GJS, Adj.6P, WI, DR, orig. **14K** or **18K** Maximus case, **NO** box, NO papers★★★	7,000	10,000	18,000
Premier Maximus, 23J, GT, **RECASED**	3,000	4,500	6,000
Railroader, 17J, M#1888, LS, NI ★★★	600	1,000	2,000
Railroad Time, 15-17J, ADJ, OF ★	300	600	900

Note: The Waltham Serial number with description book list Two runs of **Repeaters** 1st run from 3,793,001 to 3,793,400 with **chronograph** = 400 and 2nd run from 3,793,401 to 3,794,200 = 800.

Grade or Name — Description	ABP	Ex-Fn	Mint
REPEATER, 16-17J, 5 min., original **HC gold filled** case ★★	$ 2,000	$3,500	$4,500
REPEATER, 16-17J, 5 min., original **HC coin** case ★★	2,300	3,500	5,000
REPEATER, 16-17J, 5 min., original **HC 14K** case ★★★	3,200	5,000	7,500
REPEATER, 16-17J, 5 min, original **HC 18K** case ★★★★	4,500	7,000	9,500
REPEATER, 16-17J, 5 min, chronograph with register, **HC 18K** case, all original ★★★★	7,000	12,000	17,000
REPEATER, 1 minute, moon phase, M# 1872,. Perpetual Calendar, **HC 18K** case, all original ★★★★★	50,000	100,000	175,000

Grade or Name — Description	ABP	Ex-Fn	Mint
Riverside, 15-16J, M#1872, NI, OF	$100	$175	$300
Riverside, 15-16 J, M#1872, **gilded**, OF	100	175	300
Riverside, 16-17J, M#1888, NI, OF, **14K**	525	600	1,100
Riverside, 16-17 J, M#1888, NI, OF	100	175	300
Riverside, 17J, M#1888, gilded, OF	100	175	300
Riverside, 15J, M#1888, gilded, OF	100	175	300
Riverside, 17J, M#1888, checker goldtone DMK, raised gold jewel settings, OF	100	175	300
Riverside, 17J, M#1899, LS, DR, OF	100	175	300
Riverside, 17J , M#1899, LS, DR, HC	100	175	300
Riverside, 19J, M#1899, LS, DR, OF	125	225	350
Riverside, 19J, M#1908, Adj.5P, PS, DR, HC .... ★	200	300	500
Riverside, 21J , M#1888-1899-1908, LS, DR, OF	200	250	425
Riverside, 21J, M#1888-1899-1908, LS, DR, HC	250	400	600

Note: Riverside Maximus have Raised gold Jewel settings, gold train, Diamond end stones, Adj. to positions

Riverside Maximus, 21J, M#1888, Adj., G35, GT, DR, OF .....★★	675	900	1,500
Riverside Maximus, 21J, M#1888, Adj., G35, GT, DR, HC .....★★	750	1,000	1,800
Riverside Maximus, 21J, M#1888, Adj., GJS, GT, DR. HC, **14K** ....★★	1,200	1,800	2,700
Riverside Maximus, 21J, M#1899, Adj., GJS, GT, DR. OF ......★	400	600	950
Riverside Maximus, 21J, M#1899, Adj., GJS, GT, DR. HC .....★★	600	1,000	1,500
Riverside Maximus, 23J, M#1899, Adj., GJS, GT, DR. OF.........	400	700	1,000
Riverside Maximus, 23J, M#1899, Adj., GJS, GT, DR, 14K OF	850	1,500	2,200
Riverside Maximus, 23J, M#1899, Adj., GJS, GT, DR. HC	600	1,000	1,500
Riverside Maximus, 23J, M#1899 Adj., GJS, GT, DR, **Wind Ind.**, OF ....★★★★	3,500	6,000	8,000
Riverside Maximus, 23J, M#1908, Adj., GJS, DR, OF	550	700	1,100
Riverside Maximus, 23J, M#1908, Adj., GJS, DR, 14K OF	900	1,500	2,000
Riverside Maximus, 23J, M#1908, Adj., GJS, DR, HC ......★★★	700	1,000	1,700
Riverside Maximus, 23J, M#1908, Adj., GJS, GT, DR. **14KHC** ....★★★	1,100	2,000	3,000
Riverside Maximus, 23J, M#1908, Adj., GJS, GT, DR. **Wind Ind.** OF ....★★★	3,200	5,500	7,700

American Watch Co., model 1872, 16 size, 16-17-21 jewels, gold train, serial number 1,310,846. Note: 1872 models have visible winding wheels & invisible click

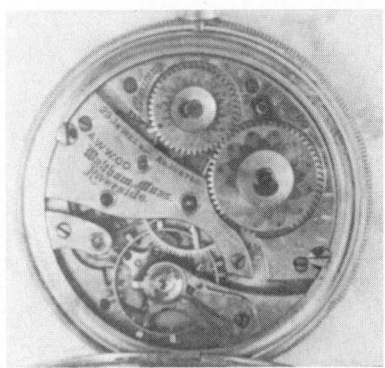

Riverside Maximus, Model 1899,16 size, 23 jewels, gold train, raised gold jewel settings, **4** diamond end stones, adjusted to 5 positions, hunting case, serial # 12,509,200.

☙ Some grades are not included. Their values can be determined by comparing with similar age, size, metal content, style, models and grades listed.

☙ A collector should expect to pay modestly higher prices at local shops.

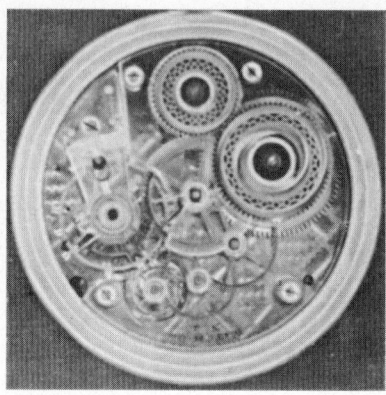

Stone Movement, 16 size, 16-17 jewels, crystal plates, Model 1872, gold train, gold jeweled settings, Adj5p, S #20.

Vanguard, 16 size, 23 jewels, Adj 6p, note pressed-in jewels rather than gold jewel settings. c. 1945.

Grade or Name — Description	ABP	Ex-Fn	Mint
Roadmaster, 17J, M#1899, LS, OF GJS ....★★	$475	$600	$1,000
Royal, 13-15J, M#1872..................................	100	150	250
Royal, 17J, M#1888, PS, OF...............................	100	150	250
Royal, 17J, M#1888,PS,HC	125	175	300
Royal, 17J, M#1899, Adj.3P, OF...........................	100	150	250
Royal, 17J, M#1899-1908,Adj.5P,OF........................	100	150	250
Royal, 17J, M#1899-1908, Adj.5P,HC	125	175	300
Royal Special, 17J, M#1888.............................	150	250	375
Santa Fe Route, M #s 1888, 1899, 1908 ....★★★	700	1,300	2,000
Sol, 7J, M#1888.......................................	100	150	250
Sol, 7J, M#1908.......................................	100	150	250
Stone Movement, 16-17J, M#1872, GT, **Crystal plates** ...★★★★★	20,000	40,000	70,000
Supremo, 17J, M#1899..................................	100	150	250
SWISS made, 17-25J	100	150	250
Traveler, 7J, M#1888, 1899, 1908 & 16 1/2 size(Equity)	100	150	250
Tennyson, 15J, M#1888, OF ....★	150	300	450
Vanguard, 19J, M#1899, PS, LS, Adj.5P, GJS, DR, OF...........	200	300	450
Vanguard, 19J, M#1899, PS, LS, Adj.5P, GJS, DR, HC	275	350	550
Vanguard, 21J, M#1899, Adj.5P, OF ....★★	275	350	550
Vanguard, 21J, M#1899, Adj.5P, **HC** ....★★	325	475	650
Vanguard, 23J, M#1899, LS, Adj.5P, GJS, DR, OF..............	250	375	525
Vanguard, 23J, M#1899, PS, Adj.5P, GJS, DR, OF.............	250	375	525
Vanguard, 23J, M#1899, Adj.6P, OF	250	375	525
Vanguard, 23J, M#1899, Adj.5P, **HC**........................	300	500	675
Vanguard, 23J, M#1899, PS, **Wind Indicator**, Adj.5P, GJS, DR .. ★	900	1,400	1,800

🖎 Watches listed in this book are priced at the collectable trade show level, as **complete** watches having an original 14k gold-filled case and *Key Wind* with silver, an original white enamel single sunk dial, and with the entire original movement in good working order with no repairs needed.

🖎 Some grades are not included. Their values can be determined by comparing with similar age, size, metal content, style, models and grades listed.

🖎 Watch **terminology** or **communication** in this book has evolved over the years, in search of better and more precise language with a effort to improve, purify, adjust itself and make it easier to understand.

🖎 **The Complete Price Guide to Watches goal is to stimulate the orderly exchange of Watches between "*buyers*" and "*sellers*".**

Grade or Name —Description	ABP	Ex-Fn	Mint
Vanguard, 19J, M#1908, LS & PS, Adj.5P, GJS, DR.	$200	$300	$425
Vanguard, 21J, M#1908, Adj.5P, GJS, DR, PS, LS, OF ★★	300	400	575
Vanguard, 21J, M#1908, Adj.5P, **Sidereal, Wind Ind.,** OF ★★★	1,200	2,500	3,500
Vanguard, 21J, M#1908, Adj.5P, GJS, DR, PS, LS, HC ★★	350	500	650
Vanguard, 23J, M#1908, LS, Adj.5P, GJS, DR, OF	275	350	575
Vanguard, 23J, M#1908, LS, Adj.5P, GJS, DR. HC	350	450	675
Vanguard, 23J, M#1908, PS, Adj.5P, GJS, DR	275	350	595
Vanguard, 23J, M#1908, Adj.5P, **Wind Indicator,** GJS, DR	850	1,100	1,500
Vanguard, 23J, M#1908, Adj.5P, GJS, Diamond end stone.	250	300	525
Vanguard, 23J, M#1908, Adj.5P, GJS, HC ★	350	425	675
Vanguard, 23J, M#1908, OF, **14K**	700	950	1,300
Vanguard, 23J, M#1908, Adj.6P, **Wind Indicator,** GJS, DR	850	1,100	1,500
Vanguard, 23J, M#1908, Adj.5-6P, **Wind Ind., Lossier,** GJS, DR	850	1,100	1,500
Vanguard, 23J, M#1912, Press Jewels	200	300	400
Vanguard, 23J, M#1912, PS, military (case), Wind Indicator ★	900	1,200	1,600
Vanguard, **24J,** & marked 9J., center sec ★★★	800	1,100	1,700
Weems, 21J, Navigation watch, **Wind Indicator** ★★★	1,100	1,600	2,200
Weems, 23J, Navigation watch, **Wind Indicator** ★★★	1,300	1,800	3,000
M#1888, G#s 650,640	100	125	250
M#1899, G#s 615, 618, 620, 625, 628,	100	125	250
M#1908, G#s 611, 613, 614, 618, 621, 623, 628,630,641,642.	100	125	250
G#637-640=3 pos., G#636=4pos., G#1617=2 pos., ALL=17J	100	125	250
G#610=7-11J., **unadjusted** & 620=15J	100	125	250
G#620-625-630-635=17J., Adj., OF	100	125	250
G#645, 21J, GCW, OF, LS	175	275	400
G#645, 21J, GCW, OF, LS, **wind indicator** ★★★	1,500	2,200	3,200
G#645, 19J, OF, LS.	175	250	400
G#665, 19J, GJS, BRG, HC	600	700	1,000
G#16-A, 22J, Adj.3P, 24 hr. dial.	200	275	400
G#16-A, & G#1024, 17J, Adj.5P	100	125	250
G#1617,1 7J, adj	100	125	250
G#1621, 21J, Adj.5P	150	250	375
G#1622, 22J, Adj.5P.	200	300	425
G#1623, 23J, Adj.5P.	250	400	575

Weems Navigation watch. 21j. Weems pat. seconds dial, pusher for seconds scale setting, ca. 1942.

Vanguard, Model 1908, 16 size, 23 jewels, diamond end stone, gold jewel settings, exposed winding gears, serial number 11,012,533.

14 SIZE
MODELS 14KW FULL PLATE, 1874,
1884, 1895,1897, COLONIAL-A

Grade or Name — Description	ABP	Ex-Fn	Mint
Adams Street, 7J, M#14KW, full plate, KW, Coin	$75	$150	$300
Adams Street, 11J, M#14KW, full plate, KW, Coin...............	100	175	350
Adams Street, 15J, M#14KW, full plate, KW	125	200	400

🙡 Generic, nameless or unmarked grades for watch movements are listed under the Company name or initials of the Company, etc. by size, jewel count and description.

A. W. Co., 7-11J, M#I4KW, full plate, **KW**	75	125	250
A. W. W. Co., 7-11J,M#1874, SW, LS, HC....................	100	150	275
A. W. Co.,7-11J,M#s P,1884,& 1895.........................	75	125	225
A. W. Co.,13J,M#1884	75	125	225
A. W. Co., 15-16J, M#1874, SW	75	125	225
A.W.Co.,17J, SW, OF	100	150	250
A.W.Co., 19J, GJS, GCW	100	150	250
Am. Watch Co.,7-11J	75	125	225
Am. Watch Co., 13J, M#1874-84, SW	75	125	225
Am. Watch Co., 15J, M#1874-84, ...	75	125	225
Am. Watch Co., 16J, M#1874, SW	100	150	250
Am. Watch Co., 7-11J, M#I4KW, **Full Plate, KW**	100	150	300
Am. Watch Co., 16J, M#1884, SW.........................	100	150	275
Am. Watch Co., 15J, M#1897, SW.........................	75	125	225
Bond St., 7-11J, M#1895, SW	75	125	225
Bond St., 9-11J, M#1884, **KW**	100	150	300
Bond St., 7J, M#1884, SW, PS	75	125	225
Beacon, 15J, M#1897, SW	75	125	225
Chronograph, 13J, 1874, **14K**, OF, **Am. W. Co. case**	1,000	2,000	3,000
Chronograph, 13J, 1874, **14K**, OF, W/ register,			
Am. W. Co. case .... ★	1,500	2,500	3,500
Chronograph, 13J, 1874, **14K, HC**, W/ register,			
Am. W. Co. case .... ★	2,000	3,000	4,000
Chronograph, 13J, 1874, **18K**, HC, W/ register,			
Am. W. Co. case .... ★	2,500	4,000	5,000
Chronograph, 13J, 1874, **SILVER HC,** *Am. W Co. case*	500	1,000	1,500
Chronograph, 16J, 1874, **double dial, "coin",** Am. W. Co. case.....	2,500	4,000	5,500
Chronograph, 16J, 1874, **double dial, 18K,** Am, W. Co. case	5,000	7,500	10,000

Chronograph, Model 1874, split-second, 14 size. Note two split second hands on dial and two pushers at 2 & 4.

Hillside, 14 size, 13 jewels, M#1674, stem wind, hunting case, Woerds Pat., serial number 1,696,188, 18K.

🙡 This book endeavours to be a guide or helpful manual and offers a wealth of material to be used as a tool not as an absolute document. Price guides are like watches, the worst may be better than none at all, but at best cannot be expected to be 100% accurate.

Grade or Name — Description		ABP	Ex-Fn	Mint
Chronograph, 13J, M# 1884 , OF		$200	$450	$650
Chronograph, 13J, M# 1884, HC		300	550	800
Chronograph, 13J, 1884, **14K**, HC, **Am. W. Co. case**		1,200	1,800	2,500
Chronograph, 13J, 1884, **18K**, HC, **Am. W. Co. case**	★	1,500	2,500	3,500
Chronograph, 15J, M#1874-1884,OF		200	450	650
Chronograph, 15J, M#1874-1884, HC		300	550	750
Chronograph, 17J, M#1874-1884 , OF		200	450	650
Chronograph, 17J, M#1874-1884, HC		300	550	750
Chronograph, 17J, split second, Am. W. Co. Case, GF,	★★★	1,200	1,500	2,500
Chronograph, 15J, split sec., **14K**, HC	★★★	4,000	5,000	8,000
Chronograph, 15J, split second, **min. register, 14K**				
Am. W. Co. HC	★★★★	5,000	7,500	11,000
Church St., 7J, M#1884		75	125	225
Crescent Garden, 7-11J, M#14KW		75	125	225
Crescent Garden, 7J, Full Plate, KW		75	125	225
Cronometro Victoria, 15J, M#1897, OF (may have sun logo) -	★★	400	550	800
Win. Ellery, 7J, M#1874, SW		75	125	225
Gentleman, 7J, M#1884, SW		75	125	225
Hillside, 7-15J, M#1874, SW		75	125	225
Hillside, 7-11J, M#FP, SW		75	125	225
Hillside, 7-13J, M#1884, KW		75	125	225
Hillside, 9-11J, M#1884, KW		75	125	225
Hillside, 15J, M#1884, SW		75	125	225
Hillside, 16J, M#1874, (calendar date only on outside chapter)				
SW, GJS, OF,(calendar sets from back with lever)	★★★	750	1,200	1,800
Hillside, 7-13J, M#1895		75	125	225
Maximus, 21J, Colonial A, Adj.5P, GT, model 1912, OF	★	125	250	400
Maximus, 21J, Colonial A, Adj.5P, GT, model 1912, **14K OF**	★	400	600	850
Night Clock, 7J, M#1884, KW		125	175	300
Perfection, 15J, M#1897, OF	★	75	125	225
Perfection, 15J, M#1897, HC	★★	150	250	375

Chronograph, M# 1884-double dial, 14 size, 15 Jewels, hunting case.

Chronograph, Model 1884-Split Second, 14 size, 15 jewels, open face, gold escape wheel, gold train, serial number 303,094.

🖝 Some watch manufacturers personalize watches for jobbers or jewelry firms, with exclusive private signed or marked movements. The valuable collectable watches are listed under the signed or marked movement. Other exclusive private signed or marked movements will have equivalent value or only slightly higher value and should be compared to Generic or Nameless movements. Railroad signed or marked (dials & movements) are usually more collectable & higher in value.

🖝 A collector should expect to pay modestly higher prices at local shops.

 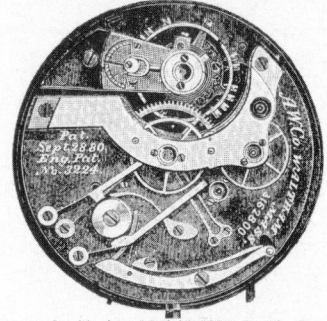

Five Minute Repeater, Model 1884,14 size, 13-15jewels, hunting case, slide activated, serial number 2,605,848. Note: estimated Total about 1,250 to 1,300.

Chronograph, 14 size, Model# 1874, Lugrin Pat., Sept. 28,1880, serial # 3,162,800. Also Pat. date (Oct. 3,1876)

Grade or Name — Description	ABP	Ex-Fn	Mint
Repeater (5 min.), 16J, M#1884, SW, LS, **14K** . . . . ★	$3,500	$5,000	$7,500
Repeater (5 min.), 16J, M#1884, SW, LS, **18K** . . . . ★	4,500	7,000	9,500
Repeater (5 min.), 16J, M#1884, split second chronograph, **18 K Case** . . . . ★★	8,000	15,000	22,000
Repeater (5 min.), 16J, M#1884, SW, LS, chronograph, with register, **14K** Am. W. Co. case	6,000	9,000	12,000
Repeater (5 min, 16J, M#1884, SW, LS, chronograph, with register, **18K** Am. W. Co. case	7,000	12,000	17,000
Repeater (5 min.), 16J, M#1884 884, SW, LS, original **Coin** case . . .	2,500	3,500	5,000
Repeater (5 min.), 16J, M#1884, SW, LS, original **gold filled** case . .	2,500	3,500	5,000
Repeater (5 Min.), **18K**, HC . . . . ★★	4,500	7,000	9,500
Repeater (**1 Min.**), perpetual calendar, moon ph., **18K** . . . . ★★★★★	60,000	100,000	175,000
Riverside, 11-15J, M#s 1874	100	175	275
Riverside, 15J, M#1884	75	125	225
Riverside, 15J, M#1885 , nickel, OF. . . . . ★★★	300	400	550
Riverside, 19J, Colonial A, Adj.5P, OF	100	175	275
Riverside, 21J, Colonial A, Adj.5P, OF . . . . ★★	200	300	450
Royal, 11-13-15J, M#s 1874, 1884	75	125	250
Seaside, 7-11J, M#1884, SW.	75	125	250
Sol, 7J, M#1897	75	125	250
Special, 7J, M#1895, HC	100	150	275
Sterling,7J,M#1884.	75	125	250
Waltham, Mass., 7J, Full Plate, KW.	100	175	275

12 SIZE
MODELS KW, 1894, BRIDGE, COLONIAL SERIES

Grade or Name — Description	ABP	Ex-Fn	Mint
A. W. W. Co., 7J, M#1894, **14K**, OF.	$200	$300	$550
A. W. W. Co., 11J, M#1894, also Colonial model	75	125	225
A. W. W. Co., 15J, M#1894, also Colonial model	75	125	225
A. W. W. Co., 15J, M#1894, Colonial, **14K**, HC	300	400	600
A. W. W. Co., 17J, M#1894, also Colonial model	75	125	225
A. W. W. Co., 17J, M#1894, also Colonial, **14K** OF	225	300	500
A. W. W. Co., 19J, OF.	75	125	225
A. W. W. Co., 21J, OF.	100	100	200
A. W. W. Co., 23J, OF.	150	225	350
P. S. Bartlett, 19J, M#1894, **14K**, HC.	300	400	700
P. S. Bartlett, 19J, M#1894	75	125	225
Bond St., 7-13J, M#1894.	75	125	225
Bridge Model, 21J, GJS, Adj.5P, GT, OF . . . . ★★	200	300	450
Bridge Model, 21J, GJS, Adj.5P, GT, **14K**, HC . . . . ★★	450	600	900
Bridge Model, 23J, GJS, Adj.5P, GT . . . . ★★	250	350	650

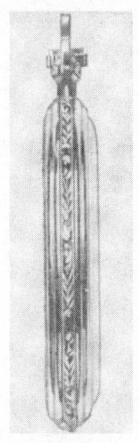

Actual size illustration or a cushion style shaped watch depicting thinness with emphasis on style and beauty. This watch was popular in the 1930s.

Grade or Name — Description	ABP	Ex-Fn	Mint
Duke, 7-15J, M#1894	$75	$125	$225
Digital Hour & Second Window, 17J	100	175	300
Elite, 17J, OF	75	125	225
Ensign, 7J, OF	75	125	225
Equity, 7J,adj	75	125	225
Martyn Square, 7-11J, M#KW	100	150	250
Maximus, 21J, GJS, GT	200	300	450
Premier, 17J, M#1894	75	125	225
Premier, 19J, M#1894	100	150	250
Premier, 21J, M#1894	125	200	300
Premier, 23J, M#1894, OF **14K**	250	400	600
Riverside, 17-19J, M#1894, Colonial	75	125	225
Riverside, 21J, M#1894, Colonial	150	250	400

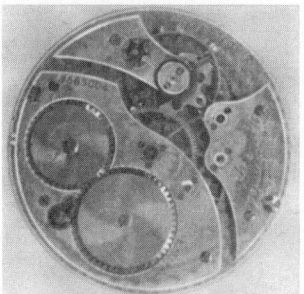

A. W. W. Co., Model 1894, 12 size, 7-11 jewels, open face, serial number 7,565.004.

Riverside, Colonial series, 12 size, 19jewels, open face or hunting, Adj5p, double roller.

Grade or Name —Description	ABP	Ex-En	Mint
Riverside, 19-21J, M#1894, also Colonial, **14K**, HC	$350	$500	$750
Riverside Maximus, 21J, M#1894, also Colonial, GT, GJS	200	300	550
Riverside Maximus, 23J, M#1894, also Colonial, GT, GJS ...... ★	250	375	550
Riverside Maximus, 23J, M#1894, also Colonial, GT, GJS, **14K** .. ★	350	500	750
Royal, 17J, OF, PS, Adj, or Adj.3P	50	75	150
Royal, 19J, OF, PS, Adj.3P	60	85	160
Secometer, 17J, (revolving seconds dial only) OF	100	175	325
G#210, 7J, G#220, 15J	50	75	150
G#225, 17J	60	95	175

THE OPERA WATCH
10-12 size case & a 6/0 size Jewel Series movement

Grade or Name — Description	ABP	Ex-Fn	Mint
12-6/0 size, 17-19J, Adj, **18K gold case**.....................★★	$475	$600	$1,000
12-6/0 size, 17-19J, Adj, **14K gold case**.....................★★	275	400	800
12-6/0 size, 17-19J, Adj, **Platinum case** ....★★★	800	1,200	1,700
12-6/0 size, 17-19J, Adj, **gold filled case**....................★	125	250	485

A unique designed Gents dress watch about 10-12 size case with a fancy framed 6/0 movement (Jewel Series).

10 SIZE
MODEL KW, 1858, 1861, 1865, 1874

Grade or Name — Description	ABP	Ex-Fn	Mint
Am. W. Co., 7-15J, M#1874-1878, KW, **14K**	$250	$400	$650
A. W. Co., 7-11J, SW OF	75	125	225
A. W. Co., 15-17J, SW OF	75	125	225
A. W. Co., 19-21J, SW OF	100	150	250
American Watch Co., 11-15J, M#1874, **14K, HC**	300	400	550
Appleton, Tracy & Co., 7-11-15J, M#1861 or 1874, **14K**, KW	300	425	600
Appleton, Tracy & Co., 7-11-15J, M#1861, **KW**			
multi-color box case, **18K**	700	1,200	1,800
P. S. Bartlett, 7-11J, M#1861, KW, **14K**	350	500	800
P. S. Bartlett, 13J, M#KW, gold balance, 1st S# 45,801,			
last 46,200, Pat. Nov. 3, 1858, **14K** ....★★★	550	700	1,000
P. S. Bartlett, 13J, M#KW, gold balance, 1st S#45,801,			
last 46,200, Pat Nov. 3, 1858, **18K**. ....★★★	700	900	1,200
P. S. Bartlett, 13J, M#1861 or 1865, KW, **14K**	350	500	625

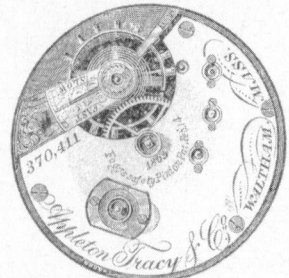

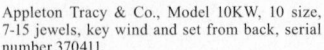

Appleton Tracy & Co., Model 10KW, 10 size, 7-15 jewels, key wind and set from back, serial number 370411.

P. S. Bartlett 10 size, 7-15 jewels, serial #181,602.

NOTE: These watches (excluding Colonial) are usually found with solid gold cases and are therefore priced accordingly. Without cases, these watches have very little value due to the fact that the cases are difficult to find. Many of the cases came in octagon, decagon, hexagon, cushion and triad shapes.

Grade or Name — Description		ABP	Ex-Fn	Mint
Crescent Garden, 7J, M#1861, KW, 14K		$200	$300	$500
Colonial R, 9J, model 1945................................		75	125	225
Colonial R, 17J, Adj.5P, model 1945		75	125	255
Colonial R, 21J, Adj.5P, model 1945		100	150	250
Colonial R, 23J, Adj.5P, model 1945	★★	100	200	325
Wm. Ellery, 7,11,15J, M#1861, KW, 14K		200	350	475
Home W. Co., 7J, M#1874, KW, 14K		200	350	475
Martyn Square, 7-11J, M#1861, 14K		200	350	475
Maximus "A",21J, model 1918, 14K.....................	★★★	250	450	600
Maximus "A", 23J, model 1918, 14K	★	225	350	550
Riverside A, 19J, Adj.5P, model 1918, GF		100	150	250

8 SIZE

MODEL 1873

NOTE: Collectors usually want solid gold cases in small watches.

Grade or Name —Description		ABP	Ex-Fn	Mint
Am. W. Co., 15-17J, M#1873,				
14K, Multi-Color Box Hinged case		$450	$650	$1,000
Am. W. Co., 15-16J, M#1873		75	100	150
P. S. Bartlett,15-16J, M#1873...........................		75	100	150
Wm. Ellery, 7-11J, M#1873		75	100	150
Wm. Ellery, 7J, **14K, HC**		300	375	475
Riverside, 7-11J, M#1873, **18K, HC**		375	500	650
Riverside,7-11J, M#1873		75	100	150
Royal, 7-16J, M#1873...................................		75	100	150
Victoria, 11-15J, tu-tone movement, **18k HC**	★	400	550	700

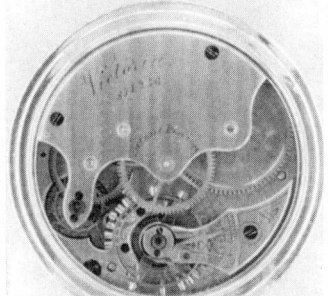

VICTORIA. 8 size 1873 model, 11-15 jewels, tu-tone high grade movement, HC, S# 871256

6 size Ladies movement. This basic model came in the following grades: J=7 jewels, gilt; Y=7 jewels, nickel; N=15 jewels, gilded or nickel; X=15 jewels, nickel, gold jewel settings; K=16 jewels nickel, raised gold settings; RIVERSIDE=17 jewels, nickel, raised gold settings.

6 SIZE

MODEL 1873,1889,1890

Grade or Name —Description	ABP	Ex-Fn	Mint
A,B,C,D,E,F,G,H,J,K....................................	$60	$100	$150
A,B,C,D,E,F,G,H,J,K, **14K, HC**	250	350	500
A. W. W. Co., 19J, **18K, HC**...........................	300	400	600
A. W. W. Co., 19J, **14K, Multi-Color gold case**	400	575	950
A. W. W. Co., 7J, M#1873................................	60	100	150

Grade or Name —Description	ABP	Ex-Fn	Mint
A. W. W. Co., 15J, **multi-color GF**, HC	$175	$275	$400
A. W. W. Co., 15J, **2 tone mvt.**, HC	75	150	250
A. W. W. Co., 11J, HC	70	125	175
Am. W. Co., 7-11J, M#1889 -1890	70	125	175
American W. Co., 7J, KW & KS from back, **10K, HC**	175	275	425
Wm. Ellery, 7J, M# 1873	70	125	175
Lady Waltham, 16J, M# 1873, Demi, HC, **14K**	250	350	535
Lady Waltham, 16J, M# 1873, **18K**	300	400	625
Riverside Maximus, 19J, GT, Adj., DR, HC ★★★	250	450	700
Riverside, 15-17J, PS	70	150	225
Seaside, 7-15J, M# 1873	70	150	225
Royal, 16J, HC	75	160	200

American Watch Co., Model 1889, 6 size 7 jewels, serial number 4,154,319.

Stone Movement or Crystal clear see through Plates, size 4,16 jewels, gold train, open face, serial number 28.

4 SIZE

Grade or Name —Description	ABP	Ex-Fn	Mint
Stone Movement or crystal movement, 4 size, 16-17 ruby jewels in gold settings, gold train, exposed pallets, compensation balance adjusted to temperature, isochronism & positions, Breguet hairspring, and crystal top plate, 14K case ★★★★	$12,000	$18,000	$35,000

1 SIZE & 0 SIZE
MODELS 1882,1891, 1900, 1907

Grade or Name —Description	ABP	Ex-Fn	Mint
A. W. Co., 7-16J, OF	$50	$75	$150
A. W. Co., 7-16J, HC	75	100	225
A. W. Co., 7-15J, multi-color **14K HC**	325	450	700
A. W. Co., 7J, **14K, HC**	200	300	550
American Watch Co., 15J, SW, OF & HC	100	150	225
"B" grade = 13J., "F" & "G" grade = 9J., 1 size	75	125	200

Right: 1 size
"B" grade = 13J., "F" & "G" grade = 9J.

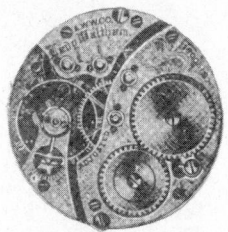

Lady Waltham, Model 1900, 0 size, 16 jewels, open face or hunting, adjusted, stem wind, pendant set.

American Watch Co., Model 1891, 0 size, 7 jewels, stem wind, originally sold for $13.00.

Grade or Name —Description	ABP	Ex-Fn	Mint
American Watch Co., 15J, S.W., **14K, HC**	$200	$300	$500
P. S. Bartlett, 11J, M# 1891, OF, 14K	150	200	300
P. 5. Bartlett, 16J, **14K, HC**	200	300	500
Cronometro Victoria, 15J ★★	300	400	600
Lady Waltham, 15J, SW, **14K, HC**	255	325	475
Lady Waltham, 15-16J, SW, HC	75	125	250
Maximus, 19J, SW, HC ★	200	300	400
Riverside, 15J, 16J,17J, SW, HC	100	175	250
Riverside, 15J, 16J,17J, SW, **14K, HC**	200	300	400
Riverside Maximus, 19J, SW, HC	175	250	400
Riverside Maximus, 19J, **14K, HC** ★	350	500	700
Royal, 13-16J, SW, HC	75	125	175
Seaside, 15J, SW, **14K, HC**	200	300	350
Seaside, 11J, SW, OF, **multi-color dial, no chips**	200	300	450
Seaside, 11J, SW, HC	75	125	200
Seaside, 7J, HC	75	125	200
Seaside, 7J, **14K, HC**	200	300	465
Special, 11J, M#1891, **14K, OF**	150	225	425
G# 61, 7J, HC	75	125	225
G# 115, 15J, HC	75	125	225

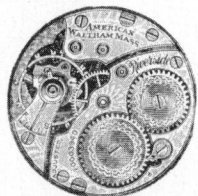

Riverside, Jewel Series, 6/0 size, 17 ruby jewels, raised gold settings, gold center wheel.

Ruby, Jewel Series, 6/0 size, 15 jewels, adjusted to temperature, open face or hunting.

JEWEL SERIES or 6/0 SIZE

Grade or Name —Description	ABP	Ex -Fn	Mint
Diamond, 17J, gold train, diamond end stone, **14K, HC** ★	$175	$250	$425
Emerald, 21J, gold train, **14K, HC** ★	225	300	475
Maximus, 17J, gold train, diamond end stone, **14K HC** ★	235	300	535
Patrician, 15J, pin set, GJS, **18K, OF** ★	225	300	525
Riverside, 17J, Jewel Series, **14K, HC** ★	225	275	425
Ruby, 15-17J, Jewel Series, **14K, OF** ★	175	200	400
Sapphire, 15J, Jewel Series, **14K, OF** ★	175	200	400

RF # 1A
gold filled : $60 - $85 - $275
dial:$40-$80-$180

RF # 2B
gold filled : $60- $85 - $285
dial:$20-$40-$100

RF # 3C
gold plate: $50 - $75 - $185
dial: $10 - $25 - $50

RF # 4D
gold filled: $60 - $85 - $260
dial: $40 - $80 - $150

RF # 5E
gold filled: $80 - $150 - $400
dial: $40 - $80 - $160

RF # 6F
gold filled : $75 - $125 - $275
dial: $20 - $40 - $100

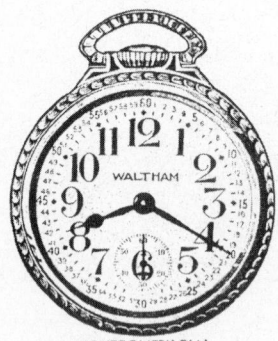

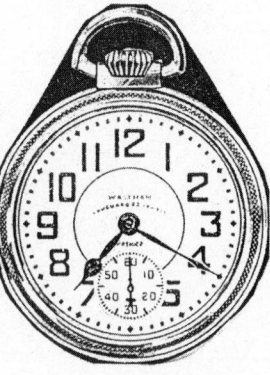

RF # 7G
LOCOMOTIVE model
gold filled: $70 - $100 - $275
dial: $40 - $65 - $120

RF # 8H
Heavy-Duty
gold filled: $80 - $150 - $325
dial: $20 - $40 - $80

RF # 9L
gold filled: $50 - $85 - $225
dial: $20 - $40 - $80

NOTE: Factory Advertised as a complete watch and was fitted with a certain matched, timed and rated movement and sold in the factory designed case style as a complete watch. The factory also sold uncased movements to jobbers such as Jewelry stores & they cased the movement in a case styles the customer requested. All the factory advertised complete watches came with a enamel dial shown or choice of other Railroad dials.

AMERICAN WALTHAM WATCH CO.
IDENTIFICATION OF MOVEMENTS
BY MODEL NUMBER

How to Identify Your Watch Size & Model: Compare the movement of your watch with the illustrations in this section. While comparing, note the location of the balance, jewels, screws, gears, and type of back plate (Full, 3/4, Bridge) these will be clues in identifying the movement you have.

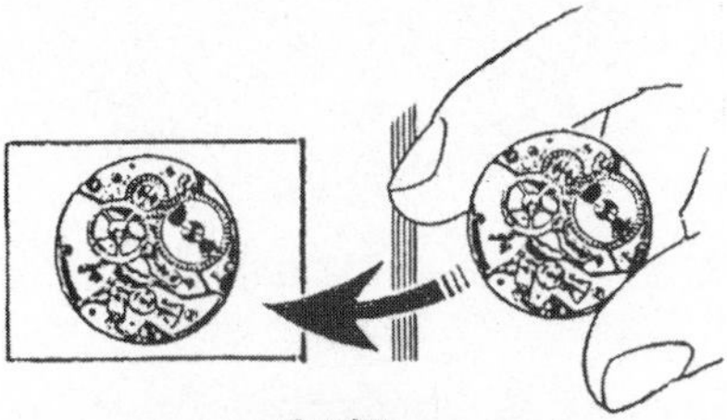

20 size, 1862 or KW 20 model. Note vibrating hairspring stud. 1st serial number 50,001

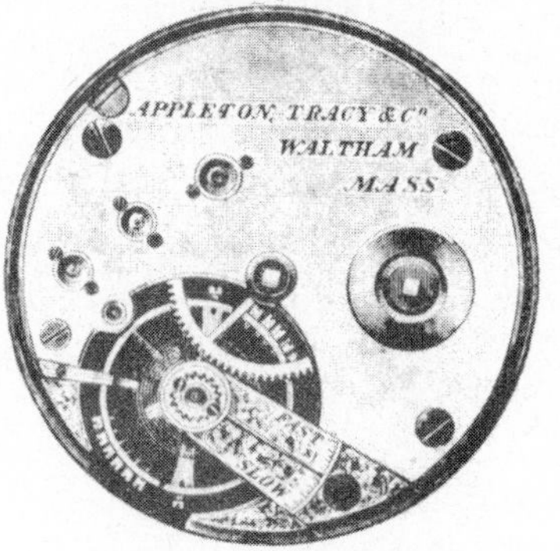

18 size, 1859 or KW 18 model. 1st serial number 28,821

Model 1857, KW, KS. 1st serial number 1,001

Model 1870, KW, KS from back 1st serial number 500,001

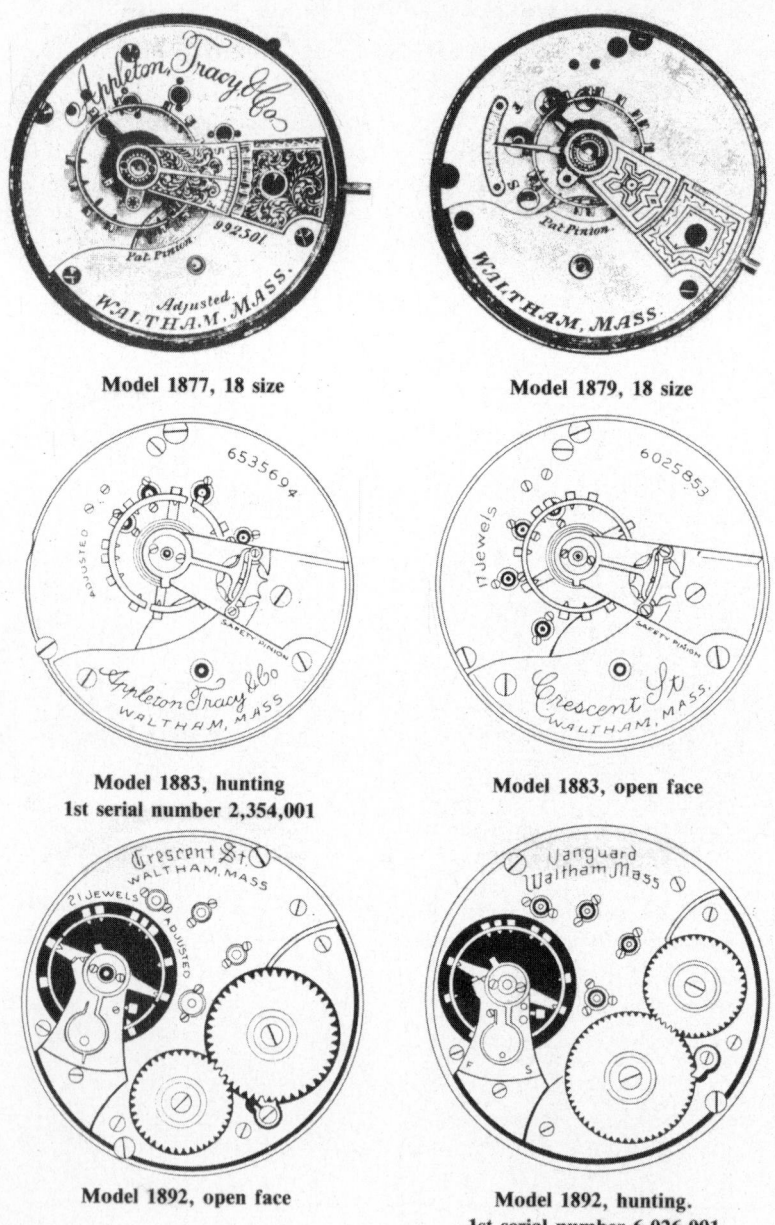

Model 1877, 18 size

Model 1879, 18 size

Model 1883, hunting
1st serial number 2,354,001

Model 1883, open face

Model 1892, open face

Model 1892, hunting.
1st serial number 6,026,001

Model is not the same defination as grade. A model may exist in different grade numbers or grade names (as Riverside-P. S. Bartlett) and may be used in many different models (as model **1892**, 18 size, open or hunting case, model **1899**, in 16 size open or hunting case, model **1894** in 12 size) etc..

16½ size, Equity open face

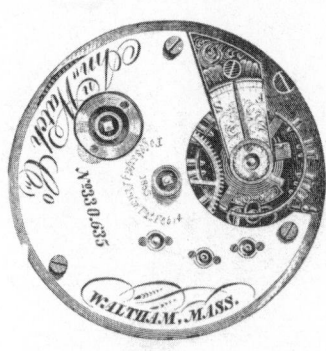

Model 1860=16KW or 1868
16 size

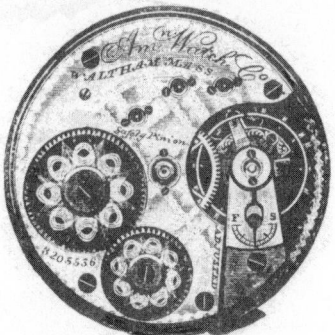

Model 1872, 16 size open face

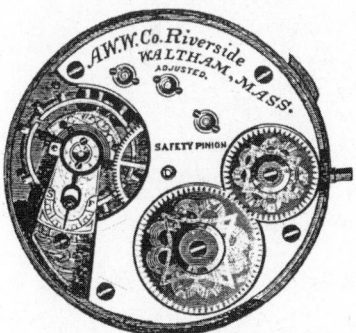

Model 1872, 16 size hunting case

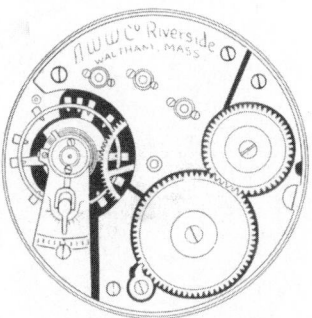

Model 1888, 16 size, hunting

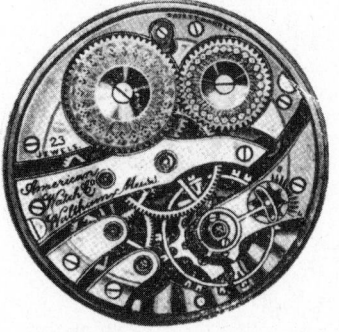

Bridge Model, 16 size

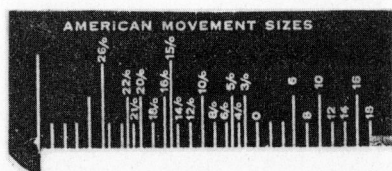

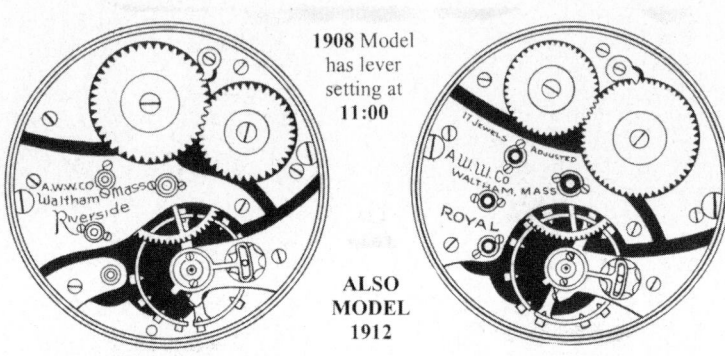

1908 Model
has lever
setting at
11:00

ALSO
MODEL
1912

**Model 1899 or Model 1908,
16 size, open face**

**Model 1899 or Model 1908,
16 size, hunting**

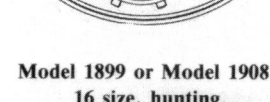

**Model 1899 or Model 1908,
16 size, open face**

Model 16-A, 16 size

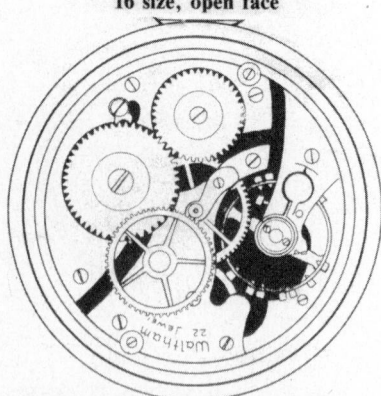

**Model 1622, Deck Watch
16 size, sweep second**

Model 1874 & 1884, 14 size

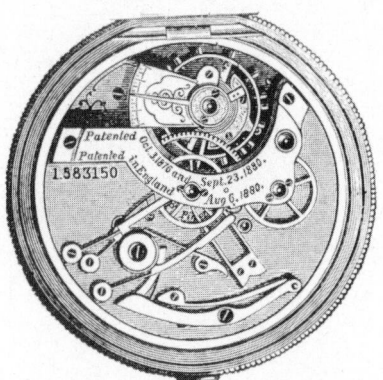

Model 1874, 14 size, hunting

Model 1884, 14 size, open face

5 Minute Repeater, 14 size

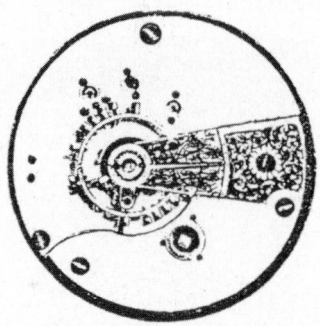

**14 SIZE FULL PLATE KW KS
1 st. SERIAL # 909,001**

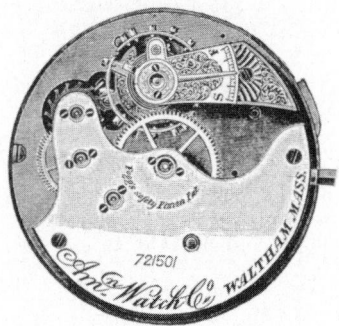

Model 1874, 14 size

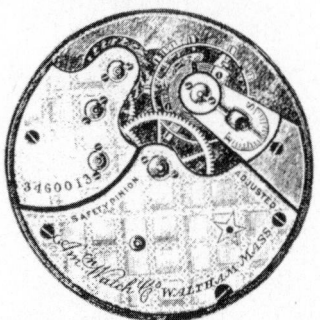

Model 1884, 14 size

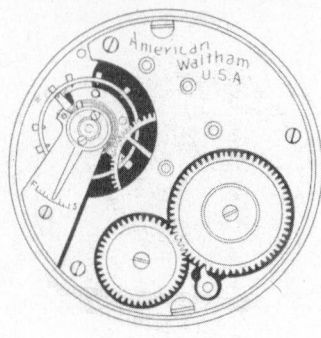

**Model 1895, 14 size,
open face**

Model 1897, 14 size

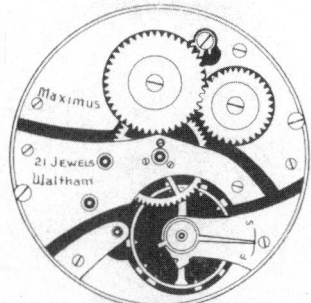

Colonial A Model, 14 size

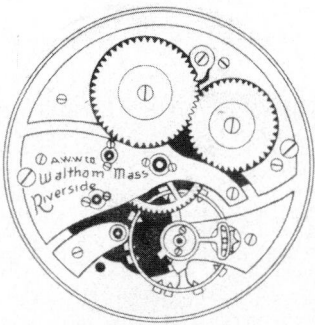

Colonial Series, 14 size

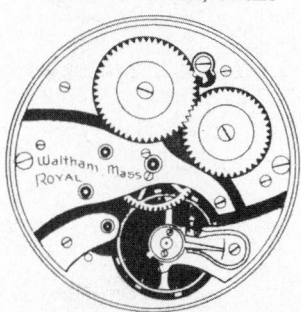

Model 1924, The Colonial

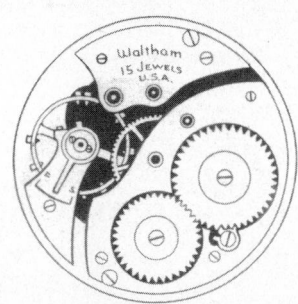

Model 1894, 12 size

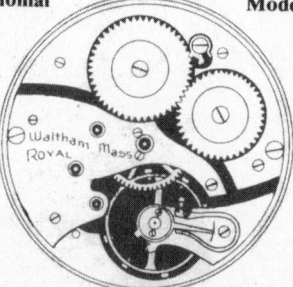

Model 1924, The Colonial

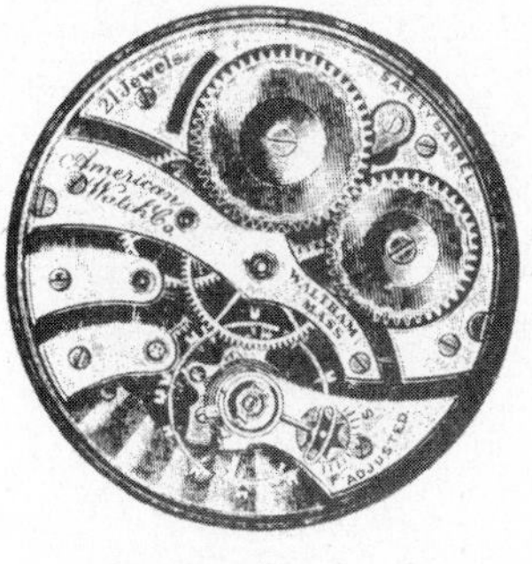

Model 1894, 12 size

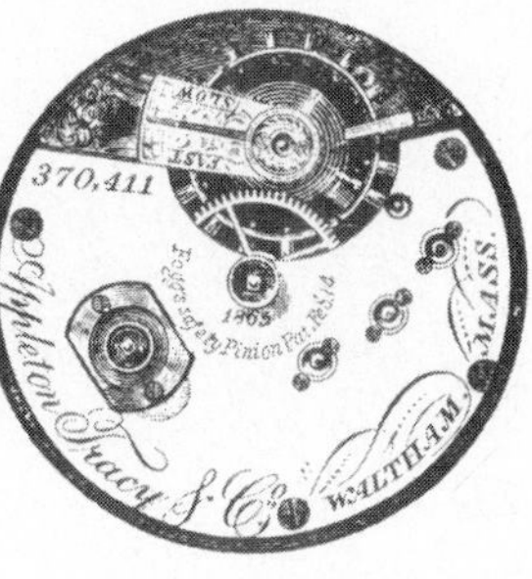

Model 10KW, 10 size

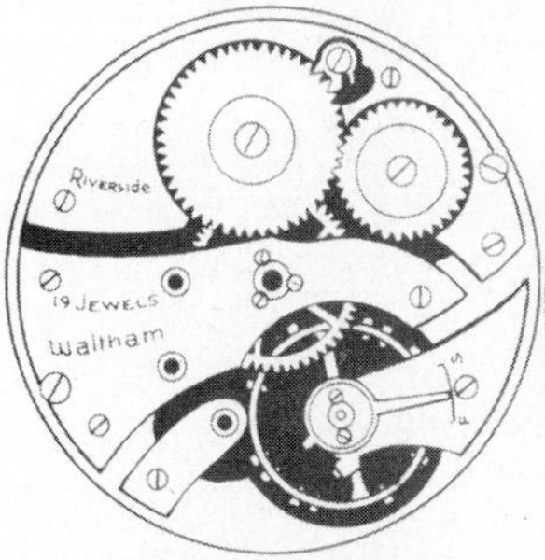

Colonial A, 10 size

Model 1873, 8 size

Model 1873, 8&6 size

Model 1889, 6 size

Model 1890, 6 size

Model 1890, 6 size

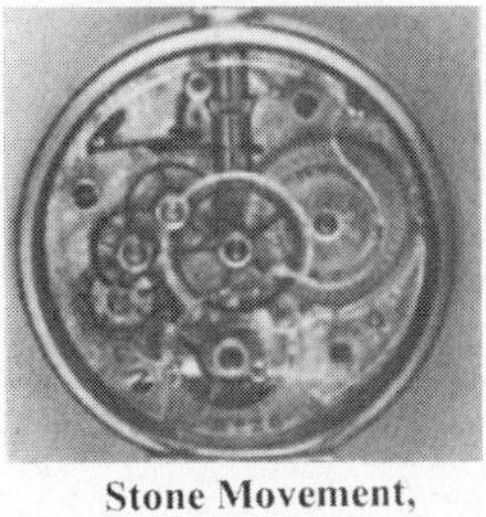

Stone Movement,
4 size

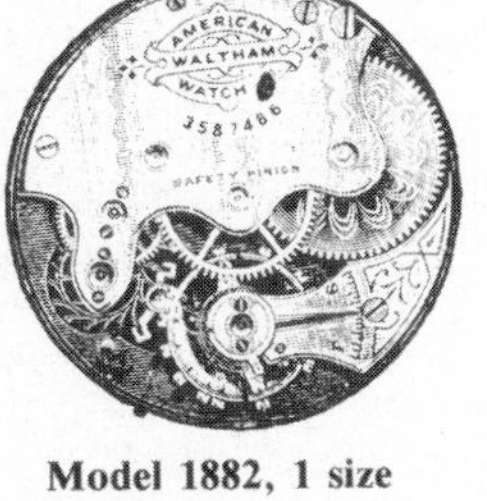

Model 1882, 1 size

Model 1891, 0 size

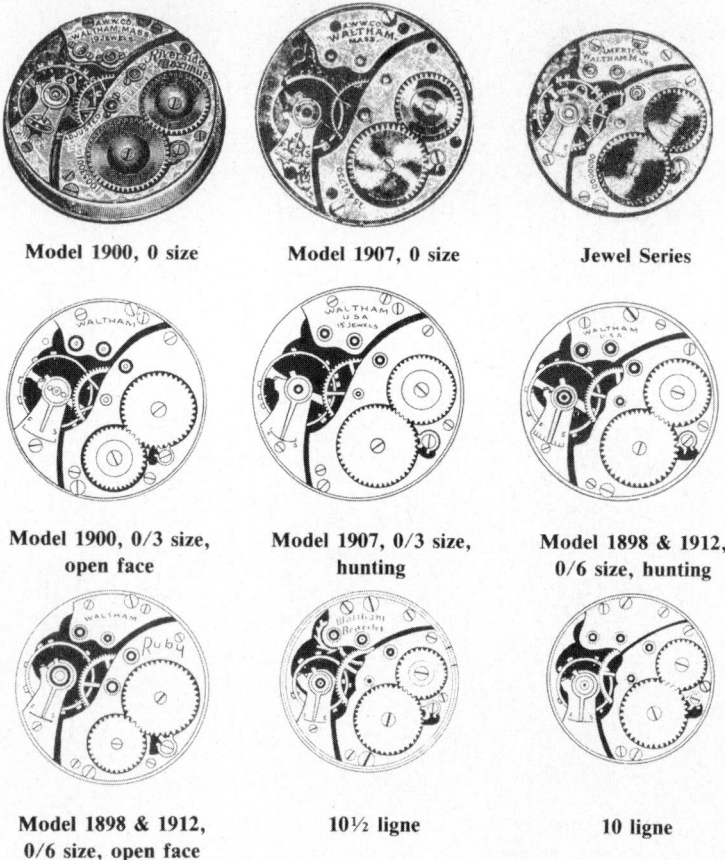

Model 1900, 0 size   Model 1907, 0 size   Jewel Series

Model 1900, 0/3 size,   Model 1907, 0/3 size,   Model 1898 & 1912,
open face   hunting   0/6 size, hunting

Model 1898 & 1912,   10½ ligne   10 ligne
0/6 size, open face

☙ Generic, nameless or unmarked grades for watch movements are listed under the Company name or initials of the Company, etc. by size, jewel count and description.

☙ Some grades are not included. Their values can be determined by comparing with similar age, size, metal content, style, models and grades listed.

☙ Watches listed in this book are priced at the collectable Trade Show level, as complete watches having an original 14k gold-filled case and Key Wind with silver, an original white enamel single sunk dial, and with the entire original movement in good working order with no repairs needed.

☙ This book endeavours to be a GUIDE or helpful manual and offers a wealth of material to be used as a tool not as an absolute document Price Guides are like watches, the worst may be better than none at all, but at best cannot be expected to be 100% accurate.

☙ Characteristics of watches differ for the same age of both case and movement. Because these features vary, it may not be accurate to date a watch by one single influence. Example: the second hand was not commonly found on watches before 1750, but common about 1800. The first second hand appeared in 1665 and another in 1690. Therefore statements are broad rather than accurate.

ANSONIA CLOCK CO.
Brooklyn, New York
1896-1929

The Ansonia Watch Co. was owned by the Ansonia Clock Company in Ansonia, Connecticut. Ansonia started making clocks in about 1850 and began manufacturing watches in 1896. They produced about 10,000,000 dollar- type watches. The company was sold to a Russian investor in 1930. "Patented April 17, 1888," is on the back plate of some Ansonia watches.

Ansonia Watch Company. Example of a basic movement, 16 size, stem wind.

Ansonia Watch Co., Sesqui-Centennial model.

Grade or Name—Description	ABP	Ex-Fn	Mint
Ansonia watch with a White Dial in Nickel case	$30	$75	$130
Ansonia watch with a Radium Dial in Nickel case	35	85	140
Ansonia watch with a Black Dial in Nickel case	50	95	150
Ascot	35	805	140
Bonnie Laddie Shoes	80	150	340
Dispatch	35	85	140
Faultless	50	95	150
Guide	50	95	150
Lenox	55	100	140
Mentor	40	85	140
Piccadilly	60	130	190
Rural	55	95	150
Sesqui-Centennial ★★★	300	500	635
Superior	55	95	150
The Auto	55	95	150
The Guide	55	95	150
Tutor	55	95	150

☞ Some grades are not included. Their values can be determined by comparing with similar age, size, metal content, style, models and grades listed.

☞ A collector should expect to pay modestly higher prices at local shops.

APPLETON WATCH CO.
(REMINGTON WATCH CO.)
Appleton, Wisconsin - 1901 - 1903

In 1901, O. E. Bell bought the machinery of the defunct Cheshire Watch Company and moved it to Appleton, Wisconsin, where he had organized the Remington Watch Company. The first watches were shipped from the factory in February 1902; production ceased in mid-1903 and the contents were sold off before the end of that year. Most movements made by this firm were modified Cheshire movements and were marked "Appleton Watch Company." Advertisements for the firm in 1903 stated that they made 16 and 18 size movements with 11, 15, or 17 jewels. Serial numbers range from 89,000 to 104,950. During the two years they were in business, the company produced about 2,000 to 3,000 watches.

 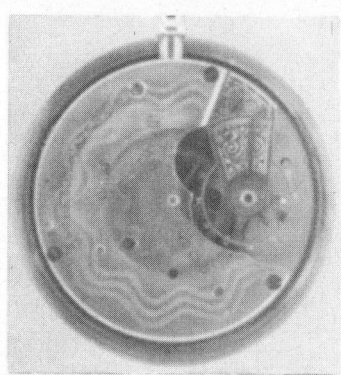

Appleton Watch Co., 18 size, 7 jewels, "The Appleton Watch Co." on dial. Engraved on movement "Appleton watch Co. Appleton, wis." Note that the stem is attached to movement. Serial number 93,106.

Description		ABP	Ex-Fn	Mint
18S, 7J, OF, NI, 3/4, DMK, SW, PS, stem attached . . . . ★★		$400	$600	$1,100
18S, 7J, OF, NI, 3/4, DMK, SW, PS, Coin, OF . . . . ★★		400	600	1,100
18S, 15J, NI, LS, SW, 3/4, M#2 . . . . ★★		500	700	1,300
16S, 7-11J, 3/4, **stem attached** . . . . ★★★		550	800	1,400

Note: With **ORIGINAL** APPLETON cases add **$300 to $400** more. This case is **difficult** to find.

AUBURNDALE WATCH CO.
Auburndale, Massachusetts
1876 - 1883

This company was the first to attempt an inexpensive watch. Jason Hopkins was issued two patents in 1875 covering the "rotary design." The rotary design eliminated the need of adjusting to various positions, resulting in a less expensive watch. The company was formed about 1876, and the first watches were known as the "Auburndale Rotary." In 1876, equipment was purchased from the Marion Watch Co., and the first rotary designed watches were placed on the market for $10 in 1877. Auburndale produced about 6,000 watches before closing in 1883. **Rotary** design as few as **500** made and **very few** known to exist. The Auburndale rotary watch, the movements whole assembly revolves once in 2 1/2 hours.

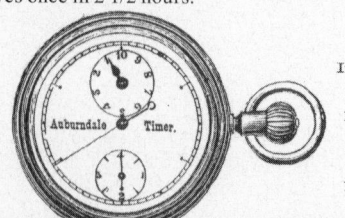

HORSE TIMERS—(only.)

In Nickel Cases.   Stem Wind.

No. 633. Auburndale Timer. Sweep Second Hand, Beats ¼ Seconds, Stop and Fly Back. (3 hands.) $17 25

No. 634. Auburndale Timer. Split Sweep Seconds, Beats ¼ Seconds, Stop and Fly Back 31 50

Auburndale Timer, 18 size, 7 jewels, stem wind, 10 minute, split seconds, fly back, 1/4 second jump timer.

Auburndale 10 min. Timer, 1/4 beat jump seconds, sweep second hand, stop & fly back, back wind.

Grade or Name —Description		ABP	Ex-Fn	Mint
Auburndale Rotary, 20S, 2-5J, SW, NI case, detent ★★★★★		$2,800	$5,500	$8,300
Auburndale Rotary, 18S, 2-5J, SW, NI case, lever. ★★★★		2,200	3,900	5,500
Bentley, 18S, 7J, LS, NI case, SW, 3/4 ★★★		1,100	2,200	3,900
Lincoln, 18S, 7J, LS, NI case, KW, 3/4 ★★★		1,100	2,200	3,900
Auburndale Timer, 18S, 5-7J, SW, NI case, 10 mm. timer, 1/4 sec. jump second		400	550	700
Auburndale Timer, 18S, 5-7J, SW, NI case, 10 mm. timer, 1/4 sec. jump seconds, with a 24 hour dial ★		450	600	800
Auburndale Timer, 18S, 5-7J, KW, NI case, 10 mm. timer, 1/4 sec. jump seconds, with split seconds ★★		700	1,000	2,000
Auburndale Timer, 18S, marked "207", gold balance, OF		350	500	800

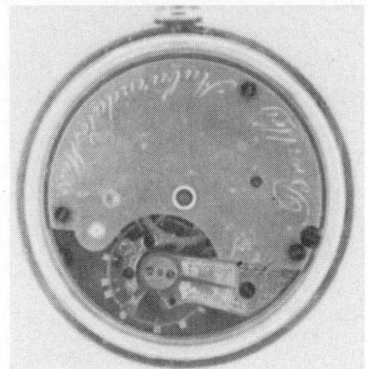

Bentley, 18 size, 7 jewels, 3/4 plate, stem wind, serial# 2.

Auburndale Rotary Mass, 16S, 2-5J., rotating once in about 2.5 hours, "Patents, Mar.30 1875, July 20 1875, June 20 1876, Jan. 30 1877". S#319. Note: Extremely RARE.

Right: Auburndale Rotary escapement, two different styles of levers used and two different styles for the escape wheel were used. Also note two banking pins in the right example.

AURORA WATCH CO.

Aurora, Illinois 1883 - 1892

Aurora Watch Co. was organized in mid-1883 with the goal of getting one jeweler in every town to handle Aurora watches. The first movements were 18S, full plate, and were first sold in the fall of 1884. There were several watches marked No. 1. Total production of 6 size watches was 7,400. For the most part Aurora produced medium to low grade(Note Waltham, Elgin, Illinois and others also made low grade watches; and at one time made about 100 movements per day. The Hamilton Watch Co. purchased the company June 19, 1890.

Aurora Watch Co.
Esimated Serial Nos. and Production Dates

1884--10,001	1888--200,000
1885--60,000	1889--215,000
1886--101,000	1891--230,901
1887--160,000	

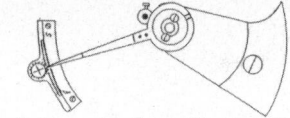

Hurd's Pat. regulator first used in early 1886.

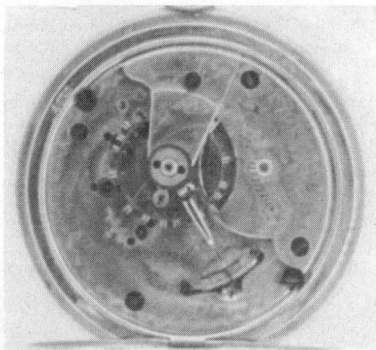

Aurora Watch Co., 18 size, 15 jewels, 'NEW MODEL', serial number 142,060. Made for railroad service.

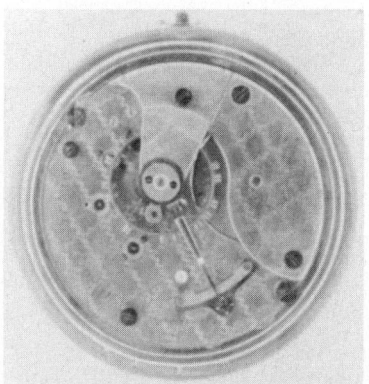

Aurora Watch Co., 18 size, 15 jewels Adj, Hurd's Pat. regulator, engraved on movement "Made expressly R. J. A." also note **5th pinion**, serial number 73,529.

Description	ABP	Ex-Fn	Mint
18S, 7J, KW, KS, Gilded, OF	$100	$200	$325
18S, 7J, KW, KS, Gilded, HC	150	225	450
18S, 7J, 5th pinion, Gilded, LS, SW, OF	100	200	325
18S, 7J, LS, SW, Gilded, new model, HC	150	225	450
18S, 11J, KW, KS, Gilded, HC	125	225	400
18S, 11J, KW, KS, Gilded, OF	125	200	400
18S, 11J, 5th pinion, LS, SW, Gilded, new model, OF	100	200	325
18S, 11J, 5th pinion, LS, SW, NI, OF	125	200	400
18S, 11J, 5th pinion, LS, SW, NI, GJS, new model, OF	125	200	400
18S, 11J, LS, SW, Gilded, **made expressly for the guild**, HC .... ★	200	325	575
18S, 11J, 5th pinion, LS, SW, NI, OF			
made expressly for the guild ★	250	375	625
18S, 15J, KW, KS, NI, GJS, DMK, OF or HC ★	175	275	450
18S, 15J, 5th pinion, LS, SW, Gilded, OF	125	200	400
18S, 15J, 5th pinion, LS, SW, NI, GJS, DMK, ADT, OF	125	200	400
18S, 15J, 5th pinion, LS, SW, NI, GJS, DMK, ADJ, new model, OF	150	200	450
18S, 15J, LS, SW, NI, GJS, DMK, ADJ, new model, HC	150	225	450
18S, 15J, LS, SW, NI, GJS, ADJ, marked **Ruby Jewels** ....★★	500	700	1,200
18S, 15J, LS, SW, NI, GJS, ADJ, 2 Tone DMK, checker-			
board or snowflake, **Ruby Jewels**, HC ....★★	600	800	1,400
18S, 15J, LS, SW, NI, GJS, ADJ, 2 Tone DMK, checker-			
board or snowflake, 5th pinion, **Ruby Jewels**, OF .....★★★	750	1,000	1,600

MARKED **"RUBY JEWELS"**, = Aurora's highest grade.

Size and Description		ABP	Ex-Fn	Mint
18S, marked **15 Ruby Jewels** but has 17J, 5th pinion, LS, SW, NI, GJS, 2 Tone, ADJ, OF	★★★	$750	$1,000	$1,500
18S, marked **15 Ruby Jewels**, only 15J, LS, SW, NI, GJS, 2 Tone DMK, ADJ, NC	★★★	700	900	1,400
18S, marked **15 Ruby Jewels**, only 15J, LS, SW, NI, GJS, ADJ, 2 Tone DMK, OF	★★★	700	900	1,400
18S, 15J, LS, SW, NI, GJS, DMK, ADJ, Railroad Time Service or Caufleld Watch, new model, NC	★★	800	1,000	1,500
18S, 15J, Chronometer, LS, SW, NI, DMK, ADJ, new model HC	★★	625	800	1,300
18S, 15J, Chronometer, LS, SW, NI, GJS, DMK, ADJ, HC	★★	600	750	1,200
18S, 15J, LS, Gilded, "Eclipse, Chicago", new model, HC		300	475	700
18S, 15J, LS, SW, NI, DMK, made expressly for the guild, HC	★	275	400	650
18S, 15J, 5th pinion, LS, SW, Gilded, made expressly for the guild, OF	★	325	500	775
18S, 15J, LS, SW, Gilded, made expressly for the "RJA" (Retail Jeweler's Assoc.), HC	★	325	500	775

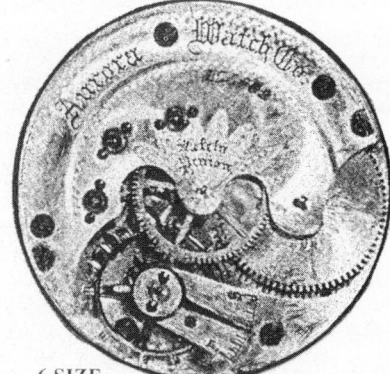

Right: **Aurora**, Total production
of 6 size watches was 7,400

6 SIZE

Size and Description	ABP	Ex-Fn	Mint
6S, 11-15J, LS, SW, Gilded, 3/4, HC	$90	$125	$250
6S, 11-15J, LS, SW, NI, GJS, DMK, 3/4, HC	100	150	300
6S, 11-15J, LS, SW, 3/4 plate, **14K, HC**	300	400	600

 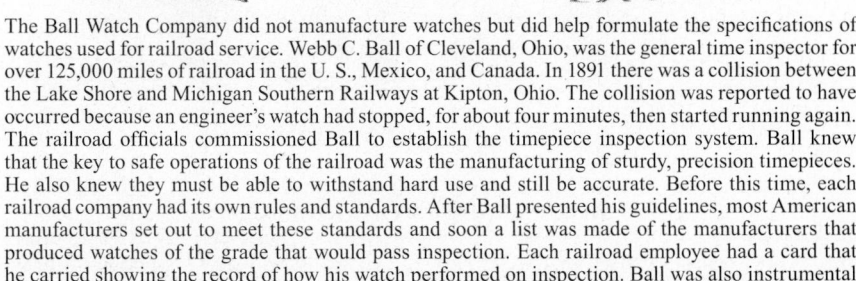

BALL WATCH CO.
Cleveland, Ohio
1879-1969

The Ball Watch Company did not manufacture watches but did help formulate the specifications of watches used for railroad service. Webb C. Ball of Cleveland, Ohio, was the general time inspector for over 125,000 miles of railroad in the U. S., Mexico, and Canada. In 1891 there was a collision between the Lake Shore and Michigan Southern Railways at Kipton, Ohio. The collision was reported to have occurred because an engineer's watch had stopped, for about four minutes, then started running again. The railroad officials commissioned Ball to establish the timepiece inspection system. Ball knew that the key to safe operations of the railroad was the manufacturing of sturdy, precision timepieces. He also knew they must be able to withstand hard use and still be accurate. Before this time, each railroad company had its own rules and standards. After Ball presented his guidelines, most American manufacturers set out to meet these standards and soon a list was made of the manufacturers that produced watches of the grade that would pass inspection. Each railroad employee had a card that he carried showing the record of how his watch performed on inspection. Ball was also instrumental in the formation of the Horological Institute of America. By 1908 Ball furnished over **100 different railroad** companies with watches.

★ Webb C. Ball started selling RR grade watches in 1893, some marked Superior Grade.

ESTIMATED SERIAL NUMBERS AND PRODUCTION DATES
FOR RAILROAD GRADE WATCHES

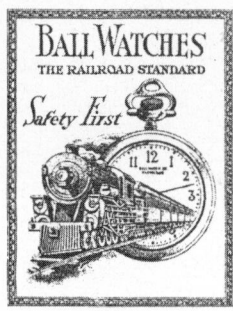

(Hamilton) Date — Serial #	(Am. Waltham) Date — Serial #	(Elgin) 1904-1906
1895 - 13,000	1900 - 060,700	S # range:
1897 - 20,500	1905 - 202,000	11,853,000
1900 - 42,000	1910 - 216,000	12,282,000
1902 - 170,000	1915 - 250,000	
1905 - 462,000	1920 - 260,000	
1910 - 600,000	1925 - 270,000	
1915 - 603,000		(E. Howard & CO.) 1893-1895
1920 - 610,000		S # range:
1925 - 620,000		226,000 - 306,000
1930 - 637,000	(Illinois)	
1935 - 641,000	Date — Serial #	(Hampden) 1890-1892
1938 - 647,000	1929 - 800,000	S# range:
1939 - 650,000	1930 - 801,000	626,750 - 657,960
1940 - 651,000	1931 - 803,000	759,720
1941 - 652,000	1932 - 804,000	
1942 - 654,000		

The above list is provided for determining the <u>APPROXIMATE</u> age of your watch. Match serial number with date. Watches were not necessarily sold in the exact order of manufactured date.

✎ NOTE: BALL WATCHES ARE PRICED AS HAVING A ORIGINAL BALL DIAL & CASE. Watches MARKED "**BALL & Co**." are more difficult to find than **BALL WATCH Co.**

BALL — AURORA
18 SIZE

Description		ABP	Ex-Fn	Mint
15-17J, marked Webb C. Ball, OF	★★★★	$2,500	$4,000	$5,500
15-17J, marked Ball, HC	★★★★	4,000	6,500	9,500

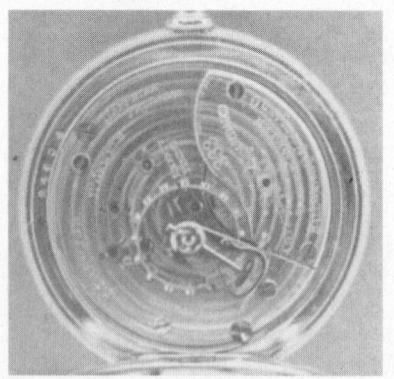

Ball-Elgin, Grade 333, 18 size, 17 jewels, rare hunting case model, serial number 11.958,002.

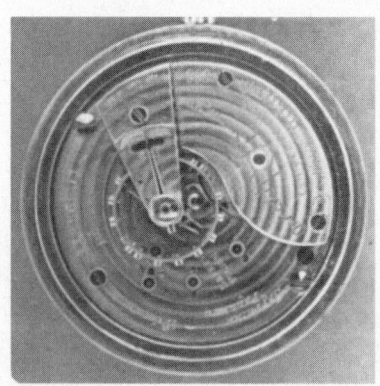

Ball-Elgin, Grade 333,18 size, 17 jewels, open face model, serial number 11,856,801.

BALL— ELGIN 18 SIZE G. F. CASES

Description		ABP	Ex-Fn	Mint
16J, G#327, Commercial Standard, LS, OF	★	$350	$500	$900
17J, G#328, Commercial Standard, LS, HC	★	450	600	1,100
17J, G#328, Coin, LS, HC	★	350	450	900

Note:18 Size Ball watches in **hunting cases** are scarce.

Description	ABP	Ex-En	Mint
17J, G#329, NI, Adj.5P, LS, HC . . . . ★★	$1,200	$1,500	$2,500
16J, G#331, NI, Adj.5P, PS, Commercial Std, OF . . . . ★★	375	450	850
16J, G#331, NI, Adj.5P, PS, Commercial Std, HC. . . . . ★★★	400	500	950
17J, G#331, NI, Adj.5P, PS, OF	250	325	550
17J, G#332, Commercial Std, OF. . . . . ★	250	325	550
17J, G#333, NI, Adj.5P, LS, OF	250	325	550
17J, G#333, NI, Adj.5P, LS, HC . . . . ★★★	1,500	2,000	3,300
21J, G#333, NI, Adj.5P, LS, OF . . . . ★	800	1,000	1,500
21J, G#333, NI, Adj.5P, LS, HC . . . . ★★	1,000	1,500	2,200
21J, G#330, LS, Official RR std., HC . . . . ★★★★	2,000	3,500	6,000
21J, G#334, NI, Adj.5P, LS, OF	900	1,200	1,800

BALL — HAMILTON
18 SIZE G. F. CASES

Description	ABP	Ex-Fn	Mint
17J, M#936, first trial run S# 601 to 625 single roller. . . . . . ★★★★	$2,500	$4,000	$6,600
17J, M#936, single roller or double roller . . . . ★	800	1,400	2,100
17J, M#936, marked Superior, Adj . . . . ★★	1,200	2,000	3,000
17J, M#-937-939, Official RR std, LS, Adj., **HC**. . . . . ★★	2,000	3,000	4,500
17J, M#938, NI, DR, OF. . . . . ★★★	800	1,200	1,800
17J, M#999, marked single roller. . . . . ★	600	800	1,000
17J, M#999, Commercial Standard	300	450	850
17J, M#999, NI, Official RR std, Adj.5P, LS, OF, Coin	300	450	850
17J, M#999, Official RR std, NI, Adj.5P, LS, OF	300	450	850
17J, M#999, "A" model adj. OF . . . . ★	350	500	900
17J, M#999, NI, Adj.5P, marked "**Loaner**" on case . . . . ★	500	600	1,100
19J, M#999, Official RR std, NI, Adj.5P, LS, OF	500	700	1,000
21J, M#999, Official RR std, NI, Adj.5P, LS, OF	600	850	1,200
23J, M#999, NI, Adj.5P, LS, Gold Filled OF Case . . . . ★★	3,500	5,000	9,000
23J, M#999, NI, Adj.5P, LS , OF, **14K case**. . . . . ★★★	6,000	7,000	11,000
23J, M#999, NI, Adj.5P, LS, **HC, 14K case** . . . . ★★★★	7,500	10,000	15,000
Early Ball & Co., 16-17J, (low serial # 13,001 to 13,400), G# 999 (second run). . . . . ★★★	1,200	2,000	3,600
Early Ball & Co., 16-17J, (low serial # 14,001 to 15,000), G# 999 (third run) . . . . ★★	1,200	1,700	3,500
Ball & Co., 16-17J, marked dial & mvt. *Railroad Watch Co* . . . . ★★	1,200	1,700	3,000
Brotherhood of Locomotive Engineers, 17J, OF . . . . ★★	3,000	4,000	6,000
Brotherhood of Locomotive Engineers, 19J, OF . . . . ★★	3,500	4,700	7,200

BALL-HAMILTON, **17J,** Webb C. Ball marked on dial, marked on movement Ball standard superior grade, also marked adjusted, G#936, serial #601, Ca. 1893-94.

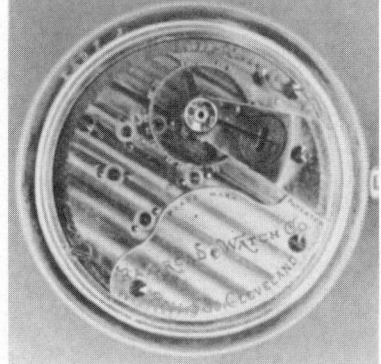

BALL-HAMILTON, Grade 999,18 size, 17 jewels, marked *"Railroad Watch Co."* Ca.June.1890, S# 20,793.

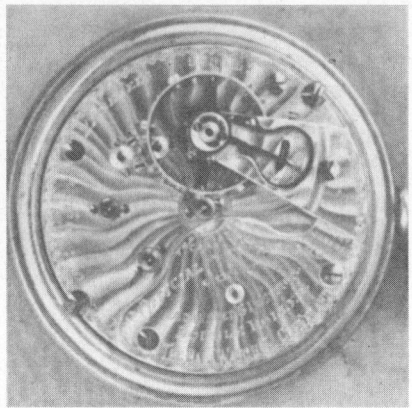

Ball Watch Co. (Hamilton). Grade 999, 18 size, 21-23 J., sun ray damaskeening, S# 548,157, Ca. Aug., 1907.

Ball Watch Co., Brotherhood of RR trainmen 18 size, 17J, movement made by Hamilton, Ca.SepL,1895 S# 13,020.

Description	ABP	Ex-Fn	Mint
Brotherhood of Locomotive Engineers, 21J, OF . . . . ★★	$3,500	$5,000	$8,000
Brotherhood of Locomotive Firemen, 17J, OF . . . . ★★	3,000	3,600	6,600
Brotherhood of Locomotive Firemen, 19J, OF . . . . ★★	3,200	4,800	7,200
Brotherhood of Locomotive Firemen, 21J, OF . . . . ★★	3,500	5,000	8,000
Brotherhood of Railroad Trainmen, 17J, OF . . . . ★★	3,000	3,500	6,600
Brotherhood of Railroad Trainmen, 19J, OF . . . . ★★	3,200	4,200	7,200
Brotherhood of Railroad Trainmen, 21J, OF . . . . ★★	3,500	5,000	8,000
Order of Railway Conductors, 17J, OF . . . . ★★	3,000	3,600	6,600
Order of Railway Conductors, 19J, OF . . . . ★★	3,200	5,000	7,700
Order of Railway Conductors, 21J, OF . . . . ★★★	3,500	5,500	8,000
Order of Railroad Telegraphers, 17J, OF . . . . ★★★★	4,000	5,500	8,800
Order of Railroad Telegraphers, 19J, OF . . . . ★★★★	4,200	5,500	9,000
Order of Railroad Telegraphers, 21J, OF . . . . ★★★★	5,000	6,800	9,900
Private Label or Jewelers name. 17J. Adj., OF . . . . ★★★	900	1,400	2,500

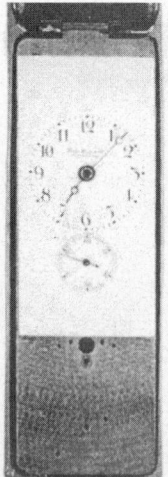

BALL WATCH Co. In line gear train, 19-21J., gold train, movement by Waltham, on dial movement by Waltham, on dial *"Ball Watch Co. Cleveland Ohio"*, rectangular **14K Case.** ($5,000 to $8,000)

BALL WATCH Co. DIAL (Order of Railway Conductors), ORC is Intertwined, 16 size.

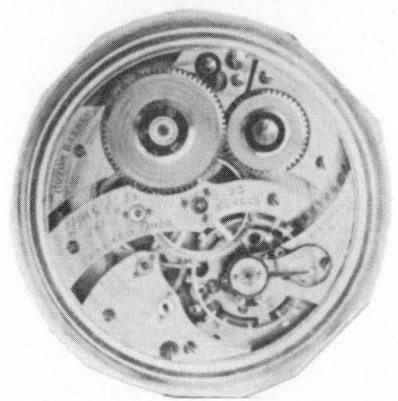
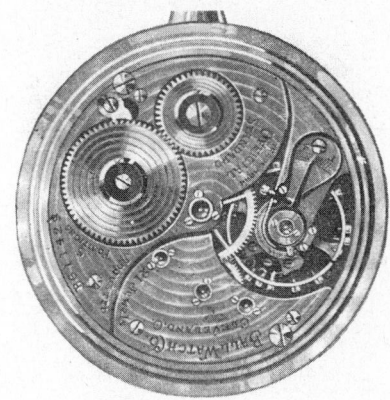

Ball-Hamilton, Model 998 Elinvar, 16 size, 23 jewels, with center bridge.

BALL W. CO. (HAMILTON), 16 size, 21 jewels, official RR standard, ADJ.5p, serial no.611429, Ca. 1908.

BALL- DeLONG ESCAPEMENT 16 SIZE

Description		ABP	Ex-En	Mint
21-23J, Adj.5P, upright **D** shaped pallets, **14K OF Case** ... ★★★★		$5,000	$7,000	$11,000
21-23J, Adj.5P, upright **D** shaped pallets, gold filled case .. ★★★★		4,000	6,000	9,000

BALL —HAMILTON
16 SIZE G. F. CASES

Description		ABP	Ex-Fn	Mint
16J, M#976, 977, 999-HC, NI, OF, LS .... ★		$350	$475	$950
17J, M#974, NI, OF, LS		200	275	575
21J, M#999, NI, Off. RR Stan., OF, LS		550	700	950
21J, M#999B-marked, Off. RR Stan., OF, marked-Adj.6P		750	1,000	1,500
21J, M#999, Off. RR Stan., Coin case		550	700	950
21J, M#999 , Off. RR Stan., marked Loaner, coin case ....★★		650	800	1,200
21J, M#992B, NI, marked 992B & Off RR Stan. Adj.6P ..... ★★★		1,000	2,000	3,200
23J, M#999, NI, Off. RR Stan., OF, LS		1,000	1,800	2,500
23J, M#998 marked-Elinvar, Off. RR Stan., Adj.5P ....★★		2,100	3,500	4,400
Brotherhood of Locomotive Engineers, OF ....★★		2,600	3,500	4,600
Brotherhood of Locomotive Firemen & Enginemen, OF ....★★		2,600	3,500	4,600
Brotherhood of Rairoad Trainmen, OF ....★★		2,600	3,500	4,600
Order of Railway Conductors, OF ....★★		2,600	3,500	4,600
Private Label or Jewelers name, 21J, Adj., OF .... ★		625	850	1,500

BALL—HAMPDEN 18 SIZE

Description		ABP	Ex-Fn	Mint
15-17J, LS, SW, HC, marked Superior Grade .... ★★★★		$2,500	$4,000	$5,500
15-17J, LS, SW, OF, marked Superior Grade.................★★		1,500	2,000	3,000
15-17J, LS, SW, OF.......................................★★		600	800	1,500
15-17J, LS, SW, HC ....★★★		600	1,000	2,000

BALL- NEW YORK WATCH CO. 18 SIZE

Description		ABP	Ex-Fn	Mint
Whitcomb & Ball, E.W. Bond style 3/4 plate, 17-19J, NI, .. ★★★★		$2,600	$3,800	$7,200

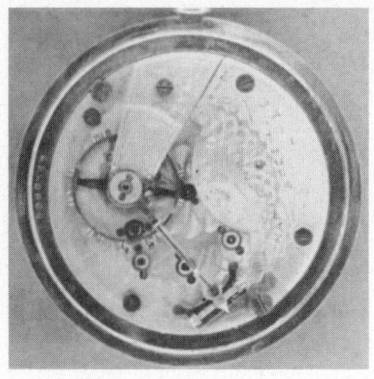

Ball-Hampden, 18 size, 17 jewels, serial number 759,728.

BALL & CO. (E. HOWARD & CO.), Series VIII, 18 size, 17 jewels. (Order of Railway Conductors), serial number 307,488. Ca. 1900.

BALL — E. HOWARD & CO.
18 SIZE

Description		ABP	Ex-Fn	Mint
VII, Ball, 17J, nickel, SW, GF, HC	★★★	$4,400	$6,600	$9,900
VII, Ball, 17J, nickel, SW, **14K** orig. HC	★★★	5,500	7,100	13,200
VII, Ball , 17J, nickel, **18K** orig. HC	★★★	8,800	11,000	16,500
VIII, Ball, 17J, nickel, SW, GF, OF	★★★	2,800	3,800	5,500
VIII, Ball, 17J, nickel, SW, **14K** orig. OF	★★★	3,800	4,900	7,700
VIII, Ball, 17J, 3/4, PS, GJS, *Brotherhood of Locomotive Engineers*, or *Order of Railway Conductors*, **gold filled** orig. OF,	★★★★	6,600	8,800	15,400
VIII, Ball, 17J, 3/4, PS, GJS, **Brotherhood of Locomotive Engineers,** or *Order of Railway Conductors*, **14K** orig. OF,	★★★★	7,700	11,000	18,700

A total of about 120=**B of LE** & about 70= **O of RC** made by E. Howard & Go., for Webb C. Ball.

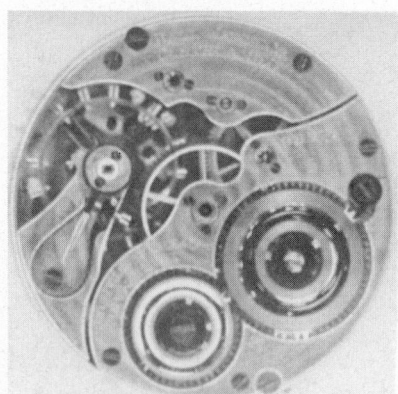

BALL W. Co. (E. HOWARD WATCH CO.), 16 size, 21J. (KEYSTONE). This watch believed to be **one-of-a kind** prototype, serial number 962,201.

Ball Watch Co., Illinois Model, 16size, 23 jewels. Note: **The CORRECT HANDS FOR BALL ILLINOIS WATCH.**

&ᔆ BALL Watches are priced as having an **ORIGINAL BALL DIAL & CASE.**

BALL —E. HOWARD WATCH CO. (Keystone)
16 SIZE

Description		ABP	Ex-Fn	Mint
17J, Keystone Howard, GJS, OF	★★★	$2,800	$3,800	$5,500
21J, Keystone Howard, Adj, GJS, OF	★★★★★	7,700	11,000	15,400

Ball Watch Co., Illinois Model #11, 16 size, 23 jewels. To identify, note back plates that circle around balance wheel, serial number B802,670.

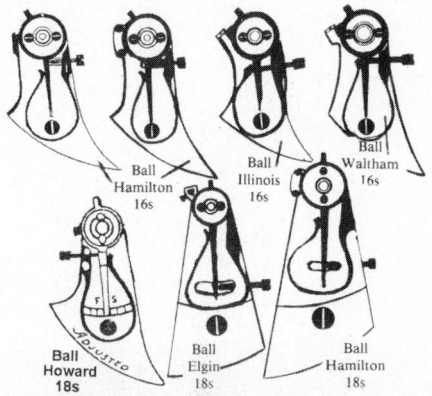

BALL regulator Identification, note: styles and location of hairspring stud. "Pat.Dec.8.08" on some balance cocks.

BALL —ILLINOIS
18 & 16 SIZE

Description		ABP	Ex-Fn	Mint
18 size, 11-15J. or (Garland model), OF		$300	$400	$600
16 size, 23J, 3/4, LS, Off. RR Stan., Adj. 5SP, GJS, OF	★	2,200	3,500	5,000

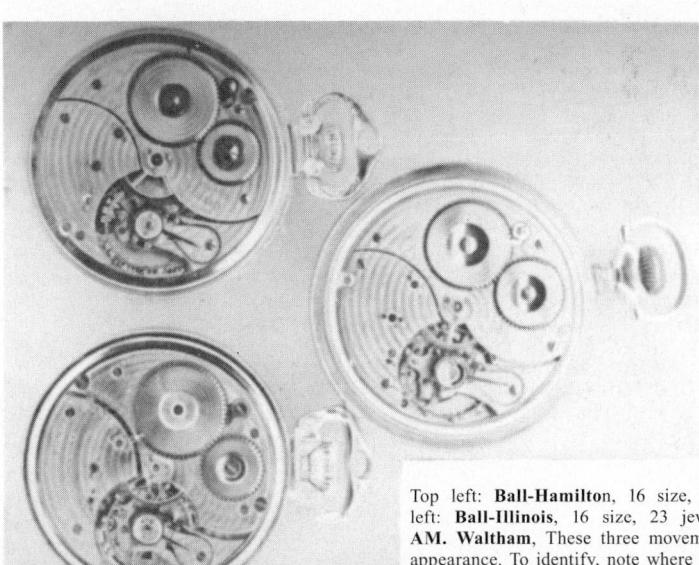

Top left: **Ball-Hamilton**, 16 size, 23 jewels. Bottom left: **Ball-Illinois**, 16 size, 23 jewels. Above: **Ball-AM. Waltham,** These three movements are similar in appearance. To identify, note where the hair spring stud attaches to the balance bridge, which is slightly different on each movement.

BALL — SETH THOMAS 18 SIZE

Description		ABP	Ex-Fn	Mint
17J, M#3, LS, OF, 3/4, GJS.	★★★★	$5,500	$9,000	$15,000

BALL — AM. WALTHAM 18 SIZE

Description		ABP	Ex-Fn	Mint
1892, 17J, OF, LS, SW,				
marked Webb C. Ball, Cleveland	★★★★	$3,000	$4,500	$7,000

BALL — AM. WALTHAM 16 SIZE

Description		ABP	Ex-Fn	Mint
15J, Commercial Std.,3/4, **HC**, GCW	★★	$300	$425	$900
15-16J, Commercial std., OF		150	300	450
16J, Commercial std., HC		225	400	650
17-19J, Commercial std., OF		150	300	450
17-19J, Commercial std., HC		225	400	650
17J, LS, 3/4, Adj.5P, Multi-color case, GF, OF		300	450	950
17J, LS, 3/4, Adj.5P, Off RR Stan., OF		225	400	650
17J, Official RR std., HC	★★	600	800	1,600

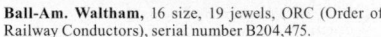

Ball-Am. Waltham, 16 size, 19 jewels, ORC (Order of Railway Conductors), serial number B204,475.

Ball-Am. Waltham, 23 jewels, Official Railroad Standard, lever set, Adjusted to 5 positions, serial# B060,915.

Description		ABP	Ex-Fn	Mint
19J, LS, Off. RR Stan., Ball stirrup style case, OF		$275	$450	$750
19J, LS, Off. RR Stan., OF, Coin		275	450	750
19J, LS, Off. RR Stan., **OF 14K**	★★	1,200	2,000	3,400
19J, Official RR. std., LS, GCW, GJS, **HC**	★★	1,000	1,500	2,200
19J, 3/4, Adj.5P, Off. RR. Stan., OF, **Wind Ind.**	★★★★	5,500	7,500	12,000
all the above, **Wind Ind., OF 14K Case.**	★★★★★	7,500	11,500	16,000
21J, Commercial std., LS, OF		300	600	800
21J, Official RR. std., LS, GCW, GJS, OF		500	700	900
21J, LS, 3/4, Adj.5P, Off. RR. Stan., OF		500	700	900
21J, LS, OF, Adj.5P, Off. RR. Stan., marked **Loaner,** OF	★	600	800	1,200
23J, LS, Adj.5P, NI, GJS, Off RR. Stand., OF,				
very rare	★★★★★	5,500	8,000	12,500

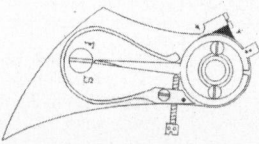

Above Am. Waltham balance cock note shape of balance cock & triangular hairspring stud.

Description		ABP	Ex-Fn	Mint
17J, Brotherhood, marked ORC, BofLF&E & *other etc. dials*, OF	★★	$2,500	$3,200	$4,900
19J, Brotherhood, marked ORC, BofLF&E & *other etc. dials*, OF	★★	2,800	3,500	4,900
17-19J, Brotherhood, marked ORC, BofLF&E & *other etc. dials*, HC	★★	4,000	5,400	8,200
21J, Brotherhood, marked ORC, BofLF&E & *other etc. dials*, OF	★★	3,000	3,800	5,000
21J, Brotherhood, marked ORC, BofLF&E & *other etc. dials*, HC	★★★	4,000	5,500	8,800

Ball Watch Co. by Illinois, Secometer, rotating digital sec, open face, 12 size, 19 jewels.

Record Watch Co. (BXC) 16 size, 17 jewels, M# 435-B, Unadjusted, Swiss made Ca.1961.

12 SIZE (NOT Railroad Grade)

Description	ABP	Ex-Fn	Mint
19J, Illinois, GCW, ADJ, OF, PS	$150	$225	$375
19J, Illinois, GCW, ADJ, **14 K** OF	275	400	600
19J, Illinois, Secometer, rotating digital sec, OF ★	250	375	600
17J, Waltham, Commercial Standard, OF, PS, ★	150	225	350

0 SIZE (NOT Railroad Grade)

Description	ABP	Ex-Fn	Mint
16j, Waltham, Queen, HC, PS.	$400	$700	$1,000
17-19J, Waltham, OF, PS	200	285	450
19J, HG, PS, "Queen" in Ball case	250	375	500

NO. 333
NO. 999

999 STANDARD

OFFICIAL RR STANDARD

OFFICIAL TIME SERVICE STANDARD

STANDARD B OF RT

The B. of L.F. & E. Standard Watch

The B. of L. E. Standard Watch.
The B. of L. F. Standard Watch.
The B. of R. T. Standard Watch.
The O. of R. C. Standard Watch.
The Official R. R. Standard Watch.
The O. of R. T. Standard Watch.

B OF LE

O OF RC

B OF LF

SAFETY FIRST

TRADE MARKS REGISTERED IN U. S. PATENT OFFICE

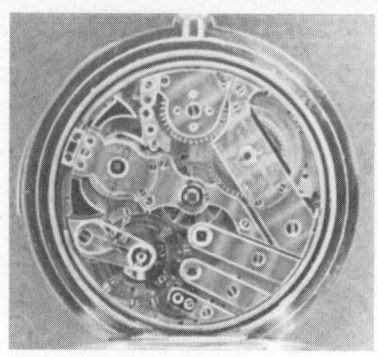

Ball-Audemars Piguet & Co., 14 size, 31 jewels, minute repeater, open face, serial number 4,220.

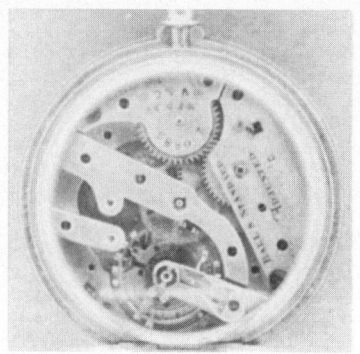

Ball-Vacheron & Constantin, 43mm, 15 jewels, hunting; note wolf-teeth winding

BALL—SWISS 12-16 SIZE

Description	ABP	Ex-Fn	Mint
17J, "Garland"	$100	$135	$275
18-21J, Longines, OF	125	150	275
21J, Time Ball Special, OF (**Swiss Fake**)	85	150	175
21J, M#435, (B or C), LS, Adj.6P, Ball case, stirrup bow, OF	150	200	300
21J, M#477-B, Adj.6P (BXC-Record Watch Co.)	150	200	300
40mm Audemar Piguet, mm. repeater, jeweled thru hammers, triple signed Webb C. Ball, **18K, OF**★★	4,500	5,500	9,500
43-44mm Vacheron & Constantin, 18J, **HC, 18K**★★	1,600	2,500	3,900
12 size, 17J, by Longines, marked "Made expressly for Webb C. Ball" Adj. temperature 2 pos. Ca. 1922 ★	200	275	350
12 size, marked *made especially for The Webb C Ball Co. extra superior Swiss* 21J., 8 adjustments, **14K** Gold OF★★★	500	650	900

PATENT SAFETY BOW

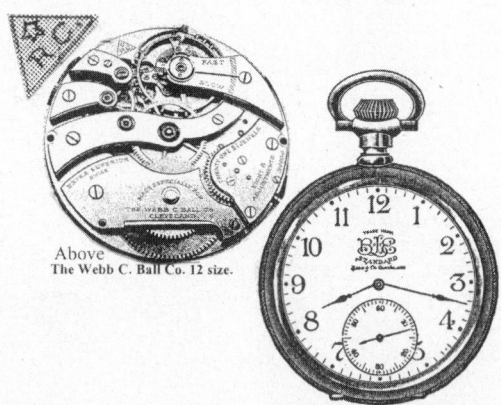

Above
The Webb C. Ball Co. 12 size.

20 th CENTURY CASE
18 size: 14K=$600 - $700 - $1,300
18 size: gold filled= $175 - $275 -$600
16 size: 14K = $500 -$600 -$1,100
16 size: gold filled= $125 - $225 - $500
16-18 size: silveroid=$100 - $200- $400

Ball RR Dials
18 size: $40 -$80- $150
16 size: $35 -$60- $125

ANTIQUE BOW
18 size: 14K=$600 - $700 - $1,400
18 size: gold filled= $175 - $270 - $600
16 size: 14K= $500 -$600 - $1,200
16 size: gold filled= $125 - $225 - $500

BLE (Brotherhood dials)
18 size: $550 -$1,100- $2,500
16 size: $500 - $1,000 - $2,000

CATALOG CASE # 106
gold filled case $100 - $185 - $400

CATALOG CASE # 110
gold filled case $150 - $200 - $475

"BOX CAR" Dial;
found on Hamilton & Illinois made Ball

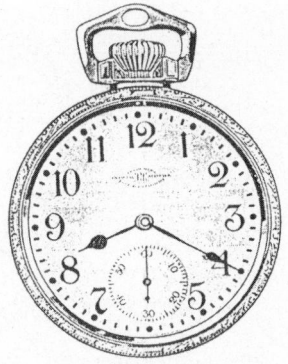

"CONVENTIONAL" Dial;
found on Waltham made Ball

CATALOG CASE # 114
gold filled case $150 - $185- $475

CATALOG CASE #118
gold filled case $175 - $200 - $500

☞ NOTE: A 1902 advertisement for Ball Watch Company read, "We do not sell movements or cases separately". Ball advertised as a complete watch with a choice of Ball dials and was fitted with a certain matched, timed and rated movement and sold in the Ball designed case style as a complete watch. All the above cases are gold filled.

CATALOG CASE # 122
gold filled case $175 - $200 - $475

CATALOG CASE# 126
gold filled case $125 - $165 - $400

OFFICIAL RR STANDARD. BALL Dial

CATALOG CASE #130
gold filled case $150 - $175 - $400

CATALOG CASE # 134
gold filled case $175 - $200 - $425

⁂ NOTE: A 1902 advertisement for Ball Watch Company read, "We do not sell movements or cases separately". Ball advertised as a complete watch with a choice of Ball dials and was fitted with a certain matched, timed and rated movement and sold in the Ball designed case style as a complete watch. All the above cases are gold filled.

BANNATYNE WATCH CO.
1905- 1911

Mr. Bannatyne had previously worked for Waterbury Clock Co., in charge of watch production. Bannatyne made non-jeweled watches that sold for about $1.50. Ingraham bought this company in 1912.

ESTIMATED SERIAL NUMBERS AND PRODUCTION DATES

Date 1906	Serial No. 40,000	Date 1908	Serial No. 140,000	Date 1910	Serial No. 250,000

Description		ABP	Ex-Fn	Mint
16-18S, OF, SW, NI- case . . . . ★★		$300	$450	$850
12-14S, OF, SW, NI- case . . . . ★★		200	300	450

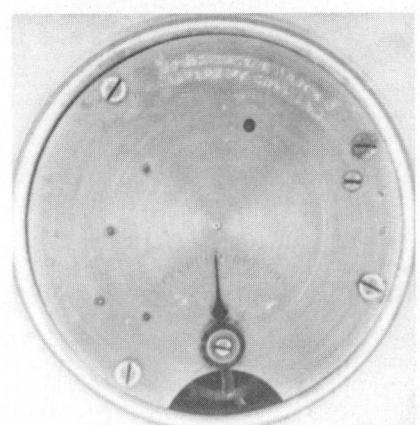 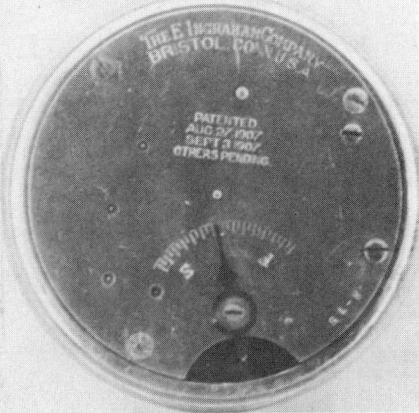

Bannatyne Watch Co. (left), Ingraham Watch Co. (right). Note similarity of movements. Both patented Aug.27th, 1907 & Sept.3rd, 1907.

BENEDICT & BURNHAM MFG. CO.
Waterbury, Connecticut 1878- 1880

The name **BENEDICT & BURNHAM MFG. CO**. will be found on back of movement on the large mainspring spring cover. D. A. A. Buck designed a rotary watch with 58 parts. The first "long wind" Waterbury watches made in 1878. These watches had skeletonized movements with open dials that made the works visible. They used 58 parts and were unique and attractive. The company was re-organized in March of 1880 as the Waterbury Watch Co. and in 1898 became the New England Watch Co.

Benedict & Burnham Mfg. Co. 18 size, long wind, 3 spoke skeletonized dial.
Benedict & Burnham Mfg. Co. will be found on back of movement on the large mainspring spring cover.

Benedict & Burnham Mfg. Co. dial & movement, 18 size, long wind, 3 spoke skeletonized dial.
Benedict & Burnham Mfg. Co. will be found on back of movement on the large mainspring spring cover.

Description		ABP	Ex-Fn	Mint
18S, duplex escapement, movement rotates as time advances, long wind				
3 spoke, Nickel OF case.	★★★	$700	$1,200	$1,500
4 spoke, Nickel OF case.	★★★★	1,000	1,500	2,200
6 spoke, Nickel OF case.	★★★	600	1,000	1,300

BOWMAN WATCH Co. 1879 - 1882

In March 1877, Ezra F. Bowman, a native of **Lancaster, Pa.,** opened a retail jewelry and watch business. He employed William H. Todd to supervise his watch manufacturing. Todd had previously been employed by the Elgin and Lancaster Watch companies. Bowman made a 17 Size, 3/4 plate, fully-jeweled movement. The escape wheel was a star tooth design, fully capped, similar to those made by Charles Frodsham, an English watch maker. They were stem wind with dials made by another company. Enough parts were made and bought for 300 watches, but only about **50** watches were completed and sold by Bowman. These watches performed very well. The company was sold to J. P. Stevens of Atlanta, Ga.

Description		ABP	Ex-Fn	Mint
★17S, 19-21J, 3/4, GJS, NI, LS, SW, made by (*Bowman W Co.*)				
marked **E. F. Bowman, (S# 1 to 50).**	★★★★	$13,000	$20,000	$35,000
18S, 17J, by Hamilton G# 928, OF, marked E. F. Bowman	★★	600	800	1,400
16S, 21J, by Hamilton G# 960, OF, marked E. F. Bowman	★★	550	750	1,300
16S, 21J, by Hamilton G# 961, HC, marked E. F. Bowman.	★★★	700	900	1,500

Bowman Watch Co., 16-18 size, 19-21 jewels, 3/4 plate, gold jewel settings, lever set, stem wind. Note free sprung balance. S# 17, Ca.1880. (made by Bowman W. Co.)

Bowman Watch Co. 16-18 size, 19-21 jewels, 3/4 plate, gold jewel settings, lever set, stem wind. Note free sprung balance. S# 19, Ca.1880. (made by Bowman W. Co.)

CALIFORNIA WATCH CO.

The Cornell Watch Co. was reorganized in early 1876 as the California Watch Co. The new company bought machinery to make watch cases of gold and silver. In a short time the company was in bad financial trouble and even paid its employees with watches. The business closed in the summer of 1876. Albert Troller bought the unfinished watches that were left. In about four months, he found a buyer in San Francisco. The factory was then closed and sold to the Independent Watch Co. Only about 5,000 watches were made by the California Watch Company.

Description		ABP	Ex-Fn	Mint
18S, 15J, FULL, KW, KS, "Berkeley"	★★★	$1,500	$2,200	$5,000
18S, 11-15J,FULL,KW,KS or SW	★	1,100	1,400	2,200
18S, 19J,FULL,KW,KS or SW	★★★	1,300	1,700	2,500

California Watch Co., 18 size, 15 jewels, full plate.　　California Watch Co., 18 size, 7 jewels, full plate, serial number 29,029.

CHESHIRE WATCH CO.

Cheshire, Connecticut
1883-1890

In October 1883, the Cheshire Watch Company was formed by George J. Capewell with D. A. A. Buck (designer of the long-wind Waterbury) as superintendent. Their first movement was 18S, 3/4 gilt plate, stem wind, stem set, with the pendant attached to the movement. It fit into a nickel case which was also made at the Cheshire factory. The first watches were completed in April 1885. A new 18S nickel movement with a second hand was made to fit standard size American cases, and was introduced in 1887. By that date production was at about 200 watches per day.

Serial numbers range from 201 to 89,650. All Cheshire watches were sold through L. W. Sweet, general selling agent, in New York City. The factory closed in 1890, going into receivership. The receiver had 3,000 movements finished in 1892. In 1901 0. E. Bell bought the machinery and had it shipped to Appleton, Wisconsin, where he had formed the Remington Watch Company. The watches produced by Remington are marked "Appleton Watch Co." on the movements.

NOTE: George J. Capewell, inventor of the Capewell horse shoe nail.

Cheshire Watch Co., 20 size, 4 jewels, model number 1. Note stem attached and will not fit standard size case, serial number 201. NOTE: Closed top plate near balance. The lowest serial number know to exist is 201.

Cheshire Watch Co., 20 size, 4 jewels, model number 1.

Description	ABP	Ex-En	Mint
20S, 4-7J, FULL, OF, SW, NI case, stem attached, low serial #			
1st **model**, closed top plate (S # **201 to 300**)........ ★★★★	$500	$1,000	$1,750
20S, 4-7J, FULL, OF, SW, NI case, stem attached,			
1st **model**, closed top plate ....★★	400	700	900
18S, 4-7J, 3/4, SW, OF, NI case, stem attached, 2nd mode .... ★	275	400	600
18S, 4-7J, HC/ OF fits standard case, 3rd model .... ★	200	300	425
18S, 11J, HC/ OF, standard case, 3rd model.................. ★	250	300	425
18S, 15J, HC/ OF, NI, ADJ, standard case, 3rd model.......... ★	275	325	450
18S, **21J**, HC / OF, SW, Coin, standard case, 3rd model ...... ★★★	350	500	700
6S,3/4, HC/OF, SW, NI case............................. ★	175	300	500

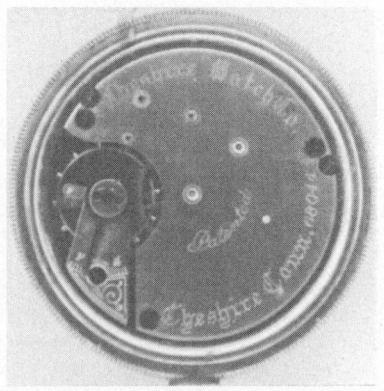

Cheshire Watch Co., 18 size, 4-7 jewels. This model number 2 was manufactured with the stem attached and requires a special case. NOTE: open top plate at Balance.

Cheshire Watch Co., 18 size, 4.7 jewels. This model fits standard 18 size cases. Model number 3.

☞ 1st & 2nd model Cheshire movements will not fit standard 18 size cases.
Model # 1, S# 201 to 15,000 - Model #2, S# 30,001 to 40,000 - Model # 3, S# 50,001 to 89,650.

CHICAGO WATCH CO.

Chicago, Illinois 1895-1903

The Chicago Watch Company's (All watches in all sizes) were made by other manufacturing companies and sold by Chicago Watch Co.

Description	ABP	Ex-Fn	Mint
18S, 7J, OF	$100	$200	$375
18S, 7-11J, HC or OF, Swiss	35	60	100
18S, 11J,KW	125	225	400
18S, 15J,OF,SW	125	225	400
18S, Made by Columbus, 15J, SW, NI, OF .... ★	150	250	425
18S, Made by Columbus, 15J, SW, NI, HC .... ★	200	300	475
18S, Made by New York Standard, marked 23J., (fake jewels)			
Locomotive on dial & movement .... ★★	100	175	300
18S, Made by Illinois, 11J, SW, NI .... ★	200	300	500
18S, Made by Waltham, 15J, SW .... ★	200	300	500
12S, 15J, OF	40	75	150
12S, 15J, YGF, HC	85	150	200

Chicago Watch Co., 18 size, 15 jewels, Hunting case, made by COLUMBUS Watch Co., nickel movement, lever set, serial #209,145.

Columbia Watch Co., 0 size, 4 jewels, stem wind, open face and hunting, duplex escapement, the escape wheel teeth were milled to give better quality than the Waterbury movements.

COLUMBIA WATCH CO.

Waltham, Massachusetts
1896-1899

The Columbia Watch Company was organized in 1896 by Edward A. Locke, formerly General Manager of the Waterbury Watch Company. The firm began manufacturing an 0-size,4-jewel gilt movement with duplex escapement in 1897. These movements were marked "Columbia Watch Co., Waltham, Mass." The firm also made movements marked "Hollers Watch Co., Brooklyn, NY," as well as nickeled movements marked "Cambridge Watch Co., New York."

Locke turned the business over to his son-in-law, Renton Whidden, in 1898, and the firm changed to an 0-size, 7-jewel nickel movement with lever escapement called the Suffolk. The firm name was not changed until early 1901.

Description	ABP	Ex-Fn	Mint
OS, 4J, SW, Duplex, gilded, HC............................	$40	$75	$175
OS, 4J, SW, Duplex, gilded, OF............................	35	65	150
OS, 7J, SW, lever escapement, OF..........................	40	75	175

COLUMBUS WATCH CO.

Columbus, Ohio

1874 -1903

Dietrich Gruen, born in Osthofen, Germany in 1847, started a business as the Columbus Watch Co. on Dec. 22, 1874 in Columbus, Ohio. At the age of 27, he received a U.S. patent for an improved safety pinion. The new company finished movements made from **Madretsch**, Switzerland, a suburb of Beil. The imported movements were made in a variety of sizes and were in nickel or gilt. The early watches usually had the initials C.W.CO. intertwined in script on the dial. The serial numbers generally ran up to around 20,000's a few examples are in the 70,000's.

D. Gruen and W. J. Savage decided in late 1882 to manufacture watches locally. By August of 1883 the first movements were being produced with a train consisting of 72 teeth on the barrel, 72 on the center wheel, 11 on the center pinion, 60 on the third wheel with a pinion of 9, 70 on the fourth wheel with a pinion of 9 with a 7 leaf escape pinion. The new manufacture primarily made 18 size movements but also pioneered the 16 size watch while reducing the size and thickness. Several new innovations were used into the design including a completely covered main spring barrel, a new micrometric regulator and the ability to change the main spring without removing the balance cock. By 1884 they were making their own dials, but no cases were ever manufactured.

The company went into receivership in 1894 with new management. That same year Frederick Gruen started again as D. Gruen & Son. They had PAUL ASSMANN to produce 18 size & 16 size movements with 18 & 21 jewels with the escapement designed by Moritz Grossman of Glasshute. Soon after this time movements were obtained from Switzerland and the new Gruen veri-thin movement was developed. In 1898 this company moved to Cincinnati, Ohio.

From 1894 through February 14, 1903 the Columbus Watch Co. produced watches both under the Columbus Watch Co. and the New Columbus Watch Co. name. The re-organized company produced the same models, but switched primarily to named grades such as Time King, Columbus King, etc. The higher grade watches were assigned a special block of serial numbers from 500,000 to 506,000. In keeping with the industry several models with 25 jewels were produced in this block of serial numbers.

In 1903 the Columbus Watch Co. was sold to the Studebakers and the South Bend Watch Co. started. The machinery, unfinished movements, parts and approximately 3/4 of the 150 employees moved to South Bend, Indiana. Some marked Columbus Watch Co. movements were finished by the South Bend W. Co. Examples exist of dials made in the South Bend style and movements marked Columbus Watch Co.

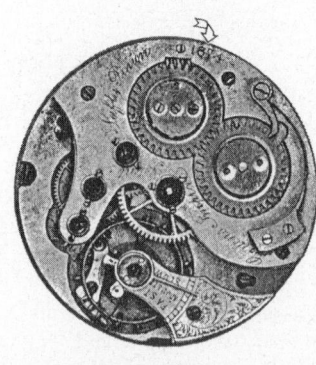

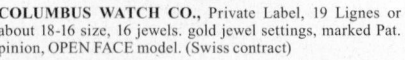

1874

COLUMBUS WATCH CO., Private Label, 19 Lignes or about 18-16 size, 16 jewels. gold jewel settings, marked Pat. pinion, OPEN FACE model. (Swiss contract)

Note: Regulator

COLUMBUS WATCH CO., 19 Lignes or about 18-16 size, 15 jewels, hunting case, engraved on movement "*1874*"

COLUMBUS
ESTIMATED SERIAL NUMBERS AND PRODUCTION DATES

DATE - SERIAL NO.	DATE— SERIAL NO.	21 jewels or more
1874—- 1	1888 — 97,000	Columbus King,
1875— 1,000	1889 — 119,000	Railway King,
1876— 3,000	1890 — 141,000	Time King,
1877— 6,000	1891 — 163,000	and Ruby.
1878— 9,000	1892—185,000	
1879— 12,000	1893 — 207 000	SPECIAL BLOCK
1880— 15,000	1894 — 229:000	OF SERIAL NOS.
1881— 18,000	1895 — 251,000	DATE—SERIAL NO.
1882— 21,000	1896 — 273,000	1894— 500,001
1883— 25,000	1897 — 295,000	1896 — 501,500
1884— 30,000	1898 — 317,000	1898 — 503,000
1885— 40,000	1899 — 339,000	1900— 504,500
1886— 53,000	1900 — 361,000	1902— 506,000
1887— 75,000	1901 — 383,000	

☞ The above list is provided for detemining the <u>APPROXIMATE</u> age of your watch. Match serial number with date. Watches were not necessarily SOLD and DELIVERED in the exact order of manufactured or production dates.

SWISS, 3/4 PLATE, & MADE FROM 1874-1883

Most marked COL. WATCH CO. with single sunk dials and may be SW/KW Transitional, serial # up to about 20,000.

Grade or Name — Description	ABP	Ex-Fn	Mint
18S, 7J, pressed J., nickel or gilded, OF/HC	$80	$125	$250
18S, 11, pressed J., nickel or gilded, OF/HC	100	150	300
18S, 15J, GJS or pressed J., nickel, Adj., OF/HC................	150	200	350
18S, 16J, **raised** GJS, 2 tone or nickel, Adj., OF/HC.............	200	275	475

Grade or Name — Description	ABP	Ex-Fn	Mint
16S, 11J, pressed J., nickel, OF/HC	$150	$200	$400
16S, 15J, pressed J. or GJS, Adj., nickel, OF/HC...............	150	200	400
16S, 16J, **raised** GJS, Adj., nickel, OF/HC	165	225	450

Private Label, KW or SW, 11-15 jewels, OF/HC

Grade or Name —Description	ABP	Ex-Fn	Mint
14S, 16J, GJS, nickel, Adj., OF/HC	$150	$200	$350

Grade or Name —Description	ABP	Ex-Fn	Mint
9S, 15J, GJS or pressed J., nickel, Adj., OF/HC................	$95	$150	$295

Grade or Name —Description	ABP	Ex-Fn	Mint
8S, 11J, pressed J., nickel, OF/HC	$95	$150	$295
8S, 15J, pressed J., nickel, OF/HC	95	150	295

FOR ABOVE HUNTING CASED MODEL ADD **$35.00 to $65.00**

NOTE: These Odd size movements are difficult to case.

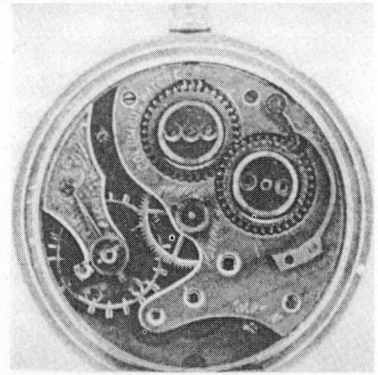

COLUMBUS WATCH CO., 19 Lignes or about 16 size, 15 jewels, exposed winding wheels, marked Gruen Patent, OPEN FACE model, serial # 1,661. (Swiss contract)

The above finished by Columbus W. Co.

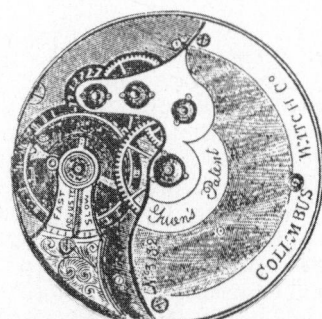

COLUMBUS WATCH CO., about 14 size, 16 jewels, gold jewel settings, nickel plates, marked Gruen's pat. pinion, HUNTING CASE model. (Swiss contract)

18 SIZE-KW, FULL PLATE, MODEL #1 & TRANSITIONAL

Serial # up to 100,000, balance cock set flush to barrel bridge and may have pinned dial.

Marked Col. watch Co., Ohio Columbus Watch Co.

Grade or Name — Description	ABP	Ex-Fn	Mint
11-13J, KW / KS, gilded, OF/HC	$250	$350	$650
13J, KW / KS, nickel, (marked 13 jewels), OF/HC .... ★★	350	450	700
15J, KW / KS, gilded, Adj., OF/HC	250	350	600
16J, KW / KS, gilded, OF/HC .... ★	325	425	700
Grade or Name — Description	**ABP**	**Ex-Fn**	**Mint**
11-13J, SW/KW, gilded or nickel, OF/HC	$135	$165	$350
15J, SW/ KW, gilded or nickel, GJS, OF/HC	150	225	400
16J, SW/ KW, gilded or nickel, GJS, OF/HC	175	265	450

FOR ABOVE HUNTING CASED MODEL ADD $25.00 to $50.00

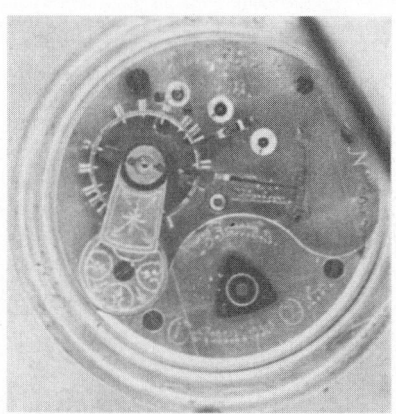 

COLUMBUS WATCH CO., 18 size, marked 13J., pressed jewels, key wind & key set, nickel plates, marked on movement Col. Watch Co. Columbus Ohio Pat. pinion, on dial *"Ohio Columbus Watch Co."*, serial #40,198.

COLUMBUS WATCH CO. 18 Size, 15 Jewels, key wind key set, hunting case, on movement "Columbus Watch Co. Columbus, Ohio Pat. Pinion" serial # 66,577.

18 SIZE, FULL PLATE, PRE-1894

Marked 'Columbus Watch Co. Columbus, Ohio", all marked Safety Pinion

Grade or Name — Description	ABP	Ex-Fn	Mint
7J, G#90, pressed J., OF	$100	$150	$200
7J, G#20, pressed J., HC	125	200	300
11J, G#92, pressed J., nickel, OF	100	150	200
11J, G#22, pressed J., nickel, HC	125	200	300
15J, G#64 /G#93, gilded, OF	100	150	200
15J, G#24/ G#32, gilded,HC	125	200	300
15J, G#63 / G#94, nickel, Adj., OF	100	175	200
15J, G#23 / G#33, nickel, Adj., HC	125	200	300
15J, G#95, nickel, Adj., D.S. dial, OF	100	150	250
15J, G#34, nickel, Adj., D.S. dial, HC	125	200	350
16J, G#97, GJS, nickel, Adj., D.S. dial, OF	125	200	250
16J, G#27, GJS, nickel, Adj., D.S. dial, HC	150	250	350
16J, G#98, raised GJS, 2 tone nickel, Adj., D.S. dial, OF	125	200	350
16J, G#28, raised GJS, 2 tone nickel, Adj., D.S. dial, HC	150	235	400
16J, G#99, raised GJS, 2 tone nickel, Adj., D.S. dial, OF	125	250	450
16J, G#18, raised GJS, 2 tone nickel, Adj., D.S. dial, HC	150	285	500

18 SIZE-FULL PLATE, POST-1894
Some Marked "New Columbus watch Co. Columbus Ohio"

Grade or Name — Description	ABP	Ex-Fn	Mint
7J, G#10, pressed J., gilded, OF	$100	$150	$200
7J, G#9, pressed J., gilded, HC	125	200	300
11J, G#8, nickel, OF	100	150	200
11J, G#7, nickel, HC	125	200	300
16J, G#6, G35, nickel, OF	100	150	200
16J, G#5, GJS, nickel, HC	125	200	300
16J, G#4, GJS, 2 tone nickel, Adj., D.S. dial, OF	150	200	350
16J, G#3, GJS, 2 tone nickel, Adj., D.S. dial, HC	175	250	400
17J, G#204, GJS, 2 tone nickel, Adj., D.S. dial, OF	175	250	400
17J, G#203, GJS, 2 tone nickel, Adj., D.S. dial, HC	200	300	450
17J, G#2, raised GJS, 2 tone nickel, Adj., D.S. dial, OF	200	300	450
17J, G#1, raised GJS, 2 tone nickel, Adj., D.S. dial, HC	250	350	475

COLUMBUS WATCH CO., with a "Choo Choo" Railway King double sunk dial.

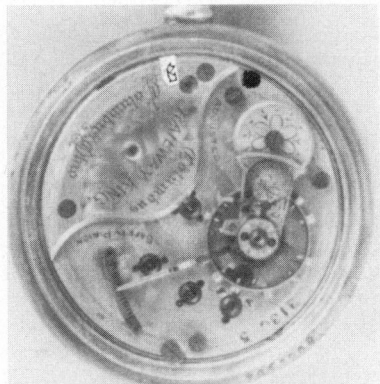

COLUMBUS WATCH CO., Railway King, 18 size, 17J,2 tone, note **missing** screw on barrel bridge, S # 313,005.

18 SIZE FULL PLATE, NAMED GRADES
Marked Names, Double Sunk Dials

Grade or Name — Description	ABP	Ex-Fn	Mint
Am. Watch Club, 15J, 2 tone, Adj., D.S. dial, OF/HC .... ★	$300	$450	$625
Burlington Route C.B. & QR.R., 153, nickel, Adj., D.S. dial, OF ....★★★★★	2,500	3,500	5,500
Champion, 15J, gilded, Adj., D.S.dial, OF	100	150	250
Champion, 15J, gilded, Adj., D.S.dial, HC	100	175	300
Champion, 15J, Nickel, Adj., D.S.dial, OF	100	150	250
Champion, 15J, Nickel, Adj., D.S.dial, HC	100	175	300
Champion, 16J, Nickel, Adj., D.S.dial, OF	100	175	300
Champion, 16J, Nickel, Adj., D.S.dial, HC	150	235	350

    ℰℒ Watches listed in this book are priced at the collectable trade show level, as complete watches having an original 14k gold-filled case & key wind with silver case, an original white enamel single sunk dial, and with the entire original movement in good working order with no repairs needed.

Grade or Name — Description	ABP	Ex-Fn	Mint
Columbus King, 17J, raised GJS, nickel, Adj., D.S. dial, OF	$200	$300	$550
Columbus King, 17J, raised GJS, nickel, Adj., D.S. dial, HC	250	400	650
Columbus King, 17J, raised GJS, nickel, Adj., **Choo Choo** D.S. dial, 2 tone, OF	500	900	1400
Columbus King, 17J, raised GJS, nickel, Adj., **Angled** Choo Choo D.S. dial, OF	500	900	1,400
Columbus King, 21J, raised GJS, nickel, Adj., D.S. dial, OF	450	600	950
Columbus King, 21J, raised GJS, nickel, Adj., D.S. dial, HC	400	700	1,100
Columbus King, 23J, raised GJS, nickel, Adj., D.S. dial, OF ..... ★	1,000	1,500	3,000
Columbus King, 23J, raised GJS, nickel, Adj., D.S. dial, HC ..... ★	1,000	1,500	3,000
Columbus King, 25J, raised GJS, nickel, Adj., D.S. dial, OF .... ★★★	3,500	4,500	6,000
Columbus King, 25J, raised GJS, nickel, Adj., D.S. dial, HC	3,000	4,000	5,500
F.C. & P.R.R., 17J, GJS, nickel, Adj., D.S. dial, OF	900	1,200	2,100
Jackson Park, 15J, 2 tone, Adj., D.S. dial, OF .... ★	450	550	950
Jay Gould, Railroad King, 15J, nickel, Adj., D.S. dial, OF .... ★★★	1,000	1,300	2,300
New York Susquehanna & Western R.R.,16J, GJS, SW/KW, gold flash, D.S. dial, OF .... ★★★★	2,500	4,000	5,000
Non-magnetic, 16J, raised GJS, 2 tone, Adj., OF/HC	300	400	700
North Star, 11J, gilded, OF	100	150	300
North Star, 11J, gilded, HC	100	175	350
North Star, 11J, nickel, OF	100	150	295
North Star, 11J, nickel, HC	100	175	350
North Star, 15J, nickel, OF	100	175	350
North Star, 15J, nickel, HC	150	200	400
The President, 17J, GJS, Adj, 2 tone, D.S. dial, OF .... ★	400	600	850
Railroad Regulator, 15J, GJS, nickel, Adj., D.S. dial, OF .... ★	450	600	950
Railroad Regulator, 16J, GJS, nickel, Adj., D.S. dial, OF .... ★	450	700	1,100
Railroad Regulator, 16J, GJS, nickel, Adj., D.S. "Special for Railway Service" on dial, 14K HC .... ★★★	1,500	2,000	2,800
Railway, 17J, GJS, 2 tone, Adj., D.S. dial, OF .... ★	300	500	675

Columbus King, 18 size, 25 jewels, open face serial number 503,094. Note two screws between balance cock & barrel bridge.

Railway King, 18 size, 23 jewels, adjusted, stem wind, **hunting case**, serial number 503,315. Note **one screw** between balance cock & barrel bridge.

꙰ Watches listed in this book are priced at the collectable Trade Show level, as complete watches having an original 14k gold-filled case & key wind with silver case, an original white enamel single sunk dial, and with the entire original movement in good working order with no repairs needed.

Grade or Name — Description	ABP	Ex-Fn	Mint
Railway King, 16J, GIS, 2 tone nickel, Adj., D.S. dial, OF	$275	$350	$575
Railway King, 16J, GJS, 2 tone nickel, Adj., D.S. dial, HC	350	500	675
Railway King, 16J, GJS, 2 tone nickel, Adj., (black red blue) **choo choo** D.S. dial, OF	400	600	1,200
Railway King, 16J, GJS, 2 tone nickel, Adj., (black red blue) **choo choo** D.S. dial, HC	400	600	1,200
Railway King, 16J, GJS, 2 tone nickel, Adj., Angled **choo choo** dial, OF	550	750	1,500
Railway King, 16J, GJS, 2 tone nickel, Adj., Angled **choo choo** dial, HC	700	1,000	1,700
Railway King, 17J, raised GJS, nickel, Adj., D.S. dial, OF	275	350	550
Railway King, 17J, raised GJS, nickel, Adj., D.S. dial, HC	300	435	600
Railway King, 21J, raised GJS, nickel, Adj., D.S. dial, OF	450	600	800
Railway King, 21J, raised GJS, nickel, Adj., D.S. dial, HC	475	650	900
Railway King, 23J, raised GJS, nickel, Adj., Railway King D.S. dial, OF ★★★	1,000	2,000	3,000
Railway King, 23J, raised GJS, nickel, Adj., Railway King D.S. dial, HC ★★★	1,000	2,000	3,000
Railway King, 25J, raised GJS, nickel, Adj., Railway King D.S. dial, OF ★★★★	2,500	4,000	5,500
Railway King, 25J, raised GJS, nickel, Adj., Railway King D.S. dial, HC ★★★★	3,000	5,000	6,500
Railway King Special, 17J, GJS, nickel, Adj., D.S. dial, OF	300	500	625
Railway Monarch, 17J, GJS, nickel, Adj., D.S. dial, OF ★	300	500	625
Railway Monarch, 17J, GJS, nickel, Adj., D.S. dial, HC ★	300	500	625
Railway Time Service, 17J, GJS, nickel, Adj., D.S. dial, OF ★	375	550	825
The Regent, 15J, D.S. dial, OF	150	250	425
R.W.K. Special, 15J, GJS, Adj., 2 tone, D.S. dial, OF	250	350	525
R.W.K. Special, 15J, GJS, Adj., 2 tone, D.S. dial, HC	250	350	525
R.W.K. Special, 16J, GJS, Adj., 2 tone, D.S. dial, OF	250	350	525
R.W.K. Special, 16J, GJS, Adj., 2 tone, D.S. dial, HC	300	400	575
Springfield Mo. W. Club, 16J, GJS, nickel, Adj., D.S. dial, HC ★	350	500	675
Special, 17J, GJS, nickel, D.S. dial, OF	200	300	475
J.P. Stevens & Co. (see listing under J.P. Stevens & Co **HEADING**)			
The New Menlo Park, 15J, HC ★★	200	400	550
The Railroader, 16J., LS, nickel, Adj., OF ★★	200	500	600
The Star, 11-15J, nickel, OF/HC	175	300	425
Time King, 21J, raised GJS, 2 tone nickel, Adj., D.S. dial, OF	300	500	650
Time King, 21J, raised GJS, 2 tone nickel, Adj., D.S. dial, HC	325	600	750
U.S. Army, 15J, nickel, HC ★	400	550	725

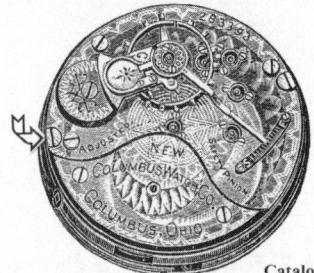 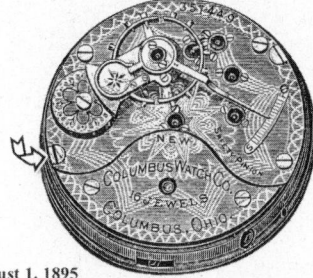

Catalog August 1, 1895

18 size **OPEN FACE** Model
NOTE: (2) SCREWS
Grade #**4**, 16J., Adjusted

18 size **HUNTING CASE** Model
NOTE: (1) SCREW
Grade #**5**, 16J.

NOTE: May not be true for KEY WIND or TRANSITIONAL MODELS

16 SIZE, 3/4 Plate

Marked "New Columbus Watch Co. Columbus Ohio"

Grade or Name — Description	ABP	Ex-Fn	Mint
7J, G#80 / G#20, gilded, OF	$50	$125	$200
7J, G#40 / G#19, gilded, HC	75	170	225
11J, G#81, gilded, OF	60	150	200
11J, G#41, gilded, HC	75	170	225
11J, G#83 / G#18, nickel, OF	60	150	195
11J, G#43 / G#17, nickel, HC	75	170	225
15J, G#84, Adj., gilded, OF	60	150	200
15J, G#44, Adj., gilded, HC	80	170	250
15J, G#86, GJS, Adj., nickel, D.S. dial, OF	70	150	225
15J, G#46, GJS, Adj., nickel, D.S. dial, HC	80	150	250
16J, G#87 / G#316, GJS, Adj., nickel, D.S. dial, OF	80	150	250
16J, G#47 / G#315, GJS, Adj., nickel, D.S. dial, HC	85	170	275
16J, G#14, GJS, Adj., 2 tone nickel, D.S. dial, OF	125	220	300
16J, G#13, GJS, Adj., 2 tone nickel, D.S. dial, HC	150	220	400
16J, G#88, raised GJS, Adj., 2 tone nickel, D.S. dial, OF	125	200	300
16J, G#48, raised GJS, Adj., 2 tone nickel, D.S. dial, HC	150	220	400
17J, G#12, raised GJS, Adj., 2 tone nickel, D.S. dial, OF	125	220	300
17J, G#11, raised GJS, Adj., 2 tone nickel, D.S. dial, HC	150	220	400
Ruby, 21J, raised GJS, Adj., 2 tone nickel, D.S. dial, OF ......★★	400	880	1,100
Ruby, 21J, raised GJS, Adj., 2 tone nickel, D.S. dial, HC ...... ★★	500	1,100	1,400

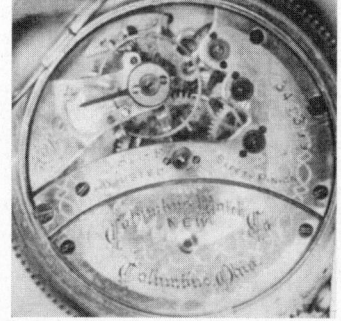
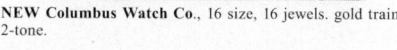

NEW Columbus Watch Co., 16 size, 16 jewels. gold train, 2-tone.

Columbus Watch Co., Ruby Model, 16 size, 21 Jewels, three quarter plate, gold jewel settings, gold train, Adj.6p.

August 1, 1895 Catalog

The following movements are all finely finished and very accurately adjusted, and will stand the most Critical Inspection of the Railway Watch Inspectors.

We are putting all of our Movements in beautiful Brass Boxes, with glass top and bottom. These boxes are made so that the movement can be wound and set without removing them from the boxes, thus enabling retail jewelers to show these Movements to their customers without the annoyance of dust or finger marks.

We buy the outside box, with original label, from the retail jeweler of the following names and numbers, at the price below:

Time King . . . . .Outside Box, $2 50	
Nos. 1 and 2 . . . " " 1 50	
" 203 and 204. . . . " " 1 00	
" 3 and 4 . . . . " " 1 00	
Ruby. . . . . . . " " 3 00	
Nos. 11 and 12 . . . . " " 2 00	
" 13 and 14 . . . . " " 1 00	
" 100 . . . . " " 1 00	

You have only to send the boxes to us, charges prepaid, and we will send you the cash. No waiting until you have sold the movements.

The New Columbus Watch Co.

Note: The following movements are all finely finished and very accurately adjusted, and will stand the most Critical Inspection of the **Railway Watch Inspectors**. Also note shipping movements In brass boxes, with glass top & will buy them back.

6 SIZE

Grade or Name — Description	ABP	Ex-Fn	Mint
7J, G#102, gilded, OF	$60	$85	$200
7J, G#102, gilded, HC	75	100	225
11J, G#101/ G#51/ G#53, nickel or gilded, HC	75	100	225
13J, G#103, nickel, HC	75	100	225
15J, G#104/ G#55, GJS, nickel, D.S. dial, HC	100	150	250
16J, G#102, raised GJS, nickel, D.S. dial, OF/HC	100	150	250
16J, G#102, raised GJS, 2 tone, D.S. dial, (marked 16J.), OF	150	225	325
16J, G#102, raised GJS, 2 tone, D.S. dial, (marked 16J.), HC	150	225	325

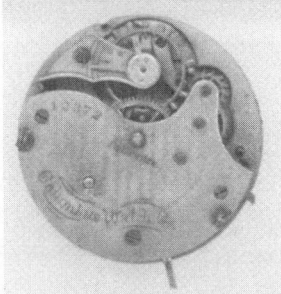

Columbus Watch Co., 8-10 size, 13 jewels, 3/4 plate, stem wind, serial number 13,372. For price see 2nd page of Columbus W. Co. under Swiss, 3/4 plate (1874-1883).

New Columbus Watch Co. Example of a basic model for 6 size, 3/4 plate, 7-16 jewels, gilded and nickel.

4 SIZE

Grade or Name — Description		ABP	Ex-Fn	Mint
11J, nickel or gilded, OF/HC	★	$100	$175	$300
15J, nickel or gilded, OF/HC	★	125	200	325

18 Size, 21 Jewels.   16 Size, Twenty=one Jewels.

NEW COLUMBUS TIME KING.   NEW COLUMBUS RUBY.

Hunting and Open Face.   Hunting and Open Face.

Nickel, 21 Genuine Ruby Jewels, set in red, Solid Gold Raised Settings, Escapement Cap Jeweled, Adjusted to temperature, Positions and Isochronism, Breguet Hair Spring, Patent Center Pinion, Patent Regulator, Polished Dust Band and Stem Wind, Beveled Steel Work, Pearled Plates; fine, white, cut and beveled edge, hard enameled, double sunk, Red marginal figured Roman or Arabic Dial; handsomely damaskeened in Gold on Nickel $25 00

Nickel, 21 Genuine Ruby Jewels, set in red Solid Gold Raised Settings, Escapement Cap Jeweled, Adjusted to Temperature, Beveled Steel Work, Positions and Isochronism, Breguet Hair Spring, Patent Center Pinion, Patent Regulator, Polished Stem Wind, Beveled Edge Steel Work, Pearled Plates; fine, white, cut and beveled edge, hard enameled, double sunk, red marginal, figured Roman or Arabic Dial; handsomely Damaskeened in Gold on Nickel..........$30 00

CORNELL WATCH CO.

Chicago, Illinois
1870-1874
San Francisco, California
1875-1876

The Cornell Watch Co. bought the Newark Watch Co. and greatly improved the movements being produced. In the fall of 1874, the company moved to San Francisco, Calif., with about 60 of its employees. The movements made in California were virtually the same as those made in Chicago. The company wanted to employ Chinese who would work cheaper, but the skilled employees refused to go along and went on strike. The company stayed alive until 1875 and was sold to the California Watch Co. in January 1876. But death came a few months later.

C. L. Kidder from 1869 to 1872 worked with F.A. Jones in Switzerland to form the *International Watch Co.*. Mr. Kidder returned to U.S.A. and took on a position with Cornell.

The Chronology of the Development of Cornell Watch Co.

Newark Watch Co. 1864-1870; S#s 6901 to about 12,000.
Cornell Watch Co., Chicago, Ill. 1870-1874; S#s 12,001 to about 23,000 or up to 25,000.
Cornell Watch Co., San Francisco, Calif. 1874-Jan. 1876; S#s 23,001 to about 35,000.
California Watch Co., Jan. 1876-mid 1876.

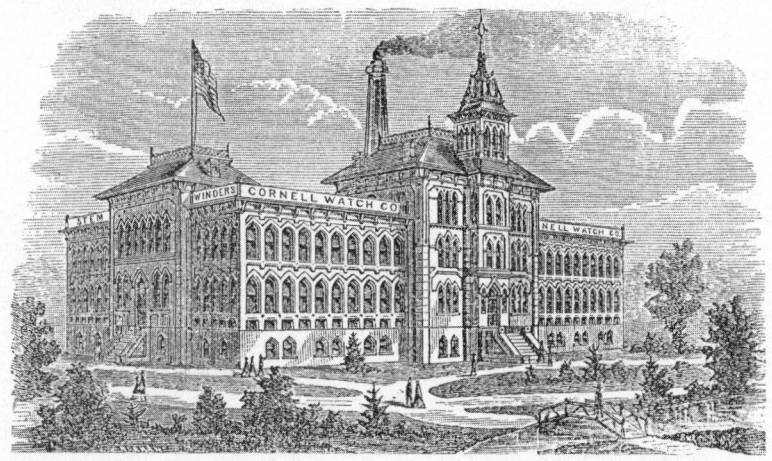

1871 AD for the Cornell Watch Co. Factory

18 SIZE

Grade or Name — Description		ABP	Ex-Fn	Mint
J. C. Adams, 11J, KW	★	$250	$385	$700
C. T. Bowen, FULL, KW	★	300	440	850
C. M. Cady, 15J, **SW**	★	400	550	900
Cornell W. Co., 7J, San Francisco on mvt, KW	★	700	1,320	2,000
Cornell W. Co., 7J, San Francisco on mvt, **SW**	★	700	1,320	2,000
Cornell W. Co., 11J, KW	★	300	440	650
Cornell W. Co., 11J, San Francisco on mvt., KW	★★	900	1,650	2,300
Cornell W. Co., 15J, KW	★	325	550	850
Cornell W. Co., 15J, San Francisco on mvt., KW	★	950	1,650	2,400
Cornell W. Co., 15J, San Francisco on mvt., SW	★★	950	1,650	2,500
Cornell W. Co., 19-20J, San Francisco on mvt, GJS, ADJ., **SW**	★★★	2,000	3,300	5,000
Paul Cornell, 19-20J, GJS, ADJ, SW	★★★	2,000	3,300	4,500
John Evans, 15J, KW		250	420	700
Excelsior, 15J, FULL, KW, KS	★	275	440	750

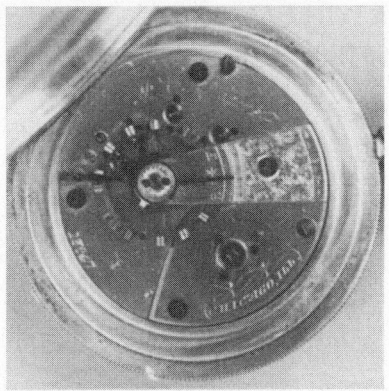

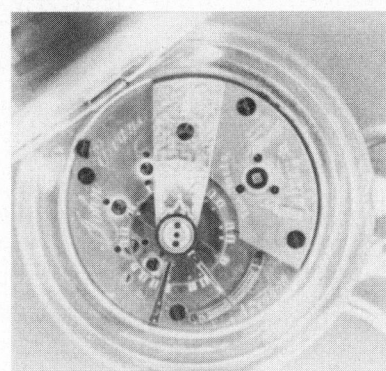

Cornell Watch Co., J. C. Adams, 18 size, 11 jewels, key wind & set, made in Chicago, Ill, serial number 13,647.

Cornell Watch Co., 18 size, 15 jewels, key wind & set, marked "John Evans," serial number 16,868.

Grade or Name — Description		ABP	Ex-Fn	Mint
H. N. Hibbard, 11J, KW, ADJ.	★	$350	$550	$800
CL. Kidder, 7J, KW, KS, OF	★	350	550	800
George F. Root, 15J, KW	★	400	605	900
George Waite, 7J, (Hyde Park), KW.	★★	350	550	875
E. S. Williams, 7J, KW.	★	250	450	700
Eugene Smith, 17J	★	450	660	900
Ladies Stemwind	★	200	375	500

JACOB D. CUSTER

Norristown, Pennsylvania 1840- 1845

At the age of 19, Jacob Custer repaired his father's watch. He was then asked to repair all the watches within his community. Custer was basically self-taught and had very little formal education and little training in clocks and watches. He made all the parts except the hairspring and fusee chains. The watches were about 14 size, and only **12 to 15** watches were made. The 14S **fusee** watches had lever escapement, 3/4 plate and were sold in his **own gold cases.** He made a few chronometers, one with a helical spring.

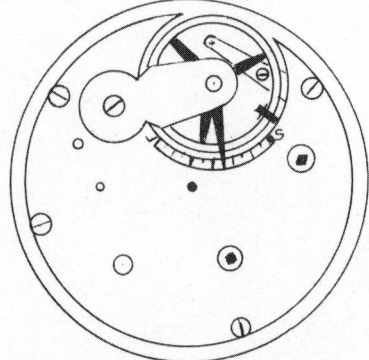

J. D. Custer, 14-16 size, engraved on movement is
J. D. Custer, Norristown, Pa. Patented Feb. 4, 1843 Key-wind Key-set, Fusee.

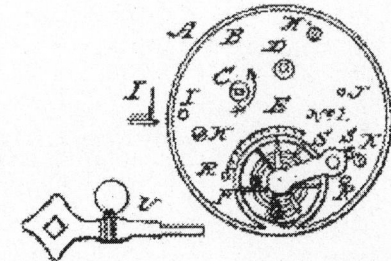

Above: J.D. Custer patent No. 2,939, with his drawing, Note the key.

Description	ABP	Ex-Fn	Mint
14S, OF, engraved on mvt. (J. D. Custer, Patented Feb. 4, 1843)			
very RARE watch, original gold case. ★★★★★	$25,000	$60,000	$110,000

DUDLEY WATCH CO.

Lancaster, Pennsylvania
1920- 1925

William Wallace Dudley became interested in watches and horology at the age of 13 and became an apprentice making ship chronometers in Canada. When he moved to America, he worked for the South Bend and Illinois Watch companies and the Trenton Watch Co. before going to Hamilton Watch Co. in Lancaster. He left Hamilton at age 69 to start his own watch company. In 1922 his first watches were produced; they were 14S, 19J, and used many Waltham Model 1894 — 1897, 14 size parts, including the train and escapement. The plates and winding mechanism were made at the Dudley plant. Dials and hands were made to Dudley's specifications in Switzerland. At first jewels were obtained from a manufacturer in Lancaster, but by 1925 they were Swiss supplied. The cases came from Wadsworth Keystone and the Star Watch Case Co. Dudley also made a 12S, 19J watch. By 1924, the company was heavily in debt, and on February 20, 1925, a petition for bankruptcy was filed. The Masonic Watch was his most unusual watch.

			ESTIMATED TOTAL
DUDLEY WATCHES			**PRODUCTION**
Dudley Watch Co.	1920-1925	Model No.1 =	S# 500— 1,900 = 1,400
P. W. Baker Co.	1925-1935	Model No.2 =	S# 2,001—4,800 = 2,800
XL Watch Co., N.Y.	1935-1976	Model No.3 =	S# 4,801—6,500 =1,700
			TOTAL = 5,900

👆 NOTE: Not all movements were finished and sold as complete watches.

Model No. 1, 14S, 19J, OF, can be distinguished by the "Holy Bible" engraved on the winding arbor plate, and a gilded pallet bridge matching the plates.

Model No. 2, 12S, 19J, used the 910 and 912 Hamilton wheels and escapement, has a flat silver-colored Bible.

Model No. 3, 12S, can be distinguished by the silver Bible which was riveted in place and was more three-dimensional. The 3rd wheel bridge was rounded off at one end.

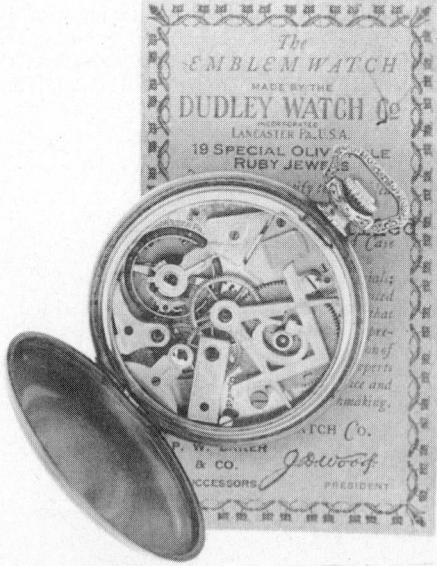

Dudley Watch Co., Model 1, 14 size, 19J., open face, Masonic form plates, flip back, serial # 1232, ca. 1924.

Dudley Watch Co., Model 2, 14 size, 19J., open face. with original paper. The watch also came with a keystone shaped box, Ca.1927.

12 SIZE-14 SIZE
"MASONS" MODEL

Grade or Name — Description		ABP	Ex-Fn	Mint
14S, Dudley, 19J, 14K, flip open back, Serial #1 (made 5 experimental models with Serial #1)	★★★	$5,500	$8,000	$15,000
14S, M#1, 19J, OF, **14K** flip open back	★★	2,800	4,000	5,000
14S, M#1, 19J, OF, **14K** flip open back, w/box & papers	★★	3,100	5,000	6,000
12S, M#2, 19J, OF, flip open back, **GF**	★	2,000	2,700	3,800
12S, M#2, 19J, OF, **14K**, flip open back case	★	2,200	3,000	4,000
12S, M#2, 19J, OF, **14K** display case	★	2,200	3,000	4,000
12S, M#3, 19J, OF, display case, **GF**	★	1,800	2,700	3,400
12S, M#3, 19J, OF, **14K** flip open case	★	2,200	3,000	4,000

 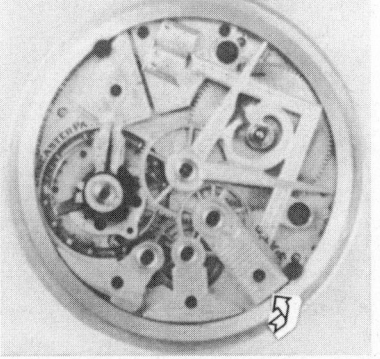

Dudley Watch Co,. Model 2, 12 size, 19jewels, open face, serial number 2,420.

Dudley Watch Co, Model 3,12 size, 19 jewels, open face. NOTE: 3rd wheel bridge is rounded off at one end.

ELGIN WATCH CO
(NATIONAL WATCH CO.)
Elgin, Illinois 1864 - 1964

Above: *B. W. Raymond*

First wooden building in Jan. 1865.(30X60)

This was the largest watch company in terms of production; in fact, Elgin produced half of the total number of pocket watches (dollar-type not included). Some of the organizers came from Waltham Watch Co., including P. S. Bartlett, D. G. Currier, Otis Hoyt, Charles H. Mason and others. The idea of beginning a large watch company for the mid-West was discussed by J. C. Adams, Bartlett and Blake. After a trip to Waltham, Adams went back to Chicago and approached Benjamin W. Raymond, a former mayor of Chicago, to put up the necessary capital to get the company started. Adams and Raymond succeeded in getting others to pledge their financial support. The National Watch Co. (Elgin) was formed in August 1864. The factory was completed in 1866, & the 1st. movement was a B. W. Raymond, 18 size.

Elgin 1st Movements

Movements	1st App.	1st S#	Movements	1st App.	1st S#
18S B. W. Raymond	April 1867	101	18S Veritas	No date	8,400,001
18S H. Z. culver	July 1867	1,001	10S Lady Elgin	Jan. 1869	40,001
18S J. T. Ryerson	Oct. 1867	5,001	10S Frances Rubie	Aug. 1870	50,001
18S H. H. Taylor	Nov. 1867	25,001	10S Gail Borden	Sept. 1871	185,001
18S G. M. Wheeler	Nov. 1167	6,001	10S Dexter Street	Dec. 1871	201,001
18S Matt Laflin	Jan. 1868	9,001			
18S W. H. Ferry	No date	30,056	1st Stem wind, H. Z. Culver	June 1873	155,000
18S J. V. Farwell	No date	30,296	1st Nickel Movement	Aug.15, 1879	
18S M. D. Ogden	No date	30,387	Convertible	Fall 1878	
18S Charles Fargo	No date	30,490	1st 16 Size watch	No date	600,000
18S Father Time	No date	2,300,001	18 size with double roller	G#214	8,400,001
18S Overland	No date	6,653,401	16 size with double roller	G#156	10,249,901

The first watch a **B. W. Raymond** was sold April 1, 1867, selling for about $115.00, and was a 18 size, KW and quick train serial # 101. This first Pocket Watch, Serial No. 101, was once again sold for $12,000.00 in 1988 at a sale in New York. The first stem wind model was an H. Z. Culver with serial No. 155,001, lever set and quick train made in June 1873. in 1874, the name was changed to the Elgin National Watch Co., and they produced watches into the 1950s. The first wrist watch made by Elgin was sold in 1910.

Some Serial Nos. have the first two numbers replaced by a letter; i.e., 49,582,000 would be F 582,000.

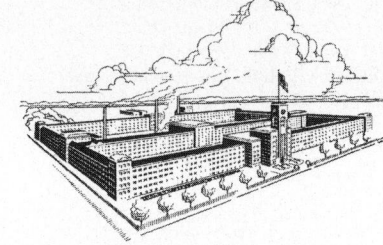

Elgin National Watch Factory
ELGIN, U. S. A.

X= 38 & 39	F= 49
C,E,T &Y= 42	S= 50
L= 43	R= 51
U= 44	P= 52
J= 45	K= 53
V= 46	I= 54
H= 47	
N= 48	

☞ If the letters do not match the list above; the movement was produced after 1954.

ELGIN ESTIMATED SERIAL NUMBERS
AND PRODUCTION DATES

DATE — SERIAL #	DATE - SERIAL #	DATE-SERIAL #
1867 - 101= April - 9,000 =Dec	1897 — 7,000,000 Oct.28th	1927 — 30,050,000
1868 - 25,001 - Nov. 20th	1898 — 7,494,001 May 14th	1928 — 31,599,001-Jan.11
1869 — 40,001-May 20th	1899 — 8,000,000 Jan. 18th	1929 — 32,000,000
1870 — 50,001-Aug.24th	1900 — 9,000,000 Nov.14th	1930 — 32,599,001-July
1871 — 185,001-Sep.8th	1901 — 9,300,000	1931 — 33,000,000
1872 — 201,001-Dec.20th	1902 — 9,600,000	1932 — 33,700,000
1873 — 325,001	1903 — 10,000,000 May 15th	1933 — 34,558,001-July 24th
1874 — 400,001-Aug.28th	1904 — 11,000,000 April 4th	1934 — 35,000,000
1875 — 430,000	1905 — 12,000,000 Oct.6th	1935 — 35,650,000
1876 — 480,000	1906 — 12,500,000	1936 — 36,200,000
1877 — 520,000	1907 — 13,000,000 April 4th	1937 — 36,978,001-July 24th
1878 — 570,000	1908 — 13,500,000	1938 — 37,900,000
1879 — 625,001-Feb.8th	1909 — 14,000,000 Feb.9th	1939 — 38,200,000
1880 — 750,000	1910 — 15,000,000 April 2nd	1940 — 39,100,000
1881 — 900,000	1911 — 16,000,000 July 11th	1941 — 40,200,000
1882 — 1,000,000-March,9th	1912 — 17,000,000 Nov.6th	1942 — 41,100,000
1883 — 1,250,000	1913 — 17,339,001- Apr.14th	1943 — 42,200,000
1884 — 1,500,000	1914 — 18,000,000	1944 — 42,600,000
1885 — 1,855,001-May 23rd	1915 — 18,587,001-Feb.11th	1945 — 43,200,000
1886 — 2,000,000-Aug. 4th	1916 — 19,000,000	1946 — 44,000,000
1887 — 2,500,000	1917 — 20,031,001 -June 27th	1947 — 45,000,000
1888 — 3,000,000 June 20th	1918 — 21,000,000	1948 — 46,000,000
1889 — 3,500,000	1919 — 22,000,000	1949 — 47,000,000
1890 — 4,000,000 Aug.16th	1920 — 23,000,000	1950 — 48,000,000
1891 — 4,449,001-Mar.26th	1921 — 24,321,001 -July 6th	1951 — 50,000,000-Sept. 7th
1892 — 4,600,000	1922 — 25,100,000	1952 — 52,000,000
1893 — 5,000,000 July 1st	1923 — 26,347,001 -Dec.28th	1953 — 53,500,000
1894 — 5,500,000	1924 — 27,000,000	1954 — 54,000,000
1895 — 6,000,000 Nov.26th	1925 — 28,421,001-July 14th	1955 — 54,500,000
1896 — 6,500,000	1926 — 29,100,000	1956 — 55,000,000

☞ The above list is provided for determining the approximate age of your watch. Match serial number with date. Watches were not necessarily made and delivered in the exact order of manufactured or production dates.

It required several months for raw material to emerge as a finished movement. All the while the factory is producing all sizes, models and grades. The numbering system was basically "consecutive", due to demand a batch of movements could be side tracked, thus allowing a different size and model to move ahead to meet this demand. Therefore, the dates some movements were sold and delivered to the trade, may not be "consecutive".

There are 129 parts & 2,145 operations in the construction of a full-plate 18 size Elgin Watch.

NOTE: Elgin starts to engrave Adjusted to 5 Positions about S# 15,158,001.

In 1950 the B. W. Raymond grade 571 made the following three changes. First, friction jewels; second, a solid balance wheel; third, a "DuraPower" mainspring. This was also the 47th model made by the Elgin Watch Co.. This model conformed with all railroad specifications as 16 size, 21 jewels and (8) eight adjustments; the movement is lever-set has a white enamel dial & black numbers. ★★ **Important note** most production DATES for this section of Elgin are from a photograph of a 4 1/2 foot display made by Elgin with **83 movements** and arranged in chronological order. For each production model and under each movement is a inscription listing model, size, serial number & date. Example of inscription: (18 Size, 6th Model, Number 1,855,001, Made May 23, 1885.)

Some collectors seek out low serial numbers and will usually pay a premium for them. The lower the number, the more desirable the watch. The table shown below lists the first serial number of each size watch made by Elgin

Size	1st Serial Nos.	Size	1st Serial Nos.
18	101	10	40,001
17	356,001	8	570,001
16	600,001	0	2,889,001
14	351,001		

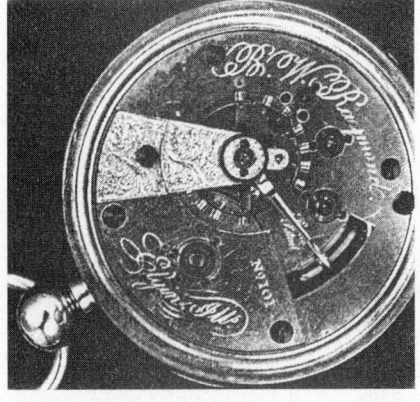 

B. W. Raymond, 18 size, 15 jewels, model # 1, key wind & set. 1st. run in April of 1867, serial number 101.

Father Time, 18 size, 21 jewels, model #8 with wind indicator, free sprung model, serial number 22,888,020

18 SIZE

Grade or Name — Description		ABP	Ex-Fn	Mint
Advance, 11J, gilded, KW, FULL, HC. ★		$100	$275	$350
Age, 7J, gilded, KW, FULL, OF/HC ★		100	275	350
Atlas Watch Co., 7J, , LS, FULL, HC (1st 7,090,001).		100	150	300
California Watch, 15J, gilded, KW, KS, FULL, HC		175	300	475
Chief, 7J, gilded, KW, FULL, HC ★		100	250	400
Convertible, 7J= G#98, 11J=G#99, gilded, 3/4, M#6		125	175	375
Convertible, 15J=G#100, gilded, 3/4, M#6		150	275	425
H. Z. Culver (Howard Z. Culver)				
H. Z. Culver, 15J, gilded, KW, KS, FULL, **ADJ**, HC, low S#		200	300	550
H. Z. Culver, 15J, gilded, KW, KS, FULL, **ADJ**, HC		150	250	400
H. Z. Culver, 15J, KW, KS, **14K, HC.**		700	1,000	1,500
H. Z. Culver, 15J, gilded, KW, KS, FULL, HC		125	250	375
H. Z. Culver, 15J, gilded, SW, FULL, HC		100	175	300
H. Z. Culver, 15J, gilded, KW, FULL, LS, HC		100	225	325

☞ **Generic, nameless or unmarked** grades for watch movements are listed under the Company name or initials of the Company, etc. by size, jewel count and description.

Grade or Name —Description	ABP	Ex-Fn	Mint
Elgin N. W. Co., 7J, OF, SW	$50	$120	$200
Elgin N. W. Co., 7J, KW, gilded, HC	100	150	300
Elgin N. W. Co., 11J, SW/KW, LS	50	120	200
Elgin N. W. Co., 11J, LS, SW, **HC, 9K-10K**	250	400	600
Elgin N. W. Co., 11J, LS, SW, HC, Silveroid	75	135	175
Elgin N. W. Co., 11J, LS, KW/SW, OF	50	135	175
Elgin N. W. Co., 13J, KW/SW, PS/LS, OF	50	135	175
Elgin N. W. Co., 13J, KW/SW, PS/LS, HC	100	150	300
Elgin N. W. Co., 15J, SW, LS, OF	50	135	200
Elgin N. W. Co., 15J, KW, LS, HC	125	175	300
Elgin N. W. Co., 15J, KW/SW, LS, HC	75	150	300
Elgin N. W. Co., 15J, KW, **hidden key, COIN silver case**	250	400	600

Elgin W. Co., engraved on movement California Watch, 18 size, 15 jewels, gilded, key wind & set, serial # 200,700.

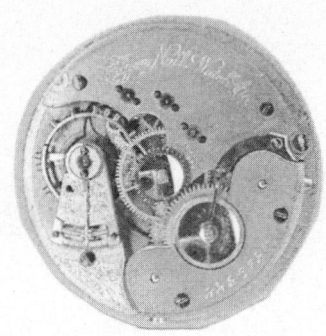

Convertible, 18 size, 15 jewels, converts to either hunting or open face, Gilded, G#100, S#2,226,720.

Grade or Name — Description	ABP	Ex-Fn	Mint
Elgin N. W. Co., 15-17J, KW/SW, LS, **box—hinge YGF, HC**	$300	$500	$800
Elgin N. W. Co., 15-17J, KW/SW, LS, **box—hinge 14K, HC**	1,200	2,000	3,500
Elgin N. W. Co., 15-17, KW/SW, LS, **Multi-color box YGF, HC**	600	1,200	2,000
Elgin N. W. Co., 15-17J, KW/SW, **14K case, OF**	400	700	1,100
Elgin N. W. Co., 15-17J, KW/SW, **14K case, HC**	600	1,000	1,500
Elgin N. W. Co., 15-17J, KW/SW, **18K case, HC**	700	1,500	2,000
Elgin N. W. Co., 15:17J, KW/ SW, **Multi-color, 14K, HC**	2,000	3,000	5,000
Elgin N. W. Co., 15-17J, KW/SW, LS, **COIN Silver** 6 oz, OF	300	500	800
Elgin N. W. Co., 15-17J, KW/SW, LS, **COIN Silver, OF**	100	175	250
Elgin N. W. Co., 17J, KW/SW, LS, OF	75	135	225
Elgin N. W. Co., 17J, SW, LS or PS, HC	125	225	350
Elgin N. W. Co., 21J, SW, LS or PS, OF	150	275	550
Elgin N. W. Co., 21J, SW, LS, **box case, GF, OF**	250	375	700
Elgin N. W. Co., 21J, LS, **HC, 14K**	700	1,000	1,500
Elgin N. W. Co., 21J, SW, LS, Silveroid	150	275	475
Elgin N. W. Co., 21t SW, LS, HC	275	400	625
Elgin N. W. Co., 21J, **Wind Indicator**	1,600	2,400	3,400
Elgin N. W. Co., 21J, **Wind Indicator, free sprung**	1,800	2,700	4,000
Elgin N. W. Co., 23J, SW, LS, OF	250	375	625
Elgin N. W. Co., 23J, SW, LS, HC ★	350	450	725

C.S. Moseley & G. Hunter
Micro. Regulator
Pat. Nov. 17, 1874

Above example of the *nameless* or unmarked *grades*. MARKED on movement **"Elgin W. Co. 17 jewels",** and listed under the Company name or initials (Elgin W. CO.) etc. as 18 Size, Elgin W. Co., 17J., & Description (KW, OF. etc.)

Above example of MARKED on movement **"Elgin W. Co. No. 349, 21 jewels Adjusted",** and is a 18 size movement and is listed under the 18 size grade **349** 21J Adj., etc.

Nameless or unmarked grades for watch movements which are listed under the Company name or initials of the Company, (Elgin W. Co.) etc. by Size, Jewel count & Description.

 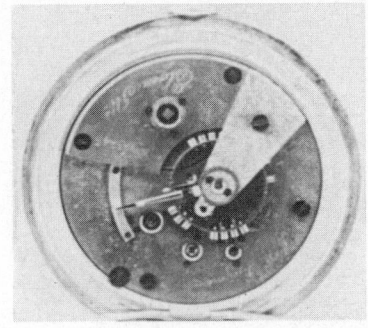

Pennsylvania Railroad Co. on dial. B.W. Raymond on movement. One of the first railroad watches commissioned by Penn. RR Co.. 18 size, 15 jewels, key wind and set, serial number 123.245, Ca. 1871. (See foot note below)

Grade or Name — Description	ABP	Ex-Fn	Mint
Charles Fargo, 7J, gilded, KW, HC	$150	$250	$425
J. V. Farwell, 11J, gilded, KW, HC ....★★	200	400	600
Father Time, 21J, NI, FULL, (up jeweled from 17J),OF	150	250	400
Father Time, 21J, SW, G266, OF	125	300	450
Father Time, 21J, SW, G995 & 274, HC.......................	275	400	600
Father Time, **20J**, NI, FULL, HC or OF ....★	300	500	700
Father Time, 21J, NI, SW, FULL, GJS, OF	200	400	575
Father Time, 21J, NI, SW, 3/4, GJS, DMK, HC.................	300	500	700
Father Time, 21J, NI, SW, 3/4, GJS, OF......................	200	350	600
Father Time, 21J, GJT, ADJ.5P, DES, **free sprung**, OF ....★	550	800	1,100
Father Time, 21J, GJT, ADJ.5P, Diamond end stone, OF	200	350	550
Father Time, 21J, NI, SW, 3/4, OF, GJS, **wind indicator**	2,000	2,200	3,000
Father Time, 21J, SW, 3/4, GJS, **wind indicator, HC** ....★★★	3,000	4,500	6,500
Father Time, G# 367, 21J, SW, 3/4, GJS, military style **wind indicator,** free sprung, sterling case.................	4,000	5,000	7,500
Father Time, G# 367, 21J, SW, 3/4, GJS, military style **wind indicator,** free sprung, **35 size with gimbals & box** ...	2,000	3,000	4,000
85 size, Model# **600**, 14J, **free sprung**, helical hair spring, dent escapement, **wind indicator, 85 size** with Gimbals & Box ....★★	3,000	4,000	6,500
W. H. Ferry, 11J, gilded, KW, HC	100	200	350
W. H. Ferry, 15J, gilded, KW, HC	125	200	350
Mat Laflin, 7J, gilded, KW, HC.............................	125	200	350
National W. Co., 7J, KW, KS	100	200	275
National W. Co., 11J, KW, KS	100	200	275
National W. Co., 15J, KW, KS	100	200	275
M.D.Ogden,15J,KW,HC....................................	125	200	350
M. D. Ogden, 11J, gilded, KW, HC	125	200	350
Order of Railway Conductors, 17J, LS, OF ....★★★	1,500	2,000	3,500
Overland, 17J, NI, KW, HC	150	300	450
Overland, 17J, NI, SW, OF.................................	150	225	400
Pennsylvania Railroad Co. on dial, B. W. Raymond on mvt., **must be ALL original,** 15J, KW, KS, (1st RR watches) ....★★★	2,500	4,000	6,500

★Below from a 1870, Elgin AD: ★

PENN'A R.R. Co.. Gen,1 Supt's Office, Altoona, *Jan. 19th, 1870.*

TM. Avery, Esq. Pres't National Watch Co., Chicago.

Dear Sir: This Company has purchased and put in the hands of its enginemen **eighty** "Raymond movements," which have given excellent satisfaction and proved to be very reliable time-keepers. In addition to these, quite a number of Elgin Watches have been purchased by officers and employees of this Company, all of whom have been well pleased with the efficiency and regularity of the movements manufactured by the National Watch Company.

Respectfully, Edward H. Williams, Gen'l Sup't.

B.W. Raymond, 18 size, 19 jewels, wind indicator. Note small winding indicator gear next to crown wheel.

H.H.Taylor, 18 size, 15 jewels, keywind&set,S#288,797.note the S# 288797, 88 larger than digits 2 & 797 (??)

Grade or Name — Description	ABP	Ex-Fn	Mint
Railway Timer, 15J, FULL, HC ....★	$400	$550	$850
B. W. Raymond, 15-17J, KW, low S# **under 200**	850	1,200	1,800
B. W. Raymond, 15-17J, KW, low S# **201 to 500**.	600	750	1,300
B. W. Raymond, 15-17J, KW, low S# **501 to 1,000**	400	550	900
B. W. Raymond, 15J, gilded, KW, FULL, HC.	150	300	350
B.W. Raymond, 15J,SW,HC.	100	200	300
B. W. Raymond, 15J, **box case 14K**	1,100	2,000	2,800
B. W. Raymond, 17J, gilded, KW, FULL, HC.	150	250	350
B. W. Raymond, 17J, NI, FULL, HC.	165	250	400
B. W. Raymond, 17J, all G#s, NI, FULL, OF	100	175	300
B. W. Raymond, 17J, gilded, or NI, SW, FULL, **ADJ**, OF	125	185	325
B. W. Raymond, 17J, **Wind Indicator**	1,400	1,700	2,500
B. W. Raymond, 19J, NI, 3/4, SW, OF, GJS, G#240, GT.	200	285	425
B. W. Raymond, 19J, 3/4, GJS, **jeweled barrel, Wind Indicator** ...	1,400	2,000	2,200
B. W. Raymond, 19J, 3/4, GJS, GT, Diamond end stone	200	300	425
B. W. Raymond, 21J, 3/4, GJS, GT, Diamond end stone, OF	200	300	475
B. W. Raymond, 21J, SW, Silveroid.	150	250	300
B. W. Raymond, 21J, SW, GJS, GT, G#274, HC ....★★	350	550	750
B. W. Raymond, 21J, NI, 3/4, SW, GJS, G#389 & 390, GT, OF	225	350	500
B. W. Raymond, 21J, NI, 3/4, SW, GJS, **Wind Indicator**, DMK	1,600	2,000	3,000
J T. Ryerson, 7J, gilded, FULL, KW, HC.	150	275	400
R.W. Sears on dial, 15J., R.W. Sears Special on movement,			
(Special order by Sears prior to Sears, Roebuck & Co.). ..★★	225	325	575
Solar W. Co., 15J, **Multi-color dial**.	165	250	500
Standard, 17J, OF, LS.	125	185	300
Sundial, 7J, SW, PS (1st 7,080,001)	100	125	250
H. H. Taylor, 15J, gilded, FULL, KW, HC.	100	250	350
H. H. Taylor, 15J, NI, FULL, KW, DMK, HC.	100	250	350
H. H. Taylor, 15J, NI, FULL, **SW**, HC, DMK, quick train	125	200	350
H. H. Taylor, 15J, SW, Silveroid.	100	145	200
H. H. Taylor, 15J, SW, slow train	100	145	200

IMPORTANT NOTE: Railroad Standards, Railroad Approved & Railroad Grade terminology, as defined and used in this book

1.**RAILROAD STANDARDS** = A commission or board appointed by the railroad companies outlined a set of **guidelines t**o be accepted or approved by each railroad line

2.**RAILROAD APPROVED** = A list of watches each railroad line would approve if purchased by their employee's. (this list changed through the years).

3.**RAILROAD GRADE** = A watch made by manufactures to meet or exceed the guidelines set by the railroad standards. Grades such as 992, Vanguard and B.W. Raymond, etc.

*Some GRADES exceeded the R.R. standards such as 23 jewels, diamond end stone, gold train, raised gold jewel settings, double sunk dial and the list goes on. Examples: such as Veritas, Sangamo,950 & Riverside Maximus and many others.

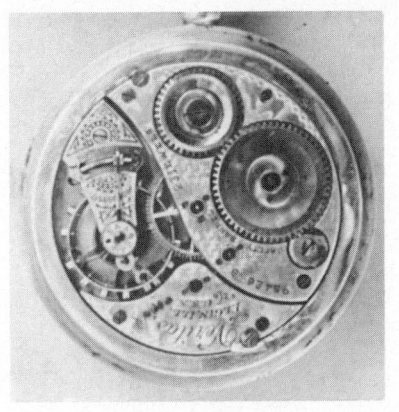

Veritas, 18 size, 23 jewels, solid gold train, gold jewel settings, diamond end stone, serial number 9,542,678.

G. M. Wheeler, Grade 369, 18 size, 17 jewels, open face, gold jewel settings, serial number 14,768,315

The word **VERITAS** translated is **"TRUTH"**.

Grade or Name — Description	ABP	Ex-Fn	Mint
Veritas, 21J, 3/4, NI, GJS, DMK, GT, G#239, OF	$265	$350	$600
Veritas, 21J, 3/4, GJS, GT, Diamond end stones	285	350	625
Veritas, 21J, SW, PS, GJS, GT, HC	300	500	675
Veritas, 21J, SW, LS, GJS, GT, HC	300	500	675
Veritas, 21J, 3/4, GJS, GT, Diamond end stones, G#274, HC	325	500	700
Veritas, 21J, 3/4, NI, GJS, Wind Indicator, DMK, G#239, OF	2,000	2,500	3,500
Veritas, 21J, 3/4, NI, GJS, Wind Indicator, DMK, G#274,HC . . . ★★	3,500	5,000	8,000
Veritas, 23J, 3/4, NI, GJS, OF, DMK, OT	350	550	800
Veritas, 23J, 3/4, NI, GJS, OF, DMK, GT, Diamond end stone.	350	550	800
Veritas, 23J, G#214, 3/4, NI, GJS, Wind Indicator, OF	2,200	3,000	3,500
Veritas, 23J, G#494, Wind Indicator, "Free Sprung", OF . . . . . ★★★	2,500	3,200	4,500
Veritas, 23J, G#214, SW, OF	450	550	800
Veritas, 23J, 3/4, SW, NI, GJS, GT, LS, HC. . . . . ★★★	600	1,000	1,500
Veritas, 23J, SW, OF, 14K	700	1,200	1,750
Wabash, 21J, G #349, Adj.5P,LS, OF . . . . ★	300	600	1,000
G. M. Wheeler, 11J, gilded, KW, HC.	100	200	300
G. M. Wheeler, 13-15J, gilded, FULL, KW, SW	100	150	200
G. M. Wheeler, 15J, NI, FULL, KW, DMK, HC.	100	200	300
G. M. Wheeler, 15J, SW, NI, FULL, DMK, OF	100	135	200
G. M. Wheeler, 17J, KW, NI, FULL, DMK, OF	100	150	250
G. M. Wheeler, 17J, SW, NI, DMK, OF.	100	135	200

MOVEMENT WITH NO NAME

Grade or Name — Description	ABP	Ex-Fn	Mint
No. 5 & No. 17, 7J, gilded, FULL, HC.	$100	$150	$300
No. 23 & No. 18, 11J, gilded, FULL, HC.	100	150	300
No. 69, 15J, M#1, KW, quick train, HC	100	200	300
No. 150, 20-21J, full plate, GJS, LS	200	300	475
No. 155, 17J, GJS, Adj.5P, HC	125	200	300
No. 274, 21J., marked 274, GT, Adj. 5p, diamond end stone	250	375	625
No. 316, 15J, NI, FULL, DMK, HC.	100	200	300
No. 317, 15J, NI, FULL, ADJ, DMK, OF.	100	135	200

🖎 Generic, nameless or unmarked grades for watch movements are listed under the Company name or initials of the Company, etc. by size, jewel count and description.

Grade or Name — Description	ABP	Ex-Fn	Mint
No. 326, 15J, OF	$100	$125	$200
No. 327, 15J, HC	100	200	300
No. 331, **16J**, M#11,NI,OF .... ★	125	150	265
No. 335, 17J, HC	110	200	300
No. 336, 17J, NI, FULL, DMK, OF	100	125	200
No. 348, 21J, NI, FULL, GJS, DMK, HC	300	500	625
No. 349, 21J, , LS, OF	250	300	450
No. 349, 21J, , LS, **MARKED LOANER**, OF .... ★	350	475	750
No. 378, 17-19J, NI, FULL, DMK, HC	125	200	325
No. 379, 17-19J, OF	125	185	300
No. 411, 21J, PS, **2-tone**, NI, OF .... ★★★	375	500	1,000

 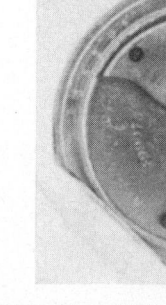

Elgin watch co., Leader, 17 size, 11 jewels, made for English market, serial number 467,255.

Elgin watch co., 17 size, 7 jewels, key wind & set, serial number 499,076. Made for Kennedy & co.

17 SIZE

Grade or Name — Description	ABP	Ex-Fn	Mint
Avery, 7J, gilded, KW, FULL, HC (1st 400,001)	$100	$200	$300
Inter-Ocean, 7J, KWKS, HC .... ★★★	400	600	1,000
Leader, 7J, gilded, KW, FULL, HC (1st 356,001)	100	200	300
Leader, 11J, gilded, KW, FULL, HC	100	200	300
Sunshine, 15J, M# 1, **KW & KS from back** .... ★	150	200	350
Grade 11, 14,15,51,59,7J, gilded, KW, FULL, HC	100	200	300
17 Size, KW, Silveroid	100	125	200

Note model # 1, 17 size is key-wind key-set both from the back.

16 SIZE

Grade or Name — Description	ABP	Ex-Fn	Mint
Braille or Blind Man's Watch, 9-17J, HC......................	$125	$200	$400
Convertible Model, 7J=G#47 & 11J=G#9J, 13J=G#48, 3/4, gilded	75	110	210	300
Convertible Model, 13J=G#90, 3F BRG	125	175	275
Convertible Model, 15J=G#49, 3/4, gilded	100	175	275
Convertible Model, 15J=G#50, 3/4, NI, ADJ	125	185	295
Convertible Model, 15J=G#50, 3/4, NI, ADJ, **14K, HC**........	900	1,000	1,800
Convertible Model, 15J=G#85, 3F BRG, gilded	175	225	375
Convertible Model, 15J=G#86, 3F BRG, NI	175	225	375
Convertible Model, 21J=G#72, 3/4, NI, ADJ, GJS .... ★★★	1,500	2,400	4,000
Convertible Model, 21J=G#72, 3/4, NI, ADJ, GJS, **14K**..... ★★★	2,200	3,200	5,000
Convertible Model, 21J=G#91, 3F BRG, NI .... ★★★	1,600	2,400	4,000
Convertible Model, 21J,G#91, 3F BRG, NI, **14K** .... ★★★	2,200	3,200	5,000

NOTE: **Convertible** = Same **movement** can be changed to either a hunting or open face case.

👉 A collector should expect to pay modestly higher prices at local shops.

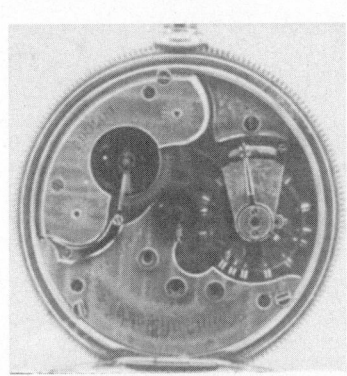

Elgin watch Co., 16 size, 21J, 3/4, convertible Model GRADE # 72, S#607,061. **Convertible** movements= can be converted to a hunting or open face case.

Elgin W.Co., convertible model, 16 Size ,15 jewels, three fingered bridge model, G # 86, adjusted, S #4,907,178. **Convertible** = can be converted to a HC or OF case.

Grade or Name — Description	ABP	Ex-Fn	Mint
Doctors Watch, 13J, 4th Model, NI, GT, sweep second hand, G#89 gilded, GF	$300	$500	$900
Doctors Watch, 15J, 4th Model, NI, GT, sweep second hand, G# 83 gilded & G#84 nickel, GF case	300	500	900
Doctors Watch, 15J, 4th Model, gilded, sweep second hand, coin silver case	350	550	950
Doctors Watch, 15J, 4th Model, sweep second hand, **14K, OF**	900	1,400	2,300
Elgin N. W. Co., Locomotive + **diamond** 1n lantern on case, **multi-color gold, 14K HC** ★	2,600	4,000	6,000

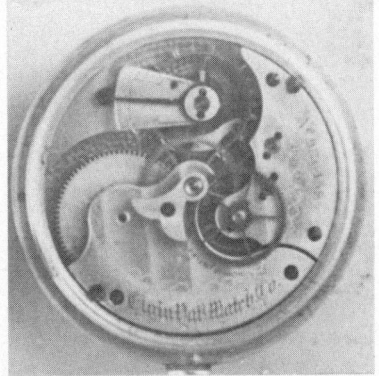

Elgin watch Co., 16 size, Multi- color Gold hunting case, the locomotive has a diamond in the lantern, the case has white, yellow, rose flowers & green leaf designs, Ca.1880

Doctors Watch, 16 size, 15jewels, fourth model, gold jewel settings, gold train, sweep second hand, serial number 926,458.

Grade or Name — Description	ABP	Ex-Fn	Mint
Elgin N. W. Co., 7-9J, OF	$40	$100	$150
Elgin N. W. Co., 7-9J, HC..............................	40	125	200
Elgin N. W. Co., 11J,OF	40	100	150
Elgin N. W. Co., 11J,HC..............................	60	125	200
Elgin N. W. Co., 13J, OF..............................	40	100	150
Elgin N. W. Co., 13J, OF, Silveroid	40	100	150
Elgin N. W. Co., 13J,HC..............................	65	125	200
Elgin N. W. Co., 15J, HC	75	135	200
Elgin N. W. Co., 15J, OF..............................	65	125	150
Elgin N. W. Co., 15J, OF **14K case**.....................	300	400	600
Elgin N. W. Co., 15J, HC, **14K**........................	450	600	900
Elgin N. W. Co., 15J, **multi-color Gold +diamond, HC, 14K**......	1,700	2,500	3,500
Elgin N. W. Co., 16J, OF..............................	85	150	225
Elgin N. W. Co., 16J, **Chronograph** M #4, LS, OF ..... ★★★★★	2,500	4,000	6,500
Elgin N. W. Co., 17J, OF..............................	75	125	200
Elgin N. W. Co., 17J, LS, **multi-color HC, YGF**	250	400	800
Elgin N. W. Co., 17J, **multi-color HC, 14K**	1,000	2,000	2,500
Elgin N. W. Co., 17J, **14K, HC**..........................	400	500	900
Elgin N. W. Co., 17J, HC..............................	95	175	300
Elgin N. W. Co., 19J,OF	100	185	310
Elgin N. W. Co., 21J, HC	175	500	600
Elgin N. W. Co., 21J, OF, **Silveroid**	95	175	300
Elgin N. W. Co., 21J, OF..............................	150	300	375
Elgin N. W. Co., 23J, OF..............................	250	400	550
3F Bridge Model, 15J, NI, DMK,, OF	95	185	300
3F Bridge Model, 15J, NI, DMK, HC	150	225	350
3F Bridge Model, 17J, NI, DMK, OF	95	165	295
3F Bridge Model, 17J, Adj., NI, DMK, GJS, HC ....★★	200	300	475
3F Bridge Model, 17J, **Adj.5P**, NI, DMK, GJS, GT, OF ....★★★	300	400	600
3F Bridge Model, 21J, Adj.5P, NI, DMK, GJS, GT, OF	550	700	900
3F Bridge Model, 21J, Adj.5P, NI, DMK, GJS, GT, **18K**..........	1,000	1,500	2,500
Father Time, 21J, 3/4, NI, GJS, DR, DMK, ADJ.5P, HC..........	225	500	600
Father Time, 21J, 3/4, NI, GJS, DR, **Wind Indicator**, OF	1,100	1,500	1,800
Father Time, 21J, 3/4, NI, GJS, DR, **pendant set**, AD3.SP, OF ... ★	200	300	500
Father Time, 21J, NI, GJS, DR, ADJ.5P, OT, OF..........	200	300	500
Lord Elgin, 21J, GJS, DR, Adj.5P, BRG, Gold filled, **OF** ....★★	800	1,400	2,000
Lord Elgin, 21J, GJS, DR, Adj.5P, BRG, Gold filled, **HC** ......★★	900	1,500	2,100
Lord Elgin, 21J, GJS, DR, Adj.5P, 3F BRG, **14K, OF** ....★★	1,500	2,600	3,250
Lord Elgin, 21J, GJS, DR, Adj.5P, 3F BRG, **14K, HC** ....★★	1,800	3,100	3,750
Lord Elgin, 23J, GJS, DR, Adj.5P, 3/4, 14K, OF ....★★	2,000	3,100	3,750
Lord Elgin, 23J, GJS, DR, Adj.5P, 3/4, Gold filled OF ....★★	1,200	1,900	2,750

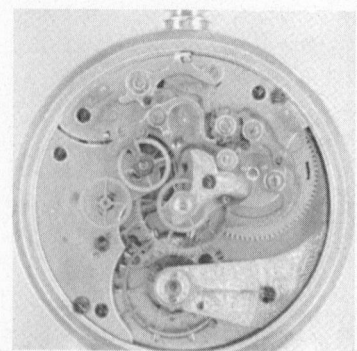

ELGIN W. Co., Chronograph. 16 size, 16 jewels, model #4, lever set. (Very rare, may be one of a kind)

Father Time, 16 size, 21 jewels, gold train; Note model 19 up and down wind indicator movement does not show the differential wheel as does the 18 size, S# 18,106,465.

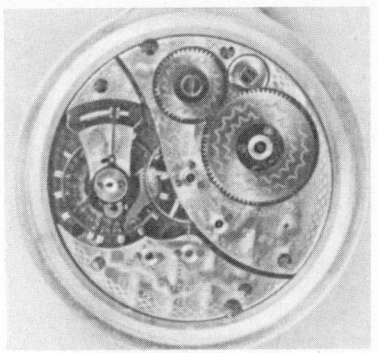

Lord Elgin, 16 Size, 21 Jewels, gold train, raised gold jewel settings, 3 finger bridge, grade 156 S# 10,249,819

B. W. Raymond, 16 Size, 19 Jewels, gold jewel settings, Grade 350, Serial number 17,822,991

Grade or Name — Description	ABP	Ex-Fn	Mint
B. W. Raymond, 17J, 3/4, GJS, **14K, OF**	$400	$500	$800
B. W. Raymond, 17J, 3/4, GJS, SW, HC.	200	335	500
B. W. Raymond, 17J, 3F BRG . . . . ★★	400	550	800
B. W. Raymond, 17J, LS, NI, **Wind Indicator** . . . . ★★	900	1,400	2,000
B. W. Raymond, 17J, GJS, SW, Adj., ALL G#s, OF	150	225	350
B. W. Raymond, 17J, 3/4, GJS, DR Adj.5P, DMK.	150	225	350
B. W. Raymond, 19J, 3/4, GJS, DR, Adj.5P, DMK, OF.	175	275	400
B. W. Raymond, 19J, (Elgin **The Railroader** on dial) Adj.5P, OF . . .	400	750	950
B. W. Raymond, 19J, OF, **14K, 30 DWT**	400	800	1,100
B. W. Raymond, 19J, 3/4, GJS, DR, Adj.5P, DMK, **Wind Indicator**.	850	1,200	1,500
B. W. Raymond, 19J, M#8, G#372, 455, Adj.5P, OF	175	225	400
B. W. Raymond, 19J, GJS, G#371, 401,Adj.5P, HC	200	300	400
B. W. Raymond, 21J, **14K, OF**	450	700	1,000
B. W. Raymond, 21J, G#472, 478, 506, 571, 581, 590, Adj.5P, OF . . .	200	300	450
B. W. Raymond, 21J, 3/4, GJS, DR, Adj.5P, HC	300	500	650
B. W. Raymond, 21J, G# 391, 3/4, GJS, DR, Adj.5P, DMK, OF.... . . .	200	300	450
B. W. Raymond, 21J, **gold flashed movement,** OF	275	350	500
B. W. Raymond, 21J, 3/4, GJS, DR, Adj.5P, DMK, **Wind Indicator**	900	1,200	1,600
B. W. Raymond, 21J, 3/4, GJS, DR, **Adj.6P,** DMK, **Wind Indicator**	900	1,200	1,600
B. W. Raymond, 22J, WWII Model, sweep second hand	250	450	550
B. W. Raymond, 22J, WWII Model, GCW sweep second hand,			
Wind Indicator . . . . ★★★★	4,000	6,000	8,500
B. W. Raymond, 23J, 3/4, GJS, DR, Adj.5P, G#376, 494, 540	350	500	650
B. W. Raymond, 23J, 3/4, GJS, DR, Adj.5P, DMK, **Wind Indicator**	1,200	1,600	2,400
B. W. Raymond, 23J, 3/4, GJS, DR, **Adj.6P,** DMK, **Wind Indicator**	1,200	1,600	2,400
B. W. Raymond, 23J, 3/4, GJS, DR, Adj.5P, DMK, **Wind Indicator**			
Military style.	1,100	1,500	2,200

14K White or Green
Gold Filled
Specially Designed
Screw Case

Price $35.30

12K-Gold Filled
Specially Designed
Screw Case

Price $31.65

10K-Gold Filled
Specially Designed
Screw Case

Price $31.65

Winding Indicator $3.50 extra

AD
Oct. 15th, 1926
and
Aug, 15th, 1927

B. W. Raymond Movement
16 Size
21 Jewels
8 Adjustments, 5 of them position
Supplied with Montgomery Dial if desired

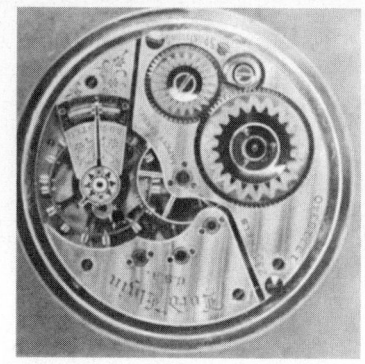

Veritas, 16 size, 23 jewels, (Veritas = TRUTH'), solid gold train, gold jeweled settings, S# 16,678,681.

Elgin Watch Co., LORD ELGIN, Grade 351, 16 size, 23J gold train, gold jewel settings, S# 12,718,340. NOTE: This watch came from the first run of G # 351, 23J. Lord Elgins.

Grade or Name — Description		ABP	Ex-Fn	Mint
Veritas, 19J, G# 401, GJS, Adj. SP., HC	★	$400	$600	$800
Veritas, 21J, GJS, DR, Adj.5P, DMK, 3/4, **Wind Indicator**		1,300	2,000	2,700
Veritas,21J,3F brg,GJS,G#360	★	350	450	725
Veritas, 21J, GJS, DR, Adj.5P, DMK, 3/4, G#401, HC		425	600	825
Veritas,21J,GJS, SW, Grade 360	★	350	450	725
Veritas, 21J, GJS, SW, Adj.5P, OF, Grade 270 & 375		300	425	675
Veritas, 23J, GJS, Adj.5P, **14K, OF**		600	800	1,200
Veritas, 23J, GJS, Adj.5P, **HC**		500	750	1,100
Veritas, 23J, GJS, DR, Adj.5P, 3/4, G#375- 376- 453, OF		375	450	700
Veritas, 23J, GJS, DR, Adj.5P, DMK, 3/4, Diamond end stone, Grade 350	★	400	600	800
Veritas, 23J, GJS, DR, Adj.5P, Grade 453 & 376 DMK, 3/4, **Wind Indicator**		1,700	2,500	3,500
G. M. Wheeler, 17J, DR, Adj.3P, DMK, 3/4.		65	110	200
G. M. Wheeler, 17J, 3F BRG		80	150	250
G.M.Wheeler,17J, **HC,14K**		350	600	750
WWII Model,17J,OF		100	200	300
WWII Model, 21J, OF		175	300	450
M#13,9J,HC		65	200	250
M#48,13J,HC		65	200	250

(Add $50 to $75 to hunting case models listed as open face)

MODELS WITH NO NAMES

Grade or Name — Description		ABP	Ex-Fn	Mint
Grade #155-160,17J, GT, GJS, HC		$100	$175	$250
Grade #156, 21J, 3/4, NI, DR, DMK, GT, GJS, HC	★	350	475	700
Grade #156, 21J, 3/4, NI, DR, DMK, GT, GJS, HC, **14K**	★	600	800	1,000
Grade#161, **17J,**SW,PS,NI,GJS,GT,OF	★★	300	425	600
Grade #162, 21J, SW, PS, NI, GJS, GT, OF		225	325	450
Grade #270, 21J, 3F BRG, GJS, **marked** 270 on mvt		275	400	600
Grade #280, 17J, 3F BRG, **marked** 280 on mvt, OF		175	250	425
Grade #290 HC & #291 ,7J, 3/4, NI, DMK, OF		65	110	150

A watch marked as 5 positions is equivalent to one marked eight adjustments (the most common found on RR watches) and will be listed in this book as: "Adj.5P" (adjusted to heat, cold, isochronism and 5 positions). A watch marked as nine adjustments is equivalent to one marked 6 positions & listed as "Adj.6P" (adjusted to heat, cold, isochronism and 6 positions). A watch that is marked as ADJUSTED only is adjusted to isochronism & in poise in all temperatures & is listed as "Adj.".

*Later some manufactures used a variations of 8 adjustments, six to position, 1-isochronism, 1-temperature or as in the Elgin grade 571 two to temperature in about 1950.

Grade or Name — Description	ABP	Ex-Fn	Mint
Grade #291, 7J, 3/4, HC, **14K**	$300	$600	$800
Grade #312 & #313, 15J,3/4, NI, DR, DMK, OF	75	120	200
Grade #340, 17J, 3 finger bridge, OF	75	120	200
Grade #372, 19J, M#15, LS, OF, Adj.5P	200	250	350
Grade #374, 21J, M#15, LS, OF, Adj.5P	250	350	450
Grade #381 & #382, 17J, 3/4, NI, DR, DMK, OF	100	165	300
Grade #401, 19J, M#17, LS, HC	200	300	425
Grade #540, **23J**, Adj.5P, OF	300	400	550
Grade #572, 19J, Adj.5P, OF	135	250	350
Grade #573, 17J, Adj.5P, OF	125	175	275
Grade #575, 15J, Adj.3P, OF	100	150	250
Grade #581, 21J, Adj.5P, **center sec, hacking, Army,** OF	250	400	550
Grade #845,23J, Adj., (by **Buren** W. Co.) Swiss	65	120	175

14 SIZE

Grade or Name — Description	ABP	Ex-Fn	Mint
Lord Elgin, 15J, G#357, OF	$65	$95	$175
Lord Elgin, 17J,G#358-3590F	70	100	200
7J, M#1, gilded, KW, **14K, HC**	250	350	575
7J, M#1, gilded, KW, YGF, HC	40	70	125
11J, M#1, gilded, KW, YGF, HC	40	70	125
11J, M#1, gilded, KW, YGF, OF	40	70	125
13J, M#1, gilded, KW, OF	40	70	125
15J, M#1, gilded, KW, OF	40	70	125
7J, M#2, SW, OF	40	70	125
15J, M#2, SW, OF	40	70	125
15J, M#2, SW, **14K, HC**	200	350	500
15J, M#1, grade #46, KW, 3/4, HC	75	100	200

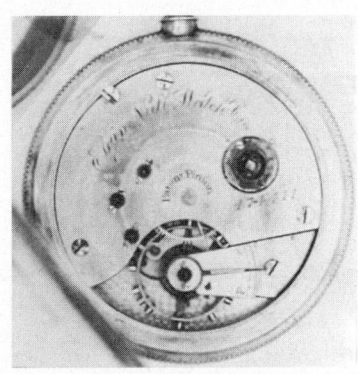

ELGIN, 14 size, model # 1, grade # 46, 3/4 plate design, key wind and key set, hunting case, serial # 474,414

ELGIN EIGHT DAY, 12 size, 21 jewels, wind indicator, bridge movement, open face, serial number 12,345,678,

12 SIZE

Grade or Name — Description		ABP	Ex -Fn	Mint
Eight Day, 21J, 8-Day Wind Indicator, BRG	★★★★★	$2,500	$3,500	$5,500
24 hour dial in one revolution	★	900	1,200	2,200
Elgin N. W. Co., Aux. dial for date of month & day of week	★	900	1,200	2,200

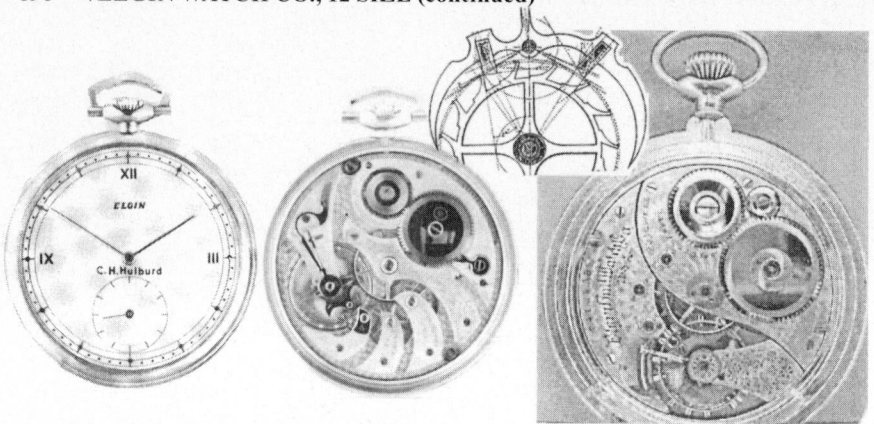

C H Hulburd 19J, thin BRG model (12 /14 size), 8 Adj. Ca 1920-1925 Advertised as **ALL in a Unique case.** Mr. Charles H Hulburd became president of Elgin in 1898.

ELGIN W.Co., 12 size,G#190,23J,GJS,Adj.5P,NI, DMK GT, M# 2, **Mustache lever,** HC, (**Hi-grade**) S# 7412238.Note the illustration of counterpoised **Mustache lever.**

Grade or Name — Description	ABP	Ex-Fn	Mint
Elgin N. W. Co. # 30, 73, gilded, **KW**, OF	$85	$145	$250
Elgin N.W.Co. #89, 19J, HC	75	110	20
Elgin N. W. Co. # 190, 23J, GJS, Adj.5P, NI, DMK, GT, M# 2,*(Hi-grade)*			
Mustache or **Standard** lever, **Gold Filled, HC**	225	300	500
Elgin N. W. Co. # 190,23J, GJS, Adj.5P, NI, DMK, GT, M# 2,(**Hi-grade**)			
Mustache lever, **18K, HC** . . . . ★	1,100	1,400	1,800
Elgin N. W. Co. # 194, 23J, GJS, Adj.5P, NI, DMK, GT, OF.	175	275	350
Elgin N. W. Co. #236, 21J, GJS, Adj.5P, NI, DMK, GT, HC . . . . . ★	150	200	275
Elgin N. W. Co. #237 or 273, 21J, GJS, Adj.5P, NI, GT, OF . . . . . . ★	125	175	250
Elgin N. W. Co. # 301 7J,HC	50	85	150
Elgin N. W. Co. #314, 15J, HC	90	145	250
Elgin N. W. Co. #384,17J,OF	60	95	175
Elgin N. W. Co., 7-15J, **14K, Multi-color**	900	1,200	1,800
Elgin N. W. Co., 7-15J OF, GF	60	85	150
Elgin N. W. Co., 7-15J, **HC, 14K**	250	350	575
Elgin N. W. Co., 17J, OF, GF	60	95	175
Elgin N. W. Co., 19J, OF, Gold filled	75	110	200
Elgin N. W. Co., 19J, HC, Gold filled.	75	110	200
Elgin N. W. Co., 19J, **HC, 14K**	250	350	625
Elgin N. W. Co., 19J, **14K, OF**	175	250	400
Elgin N. W. Co.,21J, OF, gold filled case	100	185	310
12 size movements, Model 2 & 3 were spread or made to fit a "16 size CASE"			
Elgin N. W. Co., 15-17J, Model 3, 12 size **spread** to 16 size, OF.	$75	$100	$150
Elgin N. W. Co., 15-17J, Model 2, 12 size **spread** to 16 size, HC	85	125	200
Elgin N. W. Co., 19-21J, Model 3, 12 size **spread** to 16 size, OF	85	125	200
Elgin N. W. Co., 19-21J, Model 2, 12 size **spread** to 16 size, HC	100	175	250
STANDARD 12 SIZE (continued)			
Elete, 17J, GJS, Adj,4P, OF.	$40	$75	$135
C. H. Hulburd, 19J, thin BRO model (12 /14 size) **14K case** . . . . . . ★	800	1,000	1,600
C. H. Hulburd, 19J, thin BRO model (12 /14 size) **18K case** . . . . . . ★	900	1,200	1,800
C. H. Hulburd, 19J, thin BRO model (12 /14 size) **Platinum** . . . . . ★	1,400	2,000	3,000
Lord Elgin, 17J, OF.	60	95	150
Lord Elgin,17,HC	75	120	200
Lord Elgin,19 , ADJ, OF.	75	120	200
Lord Elgin,19J,ADJ,HC	125	200	250
Lord Elgin, 21, GJS, DR, Adj.5P, DMK, NI, OF	125	200	250
Lord Elgin, 21J,G3S, DR, Adj.5P, DMK, NI, **14K, OF**	200	250	400
Lord Elgin, 21J, GJS., DR, Adj.5P, DMK, NI, HC	150	200	350
Lord Elgin ,23, G# 194, GJS, DR, Adj.5P, DMK, NI, OF.... . ★★★	150	300	400
Lord Elgin, 23J, G# 190, GJS, DR, Adj.5P, DMK, NI, HC.. . ★★★	225	400	500
Lord Elgin, 23J, GJS, DR, Adj.5P, DMK, NI, **14K,** HC . . . . . . ★★★	300	500	700

Lord Elgin, 12 size, 23 jewels, gold jewel settings, Adj.5p, originally sold for $110.00.

G. M. Wheeler, 12 size, 17 jewels, Adj3p, originally sold for $27.00.

Grade or Name —Description	ABP	Ex-Fn	Mint
Masonic dial, 15-17J, (with original Masonic dial), OF	$200	$300	$400
Pierce Arrow, 17J, (with original dial), OF	325	500	850
B. W. Raymond, 19J, G# 189, GJS, Adj.5P, DR, DMK, NI, HC	80	135	275
B. W. Raymond, 19J, G# 193, GJS, Adj.5P, DR, DMK, NI, OF	50	125	200
B. W. Raymond, 19J, G# 448, GIS, Adj.5P, DR, DMK, NI, OF	50	125	200
Transit, 17J., 2 tone, OF	80	135	275
G. M. Wheeler, 17J, DR, Adj.5P, DMK, NI, OF	30	50	125
G. M. Wheeler, 17J, DR, Adj.5P, DMK, NI, HC	40	150	200

Frances Ruble, Grade 23, 10 size, 16 jewels, key wind & set.

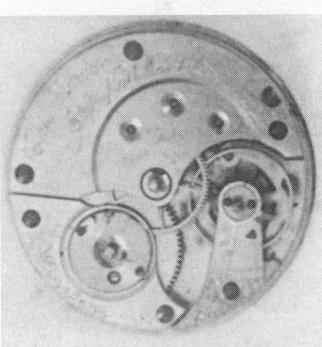

Gall Borden, Grade 22, 10 size, 11 Jewels, key wind & set, serial number 947,696.

10 SIZE

(HC)

Grade or Name — Description	ABP	Ex-Fn	Mint
Elgin, multi-color case, gold filled, HC	$225	$350	$550
Elgin, 15J, Silveroid, HC	40	60	100
Elgin, 15J, YGF, HC	65	85	150
Dexter St., 7J, KW, HC, 14K	225	350	525
Dexter St., 7J, KW, HC, 18K	250	400	625
Dexter St., 7J, gilded, KW, HC, gold filled	75	95	150
Frances Rubie, 15J, gilded, KW, HC, 14K ★	500	635	825
Frances Rubie, 15J, KW, HC, 18K ★★	600	750	950

☞ Watches listed in this book are priced at the collectable Trade Show level, as complete watches having an original 14k gold-filled case and Key Wind with silver, an original white enamel single sunk dial, and with the entire original movement in good working order with no repairs needed.

Grade or Name — Description	ABP	Ex-Fn	Mint
Gail Borden, 11J, gilded, KW, HC, **14K**	$225	$350	$500
Gail Borden, 11J, KW, HC, gold filled	65	100	150
Gail Borden, 11J KW, HC, **18K**	300	400	600
Lady Elgin, 15J, gilded, KW, HC, **14K**	225	300	500
Lady Elgin, 15J, KW, HC, **18K**	300	400	600
Grade #21 or 28, 7J, gilded, KW, HC, gold filled	65	100	175

Elgin W. Co., Grade 121, 6 size, 15 jewels, hunting, serial number 4,500,445.

Elgin W. Co., 6 size, ENGRAVED movement, enamel & gold case, fancy dial, G# 94, S# 1,866,804.

6 SIZE

(HC Only)

Grade or Name — Description	ABP	Ex-Fn	Mint
Atlas, 7J, HC	$40	$65	$150
Elgin N. W. Co. #286, 7J, HC, DMK, NI	40	65	150
Elgin N. W. Co. #295, 15J, HC, DMK, NI	40	65	150
Elgin N. W. Co. #168, **16J**, nickel, HC	100	165	275
Elgin N. W. Co., 7J, HC, **14K**	150	300	450
Elgin N. W. Co., 11J HC, **14K**	150	300	450
Elgin N. W. Co., ENGRAVED movement, **enamel & gold case** fancy dial, G# 94, **14K** HC	700	1,000	1,400
Elgin N. W. Co., 15J, YGF, HC	60	100	175
Elgin N. W. Co., 15J, YGF demi-HC	60	100	175
Elgin N. W. Co., 15J, HC, **YGF** multi-color case	200	250	400
Elgin N. W. Co., 15J, HC, **10K**	175	200	300
Elgin N. W. Co., 15J, HC, **14K**	200	300	450
Elgin N. W. Co., 15J, **14K, Multi-color HC**	400	600	900
Elgin N. W. Co., 15J, HC, **18K**	300	400	500
Elgin N. W. Co., 15J, SW, HC, **Enamel case, 18K**	500	800	1,300
Elgin N. W. Co., **16J**, G# 230, gilded or nickel, HC	95	135	265

☞ A collector should expect to pay modestly higher prices at local shops.

☞ **Generic, nameless or unmarked** grades for watch movements are listed under the Company name or initials of the Company, etc. by size, jewel count and description.

Elgin W. Co., 6 size, 15 jewels

Elgin W. Co., Grade 201-HC, 205-OF, 0 size, 19 jewels, gold train.

0 SIZE

Lady Raymond, 5/0 size. 15J.

Grade or Name —Description	ABP	Ex-En	Mint
Atlas W. Co., 7J, HC	$40	$100	$200
Elgin N. W. Co., 7J, NI, DR, DMK, OF	35	55	150
Elgin N. W. Co., 15J, NI, DR, DMK, OF	35	55	150
Elgin N. W. Co., 15J, NI, OR, DMK, HC	50	90	225
Elgin N. W. Co., 17J, NI, DR. DMK, ADJ, OF	50	90	175
Elgin N. W. Co., 19J, NI, OR, DMK, GJS, ADJ, OF	35	55	150
Elgin N. W. Co., 15J, OF, **14K**	150	200	300
Elgin N. W. Co., 15J, HC, **14K**	200	250	400
Elgin N. W. Co., 15J, HC, **multi-color GF**	150	250	350
Elgin N. W. Co., 15J, OF, **multi-color dial**	150	200	300
Elgin N. W. Co., 15J, HC, **10K**	150	200	300
Elgin N. W. Co., 15J, **14K, Multi-color case**	375	450	700
Elgin N. W. Co., 15J, **14K, Multi-color case + diamond**	400	500	800
Frances Ruble, 19J, HC. ★★	250	375	625

3/0 and 5/0 SIZE (HC ONLY)

Grade or Name — Description	ABP	Ex-En	Mint
Lady Elgin, 15J, PS, HC	$40	$75	$175
Lady Elgin, 15J, **14K**, HC	135	300	400
Lady Raymond, 15J, PS, HC	40	75	175
Elgin N. W. Co., 7J, HC	40	55	125

Style: 3056
Center: Ca. 1950s Diamond Bar Bezel
gold filled: $90 - $125 - $225
DIAL:$30 - $50 - $95

Ca. 1950s Plain Bezel
gold filled: $90 - $125 - $195
DIAL: $30 - $50 - $95

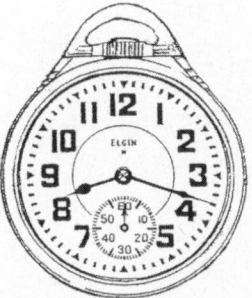

Style: 3055 - Streamline
Ca. 1950s Tear Drop Plain Bezel
gold filled: $90 - $125 - $225
DIAL: $30 - $50 - $95

Above Right: Tear Drop bezel came with a Diamond Bar Bezel.

STYLE NO. 40
gold filled : $90 - $125 - $300
DIAL:$20 - $30 - $50

STYLE NO. 39, Ca.1923
gold filled : $95 - $110 - $275
DIAL: $20 - $30 - $50

STYLE NO.38
gold filled : $95 - $110 - $285
DIAL: $ 20 - $30 - $50

STYLE NO. 19
gold filled : $95 -$125- $300
wind-ind. -DIAL: $40 - $80 - $225

STYLE NO. 18
CHROME : $25 -$40- $90
DIAL: $15 - $20 - $40

STYLE NO.25
gold filled : $95- $125 -$275
wind-ind.-DIAL: $40 - $80 - $225

STYLE NO.26
gold filled : $90 - $125 - $200
wind-ind.-DIAL: $40 - $50 - $225

ANTIQUE BOW
gold filled : $95- $125 - $250
DIAL: $30 - $50 - $95

RIGID BOW
gold filled : $95- $125 - $290
DIAL: $30 - $40 - $60

☞ NOTE: Factory Advertised as a complete watch and was fitted with a certain matched, timed and rated movement and sold in the factory designed case style as a complete watch. The factory also sold. uncased movements to jobbers such as jewelry stores & they cased the movement in a case style the customer requested. All the factory advertised complete watches came with a enamel dial shown or choice of other Railroad dials.

ELGIN NATIONAL WATCH CO.

GRADES OF MOVEMENTS
WITH
CLASSIFICATION AND DESCRIPTION
AS ORIGINALLY MADE

Grade.	Class.	Size.		Style.		Model.	Sett.	Train.	Jewels.
Advance........	5	18	F. Pl.	Htg.	Gilded	1st to 4th	Key or Lever	Slow	11
Age............	5	"	"	"	"	"	"	"	7
Avery..........	15	17	"	"	"	1st	Key	"	7
Chief..........	5	18	"	"	"	1st to 4th	Key or Lever	"	7
Culver.........	2	"	"	"	"	"	"	Quick	15
Dexter St......	48	10	¾ Pl.	"	"	1st	Key	"	7
Father Time....	1	18	F. Pl.	"	Nickel	2d to 4th	Lever	"	20–21
Father Time....	1	"	"	"	"	"	"	"	17
Father Time....	7	"	"	O. F.	"	5th	Pend.	"	20–21
Father Time....	7	"	"	"	"	"	"	"	17
Father Time....	65	"	"	"	"	7th	Lever	"	17–21
Father Time....	90	"	¾ Pl.	"	"	8th	"	"	21
Father Time....	99	"	"	Htg.	"	9th	"	"	21
Father Time....	134	"	"	O. F.	"	8th	"	"	21
Father Time....	98	16	"	"	"	15th	"	"	21
Father Time....	126	"	"	Htg.	"	14th	"	"	21
Father Time....	126	"	"	"	"	17th	"	"	21
Fargo..........	5	18	F. Pl.	"	Gilded	1st	Key	Slow	7
Farwell........	5	"	"	"	"	"	"	"	11
Ferry..........	4	"	"	"	"	"	"	"	15
Frances Rubie...	46	10	¾ Pl.	"	"	"	"	Quick	15
Frances Rubie...	76	0	"	"	Nickel	2d	Pend.	"	19
Frances Rubie...	80	"	"	O. F.	"	3d	"	"	19
Gail Borden....	48	10	"	Htg.	Gilded	1st	Key	"	11
Lady Elgin.....	47	"	"	"	"	"	"	"	15
Lady Elgin.....	133	5/0	"	"	Nickel	"	Pend.	"	15
Lady Elgin.....	96	10/0	"	O. F.	"	"	"	"	17
Lady Elgin.....	97	"	"	"	"	"	"	"	15
Lady Raymond..	133	5/0	"	Htg.	"	"	"	"	15
Lady Raymond..	136	"	"	O. F.	"	2d	"	"	15
Laflin.........	4	18	F. Pl.	Htg.	Gilded	1st to 4th	Key or Lever	Slow	7
Leader........	15	17	"	"	"	1st to 2d	"	"	7
Lord Elgin.....	36	16	¾ Pl.	Htg. Br.	Nickel	6th	Pend.	Quick	21
Lord Elgin.....	41	"	"	O. F. Br.	"	7th	"	"	21
Lord Elgin.....	41	"	"	O. F.	"	"	"	"	23
Lord Elgin.....	67	12	"	Htg.	"	2d	"	"	23
Lord Elgin.....	71	"	"	O. F.	"	3d	"	"	23
Lord Elgin.....	135	"	"	"	"	4th	"	"	17
Lord Elgin.....	135	"	"	"	"	"	"	"	21
Ogden.........	5	18	F. Pl.	Htg.	Gilded	1st to 4th	Key or Lever	Slow	11
Overland	3	"	"	"	Nickel	2d to 4th	Lever	Quick	17
Overland......	4	"	"	"	"	"	"	"	17
Overland......	8	"	"	O. F.	"	5th	Pend.	"	17
Overland......	9	"	"	"	"	"	"	"	17
Overland......	66	"	"	"	"	7th	Lever	"	17
Overland......	123	"	"	Htg.	"	2d to 4th	"	"	17
Overland......	124	"	"	O. F.	"	7th	"	"	17
Raymond......	1	"	"	Htg.	Gilded or Nickel	1st to 4th	Key or Lever	"	15–17
Raymond......	7	"	"	O. F.	"	5th	Pend.	"	15–17
Raymond......	65	"	"	"	Nickel	7th	Lever	"	17
Raymond......	91	"	¾ Pl.	"	"	8th	"	"	19
Raymond......	91	"	"	"	"	"	"	"	21
Raymond......	99	"	"	Htg.	"	9th	"	"	21
Raymond......	134	"	"	O. F.	"	8th	"	"	17
Raymond......	98	16	"	"	"	15th	"	"	19
Raymond......	98	"	"	"	"	"	"	"	21
Raymond......	102	"	"	O. F. Br.	"	9th	"	"	17
Raymond......	102	"	"	O. F.	"	13th	"	"	17
Raymond......	102	"	"	"	"	15th	"	"	17
Raymond......	125	"	"	Htg. Br.	"	8th	"	"	17
Raymond......	126	"	"	Htg.	"	14th	"	"	19
Raymond......	126	"	"	"	"	17th	"	"	19
Raymond......	68	12	"	"	"	2d	Pend.	"	19
Raymond......	72	"	"	O. F.	"	3d	"	"	19
Ryerson.......	4	18	F. Pl.	Htg.	Gilded	1st	Key	Slow	7
Taylor.........	3	"	"	"	"	2d to 4th	Lever	"	15
Taylor.........	3	"	"	"	Gilded or Nickel	1st to 4th	Key or Lever	Quick	15
Taylor.........	8	"	"	O. F.	Gilded	5th	Pend.	"	15
Veritas........	89	"	¾ Pl.	"	Nickel	8th	Lever	"	23
Veritas........	90	"	"	"	"	"	"	"	21
Veritas...	99	"	"	Htg.	"	9th	"	"	21
Veritas........	98	16	"	O. F. Br.	"	"	"	"	21
Veritas........	98	"	"	O. F.	"	13th	"	"	21
Veritas........	98	"	"	"	"	"	"	"	23
Veritas........	98	"	"	"	"	15th	"	"	21
Veritas........	132	"	"	"	"	"	"	"	23
Wheeler.......	4	18	F. Pl.	Htg.	Gilded	1st to 4th	Key or Lever	Slow	15
Wheeler.......	4	"	"	"	Gilded or Nickel	"	Lever	Quick	13–15
Wheeler.......	4	"	"	"	"	2d to 4th	"	"	15–17
Wheeler.......	9	"	"	O. F.	"	5th	Pend.	"	15–17

ELGIN NATIONAL WATCH CO.

Grades of Movements with Classification and Description as Originally Made

Grade.	Class.	Size.		Style.		Model.	Sett.	Train.	Jewels.
Wheeler	122	18	F. Pl.	O. F.	Nickel	7th	Lever	Quick	17
Wheeler	123	"	"	Htg.	"	2d to 4th	"	"	17
Wheeler	124	"	"	O. F.	"	7th	"	"	17
Wheeler	130	"	¾ Pl.	Htg.	"	9th	"	"	17
Wheeler	131	"	"	O. F.	"	8th	"	"	17
Wheeler	33	16	"	Htg. Br.	"	6th	Pend.	"	17
Wheeler	38	"	"	O. F. Br.	"	7th	"	"	17
Wheeler	127	"	"	"	"	9th	Lever	"	17
Wheeler	111	12	"	Htg.	"	2d	Pend.	"	17
Wheeler	112	"	"	O. F.	"	3d	"	"	17
No. 1	25	16	"	Htg.	Gilded	"	Lever	"	7
No. 2	25	"	"	"	"	"	"	"	13-15
No. 3	24	"	"	"	"	"	"	"	15
No. 4	24	"	"	"	Nickel	"	"	"	15
No. 5	5	18	F. Pl.	"	"	2d to 4th	"	Q. or S.	11
No. 6	6	"	"	"	Gilded	"	"	Slow	7
No. 7	6	"	"	"	"	1st	Key	"	7
No. 8	5	"	"	"	"	2d to 4th	Lever	"	7
No. 9	5	"	"	"	"	"	"	"	7
No. 10	5	"	"	"	"	"	"	Q. or S.	11
No. 11	15	17	"	"	"	2d	"	Slow	7
No. 12	5	18	"	"	"	1st	Key	"	7
No. 13	5	"	"	"	"	"	"	"	11
No. 14	15	17	"	"	"	"	"	"	7
No. 15	15	"	"	"	"	"	"	"	11
No. 16	4	18	"	"	"	"	"	"	7
No. 17	4	"	"	"	"	"	"	"	11
No. 18	5	"	"	"	"	"	"	"	11
No. 19	5	"	"	"	"	2d to 4th	Lever	"	11
No. 20	3	"	"	"	"	"	"	"	15
No. 21	48	10	¾ Pl.	"	"	1st	Key	Quick	7
No. 22	48	"	"	"	"	"	"	"	11
No. 23	47	"	"	"	"	"	"	"	15
No. 24	45	12	"	"	"	"	"	"	7
No. 25	45	"	"	"	"	"	"	"	11
No. 26	44	"	"	"	"	"	"	"	15
No. 27	1	18	F. Pl.	"	Nickel	2d to 4th	Lever	"	15-17
No. 28	48	10	¾ Pl.	"	Gilded	1st	Key	"	7
No. 29	47	"	"	"	"	"	"	"	11
No. 30	45	12	"	"	"	"	"	"	7
No. 31	45	"	"	"	"	1st	"	"	7
No. 32	44	"	"	"	"	"	"	"	11
No. 33	3	18	F. Pl.	"	Nickel	2d to 4th	Lever	"	15
No. 34	43	14	¾ Pl.	"	Gilded	1st	Key	"	7
No. 35	43	"	"	"	"	"	"	"	7
No. 36	43	"	"	"	"	"	"	"	11
No. 37	42	"	"	"	"	"	"	"	15
No. 38	3	18	F. Pl.	"	"	"	"	Slow	15
No. 39	43	14	¾ Pl.	"	"	"	"	Quick	13
No. 40	43	"	"	"	"	"	"	"	7
No. 41	42	"	"	"	"	"	"	"	13
No. 42	42	"	"	"	"	"	"	"	15
No. 43	10	18	F. Pl.	O. F.	Nickel	5th	Pend.	"	11
No. 44	9	"	¾ Pl.	Htg.	"	"	"	"	15
No. 45	51	6	¾ Pl.	Htg.	"	1st	Lever	"	13
No. 46	42	14	"	"	"	"	Key	"	15
No. 47	19	16	"	Htg. and O.F.	Gilded	"	Lever	"	7
No. 48	18	"	"	"	"	"	"	"	13
No. 49	17	"	"	"	"	"	"	"	15
No. 50	17	"	"	"	Nickel	"	"	"	15
No. 51	15	17	F. Pl.	Htg.	Gilded	1st	Key	Slow	7
No. 52	15	"	"	"	"	"	"	"	11
No. 53	48	10	¾ Pl.	"	"	"	"	Quick	7
No. 54	48	"	"	"	"	"	"	"	13
No. 55	5	18	F. Pl.	"	"	"	"	Slow	7
No. 56	4	"	"	"	"	"	"	"	11
No. 57	4	"	"	"	"	"	"	"	13
No. 58	3	"	"	"	"	"	"	"	15
No. 59	15	17	"	"	"	"	"	"	7
No. 60	5	18	"	"	"	"	"	"	7
No. 61	2	"	"	"	"	2d to 4th	Lever	Quick	15
No. 62	2	"	"	"	"	1st	Key	"	15
No. 63	4	"	"	"	"	2d to 4th	Lever	Slow	13
No. 64	51	6	¾ Pl.	"	"	1st	"	Quick	7
No. 65	51	"	"	"	"	"	"	"	13
No. 66	50	"	"	"	"	"	"	"	15
No. 67	50	"	"	"	Nickel	"	"	"	15
No. 68	5	18	F. Pl.	"	Gilded	2d to 4th	"	Slow	7
No. 69	1	"	"	"	"	1st	Key	Quick	15
No. 70	1	"	"	"	"	2d to 4th	Lever	"	15-17
No. 71	49	6	¾ Pl.	"	Nickel	1st	"	"	17
No. 72	16	18	"	Htg. and O.F.	"	"	"	"	21
No. 73	11	18	F. Pl.	O. F.	Gilded	5th	Pend.	"	7
No. 74	10	"	"	"	"	"	"	"	11
No. 75	9	"	"	"	"	"	"	"	15
No. 76	8	"	"	"	"	"	"	"	15
No. 77	7	"	"	"	"	"	"	"	15-17
No. 78	5	"	"	Htg.	Nickel	1st	Key	Q. or S.	11
No. 79	3	"	"	"	Gilded	"	"	Quick	15

ELGIN NATIONAL WATCH CO.

Grades of Movement with Classification and Description as Originally Made.

Grade.	Class.	Size.		Style.		Model.	Sett.	Train.	Jewels.
No. 80	3	18	F. Pl.	Htg.	Gilded	2d to 4th	Lever	Quick	15
No. 81	4	"	"	"	"	1st	Key	"	13–15
No. 82	4	"	"	"	"	2d to 4th	Lever	"	13–15
No. 83	27	16	¾ Pl.	S. Sec.	"	4th	"	"	15
No. 84	27	"	"	"	Nickel	"	"	"	15
No. 85	22	"	"	Htg. and O.F.	Gilded	2d	"	"	15
No. 86	22	"	"	"	Nickel	"	"	"	15
No. 87	5	18	F. Pl.	Htg.	"	1st	Key	"	11
No. 88	5	"	"	"	"	2d to 4th	Lever	"	11
No. 89	28	16	¾ Pl.	S. Sec.	Gilded	4th	"	"	13
No. 90	23	"	"	Htg. and O.F.	"	2d	"	"	13
No. 91	21	"	"	"	Nickel	"	"	"	21
No. 92	26	"	"	Htg.	Gilded	3d	"	"	11
No. 93	20	"	"	Htg. and O.F.	"	1st	"	"	11
No. 94	52	6	"	Htg.	"	"	"	"	11
No. 95	52	"	"	"	"	"	"	"	7
No. 96	6	18	F. Pl.	"	"	2d to 4th	"	"	7
No. 97	6	"	"	"	"	1st	Key	"	7
No. 98	14	"	¾ Pl.	Htg. and O.F.	"	6th	Pend.	"	7
No. 99	13	"	"	"	"	"	"	"	11
No. 100	12	"	"	"	"	"	"	"	15
No. 101	52	6	"	Htg.	Nickel	1st	Lever	"	11
No. 102	5	18	F. Pl.	"	"	2d to 4th	"	"	11
No. 103	4	"	"	"	"	"	"	"	15
No. 104	31	16	¾ Pl.	O. F.	Gilded	5th	Pend.	"	7
No. 105	31	"	"	"	"	"	"	"	11
No. 106	30	"	"	"	"	"	"	"	13–15
No. 107	29	"	"	"	"	"	"	"	15
No. 108	29	"	"	"	Nickel	"	"	"	15
No. 109	60	0	"	Htg.	Gilded	1st	"	"	7
No. 110	60	"	"	"	Nickel	"	"	"	11
No. 111	58	"	"	"	"	"	"	"	15
No. 112	57	"	"	"	"	"	"	"	17
No. 113	60	"	"	"	Gilded	"	"	"	11
No. 114	26	16	"	"	"	3d	"	"	7
No. 115	59	0	"	"	Nickel	1st	"	"	13
No. 116	7	18	F. Pl.	O. F.	"	5th	"	"	15–17
No. 117	56	6	¾ Pl.	Htg.	Gilded	2d	"	"	7
No. 118	56	"	"	"	"	"	"	"	11
No. 119	56	"	"	"	Nickel	"	"	"	11
No. 120	55	"	"	"	"	"	"	"	13
No. 121	54	"	"	"	"	"	"	"	15
No. 122	53	"	"	"	"	"	"	"	17
No. 123	9	18	F. Pl.	O. F.	Gilded	5th	"	"	15
No. 124	9	"	"	"	Nickel	"	"	"	15
No. 125	4	"	"	Htg.	Gilded	2d to 4th	Lever	"	15
No. 126	4	"	"	"	Nickel	"	"	"	15
No. 127	26	16	¾ Pl.	"	"	3d	"	"	11
No. 128	31	"	"	O. F.	"	5th	Pend.	"	11
No. 129	60	0	"	Htg.	Gilded	1st	"	"	15
No. 130	60	"	"	"	Nickel	"	"	"	15
No. 131	58	"	"	"	"	"	"	"	15
No. 132	56	6	"	"	Gilded	2d	"	"	15
No. 133	56	"	"	"	Nickel	"	"	"	15
No. 134	54	"	"	"	"	"	"	"	15
No. 135	26	16	"	"	Gilded	3d	Lever	"	15
No. 136	26	"	"	"	Nickel	"	"	"	15
No. 137	25	"	"	"	Gilded	"	"	"	13–15
No. 138	31	"	"	O. F.	"	5th	Pend.	"	15
No. 139	31	"	"	"	Nickel	"	"	"	15
No. 140	30	"	"	"	Gilded	"	"	"	13–15
No. 141	5	18	F. Pl.	Htg.	"	2d to 4th	Lever	"	15
No. 142	5	"	"	"	Nickel	"	"	"	15
No. 143	4	"	"	"	Gilded	"	"	"	15–17
No. 144	4	"	"	"	Nickel	"	"	"	15–17
No. 145	10	"	"	O. F.	Gilded	5th	Pend.	"	15
No. 146	10	"	"	"	Nickel	"	"	"	15
No. 147	9	"	"	"	Gilded	"	"	"	15–17
No. 148	9	"	"	"	Nickel	"	"	"	15–17
No. 149	1	"	"	Htg.	"	2d to 4th	Lever	"	20–21
No. 150	7	"	"	O. F.	"	5th	Pend.	"	20–21
No. 151	35	16	¾ Pl.	Htg.	Gilded	6th	"	"	7
No. 152	35	"	"	"	Nickel	"	"	"	15
No. 153	34	"	"	"	"	"	"	"	17
No. 154	33	"	"	"	"	"	"	"	17
No. 155	32	"	"	"	"	"	"	"	17
No. 156	36	"	"	Htg. Br.	"	"	"	"	21
No. 157	40	"	"	O. F.	Gilded	7th	"	"	7
No. 158	40	"	"	"	Nickel	"	"	"	15
No. 159	39	"	"	"	"	"	"	"	17
No. 160	38	"	"	"	"	"	"	"	17
No. 161	37	"	"	"	"	"	"	"	17
No. 162	41	"	"	O. F. Br.	"	"	"	"	21
No. 163	3	18	F. Pl.	Htg.	"	2d to 4th	Lever	"	17
No. 164	1	"	"	"	"	"	"	"	17
No. 165	8	"	"	O. F.	"	5th	Pend.	"	17
No. 166	7	"	"	"	"	"	"	"	17
No. 167	58	0	¾ Pl.	Htg.	"	1st	"	"	16
No. 168	54	6	"	"	"	2d	"	"	16

ELGIN NATIONAL WATCH CO.

Grades of Movements with Classification and Description as Originally Made.

Grade.	Class.	Size.		Style.		Model.	Sett.	Train.	Jewels.
No. 169	5	18	F. Pl.	Htg.	Nickel	2d to 4th	Lever	Quick	15
No. 170	10	"	"	O. F.	"	5th	Pend.	"	15
No. 171	6	"	"	Htg.	"	2d to 4th	Lever	"	7
No. 172	11	"	"	O. F.	"	5th	Pend.	"	7
No. 173	60	0	¾ Pl.	Htg.	"	1st	"	"	7
No. 174	57	"	"	"	"	"	"	"	17
No. 175	56	6	"	"	"	2d	"	"	7
No. 176	53	"	"	"	"	"	"	"	17
No. 177	..	"	"	"	..	"	"	"	7
No. 178	..	18	F. Pl.	"	..	2d to 4th	Lever	"	7
No. 179	..	"	"	O. F.	..	5th	Pend.	"	7
No. 180	65	"	"	"	Nickel	7th	Lever	"	17
No. 181	65	"	"	"	"	"	"	"	21
No. 182	31	16	¾ Pl.	"	Gilded	5th	Pend.	"	7
No. 183	1	18	F. Pl.	Htg.	Nickel	2d to 4th	Lever	"	17
No. 184	7	"	"	O. F.	"	5th	Pend.	"	17
No. 185	35	16	¾ Pl.	Htg.	Gilded	6th	"	"	15
No. 186	40	"	"	O. F.	"	7th	"	"	15
No. 187	70	12	"	Htg.	Nickel	2d	"	"	15
No. 188	69	"	"	"	"	"	"	"	17
No. 189	68	"	"	"	"	"	"	"	19
No. 190	67	"	"	"	"	"	"	"	23
No. 191	74	"	"	O. F.	"	3d	"	"	15
No. 192	73	"	"	"	"	"	"	"	17
No. 193	72	"	"	"	"	"	"	"	19
No. 194	71	"	"	"	"	"	"	"	23
No. 195	31	16	"	"	Gilded	5th	"	"	15
No. 196	70	12	"	Htg.	Nickel	2d	"	"	7
No. 197	74	"	"	O. F.	"	3d	"	"	7
No. 198	79	0	"	Htg.	"	2d	"	"	7
No. 199	78	"	"	"	"	"	"	"	15
No. 200	77	"	"	"	"	"	"	"	17
No. 201	76	"	"	"	"	"	"	"	19
No. 202	83	"	"	O. F.	"	3d	"	"	7
No. 203	82	"	"	"	"	"	"	"	15
No. 204	81	"	"	"	"	"	"	"	17
No. 205	80	"	"	"	"	"	"	"	19
No. 206	75	6	"	Htg.	"	2d	"	"	7
No. 207	61	18	F. Pl.	"	"	2d to 4th	Lever	"	7
No. 208	63	"	"	O. F.	"	5th	Pend.	"	7
No. 209	75	6	¾ Pl.	Htg.	Gilded	2d	"	"	7
No. 210	92	16	"	"	Nickel	6th	"	"	7
No. 211	94	"	"	O. F.	"	7th	"	"	7
No. 212	92	"	"	Htg.	Gilded	6th	"	"	7
No. 213	94	"	"	O. F.	"	7th	"	"	7
No. 214	89	18	"	"	Nickel	8th	Lever	"	23
No. 215	63	"	F. Pl.	"	Gilded	5th	Pend.	"	7
No. 216	75	6	¾ Pl.	Htg.	Nickel	2d	"	"	15
No. 217	61	18	F. Pl.	"	"	2d to 4th	Lever	"	15
No. 218	63	"	"	O. F.	"	5th	Pend.	"	15
No. 219	84	0	¾ Pl.	Htg.	Gilded	1st	"	"	7
No. 220	92	16	"	"	Nickel	6th	"	"	15
No. 221	94	"	"	O. F.	"	7th	"	"	15
No. 222	84	0	"	Htg.	"	1st	"	"	7
No. 223	84	"	"	"	"	"	"	"	15
No. 224	85	"	"	"	"	2d	"	"	11
No. 225	86	"	"	O. F.	"	3d	"	"	11
No. 226	5	18	F. Pl.	Htg.	Gilded	2d to 4th	Lever	"	17
No. 227	10	"	"	O. F.	"	5th	Pend.	"	17
No. 228	5	"	"	Htg.	Nickel	2d to 4th	Lever	"	17
No. 229	10	"	"	O. F.	"	5th	Pend.	"	17
No. 230	56	6	¾ Pl.	Htg.	Gilded	2d	"	"	16
No. 231	56	"	"	"	Nickel	"	"	"	16
No. 232	87	12	"	"	"	"	"	"	7
No. 233	87	"	"	"	"	"	"	"	15
No. 234	88	"	"	O. F.	"	3d	"	"	7
No. 235	88	"	"	"	"	"	"	"	15
No. 236	68	"	"	Htg.	"	2d	"	"	21
No. 237	72	"	"	O. F.	"	3d	"	"	21
No. 238	61	18	F. Pl.	Htg.	Gilded	1st	Key	"	7
No. 239	90	"	¾ Pl.	O. F.	Nickel	8th	Lever	"	21
No. 240	91	"	"	"	"	"	"	"	19
No. 241	33	16	"	Htg. Br.	"	6th	Pend.	"	17
No. 242	33	"	"	"	"	"	"	"	17
No. 243	32	"	"	"	"	"	"	"	17
No. 244	38	"	"	O. F. Br.	"	7th	"	"	17
No. 245	38	"	"	"	"	"	"	"	17
No. 246	37	"	"	"	"	"	"	"	17
No. 247	93	"	"	Htg. Br.	"	6th	"	"	15
No. 248	95	"	"	O. F. Br.	"	7th	"	"	15
No. 249	62	18	F. Pl.	Htg.	Gilded	2d to 4th	Lever	"	17
No. 250	64	"	"	O. F.	"	5th	Pend.	"	17
No. 251	61	"	"	Htg.	"	2d to 4th	Lever	"	7
No. 252	65	"	"	O. F.	Nickel	7th	"	"	21
No. 253	87	12	¾ Pl.	Htg.	Gilded	2d	Pend.	"	7
No. 254	88	"	"	O. F.	"	3d	"	"	7
No. 255	97	10/0	"	"	Nickel	1st	"	"	15
No. 256	96	"	"	"	"	"	"	"	17
No. 257	92	16	"	Htg.	"	6th	"	"	15

ELGIN NATIONAL WATCH CO.

Grades of Movements with Classification and Description as Originally Made.

Grade.	Class.	Size.		Style.		Model.	Sett.	Train.	Jewels.
No. 258	94	16	¾ Pl.	O. F.	Nickel	7th	Pend.	Quick	15
No. 259	87	12	"	Htg.	"	2d	"	"	15
No. 260	88	"	"	O. F.	"	3d	"	"	15
No. 261	61	18	F. Pl.	Htg.	"	2d to 4th	Lever	"	15
No. 262	63	"	"	O. F.	"	5th	Pend.	"	15
No. 263	77	0	¾ Pl.	Htg.	"	2d	"	"	17
No. 264	81	"	"	O. F.	"	3d	"	"	17
No. 265	66	18	F. Pl.	"	"	7th	Lever	"	17
No. 266	65	"	"	"	"	"	"	"	17–21
No. 267	85	0	¾ Pl.	Htg.	"	2d	Pend.	"	15
No. 268	86	"	"	O. F.	"	3d	"	"	15
No. 269	85	"	"	Htg.	"	2d	"	"	7
No. 270	98	16	"	O. F. Br.	"	9th	Lever	"	21
No. 271	60	0	"	Htg.	"	1st	Pend.	"	16
No. 272	56	6	"	"	"	2d	"	"	16
No. 273	65	18	F. Pl.	O. F.	"	7th	Lever	"	17
No. 274	99	"	¾ Pl.	Htg.	"	9th	"	"	21
No. 275	100	12	"	"	"	2d	Pend.	"	17
No. 276	101	"	"	O. F.	"	3d	"	"	17
No. 277	65	18	F. Pl.	"	"	7th	Lever	"	21
No. 278	4	"	"	Htg.	"	2d to 4th	"	"	17
No. 279	9	"	"	O. F.	"	5th	Pend.	"	17
No. 280	102	16	¾ Pl.	O. F. Br.	"	9th	Lever	"	17
No. 281	85	0	"	Htg.	"	2d	Pend.	"	11
No. 282	86	"	"	O. F.	"	3d	"	"	7
No. 283	66	18	F. Pl.	"	"	7th	Lever	"	17
No. 284	75	6	¾ Pl.	Htg.	Gilded	2d	Pend.	"	15
No. 285	63	18	F. Pl.	O. F.	"	5th	"	"	15
No. 286	115	6	¾ Pl.	Htg.	Nickel	2d	"	"	7
No. 287	105	18	F. Pl.	"	"	2d to 4th	Lever	"	7
No. 288	106	"	"	O. F.	"	5th	Pend.	"	7
No. 289	115	6	¾ Pl.	Htg.	Gilded	2d	"	"	7
No. 290	109	16	"	"	Nickel	6th	"	"	7
No. 291	110	"	"	O. F.	"	7th	"	"	7
No. 292	109	"	"	Htg.	Gilded	6th	"	"	7
No. 293	110	"	"	O. F.	"	7th	"	"	7
No. 294	106	18	F. Pl.	"	"	5th	"	"	7
No. 295	115	6	¾ Pl.	Htg.	Nickel	2d	"	"	15
No. 296	105	18	F. Pl.	"	"	2d to 4th	Lever	"	15
No. 297	106	"	"	O. F.	"	5th	Pend.	"	15
No. 298	116	0	¾ Pl.	Htg.	Gilded	2d	"	"	7
No. 299	109	16	"	"	Nickel	6th	"	"	15
No. 300	110	"	"	O. F.	"	7th	"	"	15
No. 301	113	12	"	Htg.	"	2d	"	"	7
No. 302	113	"	"	"	"	"	"	"	15
No. 303	114	"	"	O. F.	"	3d	"	"	7
No. 304	114	"	"	"	"	"	"	"	15
No. 305	107	16	"	Htg. Br.	"	6th	"	"	15
No. 306	108	"	"	O. F. Br.	"	7th	"	"	15
No. 307	103	18	F. Pl.	Htg.	Gilded	2d to 4th	Lever	"	17
No. 308	104	"	"	O. F.	"	5th	Pend.	"	17
No. 309	105	"	"	Htg.	"	2d to 4th	Lever	"	7
No. 310	113	12	¾ Pl.	"	"	2d	Pend.	"	7
No. 311	114	"	"	O. F.	"	3d	"	"	7
No. 312	109	16	"	Htg.	Nickel	6th	"	"	15
No. 313	110	"	"	O. F.	"	7th	"	"	15
No. 314	113	12	"	Htg.	"	2d	"	"	15
No. 315	114	"	"	O. F.	"	3d	"	"	15
No. 316	105	18	F. Pl.	Htg.	"	2d to 4th	Lever	"	15
No. 317	106	"	"	O. F.	"	5th	Pend.	"	15
No. 318	116	0	¾ Pl.	Htg.	"	2d	"	"	15
No. 319	117	"	"	O. F.	"	3d	"	"	15
No. 320	116	"	"	Htg.	"	2d	"	"	7
No. 321	111	12	"	"	"	"	"	"	17
No. 322	112	"	"	O. F.	"	3d	"	"	17
No. 323	116	0	"	Htg.	"	2d	"	"	11
No. 324	117	"	"	O. F.	"	3d	"	"	7
No. 325	115	6	"	Htg.	Gilded	2d	"	"	15
No. 326	106	18	F. Pl.	O. F.	"	5th	Lever	"	15
No. 327	118	"	"	Htg.	Nickel	10th	Lever	"	16
No. 328	118	"	"	"	"	"	"	"	17
No. 329	119	"	"	"	"	"	"	"	17
No. 330	119	"	"	"	"	"	"	"	21
No. 331	120	"	"	O. F.	"	11th	Pend.	"	16
No. 332	120	"	"	"	"	"	"	"	17
No. 333	121	"	"	"	"	"	Lever	"	17
No. 334	121	"	"	"	"	"	"	"	21
No. 335	105	"	"	Htg.	"	4th	"	"	17
No. 336	106	"	"	O. F.	"	5th	Pend.	"	17
No. 337	33	16	¾ Pl.	Htg. Br.	"	6th	"	"	17
No. 338	38	"	"	O. F. Br.	"	7th	"	"	17
No. 339	107	"	"	Htg. Br.	"	6th	"	"	17
No. 340	108	"	"	O. F. Br.	"	7th	"	"	17
No. 341	125	"	"	Htg. Br.	"	8th	Lever	"	17
No. 342	127	"	"	O. F. Br.	"	9th	"	"	17
No. 343	122	18	F. Pl.	O. F.	"	7th	"	"	17
No. 344	113	12	¾ Pl.	Htg.	"	2d	Pend.	"	17
No. 345	114	"	"	O. F.	"	3d	"	"	17
No. 346	111	"	"	Htg.	"	2d	"	"	17

ELGIN NATIONAL WATCH CO.

Grades of Movements with Classification and Description as Originally Made.

Grade.	Class.	Size.		Style.		Model.	Sett.	Train.	Jewels.
No. 347	112	12	¾ Pl.	O. F.	Nickel	3d	Pend.	Quick	17
No. 348	1	18	F. Pl.	Htg.	"	2d to 4th	Lever	"	21
No. 349	65	"	"	O. F.	"	7th	"	"	21
No. 350	98	16	¾ Pl.	"	"	13th	"	"	23
No. 351	41	"	"	"	"	7th	Pend.	"	23
No. 352	123	18	F. Pl.	Htg.	"	2d to 4th	Lever	"	17
No. 353	124	"	"	O. F.	"	7th	"	"	17
No. 354	116	0	¾ Pl.	Htg.	"	2d	Pend.	"	15
No. 355	117	"	"	O. F.	"	3d	"	"	15
No. 356	128	14	"	"	"	2d	"	"	7
No. 357	128	"	"	"	"	"	"	"	15
No. 358	128	"	"	"	"	"	"	"	17
No. 359	129	"	"	"	"	"	"	"	17
No. 360	98	16	"	"	"	13th	Lever	"	21
No. 361	102	"	"	"	"	"	"	"	17
No. 363	113	12	"	Htg.	Gilded	2d	Pend.	"	15
No. 364	114	"	"	O. F.	"	3d	"	"	15
No. 365	109	16	"	Htg.	"	6th	"	"	15
No. 366	110	"	"	O. F.	"	7th	"	"	15
No. 367	90	18	"	"	Nickel	8th	Lever	"	21
No. 368	130	"	"	Htg.	"	9th	"	"	17
No. 369	131	"	"	O. F.	"	8th	"	"	17
No. 370	102	16	"	"	"	15th	"	"	17
No. 371	126	"	"	Htg.	"	14th	"	"	19
No. 372	98	"	"	O. F.	"	15th	"	"	19
No. 373	126	"	"	Htg.	"	14th	"	"	21
No. 374	98	"	"	O. F.	"	15th	"	"	21
No. 375	98	"	"	"	"	"	"	"	21
No. 376	132	"	"	"	"	"	"	"	23
No. 377	116	0	"	Htg.	Gilded	2d	Pend.	"	15
No. 378	105	18	F. Pl.	"	Nickel	2d to 4th	Lever	"	17
No. 379	106	"	"	O. F.	"	5th	Pend.	"	17
No. 380	133	5/0	¾ Pl.	Htg.	"	1st	"	"	15
No. 381	107	16	"	Htg. Br.	"	6th	"	"	17
No. 382	108	"	"	O. F. Br.	"	7th	"	"	17
No. 383	113	12	"	Htg.	"	2d	"	"	17
No. 384	114	"	"	O. F.	"	3d	"	"	17
No. 385	134	18	"	"	"	8th	Lever	"	17
No. 386	109	16	"	Htg.	"	6th	Pend.	"	17
No. 387	110	"	"	O. F.	"	7th	"	"	17
No. 388	98	"	"	"	"	15th	Lever	"	21
No. 389	134	18	"	"	"	8th	"	"	21
No. 390	91	"	"	"	"	"	"	"	21
No. 391	98	16	"	"	"	15th	"	"	21
No. 392	135	12	"	"	"	4th	Pend.	"	17
No. 393	113	"	"	Htg.	Gilded	2d	"	"	7
No. 394	114	"	"	O. F.	"	3d	"	"	7
No. 395	113	"	"	Htg.	"	2d	"	"	15
No. 396	114	"	"	O. F.	"	3d	"	"	15
No. 397	33	16	"	Htg. Br.	Nickel	6th	"	"	17
No. 398	38	"	"	O. F. Br.	"	7th	"	"	17
No. 399	136	5/0	"	O. F.	"	2d	"	"	15
No. 400	131	18	"	"	"	8th	Lever	"	17
No. 401	126	16	"	Htg.	"	17th	"	"	19
No. 402	126	"	"	"	"	"	"	"	21
No. 403	133	5/0	"	"	"	1st	Pend.	"	7
No. 404	97	10/0	"	O. F.	"	"	"	"	15
No. 405	96	"	"	"	"	"	"	"	17
No. 406	116	0	"	Htg.	Gilded	2d	"	"	13
No. 407	135	12	"	O. F.	Nickel	4th	"	"	21
No. 408	133	5/0	"	Htg.	"	1st	"	"	15
No. 409	117	0	"	O. F.	Gilded	3d	"	"	7
No. 410	117	"	"	"	"	"	"	"	15
No. 411	106	18	F. Pl.	"	Nickel	5th	"	"	21
No. 412	91	"	¾ Pl.	"	"	8th	Lever	"	21
No. 413	116	3/0	"	Htg.	"	2d	Pend.	"	7
No. 414	117	"	"	O. F.	"	3d	"	"	7
No. 415	116	"	"	Htg.	"	2d	"	"	15
No. 416	117	"	"	O. F.	"	3d	"	"	15

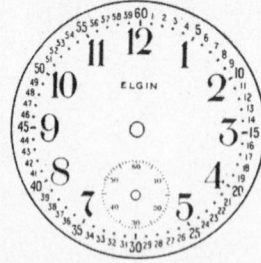

Left Dial: 18 & 16 size=$30-$50-$100
Left Dial: 12 size=$25-$35-$60
Left Dial: 6 & 0 size=$15-$2-$45

Center: wind-ind. 18 size=$55-$85-$275
Center: wind-ind. 16 size=$55-$65-$275

Right: 24 Hr. 18 size=$35-$55-$125
Right: 24 Hr. 16 size=$35-$55.$125
Right: 24 Hr. 12 size=$30-$45-$100

ELGIN NATIONAL WATCH CO.

IDENTIFICATION OF MOVEMENTS
BY MODEL NUMBER

How to Identify Your Watch Size & Model: Compare the movement of your watch with the illustrations in this section. While comparing, note the location of the balance, jewels, screws, gears, and type of back plate (Full, 3/4, Bridge) these will be clues in identifying the movement you have.

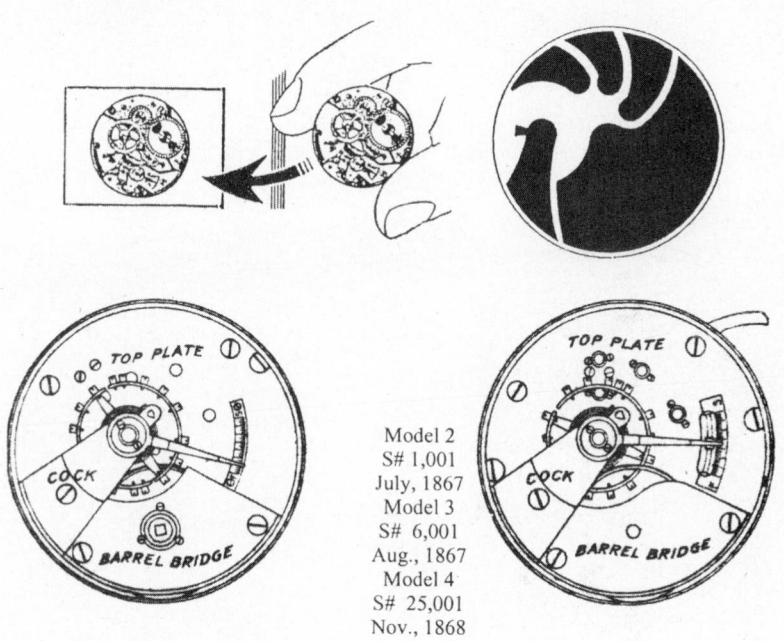

Model 2
S# 1,001
July, 1867
Model 3
S# 6,001
Aug., 1867
Model 4
S# 25,001
Nov., 1868

Model 1, 18 size, full plate, hunting, key wind & set, first serial number 101, Apr., 1867.

Model 2-4, 18 size, full plate, hunting, lever set,

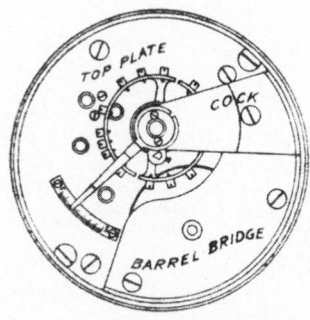

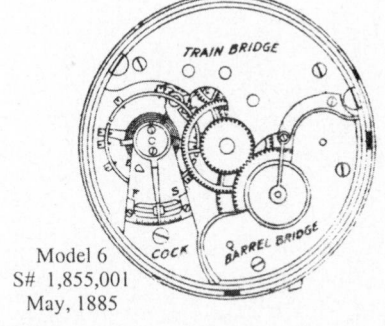

Model 6
S# 1,855,001
May, 1885

Model 5, 18 size, full plate, open face, pendant set, first serial number, 2,110,001, Grade 43, Dec., 1885.

Model 6, 18 size, three-quarter plate, hunting, open face, pendant set.

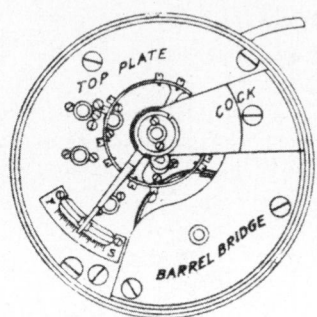

Model 7, 18 size, fu" plate, open face, lever set, first serial number 6,563,821, Grade 265, Apr., 1897.

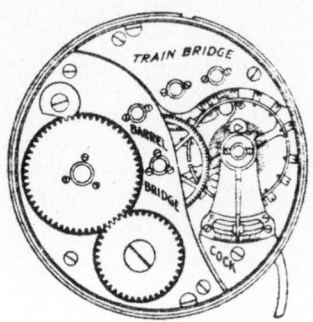

Model 8, 18 size, three-quarter plate, open face, lever set, first serial number 8,400,001, Grade 214, Dec., 1900.

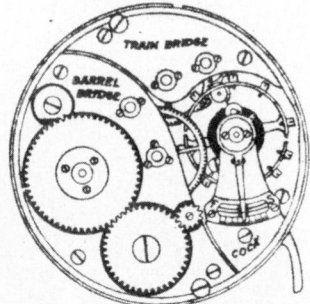

Model 8, 18 size, three-quarter plate, open face, lever set with winding indicator.

Model 9, 18 size, three-quarter plate, hunting, lever set, first serial number 9,625,001, Grade 274, May, 1904.

Model 9, 18 size, three-quarter plate, hunting, lever set with winding indicator.

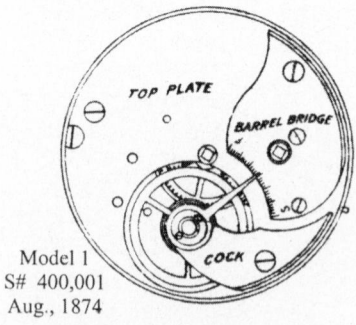

Model 1
S# 400,001
Aug., 1874

Model 1, 17 size, full plate, hunting, Key wind and set from the back.

Note: Model is not the same defination as grade. A model may exist in many different grades or grade names (as B.W. Raymond) and may be used in many different models (as model 1, 18 size, open or hunting case, model 1, in 16 size open or hunting case, model 1 in 12 size) etc..

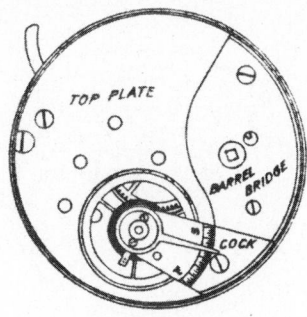

Model 2, 17 size, full plate, hunting, lever set.

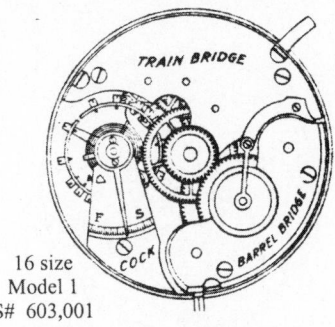

16 size
Model 1
S# 603,001

Model 1, 16 size, three-quarter plate, hunting & open face, lever set.

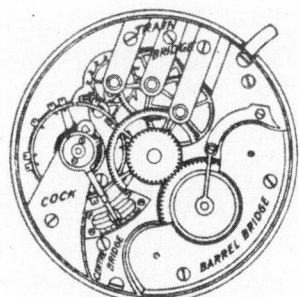

Model 2, 16 size, three-quarter plate, bridge, hunting & open face, lever set.

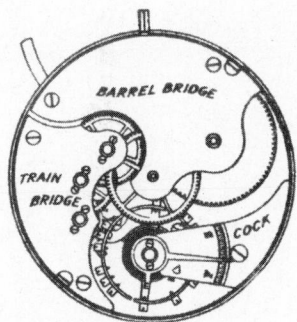

Model 3, 16 size, three-quarter plate, hunting, lever set, first serial number 625,001, Grade 1, Feb., 1879.

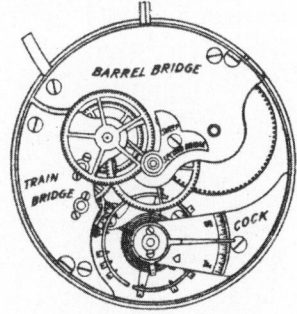

Model 4, 16 size, three-quarter plate, sweep second, hunting & open face, lever set.

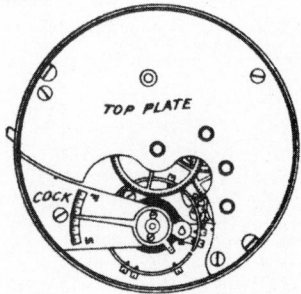

Model 5, 16 size, three-quarter plate, open face, pendant set.

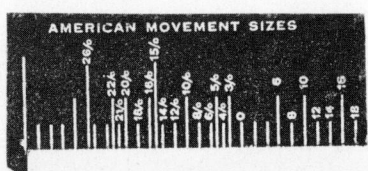

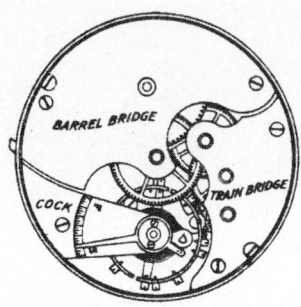

Model 5, 16 size, three-quarter plate, open face, pendant set, first serial number 2,811,001, Grade 105, Oct., 1887.

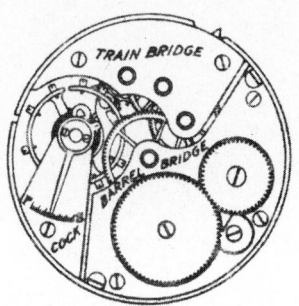

Model 6, 16 size, three-quarter plate, hunting, pendant set, first serial number 6,458,001, Grade 151, Aug., 1895.

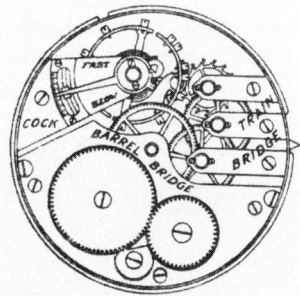

Model 6, 16 size, three-quarter plate, bridge, hunting, pendant set, first serial number 6,463,001, Grade 156, May, 1896.

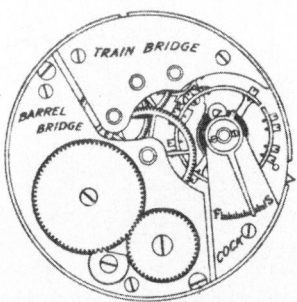

Model 7, 16 size, three-quarter plate, open face, pendant set, first serial number 6,464,001. Grade 157, Sept., 1895.

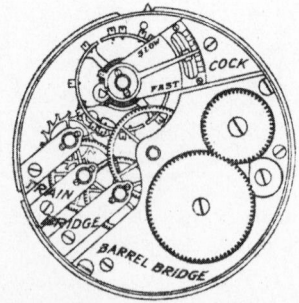

Model 7, 16 size, three-quarter plate, bridge, open face, pendant set, first serial number 6,469,001, Grade 162, Apr., 1896.

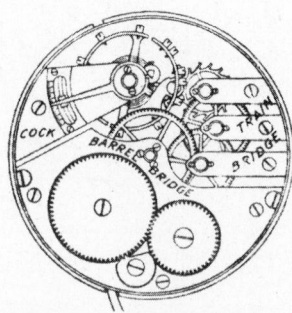

Model 8, 16 size, three-quarter plate, bridge, hunting, lever set, serial number 12,283,001, Grade 341, Jan., 1907.

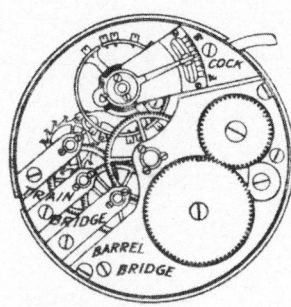

Model 9, 16 size, three-quarter plate, bridge, open face, lever set, first serial number 9,250,001, Grade 270, July, 1902.

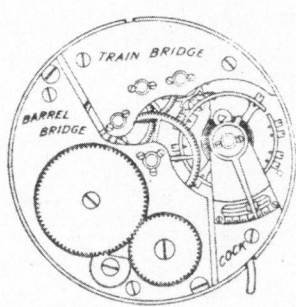

Model 13, 16 size, three-quarter plate, open face, lever set, first serial number 12,717,001, Grade 350, June, 1908.

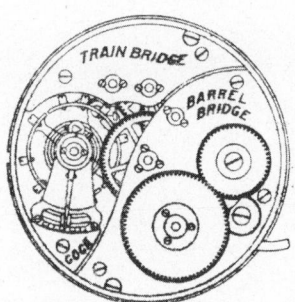

Model 14, 16 size, three quarter plate, hunting, lever set.

Model 15, 16 size, three quarter-plate, open face, lever set.

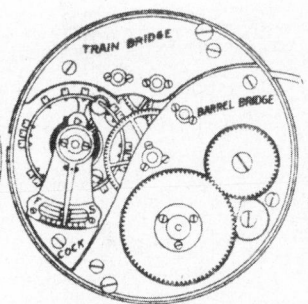

Model 17, 16 size, three quarter-plate, hunting, lever set.

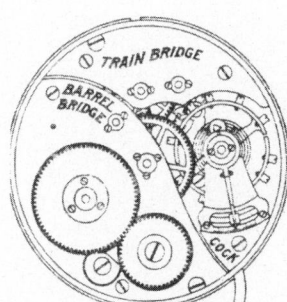

Model 19, 16 size, three quarter plate, open face, lever set with. Winding indicator.

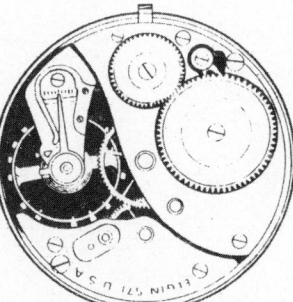

Model 20, 16 size, three quarter plate, open face, Grades 571, 572, 573, 574, 575, 616.

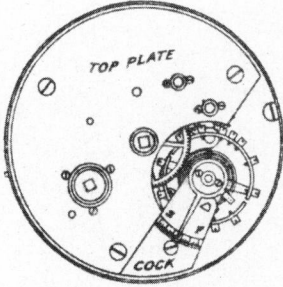

Model 1, 14 size, three quarter plate, hunting, key wind and set.

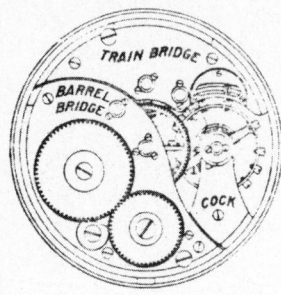

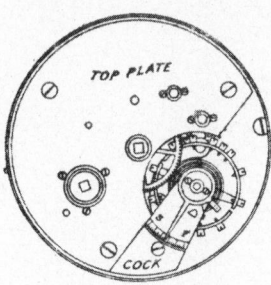

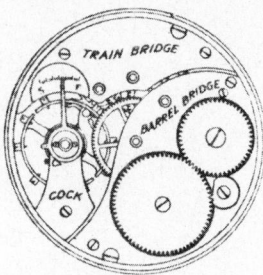

Model 2, 14 size, three quarter plate, open face, pendant set.

Model 1, 12 size, three quarter plate, hunting, key wind and set.

Model 2, 12 size, three-quarter plate, hunting, pendant set, first serial #7,410,001, Grade 188, Dec., 1897.

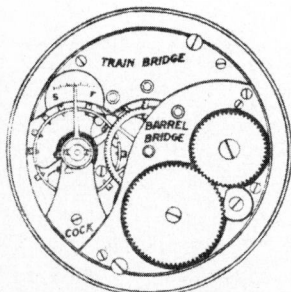

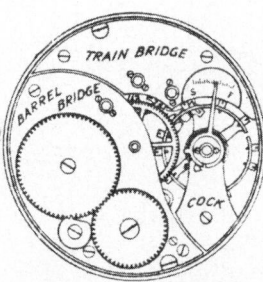

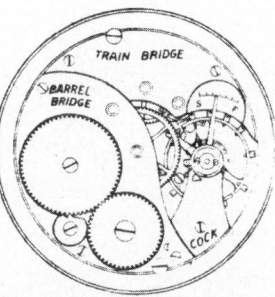

Model 2, 12 size, three-quarter plate, spread to 16 size, hunting, pendant set.

Model 3, 12 size, three quarter plate, open face, pendant set, serial number 7,423,001, Grade 192, May 1898.

Model 3, 12 size, three quarter plate, spread to16 size, open face, pendant set.

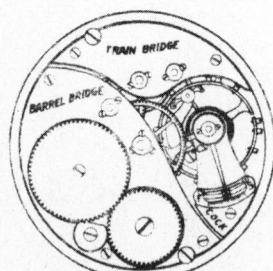

Model 4, 12 size, three-quarter plate, open face, pendant set, serial number 16,311,001, Grade 392, July, 1912.

Model 1, 10 size, three-quarter plate, style 1, hunting, key wind and set.

Model 2, 10 size, three-quarter plate, hunting, key wind and set.

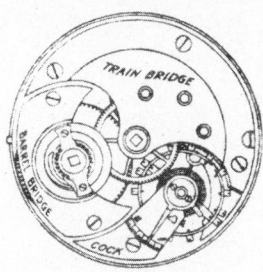

Model 3, 10 size, three-quarter plate, hunting.

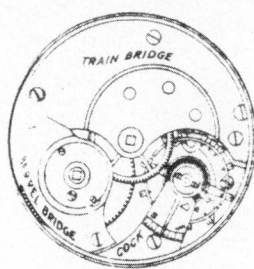

Model 4, 10 size, three-quarter plate, hunting.

Model 5 & 6, 10 size, three-quarter plate.

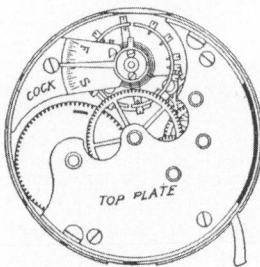

Model 1, 6 size, three-quarter plate, hunting.

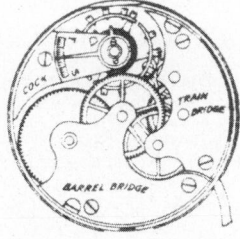

Model 1, 6 size, three-quarter plate, hunting.

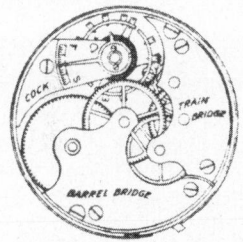

Model 2, 6 size, three-quarter plate, hunting.

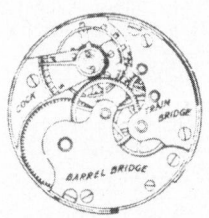

Model 1, 0 size, three-quarter plate, hunting.

Model 2, 0 size, three-quarter plate, hunting.

Model 2, 0 size, three-quarter plate, hunting.

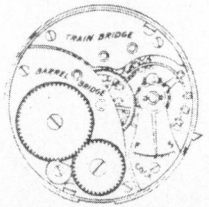

Model 3, 0 size, three-quarter plate, open face.

Model 3, 0 size, three-quarter plate, open face.

Model 2, 3-0 size, three-quarter plate, hunting.

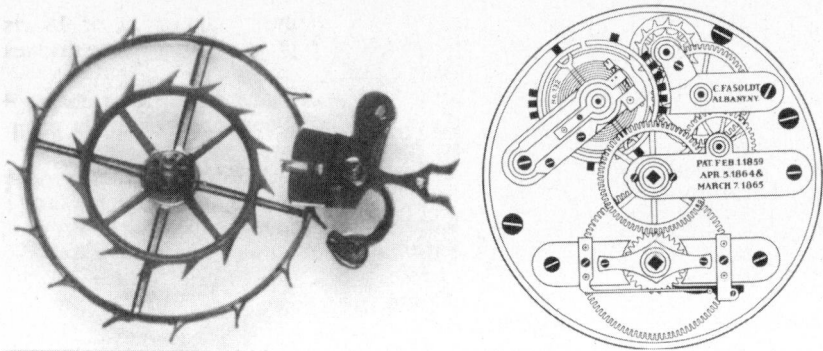

Charles Fasoldt's coaxial escape wheel with odd shaped lever. The escape wheels were designed to eliminate the use of oil on the chronometer escapement & prevent over- banking.

Charles Fasoldt, 18-20 size, 16 jewels, coaxial double escape wheel, key wind & set, bar gilded movement, Serial # 132, note patented regulator (not gold), series II.

CHARLES FASOLDT WATCH CO.

Rome, New York 1849 - 1861
Albany, New York 1861 - 1878

Charles Fasoldt came from Dresden, Germany to Rome, New York in 1848. In 1861 he moved to Albany, New York where he set up a factory to make watches and clocks and other instruments. One of his first watches, Serial No. 27, was for General Armstrong and was an eight-day movement. At about that same time, he made several large regulators and a few pocket chronometers. He displayed some of his work at fairs in Utica and Syracuse and received four First-Class Premiums and two diplomas. In 1850, he patented a micrometric regulator (generally called the Howard Regulator because Howard bought the patent). He also patented a **chronometer** escapement with a coaxial double escape wheel in 1859 & 1865, a watch regulator in 1864, and a hairspring stud in 1877.

The reliability of his coaxial double escape wheel was demonstrated when Mr. Fasoldt **strapped** one of his watches (serial # 6), along with some other brand watches, to the **drive-rod** of the Empire Express locomotive. This round trip run from Albany to New York proved his point; all the other manufacturer's watches stopped about a minute after the train started. Mr. Fasoldt's watch, serial # 6, made the entire trip running, and was within a few minutes of the correct time.

Mr. Fasoldt's coaxial double escape wheel was designed to eliminate the use of oil at the escapement and prevent over-banking. Each watch he made has minor changes making no two watches alike and these masterpieces sold for about $300.00 dollars. Mr. Fasoldt was also known for his tower clocks, for which he received many awards and medals. He made **less than 400 watches in Albany N.Y.** and **about 50 watches in Rome N.Y..** Serial numbers **200 to 299** have not been seen. Note a few movements were made **with no serial numbers.**

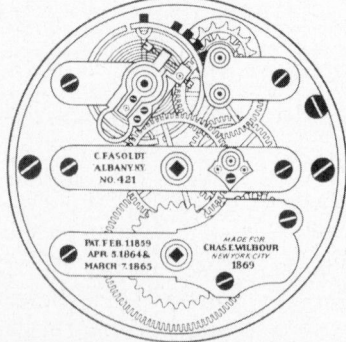

Charles Fasoldt, 18-20 size, 16 jewels, stem wind, key set, bar movement, note: the barrel ratchet wheel only having wolf tooth form, note: Single Winding Bridge, series III.

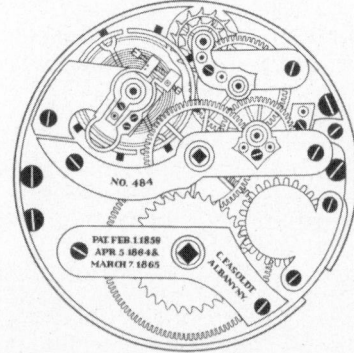

Charles Fasoldt, 16-20 size, 16 jewels, stem wind, key set, bar movement, note: the barrel ratchet wheel only having wolf tooth form, note: Double Winding Bridge, series III.

Estimated serial numbers & Production Dates
For Albany, New York MODELS (ONLY)

Year	Model	Style	Serial # Range
1861-1863	Series I	KW/KS, 1/2 plate	5-40
1864-1866	Series II	KW/KS, Bar	41-99
1867-1868	Series II	KW/KS, Bar	100-199
1868-1869	Series II	KW/KS, Bar	300-399
1869-1871	Series III	SW/KS, Bar	400-499
1872-1875	Series III	SW/KS, Bar	500-540

Serial numbers *200* to *299* have not been seen.

Serial # reported = 3, 5, 6, 27, 46, 59, 61, 64, 66, 87, 88, 90, 112, 113, 122, 124, 132, 135, 161, 166, 174, 335, 338, 349, 350, 384,385, 388, 390,395,400,402, 415,418, 421,424, 436, 437,438, 439,456, 457, 481,484,485, 496, 500, 504, 508, 510, 512 = 12 size,540.

Grade or Name — Description		ABP	Ex-Fn	Mint
18 - 20 Size, 22J, chronograph,Wind Ind., dual mainsprings &				
dual train, GJS, KW or SW, **18K case** ★★★★		$22,000	$44,000	$66,000
18 - 20 Size, 16J, GJS, **KW/ KS**, coaxial double escape wheel,				
18Kcase ★★★		16,500	33,000	55,000
*All of the above and below with a **REMONTOIRE** ★★★★★		18,000	44,000	66,000
18 - 20 Size, 16J, GJS, **KW/KS**, coaxial double escape wheel,				
Original 18K cabriolet case ★★★★★		19,800	50,000	75,000
18 - 20 Size, 16J, GJS, **SW/KS**, coaxial double escape wheel,				
18K case ★★★		16,500	33,000	55,000
18-20S, 16J, pivoted dentent, SW/KS, recased 18K ★★★★★		5,500	8,800	16,500
18 - 20 Size, 16J, GJS, double escape wheel, **original silver case**		8,800	16,500	22,000
10- 12 Size, 16J, by **C. Fasoldt**, GJS, KW & SW, KS, **14K**		3,800	6,000	9,900
by **Otto H. Fasoldt, 18S**, 15J, SW, Swiss made or American		550	1,100	1,550

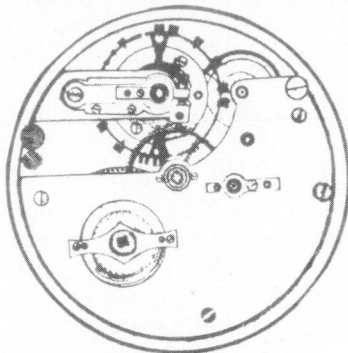

Charles Fasoldt, 18-20 size, 16 jewels, key wind, key set, half plate, coaxial double escape wheel, S. #6, series 1.

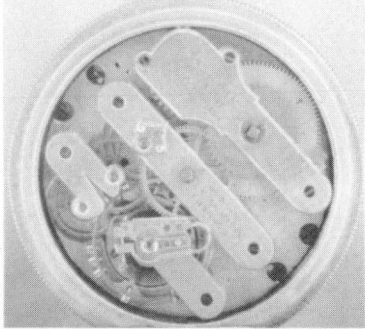

Charles Fasoldt,18-20 size, 16 jewels, stem wind, key set, patented chronometer escapement with a coaxial double escape wheel, gold regulator , Serial No.438, Series III

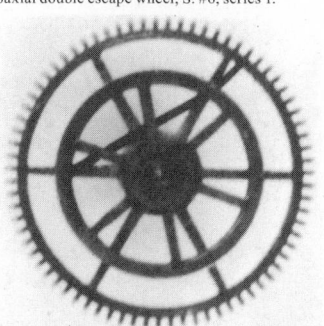

Remontoire: The constant force device is placed on the third wheel which bears two coaxial independent wheels kept in traction between themselves by a linear spring. Similar to maintaining power used on a fusee & clocks.

Fasoldt, 18-20 size , pivoted dentent, S#315, micrometric regulator, on dial & mvt. A.M. Edwards Buffalo N.Y.

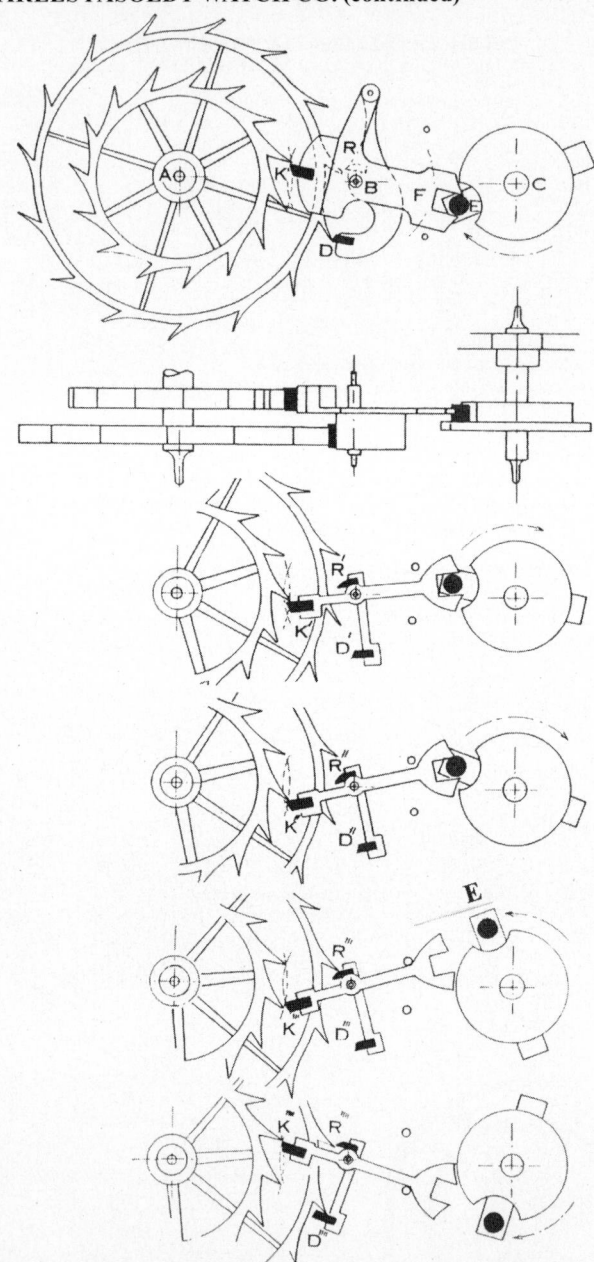

FASOLDT, CO-AXIAL DOUBLE ESCAPE WHEEL WITH ODD SHAPED LEVER

Mr. Fasoldt's coaxial double escape wheel was designed to eliminate the use of oil at the escapement and prevent over-banking. The impulse jewel **E** on its return has just unlocked pallet **D** and the smaller escape wheel is beginning impulse on **K**. At **K'** and **K''** the impulse is continuing. At **K'''** the impulse is finished and the large escape wheel locks on **R'''**. The impulse jewel having made its excursion to the right will unlock **D''''** and with some recoil in unlocking the escape wheel tooth, will begin impulse on **K''''** and continue as at **K**.

FITCHBURG WATCH CO.

Fitchburg, Massachusetts

1875-1878

In 1875, S. Sawyer decided to manufacture watches. He hired personnel from the U. S. Watch Company to build the machinery, but by 1878 the company had failed. It is not known how many, if any, watches were made. The equipment was sold to Cornell and other watch companies.

E. H. FLINT

Cincinnati, Ohio 1877-1879

The Flint watch was patented September 18, 1877, and about 100 watches were made. The serial number is found under the dial.

Grade or Name — Description		ABP	Ex-Fn	Mint
18 Size, 4—7J, KW, Full Plate, OF, Coin	★★★★	$5,500	$7,700	$11,000
18 Size, 4—7J, KW, Full Plate, **14K**, HC	★★★★	6,600	11,000	15,400

 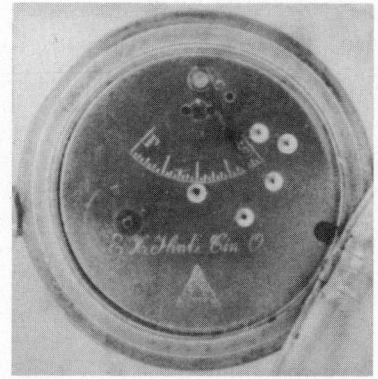

E.H. Flint dial and movement, 18 size, 4-7 jewels, open face, key wind & set, "Lancaster Pa." on dial, "Patented Sept. 18th,1877 on movement.

FREDONIA WATCH CO.

Fredonia, New York

1881 - 1885

This company sold the finished movements acquired from the Independent Watch Co. These movements had been made by other companies. The Fredonia Watch Company was sold to the Peoria Watch Co. in 1885, after having produced approximately 20,000 watches. Fredonia makes a official announcement that read as follows:

> *"Born at 2 o'clock p.m., Wednesday, Feb. 1st (1882). the "**Mark Twain**" gilt key winding movement. The child is vigorous and healthy, and there seems to be a large and increasing number of him. His parents are proud of him, and he already promises to become as universal a favorite as his illustrious namesake."*

212

Chronology of the Development of Fredonia:

Independent Watch Co.	1875 —1881
Fredonia Watch Co.	1881 —1885
Peoria Watch Co.	1885 —1889

Fredonia "Mark Twain", 18S, 11J, KW, KS, dial signed "Independent Watch Co.", S# 202,263, Ca 1883

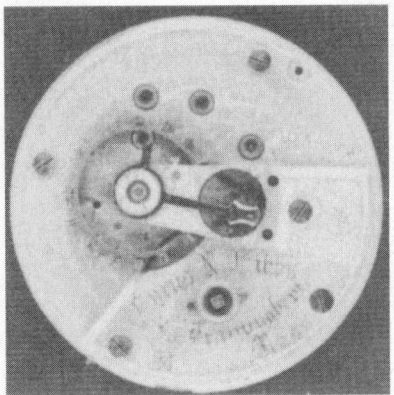

Fredonia Watch Co., 18 size, 15 jewels, signature on movement "Cyrus N. Gibbs, Mass.' key wind & set, serial number 4403.

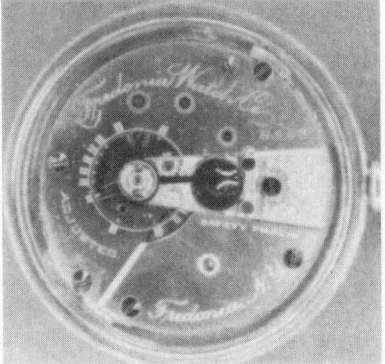

Fredonia Watch Co., 18 size, 15 jewels, adjusted, serial number 8,368. NOTE: FREDONIA Regulator disc will have teeth all around the disc.

Fredonia Watch Co., with a reversible case; changes to either hunting or open face.

Grade or Name — Description	ABP	Ex-Fn	Mint
18S, 7J, SW, OF	$200	$275	$425
18S, 7J, SW, HC	250	375	500
18S, 9J, SW, OF	200	275	425
18S, 9J, SW, HC	250	375	500
18S, 11J, SW, OF	200	275	425
18S, 11J, KW, KS, HC, Coin	250	375	500
18S, 15J, SW, Multi-color, **14K, HC**	1,600	3,000	4,000
18S, KW, **Silver Reversible case**	800	1,200	1,500
18S, 15J, SW, LS, **Gilt**, OF	225	375	500
18S, 15J, straight line escapement, NI, marked Adjusted	300	475	650
18S, 15J, SW, LS, **Gold Plated**, OF	300	475	650
18S, 15J, HC, **low serial number**	350	625	800
18S, 15J, personalized mvt	250	375	550
18S, 15J, KW, HC, marked **Lakeshore W. Co**	250	375	550
18S, 15J, Anti-Magnetic, OF	300	475	650
18S, 15J, Anti-Magnetic, HC	335	500	675
18S, 15J, Anti-Magnetic, Special, OF ★	335	475	650
18S, 15J, Anti-Magnetic, Special, HC ★	365	525	700
18S, 15J, Anti-Magnetic, Special Superior Quality, OF ★★	475	725	1,000
18S, 15J, Anti-Magnetic, Special Superior Quality, HC ★★	550	825	1,200
18S, Mark Twain, 11J, KW, KS ★★★	1,300	2,500	3,500

NOTE: Some of the above watches were marked **Quick Beat.**

FREEPORT WATCH CO.

Freeport, Illinois
1874-1875

Probably less than 20 nickel watches made by Freeport have survived. Their machinery was purchased from Mozart Co., and a Mr. Hoyt was engaged as superintendent. The building erected was destroyed by fire on Oct. 27, 1875. A safe taken from the ruins contained 300 completed brass movements which were said to be ruined.

Grade or Name — Description	ABP	Ex-Fn	Mint
18S, 19J, KW, SW, gold train, raised gold jewel settings 18K case ★★★★	$9,900	$18,700	$33,000
18S, 15J, KW, KS, gold train, friction jewels 18Kcase ★★★★	$8,800	$16,500	$30,800
Geo. P. Rose, Dubuque, Iowa, 18S, 15J, KW, KS, gold train, friction jewels, 18K case ★★★★	$6,600	$11,000	$22,000

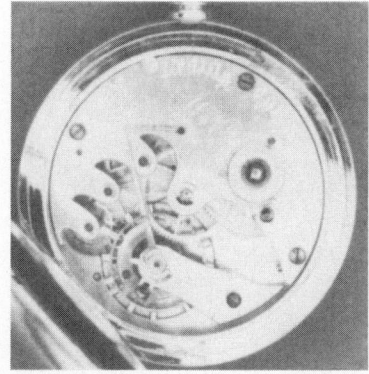 

Freeport Watch Co., Example of a basic movement, 18 size. 15 jewels, key wind & set, pressed jewels, gold train, high grade movement, serial number 11.

Freeport Watch Co., 15 jewels, gold train, damaskeened, large over coiled hairspring with a floating stud, steel lever& escape wheel with single roller.

SMITH D. FRENCH

Wabash, Indiana
1866-1878

On August 21, 1866, Mr. French was issued a patent for an improved escapement for watches. The escape wheel has triangular shaped pins and the lever has two hook-shaped pallets. The pin wheel escapement was probably first used by Robert Robin, about 1795, for pocket watches. Antoine Tavan also used this style escape wheel around 1800. Mr. French's improved pin wheel and hook shaped lever (about 70 total production) can be seen through a cutout in the plates of his watches.

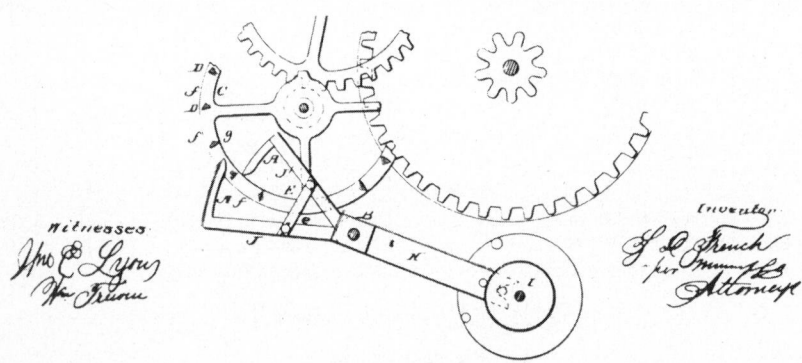

Illustration from the patent office, patent number 57,310. patented Aug. 21. 1866. Note pin wheel escapement with adjustable hook shaped lever.

Grade or Name — Description	ABP	Ex-Fn	Mint
18S, 15J, 3/4, KW, KS, gilt, pin wheel escapement, **Silver** case .... ★★★★	$9,900	$16,500	$22,000
18S, 15J, 3/4, KW, KS, gilt, pin wheel escapement, **18K** case .... ★★★★	13,200	19,800	28,600

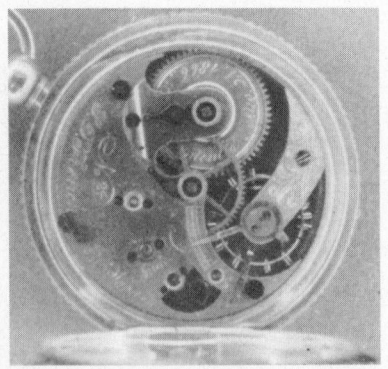

S.D. French, about 18 size, 15J.. gilt 3/4 movement, keywind & set, with pin wheel escapement, engraved on movement "S.D. French, Wabash Ind., Aug. 21, 1866, No.24."

L. Goddard, 55mm, 7 jewels, full plate movement with solid cock, chain driven fusee, flat steel balance, serial number 235, ca. 1809-1817.

LUTHER GODDARD

Shrewsbury, Massachusetts 1809-1825

The first significant attempt to produce watches in America was made by Luther Goddard. William H. Keith, who became president of Waltham Watch Co. (1861-1866) and was once apprenticed to Goddard, said that the hands, dials, round and dovetail brass, steel wire, mainsprings and hairsprings, balance, verge, chains, and pinions were all imported. However, the plates, wheels, and brass parts were cast at the Goddard shop. He also made the cases for his movements which were of the usual style; open faced, double cased and somewhat in advance of the prevalent style of thick bull's eye watches of the day. About 400+ watches were made. They were of good quality and more expensive than the imported type. The first watch was produced about 1809 and was sold to the father of ex-governor Lincoln of Worcester, Massachusetts. In 1820, his watches sold for about $60.00.

Goddard built a shop one story high with a hip roof about 18' square. It had a lean-to in the rear for casting. The building was for making clocks, but a need for watches developed. He earned the distinction of establishing the first watch factory in America. He was also one of the first to use a rack and pinion lever escapement and going barrel. A Luther Goddard & James Hamilton ad appeared on Nov.16, 1803 in NAWCC Bulletin No. 338.

Watches imported from England were signed Worcester. Watches signed Shrewsbury used brass parts (plates & wheels) & were cast at the Goddard shop. All steel parts were imported (hands, dials, mainsprings, hairsprings, balance, verge, chains, and pinions). Frank A. Knowlton purchased the company and operated it until 1933.

Chronology of the Development of Luther Goddard:

Luther Goddard, L. Goddard, L. Goddard & Son 1809-1825
P. & D. Goddard 1825-1842
D. Goddard & Son 1842-1850
Luther D. Goddard 1850-1857
Goddard & Co 1857-1860
D. Goddard & Co., & Benj'n Goddard 1860-1872

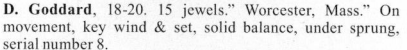

D. Goddard, 18-20. 15 jewels." Worcester, Mass." On movement, key wind & set, solid balance, under sprung, serial number 8.

L. Goddard & Co.,16-18 size, pair case, open face-thick bulls-eye type, and of high quality for the time.

NOTE: Watches listed below are with original silver cases.

Grade or Name — Description		ABP	Ex-Fn	Mint
Benj'n Goddard	◻★★★	$2,300	$3,000	$4,800
Luther Goddard, S#1-35 with **eagle** balance bridge	◻★★★★★	11,000	16,500	27,500
Luther Goddard without eagle on cock	◻★★★	7,700	11,000	16,500
Luther Goddard, L. Goddard, Luther Goddard & Son	◻★★★	6,000	8,800	16,500
L. Goddard & Co., D. Goddard & Son.	◻★★★	4,900	7,100	13,200
Luther D. Goddard, Goddard & Co., D. Goddard	◻★★★	4,400	6,600	11,000
P. Goddard, with eagle on cock	◻★★★	6,100	8,200	14,300
P & D Goddard, 7J., (Worcester), fusee, KW KS, OF	◻★★★	2,200	3,300	6,600

*Note: See other Goddard **illustrations** on previous page and also on next page.

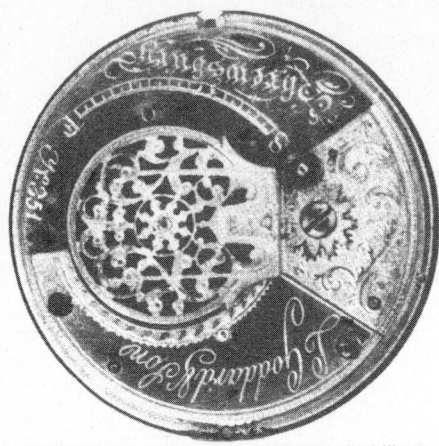

L. Goddard & Son. Example of basic movement, about 18 size, open face, pair case, S# 351, CA.1818. Note: Brass parts were made at the Goddard shop but steel parts were imported.

L. Goddard & Son, about 18 size, pair case, verge escapement, engraved on movement "L. Goddard & Son, Shrews bury, serial number 460.

JONAS G. HALL

Montpelier, Vermont 1850 - 1870
Miliwood Park, Roxbury, Vermont 1870 – 1890

Jonas G. Hall was born in 1822 in Calais, Vermont. He opened a shop in Montpelier where he sold watches, jewelry, silverware, and fancy goods. While at this location, he produced more than 60 full plate, lever style watches. Hall, later established a business in Roxbury, where he manufactured watch staking tools and other watchmaking tools. At Roxbury, he made at least one watch which was a three-quarter plate model. He also produced a few chronometers, about 20-size with a fusee and detent escapement and a wind indicator on the dial.

Hall was employed by the American Waltham Watch Co. for a short time and helped design the first lady's model. He also worked for Tremont Watch Co., B. Howard & Co., and the United States Watch Co. of Marion, New Jersey.

Style or Name—Description		ABP	Ex-Fn	Mint
18S, 15J, Full plate, KW KS	★★★	$4,400	$7,700	$11,000
18S, 15J, 3/4 plate, gilded, KW KS	★★★	5,500	8,800	12,100
20S, 15J, Detent Chronometer, KW Ks	★★★★	7,700	11,000	19,800

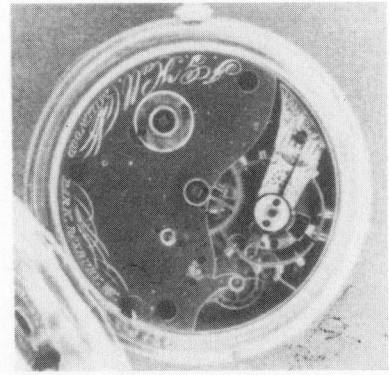

J. G. Hall, 18 size, 15 jewels, full plate, key wind & set, engraved on movement J. G. Hall, Montpelier. VT., serial number 25, ca. 1857.

J. G. Hall, 18 size, 15 jewels, 3/4 plate, key wind and set, engraved on movement J. G. Hall, Miliwood Park, Roxbury, VT, no serial number, ca. 1880.

HAMILTON WATCH CO.

Lancaster, Pennsylvania
December 14, 1892 - Present

Hamilton's roots go back to the Adams & Perry Watch Manufacturing Co. On Sept. 26, 1874, E. F. Bowman made a model watch, and the first movement was produced on April 7, 1876. It was larger than an 18S, or about a 19S. They decided to start making the watches a standard size of 18, and no more than 1,000 of the large-size watches were made. Work had commenced on Sept. 1, 1877, at the Lancaster Watch Co. The watches were designed to sell at a cheaper price than normal. It had a one-piece top 3/4 plate and a pillar plate that was fully ruby-jeweled (4 1/2 pairs). It had a gilt or nickel movement and a new stem-wind device designed by Mosely & Todd. By mid-1 878, the Lancaster Watch Co. had made 150 movements. Four grades of watches were produced: Keystone, Fulton, Franklin, and Melrose. In September 1879 the company had manufactured 334 movements. In 1880 some 1,250 movements had been made. In mid-1882, about 17,000 movements had been assembled.

THE

Hamilton Watch

940

THE
RAIL ROAD TIMEKEEPER
OF AMERICA.

LANCASTER, PA

ABOVE: AD 1910

HAMILTON
No. 950 MOVEMENT

*Without an
equal among
fine
timekeepers*

*Phenomenally
accurate
and
dependable*

A most accurate and dependable movement designed by Hamilton to meet the most exacting standards of timekeeping.

No. 950 OPEN FACE—white gold finish, bridge movement, pendant or lever set, 23 extra fine ruby and sapphire jewels in gold settings, patent motor barrel, gold train, escapement cap jeweled, steel escape wheel, double roller escapement, sapphire pallets, Breguet hairspring, micrometric regulator, compensation balance, double sunk dial, adjusted to temperature, isochronism, and five positions.

GRADE 992 ELINVAR MOVEMENT

16 size, nickel, ¾ plate, lever set, 21 extra fine ruby and sapphire jewels, double roller escapement, sapphire pallets, gold center wheel, steel escape wheel, micrometric regulator, ELINVAR hairspring, monometallic balance, friction set roller jewel, double sunk dial, two piece friction fit balance staff, beautifully damaskeened. Adjusted to five positions and automatically regulated to temperature. Sold cased only.

Note. Automatically regulated to temperature (1933 AD)

ABOVE: AD 1924
(TIME BOOK)
Note: "white gold finish"

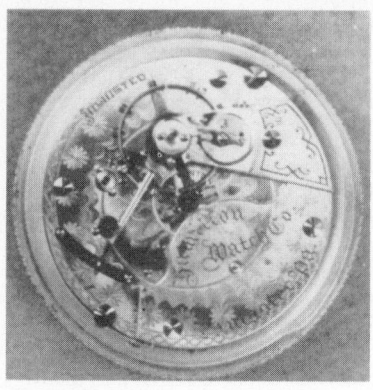

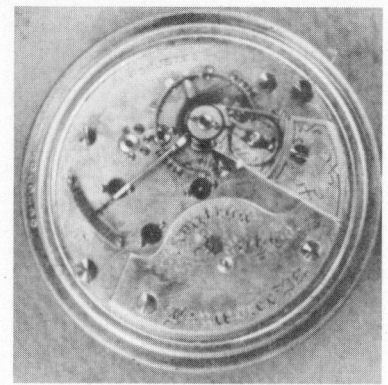

Grade 936, 18 size, 17 jewels, Note: serial number 1.   Grade 936, 18 size, 17 jewels, Serial number 2,c,1893.

The first Hamilton movement to be sold was No. 15 to W. C. Davis on January 31, 1893. The No. 1 movement was finished on April 25, 1896, and was never sold. The No.2 was finished on April 25, 1893, and was shipped to Smythe & Ashe of Rochester, N. Y. serial Nos. 1 & 2 are at the N.A.W.C.C. museum.

Chronology of the Development of Hamilton:

Adams & Perry Watch Co. . . . . .Sept 1874 - May 1876
Lancaster Penna. Watch . . . . .Aug. 1877 - May 1879
Lancaster Watch Co. . . . . May 1883 - 1886
Keystone Standard Watch Co. 1886-1890
Hamilton Watch Co. . . . . .Dec. 14, 1892 - Present

In 1893 the first watch was produced by Hamilton. The watches became very popular with railroad men and by 1923 some 53 percent of Hamilton's production were railroad watches. The 940 model watch was discontinued in 1910. Most Hamilton watches are fitted with a 42-hour mainspring.

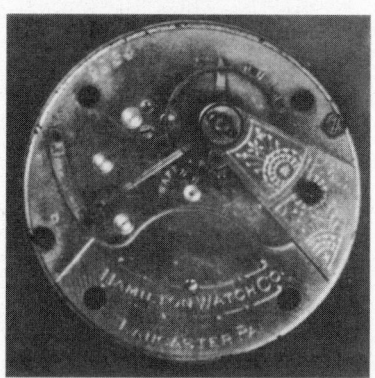

Grade 937, 18S, 17J, hunting case. Serial number 1047, Ca. Dec.,1893. **Hunting case models began with 1001.**

Hamilton   Watch   Co.,   18size,7jewels,   serial number2934.Ca. 1894. NOTE: Gilded plates.

The 950B was introduced in 1940 and by this time a total of about 25,000 grade (950) had been sold. The 992 watch sold for about $60.00 in 1929, the price remained the same $60.00 until 1940. Hamilton discontinued manufacturing pocket watches in December of 1969, the last railroad-grade watch to to be made was a 992B 21-jewel Railway Special, and sale would be discontinued when supplies were exhausted.

The Elinvar hairspring was patented in 1931 and used in all movements thereafter. Elinvar, taking its name from the words" Elasticity Invariable". On October 15, 1940, Hamilton introduced the 992B, also the Elinvar extra hairspring, all watches were fitted with the new hairspring. Elinvar and Invar are trade names and are the same 36 percent nickel steel. Although the Hamilton Watch Co. is still in business today, they last produced American made watches in about 1969.

HAMILTON ESTIMATED SERIAL NUMBERS
AND PRODUCTION DATES

Date— Serial No.	Date— Serial No.	Date— Serial No.	Date— Serial No.	
1893-1 to 2,000	1906 — 500,000	1919— 1,600,000	1932— 2,440,000	Note: The Serial
1894 — 5,000	1907 — 580,000	1920— 1,700,000	1933— 2,480,000	numbers below
1895 — 11,500	1908— 880,000	1921— 1,800,000	1934— 2,520,000	were **NOT USED:**
1896— 18,000	1909— 750,000	1922— 1,900,000	1935— 2,560,000	S#2,655,301 to
1897— 27,000	1910— 790,000	1923— 2,000,000	1936— 2,600,000	S#2,900,000
1898— 50,000	1911— 860,000	1924— 2,050,000	1937— 2,900,000	
1899— 74,000	1912— 940,000	1925— 2,100,000	1938— 3,200,000	
1900— 104,000	1913— 1,000,000	1926— 2,150,000	1939— 3,400,000	
1901— 143,000	1914— 1,100,000	1927— 2,200,000	1940— 4,000,000	**also not used:**
1902— 196,000	1915— 1,200,000	1928— 2,250,000	1941— 4,250,000	S#3,460,901 TO
1903— 260,000	1916— 1,300,000	1929— 2,300,000	1942— 4,500,000	S#4.000,000
1904— 340,000	1917— 1,400,000	1930— 2,350,000		
1905— 435,000	1918— 1,500,000	1931— 2,400,000		

The ABOVE list is provided for determining the APPROXIMATE age of your watch. Match serial number with date. Watches were not necessarily SOLD in the exact order of manufactured date.

Some serial numbers have the first numbers replaced by a (date) letter such as A, B, C, E, F, G, H, J, L, M, N, R, 5, T, V, W, X, Y, CY, HW. These letters were used from late 30's to about late 60's. The date letter "2B + Ser#' found on 950B, the date letter "C + Ser#" found on 992B, the date letter "S + Ser#" found on 950B and **HA = SWISS.**

992B with first letter of C + serial no.

1940= C001
1941= C40,000
1942= C60,000
1943= C90.000
1944= C120,000
1946= C170,000
1947= C215.000
1948= C255,000
1950= C350,000
1951 = C390,000
1954= C420,000
1956= C455,000
1959= C5OO,000
1964= C520,000
1969= C529,200

950B with first letter of 25 + serial no.

1941=2B001
1942=29400
1943=2B800

950B with first letter of S+ serial no.

1941= S001
1944= S1.500
1945= S2,800
1946= S4,000
1947= S4,500
1948= S6,500
1949= S7,500
1951= S10,000
1955= S25,000
1962= S28,000
1965= S30,000

4992B with first letter of 4C + serial no.

1941=4CXXXX
1942=4C40,000
1944=4C90.000
1950=4CI2O,000
1960=4C135,000
1968=4C145,000
1971=4C146,900
1969-70=4C148,959
3992B-made from about 1943 to 1945
992B Actual Number
1970= 4C14,432 M#15
4C148,015 M#15
4C147,146 M#16
4C147,830 M#17
4C148,959 M#15

NOTE: It required several months for raw material to emerge as a finished movement. All the while the factory is producing all sizes, models and grades. The numbering system was basically "consecutive' due to demand a batch of movements could be side tracked, thus allowing a different size and model to move ahead to meet this demand Therefore, the dates some movements were sold and delivered to the trade, the serial numbers may not be **"consecutive".**

The Hamilton Masterpiece

The adjoining illustration shows the Hamilton Masterpiece. The dial is sterling silver with raised gold numbers and solid gold hands. This watch sold for $685.00 in 1930. All 922 **MP** Models included the following: 12 size, 23 jewels, were adjusted to heat, cold, isochronism, and five positions, with a motor barrel, solid gold train, steel escape wheel, double roller, sapphire pallets and a micrometric regulator.

To help determine the size and grade of your watch, the following serial number list is provided. Serial numbers 30,001 through 32,000, which are omitted from the list, were not listed by Hamilton. To identify your watch, simply look up its serial number which will identify the grade. After determining the grade, your watch can be easily located in the pricing section.

Note: Some of the early watches were re-numbered, S# 07 re-numbered as 30,007, S# 12 re-numbered as 30,012, S# 1006 re-numbered as 31006, S# 1016 re-numbered as 31016, The above list is just a few examples also some returned and renumbered.

Serial	Grade
1-20	936
21-30	932
31-60	936
61-1000	932
401-1000	936
1001-20	937
1021-30	933
1031-60	937
1061-1100	933
1101-300	937
1301-600	933
1601-2000	937
2001-3000	7J
3001-100	931
3101-500	935
3501-600	931
3601-900	935
3901-4000	931
4001-300	930
4301-5100	934
5101-400	926
5401-600	934
5601-6000	930
6001-600	936
6601-700	938
6701-800	936
6801-7000	932
7001-10	17J
7011-600	937
7601-700	939
7701-800	937
7801-8000	933
8001-700	936
8701-800	938
8801-9000	936
9001-300	937
9301-600	939
9601-800	937
9801-900	933
9901-10000	939
10001-200	938
10201-400	936
10401-50	932
10451-500	936
10501-700	938
10701-900	936
10901-11000	938
11001-12000	936
12001-200	939
12201-13000	937
13001-400	999
13401-14000	938
14001-15000	999
15001-300	939
15301-15401	21J
15302-700	937
15701-16000	939
16001-100	931
16101-200	930
16201-300	927
16301-400	931
16401-600	927
16601-17000	931
17001-500	929
17501-18000	931
18001-200	928
18201-300	926
18301-500	928
18501-19500	930
19501-700	926
19701-20000	930
20001-300	934
20301-500	926
20501-21000	999
21001-300	935
21301-500	927
21501-800	935
21801-22500	927
22501-800	931
22801-23000	935
23001-200	928
23201-500	7J
24001-500	926
24501-25000	934
25001-100	11J
25101-400	927
25401-800	931
25801-26000	935
26001-500	930
26501-27000	928
27001-28000	929
28001-29000	999
29001-800	927
29801-30000	935
32001-300	926
32301-700	930
32701-33000	934
33001-500	931
33501-800	927
33801-34000	935
34001-500	928
34501-700	930
34701-800	926
34801-35000	934
35001-800	931
35801-36000	935
36001-37000	928
37001-38000	929
38001-500	926
38501-600	930
38601-900	934
38901-39000	926
39001-200	931
39201-500	935
39501-700	927
39701-900	935
39901-40000	931
40001-200	930
40201-500	934
40501-41000	926
41001-500	929
41501-42000	927
42001-43000	999
43001-300	941
43301-500	943
43501-700	937
43701-900	941
43901-44000	943
44001-02	21J
44003-400	938
44401-500	942
44451-45000	936
45001-46000	929
46001-500	926
46501-800	934
46801-47000	930
47001-500	927
47501-700	935
47701-48000	931
48001-05	942
48006-300	940
48301-500	942
48501-900	940
48901-49000	942
49001-400	927
49401-900	925
49901-50	11J
50071-500	962
50501-750	960
50751-50850	964
50851-51000	960
51001-51300	16s
51301-400	963
51401-650	961
51651-750	965
51751-52000	961
52001-300	16s
52301-500	975
52501-700	974
52701-800	966
52801-53000	976
53001-53070	16s
53071-53350	977
53351-900	975
53901-54000	967
54001-200	972
54201-300	974
54301-500	976
54501-700	974
54701-800	968
54801-55000	976
55001-300	973
55301-600	977
55601-700	969
55701-800	977
55801-56000	974
56001-300	976
56301-500	976
56501-600	966
56601-800	972
56801-900	974
56901-57000	976
57001-300	977
57301-500	975
57501-600	973
57601-800	975
57801-58000	977
58001-100	972
58101-200	974
58201-300	972
58301-400	966
58401-500	976
58501-600	972
58601-800	974
58801-59000	976
59001-300	973
59301-500	967
59501-700	975
59701-60000	977
60001-500	976
60501-700	974
60701-61000	976
61001-200	975
61201-500	977
61501-600	973
61601-800	975
61801-62000	977
62001-100	972
62101-300	974
62301-500	976
62501-700	974
62701-900	972
62901-63000	974
63001-500	977
63501-600	975
63601-800	977
63801-900	975
63901-64000	973
64001-100	976
64101-200	972
64201-300	974
64301-600	972
64601-700	976
64701-900	974
64901-65000	976
65001-200	973
65201-300	977
65301-400	975
65401-500	973
65501-700	977
65701-900	975
65901-66000	977
66001-200	976
66201-300	974
66301-500	972
66501-600	976
66601-700	974
66701-800	972
66801-67000	974
67001-100	977
67101-300	975
67301-600	973
67601-800	975
67801-68000	977
68001-800	960
68801-69000	964
69001-100	977
69101-200	975
69201-400	973
69401-600	975
69601-70000	977
70001-200	976
70201-400	970
70401-600	968
70601-900	972
70901-71000	974
71001-200	975
71201-500	971
71501-700	975
71701-90	973
71791-800	969
71801-900	977
71901-72000	975
72001-100	974
72101-300	976
72301-600	974
72601-700	968
72701-900	976
72901-73000	972
73001-200	975
73201-300	973
73301-74000	977
74001-400	974
74401-600	972
74601-75000	976
75001-76799	HWW*
76002-76800	HWW*
77001-100	969
77101-300	973
77301-500	975
77501-600	971
77601-700	973
77701-900	975
77901-78000	977
78001-500	970
78501-700	972
78701-900	974
78901-79000	976
79001-100	973
79101-300	975
79301-700	977
79701-900	975
79901-80000	973
80001-200	972
80201-400	974
80401-600	970
80601-700	972
80701-900	974
80901-81000	976
81001-300	961
81301-500	965
81501-82000	961
82001-300	972
82301-500	974
82501-600	970
82601-700	972
82701-800	974
82801-900	968
82901-83000	976
83001-400	977
83401-500	971
83501-700	975
83701-800	973
83801-900	975
83901-84000	969
84001-400	974
84401-500	970
84501-700	972
84701-800	968
84801-85000	976
85001-200	937
85201-900	941
85901-86000	943
86001-87000	928
87001-88000	929
88001-500	926
88501-89000	930
89001-500	941
89501-90000	937
90001-100	926
90101-950	999
91001-92000	925
92001-200	940
92201-93000	936
93001-94000	927
94001-003	934
94004-95000	928
95001-96000	923
96001-100	942
96101-700	940
96701-97000	936
97001-900	929
97901-98000	927
98001-99000	924
99001-100000	925
100001-101000	924
101001-102000	925
102001-103000	922
103001-104000	927
104001-105000	940
105001-500	925
105501-106000	927
106001-107000	940
107001-400	941
107401-500	943
107501-800	941
107801-108000	943
108001-200	928

Serial No.	Grade	Serial No.	Grade	Serial No.	Grade	Serial No.	Grade
108201-109000	926	186001-187000	942	275202-460	HWW*	322001-323000	974
109001-500	927	187001-188000	927	275462-500	HWW*	323001-700	975
109501-110000	925	188001-189000	924	276001-277000	940	323701-324000	973
110001-900	940	189001-190000	925	277001-278000	941	324001-325000	960
110901-111000	942	190001-191000	926	278001-279000	940	325001-100	965
111001-500	937	191001-192000	927	279001-280000	925	325101-326000	961
111501-112000	941	192001-193000	924	280001-281000	936	326001-327000	974
112001-200	928	193001-194000	925	281001-282000	927	327001-300	971
112201-113000	926	194001-195000	926	282001-283000	926	327301-500	973
113001-114000	925	195001-500	935	283001-284000	925	327501-328000	975
114001-003	940	195501-196000	927	284001-500	934	328001-300	992
114004-115000	936	196001-197000	926	284501-900	924	328301-500	990
115001-116000	927	197001-198000	937	284901-285000	999	328501-329000	992
116001-117000	940	198001-199000	936	285001-286000	925	329001-330000	975
117001-118000	925	199001-200000	925	286001-287000	940	330001-100	992
118001-119000	999	200001-201000	926	287001-288000	927	330101-500	990
119001-120000	925	201001-202000	925	288001-289000	940	330501-331000	992
120001-121000	924	202001-500	926	289001-290000	927	331001-200	973
121001-500	941	202501-203000	934	290001-800	936	331201-400	975
121501-122000	943	203001-204000	927	290801-291000	938	331401-500	969
122001-300	940	204001-100	934	291001-292000	925	331501-700	971
122301-400	942	204101-500	926	292001-500	940	331701-800	973
122401-123000	940	204501-205000	934	292501-293000	942	331801-332000	975
123001-124000	941	205001-206000	941	293001-294000	925	332001-200	992
124001-100	942	206001-207000	940	294001-295000	926	332201-800	972
124101-800	940	207001-208000	927	295001-296000	927	332801-333000	974
124801-125000	942	208001-900	999	296001-297000	940	333001-500	975
125001-126000	927	208901-209000	940	297001-298000	927	333501-700	971
126001-127000	924	209001-210000	925	298001-299000	940	333701-900	973
127001-128000	941	210001-211000	940	299001-300000	925	333901-334000	975
128001-129000	936	211001-212000	927	300001-300	972	334001-200	972
129001-130000	925	212001-213000	940	300301-500	970	334201-800	992
130001-500	924	213001-500	941	300501-900	974	334801-335000	990
130501-131000	926	213501-600	937	300901-301000	968	335001-600	975
131001-132000	925	213601-214000	925	301001-400	975	335601-800	971
132001-100	926	214001-215000	924	301401-500	971	335801-900	973
132101-200	934	215001-216000	973	301501-302000	973	335901-336000	975
132201-500	926	216001-217000	940	302001-100	990	336001-200	972
133001-134000	937	217001-218000	940	302101-200	992	336201-337000	974
134001-135000	924	218001-219000	940	302201-300	990	337001-338000	975
135001-136000	925	219001-220000	925	302301-900	992	338001-200	974
136001-137000	926	220001-221000	924	302901-303000	990	338201-900	992
137001-100	11J	221001-222000	927	303001-100	973	338901-339000	990
137101-138000	927	222001-223000	926	303101-300	971	339001-300	971
138001-139000	940	223001-02	927	303301-800	975	339301-500	973
139001-140000	937	223003-04	941	303801-304000	973	339501-340000	975
140001-300	938	223005	937	304001-100	970	340001-200	974
140301-141000	942	223006-224000	927	304101-400	972	340201-300	972
141001-142000	941	224001-225000	924	304401-305000	974	340301-600	970
142001-143000	940	225001-226000	927	305001-100	973	340601-341000	974
143001-100	927	226001-227000	940	305101-200	971	341001-200	973
143101-144000	925	227001-228000	925	305201-300	969	341201-342000	975
144001-145000	924	228001-229000	924	305301-900	975	342001-300	990
144501-146000	925	229001-230000	925	305901-306000	973	342301-343000	992
146001-400	934	230001-500	926	306001-400	972	343001-344000	975
146401-147000	924	230501-231000	924	306401-307000	974	344001-200	970
147001-148000	927	231001-565	937	307001-100	975	344201-400	972
147801-149000	940	231566-232000	927	307101-300	971	344401-345000	974
149001-150000	925	232001-233000	940	307301-400	975	345001-346000	975
150001-151000	924	233001-234000	941	307401-500	973	346001-300	992
151001-400	927	234001-235000	940	307501-600	975	346301-347000	974
151401-500	935	235001-236000	927	307601-700	971	347001-180	993
151501-152000	927	236001-237000	936	307701-900	975	347181-200	991
152001-153000	936	237001-238000	941	307901-308000	969	347201-300	975
153001-154000	941	238001-239000	926	308001-700	990	347301-400	973
154001-155000	936	239001-500	943	308701-309000	992	347401-700	993
155001-156000	927	239501-240000	941	309001-100	971	347701-900	991
156001-157000	940	240001-241000	940	309101-400	973	347901-348000	973
157001-158000	925	241001-242000	941	309401-310000	975	348001-200	970
158001-159000	940	242001-243000	940	310001-400	970	348201-800	974
159001-160000	941	243001-244000	927	310401-311000	974	348801-349000	972
160001-161000	940	244001-245000	936	311001-700	975	349001-350000	975
161001-162000	941	245001-246000	925	311701-312000	973	350001-300	990
162001-163000	926	246001-247000	940	312001-200	970	350301-400	974
163001-164000	943	247001-248000	927	312201-500	972	350401-600	990
164001-165000	940	248001-249000	940	312501-600	968	350601-351000	992
165001-166000	925	249001-250000	927	312601-313000	974	351001-352000	975
166001-167000	924	250001-251000	926	313001-100	973	352001-100	968
167001-168000	927	251001-252000	927	313101-400	971	352101-353000	974
168001-169000	940	252001-253000	924	313401-600	969	353001-354000	975
169001-400	935	253001-254000	940	313601-314000	975	354001-400	992
169401-170000	927	254001-255000	940	314001-600	974	354401-355000	974
170001-171000	999	255001-256000	925	314601-900	972	355001-800	975
171001-172000	925	256001-257000	926	314901-315000	970	355801-900	973
172001-100	934	257001-258000	941	315001-100	971	355901-356000	993
172101-173000	926	258001-259000	924	315101-400	973	356001-500	990
173001-174000	925	259001-260000	941	315401-316000	975	356501-357000	974
174001-175000	924	260001-261000	940	316001-200	992	357001-358000	975
175002-176000	HWW*	261001-262000	927	316201-300	972	358001-359000	974
175001-699	HWW*	262001-263000	926	316301-500	992	359001-360000	975
176001-177000	940	263001-264000	925	316501-317000	972	360001-550	960
177001-178000	927	264001-265000	940	317001-600	975	360801-361000	960
178001-179000	942	265001-266000	927	317601-700	969	361001-100	969
179001-500	935	266001-267000	940	317701-318000	973	361101-300	991
179501-180000	927	267001-268000	925	318001-100	972	361301-400	993
180001-181000	940	268001-269000	940	318101-900	974	361401-700	975
181001-182000	941	269001-270000	927	318901-319000	970	361701-20	973
182001-300	926	270001-271000	940	319001-100	971	361721-362000	975
182301-400	934	271001-272000	925	319101-320000	975	362001-900	974
182401-183000	926	272001-273000	926	320001-300	972	362901-363000	990
183001-184000	941	273001-274000	941	320301-400	968	363001-364000	975
184001-185000	940	274001-275000	924	320401-321000	974	364001-365000	974
185001-186000	925	275002-100	HWW*	321001-200	973	365001-100	975
		275102-200	HWW*	321201-322000	975	365101-300	973

Serial	Grade	Serial	Grade	Serial	Grade	Serial	Grade
365301-366000	975	441001-442000	940	568001-569000	936	667001-668000	941
366001-367000	974	442001-400	946	569001-571000	924	668001-669000	926
367001-500	975	442401-500	942	571001-576000	940	669001-670000	999
367501-368000	993	442501-443000	946	576001-200	942	670001-100	937
368001-369000	974	443001-444000	926	576201-578000	940	670501-673000	925
369001-370000	992	444001-445000	924	578001-580000	924	673001-675000	926
370001-100	990	445001-446000	927	580001-582000	926	675001-677000	940
370101-400	992	446001-447000	924	582001-584000	925	677001-678000	924
370401-500	974	447001-448000	925	584001-585000	927	678001-679200	927
370501-800	990	448001-449000	926	585001-587000	999	679201-680000	926
370801-371400	992	449001-450000	924	587001-592000	940	680001-685000	924
371401-500	972	450001-451000	926	592001-593000	926	685001-687000	940
371501-373500	974	451001-452000	925	593001-594000	924	687001-688000	925
373501-700	990	452001-453000	940	594001-601000	940	688001-689000	946
373701-374000	992	453001-454000	924	B600001-601000	999 Ball	689001-694000	940
374001-200	974	454001-456000	940	601001-601800	926	694001-696000	924
374201-700	990	456001-457000	999	B601001-601800	999 Ball	696001-697000	941
374701-375000	974	457001-458000	940	601801-602000	934	697001-700000	924
375001-100	993	458001-459000	999	B601801-602000	999 Ball	700001-702000	974
375101-500	991	459001-110	946	602001-603000	926	702001-703800	992
375501-376000	975	459111-118	942	B602001-603000	999 Ball	703801-704000	990
376001-200	972	459119-200	946	603001-604000	926	704001-400	992
376201-500	974	459201-700	942	B603001-604000	999 Ball	704401-705000	990
376501-377000	992	459701-460000	946	604001-605000	926	705001-700	972
377001-200	973	460001-461900	940	B604001-605000	999 Ball	705701-706000	974
377201-378000	975	461901-462000	940	605001-606000	925	706001-707000	990
378001-379000	974	462001-463000	999	B605001-606000	999 Ball	707001-800	972
379001-380800	992	463001-500	940	606001-607000	925	707801-708000	990
380801-381000	990	463501-464000	940	B606001-607000	999 Ball	708001-709500	975
381001-382000	992	464001-466000	926	607001-608000	925	709501-710000	973
382001-100	990	466001-467000	924	B607001-608000	999 Ball	710001-800	993
382101-383000	974	467001-468000	926	608001-613000	924	710801-711000	991
383001-300	992	468001-469000	940	B608001-613000	999 Ball	711001-300	973
383301-700	990	469001-470000	924	613001-614000	925	711301-712000	975
383701-384000	972	470001-471000	926	B613001-614000	999 Ball	712001-600	993
384001-700	974	471001-472000	946	614001-616500	924	712601-713000	991
384701-900	972	472001-473000	924	B614001-616500	999 Ball	713001-714900	975
384901-385000	974	473001-474000	940	616501-617000	934	714901-715000	991
385001-600	972	474001-475000	924	B616501-617000	999 Ball	715001-716000	993
385601-800	974	475001-476000	940	617001-619000	926	716001-100	972
385801-386000	990	476001-477000	,924	B617001-619000	999 Ball	716101-717000	974
386001-800	974	477001-478000	940	619001-620000	927	717001-200	991
386801-900	992	478001-479000	926	B619001-620000	999 Ball	717201-718000	975L
386901-387000	972	479001-480000	944	620001-622700	940	718001-721500	974
387001-100	990	480001-481000	926	B620001-622700	999 Ball	721501-722000	992
387101-900	992	481001-482000	927	622701-623000	942	722001-724000	974
387901-388000	972	482001-483000	924	B622701-623000	999 Ball	724001-725000	972
388001-400	990	483001-484000	926	623001-624000	941	725001-726000	974
388401-389000	992	484001-485000	940	B623001-624000	999 Ball	726001-727000	992
389001-391000	974	485001-486000	925	624001-625000	936	727001-728000	974
391001-300	972	486001-487000	999	B624001-625000	999 Ball	728001-729000	992
391301-392000	974	487001-489000	924	625001-626000	925	729001-730000	975
392001-800	992	488001-489000	999	B625001-626000	999 Ball	730001-731000	992
392801-393000	990	489001-492000	924	626001-627000	926	731001-732000	975
393001-400	975	492001-493000	940	B626001-627000	999 Ball	732001-734000	992
393401-600	973	493001-494000	946	627001-628000	924	734001-735000	975
393601-394000	993	494001-495000	944	B627001-628000	999 Ball	735001-736000	974
394001-200	972	495001-496000	940	628001-630800	925	736001-738000	975
394201-395000	974	496001-497000	925	B628001-630800	999 Ball	738001-739000	974
395001-100	993	497001-498000	999	631001-636000	940	739001-740000	975
395101-900	991	498001-499000	936	B631001-636000	999 Ball	740001-100	974
395901-396000	993	499001-501000	940	636001-637000	941	740101-200	972
396001-397000	992	501001-900	926	B636001-637000	999 Ball	740201-900	974
397001-200	990	501901-502000	934	637001-638000	936	740901-741000	975
397201-398000	992	502001-503000	926	B637001-638000	999 Ball	741001-742000	992
398001-200	972	503001-504000	999	638001-639000	926	742001-743000	974
398201-399000	992	504001-507000	940	B638001-639000	999 Ball	743001-300	975
399001-600	993	507001-508000	999	639001-640000	925	743301-400	993
399601-400000	975	508001-509900	940	B639001-640000	999 Ball	743401-744000	975
400001-401000	940	509901-510000	942	640001-642000	924	744001-500	974
401001-402000	940	510001-511500	940	B640001-644000	999 Ball	744501-745000	975
402001-404000	924	511501-700	942	644401-645000	940	745001-747000	975
404001-405000	926	511701-517000	940	645001-645500	927	747001-700	974
405001-406000	924	517001-519000	924	B645001-645500	999 Ball	747701-748000	972
406001-407000	940	519001-521000	925	645501-646000	925	748001-749500	992
407001-408000	926	521001-523000	944	B645501-646000	999 Ball	749501-750000	974
408001-416000	940	523001-524000	946	646001-647000	926	750001-100	961
416001-417000	926	524001-531000	940	B646001-647000	999 Ball	750101-200	961
417001-418000	940	531001-532000	926	647001-648000	940	750201-700	950
418001-419000	926	532001-10	934	B647001-648000	999 Ball	750701-751000	952
419001-420000	941	532011-533000	926	648001-649000	940	751001-752000	960
420001-421000	940	533001-535500	999	B648001-649000	998 Ball	752001-500	952
421001-422000	926	535501-536000	940	B649001-650000	998 Ball	752501-753000	950
422001-423000	924	536001-537000	936	B650001-651000	999 Ball	753001-500	952
423001-425000	926	537001-538000	924	651001-652000	998 Ball	753501-754000	950
425001-426000	924	538001-543000	940	B651001-652000	998 Ball	754001-100	960
426001-500	936	543001-544000	927	652001-652700	924	754101-500	952
426501-427000	944	544001-200	934	B652001-652700	998 Ball	754501-755000	960
427001-428000	924	544201-545000	926	652701-652800	924	755001-400	992
428001-429000	926	545201-546000	925	652801-652900	927	755401-500	974
429001-430000	925	546001-547000	924	652901-653000	937	755501-700	972
430001-431000	924	547001-548000	926	653001-655000	940	755701-900	974
431001-432000	925	548001-549000	999	B653001-655000	999 Ball	755901-756000	972
432001-433000	940	549001-551000	946	655001-655200	924	756001-757000	974
433001-434000	924	551001-553000	944	B655001-655200	999 Ball	757001-300	975
434001-500	940	553001-555000	940	655201-656000	924	757301-500	993
434501-600	942	555001-556000	936	656001-657000	926	757501-758000	975
434601-435000	946	556001-558000	924	657001-659000	927	758001-100	972
435001-436000	924	558001-560000	925	659001-660000	925	758101-759000	992
436001-438500	940	560001-561000	999	660001-661000	927	759001-760000	975
438501-800	946	561001-562000	926	661001-662000	924	760001-400	992
438801-900	942	562001-564000	924	662001-664000	940	760401-600	972
438901-440000	946	564001-565000	926	664001-666000	924	760601-800	974
440001-441000	924	565001-568000	940	666001-667000	940	760801-761000	992

Serial	Grade	Serial	Grade	Serial	Grade	Serial	Grade
761001-400	975	826001-500	975L	898001-899100	992	1051001-200	975
761401-600	993	826501-827000	993	899101-500	978	1051201-1052000	993
761601-762000	975	827001-828000	975P	899501-900000	974	1052001-500	972P
762001-200	992	828001-829000	974L	900001-902000	940	1052501-900	954
762201-300	972	829001-830000	974P	902001-904000	926	1052901-1053000	974
762301-763000	974	830001-500	990L	904001-906000	924	1053001-1054000	992
763001-300	993	830501-831000	992L	906001-914000	940	1054001-1056000	974
763301-600	973	831001-100	954P	914001-916000	926	1056001-1057000	975
763601-764000	975	831101-200	972P	916001-917000	927	1057001-1061300	992
764001-300	992	831201-500	954P	917001-919000	925	1061301-1062300	972
764301-400	972	831501-832000	974P	919001-921000	940	1062301-1066000	992
764401-765000	974	832001-400	974L	921001-923000	924	1066001-1068000	974
765001-300	992	832401-833000	992L	923001-500	999	1068001-1069000	975
765301-767000	974	833001-834000	990L	923501-924000	925	1069001-1070000	974
767001-600	992	834001-600	974P	924001-926000	940	1070001-1071000	992L
767601-800	972	834601-800	974L	926001-100	927	1071001-1073000	975P
767801-768000	974	834801-835000	974P	927001-929000	926	1073001-1075000	992
768001-769000	975	835001-600	992L	929001-933000	924	1075001-1076200	974L
769001-700	992	835601-800	990L	933001-935000	925	1076201-700	972L
769701-770000	972	835801-836000	974L	935001-937000	926	1076701-1077000	978L
770001-100	974	836001-500	974P	937001-939000	940	1077001-1079000	974P
770101-771200	992	836501-900	954P	939001-941000	924	1079001-1080000	992L
771201-400	972	836901-837000	974P	941001-944000	940	1080001-100	952L
771401-772000	974	837001-838000	975P	944001-949000	926	1080101-200	960L
772001-773000	975	838001-839000	975L	949001-952000	925	1080201-400	994L
773001-800	992	839001-400	974L	952001-958000	926	1080401-1081000	950L
773501-774000	972	839401-700	992L	958001-960000	926	1081001-1082000	978L
774001-775000	975	839701-840000	990L	960001-968000	940	1082001-400	993L
775001-500	952	840001-400	952L	968001-970000	926	1082401-1083000	973L
775501-776000	950	840401-900	950L	970001-971700	924	1083001-1084000	990L
776001-300	973	840901-841000	952L	971701-972000	948	1084001-1085000	992L
776301-700	993	841001-842000	975P	972001-973000	924	1085001-1086000	992L
776701-777000	975	842001-843000	974L	973001-974000	936	1086001-1088000	974P
777001-300	972	843001-844000	974P	974001-975400	924	1088001-1091000	992L
777301-778300	974	844001-200	993	975401-25 Spec.	926	1091001-200	978L
778301-800	992	844201-845000	975	975426-976000	924	1091201-1092000	974L
778801-900	972	845001-200	992	976001-979000	940	1092001-1093000	992L
778901-779300	974	845201-400	972	979001-100	942	1093001-1095000	974P
779301-780100	992	845401-700	954	979101-981000	940	1095001-1096000	992P
780101-300	972	845701-846000	972	981001-982000	948	1096001-400	974L
780301-781300	992	846001-500	952	982001-984000	924	1096401-1097000	974P
781301-400	972	846501-847000	950	984001-986000	940	1097001-1098000	992L
781401-500	974	847001-200	972	986001-987000	946	1098001-400	975P
781501-782000	992	847201-849000	974	987001-988000	936	1098401-1099000	975L
782001-783000	975	849001-850000	975	988001-992000	940	1099001-600	993L
783001-600	992	850001-300	992	992001-996000	924	1099601-1100000	975P
783601-784000	974	850301-800	990	996001-999999	940	1100001-1104000	992L
784001-785000	992	850801-851000	972	999999-1000000	947	1104001-1105000	974P
785001-500	952	851001-400	993	1000001-1000300	972	1105001-1106000	992L
785501-786000	950	851401-852000	975	1000301-1003000	992	1106001-500	978L
786001-787000	992	852001-853000	992	1003001-1004000	974	1106501-1107000	972L
787001-400	974	853001-854000	974	1004001-900	992	1107001-1109000	992L
787401-788000	972	854001-600	950	1004901-1007100	974	1109001-1111000	972P
788001-791300	992	854601-900	952	1007101-1008300	992	1111001-1112000	974L
791301-792600	974	854901-855100	960L	1008301-1009500	974	1112001-1113000	974P
792601-900	972	855101-856000	950L	1009501-1010700	992	1113001-1116000	992L
792901-793700	992	856001-857840	975	1010701-1011200	972	1116001-900	974P
793701-900	990	857841-858000	975L	1011201-1012700	974	1116901-1117000	974L
793901-794000	992	858001-500	974	1012701-1013000	992	1117001-1119000	992L
794001-200	972	858501-859000	972	1013001-1015000	978	1119001-1120000	978L
794201-795000	974	859001-860000	974	1015001-300	974	1120001-1122000	992L
795001-796400	992	860001-862300	992	1015301-1016000	992	1122001-1123000	974P
796401-800	972	862301-400	954	1016001-300	975	1123001-500	972P
796801-797200	974	862401-500	972	1016301-600	973	1123501-1125000	974P
797201-500	954	862501-800	954	1016601-1018000	993	1125001-1127000	992L
797501-798000	954	862601-800	972	1018001-1020000	992	1127001-1128000	972L
798001-500	990	862801-863000	974	1020001-1022000	950	1128001-1129000	972L
798501-800	972	863001-864000	992	1022601-1023000	952	1129001-1130500	974P
798801-799000	974	864001-865000	975	1023001-700	992	1130501-1131000	956P
799001-200	954	865001-866000	992	1023701-1024500	974	1131001-1132000	992L
799201-600	992	866001-600	974	1024501-600	974	1132001-1133000	990L
799601-800000	954	866601-700	954	1024601-1025000	972	1133001-1134000	978L
800001-802000	974	866701-867000	972	1025001-1027000	975	1134001-1135000	972L
802001-200	954	867001-868000	975	1027001-400	993	1135001-1137000	992L
802201-2	972	868001-869000	992	1027401-1029600	975	1137001-1138000	956P
802203-300	954	869001-870000	975	1029601-1030000	973	1138001-1139000	956P
802301-500	972	870001-872000	992	1030001-1032000	992	1139001-1140000	978L
802501-803700	974	872001-200	993	1032001-1033000	974	1140001-1141000	972L
803701-804200	954	872201-874000	975	1033001-200	972	1141001-1142000	956P
804201-806000	974	874001-800	974	1033201-800	954	1142001-500	974P
806001-807000	975	874801-875000	975	1033801-1035300	974	1142501-1145000	974L
807001-500	993	875001-300	952	1035301-600	972	1145001-1146000	975P
807501-808800	975	875301-876000	975	1035601-1036000	974	1146001-500	956P
808801-809000	993	876001-600	993	1036001-300	972	1146501-1149000	974P
809001-500	974	876601-877000	975	1036301-600	954	1149001-1150000	974L
809501-600	972	877001-400	992	1036801-1037000	992L	1150001-600	950L
809601-810000	974	877401-700	975	1037001-1038000	974	1150601-1151800	952L
810001-300	990	877701-878000	993	1038001-1039000	992	1151801-1152000	952P
810301-812000	974	878001-879400	975	1039001-200	972	1152001-900	992
812001-700	992	879401-880000	992	1039201-500	978	1152901-1153200	952P
812701-813000	974	880001-600	974	1039501-1040300	974	1153201-300	994P
813001-814000	974P	880601-882400	992	1040301-1041000	992	1153301-500	994L
814001-800	974L	882401-883400	974	1041001-1042000	974	1153501-800	960L
814801-815900	992	883401-884100	992	1042001-700	992	1153801-1154000	950L
815901-816000	974L	884101-885300	974	1042701-1043000	972	1154001-500	950P
816001-817000	974P	885301-886000	992	1043001-700	978	1154501-1155000	994L
817001-819000	974L	886001-887000	992	1043701-1044000	992	1155001-200	994P
819001-820000	974P	887001-300	974	1044001-1045000	974	1155201-500	994L
820001-821500	974L	887301-890300	992	1045001-1046000	992	1156001-1158000	996L
821501-822000	990L	890301-891000	974	1046001-1047000	975	1158001-1160000	974P
822001-700	992L	891001-600	992	1047001-1048000	974L	1160001-1162000	992L
822701-823000	974L	891601-892200	978	1048001-1049000	992	1162001-500	993L
823001-824000	974P	892201-896200	992	1049001-500	990	1162501-1164000	992L
824001-826000	975P	896201-897800	974	1049501-1051000	992	1164001-1166000	974P
		897801-898000	972				

Serial	Grade	Serial	Grade	Serial	Grade	Serial	Grade
1166001-1167000	974L	1291501-1292000	992P	1394001-1396000	992L	1569001-1571000	972L
1167001-1168000	956P	1292001-1297000	992L	1396001-500	972L	1571001-1572000	974P
1168001-1169000	975P	1297001-1298000	974P	1396501-1398000	974L	1572001-1573000	975P
1169001-1170000	974P	1298001-1299000	992L	1398001-400	974P	1573001-1575000	974P
1170001-1174000	956P	1299001-1300000	975P	1398401-1399000	956P	1575001-400	950L
1174001-1176000	974P	1300001-1301000	974P	1399001-1400000	992L	1575401-1576000	950P
1176001-1177000	992L	1301001-1302000	974L	1400001-1401000	936	1576001-1577000	950L
1177001-1178000	956P	1302001-500	992L	1401001-1403000	924	1577001-1578000	975P
1178001-1179000	974P	1302501-1303000	990L	1403001-1409000	940	1578001-1580000	992L
1179001-1181000	996L	1303001-500	972L	1409001-500	946	1580001-1581200	974L
1181001-1182000	992L	1303501-1304000	972P	1409501-1410000	940	1581201-1582000	956P
1182001-1183000	996L	1304001-1305000	978L	1410001-1414000	924	1582001-1583000	974P
1183001-1184400	974P	1305001-1306000	956P	1414001-300	941	1583001-1584000	992L
1184401-1185400	956P	1306001-1307000	974P	1414501-1415000	925	1584001-1585000	978L
1185401-1186000	974P	1307001-1308500	992L	1415001-1417000	940	1585001-1586000	972L
1186001-1187000	992L	1308501-1309000	993L	1417001-1419000	940	1586001-1587000	992L
1187001-1188000	996L	1309001-1310000	974L	1419001-1420000	924	1587001-500	992P
1188001-1189000	992L	1310001-1311000	972L	1420001-1421000	940	1587501-1589000	992L
1189001-1190000	974P	1311001-1312000	992L	1421001-1422000	924	1589001-500	956P
1190001-1192000	996L	1312001-800	974P	1422001-1424000	940	1589501-1590000	974P
1192001-1193000	975P	1312801-1313000	956P	1424001-1428000	924	1590001-1591000	974L
1193001-1194000	974P	1313001-1317000	992L	1428001-1430000	940	1591001-1592000	992L
1194001-1195000	956P	1317001-1318000	956P	1430001-200	924	1592001-1593000	974P
1195001-1196000	974P	1318001-1321000	992L	1430201-400	948	1593001-1595000	992L
1196001-1199000	992L	1321001-300	990L	1430401-1431000	924	1595001-200	974P
1199001-1201000	974P	1321301-1322000	992L	1431001-1433000	940	1595201-900	956P
1201001-1202000	975P	1322001-700	974L	1433001-1438000	924	1595901-1596000	974P
1202001-1203000	992L	1322701-1323000	972L	1438001-500	926	1596001-1611000	992L
1203001-1204000	974P	1323001-1324000	992L	1438501-1439500	924	1611001-1612000	974P
1204001-500	956P	1324001-1325000	996L	1439501-1440000	926	1612101-1613000	956P
1204501-1206000	974P	1325001-1326500	975P	1440001-1441000	940	1613001-600	996L
1206001-1207000	992L	1326501-1327000	993L	1441001-1442000	924	1614001-900	956P
1207001-1210000	974P	1327001-300	956P	1442001-500	926	1614901-1615000	974P
1210001-1212000	992L	1327301-1329000	974P	1442501-1444000	924	1615001-1625000	992L
1212001-1213000	974P	1329001-1330000	992L	1444001-1445000	940	1625001-200	950L
1213001-500	996L	1330001-1331300	974L	1445001-1447000	924	1625201-1626000	952L
1213501-1214000	992L	1331301-800	972L	1447001-1448200	940	1626001-1627000	974P
1214001-1214600	993L	1331801-1332000	978L	1448201-1449000	924	1627001-1633000	992L
1214601-1215000	975P	1332001-1334000	992L	1449001-1450500	924	1633001-1635000	950L
1215001-1216000	974L	1334001-400	974P	1500001-600	974P	1635001-1636000	992L
1216001-1219000	992L	1334401-1335000	956P	1500601-1501200	956P	1636001-1637000	956P
1219001-1220000	974P	1335001-300	978L	1501201-1502000	974P	1637001-1638000	974P
1220001-1221000	992L	1335501-1336000	972L	1502001-1503000	993L	1638001-1642800	992P
1221001-1223500	974P	1336001-1337000	992L	1503001-1504000	996L	1642801-1643000	992P
1223501-1224000	956P	1337001-1338200	996L	1504001-500	974L	1643001-1644000	992L
1224001-1227000	992L	1338201-1339000	996L	1504501-1505200	972L	1644001-1646000	974L
1227001-1228000	972L	1339001-1340000	956P	1505201-700	978L	1646001-1648000	972L
1228001-700	992L	1340001-1341000	992L	1505701-1506000	974L	1648001-1649000	992L
1228701-1229000	990L	1341001-300	972L	1506001-1507000	975P	1649001-1652000	974P
1229001-500	956P	1341301-500	974L	1507001-1508000	992L	1652001-1653000	950L
1229501-1230000	974P	1341501-1342000	978L	1508001-400	974P	1653001-1654000	956P
1230001-1231000	974L	1342001-1343000	992L	1508401-1509000	956P	1654001-1657000	974P
1231001-1232000	992L	1343001-400	956P	1509001-1510000	992L	1657001-1660000	992L
1232001-1233000	974P	1343401-1344000	974P	1510001-1511000	974L	1660001-1661000	978L
1233001-1236000	992L	1344001-1345000	992L	1511001-1512000	975P	1661001-1663000	974P
1236001-500	974P	1345001-600	974L	1512001-1513200	992L	1663001-1664000	974P
1236501-1237000	956P	1345601-1346000	972L	1513201-600	992P	1664001-1665000	950L
1237001-500	996L	1346001-1348000	975P	1513601-1514000	992L	1665001-1666000	974P
1237501-1238000	992L	1348001-1349000	974P	1514001-200	956P	1666001-1667000	956P
1238601-1239000	956P	1349001-1350000	992L	1514201-1515000	974P	1667001-1669000	974P
1239001-1241000	992L	1350001-600	972L	1515001-1516000	992L	1669001-1670000	978L
1241001-1242000	975P	1350601-1351000	974L	1516001-1517000	974P	1670001-1671000	974P
1242001-400	974L	1351001-1352000	993L	1517001-1520000	992L	1671001-300	992L
1242401-1243000	972L	1352001-1352300	974L	1520001-1521200	974L	1671301-900	992P
1243001-500	996L	1352301-800	978L	1521201-1522200	978L	1671901-1672000	992L
1243501-1244000	992L	1352801-1353000	974L	1522001-600	974P	1672001-1676000	974P
1244001-1245000	974P	1353001-500	972P	1522601-1525000	956P	1676001-1678000	992L
1245001-1246000	992L	1353501-1354200	956P	1525001-1527000	996L	1678001-1679000	974P
1246001-300	974P	1354201-700	992P	1527001-1528000	992L	1679001-1681000	974L
1246301-800	956P	1354701-1355000	974P	1528001-1531000	974P	1681001-1682000	974P
1246801-1247000	974L	1355001-1356000	992L	1531001-1533000	992L	1682001-1683000	956P
1247001-1248000	992L	1356001-1357000	974P	1533001-600	974P	1683001-1685000	974P
1248001-1249700	974P	1357001-1359800	992L	1533601-1534000	956P	1685001-1686000	992L
1249701-1250000	956P	1359801-1361000	996L	1534001-100	975P	1686001-1688000	974P
1250001-1252000	983	1361001-1362000	992L	1535101-200	975P	1688001-500	978L
1252001-1253000	985	1362001-600	974P	1535201-600	975P	1689001-600	975P
1253001-1257000	983	1362601-1363000	956P	1535601-1536000	993L	1690001-1691000	956
1257001-900	985	1363001-1364000	992L	1536001-1537000	972L	1691001-1693000	992L
1260001-970	Chro.*	1364001-1365000	975P	1537001-1538000	992L	1693001-1696000	956P
1260971-1265000		1365001-800	956P	1538001-800	956P	1696001-1699000	992L
1265001-1266000	956P	1365801-1367000	974P	1538801-1539000	974P	1699001-1703000	974P
1266001-1267000	974P	1367001-1369400	992L	1539001-1540000	992L	1703001-1704000	992L
1267001-1268200	978L	1369401-1370000	996L	1540001-500	992P	1704001-1705000	956P
1268201-1269000	978L	1370001-1371000	974L	1540501-1541000	992L	1705001-1706000	974P
1269001-600	992L	1371001-600	996L	1541001-1542200	974P	1706001-1707100	992L
1269601-1270000	992L	1371601-1373000	992L	1542201-800	956P	1708001-1714000	992L
1270001-1271700	956P	1373001-1374000	975P	1542801-1543000	974P	1714001-1715000	974P
1271701-1272000	974P	1374001-1375000	992L	1543001-1544000	996L	1715001-1717000	992L
1272001-1274000	996L	1375001-1376000	950L	1544001-1545000	992L	1717001-800	956
1274001-500	993L	1376001-1377000	992L	1545001-400	978L	1718001-1750000	992L
1274501-700	992L	1377001-1378300	974P	1545401-1546000	974L	1750001-1761000	900
1274701-1275000	992L	1378301-1379000	956P	1546001-1548000	992L	1761001-1765000	914
1275001-1276000	972L	1379001-1380200	972L	1548001-600	974L	1765001-1767000	920
1276001-1277000	974L	1380201-1381000	978L	1548601-1549000	972L	1767001-1768000	914
1277001-1278000	992L	1381001-500	956P	1549001-1550000	992L	1768001-1769000	900
1278001-1279000	975P	1381501-1383000	974P	1550001-500	972P	1769001-1770000	920
1279001-1280000	974P	1383001-1384000	992L	1550501-1552000	992L	1770001-1778200	914
1280001-1281000	992L	1384001-1386100	974P	1552001-1555000	992L	1778201-1779000	910
1281001-800	974P	1386101-1387000	956P	1555001-1557000	993P	1779001-1780000	920
1281801-1282000	956P	1387001-1388000	992L	1557001-800	972L	1780001-1782000	910
1282001-1284000	996L	1388001-400	974P	1557801-1558000	974L	1782001-500	920
1284001-1285000	992L	1388401-1389000	978L	1558001-500	956	1782501-1783000	900
1285001-1286000	956P	1389001-300	956P	1558501-1559700	956P	1783001-1808000	910
1286001-1288000	978L	1389301-1390000	956P	1559701-1560000	974P	1808001-1810000	914
1288001-500	993L	1390001-1391000	992L	1560001-1561000	975P	1810001-1811000	910
1288501-1289100	992L	1391001-500	956P	1561001-1563000	992L	1811001-1813000	900
1289101-700	990L	1391501-1392000	974P	1563001-1565000	978L	1813001-1818000	910
1289701-1290000	992L	1392001-1393000	992L	1565001-1567000	992L	1818001-1819000	914
1290001-1291500	974P	1393001-1394000	974P	1567001-1568000	974L	1819001-1821000	910
				1568001-1569000	992L		

Serial range	Grade
1821001-1822000	914
1822001-1827000	910
1827001-600	914
1827601-1829100	910
1829101-500	914
1829501-1830000	910
1830001-1831000	900
1831001-1832000	920
1832001-700	910
1832701-1833300	914
1833301-1834500	910
1834501-1835400	914
1835401-1836900	910
1836901-1837400	914
1837401-1839000	910
1839001-500	914
1839501-1844700	910
1844701-1845700	914
1845701-1848300	910
1848301-1849500	914
1849501-1851900	910
1851901-1853100	914
1853101-1856800	910
1856801-1857900	914
1857901-1860300	910
1860301-1861000	914
1861001-1863000	900
1863001-700	920
1863701-1864300	900
1864301-1865000	920
1865001-500	914
1865501-1870300	910
1870301-1871500	914
1871501-1875100	910
1875101-600	914
1875601-1876500	910
1876501-1877500	914
1877501-1878700	910
1878701-1880000	914
1880001-300	920
1880301-1881500	900
1881501-700	920
1881701-900	900
1881901-1882900	920
1882901-1885000	900
1885001-1887400	910
1887401-1888600	914
1888601-1891000	910
1891001-1892200	914
1892201-1894600	910
1894601-1895800	914
1895801-1899000	910
1899001-300	900
1899301-1900000	910
1900001-400	910
1900401-1902100	914
1902101-1907000	910
1907001-1909000	914
1909001-1910000	910
1910001-500	920
1910501-1911000	920
1911001-1913000	900
1913001-1914000	920
1914001-1920000	910
1920001-1922000	920
1922001-1924000	910
1924001-1925000	910
1925001-1936000	910
1936001-1937000	920
1937001-900	900
1940001-1941000	914
1941001-1949000	910
1949001-1950000	914
1950001-1962000	910
1962001-1963000	914
1963001-1975000	910
1975001-1976000	914
1976001-1980000	910
1980001-1981000	914
1981001-1988500	910

*Hamilton 36 size chronometer watch

Serial range	Grade
1989001-400	914
2000001-2001700	988
2001701-2002400	986
2002401-800	988
2002801-2003100	986
2004001-2035000	986
2035001-2037200	981
2040001-2064900	986
2100001-2191300	986A
2200001-2248000	987
2248001-2300000	987F
2300001-2311000	992L
2311001-2312000	974L
2312001-2321700	992L
2321701-2323000	974L
2323001-2326000	992L
2326001-2327000	974P
2327001-2333000	974P
2333001-2336000	974F
2336001-2338000	992L
2338001-2339000	974P
2339001-2340000	974L
2340001-2341000	974P
2341001-2346000	992L
2346001-2347000	974P
2347001-2356000	992L
2356001-2358000	974P
2358001-2364000	992L
2364001-2365000	974P
2365001-2374000	992L
2374001-2375000	974P
2375001-2378000	992L
2378001-2380000	974L
2380001-2383000	992L
2383001-2384000	950L
2384001-2385000	992L
2385001-2396000	974P
2386001-2390000	992L
2390001-2391000	974F
2391001-2393000	992L
2393001-2395000	974P
2395001-2397000	992L
2397001-2398000	974L
2398001-2401000	992L
2401001-2402000	974P
2402001-2407000	992L
2407001-2409000	974P
2409001-2413000	992L
2413001-2414000	974P
2414001-2415000	974L
2415001-2418000	992L
2418001-2420000	974P
2420001-2422000	992L
2422001-2423000	974P
2423001-2432000	992L
2432001-2433000	974P
2433001-2434000	992L
2434001-2435000	974P
2435001-2437000	992L
2437001-2438000	974P
2438001-2442000	992L
2442001-2445000	974P
2445001-2451000	992L
2451001-2453000	974P
2453001-2455000	992L
2455001-2456000	974P
2456001-2457000	992L
2457001-2458000	950L
2458001-2459000	974L
2459001-2461000	992L
2461001-2462000	974L
2462001-2464000	992L
2464001-2466000	974P
2466001-2468000	992L
2468001-2469000	974P
2469001-2472000	992L
2472001-2473000	974P
2473001-2474000	992L
2474001-2475000	974P

Serial range	Grade
2475001-2476000	992L
2476001-2477000	974P
2477001-2490000	992L
2490001-2492000	974L
2492001-2504000	992L
2504001-2505000	950L
2505001-300	950L
2506001-2526000	992L
2526001-2528000	974P
2528001-2533000	992L
2533001-2534000	974P
2534001-2535000	992L
2535001-2536000	974P
2536001-2537000	974L
2537001-2538000	974P
2538001-2539000	974L
2539001-2542000	974P
2542001-2543000	992L
2543001-2545000	974P
2545001-2547000	992L
2547001-2548400	974P
2548401-2548700	974L
2548701-2550000	974P
2550001-2551000	992L
2551001-2552000	974L
2552001-2555000	992L
2555001-2555600	974L
2555701-2557000	974L
2558001-2560000	992L
2560001-2561000	974L
2561001-2563000	992L
2563001-2564000	974L
2564001-2566000	992L
2566001-2566800	974L
2567001-2581000	992L
2581001-2583900	992E
2583901-2584300	992L
2584301-2596000	992E
2596001-2597000	974L
2597001-2608000	992E
2608001-2608800	974L
2609001-2611000	992E
2611001-2611400	950L
2611401-2613000	950E
2613001-2618000	992E
2618001-2619000	950E
2619001-2631000	992E
2631001-2631600	950E
2631801-2632000	950E
2632001-2639000	992E
2639001-2641000	950E
2641001-2649000	992E
2649001-2650600	950E
2651001-2655300	992E
2900001-2911500	979
2911601-2931900	979F
3000001-3002300	922
3002301-3002500	922M.P.
3002501-3003800	922
3003501-3004000	922M.P.
3004001-3006100	922
3006101-3006300	922M.P.
3006301-3008000	922
3008001-3008600	922M.P.
3008601-3010000	922
3010001-3010500	922
3010501-3010700	922M.P.
3010701-3011900	922
3011901-3012500	922M.P.
3012501-3013100	922
3013101-3013700	922M.P.
3013701-3015700	922
3050001-3054800	902
3054801-3056000	922
3056001-3060800	902
3061001-3065100	904
3100001-3133800	916
3135001-3152700	918
3200001-3460900	912
4000001-4447201	987F
4447301-4523000	987E

Serial range	Grade
A-001 to A-8900	980B
1B-001 to 1B-25300	999B
2B-001 to 2B-700	999B
2B-701 to 2B-800	950B
C-001 to C-531000	992B
E-001 to E-114000	989
E-114001 to E-140400	989E
F-101 to F-57600	995
F-57601 to F-59850	995A
F-59851 to F-62000	995
F-62001 to F-63000	995A
F-63001 to F-63800	995
F-63801 to F-286200	995A
G-001 to G-13600	980
G-13601 to G-14600	980 & 980A
G-14601 to G-44500	980
G-44501 to G-45000	980A
G-45001 to G-47400	980
G-47401 to G-48400	980A
G-48401 to G-58200	980
G-58201 to G-58700	980A
G-58701 to G-61600	980
G-61601 to G-62500	980A
G-62501 to G-67500	980
G-67501 to G-68600	980A
G-68601- to G-651700	980
H-001 to H-1000	921
H-1001 to H-1800	400 & 921
H-1801 to H-2000	921
H-2001 to H-2800	400 & 921
H-2801 to H-3500	400
H-3501 to H-51700	921
H-50001 to H-57500	401
J-001 to J-670600	982
L-001 to L-165000	997
M-001 to M-201900	982M
N-001 to N-532200	721
O-1 to O-486300	987A
R-001 to R-3600	923
S-001 to S-18700	950B
S8-001 to S8-87400	987S
T-001 to T-783000	911
V-001 to V-127200	911M
X-001 to X-197600	917
Y-001 to Y-396200	747
CY-001 to CY-176700	748
O-01A to 622700-A	750
O-01C to 126000-C	751
001E to 47400E	752
001F to 63700F	753
001H to 26800H	754

NOTE: THE serial numbers BELOW were NOT USED S# 2,655,301 TO S# 2,900,000

also not used S# 3,460,901 TO S# 4,000,000

* Hayden W. Wheeler model

NOTE: The above serial number and grade listing is an actual Hamilton factory list and is accurate in most cases. However, it has been brought to our attention that in rare cases the serial number and grade number do not match the list. One example is the Hayden W. Wheeler model.

Grade 936 single roller before S# 426,001, double roller after S# 426,000.
Grade 937 single roller before S# 652,901, double roller after S# 652,900.
Grade 940 single roller before S# 512,201, double roller after S# 512,200.
Grade 941 single roller before S# 419,101, double roller after S# 419,100.
Grade 972 single roller before S# 748,001, double roller after S# 748,000.
Grade 973 single roller before S# 711,301, double roller after S# 711,300.
Grade 992 single roller before S# 377,001, double roller after S# 379,000.
Grade 993 single roller before S# 367,801, double roller after S# 367,800.
Grade 956, 964, 965, 968, 969, 975, 976 & 977 single roller before S# 2,477,001, double roller after S# 2,477,000.
Grade 974 & 978 single roller before S# 2,490,001, double roller after S# 2,490,000,

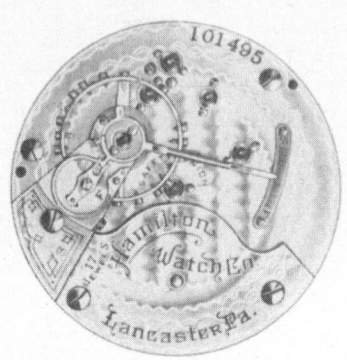

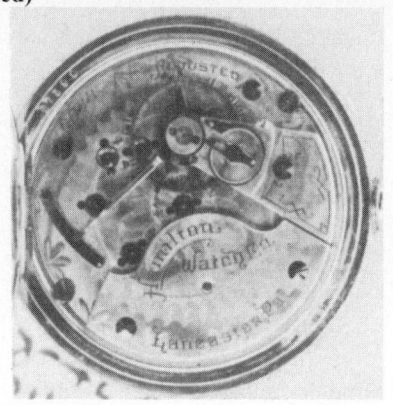

Grade 925, 18 size, 17 jewels, hunting case, serial number 101,495.

Grade 932, 18 size, 16 jewels, open face, serial number 6,888. Ca. 1894.

HAMILTON 18 SIZE

Grade or Name — Description		ABP	Ex-Fn	Mint
7J, LS, FULL, OF (total production, **1,100**)	★★	$1,600	$3,000	$3,500
11J, LS, FULL, HC (total production, **63**)	★★★★	2,200	3,500	4,500
11J, LS, FULL, OF (total production, **328**)	★★★	1,700	3,000	4,000
922, 15J, OF	★★	400	660	1,100
923, 15J, HC	★★	550	880	1,300
924, 17J, NI, OF, DMK		150	250	440
925, 17J, NI, HC, DMK		150	250	440
926, 17J, NI, OF, DMK, ADJ		150	250	440
927, 17J, NI, HC, DMK, ADJ		150	250	440
928, 15J, NI, OF		200	400	550
929, 15J, NI, HC, **14K** orig. case		650	1,200	2,000
929, 15J, NI, HC		200	400	770
930, 16J, NI, OF		200	330	770
931, 16J, NI, HC		250	440	825
932, 16J, S#**21-30 1st run** ,OF	★★★★	2,800	4,000	5,500
932, 16J, NI, OF **(S#s less than 400)**		800	1,400	2,000
932, 161, NI, OF	★★	400	660	1,200
933, 16J, NI, HC	★★	500	770	1,350
933, 16J, NI, HC *((Serial #s started at 1021-30)*		600	990	1,750
934, 17J, NI, DMK, ADJ, OF		150	275	500
934, 17J, NI, ADJ, Coin, OF		125	275	500
934 & 935 & 937, 17J, MARKED **(Main Line)**	★	350	710	1,100
935, 17J, NI, DMK, ADJ, HC	★	275	440	660
936, 17J, S# **1-20, 1st run**, OF	★★★	4,000	6,500	10,000
936, 17J, NI, DMK, SR & DR, OF		100	250	440
936, 19J, NI, DMK, SR & DR, OF	★★★★	3,000	5,000	7,500
937, 17J, NI, MARKED on Mvt.(Official Standard), HC	★	750	1,700	2,200
937, 17J, NI, DMK, SR & DR, HC		200	350	550
937, 17J, serial # 1001 to 1020 = **1st run** HC	★★	1,200	2,000	3,000
937, 17J, serial # 1031 to 1060 = **2nd run** HC	★★	600	1,400	2,200

FIRST Hunting Case serial # was **1001.**

Grade 937 *(Serial #s started at **1001**)*

Note: Some of the early watches were re-numbered - S# 07 re-numbered as 30,007, S# 12 re-numbered as 30,012, S# 1006 re-numbered as 31,006, S# 1016 re-numbered as 31,016. The above list are just a few examples, others were also returned and re-numbered

Grade or Name —Description		ABP	Ex-Fn	Mint
938, 17J, NI, DMK, DR, OF	★★	$650	$800	$1,100
939, 17J, NI, DMK, DR, HC	★★	700	850	1,200
940, 21J, NI, Mermod Jaccards St. Louis Paragon , OF Time Keeper & a hour glass on mvt	★	635	900	1,200
940, 21J, NI, DMK, SR & DR, Adj.5P, GJS, OF		225	300	450
940, 21J, NI, GF or Coin, OF		225	300	450
940, 21J, NI, SR & DR, **2-Tone**, OF	★	325	400	775
940, 21J, NI, DR. Marked **Extra**, OF	★	500	750	1,000
940, 21J, NI, DR, Marked **Special**, OF	★	500	750	1,000
940, 21J, NI, DR. Marked **Special for R R Service**, OF	★★★	2,500	3,200	4,800
940, 21J, NI, DR. Marked **Pennsylvania Special**, OF	★★	2,800	3,500	5,500
941,21J, NI, SR, GJS, HC		300	500	650
941, 21J, NI, DR. GJS, Marked **Special**, HC	★	500	750	1,200
941, 21J, NI, DMK, DR, **Adj.5P**, GJS, HC		300	500	650
942, 21J, NI, DMK, DR, Adj.5P, GJS, OF		300	500	650
942, 21J, NI, DMK, DR, Adj.5P, GJS Marked **For Railroad Service**. OF	★★	2,500	3,500	5,000
943, 21J, NI, DMK, DR, Adj.5P, GJS, HC	★	350	600	800
943, 21J, Marked Burlington Special	★★	2,600	3,500	4,500
944, 19J, NI, DMK, DR, Adj.5P, GJS, OF		300	450	700
946, Anderson, (Jobber name on movement), **14K**		1,200	1,800	2,800
946, 23J, Marked **Extra**, GJS, OF	★	1,000	1,500	2,400
946, 23J, Marked "Loaner" on case	★	800	1,200	1,800
946, 23J, NI, DMK, DR, Adj.5P, GJS, OF		1,000	1,500	1,800
946, 23J, NI, DMK, Adj.5P, GJS, unmarked, OF		1,000	1,500	1,800
947, 23J, NI, DMK, DR, Adj.5P, GJS, **14K**, HC, **NOT** MARKED "947	★★★	4,000	8,000	10,000
947, 23J, NI, DMK, DR, Adj.5P, GJS, **14K**, HC, **MARKED** "947	★★★	4,500	9,000	12,000
947, 23J, NI, DMK, DR, Adj.5P, GJS, **14K**, HC, **MARKED** "947" **EXTRA**	★★★★	5,500	10,000	15,000

*NOTE: **947 grade** is a up-jeweled version of the **943- 21J.** grade. (check serial numbers list)

MOVEMENTS WITH ODD GRADE NUMBERS ARE HUNTING CASE example **947.**
MOVEMENTS WITH EVEN GRADE NUMBERS ARE OPEN FACE example **946.**
Note: Some 18 size movements are marked with grade numbers, some are not. Collectors prefer
MARKED movement

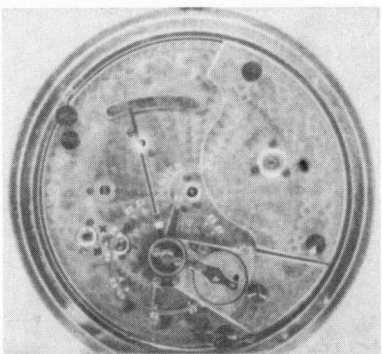

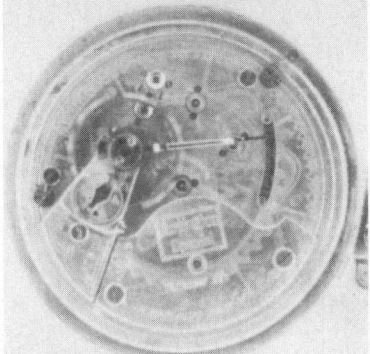

Grade 947 (marked), 18 size, 23jewels, gold jewel settings, HC, Adj5p, S# **163,219**. (From 943 run 163,001-164000) 947 grade is a up-jeweled version of the **943 21J.** grade.

Burlington Special, 18 size, 21 jewels, Grade 943, Hunting Case, serial number 121,614.

Grade or Name — Description	ABP	Ex-Fn	Mint
948, 17J, NI, DMK, DR, Adj.3P, GJS, OF .... ★	$350	$450	$950
948, 17J, NI, DMK, DR, Adj.3P, GJS, Coin, OF .... ★	350	450	950
The Banner, 928, 15J, NI, OF................................	175	300	450
The Banner, 940, 21J, NI, OF..............................	275	400	550
The Banner, 940 **special**, 21J, NI, OF	375	500	900
The Banner, 941, 21J, NI, HC..............................	325	500	650
The Banner, 17J, M#927, HC, ADJ	150	300	350
Burlington Special, 17J, Adj.5P, OF.....................★★	1,000	1,400	2,300
Burlington Special, 17J, Adj.5P, HC ....★★	1,100	1,500	2,000
Burlington Special, 21J, Adj.5P, OF ....★★	1,200	2,000	2,500
Burlington Special, 21J, Adj.5P, HC ....★★	1,400	2,500	3,500
Chesapeake & Ohio, Special, (936).....................★★★	2,500	3,500	5,000
Chesapeake & Ohio, Railway Special, (936)..............★★★	2,500	3,500	5,000
Chesapeake & Ohio, Railway Special, (937)..............★★★	2,500	3,500	5,000
Imperial Canada, GRADE 922, OF.......................★★	550	900	1,200
Imperial Canada, GRADE 923, HC.......................★★	600	1,000	1,500
Inspectors Standard, 21J, OF ....★★	900	1,500	1,800
The Union, 17J, G#924................................	175	300	450
The Union Special, 173	175	300	450
The Union, 17J, G#925, HC..............................	225	350	550

Grade 950, 16S, 23J, pendant set, gold train, gold jewel settings, white gold finish movement, OF, S# 1,020,650.

Grade 961, 16 size, 21 jewels, gold train, gold jewel settings, HC, serial number 81,848. CA. Feb, 1006.

16 SIZE

Grade or Name — Description	ABP	Ex-Fn	Mint
950, 23J, LS, BRG, DR, GT, **14K not Hamilton case OF**	$1,600	$2,200	$3,200
950, 23J, LS, BRG, DR, GT, **14K marked Hamilton case OF**	$2,000	$2,600	$3,600
950, 23J, DR, BRG, GJS, Adj.5P, NI, GCW, OF	800	1,200	1,700
950, 23J, DR, GJS, BRG, Adj.5P, NI, **Gold Train**, OF	900	1,300	1,800
950, 23J, DR, GJS, Adj.5P, NI, **PS**	700	1,100	1,600
950**B**, 23J, LS, Adj.6P, NI, DR, BRG, OF ....⬡	950	1,500	2,000
950**B**, 23J, LS, Adj.6P, NI, DR, BRG, **Gold Train**, OF........⬡	1,000	1,600	2,200
950**B**, 23J, LS, Adj.6P, NI, DR, BRG, OF, In Hamilton original two factory boxes with matching serial numbers .... ⬡★★	1,500	2,500	3,000
950**E**, 23J, LS, Adj.6P, NI, DR, BRG, marked **Elinvar**, OF ......⬡	1,100	2,000	2,500
*951, 23J, LS, BRG, Adj.5P, NI, GT, GJS, DR, HC .... ★★★★	5,000	10,000	15,000
*951, 23J, PS, BRG, Adj.5P, NI, GT, GJS, DR, HC,**14K** ... ★★★★	6,000	12,000	18,000
952, 19J, LS or PS, BRG, Adj.5P, NI, GJS, DR, OF............. ★	300	450	600
952, 19J, LS or PS, BRG, Adj.5P, OF, **14K**.................. ★	500	900	1,300

*NOTE: 951 movements were made from the **961 runs**. (check serial numbers list)

The last made American Pocket Watch was Hamiltons 992B, in 1969.

★Add $500 to 950B for 23J Railway Special mint enamel dial

🔍 Elinvar or Non Elinvar hairspring? Wind and put the watch to your ear and rock left and right. Elinvar equipped watch will thud. The non Elinvar equipped watch will ring or have a bell sound.

Grade or Name — Description	ABP	Ex-Fn	Mint
954, 17J, LS or PS, 3/4, DR, Adj., OF..........................	$125	$200	$400
956, 17J, PS, 3/4,DR, Adj., OF	100	200	350
960, 21J, PS, BRG, GJS, GT, DR, Adj.5P, OF .... ★	440	770	1,100
960, 21J, LS, BRG, GJS, OT, DR, Adj.5P, OF .... ★	440	770	1,100
961, 21J, PS & LS, BRG, GJS, GT, DR, Adj.5P, HC ....★★	495	880	1,200
962, 17J, PS, BRG, OF ....★★	525	990	1,550
963, 17J, PS, BRG, HC.................................★★★	525	990	1,550
964, 17J, PS, BRG, OF ....★★★	550	1,100	1,650
965, 17J, PS, BRG, HC.................................★★★	550	1,100	1,650
966, 17J, PS, 3/4, OF..................................★★★	550	1,100	1,650
967, 17J, PS, 3/4, HC..................................★★★	660	1,200	1,900
968, 17J, PS, 3/4, OF................................. ★	440	770	1,000
969, 17J, PS, 3/4, HC................................. ★	495	880	1,100
970, 21J, PS, 3/4, OF	250	350	600
971, 23J, Adj.5P, **SWISS MADE**.......................	75	150	200
971, 21J, PS, 3/4, HC................................. ★	300	500	700
972, 17J, PS & LS, OF, 3/4, NI, DR, GJS, Adj.5P, DMK, OF	125	200	375
973, 17J, PS & LS, 3/4, NI, DR, Adj.5P, HC	150	225	450
974, 17J, PS or LS, 3/4, NI, single roller, Adj.3P, OF.............	100	150	250
974, 17J, PS or LS, 3/4, NI, double roller, Adj.3P, OF	125	175	275
974 **special**, 17J, marked Special, double roller, Adj.3P, OF........	125	300	450
974 **special**, 17J, Electric Railway, Electric Interurban, Traffic Special or Trolly Car, Adj.3P, OF................................	175	400	550
974, 17J, Adj.3P, 2-tone, OF............................	175	200	450
2974B, 17J, Adj.3P, **hacking, U.S. GOV.**, OF	300	500	600
975, 17J, PS & LS, 3/4, NI, Adj.3P, HC	125	200	325
976, 16J, PS, 3/4, OF.................................	125	200	325
977, 16J, PS, 3/4, HC.................................	125	200	325
978, 17J, LS, 3/4, NI, DMK, OF..........................	125	185	325
990, 21J, LS, GJS, DR, Adj.5P, DMK, NI, 3/4, OT, OF...........	200	400	600
991, 21J, LS, 3/4, DR, GJS, Adj.5P, DMK, NI, GT, HC.......... ★	300	550	700

EARLY 16 size only made 670 - used a larger pillar plate

EARLY 16 size, 17J., ADJ, 1st run = 51,001 to 51,300 ...... ★★★	$500	$700	$875
EARLY 16 size, 17J., ADJ, 2nd run = 52,001 to 52,300 ..... ★★★	400	600	775
EARLY 16 size, 17J., ADJ, 3rd run = 53,001 to 53,070 ...... ★★★	300	500	675

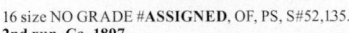

16 size NO GRADE #**ASSIGNED**, OF, PS, S#52,135. **2nd run, Ca. 1897.**

Grade 4992B, 16 size, 22 jewels, Adj.6p. Note Extra wheel for center seconds hand.

Note:Prefix before serial no. was Hamilton's method of I.D.,(C & serial no.= 992B railroad watch), (2B & serial no. = 950B railroad watch also S), (3C & serial #. = 3992B G.T.C. British & Canada), (4C & serial no.= 4992B for U.S.A. Gov't), (2K & serial no. 2974B used for comparing watch).

Grade 992E, 21 jewels, gold center wheel (<-), gold jewel settings, Adj.5P, marked Elinvar under balance wheel, Note the wide striped style Damaskeening, serial #2,595,787.

Grade 3992B, 22J, Adj.6P, 'Navigation Master', note out side chapter on dial 1—10, 5-60 in red with red minute hand. Ca. 1942. (NATO dial)

Grade or Name — Description	ABP	Ex-Fn	Mint
992, 21J, 3/4, AdJ.5P, SR & DR, NI, OF	$200	$300	$450
992, 21J, 3/4, **gold center wheel,** GJS, Adj.5P, SR & DR, NI, OF ...	225	300	475
992, 21J, 3/4, GJS, Adj.5P, DR, NI, DMK, **Mvt. 2 -Tone,** OF	265	400	675
992, 21J, **Extra,** 3/4, GJS, Adj.5P, DR, NI, DMK, OF .... ★	425	600	1,000
992, 21J, 3/4, DR, NI, **marked 8 Adj. for RR, Gold Flashed,** OF ★	600	800	1,400
992, 21J, marked **Special,** 3/4, PS & LS, GJS, Adj.5P, DR, **2-tone** NI, DMK, marked **Adj. for RR** Service on dial, OF .... ★★★	1,300	2,000	2,800
992E, 21J, marked **Elinvar, gold center wheel,** 3/4, GJS, Adj.5P . ★	450	600	950
992B, 21J, LS, Adj.6P, 3/4, OF	275	400	575
992B, 21J, Adj.6P, **2-Tone case** ....◲	300	425	675
992B, 21J, Adj.6P, 3/4, **Military** silver case, OF	325	500	675
3992B, 22J, Adj.6P, 12 hr. dial, (Canadian), Silver case ...... ★★★	600	1,000	1,200
3992B, 22J, Adj.6P, "Navigation Master", Chrome case ....★★	500	650	850
4992B, 22J, PS, 3/4, 24-hr. dial, Greenwich Civil Time, silveroid ...	250	400	550
4992B, 22J, PS, 3/4, 24-hr. dial, **Military** Silver case, OF .....◲★	350	600	800
993, 21J, LS, GJS, Adj.5P, DR, NI, DMK, HC .... ★	300	500	600
993, 21J, GJS, Adj.5P, DR, NI, DMK, HC, PS................. ★	300	500	600
993, 21J, marked **Special, tu-tone,** GJS, Adj.5P, DMK, DR, HC . ★	400	600	800
993, 21J, LS, GJS, Adj.5P, DMK, DR, NI, **14K,** HC .... ★	600	900	1,200
993, 21J, LS. GJS, Adj.5P, DMK, DR, **(GF multi color case)** HC . ★	500	800	1,000

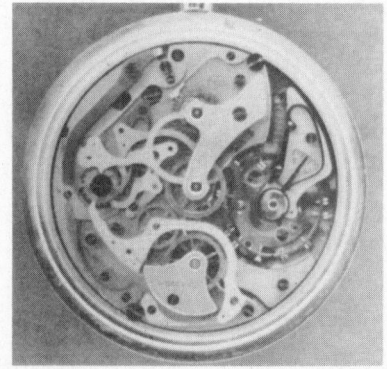

ADMIRAL,16 size, 16 jewels, Damaskeened on nickel 3/4 plate, HC, grade 977, Ca. Sept, 1898, serial no. 57821.

Chronograph, Grade 23,16 size, 19 jewels, start-stop-re-set to 0. Chronograph Grade 23 starts in 1943 ends in 1956 & total production = 23,146.

Grade or Name — Description		ABP	Ex-Fn	Mint
994, 21J, BRG, GJS, GT, DR, Adj.5P, DMK, PS, OF	★★	$900	$1,650	$2,200
994, 21J, BRG, GJS, GT, DR, Adj.5P DMK, LS, OF	★★	1,000	1,750	2,400
996, 19J, LS, 3/4 GJS, DR, Adj.5P, DMK, OF		200	300	450
Admiral, 16J., 3/4 plate, OF		125	200	350
Admiral, 16J, 3/4, NI, ADJ., DMK, HG	★	250	325	450
De Long Escapement, 21J., upright **D** shaped pallets	★★★★	4,000	6,000	9,000
Hayden W. Wheeler, 17J, OF	★	400	500	725
Hayden W. Wheeler, 17J, HC	★	450	600	900
Hayden W. Wheeler, 21J.	★	500	700	1,000
Hayden W. Wheeler, 21J, **14K & H.W.W.** on case.	★	900	1,200	1,500
Limited, 17J, G#974		200	250	350
Official Standard, 17J, OF		250	400	600
Union Special, 17J		150	250	450
Swiss Mfg., 17J, Adj.2P, G#669, OF, GF case		75	100	150
Swiss Mfg., 17J, Adj.2P, G#670, HC, GF case		100	135	200
Swiss Mfg., 23J, Adj.3P, (by Buren W. Co. G# 971), Ca. 1969-70s		125	150	250

CHRONOGRAPH
Grade 23

Grade or Name — Description	ABP	Ex-Fn	Mint
16S, 19J, chronograph with start-stop-reset to zero.	$350	$575	$725

12 SIZE
(Some cases were octagon, decagon, cushion, etc.)

Grade or Name — Description		ABP	Ex-Fn	Mint
900, 19J, BRG, DR, Adj.5P, GJS, OF, **14K**.	★	$250	$350	$525
900, 19J, BRG, DR, Adj.5P, GJS, OF		100	175	325
902, 19J, BRG, DR, Adj.5P, GJS, OF		100	175	325
902, 19J, BRG, DR, Adj.5P, GJS, **14K**	★	250	375	525

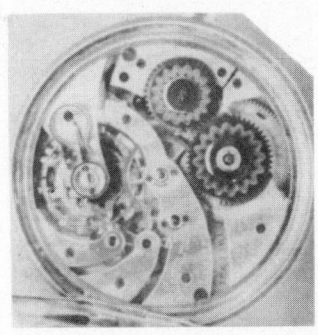

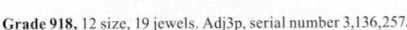

Grade 918, 12 size, 19 jewels. Adj3p, serial number 3,136,257.

Grade 920, 12 size, 23 jewels, gold train, gold jewel settings, serial number 1,863,381,

☞ A collector should expect to pay modestly higher prices at local shops.

☞ Watches listed in this book are priced at the collectableTrade Show level, as complete watches having an original 14k gold-filled case for Stem Wind and Key Wind with silver case, an original white enamel single sunk dial, and with the entire original movement in good working order with no repairs needed.

MOVEMENTS WITH ODD GRADE NUMBERS ARE HUNTING CASE ex. 951, pg. 228.
MOVEMENTS WITH EVEN GRADE NUMBERS ARE OPEN FACE ex. 950, pg. 228..

Grade or Name — Description	ABP	Ex-Fn	Mint
904, 21J, BRG, DR, Adj.5P, GJS, GT.................... ★	$150	$250	$475
910, 17J, 3/4,DR, ADJ..............................	50	100	175
912, 17J, **Digital model, rotating seconds,** OF	200	350	525
912, 17J, 3/4,DR,ADJ.............................	50	100	175
914, 17J,3/4, DR, Adj.3P, GJS	50	100	175
914, 17J, 3/4, DR, Adj.3P, GJS, **14K**..................	200	300	450
916, 17J,3/4,DR,Adj.3P............................	50	100	175
916, 17J, Adj.3P, silver case	50	100	175
918, 19J,Adj.3P,WGF	100	135	275
918, 19J, 3/4, DR, Adj.3P, GJS, OF...................	100	135	275
920, 23J, BRG, DR, Adj.5P, GJS, GT, OF	225	300	475
920, 23J, BRG, DR, Adj.5P, GJS, GT, **14K**	425	550	700
922, 23J, BRG, DR, Adj.5P, GJS, GT, **14K**	425	550	700
922, 23J, BRG, DR, Adj.5P, GJS, GT, OF	225	300	475
922 MP, 23J, marked (MASTERPIECE), 18K case .... ★	800	1,500	2,000
922 MP, 23J, marked (MASTERPIECE), Iridium Platinum...... ★	1,000	2,200	3,000
922 MP, **Gold Filled, Hamilton case**	325	500	650
400, 21J, (Illinois 13 size M#2, 5 tooth click), the Tycoon Series,			
Hamilton on dial & case, 18K, OF .... ★	450	750	900

Grade **922MP,** 12 size, 23 jewels, marked "masterpiece" serial number 3,013,390, c. 1930.

Grade **914,10**-12 size, 17J, gold jewel settings, double roller, open face, S #1,767,782.

10 SIZE

Grade or Name — Description	ABP	Ex-Fn	Mint
917, 17J, 3/4,DR, Adj.3P..................................	$50	$75	$150
917, 17J, 3/4, DR, Adj.3P, **14K**	200	300	425
921,21J,BRG,DR,Adj.5P	125	200	325
923, 23J, BRG, DR, Adj.5P, **G.F**	150	225	375
923, 23J, BRG, DR, Adj.5P, (**spread** to fit a 12 size CASE),**14K**	225	300	500
923,23J, **18K, and box**	400	700	900
923, 23J, BRG, DR, Adj.5P, **Iridium Platinum** .... ★	800	1,000	1,300
945, 23J, Adj.5P, Masterpiece on DIAL.....................	100	185	325
945, 23J, Adj.5P, spread to **12 size**.......................	100	185	325

☞ A collector should expect to pay modestly higher prices at local shops.

☞ The Complete Price Guide to Watches goal is to stimulate the orderly exchange of watches between "buyers" and "sellers".

0 SIZE

Grade or Name — Description	ABP	Ex-Fn	Mint
981, 17J, 3/4, Adj.3P, DR, **18K, HC**	$200	$400	$575
982, 17-19J, same as 981 & 983 HC but no seconds bit	75	125	200
983, 17J, Adj.3P, DR, GJS, **18K, HC**	200	400	575
985, 19J, BRG, Adj.3P, DR, GJS, GT, **18K, HC**	225	450	650
Lady Hamilton, **14K** case, OF	200	275	400
Lady Hamilton, 23J, GJS, **gold filled OF**	150	200	350

Model 22, 21 Jewels, 35 Size or 70mm, wind indicator, adjusted to 6 positions, base metal case.

Chronometer Model 22, 21 Jewels, 35 Size or 70mm, wind indicator, 54 hour mainspring, adjusted to 6 positions.

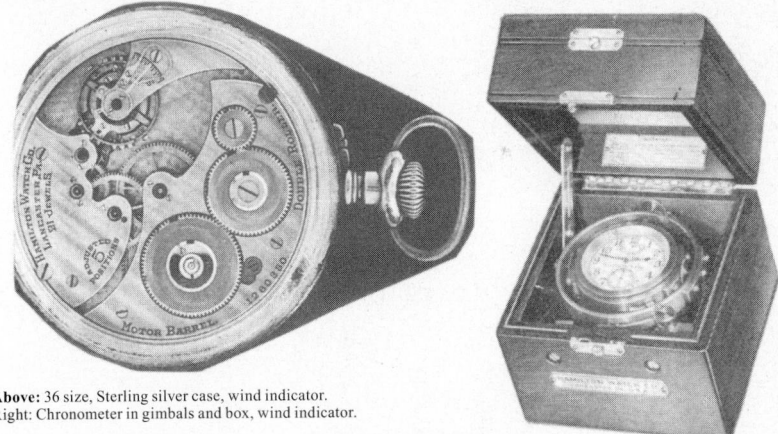

Above: 36 size, Sterling silver case, wind indicator.
Right: Chronometer in gimbals and box, wind indicator.

CHRONOMETER

Grade or Name — Description	ABP	Ex-Fn	Mint
35S, M#22, 21J, Wind Indicator, **Adj.6P,** in gimbals and box, lever	$1,000	$1,400	$2,100
35S, M#22, 21J, Wind Indicator, **Adj.6P,** in a large base metal OF case	600	800	1,200
36S, M#36, 21J, **Adj.5P,** Wind Indicator, in gimbals and box	1,300	1,800	2,600
36S, M#36, 21J, 56 hr. W. Ind., SID (sidereal), chrome case. ★	1,500	2,000	3,200
36S, M#36, 21J, Wind Indicator, in Hamilton sterling pocket watch case with bow (s# 1,260,001 to 1,260,970) ★★★	2,000	3,500	4,500
37S, 21J, 940 movement S# range= 420,001 to 421,000, ONLY 220 made for U.S. Navy, true 24 hour black dial. ★★★	1,000	1,500	3,000
85S, M#21, 14J, KW, KS, **Fusee, Detent Escapement** with helical hairspring, gimbals and box, (**all original**)	1,500	2,500	3,500

Baton
Hands
Ca.1940

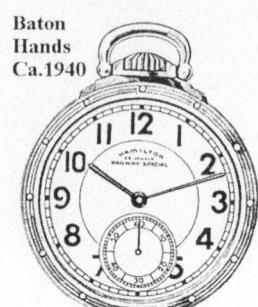

CASE MODEL # A
gold filled : $95 - $150 - $350
Dial:(23J RR)$30 - $50 - $100
Note: Baton Style hands Ca.1940

BOC = Bar Over Crown
CASE MODEL # 2,Ca.1926
gold filled : $95 - $150 - $350
14K Gold : $700 - $900 - $1,500
2 TONE case (Number 3):$150-$250-$550
Dial: RR, $20 - $40- $100

CASE MODEL #3 Ca May 1926
gold filled : $125- $200 - $375
Dial: RR, $20 - $30- $60
M#2 & M#3 first seen
Ca. May, 1926

Rigid Bow **CASE MODEL # 4**
gold filled : $125 - $200 - $375
Dial: $20 - $30 - $60
First seen Ca. Oct.1927

CASE MODEL #5
gold filled : $100- $150 -$275
Montgomery Dial: $30 - $45 - $100
First seen Ca. July, 1928

CASE MODEL #6
gold filled : $125- $200 -$350
Dial: $25 - $35 - $65
First seen Ca. Sept., 1929

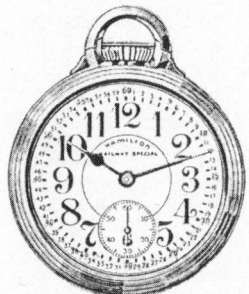

CASE MODEL # 7
White gold filled: $125 - $210 - $325
Montgomery Dial: $30 - $45 - $95
First seen Ca. May, 1930

CASE MODEL #8
gold filled : $135- $225- $400
Dial:$20-$30-$60
First seen Ca. Sept., 1931

CASE MODEL # 10
gold filled : $125- $210 - $350
Montgomery Dial: $35 - $50 - $95
First seen Ca. May 1936

Model "A" was advertised in a Gold-filled Case & advertised with a grade 950 movement.
Models 2 & 17 came in 14K solid GOLD or gold-filled, model 2 advertised with 992 or 950.
Models 3,4, 5, 6, (7 white G.F.), 8, 10, 11, Cross Bar, & Traffic Special II all gold-filled.
Model "16" gold plate and Model "15" & Traffic Special I was stainless steel case.

↝NOTE: Factory Advertised as a complete watch and was fitted with a certain matched, timed and rated movement and sold in the factory designed case style as a complete watch. The factory also sold uncased movements to JOBBERS such as Jewelry stores & they cased the movement in a case styles the CUSTOMER requested. All the factory advertised complete watches came with the dial SHOWN or CHOICE of other Railroad dials.

HAMILTON Factory Advertised 16 size Railroad Case Models

CASE MODEL # 11
gold filled : $95 - $150 - $325
Dial:$20-$40-$80

CASE MODEL # 14
Nickel: $75- $100-$175
Dial: $20 - $40 - $80

CASE MODEL # 15 Ca. 1950
S. Steel $35- $50-$100
Dial: $20 - $40 - $80

CASE MODEL # 16
gold filled: $80 - $95 - $225
M # 12 chrome:$40 - $50 - $100
Montgomery Dial: $45 - $65 - $125

CASE MODEL #17
gold filled: $125- $195 -$375
14KGold : $700 - $900 - $1,500
Dial: $30 - $50 - $100

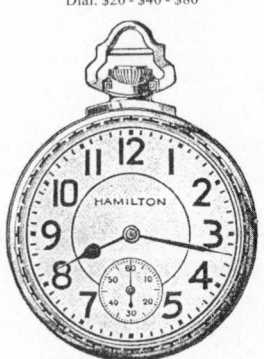

CASE MODEL Cross Bar
gold filled: $150- $300 -$500
Dial: $20 - $35 - $70
first seen in Nov. 1924

TRAFFIC SPECIAL I & #3
S. Steel : $35- $45 - $100
Montgomery Dial: $35 - $55 - $90

TRAFFIC SPECIAL II &#4
gold plated : $45- $55 - $100
Dial:$20-$30-$85

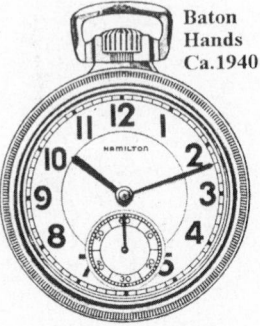

The MAINLINER
gold filled : $100 - $165 - $325
Dial:$30-$45-$80
first seen Ca 1937

*Railway Specials were packed & shipped in a plastic ivory cigarette style box & came in 12 or more different colors. **THESE PLASTIC IVORY CIGARETTE STYLE BOX** sell for **$100 -$200 -$350** +.

Model "A" was advertised in a Gold-filled Case & advertised with a grade 950 movement.
Models 2 & 17 came in 14K solid GOLD or gold-filled, model 2 advertised with 992 or 950.
Models 3, 4, 5, 6, 8, 10, 11, & Cross Bar gold-filled.
Model "16" gold plate and Model "15" & Traffic Special I was stainless steel case.
Case Model 14 = Nickel-Chrome.

HAMILTON W. CO. IDENTIFICATION OF MOVEMENTS

How To Identify Your Watch: Compare the movement with the illustration in this section. While comparing, note the location of the balance, jewels, screws, gears, and back plate (Full, 3/4, Bridge) these will be clues in identifying the movement you have. Having determined the size, the **GRADE** can also be found by looking up the serial number of your watch in the Hamilton Serial Number & Grades List. Illustrations of selected grades of the different size movements are shown to assist you in identifying movements. Hamilton movements that do not have grade numbers engraved on them do carry serial numbers which can be checked against the serial number list to secure the *grade number.*

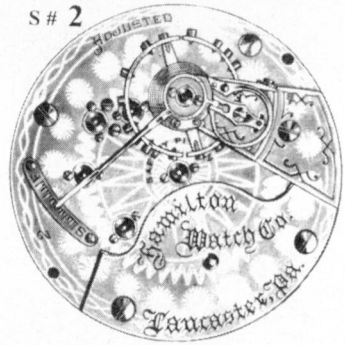

Grade 936, 18 SIZE. Full Plate, OPEN FACE SHOWN. Also grades 922, 924, 926, 928, 930, 932, 934, 938, 940. 942, 944, 946, & 948 All look SIMILAR to the above.

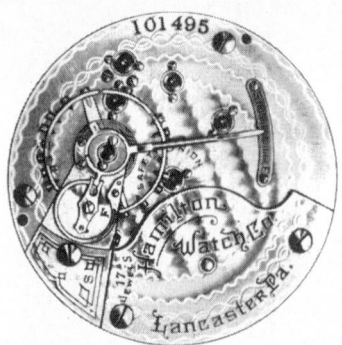

Grade 925, 18 SIZE. Full Plate, Hunting Case SHOWN. Also grades 923, 927, 929, 931, 933, 935, 937, 939, 941, 943, 945, and 947 All look SIMILAR to the above.

NOTE: 18 Size Grades 924, 925, 926, 927, 928, 929, 930, 931, 932, 933, 934, & 935 use 90% same parts but not plates. 18 Size Grades 936, 937, 938, 939, & 948 use 90% same parts but not plates. Grades 940, 941, 942, & 943 use 90% same parts but not plates. 18 Size Grades 944 & 946 use 90% same parts.

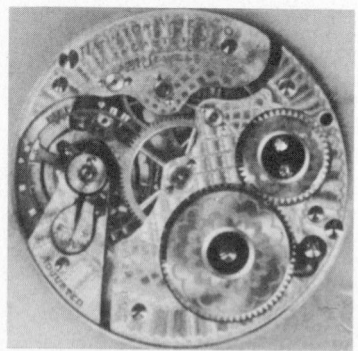

Grade 971, 16 SIZE. **Hunting Case,** 3/4 Plate, 21 jewels, Shown. Note Crown Wheel with 2 Screws this movement uses a 4 Footed Dial. Also grades 969.973,975,991, & 993 all look SIMILAR to the above. Note location of the larger ratchet wheel next to balance cock..

Grade 992, 16 SIZE. **Open Face,** 3/4 Plate, 21 jewels, 1st. model Shown. Note Crown Wheel with 2 Screws this movement uses a 4 Footed Dial. Also grades 954,968,970,972, 974, & 990 all look SIMILAR to the above. Note location of the smaller Crown wheel next to balance cock. 1st. model.

NOTE: 16 Size Grades 950, 952 & 996 use 90% same parts. 16 Size Grades 954, 962, 963, 966, 967, 972 & 973 use 90% same parts but not plates. 16 Size Grades 956, 964, 965, 968, 969, 974, 975, 976, 977, & 978 use 90% same parts. 16 Size Grades 960, 961, 970, 971, 990, 991, 992, 993, & 994 use 90% same parts but not plates. Grades 950E & 950B differ from grade 950. Grades 992E & 992B differ from grade 992.

Grade 992 Note: with narrow stripes, 18 size, 3/4 plate, 21 jewels, 5 positions, **2nd model** Shown. Note: Crown Wheel with 1 Screw. 2nd. model.

Grade 992 E = wide stripes Damaskeening with ELINVAR under balance wheel. 16 size, 3/4 plate, 21J., 5 positions, **3rd model** Shown.

Grade 992B, 16 size, 3/4 plate, 21J., **6 POSITIONS** last model, model# 4.

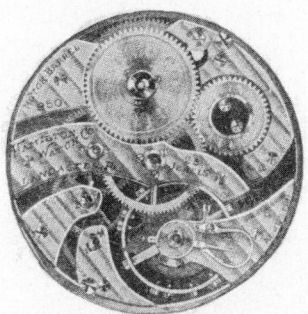

Grade 950 16 size, BRIDGE, 23J., 5 positions. Note: with narrow stripes,

Grade 950E = wide stripes Damaskeening with ELINVAR under balance wheel. 16 size, BRIDGE, 23J., 5 positions.

Grade 950B, 16 size, BRIDGE, 23J., **6 POSITIONS.**

Grade 960, <u>16 SIZE</u>. BRIDGE, OPEN FACE
SHOWN. Also GRADES 950, 952, 962, 964,
994 all look SIMILAR to the above. Note
location of the smaller Crown wheel next to
balance cock.

Grade 961, <u>16 SIZE</u> BRIDGE, Hunting Case
SHOWN. Also GRADES 951,963,965 all look
SIMILAR to the above.
Note location of the larger ratchet wheel next to
balance cock.

SWISS MADE 16size, open face, 17 to 23
jewels 3/4plate.

Grade 902, 12 size
Open face, bridge movt., 19
jewels, double roller

Grade 912, 12 size
Open face, ¾ plate move., 17
jewels, double roller

Grade 918, 12 size
Open face, ¾ plate movt., 19
jewels, double roller

Grade 922, 12 size
Open face, bridge movt., 23
jewels, double roller

Grade 917, 10 size
Open face, ¾ plate movt., 17
jewels, double roller

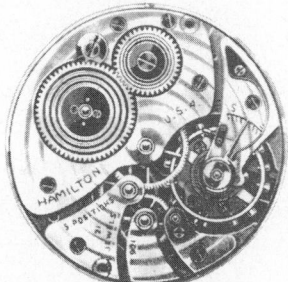

Grade 921, 10 size
Open face, bridge movt., 21
jewels, double roller

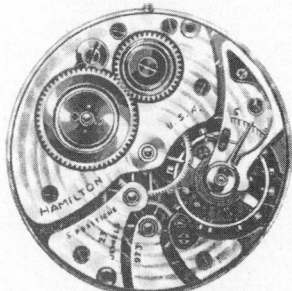

Grade 923, 10 size
Open face, bridge movt., 23
jewels, double roller

Grade 983, 0 size
Hunting, bridge movt,, 17
jewels, double roller

Grade 979,6/0 size
Hunting, 1/4 plate movt.,
19 jewels, double roller

Grade 986, 6/0 size
Open face, 3/4 plate movt.,
17 jewels, double roller

IMPORTANT NOTE: Railroad Standards, Railroad Approved & Railroad Grade **terminology**, as
defined and used *in this book*.

1. **RAILROAD STANDARDS** = A commission or board appointed by the railroad companies
outlined a set of guidelines to be accepted or approved by each railroad line.

2.**RAILROAD APPROVED** = A list of watches each railroad line would approve if purchased by
their employee's. (this list changed through the years).

3. **RAILROAD GRADE** = A watch made by manufactures to meet or exceed the guidelines set by
the railroad standards, Grades such as 992, Vanguard and B.W. Raymond, etc.

☞ Some GRADES **exceeded** the R.R standards such as 23 jewels, diamond end stone, gold train,
raised gold jewel settings, double sunk dial and the list goes on. Examples: such as Veritas, Sangamo, 950 & Riverside Maximus and many others.

HAMPDEN WATCH CO.

(DUEBER WATCH CO.)

Springfield, Massachusetts later Canton, Ohio   1877-1930

The New York Watch Co. preceded Hampden, and before that Don J. Mozart (1864) produced his three-wheel watch. Mozart was assisted by George Samuel Rice of New York and, as a result of their joint efforts, the New York Watch Co. was formed in 1866 in Providence, Rhode Island. It was moved in 1867 to Springfield, Massachusetts. Two grades of watches were decided on, and the company started with a 18S, 3/4 plate engraved "Springfield." They were sold for $60 to $75. The 18S, 3/4 plate were standard production, and the highest grade was a "George Walker" that sold for about $200 and a 16S, 3/4 plate "State Street" which had steel parts and exposed balance and escape wheels that were gold plated.

John C. Dueber started manufacturing watch cases in 1864 and bought a controlling interest in a company in 1886. At about this time a disagreement arose between Elgin, Waltham, and the Illinois Watch companies. Also, at this time, an anti-trust law was passed, and the watch case manufacturers formed a boycott against Dueber. Dueber was faced with a major decision, whether to stay in business, surrender to the watch case companies or buy a watch company. He decided to buy the Hampden Watch Co. of Springfield, Mass. By 1889 the operation had moved to Canton, Ohio. By the end of the year the company was turning out 600 watches a day. The first 16 size watch was produced in 1890 (serial number 800,xxx). In 1891 Hampden introduced the first 23J (16 size) movement made in America. Hampden assigned serial numbers at random to the New York Watch Co. movements for years after they purchased the N.Y.W.Co. Hampden W. Co. serial numbers start at about 58,000.

HAMPDEN ESTIMATED SERIAL NUMBER
AND PRODUCTION DATES

DATE- SERIAL NO		DATE-SERIAL NO.		DATE-SERIAL NO.		DATE-SERIAL NO.	
1877	59,000	1890	740,000	1903	1,768,000	1916	3,100,000
1878	70,000	1891	805,000	1904	1,896,000	1917	3,240,000
1879	100,000	1892	835,000	1905	2,024,000	1918	3,390,000
1880	140,000	1893	865,000	1906	2,152,000	1919	3,500,000
1881	180,000	1894	900,000	1907	2,280,000	1920	3,600,000
1882	215,000	1895	930,000	1908	2,400,000	1921	3,700,000
1883	250,000	1896	970,000	1909	2,520,000	1922	3,750,000
1884	300,000	1897	1,000,000	1910	2,650,000	1923	3,800,000
1885	350,000	1898	1,120,000	1911	2,700,000	1924	3,850,000
1886	400,000	1899	1,255,000	1912	2,760,000	1925	3,900,000
1887	480,000	1900	1,384,000	1913	2,850,000	1926	3,950,000
1888	560,000	1901	1,512,000	1914	2,920,000	1927	3,980000
1889	640:000	1902	1,642,000	1915	3,000,000		

The above list is provided for determining the **APPROXIMATE** age of your watch. Match serial number with date. Watches were not necessarily sold in the exact order of manufactured date.

**In 1891 Hampden introduced the first "23 Jewel" (16 size) watch made in America.

Left:**Teske's** patent round regulator, Ca.1875 Right: Tucker's patent square regulator, both were applied by watchmakers. Can be found on 18 size movements such as Hampden Springfield, Waltham, Elgin, Rockford and others.

Chronology of the Development of Hampden Watch Co.:

The Mozart Watch Co., Providence, R. I. (1864-1866)
New York Watch Co., Providence, R I. (1866-1867)
New York Watch Co., Springfield, Mass. (1867-1875)
New York Watch Mfg. Co., Springfield, Mass. (1875-1876)
Hampden Watch Co., Springfield, Mass. (1877-1886)
Hampden-Dueber Watch Co., Springfield, Mass. (1886-1888)
Hampden Watch Co., Canton, Ohio. (1888—1923)
Dueber Watch Co., Canton, Ohio. (1889—1923)
Dueber-Hampden Watch Co., Canton, Ohio. (1923—1931)
Amtorg, U.S.S.R (1930)

NR inside flag = New Railway and SR inside flag = Special Railway
D & ★D & anchor inside flag = Dueber and H inside flag = Hampden

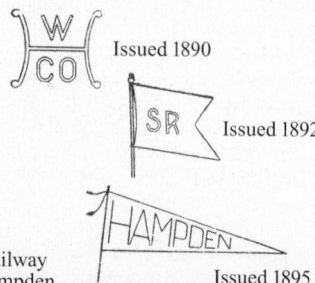

Issued 1890

Issued 1892

Issued 1895

HAMPDEN WATCH CO. (continued)

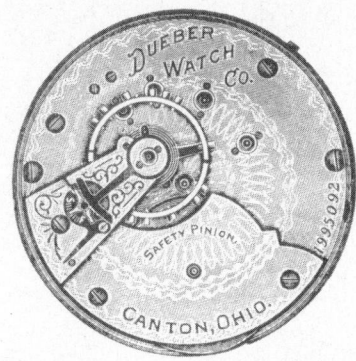

Dueber Watch Co., 18 size, 15 Jewels, nickel movement. Model 3, OF.

Canadian Pacific R. W., 17J, 18 size, Adj., Teske's patented regulator, M# 4, S# 761571, HC.

HAMPDEN 18 SIZE

Grade or Name — Description	ABP	Ex-Fn	Mint
Anchor (inside flag), 17J, ADJ, GJS, DMK	$100	$150	$225
"3 Ball", 17J, ADJ, NI, (3 Ball-damaskeening pattern)	100	150	275
Boston W. Co. 11J, KW/SW	100	150	275
Canadian Pacific R. W., 17J, Adj., M# 4, OF ★★	1,200	1,600	2,500
Canadian Pacific RR, 17J, OF ★★	1,000	1,400	2,000
Canadian Pacific RR, 21J, OF ★★	1,500	2,000	3,000
Champion, 7-11J, ADJ, FULL, gilded, or, NI, OF	100	150	175
Champion, 7-11J, ADJ, FULL, gilded, or, NI, HC	100	150	300
Correct Time, 15J, HC ★	200	300	500
Dueber Chronometer, 16-19-21J, detent escapement, (Swiss)			
Helical hairspring, LS, NI, Adj.3P, GJS, HC ★★	1,000	2,000	3,000
Dueber, 11J, gilded, DMK	100	150	175
Dueber, 15J, gilded, DMK	100	150	175
Dueber, 16J, gilded, DMK	100	150	200
Dueber, 17J, gilded, DMK	100	150	175
Dueber Grand, 17J, OF	100	150	200
Dueber Grand, 17J, ADJ, HC	125	200	300
Dueber Grand, 21J, ADJ, DMK, NI, OF	125	300	375
Dueber Grand, 21J, ADJ, DMK, NI, HC	150	550	700
John C. Dueber, 15J, gilded, DMK, OF	100	150	175
John C. Dueber, 15J, gilded, DMK, HC	125	150	300
John C. Dueber, 17J, gilded, DMK, OF	100	150	175
John C. Dueber, 17J, NI, ADJ, DMK, OF	100	150	175
John C. Dueber, 17J, NI, ADJ, DMK, HC	125	200	300
John C. Dueber, Special, 17J, ADJ, DMK, OF	100	150	200
John C. Dueber, Special, 17J, ADJ, DMK, HC	125	200	325
John C. Dueber, 21J, HC	200	500	700

Chronometer "Dueber", 16-19-21J, detent escapement, **Helical hairspring**, LS, NI, Adj.3P, GJS, S# 50200, HC. **Swiss**

John C. Dueber Special, 18 size, 17 jewels, serial number 949097.

Oriental, 18 size, 15 jewels, open face, serial number 117,825.

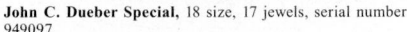

Grade or Name — Description	ABP	Ex-Fn	Mint
Dueber W. Co.,7-11J, OF	$100	$150	$175
Dueber W. Co., 15J, DMK, OF	100	150	175
Dueber W. Co., 15J, DMK, HC	125	200	300
Dueber W. Co., 16J, OF	100	150	175
Dueber W. Co., 16J, HC	125	200	300
Dueber W. Co., 17J, DMK, ADJ, OF	100	150	175
Dueber W. Co., 17J, Gilded	100	150	175
Dueber W. Co., 17J, DMK, ADJ, HC	125	200	300
Dueber W. Co., 19J, ADJ, GJS, HC ★	400	600	800
Dueber W. Co., 21J, Adj.5P, GJS, OF	150	225	350
Dueber W. Co., 21J, GJS, Adj.5P, HC	200	500	700
Forest City, 15J, KW	100	150	250
Gladiator, 7-9J, KW, OF	100	150	225
Gladiator, 9-11J, NI, DMK, OF	100	150	285
Gulf Stream Sp., 21J, R. R. grade, LS, OF ★★	750	1,000	1,600
Homer Foot, gilded, KW, OF (Early)	200	300	500

𝒢𝒢 **Generic, nameless or unmarked grades for watch movements are listed under the Company name or initials of the Company, etc. by size, jewel count and description.**

	ABP	Ex-Fn	Mint
Hampden W. Co., 7J, KW, KS, coin silver OF	$100	$150	$275
Hampden W. Co., 7J, SW, OF	100	150	175
Hampden W. Co., 11J, KW, OF	100	150	175
Hampden W. Co., 11J, KW, HC	125	200	250
Hampden W. Co., 11J, SW, OF	100	150	175
Hampden W. Co., 11J, SW, HC	125	200	250
Hampden W. Co., 15J, KW, OF	100	150	175
Hampden W. Co., 15J, KW, HC	125	200	250
Hampden W. Co., 15J, SW, HC	125	200	250
Hampden W. Co., 15J, SW, Gilded, OF	100	150	175
Hampden W. Co., 15J, SW, NI, OF	100	150	175
Hampden W. Co., 15J, **Multi-color, 14K, HC**	2,000	3,000	4,200
Hampden W. Co., 16J, OF	100	150	225
Hampden W. Co., 17J, SW, Gilded	100	150	225
Hampden W. Co., 17J, SW, NI, OF	100	150	225
Hampden W. Co., 17J, SW, HC	125	200	250
Hampden W. Co., 17J, LS, HC, **14K**	500	900	1,200
Hampden W. Co., 17J, LS, HC, **10K**	275	500	800
Hampden W. Co., 21J, SW, OF	175	300	400
Hampden W. Co., 21J, SW, HC	225	500	700

NR inside flag = New Railway and SR inside flag = Special Railway
D & ★ D & anchor inside flag = Dueber and H inside flag = Hampden

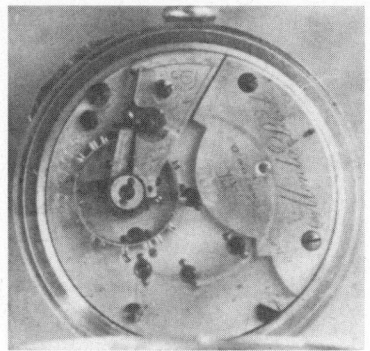

Menlo Park, 18 size, 17 jewels, serial number 1,184,116, OF.

New Railway, 18 size, 23 jewels, open face only, gold jewel settings, originally sold for $50.00, Model 3.

Grade or Name — Description	ABP	Ex-Fn	Mint
John Hancock, 17J, GJS, Adj., OF	$100	$150	$200
John Hancock, 17J, GJS, Adj., HC	125	175	275
John Hancock, 21J, GJS, Adj.5P, OF	175	300	400
John Hancock, 23J, GJS, Adj.5P, OF	300	500	600
Hayward, 11J, SW	100	150	200
Hayward, 15J, **KW**	125	200	350
Lafayette, 11J, NI, HC	125	250	375
Lafayette, 15J, NI, KW ★	200	300	500
Lafayette, 15J, NI, HC	125	225	375
Lakeside, 15J, NI, SW, HC	135	200	375
M. J. & Co. Railroad Watch Co., 15J HC ★★	400	700	1,000
Menlo Park, 11-15J	125	150	250
Menlo Park, 17J, NI, ADJ, OF	135	175	300
Menlo Park, 17J, gilded, ADJ, HC	150	225	400
Mermod, Jaccard & Co., 15J, KW, HC	150	275	400
Metropolis, 15J, NI, SW, OF	100	175	300
Wm. McKinley, 17J, Adj.3P, OF	100	150	200
Wm. McKinley, 17J, Adj.3P, HC	125	200	275
Wm. McKinley, 21J, GJS, Adj.5P	135	300	400
New Railway, 17J, GJS, Adj.5P, OF	125	175	365
New Railway, 19J, GJS, Adj.5P, OF	175	225	425
New Railway, 19J, GJS, Adj.5P, HC	200	400	550

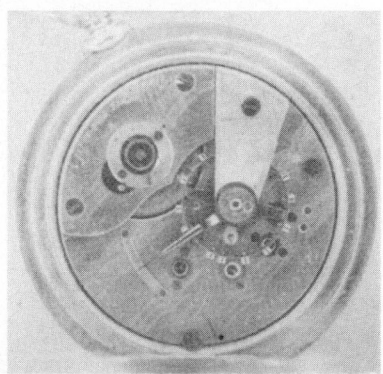

Railway, 18 size, 15-17 jewels, keywind & set, S# 115,143, early railroad watch, Ca. 1880.

Special Railway, 18 size, 23 jewels, Adj5p, serial number 3,357,284, OF.

Grade or Name — Description		ABP	Ex-Fn	Mint
New Railway, 21J, GJS, Adj.5P, OF		$175	$300	$450
New Railway, 21J, GJS, Adj.5P, HC		200	500	700
New Railway, 23J, GJS, Adj.5P		250	400	600
New Railway, 23J, GJS, Adj.5P, **14K**, OF		500	900	1,200
North Am. RW, 21J, GJS, Adj.5P, OF		225	300	500
North Am. RW, 21J, GJS, Adj, HC		250	500	700
Order of Railroad Conductors, 17J, ADJ, OF	★★★	1,800	2,500	3,500
Oriental, 15 jewels, OF		100	150	200
Pennsylvania Special, 17J, GJS, Adj.5P, DR, NI	★★★	1,500	2,500	3,500
J. G. Perry, 15J, **KW**, gilded, HC		100	175	300
J. G. Perry, 15J, NI, SW, OF		100	150	200
J. G. Perry, 15J, gilded, SW, OF		100	150	200
Railway, 11J, gilded, OF		100	200	300
Railway, 15-17J, NI, OF		125	200	400
Railway, 15-17J, KW, marked on mvt., HC	★★	700	1,000	1,600
★Railroad with R.R. names on dial and movement:				
Private Label RR. 17J, OF	★★	650	850	1,200
Special Railway, 17J, GJS, Adj.5P, NI, DR, OF		100	165	300
Special Railway, 21J, GJS, Adj.5P, NI, DR, OF		200	300	425
Special Railway, 21J, GJS, Adj.5P, NI, DR, 2-Tone, OF		250	375	600
Special Railway, 21J, GJS, Adj.5P, NI, DR, HC		225	500	700
Special Railway, 23J, GJS, Adj.5P, NI, DR, OF		300	400	550
Special Railway, 23J, GJS, Adj.5P, NI, DR, 2-Tone, OF		350	500	700
Special Railway, 23J, GJS, Adj.5P, NI, DR, HC		350	600	800
Special Railway, 23J, **14K, HC**		650	1,200	1,500
Springfield, 7-11J, KW, gilded, HC		125	200	300
Springfield, 7-11J, SW, NI, HC		125	200	300
Standard, 15J, gilded, HC		125	200	300
Train Service Standard, 17J, LS, M# 2, NI, HC	★	450	550	850
Theo. Studley, 9-15J, KW, KS, HC		125	200	300
Tramway Special, 17J, NI, OF		150	225	375
Wisconsin Central R W, 17J, LS, OF	★	650	850	1,600
Woolworth, 11-15J, KW, OF		100	150	275
Grade 30,31,45,46,54,57,65,66,70,71, **ALL =11J**		100	150	200
Grade 32,33,34,35,36,40,41,42,49,55,56,58,59,60,62, **All=15J**		100	150	200
Grade, 43,44,47,48,49,63,64,67,68,69,80,81, **ALL=16-17J**		100	165	250
Grade 85, 19J, GJS, 2-Tone, HC	★★	500	700	1,200
Grade 95, 21J, GJS, OF		175	300	450
Grade 125, 21J, Adj.3P, OF		175	300	450

**In 1891 Hampden introduced the first "23 Jewel" (16 size) watch made in America.

16 SIZE

Grade or Name — Description		ABP	Ex-Fn	Mint
Beacon, 7J, OF		$75	$110	$200
E.W. Bond & State Street models see New York W. Co. Springfield				
Champion, 7J, NI, 3/4, gilded, coin, OF		60	85	185
Champion, 7J, NI, 3/4, gilded, OF		60	85	185
Champion, 7J, NI, 3/4, gilded, HC		90	135	275
Chronometer, 21J, NI, Adj.3P, GJS, (lever Escap.), OF	★	500	650	900
Chronometer, 21J, NI, Adj.3P, GJS, (lever Escap.), HC	★	650	750	1,000
John G. Dueber, 17J, GJS, NI, Adj.5P, 3/4, LS, OF		75	110	200
John G. Dueber, 21J, GJS, NI, Adj.5P, 3/4		125	250	325
John G. Dueber, 21J, GJS, NI, Adj.5P, DR, BRG		150	275	325
Dueber Watch Co., 15-17J, ADJ, 3/4		70	110	200

NOTE: Railroad Standards, Railroad Approved & Railroad Grade **terminology**, as defined and used in this book.
1. **RAILROAD STANDARDS** = A commission or board appointed by the railroad companies outlined a set of **guidelines** to be accepted or approved by each railroad line.
2. **RAILROAD APPROVED** = A **LIST** of watches each railroad fine would approve if purchased by their employees. (this list changed through the years).
3. **RAILROAD GRADE** = A watch made by manufactures to meet or exceed the guidelines set by the railroad **standards**. Grades such as 992, Vanguard and B. W. Raymond, etc.
↝ Some GRADES **exceeded** the R.R. standards such as 23 J,. diamond end stone, gold train, raised gold jewel settings, double sunk dial and the list goes on. Examples: such as Veritas, Sangamo, 950 & Riverside Maximus and many others.

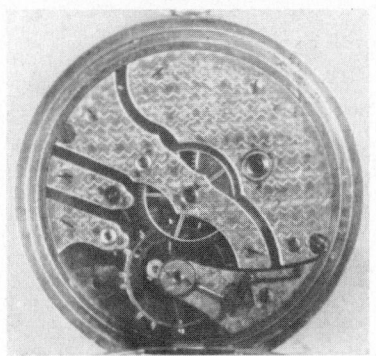

Hampden W. Co., Bridge Model, 16 size, 23 jewels, 2-tone movement, serial number 1,899,430.

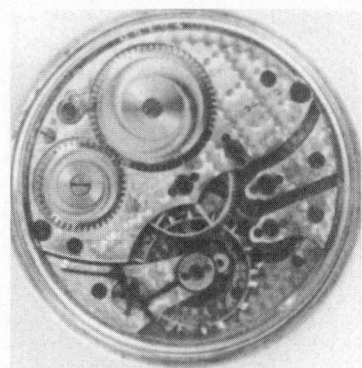

Hampden W. Co., 16 size, 17 jewels, gold jewel settings, serial number 3,075,235.

⚲ Generic, nameless or unmarked grades for watch movements are listed under the Company name or initials of the Company, etc. by size, jewel count and description.

Grade or Name — Description	Av	Ex-Fn	Mint
Hampden W. Co., 7J, SW, OF...............................	$45	$70	$135
Hampden W. Co., 7J, SW, HC	75	150	200
Hampden W. Co., 11J, SW, OF..............................	50	100	150
Hampden W. Co., 11J, SW, HC..............................	75	150	200
Hampden W. Co., 15J, SW, OF..............................	60	100	175
Hampden W. Co., 15J, SW, HC	75	150	200
Hampden W. Co., 17J, SW, OF..............................	70	100	225
Hampden W. Co., 17J, **14K, Multi-color,** HC..............	1,600	2,200	3,600
Hampden W. Co., 17J, SW, HC	90	150	275
Hampden W. Co., 21J, SW, HC	150	500	600
Hampden W. Co., 21J, SW, OF..............................	150	300	425
Hampden W. Co., 23J, Adj.5P, GJS, 3/4......................	300	450	625
Hampden W. Co., 23J, Adj.5P, GJS, bridge model, **2-tone**	325	475	675
Hampden W. Co., 23J, Series 2, **Freesprung,** GJS GT, HC ... ★★★	700	1,000	1,600
Masonic Dial, 23J, GJS, 2-Tone **enamel dial**	700	1,000	1,600

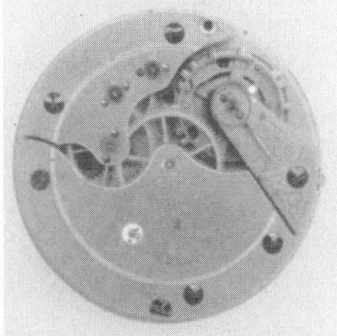

Hampden W. Co., Series 1, 16 size, 15 jewels, stem wind open face.

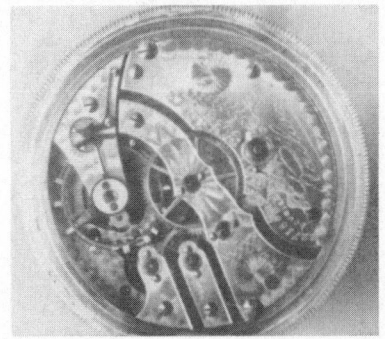

Railway, 16 size, 17 jewels, Adj.5P, gold jewel settings, serial number 2,271,866.

NR inside flag = New Railway and SR inside flag = Special Railway
D & ★D & anchor inside flag = Dueber and H inside flag = Hampden

⚲ Generic, nameless or unmarked grades for watch movements are listed under the Company name or initials of the Company, etc. by size, jewel count and description.

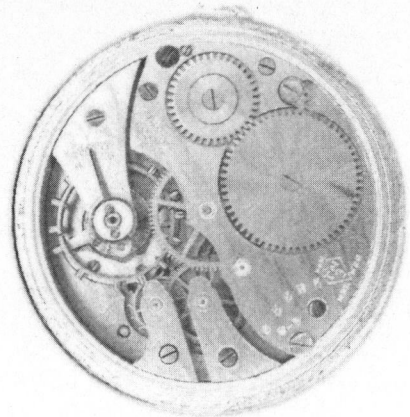

Grade 104, 16 size, 23 jewels, gold jewel settings, gold train, Adj5p, open face, serial number 2,801,184

Hampden style watch produced in Russia with the machinery purchased from Hampden W. Co. by the Russian factory. This watch is a 16 size 7 jewel movement Ca. 1935 engrave on Mvt. 7 KAMMEA 4-8, 28229 HKM MOCKER.

Grade or Name — Description	ABP	Ex-Fn	Mint
Wm. McKinley, 17J, GJS, Adj., NI, DR. 3/4	$75	$110	$200
Wm. McKinley, 21J, GJS, Adj.5P, NI, DR. OF	150	300	400
Wm. McKinley, 21J, GJS, Adj.5P, NI, DR, 3/4, Coin	150	300	400
Wm. McKinley, 21J, GJS, Adj.5P, NI, DR, HC	200	500	525
New Railway, 17J, GJS, LS, NR (in flag) .... ★★★	225	325	550
New Railway, 21J, GJS, Adj.5P	175	300	400
New Railway, 23J, GJS, Adj.5P, LS, HC	225	500	650
Ohioan, 21J, Adj., GJS, 3/4, OF & HC	150	400	500
Railway, 17-19J, GJS, Adj.5P, BRG, DR, OF	125	200	350
Special Railway, 17J, Adj, NI, BRG, DR. OF	125	200	350
Special Railway, 17J, Adj, NI, BRG, DR, HC	95	200	300
Special Railway, 23J, Adj.5P, NI, BRG, DR	300	500	675
Russian made model, 7-17J, 16 size, 3/4 plate. .... ★★	175	235	400
Garfield, 21J., Adj.5P, OF.	200	325	400
Gen'l Stark, 15J, DMK, BRG.	75	110	200
Gen'l Stark, 17J, DMK, BRG.	75	110	200
76, 21J, LS, Adj.3P	125	250	300
94-95, 21J, **marked** "94 or 95", GJS, Adj.5P	225	300	500
97 HC, 98 HC, 107 OF, 108 OF, 17J, Adj.3P, NI, 3/4	75	150	250
97, 17J., **marked** 97, Adj., HC	200	275	350
99, 15J, 3/4, HC.	75	150	250
103, 23J, GJS, Adj., NI,3/4, DR, free sprung, **2-tone**, HC .... ★★★	700	1,000	1,600
104, 17J, NI, Adj., 2-tone	250	375	600
104, 23J, GJS, Adj.5P, NI, 3\4 or BRG, DR, **marked**, OF	300	500	700
104, 23J, GJS, Adj.5P, NI, 3\4 or BRG, DR. **2-tone**, OF	350	600	800
104, 23J, GJS, Adj.5P, NI, BRG, DR, **marked**, HC.	350	575	800
105, 21J, GJS, Adj.5P, NI, 3/4, DR, marked, OF	225	300	475
105, 23J, GJS, Adj.5P, NI, 3/4, DR, HC	275	600	750
106, 107 OF, & 108, **17J**, SW, NI, **marked**	75	110	200
107, 17J, NI, Adj., 2-tone	250	350	600
109, 15J, 3/4, **marked**, OF	75	100	200
110, 11J, 3/4.	50	100	150
115, 21J, SW, NI, **marked**, OF	225	300	475
120, 21J, SW, NI, OF, **marked Chronometer on dial** .... ★	300	450	650
125, **marked**, 21J, DR, Adj.3p	200	300	375
340, 17J, SW, NI.	85	125	225
440, 15J, 2-tone.	85	125	225
555, 21J, GT, GJS, **marked 555, Chronometer on dial & mvt** .. ★	600	800	1,100
555, 21J, GT, GJS, **marked 555, Chronometer on dial ONLY** .. ★	375	500	650
600, 17J, SW, NI, **marked, 600**	75	110	200

Dueber Grand, 12 size, 17 jewels, gold jewel settings, hunting case, serial number 1,737,354.

John Hancock, 21 jewels, Adj. 5P, lever set, came in HC & OF, Movement above is Hunting Case.

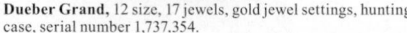

12 SIZE Standard Model

Grade or Name — Description		ABP	Ex-Fn	Mint
Aviator, 17J, Adj.4P, OF	★	$90	$150	$275
Aviator, 19J, Adj.4P, OF		75	100	200
Beacon, 17J, OF (only seen in ads)	★★★★	200	400	600
Biltmore, 17J, OF		75	100	200
Dueber Grand, 17J, BRG, OF		75	100	200
Dueber Grand, 17J, BRG, HC		100	200	275
Dueber Grand, 17J, 3/4 plate, pin set, OF		75	100	200
Dueber Grand, 17J, 3/4 plate, lever set OF	★★	100	150	250
Dueber Grand, 17J, 3/4 plate, pendant set, OF	★	100	150	250
Dueber Grand, 17J, 3/4 p late, HC		100	200	250
Dueber Grand, 17J, BRG, lever set, HC		100	200	250
Dueber Grand, 17J, BRG, lever or pendant set, OF		75	100	200
Dueber W. Co. 17J, Adj., 3/4, pendant set OF		75	100	200
Dueber W. Co. 17J, Adj., 3/4, pendant set, HC		85	175	225
Duquesne, 19J, Adj., OF	★★	95	150	275
Gen'l Stark, 15J, M#3 LS, HC		75	150	200
Gen'l Stark, 15J, M# 3 **PIN** or pendant set OF		65	95	150
Gen'l Stark, 15J, M# 3 lever set, OF	★	100	135	250
Gen'l Stark, 15J, M# 4 lever set, HC		75	150	200
Gen'l Stark, 15J, M# 4 pendant set OF		65	95	150
Gen'l Stark, 15J, M# 4 lever set OF	★	60	90	150
Hampden W. Co., 17J, **14K, Multi-color, HC**		675	1,000	1,800
John Hancock, 21J, 3/4, **PIN** set, Adj.5P, GJS, OF	★★	125	175	250
John Hancock, 21J, 3/4, lever set, Adj.5P, GJS, HC	★	150	200	300
John Hancock, 21J, BRG, pendant or lever set, Adj.5P, GJS, OF	★★	150	200	300
John Hancock, 21J, BRG, lever set, Adj.5P, GJS, HC	★	150	200	300
Minute Man, 17J., (standard size), OF		85	135	250
Ohioan, 21J, Adj.3P, GJS, 3/4, OF	★	125	175	275
Ohioan, 21J, Adj.3P, GJS, 3/4, HC	★★★	175	250	375
Viking, 17J, Adj, OF	★	75	110	200
No.10, 7J, OF		40	60	100
300, 7J, M# 3 LS, M# 5 stem set, HC		40	125	200
300,7J, M# 5 lever set, HC	★★	50	125	200
302, 73., M# 3 LS, M# 5 stem set, OF		40	60	100
302, 7J, M# 5 lever set, OF	★	50	75	135
304, 15J, HC		75	125	200
305, 17J, HC	★	75	125	225
306, I53, OF		60	85	125
307, 17J, Adj, OF		75	100	165
308, 17J, Adj, HC		85	135	200
310, 17J, Adj, OF		65	95	150
310, 17J, Adj, **marked, 14K** OF case		175	300	425
312, **marked**, 21J, 3/4, Adj.5P, DMK, HC	★★	150	200	300
314, **marked**, 21J, DR, Adj. 5P, DMK, OF	★	125	175	265
320, **marked**, 17J, DR, Adj	★★	100	165	250
366, 17J., OF	★★	85	100	170
500, 17J, **marked**, OF		85	100	170
500, 17, HC	★★★	125	165	225
603, 17J, OF	★	85	100	170
700, 15J, **marked**, OF		60	80	150
17 Jewel Special marked on Dial & Mvt., 2 tone, OF	★★	95	125	195

Example of Hampden Watch Co.'s THIN MODEL showing dial and movement, 12 size, 17-19 jewels, Adj3-5p.

12 SIZE (THIN MODEL)

Grade or Name — Description	ABP	Ex-Fn	Mint
Nathan Hale, 15J	$75	$95	$250
Minute Man, 17J ★	85	125	275
Relgis, 15J, OF ★★	75	100	200
Relgis, 17J, OF ★★★	125	150	250
Paul Revere, 17J, OF, **14K**	200	300	600
Paul Revere, 17J	95	125	275
Paul Revere, 19J	125	150	325

Hampden 12 size (thin model) case are **not** interchangeable with other American 12 style cases.

6 SIZE

Grade or Name — Description	ABP	Ex-Fn	Mint
200, 7J (add $25 for HC)	$40	$65	$150
206, 11J (add $25 for HC)	40	65	150
21J, 15J (add $25 for HC)	40	65	150
215, 16J, (add $25 for HC)	40	65	150
220, 17J (add $25 for HC)	40	65	150
Hampden W. Co., 15J, **multi-color Gold Filled, HC**	225	275	475
Hampden W. Co., 15J, **multi-color, 14K, HC**	400	650	925

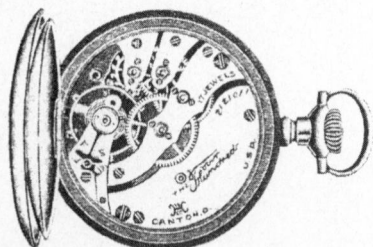

The Four Hundred, 17 jewels, raised gold jewel settings, hunting case. and originally sold for $12.00.

Molly Stark, 000 size, 7 jewels, hunting or open face,

000 SIZE

Grade or Name — Description	ABP	Ex-Fn	Mint
Diadem, 11-15J, **14K**,OF	$125	$175	$350
Diadem, 11-15J, **14K**, HC	225	300	475
Diadem, 11-15J, **Gold Filled**, HC	75	175	250
Molly Stark, 7J, **Gold Filled**, HC	75	175	250
Molly Stark, 7J, **14K**, HC	225	300	475
Molly Stark, 7J, Pin Set, OF	75	125	200
No.400, 16-17j, 14K **solid gold plates** & bridges, 14K HC ★★★★	500	800	1,200
The Four Hundred, 17J, raised gold jewel settings, HC	100	150	275
14K Multi-color, HC	400	600	900

HAMPDEN WATCH Co.
IDENTIFICATION OF MOVEMENTS

How to Identify Your Watch Size & Model: Compare the movement of your watch with the illustrations in this section. While comparing, note the location of the balance, jewels, screws, gears, and type of back plate (Full, 3/4, Bridge) these will be clues in identifying the movement you have.

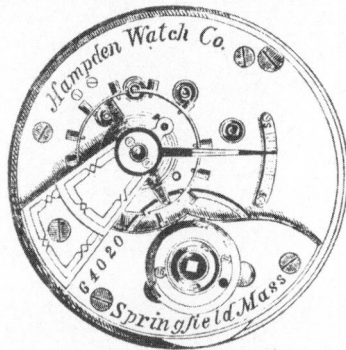

Model I, 18 size
Hunting or open face, key wind & set

Model II, 18 size
Hunting, stem wind, pendant or lever set

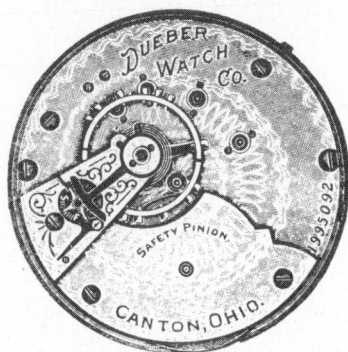

Model IV, 18 size
Hunting, stem wind, pendant or lever set

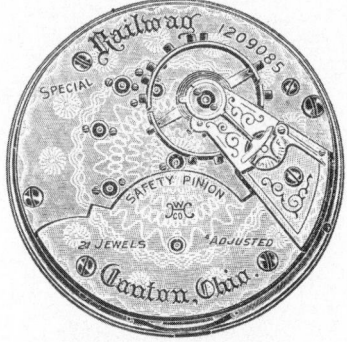

Model III, 18 size
Open face, stem wind, lever set

000 SIZE

No. 400 14 karat solid gold movement. All plates and bridges made of 14k gold. 1897 ad priced at $65.00 case extra.

Model 1, 16 size
Open face, seem wind,
pendant or lever set

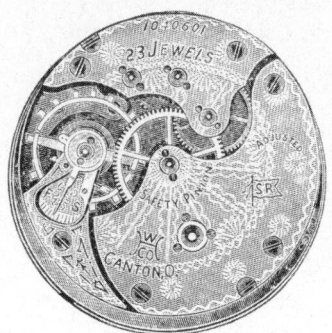

Model II, 16 size
Hunting, stem wind,
pendant or lever set

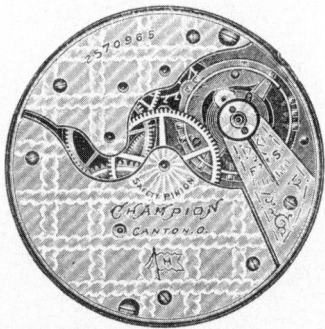

Model III, 16 size
Open face, stem wind, pendant set

Model IV, 16 size
Hunting, stem wind,
pendant or lever set

Model V, 16 size
Open face, stem wind,
pendant or lever set

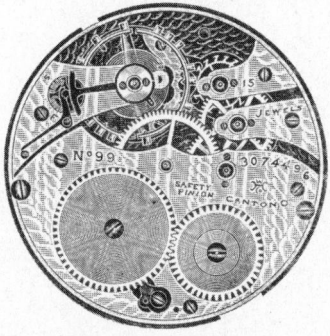

Model VI, 16 size
Hunting, stem wind, pendant set

Model VII, 16 size
Open face, stem wind, pendant set

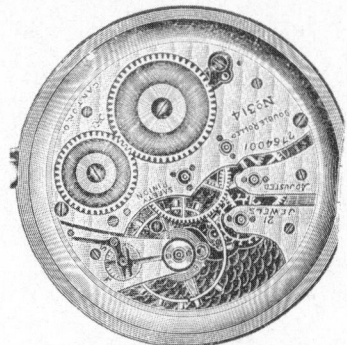

Model III, 12 size
Open face, stem wind, pendant set

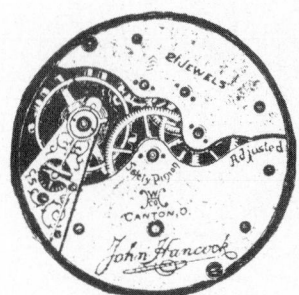

Model I, 12 size
Hunting, stem
wind, lever set

Model II, 12 size
Open face, stem
wind, lever set

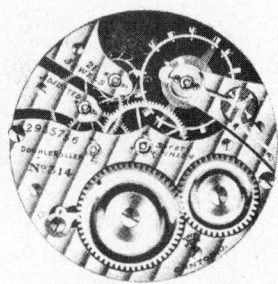

Model IV, 12 size
Open face, stem
wind, pendant

Model V, 12 size
Open face, stem
wind, pendant set

Model I, 6 size
Hunting, stem wind

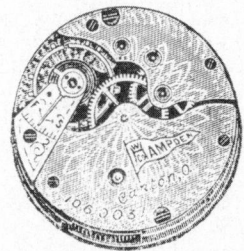

Model I, 3/0 size
Hunting, stem wind

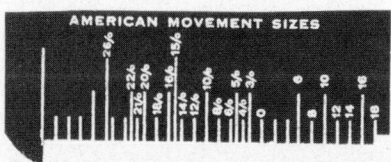

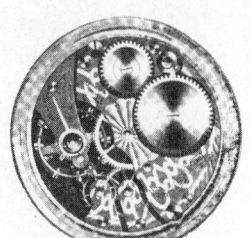

Series II, 3/0 size
Open face, stem wind, pendant

Series III, 3/0 size
Hunting, lever or pendant

Series IV, 3/0 size
Hunting, stem wind, pendant

No. 104

16 Size

Open Face and Hunting

Lever Setting

1908 AD
1922 PRICE
LIST

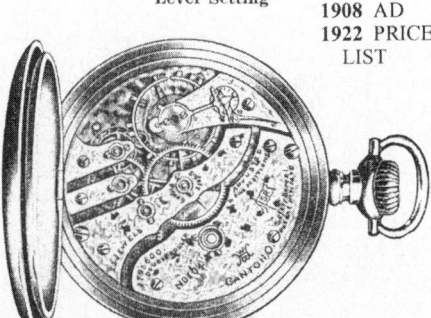

Nickel, bridge model, 23 extra fine Ruby and Sapphire jewels in solid gold settings, *Sapphire Roller Jewels* and *Pallet Stones, Steel Escape Wheel,* round arm polished train wheels, *Patent Safety Barrel No. 711476 with Main Wheel Arbor Pivots Revolving in Jewels,* patent center pinion, escape pinion and pallet arbor with conical pivots cap jeweled, patent microm. regulator, Breguet hairspring, New Model stud, compensation balance with gold screws and meantime screws, accurately *Adjusted to Temperature, Isochronism* and *5 Positions,* double sunk glass enameled dial with red marginal figures, beveled head gilt screws, elegantly engraved and damaskeened, gold lettering, highly polished steel work, first quality "Hampden" mainspring for patent barrel, and *Double Roller Escapement.*

1908 AD
1922 PRICE
LIST

Special Railway

18 Size ☞

Open Face and Hunting

Lever Setting

Nickel, 23 extra fine Ruby and Sapphire jewels in solid gold settings, barrel arbor and center staff jeweled with the finest of Sapphires, escapement cap jeweled, conical pivots, finely graduated microm. regulator, compensating balance, gold screws, *Steel Escape Wheel,* Breguet hairspring, meantime screws, New Model stud, accurately *Adjusted to Temperature, Isochronism and 5 Positions,* patent center pinion, beveled head gilt screws, highly polished steel work, fine double sunk glass enameled dial in Arabic or Roman figures, elegantly engraved and damaskeened in two colors, gold lettering.

The handsomest, most finely finished and closely timed Movement made in America.

HAMPDEN WATCH MOVEMENTS

18 SIZE

Special Railway ____21J. OF _____	$24.70
Dueber Watch Co.___21J. OF _____	20.50
No. 64 _____17J. OF _____	9.35

16 SIZE

Special Railway ____23J. OF only _____	$35.80
No. 104 _____23J. OF only _____	35.80
New Railway _____21J. OF only _____	28.70
No. 105 _____21J. OF only _____	28.70
Wm. McKinley _____21J. OF only _____	28.70
Railway _____19J. OF only _____	24.85
Wm. McKinley _____17J. Htg.-OF _____	12.25
No. 98—No. 108 ____17J. Htg.-OF _____	11.35
No. 99—No. 109 ____15J. Htg.-OF _____	9.05

12 SIZE

No. 305—No. 307 ___17J. Htg.-OF _____	$12.60
No. 304—No. 306 ___15J. Htg.-OF _____	10.65

Fancy solid silver dials fitted on 12 and 16 size
movements — extra _____$2.50

BRACELET HEADS

We make a complete line of the various popular shapes and sizes of bracelet heads in white, green and regular solid gold and gold-filled cases.

WATCH CASES

Our line of watch cases includes the same high quality of solid gold, 25-year and 20-year gold-filled and silverine cases in all standard models, including white, green and regular colored gold-filled cases.

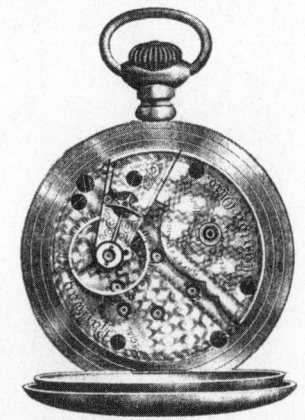

HERMAN VON DER HEYDT

CHICAGO SELF-WINDING WATCH CO.
Chicago, Illinois 1883- 1895

Herman von der Heydt patented a self-winding watch on Feb. 19, 1884. A total of about **35** watches were hand-made by von der Heydt. The watches were 18S, full plate, lever escapement and fully-jeweled. The wind mechanism was a gravity type made of heavy steel and shaped like a crescent. The body motion let the heavy crescent move, as it was connected to a ratchet on the winding arbor, resulting in self-winding. About **Five** movements were nickel and sold for about $90; the gilded model sold for about $75.

Grade or Name — Description		ABP	Ex-Fn	Mint
18S, 19J FULL, NI .... ★★★★★		$16,500	$27,500	$49,500
18S, 19J, FULL, gilded. .... ★★★★★		13,200	22,000	44,000

Herman Von Der Heydt, 18 size **self winding watch**, "Chicago S. W. Co.' on dial. H. VON DER HEYDT, PATENTED, FEB.19, 84 on auxiliary dial.

Herman Von Der Heydt, 18 size, 19jewels; Americas only self winding pocket watch. Note crescent shaped winding weight, serial number 19.

Maintaining Power

Maintaining Power is a device for driving a watch during the operation of winding. Harrison introduced the Maintaining Spring device and was used in all fusee watches. The intermediate disc carried the pawl to engage the fusee ratchet and drove the main wheel by a small curved spring. The intermediate wheel did not turn during winding, being toothed on its outer edge and resist by a pawl set between the plates of the movement. The fusee was abandoned for American pocket watches and the going barrel employed. On some early Howards & Walthams maintaining power was used. The advantage was safety against damage due to breaking of mainsprings. G.P. Reed worked for Dennison, Howard & Davis and patented on April 14, 1857 a maintaining spring barrel. This device was used by Howard up to about S# 30,000 and American Waltham W. Co. used Stratton's, Pat. Feb. 2,1864.

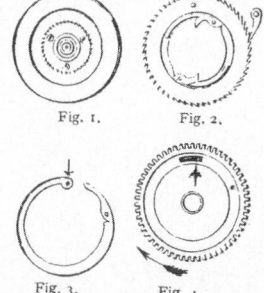

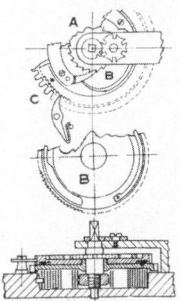

Above: Harrison's Maintaining Spring. Fig.1 end of fusee & Fig. 2 ratchet placed next to fusee, a pin passes through the ball end of the spring Fig.3, & enters a slot in wheel Fig.4.

Above: Howard's Maintaining Spring in going barrel set into the pillar plate. A turned with the arbor & collet, B carried the pawl on its top side & maintaining spring B on its under side, driving the main wheel during winding.

E. HOWARD & Co.

Boston (Roxbury), Massachusetts   December 11, 1858 - 1903

After the failure of the Boston Watch Company (1853-57), Edward Howard decided to personally attempt the successful production of watches using the interchangeable machine-made parts system. He and Charles Rice, his financial backer, were unable to buy out the defunct watch company in Waltham, however, they did remove (per a prior claim) the watches in progress, the tools and the machinery to Howard and Davis' Roxbury factory (first watch factory in America), in late 1857. During their first year, the machinery was retooled for the production of a revolutionary new watch of Howard's design. Also, the remaining Boston Watch Co. movements were completed (E. Howard & Co. dials, Howard & Rice on the movement). By the summer of 1858, Edward Howard had produced his first watch. On December 11, 1858 the firm of E. Howard & Co. was formed for the manufacture of high-grade watches. Howard's first model was entirely different from any watch previously made. It introduced the more accurate "quick beat" train to American watchmaking. The top plate was in two sections and had six pillars instead of the usual four pillars in a full plate. The balance was gold or steel at first, then later it was a compensation balance loaded with gold screws. Reed's patented barrel was used for the first time. The size, based on the Dennison system, was a little larger than the regular 18 size. In 1861 , a 3/4 plate model was put on the market. Most movements were being stamped with "N" to designate Howard's 18 size. On February 4, 1868 Howard patented a new steel motor barrel which was to supersede the Reed's, but not before some 28,000 had been produced. Also, in 1868 Howard introduced the stemwinding movement and was probably the first company to market such a watch in the U. S. By 1869, Howard was producing their "L" or 16 size as well as their first nickel movements. In 1870, G. P. Reed's micrometer regulator was patented for use by E. Howard & Co. The Reed style "whiplash" regulator has been used in more pocket watches, worldwide, than any other type. In 1878, the manufacturing of keywind movements was discontinued. Mr. Howard retired in 1882, but the company continued to sell watch movements of the grade and style set by him until 1903 and beyond. This company was the first to adjust to all six positions. Their dials were always a hard enamel and always bore the name "E. Howard & Co., Boston." In 1902, the company transferred all rights to use the name "Edward Howard," in conjunction with the production of watches, to the Keystone Watch Case Co. Most of their models were stamped "Howard" on the dial and "E. Howard Watch Co., Boston. U.S.A." on the movement. Edward Howard's company never produced its own watch cases, the great majority of which were solid gold or silver. Keystone, however, produced complete watches, many of which were gold filled.

CHRONOLOGICAL DEVELOPMENT OF E. HOWARD & CO.:
Warren Manufacturing Company, Roxbury, Mass., (1851-53)
Boston Watch Co., Roxbury, Mass., (1853-54) & Waltham, Mass., (1854-57)
Howard & Rice, Roxbury, Mass., (1857-58) with (E. Howard & Co. on dials)
E. Howard & Co., Roxbury, Mass., (1858-1903)
Keystone Watch Case Co. (Howard line), Jersey City, N. J., (1902-30)

Below: Lever with upright pallets.

Note: All E. Howards were adjusted to Isochronism.
LEFT: Balance cock unmarked =UNADJUSTED
CENTER: Balance cock marked heat &cold =adjusted to TEMPERATURE
RIGHT: Balance cock on movement marked adjusted =FULLY ADJUSTED

A list of initials for most of the Solid Gold Watch Case companies used by E. Howard & Co.

A.W.C. Co.=American Watch Case Co.	**K (Inside) U** = Keller & Untermeyer
B & T = Booz & Thomas	**K E & F. Co.**= Keller, Ettinger & Fink N.Y.
B.W.C. Co.=Brooklyn Watch Case Co.	**M B** = Margot Bros.
C & M =Crosby & Mathewson	**M & B** = Mathey Bros.
C.E.H. & Co. = C. E. Hale & Co.	**N.Y.G.W.C.Co** =New York Gold Watch Case Co.
C. W. Mfg. Co. = Courvoisier Wilcox Mfg. Co.	**P & B** = Peters & Boss
D T W & Co.= D.T. Warren & Co.	**S & D** = Serex & Desmaison
F & Co.=Fellows & Co.	**S & M B** = Serex Maitre Bros.
F & S = Fellows & Shell	**S & R**=Serex & Robert
J M H = J. M. Harper	**W & S** = Warren & Spadone
J S (Intertwined)= Jeannot & Shiebler	**W P & Co** = Wheeler Parsons & Co.
	W W C Mfg. Co =Western Watch Case Co.

	Ladd Watch Case Co.
Crescent Watch Case Co.	Marsh= Marsh Watch Case Co.
Dueber Watch Case Co.	Muhr Watch Case Co.
Keystone Watch Case Co.	Roy = Roy Watch Case Co.

NOTE: The "E.H.& Co." marking seen on cases, was put on cases by numerous different case makers, at the request of the Howard sales offices.

      NOTE: E. Howard & Co. movements will not fit standard cases properly.

E. HOWARD & CO. Series I, helical hair-spring, detent escapement , KW KS, N(18) size serial #1120

E. HOWARD & CO. (18) size, 15 jewels, chronometer escapement engraved on balance, Robin's escapement, Serial # 3126.

E. HOWARD & CO. III, 18 size, KW KS. note compensating balance above center wheel, serial # 3363.

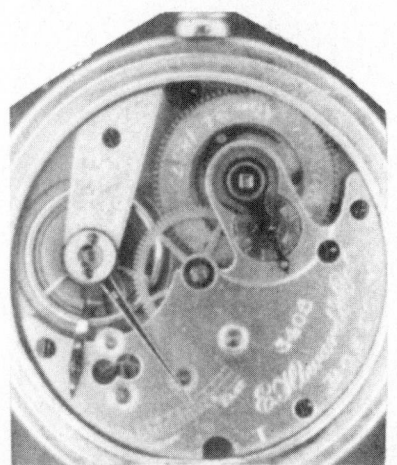

E. HOWARD & CO. I, 10 size, KW KS. Note solid balance, unique escape wheel & pallet fork, serial #3406.

256

E. HOWARD & CO.
APPROXIMATE DATES, SERIAL NOS., AND TOTAL PRODUCTION

Serial No.	Date	Series	Total Prod.
113-1,900—	1858-1860—	I (18S)—	1,800
1,901-3,000—	1860-1861—	II (18S)—	1,200
3,001-3,100—	1861 -1862—	K (14S)—	100
3101-3,300—reserved for helicals & experimentals			
3,301-3,400—	1861-1863—	III (18S)—	100
3,401-3,500—	1861-1863—	I (10S)—	100
3,501-28,000—	1861-1871—	III (18S)—	24,500
30,001-50,000—	1868-1883—	IV (18S)—	20,000
50,001-71,500—	1869-1899—	V (16S)—	21 500
100,001-105,500—	1874-1878—	VI (6S)—	5,500
200,001-227,000—	1883-1899—	VII (18S)—	27,000
*228,001,,231,000—	1893.1894—	VII (18S)—	3,000
300,001-309,000—	1884-1899—	VIII (18S)—	9,000
*309,001-310,000—	1895-1903—	VIII (18S)—	1,000
400,001-405,000—	1890-1895—	IX (18S)—	5,000
500,001-501,500—	1892-1899—	X (12S)—	1,500
*600,001-601,500—	1895-1903—	XI (16S)—	1,500
*700,001-701,500—	1896-1904—	XII (16S)—	1,500

(*) a 3/4 Split Plates & 17 J. **Possible Total - 118,500**

The above list is provided for determining the age & help identify
the Series of your watch. Match serial number with date & Series.

E. HOWARD & CO. WATCH SIZES

Letter	Inches	Approx. Size
N	1 13/16	18
L	1 11/16	16
K	1 10/16	14
J	1 9/16	12
I	1 8/16	10
H	1 7/16	8
G	1 6/16	6
F	1 5/16	4
E	1 4/16	2
D	1 3/16	0

Below: Mershon's Patent center wheel
rack regulator (April 26,1859).

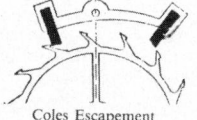
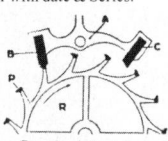
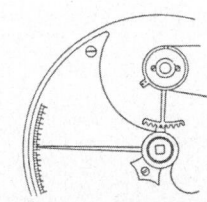

Coles Escapement
Resilient Escapement

Standard Escapement

Deer
Adjusted to
HcI6P

Horse
Adjusted to
HCI-No
positions

Hound
Unadjusted

Howard used a maintaining
power device up to serial
30,000.1st NICKEL
movement Ca. 1871.

All E. Howards were adjusted to Isochronism.

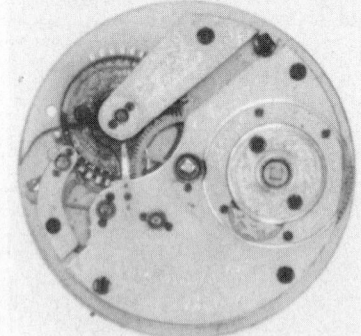
14 or K size, 15 jewels, right angle lever escapement, experimental model, serial number 3,022.

10 or I size, 15 jewels; cut-out to view escape wheel, experimental model, serial number 3,472.

E HOWARD & CO.
N SIZE (18) (In Original Cases)

Series or Name — Description		ABP	Ex-Fn	Mint
I, II or III, 15J, gilded, KW, helical hairspring.	★★★★	$14,000	$21,000	$32,000
I, 15J, marked "Howard & Rice"	★★★★	5,000	7,000	10,000

FOR, E. Howard & Co. on dial and movement, 15-16J, **1857 Model**
See American Waltham Watch Co. section for 1857 Model for prices
All Howard prices are for original factory cases

Series 1, 18 size. 17 jewels, note the compensating balance on this early movement, low serial number 133

Series II, 18 size. 15 jewels, key wind & set serial number 2,477.

Series or Name —Description		ABP	Ex-Fn	Mint
I, 15J, with serial # below 125 ⭐⭐⭐⭐⭐		$9,000	$12,000	$18,000
I, 15J, with serial # below 200 ⭐⭐⭐⭐		5,000	7,000	9,000
I, 15J, with serial # below 300 ⭐⭐⭐⭐		4,800	6,000	8,000
I, 15J, gilded, KW, **18K** HC, OF, upright or horizontal pallets ...⭐⭐		5,500	7,000	10,000
I, 15J, gilded, KW, silver HC ⭐⭐		2,800	3,500	5,500
I, 15J, (movement only) ⭐⭐		800	1,200	2,600
I, 17J, with unusual plate cut (movement only) ⭐⭐⭐		4,500	7,000	10,000
II, 15J, gilded, KW, **18K**, HC or OF ⭐⭐		2,500	4,500	6,500
II, 15J, gilded, KW, silver HC ⭐⭐		1,500	3,000	5,000
II, 15J, (movement only) ⭐⭐		700	1,000	2,500
II, 17J, with screw down jewel settings (movement only). ⭐⭐⭐⭐⭐		3,000	4,000	7,000
III, 15J, gilded, KW, **18K**, HC		1,500	2,500	3,500
III, 15J, gilded, KW, silver case		600	1,200	1,800
III, 15J, **nickel**, KW, silver case ⭐⭐⭐⭐		2,000	3,000	4,000
III, 15J, gilded, KW, **18K**, Mershon's Patent		1,200	2,000	3,800
III, 15J, gilded, KW, Coles Resilient Escapement, **18K**, ⭐⭐		1,600	2,500	4,500
III, 15J, gilded, KW, Coles Resilient Escapement, (movement only) .		300	400	600
III, 15J, nickel Coles Movement, **18K** ⭐⭐⭐⭐		3,500	5,000	7,000
III, 15J, Gold flashed DMK, Coles Movement, **18K** ⭐⭐⭐⭐		2,200	3,500	6,000
III, 15J, NI, Private label		800	1,300	2,000
III, 15J, gold flash ray DMK screw down settings (movement only) .		950	1,400	2,200
III, 15J, with RAY & nickel DMK (movement only)		500	1,100	2,000
III, 15J, SW, 4 OZ. hand engraved **18K CASE**		2,500	3,750	5,000

Series III,18 size. 15jewels, note **Mershon's Patent** center wheel rack regulator (April 26, 1859), serial # 22,693.

Series III, 18 size, 15J, Note: Maintaining spring barrel found on earlier Howard watches, advantage was safety against damage due to breaking of mainspring in going barrel. (protecting the train).

Series IV, 18 size, 15 jewels, key wind and set, serial number 37,893, Moustache Lever.

Series VII, 18 size, 15 jewels, nickel movement, note running deer on movement, 'adjusted' on bridge, serial number 216,504.

Series or Name — Description		ABP	Ex-Fn	Mint
IV, 15J, gilded, KW, **18K**, HC		$1,000	$2,000	$3,200
IV, 15J, nickel, KW, **18K**, HC	★★★	2,400	3,000	4,000
IV, 15J, gilded, SW, **18K**, HC		1,000	1,500	3,000
IV, 15J, nickel, SW, **18K**, HC		1,000	1,800	3,000
IV, personalized with jobber's name, silver	★★	450	850	1,500
IV, SW, with Transitional dial, OF **14K**		1,400	2,000	3,200
IV, 15J (movement only)		100	200	500
VII, 15J, gilded or nickel, SW, **14K**, HC		650	1,200	2,000
VII, 15J, unusual **Moorhouse** dial, **14K**		1,500	2,500	3,200
VII, 15J, complex DMK (movement only)		150	300	500
VII, 15J (movement only)		125	200	450
VII, 17J, nickel, split plate, SW, **14K**, HC	★★★	1,500	2,500	3,600
VII, 17J, nickel, split plate, SW, silver, HC	★★★	700	1,200	2,500
VII, 19J, nickel, SW, **14K**, HC	★★★	2,500	4,000	6,000
VII, 21J, 3/4 plate (movement only)	★★★★	1,600	2,500	4,500
VIII, 15J, gilded or nickel, SW, **14K**, OF		700	1,000	2,000
VIII, 15J, nickel, Complex DMK (movement only)		150	300	600
VIII, 15J, unusual **Moorhouse** dial	★★★	1,500	2,500	3,200
VIII, 15J (movement only)		125	300	500
VIII, 17J, nickel, split plate, SW, **14K**, OF	★★★	1,800	2,500	4,000
VIII, 17J, nickel, split plate, SW, **silver**, OF	★★★	700	1,000	2,200
VIII, 17J, nickel or gilded, with RR on the side of balance cock, silver, OF		1,000	1,500	3,000

BALL - HOWARDS SEE **BALL W. Co..**

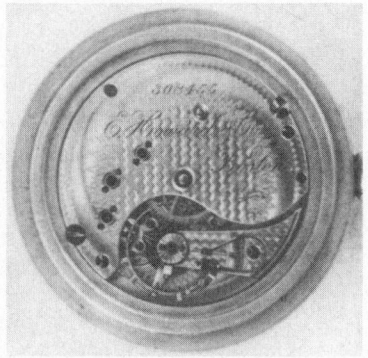

Series VII, 18 size, 17J, nickel, split plate, adjusted, Stem Wind, serial number 228,055.

Series VIII, 18 size, 15 jewels, serial number 308,455.

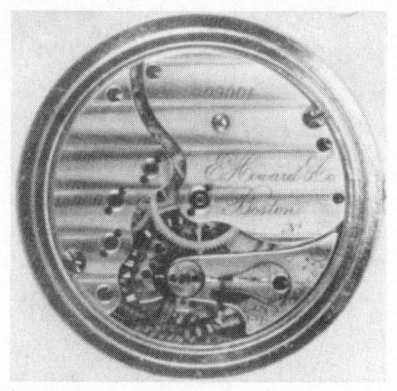

Series VIII, 18 size, 17 jewels, split plate model, gold jewel settings, serial number 309,904.

Series IX, 18 size, 15 jewels, hunting. This series is gilded only and hound grade exclusively, S #402,873.

Series or Name — Description	ABP	Ex-Fn	Mint
IX, 15J, gilded, SW, **14K**, HC.	$900	$1,500	$2,500
IX, 15J, gilded, SW, **silver**, HC	450	1,000	1,500
IX, 15J, gilded, SW, unusual **Moorhouse** dial.	1,500	2,500	3,200
IX, 15J (movement only)	100	200	500

L SIZE (16)
(In Original Cases)

Series or Name — Description	ABP	Ex-Fn	Mint
V, 15J, gilded, KW, **18K**, HC	$1,100	$2,000	$3,000
V, 15J, gilded, KW, **18K, Coles Escapement** ★★	1,300	2,500	3,500
V, 15J, nickel, **18K, Coles Escapement** ★★★★	3,000	4,500	6,500
V, 15J, gilded or nickel, SW, **14K**, HC	800	1,200	2,000
V, 15J, gilded, SW, **14K, Coles Escapement** ★★	1,000	2,000	3,000
V, 15J, SW, **14K** OF, with transitional dial. ★★	1,300	2,100	3,500
V, 15J, SW, **14K** OF, with Moorhouse dial. ★★	1,500	2,800	4,200
V, 15J, SW, **14K**, 24 Hr. dial (red/black) ★★★	1,300	2,000	3,000
V, 15J, nickel KW, (movement only)	400	600	1,000
V, 15J, gilded (movement only)	100	200	400
V, **Prescott**, 15J., gilded, LS, SW, NOTE: original case may show evidence of filled key holes on dust cover ★★★	2,500	3,500	8,000
V, Prescott, 15J., gilded, SW, (Series V **movement** only) ★★★	1,000	1,500	4,000

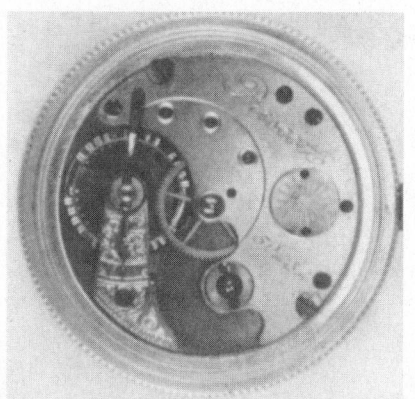

Series V, 16 or L size, Prescott Model, 15J., HC, S#50,434. NOTE: Original case may show evidence of **filled key holes on dust cover** from when watches were returned to factory & converted from KW Coles movement to stem wind & lever set.

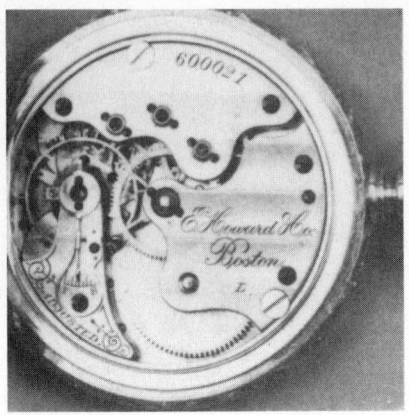

Series XI, 16 size, 17 jewels. split plate model, nickel movement, gold jewel settings, serial number 600,021.

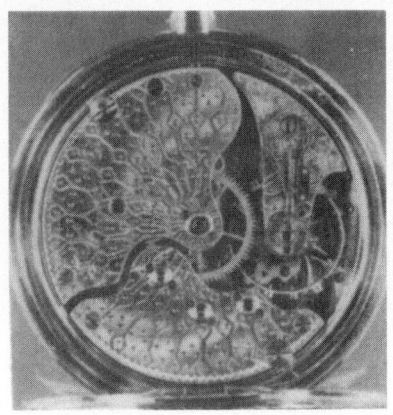

Series XII, L-16 size, 21 jewels, split plate model, nickel movement, gold lettering, gold jewel settings, serial number 700,899.

Series or Name — Description		ABP	Ex-Fn	Mint
XI, 17J, nickel, split plate, SW, **14K,** HC	★★★	$1,100	$1,800	$3,200
XI, 17J, nickel, split plate, SW, **silver**, HC	★★★	600	1,200	2,400
XI, 17J (movement only)		300	500	1,200
XII, 17J, nickel, split plate, SW, **14K**, OF	★★★	1,000	1,800	3,000
XII, 17J, nickel, split plate, SW, **silver**, OF	★★★	500	800	2,200
XII, 17J (movement only)		100	300	600
XII, 21J, nickel, split plate, SW, **14K**, OF	★★★★	4,000	6,500	9,500

K SIZE (14)
(In Original Cases)

Series or Name — Description		ABP	Ex-Fn	Mint
K, 15J, gilded, KW, **Original case 18K**, HC	★★★★★	$9,000	$18,000	$25,000
K, 15J, gilded, (movement only)	★★★★	6,000	8,000	10,000

Series K, 14 or K size, 15 jewels, key wind, serial number 3,004.

Example of Moorhouse style dial. Signed J. Moorhouse on back side of dial. Also note Mulberry style at 15–30–45-60 minutes.

J SIZE (12) (In Original Cases)

Series or Name — Description		ABP	Ex-Fn	Mint
X, 15J, nickel, hound, SW, **14K**, OF	★	$750	$1,400	$1,800
X, 15J, nickel, hound, SW, fancy Moorhouse dial, **14K**, OF		1,200	1,800	2,700
X, 15J, nickel, horse, SW, **14K**, OF	★	850	1,500	2,000
X, 15J, nickel, deer, SW, **14K**, OF	★	950	1,600	2,200
X, 15J, hound (movement only)	★	250	300	650

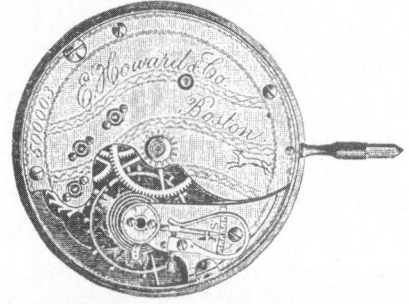

Series X, 15J, J size or 12 size, nickel, hound, SW, serial ft 500,003.

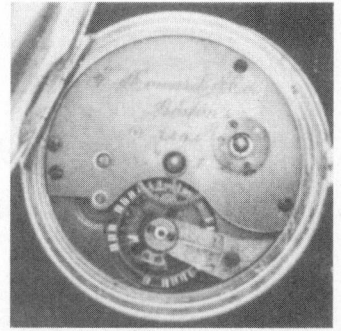

I size (10 size), 15 Jewels, gilded, key wind, serial number 3,454.

I SIZE (10) (In Original Cases)

Series or Name — Description		ABP	Ex-Fn	Mint
I size (10 size), 15J, gilded, KW, **18K** HC	★★★★	$4,000	$6,000	$9,500
I size (10 size), 15 jewels, gilded, key wind, with unique **escape wheel & pallet fork**, 18K case	★	7,000	9,000	15,000

G SIZE (6) (In Original Cases)

Series or Name — Description		ABP	Ex-Fn	Mint
VI, 15J, gilded, **KW, 18K**, HC	★★★	$2,000	$3,000	$5,000
VI, 15J, gilded or nickel, **SW, 18K**, HC		1,100	1,400	1,800
VI, 15J, gilded or nickel, Moorhouse dial, **14K**		1,100	2,000	2,700
VI, 15J, (movement only)		175	275	500
VI, 15J, (movement only) **adjusted**		300	500	900

I size (10 size), 15 jewels, gilded, key wind, with **unique escape wheel & pallet fork,** note special opening to view escapement, S# 3406

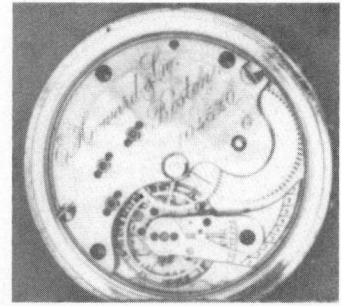

Series VI, 6 or G size, 15 jewels, stem wind, serial number 104,520.

Below 1888 AD

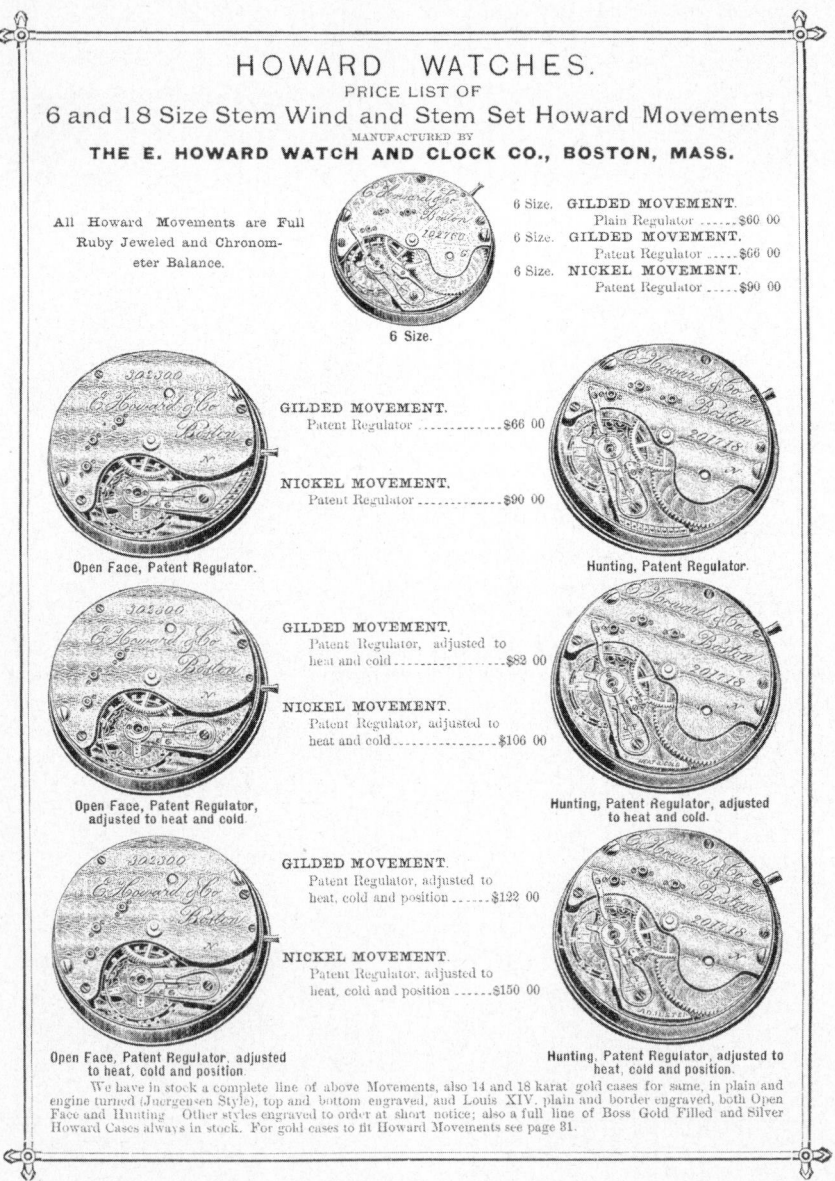

HOWARD WATCHES.
PRICE LIST OF
6 and 18 Size Stem Wind and Stem Set Howard Movements
MANUFACTURED BY
THE E. HOWARD WATCH AND CLOCK CO., BOSTON, MASS.

All Howard Movements are Full Ruby Jeweled and Chronometer Balance.

6 Size. **GILDED MOVEMENT.**
Plain Regulator $60 00
6 Size. **GILDED MOVEMENT.**
Patent Regulator $66 00
6 Size. **NICKEL MOVEMENT.**
Patent Regulator $90 00

6 Size.

GILDED MOVEMENT.
Patent Regulator $66 00

NICKEL MOVEMENT.
Patent Regulator $90 00

Open Face, Patent Regulator.

Hunting, Patent Regulator.

GILDED MOVEMENT.
Patent Regulator, adjusted to heat and cold............$82 00

NICKEL MOVEMENT.
Patent Regulator, adjusted to heat and cold............$106 00

Open Face, Patent Regulator, adjusted to heat and cold.

Hunting, Patent Regulator, adjusted to heat and cold.

GILDED MOVEMENT.
Patent Regulator, adjusted to heat, cold and position $122 00

NICKEL MOVEMENT.
Patent Regulator, adjusted to heat, cold and position $150 00

Open Face, Patent Regulator, adjusted to heat, cold and position.

Hunting, Patent Regulator, adjusted to heat, cold and position.

We have in stock a complete line of above Movements, also 14 and 18 karat gold cases for same, in plain and engine turned (Juergensen Style), top and bottom engraved, and Louis XIV. plain and border engraved, both Open Face and Hunting. Other styles engraved to order at short notice; also a full line of Boss Gold Filled and Silver Howard Cases always in stock. For gold cases to fit Howard Movements see page 81.

Note: A FULL line of Boss Gold Filled Cases and Silver Howard Cases always in stock.

E. HOWARD WATCH CO. (KEYSTONE)

Waltham, Massachusetts   1902 - 1930

The watches are marked **"E. Howard Watch Co. Boston, U. S. A."** The Howard name was purchased by the Keystone Watch Case Co. in 1902. There were no patent rights transferred, just the Howard name. The Edward Howard chronometer was the highest grade, 16 size, & was introduced in 1912 for $350 (about 300 made). All watches cased & timed at factory as a complete watch only. Keystone Howard also gained control of U. S. Watch Co. of Waltham and New York Standard Watch Company.

ESTIMATED SERIAL NUMBERS
AND PRODUCTION DATES

Date	Serial No.
1902 —	850,000
1903 —	900,000
1909 —	980,000
1912 —	1,100.000
1915 —	1,285,000
1917 —	1,340,000
1921 —	1,400,000
1930 —	1,500,000

Adjusted to Temperature & Isochronism. The arrows denote number of jewels and adjustments in each grade.

Gross =23 jewel, 5 positions

Star =21 jewel, Adj.5P, & 19J with V under star

Triangle =19 jewel, 5 positions

Circle =17 jewel, 3 positions

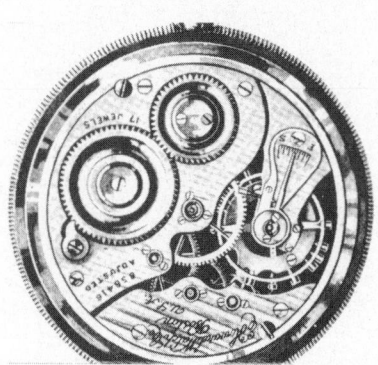

Model 1905. Series 7. 16 size, 17J., open face. This 3/4 model can be identified by the slant parallel damaskeening. This represents the 3/4 top grade, raised gold jewel settings, double roller, Adj.5P and sold for $115.00 in 1910.
The above movement (ebauche) MADE by Hamilton??

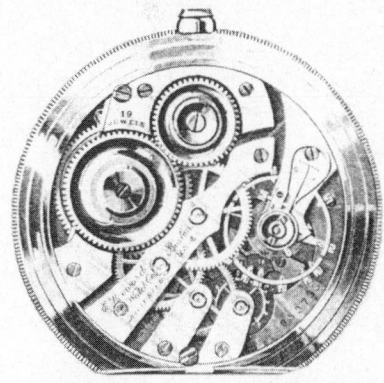

1907 Bridge Model, Series 5, 15 jewels, **open face,** Serial # 953,733. **NOTE:** The escape wheel bridge & the fourth wheel bridge is not notched out.

odel 1905, Series 9, 16 size, 17 jewels, open face. This 3/4 model can be identified by the checkerboard damaskeening. This represents the 3/4 **mid** grade, GJS, double roller, Adj.3 & 5P and sold for $105.00 in 1910.

Model 1905, Series 3, 16 size, 17 jewels open face. This 3/4 model can be identified by the circular damaskeening. This represents the 3/4 **lowest** grade of the three with single roller, Adj.3P and sold for $100.00 in 1910.

E. Howard Watch Co., Model 1907, marked Series 0, 16 size, 23 jewels. in original E. Howard Watch Co. swing-out movement Keystone Extra gold filled Open Face case.

E. HOWARD WATCH CO. Model 1907, Series 0 (not marked), 16S, 23J., Hunting Case. Under balance wheel "Special Adjusted Five Positions, Temperature".

🖙 Model 1907 **bridge** OF & HC and Series or No., 0, 1, 2, 5 & 10, see above illustrations, 1907 = Series or No. 0=23J, Series or No.1&10 =21J, Series2=17J, Series5 or No.5 =19J. Model 1905 = **3/4 plate** OF & HC and Series 3,7,9 = 17J.

Prices below are for original signed cases.

E. HOWARD WATCH CO. (KEYSTONE)
16 SIZE

Series or Name — Description		ABP	Ex-Fn	Mint
No. 0, & 1907, 23J, BRG, Adj.5P, DR, OF		$400	$600	$825
1907 model & No.0, 23J, BRG, Adj.5P, DR, HC		425	700	900
Unmarked, 23J, BRG, Adj.5P, DR, OF		350	700	900
Series 0, 23J, BRG, Adj.5P, DR, **Ruby banking pins**		800	1,000	1,500
Series 0, 23J, BRG, Adj.5P, DR, **jeweled barrel**		800	1,000	1,500
Series 0, 23J, BRG, Adj.5P, DR, **OF, 14K**		1,000	1,500	2,000
Series 0, 23J, BRG, Adj.5P, DR, **HC, 14K**		1,100	2,000	2,500
No. 1, 21J, BRG, Adj.5P, DR	★	400	550	900
Series 1, 21J, BRG, Adj.5P, DR		300	450	625
Series 2, 17J, BRG, Adj.5P, DR, HC	★	200	300	450
Series 2, 17J, BRG, Adj.5P, DR, OF	★	175	250	400

Series II, marked *Railroad Chronometer*, 16 size, 21 jewels, Adj5p, serial number 1,217,534.

Edward Howard Model, 16 size, 23 blue sapphire jewels, frosted gold bridge, wolfteeth wind, serial #77.

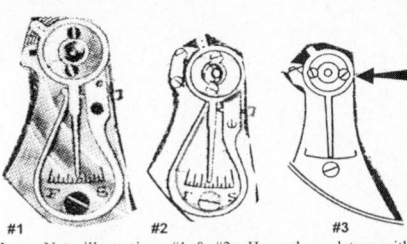

Above: Note illustrations #1 & #2= Howard regulators with the 2 jewel screws vertical or upright and #1 has a **square** hairspring stud also note #2 has a **sliding** stud & a bean shaped cover. Howard-**Waltham** regulators (#3) the 2 jewel screws are horizontal and **triangular** hairspring stud.

E. Howard Watch Co., 16 size, 23 jewels, by Waltham, raised gold jewel settings, gold train, Adj5p, open face, bridge style movement. NOTE: Bow, also note the Howard S# seen on bridge is 1,005,363. The **Waltham** S# seen under dial, is 605,363.

E. Howard Watch Co., 16S., 19J., by **Waltham, Equity** Model, Adj3p, 3/4 plate, gold center wheel.

Series or Name — Description	ABP	Ex-Fn	Mint
Series 3, 17J, 3/4, Adj.3P, circular DMK	$150	$200	$400
Series 3, 17J, Adj.3P, circular DMK, **14K** OF,...................	400	600	800
No. 5, 19J, BRG, GJS, HC .... ★	250	400	700
Series 5, 19J, BRG, Adj.5P, DR, **14K**	500	700	900
Series 5, 19J, BRG, Adj.5P, DR, 1907 Model.	200	300	500
Series 7, 17J, 3/4, Adj.5P, DR, RGJS, slant parallel DMK, OF	100	175	325
Series 7, 17J, 3/4, Adj.5P, DR, RGJS, slant parallel DMK, HC	125	300	400
Series 9, 17J, 3/4, Adj.3P, LS, checkerboard DMK, OF...........	100	200	350
Series 9, 17J, 3/4, Adj.5P, DR, checkerboard DMK, RR grade,**14K** ..	500	750	1,000
Series 10, 21J, BRG, Adj.5P, DR, **Marked Non—Magnetic** . ★★★	600	1,000	1,700
Series 10, 21J, BRG, Adj.5P, DR	400	600	800
No. 10, 21J, BRG, Adj.5P, DR	400	600	800
Series 11, 21J, **R. R. Chrono.**, Adj.5P, DR	400	650	800
Edward Howard, 23 blue sapphire pressed 5, Free Sprung, Adj.5P, DR,			
without box, **18K** Edward Howard case ....★★	6,000	10,000	13,500
Edward Howard, 23J., sapphire banking pins, Adj.5P, DR, wolf-tooth winding, Free Sprung,			
with original outer card and mahogany fitted box, extra mainspring, crystal and			
certificate, **18K** Edward Howard case .... ★★★	8,000	15,000	20,000
Glimax,7J., (made for export), gilded, OF.......................	75	135	250
23J, E. Howard W. Co. (mfg. by Waltham), **14K**, Brg model . . . . ★★	1,200	1,500	2,400
23J, E. Howard W. Co. (mfg. by Waltham), gold filled, OF	600	800	1,300
23J, E. Howard W. Co. (mfg. by Waltham), gold filled, HC	800	1,000	1,600
21J, E. Howard W. Co. (mfg. by Waltham), Bridge model, HC......	400	600	1,000
21J, E. Howard W. Co. (mfg. by Waltham), 3/4, OF	200	400	500
19J, E. Howard W. Co. (mfg. by Waltham), Bridge model, HC.....	225	350	550
19J, E. Howard W. Co. (mfg. by Waltham), 3/4, OF	200	325	500
17J, E. Howard W. Co. (mfg. by Waltham), Bridge model, HC......	200	300	500
17J, E. Howard W. Co. (mfg. by Waltham), **Equity model**, 3/4, OF..	175	250	400

12 SIZE - 1908 Model

Series or Name — Description	ABP	Ex-Fn	Mint
Series 6, 19J, BRG, DR, Adj.5P, 1908 Model, **14K**, HC	$300	$400	$650
Series 6, 19J, BRG, DR, Adj.5P, **14K**, OF	200	400	500
Series 6, 19J, BRG, DR, Adj.5P, OF	100	200	250
Series 7, 17J, BRG, DR, Adj.3P, **14K**, OF	200	300	500
Series 7, 17J, BRG, DR, Adj.3P, OF	100	150	200
Series 8, 21J, BRG, DR, Adj.5P, OF	100	250	325
Series 8, 23J, BRG, DR, Adj.5P, **14K**, OF	250	500	650
Series 8, 23J, BRG, DR, Adj.5P, OF	150	300	450
Series 8, 23J, BRG, DR, Adj.5P, **14K**, HC	450	650	800
21J,Waltham Model, BRG, HC . . . . ★★★	200	400	550
21J,Waltham Model, BRG, OF . . . . ★★★	250	400	650
19J,Waltham Model, gold center wheel, BRG, HC . . . . . ★★★	200	350	550
19J,Waltham Model, gold center wheel, BRG, OF . . . . ★★★	250	350	650
17J,Waltham Model, 3/4, HC . . . . ★★★	100	175	300
17J,Waltham Model, 3/4, OF . . . . ★★★	90	150	275

NOTE: First Serial # for 12 size with 17J.=977,001; 19J.=977,451; 21J=1,055,851.

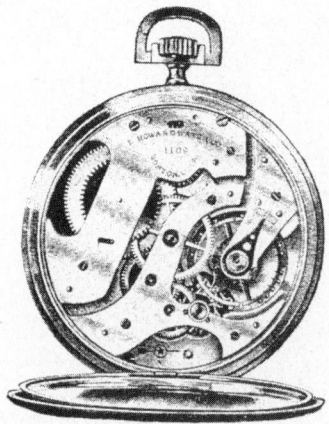

Series 8, 12 size. 21 jewels, open face, stop works, extra thin. **1908 MODEL** with 21 jewels, engraved under balance, "five positions and temperature".

E. Howard Watch Co., 10 size, 21J. Adj.,5p. (serial # started at about 1,001 on this model.)

21 Jewels 5 Positions ⊶⊛→
19 Jewels 5 Positions ⊶⊕→
17 Jewels 3 Positions ⊶○→

10 SIZE (Ca. 1921)

NOTE: 10 Size Serial numbers start at about 1,001 on this model and used their own serial numbers list.

Series or Name — Description	ABP	Ex-Fn	Mint
Thin Model, 21J, Adj.5P, **14K** case, OF	$200	$300	$425
Thin Model, 21J, Adj.5P, Gold filled, OF	100	200	250
Thin Model, 19J, Adj.5P, **14K** case, OF	200	300	400
Thin Model, 19J, Adj.5P, Gold filled, OF	100	175	225
Thin Model, 17J, Adj.3P, **14K** case, OF	175	300	400
Thin Model, 17J, Adj.3P, Gold filled, OF	100	150	175

☞ A collector should expect to pay modestly higher prices at local shops.

☞ Watches listed in this book are priced at the collectable Trade Show level, as complete watches having an original 14k gold-filled case and Key Wind with silver, an original white enamel single sunk dial, and with the entire original movement in good working order with no repairs needed.

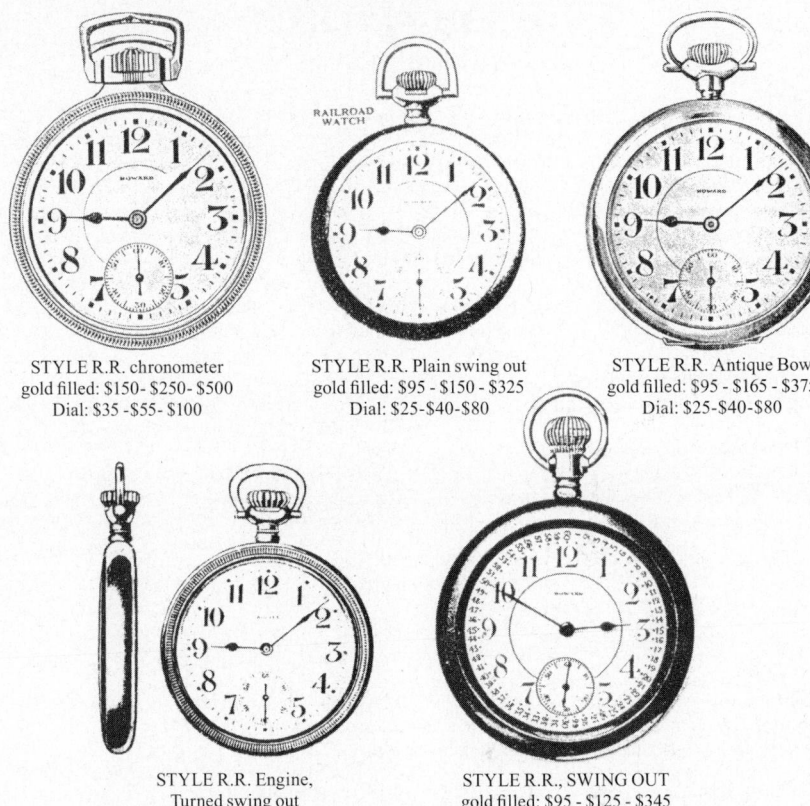

STYLE R.R. chronometer
gold filled: $150- $250- $500
Dial: $35 -$55- $100

STYLE R.R. Plain swing out
gold filled: $95 - $150 - $325
Dial: $25-$40-$80

STYLE R.R. Antique Bow
gold filled: $95 -$165 - $375
Dial: $25-$40-$80

STYLE R.R. Engine,
Turned swing out
gold filled: $95- $150 - $325
Dial: $25-$40-$80

STYLE R.R., SWING OUT
gold filled: $95 - $125 - $345
14K GOLD: $325 - $400 - $650
Montgomery Dial: $75 -$150 -$200

&ᔆ NOTE: Factory Advertised as a complete watch and was fitted with a certain matched, timed and rated movement and sold in the factory designed case style as a complete watch. The factory advertised as "Howard movements and cases are not sold separately". All the factory advertised complete watches came with a enamel dial SHOWN or CHOICE of other Railroad dials.

Howard Railroad Watches

16s. SERIES No. 0 R.R. STANDARD
— 23 J. Adj. 5 POS.

	Keystone List	Retail Price
14K Gold O. F.		
35 –14K P.P.—Cap.	$204.00	$170.
Keystone Extra O. F.		
55 –P.P.—Cap.	156.00	130.
65 –E.T.—Cap.	156.00	130.
95W –White Screw Butler	150.00	125.
95G –Green Screw—P.P. or But.	150.00	125.

16s. SERIES No. 10 R.R. STANDARD
— 21 J. Adj. 5 POS.

	Keystone List	Retail Price
14K Gold O. F.		
1035 –P.P.—Cap.	162.00	135.
Keystone Extra O. F.		
1065 –P.P.—Cap.	114.00	95.
1065 –E.T.—Cap.	114.00	96.
1095W–White Screw Butler	108.00	90.
1095G–Green Screw P.P. or But.	108.00	90.

16s. SERIES No. 11 R.R. CHRONOMETER
— 21 J. Adj. 5 POS.

	Keystone List	Retail Price
Keystone Extra O. F.		
1195W–White Screw Butler	96.00	80.
1195G –Green Screw—P.P. or But.	96.00	80.
1195 –Yellow Screw—P.P.	96.00	80.

Montgomery Dials supplied on Railroad Watches without extra charge.

ILLINOIS WATCH CO.

Springfield, Illinois
1869 - 1927

The Illinois Watch Company was organized mainly through the efforts of J. G. Adams. The first directors were J. T. Stuart, W. B. Miller, John Williams, John W. Bunn, George Black and George Passfield. In 1879 the company changed all its watches to a quick train movement by changing the number of teeth in the fourth wheel. The first nickel movement was made in 1879. The first mainspring made by the company was used in 1882. The next year soft enamel dials were used.

The Illinois Watch Co. used more names on its movements than any other watch manufacturer. To identify all of them requires extensive knowledge by the collector plus a good working knowledge of watch mechanics. Engraved on some early movements, for example, are "S. W. Co." or "I. W. Co., Springfield, Ill." To the novice these abbreviations might be hard to understand, thus making Illinois watches difficult to identify. But one saving clue is that the location "Springfield, Illinois" appears on most of these watches. It is important to learn how to identify these type watches because some of them are extremely collectible. Examples of some of the more valuable of these are: the Benjamin Franklin (size 18 or 16, 25 or 26 jewels), Paillard's Non-Magnetic, Pennsylvania Special, C & O, and B & O railroad models.

The earliest movements made by the Illinois Watch Co. are listed below. They made the first watch in early 1872, but the company really didn't get off the ground until 1875. Going by the serial number, the first watch made was the Stuart. Next was the Mason, followed by the Bunn, the Miller, and finally the Currier. The first stem-wind was made in 1875.

STUART, FIRST Run was serial numbers . . . . 1 to 100.
MASON, FIRST Run was serial numbers . . . . 101 to 200.
BUNN, FIRST Run was serial numbers . . . . 201 to 300.
MILLER, FIRST Run was serial numbers . . . . 301 to 400.
CURRIER, FIRST Run was serial numbers . . . . 401 to 500.

The Illinois Watch Company was sold to Hamilton Watch Co. in 1927. The Illinois factory continued to produce Illinois watches under the new management until 1932. After 1933 Hamilton produced watches bearing the Illinois name in their own factory until 1939.

CHRONOLOGY OF THE DEVELOPMENT OF ILLINOIS WATCH CO.:
Illinois Springfield Watch Co. 1869-1879
Springfield Illinois Watch Co. 1879-1885
Illinois Watch Co. 1885-1927
Illinois Watch Co. sold to Hamilton Watch Co. 1927

ILLINOIS WATCH CO., Bates Model. 18 size, 7 jewels, key wind & set, serial number 43,876, c.1874.

BUNN, 18 size, 16 jewels, hunting case, NOTE: Chalmer patented regulator, serial number 1,185,809.

ILLINOIS ESTIMATED SERIAL NUMBERS AND PRODUCTION DATES

DATE — SERIAL NO.	DATE — SERIAL NO.	DATE — SERIAL NO.
1872 — 5,000	1893 — 1,120,000	1914 — 2,600,000
1873 — 20,000	1894 — 1,160,000	1915 — 2,700,000
1874 — 50,000	1895 — 1,220,000	1916 — 2,800,000
1875 — 75,000	1696 — 1,250,000	1917 — 3,000,000
1876 — 100,000	1897 — 1,290,000	1918 — 3,200,000
1877 — 145,000	1898 — 1,330,000	1919 — 3,400,000
1878 — 210,000	1899 — 1,370,000	1920 — 3,600,000
1879 — 250,000	1900 — 1,410,000	1921 — 3,750,000
1880 — 300,000	1901 — 1,450,000	1922 — 3,900,000
1881 — 350,000	1902 — 1,500,000	1923 — 4,000,000
1882 — 400,000	1903 — 1,650,000	1924 — 4,500,000
1883 — 450,000	1904 — 1,700,000	1925 — 4,700,000
1884 — 500,000	1905 — 1,800,000	1926 — 4,800,000
1885 — 550,000	1906 — 1,840,000	1927 — 5,000,000
1886 — 600,000	1907 — 1,900,000	(Sold to Hamilton)
1887 — 700,000	1908 — 2,100,000	1928 — 5,100,000
1888 — 800,000	1909 — 2,150,000	1929 — 5,200,000
1889 — 900,000	1910 — 2,200,000	1931 — 5,400,000
1890 — 1,000,000	1911 — 2,300,000	1934 — 5,500,000
1891 — 1,040,000	1912 — 2,400,000	1948 — 5,600,000
1892 — 1,080,000	1913 — 2,500,000	

The above list is provided for determining the **APPROXIMATE** age of your watch. Match serial number with date. Watches were not necessarily sold in the exact order of manufactured date.

NOTE: It required several months for raw material to emerge as a finished movement. All the while the factory is producing all sizes, models and grades. The numbering system was basically "consecutive", due to demand a batch of movements could be side tracked, thus allowing a different size and model to move ahead to meet this demand. Therefore, the dates some movements were sold and delivered to the trade, may not be "consecutive".

(See Illinois Identification of Movements section located at the end of the Illinois price section to identify the movement, size and model number of your watch.)

ILLINOIS
18 SIZE (ALL FULL PLATE)

Grade or Name — Description	ABP	Ex-Fn	Mint
Alleghany, 11J, KW, gilded, OF............................	$100	$175	$250
Alleghany, 11J, M#1, NI,KW.............................	100	175	250
Alleghany, 11J, M#2, NI, Transition	100	150	250
America, 7J, M#3, Silveroid.......................... ★	100	150	250
America, 7J, M#1-2, KW............................. ★	100	200	325
America Special, 7J, M#1-2, KW....................... ★	175	275	400
Army & Navy, 19J, GJS, Adj.5P, OF	200	300	500
Army & Navy, 19J, GJS, Adj.5P, HC......................	225	400	550
Army & Navy, 21J, GJS, Adj.5P, OF	200	400	500
Army & Navy, 21J, GJS, Adj.5P, HC......................	250	575	800
Baltimore & Ohio R.R. Special, 17J, GJS, ADJ............. ★★★	1,300	2,000	3,000
Baltimore & Ohio R.R. Special, 21J, GJS, NI, ADJ .... ★★★	1,500	2,500	3,500
Baltimore & Ohio R.R. Standard, 24J, GJS, ADJ........... ★★★	2,200	4,000	5,000
Bates, 7J, M#1-2, KW.................................	175	275	525

🖝 NOTE: Numerous model 2 & 3 movements have key-wind style barrel arbors and stem wind capabilities. They are referred to as transition models. When models 2 & 3 were introduced the factory must have had a large supply of key-wind style barrel arbors; so being frugal, they were used.

🖝 Some watch manufacturers personalize watches for jobbers or jewelry firms, with exclusive private signed or marked movements. The valuable collectable watches are listed under the signed or marked movement. Other exclusive private signed or marked movements will have equivalent value or only slightly higher value and should be compared to Generic or Nameless movements. Railroad signed or marked (dials & movements) are usually more collectable & higher in value.

Illinois Watch Co., 18 size, railroad watch with a Ferguson dial with the numbers **1 through 12 in red**.
Illinois Ferguson = **18S**, Dial: $250 - $500 - $1,000

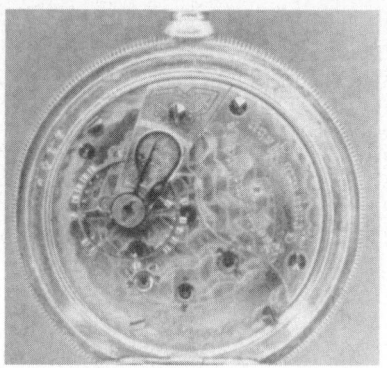

Army and Navy, 18 size, 19 jewels, engraved on movement "Washington Watch Co.," serial number 1,606,612.

Grade or Name — Description		ABP	Ex-Fn	Mint
Benjamin Franklin U.S.A., 17J, ADJ, NI	★	$425	$700	$ 1,000
Benjamin Franklin U.S.A., 21J, GJS, **Adj.6P**, NI	★	950	1,500	2,000
Benjamin Franklin U.S.A., 21J, GJS, Adj.5P, NI	★	950	1,500	2,000
Benjamin Franklin U.S.A., 24J, GJS, Adj.6P, NI	★	2,000	3,500	4,500
Benjamin Franklin U.S.A., 25J, GJS, Adj.6P, NI	★★★★	3,800	6,500	9,500
Benjamin Franklin U.S.A., 26J, GJS, Adj.6P, NI,	★★★★	4,800	8,000	11,000
Bunn, 15J, M#1, KW, KS, **1st. run S# 201 to 300**, Adj.	★★★★	2,100	3,500	4,500
Bunn, 15J, M#1, KW, KS, **2nd. run S# 2,001 to 2,500**, Adj.	★★	1,500	2,500	3,500
Bunn, 15J, M#1, KW, KS, OF	★	450	600	1,000
Bunn, 15J, M#1, KW, KS, "**ADJUSTED**"	★	500	700	1,100
Bunn, 15J, KW/SW transition		250	450	850
Bunn, 15J, M#1, KW, Coin.		375	500	900
Bunn, 15J, KW, MM, HC		375	500	900
Bunn, 15J, SW, M#2, HC		375	500	900
Bunn, 16J, KW, (not marked 16J.), OF	★	400	600	900
Bunn, 16J, KW, (not marked 16J.), HC	★	400	700	900
Bunn, 16J, SW, (not marked 16J.), HC		350	550	825
Bunn, 16J, SW, **ADJ**, (not marked **16J.**), HC.		375	575	875
Bunn, 17J, SW, NI, Coin.		150	300	400
Bunn, 17J, SW, M#3, **5th pinion**, gilded, OF		250	400	625
Bunn, 17J, M#4, SW, NI, OF		150	250	500
Bunn, 17J, M#5, SW, NI, HC		200	350	600
Bunn, 17J, SW, M#5, "**Ruby Jewels**", NI, Adj., HC	★	500	750	1,100
Bunn, 17J, M#6, SW, NI, OF		150	300	500
Bunn, 18J, SW, NI, **ADJ**., (not marked **18J.**), OF	★★	500	750	1,000
Bunn, 19J, SW, NI, DR, LS, GJS, Adj.5P, **J. barrel**, OF		200	400	500
Bunn, 19J, SW, **Adj.6P**, DR. **J. barrel**, OF		285	450	600
Bunn, 19J, SW, GJS, DR, Adj.5P, **J. barrel, HC**	★	375	600	800

IMPORTANT NOTE - Railroad Terms as defined and used in this book:

1. **RAILROAD STANDARDS** = A commission or board appointed by the railroad companies outlined a set of guidelines to be accepted or approved by each railroad line.

2. **RAILROAD APPROVED** = A list of watches each railroad line would approve if purchased by their employee's. (this list changed through the years).

3. **RAILROAD GRADE** = A watch made by manufactures to meet or exceed the guidelines set by the railroad standards. Grades such as 992, Vanguard and B.W. Raymond, etc.

☞ Some GRADES exceeded the R.R. standards such as 23 jewels, diamond end stone, gold train, raised gold jewel settings, double sunk dial and the list goes on. Examples: such as Veritas, Sangamo, 950 & Riverside Maximus and many others.

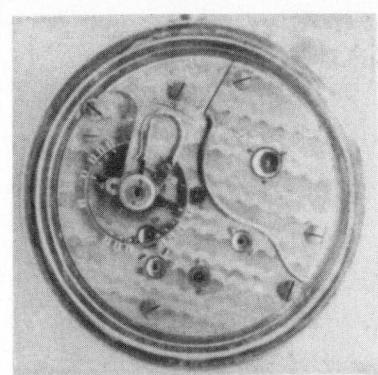

Bunn Special, 18 size, 24 Ruby Jewels, adjusted, serial number 1,413,435.

Bunn Special, 18 size, 26 Ruby Jewels, 'J. Home & Co." on dial adjusted to six positions, gold Jewel settings, serial number 2,019,415

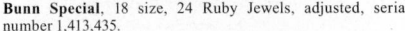

Grade or Name — Description	ABP	Ex-Fn	Mint
Bunn Special, 21J, SW, Coin	$200	$375	$600
Bunn Special, 21J, GJS, ADJ, HC	450	575	800
Bunn Special, 21J, GJS, ADJ, DR, OF	250	375	475
Bunn Special, 21J, GJS, DR, Adj.5P, OF	250	375	475
Burnt Special, 21J, GJS, DR, Adj.**6P**, OF	300	450	600
Bunn Special, 21J, GJS, Adj.5P, **HC, 14K**	1,000	1,500	2,000
Bunn Special, 21J, GJS, ADJ, **2-Tone**	325	450	700
Bunn Special, 21J, GJS, Adj.5P, DR	275	400	500
Bunn Special, 21J," **EXTRA'**, GJS ★★	1,000	1,500	2,200
Bunn Special, 23J, GJS, ADJ, DR, OF	600	900	1,200
Bunn Special, 23J, GJS, Adj.6P, DR, OF	650	900	1,200
Bunn Special, 23J, GJS, Adj.6P, DR, 2-Tone, OF ★★	700	950	1,250
Bunn Special, 23J, GJS, ADJ, DR, HC ★★★	2,000	3,500	4,800
Bunn Special, 24J, GJS, ADJ, DR, HC	1,000	1,800	2,300
Bunn Special, 24J, GJS, ADJ, DR, **14K, HC**	1,900	2,500	3,500
Bunn Special, 24J, GJS, ADJ, DR, OF	950	1,500	1,800
Bunn Special, 24J, GJS, **Adj.6P**, DR, OF	950	1,500	1,800
Bunn Special, 24J, GJS, **Adj.6P**, DR, HC	950	1,700	2,000
Bunn Special, 25J, GJS, **Adj.6P**, DR ★★★	5,000	7,500	10,000
Bunn Special, 26J, GJS, **Adj.6P**, DR ★★★	4,000	7,000	9,500
Central Truck Railroad, 15J, KW, KS ★★	700	1,200	1,800
Chesapeake & Ohio, 17J, ADJ, OF ★★	1,000	1,800	2,600
Chesapeake & Ohio Special, 21J, GJS, **2-Tone** ★★	1,400	2,200	3,500
Chesapeake & Ohio Special, 24J, NI, ADJ, GJS ★★	2,400	3,500	5,600
Chronometer, 11-15J, KW, OF ★	250	350	600
Chronometer, 15J, M#2, HC ★	285	400	700
Columbia, 11J, M#3, 5th Pinion	100	175	300
Columbia, 11J,M#1 &2,KW	100	175	300
Columbia, 11J, M#1 & 2, Silveroid	100	150	250
Columbia Special, 11J, M#1-2-3, KW	100	150	250
Columbia Special, 11J, M#1-2-3, KW/SW, transition	100	175	300
Comet, 11J, M#3, OF, LS, SW	100	150	200
Commodore Perry, 15-16J, HC	150	250	350
Criterion, 11-15J,HC	100	200	300

☞ Some watch manufacturers personalize watches for jobbers or jewelry firms, with exclusive private signed or marked movements. The valuable collectable watches are listed under the signed or marked movement. Other exclusive private signed or marked movements will have equivalent value or only slightly higher value and should be compared to Generic or Nameless movements. Railroad signed or marked (dials & movements) are usually more collectable & higher in value.

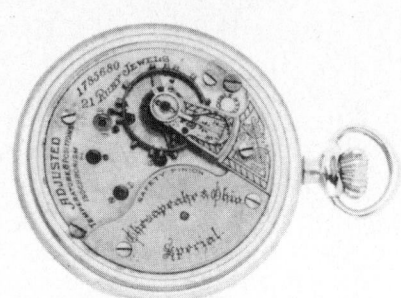
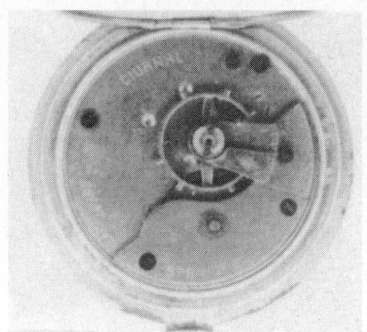

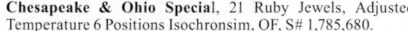

Chesapeake & Ohio Special, 21 Ruby Jewels, Adjusted Temperature 6 Positions Isochronsim, OF, S# 1,785,680.

Dlurnal, 18 size, 7 Jewels, keywind & set, only one run, total production 2,000, serial number 86,757.

Grade or Name — Description	ABP	Ex-Fn	Mint
Currier, 11-12J,KW, OF	$100	$175	$300
Currier, 11-12J,KW, HC	100	250	350
Currier, 11-12J, **1st run S# 401 to 500** ★★★	400	700	1,100
Currier, 11-12J, KW/SW, transition, OF	100	150	200
Currier, 13—15J, M#3, OF	100	150	200
Currier, 13—15J, M#3, HC	125	175	250
Dauntless, 11J	100	175	250
Dean, 15J, M#1, KW, HC ★★	300	550	1,000
Diurnal, 7J, KW, KS, HG, **Coin** ★	250	400	700
Dominion Railway, with train on dial ★★★	2,500	5,000	7,000
Eastlake, 11J, SW, KW, Transition	150	250	400
Emperor, 21J, M#6, LS, SW, ADJ	200	350	500
Enterprise, M#2, ADJ	125	200	250
Eureka, 11J	100	175	250
Favorite, 16J, LS, OF	100	175	250
Forest City, 7—11J, SW, LS, HC	100	200	300
Forest City, 17J, KW/SW, gilDed	110	200	275
General Grant or General Lee, 11J, M#1, KW ★	300	450	625
Hoyt, 7-9-11J, M#1-2, KW	100	150	200

🖎 Generic, nameless, Personalized Jobber Watches or unmarked grades for watch movements are listed under the Company name or initials of the Company, etc. by size, jewel count and description.

	ABP	Ex-Fn	Mint
Illinois Watch Co., 7-9J, M#1-2, KW	$100	$150	$200
Illinois Watch Co., 7-9J, M#2-6, SW	100	135	200
Illinois Watch Co., 11J, M#1-2, KW	100	150	200
Illinois Watch Co., 11J, M#3, SW	100	125	150
Illinois Watch Co., 12-13J, M#1-2, KW	100	150	200
Illinois Watch Co., 15J, M#1-2, KW	100	150	200
Illinois Watch Co., 15J, KW, ADJ, NI	100	150	275
Illinois Watch Co., 15J, SW, ADJ, DMK, NI	100	150	275
Illinois Watch Co., 15J, transition	100	135	150
Illinois Watch Co., 15J, SW, **Silveroid**	100	135	150
Illinois Watch Co., 15J, SW, **9K, HC**	225	500	700
Illinois Watch Co., 16J, SW, ADJ, DMK, NI	100	135	150
Illinois Watch Co., 16J, SW, ADJ, DMK, NI, marked **ADJ**	100	200	300
Illinois Watch Co., 17J, SW, Silveroid	100	135	150
Illinois Watch Co., 17J, KW/SW, transition	100	150	200
Illinois Watch Co., 17J, M#3, **5th Pinion**	100	175	300
Illinois Watch Co., 17J, SW, ADJ	100	150	200

🖎 Pricing in this Guide are fair market price for complete watches which are reflected from the NAWCC National and regional shows.

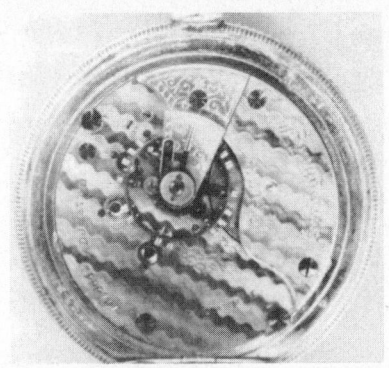

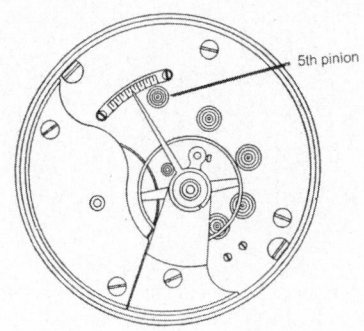

III .W. Co., 18 Size, 17 jewels, adjusted, **2-tone movement**, serial number 1,404,442.

18 Size, the 5th pinion which changed hunting case to open face.

Grade or Name — Description	ABP	Ex-Fn	Mint
Illinois Watch Co., 17J, SW, **2 tone movement**	$125	$200	$300
Illinois Watch Co., 17J, SW, **"EXTRA"**, Adj.4P . . . . ★	275	375	725
Illinois Watch Co., 19J, ADJ. **J. Barrel**, OF	150	250	450
Illinois Watch Co., 21J, Adj.3P, OF	195	300	500
Illinois Watch Co., 21J, ADJ.5-6P, ...	300	375	575
Illinois Watch Co., 23J, ADJ.6P, OF . . . . ★★★★	1,500	2,000	3,500
Illinois Watch Co., 24J, ADJ, ...	700	1,200	1,600
Inspector Special, 17J, LS, OF . . . . ★	300	500	750
Interior, 7J, KW & SW, OF.	100	150	175
Interstate Chronometer, 17J, HC, (sold by Sears) . . . . ★★★	400	500	750
Interstate Chronometer, 17J, OF . . . . ★★	300	450	650
Interstate Chronometer, 23J, Adj.5P, GJS, NI, OF . . . . ★	1,000	1,500	2,000
Interstate Chronometer, 23J, Adj.5P, GJS, NI, HC . . . . ★★	1,200	1,800	2,200
Iowa W. Co., 7-11J,M#1-2,KW.	150	225	350
King of the Road, 16 &17J, NI, OF & HC, LS, ADJ . . . . ★	400	650	950
King Special, 17J, 2-tone, OF.	150	275	500
King Philip Sp., 17J, (RR spur line). . . . . ★★★	400	700	1,000
Lafayette, 24J, GJS, Adj.6P, NI, SW, OF . . . . ★	1,000	1,500	2,000
Lafayette, 24J, GJS, Adj.6P, NI, SW, HC. . . . . ★★	1,300	2,000	2,500
Lakeshore, 17J, OF, LS, NI, SW.	125	200	300
Landis W. Co., 15-17J.	100	150	250
Liberty Bell, 17J, LS, NI, SW, OF	100	175	250
Liberty Bell, 17J, LS, NI, SW, HC	125	200	300
Lightning Express, 11-13J, KWKS . . . . ★	200	350	500
A. Lincoln, 21J, Adj.5P, NI, DR GJS, HC	400	600	800
A. Lincoln, 21J, Adj.5P, NI, DR, GJS, OF	250	400	500
Lincoln Park, 15-17J, LS, OF	100	150	200
Majestic Special, 17J, **2-tone movement,** OF	125	200	300
Locomotive, 11J, M# 2 grade 4, Locomotive engraved on Mvt	225	375	550
Maiden Lane, 16-17J, 5th Pinion	300	500	650
Manhattan, 11-13J, NI, KW, LS, HC or OF	100	200	300
Manhattan, 15—17J, NI, KW, LS, HC or OF	125	225	350
Mason,7J,KW,KS,HC.	100	200	300
Mason, 7J, KW, KS, HC, **1st run S# 101 to 200** . . . . ★★	450	600	900
Miller, 15J, **1st run S# 301 to 400** . . . . ★★	400	550	850
Miller, 15J, M#, HC, KW	100	200	300
Miller, 15J, M#, HC, KW, ADJ	125	250	350
Miller, 15J, KW, OF	100	175	275
Miller, 17J, 5th Pinion, ADJ, RR	150	275	425
Monarch W. Co., 17J, NI, ADJ, SW	125	175	325

&ᢒ Generic, nameless, Personalized Jobber Watches or unmarked grades for watch movements are listed under the Company name or initials of the Company, etc. by size, jewel count and description.

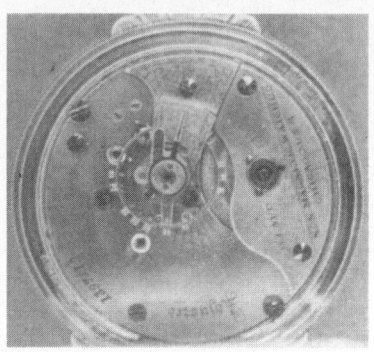

Palliard Non-Magnetic W. Co., 15 size, 24 jewels, gold jewel settings, serial number 1,397,812.

Pennsylvania Special, 18 size, 26 Ruby Jewels, Adj6p, 2-tone movement serial number 1,742,913.

Grade or Name — Description	ABP	Ex-Fn	Mint
Montgomery Ward, 15-17J, GJS, OF	$125	$225	$350
Montgomery Ward, 19J, GJS, OF...........................	200	350	450
Montgomery Ward, 21J, OF...............................	300	500	600
Montgomery Ward Timer, 21J, OF....................... ★	300	500	600
Montgomery Ward, 24J, OF...............................	1,000	1,500	1,800
Montgomery Ward, 24J, HC .... ★	1,100	1,700	2,000
Montgomery Ward, 24J, marked double roller, HC............ ★	1,100	1,700	2,000
Muscatine W. Co., 15J, LS, NI, HC	135	225	400
The National, 11J, SW, LS, OF.............................	100	150	225
North Western Special, 17J, GJS, ADJ, NI	600	850	1,100
(Paillard Non-Magnetic W. Co. SEE Non-Magnetic W. Co.)			
Pennsylvania Special, 17J, GJS, ADJ.....................★★	900	1,100	1,600
Pennsylvania Special, 21J, DR, Adj.5P ....★★	2,000	3,000	3,600
Pennsylvania Special, 24J, DR, GJS, ADJ..................★★	3,000	4,000	5,000
Pennsylvania Special, 25J, DR, GJS, ADJ, NI............★★★	4,500	6,500	9,000
Pennsylvania Special, 26J, DR, GJS, ADJ, NI ....★★★	5,500	7,500	10,000
Pierce Arrow, 17J, "automaker logo....................... ★	375	550	800
Plymouth W. Co., 15-17J, SW, (sold by Sears).................	100	150	200
Potomac, 17J,ADJ, NI, OF	150	200	375
Potomac, 17J, ADJ, NI, HC .... ★	225	300	500
The President, 15J, NI, OF	100	250	400
The President, 17J, DMK, **14K gold case**	500	1,000	1,300
Rail Road Construction, 17J, OF	225	410	575
Rail Road Dispatcher Extra or Special, 15-17J, OF............ ★	250	410	660
Rail Road Dispatcher Extra, 15-17J, HC .... ★	250	410	660
Rail Road Employee's Special, 17J, NI, LS, HC .... ★	250	440	660
Rail Road King, 15J, NI, ADJ, OF......................... ★	225	400	550
Rail Road King, 15J, NI, ADJ, HC........................ ★	300	500	770
Rail Road King, 16J, NI, ADJ, OF......................... ★	300	500	770
Rail Road King, 16J, NI, ADJ, HC........................ ★	325	525	800
Rail Road King, 17J, NI, ADJ, OF......................... ★	300	500	770
Rail Road King, 17J, NI, ADJ, HC........................ ★	350	550	825
Rail Road King, 19J, NI, ADJ, **2 tone**, OF................. ★	350	600	850
4 Railroader, 11J, (Locomotive engraved on movement) .... ★	250	550	825

"4 Railroader" 

	ABP	Ex-Fn	Mint
Rail Road Timer Extra, 17-21J, (Montgomery Ward), OF .... ★	225	375	500
Railway, 11J,KW, KS, gilt .... ★	200	300	500
Railway Engineer, 15J .... ★	275	400	625
Railway Regulator, 11-15J, LS, (R. W. Sears Watch Co.) ....★★	450	600	975
Remington W. Co. 17J, OF................................	200	275	450
Remington W. Co. 17J, HC.................................	225	285	500

The President, 18 size, 17 jewels, Chalmer regulator Pat. Dec. 19,1882, serial number 1,240,909.

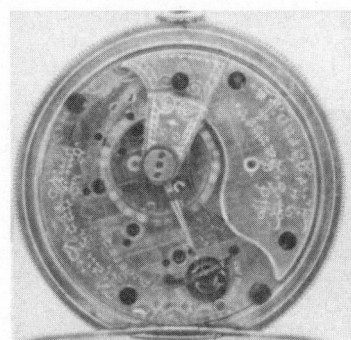

Railroad King, 18 size, 17 jewels, Fifth Pinion Model, adjusted. Note Chalmer patented regulator, S# 1,160,836.

Grade or Name — Description	ABP	Ex-Fn	Mint
Remington Special, 21J, Adj.6P, OF	250	350	575
Standard W. Co., 15J, several models .... ★	$125	$200	$300
S.W.Co.,15J,M#,KW,HC	110	200	300
R. W. Sears Watch Co. Chicago,"Defiance" model, HC........★★	500	700	1,400
Sears & Roebuck Special, 15-17J, GJS, NI, DMK, Adj...........	150	200	350
Senate, 17J, NI, DMK, Washington W. Co	150	200	350
Southern R.R. Special, 21J, LS, ADJ, OF ....★★	1,400	2,000	3,000
Southern R.R. Special, 21J, M#5, LS, Adj., HC ....★★	1,600	2,500	3,500
Star Light, 17J, 5th pinion, Chalmers Reg. OF	150	235	450
Stewart Special, 11J	100	135	175
Stewart Special, 15J, Adj	100	150	200
Stewart Special, 17J, Adj	100	200	250
Stewart Special, 21J, Adj	150	300	400
Stuart, 15J, M#1, KW, KS	300	450	950
Stuart, 15J, M#1, KW/SW, transition......................	250	400	850
Stuart, 15J, M#1, KW, KS, marked Adj..................... ★	275	350	750
Stuart, 15J, ADJ, KW, Abbotts Conversion, 18K, HC .... ★	1,200	2,000	3,000
Stuart, 15J, M#1, KW, KS, Coin .... ★	500	650	1,100
Stuart, 15J, M#1, KW, KS, 1st run S# 1 to 10".......... ★★★★	4,200	7,000	12,000
Stuart, 15J, M#1, KW, KS, 1st run S#11 to 100" .... ★★★	2,400	3,000	7,000
Stuart, 17J, M#3, 5th Pinion.......................... ★★	225	350	500
Stuart, 17J, M#3, 5th Pinion, Adj........................ ★★	250	385	600

Sears & Roebuck Special, 18 size, 17Jewels, serial number 1,481,879.

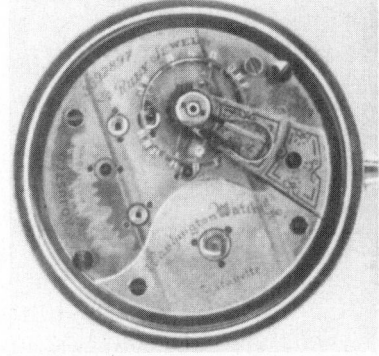

Washington W. Co., Lafayette model, 18 size, 24 Ruby jewels, gold jewel settings, adjusted, serial #3,392,897.

Grade or Name — Description	ABP	Ex-Fn	Mint
Transition Models, 17J, KW/SW, OF.........................	$75	$150	$200
Train Dispatcher Special, 17J, (Montgomery Ward), Adj, OF .... ★	275	400	625
Time King, 17J,OF, LS, NI...................................	100	150	300
Time King, 21J, OF, LS	200	400	475
Union Pacific Sp., 17J, OF .... ★★	450	700	1,400
Vault Time Lock for Mosler, 15J,72 hr....................	100	175	300
Ward's Special, 15J, NI, FULL, LS	100	150	200
George Washington,11J, HC .... ★★★	250	350	550
Washington, 11j, also (U.S.A) sold by **Montgomery Ward**	100	150	200
Washington, 17J, also (U.S.A) sold by **Montgomery Ward**, ...	125	200	275
Washington W. Co. (See Army & Navy, Liberty Bell, Lafayette, Senate)			
Wathiers Railway Watch, 15-17J, Adj., NI .... ★	450	700	1,400
NO. 5, 11J, KW KS, (**marked** No.5), HC.......................	150	235	400
65, 15J, HC, LS, M#2...	100	150	175
89, 17J, nickel, ADJ, OF	100	150	200
89, 21J, nickel, ADJ, HC.....................................	200	400	500
101, 11J, SW, KW, OF	100	150	175
101, 11J ,SW, KW, Silveroid..................................	100	150	175
101, 11J, SW, KW, HC.......................................	100	175	225
102, 13J, SW, KW, Silveroid..................................	100	175	200
102, 13J, SW, KW, OF	100	175	200
102, 13J, SW, KW, HC	100	200	275
103, 15-16J,ADJ...	100	150	250
104, 15J, M#2, HC .... ★★★	300	550	900
104, 17J, M#3, **early high grade** for RR, Ca. 1885, OF.,.... ★★★★	375	650	1,000
105, 17J, M#3, **early high grade** for RR, Ca. 1885, OF..... ★★★★	600	825	1,500
105, 15J, M#2, GJS, ADJ, KW, KS, HC .... ★★★	375	650	1,000
106, 15-17J, ADJ, KW, KS .... ★	250	350	600
107, 15-17J, NI, ADJ .... ★	285	450	800
108, 15-17J, (if it is in the "Stuart" run it is 108) .... ★★★	1,000	1,400	1,800
1908 Special, 21J, NI, Adj.5P, (**marked** 1908 special), OF.........	325	550	750

STUART, 17 jewels, Model #3,5th Pinion, Transition Model.

First Model in 14K white or green
gold filled Wadsworth case, showing
Montgomery numerical dial.

☞ A collector should expect to pay modestly higher prices at local shops.

☞ Pricing in this Guide are fair market price for complete watches which are reflected from the NAWCC National and regional shows.

ILLINOIS 16 SIZE

Grade or Name — Description	ABP	Ex-Fn	Mint
Adams Street 17J, 3/4, SW, NI, DMK	$200	$300	$550
Adams Street, 17J, 3/4, 2-tone, checkboard DMK, HC	250	400	700
Adams Street, 21J, 3F brg, NI, DMK . . . . ★	250	400	700
Ak-Sar-Ben (Nebraska backward), 17J, OF, GCW	150	250	350
Ariston,11J,OF&HC	75	150	200
Ariston, 15J, OF & HC	75	150	200
Ariston, 17J, Adj, HC	125	225	400
Ariston, 17J, Adj, OF	100	200	350
Ariston, 19J, Adj.5P, OF	150	275	400
Ariston, 21J, GJS, Adj.6P, OF	200	375	600
Ariston, 21J, GJS, Adj.6P, HC	250	500	700
Ariston, 23J, GJS, Adj.6P, OF	500	700	1,000
Ariston, 23J, GJS, Adj.6P, HC . . . . ★★	700	900	1,200
Arlington Special, 17J, OF	100	150	275
Arlington Special, 17J, OF, Silveroid	85	135	245
Army & Navy, 19J, GJS, Adj.3P, NI, 1F brg, OF	150	300	450
Army & Navy, 19J, GJS, Adj.3P, NI, 1F brg, HC	200	400	500
Army & Navy, 21J, GJS, Adj.3P, 1F brg, OF	250	400	525
Army & Navy, 21J, GJS, Adj.3P, 1F brg, HC	350	550	700
B & M Special, 17J, BRG, Adj.4P (Boston & Maine) . . . . ★	450	700	1,200
B & O Standard,21J . . . . ★★	1,100	2,000	2,600
Benjamin Franklin, 17J, ADJ, DMK, OF	300	500	700
Benjamin Franklin, 17J, ADJ, DMK, HC . . . . ★	400	600	800
Benjamin Franklin, 21J, GJS, Adj.5P, DR, GT, OF . . . . ★	700	1,200	1,500
Benjamin Franklin, 21J, GJS, Adj.5P, DR, GT, HC . . . . ★★	800	1,500	2,000
Benjamin Franklin, 25J, GJS, Adj.6P, DR, GT, OF . . . . ★★★	3,000	4,500	6,500
Benjamin Franklin, 25J, GJS, Adj.6P, DR, GT, HC . . . . ★★★	4,000	6,500	8,000

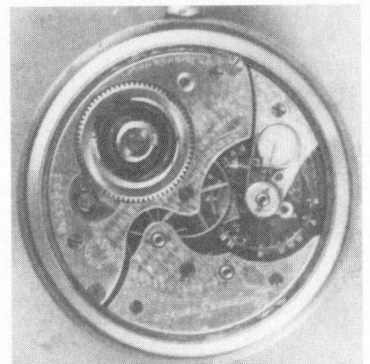

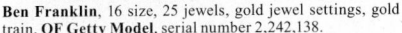

Ben Franklin, 16 size, 25 jewels, gold jewel settings, gold train, **OF Getty Model**, serial number 2,242,138.

Bunn Special, Model 163,16 size, 23J., gold jewel settings, gold train, 60 hour movement, serial #5,421,504.

Note: Bunn Special original cases were marked Bunn Special made and cased by Hamilton. Also GRADES 161 & 163 were made by Hamilton W. Co.

Special note: Some wheels or gears are gold gilded on brass and not solid gold, the appearance is rough and not as smooth as solid gold gears or wheels.

♺ Generic, nameless or unmarked grades for watch movements are listed under the Company name or initials of the Company, etc. by size, jewel count and description.

♺ Watches listed in this book are priced at the collectable fair market value at the trade show level, as complete watches having an original 14k gold filled case, KEY WIND with silver, an original white enamel single sunk dial, and with the entire original movement in good working

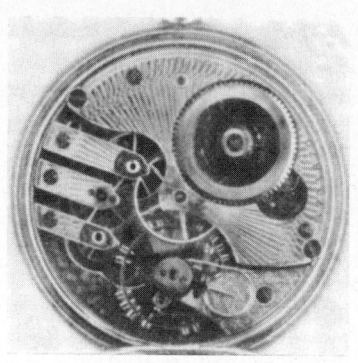

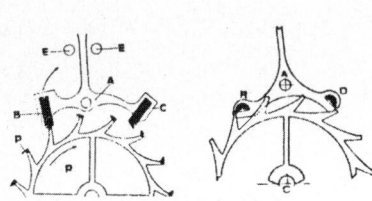

Left: standard style escapement.
Right: DeLong escapement, with upright D shaped pellets.

Illinois Watch Co., 16 size, 25J., 3 fingered bridge Getty Model, gold train, note click near balance cock = HC model, serial number S731,870.

Grade or Name — Description	ABP	Ex-Fn	Mint
Bunn, 17J, LS, NI, 3/4, GJS, Adj.5P, OF	$175	$250	$450
Bunn, 17J, LS, NI, 3/4,Adj.5P, HC .... ★★★	600	800	1,400
Bunn, 19J, LS, NI, 3/4, GJS, Adj.5P, OF	200	325	500
Bunn, 19J, LS, NI, 3/4, Adj.5P, HC .... ★★★	800	1,200	1,500
Bunn, 19J, LS, NI, 3/4, GJS, Adj.5P, 60 hour, OF	400	600	800
Bunn, 19J, **marked Jeweled Barrel,** OF......................	300	400	600
Bunn Special, 21J, NI, Adj.6P, GT, HC .... ★★	575	700	1,100
Bunn Special, 21J, LS, NI, 3/4, GJS, Adj.6P, GT, OF	250	350	525
Bunn Special, 21J, LS, GJS, Adj.6P, GT, **gold plated Mvt**..... ★★	575	700	1,100
Bunn Special, 21J, LS, NI, 3/4, GJS, Adj.6P, GT, **60** hour, OF	325	450	800
Bunn Special, 21J, 60 hr., **Bunn Special case, OF**	400	550	900
Bunn Special, 23J, LS, NI, 3/4, GJS, Adj.6P, GT, OF	500	750	1,100
Bunn Special, 23J, LS, NI, 3/4, GJS, Adj.6P, GT, **60** hour, OF	700	1,000	1,600
Bunn Special, 23J, LS, NI, 3/4, GJS, Adj.6P, GT, OF with **23J, 60-hour on dial**	1,300	2,000	2,500
Bunn Special, 23J, LS, NI, GJS, GT, Adj.6P, HC .... ★★★★	2,500	4,000	5,200
161 Bunn Special, 21J, 3/4, Adj.6P, **60** hour, OF	700	1,200	1,700
161 Bunn Special, 21J, 3/4, Adj.6P, **60** hour on dial & movement in Illinois original factory box with Bunn papers .... ★★★★	1,800	2,500	4,000
161 Elinvar Bunn Special, 21J, 3/4, Adj.6P, **60** hour (**Elinvar** signed at edge of balance cock).................	1,000	1,500	2,000
161A Bunn Special, 21J, 3/4, Adj.6P, 60 hour (Elinvar signed under balance or on train bridge)	900	1,400	1,800
161B, Bunn Special, 21J, **60** hour, pressed jewels , OF.... ... ★★★★	5,000	8,000	15,000
163 Bunn Special, 23J, GJS, Adj.6P, 3/4, **60** hour	1,600	2,200	2,800
163 Elinvar Bunn Special, 23J, GJS, Adj.6P, **60** hour, OF (**Elinvar** signed at bottom of cock, uncut balance) .... ★	2,000	2,900	3,700
163A Elinvar Bunn Special, 23J, GJS, Adj.6P, 3/4, **60** hour, OF (**Elinvar** signed under balance) .... ◁	2,100	3,200	3,900
163A Elinvar Bunn Special, 23J, Adj.6P, 3/4, **60** hour, OF (**Elinvar** signed on train bridge) .... ◁	2,200	3,700	4,200

◔◠ Some grades are not included. Their values can be determined by comparing with similar age, size, metal content, style, models and grades listed.

Grade or Name — Description		ABP	Ex-Fn	Mint
Burlington W. Co., 11-15J,OF		$100	$200	$300
Burlington W. Co., 11- 15J, HC		125	200	365
Burlington W. Co., 17J, OF		95	200	300
Burlington W. Co., 17J, HC		125	200	365
Burlington W. Co., 19J, 3/4, NI, Adj.3P		95	200	300
Burlington W. Co., 19J, BRG, NI, Adj.3P		95	200	300
Burlington W. Co., 19J, 3/4, HC		95	225	325
Burlington W. Co., 19J, 3F brg, NI, Adj.3P		90	200	275
Burlington W. Co., 21J, 3/4, NI, Adj.3P		125	275	375
Burlington W. Co., 21J, Adj.6P, GJS, Getty, 2-tone	★★	500	800	1,250
Burlington, Bull Dog- **on dial**, 21J, SW, LS, GJS, GT		275	500	750
C & O Special, 21J, 3/4, NI, ADJ	★★	900	1,500	2,000
Capitol, 17J, OF, BRG., NI., Adj., OF		95	175	250
Capitol, 19J, OF, G# 604, 3/4, NI, Adj.3P, OF	★	100	200	300
Central, 17J,SW,PS,OF		75	175	200
Commodore Perry Special, 21J, Adj.6P, GT, OF	★	250	375	700
Craftsman, 21J, Adj.3P, OF	★★★	500	650	800
D. & R. G. Special, 21J, GJS, GT, Adj.5P, (Denver & Rio Grand RR), OF	★★★★	3,100	4,000	5,500
DeLong Escapement, 21J, GJS, (Bunn Sp. or A. Lincoln) upright D shaped pallets, Adj.6P, **14K** OF	★★★★	4,000	5,500	8,000
Dependon, 17J, (J. V. Farwell)		150	250	400
Dependon, 21J, (J. V. Farwell)		200	350	525
Diamond, Ruby, Sapphire, 21J, GJS, GT, Adj.6P, BRG, OF	★★★	1,600	2,300	3,200
Diamond, Ruby, Sapphire, 23J, GJS, GT, Adj.6P, BRG, OF	★★★	3,000	4,000	5,300
Diamond, Ruby, Sapphire, 23J, GJS, GT, Adj.6P, grade# 310, tall Arabic numbers on dial, BRG, DR, **HC**	★★★★	4,000	5,500	9,000
Diamond, Ruby, Sapphire, 23J, GJS, GT, Adj.6P, BRG, OF also marked **Greenwich** (Washington W. Co.)	★★★	3,000	4,000	6,000
Diamond, Ruby, Sapphire, 23J, GJS, GT, Adj.6P, 3/4 plate, OF	★★★	2,500	3,500	5,500
Dispatcher, 19J, Adj.3P		150	300	400
Fifth Ave., 19J, Adj.3P, GT, OF		100	200	300
Fifth Ave., 21J, Adj.3P, GT, OF		125	300	400
Franklin Street, 15J, 3/4, NI, ADJ		100	200	300
Grant, 17J, ADJ, LS, **Getty Model**, OF		150	275	400
Getty Model #4&5, 17J		100	200	300
Getty Model #4&5, 21J		200	350	500

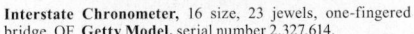

Interstate Chronometer, 16 size, 23 jewels, one-fingered bridge, OF, **Getty Model**, serial number 2,327,614.

A. Lincoln, 16 size, 21 jewels, gold jewel settings, gold train, Adj5p, OF, **Getty Model**, serial number 2,237,406.

☞ Pricing in this Guide are fair market price for complete watches which are reflected from the NAWCC National and regional shows.

Grade or Name — Description	ABP	Ex-Fn	Mint
Great Northern Special, 17J, BRG, ADJ	$200	$350	$500
Great Northern Special, 19J, BRG, ADJ	200	400	550
Great Northern Special, 21J, BRG, ADJ, Adj.3P...................	250	500	650
Illinois Central, 17-21J, 2-Tone, Adj.3P, GT....................	225	375	575
Illinois Watch Co., 7-9J, M#1-2-3	45	120	150
Illinois Watch Co., 11J., OF	45	120	150
Illinois Watch Co., 13J, 3/4, OF	45	120	150
Illinois Watch Co., 11-13J, M#7, 3/4, OF	45	120	150
Illinois Watch Co., 11-13, M#6, 3/4, HC	85	150	200
Illinois Watch Co., 15J, M#2, OF...........................	50	120	165
Illinois Watch Co., 15J, M#1, HC...........................	90	150	265
Illinois Watch Co., 15J, M#3, OF...........................	50	120	150
Illinois Watch Co., 15J, 3/4, ADJ..........................	50	120	150
Illinois Watch Co., 15J, 3F brg, GJS.......................	50	120	150
Illinois Watch Co., 16-17J, **14K, HC**......................	375	600	850
Illinois Watch Co., 16-17J, Adj.3P, OF.......................	85	140	200
Illinois Watch Co., 16-17J, M#2-3, SW, OF	85	140	200
Illinois Watch Co., 17J, M#4-6, SW, HC......................	90	200	250
Illinois Watch Co., 17J, M#7, OF	85	140	200
Illinois Watch Co., 17J, M#5, 3/4, ADJ, HC	85	200	225
Illinois Watch Co., 17J, M#4, 3F brg, GJS, Adj.5P, HC............	150	250	400
Illinois Watch Co., 19J, 3/4, GJS, Adj.5P ,**jeweled barrel**	165	275	450
Illinois Watch Co., 19J, 3/4, BRG, Adj.3-4P	95	200	250
Illinois Watch Co., 21J, Adj.3P, OF	200	300	350
Illinois Watch Co., 21J, ADJ, OF	225	300	400
Illinois Watch Co., 21J, GJS, HC	235	450	500
Illinois Watch Co., 21J, 3/4, GJS, Adj.5P....................	225	300	400
Illinois Watch Co., 21J, 3F brg, GJS, Adj.4P	200	325	400
Illinois Watch Co., 21J, 3F brg, GJS, Adj.5P	225	350	450
Illinois Watch Co., 23J, GJS, Adj.5P, OF...................★★	400	575	950
Illinois Watch Co., 23J, GJS, Adj.5P, HC...................★★	500	675	1,000
Illinois Watch Co., 25J, 4th model,3F brg, GJS, Adj.5P, HC... ★★★	3,500	5,000	7,000
Imperial Sp., 17J, SW, LS, Adj.4P, OF	125	200	375
Interstate Chronometer, 17J, GCW, Adj.3P, HC, (sold by Sears)	300	400	725
Interstate Chronometer, 17J, GCW, Adj.3P, OF	250	400	625
Interstate Chronometer, 23J, 1 F brg, ADJ, OF .... ★	800	1,200	1,600
Interstate Chronometer, 23J, 1 F brg, ADJ, HC.............. ★★	1,200	1,600	2,200
Lafayette, 23J, Washington W. Co., GJS, Adj.5P, GT, OF ... ..★★★	1,000	1,500	2,000
Lafayette, 23J, Washington W. Co., GJS, Adj.5P, GT, HC ... ..★★★	1,400	2,000	2,700
Lakeshore, 17J, OF..	75	110	200
Lakeshore, 17J, HC..	125	200	350
Landis W. Co., 15-17J.......................................	75	120	200
Liberty Bell, 15-17J, OF....................:	85	145	225
Liberty Bell, 15-17J, HC............................... ★	300	450	675
A. Lincoln, 21J, 3/4, GJS, Adj.5P, OF	225	375	500
A. Lincoln, 21J,3/4, GJS, Adj.5P, HC........................	400	600	800
The Lincoln, 15J, 3F brg...................................	125	200	300
Logan, 15J,OF..	60	120	175
Marvel, 19J, GT, GJS, Adj.3P, OF	75	140	225
Marine Special, 21J, 3/4, Adj.3P	150	300	375
Monarch W. Co., 17J, NI, ADJ, SW	125	175	300
Monroe, 17J, NI,3/4, OF (Washington W. Co.)	85	135	200
Monroe, 15J, 3/4, OF (Washington W. Co.)....................	75	120	185
Montgomery Ward, 17J, LS, Thin Model, OF	100	175	275
Montgomery Ward, 21J, "Extra RR Timer", **2 tone**, G# 179.....★★	1,000	1,200	1,700
OurNo.1, 15J, HC, M#1	100	175	300
Overland Special, 19J, Adj., OF............................	100	225	350
Pennsylvania Special, 17J, Adj.3P, HC .... ★	450	750	1,100
Pennsylvania Special, 17J, Adj., **2 tone**, G# 176, HC. .... ★	800	1,100	1,500

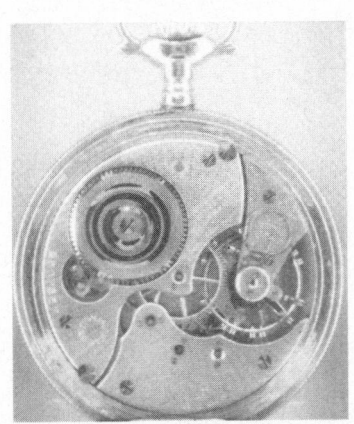

Sangamo, 16 size, 23 Jewels, Adj.6p, gold jewel settings, gold train, OF Getty Model, serial number 2,307,867.

Sangamo Special, 17S, 23J., model 13, marked motor barrel, Adj.6P, Serial # 4,628,066, Ca. 1926. NOTE: This is 60 hour movement tested and runs from 60 to 65 hours.

Grade or Name Description		ABP	Ex-Fn	Mint
Pennsylvania Special, 19J, OF	★	$600	$900	$1,300
Pennsylvania Special, 21J, Getty model, **2-tone**, Adj., OF	★	1,000	1,500	2,000
Pennsylvania Special, 21J, **2-tone**, (Finely Adj.), HC	★★★	2,000	2,500	3,500
Pennsylvania Special, 23J, 3/4, GJS, Adj.5P	★	1,400	2,100	3,000
Plymouth W. Co., 15-17J, OF (Add $50 for HC), (sold by Sears)		100	200	300
Precise, 21J, OF, LS, Adj.3P		100	200	300
Quincy Street, 17J, 3/4, NI, DMK, ADJ		95	145	275
Railroad Dispatcher, 11-17J, DMK, 3/4		175	300	425
Railroad Dispatcher Extra or Special, 15-17J, DMK, 3/4	★	225	350	550
Railroad Employee's, 17J		175	300	425
Railroad King, 16-17J, M#2 or 5-Getty model, NI, PS, OF		275	350	550
Railroad Official, 23J, 3 Finger bridge	★★★★★	2,000	2,500	3,500
Railway King, 17J, OF		175	250	425
Remington W. Co. 11-15J, OF		100	150	200
Remington W. Co. 17J, OF		125	185	265
Remington W. Co. 17J, HC		200	275	350
Rockland, 17-19J, GJS, GT, 7th model, grade GJS, OF		75	135	200
Sangamo, 19J, model #4, GJS, GT, ADJ., HC	★★★	4,000	5,500	8,500
Sangamo, 21J, GJS, Adj.6P, HC		250	400	650
Sangamo, 21J, GJS, Adj., OF		225	375	550
Sangamo, 21J, 3/4, GJS, DR, Adj.6P, OF		225	375	600
Sangamo, 21J, GJS, Adj.6P, <u>EXTRA or SPECIAL</u>. (Getty), HC	★	525	800	1,200
Sangamo, 21J, GJS, Adj.6P, <u>EXTRA or SPECIAL</u>, (Getty), OF.	★	475	700	1,100
Sangamo, 21J, GJS, Adj., <u>marked SPECIAL</u> **2-tone** Mvt., Adj.6P, **(straight ribbon** - not wavy ribbon pattern), (Getty), OF	★	475	700	1,000
Sangamo, 23J, GJS, Adj., <u>marked SPECIAL</u> **2-tone Mvt.**, Adj.6P, **(straight ribbon** - not wavy ribbon pattern), (Getty), OF	★	625	800	1,200
Sangamo, 23J, 3/4, GJS, DR, Adj.6P, OF		350	550	900
Sangamo, 23J, 3/4, GJS, DR, Adj.6P, HC		400	700	1,100
Sangamo, 25J, M#5, 3/4, GJS, DR. Adj.6P	★★★★	4,000	6,000	9,500
Sangamo, 26J, M#5, 3/4, GJS, DR. Adj.6P	★★★★	5,000	7,000	8,500
Sangamo Special, 19J, BRG, GJS, GT, Adj.6P, OF		350	500	750
Sangamo Special, 19J, BRG, GJS, GT, Adj.6P, HC	★★★	1,400	2,000	2,700
Sangamo, **Extra**, 21J, Adj.6P, gold train, Of	★★	425	600	950
Sangamo Special, 21J, M#8, BRG, HC	★★★	1,500	2,500	3,500
Sangamo Special, 21J, M#9, BRG, GJS, GT, Adj.6P, OF		400	600	900
Sangamo Special, 21J, BRG, GJS, GT, Diamond end cap		400	600	900

Grade or Name — Description	ABP	Ex-Fn	Mint
Sangamo Special, 23J, M#9-10, BRG, GJS, GT, Adj.6P,			
Sangamo Special **HINGED** case, add $300 if Fish Scale DMK	$850	$1,250	$2,000
Sangamo Special, 23J, BRG, GJS, GT, Adj.6P, Diamond			
end stone, **screw back**, Sangamo Special case..............	750	1,000	1,500
Sangamo Special, 23J, BRG, GJS, GT, Adj.6P, Fishscale Damaskeening	1,000	1,400	2,000
Sangamo Special, 23J, M#8, GJS, GT, Adj.6P, **HC** .... ★★★	1,600	2,500	3,600
Sangamo Special, 23J, BRG, GJS, GT, Adj.6P, **not marked**			
60 hour, rigid bow, Sangamo Special case.................	850	1,300	2,000
Sangamo Special, 23J, BRG, GJS, GT, Adj.6P,			
marked 60 hour, Sangamo Special case .... ★★★	1,600	3,500	4,500
Sangamo Special, 23J, BRG, GJS, GT, Adj.6P, 60 hour			
rigid bow, Sangamo Special case **14K gold case** ..... ★★★★	2,000	4,000	5,500
Santa Fe Special, 17J, BRG, Adj., (Triple Signed), OF	225	350	650
Santa Fe Special, 21J, 3/4, Adj., (Triple Signed), OF............	450	600	800
Santa Fe Special, 21J, 3/4, Adj., (Triple Signed), **HC**	500	700	950
Sears, Roebuck & Co. Special, 15-17J, ADJ	85	150	225
Senate, 17J, (Washington W. Co.), **gilt escape wheel**, NI, 3/4, Adj ..	95	150	250
Standard, 15J	75	125	200
Sterling, 17J, SW, PS, Adj.3P, OF...........................	75	125	200
Sterling, 19-21J, SW, PS, Adj.3P, OF	125	200	250
Stewart, 17J	75	140	185
Stewart Special, 21J, Adj	125	200	250
Stewart Special, 19J, Adj.3P...............................	75	150	200
Stewart Special, 15-17J, ...	60	120	165
The General, 15J, OF	75	150	200
Time King, 17J, OF.......................................	65	120	150
Time King, 19J, Adj.3P, OF	95	200	225
Time King, 21J, Adj, OF...................................../...	150	300	325
Trainmen's Special, 17J, HC .... ★	150	300	475
Union Pacific,17J, Adj., DR, 2-tone, DMK, OF..............★★	500	700	1,100
Victor, 21J, 3/4, Adj	150	250	350

Washington W. Co. (See Army & Navy, Liberty Bell, Lafayette, Senate)

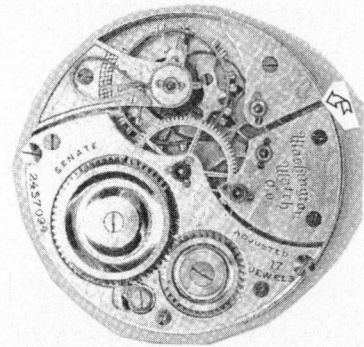

Grade 163, 16 size, 23 jewels, adjusted to 6 positions, motor barrel, 60 hour model, serial number 5,421,504.

SENATE, 17J, 16S, Washington W. CO., Adj., **gilt escape wheel & train,** HC, S# 2,457,094 (M# 6 with extra cut out.)

161 through 161A —See Bunn Special

Grade or Name — Description	ABP	Ex-Fn	Mint
167, 17J, marked	$100	$150	$250
169, 19J, Adj.3P, OF	75	200	225
174, 17J, LS, GJS, Adj., OF	60	120	185
174, 21J, LS, GJS, Adj., OF	165	300	325
174, 23J, LS, GJS, Adj., OF, **marked 174**................... ★★	500	700	925
175, 17J, RR grade & a (RR inspectors name on dial &mvt.) ...★★	600	800	1,200
176, 17J, Getty model, LS, Adj.4P, 2-tone, HC .... ★	300	400	600
177, 17J, Getty model, Ruby Jewels, Adj.5P, HC-OF ....★★	400	600	950

Grade or Name — Description	ABP	Ex-Fn	Mint
179, 21J, 3/4, GJS, GT, Adj.6P, Getty model, **marked** Ruby Jewels . .			
Getty model, HC or OF . . . . ★★	$300	$500	$725
181, 21J., ADJ, GJS, marked21 ruby jewels . . . . ★★★★	600	1,000	1,500
184, 17-19J, 3F brg, LS, OF.	95	200	250
184, 23J, 3F brg, LS, OF	500	700	1,100
186, 23J, 3F brg, LS, OF	500	700	1,100
186, 17J, 3F brg, Adj.4P, 2 tone, **marked** 186, HC	200	350	525
187, 17J, 3F brg, Adj.5P, GJS, GT, **marked** 187, HC	250	400	625
189, 21J, 3F brg, Adj.6P, GJS, DR, GT, **marked Ruby Jewels & Adjusted.**,			
Getty model, HC or OF . . . . ★	300	500	750
555, 17J, 3/4.	100	200	350
777, 17J, 3/4, ADJ . . . . ★	150	275	450
805, 17J, BRG, GJS, GT, DR, OF	75	125	200
809, 23J, Adj.6P, GT, **marked 809** . . . . ★★★	500	900	1,300
900,19J, LS, Adj.3P	125	200	300

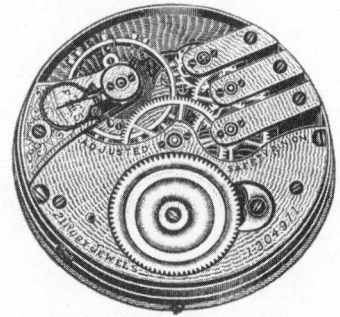

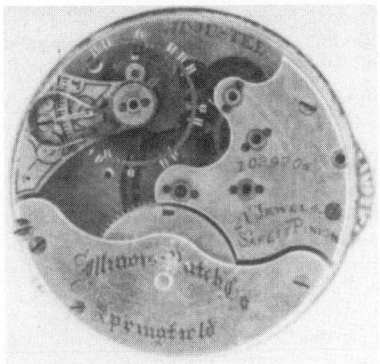

Grade 189, 21J, OF, 3 Finger bridge, GJS, DR. GT, **marked** *"Ruby Jewels" & Adjusted.*, gold balance screws including 4 timing screws, gold beveled polished train, counterpoised fork & pallet, Getty model, advertised at a cost of 20% higher than a 23J., Sangamo, Ca.1903.

Illinois Watch Co., 14 size, 21J., adjusted, nickel movement, gold jewel settings, serial number 1,029,204.

ILLINOIS 14 SIZE

Grade or Name — Description	ABP	Ex-Fn	Mint
Illinois Watch Co., 7J, M#1, **GRADE 120, KW**, OF . . . . ★	$95	$135	$275
Illinois Watch Co., 7J, M#1-2-3, SW, OF	40	100	120
Illinois Watch Co., 11J, M#1-2-3, SW, OF	45	100	125
Illinois Watch Co., 15J, M#1-2-3, SW, OF	50	100	145
Illinois Watch Co., 16J, M#1-2-3, SW, OF	70	110	165
Illinois Watch Co., 21J, M#1-2-3, SW, OF . . . . ★	125	185	325
Illinois Watch Co., 22J . . . . ★	150	300	425

NOTE: Add $35 for above watches in hunting case.

ILLINOIS 12 SIZE and 13 SIZE

Grade or Name — Description	ABP	Ex-Fn	Mint
Accurate, 21J, GJS, OF	$75	$150	$250
Aristocrat, 17J, OF	55	85	150
Aristocrat, 19J, OF	60	125	175
Ariston, 11-17J, OF	60	80	165
Ariston, 17J, Adj.3P, BRG, OF	75	110	200
Ariston, 17J, Adj.3P, G# 506, 14 size dial & 12 size mvt., HC ★★★★	225	400	800
Ariston, 19J, OF	80	135	250
Ariston, 21J, Adj.5P, OF	100	200	375
Ariston, 21J, Adj.5P, HC . . . . ★★	225	350	600
Ariston, 23J, Adj.5P, OF. . . . . ★	225	300	450
Ariston, 23J, Adj.5P, HC . . . . ★★	250	335	550
Ariston, 23J, Adj.6P, OF 18K . . . . ★★★	400	600	1,000

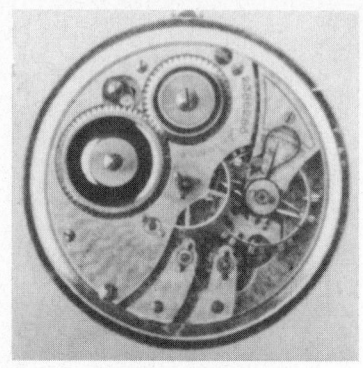

Ben Franklin, 12 size, 17J., grade 27J, open face, signed on movement Benjamin Franklin USA, S #2,386,286.

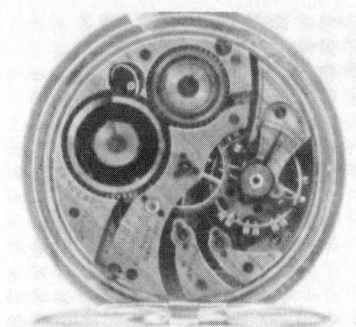

Maiden America, 12 size, 17J, serial number 2,820,499.

Grade or Name — Description	ABP	Ex-Fn	Mint
Aluminum Watch, 17J, model #3, **movement plates made or aluminum**			
G#525, S# 3,869,251 to S# 3,869,300 . . . . ★★★★★	$2,000	$3,500	$4,500
Autocrat, 17J, Adj.3P	60	85	150
Autocrat, 19J, Adj.3P	65	95	175
Banker, 17J, Adj.3P, OF	60	85	150
Banker, 21J, Adj.3P, OF	75	150	200
Benjamin Franklin, 17J, OF	150	300	475
Benjamin Franklin, 21J, OF	200	400	575
Benjamin Franklin, 21J, G# 299, HC	235	500	600
Bunn Special, 21J, Adj 3P, (by Hamilton), OF . . . . ★★	400	500	825
Burlington Special, 19J, GT, OF	75	150	200
Burlington Special, 19J, GT, HC	100	200	250
Burlington W. Co., 21J, GT, OF	75	150	200
Burlington W. Co., 21J, GT, HC	100	200	250
Central, 17J, OF, 2-Tone	50	90	125
Chronos, 21J., G# 299, GT, GJS, marked 21 Ruby Jewels . . . . ★	250	375	600
Commodore Perry Special, 17J., adj.3P . . . . ★	100	150	250
Criterion, 21J, OF	75	125	200
Dependon, 17, (J. V. Farwell), HC	70	125	185
Elite, 19J, OF.	75	150	200
Garland, 17J, Adj., GT, OF	60	85	150
Gold Metal, 17J, OF	45	85	1025

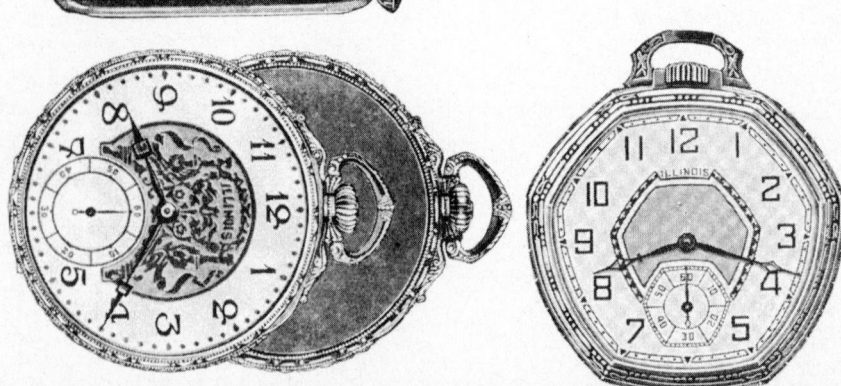

Example of Illinois Thin Model, 12 size, 17 jewels, adjusted to 3 positions.

 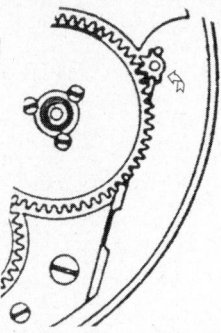 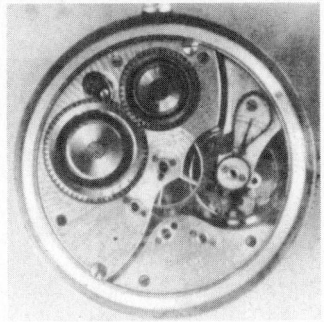

Illini, 12-13 size, 21 jewels, bridge model, serial number 3,650,129. Note five tooth pinion click & jeweled barrel.

Santa Fe Special, 12 size, 21 jewels, three-quarter plate, serial number 3,414,422.

NOTE: The "**Illini**" 5 tooth click movement is a 13 size but advertised as 12 size.

Grade or Name — Description		ABP	Ex-Fn	Mint
Illini, 13 Size, 21J, Adj.5P, jeweled barrel, 5 tooth click,				
(Hi-grade), OF, **14K** ★★		$250	$450	$600
Illini **Extra**, 13 S., 21J, Adj.5P, jeweled barrel, (Hi-grade)				
5 tooth click, OF, **14K** ★★★		350	550	750
Illini, 12 Size, 23J, Adj.6P, BRG, OF ★★★		175	300	450
Illini, 12 Size, 23J, Adj.6P, BRG, OF **14K** ★★★		250	450	600
Illinois Watch Co., 7-11-15J		40	85	100
Illinois Watch Co., 16-17J, OF, **14K**		200	300	475
Illinois Watch Co., 16-17J, GF, OF		60	100	150
Illinois Watch Co., 17J, GF, HC		80	125	200
Illinois Watch Co., 19J		80	150	200
Illinois Watch Co., 21J, OF		100	200	225
Illinois Watch Co., 21J, marked (**21 SPECIAL**), OF		110	200	265
Illinois Watch Co., 21J, HC		125	250	300
Illinois Watch Co., 23J, OF		200	275	350
Illinois Watch Co., 19J, EXTRA THIN MODEL, **14K**, OF ★★		200	300	475
Illinois Watch Co., 21J, EXTRA THIN MODEL, **14K**, OF ★★		225	350	525
Illinois Watch Co., 21J, **Marked EXTRA**,				
extra thin model, **14K**, OF ★★★		250	400	600
Interstate Chronometer, 17J, OF, (sold by Sears) ★★★		95	150	275
Interstate Chronometer, 21J, GJS, OF ★★★		175	275	425
Interstate Chronometer, 21J, GJS, HC ★★★		225	325	475
Governor, 17J, OF		60	100	150
A. Lincoln, 19J, Adj.5P, GJS, DR, OF		95	150	275
A. Lincoln, 21J, Adj.5P, DR, GIS, OF		100	175	285
A. Lincoln, 21J, Adj.5P, DR, GJS, HC ★		150	300	450
Maiden America, 17J, ADJ		60	100	125
Marquis Autocrat, 17J, OF		60	100	125
Master, 21J, GT, GJS, OF		75	100	185
Masterpiece, 19J, Adj.3P, OF		65	150	175
A. Norton, 21J, OF		100	150	250
Penn Special, 17J., Adj.3P, G# 405, OF		100	150	225
Plymouth Watch Co., 15-17J, HC, (sold by Sears)		65	100	165
Railroad Dispatch, 11-15J		55	125	175
Railroad Dispatch, 17-19J, SW, GT		75	150	200
Rockland, 17J,		50	85	125
Roosevelt, 17J, G#405, Adj.3P, OF		50	85	125
Roosevelt, 19-21J, G# 406, Adj.6P, OF		200	275	450
Santa Fe Special, 21J		200	300	450
Secometer, 19J., G# 407, OF **14K** ★★		225	375	475
Sterling, 17J, OF		40	85	100
Sterling, 19-21J,OF		60	125	175
Stewart Special, 17J, SW, Adj.3P		40	85	100
Stewart Special, 19J, SW, OF, GT		50	100	125

Grade or Name — Description	ABP	Ex-Fn	Mint
Time King, 19J, SW, Adj.3P	$50	$125	$150
Time King, 21J, SW, Adj.3P	60	150	175
Transit, 19J, OF, PS	50	125	150
Vim, 17J, ADJ, BRG, GJS, DR, OF	35	85	100
Washington W. Co., **Army & Navy**, 19J ★★	95	200	300
Washington W. Co., **Army & Navy**, 21J., G# 27J, OF ★★★	125	225	325
Washington W. Co., **Monroe**, 11J, sold by Montgomery Ward	75	125	200
Washington W. Co., **Senate**, 17J, M#2, PS ★★	60	100	175
121, 21J, Adj.3P	65	150	200
127, 17J, ADJ, (by Hamilton)	35	85	100
129, 19J, Adj.3P	45	125	175
219, 11J, M#1	30	85	100
299, 21J, Adj.5P, OF ★	75	150	200
299, 23J, Adj.5P, HC ★★★	300	400	650
299, 23J, Adj.6P, HC ★★★★	350	500	750
403, 15J, BRG	35	85	100
405, 17J, BRG, ADJ, OF	40	85	125
409, 21J, BRG, Adj.5P, GJS, OF ★	225	325	525
409, 21J, BRG, Adj.5P, GJS, HC ★★	250	385	625
410, 23J, BRG, GJS, Adj.6P, DR, OF ★	200	300	500
410, 23J, BRG, GJS, Adj.6P, DR, HC ★	250	350	600
509, 21J, BRG, Adj.5P, GJS, (spread to 14 size)	75	125	200
510, 23J, BRG, GJS, Adj.6P, DR, (spread to 14 size) ★★	100	175	275

ILLINOIS 8 SIZE

Grade or Name — Description	ABP	Ex-Fn	Mint
Arlington, 7J ★	$150	$185	$300
Rose LeLand, 13J ★★	225	285	400
Stanley, 7J ★★	195	275	450
Mary Stuart, 15J, ★★	225	285	500
Sunnyside, 11J ★	40	85	125
151-152-155, 7-11J, 3/4	30	85	100
Illinois W. Co., 11-15J, (nameless unmarked grades)	45	85	125
Illinois W. Co., 16-17J, (nameless unmarked grades)	45	75	1258

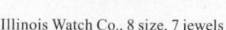

Illinois Watch Co., 8 size, 7 jewels

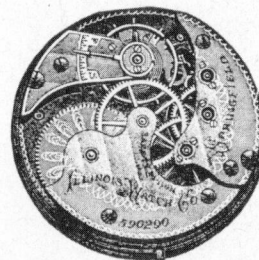

Grade 144, 6 size, 15 jewels, serial number 5,902,290.

ILLINOIS 6 SIZE

Grade or Name — Description	ABP	Ex-Fn	Mint
Illinois W. Co., 7J, LS, HC, **14K**	$200	$275	$400
Illinois W. Co., 7J, HC	45	55	125
Illinois W. Co., 7J, OF, Coin	30	45	95
Illinois W. Co., 11-12-13J, OF, HC	55	75	125
Illinois W. Co., 15J, OF, HC, **14K**	200	285	450
Illinois W. Co., 17J, OF, HC	55	65	125
Illinois W. Co., 19J, OF, HC	60	75	150
Plymouth Watch Co., 17J, OF, HC, (sold by Sears)	40	60	135
Sears & Roebuck Special, 15J, HC	55	75	110
Washington W. Co., 15J, Liberty Bell, HC	75	125	225
Washington W. Co., 11J, Martha Washington, HC ★	100	185	375

ILLINOIS
4 SIZE

Grade or Name —Description	ABP	Ex-Fn	Mint
Illinois W. Co., 7J, LS, HC	$45	$100	$125
Illinois W. Co., 11J, LS, HC	55	100	150
Illinois W. Co., 15-16J, LS, HC	55	100	150

ILLINOIS
0 SIZE

Grade or Name — Description	ABP	Ex-Fn	Mint
Accuratus, 17J, OF	$60	$100	$175
Ariste, 11-15-17J, OF & HC	95	155	225
Burlington Special, 15-17J, 3/4, OF	100	175	250
Illinois W. Co., 7 to 17J, LS, HC, 14K	200	300	425
201, 11J, BRG, NI	40	85	125
203, 15J, BRG, NI	50	85	135
204, 17J, BRG, NI	55	95	150
Interstate Chronometer, 15J, HC, SW	125	200	400
Interstate Chronometer, 17J, HC, SW	125	225	425
Lady Franklin, 15-17J, HC	65	125	200
Plymouth Watch Co., 15-17J, HC, (sold by Sears)	75	90	150
Santa Fe Special, 15-17J ★	200	275	400
Washington W. Co., Liberty Bell, 15J, ADJ	60	100	200
Washington W. Co., Mt. Vernon, 17J, ADJ	70	110	225

Washington W. Co., Mt. Vernon, 0 size, 17J, hunting case.

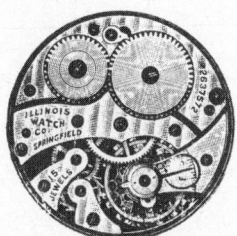

Grade 203, 0 size, 15 jewels, originally sold for $10.40

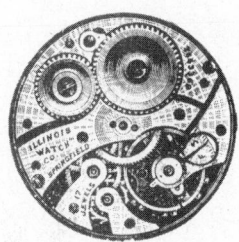

Grade 204, 0 size, 17 jewels, originally sold for $12.83.

ILLINOIS
CAPRICE

Grade or Name — Description	ABP	Ex-Fn	Mint
Caprice, 17J, handbag, pocket or desk watch, snake or ostrich	$200	$300	$500

Ca. 1929 AD

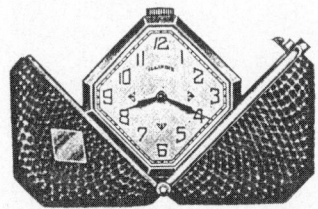

The CAPRICE
Just the watch for the handbag, pocket or desk; for sports wear or dress. It's an entirely practical timekeeper, too. In genuine coverings of snake or ostrich. 17 jewels, 14K gold filled inner case **$50**

AD for 1921 - 1924

NET PRICE LIST TO JEWELERS
Illinois-Springfield Watches

18 SIZE, Open Face and Hunting

Bunn Special, 21 Jewels Adjusted 6 Positions - - $24.00
No. 89, 17 Jewels Adj., Gilt Damsk., D. S. Dial - 10.00

16 SIZE

SANGAMO SPECIAL, Open Face Only
23 Jewels, Adj. 6 Positions, Illinois Motor Barrel

Fitted in 25 year, 14K. filled extra weight screw
back and hinged bezel case, Complete - - 50.00
Fitted in 14K. extra weight, solid gold, jointed,
inside cap case, Complete - - - - 92.50

16 SIZE, Open Face and Hunting

Bunn Special, 23J. Adj. 6 Pos., Illinois Motor Barrel 32.75
Bunn Special, 21 Jewels, Adjusted **6** Positions - 28.00
A. Lincoln, 21 Jewels, Adjusted 5 Positions - 26.00
Bunn, 19 Jewels, Adj. 5 Pos., Illinois Motor Barrel - 24.00
Bunn, 17 Jewels, Adjusted 5 Positions - - 20.00
(Special, 19 Jewels, Adjusted 4 Positions)
    Made on Special Order Only
No. 706, 17 Jewels Adjusted 4 Positions, D. S. D. - 15.00
No. 305, 17 Jewels Adj., D. R., Steel escape, D.S.D. 13.25

12 SIZE, Open Face and Hunting

No. 410, 23 Jewels, Adjusted 6 Positions - - 37.50
A. Lincoln, 21 Jewels, Adjusted 5 Positions - 26.50
(Special, 19 Jewels, Adjusted 3 Positions)
    Made on Special Order Only
No. 405, 17 Jewels, Adj., D. R., Steel escape wheel - 13.50

6-0 Size or 11 Ligne Movements

Only delivered fitted in cases supplied by the Jobbers.

No. 907, 19 Jewels, double roller, steel escape wheel 20.00
No. 903, 15 Jewels, double roller - - - - 14.50

6-0 size full open and 3-4 open face dial movements have seconds hand.
Hunting and skylight dial movements do not have seconds hand.

RETAIL PRICE LIST
The ILLINOIS WATCH
SEPTEMBER 1, 1929

	Retailer	Consumer
FACTORY CASED RAILROAD GRADES		
Sangamo Special, 23 Jewels.		
60 Hour, 6 Position, Motor Barrel, 16 Size		
14K white, green or natural solid gold hinged case, with inside cap	$92.50	$150.00
14K white, green or natural gold filled case, hinged inside cap, also screw bezel and back, plain or eng. back	50.00	90.00
Bunn Special, 23 Jewels.		
60 Hour, 6 Position, Motor Barrel, 16 Size		
Model 28, 14K white, green or comb. gold filled case	40.75	75.00
Model 28, 10K natural gold filled case	37.25	70.00
Cases with Engraved backs, extra	.75	2.00
Bunn Special, 21 Jewels.		
60 Hour, 6 Position, Motor Barrel, 16 Size		
First Model, 14K white or green gold filled case	36.00	65.00
First Model, 10K natural gold filled case	32.50	60.00
Model 29, 14K white or green gold filled case	36.00	65.00
Model 29, 10K natural gold filled case	32.50	60.00
Model 181, 14K white gold filled	36.00	65.00
Model 181, 10K natural gold filled	32.50	60.00
Cases with Engraved backs, extra	.75	2.00
DISPATCHER, 16 Size, 19 Jewels, Adj. Temp. & 3 Pos. Pend. or Lever Set.		
14K white gold filled case	21.35	45.00
10K natural gold filled case	19.85	40.00
Cases with Engraved back, extra	.50	—
16 SIZE UNCASED WATCHES, Open Face		
Lever or Pendant Setting		
No. 167, (old No. 305) 17 J., Adj., S. S. Dial	12.60	24.00
No. 169, (old No. 707) Special, 19 J. Adj., 3 pos.	16.50	32.50
12 SIZE UNCASED WATCHES, Open Face		
No. 127, (old No. 405) 17 Jewels, Adj	12.25	24.00
No. 129, (old No. 407) 19 J., Adj. 3 pos.	16.90	32.50
No. 121, (old No. 279) 21 J., Adj. 3 pos.	20.50	40.00
3/0 SIZE UNCASED WATCH.		
No. 307, (old No. 24) 17 Jewels Pat. Reg. luminous or printed dial	15.00	50.00

ILLINOIS, SPRINGFIELD MOVEMENTS,

NAMED AS FOLLOWS:

Full Plate, 18 Size.				Key Wind.	Stem-Wind
"STUART,"	15	Jew. Exp. Bal. Ad.		$44 00	$52 00
"BUNN,"	15	"	"	29 00	36 00
"MILLER,"	15	"	"	21 25	27 00
"MILLER,"	15	"	"	18 25	24 00
"CURRIER"	11	"	"	13 33	18 50
"HOYT,"	9	"	"	12 50	17 50
"DEAN,"	15	"	" half-cut	14 50	19 50
"MASON,"	7	"	" "	10 50	15 00
"BATES,"	7	" Exp. Shape, Steel Bal.		10 00	14 50
"COLUMBIA,"	11 Jew. Cut Exp. Bal.			9 05	11 80
"AMERICA,"	7	"	" "	7 55	10 25

NAMELESS MOVEMENTS.

				Key Wind	Stem-Wind
No. 25,	15	Jewels, Exp. Bal. Adj.		$21 25	$27 00
28,	15	"	"	18 25	24 00
30,	11	"	"	13 33	18 50
33,	9	"	"	12 50	17 50
35,	15	"	Half Cut Bal.	14 50	19 50
34,	7	"	Exp. Bal.	10 50	15 00
40,	7	"	Im. Exp. Bal.	10 00	14 50
1,		Cut	"	7 75	10 25
2,		"	"	9 05	11 80

ABOVE: December 2, **1878** Price List AD to Jewelers.

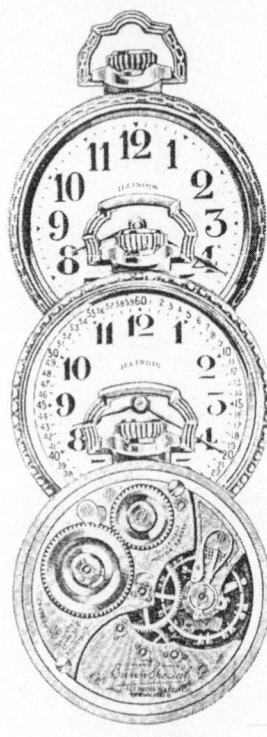

Rigid bow 60 HR MODEL
gold filled: $175 - $225 - $425
14K gold: $400 - $500 - $1,100
Dial: $35 - $75 - $125

Antique bow MODEL
gold filled: $100 - $125 - $285
14K gold: $375 - $450 - $700
Dial: $35 - $75 - $125

FIRST MODEL
gold filled: $100 - $150 - $300

Stiff bow 60 HR MODEL
gold filled: $200 - $250- $425
14K gold: $450 - $600 -$1,100
Dial:$75-$100-$150

Pyramid bow MODEL
gold filled: $95 - $150 - $325
14K gold: $400- $500 - $775
Montgomery Dial: $75 - $150 - $250

MODEL 28
gold filled: $135 - $180- $450
gold filled **2 tone**: $180 - $275 - $500
Bunn Special Dial: $75 - $150 - $275

MODEL 29
gold filled: $110 - $150 - $350
Montgomery Dial: $75 - $150 - $250

MODEL 107
gold filled: $110 -$150- $350
Dial: $50 - $100 - $125

☞ NOTE: April 1925 Factory Advertised as a complete watch and was fitted with a certain matched, timed and rated movement and sold in the factory designed case style as a complete watch. The factory also sold uncased movements to JOBBERS such as Jewelry stores & they cased the movement in a case style the CUSTOMER requested. All the factory advertised complete watches came with the dial SHOWN or CHOICE of other Railroad dials.

MODEL 108
gold filled: $110- $140 - $325
Bunn Special Dial: $100 - $150 - $275

MODEL 128
gold **filled**: $60 - $75 - $175
Dial: $50 - $75 - $125

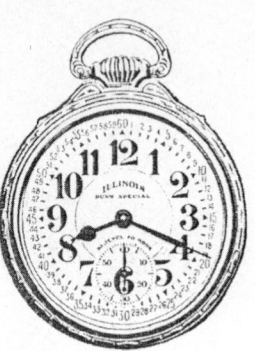

MODEL 173
gold filled: $110 - $150 - $400
gold filled **2 tone**: $175 - $250 - $500
Bunn Special Montgomery Dial: $100 - $150 - $350

MODEL 181
gold filled: $110- $150- $400
Dial: $50 - $100 - $125

17S MODEL 193
gold filled: $110- $150- $400
Dial: $50 - $100 - $125

MODEL 206
gold filled: $95 - $150 - $325
gold filled **2 tone**: $140 - $195 - $500
Dial: $50 - $100 - $125

MODEL 118, Ca.19J2
gold filled: $95 - $125 - $175
Dial: $50 - $100 - $125

SANGAMO SPECIALS &
BUNN SPECIALS were packed & shipped
in a ALUMINUM cigarette style box.
$90 —$200 —$300

NOTE: April 1925 Factory Advertised as a complete watch and was fitted with a certain matched, timed and rated movement and sold in the factory designed case style as a complete watch. The factory also sold uncased movements to JOBBERS such as Jewelry stores & they cased the movement in a case style the CUSTOMER requested. All the factory advertised complete watches came with the dial SHOWN or CHOICE of other Railroad dials.

ILLINOIS SPRINGFIELD WATCH CO.
IDENTIFICATION OF MOVEMENTS

BY MODEL NUMBER

How to Identify Your Watch Size & Model: Compare the movement of your watch with the illustrations in this section. While comparing, note the location of the balance, jewels, screws, gears, and type of back plate (Full, 3/4, Bridge) these will be clues in identifying the movement you have.

THE ILLINOIS WATCH CO. MODEL CHART

By Size-Model and **started with first serial number.**

★★

Size	Model	Plate Design	Setting	Hunting or Open Face	Type Barrel	Started w/ Serial No.	Remarks
18	1	Full	Key	Htg	Reg	1	Course train
	2	Full	Lever	Htg	Reg	38,901	Course train
	3	Full	Lever	OF	Reg	46,201	Course train, 5th pinion
	4	Full	Pendant	OF	Reg	1,050,001	Fast train
	5	Full	Lever	Htg	Reg	1,256,101	Fast train, RR Grade
	6	Full	Lever	OF	Reg	1,144,401	Fast train, RR Grade
16	1	Full	Lever	Htg	Reg	1,030,001	Thick model
	2	Full	Pendant	OF	Reg	1,037,001	Thick model
	3	Full	Lever	OF	Reg	1,038,001	Thick model
	4	¾ & brg	Lever	Htg	Reg	1,300,001	Getty model
	5	¾ & brg	Lever	OF	Reg	1,300,601	Getty model
	6	¾ & brg	Pendant	Htg	Reg	2,160,111	DR & Improved RR model
	7	¾ & brg	Pendant	OF	Reg	2,160,011	DR & Improved RR model
	8	¾ & brg	Lever	Htg	Reg	2,523,101	DR & Improved RR model
	9	¾ & brg	Lever	OF	Reg	2,522,001	DR & Improved model
	10	Cent brg	Lever	OF	Motor	3,178,901	Also 17S Ex Thin RR gr 48 hr
	11	¾	Lever & Pen	OF	Motor	4,001,001	RR grade 48 hr
	12	¾	Lever & Pen	Htg	Motor	4,002,001	RR grade 48 hr
	13	Cent brg	Lever	OF	Motor	4,166,801	Also 17S RR grade 60 hr
	14	¾	Lever	OF	Motor	4,492,501	RR grade 60 hr
	15	¾	Lever	OF	Motor	5,488,301	RR grade 60 hr Elinvar
14	1	Full	Lever	Htg	Reg	1,009,501	Thick model
	2	Full	Pendant	OF	Reg	1,000,001	Thick model
	3	Full	Lever	OF	Reg	1,001,001	Thick model
13	1	brg	Pendant	OF	Motor		Ex Thin gr 538 & 539
12	1	¾	Pendant	OF	Reg	1,685,001	
Thin	2	¾	Pendant	Htg	Reg	1,748,751	
	3	Cent brg	Pendant	OF	Reg	2,337,011	Center bridge
	4	Cent brg	Pendant	Htg	Reg	2,337,001	Center bridge
	5	Cent brg	Pendant	OF	Motor	3,742,201	Center bridge
	6	Cent brg	Pendant	Htg	Motor	4,395,301	Center bridge
12T	1	True Ctr brg	Pendant	OF	Motor	3,700,001	1 tooth click, Also 13S
	2	True Ctr brg	Pendant	OF	Motor	3,869,301	5 tooth click
	3	¾	Pendant	OF	Motor	3,869,201	2 tooth click
8	1	Full	Key or lever	Htg	Reg	100,001	Plate not recessed
	2	Full	Lever	Htg	Reg	100,101	Plate is recessed
6	1	¾	Lever	Htg	Reg	552,001	
4	1	¾	Lever	Htg	Reg	551,501	
0	1	¾	Pendant	OF	Reg	1,815,901	
	2	¾	Pendant	Htg	Reg	1,749,801	
	3	Cent brg	Pendant	OF	Reg	2,644,001	
	4	Cent brg	Pendant	Htg	Reg	2,637,001	

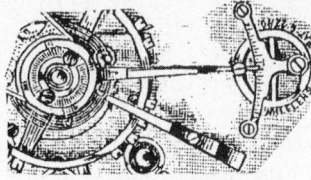

Wheelers Pat. 6, 22, 80
LEFT (patented regulator)

BELOW
Chalmers Pat. 12, 19, 82 (patented regulator)

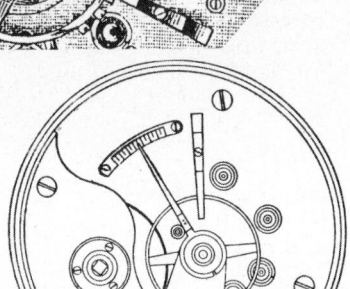

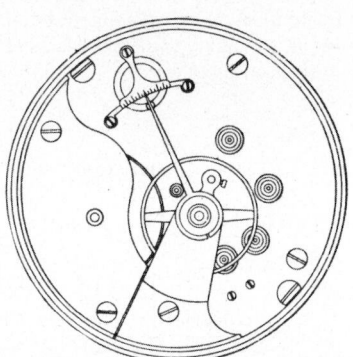

Model 1, 18 size, hunting, key wind & set.

Model 2, 18 size, hunting, lever set, coarse train.

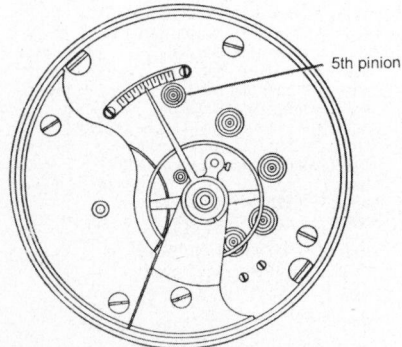

5th pinion

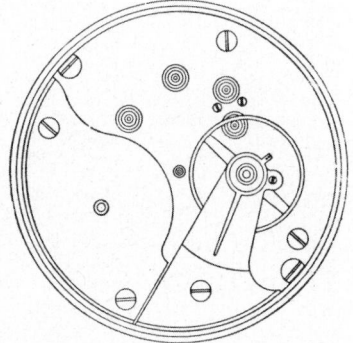

Model 3, 18 size, open face, lever set, coarse train, with fifth pinion.

Model 4, 18 size, open face, pendant set, fine train.

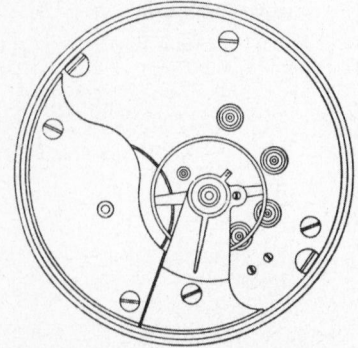

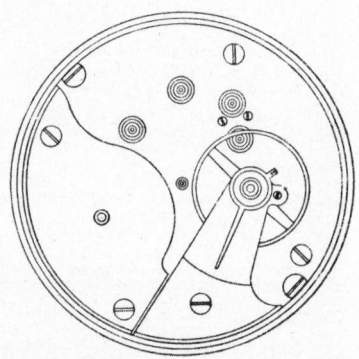

Model 5, 18 size, hunting, lever set, fine train.

Model 6, 18 size, open face, lever set, fine train.

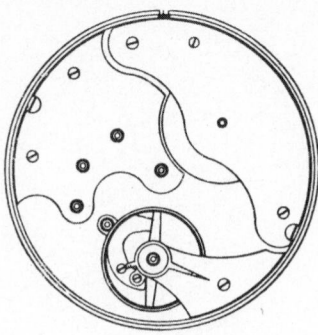

Model 1, 16 size, hunting, lever set.

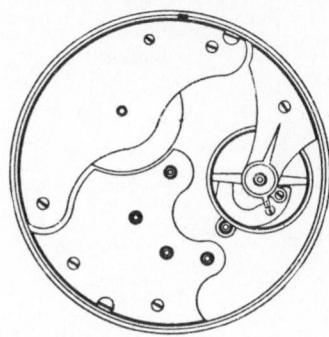

Model 2, 16 size, open face, pendant set.

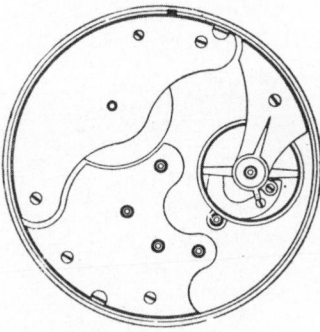

Model 3, 16 size, open face, lever set

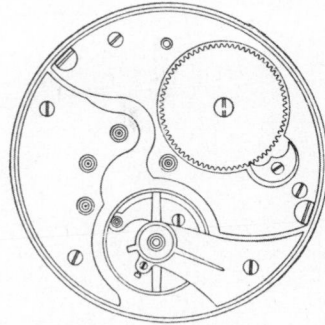

Model 4, 16 size, three-quarter plate, bridge, hunting, lever set.

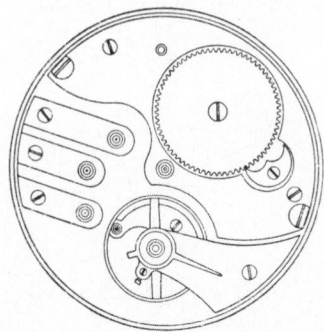

Model 4, 16 size, three-quarter plate, hunting, lever set.

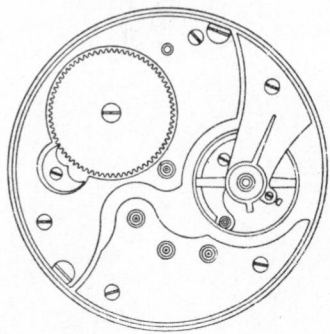

Model 5, 16 size, three-quarter plate, open face, lever set.

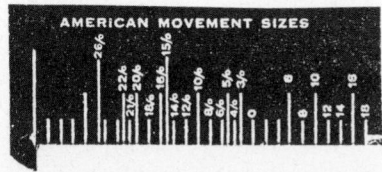

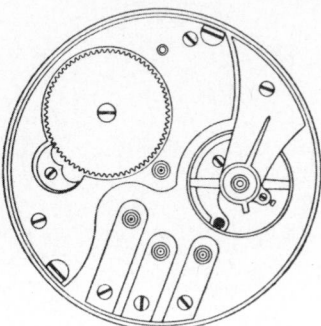

Model 5, 16 size, three-quarter plate, bridge, open face, lever set.

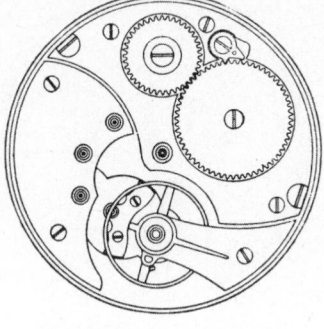

Model 6, 16 size - Pendant set
Model 8, 16 size - Lever set
hunting, three-quarter plate

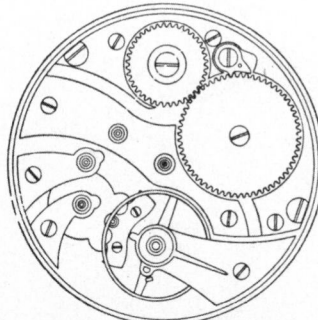

Model 6, 16 size - Pendant set
Model 8, 16 size - Lever set
hunting, bridge model

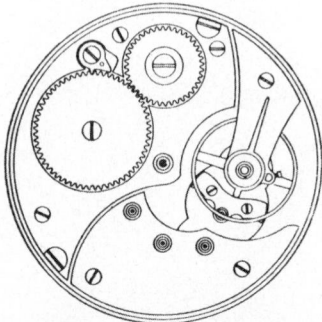

Model 7, 16 size - Pendant set
Model 9, 16 size - Lever set
open face, three-quarter plate

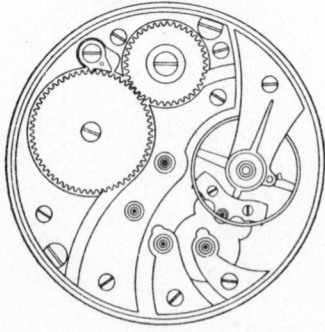

Model 7, 16 size - Pendant set
Model 9, 16 size - Lever set
open face, bridge model

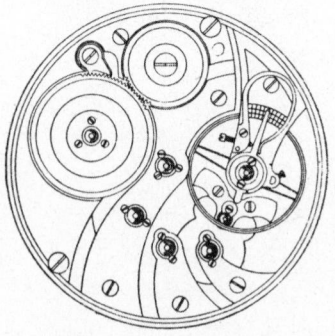

Model 10, 16 size, bridge, extra thin, open face, lever set, motor barrel.

Note: Model is not the same defination as grade. A model may exist in many different grades or grade names (as Bunn, A. Lincoln) and may be used in many different models (as model **1**, 18 size, open or hunting case, model **1**, in 16 size open or hunting case, model **1** in 12 size) etc..

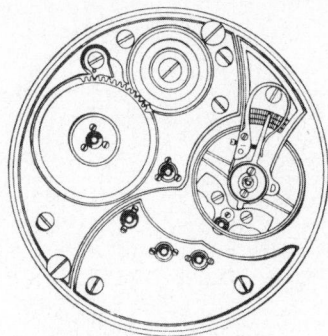

Model 11, 16 size, three-quarter plate, open face, pendant set, motor barrel.

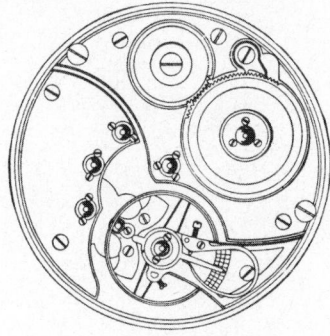

Model 12, 16 size, three-quarter plate, hunting, pendant set, motor barrel.

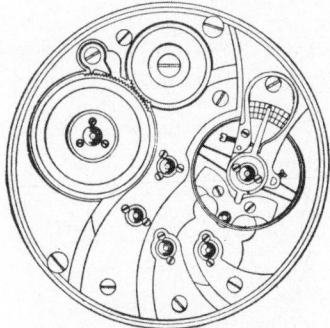

Model 13, 17 size, bridge, open face, lever set, motor barrel.(no red border on bal. cock)

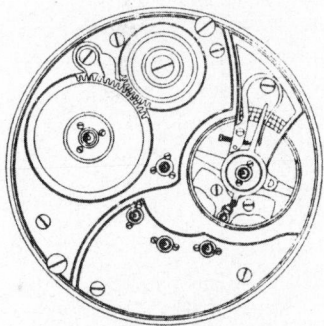

Model 14, 16 size, three-quarter plate, open face, lever set, 60-hour motor barrel.

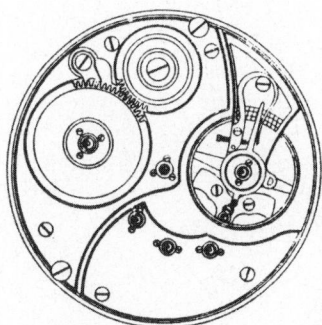

Model 15, 60 Hr. Elinvar.

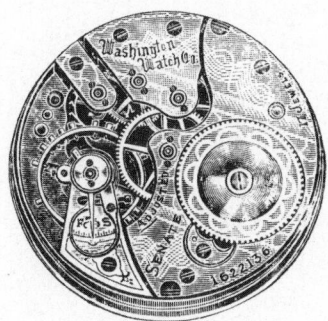

Model B, 16 size, hunting case

Model C, 16 size, open face.

Model D, 16 size, open face.

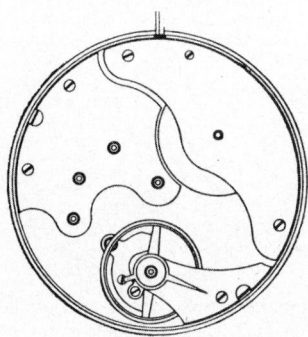

Model 1, 14 size, hunting, lever set.

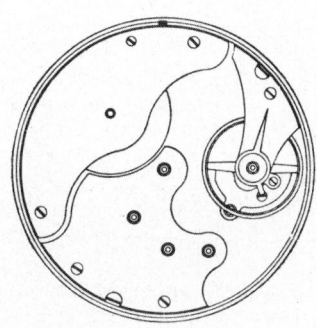

Model 2, 14 size, open face, pendant set.

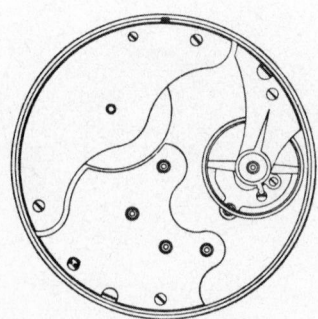

Model 3, 14 size, open face, lever set.

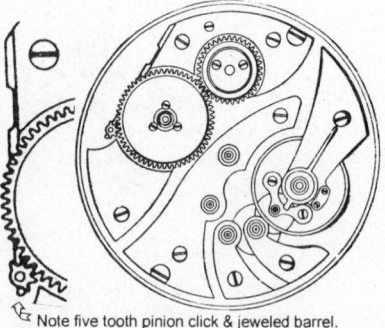

Note five tooth pinion click & jeweled barrel.

Model 1, 13 size, bridge, extra thin, open face, pendant set, motor barrel.

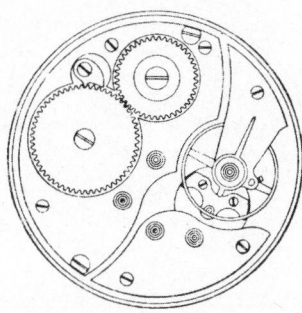

Model 1, 12 size, three-quarter plate, open face, pendant set.

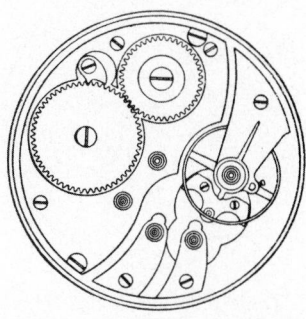

Model 1, 12 size, three-quarter plate, bridge, open face, pendant set.

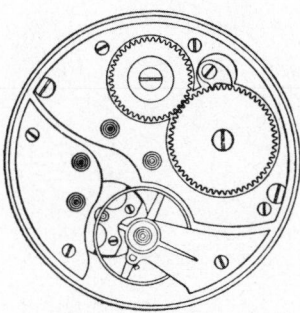

Model 2, 12 size, three-quarter plate, hunting, pendant set.

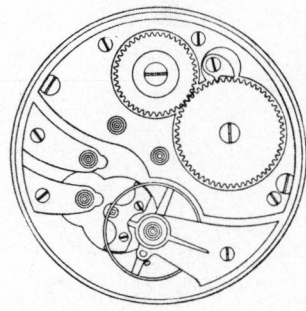

Model 2, 12 size, three-quarter plate, bridge, hunting, pendant set.

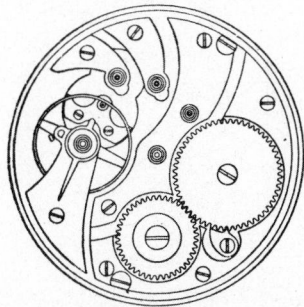

Model 3, 12 size, Model 4, 12 & 14 size, bridge, open face, pendant set.

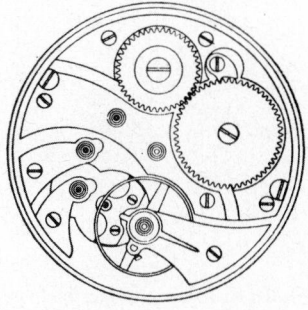

Model 4, 12 size, bridge, hunting, pendant set.

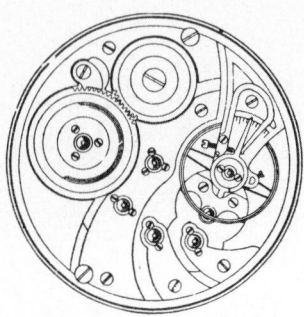

Model 5, 12 size, bridge, open face, pendant set, motor barrel.

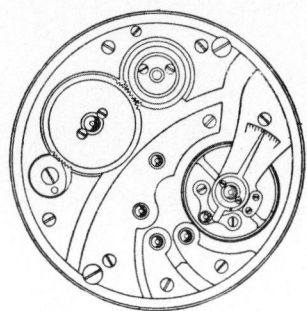

Model 1, 12 size, extra thin, bridge, open face, pendant set, motor barrel.

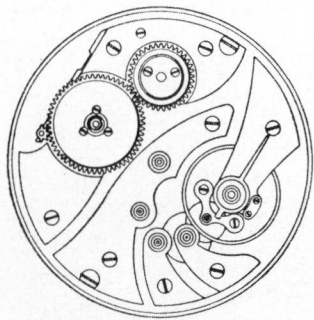

Model 2, 12 size, extra thin, bridge, open face, pendant set, motor barrel.

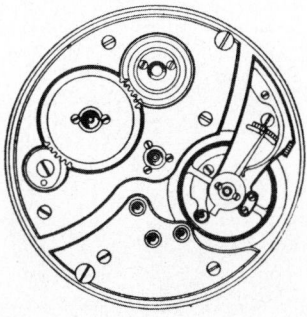

Model 3, 12 size, extra thin, three-quarter plate, open face, pendant set, motor barrel.

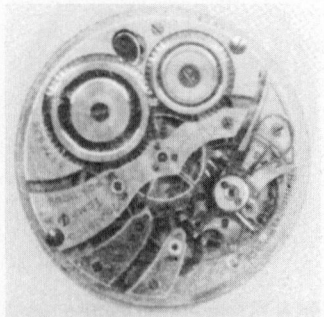

Model A, 12 size, bridge, open face.

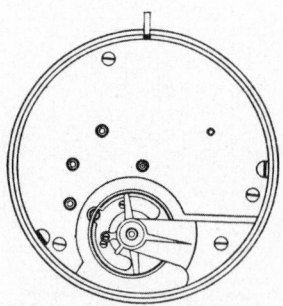

Model 1, 8 size, hunting, key or lever set.

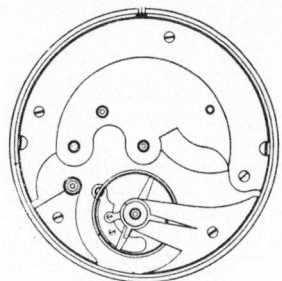

Model 2, 8 size, hunting, lever set.

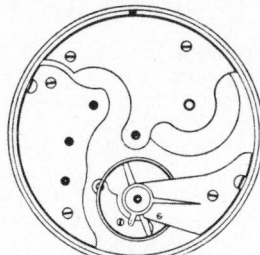

Model 1, 6 size, hunting, lever set.

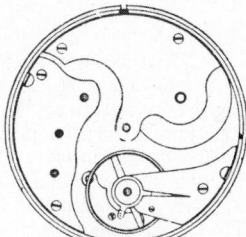

Model 1, 4 size, hunting, lever set.

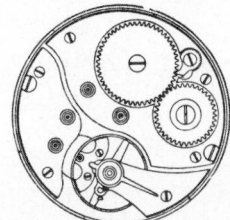

Model 1, 0 size, three-quarter plate, open face, pendant set.

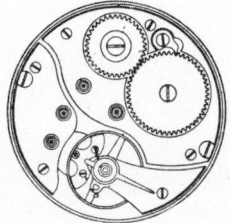

Model 2, 0 size, three quarter plate, hunting, pendant set.

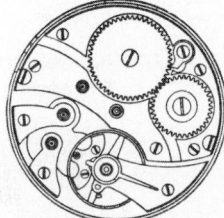

Model 3, 0 size, bridge, open face, pendant set.

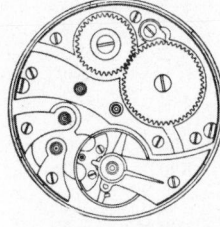

Model 4, 0 size, bridge, hunting, pendant set.

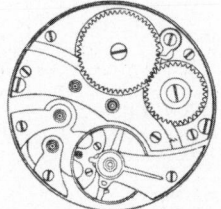

Model 3, 3/0 size, bridge, open face, pendant set.

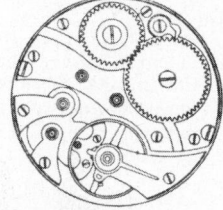

Model 4, 3/0 size, bridge, hunting, pendant set.

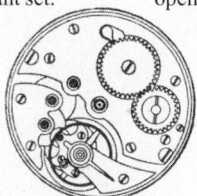

Model 1, 6/0 size, three-quarter plate, open face, pendant set.

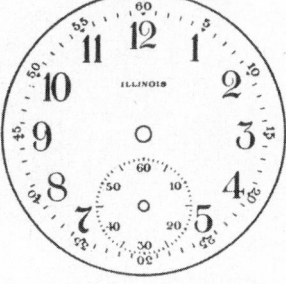

No. 5277—269-D
18, 16, 12 Sizes S. S. & D. S.
Spread 12, 8, 6, 4, 0 &
3/0 Sizes S. S. Only

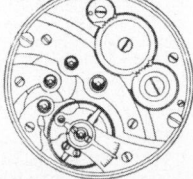

Model 2, 6/0 size, bridge, open face, pendant set.

300

INDEPENDENT WATCH CO.

Fredonia, New York 1875-1881

The California Watch Company was idle for two years before it was purchased by brothers E. W. Howard and C. M. Howard. They had been selling watches by mail for sometime and started engraving the Howard Bros. name on them and using American-made watches. Their chief supply came from Hampden Watch Co., Illinois W. Co., U. S. Watch Co. of Marion. The brothers formed the Independent Watch Co. in 1880, but it was not a watch factory in the true sense. They had other manufacturers engrave the Independent Watch Co. name on the top plates and on the dials of their watches. These watches were sold by mail order and sent to the buyer C. O D. The names used on the movements were "Howard Bros.," "Independent Watch Co.,"" Fredonia Watch Co.,"" Lakeshore Watch Co., Fredonia, N. Y." and "Empire Watch Co. Fredonia"

The company later decided to manufacture watches and used the name Fredonia Watch Co., but they found that selling watches two different ways was not very good. The business survived until 1881 at which time the owners decided to move the plant to a new location at Peoria, Illinois. Approximately 180,000 watches were made that sold for $16.00.

CHRONOLOGY OF TILE DEVELOPMENT OF INDEPENDENT WATCH CO.

Independent Watch Co . . . . 1875—1881
Fredonia Watch Co . . . . 1881—1885
Peoria Watch Co . . . . 1885—1889

18 SIZE

Grade or Name — Description	ABP	Ex-Fn	Mint
18S,7J, KW, KS, OF, made by U.S. W. Co. Marion, with expanded butterfly cutout . . . . ★★	$350	$500	$700
18S, 11J, KW, KS, by Hampden	175	330	400
18S, 11J, KW, KS, Coin	175	330	400
18S, 15J,KW,KS	175	330	400
18S, 15J, KW, KS	175	330	400
18S, Empire Watch Co. Fredonia, 11-15J, KWS . . . . ★★★★	575	880	1,100
18S, Howard Bros., 11J, KW, KS	300	440	650
18S, Independent W. Co., 11J, by Illinois W. Co . . . . ★	200	330	450
18S, Independent W. Co., 15J, transition model by Illinois . . . . . ★	225	380	500
18S, Lakeshore W. Co., 15J, KW, HC, by N.Y. W. Co . . . . ★	300	410	550

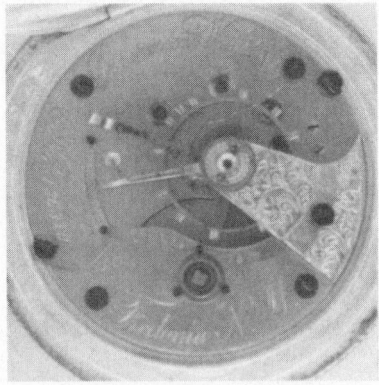 

Independent Watch Co. on movement, on dial Howard Bros. Fredonia N.Y., 18 size, 11 jewels, key wind & stem wind, improved April 10.1879, serial number 126,319.

Independent Watch Co., 16 size, 15 jewels, key wind, made by US. Watch Co. Marion, note expanded butterfly cutout, serial number 192,661.

☞ Watches listed in this book are priced as complete watches having an original 14k gold filled case, key wind with silver, an original white enamel single sunk dial, and with the entire original movement in good working order with no repairs needed, unless otherwise noted.

ROBERT H. INGERSOLL & BROS.

New York, New York
1892-1922

In 1892 Ingersoll ordered 10,000 watches from Waterbury Clock Co. to sell in their mail order catalog. The first 1,000 said "the Universal Watch" on the dial. The remainder had R.H. Ingersoll & Bro. on the dial. In 1893, they sold about 85,000 embossed watches at the Columbian Exposition. In 1896 they introduced the "Yankee" that sold for $1.00. By 1899 their output was 8,000 per day, and in 1901 Ingersoll advertised that their watches were sold by 10,000 dealers at $1.00 in U.S.A. and Canada. Ingersoll bought the Trenton W. Co. in 1908 and the New England W. Co. in 1914. Their slogan became "The Watch that Made the Dollar Famous". In 1917 they introduced the "Reliance" which had jewels. Waterbury Clock Co. took over the Ingersoll name in 1922. In 1944 U. S. Time Corp. acquired the Waterbury Co. and continued the Ingersoll name.

ESTIMATED SERIAL NUMBERS AND PRODUCTION DATES

DATE—SERIAL NO.	DATE—SERIAL NO.	DATE—SERIAL NO.	DATE-SERIAL NO.
1892 —150,000	1902— 7,200,000	1912 —38,500,000	1922 —60,500,000
1893 —310,000	1903 — 7,900,000	1913 —40,000,000	1923 —62,000,000
1894 —650,000	1904 — 8,100,000	1914 —41,500,000	1924 —65,000,000
1895 —1,000,000	1905 —10,000,000	1915 —42,500,000	1925 —67,500,000
1896 —2,000,000	1906 —12,500,000	1916 —45,500,000	1926 —69,000,000
1897 —2,900,000	1907 —15,000,000	1917 —47,000,000	1927 —70,500,000
1898 —3,500,000	1908 —17,500,000	1918 —47,500,000	1928 —71,500,000
1899 —3,750,000	1909 —20,000,000	1919 —50,000,000	1929 —73,500,000
1900 —6,000,000	1910 —25,000,000	1920 —55,000,000	1930 —75,000,000
1901 —6,700,000	1911 —30,000,000	1921 —58,000,000	1944 —95,000,000

The above list is provided for determining the APPROXIMATE age of your watch. Match serial number with date. Watches were not necessarily sold in the exact order of manufactured date.

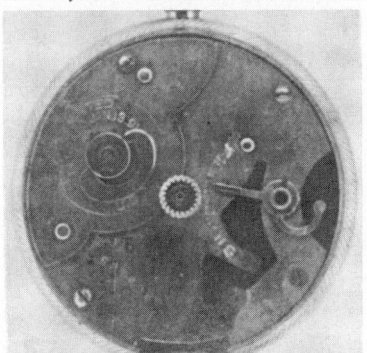

Ingersoll back Wind & Set, patent date Dec.23, 1890 and Jan.13,1891, c. late 1890s.

Ingersoll, engraved movement also pin set.

Ingersoll Celluloid Case in Black or White.

Ingersoll, Blind Man's Watch.

INGERSOLL DOLLAR TYPE

NOTE: Prices are for complete watch in **good running order**. In some specialty markets, the comic character watches may bring higher prices in top condition.

Grade or Name — Description	ABP	Ex-Fn	Mint
Ingersoll Early **Back Wind** Models, (with cover plate)	$50	$105	$150
Ingersoll **Back Wind** Models	50	105	150
Ingersoll, Pin set or **Rim set** & Fancy **engraved** movement	75	100	200
Admiral Dewey, "Flagship Olympia" on back of case . . . . . ★★★★	600	900	1,250
Advance, (revolving seconds)	40	80	100
American Pride	75	105	150
Are U My Neighbor	40	60	75
B. B. H. Special, Backwind	65	105	125
Blind Man Pocket Watch	55	105	150
Boer War, on dial Souvenir of **South African War 1900** . . ★★★★	900	1,400	2,000
Buck 40	55	90	100
Calendar (moveable calendar on back of case)	75	105	135
Celluloid Case in Black or White	100	140	200
Champion (many models)	50	80	135
Chancery	50	80	135
Chicago Expo. 1933 . . . . ★★	300	475	850
Climax	50	70	120
Cloverine	40	60	95
Colby	35	50	75
Columbus (3 ships on back of case), back wind, 1893 . . . . ★★★	500	900	1,200
Connecticut W. Co	40	60	75
Cord 40	55	90	100
Crown	40	60	75
Dan Dee	40	60	75
Defiance	40	60	75
Delaware W. Co	40	60	75
Devon Mfg. Co	40	60	75
Eclipse (many models)	40	60	75
Eclipse, back wind & set, engraved . . . . ★★	75	100	200
Eclipse Radiolite	45	70	85
Endura	40	60	75
Ensign	40	60	75
Escort	40	60	75

Scout watch (Be prepared)

Yankee watch with bicycle on dial.

NOTE:ADD $25 to $100 for original BOX and PAPERS

Ingersoll Defiance Conneticut Watch Co.

Ingersoll Triumph, note slide-pin for rim setting.

Grade or Name — Description	ABP	Ex-Fn	Mint
Fancy Dials (unfaded to be mint)	$125	$220	$400
Freedom	40	60	75
Gotham	70	90	150
Graceline	45	60	75
Gregg	40	60	75
Junior (several models)	40	60	75
Junior Radiolite	40	60	75
Kelton	40	60	75
Lapel Watches	30	60	75
Leader	30	60	75
Leeds	30	60	75
Liberty U.S.A., backwind	75	150	250
Liberty Watch Co	50	80	175
Limited, LEVER SET ON CASE RIM OF WATCH	50	80	175
Major	40	60	75
Maple Leaf	40	60	75
Master Craft	40	60	75
Mexicana	40	60	75
Midget (several models)	40	60	75
Midget, 6 size, "patd. Jan. 29 -01,," Damaskeened, fancy case	40	80	175
Monarch	40	60	75
New West	40	60	75
New York World's Fair, 1939 ★★	275	450	725
Overland	40	60	75
Pan American Expo., Buffalo, 1901 ★★★	300	550	775
Paris World Expo., 1900 ★★★★	600	900	1,250
Patrol	40	60	75
Perfection	40	60	75
Pilgram	40	60	75

NOTE ADD $25 to $75 for original BOX and PAPERS

  ✒ Pricing in this Guide are fair market price for complete watches which are reflected from the **NAWCC** National and regional shows.

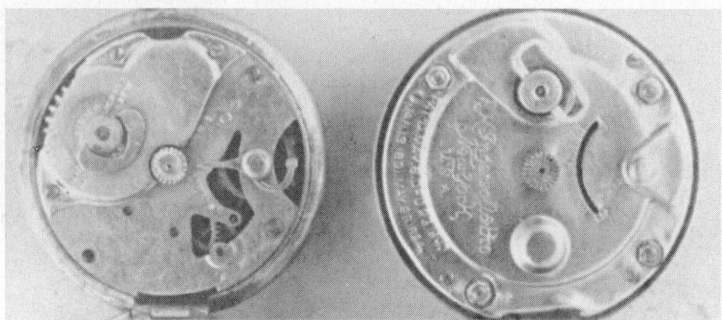

Left: Ingersoll Back Wind, c. 1895.   **Right**: Yankee Back Wind. c. 1893.

Grade or Name — Description	ABP	Ex-Fn	Mint
Premier, back wind, **eagle** on back, c. 1894. ★★★	$150	$275	$425
Premium Back Wind and Set	125	250	300
Progress, 1933 World's Fair Chicago ★★	250	350	600
Puritan	60	90	125
Quaker	60	90	125
Radiolite	45	75	85
Reliance,7J	60	85	100
Remington W. Co. USA	60	85	100
Rotary International, c. 1920	50	75	100
Royal	45	60	75
St. Louis World's Fair (two models). ★★	300	550	800
The Saturday Post.	70	150	250
Senator	40	60	75
Senior	40	60	75
Sir Leeds	35	50	65
Solar35	35	50	65
Souvenir Special.	50	85	120
Sterling	35	50	65
Ten Hune.	60	85	125
Traveler with Bed Side Stand	35	55	75
Triumph, 35 Size	150	225	300
Triumph Pin set or rim set, large crown, engine turned case (early model) with engraved barrel or movement.	200	300	400
True Test	35	50	65
Trump	35	50	65
USA (two models)	50	85	100
Universal, 1st model ★★★	250	375	500
Uncle Sam.	50	80	100
George Washington	150	200	325

Waterbury Watches & 35 size Duke or Duchess model see Waterbury W. Co. (Big Watch).

NOTE ADD $35 to $150 for original BOX and PAPERS

江 A collector should expect to pay modestly higher prices at local shops.

江 Pricing in this Guide are fair market price for complete watches which are reflected from the NAWCC National and regional shows.

Grade or Name — Description	ABP	Ex-Fn	Mint
Winner	$40	$60	$75
Winner, with Screw Back & Bezel	65	85	125
Yankee Backwind.	85	105	200
Yankee Bicycle Watch (sold for $1.00 in 1896) ....★★	200	300	400
Yankee Radiolite	55	75	100
Yankee Radiolite with Screw Back & Bezel	75	105	150
Yankee Special (many models)	75	105	150
Yankee, Perpetual calendar on back of case	100	140	200

 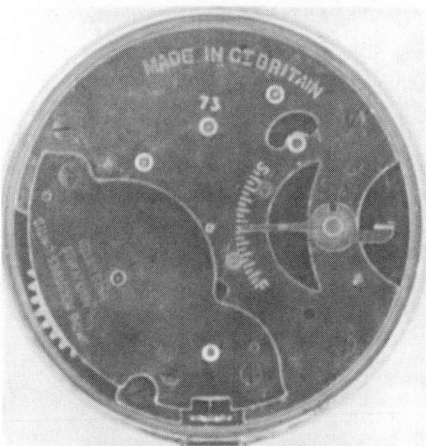

Ingersoll moveable calendar for years 1929-1951 located on back of case.   **Ingersoll** movement made in Great Britain.

INGERSOLL LTD.
(GREAT BRITAIN)

Grade or Name — Description	ABP	Ex-Fn	Mint
Ingersoll Ltd. (many models).............................	$65	$80	$100
Coronation, Elizabeth II on watch ....★	175	225	475
Coronation, June 2, 1953 on dial ....★	175	225	450
16S, 7J, 3F Brg	55	70	95
16S, 15J, 3F Brg	90	100	135
16S, 17J, 3F Brg, ADJ......................................	125	150	175
16S, 19J, 3F Brg, Adj5P	150	185	275
12S, 4J...	45	65	85

E. INGRAHAM CO.

Bristol, Connecticut 1912 – 1968

The E. Ingraham Co. purchased the Bannatyne Co. in 1912. They produced their first pocket watch in 1913. A total of about 65 million pocket watches and over 12 million wrist watches were produced before they started to import watches in 1968.

Grade or Name — Description	ABP	Ex-Fn	Mint
Ingraham W. Co. (many models)	$30	$45	$65
Allure	30	45	65
Aristocrat Railroad Special	50	70	100
Autocrat	30	50	75
Basketball & Football Timer	50	70	100
Beacon	30	45	65
Biltmore	30	45	75
Biltmore Radium dial	50	70	100
Bristol	30	45	65
Clipper	30	45	65
Co-Ed	30	45	65
Comet	50	70	100
Companion, sweep second hand	50	70	100
Cub	25	35	55
Dale	30	45	65
Demi—hunter style cover	65	80	150
Digital seconds dial, (no second hand but a digital seconds on dial)	60	75	100
Dixie	35	50	70
Dot	35	50	60
Endura	35	50	60
Everbrite (all models)	40	60	75
Graceline	30	50	65
Ingraham USA	30	50	65
Jockey	30	50	65
Laddie	25	35	50
Laddie Athlete	40	50	65
Lady's Purse Watch, with fancy bezel	50	70	100
Lendix Extra	30	50	60
Master	25	35	50
Master Craft	30	50	60
Miss Ingraham	25	35	50
New York to Paris(with box for mint) ★★	250	400	725
Overland	45	60	80
The Pal	30	50	65

INGRAHAM, Seven Seas, shows standard time, & Nautical time.

New York to Paris, with airplane model on dial, engraved bezel, commemorating Lindbergh's famous flight.

NOTE : ADD $25 to $75 for original BOX and PAPERS.

Pastor Stop Watch, Sterling W. Co. printed on dial, with start stop & fly back to zero function.
The Sterling Watch Company, Inc. Waterbury, Conn. U.S.A. on movement

Grade or Name —Description		ABP	Ex-Fn	Mint
Pastor Stop Watch, (Sterling W. Co), fly back to zero.	★	$125	$200	$350
Pastor on dial & E. Ingraham on movement, fly back to zero.	★	125	200	350
Pathfinder, compass on pendant (14 size).		95	150	250

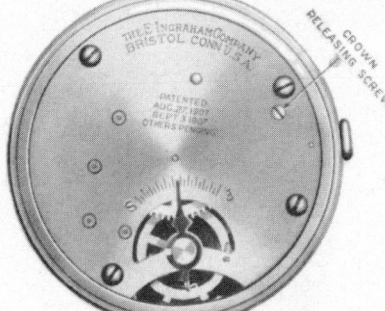

Path Finder showing compass in crown

E. Ingraham Co. on movement, **14 SIZE.**

Grade or Name — Description	ABP	Ex-Fn	Mint
Patriot.	$125	$200	$275
Peerless.	30	45	60
Pilot	40	50	75
Pocket Pal	30	45	60
Pony	30	45	60
Pride	30	45	60
Princess.	30	45	60
Prince.	30	45	60
Professional	30	45	60
Pup	30	45	60
Reliance	40	50	75
Rex	30	45	60
Rite Time	30	45	60
St Regis.	30	45	60
Secometer	40	50	75
Sentinel, Sentinel Click	30	45	60
Sentinel Fold Up Travel	50	70	100
Sentry	30	45	60
Seven Seas, 24 hr. dial & nautical dial.	55	90	150
Silver Star.	30	45	60
Sturdy.	30	45	60

Grade or Name — Description	ABP	Ex-Fn	Mint
Target	$30	$45	$60
The Best, The Pal	30	45	60
Time Ball	40	55	80
Time &Time	30	45	60
Tommy Ticker	30	45	60
Top Flight	30	45	60
Top Notch	30	45	60
Tower	30	45	60

Trail Blazer Commemorating Byrd's Antarctic Expedition.

Showing back side of **Trail Blazer**, also depicted on box.

Fob

ABOVE, BOX - Same as depicted on BACK of watch.

Grade or Name — Description		ABP	Ex-Fn	Mint
Trail Blazer, Commemorating BYRD'S Antarctic Expedition	★	$250	$500	$700
Trail Blazer, Commemorating BYRD'S Antarctic Expedition, *all original* *watch*, with **fob** (wings over the pole), + **box**	★★★	600	1,000	1,750
Treasure		15	25	35
Unbreakable Crystal		40	55	75
Uncle Sam (all models)		50	80	125
Uncle Sam Backwind & Set		125	175	265
United		30	40	55
Viceroy		30	45	60
Victory		30	45	60
Vogue about 14 size		30	45	60
Wings		40	55	75

Example of a basic **International Watch Co.** movement with
patent dates of Aug. 19, 1902. Jan. 27,1903 & Aug. 11,1903.

International Watch Co., "Highland" on dial.

INTERNATIONAL WATCH CO.

Newark City, New Jersey
1902-1907

This company produced only non-jeweled or low-cost production type watches that were inexpensive and nickel plated. Names on their watches include: Berkshire, Madison, and Mascot.

Grade or Name — Description		ABP	Ex-Fn	Mint
18 Size, skeletonized, pinlever escape., first model	★★	$200	$300	$425
Berkshire, OF	★	80	110	225
Highland	★	80	110	225
Madison, 18S, OF	★	80	110	225
Mascot, OF	★	80	110	225

KANKAKEE WATCH CO.

Kankakee, Illinois
1900

This company reportedly became the McIntyre Watch Co. Little or no information is available.

Grade or Name — Description		ABP	Ex-Fn	Mint
16S, BRG, NI	★★★★	$5,000	$8,000	$12,500

⚲ Watches listed in this book are priced at the **collectable fair market value** at the Trade Show level, as complete watches having an original 14k gold filled case, KEY WIND with silver, an original white enamel single sunk dial, and with the entire original movement in good working order with no repairs needed, unless otherwise noted.

KELLY WATCH Co.

Chicago, Illinois
c. 1900

Grade or Name — Description	ABP	Ex-Fn	Mint
16S, **aluminum** movement and OF case . . . .★★★★★	$500	$900	$1,500

Very Rare (About **10**)

Kelly Watch Co., 16 size, aluminum movement, straight line lever, quick train, porcelain dial, stem set, reversible ratchet stem wind, originally sold for $2.20. Ca. 1900.

KEYSTONE STANDARD WATCH CO.

Lancaster, Pennsylvania
1886-1891

Abram Bitner agreed to buy a large number of stockholders' shares of the Lancaster Watch Co. at 10 cents on the dollar; he ended up with 5,625 shares out of the 8,000 that were available. Some 8,900 movements had been completed but not sold at the time of the shares purchase. The company Bitner formed assumed the name of Keystone Standard Watch Co. as the trademark but in reality existed as the Lancaster Watch Co. The business was sold to Hamilton Watch Co. in 1891.

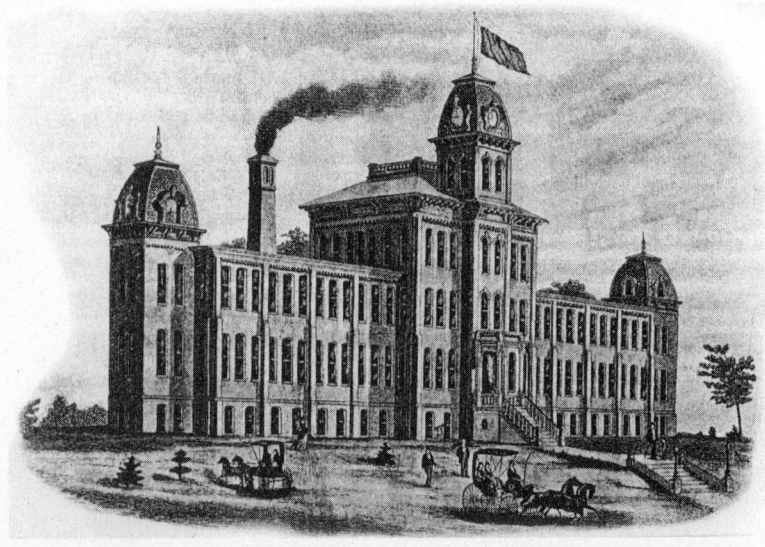

Grade or Name —Description	ABP	Ex-Fn	Mint
18S, 7-15J, OF, **KW**	$100	$175	$275
18S, 7-15J, OF, SW, 3/4, LS	100	125	175
18S, 15J, dustproof, ADJ	100	175	275
18S, 11-15J, dustproof, OF	100	150	200
18S, 11-15J, dustproof, HC	125	175	275
18S, 17J, dustproof, HC	150	200	285
18S, 20J, dustproof, HC ★★	350	500	775
18S, WestEnd, 15J, HC	100	150	200
8S, 11J, dustproof	100	150	200
6S, 7-10J, HC ★	100	200	275

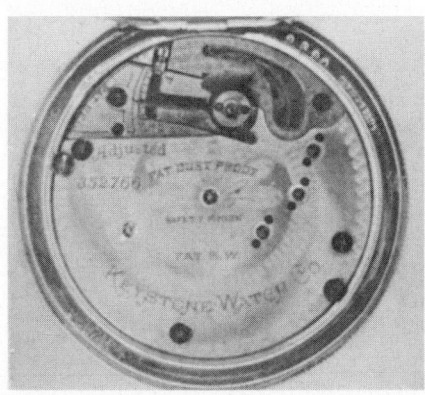

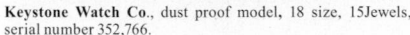

Keystone Watch Co., dust proof model, 18 size, 15Jewels, serial number 352,766.

Knickerbocker movement 16-18 size, 7 jewels, duplex escapement.

KNICKERBOCKER WATCH CO.

New York, New York
1890-1930

This company imported and sold Swiss and low-cost production American watches by New England Watch Co.

Grade or Name — Description	ABP	Ex-Fn	Mint
18S, 7J, OF, PS, NI, duplex escapement	$60	$100	$175
16S, 7J	40	75	100
12S, 7J, OF	50	85	115
10S, Barkley " **8Day** " ★★★	150	250	330
6S, Duplex	40	75	100

🖝 Some grades are not included. Their values can be determined by comparing with **similar** age, size, metal content, style, models and grades listed.

🖝 Watches listed in this book are priced at the collectable fair market value at the Trade Show level, as complete watches having an original 14k gold filled case, KEY WIND with silver, an original white enamel single sunk dial, and with the entire original movement in good working order with no repairs needed, unless otherwise noted.

🖝 Pricing in this Guide are fair market price for complete watches which are reflected from the NAWCC National and regional shows.

LANCASTER WATCH CO.

Lancaster, Pennsylvania
1879-1886

Work commenced on Sept. 1, 1877, at the Lancaster Watch Co. The watches produced there were designed to sell at a cheaper price than normal. They had a solid top, 3/4 plate, and a pillar plate that was fully ruby-jeweled (4 pairs). They had a gilt and nickel movement and a new stem-wind device, modeled by Mosly & Todd. By mid-1878 the Lancaster Watch Co. had produced 150 movements. Four grades of watches were made: Keystone, Fulton, Franklin, and Melrose. In September 1879 the company had made 334 movements. In 1880 the total was up to 1,250 movements, and by mid-1882 about 17,000 movements had been produced. About 200,000 watch movements were made.

CHRONOLOGY OF THE DEVELOPMENT OF THE LANCASTER WATCH CO.

Adams and Perry Watch Mfg. Co	1874-1876
Lancaster Penna. Watch Co	1877-1879
Lancaster Watch Co	1879-1886
Keystone Standard Co	1886-1891
Hamilton Watch Co	1892 to present

LANCASTER
18 SIZE
(All 3/4 Plate)

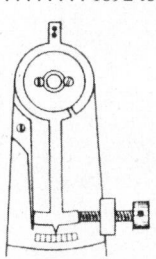

Grade or Name — Description	ABP	Ex-Fn	Mint
Chester, 7-11J, KW, dust proof, gilded	$125	$200	$350
Comet, 7J, NI	125	200	350
Delaware, 20J, ADJ, SW, dust proof, gilded .... ★	300	400	500
Denver, 7J, dust proof, gilded	100	175	250
Denver, 7J, gilded, dust proof, Silveroid	100	175	250
Elberon, 7J, dust proof	125	200	350
Ben Franklin, 7J, KW, gilded	150	300	500
Ben Franklin, 11J, KW, gilded	175	350	550
Fulton, 7J, ADJ, KW, gilded	100	175	300
Fulton, 11J, ADJ, KW, gilded	100	175	300
Girard, 15J, ADJ, dust proof, gilded	100	175	300
Hoosac, 11J, OF	100	200	350
Keystone, 15J, ADJ, gilded, GJS, dust proof	100	200	350
Keystone, 15J, ADJ, gilded, GJS, Silveroid	100	175	200
Keystone, 24 hour dial, Coin HC, c.1886 ....★★	900	1,500	2,200
Lancaster, 7J, SW	100	150	200
Lancaster, 15J, SW, Silveroid	100	150	150
Lancaster, 15J, OF	100	175	225
Lancaster Pa., 20J, Adj. nickel, LS, OF .... ★★★	400	600	800

"LANCASTER Watch PENNA. ", 20J, ADJ, GJS, 19 size, low serial No.
Referred to as (Adams Perry model**), for pricing see Adams Perry W. Co.** section.

𝒢𝒻 Some grades are not included. Their values can be determined by comparing with similar age, size, metal content, style, models and grades listed.

𝒢𝒻 A collector should expect to pay modestly higher prices at local shops.

Lancaster Watch PENNA., 19 size, 2Ojewels, gold jeweled settings. Referred to as Adams Perry model S# 1747.

Stevens Model, 18 size, 15 Jewels, adjusted, **dust proof** model, swing-out movement, S# 153044, ca.1836.

Above watch is *Lancaster Watch PENNA.,* 20J, ADJ, GJS, about 19 size, low serial No. Referred to as (Adams Perry model), **for pricing see Adams Perry W. Co.** section.

Grade or Name — Description	ABP	Ex-Fn	Mint
Malvern, 7J, dust proof, gilded	$100	$150	$200
Melrose, 15J, NI, ADJ, GJS	125	200	250
Nation Standard American Watch Co., 7J, HC	200	300	450
New Era, 7J, gilded, KW, HC	100	175	200
New Era, 7J, gilded, KW, Silveroid........................	100	150	175
Paoli, 7J, NI, dust proof..................................	100	125	225
Wm. Penn, 20J, ADJ, NI, dust proof ....★★	400	800	1,000
Radnor, 7J, dust proof, gilded	100	150	225
Record, 7J, dust proof, Silveroid	100	150	225
Record, 15J, NI	100	150	225

Lancster Keystone Rare 24 hour dial, 18s, Coin HC, C. 1886

Lancaster **movement,** 8-10 size, 15 jewels, serial number 317,812.

✑ A collector should expect to pay modestly higher prices at local shops.

✑ Pricing in this Guide are fair market price for **complete** watches which are reflected from the **"NAWCC"** National and regional shows.

Grade or Name — Description	ABP	Ex-Fn	Mint
Ruby, 7-16J, NI	$100	$175	$275
Sidney, 15J, NI, dust proof	125	225	285
Stevens, 15J, ADJ, NI, dust proof.	150	250	325
West End, 19J, HC, **KW**, gilded	450	600	800
West End, 15J, HC, **KW, KS**	125	225	325
West End, 15J, SW	110	200	275
West End, 15J, SW, Silveroid	100	150	200

8 SIZE

Grade or Name — Description	ABP	Ex-Fn	Mint
Cricket, 11J	$50	$100	$125
Diamond, 15J	50	100	125
Echo, 11J	50	100	125
Flora, 7-11J, gilded	50	100	125
Iris, 13J	50	100	125
Lady Penn, 20J, GJS, ADJ, NI ★★	375	550	810
Lancaster W. Co., 7J	50	100	125
Pearl, 7J	50	100	125
Red Rose, of Lancaster, 15J	50	100	125
Ruby, 15J	50	100	125

MANHATTAN WATCH Co.

New York, New York 1883 -1891

The Manhattan Watch Co. made mainly low cost production watches. A complete and full line of watches was made, and most were cased and styled to be sold as a complete watch. The watches were generally 16S with full plate movements. The patented winding mechanism was different. These watches were both in hunter and open-face cases and later had a sweep second hand. Total production was 160,000 or more watches.

Manhattan Watch Co., stop watch, 16 size, note the escapement uses upright "D"—shaped pallets (steel), serial number 117,480.

Manhattan Watch Co., 16 size, stop watch. Note the two buttons on top: the right (at 2 o'clock) one sets the hands, the left (at 10 o'clock) starts and stops the watch.

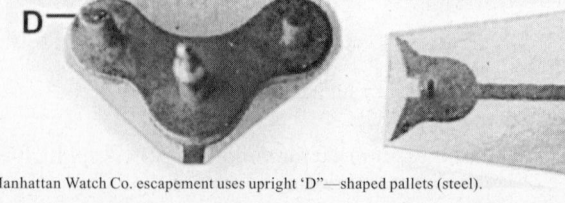

Right: Manhattan Watch Co. escapement uses upright 'D"—shaped pallets (steel).

16 SIZE

Grade or Name — Description		ABP	Ex-Fn	Mint
OF, with back wind, base metal case	★	$150	$275	$450
OF, 2 button stop watch, screw back & bezel, enamel dial, gold-filled case	★★★	275	450	800
OF, 2 button stop watch, snap back & bezel, paper dial, base metal case	★	150	325	550
HC, 2 button stop watch, snap back & bezel, paper dial, base metal case	★★	200	375	625
OF, 1 button, sweep sec., base metal case , paper dial	★	125	250	300
HC, 1 button, sweep sec., base metal case, paper dial	★	175	325	400
Ship's Bell Time Dial, OF or HC	★★★★	325	525	800
Twenty-Four Hour Dial, OF or HC	★★★★	325	525	800
Stallcup, 7J, OF	★	100	225	350

12 SIZE

Grade or Name — Description		ABP	Ex-Fn	Mint
12S	★	$80	$150	$350

Manhattan Watch Co., 16 size, time only watch & note no second hand, the button at Right sets the hands.

Manhattan Watch Co., 16 size, tine only with Sweep-Second hand, the button at Right sets the hands.

Manhattan Watch Co., 16 size, Ship's Bell Time DIAL for NAUTICAL USES & sweep second hand. Hunting Case.

Manhattan Watch Co., 16 size, with a 24-HOUR D IAL & sweep second hand, Hunting Case.

MANISTEE WATCH CO.

Manistee, Michigan 1908-1912

The Manistee watches, first marketed in 1909, were designed to compete with the low-cost production watches. Dials, jewels, and hairsprings were not produced at the factory. The first movement was 18S, 7J, and sold for about $5. Manistee also made 5J, 15J, 17J, and 21J watches in cheap cases in sizes 16 and 12. Estimated total production was 60,000. Most were sold by Star Watch Case Co.

18 SIZE

Grade or Name —Description		ABP	Ex-Fn	Mint
18S, 7J, 3/4, LS, HC .... ★		$300	$400	$500
18S, 7J, 3/4, LS, OF .... ★		200	300	400
18S, 7J, 3/4, LS, OF, **gold train** .... ★★★		375	500	700
18S, 7J, **cut out** movement .... ★★		200	300	400

16 TO 12 SIZE

Grade or Name —Description		ABP	Ex-Fn	Mint
16S, 7J, OF .... ★		$200	$250	$325
16S, 15J, OF .... ★		225	275	400
16S, 15J, HC .... ★		250	300	425
16S, 17J, OF .... ★		225	275	400
16S, 19J, HC .... ★		300	350	525
16S, 21J, OF .... ★		350	400	600
12S, 15J. .... ★		150	200	300

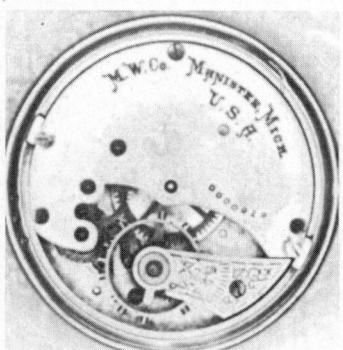

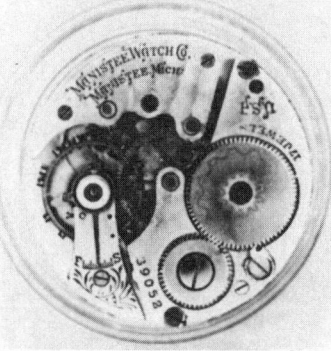

Manistee movement, 18 size. 7 jewels. 3/4 plate, open face, serial number 0000919.

Manistee movement, 16 size. 17 jewels, three-quarter plate, open face, serial number 39,052.

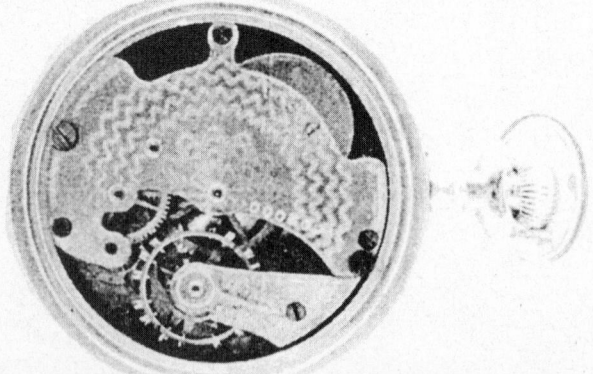

Manistee cut out movement, 18 size, 7 jewels, open face, serial number 0006094.

McINTYRE WATCH CO.

Kankakee, Illinois
1908-1911

This company probably bought the factory from Kankakee Watch Co. In 1908 Charles DeLong was made master watchmaker, and he designed and improved the railroad watches. Only a few watches were made, estimated total production being about eight watches.

Grade or Name — Description	ABP	Ex-Fn	Mint
16S, 21J, BRG, NI, WI	★★★★ $8,000	$18,000	$22,000
16S, 25J, ERG, WI, Adj.5P, equidistant escapement	★★★★ 10,000	25,000	35,000
12S, 19J, BRG	★★★★ 5,000	10,000	12,000

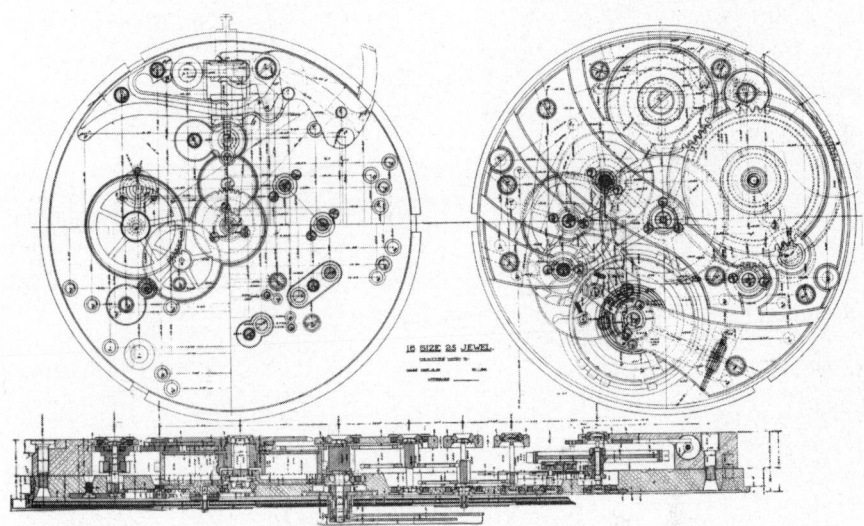

Mcintyre Watch Co., 16 size, 25 jewels, adjusted to 5 positions with wind indicator, with equidistant escapement, manufactured about 1909. Above illustration taken from a blue print.

EXAMPLE OF A BREGUET STYLE DIAL

EXAMPLE OF A BOX CAR STYLE DIAL

MELROSE WATCH CO.

Melrose, Massachusetts (1866- 1868)

In late 1866 the Tremont Watch Co. moved from Boston, Mass., and changed its name to Melrose Watch Co., and started making the complete watch movements, movement engraved 'Melrose Watch Co. and dials marked Tremont W. Co. About 3,000 were produced. Serial # range 30,000 and higher. In about 1870 sold to the English and used the name Anglo-American Watch Co.

Factory at Melrose, Mass. General Agents, Messrs. WHEELER, PARSONS & CO.,New York, Messrs. BIGELOW BROS. & KENNARD, Boston, and for sale by the trade generally. Every movement warranted.

The TREMONT WATCH CO. manufacture the only DUST-PROOF Watch movement in this country. They have a branch establishment in Switzerland, under the personal superintendence of Mr. A. L. DENNISON, (the ORIGINATOR of the American system of watch-making), where they produce their Balances and Escapements of a superior quality. The cheap skilled labor of Europe, working thus on the AMERICAN SYSTEM, enables them to offer a superior article at a low rate.

Melrose Watch Co. movement, 18 size, 15 jewels, Key wind & set. Melrose W. Co. serial # range 30,000 and higher.

Above: 1867 ADVERTISEMENT

Grade or Name — Description		ABP	Ex-Fn	Mint
18S, 7J, KW, KS . . . . ★★		$275	$425	$600
18S, 11J, KW, KS, OF. . . . . ★★		275	425	600
18S, 15J, KW, KS . . . . ★★		330	525	700
18S, 15J, KW, KS, Silveroid. . . . . ★★		275	425	550

MOZART WATCH CO.

Providence, Rhode Island to Ann Arbor, Michigan (1864 - 1870)

In 1864 Don J. Mozart started out to produce a less expensive three-wheel watch in Providence, R. I. Despite his best efforts, the venture was declared a failure by 1866. Mozart left Providence and moved to Ann Arbor, Mich. There, again, he started on a three-wheel watch and succeeded in producing thirty. The three-wheel watch was not a new idea except to American manufacturers. Three-wheel watches were made many decades before Mozart's first effort, but credit for the first American-made three-wheel watch must go to him. The size was about 18 and could be called a 3/4 or full plate movement. The balance bridge was screwed on the top plate, as was customary. The round bridge partially covered the opening in the top plate and was just large enough for the balance to oscillate, The balance was compensated and somewhat smaller in diameter than usual. Mozart called it a chrono-lever, and it was to function so perfectly it would be free from friction, but no way was this true.

Mozart Chrono-lever; The escape wheel has 30 teeth and receives its impulse directly from the roller on the staff, while the escape tooth locked on the intermediate lever pallet. The escape pinion had a long pivot that carries the second hand, which made a circuit of the seconds dial, once in 12 seconds. The balance wheel has sliding weights, instead of screws.

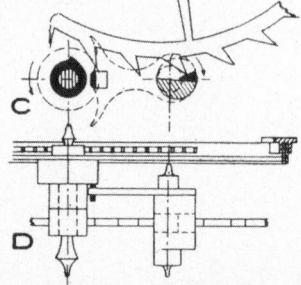

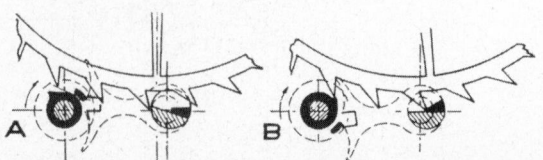

The watch is about 18 size with a train that had a main wheel with the usual number of teeth and a ten-leaf center pinion, but it had a large center wheel of 108 teeth and a third wheel of 90 teeth, with a six-leaf third (escape) pinion. The escape wheel had 30 teeth and received its impulse directly from the roller on the staff, while the escape tooth locked on the intermediate lever pallet. The escape pinion had a long pivot that carried the second hand, which made a circuit of the dial, once in 12 seconds. The total number of Mozart watches produced was about 165 and only a few were ever finished.

Grade or Name — Description		ABP	Ex-Fn	Mint
18S, 3/4, KW & KS from back, 3-wheel .... ★★★★★	$25,000	$60,000	$110,000

Mozart Watch Co. movement, 18 Size, three-quarter plate, keywind & set, three wheel train, "Patent Dec. 24th, 1868" & Patent # 72,528. Note sliding weights on balance wheel.

J. H. Mulford, 18 size, about 10 jewels, key wind, and is marked, "J. H. Mulford, patent, Albany, N.Y. S# 25".

J. H. MULFORD

Albany, New York (1842 - 1876)

John Mulford started out as a jeweler and by about 1842 was listed as a watchmaker. Mulford was granted a patent on Feb. 21, 1842 (no. 2465) for his style escapement. It appears that the basic movement was imported. Most were 18 size, key wind & set with a going barrel, and he used gold jewel screwed down settings. The verge style escapement and on the balance staff instead of pallets, he used two cylindrical jewels, and each jewel had a notch.

Grade or Name — Description		ABP	Ex-Fn	Mint
18S, 10-12J., ¾,KW, KS .... ★★★★	$9,000	$15,000	$25,000

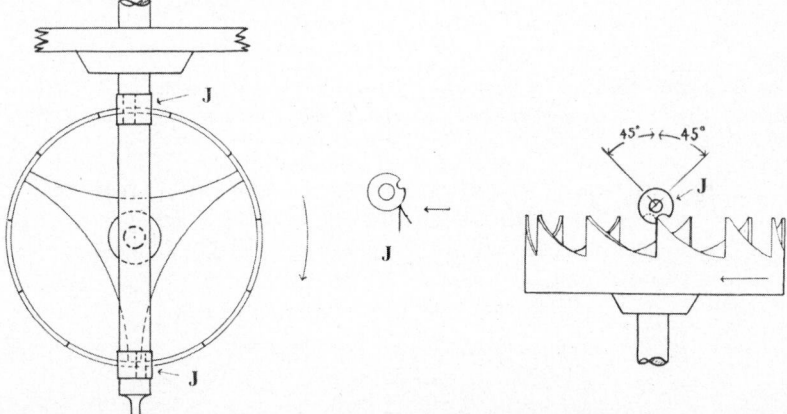

J. H. Mulford, drawing of his patented escapement. (Pat. # 2465 date Feb.21, 1842) On the balance staff, instead of flag style pallets, there are two cylindrical jewels "J" each jewel has a notch similar to the notch of a duplex escapement. When the tip of the escape wheel tooth drops on the jewel it imparts a impulse against the side of the notched jewel.

320

NASHUA WATCH CO.

Nashua, New Hampshire
1859 – 1862

One of the most important contributions to the American Watch industry was made by the Nashua Watch Co. of Nashua, New Hampshire. Founded in 1859 by B. D. Bingham, the company hired some of the most innovative and creative watchmakers in America and produced an extremely high grade American pocket watch.

Since almost all the production material made by Nashua from 1859 until its incorporation into the American Watch Co. in 1862 was unfinished by Nashua, only about four examples of the 20-size keywind keyset from the back signed Nashua Watch Co. are known to exist.

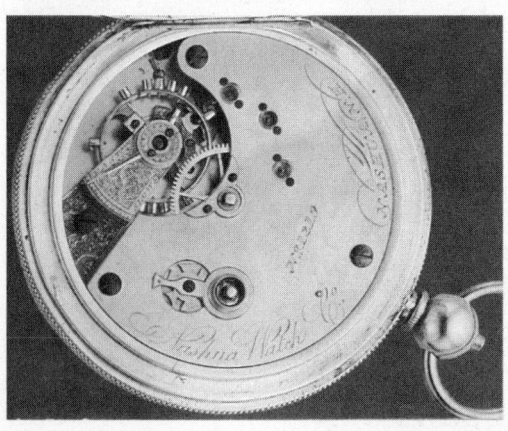

NASHUA WATCH CO. (marked), 20 size, 19 jewels, gold jewel settings, key wind & set from back, stop work, serial number 1,219.

20-size keywind keyset from the back signed Nashua Watch Co.

Grade or Name — Description	ABP	Ex-Fn	Mint
Nashua (marked), 19J, KW, KS, 3/4, 18K .... ★★★★★ $20,000		$40,000	$50,000
Nashua (marked), 15J, KW, KS, 3/4, silver case .... ★★★★ 17,000		30,000	40,000

NEWARK WATCH CO.

Newark, New Jersey
1864- 1870

Arthur Wadsworth, one of the designers for Newark Watch Co., patented an 18 Size full plate movement. The first movements reached the market in 1867. This company produced only about 8,000 watches before it was sold to the Cornell Watch Co.

CHRONOLOGY OF THE DEVELOPMENT OF NEWARK WATCH CO.
Newark Watch Co. 1864-1870; S#s 4,301 to 12,000;
Cornell Watch Co., Chicago, Ill. 1870-1874; S#s 12,001 to 25,000;
Cornell Watch Co., San Francisco, Calif 1874-Jan. 1876; S#s 25,001 to 35,000;
California Watch Co., Jan. 1876-mid 1876.

The Complete Price Guide to Watches goal is to stimulate the orderly exchange of watches between "buyers" and "sellers ".

Newark Watch Co. Robert Fellows grade movement, 18 size, 15jewels, key wind & set, serial number 12, 044.

Grade or Name — Description		ABP	Ex-Fn	Mint
18S, 15J, KW, KS, **HC**	★★	$360	$475	$700
18S, 15J, KW, KS, OF.	★★	330	450	650
18S, 7J, KW, KS	★★	275	375	500
J.C. Adams, 11J, KW, KS	★★	330	450	600
J.C. Adams, 11J, KW, KS, Coin	★★	360	475	700
Edward Biven, 11-15J, KW, KS	★★	385	525	750
Robert Fellows, KW, KS	★★★	440	625	950
Keyless Watch Co., 15J, LS, SW	★★★	440	775	1,150
Newark Watch Co., 7-15J, KW, KS	★★	330	475	700
Arthur Wadsworth, SW	★★★	660	925	1,650
Arthur Wadsworth, 18S, 15J, 18K, HC, *"Arthur Wadsworth, New York"* on dial; *"Keyless Watch, Patent #3655. June 19, 1866"* engraved on movement	★★★	1,600	2,500	3,500

NEW ENGLAND WATCH CO.

Waterbury, Connecticut 1898- 1914

The New England Watch Co., formerly the Waterbury Watch Co., made a watch with a duplex escapement, gilt, 16S, open faced. Watches with the skeletonized movement are very desirable. The company later became Timex Watch Co.

Grade or Name — Description		ABP	Ex-Fn	Mint
16S, OF, duplex, **SKELETON**, good running order	★	$300	$500	$700
12S, 16S, 18S, OF, pictures on dial: ladies, dogs, horses, trains, flags, ships, cards, etc		150	300	525
12S, 16S, 18S, OF, duplex escapement, good running order		65	100	150
12S, 16S, 18S, OF, pin lever escapement, good running order		50	100	125

Above: Pictures on dial: ladies, dogs, horses, trains, flags, ships, cards, etc

Front & back view of a **skeletonized** New England Watch Co. movement. This watch is fitted with a glass display back and front, making the entire movement and wheels visible, 4 jewels, silver hands, black numbers, originally sold for $10-13.

Grade or Name — Description	ABP	Ex-Fn	Mint
6S, duplex	$40	$60	$75
6S, duplex, **SKELETON** model, OF	300	425	550
0 S, 15-17 J, lever escapement	55	110	125
Addison, (all sizes)	55	110	125
Alden, (all sizes)	35	85	85
Ambassador, 12S, duplex	35	85	85
Americus, duplex escapement	40	85	95
Berkshire, duplex escapement, **GF**	55	110	125

New England Watch Co., 16 size, 7 jewels, open face, double roller, Dan Patch stop watch.

New England Watch Co., Scout, about 16 size, 4 jewels, duplex escapement, New England base metal case.

⚬ A collector should expect to pay modestly higher prices at local shops.

⚬ Pricing in this Guide are fair market price for complete watches which are reflected from the NAWCC National and regional shows.

Addison, Duplex Escapement

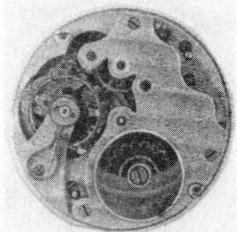

New England Watch Co., multi-colored paper dials, showing poker style playing cards. Watches complete with these type dials bring **$425 -$675 -$1,500.**

New England Watch Co., **Lady Mary**, 0 size, 17 Jewels, lever escapement, serial # 1,000,283.

Grade or Name — Description	ABP	Ex-Fn	Mint
Cadish, duplex escapement	$35	$80	$85
Cavour, duplex escapement	35	80	85
Columbian	40	85	95
Chronograph, 7J, Start, Stop & Reset	125	225	300
Cruiser, duplex	40	85	85
Dan Patch, Chronograph, 7J, Start, Stop & Reset ★	275	525	600
Dominion, **0 size**	35	75	75
Elf, **series 55**, duplex	45	80	85
Excelsior, 7J	60	110	125
Enamel, full enamel cased watches back and bezel, blue, red, green, sizes from 6 size to 0 size	150	275	350
Embossed, base metal cases with duplex escapement	75	135	225
Fancy, **"unfaded dial"**	125	220	300
Fire Fly, about 8 size	40	80	85
Gabour	60	90	125
General	35	80	85
Hale, 7J	35	80	85
Jockey, duplex escapement	60	90	125
Lady Mary	60	90	125
Oxford	35	80	85
Padishah also Pilgram, both duplex escapement	60	90	125
Putnam	40	85	95
Queen Mab, duplex escapement - **0 size**, 4J	35	80	85
Rugby, stop watch	65	95	125
Scout, 12 Size, duplex escapement, HC	35	80	85
Senator, duplex escapement	35	80	85
Standish, about 12 size	35	80	85
Trump, duplex escapement	35	80	85
Tuxedo	35	80	85
Tuxedo, duplex escapement	60	90	125

☞ Some grades are not included. Their values can be determined by comparing with similar age, size, metal content, style, models and grades listed.

NEW HAVEN CLOCK AND WATCH Co.

New Haven, Connecticut 1853-1956

The company started making Marine clock movements with a balance wheel in about 1875, and a used similar smaller movement to make watches in early 1880. The company soon reached a production of about 200 watches per day, making a total of some 40 million watches.

NEW HAVEN Clock & Watch Co., Angelus, with rotating dials, patented Jan 23,1900.

NEW HAVEN, Ships Time, Ben Franklin style dial. Note this watch uses only one hand.

Grade or Name —Description	ABP	Ex-Fn	Mint
Always Right	$35	$80	$85
The Angelus, 2 rotating dials ★	135	325	400
Beardsley Radiant	55	85	115
Buddy	35	60	75
Bull Dog	30	60	70
Compensated	35	60	75
Captain Scout	75	110	160
Celluloid case (bold colors)	100	145	200
Chronometer	60	95	175
Earl 35	50	85	95
Elite 35	50	85	95
Elm City	35	60	75
Fancy dials, no fading	100	160	325
Football Timer ★	75	110	200
Ford Special	60	85	95
Hamilton	40	65	75
Handy Andy	65	95	165
Jerome USA	40	65	75

Traveler, with travel case.

Example of Kaiser Wilhelm.

Sport Timer + RED BOX and White Letters.

Grade or Name —Description	ABP	Ex-Fn	Mint
Kaiser Wilhelm .... ★★★	$500	$800	$1,200
Kermit...	35	55	65
Laddie...	25	35	50
Leonard Watch Co	30	45	60
Leonard...	35	55	75
Mastercraft Rayolite...................................	50	75	95
Miracle...	35	55	75
Motor	30	45	60
Nehi50...	70	100	150
New Haven, pin lever, SW	60	80	125
New Haven, back wind.................................	100	155	200
Panama Official Souvenir, 1915........................ ★★★	350	600	850
Paul Pry, 14 size with a Locomotive on back of case.............	40	55	75
Pedometer, 14 size, OF..................................	40	55	75
Pentagon-shaped case...................................	40	55	75
Playing cards on dial ....★★	400	700	975
Service	25	35	50
Ships Time, Franklin style dial (one hand) .... ★	75	105	175
Sports **Timer**	65	80	150
Sports **Timer** +**Box**	75	105	185
Surity	35	55	75
Teller...	30	50	70
Tip Top	20	35	60
Tip Top Jr	20	35	60
The American..	40	60	85
The JAP 12size.......................................	35	45	65
The Midget about 4 size	25	35	50
The Lady Clare 6 size.................................	30	40	50
Tommy Ticker..	30	40	50
Tourist...	40	55	75
Traveler, with travel case	55	70	100
True Time...	30	50	70
United	25	35	50
USA30	40	65	75
Victor	25	35	50

NOTE ADD $25 to $70 for original BOX and PAPERS

NEW HAVEN WATCH CO.

New Haven, Connecticut
1883-1887

This company was organized October 16, 1883 with the intention of producing W. E. Doolittle's patented watch; however, this plan was soon abandoned. They did produce a "Model A" watch, the first was marketed in the spring of 1884. Estimated total production is **200**. The original capital became absorbed by Trenton W. Co.

"The New Haven Watch Co. Alpha, 149, Pat. Dec. 27-81," engraved on movement, lever escapement, open face, extremely rare watch.

Grade or Name —Description		ABP	Ex-Fn	Mint
"A" Model, about 18S, pat. Dec. 27, '81 . . . . ★★★★★		$900	$2,000	$3,000
Alpha Model, pat. Dec. 27, '81 . . . . ★★★★★		900	2,000	3,000

NEW YORK CITY WATCH CO.

New York, New York
1890-1897

This company manufactured the Dollar-type watches, which had a pendant-type crank. The watch is wound by **cranking the pendant**, and has a pin lever escapement. The hands are set from the back of the watch movement. **"Patent number 526,871"**, is engraved on the movement and patent is dated October 1894, and was held by S. Schisgall. The New York City Watch Co., 20 size watch has the words "Lever Winder" printed on the paper dial.

☞ A collector should expect to pay modestly higher prices at local shops.

☞ Watches listed in this book are priced as complete watches having an original 14k gold filled case, KEY WIND with silver, an original white enamel single sunk dial, and with the entire original movement in good working order with no repairs needed, unless noted.

Grade or Name —Description		ABP	Ex-Fn	Mint
18-20S, no jewels, "**Lever Winder**" on dial . . . . ★★★★		$1,500	$3,000	$4,000
18-20S, no jewels, "**SUN DIAL**" on dial . . . . ★★★★		$800	$1,500	$2,500

New York City Watch Co., about 18-20 size, "**Lever Winder**" printed on paper dial. This watch is **WOUND by cranking the pendant back and forth**, pin lever escapement, also **back set**, & *"New York City Watch Co., patent No. 526,871"* engraved on movement.

NEW YORK CHRONOGRAPH WATCH CO.

NEW YORK NEW YORK
1883 –1885

This company sold about 800 watches marked "New York Chronograph Watch Co." The 18 size stop watch was manufactured by Manhattan Watch Co. 16 size made by?

Grade or Name —Description		ABP	Ex-Fn	Mint
18S, 7J, stopwatch, HC . . . . ★		$125	$200	$275
18S, 7J, stopwatch, OF . . . . ★		100	175	200
16S, 7J, SW, time only, OF . . . . ★		150	200	275
16S, 9-11J, SW, time only, OF . . . . ★		150	200	275
16S, 7-11J, SW, time only with sweep sec. hand, OF . . . . ★		175	225	300
16S, 11J, SW, **true CHRONOGRAPH**, OF . . . . ★★★★★		600	1,200	2,000

 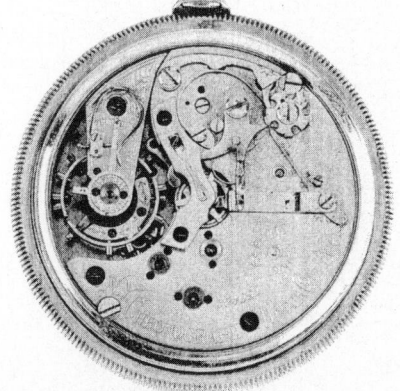

N.Y. Chronograph Watch Co., dial and movement, 16 size, 11 Jewels, open face. chronograph.

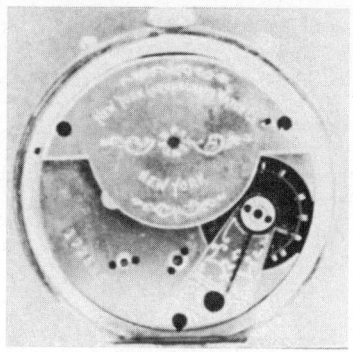

New York chronograph Watch CO. dial and movement, 7 jewels, open face, buttons at the top of case set hands and stop watch.

No.30

Hunting also seen Key Wind & Set

Open Face

NEW YORK STANDARD WATCH CO.

(CROWN WATCH CO.)
Jersey City, New Jersey 1885 – 1929

The first watch reached the market in early 1888 and was a 18S. The most interesting feature was a straight line lever with a "worm gear escapement." This was patented by R. J. Clay. All watches were quick train and open-faced. The company also made its own cases and sold a complete watch. Total production maybe, as high as, 30,000,000. A prefix number was added to some serial numbers.

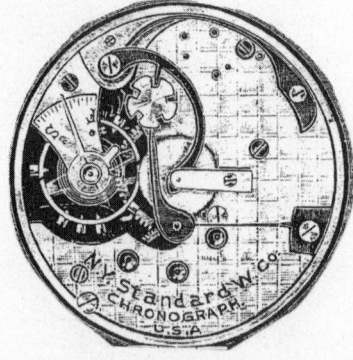

New York Standard, Chronograph, 18 size, 7 jewels, stem wind, second hand start-stop and fly back, 3/4 plate.

New York Standard, converts to a hunting case movement or a open face movement, serial number 502,619.

N.Y. STANDARD 16 AND 18 SIZE

Grade or Name —Description	ABP	Ex-Fn	Mint
18S, 7J, N. Y. Standard, **KW, KS** ★★★	$250	$350	$500
18S, 7J, N. Y. Standard, SW	50	90	125
18S, 15J, N. Y. Standard, SW, LS, HC	100	125	175
Chicago, U.S.A., **17-23 fake jewels**, with a **Locomotive** on Movement & Dial	100	150	235
Chronograph, 7-11J, 3/4, NI, DMK, SW, fly back hand	150	225	400
Chronograph, 10J, (marked 10J), fly back hand ★	185	275	425
Chronograph, 13J, sweep sec., stop & fly back hand	150	250	400
Chronograph, 15J, 3/4, NI, DMK, SW, fly back hand	150	250	400
Convertible, 15J., 16 size, can be changed to HC or OF ★★★★	300	500	850
Crown W. Co., 7J, OF or HC	50	90	125
Crown W. Co., 15J, HC	60	100	150
Dan Patch, 7J, stop watch (pat DEC. 22 '08) ★	250	450	575
Dan Patch, 17J, stop watch (pat. DEC. 22 '08) ★★	375	550	675
Edgemere, 7J, OF & HC	45	80	110
Excelsior, 7J, OF or HC	45	80	110

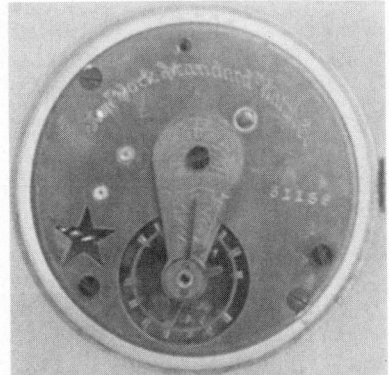

New York Standard, with **WORM GEAR** (located under cutout star). 18 size, OF, 5-7 jewels, there was 2 or 3 runs of the worm-drive model. 52,000 made, S# 31,138.

Remington W. Co. (marked on movement & case), 16 size, 11 jewels, 2-tone damaskeening, NOTE crown wheel & ratchet (no click)' serial # CC 021,331.

Grade or Name — Description	ABP	Ex-Fn	Mint
Harvard W. Co., 7—11J	$40	$80	$110
Hi Grade	50	80	110
Ideal 50	50	80	110
Jefferson, 7J	50	80	110
La Salle, 7J	35	80	110
New Era, 7J., **skeletonized** (Poor Man's Dudley) OF- HC	250	350	550
New Era,7—11J	40	80	110
New York Standard W. Co., 11J, 3/4	60	90	125
New York Standard, 7J, 3/4	60	90	125
New York Standard, 15J, BRG	75	100	150
N. Y. Standard, with (**" WORM GEAR"**)' OF ★	600	1,000	1,200
N. Y. Standard, with (" **WORM GEAR"**) multi-color dial ★	700	1,200	1,500
N. Y. Standard, with (**" WORM GEAR"**), HC ★★★	1,000	2,000	2,500

Also **Watch Co.** names also signed **USA** as: Bay State, Chicago, Crown, Eldridge, Excelsior, Gloria, Hamlet, Hercules, Highgrade, Jefferson, LaSalle, New Era, Pacific, Remington, Rosemere, Solar, Tribune, Waldemar, Washington, & Wilmington Special etc.. $60 $90 $120

🕰 Note: Some styles, models and grades are not included. Their values can be determined by comparing with similar styles, size, age, models and grades listed.

🕰 A collector should expect to pay modestly higher prices at local shops.

Grade or Name —Description	ABP	Ex-Fn	Mint
Pan- America, 7J, OF	$60	$100	$150
Perfection, 7J, OF or HC	45	90	110
Perfection, 15J, OF or HC, NI	55	90	110
Remington W. Co., 11J, marked mvt. & case	75	100	160
Solar W. Co., 7J	50	90	110
Special USA, 7J	45	90	110
18S Tribune USA, **23J**, HC or OF, Pat Reg. Adj . . . . ★	150	185	300
Washington, 7-11J	50	90	110
William Penn, 7-11J	50	90	110
Wilmington, 7-11J	45	90	110

For watches with <u>O'Hara Multi-Color</u> Dials, add $75 -$100 to value in mint condition; add $40-$60 for Hunting Cases.

12 SIZE

Grade or Name —Description	ABP	Ex-Fn	Mint
N. Y. Standard, 7J-11J, OF	$25	$30	$45
N. Y. Standard, 7J-11J, HC	40	50	65
N. Y. Standard, 7J, Multi-Color dial	75	125	250
N. Y. Standard, 15J, OF	35	40	55
N. Y. Standard, 15J, HC	45	55	75
Columbia, 7J	50	65	85
Crown W. Co., 7J, OF or HC	30	40	55

New York Standard W. Co., 12 size, 7J., open face, S# 1,021,224. Note similarity to Keystone Howard Railroad chronometer.

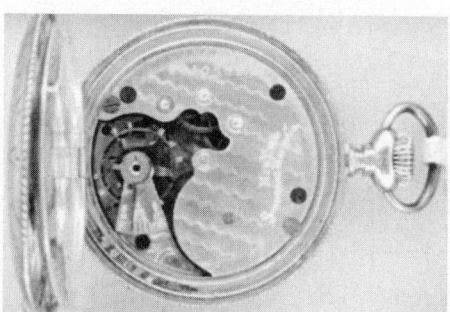

New York Standard W.Co., 6 size G# 144, Hunting case.

6 SIZE – 0 SIZE –3/0 SIZE

Grade or Name — Description	ABP	Ex-Fn	Mint
Alton, 7-15J.	$35	$40	$55
American, 7J.	35	40	55
Empire State W. Co., 7J	45	55	80
Excelsior, 7J, HC.	50	70	100
6S, Columbia, 7J, HC	55	70	100
Crown W. Co., 7J, 6 size & 0 size, OF or HC	40	50	65
Standard USA, 7J	35	40	55
6S, N.Y. Standard, 7J, HC.	60	80	110
6S, Orient, SW	30	40	60
Tribune, 11J., (some spread or oversized)	50	65	100
6S, Progress, 7J.	40	50	65
0S, Ideal, 7J, HC	55	70	90
0S, N. Y. Standard, 7J, HC	55	70	90

🖙 Pricing in this Guide are fair market price for complete watches which are reflected from the NAWCC National and regional shows.

How to Identify Your Watch Size & Model: Compare the movement of your watch with the illustrations in this section. While comparing, note the location of the balance, jewels, screws, gears, and type of back plate (Full, 3/4, Bridge) these will be clues in identifying the movement you have.

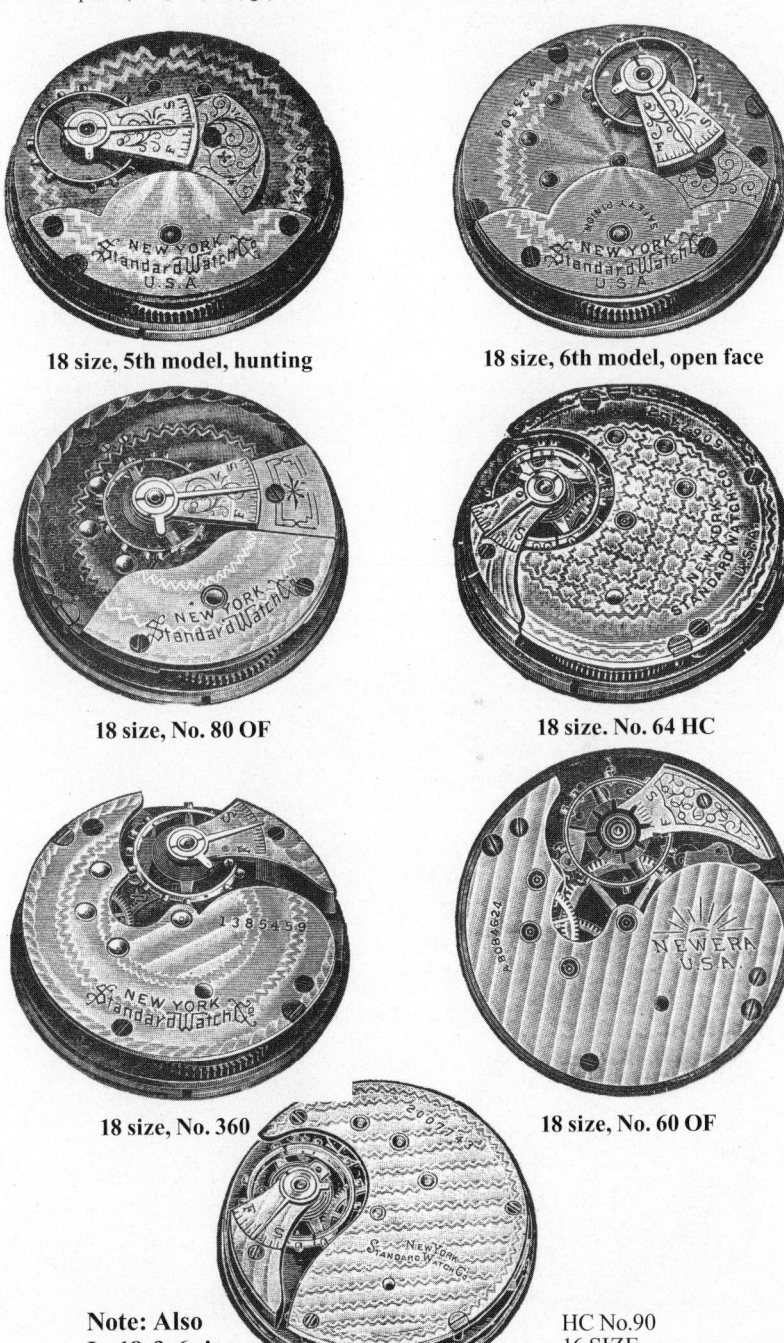

18 size, 5th model, hunting

18 size, 6th model, open face

18 size, No. 80 OF

18 size. No. 64 HC

18 size, No. 360

18 size, No. 60 OF

Note: Also In 18 & 6 size

HC No.90
16 SIZE

18 Size, No.165 OF

18 size, 4th Model OF

16 size, No. 94 OF

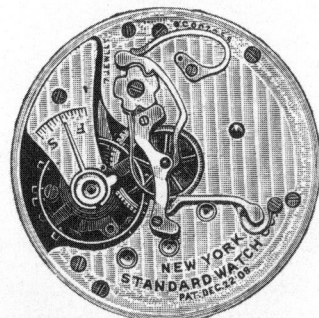

16 size, No. 91

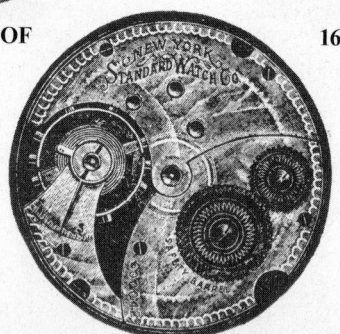

16 Size, 1st Model
converts to open
or hunting.

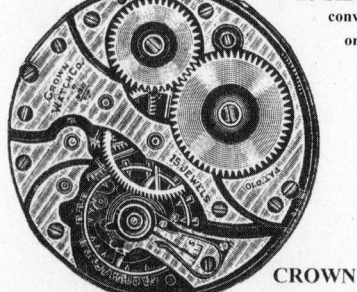

CROWN

16 size, No. 1516 HC

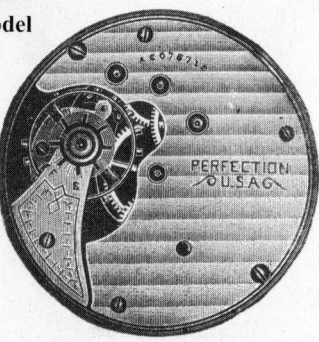

16 size, No. 390 HC

12 size, No. 170 HC

12 size, No. 1570 HC

12 size, hunting

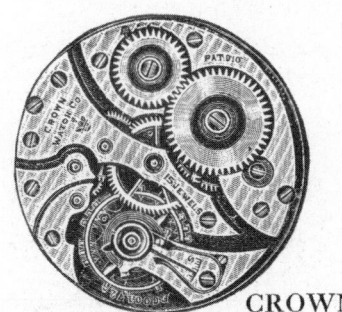

CROWN

12 size, No. 1512 HC

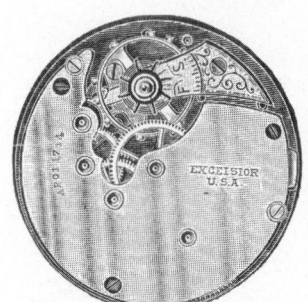

12 size, No. 370 OF

6 size, No. 146 OF

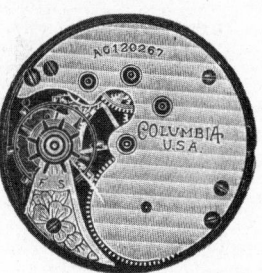

6 size, No. 44 HC

0 size, No.300   OF

3/0 size, No.730 HC

10/0 size, No. 1015   OF

NEW YORK SPRINGFIELD WATCH CO.

Springfield, Massachusetts
1866-1876

The New York Watch Co. had a rather difficult time getting started. The name of the company was changed from the Mozart Watch Co. to the New York Watch Co., and it was located in Rhode Island. Before any watches had been sold, they moved to Springfield, Mass., in 1867. A factory was built there, but only about 100 watches were produced before a fire occurred on April 23, 1870. Shortly after the fire, in 1870, a newly -designed watch was introduced. The first movements reached the market in 1871, and the first grade was a fully -jeweled adjusted movement called "Frederick Billings." The standard 18 S and the Swiss Ligne systems were both used in gauging the size of these watches. The New York Watch Co. used full signatures on its movements. The doors closed in the summer of 1876.

In January 1877, the Hampden Watch Co. was organized and commenced active operation in June 1877.

CHRONOLOGY OF THE DEVELOPMENT OF NEW YORK WATCH CO.

The Mozart Watch Co., Providence, R. I	1864-1866
New York Watch Co., Providence, R. I	1866-1867
New York Watch Co., Springfield, Mass	1867-1875
New York Watch Mfg. Co., Springfield, Mass.	1875-1876
Hampden Watch Co., Springfield, Mass	1877-1886
Hampden-Dueber Watch Co., Springfield, Mass.	1886-1888
Hampden Watch Co. Works, Canton, Ohio	1888-1923
Dueber-Hampden Watch Co., Canton, Ohio	1923-1930
Amtorg, U.S.S.R	1930

NEW YORK WATCH CO.SPRINGFIELD
ESTIMATED SERIAL NUMBERS
AND PRODUCTION DATES

DATE	SERIAL NO.		DATE	SERIAL NO.
1866	1,000		1871	20,000
1867	3,000		1872	30,000
1868	5000		1873	40,000
1869	7,000		1874	50,000
1870	10,000		1875	60.000

The above list is provided for determining the APPROXIMATE age of your watch. Match serial number with date. Watches were not necessarily sold in the exact order of manufactured date.

N.Y. W. SPRINGFIELD
SPRINGFIELD
18 TO 20 SIZE

Grade or Name — Description		ABP	Ex-Fn	Mint
Aaron Bagg, 7J, KW, KS	★	$225	$450	$575
Frederick Billings, 15J, KW, KS	★	225	450	575
E. W. Bond, 15-17J, 3/4	★★★	500	800	1,100
E. W. Bond, 18J, Adj., GJS, 3/4	★★★	600	900	1,200
J. A. Briggs, 11J, KW, KS, from back	★★	300	600	775

🕭 Some grades are not included. Their values can be determined by comparing with similar age, size, metal content, style, models and grades listed.

🕭 Watches listed in this book are priced at the collectable trade show level, as complete watches having an original 14k gold-filled case and *Key Wind* with silver, an original white enamel single sunk dial, and with the entire original movement in good working order with no repairs needed.

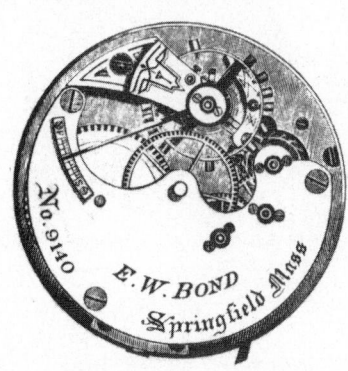

E.W. Bond movement, 18 size, 15 jewels, three-quarter plate.

Chas. E. Hayward, 18 size, 15jewels, key wind & set, note the hidden key, serial number 18733.

Grade or Name —Description	ABP	Ex-Fn	Mint
Albert Clark, 11-15J, KW, KS, from back, 3/4. ★★	$300	$425	$700
Homer Foot, 11-15J, KW, KS, from back, 3/4 ★	225	375	500
Herman Gerz, 11J, KW, KS ★	225	375	500
John Hancock, 7J, KW, KS	125	225	300
John Hancock, 7J, KW, KS, Silveroid	100	200	250
John Hancock, 7J, KW, KS, Coin.	100	225	300
Chas. E. Hayward, 11-15J, KW, KS, long balance cock	175	325	400
Chas. E. Hayward, 11-15J, KW, KS, Coin	175	325	400
J. L. King, 15-17J, KW, KS, from back, 3/4. ★	400	625	900
New York Watch Co., 7 11J, KW, KS. ★	200	325	500
New York Watch Co., 15-19J, KW, KS, **Wolf's Teeth winding,** (Serial #s below 75) (20 lignes) ★★★★★	1,200	2,025	2,750
New York Watch Co., 15-19J, KW, KS, **Wolf's Teeth winding,** all original (20 lignes) ★★★★	850	1,225	1,800
H. G. Norton, 15J, KW, KS, from back, 3/4. ★	165	325	400
H. G. Norton, 17J, KW, KS, from back, 3/4. ★	165	325	400
H. G. Norton, 19J, KW, KS, from back, 3/4. ★★★	475	625	825

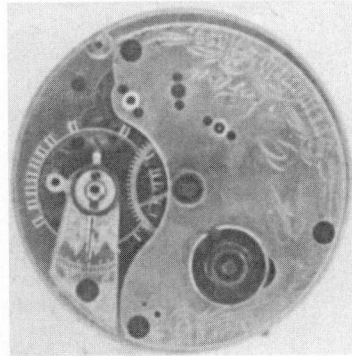

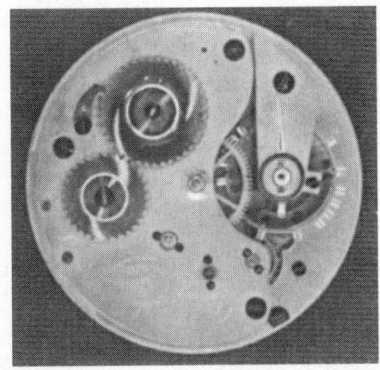

H. G. Norton, 18 size, 15 Jewels, three-quarter plate, gold escape wheel, serial number 6592.

SPRINGFIELD, (20 lignes), 15-19 jewels, stem wind, hunting case, note wolf teeth winding, serial number 978.

State Street movement, 18 size, 15 jewels, three-quarter plate.

Theo E. Studley movement, 18 size, 15 jewels, key wind & set, full plate.

Grade or Name — Description		ABP	Ex-Fn	Mint
J.C.Perry, 15J	★	$100	$225	$350
J. C. Perry, 15J, Silveroid	★	100	200	250
Railway, 15J, KW, FULL, Coin	★★★	750	1,025	1,600
Railway, 15J, KW, KS, FULL	★★★	650	925	1,500
William Romp, 15J, KW, KS from back, 3/4	★★	300	525	775
Geo. Sam Rice, 7J, KW, KS	★	150	325	400
Springfield, 15J, KW, KS, from back, ADJ, **Wolf teeth winding**, serial Nos. below 1, 000, (20 lignes)	★★★	800	1,125	1,550
Springfield, 19J, KW, KS, from back, ADJ, **Wolf teeth winding**, serial Nos. below 1, 000, (20 lignes)	★★★	900	1,425	1,800
State Street, 11J, 3/4, SW	★★	200	425	525
State Street, 15J, 3/4, SW	★★	250	450	650
Theo E. Studley, 15J, KW, Coin		125	225	300
Theo E. Studley, 15J, KW, KS		125	225	300
George Walker, 17J, KW, 3/4, ADJ	★	275	375	550
Chester Woolworth, 15J, KW, KS		125	225	300
Chester Woolworth, 11J, KW, KS		100	175	250
Chester Woolworth, 11J, KW, KS, Silveroid		100	175	200
Chester Woolworth, 11J, KW, KS, ADJ		110	200	275
#4, 15J, ADJ, KW, KS		110	175	275
#5, 15J, KW, KS		100	160	200
#6, 11J, KW, KS		100	160	200
#6, 11J, KW, KS, Silveroid		100	160	200

🕮 Some KW, KS watches made by the New York Watch Co. have a hidden key. If you unscrew the crown, and the crown comes out as a key, add $100 to the listed value.

🕮 Watches listed in this book are priced at the collectable trade show level, as **complete** watches having an original 14k gold-filled case and *Key Wind* with silver, an original white enamel single sunk dial, and with the entire original movement in good working order with no repairs needed.

🕮 This book endeavours to be a GUIDE or helpful manual and offers a wealth of material to be used as a tool not as a absolute document. Price Guides are like watches the worst may be better than none at all, but at best cannot be expected to be 100% accurate.

🕮 Characteristics of watches differ for the same age of both case and movement, because these features vary it may not be accurate to date a watch by one single influence. Example: the second hand was *not* commonly found on watches before 1750, but common about 1800. The first second hand appeared in 1665 and another in 1690. Therefore statements are broad rather than accurate.

🕮 A collector should expect to pay modestly higher prices at local shops.

NON-MAGNETIC WATCH CO.

Geneva and America
1887-1905

The Non-Magnetic Watch Co. sold and imported watches from the Swiss as well as contracted watches made in America. Geneva Non-Magnetic marked watches appear to be the oldest type of movement. This company sold a full line of watches, high grade to low grade, as well as repeaters and ladies watches. An advertisement appeared in the monthly journal of "Locomotive Engineers" in 1887. The ad states that the "Paillard's patent non-magnetic watches are uninfluenced by magnetism of electricity." Each watch contains the Paillard's patent non-magnetic, inoxidizable compensation balance and hairspring. An ad in 1888 shows prices for 16 size Swiss style watches as low as $15 for 7 jewels and as high as $135 for 20 jewels.

18 SIZE
(must be marked Paillard's Patent)

Grade or Name —Description	ABP	Ex-Fn	Mint
Elgin, 17J, FULL, SW, LS, OF	$95	$175	$200
Elgin, 17J, FULL, SW, LS, HC	125	225	300
Elgin, 15J, FULL, SW, LS, OF	100	150	200
Elgin, 15J, FULL, SW, LS, HC	125	225	300
Illinois, 24J, GJS, NI, Adj.5P, OF	800	1,225	1,800
Illinois, 24J, GJS, NI, Adj.5P, HC ★★	1,000	1,525	2,200
Illinois, 23J, GJS, NI, Adj.5P, OF	700	925	1,200
Illinois, 23J, GJS, NI, Adj.5P, HC ★★★	1,600	2,025	2,600
Illinois, 21J, GJS, NI, Adj.5P, OF	350	475	700
Illinois, 21J, GJS, NI, Adj.5P, HC	400	525	800
Illinois, 17J, NI, ADJ, OF	125	200	250
Illinois, 17J, NI, ADJ, HC	175	275	350
Illinois, 15J, NI, OF	100	175	200
Illinois, 15J, NI, HC	125	225	250
Illinois, 11J, OF	100	150	185
Illinois, 11J, HC	125	200	225

Non-Magnetic watch Co., 15 size, 15 jewels, gold jewel settings, Adj.5p, Hunting Case, by Peoria Watch Co.

Non-Magnetic Watch Co., 18size, 21 Ruby jewels,Adj.5p, open face, note "Paillard engraved on movement, made by Illinois Watch Co.

𝒢𝒻 Watches listed in this book are priced at the collectable trade show level, as complete watches having an original 14k gold-filled case and *Key Wind* with silver, an original white enamel single sunk dial, and with the entire original movement in good working order with no repairs needed.

Non-Magnetic Watch Co., 18 size, min repeater, jeweled through to the hammers, s#6,870

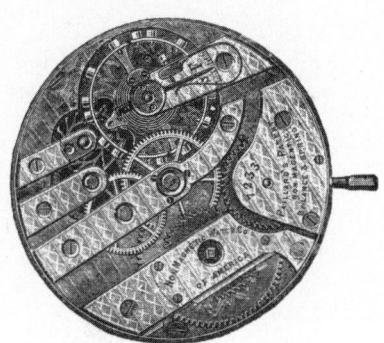

Non-Magnetic Watch Co., 18 size, 16 jewels, Bar bridge model, example of a Swiss Ebauche.

Grade or Name — Description	ABP	Ex-Fn	Mint
Peoria, 17J, FULL, SW, LS, Adj., OF	$175	$375	$600
Peoria, 15J, FULL, SW, LS, Adj., OF	150	325	475
Peoria, 15J, FULL, SW, LS, Adj., HC	250	425	525
Peoria, 11J, FULL, SW, LS, OF	110	275	325
Peoria, 11J, FULL, SW, LS, HC	175	325	375
Swiss, 16J, 3/4 plate, SW, LS, Adj., OF	100	175	200
Swiss, 16J, 3/4 plate, SW, LS, Adj., HC	100	200	225
Swiss, 15-16J, bar bridge, SW, LS, Adj., OF	100	175	210
Swiss, 15-16J, bar bridge, SW, LS, Adj., HC	100	200	225
Swiss, 11J, 3/4 plate, SW, LS, OF, HC	100	200	225
Swiss, 11J, bar bridge, SW, LS, OF, HC	100	200	225
Swiss, **min repeater**, jewelled through to the hammers, 14K case, OF, HC	2,200	3,500	5,000

Non-Magnetic Watch Co., 18 size, 17 Ruby jewels, HC, adjusted, made by Elgin Watch Co.

Non-Magnetic Watch Co., 16 size, 21 Ruby jewels, OF, adjusted, made by Illinois Watch Co. **Model 5, G# 179.**

🕰 Watches listed in this book are priced at the collectable fair market value at the Trade Show level, as complete watches having an original 14k gold filled case, KEY WIND with silver, an original white enamel single sunk dial, and with the entire original movement in good working order with no repairs needed, unless otherwise noted.

Non-Magnetic Watch Co., 16 size, 3/4 plate, 16 jewels, lever set, gilded, hunting case, adjusted, "Paillard's Patent, Balance And Spring" engraved on movement, S# 251568. Swiss made.

Non-Magnetic Watch Co., 16 size, 1/2 plate, 15-20 jewels, note "Paillard's Patent. HC Balance And Spring" engraved on movement. Swiss made.

16 SIZE
(must be marked Paillard's Patent)

Grade or Name —Description	ABP	Ex-Fn	Mint
Elgin, 21J, ADJ 5P, OF	$175	$325	$425
Elgin, 21J, ADJ 5P, HC	300	525	625
Elgin, 17J, ADJ 5P, OF	75	175	275
Elgin, 17J, ADJ 5P, HC	100	225	375
Illinois, 21J, GJS, 3/4, DR, Adj.6P, OF	200	375	525
Illinois, 21J, GJS, 3/4, DR, Adj.6P, HC	300	525	825
Illinois, 17J, 3/4, DR, ADJ, OF	75	175	300
Illinois, 17J, 3/4, DR, ADJ, HC	125	250	375
Illinois, 15J, HC	95	175	275
lllinois, 15J, OF	60	125	200
Illinois, 11J, OF	55	125	200
Illinois, 11J, HC	70	175	250
Swiss, 20J, GJS, DR, Adj.6P, NI, 1/2 , OF	80	175	250
Swiss, 20J, GJS, DR, Adj.6P, NI, 1/2, HC	80	175	275
Swiss, 18J, GJS, DR, Adj.6P, NI, 1/2, OF	100	175	275
Swiss, 18J, GJS, DR, Adj.6P, NI, 1/2, HC	150	200	310
Swiss, 16J, GJS, DR, Adj.6P, NI, 1/2, OF	70	125	200
Swiss, 16J, GJS, DR, Adj.6P, NI, 1/2, HC	90	150	225
Swiss, 16J, DR, adjusted, gilded, 3/4, OF	50	125	200
Swiss, 16J, DR, adjusted, gilded, 3/4, HC	70	175	250
Swiss, 7-11J, gilded, 3/4, OF	40	100	150
Swiss, 7-11J, gilded, 3/4, HC	70	150	225

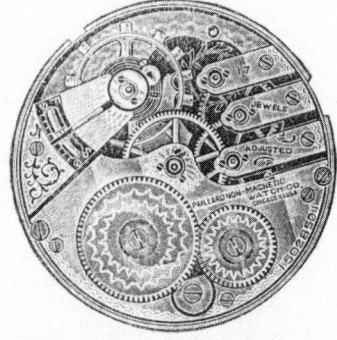

Non-Magnetic Watch Co., 16 size, 17J., Three finger bridge design, HC, by Elgin W. Co.

Non-Magnetic Watch Co., 16 size, 17J., 3/4 Plate design, HC,. by Elgin W. Co

OTAY WATCH CO.

Otay, California
1889-1894

This company produced about 1,000 watches with a serial number range of 1,000 to 1,500 and 30,000 to 31,000. The company was purchased by a Japanese manufacturer in 1894. Names on Otay movements include: Golden Gate, F. A. Kimball, Native Sun, Overland Mail, R. D. Perry, and P. H. Wheeler. Machinery sold to Osaka of Japan. Only a few watches were made. Osaka watches look about the same as Otay watches.

Otay Watch Co. Dial; note hunting case style and lever for setting hands.

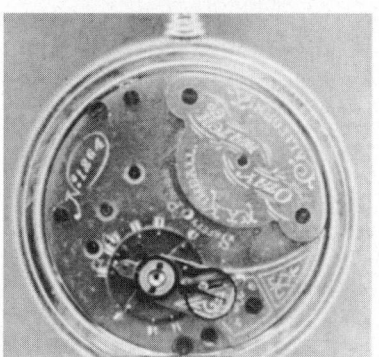

Otay Watch Co., F. A. Kimball, 18 size, 15 jewels, lever set, hunting, serial number 1,264.

18 SIZE

Grade or Name —Description		ABP	Ex-Fn	Mint
California, 15J., LS, NI, HC	★★★	$2,000	$3,750	$4,750
Golden Gate, 15J, LS, NI, HC	★★★	2,200	4,250	5,250
F. A. Kimball, 15J, LS, Gilt, HC	★★	1,500	2,750	3,250
Native Son, 15J, LS, NI, NC	★★	3,000	4,750	5,750
Native Son, 15J, LS, NI, **2-tone** movement, NC	★★★★	3,500	5,250	6,250
Overland Mail, 15J, LS, NI, NC	★★★	2,600	4,250	5,250
R. D. Perry, 15J, LS, Gilt, NC	★★	1,500	2,450	3,250
P. H. Wheeler, 15J, LS, Gilt, NC	★★	1,500	2,450	3,250
Sunset, 7J, Gilt, NC	★★	1,800	2,850	3,750
Osaka W. Co., 15J, NI, or gilt, (made in Japan)	★★★★	3,200	5,250	6,250

D.D.PALMER WATCH CO.

Waltham, Massachusetts
1864-1875

In 1858, at age 20, Mr. Palmer opened a small jewelry store in Waltham, Mass. Here he became interested in pocket chronometers. At first he bought the balance and jewels from Swiss manufacturers. In 1864 he took a position with the American Watch Co. and made the chronometers in his spare time (only about 25 produced). They were,18S, 3/4 plate, gilded, key wind, and some were nickel. At first they were fusee driven, but he mainly used going barrels. About 1870, Palmer started making lever watches and by 1875 he left the American Watch Co. and started making a 105 keywind, gilded movement, and a 16S, 3/4 plate, gilt and nickel, and a stem wind of his own invention (a vibrating crown wheel). In all he made about 1,500 watches. The signature appearing on the watches was "Palmer W. Co. Wal., Mass".

He basically had three grades of watches: Fine-Solid Nickel; Medium-Nickel Plated; and Medium-Gold Gilt. They were made in open-face and hunter cases.

D. D. Palmer Watch Co., 18 size, 15 jewels, Palmer's Pat. Stem Winder on movement, serial number 1098.

Grade or name —Description	ABP	Ex-Fn	Mint
10-16S, 15-17J, 3/4 plate, spring detent chronometer ...... ★★★★	$4,000	$6,000	$8,500
16-18S, 15-17J, NI, OF, 18K .... ★★★	2,600	3,500	6,500

PEORIA WATCH CO.

Peoria, Illinois
1885- 1895

The roots of this company began with the Independent Watch Co. (1875 - 1881). The watches marked Mark Twain were made by the Fredonia Watch Co. (1881 - 1885). Peoria Watch Co. opened Dec. 19, 1885, and made one model of railroad watches in about 1887.

Peoria watches were 18S, quick train, 15 jewel, and all stem wind. These watches are hard to find, as only about 3,000 were made. Peoria also made railroad watches for A. C. Smith's Non-Magnetic Watch Co. of America, from 1884-1888. The 18 size watches were full plate, adjusted, and had a whiplash regulator.

The Peoria Watch Co. closed in 1889, having produced about 47,000 watches.

Peoria Watch Co., 18 size, 15 jewels, nickel damaskeening plates, hunting, note patented regulator, teeth only part way around the wheel, serial number 11,532.

Grade or Name — Description	ABP	Ex-En	Mint
18S, 9-11J,SW,OF	$150	$325	$425
18S, 15J, SW, personalized name	250	425	525
18S, Peoria W. Co., 15J, SW, OF	200	375	475
18S Peoria W. Co., 15J, SW, HC	250	425	550
18S, Peoria W. Co., 15J, SW, low S# . . . . ★	450	725	925
18S, Anti-Magnetic, 15J, OF	200	375	475
18S, Anti-Magnetic, 15J, HC	285	475	575
18S, Anti-Magnetic, 15J, For Railway Service, OF . . . . ★	385	725	925
18S, Anti-Magnetic, 15J, For Railway Service, HC . . . . ★	475	825	1,025
18S, Superior Quality Anti-Magnetic, 15J, NI, SW, GJS, AdJ.5P, OF . . . . ★★	500	825	1,125
18S, Superior Quality Anti-Magnetic, 15J, NI, SW, GJS, Adj.5P, HC . . . . ★★★	550	925	1,225
18S, For Railway Service, 15J, NI, GJS, Adj.5P, OF . . . . ★	385	725	925
18S, For Railway Service, 15J, NI, GJS, Adj.5P, HC . . . . ★	450	825	1,025

PHILADELPHIA WATCH Co.

Philadelphia, Pennsylvania
1868-1886

Eugene Paulus organized the Philadelphia Watch Co. about 1868. Most all the parts were made in Switzerland, and finished and cased in this country. The International Watch Co. is believed to have manufactured the movements for Philadelphia Watch Co. Estimated total production of the company is 12,000 watches.

Issued by the U.S. Patent Office, August 25, and November 3, 1808.

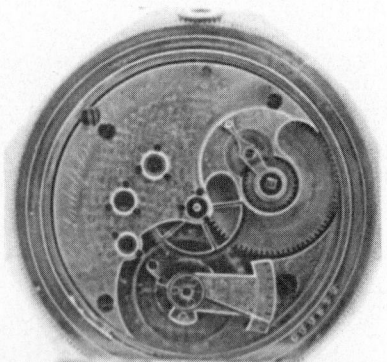

Philadelphia Watch Co., 16 size, 15 jewels, gold jewel settings, hunting case model. "Paulus Patents 1868. Aug. 25th, Nov. 3rd" on movement, serial number 5751.

NOV. 1871 advertising 15,16,19, &21 size watches for sale at their New York City and Philadelphia offices.

Grade or Name —Description	ABP	Ex-Fn	Mint
18S, 15J, SW, HC . . . . ★	$225	$350	$500
18S, 15J, KW, KS . . . . ★	225	350	500
18S, 15J, SW, OF . . . . ★	200	300	450
18S, HC, KW, KS, **18K** original case marked Philadelphia Watch Co . . . . ★★	1,000	1,500	2,000
18S, 11J, KW, KS . . . . ★	100	150	250
16S, 15J, KW, KS . . . . ★	150	200	275
16S, 19J, KW, KS, GJS . . . . ★	300	550	700
8S-6S, 11J, HC . . . . ★	100	200	250
8S-6S, 15J, HC . . . . ★	125	225	275
8S-6S, Paulus, 19J, KW, KS . . . . ★	200	300	475
OOO/ S, 7J, HC, PS . . . . ★	125	250	300

JAMES & HENRY PITKIN

Hartford, Connecticut
New York, New York
1838-1852

Henry Pitkin was the first to attempt to manufacture watches by machinery. The machines were of Pitkin's own design and very crude, but he had some brilliant ideas. His first four workers were paid $30 a year plus their board. After much hardship, the first watches were produced in the fall of 1838. The watches had going barrels, not the fusee and chain, and the American flag was engraved on the plates to denote they were American made and to exemplify the true spirit of American independence in watchmaking.

The first 50 watches were stamped with the name "Henry Pitkin." Others bore the firm name "H. & J. F. Pitkin." The movements were about 16S and 3/4 plate. The plates were rolled brass and stamped out with dies. The pinions were lantern style with eight leaves. The movement had a slow train of 14,400 beats per hour. Pitkin's first plan was to make the ends of the pinions conical and let them run in the ends of hardened steel screws, similar to the Marine clock balances. A large brass setting was put in the plates and extended above the surface. Three screws, with small jewels set in their ends, were inserted so that they closed about the pivot with very small end shake. This proved to be too expensive and was used in only a few movements. Next, he tried to make standard type movements extend above the plates with the end shake controlled by means of a screw running down into the end of the pivots, reducing friction. This "capped jewel train" was used for a while before he adopted the standard ways of jeweling. The escape wheels were the star type, English style. The balance was made of gold and steel. These movements were fire gilded and not interchangeable. The dials, hands, mainsprings and hairsprings were imported. The rounded pallets were manufactured by Pitkin, and the cases for his watches were made on the premises. As many as 900 watches could have been made by Pitkin.

Grade or Name —Description		ABP	Ex-Fn	Mint
Henry Pitkin S#1-50	★★★★★	$30,000	$66,000	$110,000
H. & J. F. Pitkin, S#51-377	★★★★	20,000	33,000	66,000
Pitkin & Co., **New York**, S#378-900	★★★★	6,000	13,200	22,000
W. Pitkin, Hartford, Conn., S# approx. 40,000, fusee lever, KW, Coin	★★	1,400	2,200	3,850

H. & J. F. Pitkin, about 16 size, engraved on movement.
"H & J. F. PITKIN DETACHED LEVER", key wind & set.

Movements marked with New York are English made. (Imports)

ALBERT H. POTTER WATCH Co.

New York, New York 1855 – 1875

Albert Potter started his apprenticeship in 1852. When this was completed he moved to New York to take up watchmaking on his own. He made about 35 to 40 watches in USA that sold for $225 to $350. Some were chronometers, some were lever escapements, key wind, gilded movements, some were fusee driven, both bridge and 3/4 plate. Potter was a contemporary of Charles Fasoldt and John Mulford, both horological inventors from Albany, N. Y. Potter moved to Cuba in 1861 but returned to New York in 1868. In 1872 he worked in Chicago and formed the Potter Brothers Company with his brother William. He moved to Geneva in about 1876 to make his high grade Swiss timepieces and about 600 of these watches were made.(For futher information on Potter Geneva timepieces, SEE European Section)

Below U.S. mfg.

Grade or Name — Description		ABP	Ex-Fn	Mint
18S, BRG lever, Chronometer, signed A. H. Potter,				
New York 18K Potter case, **U.S. mfg** . . . . ★★★★★	$12,000	$22,500	$32,500
18S, BRG lever with wind indicator, **18K** Potter case . . . . ★★★	7,000	17,500	22,500
18S-20S, **Tourbillon**, signed A. H. Potter, **Boston**, gilded,				
18K Potter case, **U.S. mfg** . . . . ★★★★★	30,000	52,500	77,500

below GENEVA Mfg. (Dollar Watch)

Grade or Name — Description		ABP	Ex-Fn	Mint
16S, "Charmilles," 3/4 plate, Geneva, (Dollar Watch) . . . . ★★	$325	$500	$850

(Note: For futher information on Potter **Geneva** timepieces, **SEE European Section**)

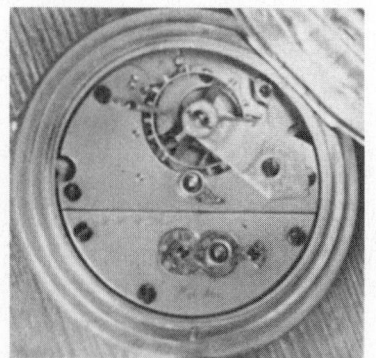

A.H. Potter Watch co., BOSTON, 18 size, S#5, about 6J., detent escapement, note similarity to E. Howard & CO.(early ebauche?), not a typical A.H.Potter movement.

"Charmilles Geneva" on dial, made in Charmilles Switzerland by J.J.Badollet Co factory, 165, 7-1J., 3/4 plate, Gun Metal case, (dollar watch), Ca. 1890-95.

THE "CHARMILLES" MOVEMENT

is made of **solid nickel**, handsomely damaskeened. The center of the case is a part of the movement, thus insuring greater strength and reducing cost. It is 16 size ¾ plate, Open Face, Stemwinding and Pendant Hand Setting; Straight line Lever Escapement; Seven Jewels; Non-Magnetic Balance, Hair Spring and Escapement; is non-magnetic and non-oxidizable. The wheels and pinions as well as all parts are better finished than in higher priced movements, *and guaranteed perfect timekeepers.*

"Charmilles" **AD Ca. 1896**. In Marshall Field & Co. sales catalog prices from $8.00 to $15.00.

GEORGE P. REED

Boston, Massachusetts 1865 – 1885

In 1854, George P. Reed entered the employment of Dennison, Howard and Davis, in Roxbury, Mass., and moved with the company to Waltham, Mass. Here he was placed in charge of the pinion finishing room. While there he invented and received a patent for the mainspring barrel and maintiming power combination. This patent was dated February 18, 1857. Reed returned to Roxbury with Howard who purchased his patented barrel. He stayed with the Howard factory as foreman and adjuster until 1865, when he left for Boston to start his own business.

He obtained a patent on April 7, 1868, for an improved chronometer escapement which featured simplified construction. He made about 100 chronometers with his improved escapement, to which he added a stem-wind device. His company turned out about 100 watches the first three years. Many of his watches run for two days and have up and down indicators. They are both 18S and 16S, 3/4 plate, nickel, and are artistically designed. Reed experimented with various combinations of lever and chronometer escapements. In all, about 350 watches were made.

Grade or Name —Description		ABP	Ex-Fn	Mint
18S, 15J, **pivoted detent** escapement, **18K case** . . . . ★★★★	$12,000	$32,000	$47,000
16S, 15J, LS, OF or HC, **with** chronometer, **18K case** . . . . . . ★★★	8,000	17,000	27,000
16S, 15J, LS, OF or HC, not chronometer, **18K case** . . . . ★★★	7,000	14,000	22,000
16S, 15J, LS, OF, 31 day calendar, "Monitor", **18K case** . . . . . . ★★★	8,000	17,000	24,000
16S, 15-17J, Wind Indicator, "Monitor", **14K, OF** . . . . ★★★	7,000	15,000	22,000

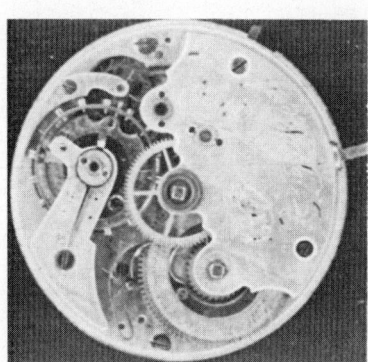

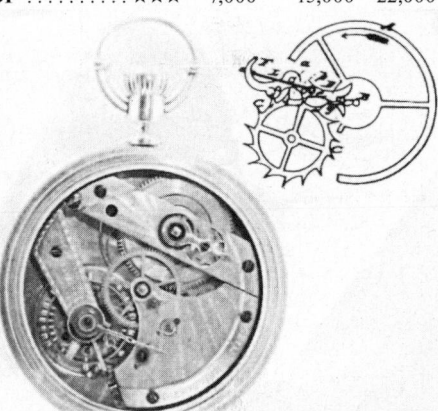

George P Reed, 18 size, 15 jewels. key & stem wind, key & lever set, lever escapement, 48 hour up and down wind indicator, serial number 262.

George P. Reed, 18 size, 15 jewels, key & stem wind, key & lever set, Chronometer escapement, serial number 5. Note: This escapement was used on maybe 20 watches.

George P. Reed, Reeds Two Days, Monitor, No. 335, engraved on movement, 31 calendar, 18-16 Size.

George P. Reed Boston, Monitor, 18-16 size, 15 jewels wind indicator, serial # 322.

ROCKFORD WATCH CO.
Rockford, Illinois
1873-1915

The Rockford Watch Company's equipment was bought from the Cornell Watch Co., and two of Cornell's employees, C. W. Parker and P. H. Wheeler, went to work for Rockford. The factory was located 93 miles from Chicago on the Rock River. The first watch was placed on the market on May 1, 1876. They were key wind, 18S, full plate expansion balance & dials made by outside contract. By 1877 the company was making 3/4 plate nickel movements that fit standard size cases. Three railroads came through Rockford, and the company always advertised to the railroad and the demand was very popular with them. The company had some problems in 1896, and the name changed to Rockford Watch Co. Ltd. It closed in 1915.

ROCKFORD ESTIMATED SERIAL NUMBERS & PRODUCTION DATES

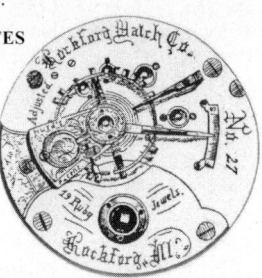

DATE—SERIAL #	DATE—SERIAL #	DATE-SERIAL #	DATE-SERIAL #
1876— 1,200	1886—267,100	1896—470,000	1906—670,000
1877— 22,600	1887—287,200	1897—490.000	1907—690,000
1878— 43,000	1888—308,300	1898—510,000	1908—734,000
1879— 64,000	1889—328,400	1899—530,000	1909—790,000
1880—95,000	1890—349,500	1900—550,000	1910—824,000
1881— 136,000	1891—369,600	1901—570,000	1911—880,000
1882—167,000	1892—390,700	1902—590,000	1912—936000
1883—208.000	1893—410,800	1903—610,000	1913—958000
1884—229,000	1894—430,900	1904—630,000	1914—980,000
1885—240,000	1895—450,000	1905—650,000	1915-1,000,000

The above list is provided for detemining the APPROXIMATE age of your watch. Match serial number with date. Watches were not necessarily sold in the exact order of manufactured date.

ABOVE:
Early Rockford, note RUBY JEWELS made in both nickel & gilt, stem-wind only, Ca. 1876

From Rockford Catalog
Early 18 Size Regulators

Grade or Name —Description	ABP	Ex-Fn	Mint
Belmont USA, 21J, LS, OF, NI, M#7	$250	$400	$500
Chronometer, 17J, ADJ, OF, G925. .... ★	400	600	850
Dome Model, 9J, brass plates. .... ★	150	300	425

Rockford Watch Co., Enamel Railroad double sunk dial, with two hour hands for a second time zone the hour hand at 2 O'clock is BLUE, the hour hand at 3 O'clock is RED.

16-SIZE ROCKFORD

OUR SPECIAL No. 1000 21 JEWELS

Hunting or Open Face, nickel, 21 ruby and sapphire jewels in settings, **adjusted to heat and cold.** Compensating balance, Breguet hair spring, safety pinion, patent micrometric regulator, gold lettering, handsomely damaskeened, double sunk glass enameled dial, **pendant set.**

Above: 1913 AD

Note: S # 825,020, about the same as grade 645.

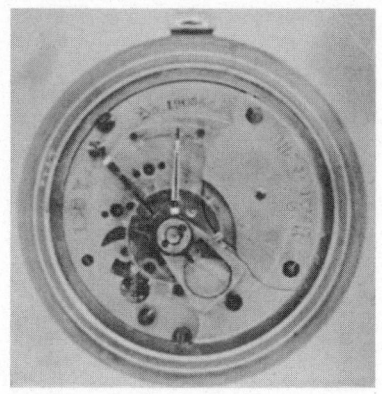

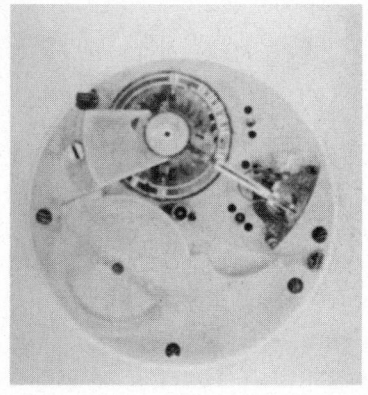

Rockford Watch Co., 18 size, 11 jewels, hunting, Model number 6, exposed escapement, serial number 190,564

Special Railway 18 size, 17 jewels, hunting, Model number 8, serial number 344,551.

Grade or Name —Description	ABP	Ex-Fn	Mint
King Edward, 21J, **Plymouth W. Co., 14K HC**	$675	$1,200	$1,600
King Edward, 21J, **(Sears) Plymouth W. Co.** GJS, ADJ, NI, OF.	350	600	800
King Edward, 21J, **(Sears), Plymouth. W. Co.** GJS, ADJ, NI, HC	400	800	900
Nacirema is American backward, on dial Nacirema Watch Co	125	200	300
Paxton's, 21J, **(Special on dial),** OF	350	500	725
Pennsylvania Special, 17J, LS, Adj., OF ★★★	2,000	3,500	4,500
Pennsylvania Special, 25J, LS, Adj.6P, tu-tone, OF ★★★★	6,000	10,000	15,000
Railway King, 21J,OF. ★	425	800	1,200
The Ramsey Watch, 11J, NI, KW or SW	125	200	300
The Ramsey Watch, 15J, NI, KW or SW	125	200	300
The Ramsey Watch, M#7, 21J, OF, NI, ADJ	350	600	750

↩ Generic, nameless or unmarked grades for watch movements are listed under the Company name or initials of the Company, etc. by size, jewel count and description.

	ABP	Ex-Fn	Mint
Rockford Early KW-KS, M#1 -2, with low Serial #S less than 500 ★★	$800	$1,200	$1,700
Rockford Early KW-KS, M#1 -2, with low Serial #S from 500-1,000 ★	425	650	950
Rockford Early KW-KS, M#1 -2, with **reversible case**	500	700	1,000
Rockford,7J,KW,FULL,OF	100	200	300
Rockford, 7J, KW, FULL, Silveroid	100	200	300
Rockford, 9J, SW, FULL, HC	100	200	300
Rockford, M#1, 9J, KW, FULL, HC	100	200	300
Rockford, 11J, KW, Coin HC	150	250	350
Rockford, 11J,SW,FULL,OF	100	175	225
Rockford,13J,HC	125	200	300
Rockford, 11-13J, M#6, exposed escape wheel, FULL, HC ★	250	400	650
Rockford, M#1-2, 11J, KW, FULL.	150	250	350
Rockford, M#1-2, 11J, transition case, FULL	100	200	250
Rockford, 9J,SW/ KW, **M#5, 3/4 Plate**, HC Coin	250	400	550
Rockford, 11J, SW/KW, **M#5, 3/4 Plate**, HC Coin	275	450	600
Rockford, 15J, SW/KW, **M#5, 3/4 Plate**, HC Coin	350	475	650
Rockford, 15J, SW, FULL	100	200	225
Rockford, 15J, KW, FULL, **multi-color dial**	400	600	1,100
Rockford, 15J, SW, 2-Tone movement	150	250	400
Rockford, 15J, KW, FULL, marked- **ADJ**.	150	250	400
Rockford, 15J, KW/SW	100	200	275
Rockford, 15J, KW/SW, Silveroid	100	175	225

Rockford movement, 18 size, 7 jewels, model 5, hunting, lever set, three-quarter plate.

Grade 900, 18 size, 24J., gold jewel settings, Adj.5p.OF Warning: 24J. fakes have been made from 21J. movements. The fakes are missing the eliptical jewel setting on the barrel bridge.

Grade or Name — Description	ABP	Ex-Fn	Mint
Rockford, 15J, M#6, exposed escapement wheel, FULL, HC, LS, nickel mvt .... ★	$300	$400	$600
Rockford, 15J, M#6, exposed escapement wheel, FULL, HC, LS, gilded mvt .... ★	225	300	500
Rockford, 15J, M#6, exposed wheel, nickel mvt., Coin	175	275	400
Rockford, M#1, 15J, KW, FULL	100	200	250
Rockford, 16J, GJS, NI, DMK, SW	100	200	250
Rockford, 16J, GJS, NI, DMK, SW, Silveroid	100	175	225
Rockford,16J,GJS,NI,DMK,SW,COin	100	175	225
Rockford,17J,NI,DMK,SW,OF	100	175	225
Rockford, 17J, GJS, NI, DMK, SW, Adj.5P	110	200	275
Rockford, 17J, GJS, NI, SW, 2-Tone, OF	200	300	425
Rockford Early,19J, SW-KS, M#1-2, nickel, marked Ruby Jewels, ADJ, Serial # less than 100 .... ★★★★	2,600	3,500	5,200
Rockford, M#1-2, 19J, KS, gilt, marked Ruby Jewels, ADJ, HC .... ★★	1,800	2,500	3,000
Rockford, 21J, SW, Silveroid	225	350	500
Rockford, 21J, GJS, OF, Adj.5P, **wind indicator** .... ★★★	3,000	4,500	5,600
Rockford, 21J, SW, DMK, ADJ, HC	400	600	700
Rockford,21J,NI,DMK,ADJ,OF	300	400	600
Rockford, 21J, GJS, NI, DMK, Adj.5P, marked "RG' OF	400	500	650
Rockford, ("22J", marked,) GJS, Adj.5P, 2 tone, HC ..... ★★★	1,450	1,800	2,600
Rockford, ("22J", marked,) Adj, NI, SW, "RG," OF ..... ★★★	800	1,100	1,700
Rockford, 24J,GJS,SW,LS,Adj,5P,NI,DMK. .... ★★	1,500	2,500	3,500
Rockford, 25J, G#25, GJS, SW, LS, Adj.5P, NI, DMK ..... ★★★★	4,000	5,500	8,500
Rockford, 26J, G#25, GJS, SW, LS, Adj.5P, NI, DMK .... ★★★★★	9,000	12,000	21,000
R.W. Co., 7-9-11J, NI or Gilded	100	150	175
R.W. Co., 15J, NI or Gilded, OF	100	150	200
R.W. Co., 15J, NI or Gilded, HC...........................	100	175	225
R.W. Co., 15J, SW, **multi-color box hinged**, 14K, HC	2,000	3,500	4,000
R.W. Co., 16-17J, Adj, NI, OF.............................	100	175	225
R.W. Co., 16-17J, Adj, NI, HC	125	200	265
R.W. Co., 21J, Adj, NI, SW, OF	175	300	400
R.W. Co., 21J, Adj, NI, SW, HC	250	500	600

Note: Model is not the same defination as grade. A model may exist in many different grades or grade names (as Winnebago) and may be used in many different models (as model 1, 18 size, open or hunting case, model 1, in 16 size open or hunting case, model 1 in 12 size) etc..

LS/PS
SWITCH

Rockford Watch Co.. 18 size, 15 jewels, model #5, 3/4 plate, key & stem wind.

Rockford Watch Co., 18S, 11-15J., M# 7 & 8, SW, Note: LS/PS screw switch, G#68-69-85 HC & G#66-67-89 OF.

Grade or Name — Description	ABP	Ex-Fn	Mint
Special Railway, 17J, ADJ, 2-tone, SW, HC .... ★	$425	$575	$825
The Syndicate Watch Co., M#7, 15J, LS, NI, HC	175	300	400
Winnebago, 17J, LS, GJS, Adj.5P, DR, NI, DMK, HC	300	400	650
Winnebago, 17J, LS, GJS, Adj.5P, DR, NI, DMK, OF	200	350	500
24 Hour Dial, 15J,SW or KW............ ★★	250	600	750
40, 15J, M#3, HC .... ★★	275	450	650
43, 15J, M#3, HC, **2-Tone**................	135	200	325
60, 7J., **2-tone**.................	125	175	275
66 & 67=11J, 89=15J., M#7, **LS/PS screw switch, OF**........	100	150	225
66, 11J, M#7, HC, Silveroid	100	175	200
68=11J, 69-85=15J., M#8, **LS/PS screw switch**, HC	100	200	300
72, 15J, KW-SW, **exposed escapement**, HC........ ★	600	775	1,200
81, 9J, M#3, Gilt, HC	100	200	300
82, **Special**, 21J, SW................ ★★★	700	900	1,500
83, 15J, M#8, 2-Tone, HC................	150	250	370
93, 9J, M#8, Gilt, HC	125	200	300
94, 9J, M#7, OF..................	100	150	225
200, 17J, M#9, NI, LS, HC	125	200	300
205, 17J, M#9, NI, LS, OF	100	175	225
800, 24J, GJS, DR, Adj.5P, DMK, HC........ ★	1,500	2,000	3,000
805, 21J, GJS, Adj.5P, NI, DMK, marked "**RG**" HC	425	500	800
810, 21J, NI, DMK, ADJ, HC........	400	550	700
820, 17J, SW, HC .... ★★	300	400	600
825, 17J, FULL, HC	100	200	300
830, 17J, FULL, HC	100	200	300
835, 17J, FULL, HC................ ★	125	200	300
845, 21J, GJS, FULL, HC................ ★	425	550	800
870, 7J, FULL, HC................	100	200	300

IMPORTANT NOTE - Railroad terms as used in this book:

1. **RAILROAD STANDARDS** = A commission or board appointed by the railroad companies outlined a set of **guidelines** to be accepted or approved by each railroad line.

2. **RAILROAD APPROVED** = A **LIST** of watches each railroad line would approve if purchased by their employee's. (this list changed through the years).

3. **RAILROAD GRADE** = A watch made by manufactures to meet or exceed the guidelines set by the railroad **standards**. Grades such as 992, Vanguard and B.W. Raymond, etc.

☞ Some GRADES exceeded the R.R. standards such as 23 jewels, diamond end stone, gold train, raised gold jewel settings, double sunk dial and the list goes on. Examples: such as Veritas, Sangamo, 950 & Riverside Maximus and many others.

Grade or Name — Description		ABP	Ex-Fn	Mint
890, **24J**, GJS, DR, Adj.5P, NI, DMK, **HC**	★★	$1,500	$2,200	$2,700
900, **24J**, GJS, DR, Adj.5P, NI, DMK, OF	★★	1,500	2,200	2,700
900, **24J**, GJS, DR, Adj.5P, **14K**, OF case	★★	2,000	3,000	3,500
905, 21J, GJS, DR, Adj.5P, NI, DMK, OF	★	300	400	600
910, 21J, NI, DMK, ADJ, OF		250	350	500
912, 21J, Adj.5P, LS, OF	★★	485	650	850
915, 17J, M# **7 & 9**, SW, OF	★★★	700	900	1,400
918, **24J**, GJS, DR, Adj.5P, NI, DMK, OF	★★	1,500	2,000	2,500
918, 21J, NI, GJS, Adj.5P, DR, OF		300	400	600
918, 21J, NI, GJS, Adj-SP, DR, , OF Coin		275	350	450
920&930,17J,OF		175	250	350
925&935,17J,OF		100	175	200
945, 21J, M#9, SW, OF		225	300	425
950-marked, 21J, GJS, Adj.5P, DR, OF, **Wind Indicator**	★★★	3,000	4,500	6,000
970, 7J, OF		100	125	175
970, 7J, OF Silveroid case		100	125	150

16 SIZE
(most HC grade numbers end with 0 & most OF grade numbers end with 5

Grade or Name — Description		ABP	Ex-Fn	Mint
Commodore Perry, 21J, GJS, GT, marked "**RG**", OF	★	$300	$400	$625
Commodore Perry, 15-17J, ADJ.		125	200	275
Cosmos, 17J, OF, GJS, LS, DMK, marked dial & mvt		250	350	600
Cosmos, 17J, **HC**, GJS, LS, DMK, marked dial & mvt		300	400	700
Doll Watch Co., 17J, marked dial & mvt., OF.	★★★	850	1,300	2,000
Doll Watch Co., 21J, marked dial & mvt., OF.	★★★	1,000	1,500	2,200
Doll Watch Co., 23J, marked dial & mvt., OF	★★★	1,500	2,500	3,000
Doll Watch Co-, 23J, (G#504-M# 4), triple signed, HC	★★★★	1,700	3,000	4,000
Dome Model, 15J		75	150	200
Dome Model, 17J		85	170	225
Dome Model, 17J, **2-tone**, HC		150	300	450
Herald Square, 7J, 3/4, OF		100	170	225
Iroquois, 17J, G# 630, DR, **14K, HC**		550	800	1,200
Iroquois, 17J, G# 635, DR, OF		200	300	400
Peerless, 17J, OF, NI, LS, DMK	★	150	285	400
Pocahontas, 17J, GJS, Adj.5P, DR, OF	★	200	350	550
Pocahontas, 17J, GJS, Adj.5P, DR, HC	★	275	450	700
Pocahontas, 21J, GJS, Adj.5P, DR, OF	★	300	600	750
Pocahontas, 21J, GJS, Adj.5P, DR, HC	★★	500	800	975
Prince of Wales (Sears), 21J, Plymouth W. Co., OF	★★	300	450	700
Prince of Wales (Sears), 21J, Plymouth W. Co., HC	★★	375	550	800

Grade 103, 16 size, 17 jewels, model 1, hunting case, serial number 384,857.

Cosmos movement, 16 size, 17 jewels, open face, gold jewel settings, grade 565, model 2.

Grade 500-HC, model 4, 16 size, 21 jewels, gold jewel settings, gold train, Adj6p, marked "RG," serial number 546,617, originally sold for about $100.00.

Grade 505-OF, model 5,16 size, 21 jewels, gold jewel settings, gold train, Adj6p, marked "RG," serial number 593,929, originally sold for about $100.00.

Grade or Name —Description	ABP	Ex-Fn	Mint
Rockford, 7J, 3/4, HC	$75	$200	$300
Rockford, 9J, 3/4, SW, OF	65	125	185
Rockford, 9J, SW, Silveroid	65	125	165
Rockford, 9J, SW, HC	85	200	300
Rockford, 11J, SW, Silveroid	65	125	175
Rockford, 11J, 3/4, HC	75	200	300
Rockford, 15J, 3/4, ADJ, OF	70	135	200
Rockford, 15J, 3/4, ADJ, Silveroid	65	125	175
Rockford, 15J, 3/4, ADJ, HC	75	200	325
Rockford, 16J, 3/4, SW, Silveroid	65	125	165
Rockford, 16J, 3/4, AD3, NI, DMK	65	125	175
Rockford, 17J, 3/4	65	125	175
Rockford, 17J, 3/4, **2-Tone**, marked **"RG"** ★	250	350	650
Rockford, 17J, BRG, Adj.3P, DR	125	175	250
Rockford, 17J, BRG, Silveroid	70	135	175
Rockford, 17J, 3/4, Silveroid	70	135	170
Rockford, 21J, 3/4, SW, Silveroid	250	300	400
Rockford, 21J, BRG, SW, Silveroid	250	300	400
Rockford, 21J, 3/4, GJS, Adj.5P	300	400	550
Rockford, 21J, BRG, GJS, Adj.5P, GT, DR	350	450	700
Winnebago, 17J, G#400, BRG, GJS, Adj.5P, NI, HC ★	250	400	650
Winnebago, 17J, G#405, BRG, GJS, Adj.5P, NI, OF	200	300	400
Winnebago, 21J, BRG, GJS, Adj.5P,NI ★	325	600	750
100, 16-17J, M#1, 3/4, **2-Tone**, HC	250	300	450
100S, 21J, Special, 3/4, LS, OF	300	400	575
102, 15J, M#1,HC ★	150	200	300
103, 15-17J, M#1,HC ★★	275	350	450
104, 11J, M#1,HC	75	200	250
110, 17J, 2 tone dome style mvt., HC ★	325	385	600
115-125, 17J, **Special**, HC ★★★	525	700	1,000
120-130, 17J, HC ★★★	425	550	875

𝒢 Generic, nameless or unmarked grades for watch movements are listed under the Company name or initials of the Company, etc. by size, jewel count and description.

𝒢 Pricing in this Guide are fair market price for complete watches which are reflected from the NAWCC National and regional shows.

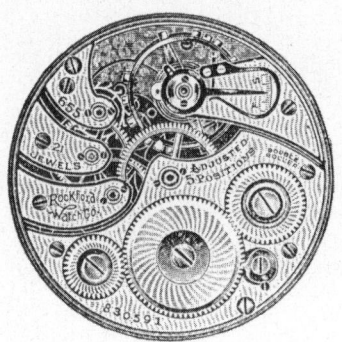

Rockford Watch Co., Pocahontas, 21 jewels., hunting case, bridge model, Adj.5P, serial # 670,203

Rockford Watch Co., 21j. Wind indicator, marked 655, adjusted to 5 positions, gold jewel settings, gold center wheel, double roller, Serial # 830,591.

Grade or Name —Description		ABP	Ex-Fn	Mint
400, 17J, NI, Adj.5P, GJS, DR, BRG, HC		$125	$200	$275
405, 17J, NI, Adj.5P, GJS, DR, BRG, OF		100	175	250
440, 17J, GJS, HC		125	200	275
445, 19J, GJS, OF	★★	900	1,000	1,300
500-501, 21J, BRG, NI, GJS, Adj.5P, GT, HC	★★★	600	800	1,200
505, 21J, BRG, NI, GJS, Adj.5P, GT, OF	★★★	600	800	1,200
510, 21J, BRG, NI, GJS, Adj.5P, GT, HC	★★★	600	900	1,200
515-525-545, 21J, 3/4, OF		350	450	725
520, 21J, 3/4, HC		400	550	800
520-540, 21J, BRG, NI, GJS, Adj.5P, HC		450	600	800
525, 21J, M#5, GT, Adj.5P, OF	★	350	450	625
530, 21J, GJS, Adj.5P, marked "RG", 1W	★	450	550	900
535, 21J, 3/4, OF	★	300	400	600
537, 21J, OF, GJS, Adj.5P	★★★	1,000	1,200	1,900
540, 21J, GT, BRG, Adj.5P, HC	★	300	500	600
545, 21J, GT, BRG, Adj.5P, OF		275	400	550
561, 17J, BRG, HC		150	200	400
566, 17J, BRG, OF		150	200	325
572, 17J, BRG, NI, HC		150	200	350
573-575, 17J, 3/4 & BRG, NI, OF		150	200	325
578-579, 17J, PS, GJS	★★	300	400	600
584 15J, 3/4 NI, HC		100	200	300
585, 15J, 3/4, NI, OF		65	100	150
620, 21J, 3/4, HC	★	325	500	650
625, 21J, 3/4, OF	★	300	400	600
640, 21J, GT, 3/4, Adj.5P, HC	★	275	500	600
645, 21J, GT, 3/4, Adj.5P, OF		275	375	525
655, 21J, **Wind Indicator**, Adj.5P, **marked 655**, OF	★★	1,200	2,500	3,500
665, 17J, **Wind Indicator**, Adj, 5P, OF	★	1,000	2,000	3,000
700, 21J, Adj., BRG, HC		275	500	600
705, 21J, Adj., BRG, OF		250	375	475
810, 21J, 3/4, Adj. heat & cold, OF		275	375	500
1000, 21J, 3/4, Adj. heat & cold, OF	★★	325	485	750

☞ Watches listed in this book are priced at the collectable Trade Show level, as complete watches having an original 14k gold-filled case and Key Wind with silver, an original white enamel single sunk dial, and with the entire original movement in good working order with no repairs needed.

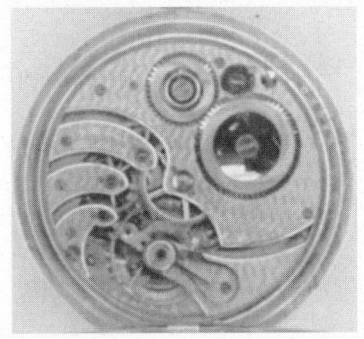

Rockford Watch Co., 12 size, 15 jewels, model 1, hunting, pendant set.

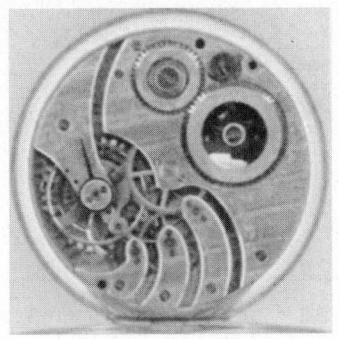

Rockford Watch Co., 12 size, 15 jewels, model 2, open face, pendant set.

12 SIZE
All 3/4 Bridge

Grade or Name — Description	ABP	Ex-Fn	Mint
Doll Watch Co., 21J, marked on dial & movement, OF ....★★	$275	$400	$700
Iroquois, 17J, BRG, DR, ADJ.	100	200	350
Pocahontas, 21J, GJS, Adj.5P, BRG, DR	200	300	500
Rockford, 15J, BRG	45	100	150
Rockford, 17J, BRG, NI, DR, ADJ.	45	100	150
Rockford, 21J, BRG, NI, DR, ADJ.	100	200	300
Rockford, 21J, BRG, NI, DR, ADJ, Silveroid	75	125	200
300, 23J, 3/4, GJS, Adj.5P, HC ....★★★	300	400	600
305, 23J, BRG, NI, GJS, Adj.5P, OT, OF ....★★★	300	400	600
310Q-IC)-315(OF), 21J, BRG, NI, GJS, Adj.5P ....★★	125	200	300
320(HC)-325(OF), 17J, BRG, NI, ADJ, DR.	60	100	125
330, 17J, BRG, NI, DR, HC	70	100	150
335, 17J, BRG, NI, DR, OF.	60	100	125
340(HC)-345(OF), 21J, M#1 ....★	225	275	400
350, 17J, OF.	60	100	125
355, 17J, HC	65	100	150

Note: Add $10 to $25 to above watches with hunting case.

0 - Size movement in 12- Size Case *("Xtremethin")*

Grade or Name —Description	ABP	Ex-Fn	Mint
0 - Size movement in 12 - Size Case, 15J., Plain OF case	$65	$85	$150
0 - Size movement in 12 - Size Case, 15J., OF case & ENAMELED .	125	175	250

8 SIZE

Grade or Name —Description	ABP	Ex-Fn	Mint
15J, 3/4, HC, LS, **14K, 40 DWT**.	$500	$800	$1,000
9-15J, 3/4, KW or SW, LS, OF or HC, ...	70	100	175

&ᕫ A collector should expect to pay modestly higher prices at local shops.

&ᕫ Pricing in this Guide are fair market price for complete watches which are reflected from the NAWCC National and regional shows.

0 Size
Pendant Set

1906 AD $37.00

No. 140

Rockford movement, 6 size, 17 jewels, quick train, straight line escapement, compensating balance, adjusted to temperature, micrometric regulator, 3/4 damaskeened plates.

Hunting, Nickel, 17 ruby jewels adjusted to temperature and position, gold round center wheel, steel escape wheel, double roller escapement, compensating balance, Breguet hair spring, micrometric regulator, gold lettering, handsomely damaskeened, sunk second glass enamel dial.

6 SIZE

Grade or Name —Description	ABP	Ex-Fn	Mint
9J, NI, **HC**	$90	$125	$225
15J, 3/4, NI	75	100	200
16J, 3/4, NI	75	100	200
17J, 3/4, ADJ, NI	75	100	200

0 SIZE

Grade or Name — Description	ABP	Ex-Fn	Mint
Iroquois, 17J., HC	$125	$200	$350
Plymouth Watch Co., 15-17J, HC	200	250	375
Winona, 15J., HC	125	200	350
7J, BRG, NI, DR, HC	75	100	200
11J, BRG, NI, DR, HC	75	100	200
15J, BRG, NI, DR, HC	85	125	250
17J, BRG, NI, DR, HC	85	125	250

ROCKFORD
1906 AD

16 Size

No. 500 Hunting } Bridge $100.00
No. 505 Open Face }

Nickel, 21 high colored ruby jewels, gold settings, accurately adjusted to temperature, all positions and isochronism. Closely rated in pocket position. Compensating balance with gold screws, also mean time screws, gold beveled polished train, double roller escapement, sapphire jewel pin, steel escape wheel ground and highly polished on all frictional surfaces. Red ruby pallet stone, patent micrometric regulator, positive action. Breguet hair spring of best quality. Beveled and rayed winding wheels, all steel work elegantly polished and cornered. First quality mainspring, double sunk glass, enamel dial, bronzed hands, gold lettering and artistically damaskeened.

WINNEBAGO   16 Size

Hunting }
Open Face } Bridge $37.50

Nickel, 17 Ruby and Sapphire jewels in gold settings, accurately adjusted to temperature, isochronism and five positions. Compensating balance with gold screws, also mean time screws. Red beveled train, double roller escapement, sapphire pallet stone, steel escape wheel, ground and polished on all acting surfaces, patent micrometric regulator. Breguet hair spring, beveled winding wheel, steel work highly polished and cornered. Double sunk glass enamel dial, gold lettering, attractively damaskeened. A 17 jewel watch elegantly finished and equipped with all modern improvements. Certificate of Rating furnished on application.

The Rockford Watch Company, Ltd.

JANUARY 1907
NUMBER AND GRADE

WITH

DESCRIPTION OF MOVEMENTS MANUFACTURED TO DATE

Number and Grade of Movement	GRADE	Size	Style		Jewels	Wind	Sett	Model
1 to 114,000		18	Htg.	F. Pl.		Key	Key	1
114,001 " 115,000		"	"	¾ Pl.		Stem	Lever	5
115,001 " 126,000		"	"	F. Pl.		"	"	2
126,001 " 127,000		"	"	¾ Pl.		"	"	5
127,001 " 130,000		"	"	F. Pl.		"	"	2
130,001 " 131,000		"	"	¾ Pl.		"	"	5
131,001 " 133,000		"	"	F. Pl.		"	"	3
133,001 " 134,000		"	"	¾ Pl.		"	"	5
134,001 " 138,000		"	"	F. Pl.		"	"	3
138,001 " 139,000		"	"	¾ Pl.		"	"	5
139,001 " 143,000		"	"	F. Pl.		"	"	3
143,001 " 144,000		"	"	¾ Pl.		"	"	5
144,001 " 145,000		"	"	F. Pl.		"	"	3
145,001 " 146,000		"	"	¾ Pl.		"	"	5
146,001 " 149,000		"	"	F. Pl.		"	"	3
149,001 " 151,000		"	"	¾ Pl.		"	"	5
151,001 " 153,000		"	"	F. Pl.		"	"	3
153,001 " 154,000		"	"	¾ Pl.		"	"	5
154,001 " 158,000		"	"	F. Pl.		"	"	3
158,001 " 159,000		"	"	¾ Pl.		"	"	5
159,001 " 169,000		"	"	F. Pl.		"	"	3
170,001 " 170,100		"	"	¾ Pl.	15	"	"	5
170,101 " 177,000		"	"	F. Pl.		"	"	3
177,001 " 177,800		"	"	"		"	"	6
177,901 " 189,500		"	"	"		"	"	3
189,601 " 190,900		"	"	"		"	"	6
191,001 " 191,100		"	"	"		"	"	3
191,101 " 196,400		"	O. F.	"		"	"	4
196,501 " 197,000		"	Htg.	"		"	"	6
197,101 " 197,500		"	"	"		"	"	3
197,601 " 198,000		"	"	"		"	"	6
198,101 " 199,100		"	O. F.	"		"	"	4
199,201 " 199,500		"	Htg.	"		"	"	6
199,600 " 200,000		"	"	¾ Pl.		"	"	5
200,001 " 213,100		8	"	"		"	"	1
213,101 " 218,900		6	"	"		"	"	
219,001 " 219,500		18	"	"		"	"	5
219,501 " 224,500		"	"	F. Pl.		"	"	3
224,501 " 228,900		"	O. F.	"		"	"	4
229,001 " 232,000		"	Htg.	"		"	"	3
232,001 " 233,000		"	"	¾ Pl.		"	"	5
233,001 " 234,000	47	"	O. F.	F. Pl.	Nickel	15	"	"	4
234,001 " 235,000	45	"	"	"	"	"	"	"
235,001 " 236,000	43	"	Htg.	F. Pl.	"	"	"	"	3
236,001 " 237,000	44	"	"	"	Gilt	"	"	"
237,001 " 238,000	45	"	O. F.	F. Pl.	"	"	"	"	4
238,001 " 239,000		"	"	"	"	9	"	"	"
239,001 " 240,000	45	"	"	"	"	15	"	"	
240,001 " 241,000	46	"	"	"	"	11	"	"	
241,001 " 241,800	47	"	"	"	Nickel	15	"	"	
241,801 " 242,000	40	"	Htg.	"	"	"	"	"	3
242,001 " 243,000	43	"	"	"	"	"	"	"	
243,001 " 244,000	44	"	"	"	Gilt	"	"	"	
244,001 " 244,300	49	"	"	"	Nickel	"	"	"	6
244,301 " 244,400	72	"	"	"	"	"	"	"	
244,401 " 245,000	62	"	"	"	"	11	"	"	8
245,001 " 246,000	81	"	"	"	Gilt	9	"	"	3
246,001 " 247,000	44	"	"	"	"	15	"	"	
247,001 " 248,000	64	"	O. F.	"	"	11	"	"	4
248,001 " 249,000	46	"	Htg.	"	"	15	"	"	6
249,001 " 250,000	49	"	"	"	Nickel	"	"	"	
250,001 " 250,500	62	"	"	"	"	11	"	"	
250,501 " 251,000	60	"	O. F.	"	"	"	"	"	7
251,001 " 252,000	66	"	"	"	"	"	"	"	
252,001 " 253,000	67	"	"	"	Gilt	"	"	"	
253,001 " 253,500	83	"	Htg.	"	Nickel	15	"	"	8
253,501 " 253,700	77	"	"	"	"	"	"	"	
253,701 " 254,000	68	"	"	"	Gilt	11	"	"	
254,001 " 254,600	86	"	O. F.	"	Nickel	15	"	"	7
254,601 " 254,800	76	"	"	"	"	"	"	"	
254,801 " 255,000	78	"	"	"	Gilt	"	"	"	
255,001 " 256,000	89	"	"	"	"	"	"	"	
256,001 " 257,000	68	"	Htg.	"	"	11	"	"	8
257,001 " 258,000	93	"	"	"	"	9	"	"	"
258,001 " 259,000	69	"	"	"	Nickel	11	"	"	"

The Rockford Watch Company, Ltd.

Number and Grade of Movement	GRADE	Size		Style		Jewels	Wind	Sett	Model
259,001 to 260,000	66	18	O. F.	F. Pl.	Nickel	11	Stem	Lever	7
260,001 " 261,000	68	"	Htg.	"	Gilt	"	"	"	8
261,001 " 262,000	86	"	O. F.	"	Nickel	15	"	"	7
262,001 " 263,000	67	"	"	"	Gilt	11	"	"	"
263,001 " 264,000	83	"	Htg.	"	Nickel	15	"	"	8
264,001 " 265,000	69	"	"	"	"	"	"	"	"
265,001 " 266,000	68	"	"	"	Gilt	11	"	"	"
266,001 " 267,000	93	"	"	"	"	9	"	"	8
267,001 " 267,800	83	"	"	"	Nickel	15	"	"	"
267,801 " 268,000	77	"	"	"	"	..	"	"	"
268,001 " 269,000	68	"	"	"	Gilt	11	"	"	"
269,001 " 270,000	67	"	O. F.	"	"	"	"	"	7
270,001 " 270,800	85	"	Htg.	"	"	15	"	"	8
270,801 " 271,000	79	"	"	"	"	"	"	"	"
271,001 " 272,000	66	"	O. F.	"	Nickel	11	"	"	7
272,001 " 272,100	77	"	Htg.	"	"	15	"	"	8
272,101 " 272,200	83	"	"	"	"	"	"	"	"
272,201 " 272,300	77	"	"	"	"	"	"	"	"
272,301 " 272,600	83	"	"	"	"	"	"	"	"
272,601 " 272,700	77	"	"	"	"	"	"	"	"
272,701 " 272,900	83	"	"	"	"	"	"	"	"
272,901 " 273,000	77	"	"	"	"	"	"	"	"
273,001 " 274,000	69	"	"	"	"	"	"	"	"
274,001 " 275,000	83	"	"	"	"	"	"	"	"
275,001 " 276,000	69	"	"	"	"	11	"	"	"
276,001 " 277,000	83	"	"	"	"	15	"	"	"
277,001 " 278,000	85	"	"	"	Gilt	"	"	"	"
278,001 " 279,000	66	"	O. F.	"	Nickel	11	"	"	7
279,001 " 279,200	76	"	"	"	"	15	"	"	"
279,201 " 280,000	86	"	"	"	"	"	"	"	"
280,001 " 281,000	66	"	"	"	"	11	"	"	"
281,001 " 282,000	85	"	Htg.	"	Gilt	15	"	"	8
282,001 " 283,000	83	"	"	"	Nickel	"	"	"	"
283,001 " 284,000	93	"	"	"	Gilt	9	"	"	"
284,001 " 285,000	89	"	O. F.	"	"	15	"	"	7
285,001 " 286,000	69	"	Htg.	"	Hickel	11	"	"	8
286,001 " 286,200	83	"	"	"	Nick.& Gilt	15	"	"	.
286,201 " 286,500	84	"	"	"	"	"	"	"	"
286,501 " 287,000	83	"	"	"	Nickel	"	"	"	"
287,001 " 288,000	66	"	O. F.	"	"	11	"	"	7
288,001 " 289,000	67	"	"	"	Gilt	"	"	"	"
289,001 " 289,500	84	"	Htg.	"	Spot Gilt	15	"	"	8
289,501 " 291,000	83	"	"	"	Nickel	"	"	"	"
291,001 " 292,000	69	"	"	"	"	11	"	"	"
292,001 " 293,000	67	"	O. F.	"	Gilt	"	"	"	7
293,001 " 294,000	85	"	Htg.	"	"	15	"	"	8
294,001 " 295,000	93	"	"	"	"	9	"	"	"
295,001 " 296,000	66	"	O. F.	"	Nickel	11	"	"	7
296,001 " 297,000	89	"	"	"	Gilt	15	"	"	"
297,001 " 298,000	69	"	Htg.	"	Nickel	11	"	"	8
298,001 " 299,000	67	"	O. F.	"	Gilt	"	"	"	7
299,001 " 300,000	93	"	Htg.	"	"	9	"	"	8
300,001 " 300,500	84	"	"	"	Nick.& Gilt	15	"	"	"
300,501 " 300,700	83	"	"	"	Nickel	"	"	"	"
300,701 " 301,000	70	"	"	"	Nick.& Gilt	16	"	"	"
301,001 " 302,000	66	"	O. F.	"	Nickel	11	"	"	7
302,001 " 303,000	93	"	Htg.	"	Gilt	9	"	"	8
303,001 " 304,000	69	"	"	"	Nickel	11	"	"	"
304,001 " 304,500	84	"	"	"	Nick.& Gilt	15	"	"	"
304,501 " 305,000	83	"	"	"	Nickel	"	"	"	"
305,001 " 305,500	84	"	"	"	Nick.&Gilt	"	"	"	"
305,501 " 306,000	83	"	"	"	Nickel	"	"	"	"
306,001 " 307,000	66	"	O. F.	"	"	11	"	"	7
307,001 " 308,000	83	"	Htg.	"	"	15	"	"	8
308,001 " 309,000	93	"	"	"	Gilt	9	"	"	"
309,001 " 310,000	83	"	"	"	Nickel	15	"	"	"
310,001 " 310,500	87	"	O. F.	"	Nick.& Gilt	"	"	"	7
310,501 " 310,700	88	"	"	"	Nickel	16	"	"	"
310,701 " 311,000	86	"	"	"	"	15	"	"	"
311,001 " 312,000	69	"	Htg.	"	"	11	"	"	8
312,001 " 313,000	93	"	"	"	Gilt	9	"	"	"
313,001 " 314,000	83	"	"	"	Nickel	15	"	"	"
314,001 " 317,000	93	"	"	"	Gilt	9	"	"	"
317,001 " 318,000	85	"	"	"	"	15	"	"	"
318,001 " 319,000	93	"	"	"	"	9	"	"	"
319,001 " 320,000	85	"	"	"	"	15	"	"	"
320,001 " 321,000	84	"	"	"	Nick.& Gilt	"	"	"	"
321,001 " 322,000	83	"	"	"	Nickel	"	"	"	"
322,001 " 323,000	84	"	"	"	Nick.& Gilt	"	"	"	"
323,001 " 325,000	83	"	"	"	Nickel	"	"	"	"
325,001 " 326,000	85	"	"	"	Gilt	"	"	"	"
326,001 " 327,000	93	"	"	"	"	9	"	"	"
327,001 " 328,000	83	"	"	"	Nickel	15	"	"	"
328,001 " 329,000	89	"	O. F.	"	Gilt	"	"	"	7
329,001 " 329,100	84	"	Htg.	"	Nick.& Gilt	"	"	"	8
329,101 " 329,200	83	"	"	"	Special	.....	"	"	"
329,201 " 329,700	84	"	"	"	Nick.& Gilt	15	"	"	"
329,701 " 330,000	70	"	"	"	"	16	"	"	"
330,001 " 330,800	87	"	O. F.	"	Nickel	15	"	"	7

The Rockford Watch Company, Ltd.

Number and Grade of Movement	GRADE	Size		Style		Jewels	Wind	Sett	Model
330,801 to 331,000	88	18	O. F.	F. Pl.	Nick.& Gilt	16	Stem	Lever	7
331,001 " 332,000	68	"	Htg.	"	Gilt	11	"	"	8
332,001 " 333,000	86	"	O. F.	"	Nickel	15	"	"	7
333,001 " 334,000	69	"	Htg.	"	"	11	"	"	8
334,001 " 335,000	66	"	O. F,	"			"	"	7
335,001 " 336,000	94	"	"	"	Gilt	9	"	"	"
336,001 " 337,000	68	"	Htg.	"	"	11	"	"	8
337,001 " 338,000	94	"	O. F.	"	"	9	"	"	7
338,001 " 338,500	88	"	"	"	Nick.& Gilt	16	"	"	"
338,501 " 339,000	86	"	"	"	Nickel	"	"	"	"
339,001 " 339,500	70	"	Htg.	"	Nick.& Gilt	"	"	"	8
339,501 " 340,000	84	"	"	"	"	15	"	"	"
340,001 " 341,000	66	"	O. F.	"	Nickel	11	"	"	7
341,001 " 342,000	85	"	"	"	Gilt	15	"	"	8
342,001 " 343,000	89	"	O. F.	"	"	"	"	"	7
343,001 " 344,000	94	"	"	"	"	9	"	"	"
344,001 " 345,000	84	"	Htg.	"	Nick.& Gilt	15	"	"	8
345,001 " 346,000	68	"	"	"	Gilt	11	"	"	"
346,001 " 347,000	87	"	O. F.	"	Nick.& Gilt	15	"	"	7
347,001 " 348,000	94	"	"	"	Gilt	9	"	"	"
348,001 " 348,300	88	"	"	"	Nick.& Gilt	16	"	"	"
348,301 " 348,500	87	"	"	"	"	15	"	"	"
348,501 " 349,000	86	"	"	"	Nickel	"	"	"	"
349,001 " 349,500	67	"	"	"	Gilt	11	"	"	"
349,501 " 350,000	89	"	"	"	"	15	"	"	"
350,001 " 350,500	70	"	Htg.	"	Nick.& Gilt	16	"	"	8
350,501 " 351,000	85	"	"	"	Gilt	15	"	"	"
351,001 " 352,000	87	"	O. F.	"	Nick & Gilt	"	"	"	7
352,001 " 352,500	88	"	"	"	"	16	"	"	"
352,501 " 353,000	67	"	"	"	Gilt	11	"	"	"
353,001 " 353,500	100	16	Htg.	¾ Pl.	Nick.& Gilt	16	"	"	1
353,501 " 353,800	101	"	"	"	Nickel	15	"	"	"
353,801 " 354,000	102	"	"	"	"	"	"	"	"
354,001 " 354,500	103	"	"	"	"	"	"	"	"
354,501 " 355,000	104	"	"	"	"	11	"	"	"
355,001 " 355,500	111	"	"	"	Gilt	15	"	"	"
355,501 " 356,000	112	"	"	"	"	"	"	"	"
356,001 " 356,500	113	"	"	"	"	11	"	"	"
356,501 " 357,000	114	"	"	"	"	9	"	"	"
357,001 " 358,500	68	18	"	F. Pl.	"	11	"	"	8
358,501 " 359,000	67	"	O. F.	"	"	"	"	"	7
359,001 " 359,500	87	"	"	"	Nick.& Gilt	15	"	"	"
359,501 " 360,000	86	"	"	"	Nickel	"	"	"	"
360,001 " 360,500	101	16	Htg.	¾ Pl.	Nick.& Gilt	"	"	"	1
360,501 " 361,000	102	"	"	"	Nickel	"	"	"	"
361,001 " 361,500	103	"	"	"	"	"	"	"	"
361,501 " 362,000	104	"	"	"	"	11	"	"	"
362,001 " 364,000	67	18	O. F.	F. Pl.	Gilt	"	"	"	7
364,001 " 365,000	112	16	Htg.	¾ Pl.	"	15	"	"	1
365,001 " 366,000	102	"	"	"	Nickel	"	"	"	"
366,001 " 367,000	103	"	"	"	"	"	"	"	"
367,001 " 368,000	67	18	O. F.	F. Pl.	Gilt	11	"	"	7
368,001 " 368,500	112	16	Htg.	¾ Pl.	"	15	"	"	1
368,501 " 369,000	101	"	"	"	Nick.& Gilt	"	"	"	"
369,001 " 370,000	104	"	"	"	Nickel	11	"	"	"
370,001 " 370,500	86	18	O. F.	F. Pl.	"	15	"	"	7
370,501 " 371,000	87	"	"	"	Nick.& Gilt	"	"	"	"
371,001 " 371,500	89	"	"	"	Gilt	"	"	"	"
371,501 " 372,000	94	"	"	"	"	9	"	"	"
372,001 " 372,500	113	16	Htg.	¾ Pl.	"	11	"	"	1
372,501 " 373,000	114	"	"	"	"	9	"	"	"
373,001 " 374,000	113	"	"	"	"	11	"	"	"
274,001 " 374,500	68	18	"	F. Pl.	"	"	"	"	8
374,501 " 375,000	94	"	O. F.	"	"	9	"	"	7
375,001 " 376,000	87	"	"	"	Nick.& Gilt	15	"	"	"
376,001 " 376,200	100	16	Htg.	¾ Pl.	"	16	"	"	1
376,201 " 376,700	101	"	"	"	"	15	"	"	"
376,701 " 377,000	102	"	"	"	Nickel	"	"	"	"
377,001 " 377,500	104	"	"	"	"	11	"	"	"
377,501 " 378,000	103	"	"	"	"	15	"	"	"
378,001 " 379,000	94	18	O. F.	F. Pl.	Gilt	9	"	'	7
379,001 " 379,500	86	"	"	"	Nickel	15	"	"	"
379,501 " 380,000	84	"	Htg.	"	Nick.& Gilt	"	"	"	8
380,001 " 380,500	101	16	"	¾ Pl.	"	"	"	"	1
380,501 " 381,000	104	"	"	"	Nickel	11	"	"	"
381,001 " 381,300	102	"	"	"	"	15	"	"	"
381,301 " 382,000	103	"	"	"	"	"	"	"	"
382,001 " 382,200	111	"	"	"	Gilt	"	"	"	"
382,201 " 383,000	112	"	"	"	"	"	"	"	"
383,001 " 383,500	113	"	"	"	"	11	"	"	"
383,501 " 384,000	114	"	"	"	"	9	"	"	"
384,001 " 384,500	100	"	"	"	Nick.& Gilt	16	"	"	"
384,501 " 385,000	103	"	"	"	Nickel	15	"	"	"
385,001 " 385,500	104	"	"	"	"	11	"	"	"
385,501 " 386,000	103	"	"	"	"	15	"	"	"
386,001 " 387,000	112	"	"	"	Gilt	"	"	"	"
387,001 " 387,500	93	18	"	F. Pl.	"	9	"	"	8
387,501 " 388,000	68	"	"	"	"	11	"	"	"

The Rockford Watch Company, Ltd.

Number and Grade of Movement	GRADE	Size		Style		Jewels	Wind	Sett	Model
388,001 to 388,500	94	18	O. F.	F. Pl.	Gilt	9	Stem	Lever	7
388,501 " 389,000	89	"	"	"	"	15	"	"	"
389,001 " 389,100	76	"	"	"	Nickel	"	"	"	"
389,101 " 390,000	86	"	"	"	"	"	"	"	"
390,001 " 391,000	69	"	Htg.	"	"	11	"	"	8
391,001 " 391,400	162	6	"	¾ Pl.	Gilt	9	"	"	2
391,401 " 391,700	161	"	"	"	"	11	"	"	"
391,701 " 392,000	160	"	"	"	"	15	"	"	"
392,001 " 392,300	154	"	"	"	Nickel	9	"	"	"
392,301 " 392,500	153	"	"	"	"	11	"	"	"
392,501 " 392,700	152	"	"	"	"	15	"	"	"
392,701 " 392,900	151	"	"	"	Nick.& Gilt	"	"	"	"
392,901 " 393,000	150	"	"	"	"	16	"	"	"
393,001 " 393,500	154	"	"	"	Nickel	9	"	"	"
393,501 " 394,000	153	"	"	"	"	11	"	"	"
394,001 " 394,500	152	"	"	"	"	15	"	"	"
394,501 " 394,800	151	"	"	"	Nick.& Gilt	"	"	"	"
394,801 " 395,000	150	"	"	"	"	16	"	"	"
395,001 " 396,000	162	"	"	"	Gilt	9	"	"	"
396,001 " 396,500	161	"	"	"	"	11	"	"	"
396,501 " 397,000	160	"	"	"	"	15	"	"	"
397,001 " 397,800	162	"	"	"	"	9	"	"	"
397,801 " 398,600	161	"	"	"	"	11	"	"	"
398,601 " 399,000	160	"	"	"	"	15	"	"	"
399,001 " 400,200	153	"	"	"	Nickel	11	"	"	"
400,201 " 400,700	152	"	"	"	"	15	"	"	"
400,701 " 401,000	152	"	"	"	Nick.& Gilt	"	"	"	"
401,001 " 401,500	93	18	"	F. Pl.	Gilt	9	"	"	8
401,501 " 402,000	68	"	"	"	"	11	"	"	"
402,001 " 402,500	69	"	"	"	Nickel	"	"	"	"
402,501 " 403,000	85	"	"	"	Gilt	15	"	"	"
403,001 " 403,500	94	"	O. F.	"	"	9	"	"	7
403,501 " 404,000	86	"	"	"	Nickel	15	"	"	"
404,001 " 404,300	60	"	"	"	Nick.& Gilt	11	"	"	"
404,301 " 405,000	66	"	"	"	Nickel	17	"	"	"
405,001 " 405,500	86	"	"	"	"	15	"	"	"
405,501 " 406,000	83	"	Htg.	"	"	"	"	"	8
406,001 " 407,000	69	"	"	"	"	11	"	"	"
407,001 " 407,500	68	"	"	"	Gilt	"	"	"	"
407,501 " 408,000	85	"	"	"	"	15	"	"	"
408,001 " 408,500	93	"	"	"	"	9	"	"	"
408,501 " 409,000	94	"	O. F.	"	"	"	"	"	7
409,001 " 410,000	69	"	Htg.	"	Nickel	11	"	"	8
410,001 " 410,500	93	"	"	"	Gilt	9	"	"	"
410,501 " 411,000	68	"	"	"	"	11	"	"	"
411,001 " 411,500	94	"	O. F.	"	"	9	"	"	7
411,501 " 412,000	67	"	"	"	"	11	"	"	"
412,001 " 412,500	86	"	"	"	Nickel	15	"	"	"
412,501 " 413,000	69	"	Htg.	"	"	11	"	"	8
413,001 " 414,000	93	"	"	"	Gilt	9	"	"	"
414,001 " 415,000	94	"	O. F.	"	"	"	"	"	7
415,001 " 415,200	81	"	Htg.	"	Plain	17	"	"	8
415,201 " 415,500	83	"	"	"	Nickel	15	"	"	"
415,501 " 415,600	80	"	"	"	Spot Gilt	17	"	"	"
415,601 " 416,000	82	"	"	"	Plain	"	"	"	"
416,001 " 416,100	61	"	O. F.		....	"	"	"	7
416,101 " 416,500	86	"	"	"	Nickel	15	"	"	"
416,501 " 417,000	62	"	"	"	Plain	17	"	"	"
417,001 " 417,500	66	"	"	"	Nickel	11	"	"	"
417,501 " 418,000	83	"	Htg.	"	"	17	"	"	8
418,001 " 419,000	93	"	"	"	Gilt	9	"	"	"
419,001 " 419,500	94	"	"	"	"	"	"	"	"
419,501 " 420,500	153	6	"	¾ Pl.	Nickel	11	"	"	2
420,501 " 421,500	161	"	"	"	Gilt	"	"	"	"
421,501 " 422,500	162	"	"	"	"	9	"	"	"
422,501 " 423,000	66	18	O. F.	F. Pl.	Nickel	11	"	"	7
423,001 " 424,000	93	"	Htg.	"	Gilt	9	"	"	8
424,001 " 425,000	69	"	"	"	Nickel	11	"	"	"
425,001 " 425,500	94	"	O. F.	"	Gilt	9	"	"	7
425,501 " 426,000	66	"	"	"	Nickel	11	"	"	"
426,001 " 427,000	83	"	Htg.	"	"	15	"	"	8
427,001 " 428,000	69	"	"	"	"	11	"	"	"
428,001 " 429,000	66	"	O. F.	"	"	"	"	"	7
429,001 " 430,000	83	"	Htg.	"	"	15	"	"	8
430,001 " 431,000	68	"	"	"	Gilt	11	"	"	"
431,001 " 431,500	66	"	O. F.	"	Nickel	"	"	"	7
431,501 " 432,000	82	"	Htg.	"	Plain	17	"	"	8
432,001 " 433,000	67	"	O. F.	"	Gilt	11	"	"	7
433,001 " 433,100	83	"	Htg.	"	Nickel	15	"	"	8
433,101 " 433,140	82a	"	"	"	"	"	"	"	"
433,141 " 433,400	82	"	"	"	"	"	"	"	"
433,401 " 433,500	82	"	"	"	"	17	"	"	"
433,501 " 433,600	83	"	"	"	"	15	"	"	"
433,601 " 433,700	82	"	"	"	Plain	17	"	"	"
433,701 " 433,750	80	"	"	"	Spot Gilt	"	"	"	"
433,751 " 433,800	81	"	"	"	Plain	"	"	"	"
433,801 " 434,000	83	"	"	"	Nickel	15	"	"	"
434,001 " 434,500	69	"	"	"	"	"	"	"	"

The Rockford Watch Company, Ltd.

Number and Grade of Movement	GRADE	Size			Style	Jewels	Wind	Sett	Model
					Description of Movement				
434,501 to 434,600	86	18	O. F.	F. Pl.	Nickel	15	Stem	Lever	7
434,601 " 434,700	62	"	"	"	Plain	17	"	"	"
434,701 " 435,000	86	"	O. F.	"	Nickel	15	"	"	"
435,001 " 435,500	85	"	Htg.	"	Gilt	"	"	"	8
435,501 " 436,000	94	"	O. F.	"	"	9	"	"	7
436,001 " 436,100	67	"	"	"	"	11	"	"	"
436,101 " 436,200	89	"	"	"	"	15	"	"	"
436,201 " 436,300	67	"	"	"	"	11	"	"	"
436,301 " 437,000	89	"	"	"	"	"	"	"	"
437,001 " 437,800	82	"	Htg.	"	Nickel	17	"	"	8
437,801 " 438,000	81	"	"	"	Plain	"	"	"	"
438,001 " 438,500	83	"	"	"	"	15	"	"	"
438,501 " 438,900	62	"	O. F.	"	"	17	"	"	7
438,901 " 439,000	86	"	"	"	Nickel	15	"	"	"
439,001 " 439,500	82	"	Htg.	"	"	17	"	"	8
439,501 " 439,550	80	"	"	"	Nick.& Gilt	"	"	"	"
439,551 " 439,650	82a	"	"	"	Nickel	"	"	"	"
439,651 " 439,700	81	"	"	"	"	"	"	"	"
439,701 " 439,750	62a	"	O. F.	"	"	"	"	"	7
439,751 " 439,850	62	"	"	"	"	"	"	"	"
439,851 " 439,900	61	"	"	"	"	"	"	"	"
439,901 " 439,950	86	"	"	"	"	15	"	"	"
439,951 " 440,000	62a	"	"	"	"	17	"	"	"
440,001 " 441,000	93	"	Htg.	"	Gilt	9	"	"	8
441,001 " 441,500	62	"	O. F.	"	Nickel	17	"	"	7
441,501 " 442,000	83	"	Htg.	"	Plain	15	"	"	8
442,001 " 442,050	80	"	"	"	Nick.& Gilt	17	"	"	"
424,051 " 442,150	81	"	"	"	Plain	"	"	"	"
442,151 " 442,500	82	"	"	"	Nickel	"	"	"	"
500,001 " 500,054	930	"	O. F.	"	"	"	"	"	9
500,055...	935	"	"	"	"	"	"	"	"
500,056 to 500,250	930	"	"	"	"	"	"	"	"
500,251 " 500,260	920	"	"	"	"	"	"	"	7
500,261 " 500,300	930	"	"	"	"	"	"	"	9
500,301 " 500,400	935	"	"	"	"	"	"	"	"
500,401 " 500,800	830	"	Htg.	"	"	"	"	"	10
500,801 " 500,900	835	"	"	"	"	"	"	"	"
500,901 " 501,100	830	"	"	"	"	"	"	"	"
501,101 " 501,900	835	"	"	"	"	"	"	"	"
501,901 " 502,400	830	"	"	"	"	"	"	"	"
502,401 " 502,481	930	"	O. F.	"	"	"	"	"	9
502,482 " 502,489	935	"	"	"	"	"	"	"	"
502,490 " 502 592	930	"	"	"	"	"	"	"	"
502,593...	935	"	"	"	"	"	"	"	"
502,594 to 502,700	930	"	"	"	"	"	"	"	"
502,701 " 503,200	935	"	"	"	"	"	"	"	"
503,201 " 503,460	830	"	Htg.	"	"	"	"	"	10
503,461 " 503,470	820	"	"	"	"	"	"	"	8
503,471 " 503,483	830	"	"	"	"	"	"	"	10
503,484 " 503,489	820	"	"	"	"	"	"	"	8
503,490 " 503,520	830	"	"	"	"	"	"	"	10
503,521 " 503,531	820	"	"	"	"	"	"	"	8
503,532 " 503,536	830	"	"	"	"	"	"	"	10
503,537 " 503,540	820	"	"	"	"	"	"	"	8
503,541 " 503,550	825	"	"	"	"	"	"	"	10
503,551 " 503,610	830	"	"	"	"	"	"	"	"
503,611 " 503,620	820	"	"	"	"	"	"	"	8
503,621 " 503,700	830	"	"	"	"	"	"	"	10
503,701 " 504,000	835	"	"	"	"	"	"	"	"
504,001 " 504,100	830	"	"	"	"	"	"	"	"
504,101 " 505,150	835	"	"	"	"	"	"	"	"
505,151 " 505,200	830	"	"	"	"	"	"	"	"
505,201 " 505,300	835	"	"	"	"	"	"	"	"
505,301 " 505,350	830	"	"	"	"	"	"	"	"
505,351 " 505,360	835	"	"	"	"	"	"	"	"
505,361 " 505,370	830	"	"	"	"	"	"	"	"
505,371 " 505,398	835	"	"	"	"	"	"	"	"
505,399 " 505,400	830	"	"	"	"	"	"	"	"
505,401 " 505,700	835	"	"	"	"	"	"	"	"
505,701 " 506,000	830	"	"	"	"	"	"	"	"
506,001 " 506,800	935	"	O. F.	"	"	"	"	"	9
506,801 " 506,810	910	"	"	"	"	21	"	"	"
506,811 " 507,600	930	"	"	"	"	17	"	"	"
507,601 " 507,900	830	"	Htg.	"	"	"	"	"	10
507,901 " 508,500	835	"	"	"	"	"	"	"	"
508,501 " 509,000	830	"	"	"	"	"	"	"	"
509,001 " 509,100	820	"	"	"	"	"	"	"	8
509,101 " 509,700	925	"	O. F.	"	"	"	"	"	9
509,701 " 509,729	920	"	"	"	"	"	"	"	7
509,730...	915	"	"	"	"	"	"	"	"
509,731 to 509,759	920	"	"	"	"	"	"	"	"
509,760...	915	"	"	"	"	"	"	"	"
509,761 to 509,791	920	"	"	"	"	"	"	"	"
509,792...	915	"	"	"	"	"	"	"	"
509,793 to 509,900	920	"	"	"	"	"	"	"	"
509,901 " 510,200	810	"	Htg.	"	"	21	"	"	10
510,201 " 510,700	825	"	"	"	"	17	"	"	"
510,701 " 511,300	830	"	"	"	"	"	"	"	"
511,301 " 511,600	835	"	"	"	"	"	"	"	"

The Rockford Watch Company, Ltd.

Number and Grade of Movement	GRADE	Size		Style		Jewels	Wind	Sett	Model
				F. Pl.	Nickel				
511,601 to 512,500	935	18	O. F.	F. Pl.	Nickel	17	Stem	Lever	9
512,501 " 512,600	910	"	"	"	"	21	"	"	"
512,601 " 512,700	920	"	"	"	"	17	"	"	7
512,701 " 512,800	930	"	"	"	"	"	"	"	9
512,801 " 512,850	920	"	"	"	"	"	"	"	7
512,851 " 512,872	830	"	Htg.	"	"	"	"	"	10
512,873	915	"	O. F.	"	"	"	"	"	7
512,874 to 512,875	920	"	"	"	"	"	"	"	"
512,876	915	"	"	"	"	"	"	"	"
512,877 to 512,900	920	"	"	"	"	"	"	"	"
512,901 " 513,101	830	"	Htg.	"	"	"	"	"	10
513,102 " 513,181	820	"	"	"	"	"	"	"	8
513,182	815	"	"	"	"	"	"	"	"
513,183 to 513,251	820	"	"	"	"	"	"	"	"
513,252 " 513,259	810	"	"	"	"	21	"	"	10
513,260 " 513,300	820	"	"	"	"	17	"	"	8
513,301 " 513,400	830	"	"	"	"	"	"	"	10
513,401 " 513,500	835	"	"	"	"	"	"	"	"
513,501 " 513,600	830	"	"	"	"	"	"	"	"
513,601 " 513,900	835	"	"	"	"	"	"	"	"
513,901 " 514,000	930	"	O. F.	"	"	"	"	"	9
514,001 " 514,100	935	"	"	"	"	"	"	"	"
514,101 " 514,150	825	"	Htg.	"	"	"	"	"	10
514,151 " 514,500	835	"	"	"	"	"	"	"	"
514,501 " 514,600	930	"	O. F.	"	"	"	"	"	9
514,601 " 514,900	935	"	"	"	"	"	"	"	"
514,901 " 515,100	835	"	Htg.	"	"	"	"	"	10
515,101 " 515,400	935	"	O. F.	"	"	"	"	"	9
515,401 " 515,500	810	"	Htg.	"	"	21	"	"	10
515,501 " 515,600	910	"	O. F.	"	"	"	"	"	9
515,601 " 516,000	935	"	"	"	"	17	"	"	"
516,001 " 516,300	925	"	"	"	"	"	"	"	"
516,301 " 516,400	935	"	"	"	"	"	"	"	"
516,401 " 516,500	925	"	"	"	"	"	"	"	"
516,501 " 517,200	825	"	Htg.	"	"	"	"	"	10
517,201 " 519,300	910	"	O. F.	"	"	21	"	"	9
519,301 " 519,400	900	"	"	"	"	24	"	"	"
519,401 " 519,500	800	"	Htg.	"	"	"	"	"	10
519,501 " 519,600	805	"	"	"	"	21	"	"	"
519,601 " 519,700	905	"	O. F.	"	"	"	"	"	9
519,701 " 520,000	835	"	Htg.	"	"	17	"	"	10
520,001 " 521,000	935	"	O. F.	"	"	"	"	"	9
521,001 " 522,000	870	"	Htg.	"	"	7	"	"	10
522,001 " 522,400	970	"	O. F.	"	"	"	"	"	9
522,401 " 523,500	870	"	Htg.	"	"	"	"	"	10
523,501 " 524,800	970	"	O. F.	"	"	"	"	"	9
524,801 " 525,000	935	"	"	"	"	17	"	"	"
525,001 " 525,100	900	"	"	"	"	24	"	"	"
525,101 " 525,400	935	"	"	"	"	17	"	"	"
525,401 " 525,900	925	"	"	"	"	"	"	"	"
525,901 " 526,700	825	"	Htg.	"	"	"	"	"	10
526,701 " 526,900	930	"	O. F.	"	"	"	"	"	9
526,901 " 527,900	935	"	"	"	"	"	"	"	"
527,901 " 528,800	930	"	"	"	"	"	"	"	"
528,801 " 529,800	935	"	"	"	"	"	"	"	"
529,801 " 530,800	925	"	"	"	"	"	"	"	"
530,801 " 531,800	835	"	Htg.	"	"	"	"	"	10
531,801 " 532,450	825	"	"	"	"	"	"	"	"
532,451 " 532,500	835	"	"	"	"	"	"	"	"
532,501 " 533,400	925	"	O. F.	"	"	"	"	"	9
533,401 " 534,000	935	"	"	"	"	"	"	"	"
534,001 " 534,012	920	"	"	"	"	"	"	"	7
534,013	915	"	"	"	"	"	"	"	"
534,014 to 534,035	920	"	"	"	"	"	"	"	"
534,036	915	"	"	"	"	"	"	"	"
534,037 to 534,039	920	"	"	"	"	"	"	"	"
534,040	915	"	"	"	"	"	"	"	"
534,041 to 534,064	920	"	"	"	"	"	"	"	"
534,065	915	"	"	"	"	"	"	"	"
534,066 to 534,112	920	"	"	"	"	"	"	"	"
534,113 " 534,115	915	"	"	"	"	"	"	"	"
534,116 " 534,119	920	"	"	"	"	"	"	"	"
534,120	915	"	"	"	"	"	"	"	"
534,121	920	"	"	"	"	"	"	"	"
534,122 to 534,123	915	"	"	"	"	"	"	"	"
534,124 " 534,127	920	"	"	"	"	"	"	"	"
534,128	915	"	"	"	"	"	"	"	"
534,129 to 534,130	920	"	"	"	"	"	"	"	"
534,131	915	"	"	"	"	"	"	"	"
534,132	920	"	"	"	"	"	"	"	"
534,133	915	"	"	"	"	"	"	"	"
534,134	920	"	"	"	"	"	"	"	"
534,135	915	"	"	"	"	"	"	"	"
534,136 to 534,138	920	"	"	"	"	"	"	"	"
534,139	915	"	"	"	"	"	"	"	"
534,140 to 534,144	920	"	"	"	"	"	"	"	"
534,145	915	"	"	"	"	"	"	"	"
534,146 to 534,147	920	"	"	"	"	"	"	"	"
534,148	915	"	"	"	"	"	"	"	"

The Rockford Watch Company, Ltd.

Number and Grade of Movement	GRADE	Size		Style		Jewels	Wind	Sett	Model
534,149	920	18	O. F.	F. Pl.	Nickel	17	Stem	Lever	7
534,150	915	"	"	"	"	"	"	"	"
534,151 to 534,155	920	"	"	"	"	"	"	"	"
534,156 " 534,157	915	"	"	"	"	"	"	"	"
534,158 " 534,163	920	"	"	"	"	"	"	"	"
534,164	915	"	"	"	"	"	"	"	"
534,165 to 534,171	920	"	"	"	"	"	"	"	"
534,172	915	"	"	"	"	"	"	"	"
534,173	920	"	"	"	"	"	"	"	"
534,174	915	"	"	"	"	"	"	"	"
534,175	920	"	"	"	"	"	"	"	"
534,176 to 534,179	915	'	"	"	"	"	"	"	"
534,180 " 534,182	920	"	"	"	"	"	"	"	"
534,183	915	"	"	"	"	"	"	"	"
534,184	920	"	"	"	"	"	"	"	"
534,185	915	"	"	"	"	"	"	"	"
534,186 to 534,188	920	"	"	"	"	"	"	"	"
534,189	915	"	"	"	"	"	"	"	"
534,190 to 534,196	920	"	"	"	"	"	"	"	"
534,197	915	"	"	"	"	"	"	"	"
534,198	920	"	"	"	"	"	"	"	"
534,199	915	"	"	"	"	"	"	"	"
534,200	920	"	"	"	"	"	"	"	9
534,401 to 534,600	930	"	"	"	"	"	"	"	9
534,601 " 535,200	910	"	"	"	"	21	"	"	"
535,201 " 535,400	900	"	"	"	"	24	"	"	"
535,401 " 535,600	910	"	"	"	"	21	"	"	"
535,601 " 535,700	800	"	Htg.	"	"	24	"	"	10
535,701 " 535,800	805	"	"	"	"	21	"	"	"
535,801 " 536,300	910	"	O. F.	"	"	..	"	"	9
536,301 " 536,600	930	"	"	"	"	17	"	"	"
536,601 " 536,700	945	"	"	"	"	21	"	"	Special
536,701 " 537,400	910	"	"	"	"	..	"	"	9
537,401 " 539,400	935	"	"	"	"	17	"	"	"
539,401 " 540,400	910	"	"	"	"	21	"	"	"
540,401 " 541,400	935	"	"	"	"	17	"	"	"
541,401 " 541,500	905	"	"	"	"	21	"	"	"
541,501 " 542,000	835	"	Htg.	"	"	17	"	"	10
542,001 " 542,300	800	"	"	"	"	24	"	"	"
542,301 " 542,500	810	"	"	"	"	21	"	"	"
542,501 " 542,700	900	"	O. F.	"	"	24	"	"	9
542,701 " 542,800	905	"	"	"	"	21	"	"	"
542,801 " 543,300	805	"	Htg.	"	"	..	"	"	10
543,301 " 543,500	905	"	O. F.	"	"	..	"	"	9
543,501 " 544,000	835	"	Htg.	"	"	17	"	"	10
544,001 " 544,100	560	16	"	¾ Pl.	"	"	"	"	3
544,101 " 544,200	570	"	"	"	"	"	"	"	"
544,201 " 544,400	560	"	"	"	"	"	"	"	"
544,401 " 544,500	530	"	"	"	"	21	"	"	"
544,501 " 544,800	550	"	"	"	"	17	"	"	4
544,801 " 545,000	540	"	"	"	"	21	"	"	"
545,001 " 545,500	535	"	O. F.	"	"	..	"	"	2
545,501 " 546,500	570	"	Htg.	"	"	17	"	"	3
546,501 " 546,600	540	"	"	"	"	21	"	"	4
546,601 " 546,700	500	"	"	"	"	..	"	"	"
546,701 " 546,800	510	"	"	"	"	"	"	"	"
546,801 " 546,900	520	"	"	"	"	"	"	"	"
546,901 " 547,000	530	"	"	"	"	"	"	"	3
547,001 " 548,000	560	"	"	"	"	17	"	"	"
548,001 " 549,000	565	"	O. F.	"	"	..	"	"	2
549,001 " 550,000	575	"	"	"	"	"	"	"	"
550,001 " 550,500	560	"	Htg.	"	"	"	"	"	3
550,501 " 550,600	515	"	O. F.	"	"	21	"	"	5
550,601 " 550,700	525	"	"	"	"	"	"	"	"
550,701 " 550,900	545	"	"	"	"	"	"	"	"
550,901 " 551,200	555	"	"	"	"	17	"	"	"
551,201 " 551,700	530	"	Htg.	"	"	21	"	"	3
551,701 " 552,700	575	"	O. F.	"	"	17	"	"	2
552,701 " 553,200	565	"	"	"	"	..	"	"	"
553,201 " 554,200	570	"	Htg.	"	"	"	"	"	3
554,201 " 554,700	565	"	O. F.	"	"	"	"	"	2
554,701 " 554,900	555	"	"	"	"	"	"	"	5
554,901 " 554,920	535	"	"	"	"	21	"	"	3
554,921 " 554,927	570	"	Htg.	"	"	17	"	"	2
554,928 " 554,930	575	"	O. F.	"	"	"	"	"	3
554,931 " 554,940	560	"	Htg.	"	"	11	"	"	3
554,941 " 554,960	605	"	O. F.	"	"	11	"	Pend.	Special
554,961		"	"	"	Gilt	..	"	"	"
554,962		"	"	"	"	"	"	"	"
554,963		"	"	"	"	"	"	"	"
554,964		"	Htg.	"	Nickel	17	"	"	"
554,965		"	"	"	Gilt	"	"	"	"
554,966		"	"	"	"	..	"	"	"
554,967		"	"	"	Nickel	"	"	"	"
554,968		"	"	"	Gilt	15	"	"	"
554,699		"	O. F.	"	....	..	"	"	"
554,970		"	"	"	"	"	"	"	"
554,971		"	Htg.	"	....	"	"	"	"
554,972		"	"	"	"	"	"	"	"

The Rockford Watch Company, Ltd.

Number and Grade of Movement	GRADE	Size		Style		Jewels	Wind	Sett	Model
554,973	....	16	Htg.	¾ Pl.	Gilt	11	Stem	Pend.	Special
554,974	935	18	O. F.	F. Pl.	Nickel	17	"	Lever	9
554,975	....	16	Htg.	¾ Pl.	Nickel	11	"	Pend.	Special
554,976	....	"	"	"	"	"	"	"	"
554,977	....	"	"	"	....	"	"	"	"
554,978	....	"	O. F.	"	Nickel	17	"	"	"
554,979	....	"	"	"	"	"	"	"	"
554,981 to 554,992	25	18	"	F. Pl.	"	25	"	Lever	"
555,001 " 556 000	560	16	Htg.	¾ Pl.	"	17	"	"	3
556,001 " 558,000	575	"	O. F.	"	"	"	"	"	2
558,001 " 558,500	550	"	Htg.	"	"	"	"	"	4
558,501 " 559,000	540	"	"	"	"	21	"	"	"
559,001 " 560,000	560	"	"	"	"	17	"	"	3
560,001 " 560,500	545	"	O. F.	"	"	21	"	"	5
560,501 " 561,000	555	"	"	"	"	17	"	"	"
561,001 " 562,000	835	18	Htg.	F. Pl.	"	"	"	"	10
562,001 " 563,000	935	"	O. F.	"	"	"	"	"	9
563,001 " 565,000	570	16	Htg.	¾ Pl.	"	"	"	"	3
565,001 " 566,000	575	"	O. F.	"	"	"	"	"	2
566,001 " 566,500	918	18	"	F. Pl.	"	24	"	"	9
566,501 " 566,600	930	"	"	"	"	17	"	"	"
566,601 " 566,800	935	"	"	"	"	"	"	"	"
566,801 " 566,900	830	"	Htg.	"	"	"	"	"	10
566,901 " 566,940	500	16	"	¾ Pl.	"	21	"	"	4
566,941 " 567,000	501	"	"	"	"	"	"	"	"
567,001 " 568,000	575	"	O. F.	"	"	17	"	"	2
568,001 " 570,000	570	"	Htg.	"	"	"	"	"	3
570,001 " 571,000	575	"	O. F.	"	"	"	"	"	2
571,001 " 571,300	545	"	"	"	"	21	"	"	5
571,301 " 571,500	575	"	"	"	"	17	"	"	2
571,501 " 571,530	505	"	"	"	"	21	"	"	5
571,531 " 571,600	515	"	"	"	"	"	"	"	"
571,601 " 571,700	570	"	Htg.	"	"	17	"	"	3
571,701 " 571,900	575	"	O. F.	"	"	"	"	"	2
571,901 " 572,000	585	"	"	"	"	15	"	"	"
572,001 " 572,700	565	"	"	"	"	17	"	"	"
572,701 " 573,000	560	"	Htg.	"	"	"	"	"	3
573,001 " 573,500	810	18	"	F. Pl.	"	21	"	"	10
573,501 " 573,510	590	16	"	¾ Pl.	"	.11	"	"	3
573,511 " 574,000	584	"	"	"	"	15	"	"	"
574,001 " 574,500	905	18	O. F.	F. Pl.	"	21	"	"	9
574,501 " 575,000	835	"	Htg.	"	"	17	"	"	10
575,001 " 577,000	570	16	"	¾ Pl.	"	"	"	"	3
577,001 " 577,500	584	"	"	"	"	15	"	"	"
577,501 " 577,800	565	"	O. F.	"	"	17	"	"	2
577,801 " 577,900	520	"	Htg.	"	"	21	"	"	4
577,901 " 578,000	525	"	O. F.	"	"	"	"	"	5
578,001 " 579,150	835	18	Htg.	F. Pl.	"	17	"	"	10
579,201 " 379,370	935	"	O. F.	"	"	"	"	"	9
579,401 " 379,500	570	16	Htg.	¾ Pl.	"	"	"	"	3
579,501 " 579,600	575	"	O. F.	"	"	"	"	"	2
579,601 " 579,700	560	"	Htg.	"	"	"	"	"	3
579,701 " 579,735	565	"	O. F.	"	"	"	"	"	2
579,801 ' 579,900	830	18	Htg.	F. Pl.	"	"	"	"	10
579,901 " 580,000	930	"	O. F.	"	"	"	"	"	9
580,001 " 580,200	560	16	Htg.	¾ Pl.	"	"	"	"	3
580,201 " 580,300	565	"	O. F.	"	"	"	"	"	2
580,301 " 580,500	570	"	Htg.	"	"	"	"	"	3
580,501 " 580,600	575	"	O. F.	"	"	"	"	"	2
580,601 " 581,000	930	18	"	F. Pl.	"	"	"	"	9
581,001 " 582,000	585	16	"	¾ Pl.	"	15	"	"	2
582,001 " 583,000	584	"	Htg.	"	"	"	"	"	3
583,001 " 584,000	560	"	"	"	"	17	"	"	"
584,001 " 585,000	584	"	"	"	"	15	"	"	"
585,001 " 585,500	935	18	O. F.	F. Pl.	"	17	"	"	9
585,501 " 585,600	515	16	"	¾ Pl.	"	21	"	"	5
585,601 " 585,700	525	"	"	"	"	"	"	"	"
585,701 " 585,800	830	18	Htg.	F. Pl.	"	17	"	"	10
585,801 " 585,900	930	"	O. F.	"	"	"	"	"	9
585,901 " 586,000	835	"	Htg.	"	"	"	"	"	10
586,001 " 588,000	584	16	"	¾ Pl.	"	15	"	"	3
588,001 " 590,000	835	18	"	F. Pl.	"	17	"	"	10
590,001 " 591,000	570	16	"	¾ Pl.	"	"	"	"	3
591,001 " 592,000	584	"	"	"	"	15.	"	"	"
592,001 " 593,000	835	18	"	F. Pl.	"	17	"	"	10
593,001 " 593,100	560	16	"	¾ Pl.	"	"	"	"	3
593,101 " 593,200	570	"	"	"	"	"	"	"	"
593,201 " 593,300	100	"	"	"	"	21	"	Pend.	Special
593,301 " 593,400	101	"	O. F.	"	"	"	"	"	"
593,401 " 593,600	925	18	"	F. Pl.	"	17	"	Lever	9
593,601 " 593,700	835	"	Htg.	"	"	"	"	"	10
593,701 " 593,800	825	"	"	"	"	"	"	"	"
593,801 " 593,900	520	16	"	¾ Pl.	"	21	"	"	4
593,901 " 594,000	505	"	O. F.	"	"	"	"	"	5
594,001 " 596,000	590	"	Htg.	"	"	11	"	Pend.	3
596,001 " 597,000	595	"	O. F.	"	"	"	"	"	2
597,001 " 598,000	590	"	Htg.	"	"	"	"	"	3
598,001 " 599,000	586	"	"	"	"	15	"	"	5
599,001 " 599,500	587	"	O. F.	"	"	"	"	"	2

The Rockford Watch Company, Ltd.

Number and Grade of Movement	GRADE	Size	Style		Jewels	Wind	Sett	Model
				Description of Movement				
599,501 to 599,502	575	16	O. F.	¾ Pl. Nickel	17	Stem	Lever	2
599,503 " 599,504	565	"	"	" "	"	"	"	"
599,505	575	"	"	" "	"	"	Pend.	"
599,506 to 600,000	587	"	"	" "	15	"	Pend.	"
600,001 " 601,000	935	18	"	F. Pl. "	17	"	Lever	9
601,001 " 602,000	590	16	Htg.	¾ Pl. "	11	"	Pend.	3
602,001 " 603,000	595	"	O. F.	" "	"	"	"	2
603,001 " 605,000	561	"	Htg.	" "	17	"	"	4
605,001 " 605,700	573	"	O. F.	" "	"	"	"	5
605,701 " 605,850	845	18	Htg.	F. Pl. "	21	"	Lever	Special
605,851 " 605,900	945	"	O. F.	" "	"	"	"	"
605,901 " 605,950	540	16	Htg.	¾ Pl. "	"	"	"	4
606,001 " 608,000	935	18	O. F.	F. Pl. "	17	"	"	9
608,001 " 609,000	572	16	Htg.	¾ Pl. "	"	"	Pend.	4
609,001 " 610,000	566	"	O. F.	" "	"	"	"	5
610,001 " 613,000	605	"	"	" "	11	"	"	2
613,001 " 614,000	587	"	"	" "	15	"	"	"
614,001 " 615,000	600	"	Htg.	" "	11	"	"	3
615,001 " 617,000	605	"	O. F.	" "	"	"	"	2
617,001 " 617,500	586	"	Htg.	" "	15	"	"	3
617,501 " 617,800	845	18	"	F. Pl. "	21	"	Lever	Special
617,801 " 618,000	810	"	"	" "	"	"	"	10
618,001 " 618,500	587	16	O. F.	¾ Pl. "	15	"	Pend.	2
618,501 " 618,600	578	"	Htg.	" "	17	"	"	3
618,601 " 618,700	579	"	O. F.	" "	"	"	"	2
618,701 " 618,800	600	"	Htg.	" "	11	"	"	3
618,801 " 618,900	586	"	"	" "	15	"	"	"
618,901 " 618,950	120	"	"	" "	17	"	"	Special
618,951 " 619,000	125	"	O. F.	" "	"	"	"	"
619,001 " 619,300	525	"	"	" "	21	"	Lever	5
619,301 " 619,700	600	"	Htg.	" "	11	"	Pend.	3
619,701 " 619,900	565	"	O. F.	" "	17	"	Lever	"
619,901 " 620,000	101	"	"	" "	21	"	Pend.	Special
620,001 " 621,000	545	"	"	' "	"	"	Lever	5
621,001 " 622,000	935	18	"	F. Pl. "	17	"	"	9
622,001 " 622,300	160	0	Htg.	¾ Pl. "	15	"	Pend.	1
622,301 " 622,350	140	"	"	" "	17	"	"	"
622,351 " 622,500	150	"	"	" "	"	"	"	"
622,501 " 623,000	160	"	"	" "	15	"	"	"
623,001 " 623,100	200	18	O. F.	F. Pl. "	17	"	Lever	10
623,101 " 623,500	605	16	"	¾ Pl. "	11	"	Pend.	2
623,501 " 624,000	160	0	Htg.	" "	15	"	"	1
624,001 " 624,200	205	18	O. F.	F. Pl. "	17	"	Lever	10
624,201 " 624,300	945	"	"	" "	21	"	"	Special
624,301 " 624,400	930	"	"	" "	17	"	"	9
624,401 " 624,450	110	16	Htg.	¾ Pl. "	"	"	Pend.	Special
624,451 " 624,500	115	"	O. F.	" "	"	"	"	"
624,501 " 624,525	130	"	Htg.	" Gilt	"	"	"	"
624,526 " 624,550	135	"	O. F.	" "	"	"	"	"
624,601 " 624,800	540	"	Htg.	" Nickel	21	"	Lever	4
625,001 " 625,400	400	"	"	" "	17	"	Pend.	"
626,001 " 626,200	405	"	"	" "	21	"	"	5
626,201 " 626,400	510	"	"	" "	"	"	Lever	4
626,401 " 626,600	515	"	O. F.	" "	"	"	"	5
626,601 " 626,700	520	"	Htg.	" "	"	"	"	4
626,701 " 626,900	525	"	O. F.	" "	"	"	"	5
626,901 " 627,000	845	18	Htg.	F. Pl. "	"	"	"	Special
627,001 " 627,300	572	16	"	¾ Pl. "	17	"	Pend.	4
628,001 " 628,100	500	"	"	" "	21	"	Lever	"
628,101 " 628,300	520	"	"	" "	"	"	"	"
628,301 " 628,500	515	"	O. F.	" "	"	"	"	5
628,501 " 628,600	505	"	"	" "	"	"	"	5
628,601 " 628,800	510	"	Htg.	" "	"	"	"	4
628,801 " 628,950	100	"	"	" "	"	"	Pend.	Special
628,951 " 629,000	101	"	O. F.	" "	"	"	"	"
629,001 " 630,000	935	18	"	F. Pl. "	17	"	Lever	9
630,001 " 630,600	835	"	Htg.	" "	"	"	"	10
630,601 " 630,700	162	0	"	¾ Pl. "	"	"	Pend.	1
630,701 " 630,800	150	"	"	" "	"	"	"	"
630,801 " 631,000	160	"	"	" "	15	"	"	"
631,001 " 632,000	586	16	"	" "	"	"	"	3
632,001 " 632,500	825	18	"	F. Pl. "	17	"	Lever	10
633,001 " 633,500	925	"	O. F.	" "	"	"	"	9
634,001 " 635,000	587	16	"	¾ Pl. "	15	"	Pend.	2
635,001 " 636,000	935	18	"	F. Pl. "	17	"	Lever	9
636,001 " 636,500	160	0	Htg.	¾ Pl. "	15	"	Pend.	1
636,501 " 636,600	150	"	"	" "	17	"	"	"
636,601 " 638,000	160	"	"	" "	15	"	"	"
638,001 " 639,000	600	16	"	" "	11	"	"	3
639,001 " 640,000	160	0	"	" "	15	"	Pend.	1
640,001 " 641,000	162	"	"	" "	"	"	"	"
641,001 " 642,000	610	16	"	" "	7	"	"	Special
642,001 " 643,000	615	"	O. F.	" "	"	"	"	3
643,001 " 644,000	587	"	"	" "	15	"	"	2
644,001 " 644,500	142	0	Htg.	" "	17	"	"	1
645,001 " 646,600	162	"	"	" "	15	"	"	1
646,001 " 647,000	610	16	"	" "	7	"	"	Special
647,001 " 648,000	615	"	O. F.	" "	"	"	"	3
648,001 " 649,000	160	0	Htg.	" "	15	"	Pend.	1
649,001 " 650,000	605	16	O. F.	" "	11	"	"	2

The Rockford Watch Company, Ltd.

Number and Grade of Movement	GRADE	Description of Movement						
		Size	Style		Jewels	Wind	Sett	Model
650,001 " 651,000	573	16	O. F.	¾ Pl.	Nickel	17	Stem	Pend.	5
651,001 to 656,000	160	0	Htg.	"	"	15	"	"	1
656,001 " 656,100	152	"	"	"	"	17	"	"	Special
657,001 " 657,200	182	"	"	"	"	7	"	"	"
658,001 " 659,000	600	16	"	"	"	11	"	"	3
659,001 " 659,200	930	18	O. F.	F. Pl.	"	17	"	Lever	9
660,001 " 660,100	910	"	"	"	"	21	"	"	"
661,101 " 661,200	810	"	Htg.	"	"	"	"	"	10
662,001 " 662,600	100	16	O. F.	¾ Pl.	"	"	"	Pend.	Special
663,001 " 663,100	101	"	O. F.	"	"	"	"	"	"
664,001 " 664,100	845	18	Htg.	F. Pl.	"	"	"	Lever	"
665,001 " 665,100	830	"	"	"	"	17	"	"	10
666,001 " 666,100	900	"	O. F.	"	"	24	"	"	9
667,001 " 667,100	905	"	"	"	"	21	"	"	"
668,001 " 669,000	605	16	"	¾ Pl.	"	11	"	Pend.	2
669,001 " 669,100	912	18	"	F. Pl.	Spot Gilt	21	"	Lever	9
670,001 " 670,100	537	16	"	¾ Pl.	"	"	"	"	2
671,001 " 671,300	200	18	"	F. Pl.	Nickel	17	"	"	10
672,001 " 673,000	205	"	"	"	"	"	"	"	"
674,001 " 675,000	405	16	"	¾ Pl.	"	"	"	Pend.	5
675,001 " 675,500	525	"	"	"	"	21	"	Lever	"
676,001 " 677,000	566	"	"	"	"	17	"	Pend.	"
677,001 " 678,000	573	"	"	"	"	"	"	"	"
678,001 " 678,500	586	"	"	"	"	15	"	"	3
679,001 " 680,500	587	"	"	"	"	"	"	"	2
681,001 " 682,000	600	"	Htg.	"	"	11	"	"	3
682,001 " 686,000	605	"	O. F.	"	"	"	"	"	2
686,001 " 693,000	615	"	"	"	"	7	"	"	"
693,001 " 694,000	610	"	Htg.	"	"	"	"	"	3
694,001 " 694,500	935	18	O. F.	F. Pl.	"	17	"	Lever	9
695,001 " 695,500	945	"	"	"	"	21	"	"	Special

(More Serial Numbers and Grade of Movement next page.)

STYLE & NAMES OF U.S.A. HANDS

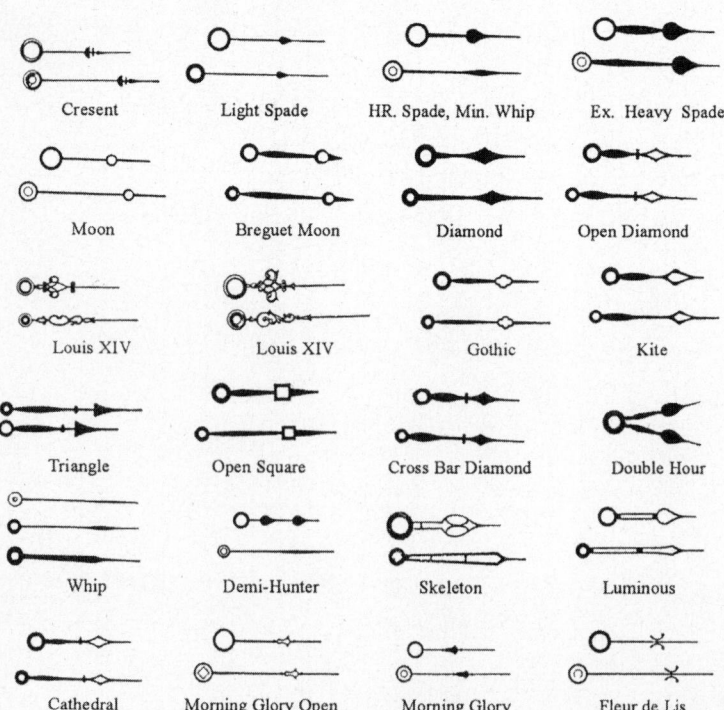

Cresent   Light Spade   HR. Spade, Min. Whip   Ex. Heavy Spade

Moon   Breguet Moon   Diamond   Open Diamond

Louis XIV   Louis XIV   Gothic   Kite

Triangle   Open Square   Cross Bar Diamond   Double Hour

Whip   Demi-Hunter   Skeleton   Luminous

Cathedral   Morning Glory Open   Morning Glory   Fleur de Lis

SERIAL NUMBER — Grade, Size, Style, Jewels, Model #

695501-696000=945,18S.O.F.21J,M#SP.
696001-697000=838,18S.H.C.17J,M#10
697001-698000=938,18S.O.F.17J,M# 9
698001-699000=150, 0S. H.C.17J.M# 1
699001-700000=140, 0S. H.C.17J.M# 1
700001-702100=180, 0S. H.C. 7J,M# 1
702101-703000=160, 0S. H.C.15J.M# 1
703001-703500=170, 0S. H.C.11J.M# 1
703501-704000=160, 0S. H.C.15J.M# 1
704001-704300=935,18S.O.F.17J.M# 9
704301-704400=930,18S.O.F.17J.M# 9
704401-704500=935,18S.O.F.17J.M# 9
704501-704600=930,18S.O.F.17J.M# 9
704601-705000=935,18S.O.F.17J.M# 9
705001-706000=572,16S.H.C.17J.M# 4
706001-707000=600,16S.H.C.11J.M# 3
707001-708000=918,18S.O.F.21J.M# 9
708001-709000=586,16S.H.C.15J.M# 4
709001-710000=587,16S.O.F.15J.M# 3
710001-710100=930,18S.O.F.17J.M# 9
710101-710600=935,18S.O.F.17J.M# 9
710601-710700=930,18S.O.F.17J.M# 9
710701-711000=935,18S.O.F.17J.M# 9
711001-711100=830,18S.H.C.17J.M# 9
711101-711500=835,18S.H.C.17J.M#10
711501-711600=830,18S.H.C.17J.M#10
711601-712000=835,18S.H.C.17J.M#10
712001-712700=573,16S.O.F.17J.M# 5
712701-713000=635,16S.O.F.17J.M# 5
713001-714000=610,16S.O.F. 7J.M#SP.
714001-715000=572,16S.H.C.17J.M# 4
715001-716000=586,16S.O.F.15J.M# 3
716001-717000=587,16S.O.F.15J.M# 2
717001-718000=600,16S.O.F.11J.M# 3
718001-719000=605,16S.O.F.11J.M# 3
719001-720000=615,16S.O.F. 7J.M# 3
720001-721000=610,16S.O.F. 7J.M#SP.
721001-721500=600,16S.H.C.11J.M# 3
721501-722000=586,16S.H.C.15J.M# 3
722501-722700=573,16S.O.F.17J.M# 5
722701-722800=635,16S.O.F.17J.M# 5
722801-722900=573,16S.O.F.17J.M# 5
722901-723000=635,16S.O.F.17J.M# 5
723001-724000=935,18S.O.F.17J.M#10
724001-725000=205,18S.O.F.17J.M# 9
725001-725100=930,18S.O.F.17J.M# 9
725101-726000=935,18S.O.F.17J.M# 9
726001-727000=405,16S.O.F.17J.M# 5
727001-728000=587,16S.O.F.15J.M# 2
728001-728500=573,16S.O.F.17J.M# 5
728501-728600=635,16S.O.F.17J.M# 5
728601-728800=573,16S.O.F.17J.M# 5
728801-729000=635,16S.O.F.17J.M# 5
729001-729800=600,16S.H.C.11J.M# 3
729801-730000=586,16S.O.F.15J.M# 3
730001-730700=610,16S.O.F. 7J.M#SP.
730701-731000=586,16S.O.F.15J.M# 3
731001-732000=615,16S.O.F. 7J.M# 3
732001-732500=162, 0S.H.C.17J.M# 1
732501-733000=150, 0S.H.C.17J.M# 1
733001-734000=572, 6S.H.C.17J.M# 4
734001-735000=586,16S.O.F.15J.M# 2
734501-735200=610,16S.H.C. 7J.M#SP.
735201-736000=586,16S.O.F.15J.M# 2
736001-738000=935,18S.O.F.17J.M# 9
738001-739000=938,18S.O.F.17J.M#10
739001-740000=925,18S.O.F.17J.M# 9
740001-740200=830,18S.H.C.17J.M#10
740201-741000=835,18S.H.C.17J.M#10
741001-741100=600,16S.H.C.11J.M# 3
741101-742000=586,16S.H.C.15J.M# 3
742001-742500=605,16S.O.F.11J.M# 2
742501-743000=587,16S,O,F.15J.M# 2
743001-745000=935,18S.O.F.17J.M# 9
745001-746000=930,18S.O.F.17J.M# 9
746001-747000=586,16S.O.F.15J.M# 2
747001-748000=935,18S.O.F.17J.M# 9
748001-749000=938,18S.O.F.17J.M#10
749001-749600=572,16S.H.C.17J.M# 4
749601-750000=630,16S.H.C.17J.M# 4
750001-750200=573,16S.O.F.17J.M# 5
750201-750600=635,16S.O.F.17J.M# 5
750601-751000=573,16S.O.F.17J.M# 5
751001-751200=605,16S.O.F.15J.M# 2
752001-752100=572,16S.H.C.17J.M# 4
752101-752200=630,16S.H.C.17J.M# 4
752201-753000=572,16S.H.C.17J.M# 4
753001-754000=573,16S.O.F.17J.M# 5
754001-755000=586,16S.H.C.15J.M# 3
755001-756000=587,16S.O.F.15J.M# 2
756001-757000=935,18S.O.F.17J.M# 9
757001-758000=925,18S.O.F.17J.M# 9
758001-759000=150, 0S.H.C.17J.M# 1
759001-759500=572,16S.H.C.17J.M# 4

**FROM
ROCKFORD
PARTS CATALOG
1907 to 1910**

SERIAL NUMBER — Grade, Size, Style, Jewels, Model #

759501-756000=620,16S.H.C.21J.M# 5
760001-760500=573,16S.O.F.17J.M# 5
760501-761000=625,16S.O.F.21J.M# 5
761001-762000=160, 0S.H.C.15J.M# 1
762001-762500=400,16S.H.C.17J.M# 4
762501-764000=405,16S.O.F.17J.M# 5
764001-765000=205,18S.O.F.17J.M#10
765001-765500=515,16S.O.F.21J.M# 5
765501-766000=545,16S.O.F.21J.M# 5
760010-767000=930,18S.O.F.17J.M# 9
767001-768000=572,16S.H.C.17J.M# 4
768001-769000=935,18S.O.F.17J.M# 9
769001-770000=918,18S.O.F.21J.M#10
770001-770500=938,18S.O.F.17J.M#10
770501-771000=835,18S.H.C.17J.M#10
771001-772000=586,16S.O.F.15J.M# 3
772001-772100=320,12S.H.C.17J.M# 1
772001-772200=330,12S.H.C.17J.M# 1
772201-772300=310,12S.H.C.21J.M# 1
772301-772400=300,12S.H.C.23J.M# 1
772401-772600=325,12S.O.F.17J.M# 2
772601-772800=335,12S.O.F.17J.M# 2
772801-772900=315,12S.O.F.21J.M# 2
772901-773000=305,12S.O.F.23J.M# 2
773001-773100=300,12S.H.C.23J.M# 1
773101-773200=310,12S.H.C.21J.M# 1
773201-773400=320,12S.H.C.17J.M# 1
773401-773500=305,12S.O.F.23J.M# 2
773501-773600=315,12S.O.F.21J.M# 2
773601-773800=325,12S.O.F.17J.M# 2
773801-774000=330,12S.H.C.17J.M# 1
774001-774500=335,12S.O.F.17J.M# 1
774501-774700=325,12S.O.F.17J.M# 2
774701-774000=330,12S.H.C.17J.M# 1
774901-775000=320,12S.H.C.17J.M# 1
775001-776000=587,16S.O.F.15J.M# 2
776001-777000=630,16S.H.C.17J.M# 5
777001-778000=635,16S.O.F.17J.M# 5
778001-779000=838,18S.H.C.17J.M#10
779001-779500=938,18S.H.C.17J.M#10
779501-780000=935,18S.O.F.17J.M# 9
780001-781000=835,18S.H.C.17J.M#10
781001-782000=545,16S.O.F.21J.M# 5
782001-783000=404,16S.O.F.17J.M# 5
783001-784000=561,16S.H.C.17J.M# 4
784001-785000=930,18S.O.F.17J.M# 9
785001-786000=205,18S.O.F.17J.M# 9
786001-787000=935,18S.O.F.17J.M# 9
787001-787200=310,12S.H.C.21J.M# 1
787201-788000=335,12S.O.F.17J.M# 2
788001-788100=315,12S.O.F.21J.M# 2
788101-789000=335,12S.O.F.17J.M# 2
789001-789100=330,12S.H.C.17J.M# 1
789001-789500=320,12S.H.C.17J.M# 1
789501-790000=330,12S.H.C.17J.M3 1
790001-791000=325,12S.O.F.17J.M# 2
791001-792000=330,12S.H.C.17J.M# 1
792001-792900=335,12S.O.F.17J.M# 2
722901-793000=355,12S.O.F.17J.M# 2
793001-796000=935,18S.O.F.17J.M# 9
796001-797000=930,18S.O.F.17J.M# 9
797001-798000=938,18S.O.F.17J.M# 9
798001-799000=830,18S.H.C.17J.M# 8
799001-800000=587,16S.O.F.15J.M# 2
800001-801000=572,16S.H.C.17J.M# 4
801001-802000=573,16S.O.F.17J.M# 5
802001-802500=573,16S.O.F.17J.M# 5
802501-803000=566,16S.O.F.17J.M# 5
803001-804000=573,16S.O.F.17J.M# 5
804001-805000=150, 0S.H.C.17J.M# 1
805001-806000=335,12S.O.F.17J.M# 2
806001-806100=300,12S.H.C.23J.M# 1
806101-807000=335,12S.O.F.17J.M# 2
807001-807100=305,12S.O.F.23J.M# 2
807101-808000=335,12S.O.F.17J.M# 2
808001-810000=573,16S.O.F.17J.M# 5
810001-811000=572,16S,H,C.17J.M# 4
811001-812000=160, 0S.H.C.15J.M# 1
812001-813000=330,12S.H.C.17J.M# 1
813001-814000=355,12S.O.F.17J.M# 1
814001-814500=350,12S.H.C.17J.M# 1
814501-814600=345,12S.H.C.21J.M# 1
814601-814700=340,12S.O.F.21J.M# 2
814701-815000=350,12S.H.C.17J.M# 1
815001-816000=335,12S.O.F.17J.M# 1
816001-817000=190, 0S.H.C.15J.M# 1
817001-818000=185 0S.H.C.17J.M# 1
818001-819000=335,12S.O.F.17J.M# 2
819001-820000=355,12S.O.F.17J.M# 2
820001-821000=190, 0S.H.C.15J.M# 1
821001-822000=335,12S.H.C.17J.M# 1
822001-823000=350,12S.H.C.17J.M# 1
823001-824000=330,12S.H.C.17J.M# 1

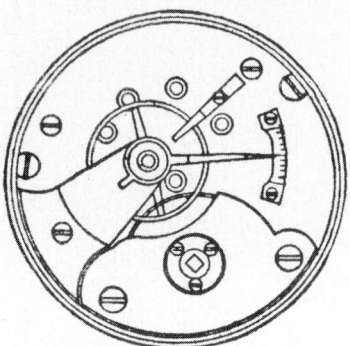

Model 1, 18 size, full plate, hunting, key wind & set.

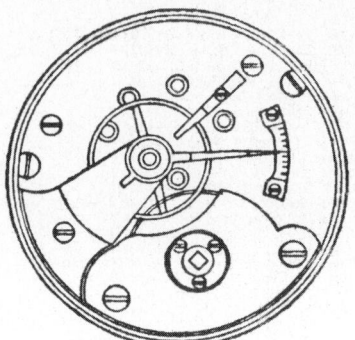

Model 2, 18 size, full plate, hunting, lever set.

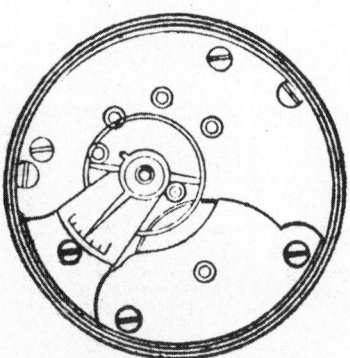

Model 3, 18 size, full plate, hunting, lever set.

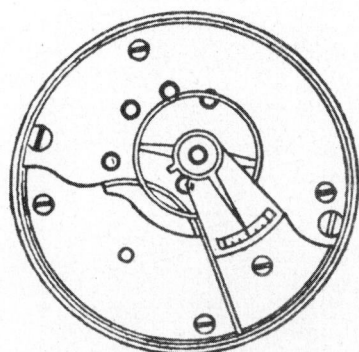

Model 4, 18 size, full plate, open face, lever set.

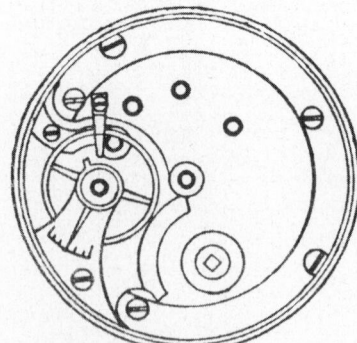

Model 5, 18 size, three-quarter plate, hunting, lever set.

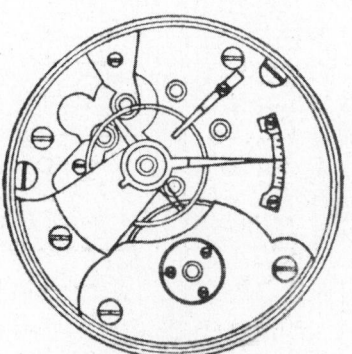

Model 6, 18 size, full plate, hunting, lever set, exposed escapement.

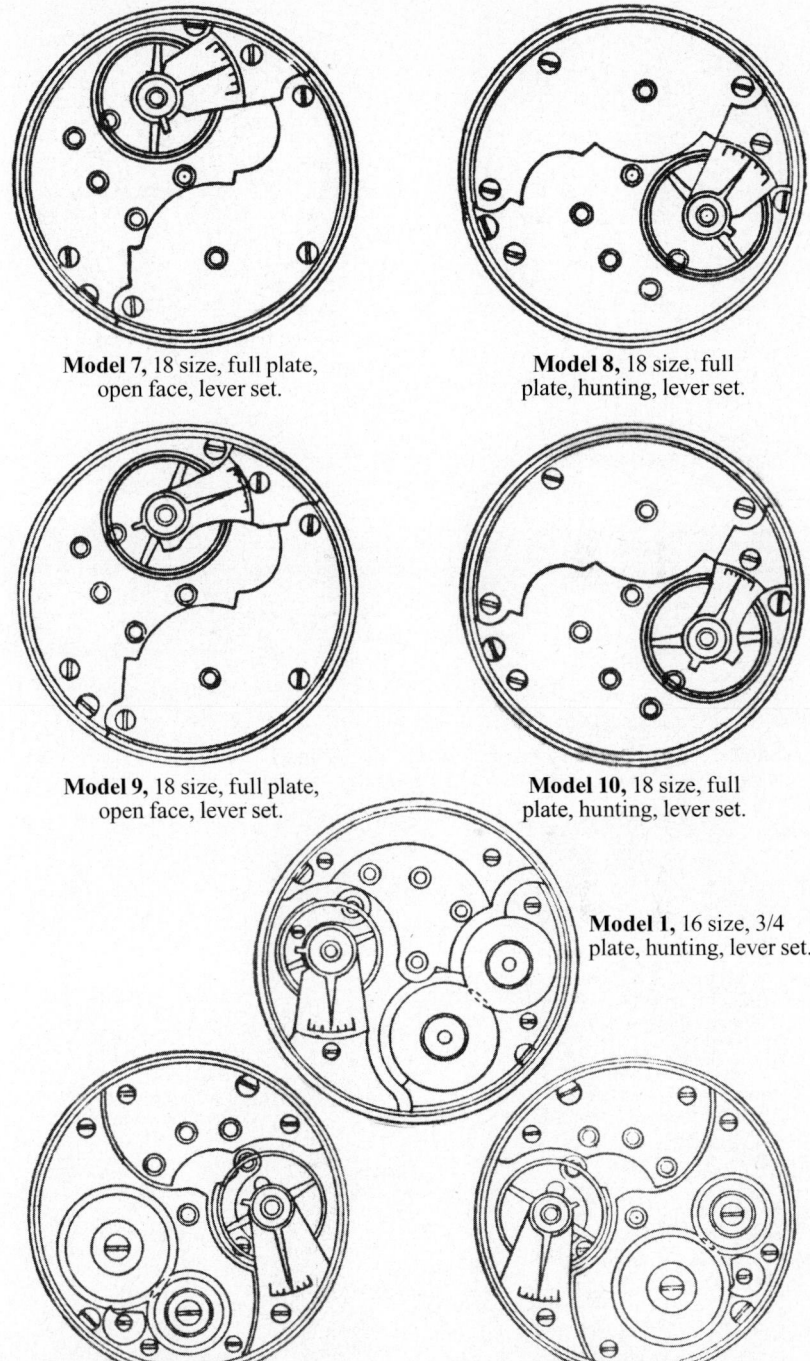

Model 7, 18 size, full plate, open face, lever set.

Model 8, 18 size, full plate, hunting, lever set.

Model 9, 18 size, full plate, open face, lever set.

Model 10, 18 size, full plate, hunting, lever set.

Model 1, 16 size, 3/4 plate, hunting, lever set.

Model 2, 16 size, three-quarter plate, open face, pendant & lever set.

Model 3, 16 size, three-quarter plate, hunting, pendant & lever set.

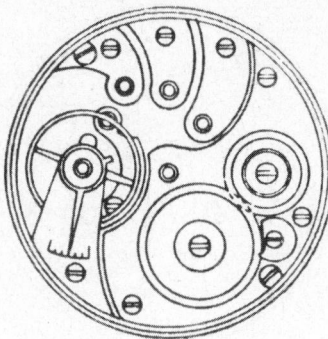

Model 4, 16 size, three-quarter plate, bridge, hunting, pendant & lever set.

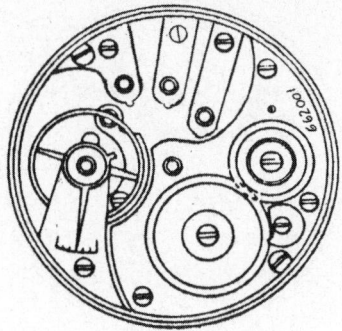

Model 4 "SPECIAL", 16 size, 3/4 plate, hunting, pendant set.

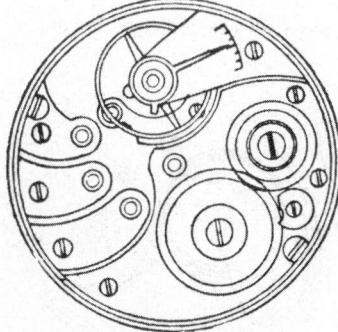

Model 5, 16 size, three quarter plate, bridge, open face pendant & lever set.

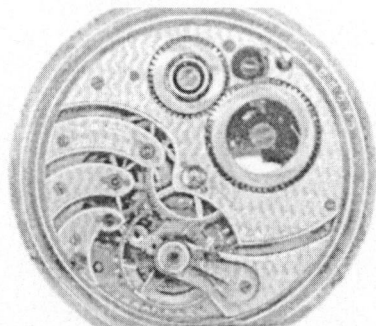

Model 1, 12 size, three quarter plate bridge, hunting, pendant set.

Model 2, 12 size, three quarter plate bridge, open face, pendant set.

Model 1, 6 & 8 size, three quarter plate, hunting, lever set.

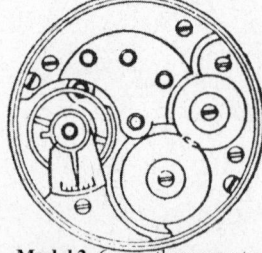

Model 2, 6 size, three quarter plate, hunting, lever set.

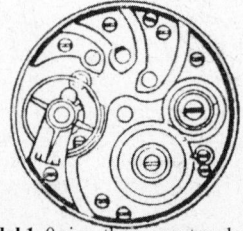

Model 1, 0 size, three quarter plate, bridge, hunting, pendant set.

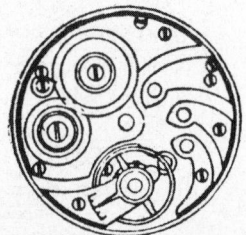

Model 2, 0 size, three quarter plate, bridge, open face, pendant set.

SAN JOSE WATCH CO.

California 1891

Very few watches were made by the San Jose Watch Co., and very little is known about them. The company purchased the Otay Watch Company and machinery and remaining watch movements. The San Jose Watch Co. produced a few dozen watches. Engraved on a San Jose Watch Co. movement S# 30,656 (First watch manufactured by San Jose Watch Co. November 1891). The San Jose W. Co was sold to Osaka, in Japan.

Grade or Name — Description		ABP	Ex-Fn	Mint
18S, 15J, LS, SW	★★★	$2,400	$4,000	$5,000

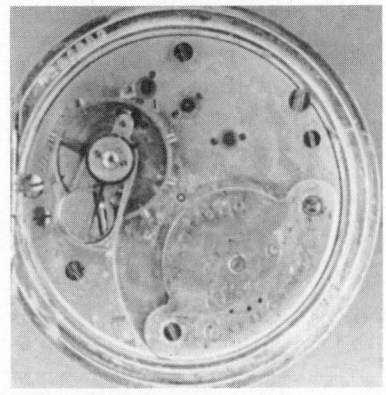 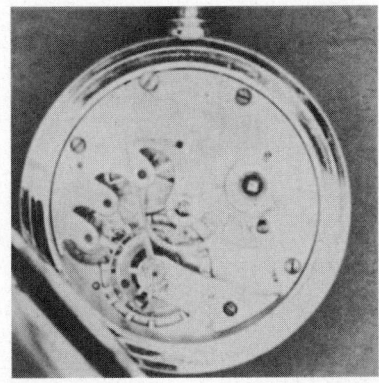

SAN JOSE WATCH CO. movement 18 size 15 jewels, Otay W. Co. material & machinery used to produce movement.

M. S. Smith & Co. movement Freeport style or Model, 18 size, 19 jewels, three-quarter plate, key wind & set.

M. S. SMITH & CO.

Detroit, Michigan 1870 - 1874

Eber B. Ward purchased the M. S. Smith & Co. which was a large jewelry firm. These watches carried the Smith name on them. A Mr. Hoyt was engaged to produce these watches and about 100 were produced before the Freeport Watch Co. purchased the firm. These watches are very similar to the **"J. H. Allison"** movements.

Grade or Name — Description		ABP	Ex-En	Mint
18S, 19J, 3/4, KW, KS, Freeport Model, **18K** case	★★★★	$3,500	$6,000	$10,000
18S, 19J, 3/4, KW, KS, Freeport Model	★★★★	2,000	3,000	5,000
18S, 15J, 3/4, wolf's tooth -wind, Swiss, **14K** HC	★	800	1,200	1,500
6S, 15J, KW, KS, HC **18K** case	★	500	800	1,200
6S, 15J, SW	★	200	400	500

 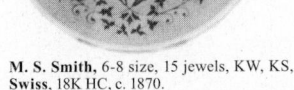

M. S. Smith & Co., 18S, 15J, 3/4, wolf's tooth-wind, Swiss, c. 1874.

M. S. Smith, 6-8 size, 15 jewels, KW, KS, Swiss, 18K HC, c. 1870.

SOUTH BEND WATCH CO.

South Bend, Indiana - March 1902 - 1929

Brothers George, Clement & uncle John M. Studebaker, purchased the successful Columbus W. Co. The serial numbers started at 380,501 where the Columbus serial numbers stopped. Early South Bend full plate watches, some of which were actually assembled in Columbus, Ohio in 1902, they are re-worked Columbus designs. The Polaris, a 16 size, 21 jeweled watch came only in a solid gold case and The Studebaker 223 & 229 also grades 227, 292, 293, 294 and 295 were all Railroad grade watches, and the 18 size grades, The Studebaker 323, 328, and 329 as well as grade 327. The 12 size grade 431 is also a very high grade. Movement models are known by grade numbers 100 through 431. The first digit in the grade number as: 1 denotes 0 & 6 size, 2 denotes 16 size, 3 denotes 18 size and 4 denotes 12 size, the last digit denotes movement type, even 4 denotes hunting case (HC) & odd 4 denotes open face (OF). Example: Grade 4 431 the first digit (4) denotes 12 size & the last digit (1) denotes open face (OF). They made over 850,000 watches in 71 grades, S sizes & 17 models.

SOUTH BEND ESTIMATED SERIAL NUMBERS AND PRODUCTION DATES

DATE -SERIAL NO.	DATE —SERIAL NO.	DATE -SERIAL NO.	DATE -SERIAL NO.
1903 — 380,501	1910 — 600,000	1917 — 860,000	1924 — 1,070,000
1904 — 390,000	1911 — 660,000	1918 — 880,000	1925 — 1,105,000
1905 — 405,000	1912 — 715,000	1919 — 905,000	1926 — 1,140,000
1906 — 425,000	1913 — 765,000	1920 — 935,000	1927 — 1,175,000
1907 — 460,000	1914 — 800,000	1921 — 975,000	1928 — 1,210,000
1908 — 500,000	1915 — 820,000	1922 — 1,000,000	1929 — 1,240,000
1909 — 550,000	1916 — 840,000	1923 — 1,035,000	

The above list is provided for determining the APPROXIMATE age of your watch. Match serial number with date. Watches were not necessarily sold in the exact order of manufactured date.

SOUTH BEND
18 SIZE (Lever set)

Grade or Name — Description	ABP	Ex-Fn	Mint
South Bend, 15J, OF......................................	$85	$150	$175
South Bend, 15J, HC......................................	125	200	250
South Bend, 17J, OF......................................	100	150	200
South Bend, 17J, HC......................................	135	200	265
South Bend, 21J, OF......................................	375	500	700
South Bend, 21J, HC, **14K**	650	1,200	1,500
South Bend, 21J, OF, HC, Silveroid.........................	300	400	500
South Bend, 21J, SW, HC...................................	500	600	900
The Studebaker, G#323, 17J, GJS, NI, Adj.5P, OF	500	900	1,200
The Studebaker, G#328, 21J, GJS, NI, FULL, Adj.5P, HC.... ★★★	900	1,500	2,000
The Studebaker, G#329, 21J, GJS, NI, FULL, Adj.5P, OF	700	1,200	1,600

The **last** digit of Grade # denotes style of movement Even # = Hunting & Odd # = Open Face.

	MINIMUM PRICE	COST	JEWEL	SIZE	GRADE O.F.	Hg.
	$ 9.00		7	0		100
	12.50		15	0		110
	16.00		17	0		120
	6.50		7	16	261	260
	11.00		15	16	281	280
	14.50		17 Adj.	16	291	290
	20.00		17 Adj.	16	299	298
	26.00		19 Adj.	16	293	292
	35.00		21 Adj.	16	295	294
	8.00		15	18	331	330
	8.50		15	18	333	332
	12.25		17 Adj.	18	341	340
	14.00		17 Adj.	18	313	
	20.00		17 Adj.	18	345	344
	26.00		17 Adj.	18	323	
	35.00		21 Adj.	18	329	
	11.25		17	18	343	342
	11.50		17	18	347	346

FORM 78-5M-5-1-10   SOUTH BEND WATCH CO.
PRICE LIST

Above: South Bend Price List for movement only Ca. about **1910**

South Bend movement, 18 size, 17 jewels, stem wind, hunting, serial number 426,726.

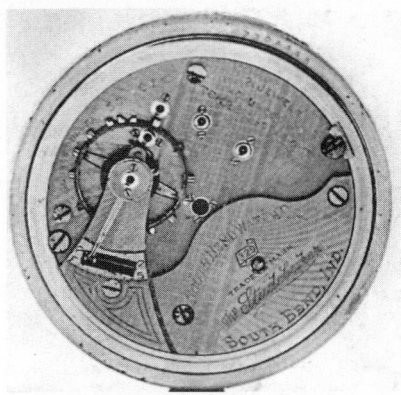

The Studebaker in (in SCRIPT), 18 size, 21 jewels, gold jewel settings, marked 329, stem wind.

Grade or Name —Description	ABP	Ex-Fn	Mint
302, 15J, M#1, HC, (not seen) ....★★★★★	$500	$800	$1,200
304, 15J, HC	110	200	330
305, 15J, OF	110	175	200
305, 15J, Silveroid, OF	110	175	200
309, 17J, OF	110	175	245
312, 17J, NI, ADJ, HC...........................★★	165	250	350
313, 17J, NI, ADJ, **marked 313** OF ....★	220	325	475
313, 17J, NI, ADJ, **Not Marked**, OF	135	225	350
315, 17J, NI, Adj.3P, OF	110	175	250
For - G#s 323, 328 & 329 see *"The Studebaker"*			
327, 21J, Adj.5P, marked 327, OF.................★★★	500	600	1,000
330, 15J, M#1, LS, HC	110	220	330
331, 15J, M#1, LS, OF...............................	110	175	220
332, 15J, HC	110	200	330
333, 15J, OF..	110	175	220
337, 17J, OF..	110	175	245
340, 17J, M#1, Adj.3P, NI, HC.........................	135	200	330
341, 17J, M#1, ADJ, NI, Adj.3P, OF.....................	110	175	245
342, 17J, M#1, LS	110	175	245
343, 17J, M#1, LS, OF	110	175	245
344, 17J, NI, Adj.3P, HC........................★★	410	525	770
345, 17J, NI, Adj.3P, OF ....★	355	425	715
346, 17J, NI, HC.................................★★	385	490	660
347, 17J, NI, OF	121	200	300

Grade # s are conveniently numbered if the starting digit is 1 it is for 0 & 6 sizes, starting digit 2=16 size, starting digit 3=18 size, starting digit 4=12 size. The final digit of the Grade # if it is Even it is a Hunting Case. if final digit is Odd it is Open Face. Example: G# 347, 3=18 size, 7=open faced.

Note: Gold Filled cases marked, South Bend or Pyramid - **30yr.,** =$60- $100 - $250
            Gold Filled cases marked, South Bend or Pilgrim - **25yr.,** =$50 - $80 - $180
            Gold Filled cases marked, South Bend or Panama - **20yr.,** =$40 - $70 - $150

☞ Generic, nameless or unmarked grades for watch movements are listed under the Company name or initials of the Company, etc. by size, jewel count and description.

☞ A collector should expect to pay modestly higher prices at local shops.

☞ Pricing in this Guide are fair market price for complete watches which are reflected from the NAWCC National and regional shows.

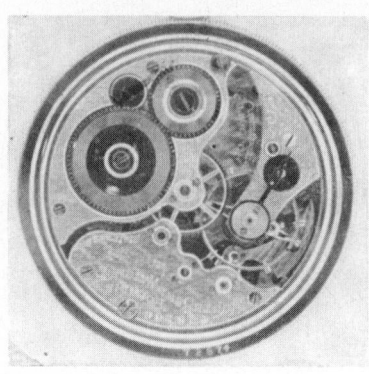

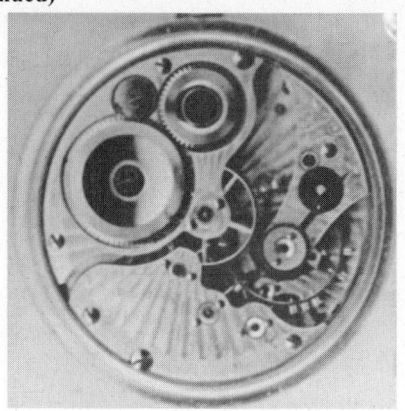

South Bend Watch Co. **Polaris**, 16 size, 21 jewels, model number 1, Adj.5p, gold jewel setting, gold train, open face, 14K case, serial number 518,236. (made from grade 295)

Grade marked **295**, 16S, 21J., first model, gold jewel settings, Adj.5p, gold train, OF, S# 518,022. Example left & right came from same run(518001-518500)

Grade # s are conveniently numbered if the starting digit is 1 it is for 0 & 6 sizes, starting digit 2 = 16 size, starting digit 3 = 18 size, starting digit 4 = 12 size. The final digit of the Grade # if it is Even it is a Hunting Case. if final digit is Odd it is Open Face. Example: G# 347 =18 size, open faced.

16 SIZE

Grade or Name — Description	ABP	Ex-Fn	Mint
Polaris, 21J, M#1, Adj.5P, 3/4, NI, DR, GJS, GT,			
14K South Bend case marked Polaris on dial & MVT ★★★★	$2,200	$3,500	$5,000
South Bend, 7J, OF.......................................	70	125	150
South Bend, 7J, HC.......................................	100	150	200
South Bend, 9J, OF.......................................	70	125	150
South Bend, 9J, HC.......................................	100	150	200
South Bend, 15J, OF......................................	70	125	150
South Bend, 15J, HC......................................	100	150	225
South Bend, 15J, OF, Silveroid............................	70	125	150
South Bend, 17J, OF......................................	70	125	150
South Bend, 17J, HC, ADJ.................................	125	175	250
South Bend, 17J, **14K HC**...............................	450	550	850
The Studebaker 223, 17J, M#2, Adj.5p., GJS, DR, GT............	600	900	1,300
The Studebaker 229, 21J, M#2, Adj.5p., GJS, DR, GT............	850	1,200	1,600
* Movements marked "**Studebaker 8-adjustments**" should not be confused with *The Studebaker*.			
Studebaker, 21J, PS, 8Adj, OF............................	300	500	600
203, 7J, 3/4, NI, OF......................................	70	125	150
204, 15J, 3/4, NI, HC	90	150	200
207, 15J, PS...	70	125	150
209, 9J, M#2, PS, OF	65	125	150
211, 17J, M#2,3/4,NI,OF	75	125	175
212, 17J, M#2, LS, heat & cold, HC.......................	125	175	250
215, 17J, M#2, LS, heat & cold, OF	70	125	150
217, 17J, M#2, NI, BRG, DR, GT, ADJ.3P, OF	95	150	200
219 marked 219, 19J, DR, ADJ.4P, OF	150	200	350

A watch marked as 5 positions is equivalent to one marked eight adjustment (the most common found on RR watches) and will be listed in this book as: "Adj.5P" (adjusted to heat, cold, isochronism and 5 positions). A watch marked as nine adjustments is equivalent to one marked 6 positions & listed as "Adj.6P" (adjusted to heat, cold, isochronism and 6 positions). A watch that is marked as ADJUSTED only is adjusted to isochronism & in poise in all temperatures & is listed as "Adj.".
*Later some manufactures used a variations of 8 adjustments, six to position, 1-isochronism, 1-temperature or as in the Elgin grade 571 two to temperature in about 1950.

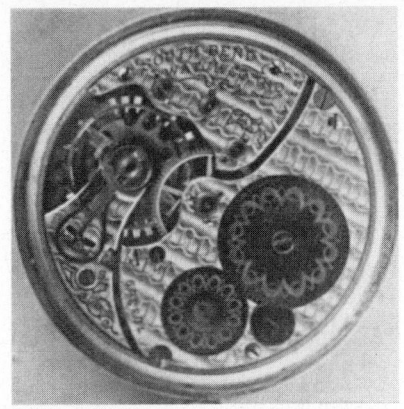

Grade 211, 16 size, 17 jewels, three-quarter plate, marked 211, serial number 703,389.

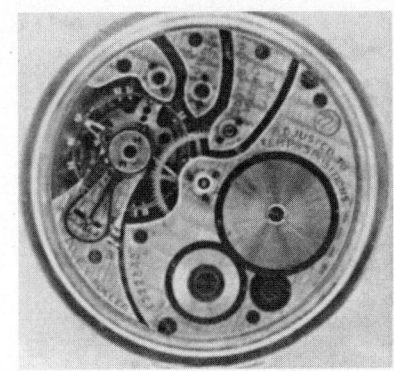

Grade 227, 16 size, 21 jewels, RR approved, gold jewel settings, Adj5p, marked 227, serial number 1,222,843.

Grade or Name —Description	ABP	Ex-Fn	Mint
223, 17J, M#2, LS, ADJ.5P, OF	$75	$150	$200
227, 21J, M#2, 3/4, NI, LS, DR, ADJ.5P, marked 227, OF	225	375	500
260, 7J, M#1, HC	100	150	200
261, 7J, M#1, OF	70	125	150
280, 15J, M#1, HC	100	150	200
281, 15J, M#1, OF	70	125	150
290, 17J, M#1, LS, Adj..3P, HC	165	225	350
291, 17J, M#1, Adj.3P, OF	185	250	400
292, 19J, M#1, 3/4, GJS, NI, DR, Adj.5P, HC ★★	250	350	600
293, 19J, M#1, 3/4, GJS, NI, DR, Adj,5P, OF. ★	200	300	500
294, 21J, M#1, ADJ.5P, GJS, GT, HC, marked 294, HC ★★	700	900	1, 400
295, 21J, M#1, LS, ADJ.5P, GJS, GT, marked 295, OF ★★	650	800	1, 100
298, 17J, M#1, ADJ.3P, HC ★	225	300	425
299, 17J, M#1, ADJ.3P, OF ★	175	250	375

12 SIZE Extra Thin
Chesterfield Series style cases (OF Only)

Grade or Name —Description	ABP	Ex-Fn	Mint
407, 15J, DR, Gold Filled case	$65	$70	$95
411, 17J, DR, GJS, Gold Filled case	70	85	110
415, 17J, ADJ to temp, Gold Filled case	80	95	150
417 marked, 17J, DR, Adj.5P, GJS, South Bend G. F. OF ★★★	125	200	325
419, 17J, Adj.3P, Gold Filled Case ★	90	110	200
429, 19J, Adj.4P, DR, GJS, Gold Filled	100	150	235
14K case	185	300	400
429, South Bend **Digital**, 19J, BRG, NI, DR, GJS, ADJ.4P (marked 411 &429), 12 size ▱	225	300	450
431, 21J, Adj.5P, DR, GJS, Gold Filled Case	150	185	265
14K Case	225	300	450
18K Case ★★★	300	400	700
Studebaker, 21J, 8 Adj., OF ▱	175	250	475

*Movements marked "Studebaker 8-adjustments" should not be confused with *The Studebaker*.

  ☞ Chesterfield Series (OF Only) comprises of a variety of case and dial combinations. Case styles such as Delmar, Carlton, Fairfax, Girard, Savoy, Senior, Tremont, Warwick, & Wellington. Chesterfield Series were cased and timed at the factory only as complete watches. Chesterfield Series case are **not** interchangeable with other American 12 standard style cases.

  ☞ Pricing in this guide are fair market price for complete watches which are reflected from the NAWCC National and regional shows.

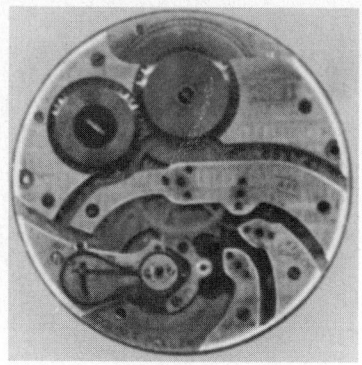

Grade 411, 12 size, 17 jewels, open face, double roller.

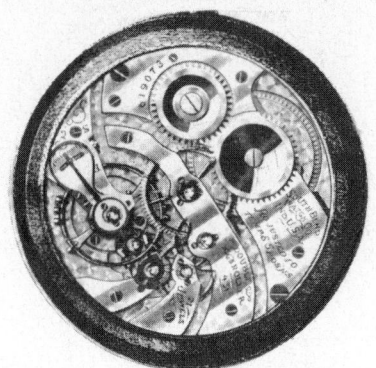

Chesterfield, 12 size, 21 jewels, grade #431, bridge, gold jewel settings, pendant set, double roller, Adj5p.

6 SIZE Hunting Case

Grade or Name —Description		ABP	Ex-Fn	Mint
South Bend, 11J, G#160, HC ....★★		$75	$150	$225
South Bend, 15J, G#170, HC .... ★		90	175	225
South Bend, 17J, G#180, HC ....★★★		100	200	300
South Bend, 17J, G#180, **14K, HC**....................★★★★		250	350	500

ALL 6 size movements were re-worked Columbus movements.

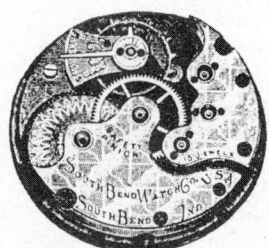

South Bend, 6 size, grade # 170 15 jewels

Grade 120-HC, 121-OF, 0 size, 17 jewels, bridge, nickel, double roller, pendant set.

0 SIZE

Grade or Name Description		ABP	Ex-Fn	Mint
South Bend, 7J, M# 1, PS, HC		$95	$125	$250
South Bend, 15J, M#1, PS, HC.........................★★★		110	150	275
Grade 100 HC & 101 OF, 7J, PS............................		75	100	200
Grade 102 HC & 103 OF, 7J, BRG (some marked 102)......★★★		100	150	300
Grade 110 HC & 111 OF, 15J, 3F Brg, DR		90	125	200
Grade 120 HC & 121 OF, 17J, BRG, NI, DR, PS..............★		90	150	250
Grade 150 HC & 151 OF, 17J, M# 3, BRG, NI, PS............★★		100	175	300

IDENTIFICATION OF MOVEMENTS BY MODEL NUMBER

How to Identify Your Watch: Compare the movement of your watch with the illustrations in this section. Upon matching the movement exactly, the model number and size can be determined. While comparing, note the location of the balance, jewels, screws, gears, and type of back plate (Full, 3/4, Bridge) these will be clues in identifying the movement you have. Having determined the size and model number, you can now find your watch in the main price listing by name or number (engraved on the movement).

Record of Serial and Grade Numbers of South Bend Watch Movements

1915

Serial Number	Grade	Size	Model	Jewels	Serial Number	Grade	Size	Model	Jewels
1000 to 4000	Htg.	18	1	7	400001 to 401200	331	18	1	15
4001 to 7000	"	18	1	7	401201 to 403200	330	18	1	16
7001 to 10000	"	16	1	15	403201 to 407200	341	18	1	17
10001 to 21000	"	18	1	15	407201 to 408600	340	18	1	17
21001 to 29500	"	16	1	7	408601 to 408700	342	18	1	17
29501 to 37000	"	18	1	7	408701 to 409200	342	18	1	17
37001 to 41000	"	16	1	15	409201 to 412200	330	18	1	15
41001 to 52000	"	18	1	15	412201 to 413800	290	16	1	17
52001 to 61000	"	18	1	7	413801 to 414800	342	18	1	17
61001 to 76000	"	18	1	15	414801 to 415800	291	16	1	17
76001 to 83000	"	16	1	15	415801 to 417700	331	18	1	15
83001 to 92000	"	16	1	7	417701 to 418700	342	18	1	17
92001 to 97000	"	18	1	7	418701 to 419700	343	18	1	17
97001 to 105000	"	18	1	15	419701 to 420600	290	16	1	17
105001 to 114000	"	16	1	17	420601 to 421900	291	16	1	17
114001 to 127000	"	18	1	15	421901 to 422400	281	16	1	15
127501 to 138000	"	18	1	17	422401 to 423200	280	16	1	15
138001 to 156000	"	16	1	7	423201 to 423800	343	18	1	17
156001 to 165000	"	18	1	15	423801 to 425800	261	16	1	7
165001 to 171000	"	16	1	7	425801 to 426100	281	16	1	15
171001 to 196000	"	16	1	17	426101 to 428100	342	18	1	17
196001 to 201000	"	18	1	7	428101 to 431100	260	16	1	7
201001 to 214000	"	16	1	15	431101 to 431600	280	16	1	15
214001 to 218000	"	16	1	7	431601 to 432100	281	16	1	15
218001 to 220000	"	18	1	15	432101 to 433100	342	18	1	17
220001 to 232000	"	16	1	15	433101 to 435100	340	18	1	17
232001 to 250000	"	18	1	7	435101 to 436600	280	16	1	15
250001 to 261000	"	16	1	7	436601 to 437900	281	16	1	15
261001 to 267000	"	16	1	15	437901 to 438200	280	16	1	15
267001 to 271000	"	18	1	15	438201 to 438500	290	16	1	17
271001 to 274000	"	16	1	15	438501 to 439500	293	16	1	19
274001 to 281000	"	16	1	7	439501 to 440500	280	16	1	16
281001 to 292000	"	16	1	7	440501 to 441500	290	16	1	17
292001 to 294000	"	16	1	17	441501 to 441600	260	16	1	7
294001 to 295500	"	18	1	17	441601 to 441700	261	16	1	7
295501 to 299100	"	18	1	7	441701 to 441800	290	16	1	17
299101 to 302000	"	18	1	7	441801 to 441850	293	16	1	17
302001 to 311000	"	16	1	7	441851 to 445900	280	16	1	15
311001 to 314000	"	16	1	15	445901 to 446000	Htg.	16	1	21
314001 to 321000	"	18	1	15	446001 to 447000	261	16	1	7
321001 to 329000	"	16	1	7	447001 to 450000	260	16	1	7
329001 to 334000	"	18	1	7	450001 to 451000	261	16	1	7
334001 to 341000	"	16	1	15	451001 to 453000	260	16	1	7
341001 to 347000	"	16	1	7	453001 to 455000	261	16	1	7
347001 to 349500	"	16	1	17	455001 to 457000	343	18	1	17
349501 to 354000	"	16	1	15	457001 to 461000	260	16	1	7
354001 to 361000	"	18	1	7	461001 to 462500	331	18	1	15
361001 to 366000	"	16	1	7	462501 to 464000	281	16	1	15
366001 to 368000	"	18	1	17	464001 to 465300	331	18	1	15
368001 to 371000	"	16	1	15	465301 to 467300	261	16	1	7
371001 to 374000	"	18	1	15	467301 to 468800	331	18	1	15
374001 to 376000	"	16	1	17	468801 to 469300	290	16	1	17
376001 to 377000	"	16	1	15	469301 to 469800	294	16	1	21
377001 to 378000	"	18	1	17	469801 to 470100	295	16	1	21
378001 to 379500	"	18	1	15	*470101 to 470200	295	16	1	21
379501 to 380500	"	16	1	15	470201 to 470300	295	16	1	21
380501 to 381000	160	6	1	11	470301 to 471300	281	16	1	15
381001 to 381500	170	6	1	15	471301 to 472300	280	16	1	15
381501 to 382500	330	18	1	15	472301 to 473300	281	16	1	15
382501 to 383000	160	6	1	11	473301 to 474800	330	18	1	15
383001 to 383500	170	6	1	15	474801 to 475800	331	18	1	15
383501 to 384000	302	18	1	15	475801 to 476800	290	16	1	17
384001 to 384500	160	6	1	11	477001 to 478000	261	16	1	7
384501 to 384900	291	16	1	17	478001 to 479000	330	18	1	15
384901 to 385200	281	16	1	15	479001 to 480000	261	16	1	7
385201 to 385500	291	16	1	17	480001 to 480200	295	16	1	21
385501 to 386400	290	16	1	17	*480201 to 480500	295	16	1	21
386401 to 386900	280	16	1	15	480501 to 481500	290	16	1	17
386901 to 387400	170	6	1	15	481501 to 483500	291	16	1	17
387401 to 387900	330	18	1	15	483501 to 485000	280	16	1	15
387901 to 388400	331	18	1	15	485001 to 486000	331	18	1	15
388401 to 389400	180	6	1	17	486001 to 487000	330	18	1	15
389401 to 389900	170	6	1	15	487001 to 489000	331	18	1	15
389901 to 390400	341	18	1	17	489001 to 490000	341	18	1	17
390401 to 390900	331	18	1	15	*490001 to 490500	294	16	1	21
390901 to 391200	330	18	1	15	490501 to 490800	293	16	1	19
391201 to 391700	341	18	1	17	*490801 to 490900	293	16	1	19
391701 to 392600	330	18	1	15	490901 to 491000	293	16	1	19
392601 to 394100	331	18	1	15	491001 to 492000	281	16	1	15
394101 to 396000	330	18	1	15	492001 to 493000	330	18	1	15
396001 to 400000	340	18	1	17	493001 to 494000	340	18	1	17

Although grade numbers appear in this list some of the earlier watches did not have grade numbers stamped upon them. In all instances odd grade numbers indicate open face movement, even grade numbers indicate hunting movement.

*Watches with these serial numbers have double roller.

Serial Number	Grade	Size	Model	Jewels
494001 to 495000...	290	16	1	17
495001 to 497000...	331	18	1	15
497001 to 498000...	291	16	1	7
498001 to 499000...	291	16	1	17
499001 to 500000...	261	16	1	7
500001 to 501000...	281	16	1	15
501001 to 502000...	290	16	1	17
502001 to 503000...	331	18	1	15
503001 to 503500...	341	18	1	17
503501 to 504000...	343	18	1	17
504001 to 505000...	290	16	1	17
505001 to 505100...	293	16	1	19
*505101 to 505500...	293	16	1	19
505501 to 506500...	261	16	1	7
506501 to 507500...	280	16	1	15
507501 to 508500...	261	16	1	7
508501 to 509500...	280	16	1	15
509501 to 510500...	281	16	1	15
510501 to 511400...	291	16	1	17
511401 to 511500...	299	16	1	17
511501 to 511900...	292	16	1	19
*511901 to 512000...	292	16	1	19
512001 to 513000...	333	18	2	15
513001 to 514000...	280	16	1	15
514001 to 515000...	261	16	1	7
515001 to 516000...	260	16	1	7
516001 to 516500...	298	16	1	17
*516501 to 516600...	298	16	1	17
516601 to 516800...	298	16	1	17
*516801 to 516900...	298	16	1	17
516901 to 517000...	298	16	1	17
517001 to 517700...	346	18	2	17
*517701 to 518000...	345	18	2	17
*518001 to 518500...	295	16	1	21
*518501 to 519000...	294	16	1	21
519001 to 520000...	347	18	2	17
520001 to 521000...	332	18	2	15
*521001 to 522000...	329	18	2	21
*522001 to 523000...	293	16	1	19
523001 to 523400...	299	16	1	17
*523401 to 524000...	299	16	1	17
524001 to 524300...	344	18	2	17
*524301 to 524800...	344	18	2	17
524801 to 525000...	344	18	2	17
525001 to 526000...	346	18	2	17
526001 to 527000...	333	18	2	15
527001 to 528000...	347	18	2	17
*528001 to 529000...	345	18	2	17
*529001 to 530000...	292	16	1	19
530001 to 531000...	260	16	1	7
531001 to 532000...	281	16	1	15
532001 to 533000...	333	18	2	15
*533001 to 534000...	323	18	2	17
*534001 to 535000...	345	18	2	17
535001 to 536000...	347	18	2	17
536001 to 537000...	333	18	2	15
537001 to 538000...	312	18	2	17
538001 to 539000...	332	18	2	15
*539001 to 539500...	298	16	1	17
539501 to 539700...	298	16	1	17
*539701 to 540000...	298	16	1	17
540001 to 540400...	299	16	1	17
540401 to 541000...	299	16	1	17
*541001 to 542000...	328	18	2	21
*542001 to 543000...	313	18	2	17
543001 to 544000...	261	16	1	7
544001 to 545000...	260	16	1	7
*545001 to 546000...	333	18	2	15
546001 to 547000...	332	18	2	15
*547001 to 548000...	333	18	2	15
548001 to 549000...	346	18	2	17
549001 to 550000...	261	16	1	7
550001 to 551000...	280	16	1	15
551001 to 552000...	281	16	1	15
552001 to 553000...	347	18	2	17
*553001 to 554000...	313	18	2	17
*554001 to 555000...	323	18	2	17
*555001 to 556000...	327	18	2	21
*556001 to 557000...	298	16	1	17
*557001 to 558000...	299	16	1	17
558001 to 559000...	347	18	2	17
559001 to 560000...	346	18	2	17
*560001 to 561000...	313	18	2	17
561001 to 562000...	333	18	2	15
562001 to 563000...	332	18	2	15
563001 to 564000...	261	16	1	7
564001 to 565000...	347	18	2	17
565001 to 566000...	260	16	1	7
566001 to 567000...	211	16	2	17
567001 to 569000...	333	18	2	15
*569001 to 570000...	215	16	2	17

Serial Number	Grade	Size	Model	Jewels
*570001 to 571000...	261	16	1	7
*571001 to 572000...	313	18	2	17
572001 to 573000...	280	16	1	15
573001 to 574000...	347	18	2	17
*574001 to 575000...	323	18	2	17
*575001 to 576000...	217	16	2	17
576001 to 577000...	333	18	2	15
577001 to 578000...	281	16	1	15
*578001 to 579000...	293	16	2	17
*579001 to 580000...	329	18	2	21
*580001 to 581000...	212	16	2	17
*581001 to 582000...	333	18	2	15
582001 to 583000...	261	16	1	7
*583001 to 584000...	227	16	2	21
*584001 to 585000...	229	16	2	21
585001 to 586000...	207	16	2	15
586001 to 587000...	211	16	2	17
*587001 to 588000...	215	16	2	17
588001 to 589000...	260	16	1	7
*589001 to 590000...	217	16	2	17
590001 to 591000...	204	16	2	15
591001 to 592000...	203	16	2	7
592001 to 593000...	207	16	2	15
*593001 to 594000...	212	16	2	17
594001 to 595000...	203	16	2	7
595001 to 596000...	332	18	2	15
*596001 to 597000...	215	16	2	17
*597001 to 598000...	223	16	2	17
*598001 to 599000...	229	16	2	21
599001 to 600000...	260	16	1	7
*600001 to 601000...	211	16	2	17
*601001 to 602000...	313	18	2	17
602001 to 603000...	203	16	2	7
603001 to 604000...	204	16	2	15
604001 to 605000...	207	16	2	15
605001 to 606000...	333	18	2	15
606001 to 607000...	347	18	2	17
*607001 to 608000...	215	16	2	17
608001 to 609000...	211	16	2	17
609001 to 610000...	203	16	2	7
*610001 to 611000...	215	16	2	17
611001 to 612000...	207	16	2	15
612001 to 613000...	203	16	2	7
*613001 to 614000...	212	16	2	17
614001 to 615000...	305	18	2	15
615001 to 616000...	204	16	2	15
616001 to 617000...	207	16	2	15
617001 to 618000...	203	16	2	7
*618001 to 619000...	415	12	1	17
*619001 to 620000...	431	12	1	21
620001 to 621000...	211	16	2	17
*621001 to 622000...	223	16	2	17
*622001 to 623000...	229	16	2	21
*623001 to 624000...	411	12	1	17
*624001 to 625000...	215	16	2	17
625001 to 626000...	203	16	2	7
626001 to 627000...	305	18	2	15
627001 to 628000...	207	16	2	15
*628001 to 629000...	419	12	1	17
629001 to 630000...	260	16	1	7
*630001 to 631000...	407	12	1	15
*631001 to 632000...	217	16	2	17
632001 to 633000...	204	16	2	15
633001 to 634000...	347	16	2	17
*634001 to 635000...	329	18	2	21
635001 to 636000...	203	16	2	7
*636001 to 637000...	217	16	2	17
*637001 to 638000...	411	12	1	17
638001 to 639000...	211	16	2	17
*639001 to 640000...	212	16	2	17
*640001 to 641000...	217	16	2	17
*641001 to 642000...	415	12	1	17
642001 to 643000...	203	16	2	7
*643001 to 644000...	229	16	2	21
644001 to 645000...	260	16	1	7
*645001 to 646000...	215	16	2	17
646001 to 647000...	207	16	2	15
*647001 to 648000...	407	12	1	15
*648001 to 649000...	419	12	1	17
649001 to 650000...	207	16	2	15
650181 to 655200...	Htg.	0	1	7
655201 to 656200...	"	0	1	15
656201 to 659700...	"	0	1	7
659701 to 662400...	"	0	1	7
662401 to 662500...	O.F.	0	2	7
662501 to 665400...	Htg.	0	2	7
665401 to 665500...	O.F.	0	2	7
665501 to 666000...	Htg.	0	2	7
666001 to 666500...	"	0	2	7
666501 to 666600...	"	0	2	17
666601 to 666650...	O. F.	0	2	15

Although grade numbers appear in this list some of the earlier watches did not have grade numbers stamped upon them. In all instances odd grade numbers indicate open face movement, even grade numbers indicate hunting movement.
*Watches with these serial numbers have double roller.

Serial Number	Grade	Size	Model	Jewels
666651 to 667500...	Htg.	0	2	15
667501 to 671500...	"	0	2	7
671501 to 671600...	O. F.	0	2	7
671601 to 672800...	Htg.	0	2	7
672801 to 672900...	O. F.	0	2	7
672901 to 673000...	Htg.	0	2	7
673001 to 674000...	"	0	2	15
674001 to 675000...	"	0	2	17
675001 to 676000...	"	0	2	7
676001 to 679400...	"	0	2	15
679401 to 679500...	O. F.	0	2	15
679501 to 680400...	Htg.	0	2	15
680401 to 680500...	O. F.	0	2	15
680501 to 681000...	Htg.	0	2	15
681001 to 682000...	"	0	2	17
682001 to 682280...	"	0	2	15
682801 to 682900...	O. F.	0	2	15
682901 to 683000...	Htg.	0	2	15
683001 to 684000...	"	0	2	17
684001 to 684600...	"	0	2	7
684601 to 684700...	O. F.	0	2	7
684701 to 685000...	Htg.	0	2	7
685001 to 686000...	'	0	2	15
686001 to 686100...	101	0	2	7
686101 to 687000...	100	0	2	7
687001 to 687100...	111	0	2	15
687101 to 688000...	110	0	2	15
688001 to 688100...	101	0	2	7
688101 to 689000...	100	0	2	7
689001 to 689100...	111	0	2	15
689101 to 690000...	110	0	2	15
690001 to 690100...	101	0	2	7
690101 to 691000...	100	0	2	7
691001 to 691100...	101	0	2	7
691101 to 692000...	100	0	2	7
692001 to 692100...	111	0	2	15
692101 to 693000...	110	0	2	15
693001 to 693100...	101	0	2	7
693101 to 694000...	100	0	2	7
*694001 to 695000...	217	16	2	17
695001 to 696000...	305	18	2	15
696001 to 696100...	111	0	2	15
696101 to 697000...	110	0	2	15
697001 to 697100...	101	0	2	7
697101 to 698000...	100	0	2	7
*698001 to 699000...	215	16	2	17
*699001 to 700000...	415	12	1	17
*700001 to 701000...	431	12	1	21
*701001 to 702000...	313	18	2	17
702001 to 702100...	111	0	2	15
702101 to 703000...	110	0	2	16
703001 to 704000...	211	16	2	17
*704001 to 705000...	212	16	2	17
705001 to 706000...	305	18	2	15
*706001 to 707000...	215	16	2	17
707001 to 708000...	203	16	2	7
*708001 to 709000...	407	12	1	15
709001 to 710000...	204	16	2	15
710001 to 711000...	305	18	2	15
711001 to 712000...	260	16	1	7
712001 to 713000...	207	16	2	15
*713001 to 713900...	111	0	2	15
*713101 to 714000...	110	0	2	15
*714001 to 715000...	227	16	2	21
715001 to 716000...	211	16	2	17
*716001 to 717000...	411	12	1	17
*717001 to 717100...	101	0	2	7
*717101 to 718000...	100	0	2	7
*718001 to 719000...	215	16	2	17
719001 to 720000...	309	18	2	17
720001 to 721000...	203	16	2	7
*721001 to 722000...	227	16	2	21
722001 to 723000...	204	16	2	15
723001 to 724000...	207	16	2	15
724001 to 725000...	211	16	2	17
*725001 to 726000...	217	16	2	17
*726001 to 727000...	227	16	2	21
*727001 to 728000...	223	16	2	17
*728001 to 729000...	212	16	2	17
729001 to 730000...	305	18	2	15
730001 to 731000...	304	18	2	15
*731001 to 732000...	313	18	2	17
732001 to 733000...	309	18	2	17
733001 to 734000...	211	16	2	17
*734001 to 735000...	215	16	2	17
*735001 to 736000...	217	16	2	17
*736001 to 737000...		0	2	17
*737001 to 738000...	227	16	2	21
*738001 to 739000...	215	16	2	17

Serial Number	Grade	Size	Model	Jewels
*739001 to 740000...	217	16	2	17
*740001 to 740200...	101	0	2	7
*740201 to 741000...	100	0	2	7
*741001 to 741200...	111	0	2	15
*741201 to 742000...	110	0	2	15
742001 to 743000...	207	16	2	15
743001 to 744000...	203	16	2	7
*744001 to 745000...	212	16	2	17
*745001 to 746000...	227	16	2	21
*746001 to 746100...	111	0	2	15
*746101 to 747000...	110	0	2	15
747001 to 748000...	305	18	2	15
748001 to 749000...	309	18	2	17
*749601 to 750000...	223	16	2	17
750001 to 751000...	207	16	2	15
*751001 to 751100...	101	0	2	7
*751101 to 752000...	100	0	2	7
752001 to 753000...	211	16	2	17
*753001 to 754000...	229	16	2	21
754001 to 755000...	203	16	2	7
*755001 to 756000...	215	16	2	17
*756001 to 757000...	313	18	2	17
*757001 to 758000...	323	18	2	17
758001 to 759000...	204	16	2	15
*759001 to 759500...	Htg.	0	2	17
759501 to 759510...	150	0	3	17
759511 to 759520...	103	0	3	7
759521 to 759530...	102	0	3	7
759531 to 759540...	151	0	3	17
759541 to 760000...	Htg.	0	2	17
760001 to 761000...	305	18	2	15
761001 to 762000...	207	16	2	15
*762001 to 762100...	111	0	2	15
762101 to 763000...	110	0	2	17
763001 to 764000...	203	16	2	7
*764001 to 765000...	215	16	2	17
*765001 to 766000...	217	16	2	17
766001 to 767000...	211	16	2	17
*767001 to 768000...	217	16	2	17
*768001 to 769000...	212	16	2	17
*769001 to 770000...	217	16	2	17
*770001 to 771000...	151	0	3	17
*771001 to 772000...	217	16	2	17
*772001 to 773000...	150	0	3	17
*773001 to 774000...	215	16	2	17
*774001 to 776000...	107	0	3	15
*775001 to 776000...	106	0	3	15
*776001 to 777000...	207	16	2	15
*777001 to 778000...	102	0	3	7
*778001 to 779000...	103	0	3	7
779001 to 780000...	211	16	2	17
780001 to 781000...	203	16	2	7
781001 to 782000...	305	18	2	16
*782001 to 783000...	217	16	2	17
*783001 to 784000...	215	16	2	17
784001 to 785000...	207	16	2	15
*785001 to 786000...	215	16	2	17
*786001 to 787000...	227	16	2	21
*787001 to 788000...	407	12	1	15
*788001 to 789000...	217	16	2	17
789001 to 790000...	211	16	2	17
*790001 to 791000...	215	16	2	17
*791001 to 792000...	217	16	2	17
*792001 to 793000...	407	12	1	15
*793001 to 794000...	215	16	2	17
*794001 to 795000...	212	16	2	17
*795001 to 796000...	411	12	1	17
796001 to 797000...	203	16	2	7
*797001 to 798000...	407	12	1	15
*798001 to 799000...	429	12	1	19
*799001 to 800000...	411	12	1	17
*800001 to 801000...	219	16	2	19
*801001 to 802000...	429	12	1	19
*802001 to 804000...	219	16	2	19
*804001 to 805000...	411	12	1	17
*805001 to 806000...	407	12	1	15
*806001 to 808000...	429	12	1	19
*808001 to 809000...	219	16	2	19
*809001 to 810000...	411	12	1	17
*810001 to 811000...	429	12	1	19
*811001 to 812000...	211	16	2	17
*812001 to 814000...	219	16	2	19
*814001 to 816000...	429	12	1	19
*815001 to 816000...	407	12	1	15
*816001 to 817000...	219	16	2	19
*817001 to 818000...	429	12	1	19
*818001 to 819000...	219	16	2	19
*819001 to 820000...	429	12	1	19

Although grade numbers appear in this list some of the earlier watches did not have grade numbers stamped upon them. In all instances odd grade numbers indicate open face movement, even grade numbers indicate hunting movement.

*Watches with these serial numbers have double roller.

A-112

by -Lyle & Donna Stratton (below all double roller)

SERIAL NUMBER-GRADE-SIZE-M#- Jewels		SERIAL NUMBER-GRADE-SIZE-M#- Jewels	
820001-821000	= 215 - 16 - 2 - 17j	897001-898000	= 315 - 18 - 2 - 17j < last 18 size
821001-822000	= 415 - 12 - 1 - 17j	898001-899000	= 207 - 16 - 2 - 15j
822001-823000	= 411 - 12 - 1 - 17j	899001-900000	= 429 - 12 - 1 - 19j
823001-825000	= 429 - 12 - 1 - 19j	900001-901000	= 227 - 16 - 2 - 21j
825001-826000	= 209 - 16 - 2 - 9j	901001-902000	= 219 - 16 - 2 - 19j
826001-827000	= 207 - 16 - 2 - 15j	902001-903000	= 211 - 16 - 2 - 17j
827001-828000	= 407 - 12 - 1 - 15j	903001-904000	= 227 - 16 - 2 - 21j
828001-830000	= 429 - 12 - 1 - 19j	904001-905000	= 411 - 12 - 1 - 17j
830001-831000	= 211 - 16 - 2 - 17j	905001-906000	= 407 - 12 - 1 - 15j
831001-832000	= 407 - 12 - 1 - 15j	906001-907000	= 429 - 12 - 1 - 19j
832001-833000	= 207 - 16 - 2 - 15j	907001-908000	= 411 - 12 - 1 - 17j
833001-834000	= 429 - 12 - 1 - 19j	908001-910000	= 209 - 12 - 1 - 9j
834001-835000	= 219 - 16 - 2 - 19j	910001-911000	= 207 - 16 - 2 - 15j
835001-837000	= 429 - 12 - 1 - 19j	911011-912000	= 219 - 16 - 2 - 19j
837001-838000	= 219 - 16 - 2 - 19j	912001-913000	= 429 - 12 - 1 - 19j
838001-839000	= 209 - 16 - 2 - 9j	913001-914000	= 207 - 16 - 2 - 15j
839001-840000	= 211 - 16 - 2 - 17j	914001-915000	= 209 - 16 - 2 - 9j
840001-841000	= 219 - 16 - 2 - 19j	915001-916000	= 219 - 16 - 2 - 19j
841001-842000	= 209 - 16 - 2 - 9j	916001-917000	= 211 - 16 - 2 - 17j
842001-843000	= 207 - 16 - 2 - 15j	917001-918000	= 207 - 16 - 2 - 15j
843001-844000	= 429 - 12 - 1 - 19j	918001-919000	= 407 - 12 - 1 - 15j
844001-845000	= 411 - 12 - 1 - 17j	919001-920000	= 219 - 16 - 2 - 19j
845001-846000	= 429 - 12 - 1 - 19j	920001-921000	= 209 - 16 - 2 - 9j
846001-847000	= 209 - 16 - 2 - 9j	921001-923000	= 429 - 12 - 1 - 19j
847001-848000	= 227 - 16 - 2 - 21j	923001-924000	= 407 - 12 - 1 - 15j
848001-849000	= 429 - 12 - 1 - 19j	924001-925000	= 227 - 16 - 2 - 21j
849001-850000	= 407 - 12 - 1 - 15j	925001-926000	= 219 - 16 - 2 - 19j
850001-851000	= 211 - 16 - 2 - 17j	926001-927000	= 429 - 12 - 1 - 19j
851001-852000	= 209 - 16 - 2 - 9j	927001-928000	= 227 - 16 - 2 - 21j
852001-853000	= 429 - 12 - 1 - 19j	928001-929000	= 204 - 16 - 2 - 15j
853001-854000	= 219 - 16 - 2 - 19j	929001-930000	= 209 - 16 - 2 - 9j
854001-855000	= 429 - 12 - 1 - 19j	930001-931000	= 217 - 16 - 2 - 17j
855001-856000	= 207 - 16 - 2 - 15j	931001-932000	= 219 - 16 - 2 - 19j
856001-857000	= 209 - 16 - 2 - 9j	932001-933000	= 407 - 12 - 1 - 15i
857001-858000	= 407 - 12 - 1 - 15j	933001-934000	= 411 - 12 - 1 - 17j
858001-859000	= 429 - 12 - 1 - 19j	934001-935000	= 211 - 16 - 2 - 17j
859001-860000	= 204 - 16 - 2 - 15j	935001-937000	= 429 - 12 - 1 - 19j
860001-861000	= 211 - 16 - 2 - 17j	937001-938000	= 207 - 16 - 2 - 15j
861001-862000	= 411 - 12 - 1 - 17j	938001-939000	= 227 - 16 - 2 - 21j
862001-863000	= 209 - 16 - 2 - 9j	939001-940000	= 407 - 12 - 1 - 15j
863001-864000	= 429 - 12 - 1 - 19j	940001-941000	= 209 - 16 - 2 - 9j
864001-865000	= 219 - 16 - 2 - 19j	941001-942000	= 211 - 16 - 2 - 17j
865001-866000	= 209 - 16 - 2 - 9j	942001-943000	= 219 - 16 - 2 - 19j
866001-867000	= 429 - 12 - 1 - 19j	943001-944000	= 209 - 16 - 2 - 9j
867001-868000	= 411 - 12 - 1 - 17j	944001-946000	= 429 - 12 - 1 - 19j
866001-869000	= 211 - 16 - 2 - 17j	946001-947000	= 219 - 16 - 2 - 19j
869001-871000	= 227 - 16 - 2 - 21j	947001-948000	= 207 - 16 - 2 - 15j
871001-872000	= 207 - 16 - 2 - 15j	948001-949000	= 411 - 12 - 1 - 17j
872001-873000	= 209 - 16 - 2 - 9j	949001-950000	= 429 - 12 - 1 - 19j
873001-874000	= 219 - 16 - 2 - 19j	950001-951000	= 407 - 12 - 1 - 15j
874001-875000	= 407 - 12 - 1 - 15j	951001-952000	= 219 - 16 - 2 - 19j
875001-876000	= 411 - 12 - 1 - 17j	952001-953000	= 211 - 16 - 2 - 17j
876001-877000	= 429 - 12 - 1 - 19j	953001-954000	= 209 - 16 - 2 - 9j
877001-878000	= 207 - 16 - 2 - 15j	954001-955000	= 227 - 16 - 2 - 21j
878001-879000	= 211 - 16 - 2 - 17j	955001-956000	= 429 - 12 - 1 - 19j
879001-880000	= 219 - 16 - 2 - 19j	956001-957000	= 209 - 16 - 2 - 9j
880001-882000	= 407 - 12 - 1 - 15j	957001-958000	= 227 - 16 - 2 - 21j
882001-883000	= 217 - 16 - 2 - 17j	958001-959000	= 407 - 12 - 1 - 15j
883001-884000	= 209 - 16 - 2 - 9j	959001-960000	= 411 - 12 - 1 - 17j
884001-885000	= 411 - 12 - 1 - 17j	960001-961000	= 429 - 12 - 1 - 19j
885001-886000	= 229 - 16 - 2 - 21j	961001-962000	= 207 - 16 - 2 - 15j
886001-887000	= 429 - 12 - 1 - 19j	962001-963000	= 211 - 16 - 2 - 17j
887001-868000	= 209 - 16 - 2 - 9j	963001-964000	= 407 - 12 - 1 - 15j
888001-889000	= 217 - 16 - 2 - 17j	964001-965000	= 429 - 12 - 1 - 19j
889001-890000	= 219 - 16 - 2 - 19j	965001-966000	= 204 - 16 - 2 - 15j
890001-891000	= 209 - 16 - 2 - 9j	966001-967000	= 219 - 16 - 2 - 19j
891001-892000	= 207 - 16 - 2 - 15j	967001-968000	= 407 - 12 - 1 - 15j
892001-893000	= 227 - 16 - 2 - 21j	968001-969000	= 209 - 16 - 2 - 9j
893001-694000	= 315 - 18 - 2 - 17j	969001-970000	= 431 - 12 - 1 - 21j
894001-895000	= 211 - 16 - 2 - 17j	970001-971000	= 227 - 16 - 2 - 21j
895001-896000	= 204 - 16 - 2 - 15j	971001-972000	= 411 - 12 - 1 - 17j
896001-897000	= 219 - 16 - 2 - 19j	972001-973000	= 219 - 16 - 2 - 19j

(below all double roller)

SERIAL NUMBER-GRADE-SIZE-M#- Jewels		SERIAL NUMBER-GRADE-SIZE-M#- Jewels	
973001-974000	= 207 - 16 - 2 - 15j	1032001-1033000	= 429 - 12 - 1 - 19j
974001-975000	= 209 - 16 - 2 - 9j	1033001-1034000	= 227 - 16 - 2 - 21j
975001-977000	= 429 - 12 - 1 - 19j	1034001-1036000	= 429 - 12 - 1 - 19j
977001-978000	= 219 - 16 - 2 - 19j	1036001-1037000	= 411 - 12 - 1 - 17j
978001-979000	= 211 - 16 - 2 - 17j	1037001-1038000	= 219 - 16 - 2 - 19j
979001-980000	= 227 - 16 - 2 - 21j	1038001-1040000	= 429 - 12 - 1 - 19j
980001-981000	= 429 - 12 - 1 - 19j	1040001-1041000	= 227 - 16 - 2 - 21j
981001-982000	= 407 - 12 - 1 - 15j	1041001-1046000	= 429 - 12 - 1 - 19j
982001-983000	= 209 - 16 - 2 - 9j	1046001-1047000	= 411 - 12 - 1 - 17j
983001-984000	= 219 - 16 - 2 - 19j	1047001-1049000	= 429 - 12 - 1 - 19j
984001-985000	= 207 - 16 - 2 - 15j	1049001-1050000	= 411 - 12 - 1 - 17j
985001-986000	= 411 - 12 - 1 - 17j	1050001-1051000	= 429 - 12 - 1 - 19j
986001-987000	= 429 - 12 - 1 - 19j	1051001-1052000	= 407 - 12 - 1 - 15j
987001-988000	= 211 - 16 - 2 - 17j	1052001-1053000	= 429 - 12 - 1 - 19j
988001-989000	= 219 - 16 - 2 - 19j	1053001-1054000	= 211 - 16 - 2 - 17j
989001-990000	= 209 - 16 - 2 - 9j	1054001-1056000	= 429 - 12 - 1 - 19j
990001-991000	= 207 - 16 - 2 - 15j	1056001-1062000	= 219 - 16 - 2 - 19j
991001-992000	= 211 - 16 - 2 - 17j	1062001-1069000	= 211 - 16 - 2 - 17j
992001-993000	= ? - ? - ? - ?	1069001-1072000	= 209 - 16 - 2 - 9j
993001-994000	= 411 - 12 - 1 - 17j	1072001-1075000	= Studbebaker 12 - 1 - 21j
994001-995000	= 407 - 12 - 1 - 15j	1075001-1075100	= for directors 12 - 1 - 19j
995001-996000	= 219 - 16 - 2 - 19j	1075101-1076000	= 429 - 12 - 1 - 19j
996001-999000	= 429 - 12 - 1 - 19j	1076001-1083000	= Studbebaker 12 - 1 - 21j
999001-1001000	= 209 - 16 - 2 - 9j	1083001-1088000	= 411 - 12 - 1 - 17j
1001001-1002000	= 411 - 12 - 1 - 17j	1088001-1093000	= 227 - 16 - 2 - 21j
1002001-1003000	= 207 - 16 - 2 - 15j	1093001-1098000	= Studbebaker 12 - 1 - 21j
1003001-1004000	= 211 - 16 - 2 - 17j	1098001-1103000	= 429 - 12 - 1 - 19j
1004001-1005000	= 407 - 12 - 2 - 15j	1103001-1108000	= Studbebaker 12 - 1 - 21j
1005001-1006000	= 204 - 16 - 2 - 15j	1108001-1113000	= 211 - 16 - 2 - 17j
1006001-1007000	= 219 - 16 - 2 - 19j	1113001-1118000	= 411 - 12 - 1 - 17j
1007001-1008000	= 227 - 16 - 2 - 21j	1118001-1128000	= Studbebaker 12 - 1 - 21j
1008001-1009000	= 207 - 16 - 2 - 15j	1128001-1133000	= 227 - 16 - 2 - 21j
1009001-1010000	= 209 - 16 - 2 - 9j	1133001-1138000	= 429 - 12 - 1 - 19j
1010001-1011000	= 429 - 12 - 1 - 19j	1138001-1143000	= Studbebaker 16 - 2 - 21j
1011001-1012000	= 209 - 16 - 2 - 9j	1143001-1153000	= Studbebaker 12 - 1 - 21j
1012001-1014000	= 429 - 12 - 1 - 19j	1153001-1158000	= 411 - 12 - 1- 17j
1014001-1015000	= 407 - 12 - 1 - 15j	1158001-1163000	= Studbebaker 16 - 2 - 21j
1015001-1016000	= 219 - 16 - 2 - 19j	1163001-1168000	= Studbebaker 12 - 1 - 21j
1016001-1018000	= 429 - 12 - 1 - 19j	1168001-1173000	= Studbebaker 16 - 2 - 21j
1018001-1019000	= 209 - 16 - 2 - 9j	1173001-1178000	= 429 - 12 -1 -19j
1019001-1020000	= 227 - 16 - 2 - 21j	1178001-1183000	= Studbebaker 16 - 2 - 21j
1020001-1021000	= 411 - 12 - 1 - 17j	1183001-1188000	= Studbebaker 12 - 1 - 21j
1021001-1022000	= 211 - 16 - 2 - 17j	1188001-1193000	= 227 - 16 - 2 - 21j
1022001-1023000	= 429 - 12 - 1 - 19j	1193001-1198000	= Studbebaker 12 - 1 - 21j
1023001-1024000	= 411 - 12 - 1 - 17j	1198001-1203000	= Studbebaker 16 - 2 - 21j
1024001-1025000	= 207 - 16 - 2 - 15j	1203001-1208000	= 211 - 16 - 2 - 17j
1025001-1026000	= 227 - 16 - 2 - 21j	1208001-1213000	= Studbebaker 16 - 2 - 21j
1026001-1027000	= 219 - 16 - 2 - 19j	1213001-1218000	= 429 - 12 - 1 - 19j
1027001-1029000	= 429 - 12 - 1 - 19j	1218001-1223000	= 227 - 16 - 2 - 21j
1029001-1030000	= 407 - 12 - 1 - 15j	1223001-1228000	= 211 - 16 - 2 - 17j
1030001-1031000	= 204 - 16 - 2 - 15j	1228001-1233000	= 411 - 12 - 1 - 17j
1031001-1032000	= 209 - 16 - 2 - 9j	1233001-1238000	= Studbebaker 12 - 1 - 21j
		1238001-1241000	= 429 - 12 - 1 - 19j

The **last** digit of Grade # denotes style of movement Even # = Hunting & Odd # = Open Face.

For information about the South Bend W. Co. complete serial & grade book contact:

Lyle and Donna Stratton
1314 N. Gay St.
Longmont, CO 80501
303-776-7531

The authors of The Complete Price Guide to Watches recommend this book.

18 SIZE—MODEL 1
Open Face and Hunting Lever Set

No. 302—Hunting, 15 Jewels, Lever Set (Factory listed but never seen)
No. 341—Open Face, 17 Jewels, Lever Set, Adjusted to Temperature & 3 Positions.
No. 340—Hunting, 17 Jewels, Lever Set, Adjusted to Temperature & 3 Positions.
No. 343—Open Face, 17 Jewels, Lever Set.
No. 342—Hunting, 17 Jewels, Lever Set
No. 331—Open Face, 15 Jewels, Lever Set.
No. 330—Hunting, 15 Jewels, Lever Set

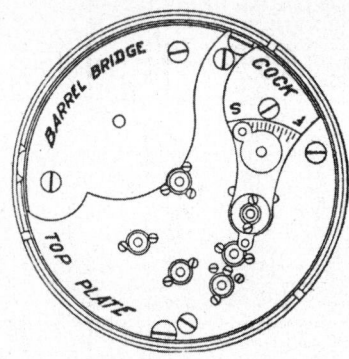 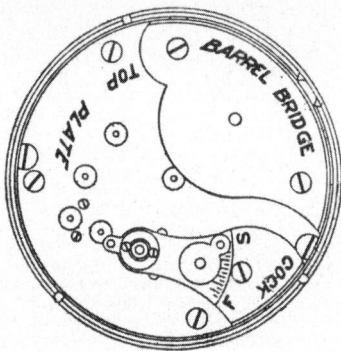

Model 1, Full Plate, Open face.   Model 1, Full Plate, Hunting

18 SIZE—MODEL 2
Open Face and Hunting, Lever Set

No. 329—21J, Open Face, "Studebaker," Adjusted to Temperature and 5 Positions.
No. 328—21J, Hunting, "Studebaker," Adjusted to Temperature and 5 Positions.
No. 327—21J, Open Face, Adjusted to Temperature and 5 Positions.
No. 323—17J, Open Face, "Studebaker," Adjusted to Temperature and 5 Positions.
No. 345—17J, Open Face, Adjusted to Temperature and 3 Positions.
No. 344—17J, Hunting, Adjusted to Temperature and 3 Positions.
No. 313—17J, Open Face, Adjusted to Temperature.
No. 312—17J, Hunting, Adjusted to Temperature.
Nos. 309, 337, 347—17J, Open Face.
No. 346—17J, Hunting.
Nos. 333, 305—15J, Open Face.
Nos. 332, 304—15J, Hunting.

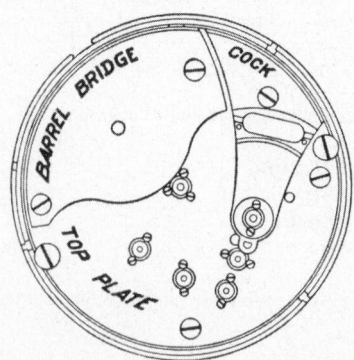 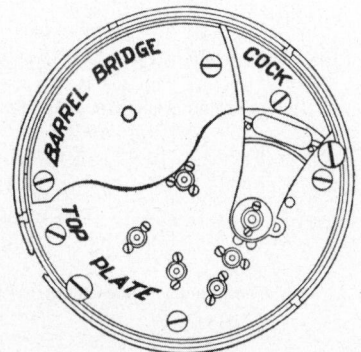

Model 2, Full Plate, Open face.   Model 2, Full Plate, Hunting.

16 SIZE—MODEL 1 Open Face and Hunting, Lever Set

No. 295—Open Face, 21 Jewels, Adjusted to Temperature and 5 Positions.
No. 294—Hunting, 21 Jewels, Adjusted to Temperature and 5 Positions.
No. 293—Open Face, 19 Jewels, Adjusted to Temperature and 5 Positions.
No. 292—Hunting, 19 Jewels, Adjusted to Temperature and 5 Positions.
No. 299—Open Face, 17 Jewels, Adjusted to Temperature and 3 Positions.
No. 298—Hunting, 17 Jewels, Adjusted to Temperature and 3 Positions.
No. 291 —Open Face, 17 Jewels, Adjusted to Temperature and 3 Positions.
No. 290—Hunting, 17 Jewels, Adjusted to Temperature and 3 Positions.
No. 281-Open ace, 15 Jewels,&No.280—Hunting, 15 Jewels.
No. 261—Open Face, 7 Jewels, & No. 260—Hunting, 7 Jewels.

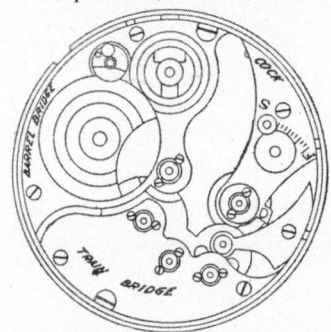 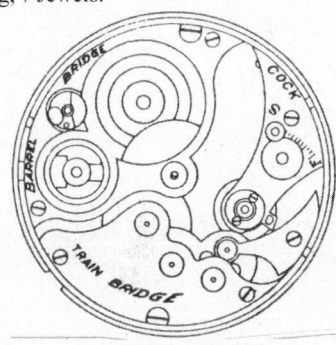

Model 1, 3/4 Plate, Open Face.   Model 1, 3/4 Plate, Hunting.

16 SIZE—MODEL 2 Open Face and Hunting, Pendant and Lever Set.

No. 229—21J, Open Face, Lever Set, "Studebaker," Adjust. to Temp. and 5 Positions.
No. 227—21J, Open Face, Lever Set, Adjusted to Temperature and 5 Positions.
No. 219—19J, Open Face, Pendant Set, Adjusted to Temperature and 4 Positions.
No. 223—17J, Open Face, Lever Set, "Studebaker," Adjust. to Temp. and 5 Positions.
No. 217—17J, Open Face, Lever Set, Adjusted to Temperature and 3 Positions.
No. 215—17J, Open Face, Pendant Set, Adjusted to Temperature.
No. 212—17J, Hunting, Lever Set, Adjusted to Temperature.
No. 211—17J, Open Face, Pendant Set
No. 207—15J, Open Face, Pendant Set, & No. 204—15J, Hunting, Lever Set.
No. 209—9J, Open Face, Pendant Set, & No. 203—7J, Open Face, Pendant Set.

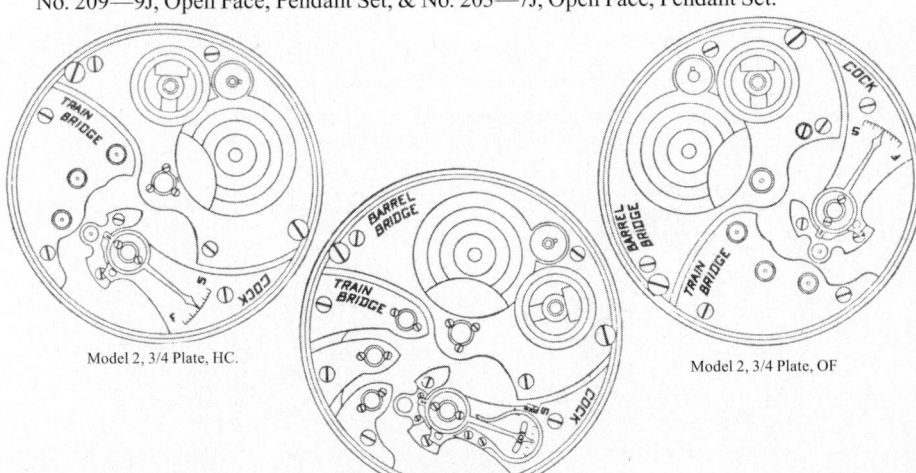

Model 2, 3/4 Plate, HC.   Model 2, 3/4 Plate, OF

Model 2, Bridges, Open Face.

12 SIZE—MODEL 1
Chesterfield Series and Grade 429 Special
Made in Pendant Set, Open Face Only

No. 431—21J, Adjusted to Temperature and 5 Positions.
No. 429—19J, Adjusted to Temperature and 4 Positions.
No. 419—17J, Adjusted to Temperature and 3 Positions.
No. 415—17J, Adjusted to Temperature.
No. 411—17J.
No. 407—15J.

Model 1, Bridges, Open Face.

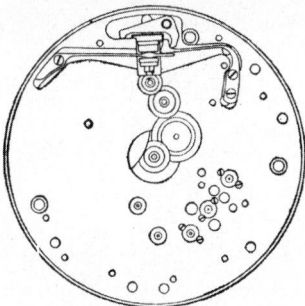

Model 1, Lower Plate, Dial Side.

6 SIZE— MODEL 1
Hunting

Grade No. 180, 17 Jewels
Grade No. 170, 15 Jewels
Grade No. 160, 11 Jewels
Serial Number Range
380,501 to 389,900
Model 1, 3/4 Plate, 6 size

0 SIZE—MODEL 1
Open Face, No second hand, Hunting has second hand

Model numbers 1 & 2 serial numbers under 659,700. All open face and hunting, parts for this model except dial and fourth pinion are interchangeable.

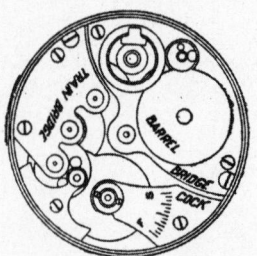

Model 1, Open Face, 3/4 Plate. 7 jewels.

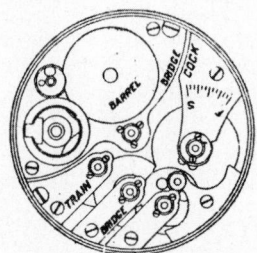

Model 1, Hunting, Bridges, 15-17 jewels.

0 SIZE—MODEL 2
Open Face, No second hand, Hunting has second hand

No. 100—7 Jewels, Hunting, Bridge.
No. 101—7 Jewels, Open Face, 3/4 Plate.
No. 110— 15 Jewels, Hunting, Bridge.
No. 111— 15 Jewels, Open Face, 3/4 Plate.
No. 120— 17 Jewels, Hunting, Bridge.
No. 121— 17 Jewels, Open Face, 3/4 Plate.

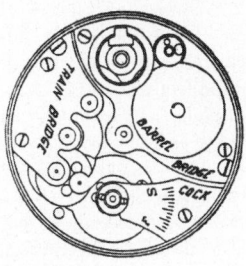

Model 2, Open Face, 3/4 Plate.

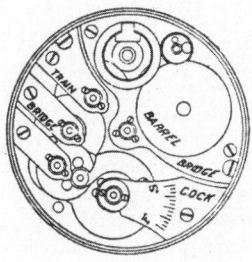

Model 2, Hunting, Bridge.

Model numbers 1 & 2 serial numbers under 659,700. All open face and hunting, parts for this model except dial and fourth pinion are interchangeable.

0 SIZE—MODEL 3
Both Open Face and Hunting have second hand

No. 151— 21J, Open Face, Bridge Model.
No. 150— 21J, Hunting, Bridge Model.
No. 121— 17J, Open Face, Bridge Model.
No. 120— 17J, Hunting, Bridge Model.

Model 3, Open Face, Bridges.

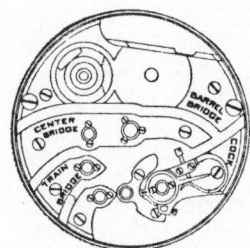

Model 3, Hunting, Bridges.

𝒢𝒪 Pricing in this Guide are fair market price for complete watches which are reflected from the NAWCC National and regional shows.

J. P. STEVENS & Co.

J. P. STEVENS & BRO.
J. P. STEVENS WATCH CO.
Atlanta, Georgia
1882-1887

In mid-1881 J. P. Stevens bought part of the Springfield Watch Co. of Massachusetts; and some unfinished watch components from F. F. Bowman. He set up his watchmaking firm above his jewelry store in Atlanta, Ga., and started to produce the Bowman unfinished watches which were 16 size and 18 size, to which was added the "Stevens Patent Regulator." This regulator is best described as a simple disc attached to the plate which has an eccentric groove cut for the arm of the regulator to move in. This regulator is a prominent feature of the J. P. Stevens, and only the top is jeweled. These watches were 16S, 3/4 plate, stem wind and had a nickel plate with damaskeening. The pallets were equidistant locking and needed greater accuracy in manufacturing. About 50 of these watches were made. A line of gilt movements was added. The pallet and fork are made of one piece aluminum. The aluminum was combined with 1/10 copper and formed an exceedingly tough metal which will not rust or become magnetized. The lever of this watch is only one-third the weight of a steel lever. The aluminum lever affords the least possible resistance for overcoming inertia in transmitting power from the escape wheel to the balance. In 1884, the company was turning out about ten watches a day at a price of $20 to $100 each. In the spring of 1887 the company failed. Only 169 true Stevens watches were made, but other watches carried the J. P. Stevens name.

J.P. Stevens Watch Co. movement by Columbus Watch Co., 18 size, 11-15 jewels.

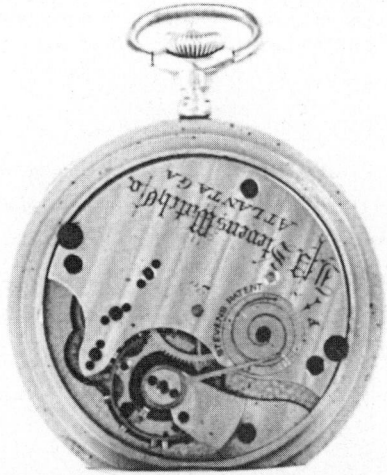

Original "J. P. Stevens Atlanta, Ga.", nickel movement, 16 size, 3/4 plate, lever set, gold jewel settings, note patented spiral grooved regulator, serial number 26.

16 TO 18 SIZE

Grade or Name — Description		ABP	Ex-Fn	Mint
Original Model, Serial Nos. 1 to 174, ALL original with J. P.				
Stevens dial & **18K** case .... ★★★★		$6,000	$7,500	$12,500
Original Model, Serial Nos. 1 to 174,(recased)............ ★★★		1,500	2,500	3,250
Aurora, 15-17J .... ★		400	600	950
Chronograph, 17J, Swiss made, fly back hand .... ★★		500	700	1,100
Columbus W. Co., 15-17J .... ★		400	600	900

🖝 Watches listed in this book are priced at the collectable Trade Show level, as complete watches having an original 14k gold-filled case and *Key Wind* with silver, an original white enamel single sunk dial, and with the entire original movement in good working order with no repairs needed.

J. P. Stevens & Bro., on movement & dial, made by Aurora, 18 size, 15 jewels, Hunting Case, S #39806.

J. P. Stevens & Bro., Swiss chronograph movement, about 18 size, with fly back hand.

Grade or Name —Description		ABP	Ex-Fn	Mint
Elgin, 15-17J	★	$300	$400	$600
Hamilton, 17J	★	400	650	900
Hampden, 15-17J		300	450	700
Illinois, 15-17J	★	600	850	1,100
N. Y. W. Co., 17J, Full Plate, S# range in 500s.	★	700	1,000	1,500
N. V. W. Co. "Bond" Model, S# range in 500s	★★	900	1,200	2,000
Albert H. Potter, **14K case**, Swiss made	★★★★	3,000	5,000	8,000
Rockford, 15J, Full Plate, HC	★	450	750	1,100
18S Swiss, 15-17J, by "Vacheron & C.", wolf teeth winding		400	650	1,100
16S Swiss, 15-17J, Longines.		175	300	350
16S Swiss, 15-17J, 3/4 plate		175	300	350
Waltham, 11-15-17J.	★	425	650	900

J.P. Stevens & Bro., about 18 size, 17 jewels, Note: by "Vacheron & Constantin", wolf teeth winding, Ca. 1889.

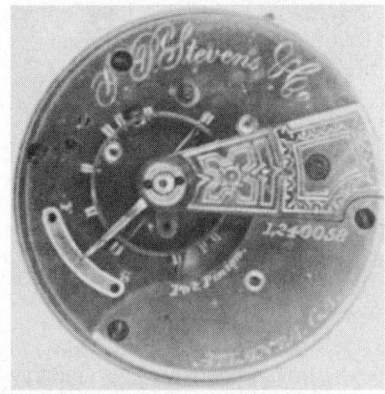

J.P. Stevens Watch Co. movement by Waltham, 18 size, 11 jewels, serial number 1,240,058.

J.P. Stevens movement made oy Hampden, 18 size, 17 jewels, note eccentric style regulator, serial # 515.

J. P. Stevens & Bro., movement made by Hampden, 18 size, 17 jewels, model 4, S#732,085.

6 SIZE

Grade or Name — Description	ABP	Ex-Fn	Mint
Ladies Model, 15J, LS, HC, **14K** . . . . ★	$475	$650	$900
Ladies Model, 15J, LS, GF case, HC	225	300	450
Ladies Model, 15J, LS, GF cases, OF	200	275	325
Ladies Model, 15J, LS, GF cases, Swiss made	150	200	300

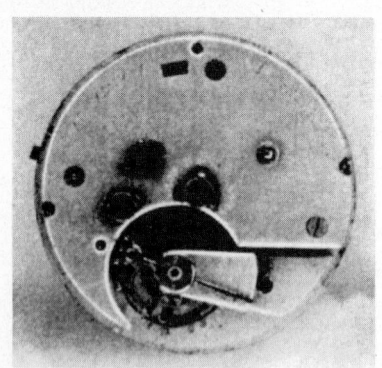

J.P. Stevens Watch Co., 16 size, 15 jewels, Adjusted to temperature & positions, serial number 21,814.

J.P. Stevens Watch Co., 6 size, 11 jewels, exposed winding gears.

⚭ Generic, nameless or unmarked grades for watch movements are listed under the Company name or initials of the Company, etc. by size, jewel count and description.

⚭ Watches listed in this book are priced at the collectable Trade Show level, as complete watches having an original 14k gold-filled case and Key Wind with silver, an original white enamel single sunk dial, and with the entire original movement in good working order with no repairs needed.

SUFFOLK WATCH CO.

Waltham, Massachusetts 1899 -1901

The Suffolk Watch Company officially succeeded the Columbia Watch Company in March 1901. However, the Suffolk 0-size, 7-jewel nickel movement with lever escapement was being manufactured in the Columbia factory before the end of 1899. More than 25,000 movements were made . The factory was closed after it was purchased by the Keystone Watch Case Company on May 17, 1901. The machinery was moved to the nearby factory of the United States Watch Company (purchased by Keystone in April 1901), where it was used to make the United States Watch Company's 0-size movement, introduced in April 1902. Both the Columbia Watch Company and the Suffolk Watch Company made 0-size movements only.

Grade or Name —Description		ABP	Ex-Fn	Mint
0S, 7J, NI, HC.. ★		$125	$200	$350

Suffolk Watch Co., 0 Size, 7 jewels, serial number216,841.

Seth Thomas, *Colonial U.S.A.* on movement, 18 size, 7 jewels, model # 11.

SETH THOMAS WATCH CO.

Thomaston, Connecticut
1883-1915

Seth Thomas was a very prominent clock manufacturer, and in early 1883, the company made a decision to manufacture watches. The watches were first placed on the market in 1885. They were 18S, open face, stem wind, 3/4 plate, and the escapement was between the plates. The compensating balance was set well below the normal. They were 11J, 16,000 beats per minute train, but soon went to 18,000 or quick train. In 1886, the company started to make higher grade watches and produced four grades: 7J, 11J, 15J, and 17J. That year the output was 100 watches a day.

SETH THOMAS ESTIMATED SERIAL NUMBERS AND PRODUCTION DATES

DATE - SERIAL NO.	DATE - SERIAL NO.	DATE-SERIAL NO.	DATE - SERIAL NO.
1885 — 5,000	1893 — 510,000	1901 — 1,230,000	1909 — 2,500,000
1886 — 20,000	1894 — 600,000	1902 — 1,320,000	1910 — 2,725,000
1887— 40,000	1895 — 690,000	1903 — 1,410,000	1911 — 2,950,000
1888 — 80,000	1896 — 780,000	1904 — 1,500,000	1912 — 3,175,000
1889 — 150,000	1897 — 870,000	1905 — 1,700,000	1913 — 3,490,000
1890 — 235,000	1898 — 960,000	1906 — 1,900,000	1914 — 3,600,000
1891 — 330,000	1899 — 1,050,000	1907 — 2.100,000	
1892 — 420,000	1900 — 1,140,000	1908 — 2,300,000	

The above list Is provided for determining the approximate age of your watch. Match serial number with date. Watches were not necessarily sold in the exact order of manufactured date.

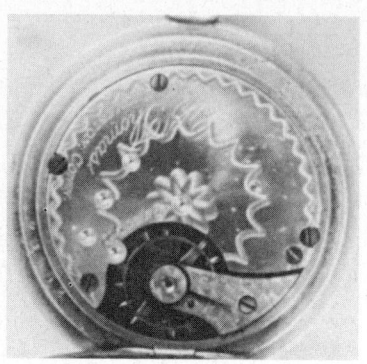

Seth Thomas movement, 18 size, 17 jewels, Molineux model, 2 tone yellow gold, heavy damaskeening, H. C.

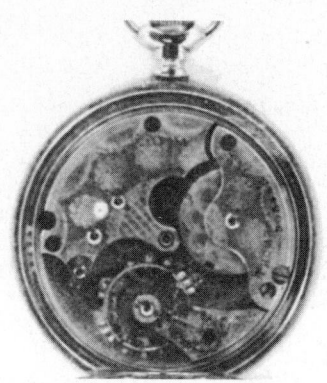

Seth Thomas 18 size, "Molineux" 17 J., 2 tone yellow gold gilt & nickel heavy damaskeening model #2, HC

18 SIZE

Grade or Name — Description	ABP	Ex-Fn	Mint
Century, 7J, OF	$100	$150	$200
Century, 7J, HC	100	225	325
Century, 15J, OF	100	150	210
Century, 15J, HC	100	225	325
Chautauqua, 15J, GJS, M#5 ★	150	275	475
Colonial U.S.A., 7J, model # 11	100	150	175
Cordnia Watch Co., 7J	100	150	175
Early model # 1, low serial # under **1,000** ★	300	525	825
Eagle Series, No. 36, 7J, OF	110	175	190
Eagle Series, No. 37, 7J, HC	110	225	355
Eagle Series, No. 106, 11J, OF	110	175	190
Eagle Series, No. 107, 11J, HC	110	225	355
Eagle Series, No. 206, 15J, OF	110	175	205

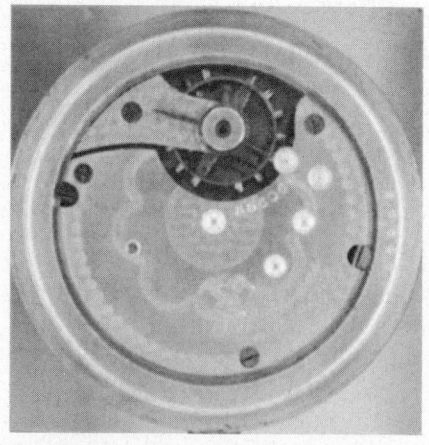

Liberty, Eagle Series, 18 size, 7 jewels, hunting or open face, eagle on movement,.

Seth Thomas, 18 size, 28 jewels, gold jewel settings, engraved dated =8.1.99. No serial number.(note regulator) Note: Cooksey Shugart & Tom Engle counted 28 jewels with dial off. Just before this watch was photographed.

☞ Pricing in this Guide are fair market price for complete watches which are reflected from the NAWCC national and regional shows.

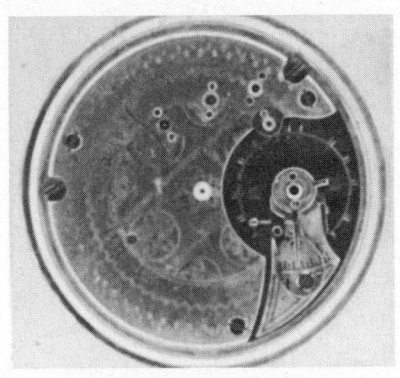

Henry Molineux, 18 size, 17 jewels, "Corona W. Co. USA" on dial, open face, serial number 54,951.

Maiden Lane, 18 size, 25 jewels, 2-tone, gold jewel settings, DR., adj.5P, M# 5, S# 350872. A Double Roller grade is identified by a recessed area under balance wheel.

Grade or Name — Description	ABP	Ex-Fn	Mint
Eagle Series, No.207,15J, HC	$165	$250	$325
Eagle Series, 15J, M#2, HC	135	225	300
Eagle Series, No. 210, 17J, OF	110	175	245
Eagle Series, No. 211, 17J, HC	165	225	380
Eagle Series, 17J, NI, 3/4, OF	110	175	245
Edgemere, 11J	100	150	175
Edgemere, 17J	100	150	200
Keywind M#2, 7J, 11J, & 15J, 3/4	165	325	425
Keywind M#4, 7J, 11J, & 15J, 3/4	165	325	425
Lakeshore, 17J, GJS, ADJ, NI	150	275	375
Liberty, 7J, 3/4, eagle on back plate	110	225	350

A **Double Roller grade** is identified by a recessed area under balance wheel.

Grade or Name — Description	ABP	Ex-Fn	Mint
Maiden Lane, 17J, GJS, DR, Adj.6P, NI, marked, OF ★★★	1,200	1,500	2,200
Maiden Lane, 19J, GJS, DR, Adj.6P, NI, marked, OF ★★★	1,300	1,600	2,400
Maiden Lane, 21J, GJS, DR, Adj.6P, NI, marked, OF ★★★	1,400	1,700	2,500
Maiden Lane, 24J, GJS, DR, Adj.6P, marked, OF ★★★	1,600	2,000	2,600
Maiden Lane, 25J, GJS, DR, Adj.6P, NI, marked, OF ★★★	2,000	2,700	3,500
Maiden Lane, 25J, GJS, DR, Adj.6P, NI, **2 tone**, OF ★★★	2,200	3,000	3,800
Maiden Lane "grade", **28J**, GJS, DR, Adj.5P, NI, OF ★★★★★	15,000	22,000	35,000
Henry Molineux, M#3, 20-21J, 3/4, GJS, ADJ, OF ★★	575	750	900
Henry Molineux, M#2, 17-18J, GJS, ADJ, HC ★★	500	700	850
Henry Molineux, M#2, 19-21J, GJS, ADJ, HC ★★★	750	1,000	1,500
Monarch Watch Co., 7-15J, **2-tone**	125	225	310
R. R. Special USA, 7J, with a **locomotive** on dial	125	225	275
Republic USA, 7J, OF also 15J, OF	100	150	175

☞ Generic, nameless or **unmarked** grades for watch movements are listed under the Company name or initials of the Company, etc. by size, jewel count and description.

Grade or Name — Description	ABP	Ex-Fn	Mint
S. Thomas, 7J, 3/4, **multi-color dial**	$175	$425	$675
S. Thomas, 7J, 3/4	100	150	200
S. Thomas, 11J, 3/4, HC	125	225	325
S. Thomas, 11J, 3/4, OF	100	150	200
S. Thomas, 15J, 3/4, HC	125	225	325
S. Thomas, 15J, 3/4, gilded, OF	100	150	200
S. Thomas, 15J, 3/4, OF	100	150	200
S. Thomas, 16J, 3/4	100	150	200
S. Thomas, 17J, 3/4, OF, nickel	125	175	225

☞ Pricing in this Guide are fair market price for complete watches which are reflected from the NAWCC national and regional shows.

Grade or Name — Description	ABP	Ex-Fn	Mint
S. Thomas, 17J, 3/4, **2-Tone**	$175	$275	$425
S. Thomas, 17J, 3/4, OF, gilded	100	150	200
S. Thomas, 17J, 3/4, HC	125	250	375
S. Thomas, 19J, GJS, DR, Adj.5P, OF ★★	700	875	1,175
S. Thomas, 21J, GJS, DR, Adj.5P.	500	675	875
S. Thomas, 23J,GJS, DR, Adj., OF ★★★	1,200	1,700	2,400
S. Thomas, G# 33, 7J, 3/4, gilded, OF	100	150	175
S. Thomas, G# 34, 7J, 3/4, gilded, HC	100	225	325
S. Thomas, G# 37, 7J, 3/4, NI, HC	100	225	325
S. Thomas, G# 44, 11J, 3/4, gilded, OF	100	150	175
S. Thomas, G# 47, 7J, gilded, FULL, OF	100	150	175
S. Thomas, G# 58, 11J, FULL, gilt, OF	100	150	175
S. Thomas, G# 70, 15J, 3/4, gilded, OF	100	150	175
S. Thomas, G# 71, 15J, 3/4, gilded, HC	110	225	325
S. Thomas, G# 80, 17J, 3/4, gilded, ADJ, HC	135	225	350
S. Thomas, G# 101, 15J, 3/4, gilded, ADJ, OF	100	150	175
S. Thomas, G# 149, 15J, gilded, FULL, OF	100	150	175
S. Thomas, G# 159, 15J, NI, FULL, OF	100	150	175
S. Thomas, G# 169, 17J, NI, FULL, OF	100	150	190
S. Thomas, G# 170, 15J, 3/4, NI, OF	100	150	175
S. Thomas, G# 171, 15J, 3/4, NI, HC	110	225	325
S. Thomas, G# 179, **16-18J**, 3/4, NI, ADJ, HC	175	250	375
S. Thomas, G# 180, 17J, 3/4, NI, HC	135	225	350
S. Thomas, G# 182, 17J, DR, NI, FULL, OF	100	150	200
S. Thomas, G# 201, 15J, 3/4, NI, ADJ, OF	100	150	175
S. Thomas, G# 202, 15J, 3/4, NI, ADJ, HC	100	225	325
S. Thomas, G# 245, 19J, GJS, **2-Tone**, HC ★★	1,000	1,300	1,800
S. Thomas, G# 248, 17-21J, FULL, DR, Adj.3P, OF, **2-tone**	250	325	425
S. Thomas, G# 260, 21J, DR, Adj.6P, NI, FULL, OF	400	575	825
S. Thomas, G# 281, 17J, FULL, DR, Adj.3P, OF, **2-tone**	250	325	425
S. Thomas, G# 282, 17J, FULL, DR, Adj.5P, OF	195	275	375
S. Thomas, G# 382, 17J, FULL, DR, Adj.5P, OF, **2-tone**	200	275	425
S. Thomas, G# 406-408, 17J, FULL, Adj., OF	200	275	375
S. Thomas, G# 408-508, 17J, FULL, Adj., HC	225	325	425
Special Motor Service,17J, LS, **2 tone**, OF ★★	400	525	775
Trainmens Special, **fake "17-23"J** Adj, seen in model 10, 12, 13	100	150	275
20th Century (Wards), 11J	100	150	210
20th Century (Wards), 11J, **2-Tone**	125	275	300
Wyoming Watch Co., 7J, OF	100	175	275

Trainmens Special Chicago U.S.A .23 jewels adjusted marked on movement, fake 23 jewels made of glass & is not adjusted, 18 size, model 10, 12 or 13, (7 operating jewels).

Grade 36, 16 size, 7 jewels, open face, three-quarter nickel plate.

16 SIZE
(OF Only)

Grade or Name — Description	ABP	Ex-Fn	Mint
Centennial, 7J, 3/4, NI, OF................................	$50	$125	$150
Locust, 7J, NI, 3/4, OF	50	125	150
Locust, 17J, NI, ADJ, 3/4, OF	60	125	175
Republic USA, 7J, OF.......................................	50	125	150

☞ Generic, nameless or unmarked grades for watch movements are listed under the Company name or initials of the Company, etc. by size, jewel count and description.

	ABP	Ex-Fn	Mint
S. Thomas, G# 25, 7J, BRG, OF..........................	$45	$125	$150
S. Thomas, G# 26, 15J, BRG, GJS, OF	50	125	150
S. Thomas, G# 27, 17J, BRG, GJS, OF..................	65	150	175
S. Thomas, G# 28, 17J, BRG, Adj.3P, GJS, OF	75	150	225
S. Thomas, G# 326, 7J, 3/4, NI, OF	45	125	150
S. Thomas, G# 328, 15J, 3/4, NI, OF	50	125	150
S. Thomas, G# 332, 7J, 3/4, NI, OF	45	125	150
S. Thomas, G# 334, 15J, NI, ADJ, 3/4, DMK, OF......	50	125	150
S. Thomas, G# 336, 17J, ADJ, 3/4, DMK, OF	75	125	175

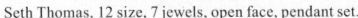

Seth Thomas, 12 size, 7 jewels, open face, pendant set.

Seth Thomas, 12 size, 17 jewels, gold jewel settings, gold center wheel, open face, Adj3p.

12 SIZE
(OF Only)

Grade or Name —Description	ABP	Ex-Fn	Mint
Centennial, 7J..	$35	$75	$115
Republic USA, 7J, OF.......................................	35	80	125
S. Thomas, G# 25, 7J, BRG, OF...........................	35	75	115
S. Thomas, G# 26, 15J, BRG, GJS, OF	40	80	125
S. Thomas, G# 27, 17J, BRG, GJS, OF...................	45	90	140
S. Thomas, G# 28, 17J, OF, BRG, Adj.3P, GJS	50	90	165
S. Thomas, G# 326, 7J, OF, 3/4, NI	35	75	115
S. Thomas, G# 328, 15J, OF, 3/4, NI	40	80	135

☞ Watches listed in this book are priced at the collectable Trade Show level, as complete watches having an original 14k gold-filled case and Key Wind with silver, an original white enamel single sunk dial, and with the entire original movement in good working order with no repairs needed.

☞ Generic, nameless or unmarked grades for watch movements are listed under the Company name or initials of the Company, etc. by size, jewel count and description.

Seth Thomas movement, 6 size, 7 jewels, serial number 441,839. Sometimes appears in a 12 size case.

SETH THOMAS, 0 size, 15 jewels, pendant set, hunting case, serial number 200,449.

6 SIZE
(Some 6 Size were spread to fit 16-12 Size cases)

Grade or Name — Description	ABP	Ex-Fn	Mint
Century, 7J, NI, 3/4	$35	$60	$100
Countess Janet, 17J, Adj., HC.	75	125	200
Eagle Series, 7J, No. 45, 3/4, NI, DMK, OF	50	65	100
Eagle Series, 7J, No. 205, 3/4, HC	60	125	150
Eagle Series, 15J, No. 35, 3/4, NI, DMK, OF.	55	75	125
Eagle Series, 15J, No.245, 3/4, HC.	70	125	150
Edgemere, 7-11J	55	75	125
Republic USA, 7J	50	65	100
Seth Thomas, 7J, 3/4, **14K, 26 DWT, HC**	400	500	700
Seth Thomas, 11J, 3/4, HC	70	80	150
Seth Thomas, 11J, 3/4, OF	55	75	125
S. Thomas, G# 35, 7J, NI, DMK,3/4, HC.	75	135	165
S. Thomas, G#119, 16J, GJS, NI, DMK, 3/4, I-IC	70	125	150
S. Thomas, G#205, 15J, HC	70	125	150
S. Thomas, G#320, 7J, NI, DMK, 3/4, OF	50	65	100
S. Thomas, G#322, 15J, OF	55	70	110

NOTE: Add **$25** to **$50** for HC.

0 -3/0 SIZE

Grade or Name —Description	ABP	Ex-Fn	Mint
Seth Thomas, 7J, No. 1, OF	$60	$75	$150
Seth Thomas, 7J, No. 1, HC	70	135	225
Seth Thomas, 15J, GJS, No. 3, OF	60	80	150
Seth Thomas, 15J, No. 3, HC	75	100	225
Seth Thomas, 17J, GJS, PS, No. 9, OF	60	80	150
Seth Thomas, 17J, GJS, PS, No. 9, HC.	75	135	225

☞ A collector should expect to pay modestly higher prices at local shops.

☞ Pricing in this Guide are fair market price for complete watches which are reflected from the NAWCC national and regional shows.

Number	Model	Number	Model	Number	Model	Number	Model
1 to 10900	1	87601 " 87900	3	540001 " 541000	2	710601 " 712400	8
10901 " 25100	3	87901 " 89100	2	541001 " 542000	6	712401 " 713700	9
25101 " 25200	2	89101 " 89600	4	542001 " 544000	2	713701 " 715200	8
25201 " 25300	3	89601 " 90800	2	544001 " 547000	6	715201 to 715300	9
25301 " 25400	2	90801 " 90900	4	547001 " 549000	2	715301 " 715600	8
25401 " 28000	3	90901 " 91500	2	549001 " 551000	7	715601 " 717000	9
28001 " 29000	2	91501 " 92000	4	551001 " 556000	6	717001 " 718000	8
29001 " 34900	3	92001 " 94400	2	556001 " 558000	7	718001 " 718100	9
34901 " 35000	2	94401 " 94600	3	558001 " 559000	2	718101 " 718200	4
35001 " 36200	4	94601 " 95200	2	559001 " 562000	6	718201 " 721500	8
36201 " 40000	3	95201 " 95300	3	562001 " 568000	7	721501 " 722000	9
40001 " 41200	3	95301 " 95500	2	568001 " 569000	6	722001 " 722200	8
41201 " 41500	2	95501 " 95800	3	569001 " 570000	7	722201 " 722900	9
41501 " 42100	3	95801 " 96500	2	570001 " 571000	6	722901 " 725600	8
42101 " 44800	2	96501 " 97100	3	571001 " 575000	7	725601 " 725700	9
44801 " 46000	4	97101 " 98200	2	575001 " 577000	6	725701 " 727000	8
46001 " 47200	2	98201 " 98225	3	577001 " 579000	7	727001 " 728600	9
47201 " 47300	3	98226 " 98700	2	579001 to 581000	6	728601 " 729500	8
47301 " 48200	2	98701 " 99300	3	581001 " 582600	7	729501 " 730100	9
48201 " 48300	3	99301 " 100000	2	582601 " 582800	4	730101 " 730300	8
48301 " 48600	2	100001 " 128000	14	582801 " 584100	7	730301 " 730800	9
48601 " 49000	3	128001 " 137000	15	584101 " 585000	6	730801 " 731000	8
49001 " 50300	2	137001 " 138000	14	585001 " 585400	7	731001 " 731200	9
50301 " 50400	4	138001 " 139000	15	585401 " 585600	4	731201 " 734900	8
50401 " 51100	2	139001 " 141000	14	585601 " 586000	7	734901 " 735100	9
51101 " 52000	4	141001 " 142000	15	586001 " 590000	6	735101 " 736700	8
52001 " 53300	2	142001 " 144000	14	590001 " 591000	7	736701 " 737800	9
53301 " 54500	4	144001 " 160000	15	591001 " 592000	6	737801 " 738400	8
54501 " 54900	2	160001 " 165000	16	592001 " 592300	7	738401 " 738600	9
54901 " 55000	3	165001 " 166000	14	592301 " 592800	4	738601 " 740500	8
55001 " 55400	2	166001 " 200000	16	592801 " 593000	7	740501 " 741200	9
55401 " 55700	4	200001 " 400000	5	593001 " 607000	6	741201 " 743100	8
55701 " 56600	3	400001 " 420000	16	607001 " 608000	7	743101 " 744200	9
56601 " 57700	4	420001 " 500000	17	608001 " 610000	6	744201 " 747000	8
57701 " 58900	2	500001 " 500500	2	610001 " 612000	7	747001 " 747300	9
58901 " 59200	3	500501 " 502400	3	612001 " 615000	6	747301 " 747500	8
59201 " 59300	2	502401 " 503500	2	615001 " 616000	7	747501 " 747600	9
59301 " 60500	4	503501 to 505600	3	616001 " 617000	6	747601 " 747700	8
60501 " 60800	2	505601 " 506200	2	617001 " 618000	7	747701 " 747800	9
60801 " 61800	3	506201 " 507900	3	618001 " 620000	6	747801 " 748000	8
61801 " 62400	2	507901 " 508000	2	620001 " 621800	7	748001 " 748200	8
62401 " 63800	4	508001 " 509000	7	621801 " 622000	4	748201 " 749100	8
63801 " 64800	2	509001 " 509800	2	622001 " 632000	6	749101 " 749200	9
64801 " 65100	3	509801 " 510000	4	632001 " 633000	7	749201 " 750000	8
65101 " 65700	2	510001 " 512300	2	633001 " 640000	6	750001 " 752600	9
65701 " 65800	4	512301 " 513500	7	640001 " 640100	7	752601 " 753300	8
65801 " 66200	2	513501 " 514300	2	640101 " 640800	6	753301 " 754100	9
66201 " 67300	3	514301 " 514800	3	640801 " 641100	7	754101 " 758400	8
67301 " 68100	2	514801 " 515300	2	641101 " 641700	6	758401 " 758700	9
68101 " 68200	3	515301 " 516100	6	641701 " 642000	7	758701 " 759600	8
68201 " 68800	2	516101 " 516600	7	642001 " 642400	6	759601 " 760600	9
68801 " 69800	3	516601 " 516800	4	642401 " 642500	7	760601 " 761800	8
69801 " 70540	2	516801 " 517400	7	642501 " 647100	6	761801 " 762000	9
70541 " 70550	3	517401 " 517500	3	647101 " 647300	7	762001 " 769000	8
70551 " 71700	2	517501 " 518200	6	647301 " 647600	6	769001 " 769200	9
71701 " 71950	3	518201 " 519300	7	647601 " 647800	7	769201 " 770100	8
71951 " 72000	2	519301 " 519800	6	647801 " 700000	6	770101 " 770600	9
72001 to 73200	2	519801 " 521800	7	700001 " 700100	7	770601 " 777600	8
73201 " 73500	3	521801 " 523300	6	700101 " 700300	9	777601 " 778700	9
73501 " 74900	2	523301 " 523800	4	700301 " 700800	8	778701 " 778900	8
74901 " 75700	3	523801 " 523834	6	700801 " 700900	9	778901 " 784600	9
75701 " 77000	2	523835 " 528100	7	700901 " 701900	8	784601 " 784700	8
77001 " 78000	3	528101 " 528600	6	701901 " 702400	9	784701 " 785800	9
78001 " 79900	2	528601 " 528900	7	702401 " 702900	8	785801 " 786400	8
79901 " 80100	3	528901 " 529900	6	702901 " 703200	9	786401 " 786800	9
80101 " 80500	2	529901 " 530500	7	703201 " 703300	8	786801 " 786900	8
80501 " 81000	3	530501 " 530700	6	703301 " 703800	9	786901 to 788700	8
81001 " 82100	2	530701 " 530800	2	703801 " 703900	8	788701 " 790000	9
82101 " 82300	3	530801 " 531000	6	703901 " 704300	9	790001 " 795300	8
82301 " 84000	2	531001 " 531100	7	704301 " 705800	8	795301 " 795350	9
84001 " 84500	4	531101 " 532600	6	705801 " 706000	9		
84501 " 84900	2	532601 " 535000	7	706001 " 707400	8		
84901 " 85500	3	535001 " 536000	2	707401 " 708000	9		
85501 " 86000	4	536001 " 537000	7	708001 " 709100	8		
86001 " 87000	2	537001 " 538000	6	709101 " 709300	9		
87001 " 87500	4	538001 " 539000	7	709301 " 710200	8	900001 to 950000	17
87501 " 87600	2	539001 " 540000	6	710201 " 710600	9	950001 " 1000000	18

SETH THOMAS WATCH CO.
IDENTIFICATION OF MOVEMENTS
BY MODEL NUMBER

How to Identify Your Watch Size & Model: Compare the movement of your watch with the illustrations in this section. While comparing, note the location of the balance, jewels, screws, gears, and type of back plate (Full, 3/4, Bridge) these will be clues in identifying the movement you have.

Model 1, 18 size, Open Face

Model 2, 18 size, Hunting

Model 3, 18 size, Open Face

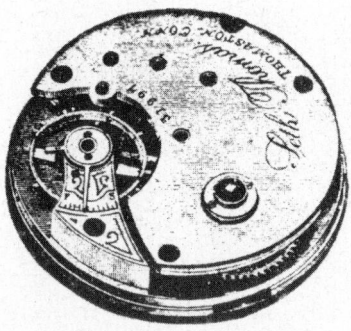

Model 4, 18 size, Key Wind

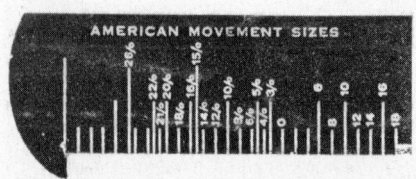

Model 5, 18 size, Maiden
Lane Series, Open Face.

Model 6, 18 Size, Open Face

Model 7 & 9, 18 size

Model 8, 18 size

Model 10, 18 size, Open Face

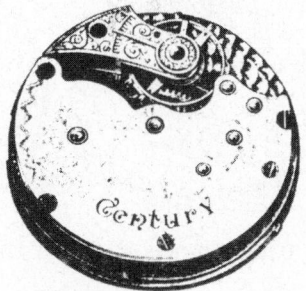

Model 11, 18 size, Hunting

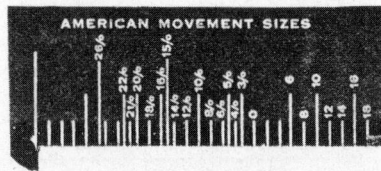

Model 13. 18 size, Hunting

16 Size

16 Size, Open Face

12 size, Open Face

6 Size, Open face

Model 14, 6 siz

Model 16 & 17, 6 size

0 SIZE
No. 9=17 J.
No. 3=15 J.
No. 1=7J.

TREMONT WATCH CO.

Boston, Massachusetts 1864 - 1866

In 1864 A. L. Dennison thought that if he could produce a good movement at a reasonable price, there would be a ready market for it. Dennison went to Switzerland to find a supplier of cheap parts, as arbors were too costly in America. He found a source for parts, mainly the train and escapement and the balance. About 600 sets were to be furnished. Dials were first made by Mr. Gold and Mr. Spear, then later by Mr. Hull and Mr. Carpenter. Tremont had hoped to produce 600 sets of trains per month. In May of 1865, the first movements were ready for the market. They were 18S, key wind, 7-15 jewels, and engraved "Tremont Watch Co." In the late 1866, the company moved to Melrose. The Melrose Watch Co. produced about 5,000 watches. Serial number range from 1 to about 10-11,000. (See Melrose W. Co.)

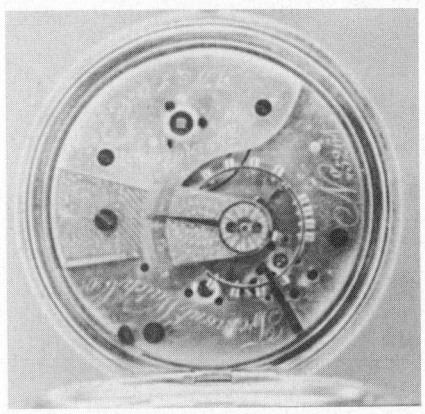

Tremont Watch Co., with "Washington Street Boston" engraved on movement. 18 size, 15 jewels, key wind and set, serial number 5,264.

Tremont movement, 18 size, 15 jewels, key wind & set, serial number 8,875.

Grade or Name —Description	ABP	Ex-Fn	Mint
18S, 7J, KW, KS	$250	$375	$475
18S, 11J, KW, KS	250	375	475
18S, 7-11-15J, KW, KS, gilded Silveroid	200	325	425
18S, 7-11-15J, KW, KS, gilded, marked **LONDON**	250	425	625
18S, 15J, KW, KS, gilded	250	375	500
18S, 15J, KW, KS, HC, **14K**	800	1,400	1,800
18S, 15J, KW, KS, gilded, Washington Street ★★	500	825	1,425
18S, 17J, KW, KS, gilded	300	425	525
18S, 7-15J, KW, **KS from back**, 3/4 plate,(English style) .... ★★★	1,800	2,500	3,700

Signed on movement Tremont Watch Co.,
18S. 3/4 plate, 15J, KW, KS from back, (English style)

TRENTON WATCH CO.

Trenton, New Jersey
1885-1908

Trenton watches were marketed under the following labels: Trenton, Ingersoll, Fortuna, Illinois Watch Case Company, Calumet U.S.A., Locomotives Special, Marvel Watch Co., Reliance Watch Co.

Serial numbers started at 2,001 and ended at 4,100,000. Total production was about 1,934,000.

CHRONOLOGY OF THE DEVELOPMENT OF TRENTON WATCH CO.:

New Haven Watch Co., New Haven, Conn. 1883-1887
Trenton Watch Co., Trenton, N. J. 1887-1908
Sold to Ingersoll 1908-1922

TRENTON MODELS AND GRADES
With Years of Manufacture and Serial Numbers

Date	Numbers	Size	Model	Date	Numbers	Size	Model
1887-1889	2,001-61,000	18	1	1900-1903	2,000,001-2,075,000	6	2
1889-1891	64,001-135,000	18	2	1902-1905	2,075,001-2,160,000	6	3 LS
1891-1898 *1	135,001-201,000	18	3	"	"	12	2 LS
1899-1890	201,001-300,000	18	6	1905-1907	2,160,001-2,250,000	6	3 PS
1891-1900	300,001-500,000	18	4	"	"	12	2 PS
1892-1897	500,001-600,000	6	1	1899-1902	2,500,001-2,600,000	3/0	1
1894-1899	650,001-700,000	16	1	ca. 1906	2,800,001-2,850,000	6	3 PS
1898-1900	700,001-750,000	6	2	"	"	12	2 PS
1900-1904 *2	750,001-800,000	18	4	1900-1904	3,000,001-3,139,000	16	2
1896-1900	850,001-900,000	12	1	1903-1907	3,139,001-3,238,000	16	3 OF
1898-1903	900,001-1,100,000	18	5	1903-1907	3,500,001-3,600,000	16	3 HC
1902-1907	1,300,001-1,400,000	18	6	1905-1907	4,000,001-4,100,000	0	1

1—7 jewel grades made only during 1891; 9 jewel chronograph Pat. Mar. 17, 1891, made 1891-1898.
2—A few examples are KWKS for export to England.

Trenton movement, 18 size, 4 jewels, model # 1, serial number 4,744. (New Haven STYLE.) Model #2 is similar.

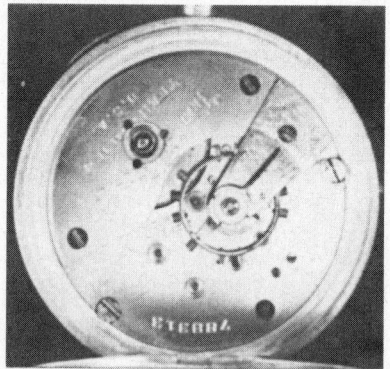

Trenton movement, 18 size, 7 jewels, 4th model, serial number 788,313.

⚖ A collector should expect to pay modestly higher prices at local shops.

⚖ Pricing in this Guide are fair market price for complete watches which are reflected from the NAWCC national and regional shows.

18 SIZE

Grade or Name —Description		ABP	Ex-Fn	Mint
Trenton W. Co., M# 1-2, gilded, OF	★	$150	$200	$300
Trenton W Co., 7J, KW, KS	★	175	250	500
Trenton W. Co., M#3, 7J, 3/4		75	100	125
Trenton W. Co., M#3, 9J, 3/4		75	100	125
Trenton W. Co., M#4, 7J, FULL		75	100	125
Trenton W. Co., M#4, 11J, FULL		75	100	125
Trenton W. Co., M#4, 15J, FULL		75	100	125
Trenton W. Co., M#4-5, FULL, OF, NI		75	100	125
A. C. Roebuck, M#2, Gilded HC	★★	375	550	800
Chronograph, 9J, start stop, & fly back, **DMK**	★★★★	275	800	1,000
Chronograph, 9J, start, stop, & fly back, **Gilded**	★★★★	275	800	1,000
Engineers Special, Chicago, U.S. of America, **17-23 fake jewels,** with a **Locomotive** on Movement & Dial		100	175	250
Locomotive Special, tu-tone, **marked 23J**, also 17J., 7 working jewels, a locomotive on dial & movement (fake jewels)	★	125	200	300
Marvel W. Co. **Marked 23 jewels** (fake jewels) 7 working jewels		60	80	125
New Haven Watch Co. STYLE, M# 1, 4J.	★★★	250	375	500

Note: Add $25 to value of above watches in hunting case.

Chronograph, 18 size, 9 jewels, third model; Gilded, start, stop & fly back, S# 135,069, pat.mar.17.91.

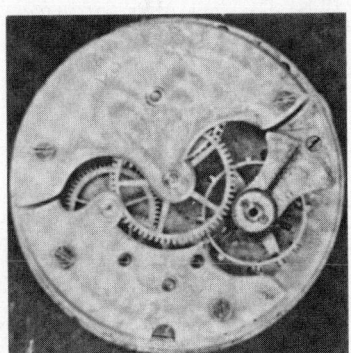

Trenton movement, 18 size, 7 jewels, model #3, serial number 148,945.

16 SIZE

Grade or Name — Description		ABP	Ex-Fn	Mint
Railroad Reliance, 17J, M# 5, OF	★	$100	$125	$250
Trenton W. Co., M#1-2, 7J, 3/4, NI, OF		40	75	125
Trenton W. Co., M#3, 7J, 3F BRG		40	75	125
Trenton W. Co., M#3, 11J, 3F BRG		40	75	125
Trenton W. Co., M#3, 15J, 3F BRG		45	85	135
Trenton W. Co., 7, 11, 15J, 3F BRG, NI		45	85	135
Trenton W. Co., Grade #30 & 31, 7J		40	75	125
Trenton W. Co., Grade #35,36 & 38, 11J		40	75	125
Trenton W. Co., Grade #45, 16J		60	100	150
Trenton W. Co., Grade #125, 12J		40	75	125
Trenton W. Co., 7J., **convertible model** converts to open face or hunting case	★★★	200	350	550

☞ Generic, nameless or unmarked grades for watch movements are listed under the Company name or initials of the Company, etc. by size, jewel count and description.

☞ A collector should expect to pay modestly higher prices at local shops.

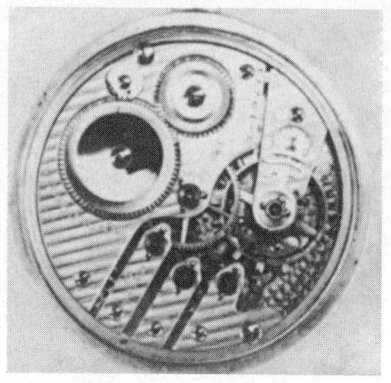

Ingersoll Trenton movement, 16 size, 19 jewels, three fingered bridge, adjusted, serial number 3,419,771.

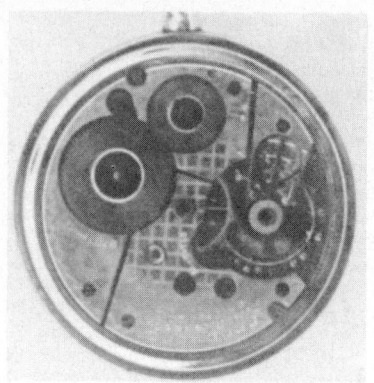

Ingersoll Trenton movement, 16 size, 12 jewels: "Edgemere" engraved on movement.

Grade or Name — Description	ABP	Ex-Fn	Mint
Ingersoll Trenton, 7J, 3F BRG	$40	$60	$125
Ingersoll Trenton, 15J, 3F BRG, NI, ADJ	75	100	150
Ingersoll Trenton, 17J, 3F BRG, NI, ADJ	85	110	160
Ingersoll Trenton, 19J, 3F BRG, NI, Adj.5P, OF ★	150	225	350
Ingersoll Trenton, 19J, 3F BRG, NI, Adj.5P, HC ★★	175	250	400
Peerless, 7J, SW, LS	40	65	85
Reliance, 7J	40	65	85

Note: Add $25 to value of above watches in hunting case.

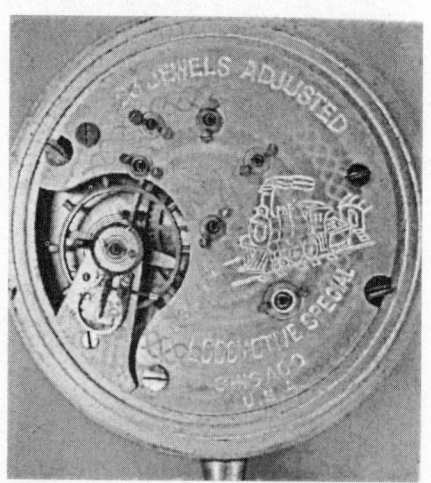

Locomotive Special Chicago U.S.A. 23 jewels adjusted Marked on movement, 16 size, OF, tu-tone, locomotive on dial & movement model # 6, S# 1,366,044. This is a fake 23J., and is not adjusted, it implies it is a railroad watch.

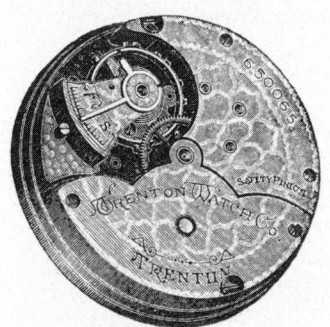

Trenton movement, convertible model converts to open face or hunting case, 16 size, 7 J.

☞ A collector should expect to pay modestly higher prices at local shops.

☞ Pricing in this Guide are fair market price for complete watches which are reflected from the NAWCC national and regional shows.

10-12 SIZE

Grade or Name —Description	ABP	Ex-Fn	Mint
"Fortuna," 7J, 3 finger BRG.	$35	$40	$75
Trenton W. Co., M#1, 7J, 3/4	35	40	75
Monogram, 7-15J, SW	35	40	75

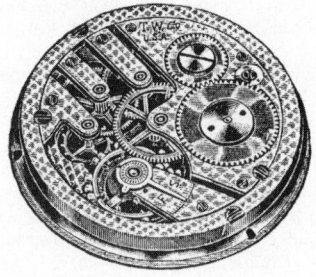 

Trenton Watch Co. movement, 12 size, *Fortuna*. 7jewels, 3 finger BRG., quick train, cut expansion balance.

Trenton Watch Co. movement, 6 size, 7 jewels, open face & hunting, nickel damaskeened.

6 SIZE

Grade or Name —Description	ABP	Ex-Fn	Mint
Trenton W. Co., 7J, 3/4, NI	$25	$40	$70
Trenton W. Co., 7J, 3Finger BRG.	25	40	70
Trenton W. Co., 15J, 3Finger BRG.	35	50	100
"Fortuna," 7J, 3 Finger Bridge	30	40	70

Note: Add $25 to value of above watches in hunting case.

0 SIZE

Grade or Name —Description	ABP	Ex-Fn	Mint
Trenton W. Co., 7J, 3F BRG	$25	$45	$75
Trenton W. Co., 15J,3F BRG	35	50	100

Note: Add $25 to value of above watches in hunting case.

Trenton Chronograph, 18 size, 9J, start, stop, & fly back, Model # 3, Ca. 1892-98. The Trenton chronograph, basically the grade 40 or 41 with modifications of chronograph which was patented by Charles Schlatter on March 17, 1891 (#448,549).

UNITED STATES WATCH CO.

Marion Watch Co.

Marion, New Jersey 1865- 1877

The United States Watch Company was chartered in 1865, and the factory building was started in August 1865 and was completed in 1866. The first watch, called the "Frederic Atherton," was not put on the market until July 1867. It was America's first mass produced stem winding watch. This first grade was 18S, 19J, full plate and a gilt finish movement. A distinctive feature of the company's full plate movements was the butterfly shaped patented opening in the plate which allowed escapement inspection. That same year a second grade called the "Fayette Stratton" was introduced. It was also a gilt finish, full plate movement.

Most of these were 15J, but some of the very early examples have been noted in 17J. In 1868 the "George Channing," "Edwin Rollo," and "Marion Watch Co." grades were introduced. All were 18S, 15J, full plate movements in a gilt finish. In February 1869 the gilt version of the "United States Watch Co." grade was introduced, It was 18S, 19J, full plate and was the company's first entry into the prestige market. Later that year the company introduced their first nickel grade, a 19J, 18S, full plate movement called the "A. H. Wallis." About this same time, in December 1869, they introduced America's most expensive watch, the first nickel, 19J, 18S, full plate "United States Watch Co." grade. Depending on case weight, these prestige watches retailed between $500 and $600, more than the average man earned in a year at that time. The company also introduced damaskeening to the American market; first on gilt movements and later on the nickel grades. The damaskeening process was later improved by using **IVORY** disc in place of wooden disc. The United States and Wallis 19J prestige grades were beautifully finished with richly enameled engraving including a variety of unique designs on the balance cock. It is significant to note that no solid gold trains have been seen with these prestige items in the extant examples presently known.

Below butterfly cut-out.

FREDERIC ATHERTON & Co., 18 size, 19 J., gold Jewel settings, key wind, also note the pin set on rim which will bring a HIGHER price. Note butterfly cut - out.

United States Watch Co. Marion, N.J., 1871 advertisement. Note the butterfly cut - out exposing the escapement.

In 1870 the company introduced their first watch for ladies, a 10S, 15J, plate, cock & bridge movement which was made to their specifications in Switzerland. This model was first introduced in two grades, the "R. F. Pratt" and "Chas. G. Knapp," both in a 15J, gilt finish movement. Later it was offered in a high grade, 19J "I. H. Wright" nickel finish movement. During 1870 and 1871 several other full plate grades in both gilt and nickel finish were introduced. In 1871 development on a new line of full plate, 3/4 plate, and plate & bridge was started but not introduced to the market until late in 1872 and early 1873. The 10S and 16S new grades in 3/4 plate and bridge were probably delayed well into 1873 and were not available long, just before the "Panic of 1873" started in September; this explains their relative scarcity.

By July 1874 the "Panic" had taken its toll and it was necessary for the company to reorganize as the Marion Watch Company, a name formerly used for one of their grades. At this time jewel count finish standards, and prices were lowered on the full plate older grades, but this proved to be a mistake. That same year they introduced a cased watch called the "North Star", their cheapest watch at $15 retail.

The year of 1875 hit the watch industry the hardest; price cutting was predatory and the higher priced watches of the United States Watch Co. were particularly vulnerable. Further lowering of finish standards and prices did not help and in 1876 the company was once again reorganized into the Empire City Watch Co. and their products were displayed at the Centennial that year. The Centennial Exhibition was not enough to save the faltering company and they finally closed their doors in 1877. The Howard brothers of Fredonia, New York (Independent and Fredonia Watch Co.) purchased most of the remaining movements in stock and machinery. In the ten year period of movement production current statistical studies indicate an estimated production of only some 60,000 watches, much smaller than the number deduced from the serial numbers assigned up to as high as 289,000.

NOTE: The above historical data and estimated production figures based on data included in the new NAWCC book *MARION, A History of the United States Watch Company,* by William Muir and Bernard Kraus. This definitive work is available from NAWCC, Inc., 514 Poplar St. Columbia, PA. (Courtesy, Gene Fuller, MARION book editor.) This book is recommended for your library.

EMPIRE CITY W. CO. & EQUIVALENT U. S. W. CO. GRADES

Empire City W. Co	United States W. Co.
W. S. Wyse	A. H. Wallis
L. W. Frost	Henry Randel
Cyrus H. Loutrel	Wm. Alexander
J. L. Ogden	S. M. Beard
E. F. C. Young	John W. Lewis
D. C. Wilcox	George Channing
Henry Harper	Asa Fuller
Jesse A. Dodd	Edwin Rollo
E. C. Hine	J. W. Deacon
New York Belle	A. J. Wood
The Champion	G. A. Read
Black Diamond	Young America

NOTE: Courtesy Gene Fuller, NAWCC "MARION" book editor.

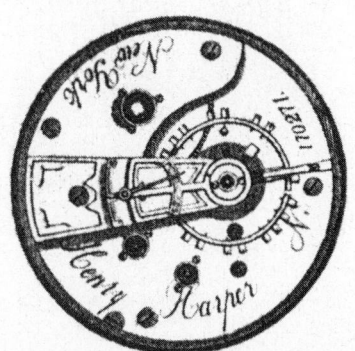

Empire city W. Co., Henry Harper, note: movement does not have **Butterfly Cut-out.**

United States Watch Co. movement, 18 size, 19 jewels, gold jewel settings, key wind. Their highest grade watch.

United States Watch Co., Henry Randel, 15 jewels, KWKS, FROSTED plates, S # 24,944

MARION
18 SIZE
(All with Butterfly Cut-out Except for 3/4 Plate)

Grade or Name — Description		ABP	Ex-Fn	Mint
Win. Alexander, 15J, NI, KW, HC	★	$300	$400	$600
Win. Alexander, 15J, NI, KW, OF	★	300	400	600
Win. Alexander, 15J, NI, SW, OF	★	300	400	600
Frederic Atherton & Co., 15J, SW, gilded		275	350	500
Frederic Atherton & Co., 17J, KW, gilded, HC		350	400	600
Frederic Atherton & Co., 17J, KW, gilded, OF		285	400	550
Frederic Atherton & Co., 17J, SW, gilded, HC		300	400	575
Frederic Atherton & Co., 17J, SW, gilded, OF		285	400	535

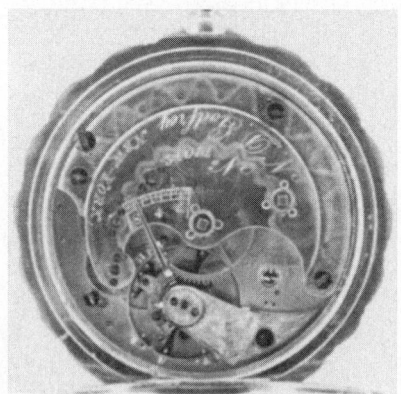

U.S. Watch Co., dial and movement, 18 size, 20 jewels, hunting case, 3/4 plate, engraved on movement "N.D. Godfrey," serial number 72,042. Painted on the dial "New York 1873." The dial consists of day-date-month and moon phases.

NOTE: The **PIN** or **NAIL** set feature is considered more desirable & will bring a **HIGHER** price.

Grade or Name —Description		ABP	Ex-Fn	Mint
Frederic Atherton & Co., 19J, SW, gilded	★★	$600	$800	$1,200
Frederic Atherton & Co., 19J, KW, gilded	★★	650	1,000	1,400
BC & M R.R, 11J, KW	★★★★	2,000	3,500	5,000
BC & M R.R., 15J, gilded, KW	★★★★	2,000	3,500	5,000
S. M. Beard, 15J, KW, NI, OF	★	200	350	450
S. M. Beard, 15J, SW, NI, OF	★	200	350	450
S. M. Beard, 15J, SW or KW, HC	★	250	400	500
Centennial Phil., 11-15J, SW or KW, NI	★★★★	2,500	4,000	6,000
George Channing, 15J, KW, NI		200	350	450
George Channing, 15J, KW, gilded		200	350	450
George Channing, 15J, KW, NI, 3/4 Plate		250	400	500
George Channing, 17J, KW, NI		250	400	500
J. W. Deacon, 11-13J, KW, gilded		175	300	350
J. W. Deacon, 15J, KW, gilded		200	350	450
J. W. Deacon, 11-15J, KW, 3/4 Plate	★	300	400	650
Empire City Watch Co., 11J, SW, **NO butterfly cut-out**	★★★★	2,000	4,000	6,500
Empire Combination Timer, 11J, FULL, time & distance on dial	★★★	1,600	3,500	4,900
Empire Combination Timer, 15J, 3/4, time & distance on dial	★★★	1,500	3,500	5,000
Fellows, 15J, NI, KW	★	400	600	750
Benjamin Franklin, 15J, KW	★★	425	700	900
Asa Fuller, 7-11J, gilded, KW		200	300	400
Asa Fuller, 15J, gilded, KW		200	300	400
Asa Fuller, 15J, gilded, KW, 3/4 Plate	★★	275	400	500
N. D. Godfrey, 20J, NI, 3/4 plate, day date month, moon phases, c. 1873, HC, 18K	★★★★	6,000	11,500	16,500
John W. Lewis, 15J, NI, KW	★	200	300	400
John W. Lewis, 15J, NI, SW	★	250	400	500
John W. Lewis, 15J, NI, 3/4 Plate	★	250	400	500

Edwin Rollo, 18 size, 15 jewels, gilded, key wind & set, note butterfly cut-out, serial number 110,214.

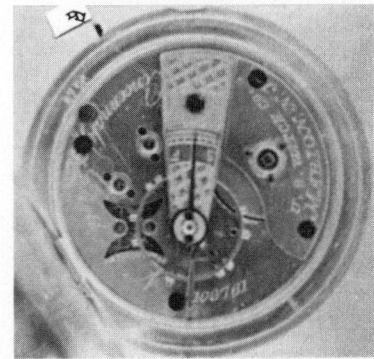

Marion Watch Co. personalized Watch, 18 size, about 15J., pin set, note butterfly cut-out, serial # 106,761.

☞ Watches listed in this book are priced at the collectable Trade Show level, as complete watches having an original 14k gold-filled case and Key Wind with silver, an original white enamel single sunk dial, and with the entire original movement in good working order with no repairs needed.

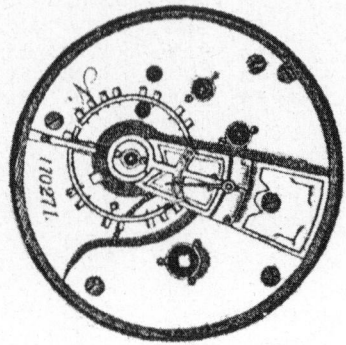

Empire City Watch Co. on movement, U.S. Marion Watch Co. on dial, 18 size, 15 jewels, note **NO butterfly cut - out** on this model. Second Quality

United States Watch Co., 18 size, 19 jewels, gold jewel settings, key wind & pin set, serial number 24,054.

Grade or Name — Description	ABP	Ex-Fn	Mint
Marion Watch Co., 11J, KW, gilded......................★	$175	$250	$375
Marion Watch Co., 15J, KW, gilded......................★	200	275	400
Marion Watch Co., 15J, SW, gilded, 3/4 Plate.............★★	300	400	600
Marion Watch Co., 17-19J, KW, gilded ....★	400	500	750
N.J. R. R. & T. Co., 15J, gilded, KW ....★★★	1,300	2,500	3,300
Newspaper Special Order, 11-15J, gilded, SW or KW..........★	500	700	1,100
North Star, 7J, KW, NI case ....★	300	400	550
North Star, 7J,SW, KS ....★	300	400	500
North Star, 7J, 3/4 Plate ....★	375	450	600
Pennsylvania R.R., 15J, NI, KW, HC ....★★★★	2,500	4,500	6,500
Personalized Watches, 7-11J, KW, 3/4 Plate ....★	250	375	500
Personalized Watches, 11J, KW; gilded....................★	250	375	500
Personalized Watches, 15J, KW, gilded....................★	250	375	500
Personalized Watches, 15J, KW, NI......................★	250	375	500
Personalized Watches, 15J, KW, 3/4 Plate.................★	250	375	500
Personalized Watches, 19J, KW, Full Plate.................★	400	500	850
Henry Randel,15J,KW,NI ....★	225	300	450
Henry Randel, 15J, KW, **frosted plates** ....★	300	400	575
Henry Randel,15J,SW,NI..............................★	250	350	450
Henry Randel, 15J, 3/4 Plate ....★	300	425	600
Henry Randel, 17J, KW, NI ....★	300	400	600
G. A. Read, 7J, gilded, KW	175	275	400
G.A.Read,7J,3/4Plate................................	200	300	425
Edwin Rollo, 11J, KW, gilded	150	225	400
Edwin Rollo, 15J, KW, gilded	175	300	425
Edwin Rollo, 15J, SW, gilded..........................	175	300	425
Edwin Rollo, 15J, 3/4 Plate...........................★	225	300	475
Royal Gold, 11J, KW ....★	400	525	850
Royal Gold, 15J, KW ....★	450	600	950
Royal Gold, 15J, 3/4 Plate.........................★★	500	700	1,300

𝒢ꞁ A collector should expect to pay modestly higher prices at local shops.

𝒢ꞁ Watches listed in this book are priced at the collectable Trade Show level, as complete watches having an original 14k gold-filled case and *Key Wind* with silver, an original white enamel single sunk dial, and with the entire original movement in good working order with no repairs needed.

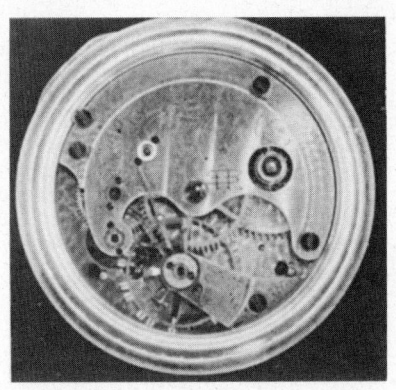

A.H. Wallis on movement, Empire City Watch Co. on dial, 18 size, 19 jewels, three-quarter plate, hunting. This combination timer has listed on the dial, 16 cities showing the time of day and distance in comparison with New York City, serial number 54,409.

Grade or Name —Description	ABP	Ex-Fn	Mint
Rural New York, 15J, gilded .... ★	$400	$550	$800
Fayette Stratton, 11J, gilded............................. ★	200	300	425
Fayette Stratton, 15J, KW, gilded....................... ★	200	300	425
Fayette Stratton, 15J, SW, gilded....................... ★	175	225	400
Fayette Stratton, 17J, KW, gilded....................... ★	275	400	500
Fayette Stratton, 17J, SW, gilded....................... ★	275	400	500
Union Pacific R.R., 15J, KW, gilded .... ★★★	2,200	3,500	5,100
United States Watch Co., 15J, NI, KW.................. ★	750	900	1,400
United States Watch Co., 15J, NI, SW.................. ★	800	950	1,500
United States Watch Co., 15J, 3/4 Plate, NI.......... ★	800	950	1,500
United States Watch Co., 15J, 3/4 Plate, gilded...... ★	800	950	1,500
United States Watch Co., 19J, GJS, Adj.5P, **18K HC**, dial, mvt. & case all marked, Pin Set, SW .... ★★★	3,800	5,000	8,500
United States Watch Co., 19J, NI, KW................ ★★	1,300	2,500	3,000
United States Watch Co., 19J, NI, SW................ ★★	1,400	2,600	3,200
A. H. Wallis, 15J, KW, NI .... ★	200	300	400
A. H. Wallis, 15J, SW, NI.............................. ★	200	300	400
A. H. Wallis, 17J, KW, NI.............................. ★	200	300	450
A. H. Wallis, 17J, SW, NI.............................. ★	200	300	450
A. H. Wallis, 19J, KW, NI........................... ★★★	450	600	900
A. H. Wallis, 19J, SW, NI........................... ★★★	450	600	900
D. G. Wilcox, 15J, SW, **NO** butterfly cut-out .... ★	300	525	775
I. H. Wright, 11J, KW, gilded........................... ★	200	300	400
I. H. Wright, 15J, KW, gilded........................... ★	200	300	400

&↷ A collector should expect to pay modestly higher prices at local shops.

&↷ Watches listed in this book are priced at the collectable Trade Show level, as complete watches having an original 14k gold-filled case and Key Wind with silver, an original white enamel single sunk dial, and with the entire original movement in good working order with no repairs needed.

&↷ Some grades are not included. Their values can be determined by comparing with similar age, size, metal content, style, models and grades listed.

&↷ Pricing in this Guide are fair market price for complete watches which are reflected from the NAWCC national and regional shows.

16 SIZE
1/4 Plate

Grade or Name — Description		ABP	Ex-Fn	Mint
S. M. Beard, 15J, NI, KW	★★★	$300	$450	$600
Marion Watch Co., 11-15J., KW	★★★	300	450	600
John W. Lewis, 15J, NI, KW	★★★	300	450	600
Personalized Watches, 15J, NI, SW	★★★	300	450	600
Edwin Rollo, 15J, KW	★★★	300	450	600
United States Watch Go., 15J, NI, SW	★★★	700	1,100	1,800
A. H. Wallis, 19J, NI, SW	★★★	700	1,100	1,800

Note: 16S, 1/4 plate fewer % made of the U.S.W.Co.—Marion watches.

Ass Fuller, 16 size, 15 jewels, stem wind, one-quarter plate, serial number 280,016. Note: 3 screws on barrel bridge.

United States Watch Co., 14 size, 15 jewels, three-quarter plate, engraved on movement "Royal Gold American Watch, New York, Extra Jeweled."

14 SIZE
3/4 Plate

Grade or Name — Description		ABP	Ex-Fn	Mint
Centennial Phil., 11J, KW, gilded	★★★★	$900	$1,200	$2,200
J. W. Deacon, 11J	★★	150	250	400
Asa Fuller, 15J	★★	275	400	500
John W. Lewis, 15J, NI	★★	275	400	500
Marion Watch Co., 15J., KW	★	200	300	450
North Star, 15J	★★	300	400	550
Personalized Watches, 7-11J	★★	300	400	550
Edwin Rollo, 15J	★	275	375	500
Royal Gold, 15J	★	375	500	750
Young America, 7J, gilded	★	250	375	500

⚿ A collector should expect to pay modestly higher prices at local shops.

⚿ Watches listed in this book are priced at the collectable Trade Show level, as complete watches having an original 14k gold-filled case and Key Wind with silver, an original white enamel single sunk dial, and with the entire original movement in good working order with no repairs needed.

⚿ Some grades are not included. Their values can be determined by comparing with similar age, size, metal content, style, models and grades listed,

10 SIZE
1/4 Plate

Grade or Name — Description	ABP	Ex-Fn	Mint
Wm. Alexander, 15J, KW, NI	$135	$200	$375
S. M. Beard, 15J, KW, NI, 1/4 Plate.........................	135	200	375
Empire City Watch Co., 15J, KW .... ★★★	600	1,000	1,300
Chas. G. Knapp, 15J, **Swiss**, 1/4 Plate, KW	100	150	275
Marion Watch Co., 11-15J., 1/4Plate	125	200	350
Personalized Watches, 11-15J, 1/4 Plate	135	200	350
R. F. Pratt, 15J, **Swiss**, 1/4 Plate, KW.........................	100	150	250
Edwin Rollo, 11-15J, 1/4 Plate	150	250	400
A.H.Wallis, 17-19J,KW,1/4Plate............................ ★	185	300	450
A. J. Wood, 15J, 1/4 Plate, KW ....★★	275	400	500
I. H. Wright, 19J, **Swiss**, NI, Plate, KW ....★★	175	300	475

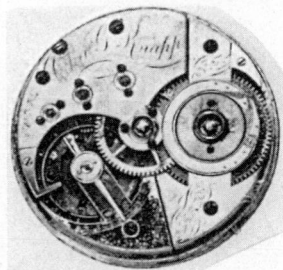

S. M. Beard, 10 size, 15 jewels, key wind, quarter plate, serial number 248,407. Note: 2 screws on barrel bridge.

Chas. G. Knapp, 10 size, 15 jewels, Swiss, quarter plate, key wind.

U. S. WATCH CO. OF WALTHAM

Waltham, Massachusetts
1885-1905

The business was started as the Waltham Watch Tool Co. in 1879. It was organized as the United States Watch Co. in about 1885. The first watches were 16S, 3/4 plate pillar movement in three grades. They had a very wide mainspring barrel (the top was thinner than most) which was wedged up in the center to make room for the balance wheel. These watches are called dome watches and are hard to find. The fork was made of an aluminum alloy with a circular slot and a square ruby pin. The balance was gold at first, as was the movement which was a slow train, but the expansion balance was changed when they went to a quick train. The movement required a special case which proved unpopular. By 1887, some 3,000 watches had been made. A new model was then produced, a 16S movement that would fit a standard case. These movements were quick train expansion balance with standard type lever and 3/4 plate pillar movement. This company reached a top production of 10 watches a day for a very short period. The company was sold to the E. Howard Watch Co. (Keystone) in 1903. The United States Watch Co. produced watches with serial number as high as 890,000 so *possible* total is 890,000. Its top grade watch movement was the "**The President.**"

𝒢𝒻 Pricing in this Guide are fair market price for complete watches which are reflected from the NAWCC national and regional shows.

U.S. WATCH CO. OF WALTHAM
ESTIMATED SERIAL NUMBERS
AND PRODUCTION DATES

Date	Serial No.	Date	Serial No.
1887	3,000	1896	300,000
1811	6,500	1897	350,000
1889	10,000	1891	400,000
1890	30,000	1899	500,000
1891	60,000	1900	600,000
1892	90,000	1901	700,000
1893	150,000	1902	750,000
1894	200,000	1903	800,000
1895	250,000		

Acid Etched, 18 Size, 7-15J., HC

U.S. Watch Co. of Waltham, The President on dial & movement 18 size, 17J, hunting case, marked Adjusted, serial # 150,020, produced in late 1893 or early 1894.

U.S. watch Co. of Waltham, The President, 18 size, 17 jewels, open face, 2-tone, adj., note regulator, serial number 150,350. Note: A.C. Roebuck 17J. similar to President.

18 SIZE

Grade or Name — Description	ABP	Ex-Fn	Mint
A.C. Robuck 15-17J, Adjusted Special (similar to The President)★★	$375	$600	$800
Acid Etched movement, 7-15J, (with good Finish)..........★★	200	325	450
Express Train, 15J, ADJ, NI, OF ....★	400	500	750
Express Train, 15J, ADJ, NI, HC ....★	625	800	975
The President, 17J, GJS, Adj.6P, DR, NI, DMK, HC........★★★	375	600	800
The President, 17J, GJS, Adj.6P, DR, NI, DMK, OF..........★★	350	600	725
The President, 21J, GJS, Adj.6P, DR, NI, DMK, OF ......★★★★	800	1,200	1,500
The President, 21J, GJS, Adj.6P, DR, **14K**..............★★★★	1,200	2,000	2,500

Note: A Feb. 1st, **1894** ad states: The only 18 size **Double Roller,** Lever set movement on the market & guarantees that this (The President) movement will vary *less than six seconds a month.*

| Washington Square, 15J, HC ....★ | $200 | $300 | $400 |

Generic, **nameless** or unmarked grades for watch movements are listed under the Company name or initials of the Company, etc. by size, jewel count and description.

U. S. Watch Co., 15J, OF, **2-tone, stem attached** ....★	$300	$400	$575
U. S. Watch Co., 39 (HC) & 79 (OF), 17J, GJS,			
ADJ, NI, DMK, Adj.5P, BRG........................	100	175	275
U. S. Watch Co., 40 (HC) & 80 (OF), 17J, GJS	100	175	275
U. S. Watch Co., 48 (HC) & 88 (OF), 7J, gilded, FULL	100	175	200
U. S. Watch Co., 48 (HC) & 88 (OF), 7J, gilded, FULL,Silveroid ...	100	150	175

☜ Some grades are not included. Their values can be determined by comparing with similar age, size, metal content, style, models and grades listed.

Grade or Name —Description	ABP	Ex-Fn	Mint
U. S. Watch Co., 52(HC)	$100	$225	$325
U. S. Watch Co., 92 (OF), 17J, Silveroid	100	150	175
U.S. Watch Co., 52 (HC) & 92 (OF), 17J	100	225	325
U. S. Watch Co., 53 (HC) & 93 (OF), 15J, NI, FULL, DMK........	100	225	325
U. S. Watch Co., 54 (HC) & 94 (OF), 15J.....................	100	225	325
U.S. Watch Co., 56(HC)&96(OF),11J	100	225	275
U.S. Watch Co., 57(HC)&97(OF), 11J........................	100	225	325
U. S. Watch Co., 58 (HC) & 98 (OF), 11J, NI, FULL, DMK........	100	200	275
U. S. Watch Co., 7-15J, note **3/4 plate** and 18 size...............	125	225	300

U.S. Watch Co. of Waltham, 16 size, 7 jewels, gilded, note raised dome on center of movement, engraved on movement 'Chas. V. Woerd's Patents," serial number 3,564.

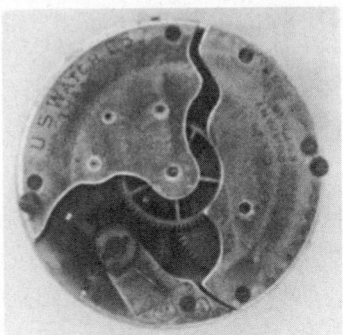

U.S. Watch Co. of Waltham, 16 size, Hunting case, 7 jewels. 'A New Watch Company At Waltham, Est'd 1885" on movement, serial number 770,771.

16SIZE

Grade or Name — Description	ABP	Ex-Fn	Mint
Acid Etched , 7-15J, (with good Finish)....................★★	$150	$300	$400
Dome plate style movement, 7J, gilded	100	225	350
U. S. Watch Co., 103, 17J, NI, 3/4, ADJ......................	65	125	175
U.S. Watch Co., 104, 17J,NI,3/4..........................	65	125	175
U.S. Watch Co., 104, 17J, NI, 3/4, Silveroid	65	125	175
U.S. Watch Co., 105, 15J, NI, 3/4, HC........................	75	150	250
U. S. Watch Co., 105, 15J, NI, 3/4, OF	65	125	175
U. S. Watch Co., 105, 15J, NI, 3/4, Silveroid	65	125	175
U, S. Watch Co., 106, 15J, gilded,3/4, Silveroid	65	125	175
U. S. Watch Co., 106, 15J, gilded,3/4..........................	65	125	175
U.S. Watch Co., 108, 11J, gilded, 3/4	65	125	175
U.S. Watch Co., 109, 7J, NI, 3/4.............................	65	125	175
U. S. Watch Co., 110,7J,3/4,HC	75	175	225
U. S. Watch Co., 110,7J,3/4,OF.............................	65	125	175

Note: Add $25 - $50 to value of above watches in hunting case.

☞ Generic, nameless or unmarked grades for watch movements are listed under the Company name or initials of the Company, etc. by size, jewel count and description.

☞ Watches listed in this book are priced at the collectable Trade Show level, as complete watches having an original 14k gold-filled case and Key Wind with silver, an original white enamel single sunk dial, and with the entire original movement in good working order with no repairs needed.

☞ Pricing in this Guide are fair market price for complete watches which are reflected from the NAWCC national and regional shows.

U.S. Watch Co., 18 or 16 size, 15 jewels, three-quarter plate.

U.S. Watch Co.,16 size, Open Face, 7 jewels, S# 15761.

6 SIZE

Grade or Name —Description	ABP	Ex-Fn	Mint
U.S. Watch Co., 60, 17J, GJS, NI, 3/4, Adj.3P	$50	$75	$150
U.S. Watch Co., 60, 17J, GJS, NI, 3/4, Adj.3P, **HC, 14K**	250	350	575
U. S. Watch Co., 62, 15J, NI, 3/4	40	75	100
U. S. Watch Co., 63, 15J, gilded	40	75	100
U.S. Watch Co., 64,11J,NI	40	75	100
U. S. Watch Co., 65, 11J, gilded	35	60	75
U. S. Watch Co., 66, 7J, gilded	35	60	75
U. S. Watch Co., 66, 7-11J, NI, 3/4	40	75	100
U. S. Watch Co., 68, 16J, GJS, NI, 3/4	45	90	125
U. S. Watch Co., 69, 7J, NI, HC	50	95	150
U. S. Watch Co., 69, 7J, NI, OF	40	75	100

Note: Add $25 - $50 to value of above watches in hunting case.

Grade 64, 6 size, 11 jewels

U.S. Watch Co. of Waltham, 0 size, 7 jewels, serial number 805,231. Engraved on movement United States Watch Co. New York USA, 808,231.

0 SIZE

Grade or Name — Description	ABP	Ex-Fn	Mint
Betsy Ross, HC, GF case	$100	$175	$300
U. S. Watch Co., 15J, HC, GF case	90	125	250
U.S. Watch Co., 7-11J, HC, GF case	90	125	250

THE WASHINGTON WATCH CO.

Washington, D.C. 1872-1874

NOTE: Check your watch for a grade name, such as Liberty Bells, Potomac, Lafayette, Army & Navy, Senate, Monroe, and others which are listed under the **Illinois section.** Washington Watch Co. was Montgomery Ward's private label and made by Illinois Watch Co.

J.P. Hopkins, though better known as the inventor of the Auburndale Rotary Watch, was also connected with the Washington Watch Co., they may have produced about 50 watches. They were 18S, key wind, 3/4 plate and had duplex escapements. Before Hopkins came to Washington Watch Co. he had handmade about six fine watches. The company had a total production of 45 movements with duplex escapements.

Grade or Name —Description	ABP	Ex-Fn	Mint
18S, 15J, 3/4,KW, KS .... ★★★★ $5,200		$7,000	$15,000

WATERBURY WATCH CO.

Waterbury, Connecticut

In 1880 Benedict & Burnham was renamed Waterbury W. Co.. D. A. A. Buck designed a rotary watch with 58 parts for Series A & 57 for B. The rotary long wind takes about 120 to 140 turns of the crown to fully wind. It had a two-wheel train rather than the standard four-wheel train. The Waterbury rotary long wind movement revolved once every hour & has a duplex escapement and paper dial, the watch was priced at $3.50 to $4.00 with case. In 1898 became the New England Watch Co.

in our new improved spring box, *satin lined.*

WATERBURY WATCH CO.

Waterbury, Conn., Nov. 1, 1881.

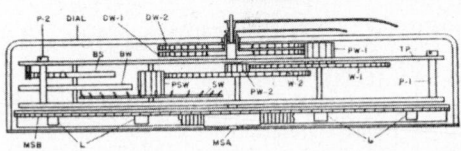

DW-1	Hour wheel	MSA	Mainspring arbor
DW-2	Fixed dial wheel	W-1	First wheel
PW-1	Pinion of 1st wheel	W-2	Second wheel
SW	Escape wheel	PW-2	Pinion of 2nd wheel
BS	Balance spring	PSW	Escape wheel pinion
BW	Balance wheel	P-1	Pillar
MSB	Mainspring barrel	TP	Top plate
MS	Mainspring	P-2	Pillar screw
L,L	Lugs		

Above: Waterbury **Rotary** movement.

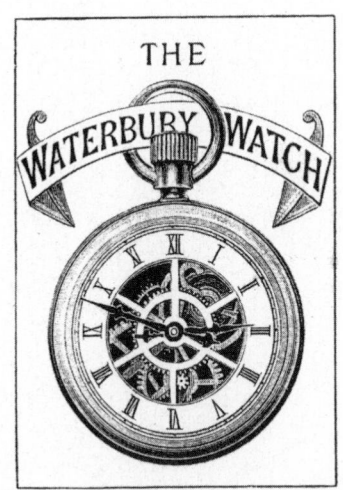

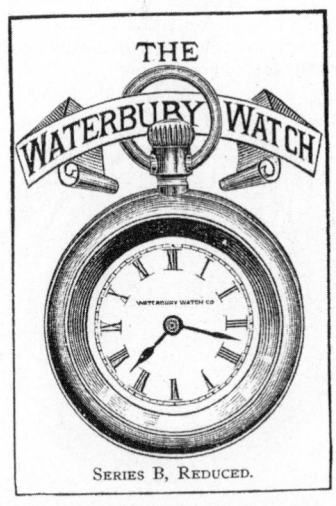

SERIES B, REDUCED.

Above extracted at 100% from 2 small catalogs, Nov 1, 1881 Series A and Oct 1, 1882 for Series B

Waterbury Watch Co., skeletonized movement; so called a poor man's tourbillon due to the fact it rotated as a tourbillion does. Patented May 21,1878 on top of crown. Note: The six spokes on dial and **CELLULOID** case.

Rotary long wind movement Note tour spokes on dial. For 3 & 4 spokes listing see **Benedict & Burnham** section.

18 TO 16 SIZES

Grade or Name — Description		ABP	Ex-Fn	Mint
Series A, **rotary long wind**, skeletonized, 6 spokes	★★	$300	$550	$750
Series A, **rotary long wind, skeletonized**, 6 spokes, celluloid case	★★★★	600	1,100	1,750
Series B, solid plates, **rotary long wind**	★★	150	350	450
Series C or E, solid plates, **rotary long wind**	★★	150	350	450
Series C or E, **rotary long wind**, advertising embossed on back Example Old Honesty	★★	250	500	650
Series D, patented Feb. 5, 1884 engraved on Movement (4 times)	★★★★	400	650	1,050
Series F, Duplex escapement		150	300	450
Series G, 3/4 lever escapement (key wind)	★	200	400	525
Series H, Columbian. Duplex	★★	200	450	650

Series E, note on back of watch (do'nt remove this cap unless you are a practical watch repairer).

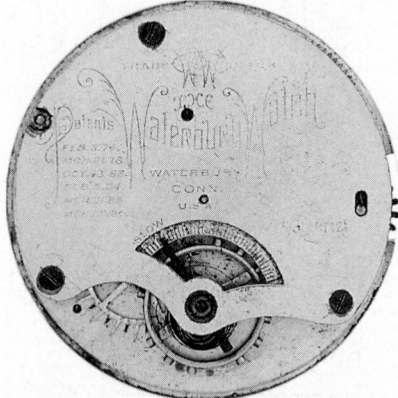

Series J, Waterbury Watch Company.

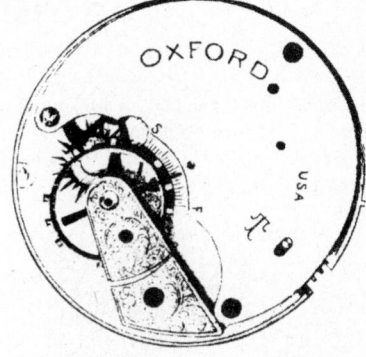

Series I, The Trump, about 18 size, 2 jewels with Duplex Escapement.

Series T, Oxford Duplex escapement about 18 size.

18 to 0 Size

Grade or Name —Description	ABP	Ex-Fn	Mint
Series I, 2J., Trump, Duplex, 18 size	$55	$100	$150
Series J, 4J., Americus, full plate, 18 size	55	100	150
Series J, 4J., Americus, Duplex, 3/4 plate, 18 size.............	75	125	175
Series K, 6J., Charles Benedict, 18 size...................★	125	225	375
Series K, Addison,18size ....★	125	225	375
Series L, 4J., gilt, Duplex 8 size...........................	85	125	175
Series L, 4J., **aluminum** movement, Duplex, 8 size ....★★	125	200	275
Series N, Addison, Duplex, 18 size ....★	125	175	225
Series N, Addison, 4J., Duplex, gilt, 4 size	65	100	135
Series N, Addison, 4J., **aluminum** movement, 4 size ....★★	125	225	300
Series P, 4J., Rugby, Duplex, 10 size	60	100	175
Series R, 9J., Tuxedo, Duplex, 14 size	60	100	175
Series S, 6J., Elfin, 6/0 size	60	95	120
Series T, Oxford, Duplex	60	95	120
Series W, 6J., Addison, Duplex, 3/4 plate, 4 size..............	65	100	160
Series Z, Cavour	60	95	120
Waterbury Clock Co. 35 size Pat Jan.15, 1878, May 6, '90, Dec.23,'90, Jan. 13,'91, on movement			
Jumbo, (seconds bit at the 12:00 o'clock position) ....★★★★	$300	$475	$650
Duke, 35 size back-wind and back-set	150	225	350
Duchess, same as duke with a fancier case................	150	225	350

NOTE: Dollar -watches must be in good running order to bring these prices.

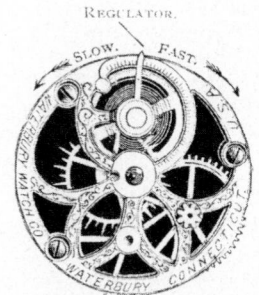

Old Honesty, Series C, rotary longwind.

Waterbury Watch Co. **"ROTARY"** movement

416

E. N. WELCH MFG. CO.

Bristol, Connecticut
1834-1897

Elisha Welch founded this company about 1834. His company failed in 1897, and the Sessions Clock Co. took over the business in 1903. E. N. Welch Mfg. Co. produced the large watch which was displayed at the Chicago Exposition in 1893. This watch depicted the landing of Columbus on the back of the case.

E.N. Welch Mfg. Co., 36 size, back wind & set, made for the Chicago Exposition in 1893. Die debossed back depicting the landing of Columbus in America, Oct. 12th, 1492.

Grade or Name — Description		ABP	Ex-Fn	Mint
36S, Columbus Exhibition watch.........................★★		$500	$800	$1200

WESTCLOX

United Clock Co. — Western Clock Mfg. Co.— General Time Corp.
Athens, Georgia
1899- Present

The first Westclox pocket watch was made about 1899; however, the Westclox name did not appear on their watches until 1906. In 1903 they were making 100 watches a day, and in 1920 production was at 15,000 per day.

Grade or Name —Description	ABP	Ex-Fn	Mint
M#1, SW, push to set, GRO	$50	$75	$135
M#2, SW, back set, GRO	50	65	100
18S, Westclox M#4, OF; GRO	45	55	75
1910 Models to 1920, GRO.................................	35	40	60
Anniversary	35	40	60
Antique...	20	25	45
Boy Proof..	50	55	90
Bingo...	30	35	55
Bulls Eye (several models).................................	15	20	25
Campus...	15	20	25
Celluloid case, 70mm.......................................	25	30	45
Coronado	15	20	25
Country Gentleman	35	45	70

Boy Proof Model, about 16 size, designed to be tamper proof.

Westclox movement, stem wind, back set.

Grade or Name — Description	ABP	Ex-Fn	Mint
Dax(many models)	$10	$15	$20
Dewey	10	15	30
Elite	25	30	40
Everbrite (several models)	30	45	65
Explorer ★	200	325	500
Farm Bureau	55	65	95
Glo Ben	55	65	95
Glory Be	20	25	35
Johnny Zero (several models)	125	165	300
I Want You to Vote	65	85	125
Ideal	30	35	45
Lighted Dial	25	30	40
Magnetic	20	25	30
Major	25	30	40
Man Time	15	20	25
Mark IV	35	40	55
Mascot	20	25	30
Maxim	30	35	50

Zep, about 16 size with radiant numbers and hands, c. 1929.

Explorer, back of case and dial, Wings Over The Pole, The Explorer on back of case.

World's Fair watch & fob, (1982 -Knoxville Tn.){Wagner Time Inc.}, total production for watch 4,200 and 200 for the FOB, 16 size, dial in red, white & blue, sold for $30.00 in 1982.

Grade or Name —Description	ABP	Ex-Fn	Mint
Military Style, 24 hour	$65	$75	$100
Monitor	15	20	25
Mustang	35	40	60
NAWCC, total production = **1,000**, Ca.1968	65	100	145
above wth box (25th. Anniversary)	85	125	185
Panther	35	40	60
Pocket Ben (many models)	10	15	30
Ruby	25	30	45
Scepter	20	25	40
Scotty (several models)	15	20	30
Silogram	15	20	30
Smile	25	30	45
Solo	15	20	30
St Regis	20	25	35
Sun Mark	30	35	40
Team Mate (various major league teams)	25	35	50
Tele Time	25	30	45
Texan	35	45	65
The Airplane	35	45	65
The American, **back SET**	50	80	195
The Conductor	45	55	85
Tiny Tim	150	175	300
Trail Blazer	60	100	265
Uncle Sam	40	45	60
Victor	80	95	130
Vote	25	30	45
Westclox	15	20	25
World's Fair (1982 -Knoxville Tn.){Wagner Time Inc.)	60	75	95
above wth box & (**FOB** total production =200) .... ★★★	95	200	400
Zep,(Zepplin) .... ★	225	400	550
Zodiak Time	35	40	55

☞ Pricing in this Guide are fair market price for complete watches which are re-flected from the NAWCC national and regional shows.

WESTERN WATCH CO.

Chicago, Illinois
1880

Albert Trotter purchased the unfinished watches from the California Watch Co. Mr. Trotter finished and sold those watches. Later he moved to Chicago, and with Paul Cornell and others, formed the Western Watch Company. Very few watches were completed by the Western Watch Co.

Grade or Name — Description		ABP	Ex-Fn	Mint
Western Watch Co., 18S, FULL.................... ★★★★		$2,000	$3,000	$5,500

Western Watch Co. movement, 18 size, 15 jewels, key wind & set.

WICHITA WATCH CO.

Wichita, Kansas
July, 1887- 1888

This company completed construction of their factory in Wichita, Kansas in June 1st., 1888, maybe a half dozen watches were produced during the brief period the company was in operation. The president was J. R. Snively. These watches are 18S, 1/2 to 3/4 plate, adjusted, 15 jewels, Savage 2 pin **style** escapement.

Grade or Name — Description		ABP	Ex-Fn	Mint
18S, 15J, 3/4 plate, ADJ, Savage 2 pin style escapement.... ★★★★		$3,500	$6,000	$9,000

ᐸ Watches listed in this book are priced at the collectable trade show level, as **complete** watches having an original 14k gold-filled case and *Key Wind* with silver, an original white enamel single sunk dial, and with the entire original movement in good working order with no repairs needed.

ᐸ Pricing in this Guide are fair market price for **complete** watches which are reflected from the **NAWCC** national and regional shows.

COMIC AND CHARACTER WATCHES

When discussing the topic of watches and someone mentions Comic Character Watches, we immediately picture a watch with Mickey Mouse. Isn't Mickey Mouse the most famous of all watches in the world? Before Mickey appeared in the 1930's there were a handful of lesser known comic watches with characters like Skeezix, Smitty and Buster Brown, but it was the Mickey Mouse Watch that paved the way for all other comic character watches. As a collaboration between Walt Disney (the creator of Mickey Mouse) and Robed Ingersoll and his brother the founders of the Ingersoll-Waterbury Watch Company, the Mickey Mouse Watch was one of this century's greatest marketing concepts. In a two year period Ingersoll had sold nearly 2.5 million Mickey Mouse wrist and pocket watches. Throughout the 1930's they also introduced other watches with Disney characters such as Big Bad Wolf in 1934, as well as, the Donald Duck wrist watch. The Donald Duck pocket watch was produced several years later in 1939. The Mickey Lapel and Mickey Deluxe Wrist were produced in the late 1930's.

Ingersoll dominated the character watch market in the early 1930's due to the incredible popularity of the Disney characters, however by the mid 1930's other companies mainly Ingraham and New Haven secured the rights to other popular characters. Throughout the 1930's kids fell in love with these watches featuring their favorite comic character or hero, such as, Popeye, Superman, Buck Rogers, Orphan Annie, Dick Tracy and The Lone Ranger. There was also a couple of other well known characters, Betty Boop and Cowboy Tom Mix produced, but for some reason these watches did not become popular like all the others, so very small quantities were produced.

During World War II production of comic watches ceased, but after the war comic watches came back stronger than ever. Once again Disney was the overall leader. The Ingersoll name only appeared on some watches to keep the trade name still familiar, as Ingersoll was sold to U.S. Time Watch Co.

The   late 1940's was very good to the character watch market and proof being the many character produced as the Twentieth Birthday Series for Mickey in 1948 that included with Mickey, Donald Duck, Pinocchio, Pluto, Bambi, Joe Carioca, Jimmy Cricket, Bongo Bear and Daisy Duck.Other watches from this time include Porky Pig, Puss-N-Boots, Joe Palooka, Gene Autry, Captain and Mary Marvel and others featuring characters of the comic and cartoons, space and western heroes.

The early to mid 1950's was also a vibrant time for character watch production with more Disney characters, western heroes and comic characters than ever before, but by 1958 manufacturing of character watches had almost completely stopped as manufacturing costs went up, popularity of some characters faded and many other circumstances led to a complete stop of any of these watches until the late 1960's. The watches were never the same again.

In the 1970's the Comic Character Watch once again made it's come back with the Bradley Watch Company (Elgin W. Co.) leading the way just as Ingersoll did in the first years of comic watches. Today there are hundreds of character watches to choose from, Disney Super Hero movie characters like E.T., and Roger Rabbit and a wealth of others, but today's fascination is not just with the new but with the old as we see in the re-issue of the original Mickey watches. There is a growing awareness and appreciation for all the originals. It is a very unusual attraction that draws people to love and collect the character watches of the past. Collectors appreciate the original boxes (that are fascinating works of ad) and the face of the watch that features the character that we love. The manufacturing method of these simple pin lever movements were not the best of timekeepers, but were solidly constructed. All in all, when you put together the watches and boxes they are pieces of functional art and history that brings back memories of our youth. Something that no other kind of watch can do.

Tom Mix pocket watch on back 'Always Find Time For A Good Deed / Tom Mix', & BOX inside color illo. of Tom on Tony.

Babe Ruth, by Exact Time. ca. 1948

Betty Boop, by Ingraham, ca. 1934.

Style or Grade —Description	ABP	Ex-Fn	Mint	Mint +Box
Alice in Wonderland, WW, c. 1951, by U.S. Time	$45	$60	$120	$350
Alice, Red Riding Hood, & Marjory Daw, WW, c. 1953, by Bradley	45	70	120	350
Alice in Wonderland, WW, c. 1958, by Timex	30	50	90	275
Alice in Wonderland & Mad Hatter, WW, c. 1948, by New Haven	60	100	175	350
All★Stars, c.1965, autograped by Mickey Mantel, Rodger Maris, Willie Mays, Sandy Koufax, Swiss, GREEN DIAL	100	250	350	600
All★Stars, c.1965, autograped by Mickey Mantel, Rodger Maris, Willie Mays, Sandy Koufax, Swiss, BLACK DIAL	90	150	225	500
Annie Oakley, WW, (Action Gun) c. 1951, by New Haven	130	225	300	525
Archie, WW, c.1970s, Swiss	45	60	90	250
Babe Ruth, WW, c. 1948, by Exact Time, box, baseball, pledge card ★	150	300	600	1,500
Ballerina, WW, c.1955, Ingraham, Action legs	30	45	60	90
Bambi, WW, c. 1949, by U.S. Time, Birthday series	90	180	300	550
Barbie, WW, c.1964, by Bradley, facing "3",	70	110	225	350
Barbie, WW, c.1970, by Bradley, action arms	70	100	225	350
Batman, WW, c. 1966 by Gilbert (band in shape of bat)	130	300	450	900
Batman, WW, c. 1978, by Timex	90	120	180	350
Betty Boop, PW, c. 1934, by Ingraham, (all original) (with diedebossed back) ★★★★	450	700	1,500	3,500
Betty Boop, WW, c.1980s, with hearts on dial & band	30	45	60	90
Bert & Ernie, WW, c.1970s, swiss	30	45	60	90
Big Bad Wolf & 3 Pigs, PW, c. 1936, by Ingersoll ★	400	800	1,500	2,500
Big Bad Wolf & 3 Pigs, WW, c. 1936, by Ingersoll ★	500	1,000	1,500	3,000
Big Bird, WW, c.1970s, Swiss, action arms, (pop up box)	30	45	60	90
Blondie & Dagwood, WW, c.1950s, Swiss	130	180	250	450
Bongo Bear, WW, c.1946, Ingersoll, Birthday series	90	130	210	350
Boy Scout, PW, c.1937, by Ingersoll, be prepared hands	250	285	450	800
Boy Scout, WW, c.1938, by New Haven	70	85	130	270
Buck Rogers, PW, c.1935, Ingraham (lightning bolt hands)	310	600	1,200	2,000
Bud Man, WW, Swiss, c.1970s	30	45	60	90
Bugs Bunny, WW, c. 1951, Swiss, (carrot shaped hands)	90	180	325	575
Bugs Bunny, WW, c. 1951, Swiss, (without carrot hands)	70	100	200	310
Bugs Bunny, WW, c. 1970, Swiss, (standing bugs)	30	50	70	130

☞ NOTE: Beware **COLOR COPY DIALS** are being faked as Buck Rogers, Babe Ruth, Hopalong Cassidy and others. BUYER BEWARE

BIG BAD WOLF & 3 PIGS + FOB INGERSOLL

BUSTER BROWN, INGERSOLL, Ca. 1925

BUGS BUNNY, EXACT TIME,
Ca. 1949 3 styles of hands.

BUCK ROGERS, INGRAHAM. Ca. 1935

Ingersoll (1934)
BIG BAD WOLF & 3 PIGS

-DICK TRACY, NEW
HAVEN, Ca. 1948

-DICK TRACY, (six shooter
action arm) ca, 1952.

DIZZY DEAN, By Everbright W. Co.

DONALD, with mickey seconds hand, 3 grades.

Left: DONALD DUCK, by INGERSOLL, C. 1947.   Center; Snoopy, Ca.1968   DALE EVANS, INGRAHAM

DAN DARE, INGERSOLL made in England

FROM OUTER SPACE, INGERSOLL made in England

Style or Grade — Description	ABP	Ex-Fn	Mint	Mint +Box
Adolf Hitler, WW, c. 1935, Swiss	$150	$250	$500	$950
Buster Brown, PW, c. 1928, by Ingersoll	$110	$160	$300	$610
Buster Brown, PW, c. 1928, by Ingersoll (Buster in circle)	110	180	400	650
Buster Brown, WW, c.1930, engraved case	110	130	250	450
Buzz Corey, WW, c. 1952, by U.S. Time	70	110	180	400
Buzzy the Crow, in red hat	30	45	70	110
Captain Liberty, WW, c. 1950, by U. S. Time, multi-color band	45	100	200	425
Captain Marvel, PW, c. 1945, by New Haven	180	300	600	900
Captain Marvel, WW, c.1948, New Haven (small w.w.)	75	150	300	625
Captain Marvel, WW, c.1948, by New Haven (larger size)	90	200	400	720
Captain Marvel, WW, c.1948, Swiss made	90	225	400	750
Captain Marvel Jr., c. 1948, Swiss, small size	150	300	550	1,300
Captain Midnight, PW, c. 1948, by Ingraham	250	400	600	1,350
Casper, WW, c.1970s, Swiss, Action arms	40	50	100	130
Cat In The Hat, WW, c.1970s, Swiss, Action arms	30	45	60	110
Cinderella, WW, c. 1950, by U.S. Time (slipper box)	30	40	85	350
Cinderella, WW, c. 1955, by Timex (box with imitation cell)	30	40	85	350
Cinderella, WW, c. 1958, by Timex (box with plastic statue)	30	40	85	350
Cinderella, WW, c. 1958, by Timex (box & porcelain statue)	35	50	100	360
Coca Cola, PW, c. 1948, by Ingersoll	60	150	225	360
Cowboy, WW, c.1955, by Muros, Swiss, Action Gun	30	50	100	140
Cowgirl, WW, c.1951, by New Haven, Action Gun	30	50	100	140
Cub Scout, WW, by Timex	30	45	60	130
Daisy Duck, WW, c. 1947, by Ingersoll (tonneau style)	90	150	250	450
Daisy Duck, WW, c. 1948, by U.S. Time (fluted bezel, birthday series)	90	150	250	450
Daisy Duck, WW, c. 1949, by U.S. Time, (grooved bezel)	75	125	160	360
Dale Evans, WW, c.1949, by Ingraham, Dale standing, (tonneau)	70	125	200	360
Dale Evans, WW, c. 1950, by Bradley (western style leather band & necklace &lucky horseshoe), tonneau style case	65	100	175	360
Dale Evans, WW, c. 1960, by Bradley (round)	30	45	75	225
Dan Dare, PW, c. 1950, by Ingersoll Ltd England, action arm	180	300	400	1,000
Davy Crockett, WW, c. 1951, by Bradley (round dial)	70	100	225	540
Davy Crockett, WW, c. 1954, Action gun, (round dial)	65	75	180	450
Davy Crockett, WW, c. 1954, Liberty , (round dial)	45	70	160	400
Davy Crockett, WW, c. 1955, by U.S. Time (& powder horn)	110	200	300	700
Davy Crockett, WW, c. 1956, by Bradley (barrel shaped dial)	45	70	180	400
Dennis the Menace, WW, c. 1970, by Bradley	40	50	80	130
Dick Tracy, PW, c. 1948, by Ingersoll	225	350	500	1,350
Dick Tracy, WW, c. 1948, by New Haven (round dial)	75	100	200	475
Dick Tracy, WW, c. 1948, by New Haven (small tonneau)	65	100	200	425
Dick Tracy, WW, c. 1935, by New Haven (large)	130	200	300	600
Dick Tracy, WW, c. 1951, by New Haven (6 shooter action)	180	250	350	720
Dizzy Dean, PW, c. 1935, by Ingersoll ★★	180	300	500	1,050
Dizzy Dean, WW, c. 1938, by Everbright W. Co ★★	180	300	500	1,050

✍ Note: To be mint condition, character watches must have **unfaded dials**, and boxes must have ALL inserts. (PW=Pocket Watch; WW=Wrist Watch)

COCA COLA, PW, Ca. 1948, by Ingersoll.

ADOLF HITLER, character wrist watch, Swiss movement 'Roskopf' caliber, Ca. 1935.

Dizzy Dean, Ingersoll, ca, 1935

Donald Duck, Ingersoll, ca, 1940. Mickey on back of case.

Style or Grade — Description	ABP	Ex-Fn	Mint	Mint +Box
Donald Duck, PW, c. 1939, by Ingersoll (Mickey on back) .... ★★	$350	$500	$1,200	$2,200
Donald Duck, PW, Ward W. Co., c. 1954, Swiss made..........	70	130	300	540
Donald Duck, WW, c. 1935, by Ingersoll (Mickey on second hand) .... ★★	500	800	1,800	2,600
Donald Duck, WW, c. 1942, by U.S. Time (tonneau style, silver tone)..................................	90	130	400	800
Donald Duck, WW, c. 1948, by U.S. Time (tonneau style, gold tone)	125	180	400	850
Donald Duck, WW, c. 1948, by Ingersoll (fluted bezel, birthday series) with metal mickey bracelet	125	180	400	850
Donald Duck, WW, c. 1955, by U.S. Time, (plain bezel, pop-up in box) with leather band & Donald metal decal....	70	90	250	550
Dopey, WW, c. 1948, by Ingersoll (fluted bezel, birthday series).................................	90	130	300	630
Dudley Do Right, WW, 17J (Bullwinkle & Rocky) ....★	180	250	500	900
Elmer Fudd, WW, c.1970s, Swiss.........................	50	90	150	325
Elvis WW c.1970s, Bradley.............................	50	65	100	180
Flash Gordon, PW, c. 1939, by Ingersoll ....★	310	450	900	1,700
Flash Gordon, WW, c.1970, Precision	80	180	400	650
From Outer Space, PW, Ingersoll G. Britian, ...	70	130	250	450
Fred Flintstone, WW, (Fred on dial)	70	150	225	360
Garfield WW, (The Cat Jumped Over The Moon).............	35	50	100	180
Gene Autry, WW, c. 1939, by Ingersoll (Gene and Champion on dial)	90	200	400	750

Mickey, 32MM. Ca.1930.
Maybe HOAX??

—Gene Autry, (action gun),
by Ingersoll, ca.1950.

— Howdy with moving eyes ca.1954.

MICKEY MOUSE, by Ingersoll, original band, Ca.1933-34

MICKEY MOUSE, by Ingersoll, Ca. 1947

Mickey Mouse by Ingersoll,
center lugs, Ca.1938.

Reproduction Box & Watch.

Mickey Mouse by Bradley, 1972-85.

MICKEY MOUSE, made in England by Ingersoll, Ca.1934

Who's afraid of the Big Bad Wolf. Maybe 'Proto Type"

Hopalong Cassidy, U.S. Time, ca. 1950s. Maybe HOAX??

Hopalong Cassidy, Ingersoll, ca. 1955.

Style or Grade —Description	ABP	Ex-Fn	Mint	Mint +Box
Gene Autry, WW, c. 1939, by Ingersoll	$90	$200	$350	$765
Gene Autry, WW, c. 1950, by New Haven, (action gun)	180	250	400	700
Gene Autry, WW, c. 1956, Swiss made	60	85	200	400
Girl Scouts, WW, c.1955, byTimex	30	45	50	120
Goofy, WW, c. 1972, by Helbros, 17J (watch runs backward)	270	400	550	1,050
Hoky Poky, WW, c.1950, **action arm**	30	45	70	200
Hopalong Cassidy, WW, by U.S. Time (metal watch, box with saddle)	45	70	200	475
Hopalong Cassidy, WW, by U.S. Time (plastic watch, box with saddle)	45	70	200	475
Hopalong Cassidy, WW, by U.S. Time (small watch, leather Western band, flat rectangular box)	40	55	125	425
Hopalong Cassidy, WW, by U.S. Time (regular size watch, black leather cowboy strap), flat box	45	60	150	450
Hopalong Cassidy, PW, c. 1955, by U.S. Time (rawhide strap and fob)	110	200	270	650
Hot Wheels, WW, c.1971, Bradley -Swiss, checkered hands.	40	50	70	150
Hot Wheels, WW, c.1971, Bradley-Swiss, rotating bezel.	30	40	60	160
Hot Wheels, WW, c.1983, Swiss, LCD QUARTZ	20	30	40	90
Howdy Doody, WW, c. 1954, Swiss (with moving eyes)	90	180	400	800
Howdy Doody, WW, c. 1954, by Ingraham (with friends)	85	130	400	720
Jamboree, PW, c. 1951, by Ingersoll, Ltd	70	100	225	450

Robin Hood, Ca.1958

BUD MAN Ca.1970s

Li'l Abner (waving flag)

LONE RANGER, New Haven, ca.1939

LONE RANGER, New Haven, ca.1939. 2 styles of backs

MICKEY MOUSE Ingersoll, ca.1933

MICKEY MOUSE Ingersoll, ca.1933

HOAX??

LEFT: Mickey Mouse, Ingersoll, w/ Mickey seconds, ca.1938. **CENTER**: Mickey Mouse, 1947 Ingersoll dial in a 1938 Ingersoll case. **RIGHT**: Mickey Mouse, Ingersoll, grooved bezel NOT birthday series, ca.1948

Note: To be **mint** condition, character watches must have unfaded dials, and boxes must have all inserts. (PW=Pocket Watch; WW=Wrist Watch)

Style or Grade —Description	ABP	Ex-Fn	Mint	Mint +Box
James Bond 007, WW, c. 1972, by Gilbert	$80	$130	$225	$720
Jeff Arnold, PW, c. 1952, by Ingersoll (English watch with moving gun)	130	180	300	540
Jimmy Cricket, WW, c.1948, Ingersoll, Birthday series (fluted). .	70	100	270	600
Jimmy Cricket, WW, c.1949, Ingersoll, Not Birthday (grooved). .	70	100	270	600
Joe Carioca, WW, c. 1948, by U.S. Time (fluted bezel, birthday series)	70	75	250	475
Joe Palooka, WW, c. 1948, by New Haven	130	180	300	550
Li'l Abner, WW, c. 1948, by New Haven (waving flag)	130	180	250	550
Li'l Abner, WW, c. 1948, by New Haven (moving mule)	130	160	225	475
Li'l Abner, WW, c. 1955, all black dial	85	120	165	360
Little King, WW, c. 1968, by Timex	50	110	200	375
Little Pig Fiddler, WW, c.1947, by Ingersoll.	110	180	270	560
Lone Ranger, PW, c. 1939, by New Haven (with fob). . . . . ★	130	250	400	900
Lone Ranger, WW, c. 1938, by New Haven (large)	90	200	350	600
Lone Ranger, WW, c. 1948, New Haven, (Fluted lugs)	70	110	225	450
Lone Ranger, WW, c. 1950's, round case	60	90	180	360
Louie, WW, c.1940s, by Ingersoll, (Donalds nephew)	85	130	225	450
Mary Marvel, WW, c. 1948, by U.S. Time (paper box)	60	75	150	450
Mary Marvel, WW, c. 1948, by U.S. Time (plastic box)	60	75	125	360
Mickey Mouse, PW, c.1933, by Ingersoll, #1&2 (tall stem)	250	400	600	900
Mickey Mouse, PW, c.1936, by Ingersoll, #3 & 4(short stem).. . . .	180	270	400	825
Mickey Mouse, PW, c. 1936, by Ingersoll, #4 lapel watch (short stem) with **rare FOB**	200	350	700	1,250
Mickey Mouse, PW, c. 1938, by Ingersoll (Mickey decal on back)	250	400	650	1,000
Mickey Mouse, PW, c. 1933, by Ingersoll Ltd. (English)	300	450	800	1,600
Mickey Mouse, PW, c. 1934, by Ingersoll (Foreign)	250	300	400	600
Mickey Mouse, PW, c.1976, by Bradley (bicentennial model). . . .	35	45	100	270
Mickey Mouse, PW, c. 1974, by Bradley (no second hand)	35	45	55	100
Mickey Mouse, PW, c. 1974, by Bradley ("Bradley" printed at 6).	35	45	55	100
Mickey Mouse, small 32 MM PW, Ingersoll, s. steel, Ca. 1930s . .	75	110	225	375

MICKEY MOUSE, Ingersoll, model no.3 on the left.   Right: Model no.4 is called a lapel watch, Very RARE FOB.

NOTE: Beware (COLOR COPY DIALS) are being FAKED as Buck Rodgers, Babe Ruth, Hopalong Cassidy and others. BUYER BEWARE

Style or Grade —Description	ABP	Ex-Fn	Mint	Mint +Box
Mickey Mouse, WW, c. 1933, by Ingersoll (metal band with 3 Mickeys' on seconds disc)	$200	$400	$650	$1,400
Mickey Mouse, WW, c. 1933, by Ingersoll (English Mickey with 3 Mickeys' on seconds disc, 24 hr. outer dial)	200	400	600	1,100
Mickey Mouse, WW, c. 1938-9, by Ingersoll (one Mickey for second hand)	110	300	400	875
Mickey Mouse, WW, c. 1939, by Ingersoll, plain seconds	75	150	250	475
Mickey Mouse, WW, c. 1938-9, by Ingersoll (girl's and boys style watch, 1 Mickey for second hand).	160	300	400	850
Mickey Mouse, WW, c. 1948, by Ingersoll (fluted Bezel, birthday series, 2 styles Mickey in a circle & no circle)	130	200	400	610
Mickey Mouse, WW, c. 1949, by Ingersoll, grooved bezel	110	150	300	400
Mickey Mouse, WW, c. 1946, by U.S. Time (10k gold plated). . . .	85	110	200	400
Mickey Mouse, WW, c. 1946, **Kelton**.	85	110	200	400
Mickey Mouse, WW, c. 1947, by U.S. Time (tonneau, plain, several styles).	70	100	160	375
Mickey Mouse, WW, c. 1947, by U.S. Time (same as above, gold tone)	75	100	175	400
Mickey Mouse, WW, c. 1950s, by U.S. Time (round style)	35	50	125	310
Mickey Mouse, WW, c. 1958, by U.S. Time (**statue** of Mickey in box)	70	90	200	475
Mickey Mouse, WW, c. 1965 to 1970, by Timex (Mickey Mouse electric).	85	110	210	400
Mickey Mouse, WW, c. 1965-70s, Timex (manual wind)	50	60	125	160
Mickey Mouse, WW, c. 1975, Elgin (**ELECTRIC MODEL**) **14K** GOLD CASE & leather band, 13 jewels . . . . ★	375	500	775	1,250
Mickey Mouse, WW, c. 1970s, by Bradley.	35	45	75	110
Mickey Mouse, WW, c. 1980, by Bradley (colored mm. chapter) .	55	65	100	130
Mickey Mouse, WW, c. 1983, by Bradley (limited commemorative model)	55	70	110	160

Mickey Mouse, Bradley, ca. 1969.

Mickey Mouse, with wide bezel, Ingersoll, it is believed dealers have used a Wrist Watch dial in a Hopalong case, ca. 1955. **Maybe HOAX??**

Note: To be **mint** condition, character watches must have unfaded dials, and boxes must have all inserts. (PW=Pocket Watch; WW=Wrist Watch)

Left: Captain Marvel, Ca. 1948.

Center: Minnie Mouse, U. S. Time, Ca.1968.

Right: Orphan Annie, New Haven, Ca.1939

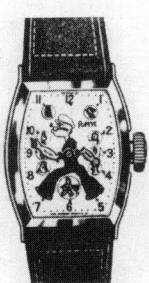

ORPHAN ANNIE, New Haven, in 1940 sold for $5.95.

2 case styles of POPEYE & friends, New Haven, Ca. 1936

POPEYE, New Haven, (with friends), Ca. 1935

POPEYE, New Haven, Ca. 1936, (Wimpy only), originally sold for .80 In 1936.

Note: To be **mint** condition, character watches must have unfaded dials, and boxes must have all inserts. (PW=Pocket Watch; WW=Wrist Watch)

LEFT: GOOFY watch runs backward.

CENTER: Little Pig & fiddle.

RIGHT: Porky Pig

Left: Pluto, Birthday Series, by Ingersoll.

Center: Rocky Jones, Ca.1955.

Right: Speedy Gonzales, Swiss

DONALD DUCK, Ward W. Co. made for
the Austria market, Ca. 1940s.

Ingraham tonneau-shaped movement Ca. 1934.

Rare Dan Winslow watch front and back.

Style or Grade — Description	ABP	Ex-Fn	Mint	Mint +Box
Mickey Mouse, WW, c. 1985, by ETA (clear plastic bezel and band)	$35	$45	$60	$90
Mickey Mouse, WW, c.1980s, Bradley, (Tachometer dial)	40	45	55	75
Mighty Mouse, WW, c.1980s, Swiss, (Plastic case)	20	25	30	45
Minnie Mouse, WW, c. 1958, by U.S. Time (statue of Minnie inbox)	45	60	180	425
Moon Mullins, PW, c. 1930, by Ingersoll ★	200	400	650	1,300
Orphan Annie, WW, c. 1939, by New Haven (fluted bezel)	70	100	200	450
Orphan Annie, WW, c. 1935, by New Haven (large style)	60	100	200	425
Orphan Annie, WW, c. 1948, by New Haven smaller model)	45	60	130	300
Orphan Annie, WW, c. 1968, by Timex	40	70	100	150
Pee Wee Herman, WW, (Swiss), FLIP TOP	20	50	100	125
Peter Pan, PW, c. 1948,by Ingraham	130	180	270	650
Pinocchio, WW, c. 1948, by Ingersoll (fluted bezel, birthday series)	110	130	250	500
Pinocchio, WW, c. 1948, by U.S. Time (Happy Birthday cake box)	110	130	300	600
Pluto, WW, c. 1948, by U.S. Time(birthday series)	90	120	225	450
Popeye, PW, c. 1935, by New Haven (with friends on dial) ★	250	500	700	1,200
Popeye, PW, c. 1936, by New Haven (plain dial)	200	350	500	1,000
Popeye, WW, c. 1936, by New Haven (tonneau style, with friends on dial) ★	250	375	775	1,500
Popeye, WW, c. 1966, by Bradley (round style)	70	100	125	180
Popeye, WW, c. 1948, Swiss, Olive Oyl at 3	70	130	225	400
Porky Pig, WW, c. 1948, by Ingraham (tonneau)	90	150	225	475
Porky Pig, WW, c. 1949, by U.S. Time (round)	90	150	225	475
Punkin Head, WW, c.1946, Ingraham	50	60	80	130
Puss-N-Boots, WW, c. 1959, by Bradley	85	150	225	360
Red Ryder, WW, c.1949, Swiss, (with Little Beaver)	85	130	270	675
Quarterback, WW, c.1965, Swiss, (Football action arm)	60	70	100	130
Robin,WW,c.1978,byTimex	35	40	80	130
Robin Hood, WW, c. 1955, by Bradley (tonneau style)	90	150	250	475
Robin Hood, WW, c. 1958, by Viking (round)	80	120	250	450
Rocky Jones Space Ranger, WW, c. 1955, by Ingraham	110	210	350	700
Roy Rogers, PW, c. 1960, by Ingraham, (stop watch) rim set	130	310	600	1,050
Roy Rogers, WW, c. 1954, by Ingraham (Roy and rearing Trigger)	60	125	300	600
Roy Rogers, WW, c. 1954, by Ingraham (Roy and Trigger)	65	110	300	600
Roy Rogers, WW, c. 1954, by Ingraham (expansion band)	65	110	300	600
Roy Rogers, WW, c. 1956, by Ingraham (round dial)	65	110	200	475

Joe Palooka, Ca.1948.

Snow White U.S.Time.

Roy Rogers, Ingraham, ca. 1954.

ROY ROGERS, Ingraham note rim set, Ca. 1960.

ROY ROGERS, Ingraham (large), Ca. 1951.

Left: ROY ROGERS, Note: This watch is a 1950s Ingraham dial in a 1938 Ingersoll case.

Center: Tom Corbett, Space Cadet, New Haven, Ca. 1935

Right: SKEEZIX, Ingraham, Ca. 1936.

Left:Smitty, New Haven, Ca.1936.

Center: Superman, New Haven, Ca.1939.

Right: Superman, New Haven, Ca.1939.

Style or Grade — Description	ABP	Ex-Fn	Mint	Mint +Box
Rudolf the Red Nose Reindeer, c.1946, Ingraham	75	110	270	550
Rudy Nebb, PW, c. 1930, by Ingraham ★★	130	175	450	810
Shirley Temple, PW, c.1958, by Westclox ★★	250	350	400	720
Skeezix, PW, c. 1928, by Ingraham ★★	300	400	700	1,200
Sky King, WW, (action gun)	70	80	150	375
Smitty, PW, c.1928, by New Haven	200	250	350	630
Smitty, WW, c. 1936, by New Haven	130	180	300	550
Smokey Stover, WW, c. 1968, by Timex	70	100	150	270
Snoopy, WW, c. 1958 (tennis racket)	25	35	70	130
Snoopy, WW, c. 1958 (Woodstock)	25	35	70	130
Snow White, WW, c. 1938, by Ingersoll (tonneau)	90	110	225	500
Snow White, WW, c. 1952, by U.S. Time (round)	40	45	60	165
Snow White, WW, c. 1956, by U.S. Time (statue in box)	35	40	70	360
Snow White, WW, c. 1962, by U.S. Time (plastic watch)	35	45	60	270
Space Explorer, c.1953, COMPASS watch	70	90	200	375
Speedy Gonzales, WW, Swiss	70	85	150	250
Spiro Agnew, WW, c.1970s, Swiss	55	70	150	250
Superman, PW, c. 1956, by Bradley (stop watch)	130	175	400	675
Superman, WW, c. 1938, by New Haven	175	225	400	800
Superman, WW, c.1946, by Ingraham (lightning bolt hands)	125	165	300	525
Superman, WW, c. 1978, by Timex (large size)	45	60	100	150
Superman, WW, c. 1978, by Timex (small size)	40	45	100	125
Superman, WW, c.1975, Dabs & Co., yellow mm chapter	35	40	75	115
Superman, WW, c.1965, Swiss, rotating superman	50	70	150	270
Superman, WW, c.1976, Timex, sweep sec. hand	55	60	80	180
Texas Ranger, WW, c.1950, by New Haven, action gun	85	110	200	400
Three Little Pigs, PW, c. 1939, by Ingersoll ★★	400	600	1,200	2,000
Tom Corbett, WW, c. 1954, by New Haven ★	180	300	600	1,050
Tom Mix, PW, c. 1934-5, by Ingersoll (with fob) ★★★	1,000	1,500	2,200	3,800
Tom Mix, WW, c. 1934-5, by Ingersoll ★★★	360	550	900	2,900
Winnie the Pooh Bear, c.1970s, Swiss	35	45	75	110
Wizard of Oz, c.1972, swiss	35	50	100	130
Wonder Woman, WW, c.1975, stars at 1,2,4,5,7,8,10,11	60	65	150	200
Wonder Woman, WW, c.1975, Dabs & Co	45	60	150	200
Woody Woodpecker, WW, c. 1948, by Ingersoll (tonneau)	90	110	300	650
Woody Woodpecker, WW, c. 1952, by Ingraham (round dial)	85	110	200	550
Yogi Bear, WW, c. 1964, by Bradley	45	50	100	180
Zorro. WW. a 1956, by U.S. Time	55	100	200	375

Left: Tom Mix wrist watch, came with metal link band.   **Center: Tom Mix, Ingersoll,** Ca. 1934-5. TOM MIX on TONY   **Right**: Woody Woodpecker, U.S. Time, ca. 1948.

Moon Mullins, by Ingersoll, ca. 1928 **Reproductions seen**

Rudy Nebb, by Ingersoll, ca. 1928

Shirley Temple, by Westclox, ca. 1958

1952 AD, by Ingersoll, Dan Dare Watch and Box.

CUB SCOUT by Timex

BOY SCOUT by New Haven

DAVY CROCKETT, by Ingraham

ADVERTISEMENTS FROM THE 1930's

MICKEY MOUSE WRIST WATCH with metal or leather strap bearing Mickey's picture. The watch itself is smartly styled . . . round and therefore entirely practical for a very little girl's wrist. Packed in Mickey Mouse display carton. Retails $2.75.
List $3.90

MICKEY MOUSE WATCH AND FOB— a wonderful buy at $1.50 complete. Mickey on the dial of the watch pointing out the time—Mickey on the fob—three little Mickies on the second-circle chasing each other around. List $2.20

New Mickey Mouse Lapel Watch. A handsome lapel model with Mickey's hands telling time on small dial. Mickey on dial and back of a black glossy finished case with nickel trim. Black lapel cord and button. Each in a display box.

No. 1W61. Each.......................$2.10

LONE RANGER FOB WATCH

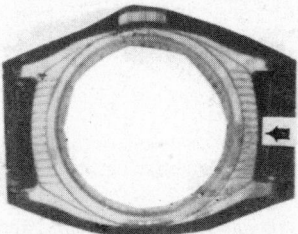

ABOVE: 20th Birthday series style case note fluted bezel. The Birthday series used ten different characters & sold for $6.95. The TEN CHARACTERS are: Mickey Mouse, Daisy Duck, Pluto, Bambi, Joe Carioca, Bongo, Donald Duck, Pinnochio, Dopey, and Jimmy Cricket.

New De Luxe Mickey Mouse Wrist Watch. A smarter thinner chromium plated rectangular case. Mickey appears in bright colors on the dial. Fitted with a perspiration proof leather band. Each in display box.

No. 11W440. Each $5.54

Above: From a 1938 ad

EARLY ANTIQUE WATCHES

Early German Alarm Iron movement, note Stackfreed with contoured cam, dumbbell foliot style balance, scroll cock, hand-form index arm with a bristle regulator, 70MM, made in Augsburg, Ca. 1570.

The early antique watches looked quite similar to small table clocks. The mainspring was introduced to clocks in about 1450. These drum-shaped watches were about two inches in diameter and usually over one-half inch thick. The drum-shaped watch lost popularity in the late 1500s. The earliest portable timepieces did not carry the maker's name, but initials were common. The cases generally had a hinged lid which covered the dial. This lid was pierced with small holes to enable ready identification of the position of the hour hand. They also usually contained a bell. The dial often had the numbers "I" to "XII" engraved in Roman numerals and the numbers "13" to "24" in Arabic numbers with the "2" engraved in the form of a "Z." Even the earliest of timepieces incorporated striking. The oldest known watch with a date engraved on the case was made in 1548. A drum-shaped watch with the initials "C. W.," it was most likely produced by Casper Werner, a protege of Henlein.

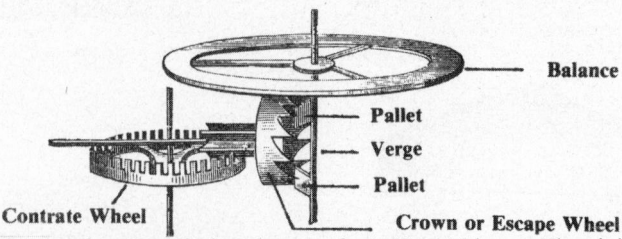

Early pocket watches were designed to run from 12 to 16 hours. The pinions usually bore five leaves, the great wheel 55 teeth, the second wheel 45 teeth, the third wheel 40 teeth, and the escape wheel 15 teeth. With one less pinion and wheel the escape wheel ran reverse to a standard four-wheel watch. During the 1500s, 1600s, and much of the 1700s, it was stylish to decorate not only the case and balance cock but all parts including the clicks, barrel, studs, springs, pillars, hands, and stackfreed.

The plates themselves were decorated with pierced and engraved metal scrolls, and in some instances the maker's name was engraved in a style to correspond with the general decoration of the movement. During these periods the most celebrated artists, designers, and engravers were employed. The early watches were decorated by famous artists such as Jean Vauquier 1670, Daniel Marot 1700, Gillis l'Egare 1650, Michel Labon 1630, Pierre Bourdon 1750, and D. Cochin 1750. Most of the artists were employed to design and execute pierced and repousse cases.

Alarm watch made by Bockel of London Ca. 1648.

THE MID-1700s

In the mid- 1700s relatively minor changes are noticed. Decoration became less distinctive and less artistic. The newer escapements resulted in better time keeping, and a smaller balance cock was used. The table and foot became smaller. The foot grew more narrow, and as the century and the development of the watch advanced, the decoration on the balance cock became smaller and less elaborate. About. 1720 the foot was becoming solid and flat. No longer was it hand pierced; however, some of the pierced ones were produced until about 1770. Thousands of these beautiful hand pierced watch cocks have been made into necklaces and brooches or framed. Sadly, many of the old movements were destroyed in a mad haste to cater to the buyers' fancy.

THE 1800s

As the 1800s approached the balance cocks became less artistic as the decoration on movements gradually diminished. Breguet and Berthoud spent very little time on the beauty or artistic design on their balance cocks or pillars. But the cases were often magnificent in design and beauty, made with enamels in many colors and laden with precious stones. During this period the movements were plain and possessed very little artistic character.

As early as 1820 thee-quarter and one-half plate designs were being used with the balance cock lowered to the same level as the other wheels. The result was a slimmer watch. **Flat enamel** dials are being used in about 1810.

The DUST CAP Ca. 1685 to 1875
Popular in England.
Note: To remove dust cap from Movement,
Slide crescent shaped catch or latch
right or Left. Daniel Quare may have
been the first to use a Dust Cap.

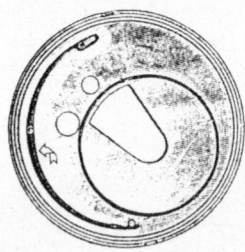

WATCH-MAKER

The term watch-maker might originally denote the *maker* of *watches* from base material or one who manufactures watches. But as we shall see a watchmaker may better be described as the expert in charge of producing watches. One other note before we move on, a watch may be considered as a miniature spring driven clock, so early on many clock-makers were also watch-makers.

There are surviving artifacts that make it possible to make certain assumptions. Thomas Tompion (also a English clock-maker) born 1639, death 1713, used a production system for making watches. About 1675-80 Tompion divided and sub-divided laborers into various branches of manufacturing of watches. This meant each craftsman specialized in making single watch parts, thus the division of labor led to a faster rate of production, with higher quality and a lower cost to the ebauche movement. About 1775 John Elliott and John Arnold had much of their work done by other sub-divided workers. The quality of the employees work depends upon the watch-maker. Thus, the PRICE depends on the reputation of the master (watch-maker). The same holds true for todays prices, the reputation of the maker helps to determine the price they can fetch for the timepieces. The parts and materials are of little value in their original state, but the various pieces require such delicacy of manipulation and the management of production of watches, thus the responsibility for the action of the watch depends on the committee in the house of the maker. Prior to 1870 rough movements were 99% produced in the Prescot area then finished in London, Liverpool, & etc.

In about 1760 to 1765 Lepine introduced the French or Lepine style calibre of ebauche movements. The Lepine style used separate bridges instead of the single top plate design. Frederic Japy (Japy Freres & Cie.) of Beaucourt, France,

later manufactured ebauche Swiss bar style movements in the early 1770's.

About 1776, Japy aids in setting up a factory in the LeLocle area and latter in England. Japy Freres & Co. were producing 30,000 movements each year by 1795, and over 60,000 ebauche style movements each year by 1860. Other "BAR" style Ebauche Companies: 1804-Sandoz & Trot of Geneva, 1840-G.A. Leschot with Vacheron & Constantin and about 1850- LeCoultre. These bar style ebauche movements were imported into the U.S.A. about 1850 and were used in the jewelry trade with the jewelers name on the case and dial until about 1875.

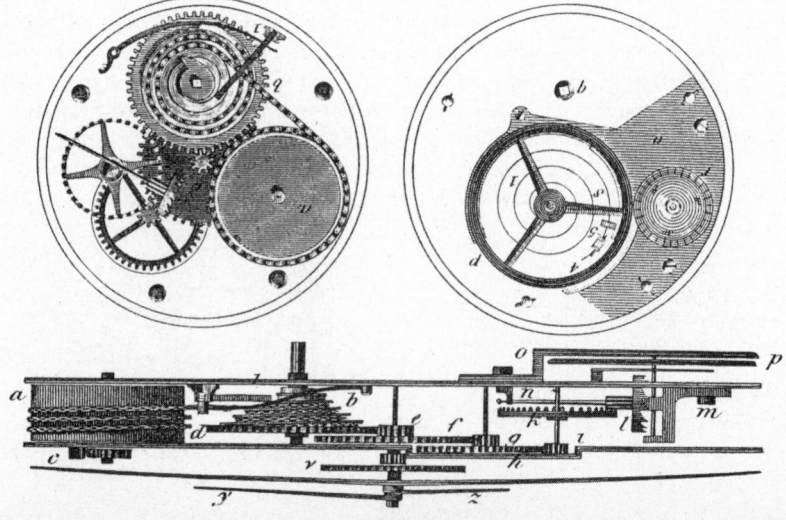

MOVEMENTS "IN THE GRAY"

Movements in an early stage of manufacture.

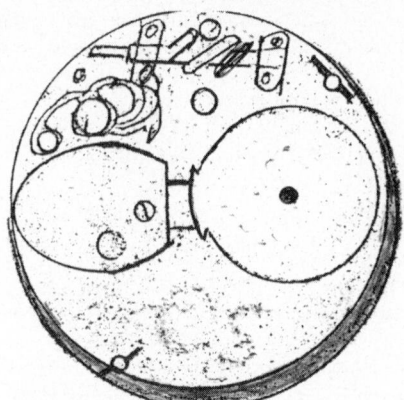

ABOUT MID 1600'S

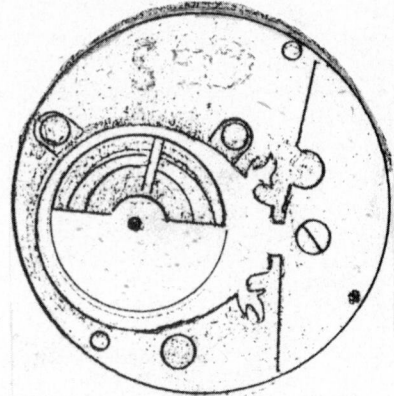

ABOUT 1675-80

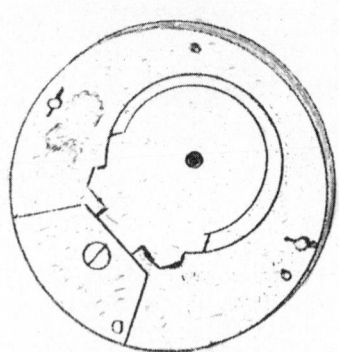

ABOUT 1790—1830 ENGLISH STYLE

EBAUCHE style movement with verge, chain driven fusee, under sprung, KW, **ABOUT 1810—1860.**

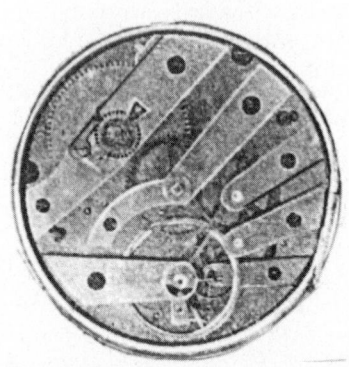

BAR STYLE movement, cylinder, ABOUT 1840 to 80.

Le Locle style EBAUCHE **1870 to 1890.**

☞ **Multi-color** cases became popular by 1800, 1st. used in 1760 & **Engine Turning** rarely found before early 1760s. **Tortoise Shell** 1st. used in 1620, but did not become popular till about 1780.

The ebauche makers and the cottage industry made different models designed to conform or answer the needs of each country to which they were trying to do business with such as French style, English style, Chinese style, etc. This makes it hard to determine the origin of the ebauche watch. The case may be made in England, the movement Swiss, and the dial French.

Below are some of the principle workmen employed in the sub-divided production of plain parts or ebauche simple watch movements (in the rough) from about 1800s. Some of these were small family specialist that formed a **cottage** industry, (some being females) they usually produced only one product.

1. Cock-maker (made brass blanks)	8.Fusee-maker
2. Pillar-maker (turn the pillars, etc.)	9. Verge-makers
3. Frame-maker (full plates, bars, bridges, etc.)	10. Chain-makers
4. Wheel-maker (small and large)	11. Pinion- maker
5. Wheel-cutter (cuts the teeth on the wheels)	12. Escapement-maker
6. Balance-makers (made of steel or brass)	13. Hand-maker
7. Spring-maker(hair & main springs)	14. Dial-maker

Below a list of craftsman making cases.
1.Case-maker (makes cupped lids for cases)
2.Side-maker (makes the side of the case)
3.Cap-maker (makes the lids of the case)
4.The joint-finisher (joints for cases)
5.Glass-maker (made crystals for bezels)
6.Bezel-makers & Pendant-maker
RIGHT: A English made movement,
      Ca. 1750s.

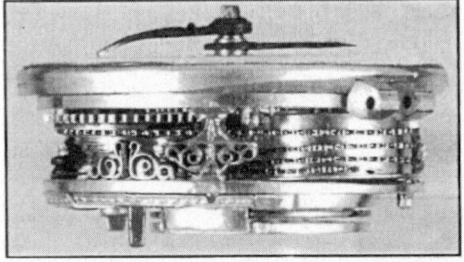

These blank movements, parts, dials and cases were bought, then shipped on to the final destination. The *watch-maker or finisher,* such as, the house of (CARTIER). The Finisher would often house or contract decorators to finish the cases. The Finisher completed, polished, engraved, timed, regulated and made all the adjustments to the movements. They added and fined the case to the movement. They added and fitted the complications such as repeaters to the movements. The *finished* watch is now ready for sale.

This type of system of producing watches left time for the Master watchmakers or famous watch-makers to invent, design new and better ways to make watches, such as, Abraham Louis Breguet. In early 1800's Breguet firm received parts and Swiss ebauches from 18 different suppliers. Thus the more famous the maker the higher the price of the 'watch even though the watch-maker may not have **made** & the smallest piece for the *finished* watch.

The cottage industry with its one man, one task system, make it difficult to establish who, when and where some watches were actually made. It is some what simpler to determine the origin or area, as Swiss, English, French or American, however it is rewarding with further research to unmask the disguise of watch-making. Close study, inspection and comparing movements over the years will prove helpful and may reveal the origin and age of your watch.

Most Swiss manufactures do not make the complete watch on their own premises. Some parts are supplied by specialized firms, such as; balance wheels, escape wheels, jewels, hairsprings, mainsprings, pendant bows and crowns, crystals, hands, cases, screws, pins and other small parts. There were a few factories in Le Lode, Switzerland that manufactured the Cylinder and escape wheel but most were made in the *Maiche district of France*. Brass plates were plated with RHODIUM for the most part in Swiss Industry. Ebauche or rough movements were made in the Valley of Joux and the Val-de-Ruz regions, in and around towns such as Granges, Bienne, Solothurn, La Chaux- de-Fonds also near by Le Locle, in the Bernese Jura, the Valley of St.Imier, and elsewhere.

CLUES TO DATING YOUR WATCH

To establish the age of a watch there are many points to be considered. The dial, hands, pillars, balance cock and pendant, for example, contain important clues in determining the age of your watch. However, no one part alone should be considered sufficient evidence to draw a definite conclusion as to age. The watch as a whole must be considered. For example, an English-made silver-cased watch will have a hallmark inside the case. It is quite simple to refer to the London Hallmark Table for hallmarks after 1697. The hallmark will reveal the age of the case only. This does not fix the age of the movement. Many movements are housed in cases made years before or after the movement was produced.

An informed collector will note that a watch with an **enamel dial**, for instance, could not have been made before 1635. **A pair of cases** indicates it could not have been made prior to 1640. A **dust cap** first appeared in 1680. The **minute hand** was introduced about 1680. The presence of a **cylinder escapement** would indicate it was made after 1710. **1750 the duplex escapement** was first used. *1776 Lepine* introduced the **thin** watch. **Flat enamel dial** being used in about 1810. **Keyless winding** came into being after 1820, but did not gain widespread popularity until *after* about 1860. All of these clues and more must be considered before accurately assessing the age of a watch. *Some watches were also updated suck as minute hand added, enamel dial or new style escapement added.*

Example of an early pocket watch (Ca. 1548) with a stackfreed tear shaped cam design to equalize power much as a fusee does. Note dumbbell shaped foliot which served as a balance for verge escapement.

Thomas Tompion called the Father of English Watchmaking. Under his improvements, watches began to embody sound principles and accuracy. He introduced the division of labor, standardized parts, **spiral** balance spring, wide firm foot to the large balance cock and key actuated regulator for balance spring. The minute hand, the second wheel planted at center of movement, enamel dials, milled teeth for wheels and pinions and a general appearance in the steel finish. He started to number his watches in about **1680** and apparently the first watchmaker to do so, therefore there are no earlier serial numbers higher than the Tompion serial numbers listed below for **approximated** year produced.

T. Tompion (time only watch) Year — Serial#	G. Graham Continues Year — Serial #
1682 — 400	1715— 4,600
1685 — 900	1725— 5,200
1690— 1,600	1735— 5,600
1695— 2100	1745— 6,100
1700 — 2,800	1750 — 6,400
1705— 3,500	
1710— 4,000	

IMPORTANT NOTE: **FORGED** Watches signed T. Tompion and G. Graham, watches were **forged** in their life-time. These watches are the same age, style, hallmarks and **difficult** to tell from the true authentic watches.

PILLARS

Pillars are of interest and should be considered as one of the elements in determining age. Though the years small watches used round pillars, and the larger watches generally used a square type engraved pillar.

(*Illus.* 1) This pillar is one of the earliest types and used in the 1800s as well. This particular pillar came from a watch which dates about 1550. It is known that this type pillar was used in 1675 by Gaspard Girod of France and also in 1835 by James Taylor of England.

(*Illus.* 2) This style pillar is called the tulip pattern. Some watchmakers preferred to omit the vertical divisions. This style was popular between 1660 and 1750 but may be found on later watches. It was common practice to use ornamentation on the tulip pillar.

(*Illus.* 3) The ornament shown was used by Daniel Quare of London from 1665 to 1725 and by the celebrated Tompion, as well as many others.

(*Illus.* 4) This type pillar is referred to as the Egyptian and dates from 1630 to the 1800s. The squared Egyptian pattern was introduced about 1630 and some may be found with a wider division with a head or bust inserted. This style was used by D. Bouquet of London about 1640 and by many other watchmakers.

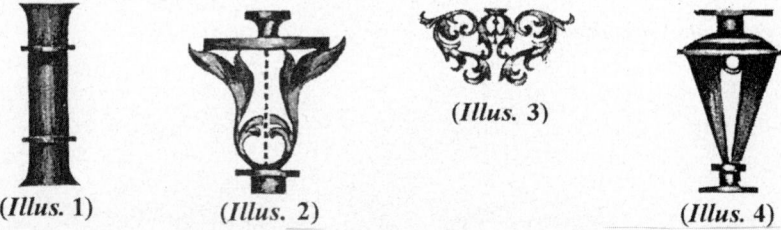

(*Illus.* 1)   (*Illus.* 2)   (*Illus.* 3)   (*Illus.* 4)

(*Illus. 5*) This pillar was used by Thomas Earnshaw of London about 1780. The plain style was prominent for close to two hundred years 1650 to 1825.

(*Illus.* 5)   (Illus. 6)   (Illus. 7)   (Illus. 8)

(**Illus. 6**) This style was popular and was used by many craftsmen. Nathaniel Barrow of London put this in his watches about 1680.

(**Illus. 7**) This pillar may be seen in watches made by Pierre Combet of Lyons, France, about 1720. It was also used by many others.

(**Illus. 8**) This style pillar and the ornament were used by John Ellicott of England and other watchmakers from 1730 to 1770.

These illustrations represent just a few of the basic pillars that were used. Each watchmaker would design and change details to create his own individual identity. This sometimes makes it more difficult to readily determine the age of watches.

⟋ **Multi-color** cases became popular by 1800, 1st. used in 1760 & **Engine Turning** rarely found before early 1760s. **Tortoise Shell** 1st. used in 1620, but did not become popular till about 1780. **Flat enamel** dials are being used in about 1810.

Example of 2 Egyptian pillars left & right also a hand pierced ornament that is not a pillar. (Ca.1700)

BALANCE COCKS OR BRIDGES

The first balance cocks or bridges used to support the balance staff were a plain "S" shape. The cocks used on the old three-wheel watches were very elaborate; hand-pierced and engraved. At first no screws were used to hold the cock in place. It is noteworthy that on the three wheel watch the regulator was a ratchet and click and was used on these earlier movements to adjust the mainspring. About 1635 the balance cock was screwed to the plate and pinned on its underside, which helped steady the balance. The first cock illustrated is a beautifully decorated example made by Josias Jeubi of Paris about 1580. Note that it is pinned to a stud which passes through a square cut in the foot of the cock. Next is a balance cock made by Bouquet of London about 1640. The third balance cock is one made by Jean Rousseau and dates around 1650. The fourth one dates around 1655.

The next two bridges are supported on both sides of the balance bridge by means of screws or pins. They are strikingly different and usually cover much of the plate of the movement. This French & Swiss style of balance bridge was used around 1665 and was still seen as late as 1765.

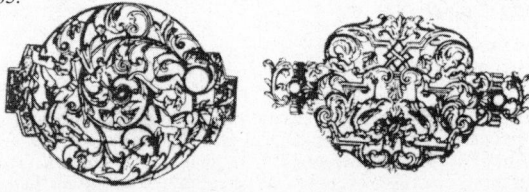

The beautiful balance cock below at left, with the ornate foot, dates about 1660-70.The next illustrated balance cock with the heavy ornamentation was used from about 1675 to 1720 or longer. By 1720 a face was added to the design. The face shows up where the table terminates on most balance cocks.

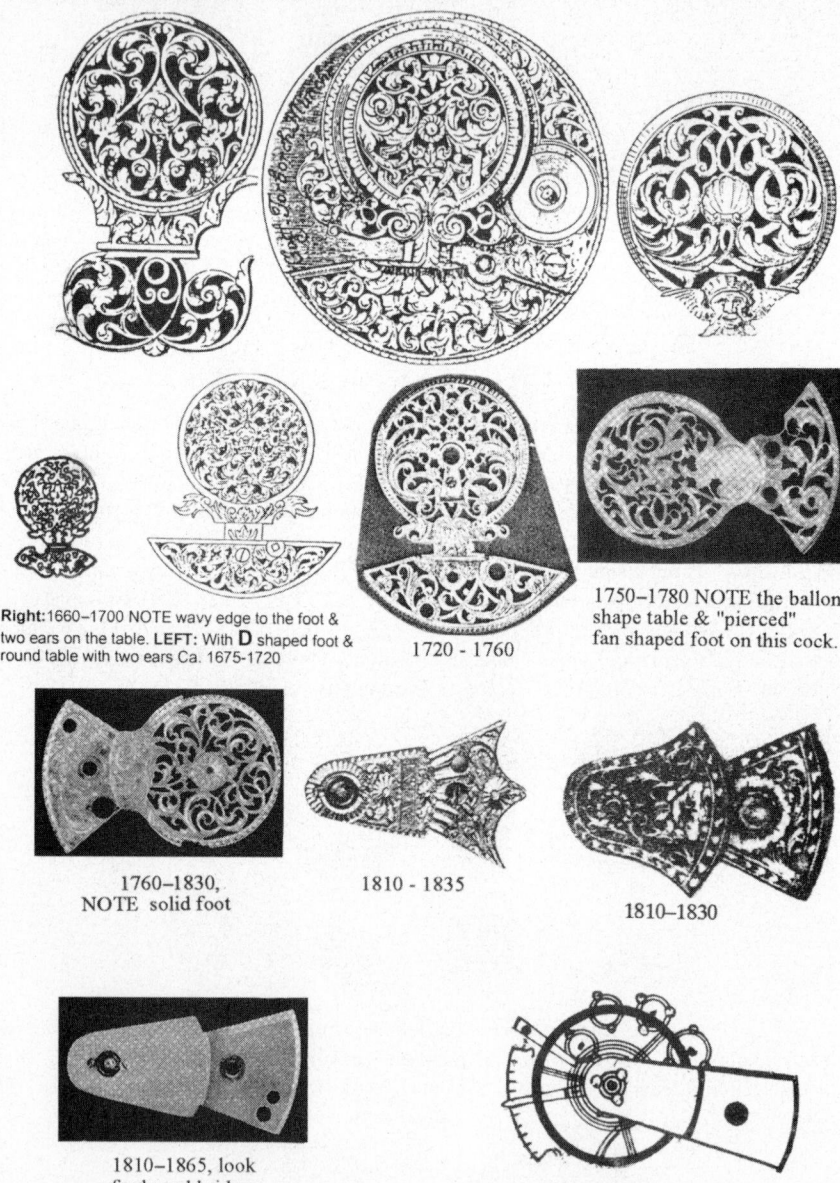

Right:1660–1700 NOTE wavy edge to the foot & two ears on the table. **LEFT:** With **D** shaped foot & round table with two ears Ca. 1675-1720

1720 - 1760

1750–1780 NOTE the ballon shape table & "pierced" fan shaped foot on this cock.

1760–1830, NOTE solid foot

1810 - 1835

1810–1830

1810–1865, look for barrel bridge

1850 NOTE under-sprung

Characteristics of watches differ for the same age of both case and movement, because these features vary it may not be accurate to date a watch by one single influence. Example: the second hand was not commonly found on watches before 1750, but common about 1800. The first second hand appeared in 1665 and another in 1690. Therefore statements are **broad** rather than absolute.

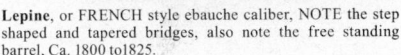

Lepine style movement Ca. 1790 to1820, with free standing barrel, also note the horse shoe shaped bridge, this denotes center seconds. (Virgule Escapement)

Lepine, or FRENCH style ebauche caliber, NOTE the step shaped and tapered bridges, also note the free standing barrel, Ca. 1800 to1825.

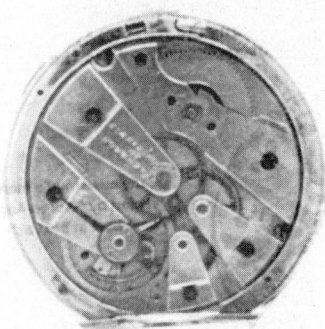

Lepine, or FRENCH style ebauche caliber, NOTE the step shaped and tapered bridges, also note the COVERED barrel bridge, this style movement was popular from Ca, 1820 to 1840.

Lepine, or FRENCH style ebauche caliber, NOTE the step shaped and tapered bridges, also note the CURVED barrel bridge, this style movement was popular from Ca.1830 to 1845.

☞ Characteristics of watches differ for the same age of both case and movement, because these features vary it may not be accurate to date a watch by one single influence. Example: the second hand was not commonly found on watches before 1750, but common about 1800. The first second hand appeared in 1665 and another in 1690. Therefore statements are **broad** rather than absolute.

Muti-colored cases became popular by 1800, 1st used in 1760 & **EngineTurning** rarely found before early 1760s. **Tortoise Shell** 1st. used in 1620, but did not become popular till about 1780. An informed collector will note that a watch with an enamel dial, for instance, could not have been made before 1635. A pair of cases indicates it could not have been made prior to 1640. The minute hand was introduced in 1650. The presence of a cylinder escapement would indicate it was made after 1710. 1750 the duplex escapement was first used. A dust cap first appeared in 1774. 1776 Lepine introduced the thin watch. **Flat enamel** dials are being used in about 1785. Keyless winding came into being after 1820 but did not gain widespread popularity until after about 1860. All of these clues and more must be considered before accurately assessing the age of a watch. Some watches were also **updated** such as minute hand added or new style escapement added.

448

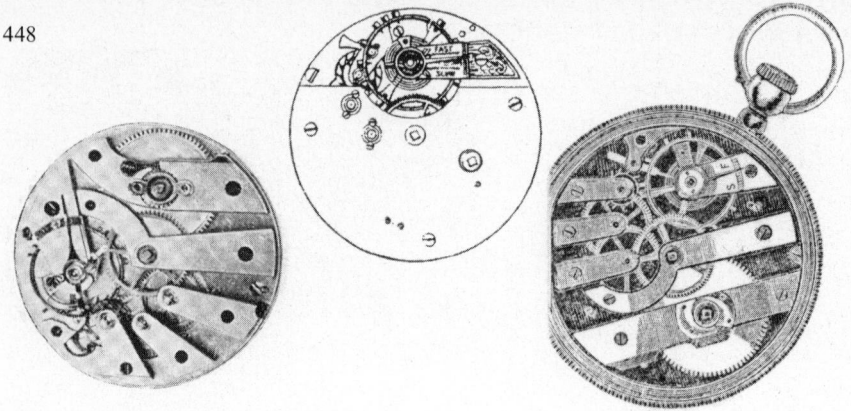

Left: Bar (Le Coultre) SWISS style ebauche caliber, NOTE the flat straight bridges and parallel design, also the CURVED barrel bridge. This movement was popular c. 1830 to 1875. **Middle**: New England style c. 1840-1885. **Right**: Bar (Le Coultre) SWISS style ebauche caliber, NOTE the flat straight bridges and parallel design, also the STRAIGHT barrel bridge. This movement was popular c.1840 to 1885. JULES JURGENSEN Style Bar SWISS a Chaux de Fonds ebauche caliber, c.1870 to 1895.

JULES JURGENSEN Style Bar SWISS
La Chaux de Fonds ebauche caliber, Ca.1870 to 1895.

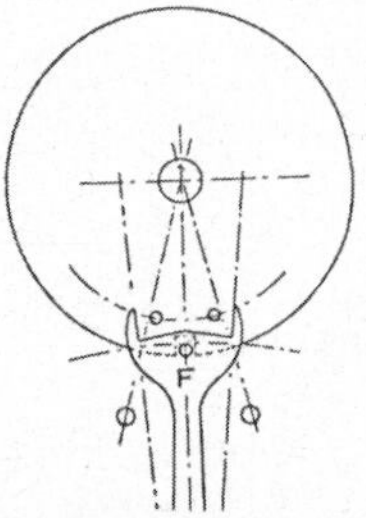

SAVAGE, two pin.

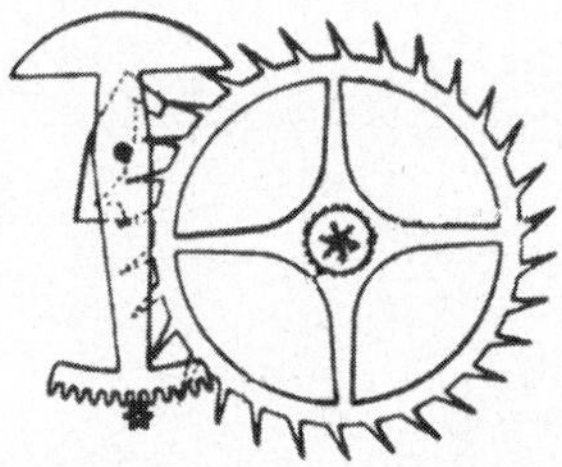

Rack and lever escapement

Invented in 1722

ESCAPEMENTS

Virgule Escapement

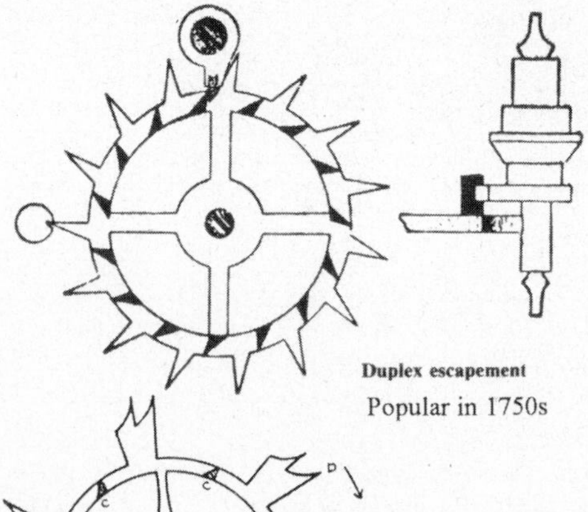

Duplex escapement
Popular in 1750s

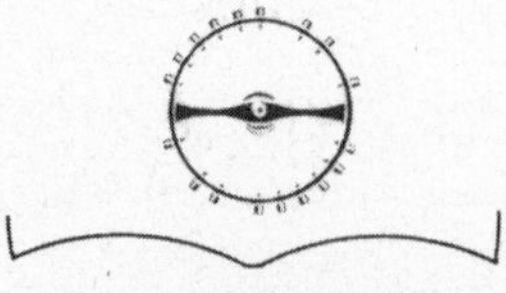

The "Glucydur" Balance can be recognized by the **shape** of its spokes.

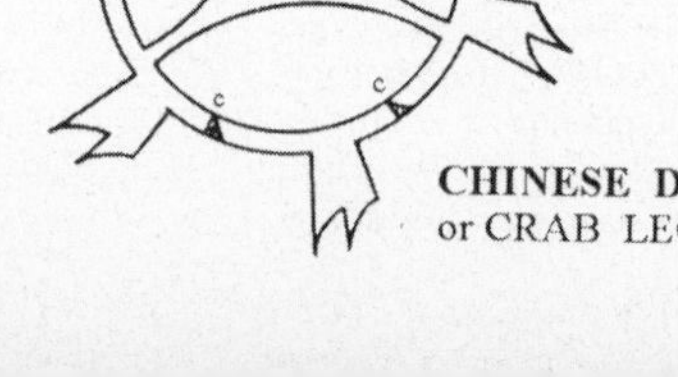

CHINESE DUPLEX
or CRAB LEG DUPLEX

CHRONOLOGICAL LIST TO HELP ESTABLISH THE AGE OF YOUR WATCHES
DATES BELOW ARE WHEN COMPONENTS WERE FIRST INTRODUCED OR BECAME POPULAR.

1450 - Mainspring, also large watches made entirely of IRON & were round in shape.

1525 - Fusee by Jacob of Prague.

1530- 1545 - Brass plates.

1550 - Screws & Oval shaped watches.

1564 - Swiss Watchmaking begins.

1570 - Hexagonal wand octagonal shapes.

1590- Rock Crystal & Form style watches.

1590 - Fusee CHAIN being used.

1590 - English Watchmaking.

1615 - Glass crystal to protect dials.

1620 - Tortoise shell covered cases & used till 1800.

1625 - Colored enamel cases and balance cock screwed to plate.

1635 - Enamel dial invented by Paul Viet, of Blois, France.

1640 - Pair cased watches.

1650 - 80-Repousse Cases & Form watches.

1657 - Hair-spring. (Not Spiral)

1660 - Virgule escapement.

1675 - Large Bulb shaped or Oignon watches, shagreen cases being seen.

1675 - Spiral balance hair- spring. also Watchmaking in Scotland.

1677 - Subdivision of labor, cottage industry.

1680 - Minute hands & Serial appear on movements. Watches now run for numbers first about 24 hours. On English watches.

1685- 90 - Repeating watches.

1690 to 1720 - All white Enamel watch dials now being used in ENGLAND.

1695- Cylinder escapement by Edward Booth, William Houghton and Thomas Tompion.

1700 - Pinchbeck "Gold" (Zink & Copper)

1704 - Watch JEWELS invented.

1715 - Repousse, dust band also seconds hand with tails.

1720 - Improved cylinder escapement by Graham, but not popular.

1722 - Rack lever escapement.(non-detached)

1724 - Duplex escapement invented.

1750 - Duplex escapement popular.

1759 - Detached Lever escapement by Mudge.

1760 - Engine Turning & multi-color gold found on cases.

1761 - John Harrison's chronometer # 4 went to sea for first trial.

1765 - Center seconds.

1766 - Compensation balance by Le Roy.

1767 - Virgule escapement.

1770 - Ebauche style watches by Japy.

1773- Detached escapement (Berthound)

1775 - Helical balance spring by Arnold.

1776 - Thin modern watches by Lepine.

1785 - Flat Enamel dials being used.

1780 - Overcoil balance spring.

1782 - Spring detent by Arnold & Earnshaw.

1790 - Musical works & Automaton style watches, 4 color gold dials.

1800 - Watches decorated with pearls.

1820 - Reproduction of 1600 Form watches. Prest patent for winding only by pendant.

1825 - Single sunk Dial.

1830 - Club tooth escape wheel. Mm repeater

1838- Louis Audemars 1st crown wind & set.

1835 - Chinese Duplex.

1844 - Heart shaped cam for chronograph.

1848 - Rocking bar keyless winding.

1867 - Roskopf (Dollar) watches.

1896 - Invar "Guillaume" balance.

1900 - Wrist Watches being used.

1924 - Auto-wind Wrist Watch.

1957 - 1st electric W. W. by Hamilton.

1960 - First Electronic Wrist Watch by Max Hetzel & by Bulova Accutron.

1967 - Quartz crystal watch developed.

Jan. 1675 Isaac Thuret introduced a **model** of a escapement that had a regulatory **spiral hairspring**. Thomas Tompion made watches with a **Minute hand**, Ca. 1680.

EARLY EUROPEAN WATCHMAKERS

NOTE ABBREVIATIONS USED
art = maker used this enamel case painter, enamel = enamel case painter or artist
pat. = patent or inventor, ca. = circa or about, since = founded to present
This list of EARLY EUROPEAN WATCHMAKERS is a small %.

Achard, J. Francois (Geneva, ca. 1750)
Addison, J. (London, 1760-1780)
Adamson, Gustave (Paris, 1775-1790)
Alfred, W. Humphreys (London, ca. 1905)
Alibut (Paris, ca. 1750s)
Alliez, Buchelard & Teron Co. (French, ca. 1830)
Amabric, Abraham (Geneva, ca. 1750-1800)
Amabric, Freres (Geneva, ca. 1760-1795)
Amon (Paris, 1913)
Andre, Jean (enamel) (Geneva, 1660-1705)
Anthony, Willams (London, 1785-1840)
Antram, J. (London, ca. 1700-1730)
Appleby, Edward (London, ca. 1675)
Appleby, Joshua (London, ca. 1720-1745)
Ardin, Coppet (ca. 1710)
Arlaud, Benjamin (London, c. 1680)
Arlaud, Louis (Geneva, ca 1750)
Anord & Dent (London) ca. 1839
Arnold & Frodsham, Charles (London, 1845)
Arnold, Henery (London, ca. 1770-1780)
Arnold, John (London, ca 1760-1790)
Arnold, John Roger, son of (London, ca. 1800-1830)
Arnold, Nicolas (ca. 1850)
Arnold & Lewis, Lose Simmons (Manchester, ca 1860)
Arnold & Son (London, ca. 1787.1799)
Assman, Julius (Glasshutte, 1850-1885)
Auber, Daniel (London, ca. 1750)
Aubert, D. F. (Geneva, ca. 1825)
Aubert, Ferdinand (1810-1835)
Aubert & Co. (Geneva, ca. 1850)
Aubry, Irenee (Geneva, 1885-1910)
Audebert (Paris,1810-1820)
Audemars, Freres (Swiss, 1810 until Co. splits in 1885)
Audemars, Louis-Benjamin (Swiss, 1811-1867)
Aureole (Swiss, 1921)
Auricoste, Jules (Paris, ca. 1910)
Bachhofen, Felix (Swiss, 1675-1690)
Badolles, Jean-Jacques (Geneva, 1779-1891)
Baillon, Jean-Hilaire (Paris, ca. 1727)
Baird, Wm. (London, 18 15-1825)
Balsiger & Fils (ca. 1825)
Barberet, J. (Paris, ca 1600)
Barbezat, Bole (Swiss, 1870)
Baronneau, Jean-Louis (France, 1675-1700)
Barnett, John (England) 1690
Barraud & Lunds (England) 1872
Barraud & Lunds (1812-1840)
Barraud, Paul-Philip (London, 1752-1820)
Barrow, Edward (London, ca. 1650-1710)
Barrow, Nathaniel (London, 1653-1689)
Barry, M. (French, ca. 1620)
Bartholony, Abraham (Paris, 1750-1752)
Barton, J. (London, 1760-1780)
Barwise J.(London, 1800)
Bassereau, Jean-Hilaire (Paris, ca. 1800-1810)
Bautte, Jean-Francois (Geneva, 1800-1835)
Bautte & Moynier (Geneva, ca 1825)
Beaumarchais, Caron (Paris, 1750-1795)
Beauvais, Simon (London, ca 1690)
Beckman, Daniel (London, 1670-1685)
Beckner, Abraham (London, ca. 1640)
Beliard, Dominique (Paris, ca. 1750)
Bell, Benj. (London, 1650-1668)
Bennett, John (London, 1850-1895)
Benson, J. W. (London, 1825-1890)
Benson, J. W. (London, 1850-1900)
Bergstein, L. (London, ca 1840)
Bernard, Nicholas (Paris, 1650-1690)

Bernoulli, Daniel (Paris, 1720-1780)
Berrollas, J. A. (Denmark, 1800-1830)
Berthoud, Augusta-Louis (Paris, ca. 1875)
Berthoud, Ferdinand (Paris, 1750-1805)
Beihler & Hartmann (Geneva, ca. 1875)
Blanc, Henri (Geneva, ends 1964)
Blanc, Jules (Geneva, 1929-1940)
Blanc & Fils (Geneva, 1770-1790)
Bock, Johann (German, 1700-1750)
Bockel (London, ca. 1650)
Bolslandon, Metz (ca. 1780)
Bolviller, Moise (Paris, 1840-1870)
Bommelt, Leonhart (Nuremburg, Ger., ca. 1690)
Bonney (London, ca. 1790)
Bonniksen, Bahne (England, 1890-1930) invented karrusel
Booth, Edward (name change to Barlow)
Bordier, Denis (France, ca. 1575)
Bordier, Freres (Geneva, 1787-1810)
Bordier, Jacques (enamel) (ca. 1670)
Bornand, A. (Geneva, 1895-1915)
Boubon (Paris, 1810-1820)
Bouquet, David (London, ca 1630-1650)
Bovet (England) 1815 (used ,J. L. Richer Art)
Bovet, Edouard (Swiss, 1820-1918)
Bovier, G. (enamel painter) (Paris, c. 1750)
Brands, Iacob (Swiss, ca. 1700)
Brandt, Robert & Co. (Geneva, ca 1820)
Breitling, "Leon" (Swiss, since 1884)
Brookbank (London, 1776)
Brocke (London, ca 1640)
Brodon, Nicolas (Paris, 1674-1682)
Bronikoff, a Wjatka (Russia, 1850 "watches of wood")
Bruguier, Charles A. (Geneva, 1800-1860)
Bull, Rainulph (one of the first British) (1590-1617)
Burgis, Eduardus (London, 1680-1710)
Burgis, G. (London, 1720-1740)
Burnet, Thomas (London, ca. 1800)
Busch, Abraham (Hamburg, Ger., ca 1680)
Buz, Johannes (Augsburg, Bavaria, ca 1625)
Cabrier, Charles (London, ca. 1690-1720)
Capt, Henry Daniel (Geneva, 1802-1880)
Caron, Augustus (Paris, ca 1750-1760)
Caron, Francois-Modeste (Paris, 1770-1788)
Caron, Pierre (Paris, ca. 1700)
Caron, Pierre Augustin (pat. virgule escap.) (Paris,1750-1795)
Carpenter, William (London, 1750-1800)
Carte, John (England, 1680-1700)
Champod, P. Amedee (enamel) (Geneva, 1850-1910)
Chapeau, Peter (England) 1746
Chapponier, Jean (Geneva, 1780-1800)
Charlton, John (England) 1635
Charman (London, 1780-1800)
Charrot (Paris, 1775-1810)
Chartiere (enamel) (France, ca 1635)
Chaunes (Paris, ca. 1580-1600)
Chauvel, J. (England) 1720-25
Chavanne & Pompejo (Vienna, 1785-1800)
Cheneviere, Louis (Geneva, 1710-1740)
Cheneviere, Urbain (Geneva, 1730-1760)
Cheriot or Cherioz, Daniel (ca. 1750-1790)
Cheuillard (Blois, France, ca 1600)
Chevalier & Co. (Geneva, 1795-1810)
Cisin, Charles (Swiss, 1580-1610)
Clark, Geo. (London, 1750-1785)
Clay, Charles (England) 1750
Clerc (Swiss, ca 1875)
Clouzier, Jacques (Paris, 1690-1750)
Cochin, D. (Paris, ca. 1800)

Cocque, Geo. (ca. 1610)
Cogniat (Paris, ca. 1675)
Coladon, Louis (Geneva, 1780-1850)
Cole, James Ferguson (London, 1820-1875)
Cole, Thomas (London, 1820-1864)
Collins, Clement (London, ca. 1705)
Collins, John (London, ca. 1720)
Collins, R. (London, ca. 1815)
Colondre & Schnee (ca. 1875)
Combret, Pierre (Lyons, France, ca. 1610-1625)
Cooper, T. F. (England) 1842-80 later "TM."
Cotton, John (London, Ca. 1695-1715)
Coulin, Jaques & Bry, Amy (Paris & Geneva, 1780-1790)
Court, Jean-Pierre (ca. 1790-1810)
Courvosier, Freres (Swiss, 1810-1852)
Courvoisier & Houriet (Geneva, ca. 1790)
Cox, James (London, 1760-1785)
Crofswell J. N. (London), ca. 1825
Csacher, C. (Prague, Aus., ca. 1725)
Cumming, Alexander (London, 1750-1800)
Cummins, Charles (London, 1820)
Cuper, Barthelemy (French, 1615-1635)
Curtis, John (London, ca. 1720)
Cusin, Charles (Geneva, ca. 1587)
Darling, William (British, ca. 1825)
Daniel, de St. Leu (England) 1815
De Baghyn, Adriaan (Amsterdam, ca. 1750)
Debaufre, Peter (French, 1690-1720) (Debaufre escap.)
Debaufre, Pierre (Paris, London, Geneva, 1675-1722)
De Bry, Theodore (German, 1585-1620)
De Charmes, Simon (London, France, 1690-1730)
De Choudens (Swiss & French, 1760-1790)
Decombaz, Gedeon (Geneva, 1780-1820)
Degeilh & Co. (ca. 1880-1900)
De Heca, Michel (Paris, ca. 1685)
De L Garde, Abraham (Paris, "Blois," ca 1590)
Delynne, F. L. (Paris, ca. 1775)
"Dent", (Edward John)(London, 1815-1850)
Denham, Go. (London, 1750)
Derham, William (English, ca. 1677-1730)
Deroch, F. (Swiss, 1730-1770)
Des Arts & Co. (Geneva, 1790-1810)
Desquivillons & DeChoudens (Paris, ca. 1785)
Destouches, Jean-Francois-Albert (Holland, ca. 1760)
Devis, John (London, 1770-1785)
Dimier & Co. (Geneva, 1820-1925)
Dinglinger (enamel) (Dresden, Ger., ca. 1675)
Ditisheim & Co. "Maurice" (Swiss, 1894)
Ditisheim, Paul (Swiss, 1892)
Dobson, A. (London, 1660-1680)
Droz, Daniel (Chaux-de-Fonds, Sw., ca. 1760)
Droz, Henri (Chaux-de-Fonds, Sw., ca. 1775)
Droz, Pierre Jacquet (Chaux-de-Fonds, Sw., 1750-1775)
Droz, Pierre (Swiss, 1740-1770)
Droz & Co. (Swiss, ca. 1825)
Dubie (enamel) (Paris, ca. 1635)
Dubois & Fits (Paris, ca. 1810)
Duchene & Co. "Louis" (Geneva, 1790-1820)
Duvommun, Charles (Geneva, ca. 1750)
Duduict, Jacques (Blois, France, ca. 1600)
Dufalga, Philippe (Geneva, 1730-1790)
Dufalga, P. F. (Geneva, ca. 1750)
Dufour, Foll & Co. (Geneva, 1800-1830)
Dufour, J. E. & Co. (ca. 1890)
Dufour & Ceret (Ferney, Fr., ca. 1770-1785)
Dufour & Zentler (ca. 1870)
Duhamel, Pierre (Paris, ca. 1680)
Dunlop, Andrew (England) 1710
Dupin, Paul (London, 1730-1765)
Dupont (Geneva, ca. 1810-1830)
Dupont, Jean (enamel) (Geneva, 1800-1860)
Duru (Paris, ca. 1650)
Dutertre, Baptiste (ca. 1730) (pat. duplex escapement)
Dutton, William (London, 1760-1840)

Dyson, John & Sons (England) 1816
Earnshaw, Thomas (London, 1780-1825)
East, Edward (London, 1630-1670)
Edmonds, James (London to U.S.A., 1720-1766)
Edward, George & Son (London, Ca. 1875)
Ekegren, Henri-Robert (Geneva, 1860)
Ellicott, John (London, 1728-1810)
Emanuel, E.& E (England) 1861
Emery, Josiah (Geneva, 1750-1800)
Etherington, George (England) 1700
Esquivillon & Dc Choudens (Paris, 1710-1780)
Ester, Jean Henry (Geneva, 1610-1665)
Etherington, George (London, 1680-1730)
Etienne Guyot & Co. (Geneva, ca. 1880)
Facio De Duillier, Nicholas (British, 1665-1710)
Fallery, Jacques (Geneva, ca. 1760)
Farmer, G. W. (wooden watches) (Germany, 1650-1675)
Fatio, Alfred (Geneva, 1920-1940)
Fatton, Frederick Louis (London, ca. 1822)
Favre Marius & Fils (Geneva, 1893)
Fenie, M. (ca. 1635)
Ferrero, J. (ca. 1854-1900)
Fiarce, Clement (Paris, ca. 1700)
Fitter, Joseph (London, ca. 1660)
Fontac (London, ca. 1775)
Forfaict, Nicolas (Paris, 1573-1619)
Fowles, Allen (Kilmarnock, Scot., ca. 1770)
French (London, 1810-1840)
Fureur (Swiss, 1910)
Gallopin "Henri Caps" (Geneva, 1875)
Gamod, G. (Paris, ca. 1640)
Gamier, Paul (Paris, 1825) (pat. Gamier escapement)
Garon, Peter (England) 1700
Garrault, Jacobus (Geneva, ca. 1650)
Garty & Constable (London, ca. 1750)
Gaudron, Antoine (Paris, 1675-1707)
Gaudron, Pierre (Paris, 1695-1740)
Geissheim, Smod (Augsburg, Ger., ca. 1625)
Gent, James & Son (London, 1875-1910)
Gerbeau, V. (Paris, 1900-1930)
Gerrard (British, 1790-1820)
Gibs, William (Rotterdam, ca. 1720)
Gibbons Joshua (London), ca. 1825
Gibson & Co., Ltd. (Ireland, ca. 1875-1920)
Gidon (Paris, ca. 1700)
Gillespey, Charles (Ireland, 1774-1171)
Girard, Perregaux (Swiss, 1856)
Girard, Theodore (Paris, 1623-1670)
Girardier, Charles (Geneva, 1780-1815)
Girod, B. (Paris, ca. 1810)
Girod, Gaspard (Paris, ca. 1670-1690)
Godod, E. (Paris, ca. 1790)
Godon, F. L. (Paris, ca. 1787)
Golay, A. Leresche & Fils (Geneva, 1844-1857)
Golay, H. (Swiss, 1969-1911)
Golay, Stahl & Fils (1878-1914)
Gollons (Paris, ca. 1663)
Gould, Christopher (England) 1650
Gounouilhou, P. S. (Geneva, 1815-1840)
Gout, Ralph (London, 1790-1830)
Graham, George (London, 1715-1750)
Grandjean, Henri (Swiss, 1825-1880)
Grandjean, L. C. (Swiss, 1890-1920)
Grant, John & Son (English, 1780-1867)
Grantham, William (London, ca. 1850-60)
Grasses, Isaac (Geneva, ca. 1896)
Gray & Constable (London, ca. 1750-90)
Grazioza (Swiss, ca. 1901)
Grebauval, Hierosme (ca. 1575)
Gregory, Jermie (London, ca 1652-1680)
Gregson, Jean P. (Paris, 1770-1790)
Grendon, Henry (England) 1645
Griblin, Nicolas (French, 1650-1716)
Griessenback, Johann G. (Bavaria, ca. 1660)

Grignion "family" (London, 1690-1825)
Grignion, Daniel & Thomas (London, 1780-1790)
Grinkin, Robert (England) 1625
Grosclaude, Ch. & Co. (Swiss, ca. 1865)
Grosjean, Henry (French, Ca. 1865)
Gruber, Hans (Nurnberg, Ger., ca. 1520-1560)
Gruber, Michel (Nurnberg, Ger., ca. 1605)
Gruet (Geneva, Sw., Ca. 1664)
Gubelin, E. (Lucern, Switzerland, Ca. 1832)
Guillaume, Ch. (pat. Invar, Elinvar)
Haas Nevevx & Co. (founder B. J. Haas) (Swiss, 1828-1925)
Hagen, Johan (German, Ca. 1750)
Haley, Charles (London, 1781-1825)
Hallewey (London, 1695-1720)
Hamilton & Co. (London, 1865-1920)
Hamilton G.(London), Ca 1800s
Harper, Henry (London, ca. 1665-1700)
Harrison, John (England, b.1693-1776) **Marine No.1-2-3-4**
Hasluck Brothers (London, Ca. 1695)
Hautefeuille, Jean (Paris, 1670-1722)
Hautefeuille, John (Paris, 1660-1700)
Hawley, John (London, Ca. 1850)
Hebert, Juliette (enamel) (Geneva, Ca. 1890)
Helbros (Geneva, since 1918)
Hele or Henlein, Peter (Nurnberg, 1510-1540)
Heliger, J. (Zug, Sw., ca. 1575)
Henner, Johann (Wurtzburg, Ger., ca 1730)
Henry, F. S. (Swiss, Ca. 1850)
Hentschel, J. J. (French, ca. 1750)
Hess, L. (Zurich, Sw., ca. 1780)
Hessichti, Dionistus (ca. 1630)
Higgs & Evans (London, 1775-1825)
Hill, Ben. (London, 1640-1670)
Hindley, Henry (England) 1758
Hoddell, James, & Co. (England) 1869
Hoguet, Francois (Paris, Ca. 1750)
Hooke, Robert (England, 1650-1700)
Hoseman, Stephen (London, Ca. 1710-1740)
Houghton, James (England, Ca. 1800-1820)
Houghton, Thomas (Chorley, England, Ca. 1820-1840)
Houriet, Jacques Frederic (Paris 1810-1825)
Howells & Pennington (England) 1795
Huaud, Freres (enamel) (Geneva, ca. 1685)
Huber, Peter (German, ca. 1875)
Hubert, David (London, 1714-1747)
Hubert, James (England) 1760
Hubert, Oliver (London, ca. 1740)
Hubert, Etienne (French, 1650-1690)
Hues, Peter (Augsburg, Ger., ca. 1600)
Huguenin, David L. (Swiss, 1780-1835)
Humbert-Droz, David (Swiss, ca. 1790)
Hunt & Roskell (England) 1846
Huygens, Christian (Paris, 1657-1680)
Iaquier or Jacquier, Francois (Geneva, 1690-1720)
Ilbery, William (London, 1800-35) (used J. L. Richer art)
Ingold, Pierre-Frederic (Swiss, Paris, London, 1810-1870)
Invicta ("R. Picard") (Swiss, 1896)
Jaccard, E. H. & Co. (Swiss, Ca. 1850)
Jacot, Charles-Edouard (Swiss, 1830-1860) (pat Chinese duplex)
Jaeger, Edmond (Paris, 1875-1920)
Jaeger Le Coultre & Co. (Swiss, since 1833)
Jamison, Geo. (London, 1786-1810)
Janvier, Antide (Paris, 1771-1834)
Japy, Frederic & Sons "family" (French, Swiss, Ca. 1776)
Jaquet, Pierre (Swiss, 1750-1790)
Jean Richard, Daniel (Swiss, 1685-1740)
Jean Richard, Edouard (Swiss, 1900-1930)
Jeannot, Paul (ca. 1890)
Jefferys & Gildert (London, 1790)
Jessop, Josias (London, 1780-1794)
Jeubi, Josias (Paris, Ca. 1575)
Joly, Jacques (Paris, ca. 1625)
Jovat (London, Ca. 1690)

Johnson Joseph. Liverpool (English), ca.1805-1855
Jones, Henry (London, Ca. 1665-1690)
Jump, Joseph (English, Ca. 1827-1850)
Junod, Freres (Geneva, Ca. 1850)
Jurgensen, Urban & Jules (Copenhagen, Swiss,1745-1912)
Just & Son (London, 1790-1825)
Juvet, Edouard (Swiss, 1844-1880)
Juvet, Leo (Swiss, 1860-1890)
Keates, William (London, Ca. 1780)
Keely, W. (London, ca. 1790)
Kendall, Larcum (London, Ca. 1786)
Kendall, James (London 1740-1780)
Kessels, H. J. (Holland, 1800-1845)
Kirkton, R. (London, Ca. 1790)
Klein, Johann Heinr (Copenhagen, Den., Ca. 1710)
Klentschi, C. F. (Swiss, 1790-1840)
Koehn, Edward (Geneva, 1860-1908)
Kreizer, Conard (German, 1595-1658)
Kuhn, Jan Hendrik (Amsterdam, 1775-1800)
Kullberg, Victor (Copenhagen to London, 1850-1890)
Lamy, Michel (Paris, 1767-1800)
Lang & Padoux (ca. 1860)
Larcay (Pads, ca 1725)
Lardy, Francois (Geneva, Ca. 1825)
Larpent, Isacc & Jurgensen (Copenhagen, 1743-1811)
Laurier, Francois (Paris, 1654-1675)
Le Baufre (Paris, ca. 1650)
Lebet (Geneva, Ca. 1850)
Lebet & Fils (Swiss, 1830-1892)
Le Coultre, Ami (Geneva, Ca. 1887)
Le Coultre, Eugene (Geneva, ca. 1850)
Leekey, C. (London, ca. 1750)
Leeky, Gabriel (London, Ca. 1775-1820)
Lepaute, Jean-Andre (Paris, 1750-1774)
Lepine or L'Epine, Jean-Antoine (Pads, 1744-1814)
Le Prevost (Swiss), ca. 1810
Le Puisne, Huand (enamel) (Blois, Fr., Ca. 1635)
Leroux, John (England, 1758-1805)   /
Le Roy & Co. (Pads, ca. 1853)
Le Roy, Charles (Paris, 1733-1770)
Le Roy, Julien (Paris, 1705-1750)
Le Roy, Pierre (French, 1710-SO) (improved duplex escap.)
Levy, Hermanos (Hong Kong, "Swiss," 1880-1890)
L'Hardy, Francois (Geneva. 1790-1825)
Lichtenauer (Wurzberg, Ger., Ca. 1725)
Lindesay, G. (London, ca. 1740-1770)
Lindgren, Erik (England, 1735-1775) (pat. rack lever)
Litherland, Peter (English, 1780-1876)
Loehr, (Von) (Swiss, Ca. 1880)
Long & Drew (enamel) (London, Ca. 1790-1810)
Losada, Jose R. (London, 1835-1890)
Lowndes, Jonathan (London, Ca. 1680-1700)
MacCabe, James (London, 1778-1830)
Maillardet & Co. (Swiss, Ca. 1800)
Mairet, Sylvain (Swiss, 1825-1885) (London, 1830-1840)
Malignon, A. (Geneva, ca. 1835)
Marchand, Abraham (Geneva, 1690-1725)
Margetts, George (London, 1780-1800)
Markwick Markham, "Perigal" "Recordon" (London, 1780-1825)
Marshall, John (London, Ca. 1690)
Martin (Paris, Ca. 1780)
Martin, Thomas (London, Ca. 1870)
Martineau, Joseph (London, 1765-1790)
Martinot, "family" (Paris, 1570-1770)
Martinot, James (London, ca. 1780)
Mascarone, Gio Batt (London, ca. 1635)
Massey, Edward (England. 1800-1850)
Massey, Henry (London, 1692-1745)
E. Mathey-Tissot & Co. (Swiss, 1886-1896)
Matile, Henry (Swiss, Ca. 1825)
Maurer, Johann (Fiessna, Ger., Ca. 1640-1650)
May, George (English, 1750-1770)
Mayr, Johann Peter (Augsburg, Ger., Ca. 1770)

McCabe, James (London, 1780-1710)
McDowall, Charles (London, ca. 1820-1860)
Met, John (London, ca. 1825)
Mecke, Daniel (ca. 1760) . ,
Melly, Freres (Geneva, Paris, 1791-1844)
Mercier, A. D. (Swiss, 1790-1820)
Mercier, Francois David (Paris, ca. 1700)
Meuron & Co. (Swiss, ca. 1784)
Meylan, C. H. "Meylan W. Co." (Swiss, ca. 1880)
Michel, Jean-Robert (Paris, ca. 1750)
Miller, Joseph (London, ca. 1728)
Milleret & Tissot (ca. 1835)
Miroir (London, ca. 1700-1725)
Mistral (Swiss, ca. 1902)
Mobilis (Swiss, ca. 19!0)
Modernists (Swiss, ca 1903)
Moillet, Jean-Jacques (Paris, 1776-1789)
Molina, Antonio (Madrid, Spain, ca. 1800)
Molinie (Swiss, ca. 1840)
Molyneux, Robert (London, ca. 1825-1850)
Montandon, Chs. Ad. (Swiss, 1800-1830)
Morand, Pierre (Paris, ca. 1790)
Moricand & Co. (Swiss, ca. 1780)
Moricand & Desgranges (Geneva, 1828-1835)
Moricand, Christ (Geneva, 1745-1790)
Morin, Pierre (English, French & Dutch style, ca. 1700)
Morliere (enamel) (Blois, Fr., ca. 1636-1650)
Moser, George Michael (London, ca. 1716-1730)
Motel, Jean Francois (French, 1800-1850)
Moulineux, Robert (London, 1800-1840)
Moulinier, Aine & Co. (Swiss, 1828-1851)
Moulinier, Freres & Co. (Swiss, ca. 1822)
Mudge, Thomas (London, 1740-1790)
Mulsund (enamel) (Paris, ca. 1700)
Munoz, Blas (Madrid, Spain, ca. 1806-1823)
Mussard, Jean (Geneva, 1699-1727)
Musy Padre & Figlo (Paris, 1710-1760)
Myrmecide (Paris, ca. 1525)
Nardin, Ulysse (Swiss, ca. 1846)
Nelson, W. (London, 1777-1818)
Nocturne (ca. 1920)
Noir, Jean-Baptiste (Paris, 1680-1710)
Norris, J. (Dutch, 1680-1700)
Norton (London), ca. 1805
Nouwen, Michael (1st English, 1580-1600)
Noyean (ca. 1850)
Oldnburg, Johan (German, ca. 1648)
Oudin, Charles (Paris, 1807-1900)
Owen, John (English, ca. 1790)
Palmer, Samuel (London, ca. 1790-1810)
Panier, Iosue "Josue" (Paris, ca. 1790)
Papillon (ca. 1690)
Papillon, Francesco (Florence, ca. 1705)
Parr, Thomas (London, ca. 1735-1775)
Payne, H. & John (London, ca. 1735-1775)
Pellaton, Albert (Swiss, ca. 1873)
Pellaton, James (Swiss, 1903) (Tourbillon)
Pendleton, Richard (London, 1780-1805)
Pennington, Robert (English, 1780-1816)
Perigal, Francis (English, 1770-1790)
Pernetti, F. (Swiss, ca. 1850)
Perrelet, Abram (Swiss, 1780) (self wind)
Perret, Edouard (Swiss, 1850)
Perrin, Freres (Swiss, 1810)
Phillips, Edouard (Paris, ca. 1860)
Phleisot (Dijon, Fr., ca. 1540)
Piaget, George (Swiss, ca. 1881)
Picard, James (Geneva, ca. 1850)
Piguet & Capt (Geneva, 1802-1811)
Piguet & Meylan (Geneva, 1811-1828)
Piguet, Victorin-Emile (Geneva, 1870-1935)
Plairas, Solomon (Blois, Fr., ca. 1640)
Plumbe, David (ca. 1730)
Poitevin, B. (Paris, 1850-1935)

Poncet, J. F. (Dresden, 1750)
Poncet, Jean-Francois (Swiss, 1740-1800)
Potter, Harry (London, 1760-1800)
Pouzait, Jean-Moise (Geneva, 1780-1800)
Poy, Gottfrey (London, ca. 1725-1730)
Press, Thomas (English, 1820-1855)
Prevost, Freres (ca. 1820)
Prior, Edward (London, 1825-1865)
Prior, George (London, 1800-1830) (used J. L. Richer art)
Pyke, John (English, 1750-1780)
Quare, Daniel (London, 1700-1724)
Quarella, Antonio (ca. 1790)
Ravine, Cesar (Swiss, ca. 1902)
Ravine, C. Frederic (Is Chaux-de-Fonds, Swiss, cal 810-32)
Raillard, Claude (Paris, 1662-1675)
Raiss (1890-1910) (enamel)
Rait, D. C. (German, ca. 1866)
Ramasy, David (Scotland, France, London, 1590-1654)
Ramuz, Humbert U. & Co. (Swiss, ca 1882)
Ratel, Henri (Paris, 1850-1900)
Recordon, Louis (London, 1778-1824)
Redier, Antoine (Paris, 1835-1883)
Renierhes (London, ca. 1850)
Rey, Jn. Ante, & Fils (Paris, 1790-1810)
Reynaud, P. & Co. (1860)
Rich, John (Geneva, London, 1795-1825)
Richard, Daniel Jean (1685-1740)
Richer, J. L. (outstanding enamel artist) (Geneva, 1786-1840)
Rigaud, Pierre (Geneva, 1750-1800)
Rigot, Francois (Geneva, ca. 1825)
Robert & Courvoisier & Co. (Paris, 1781-1832)
Robin, Robert (Paris, 1765-1805)
Robinet, Charles (Paris, ca. 1640)
Robinson, Olivier & Fredmahn (Naples, 1727-1790)
Robinson William (Liverpool), ca. 1850
Rogers, Isaac (London, 1770-1810)
Romilly, Sieur (Geneva, ca. 1750-1775)
Rooker, Richard (London, 1790-1810)
Rose, Joseph (London, 1752-1795)
Rosier, John (Geneva, ca. 1750)
Roskell, Robert (London, 1798-1830) (rack-lever)
Roskopf, G. (German to Swiss, 1835-1885)
Rosselet, Louis (Geneva, 1855-1900) (enamel)
Rousseau, Jean (Paris, 1580-1642)
Roux, Bordier & Co. (Geneva, ca. 1795)
Ruegger, Jacques (ca. 1800-1840)
Ruel, Samuel (Rotterdam, ca. 1750)
Rugendas, Nicholas (Augsburg, Ger., ca. 1700-1750)
Rundell & Bridge (London, ca. 1772-1825)
Russel, Thomas & Son (England) 1898
Sailler, Johann (Vienna, Aus., ca. 1575)
Sanchez, Cayetano (Madrid, Spain, c. 1790-1800)
Sandoz, Henri F. (Tavannes W. Co.) (ca. 1840)
Savage, George (London, 1808-1855) (Inv. pin lever)
Savage, William (London 1800-1850)
Savile, John (London, ca. 1656-1679)
Schatck, Johann Engel (Prague, ca. 1650)
Schultz, Michael (ca. 1600-1650)
Schuster, Caspar (Nunburg, ca. 1570)
Sermand, J. (Geneva, ca. 1640)
Sellar - Reading (England) 1854
Shepherd, Thomas (England) 1632
Sherman De Neilly (Belfort, ca. 1910)
Sherwood, J. (London, ca. 1750-1775)
Sidey, B. (England) 1770
Solson (London, 1750)
Soret (Geneva, ca. 1810)
Soret, Frederic II (1735-1806)
Soret, Jean & Co. (1690-1760)
Sleightholm & Co. (England) 1800
Smith, C. (England) 1829
Smith, George (England) 1630
Smith, S, & Son (England) 1910
Snelling, J.50

Speakman, Edward (England) 1690
Spencer & Perkins (London, 1770-1808)
Stadlin, Francois (Swiss, 1680-1735)
Staples, James (1755-1795)
Stuffer, M. T. (Swiss, 1830-1855)
Stauffer "Stauffer Son & Co." (London, 1880)
Strasser & Rohde (Glashutte, 1875)
Sudek, J. (ca. 1850)
Sully, Henry (French, London, 1700-1725)
Swift, Thomas (London, ca. 1825-1865)
Tavan, Antoine (Geneva, 1775-1830)
Tavernier, Jean (Paris, 1744-1795)
Tempor Watch Co. (1930) (Masonic watch)
Terond, Allier & Bachelard (ca. 1805-1830)
Terrot & Fazy (ca. 1767-1775)
Terrot, Philippe (Geneva, ca. 1732)
Terroux (ca. 1776)
Theed & Pikett (ca. 1750)
Thierry, J. (London, ca. 1760)
Thierry, Niel (ca. 1810)
Thiout, Antoine (Paris, 1724-1760)
Tobias & Co. M.I. (England) 1805-68 (Michael Isac)
Tobias large family very active in exporting watches
Thomlinson, George (England) 1675
Thorne, Robert (London, 1850)
Thoroton, James (London, 1860)
Thuret, Jacques (Paris, ca. 1695)
Thomason J. N. (Edinburgh), ca.1830
Timing & Repeating W. Co. (Geneva, 1900)
Tompion, Thomas (English, 1671-1715)
Tonkin, Tho. (London, ca. 1760)
Torin, Daniel (England) 1750
Toutaia, Henri (French, 1650) (enamel)
Toutin, Jean (enamel) (Blois, Fr., ca. 1630)
Treffler, Sebastain (ca. 1750)
Tregent, J. (English, 1765-1800)
Truitte, Louis & Mourier (Geneva, ca. 1780)
Tupman (England) 1828
Tyrer, Thomas (London, ca. 1782)
Uhren Fabrik Union (Glashutte, 1893-1970)
Uliman, J. & Co. (Swiss, 1893)
Ulrich, Johann (London, 1820-1870)
Upjohn, W. J. (London, 1815-1824)
Vacheron, Abraham Girod (German, 1760-1843)
Valere (Paris, 1860)

Vallier, Jean (Lyons, Fr., ca. 1630)
Valove, James (London, ca. 1740)
Vanbroff, James (Germany, ca. 1600)
Van Ceule, J. (ca. 1799-1725)
Vandersteen (ca. 1725)
Vaucher, C. H. (Geneva, ca. 1835)
Vaucher, Daniel (Paris, 1767-1790)
Vaucher, Freres (Swiss, 1850)
Vauquer, Robert (French, ca. 1650) (enamel)
Veigneur, F. I. (ca. 1780)
Verdiere A. (Paris), ca. 1810
Vernod, Henriette (Paris, ca. 1790)
Vigne, James (London, ca. 1770)
Viner (England) 1834
Vrard, L., & Co. (Pekin, 1860-1872)
Vulliamy, Justin (London, ca. 1830-1854)
Vully, Jaques (ca. 1890-1900)
Vuolf (Swiss, ca. 1600)
Waldron, John (London, 1760)
Wales, Giles & Co. (Swiss, ca. 1870)
Walker, Allen (England) 1784
Waltrin (Paris, ca. 1820)
Webb, Benjamin (England) 1799
Weston, D. & Willis (enamel) (London, ca. 1800-1810)
Welldon, I. (England) 1731
Wichcote, Samuel (England) 1733
Widenham (England) 1824
Windmills, J. (England) 1710
Whitney, A. (Enniscorthy- S. of Dublin) Ca. 1810-1830
Whitthorne, James (Dublin, since 1725)
Willats, John (London, ca. 1860)
Williamson, Timothy (London, 1770-1790)
Wilter, John (London, ca. 1760)
Winckles, John (London, 1770-1790)
Winnerl, Joseph Thaddeus (Paris, 1829-1886)
Wins, Freres & Menu (Swiss, ca. 1787-18 10)
Wiss, G. (Geneva, ca. 1750)
Wood, William (England) 1860
Wright, Charles (London, 1760-1790)
Wright, Thomas (English, ca. 1770-1790)
Yates, Thomas (England) 1855
Young, Richard (London, 1765-1785)
Zech, Jacob (Prague, Ass. 1525-1540)
Zolling, Ferdinand (Frankfurt, Ger. ca. 1750)

Tambour style case, probably Nuremburg, Ca. 1575, hinged cover, pierced to revel engraved Roman chapter I-XII and Arabic 13-24 Center chapter, 60mm.

HALLMARKS OF ENGLAND

Hallmarks were used only on gold and silver **cases** made in England. These case marks, when interpreted, will help determine **age** of the **case** and location of the assay office. Hallmarks were used to denote information for the case only. The Maker's Mark **W. C. Co.** when interpreted is who made the **case only.**

The *London* date-marks (a single letter) used 20 letters, A-U, never using the letters W, X, Y, or Z. The letters J & I or U & V, because of their similarity in shape, were never used together within the same 20-year period. A total of four marks maybe found on English **cases**, which are:

The **CASE MAKER'S MARK** with two or more letters was used to denote the manufacturer of the case **ONLY.**
The **STANDARD MARK** was used to denote a guarantee of the quality of the metal.
The **ASSAY OFFICE MARK** (also known as the town mark) was used to denote the location of the assay office.
The **DATE LETTER MARK** was a letter of the alphabet used to denote the year in which the article was stamped.
The stamp was used on gold and silver cases by the assay office.

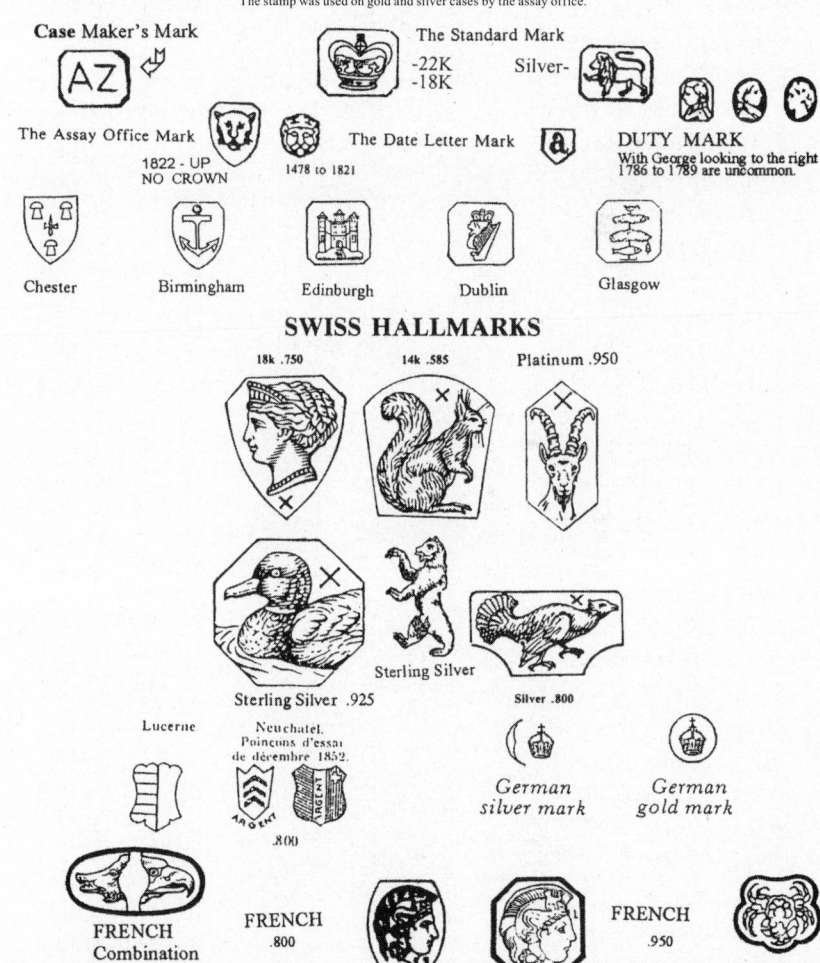

Case Maker's Mark

The Standard Mark
-22K
-18K
Silver-

The Assay Office Mark
1822 - UP
NO CROWN

The Date Letter Mark
1478 to 1821

DUTY MARK
With George looking to the right 1786 to 1789 are uncommon.

Chester   Birmingham   Edinburgh   Dublin   Glasgow

SWISS HALLMARKS

18k .750   14k .585   Platinum .950

Sterling Silver

Sterling Silver .925   Silver .800

Lucerne   Neuchâtel. Poinçons d'essai de décembre 1852.

German silver mark   German gold mark

.800

FRENCH Combination Silver & Gold   FRENCH .800   FRENCH .950

TROY WEIGHT =24 grains=1 dwt., 1 Grain= 0.0648 grams, 31.1 grams=1 Troy oz. 20dwt = 1 OZ., 12oz = 1 LB.
NOTE: Gold & Silver Standards vary from Country to Country. U.S.A. Coin Gold =.900 or 21 3/5K, Silver Coin=.900.
Gold Standards: 24K=1,000% or 1.0, 23K=.958 1/3, 22K=.916 2/3, 21K=.875, 20K=.833 1/3, 19K=.791 2/3, 18K=.750, 17K=.708 1/3, 16K=.666 2/3, 15K=.625, 14K=.583 1/3, 13K=.541 2/3, 12K=.500, 11=.458 1/3, 10K=.416 2/3, 9K=.375. 8K=.333 1/3, 7K=.291 2/3, 6K=.250, 5K=.208 1/3, 4K=.166 2/3, 3K=.125, 2K=.083 1/3, 1K=.0416 2/3.

 LONDON DATE LETTER MARKS

Year	Year	Year	Year	Year	Year	Year	Year	Year
1551	1589	1627	1666	1709	1752	1797	1841	1884
1552	1590	1628	1667	1710	1753	1798	1842	1885
1553	1591	1629	1668	1711	1754	1799	1843	1886
1554	1592	1630	1669	1712	1755	1800	1844	1887
1555	1593	1631	1670	1713	1756	1801	1845	1888
1556	1594	1632	1671	1714	1757	1802	1846	1889
1557	1595	1633	1672	1715	1758	1803	1847	1890
1558	1596	1634	1673	1716	1759	1804	1848	1891
1559	1597	1635	1674	1717	1760	1805	1849	1892
1560	1598	1636	1675	1718	1761	1806	1850	1893
1561	1599	1637	1676	1719	1762	1807	1851	1894
1562	1600	1638	1677	1720	1763	1808	1852	1895
1563	1601	1639	1678	1721	1764	1809	1853	1896
1564	1602	1640	1679	1722	1765	1810	1854	1897
1565	1603	1641	1680	1723	1766	1811	1855	1898
1566	1604	1642	1681	1724	1767	1812	1856	1899
1567	1605	1643	1682	1725	1768	1813	1857	1900
1568	1606	1644	1683	1726	1769	1814	1858	1901
1569	1607	1645	1684	1727	1770	1815	1859	1902
1570	1608	1646	1685	1728	1771	1816	1860	1903
1571	1609	1647	1686	1729	1772	1817	1861	1904
1572	1610	1648	1687	1730	1773	1818	1862	1905
1573	1611	1649	1688	1731	1774	1819	1863	1906
1574	1612	1650	1689	1732	1775	1820	1864	1907
1575	1613	1651	1690	1733	1776	1821	1865	1908
1576	1614	1652	1691	1734	1777	1822	1866	1909
1577	1615	1653	1692	1735	1778	1823	1867	1910
1578	1616	1654	1693	1736	1779	1824	1868	1911
1579	1617	1655	1694	1737	1780	1825	1869	1912
1580	1618	1656	1695	1738	1781	1826	1870	1913
1581	1619	1657	1696	1739	1782	1827	1871	1914
1582	1620	1658	1697	1739	1783	1828	1872	1915
1583	1621	1659	1698	1740	1784	1829	1873	1916
1584	1622	1660	1699	1741	1785	1830	1874	1917
1585	1623	1661	1700	1742	1786	1831	1875	1918
1586	1624	1662	1701	1743	1787	1832	1876	1919
1587	1625	1663	1702	1744	1788	1833	1877	1920
1588	1626	1664	1703	1745	1789	1834	1878	1921
		1665	1704	1746	1790	1835	1879	1922
			1705	1747	1791	1836	1880	1923
			1706	1748	1792	1837	1881	1924
			1707	1749	1793	1838	1882	1925
			1708	1750	1794	1839	1883	1926
				1751	1795	1840		
					1796			

DATE LETTER MARKS FOR
BIRMINGHAM & CHESTER

BIRMINGHAM ASSAY OFFICE DATE LETTERS

A 1773	a 1798	A 1824	A 1849	a 1875
B 1774	b 1799	S 1825	B 1850	b 1876
C 1775	C 1800	C 1826	C 1851	c 1877
D 1776	d 1801	D 1827	D 1852	d 1878
E 1777	e 1802	E 1828	E 1853	e 1879
F 1778	f 1803	F 1829	F 1854	f 1880
G 1779	g 1804	G 1830	G 1855	g 1881
H 1780	h 1805	h 1831	H 1856	h 1882
I 1781	i 1806	J 1832	I 1857	i 1883
K 1782	J 1807	R 1833	J 1858	k 1884
L 1783	k 1808	U 1834	K 1859	l 1885
M 1784	l 1809	M 1835	L 1860	m 1886
N 1785	m 1810	A 1836	M 1861	n 1887
O 1786	n 1811	A 1837	N 1862	o 1888
P 1787	o 1812	P 1838	O 1863	p 1889
Q 1788	p 1813	Q 1839	P 1864	q 1890
R 1789	q 1814	R 1840	Q 1865	r 1891
S 1790	r 1815	S 1841	R 1866	s 1892
T 1791	s 1816	T 1842	S 1867	t 1893
U 1792	t 1817	U 1843	T 1868	u 1894
V 1793	u 1818	W 1844	U 1869	v 1895
W 1794	v 1819	W 1845	V 1870	w 1896
X 1795	w 1820	V 1846	W 1871	x 1897
Y 1796	X 1821	Y 1847	X 1872	y 1898
Z 1797	Y 1822	Z 1848	Y 1873	z 1899
	Z 1823		Z 1874	

CHESTER ASSAY OFFICE DATE LETTERS

A 1701	a 1726	a 1751	a 1776	A 1797	A 1818	A 1839	a 1864
B 1702	b 1727	b 1752	b 1777	B 1798	B 1819	B 1840	b 1865
C 1703	c 1728	c 1753	c 1778	C 1799	C 1820	C 1841	c 1866
D 1704	d 1729	d 1754	d 1779	D 1800	D 1821	D 1842	d 1867
E 1705	e 1730	e 1755	e 1780	E 1801	E 1822	E 1843	e 1868
F 1706	f 1731	f 1756	f 1781	F 1802	F 1823	F 1844	f 1869
G 1707	g 1732	G 1757	G 1782	G 1803	G 1824	G 1845	g 1870
H 1708	h 1733	h 1758	h 1783	H 1804	G 1825	h 1846	h 1871
I 1709	i 1734	i 1759	i 1784	I 1805	H 1826	I 1847	i 1872
K 1710	k 1735	k 1760	k 1785	K 1806	I 1827	K 1848	k 1873
L 1711	l 1736	l 1761	l 1786	L 1807	K 1828	L 1849	l 1874
M 1712	m 1737	m 1762	m 1787	M 1808	L 1829	M 1850	m 1875
N 1713	n 1738	n 1763	n 1788	N 1809	M 1830	N 1851	n 1876
O 1714	o 1739	o 1764	O 1789	O 1810	N 1831	O 1852	o 1877
P 1715	p 1740	P 1765	B 1790	P 1811	O 1832	P 1853	p 1878
Q 1716	q 1741	Q 1766	q 1791	Q 1812	P 1833	Q 1854	q 1879
R 1717	r 1742	R 1767	r 1792	R 1813	Q 1834	R 1855	r 1880
S 1718	s 1743	S 1768	S 1793	S 1814	R 1835	S 1856	s 1881
T 1719	t 1744	T 1769	t 1794	T 1815	S 1836	T 1857	t 1882
U 1720	u 1745	U 1770	u 1795	U 1816	T 1837	U 1858	u 1883
V 1721	v 1746	U 1771	V 1796	V 1817	U 1838	V 1859	A 1884
W 1722	w 1747	V 1772				W 1860	B 1885
X 1723	X 1748	W 1773				T 1861	C 1886
Y 1724	W 1749	X 1774				W 1862	D 1887
Z 1725	W 1750	Y 1775				Z 1863	E 1888
							F 1889

The following will explain the French days of the week abbreviations, Sunday = **DIM** (Dimanche), Monday = **LUN** (Lundi), Tuesday = **MAR** (Mardi), Wednesday = **MER** (Mercedi), Thursday = **JEU** (Jeudi), Friday = **VEN** (Vendredi), Saturday = **SAM** (Samedi).

English Watch-Making Evolution

In about 1675-80 the watch trade divided into two segments. (1.) **99%** of Ebauche or rough movements were made at Prescot in Lancashire. (2.) These rough movements were then sold to finishers (watchmakers) in London, Liverpool, Coventry also to **America** and **Ireland**. This style of manufacturing of the movements, made the different components not interchangeable. By 1780 they were producing about 200,000 rough movements per year. This type of system, the quality of the watch depends on the watchmaker thus his reputation helped to determine the price of the finished product.

By mid 1870s watchmaking changed to factory-made watches. Larger volumes of watches were made and to dispose of their product. There were wholesalers who dealt with the retail trade. It is common to find identical retail watches from such firms as English Watch Co. (1874-95), William Ehrhardt (1874-1924), Rotherham & Sons (1880-1930), P. & A. Guye (1880 - 1900), Nicole, Nielsen & Co. (1887 - 1914), Lancashire Watch Co. (1888 - 1910), Coventry Watch Movement Co. (1892-1914), J. W. Benson (1892-1941) and H. Williamson (1897-1931). Below are some of the trademarks for identification of the factory-maker.

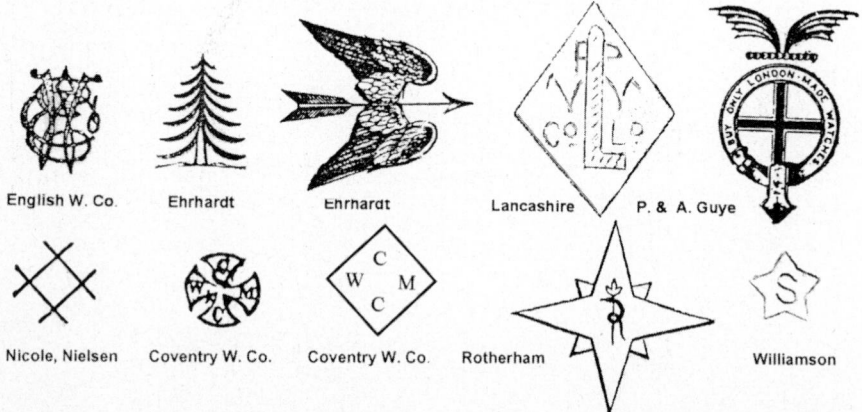

In 1812 Edward Massey invented a form of detached escapement. The Massey styles of escapement became popular and widely used. They became known as Massey style or type levers 1, 2, 3, 4, & 5. Below are some illustrations of the right angle lever with different forms of the impulse pin.

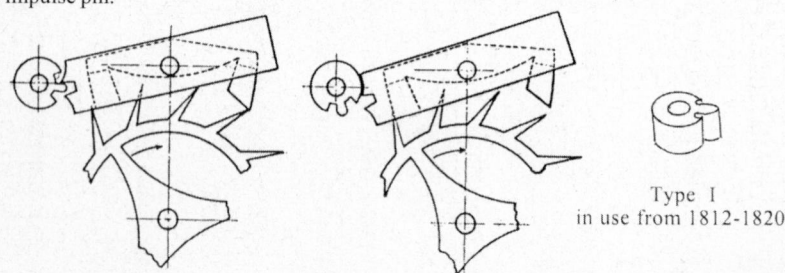

Original **Massey** (type 1) one tooth pinion (on balance staff) & the impulse slot at one end of lever.

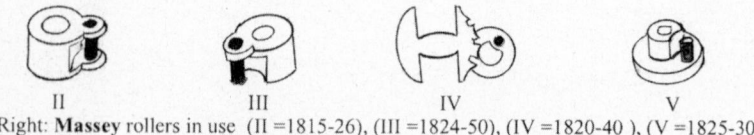

Left to Right: **Massey** rollers in use (II =1815-26), (III =1824-50), (IV =1820-40), (V =1825-30)

Note: Prior to 1870 English Watch-Making the rough movements were **99%** produced in the **Prescot** area then finished in London, Liverpool, & etc.

REPEATING WATCHES

Repeaters are those watches with an attachment added that will sound the time at the wish of the user. The repeating mechanism is operated by either a slide, plunger, or button in the case of the watch. There are basically five types of repeating mechanisms, some more common than others:

(1). **QUARTER REPEATERS**— The quarter repeater strikes the previous hour and quarter hour. In the older watches, usually verge, the striking is on a single bell attached to the inside of the case and the hour and quarter striking uses the same tone. There is first a series of hammer blows on the bell to indicate the hours, followed, after a short pause, by up to three twin strikes to denote the number of quarters elapsed. In later watches the striking is on wire gongs attached to the movement itself. The hours are struck on a single deep gong and the quarters on a higher-pitched gong followed by the deeper gong, producing a "ting-tang" sound.

(2). **HALF-QUARTER REPEATERS** -These strike the hours, followed by the quarters also an additional single blow to denote the passing of an additional **7 1/2** minutes. Half-quarter repeaters are mostly verge escapement and may be found on cylinder escapement watches. (uncommon)

(3). **FIVE-MINUTE REPEATERS**—These fall into two types. One system is similar to the half-quarter repeater but follows the 1/4 "ting-tang" by a single higher-pitched strike for each 5 minute interval elapsed since the last quarter. The other system strikes the hours on a deep gong and follows this with a single higher note for each 5 minute period after the hour, omitting a 1/4 striking.

(4).**MINUTE REPEATERS**— The most complicated of the repeater is similar to the 1/4 repeater with the addition of the minutes. The minute repeater strikes the last recorded hour, quarter and minutes. At 10:52; a minute repeater will strike 10 deep chimes for the hour, 3 double chimes (deep & high) producing a "ting-tang" for 3/4 hours & 7 high pitched chimes for 7 minutes (45+7=52).

Example of Split Second & Fly-Back Movement with a minute repeater, c. 1890. Note: ☐ Showing Hammer.

Example of English Clock Watch, 20 size, jeweled through hammers, minute repeater.

(5). **CLOCK WATCHES**— The clock watch is essentially a repeater with the features of a striking clock. Where as the above-mentioned repeaters are all operated by a plunger or slide which winds the repeating function and runs down after the last strike, the clock watch is wound in the same way as the going train usually with a key and is operated by the touch of a button in the case. The repeat function can be operated many times before the watch needs to be rewound. The **CLOCK** part of the name comes from the watch also striking the hours & sometimes the quarters or half hour in passing. The clock watch is easily recognizable by the two winding holes in either the case or the dial.

In addition to the five types described above, the features of striking are sometimes found with not only two but three and even four gongs, this producing a peal of notes. These repeaters are known as **"CARILLONS."**

At the other end of the scale from the carillon is the "dumb" repeater. This strikes on a block of metal in the case or on the movement and is felt rather than heard. It is said that the idea was to produce a watch that would not embarrass its owner when he wished to know when to slip away from boring company. Although the dumb repeater is less desirable for the average collector, it certainly should not be avoided— Breguet himself made dumb repeaters.

Grande Sonnerie and **Petite Sonnerie** have been used since early 1700's. The clock watch striking system at first was called *Dutch Striking* because it was used in clock making about 1665. The older system used striking on bells and struck the hours of the day. Then came the Dutch Striking which also struck the half-hour. This system later developed into a chiming function called **Grande Sonnerie** (grand strike or tone) which struck both the hour and quarter hours are struck ever 15 minutes (thus the hour is repeated every 15 minutes). The **Petite Sonnerie** limited to automatic strike of hours only.

L. Audemars 2 train Grande or Petite Sonnerie minute repeating clock watch. Note: Harked on bezel sonne & silence at 12 o'clock also Petite Sonnerie & Grande Sonmerie at 6 o'clock, Ca. 1870's.-

L. Audemars 2 train Grande or Petite Sonnerie 1/4 repeating clock watch. Note: The push button in the pendant that activate the repeating gongs, Ca. 1850.

A BIT OF HISTORY

Now that we have seen what repeaters are supposed to do, it might be in order to look briefly at their origins. Before the days of electric light, it was a major project to tell the time at night, since striking a tinderbox was said to have taken up to fifteen minutes to accomplish. Clocks, of course, had striking mechanisms, but they tended to keep the occupants of the house awake listening for the next strike. The repeating addition to the clock meant that the master of the house could silence the passing strike at night and, at his whim, simply pull a cord over his bed to activate the striking in another part of the house and thus waking everyone. To silence those members of the household who did not appreciate a clock booming out in the early hours of the morning, the horologists of the day turned their thoughts to the idea of a repeating watch.

The first mention of repeating watches is in the contest between Daniel Quare (1649-1724) and the Rev. Edward Barlow (1639-1719) to miniaturize the repeating action of a clock. Barlow, who for some reason had changed his name from Booth, was a theoretical horologist of outstanding ability. Barlow's design made for him by Thomas Tompion and Quare's watch were both submitted to King James II and the Privy Council for a decision as to whom should be granted a patent. The King chose Quare's design because the repeating mechanism was operated by a single push-button, whereas Barlow's required two. Quare was granted a patent in 1687. Barlow had his share of fame earlier with the invention of rack-striking for clocks in 1676.

Quare went into production with his new repeater watches, but changed the design to replace the push-button in the case with a pendant that could be pushed in. The first of these watches showed a fault that is still found on the cheaper repeaters of this century — that is, if the pendant was not pushed fully in, then the incorrect hours were struck. To overcome this problem, he invented the so-called "all-or-nothing" piece. This is a mechanism whereby if the pendant was not pushed fully home, then the watch would not strike at all.

The half-quarter appeared shortly after the all-or-nothing piece, around 1710 the five-minute repeater was on the market. Some five years after this, a "deaf-piece" was often fitted to the watch. This was a slide or pin fitted to the case when activated, caused the hammers to be lifted away from the bell and had the same effect as a dumb repeater.

Sometime around 1730, Joseph Graham decided to dispense with the idea of a bell and arranged for the hammers to strike a dust-cover, thus making the watch slimmer and preventing dust from entering the pierced case.

About the middle of the century, the French master Le Roy carried the idea a stage further and dispensed with both bells and dust covers, and used a metal block which revolutionized the thickness of the repeating watch and introduced the dumb repeater. Breguet used wire gongs around 1789 and the pattern for the modern repeater was set. The minute repeater came into more common use after 1800, and earlier examples are definitely very rare, although it is known that Thomas Mudge made a complicated watch incorporating minute repeating for Ferdinand VI of Spain about 1750.

By the last quarter of the 1700s, Switzerland had gone for the repeater in a big way and the center of fine craftsmanship for complicated watches was in the Vallee de Joux. Here the principle of division of labor was highly refined and whole families were hard at work producing parts for repeating and musical watches. Since one person concentrated only on one part of the watch, it is hardly surprising that parts of excellent quality were turned out. The basic movements were then sold to watchmakers/finishers all over the Continent and even to England, where the principle of one man, one watch, among the stubborn majority eventually led to the downfall of what had once been the greatest watchmaking nation in history. Minute repeaters first appeared about 1830.

The greatest popularity of the repeater came, however, in the last quarter of the 1800s, when Switzerland turned them out in the tens of thousands. Although there were many different names on the dials of the watches, most seem to have been produced by the company "Le Phare" and only finished by the name on the dial. The production of repeaters in quantity seems to have ground to a finish around 1921 due to (a) the invention of luminous dials and universal electric or gas lighting, and (b) a lack of watchmakers willing to learn the highly demanding skills. The interest in horology over the past decade has, however, revived the idea of the repeater and several companies in Switzerland are now producing limited editions of expensive models.

BUYING A REPEATER

Since so many repeaters seem to have been repaired at some time in the past by incompetent watchmakers, it is often too expensive a purchase if the buyer does not know what he is doing. **Important: only SET hands clockwise.**

Rule One should be: if it does not work perfectly, avoid it like the plague unless a competent repairer first gives you an estimate which suits your pocket. All too often in the past the repairer was under the impression that metal grows with age and he has filed the teeth of a rack in order to get the full striking to work again. When it dawned on him that the problem was a worn bearing, the tooth was stretched with a punch and refiled, making it weak. It was then goodbye to a fine piece of craftsmanship. **Important only: SET hands clockwise.**

A better quality repeater is usually one which is "jeweled to the hammers." This simply means that the hammers have jeweled bearings which can be seen by searching the movement for the hammers, locating the pivots around which they swing, and looking for the jeweled bearing in which they sit.

All repeaters have some system for regulating the speed of the repeating train. On the older fusee types, there was usually a rather primitive arrangement of a pinion in an eccentric bushing which could be turned to increase or decrease the depth of engagement of the pinion with the next wheel. Another system, a little better, uses an anchor and a toothed wheel as in an alarm clock. This system is usually located under the dial but can be detected by the buzzing sound it makes when the train is operated. The far superior system is the centrifugal governor that can be seen whizzing around in the top plate of the watch when the repeating action is operated. On the whole, the watch with the centrifugal governor is more desirable, although it must be mentioned that the Swiss turned out some inferior watches with this system.

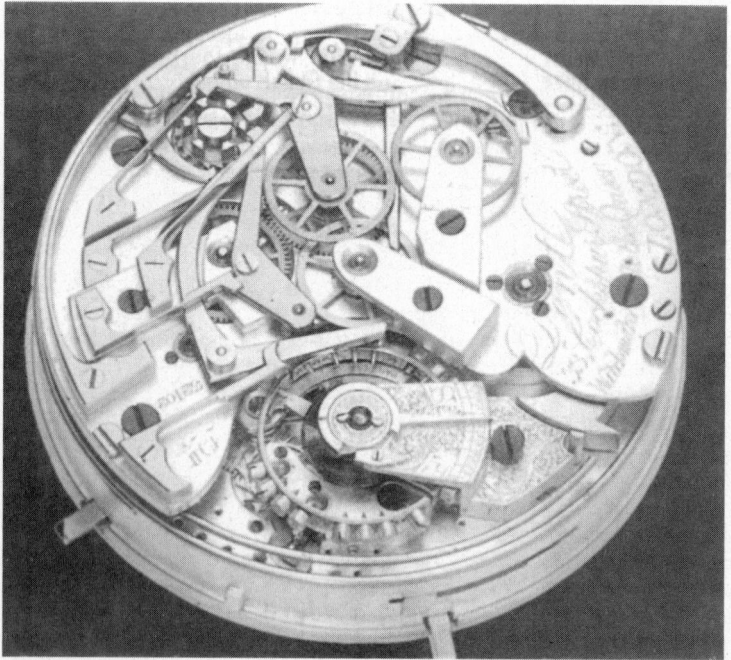

Minute repeating movement by Dent of London. Minute repeating on two gongs and slide activated. Also note the watch has a split second chronograph, Ca. early 1900s.
IMPORTANT NOTE: If possible & it should be possible if you are investing a lot of money have a watchmaker check it.

Test the watch by operating the repeating train over a full hour, seeing that the quarters and minutes function correctly, then test each individual hour. Finally, set the hands to just before 1 o'clock (about 12:45) and test the striking. Any defect due to dirt or worn bearings will show up by the final blow(s), being either sluggish or not striking at all. If there is incorrect striking, have an expert look at it before you buy. **Important: only set hands clockwise.**

Try a partial operation of the slide or push-piece. If the watch has an all-or-nothing piece (as a reasonable grade movement should have), then the watch will not strike. Partial striking indicates either a low grade watch or a non-functioning all-or-nothing piece.

Note: Additional features such as chronograph functions, calendar, moon phase, etc., and will obviously affect the price of the watch.

Important note: Remember Rule One, if any function does not work, **BUYER BEWARE!**

   🖋 The earth's orbit around the sun is 365 days, 5 hours, 48 minutes and 45.967685 seconds.

TOURBILLON

Breguet invented the tourbillon in 1795. A tourbillon is a device designed to reduce the position errors of a watch. This device has the escape wheel, lever and balance wheel all mounted in a carriage of light frameworks. The **carriage** turns 360 degrees at regular intervals (usually once per minute). The fourth wheel is fixed and is concentric with the carriage pinion and arbor. The escape wheel pinion meshes with the fourth wheel and will **rotate** around the fixed fourth wheel in the manner of a satellite. The escape wheel and lever are mounted on the carriage, and the third wheel drives the carriage pinion, turning the carriage once every minute. This rotation of the escapement will help reduce the position errors of a watch. One of the major objections is that the carriage and escapement weight mass must be stopped and started at each release of the escapement. The tourbillon design requires extreme skill to produce and is usually found on watches of high quality. Somewhat similar to the tourbillon is the *karrusel*, except it rotates about once per hour and the fourth wheel is not fixed. The escape pinion in a karrusel watch is driven in the normal manner by the fourth wheel.

Charles Frodsham, TOURBILLON escapement, minute repeating, split second chronograph, about 600 to 700 tourbillons are known to exist. About 85% of the English tourbillon movements were made by Albert Pellaton, Favre and Nicole Nielson & C. as in this watch. The TOURBILLON escapement, is located near the top of this movement.

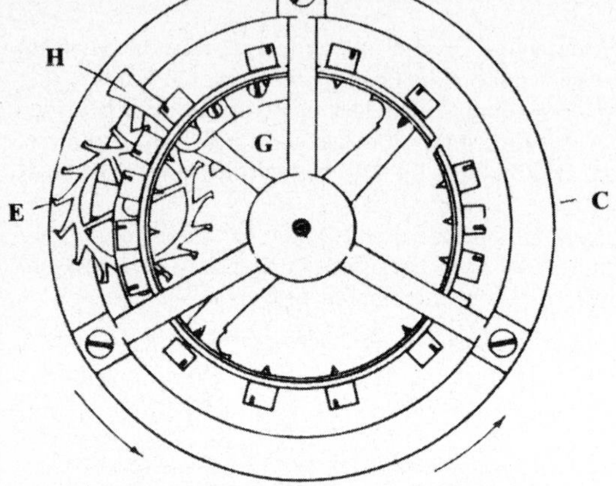

464

Tourbillon

A. Fixed fourth wheel
B. Third wheel
C. Carriage (one revolution per minute)
D. Carriage pinion
E. Escape Wheel & pinion
F. Arbor for seconds hand
G. Escape cock
H. Lever & pallets

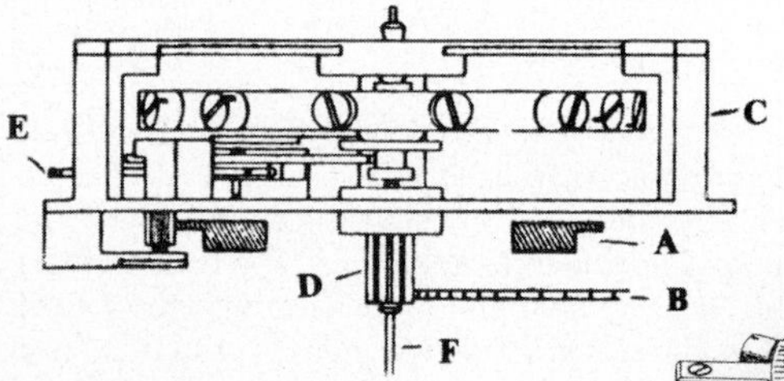

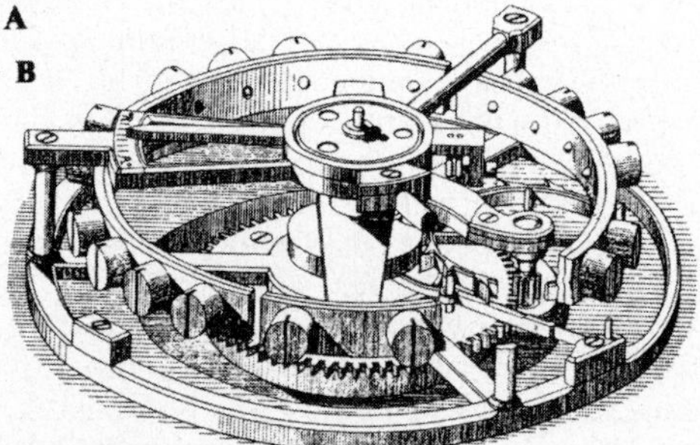

Right:
One minute Tourbillon
Chronometer Escapement
with Spring Detent

MUSICAL WATCHES
(Three basic types)

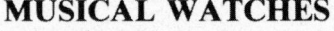

Stacked Tooth

**Disc Type with
individual teeth**

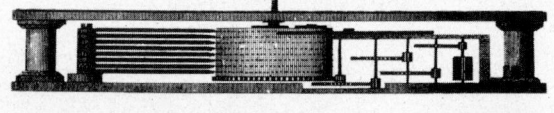

Pinned Cylinder & Comb

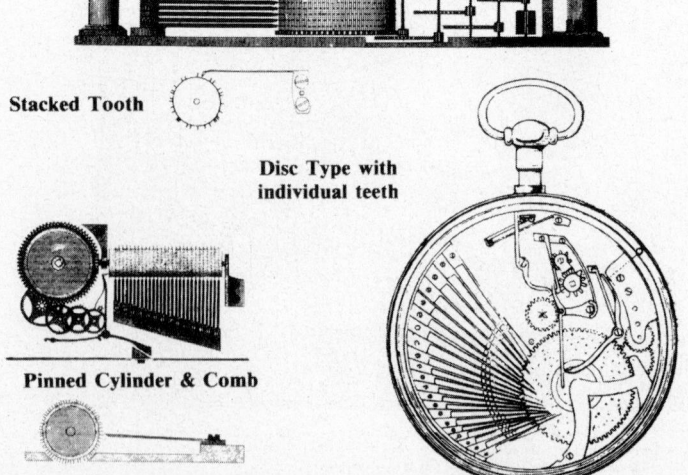

The *watch* has two *distinct* frames, one of which takes all parts but the escapement, the other taking the escapement. The *escapement frame* is made to *revolve* in the main frame at a uniform rate of about once per hour. The position of the escapement frame's bearing in the main frame is the same as that of the fourth wheel,—the axle of the escapement frame being large and having a hole through it of such a size that it admits the fourth pinion through freely, in order that the fourth wheel can run in its own jewelled holes without *interference*. The fourth wheel, C, will be seen inside the *escapement frame*, while the pinion of the fourth wheel A goes outside, so as to be *geared with* and *driven by* the 3rd wheel H.

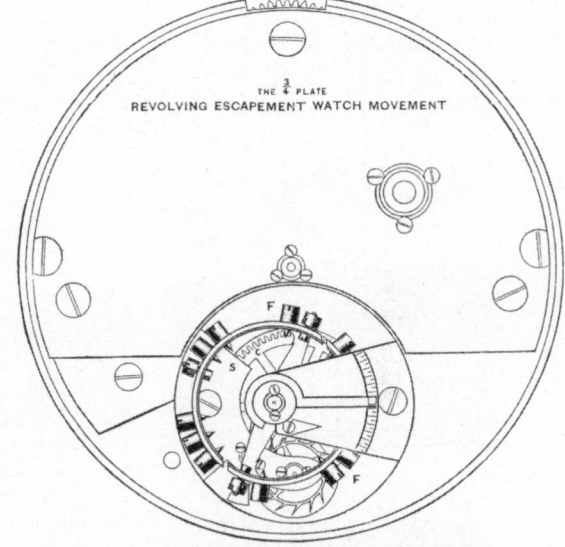

THE ¾ PLATE
REVOLVING ESCAPEMENT WATCH MOVEMENT

F F B B is the *bed-plate* of the escapement frame: B B being its axle; F F B B is turned out of *one piece*; B B goes through a hole in the main frame, and to the end of B B is screwed the wheel D D, making this wheel *practically* one with F F B B.

Now as D D has teeth upon it and is just large enough to make a correct gearing with G, the third pinion, it follows that as the *third* pinion turns round it will take the wheel D D with it, and thus the *whole escapement* must go round for D D is fixed to the axle of the escapement frame.

All will now be plain on merely naming the parts in the illustration, which are as follows :—

P P is the pillar plate.

H and G are third wheel and pinion respectively.

M is the bar under dial.

L is the third wheel top cock.

D D is the wheel fixed to B B, and driven by G.

F F B B bed-plate of the escapement frame.

K is the fourth top cock which also takes bottom balance pivot.

S is the escape-cock, the escapement is left out of the illustration.

E the balance.

N the balance cock.

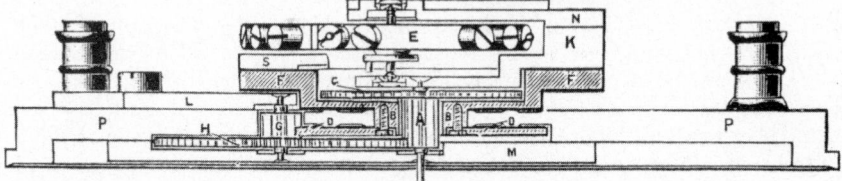

Above 1895-98 AD

The karrusel rotates slower than a tourbillon but the object is the same to average errors in the vertical position. A tourbillon uses a carriage which forms part of the train, in a karrusel the escapement is mounted on a revolving platform like a carousel, which is driven separately by the train. A tourbillon has a fixed fourth wheel and a karrusel does not have a fixed wheel. Other watch makers used ebauche movements made by Bonniksen. (Bonniksens' Karrusel invented in **1894**)

Where Watches Are Born

A trip to *"Where Watches Are Born,"* is recommended. In this area persists a strong cottage industry where in every small village and almost every street corner, a famous watch-maker or watch factory was born, and after this modern age of electronic and quartz watches still some survive. This area is the Jura Mountain chain which borders the French & Swiss countryside.

A micro-techniques route may start at Montbeliard, France and go south to Geneva Switzerland. This micro-techniques route adjacent to the French & Swiss borders should include Factories, Museums, Workshops, and *Antique watch shops galore*. In Besancon, France its Fine Arts Museum with a collection that includes the LeRoy watch that has 25 indicators in addition to the time, also the Museum of Time. This is also home of the Lip watch factory. Next to Beaucourt, France to see the Frederic Japy Museum. Japy, a very productive maker which at one time produced 3,500 Ebauches a month. On to Valdahon and Morteau (Villers-le-Lac) and visit the Museum of Clock and Watch Making (Musee de Horlogerie du Haut-Doubs). Next LeLocle, Switzerland, home of Cyma, Ulysse Nardin, Tissot and Zenith also see the Watch Museum of the Chateau des Monts. Then La Chaux-de-Fonds home of Corum, Ebel, Girard-Perregaux and many more watch factories. Also visit the International Museum of Horology with a wealth of items also near by Antique Watch & Clock shops. In Neuchatel the Art Museum with the Jaquet Droz collection of mechanical dolls. Now go North to the area of Solothurn , Grenchen & Biel (Bienne) where the Rolex, Omega movement factory and many more as Mido, Urban Jurgensen, Swatch, Breitling, Movado and ETA factory. Further south the Vallee de Joux to see watch factories as Jaeger-LeCoultre, also smaller watchmakers as Daniel Roth & Philippe Dufour in LeSentier. Near by Le Brassus to see Audemars Piguet, Blancpain, and Breguet. On south to Geneva home of Patek Philippe, Rolex, Vacheron Constantin and many more also the see the Patek Philippe Museum in Geneva. You may wish to start in Geneva and reverse the above trip. The *Basel Watch Fair* is usually in the Spring.

NOTE: **Nick Lerescu of Advantage Tours** has a Horological tour & seminar each year in late Spring or early Summer. *ADVANTAGE TOURS - P.O. BOX 401 - Glenwood, NJ 07418* or call Nick at 1-800-262-4284. Ask about the next trip for the **<u>TIME TRIPPER</u>**

EUROPEAN POCKET WATCH LISTINGS
(Complete Watches Only)

The prices shown in this book are averaged from dealers listings, catalog sales, auction results, trade shows and internet transactions. Each entry is followed by three prices: A, B and C. The three levels represent watches as follows:

A   B   C

A - **An approximate dealer buying price, ABP, for a watch which is running and complete.** (ABP)

B - **A dealer selling price for a watch, fully restored, good case and dial.** (Ex-Fn)

C - **A dealer selling price for a mint condition watch, all original.** (Mint)

Variations can take place in the pricing structure due to several factors. The cost of restoration, for example, can be quite high and some lower level watches may not warrant the restoration cost. Also, complicated watches such as repeaters, chronographs, etc., as well as early watches, especially verge and other early escapements, can also be very costly to restore. Therefore, the variations in the A level price and the C level price can vary widely if the restoration costs are excessive. The availability of parts for certain vintage and antique watches is becoming more endangered as every year passes. Some watches are simply not restorable do to this parts dilemma. The ease of sale for certain type of watches will aslo have an effect on pricing at a dealers or wholesale level. Certain watches are simply more in demand and can be sold at a quicker rate to eager collectors. Watches which are slow to sell must be held in inventory; therefore, the A level prices will be lower to offset the inventory holding cost. All watches can bring significantly higher prices when the condition is outstanding. Watches which are in virtually new condition with pristine original dials, original boxes, certificates or bills of sale (especially rare wrist watches) will often bring record price levels above the top indicator listed in this publication.

᷎ Descriptions and serial number ranges listed for early watches cannot be considered 100 percent accurate due to the manner in which records were kept by these companies. Watches were not necessarily sold in the exact order of manufactured date.

Important Notice. All of the information, including valuations, in this book has been compiled from the most reliable sources, and every effort has been made to eliminate errors and questionable data. Nevertheless, the possibility of error, in a work of such immense scope, always exists. The publisher or authors will not be held responsible for losses which may occur in the purchase, sale, statements of its advertisers, or other transaction of items, because of information contained herein. Readers who feel they have discovered errors are invited to write and inform the publishers, so that they may be corrected in subsequent editions.

᷎ WATCH terminology or communication in this book has evolved over the years, in search of better and more precise language with a effort to improve, purify, adjust itself and make it easier to understand

468

AGASSIZ (Swiss)

Auguste Agassiz of Saint Imier & Geneva started manufacturing quality watches in 1832. They later became interested in making a flat style watch which proved to be very popular. The company was inherited by Ernest Francillion who built a factory called **Longines.**

+**Agassiz**, 45mm or about 16 size, adjusted ca. 1885.　　　**Agassiz**, 45mm or about 16 size, ca. 1865.

TYPE - Description	ABP	Ex-Fn	Mint
Early, KW KS, Swiss bar Mvt., time only, Ca.1870, Silver case	$85	$100	$150
Time only, gold, 25-38mm, OF	175	225	300
HC	200	300	400
Time only, gold, 45-50mm, OF..............................	225	300	400
HC	250	400	500
Time only, gold & **enamel,** 45- 50mm, OF	400	650	1,000
HC	475	700	1,200
Cole's Resilient Escapement, 20J, gold, 45mm, Of.............	600	800	1,300
8 day, 21J, wind indicator, **18K gold,** 44mm, OF	1,000	1,500	2,000
14K gold, OF.......................................	600	1,200	1,500
S. S. case, OF......................................	350	600	1,000

Agassiz, Time only, gold & enamel, 45- 50mm, OF

Agassiz, 40mm, 21 jewels, 8 day with wind indicator.

Agassiz, $20 gold 22 / 18K coin watch, ca. 1950s.   Agassiz, 43mm, 17 jewels, World Time, 42 cities, ca. 1940.

TYPE - Description	ABP	Ex-Fn	Mint
$20 gold 22 to **18K** coin watch, 34mm, Ca. 1950s.	$1,200	$2,500	$3,000
World Time, 42 Cities, gold, 43mm, OF	2,500	4,000	5,500
Chronograph, gold, 45-50mm, register, OF	475	700	1,000
HC	675	1,000	1,500
Split second chronograph, register, gold, OF	700	1,500	2,000
HC	850	1,800	2,500
1/4 hr. repeater, gold, 46-52mm, OF	850	1,500	2,000
HC	1,200	2,000	2,500
Minute repeater, gold, 46-52mm, OF.	1,500	3,000	3,500
HC	2,000	3,500	4,500
Minute repeater, w/chrono., gold, 46-52mm, OF	2,200	3,500	4,500
HC	2,400	4,500	5,000
Minute repeater, Split sec. chrono & register, gold, 46-52mm, OF	3,000	8,000	9,000
HC	4,000	9,000	12,000

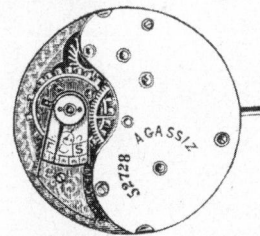

Left: *Agassiz*, 30mm or about 8 size, c. 1885

ASSMANN

Glasshute - Dresden

Julius Assmann began producing watches with the help of Adolf Lange in 1852. His watches are stylistically similar to those produced by Lange. Later on he adopted his own lever style. Assmann made highly decorative watches for the South American market that are highly regarded by some collectors.

TYPE - Description	ABP	Ex-Fn	Mint
Time only, 45- 50mm, **1st Quality**, 18K OF	$2,500	$4,000	$6,000
18K HC	3,000	5,000	8,000
Time only, 45- 50mm, **2nd Quality**, 14K OF	2,000	3,500	4,000
14K HC	2,200	4,000	5,000
Chronograph, **1st Quality**, 55mm, 18K OF	4,000	7,000	9,000
18K HC	5,000	8,000	11,000

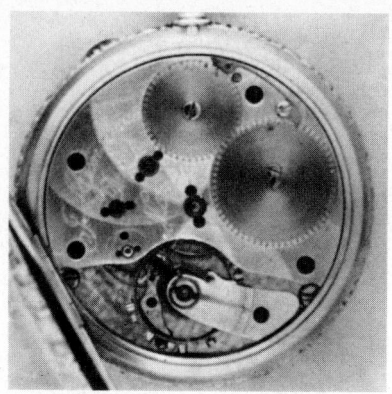

Assmann, 50mm, 19 jewels, diamond cap jewels, gold jewel settings, gold lever escapement, serial number 3,086, BRIDGE MODEL, 1st Quality, ca. 1875.

Assmann, 50mm, 19 jewels, diamond cap jewels, gold jewel settings, gold lever escapement, serial number 3,739, 1st Quality, ca. 1877.

TYPE - Description	ABP	Ex-Fn	Mint
Split second chronograph, **1st Quality,** 57mm, 18K OF	5,500	10,000	15,000
18K HC	6,200	12,000	18,000
1/4 hr. repeater, gold, 50-55mm, OF	8,000	12,000	15,000
HC	8,500	15,000	20,000
Minute repeater, gold, 50-55mm, OF	10,000	18,000	25,000
HC	12,000	20,000	30,000
Perp. moonph. cal. w/min. repeater, gold, HC	50,000	80,000	150,000
Alpina, 15J., moustache lever, Glashutte, Gold, 52mm, OF	1,000	2,000	3,000

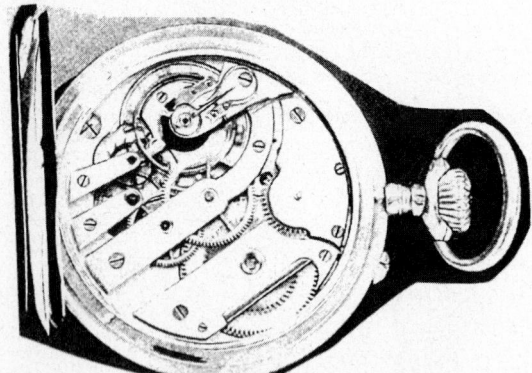

Assmann, OF, 52mm, 15 jewels, moustache lever, signed "H. Assmann Glashutte" case signed "J. Assmann Glashutte". The above movement is by ALPINA. In 1909 Alpina founded a company in Glashutte by the name "Pracisions Uhrenfabrik Alpina". Movements usefully high grade. Alpina also had factories in Geneva, Bienne, Besancon France, Glashutte.

AUDEMARS, PIGUET & CIE

Swiss

Audemars, Piguet & Cie was founded in 1875 by Jules Audemars and Edward Piguet, both successors to fine horological families. This company produced many fine high grade and complicated watches, predominantly in nickel and, with a few exceptions, fully jeweled. Their complicated watches are sought after more than the time only pocket and wrist watches.

Jules Audemars was born in Le Brassus in 1851 and trained by local master watchmakers. He began work as a "repasseur" after his apprenticeship. In 1874, he moved to Gimel and opened up a small business but he did not achieve the sucess he had hoped for. Within a short time, he moved back to Le Brassus, hoping to find a situation more fitting to his skills.

Edward Auguse Piguet was born in 1853 and received a similar eduaction as his future partner. Under the guidence of Charles Capt. he became a "repasseur".

In 1875, the two met in Le Brassus and began working together unofficially. In 1880, they moved their business to Geneva. In 1882, the name "Audemars, Piguet & Cie" was finally registered in Bern as producing movements and watch cases.

registered in Bern as producing movements and watch cases.

Jules Audemars was the technical manager while Edward Piguet was the financial specialist, This division of labor served them well for many years, working together until 1918 when Audemars died at the age of 67. Piguet died the following year. The name of Audemars Piguet became synonymous with extremely high quality, superbly thin movements and incredible complications.

PRODUCTION TOTALS

Date-	Serial #	Date-	Serial #	Date-	Serial #	Date-	Serial #	Date-	Serial #
1882 -	2,000	1905 -	9,500	1925 -	33,000	1945 -	48,000	1965 -	90,000
1890 -	4,000	1910 -	13,000	1930 -	40,000	1950 -	55,000	1970 -	115,000
1895 -	5,350	1915 -	17,000	1935 -	42,000	1955 -	65,000	1975 -	160,000
1900 -	6,500	1920 -	25,000	1940 -	44,000	1960 -	75,000	1980 -	225,000

Audemars Piguet, 40mm, about 10 size, 19 jewels, cabochon on winding stem, Platinum, OF.

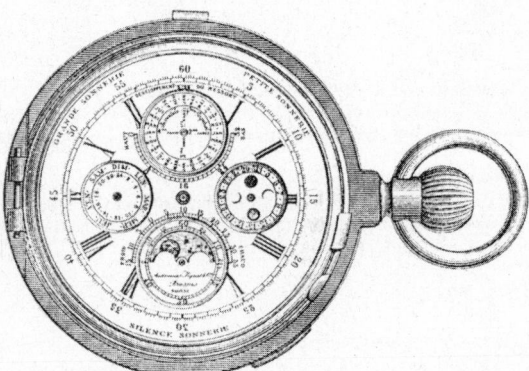

Audemars Piguet, 50mm, hunting case, Grand, Petite & Silence Sonnerie, minute repeater on demand, split-second Chronograph, Perpetual Calendar, wind indicator & thermometer, taken from a French ad, ca. 1900.

TYPE - Description	ABP	Ex-Fn	Mint
Early, KW KS, Swiss bar Mvt., time only, Ca.1870, **Gold case**	$300	$500	$600
Time only, gold, 25-38mm, OF	300	600	800
Time only, gold, 40-44mm, OF	600	1,200	1,500
HC	750	1,700	2,200
Platinum, OF	1,000	2,000	3,000
Platinum, Diamond Dial & on hands, OF	1,500	3,500	4,500
Time only, gold, 45- 50mm, OF	1,000	2,000	2,500
HC	1,200	2,500	3,200
Jumping hour w/ day-date-month, gold, 43mm., ca. 1925	3,000	5,500	7,500

Audemars Piguet, (Bras en L'Air) a push-piece on rim of watch, lifts the arms of the bronze, one points to the hour and the other points to the minutes, 44mm, 15K, OF.

Audemars Piguet, Perpetual moon phase calendar, Astronomic watch showing the moon phases, and perpetual calendar showing day, date, & month, Ca. 1920s.

AUDEMARS PIGUET, 46mm, 36 jewels, minute repeater, split-second chronograph, serial #3853, Ca.1888.

AUDEMARS PIGUET, 46mm, repeater, moon-phase, Chronograph, 18K, Ca. 1928.

TYPE - Description	ABP	Ex-Fn	Mint
Rising Arms (Bras en L'Air), 44mm, one arm points to the hours & the other to the minute, 18K, OF	$5,000	$7,000	$10,000
Chronograph, gold, 45-50mm, OF	1,500	2,500	3,500
HC	2,000	3,000	4,000
OF w/register	2,000	3,000	4,000
HC w/register	2,500	3,500	4,500
Split second chronograph, gold, 45-52mm, OF	3,500	5,000	7,000
HC	4,000	6,000	8,000
OF w/register	4,000	5,500	8,000
HC w/register	5,000	7,000	10,000
5 minute repeater, gold, 46-52mm, OF	3,000	5,000	6,000
HC	4,000	5,500	6,500
Minute repeater, gold, 46-52mm, OF	4,000	7,000	8,500
HC	5,000	8,000	10,000
OF w/chrono	4,500	6,000	7,500
HC w/chrono	5,500	9,000	12,000
OF w/chrono. & register	5,500	6,500	10,000
HC w/chrono. & register	6,000	10,000	15,000
OF w/split chrono. & register	7,000	12,000	15,000
HC w/split chrono. & register	8,000	15,000	18,000
Perpetual moonphase calendar, gold, OF	7,000	12,000	15,000
HC	8,000	14,000	18,000
Perp. moonphase cal. w/min. repeater, chronograph, gold, OF	30,000	45,000	60,000
HC	32,000	50,000	75,000
Grand & Petite Sonnerie, min. repeater, split-second Chron., Perp.Calendar, wind ind. & thermometer, 52-54mm, HC ★★★★	100,000	150,000	250,000

REPEATER IDENTIFICATION

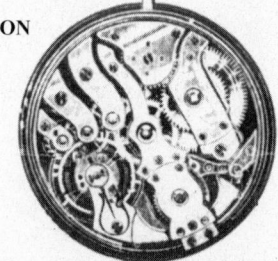

Calibre SMV   Calibre SMS

BARRAUD & LUNDS

LONDON (1750-1929)

The Barraud family (of which) there were several makers, one of them being Paul Philip Barraud. Paul was in the trade at 86 Cornhill from about 1796 to 1813. His sons John and James, traded at 41 Cornhill as Barraud & Sons from 1813 till 1838. After 1838 the firm became known as Barraud & Lunds. Circa 1885 their address was 49 Cornhill, by 1895 the firm moved to 14 Bishopsgate. Barrauds & Lunds advertised "machine-made" watches from 1880 to 1929.

TYPE - Description	ABP	Ex-Fn	Mint
Time only, gold, 45- 50mm, OF	$400	$550	$700
HC	550	700	850
Time only, gold, 45- 50mm, (**wind indicator**), OF	650	1,200	1,500
Chronograph, gold, 45-50mm, OF	800	1,200	1,500
HC	900	1,500	2,000
Split second chronograph, gold, 45-52mm, OF	1,500	2,000	2,500
HC	1,600	2,500	3,500
1/4 hr. repeater, gold, 46-52mm, OF	1,000	1,500	2,000
HC	1,200	1,700	2,200
Minute repeater, gold, 46-52mm, OF	1,800	3,500	4,500
HC	2,200	4,000	5,000
OF w/chrono	2,600	4,500	6,000
HC w/chrono	3,000	5,000	7,000
OF w/clock watch	8,000	15,000	20,000
HC w/clock watch	10,000	20,000	25,000

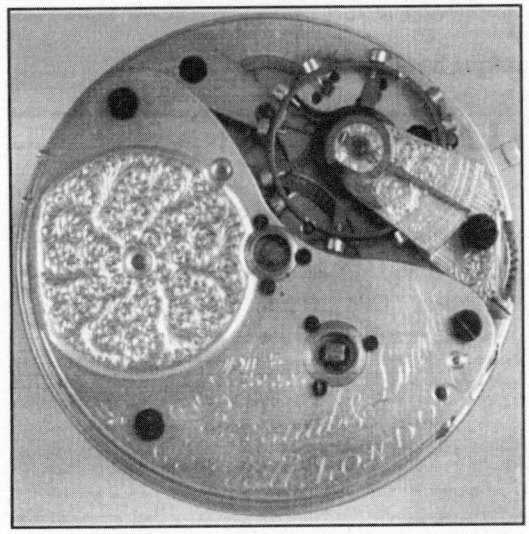

Barraud & Lunds, English lever and movement signed *"Barraud & Lunds 49 Cornhill London 3/3333",* 3/4 plate with a fusee and chain, stem wind, Note: Engraved and raised barrel. with a white enamel signed *"Barraud & Lunds-Cornhill London 3/3333",* with wind-indicator, Ca. 1886.

☞ Some models and grades are not included. Their values can be determined by comparing with similar age, size, metal content, style, models and grades listed.

BARWISE

LONDON

John Barwise a leading watchmaker born 1790 died 1843. Dealer at 29 St. Martin's Lane, and with Weston Barwise from 1820 to 1842. John Barwise was also the chairman of British Watch Co., 1842 to 1843. The firm moved back to 29 St. Martin's Lane, 1845 to 1851, and 69 Piccadilly from 1856 to 1875.

TYPE - Description	ABP	Ex-Fn	Mint
Time only, gold, 45- 50mm, OF............................	$800	$1,200	$1,400
HC..	1,000	1,400	1,800
Chronograph, gold, 45-50mm, OF...........................	1,200	1,500	2,000
HC..	1,400	1,600	2,300
7-1/2 Mm. Repeater, gold, 46-52mm, **18K**, OF............... ★	4,000	5,000	6,000
1/4 hr. repeater, gold, 46-52mm, OF	2,000	3,000	3,500
HC..	2,500	3,200	4,000
Minute repeater, gold, 46-52mm, OF.........................	3,000	4,000	4,500
HC..	3,500	5,000	6,000
Detent Chronometer, gold, 48-52mm, OF.....................	3,000	4,000	5,500
HC..	4,000	5,000	7,000

BARWISE, Rare 7-1/2 MINUTE REPEATER with ruby cylinder escapement, open face, key wind & key set, Signed BARWISE LONDON No. 5369, Ca. 1800.

COMPARISON OF WATCH CASE SIZES

U. S. A.	EUROPEAN
10-12 SIZE	40—44 MM
16 SIZE	45—49 MM
18 SIZE	50—55 MM

J. W. BENSON
LONDON (1749)

The Benson signature is found on many medium to extremely high grade gilt movements. Factory English machine-made market circa 1870-1930. "Makers to the Admiralty" & "By Warrant to H. M. the Queen" can be found signed on the movements. Named models ("Bank", "Field", "Ludgate") 16 or 14 size.

TYPE —Description	ABP	Ex-Fn	Mint
KWKS, side lever, Silver hallmarked, 48-52mm, OF, C. 1875	$125	$150	$200
SW, 15-17J, side lever, (**"Bank", "Field", "Ludgate"**)			
Silver, 49mm, C. 1870-1930	150	200	250
Gold, 49mm, C. 1870-1930	200	350	500
Fusee, lever escape., high grade, SW, **18K**, 54mm, OF, C.1875	500	800	1,000
Fusee **w/indicator**, KWKS, side lever, Silver, 54mm, OF, C.1870	450	700	900
Fusee, **w/indicator, free spring**, lever escape.,**18K**, 50mm, OF	750	1,500	2,500
Time only, gold, 45-48mm, OF	425	600	800
HC	550	900	1,200
Chronograph, gold, 45-52mm, OF	800	1,300	1,800
HC	1,100	1,500	2,000
Split second chronograph, gold, 45-52mm, OF	1,300	2,500	3,000
HC	1,500	3,000	4,000
Perpetual moonphase calendar, gold, OF	7,000	10,000	12,000
HC	9,000	12,000	15,000
Minute repeater, gold, 46-52mm, OF	3,000	4,000	5,000
HC	4,000	6,000	7,000
Minute, Clock watch, OF	10,000	15,000	20,000
Minute, Clock Watch, HC	12,000	18,000	25,000
Minute, Perpetual, Clock Watch, OF	60,000	90,000	125,000
HC	90,000	110,000	150,000
Karrusel, gold, 48-55mm, OF	4,000	6,000	8,500
Karrusel, silver, 48-55mm, OF	3,000	4,000	5,000

J. W. Benson, 13-15 jewels, 3/4 plate. "The Field, Best London Make, By Warrant to H. M. the Queen" engraved on Movement. Serial Number C8764.

J. W. Benson, 45mm, Split Second chronograph, 20 jewels, 3/4 plate, free sprung, hunting case, ca. 1890.

COMPARISON OF WATCH CASE SIZES

U. S. A.	EUROPEAN
10-12 SIZE	40—44 MM
16 SIZE	45—49 MM
18 SIZE	50—55 MM

BOREL & COURVOISIER

NEUCHATEL, SWITZERLAND

Founded in 1859 by Jules Borel & first introduced into the United States in 1860. For some of their higher grade movements they used Girard - Perregaux.

BOREL & COURVOISIER, 15J, nickel movement with counterpoised lever, HC, Ca. 1889.

TYPE - Description	ABP	Ex-Fn	Mint
Time only, KW, **SILVER**, 45- 50mm, OF	$125	$150	$200
HC	150	200	300
Time only, KW, **Gold**, 45- 50mm, OF	250	400	500
HC	300	500	600
Time only, SW, nickel, **GF**, 45- 50mm, OF	175	200	275
HC	200	250	325
Time only, SW, nickel, **Gold**, 45- 50mm, OF	325	500	600
HC	350	600	750
Captains Watch, **SILVER**, 2 hour dials, 2 trains, Key Wind,			
center seconds, 50mm, OF	500	800	1,000
(SAME AS ABOVE) HC	525	900	1,200
Captains Watch, **GOLD**, 2 hour dials, 2 trains, Key Wind,			
center seconds, 50mm, OF	900	1,700	2,000
(SAME AS ABOVE) HC	1,000	1,800	2,000
1/4 hr. repeater, **SILVER**, 46-52mm, OF	600	800	1,000
1/4 hr. repeater, **GOLD**, 46-52mm, OF	900	1,500	2,000
Detent Chronometer, gold, 48-52mm, OF	1,800	3,000	4,000
HC	2,000	3,000	4,000

BOREL & COURVOISIER, both KW movements came in 15 - 21 lignes and four grades, extra, 1st, 2nd, and 3rd quality, Ca. 1860-75.

BOVET

FRENCH & SWISS

Edouard Bovet started a company in the village of Fleurier, Switzerland circa 1818 and another firm in Besancon, France, in 1832. The Bovet firm specialized in watches for the chinese market, The Bovet Companies were purchased by Leuba Freres (Cesar & Charles). Bovet also signed watches "TEVOB" making his signature easily read by the Chinese. The new Bovet firm discontinued making watches for the Chinese market. The company was purchased by the Ullmann & Co. in 1918. **Fleurier** is a village in Switzerland with **Superior Enamel** artists.

Above: *Superior FLEURIER quality* finely painted turquoise enamel watch set in pearls, 18K, 58mm, time only, Chinese Duplex Escapement, signed **BOVET - FLEURIER,** Ca. 1835.

TYPE — Description	ABP	Ex-Fn	Mint
Time only, LEVER escapement, KW, Silver, 58mm, OF	$200	$300	$500
HC	225	400	550
Time only, DUPLEX escapement, KW, Silver, 58mm, OF.........	225	350	550
HC	250	400	600
Time only, DUPLEX escapement, KW, GOLD, 58mm, OF	700	900	1,200
HC	800	1,000	1,300
Enamel, Time only, DUPLEX, KW, **Silver/gilded,** 58mm, OF.....	1,200	4,000	5,000
HC	1,500	5,000	6,000
(below *SUPERIOR FLEURIER QUALITY* Gold & Enamel, with **Chinese Duplex**)			
Gold &Enamel, Time only, Landscape or Floral, 55- 58mm, OF ...	8,000	25,000	35,000
HC	10,000	30,000	40,000

☞ Some models and grades are not included. Their values can be determined by comparing with similar age, size, metal content, style, models and grades listed.

ABRAHAM-LOUIS BREGUET

BREGUET ET FILS
Paris

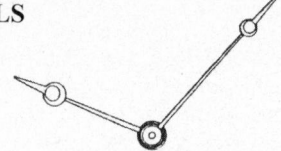

Abraham-Louis Breguet, one of the worlds most celebrated watchmakers.

Right: Breguet famous hands he called "a pomme".

Abraham-louis Breguet was born in Neuchatel Switzerland on Jan., 10, 1747. He was perhaps the greatest horologist of all time in terms of design, elegance, and innovation. He is responsible for the development of the tourbillon, the perpetual calendar, the shock-proof parachute suspension, the isochronal overcoil, and many other improvements. Abraham-Louis Breguet died on 17th day of September, 1823. It is difficult to include him in this section because of the complexity surrounding identification of his work which was frequently forged, and the fact that so many pieces produced by his shop were unique. Suffice it to say that the vast majority of watches one encounters bearing his name were either marketed only by his firm or are outright fakes made by others for the export market. Much study is required for proper identification. The first **Souscription** watch was sold in 1796. The Breguet firm continues today with the tradition started by Abraham-Louis. At first in the hands of his immediate successors and now under the guidance of the "**Swatch Group**".

The prices listed in this section give basic guidelines for Breguet watches. However, keep in mind that it is virtually impossible to give definitive values due to the many factors, including auction results, which come into play when pricing Breguet's. Auction results can be both misleading and informative at the same time. For instance, if a major watch firm wants a certain piece for their museum, a record price will likely be set. Yet, when a similiar watch is auctioned, the price may be substantially lower. Auction prices for certain Breguet's can also sky rocket if there are two or three well financed competitors wanting the same piece. Provenance, condition and certification also influence pricing. A Breguet with extract papers is always more valuable as is a watch made specifically for a historically important person.

Condition is also a key with near new watches bringing premium prices. Watches made individually by Breguet will also sell for much higher prices than those finished or made by his apprentices or other members. Breguet was also prone to redoing his watches with escapement upgrades or other variations made at a later date. These alterations can also affect value. An important Breguet must be researched fully. You should always contact a professional, reputable dealer for proper advice and insight.

A short list of terms used by Breguet. A'tact=time by touch, a'toc=dumb repeater, parachute=shock protection, pull-twist piston=a plunger in the pendant first pull out & then twisted to engage lever to repeat, jump hour hand=hour hand used a 12 tooth star to jump forward the hour hand, Souscription=made by subscription or agreement, slotted teeth=slots drilled in the escape wheel teeth to assist with oil retention, Breguet balance spring=over-coiled balance spring.

Abraham-Louis Breguet, Production Totals

Date —	Serial #	Date —	Serial #
1795 —	250	1815 —	2700
1800 —	500	1820 —	3500
1805 —	1500	1825 —	4000
1810 —	2000	1830 —	4500

The year a watch was sold may differ from the year it was **produced**.
Right: **Breguet's** Hanging Ruby Cyclinder Escapement.

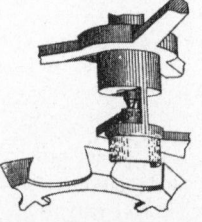
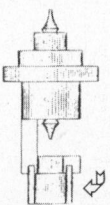

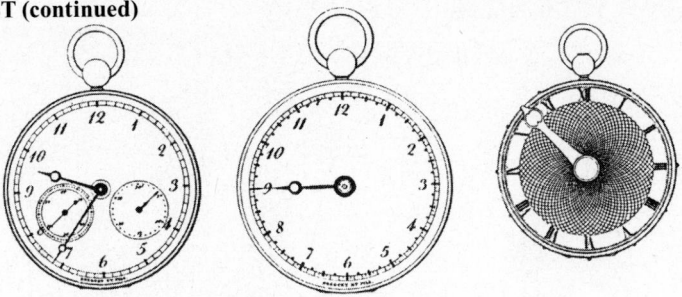

Above: Reprints (Reduced) issued by the firm Breguet Ca. 1820s.

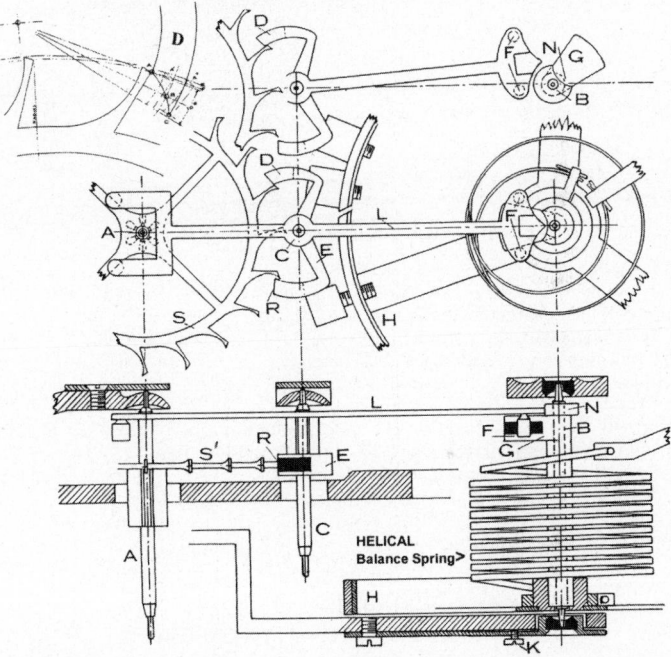

Above: Escapement by Breguet, Twenty tooth escape wheel with oil slots in each tooth, the lever **E** has circular locking and ruby pallets enclosed and pallet **R** is slightly convex and pallet **D** is concaved (see upper left), Ca. 1793. (S' note oil slot)

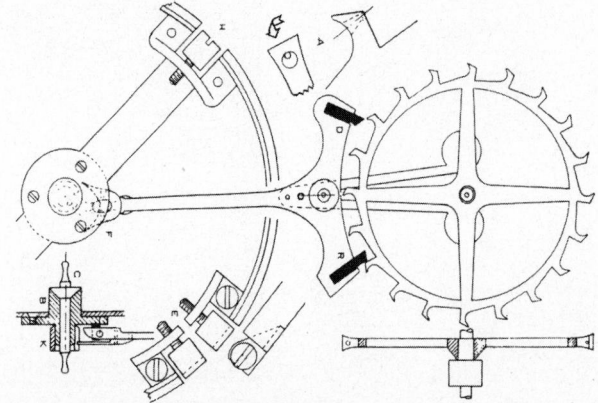

Above: Escapement by Breguet, Twenty tooth escape wheel with oil pockets in every other tooth, A=oil pockets are also in the fork of the lever where it contacts the escape wheel roller table, Ca. 1811.

60 to 62mm. Example of Breguet **SOUSCRIPTION** style face and movement. Gilt movement with central winding arbor, balance with parachute suspension, HANGING ruby cylinder escapement. White enamel dial with secret signature at 12 o'clock. **NOTE:** Winds from center either front or back, also most had a silver case and gold bezel. Total production of **SOUSCRIPTION** style watches about 1,600. **"The above Example is actual size".** (illo.A)

TYPE - Description	ABP	Ex-Fn	Mint
Hanging ruby cylinder, parachute, KW, 18K, 49mm, OF, C.1 800. . .	$5,000	$10,000	$18,000
Hanging ruby cylinder, enamel *Souscription* style dial, center wind, all original,18K, 60 to 62mm, OF, C. 1800,(**illo.A**)	15,000	30,000	35,000
1/4 repeater, **Hanging ruby cylinder**, jeweled parachute, 18K, 60-65mm, C.1795, C.1800 (**illo.B**).	15,000	30,000	40,000
1/4 Repeater Horologer De La Marine , silver dial, 2 gongs, Hanging ruby cylinder escapement, 18K OF, C.1800 (**illo.C**) . .	15,000	30,000	40,000
1/2-1/4 Repeater Horologer De La Marine , silver dial, **jump hour hand**, Hanging ruby cylinder escapement, 18K **HC**, C.1800	20,000	40,000	50,000
Montre'a tact, 6J ruby cylinder, pearl & enamel case, 18K, 36mm, C. 1790-1820, (**illo.D**).	15,000	45,000	65,000
Min. repeater, perpetual calendar chronograph, sector- wind indicator, 18K, 51mm, OF, C. 1932, (**illo.E**)	50,000	80,000	130,000
Min. repeater, split sec. chrono., mm. register 18K, 2 tone case, 53mm, OF, C. 1945, (**illo.F**)	20,000	30,000	40,000

Note: Abraham Louis Breguet, made about **150 HUNTING CASE** watches.

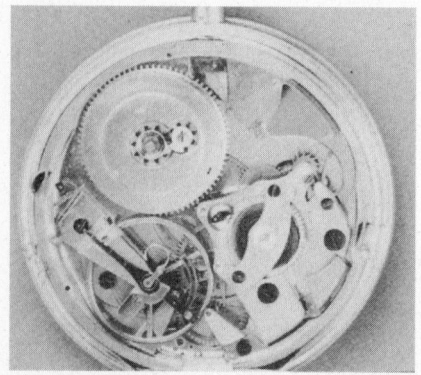
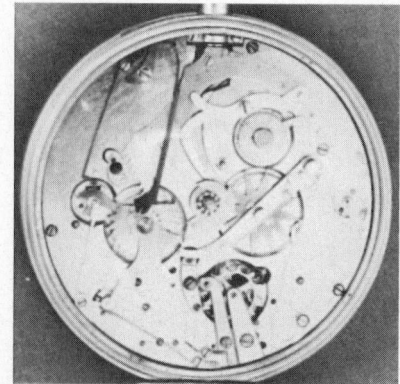

Abraham Louis Breguet, repeating, ruby cylinder watch. **Left:** gilt movement with standing barrel. Note jeweled parachute suspension. **Right:** Dial side of movement, repeating train with exposed springs. (illo.B)

Important OF, 1/4 repeater Horologer **De La Marine by Breguet.** Left: Guilloche silver dial with roman numerals and typical Breguet hands. Right: Gilt brass movement with hanging ruby cylinder escapement and triple arm balance, parachute suspension, 2 gongs, open face. Note the pull and twist piston on pendant, to operate repeating train, Ca. 1800-25. (illo.C)

Breguet "montre a tact" or touch time watch, 36mm. Case embellished with 12 pearls for tactile hours (Braille style watch). The arrow on case revolves. Center: Key with a ratchet in its shaft to prevent turning the winding arbor the wrong way. Souscription movement with 6 jewels, central barrel, ruby cylinder escapement. (illo.D)

BREGUET, 51mm, chronograph with perpetual calendar and minute repeater. Note sector style wind indicator. (illo.E)

BREGUET, 53mm, minute repeating, split-second chronograph. Chronograph activated by c rown and button on band. Repeater activated by slide. (illo.F)

Generic Breguet, 45-48mm, ruby cylinder, KW KS, Swiss bar Mvt., time only, Ca. 1830, 18K case. (illo. G)

TYPE - Description	ABP	Ex-Fn	Mint
Jump hr.w/ aperture, revolving min.disc, 18K, 46mm, OF, C.1930 ..	$6,500	$15,000	$20,000
Mm. repeater, split sec. chronograph,			
two tone gold case, 53mm, C.1948	12,000	25,000	30,000
Perpetual calendar, thin digital watch, 18K case, 45mm..........	7,500	20,000	25,000
Small keyless watch, platinum balance, gold case, 18mm	12,000	20,000	25,000
Early, KW/ KS, **generic Swiss bar Mvt.,** time only, Ca.1830,			
18K case, NOT TRUE BREGUET (illo. G)	200	325	550

BULOVA

U.S.A. & Swiss

Bulova was a leader in the mass production of quality wristwatches; however, their pocket watch output was small and limited to mostly basic time only varieties. The ultra thin "Phantom" was one of their limited production models.

Joseph Bulova started with a wholesale jewelry business in 1875. The first watches were marketed in the early 1920s. Bulova manufactured millions of movements in their own Swiss plant. The company cased these movements in the U.S.A. and imports all production today. The ACCUTRON was introduced in 1960 and sold about 5 million watches.

BULOVA Accutron, with date, gold filled hunting case, about 43mm, ca. 1970s.

BULOVA (continued)

TYPE - DESCRIPTION	ABP	Ex-Fn	Mint
GF, 17J, 42mm, OF, Ca. 1940	$50	$70	$95
Rose GF, art deco, 17J, 42mm, OF, Ca. 1930	75	100	145
14K, 17J, 42mm, OF, Ca. 1950	165	250	300
Platinum, "Phantom", ultra-thin, 18-21J., Adj.,43mm, OF, Ca.1920	400	1,000	1,200
Accutron, date, GF, 43mm, **pocket watch,** HC	135	150	200

HENRY CAPT

Geneva

Henry Daniel Capt of Geneva was an associate of Isaac Daniel Piguet for about 10 years from 1802 to 1812. Their firm produced quality watches and specialized in musicals, repeaters and chronometers. By 1844, his son was director of the firm and around 1880 the firm was sold to Gallopin.

TYPE —DESCRIPTION	ABP	Ex-Fn	Mint
Early, KW KS, Swiss bar Mvt., time only, Ca.1870, Silver case	$125	$150	$200
Early, KW KS, Swiss bar Mvt., time only, Ca.1870, Gold	300	450	600
Time only, gold, 45- 50mm, OF	400	600	700
HC	500	800	1,000
Chronograph, gold, 45-50mm, register, OF	700	1,000	1,200
HC	750	1,200	1,500
Split second chronograph, gold, 45-52mm, register, OF	1,000	1,800	2,000
HC	1,100	2,000	2,500
1/4 hr. repeater, gold, 46-52mm, OF	1,500	2,500	3,000
HC	1,700	3,000	4,500
Minute repeater, gold, 46-52mm, OF	2,000	3,000	4,000
HC	2,200	4,000	6,500
OF, w/split chrono	4,000	6,000	8,000
HC, w/split chrono	5,000	8,000	10,000
Minute repeater, w/ clock watch, OF	7,000	14,000	17,000
HC	9,000	17,000	22,000
Perpetual moonphase calendar, gold, OF	7,000	10,000	12,000
HC	8,000	12,000	15,000
Perp. moonphase cal., w/min.repeater, gold, OF	18,000	25,000	35,000
Perp. moonphase cal. ,w/min.repeater and chrono., gold, HC	20,000	35,000	45,000

HENRY CAPT, jeweled thru hammers, minute repeater, 53mm, Ca. 1900.

HENRY CAPT. 52mm, 32 jewels, minute repeater, serial number 34711, ca. 1900.

484

CARTIER

Paris

CARTIER was a famous artisan from Paris who first made powder flasks. By the mid-1840s the family became known as the finest goldsmiths of Paris. Around the turn of the century, the Cartier firm began designing watches and in 1904, the first wrist watches were being made.

Cartier, 52mm, 40 jewels, triple complicated-perpetual calendar, minute repeater, split-second chronograph.

Cartier, 45mm, 18 jewels, flat, astronomic with moon phases triple calendar, platinum watch, ca. 1930s.

TYPE — DESCRIPTION	ABP	Ex-Fn	Mint
Time only, gold, 40- 44mm, signed E.W.C., OF	$1,400	$2,200	$2,800
HC	1,600	2,500	3,200
Time only, gold, 45- 50mm, signed E.W.C., OF	1,500	2,500	3,000
HC	1,700	3,000	3,500
Flat, astronomic w/ moon ph. triple calendar, signed E.W.C., platinum, OF	7,000	12,000	15,000
Chronograph, gold, 45-50mm, signed E.W.C., OF	2,500	5,000	6,000
5 minute repeater, gold, 46-52mm, signed E.W.C., OF	3,500	5,000	7,000
HC	4,000	5,500	7,500
Minute repeater, gold, 46-52mm, signed E.W.C., OF	7,500	10,000	15,000
HC	8,000	12,000	18,000
Triple complicated, astronomical moon ph. perpetual triple cal., signed E.W.C. min. repeater, split sec. chron. w/min. recorder, 18 K	60,000	100,000	125,000

Above: Cartier, 43mm, 18 jewels, dial has raised gold Arabic numbers, 18k, OF, Ca.1930s.

T. F. COOPER

Liverpool

The Cooper name is usually marked on inner dust covers which protect Swiss ebauche keywind bar movements. Numerous watches produced from 1850-1890 are found with this Liverpool name. The T. F. Cooper & later the T. W. Cooper firms supplied the U.S. market with low cost silver-cased keywinds.

TYPE - DESCRIPTION	ABP	Ex-Fn	Mint
KWKS, "full-jeweled", Silver, 44-48mm, OF, Ca.1850-1875	$75	$100	$145
KWKS, 15J, Silver, 46-50mm, HC, Ca.1850-1870	85	125	200
KW, Fusee, lever, silver, 48mm, OF, C. 1870	135	250	300
KW, 15J, metal dust cover, gilt dial, 18K, OF, C. 1875	250	350	450
KW, 15J, Lady's, 18K, 44mm, fancy HC, C. 1875	300	400	550
KW, gold dial, bar movement w/side lever escap., parachute shock on balance, 18K, 50mm, OF, C. 1870	250	400	500
Captains double time, 15J, KWKS, silver, 48mm, OF, C.1865	400	800	1,000
18K, OF	600	1,500	1,800
18K, HC	800	1,800	2,200

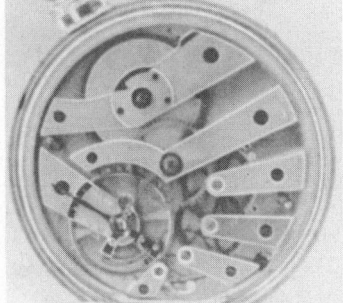  

T. F. Cooper, KW. bar movement with right angle lever escapement, parachute shock on balance, 18K, 50mm, OF, Ca. 1852.

Courvoisier, Freres, 37mm, cylinder escap. with wolf-tooth winding, front & back view, 18K & enamel HC, Ca. 1880.

COURVOISIER, Freres

SWISS (La Chaux de Fonds)

Started as Courvoisier & Cie in 1810-11, by 1845 Henri-Louis and Philippe-Auguste became owners. In 1852 name changes to Courvoisier, Freres. The watches circa 1810 are signed with the older signature. They exported very ornate pieces for the Chinese market (Lepine bar caliber).

TYPE - DESCRIPTION	ABP	Ex-Fn	Mint
Time only, KW, SILVER, 45- 50mm, OF	$125	$150	$200
HC	135	175	250
Time only, KW, Gold, 45- 50mm, OF	200	325	450
HC	300	400	550
Time only, SW, Gold, 45- 50mm, OF	225	325	450
HC	300	400	550
Captains Watch, SILVER, 2 hour dials, 2 trains, Key Wind, center seconds, 50mm, OF	500	800	1,000
HC, (SAME AS ABOVE)	550	900	1,200
Captains Watch, GOLD, 2 hour dials, 2 trains, Key Wind, center seconds, 50mm, OF	1,000	1,800	2,200
HC, (SAME AS ABOVE)	1,200	2,000	2,500
1/4 hr. repeater, SILVER, 46-52mm, OF	600	750	1,000
1/4 hr. repeater, GOLD, 46-52mm, OF	850	1,500	2,000
Detent Chronometer, gold, 48-52mm, OF	1,800	3,000	3,500
HC	2,000	3,500	4,000

E. J. Dent

LONDON

Edward John Dent, born in 1790 died in 1853. Edward was in partnership with J. R. Arnold, at 84 Strand, from 1830-1840 and worked alone at 82 Strand from 1841 to 1849. Then moved to 61 Strand 1850 till 1853. The year before his death the Westminster Palace gave Dent the contract for making BIG BEN with a big bell weighing over 13 tons. The clock was built by Frederick Rippon Dent. E. Dent & Co. Ltd. was in business until about 1968 at 41 Pall Mall London.

DENT, PIVOTED Detent chronometer, about 15 jewels, fusee, gold. 48-52mm. Ca. 1570, open face. (illo.1A)

DENT, 1/4 hr. repeater, marked "Dent Watch Maker to the Queen 61 strand London", S# 30077, note early winding **system** by Nicole Nilson, 46-52mm, OF, Ca. 1850. (illo. 2A)

TYPE - DESCRIPTION	ABP	Ex-Fn	Mint
Time only, gold, 45- 50mm, OF	$500	$700	$850
HC	600	1,000	1,200
Chronograph, gold, 45-50mm, OF	900	1,200	1,800
HC	1,000	1,500	2,000
Split second chronograph, gold, 45-52mm, OF	1,500	2,500	3,500
HC	1,800	3,000	4,000
Early stem wind, 1/4 hr. repeater, gold, 46-52mm, OF (illo. 2A)	2,000	3,000	4,200
1/4 hr. repeater, gold, 46-52mm, OF	1,800	2,500	3,500
HC	2,000	2,800	4,200
HC w/chrono., cal. & moonphase	5,000	7,000	9,000
Minute repeater, gold, OF	2,500	4,000	5,500
HC	3,000	5,500	7,000
OF w/chrono	3,000	5,000	7,000
HC w/split chrono	5,000	8,000	12,000
HC w/cal. & moonphase	7,000	12,000	18,000
Minute, w/clock watch	12,000	20,000	25,000
Pivoted Detent chronometer, fusee, gold, 48-52mm, OF (illo. 1A)	3,000	5,000	7,000
Perpetual moonphase calendar, gold, OF	8,000	11,000	16,000
HC	9,000	12,000	18,000
Perp. moonphase cal. **w/min. repeater**, OF	22,000	30,000	35,000
HC	24,000	35,000	45,000
w/split sec., OF	40,000	55,000	75,000
w/split sec., HC	50,000	65,000	100,000

PAUL DITISHEIM

La Chaux de Fonds - Swiss

In 1892 Paul Ditisheim founded his own firm, which later became Vulcain. He made precision and novelty type watches. He gained many Prizes and awards also wrote many articles for improving watches. His research of new ideas were successful with oil and balances. Found on some watches, a balance, he called **"affix"**. In about 1920 he formed the Solvil movement and later Titus.

TYPE —DESCRIPTION	ABP	Ex-Fn	Mint
Time only, gold, 40-44mm, OF	$300	$400	$550
HC	450	600	700
Time only, gold, 40-50mm, **Flat** or **Thin**, OF	450	625	700
Time only, gold, **"Affix"** balance, 45- 50mm, OF	600	700	875
HC	700	850	1,000
Time only, **platinum & diamond,** art deco, 41-42mm, OF	1,500	2,500	3,000
Chronograph, gold, 45-50mm, OF	700	900	1,200
HC	775	1,000	1,300
Split second chronograph, gold, 45-52mm, OF	900	1,700	2,000
HC	1,000	2,000	2,500
Deck chronometer w/box, detent chronometer, C. 1905	1,300	1,700	2,200
Pocket chronometer, **wind-indicator,** 21J., GJS, OF, C. 1920	1,200	1,500	1,800
Pocket chronometer, **pivoted detent,** gold, 57mm	3,000	5,000	6,500
Pocket chronometer, with **TOURBILLON**	22,000	40,000	50,000
1/4 hr. repeater, gold, 46-52mm, OF	1,800	2,200	2,800
HC	2,000	3,000	3,500
Minute repeater, gold, OF	3,000	4,000	5,500
HC	3,200	5,000	6,000

AFFIX Balance

Art Deco-style, 41mm, black onyx bezel, Ca. 1920.

Pocket chronometer, Wind-Indicator, 21J., OF, C.1920

Solvil, 17J., with **"Affix"** balance, 49mm, OF, ca. 1920s.

DUBOIS et FILS

Le Locle (SWISS)

Dubois a active merchant in the Le Lode region. In about 1761 Philippe Dubois began selling watches. They exported all over the world & specialized in repeater, automaton, skeleton watches also watches with false pendulums. They provided the Courvoisier Freres with movements. (Dew-bwah)

TYPE - Description	ABP	Ex-Fn	Mint
Verge, KW, pair case, silver, 48-52mm	$275	$450	$500
Verge, **enamel** w/scene & automata windmill, silver or gilt, 48-52mm	1,100	3,000	4,000
Verge w/mock pendulum, chain & fusee, silver, OF, 48-52mm	700	1,500	2,000
All above with **large** one second-beating balance wheel, **Pirouette** gearing			
and double escape wheel, Friction Rest Escapement . ★★★★	4,000	8,000	12,000
Verge w/mock pendulum, chain & fusee, 18K, OF, 48-52mm, **large** one			
second-beating balance wheel, **Pirouette** gearing **and double escape**			
wheel, Friction Rest Escapement . . . . ★★★★★	8,000	15,000	25,000
Verge, KW, GOLD, OF, 50-54mm.	600	900	1,200
Verge, KW, GOLD w/enamel, OF,52mm	900	2,000	2,500
1/4 hr. repeater, SILVER, OF, 50-54mm	650	1,000	1,500
1/4 hr. repeater, GOLD, OF, 50-54mm	900	1,500	2,000
1/4 hr. repeater w/automaton, **18K**, OF, 50-52mm	3,000	5,000	7,000
Minute **pump** repeater, gold, OF, 50-52mm . . . . ★★	8,000	15,000	20,000

Pirouette gearing

DuBois & Fils, Verge with mock pendulum, chain & fusee, silver, OF, enamel dial, 48-52mm, ca. 1800. **Note:** This movement used a large seconds-beating balance wheel, with pirouette gearing and double escape wheel.

DuBois et Fils, Verge, enamel w/scene, silver or gilt, OF, painted enamel scene with windmill automata, 48-52mm. ca. 1810.

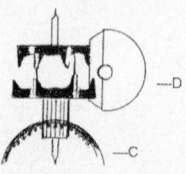

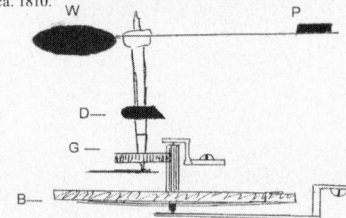

Frictional rest escapement, Double escape wheel with 6 teeth on each escape wheel for a total of 12, also note the pinion to drive double escape wheel.

D = D-shaped **pallet**, inclined for impulse. B = Balance. C = **Contrate** wheel. G= gear with 26 teeth at bottom. W = counter **Weight**. P = false pendulum.

Note: Movement has a large seconds-beating balance wheel, **pirouette** gearing, double escape wheel & a single pallet. This DuBois pirouette is unlike most DeBaufre or Pauzait ect. where balance wheel was central to movement.

DUCHENE L., & Fils

GENEVA

Watchmaker, well known for their large and small pieces, including coach clocks, calendar watches and minute repeater watches. The firm was known also for decorative work with polychrome champleve enamel and painted enamel, and fantasy watches. The movements are classically-designed, with fusee & verge escapements. Cases are in "Empire-style", engraved or guilloche.

TYPE—DESCRIPTION	ABP	Ex-Fn	Mint
KW, cylinder, silver, 46mm, OF	$85	$125	$200
HC	100	150	225
KW, verge fusee, silver, 46-52mm, OF	275	450	500
KW, verge fusee, enamel case ,gilt, 52mm, OF	600	1,200	2,000
1/4 hr. repeater, silver, 54mm, OF	500	800	1,000
1/4 hr. repeater, gold, 52mm, OF	900	1,800	2,500
1/4 hr. repeater, w/**automata**, gold, 52mm, OF	3,000	5,000	7,000
Ball form, KWKS, cylinder, 29mm, **18K** OF	450	700	1,200

Duchene L. & Fils, 1/4 Hour Repeater, fusee and cylinder escapement, repeats on gongs, 52mm, ca. 1820.

Dunand, 1/4 hour repeater, about 15 jewels, repeater is slide activated, 49MM, OF, ca. 1905

DUNAND

Swiss

The Dunand factory produced repeaters, timers & chronographs during the 1890-1930 time period.

TYPE - DESCRIPTION	ABP	Ex-Fn	Mint
Time only, gold, 45-50mm, OF	$185	$300	$400
HC	300	400	600
Chronograph, gold, 45-50mm, OF	400	550	700
HC	450	600	800
Split second chronograph, gold, 45-52mm, OF	800	1,000	1,200
HC	900	1,200	1,500
1/4 hr. repeater, gold, 46-52mm, OF	750	1,000	1,200
HC	800	1,200	1,800
OF w/chrono	900	1,300	1,500
HC w/chrono	1,100	1,500	2,000
Minute repeater, gold, 46-52mm, OF	1,500	2,500	3,000
HC	1,800	2,700	3,500

EARNSHAW, THOMAS

LONDON

Thomas Earnshaw born in 1749 died in 1829. In about 1781 he improves the spring detent. Earnshaw also contributed to the development of the chronometer. He pioneered the method of fusing brass and steel together to form a laminate of the compensation rims as in the modern method of today. Known for his chronometers he also made 1/4 and 1/2 hour repeaters with cylinder and duplex escapements.

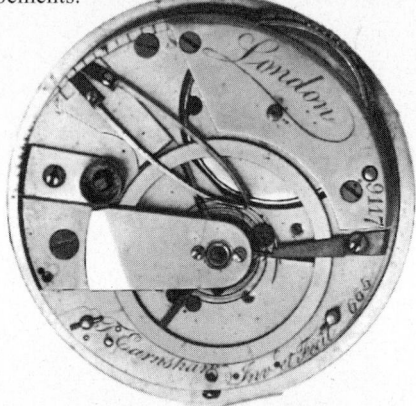

THOMAS EARNSHAW, chronometer, KWKS, spring detent, Z or S balance with trapezoidal weights, helical hair spring, serial # 589, silver case , Ca. 1810.

Signed: "T. EARNSHAW Invt et Fecit 665 London 9117" KW KS, spring detent chronometer, NOTE: compensation curb so called "sugar-tongs", silver case, ca.1803.

Right: Earnshaw spring detent escapement.

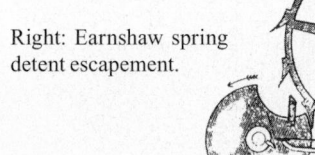

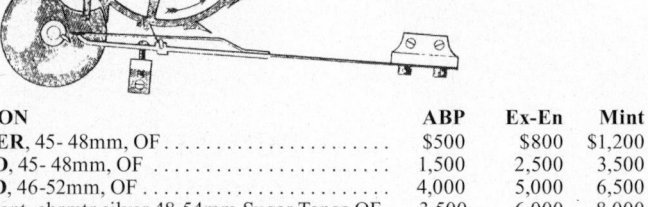

TYPE - DESCRIPTION	ABP	Ex-En	Mint
Time only, KW, **SILVER**, 45- 48mm, OF	$500	$800	$1,200
Time only, KW, **GOLD**, 45- 48mm, OF	1,500	2,500	3,500
1/4 hr. repeater, **GOLD**, 46-52mm, OF	4,000	5,000	6,500
Spring detent escapement, chrmtr,silver,48-54mm,Sugar-Tongs,OF	3,500	6,000	8,000
Spring detent escapement, chronometer, gold,Sugar-Tongs,OF	7,500	18,000	25,000

H. R. EKEGREN

Copenhagen & Geneva

Henry Robert Ekegren, a Swiss maker of quality watches, started in business around 1870. The firm specialized in flat watches, chronometers and repeaters. Ekegren became associated with **F. Koehn** in 1891.

TYPE - DESCRIPTION	ABP	Ex-Fn	Mint
Time only, gold, 45- 50mm, register, OF	$550	$700	$950
HC	650	1,000	1,300
Chronograph, gold, 45-50mm, register, OF	800	1,200	1,800
HC	900	1,500	2,500
Split second chronograph, gold, 45-52mm, OF	1,200	1,800	2,500
HC	1,300	2,000	3,000
FIVE-Minute repeater, gold, 46-52mm, OF	1,800	2,500	3,000
HC	2,000	3,000	3,500

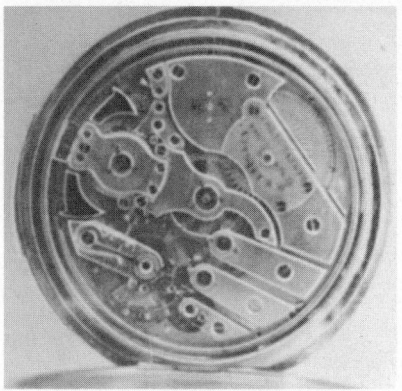

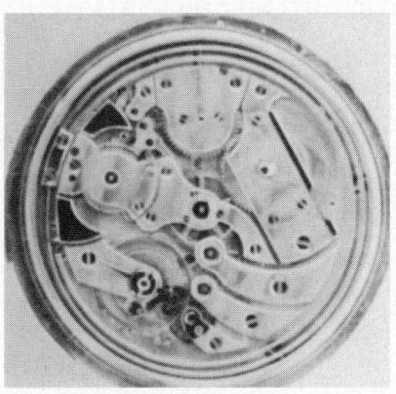

H. R. EKEGREN 46mm, minute repeater, slide activated, jeweled through hammers, open face, serial no. 78,268.

H. R. EKEGREN, 47mm, minute repeater, jeweled through hammers, hunting case.

TYPE - DESCRIPTION	ABP	Ex-Fn	Mint
Minute repeater, gold, 46-52mm, OF	$2,400	$4,000	$5,000
HC	2,800	4,500	6,500
OF w/chrono	2,500	4,500	5,500
HC w/chrono	3,000	5,000	7,000
OF w/split chrono	4,000	7,000	9,000
HC w/split chrono	4,500	9,000	15,000
Perpetual moonphase calendar, gold, OF	8,000	12,000	15,000
Perpetual moonphase cal. w/ mm. repeater, OF	18,000	30,000	35,000
HC	20,000	35,000	40,000
Perp. moonphase cal. w/min. rep. and chrono., OF	22,000	32,000	37,000
HC	25,000	40,000	50,000
Karrusel, gold, 48-55mm, OF	8,000	12,000	15,000
Tourbillon, gold, 48-55mm, OF	40,000	55,000	80,000
Detent chronometer, gold, 48-52mm, OF	4,500	5,500	6,500
World time watch, gold, 48-52mm, OF	4,000	5,500	8,000

FAVRE-LEUBE

Le Locle & Geneva

Favre-Leube firm is still active and production has covered more than eight generations of watchmakers. The company has made watches since 1815.

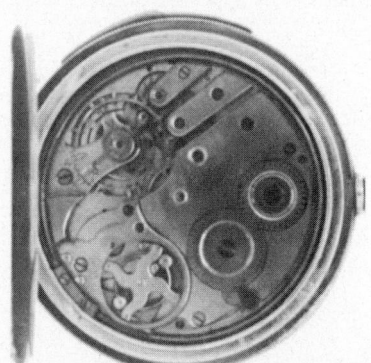

FAVRE-LEUBE, 53mm, Minute repeater, 15 jewels, slide on rim activates the repeater mechanism, ca.1895.

TYPE - DESCRIPTION	ABP	Ex-Fn	Mint
Early, KW KS, Swiss bar Mvt., time only, Ca.1870, Silver case.....	$100	$125	$195
KW, Gold w/enamel, 35-40mm, HC	700	900	1,000
KW, silver w/enamel, 45mm, HC...........................	200	300	400
KW, Gold w/enamel, 45-48mm, OF	500	750	1,000
Chronograph, gold, 45-50mm, OF...........................	500	700	800
HC	600	800	1,000
Split second chronograph, gold, 45-52mm, OF.................	700	1,000	1,200
HC	800	1,200	1,500
1/4 hr. repeater, gold, 46-52mm, OF	800	1,200	1,500
HC	950	1,800	2,200
Minute repeater, gold, 46-52mm, OF.......................	1,200	2,000	2,500
HC	1,500	2,800	3,500

CHARLES FRODSHAM

London

Charles Frodsham followed in the footsteps of his father, William, whose father was close with Earnshaw. Charles became the most eminent of the family, producing very fine chronometers and some rare tourbillon and complicated watches. He died in 1871. After about 1850 his quality 3/4 plate movements endorse the letters **A.D. FMSZ. Arnold & Frodsham** signed watches and located at 84 Strand, London are from 1843-44 until 1857-58. He later moved to New Bond Street, London.

Arnold Chas Frodsham 9139 *AD FMSZ on* dial, 84 Strand, London on movement & dust cover, 16-18J., 2 platinum balance screws, S# 9139, Ca.1856

Chas. Frodsham, 84 Strand London, 25 jewels, Fusee, Freesprung, Diamond end stone, serial number 3520.

TYPE —DESCRIPTION	ABP	Ex-Fn	Mint
Time only, early mvt. **84 Strand,** silver, 45- 48mm, OF, C.1850	$250	$350	$485
Time only, early mvt. **84 Strand, gold,** 45- 48mm, OF, C.1850	700	1,000	1,300
Time only, gold, 45- 50mm, OF............................	700	1,000	1,300
HC	900	1,200	1,500
Chronograph, gold, 45-50mm, OF...........................	1,600	2,500	3,000
HC	1,800	3,000	3,500
Split second chronograph, gold, 45-52m, OF	2,800	5,500	7,000
HC	3,200	6,000	7,500

☞ **The Complete Price Guide to Watches goal is to stimulate the orderly exchange of watches between buyers and sellers.**

Frodsham, 46-50mm, jeweled through the center wheel, stem wind, 10K case, 84 Strand, S#8132Ca. 1858.

Frodsham, 59mm, 60 minute Karrusel, 15J., stem wind, open face, S#09050/56906, 18K case, Ca. 1895.

TYPE - DESCRIPTION	ABP	Ex-Fn	Mint
Minute repeater, gold, 46-52mm, OF	$4,500	$8,000	$11,000
HC	5,000	10,000	13,000
OF w/split chrono	10,000	15,000	25,000
HC w/split chrono	15,000	20,000	30,000
Perpetual moonphase calendar, gold, OF	18,000	22,000	28,000
Perp. moonphase cal. w/min. repeater, OF	35,000	50,000	70,000
HC	40,000	70,000	90,000
Karrusel, 16J, (59 to 60 mm. Karrusel), 18K, C.1895	5,500	20,000	25,000
Tourbillon, gold, 48-55mm, OF	45,000	75,000	100,000
Marine chronometer, Parkinson-Frodsham, helical hairspring, w/ detent escape., 48 hr. WI, C. 1840, 97mm deck box	2,400	2,900	3,500
Detent chronometer, w/wind ind., 18K, OF, KWKS, C. 1850	3,000	8,000	15,000
Box Chronometer, helical hair spring, with box	15,000	17,000	20,000
Clock Watch, Minute repeater, OF	10,000	25,000	30,000
HC	13,000	30,000	35,000

GIRARD-PERREGAUX

La Chaux-de-Fonds Switzerland

In 1856, The Constant Girard and Henry Perregaux families founded the Swiss firm of Girard-Perregaux. About 1860, the firm made a tourbillon with three golden bridges. A replica of this watch was made in 1982. Both were a supreme expression of horological craftsmanship. Girard-Perregaux said about 1880 the first wrist watches were made for the German Navy officers. In 1906, the company purchased the Hecht factory in Geneva. Girard-Perregaux has been recognized many times and still makes prestigious watches.

TYPE - DESCRIPTION	ABP	Ex-Fn	Mint
Skeletonized "Shell' (Shell Oil Co. advertising watch), 7J, Base metal display case, total production = 30,000 Ca.1940	$125	$300	$375

Skeletonized **"Shell Watch"** (Golden Shell Oil) advertising a watch filled with Shell car motor oil they wanted to prove even a watch would run on this top quality car motor oil. Most stopped with heavy car oil, so the oil was removed from some watches. Girard-Perregaux used a ebauche by A. Scheld calibre 1052, Base metal display case, only 7J, total production = 30,000, & sold for $5.00. Ca. June 5,1940.

GIRARD-PERREGAUX, three gold bridges movement patented March 25th, 1884.

GIRARD-PERREGAUX, Chronometer, with pivoted dentent, gold train, 20 jewels, nickel movement, Ca. 1878.

Note: Watches with Gold embossed dial add $200.

TYPE — DESCRIPTION	ABP	Ex-Fn	Mint
Time only, gold 40-44mm, OF	$250	$400	$500
HC	350	500	700
Time only, gold 45- 50mm, OF	325	500	600
HC	475	600	800
3 gold bridges, with silver case, C. 1884.	3,500	6,000	7,500
with gold case, lever esc.	6,000	15,000	20,000
Chronometer, pivoted detent, 20J., gold train, 18K, C.1878	2,000	5,000	7,000
Chronograph, gold, 45-50mm, OF	800	1,200	1,500
HC	1,000	1,500	2,000
1/4 hr. repeater, gold, 45-52mm, OF	1,400	2,000	2,500
HC	1,600	3,000	3,500
HC w/chrono., cal. & moonphase	2,200	5,000	7,000
Minute repeater, gold, 46-52mm, OF.	2,000	3,000	3,500
HC	2,700	4,000	4,500
OF w/chrono	2,800	4,500	5,000
OF w/split chrono	4,000	6,000	8,000
HC w/cal. & moonphase	4,800	10,000	15,000
Detent chronometer, 3 bridge, gold, 48-54mm, OF	15,000	30,000	40,000
3 bridge, HC.	18,000	35,000	45,000
Tourbillion, gold, 3 bridge gold, 48-54mm, OF/HC	50,000	125,000	175,000

☞ Note: Some models and grades are not included. Their values can be determined by comparing with similar age, size, metal content, style, models and grades listed.

COMPARISON OF WATCH CASE SIZES

U.S.A.	EUROPEAN
10-12 SIZE	40—44MM
16 SIZE	45—49MM
18 SIZE	50—55 MM

GOLAY A., LERESCHE & Fils

SWISS

Manufactured under the name Golay-Leresche from 1844-1857, then his son changed the name to Golay *A.,* Leresche & Pus, he worked until the beginning of the 20th Century. Watches were primarily exported to U.S.A. He was well known for watches of all kinds and "grande complications".

TYPE - DESCRIPTION	ABP	Ex-Fn	Mint
Time only, gold, 45- 50mm, OF	$300	$500	$625
HC	400	600	725
Chronograph, gold, 45-50mm, OF	500	750	950
HC	700	1,000	1,200
Split second chronograph, gold, 45-52mm, OF	775	1,500	1,800
HC	900	2,000	2,500
1/4 hr. repeater, gold, 46-52mm, OF	1,400	2,000	2,500
HC	1,500	2,200	2,800
HC w/chrono., cal. & moonphase	3,000	4,000	5,500
Minute repeater, gold, OF	1,800	2,500	3,500
HC	2,000	3,000	3,700
OF w/chrono	2,200	3,000	3,500
HC w/split chrono	3,500	6,000	7,500
HC w/cal. & moonphase	4,000	6,000	10,000
Detent chronomter, gold, 48-52mm, OF	2,000	3,500	4,000
Perpetual moonphase calendar, gold, OF	7,000	12,000	15,000
HC	8,000	13,000	16,000
Perp. moonphase cal. w/min. repeater, OF	15,000	25,000	30,000
HC	18,000	28,000	32,000
Clock Watch, gold, 48-52mm, OF	6,000	10,000	12,000
HC	7,000	11,000	15,000

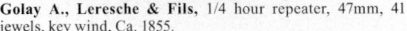

Golay A., Leresche & Fils, 1/4 hour repeater, 47mm, 41 jewels, key wind, Ca. 1855.

Golay A., Leresche & Fils, minute repeater, split seconds chronograph, moon phases, day date month, open face, Ca. 1896.

COMPARISON OF WATCH CASE SIZES

U. S. A.	EUROPEAN
10-12 SIZE	40—44MM
16 SIZE	45—49MM
18 SIZE	50—55 MM

H. GRANDJEAN

The son of David-Henri (1774-1845), this respected maker produced high quality complicated watches, chronometers and ornately decorated watches for the South American market. A Grandjean specialty was magnificent enamel and gem set ladies watches.

Note: Watches with Gold embossed dial add $500.

TYPE - DESCRIPTION	ABP	Ex-Fn	Mint
Time only, gold, 45- 50mm, OF	$500	$700	$850
HC	600	1,000	1,200
Chronograph, gold, 45-50mm, OF	650	1,000	1,200
HC	750	1,200	1,500
Split second chronograph, gold, 45-52mm, OF	1,100	1,800	2,200
HC	1,300	2,000	2,500
1/4 hr. repeater, gold, 46-52mm, OF	1,200	1,800	2,000
HC	1,600	2,200	2,800
HC w/chrono., cal. & moonphase	2,500	4,000	4,500
Minute repeater, gold, OF	2,200	3,000	3,500
HC	2,800	5,000	6,000
OF w/chrono	2,400	3,500	4,000
HC w/split chrono	3,800	7,000	9,000
HC w/cal. & moonphase	5,800	9,000	12,000
Detent chronometer, gold, 48-52mm, OF	3,000	5,000	5,500
Perpetual moonphase calendar, gold, OF	7,000	12,000	15,000
HC	8,500	14,000	18,000
Perp. moonphase cal. w/min. repeater, OF	20,000	30,000	35,000
HC	24,000	35,000	40,000
Grande & Petite Sonnerie repeating clock watch, 38J, fancy dial, 18k gold, 53mm, HC	10,000	15,000	22,000

H. GRANDJEAN, Grande & Petite Sonnerie repeating clock watch, 38 Jewels, with tandem wind mechanism, fancy dial, 18k gold, 53mm, HC.

GRUEN WATCH CO.

Swiss & U. S. A. (1874- 1953)

The early roots of the Gruen Company are found in Columbus, Ohio where Dietrich Gruen and W. J. Savage formed a partnership in 1876. The D. Gruen & Son legacy began in 1894 and flourished with the introduction of fine quality "Precision" movements. Curvex movements, ultra-thins and the prestigious 50th anniversary model are highlights of this prolific company.

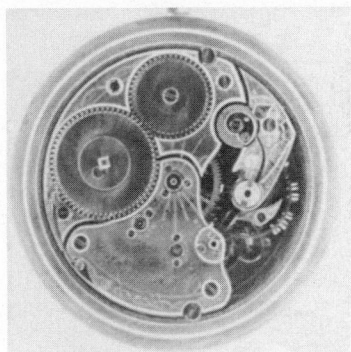

D. Gruen & Son, OF, 44mm, 19-21J., by Assmann, plates are Argentan (silver & nickel), Adj. to HCIP on bal. bridge, gold moustache lever & escape wheel, 5462,428, Ca.1895

Gruen 50th Anniversary Watch, 10 size, 23J., 12K gold plates engraved, 600 made - 1 for each month & marked all adjts 8 eight, 50 made later 1 for each year (S#01-050).

TYPE - Description	ABP	Ex-Fn	Mint
17-21J, veri-thin or precision, 40-43mm, Grades			
V1 - V2 - V3 - V4 - V5, C.1920-40, OF-**GF** case	$100	$150	$250
17-21J, veri-thin or precision, 40-43mm, Grades			
V1 - V2 - V3 - V4 - V5, C.1920-40, OF-**14K** case.	250	350	500
17-21J, ultra-thin, 40-43mm, OF, C.1920-40	125	200	275
Pentagon case ,17-21J, **GF**, 40-43mm, OF, 14K or 18K case.	250	350	500
Pentagon case, 17-21J, precision, **14K**, 40-43mm, C.1920-40	300	500	700
23J., GJS, 47mm, wind indicator, micrometer regulator, **14K**	550	1,000	1,200
Madretsch Model, 21J., 16 size, **GF** OF . . . . ★	250	400	500
21-23J, D. Gruen & Son, Swiss, Gold, 45-54mm, OF, C. 1900-20	275	400	650
21J, D. Gwen, (by Assmann), **14K**, OF, C. 1905	500	900	1,200
21J, D. Gwen, (by Assmann), **14K**, HC, C. 1905.	750	1,500	1,800
50th anniversary, 12K gold movement, 21J + 2 diamonds = 23J,			
pentagon case, **18K**, 40mm, OF, C. 1924 . . . . ★★	3,000	5,500	7,500
Platinum . . . . ★★★★	4,000	9,000	12,000

Gruen W. Co., Swiss made, 23 jewels in screwed settings, 47mm, wind indicator, micrometer regulator, Ca.1900's.

D. Gruen & Son, "Madretsch marked", 16 size, 21 jewels, open face, with end-less screw style regulato r, Ca. 1905.

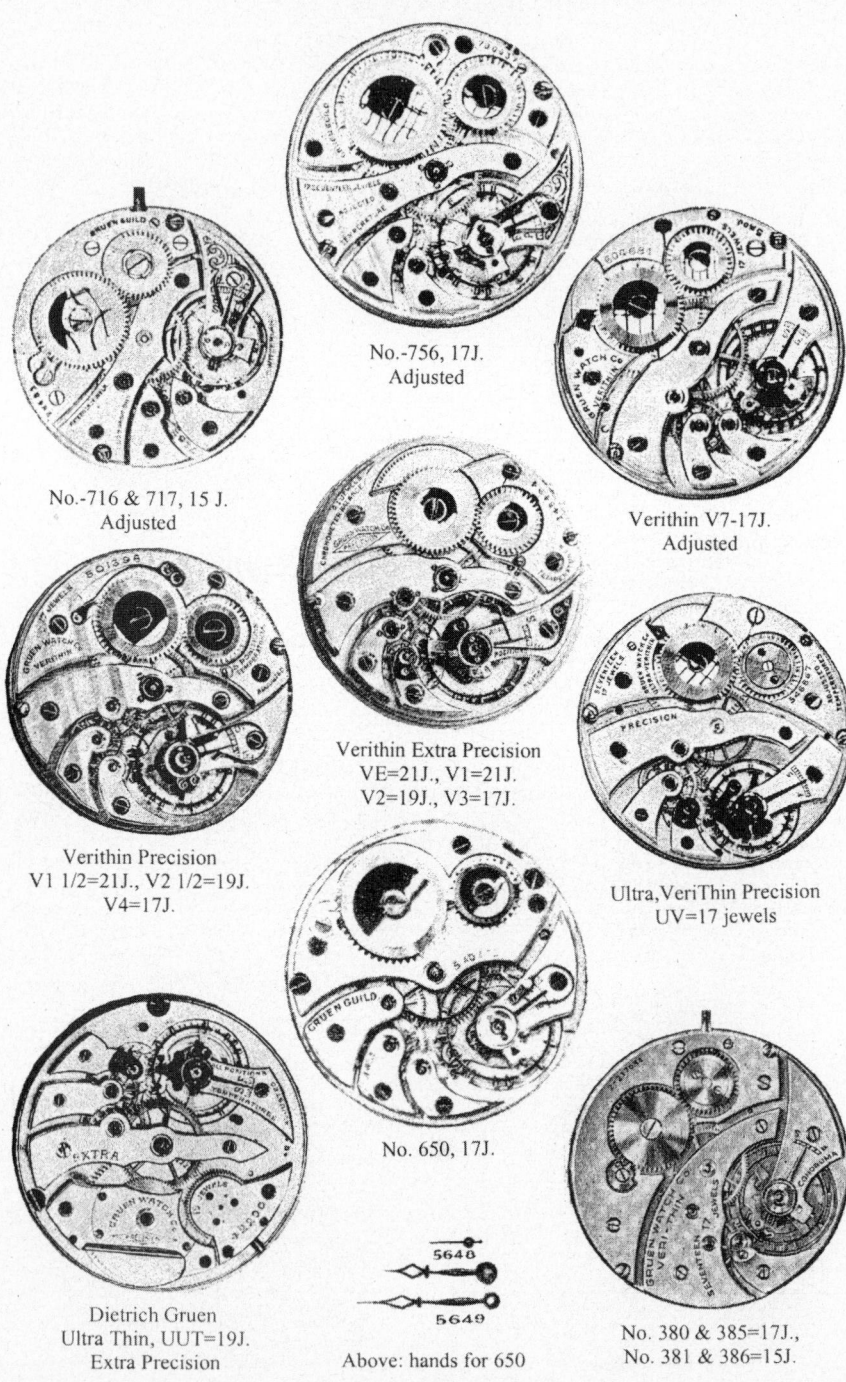

No.-756, 17J.
Adjusted

No.-716 & 717, 15 J.
Adjusted

Verithin V7-17J.
Adjusted

Verithin Extra Precision
VE=21J., V1=21J.
V2=19J., V3=17J.

Verithin Precision
V1 1/2=21J., V2 1/2=19J.
V4=17J.

Ultra,VeriThin Precision
UV=17 jewels

No. 650, 17J.

Dietrich Gruen
Ultra Thin, UUT=19J.
Extra Precision

5648

5649

Above: hands for 650

No. 380 & 385=17J.,
No. 381 & 386=15J.

E. GUBELIN

Swiss

Jacques Edouard Gubelin joined the firm of Maurice Breitschmid in Lucerne around 1854. By 1919, Edouard Gubelin headed the firm. In 1921 they opened an office in New York & produced fine jewelry and watches for 5 generations.

E. GUBELIN, 50mm, 29J., min. repeater, chronograph, Perpetual day-date-month-moon phase, by Audemars, Piguet.

E. GUBELIN, 48mm, world time with 68 cities on outside bezel 24 hour on inter bezel, Gold Filled open face.

TYPE - Description	ABP	Ex-Fn	Mint
Time only, gold, 40- 44mm, OF	$300	$400	$500
HC	400	600	700
Time only, gold, 45- 50mm, OF	350	600	700
HC	550	800	1,000
Chronograph, gold, 45-50mm, OF	500	800	900
HC	600	900	1,100
Split second chronograph, gold, 45-52mm, OF	750	1,500	1,800
HC	900	1,700	2,500
1/4 hr. repeater, gold, 46-52mm, OF	1,200	2,300	2,800
HC	1,400	2,500	3,100
OF w/chrono	1,300	2,300	2,800
HC w/chrono	1,500	2,700	3,300
HC w/chrono., calendar & moonphase	3,000	4,000	4,500
5 minute repeater, gold, 46-52mm, OF	1,800	3,000	3,500
HC	2,000	3,200	4,000
Minute repeater, gold, 46-52mm, OF	2,200	3,500	4,000
OF w/chrono	2,500	3,700	4,500
OF w/split chrono	4,000	6,500	8,500
OF w/chrono., calendar & moonphase	4,800	9,500	12,500
World time watch, **Gold Filled**, 48-52mm, OF	700	1,300	1,500
World time watch, **18K Gold**, 48-52mm, OF ★★	3,500	4,000	5,000
Perpetual moonphase calendar, gold, OF	8,500	12,000	15,000
Perp. moonphase cal. w/min. repeater, OF/HC	24,000	28,000	35,000
Perp. moonphase cal. w/min. rep. and chrono., OF/HC	26,000	32,000	40,000
Gold Clock Watch, OF	5,000	10,000	15,000
HC	7,000	15,000	20,000

The following will explain the French days of the week abbreviations, Sunday =**DIM** (Dimanche), Monday = **LUN** (Lundi), Tuesday = **MAR** (Mardi), Wednesday = **MER** (Mercedi), Thursday = **JEU** (Jeudi), Friday = **VEN** (Vendredi), Saturday = **SAM** (Samedi).

C. L. GUINAND & CO.

Swiss

Founded Ca. 1865 and became know for their Timers and Chronographs.

TYPE - Description	ABP	Ex-Fn	Mint
Timer, with register, base metal, OF, 46mm	$55	$75	$90
Timer, split second, register, base metal, OF, 46mm	75	200	250
Chronograph, 30 mm register,14K, 50mm, OF, C. 1910	400	600	850
HC	600	800	950
Split sec. chrono., 30 mm. register, 14K, OF, 50mm, C. 1915	900	1,300	1,600
Minute repeater, **18K**, OF, 50mm, C. 1915	2,000	3,000	3,500
HC	2,500	3,500	4,000
Minute repeater, split sec. chrono., 18K, OF, 50mm, C. 1915	4,000	8,000	10,000

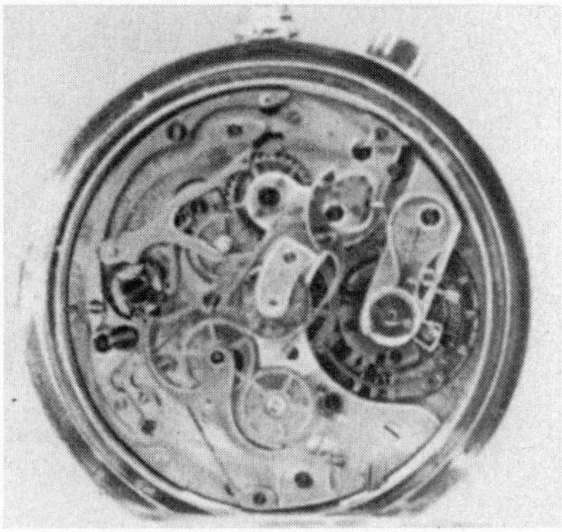

C. L. Guinand, 50mm, split-second chronograph. serial number 44,109.

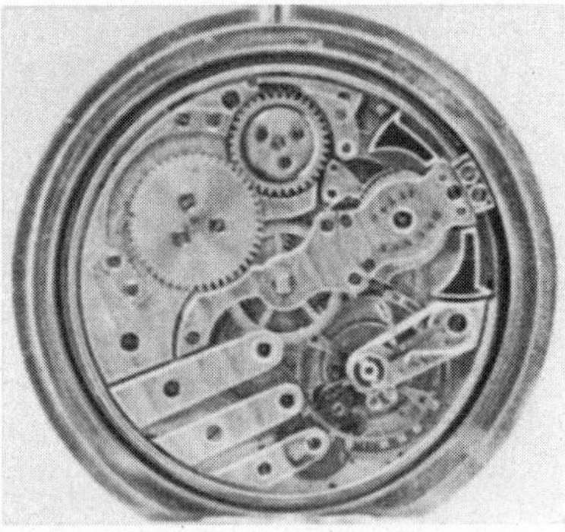

Haas, Neveux & Co., 40mm, 31 jewels, minute repeater, 18k open face case, serial number 11,339.

HAAS, NEVEUX

Swiss

The Haas Neveux firm is one of the oldest in Switzerland, founded by Leopold & Benjamin Haas in 1848. High grade precision timepieces and chronometers were characteristic of this reputable firm's output.

TYPE - Description	ABP	Ex-Fn	Mint
Time only, gold, 40- 44mm, OF	$300	$440	$575
HC	400	600	710
Time only, gold, 45- 50mm, OF	400	600	710
HC	600	880	1,050
Chronograph, gold, 45-50mm, OF	700	880	1,050
HC	800	1,100	1,320
Split second chronograph, gold, 45-52mm, OF	1,000	1,400	1,700
HC	1,200	1,800	2,200
1/4 hr. repeater, gold, 46-52mm, OF	900	1,500	1,800
HC	1,100	1,800	2,200
Minute repeater, gold, 46-52mm, OF	1,500	2,200	2,700
OF w/split chrono	3,500	6,000	8,000
OF w/cal. & moonphase	4,000	7,000	10,000
Perpetual moonphase calendar, gold, OF	7,000	10,000	12,000
Perp. moonphase cal. w/min. repeater, OF	20,000	25,000	30,000
HC	22,000	27,000	32,000
Perp. moonphase cal. w/min. rep. and chrono., OF	24,000	28,000	33,000
Clock Watch, Gold, OF	5,000	9,000	13,000
HC	7,000	11,000	16,000

HEBDOMAS

Swiss

The Hebdomas name is commonly found on imported Swiss novelty "8" day watches. Produced from the early 1900's to the 1960's, these popular timepieces featured fancy colored dials with an opening at the bottom of dial to expose the balance wheel and pallet-fork. This style watch is now being -made by Amex Time Corp. under the name of (Lucien Piccard) & other Co. names.

Hebdomas, 8 day (JOURS) 6 jewels, balance seen from the face of the watch. Ca.1920s. This style watch is now being made by Amex Time corp. (Lucien Piccard).

Hebdomas, 8 day (JOURS) 6 jewels, 1 adjustment, exposed balance, day date, center seconds, Ca. 1920s.

TYPE -DESCRIPTION	ABP	Ex-Fn	Mint
8 day, exposed balance, 7J, gun metal, 50mm, OF, C. 1920	$150	$275	$325
8 day, exposed balance, 7J, base metal, fancy dial, 50mm, OF, C.1920	185	300	350
8 day, exposed balance, 7J, silver, 50mm, OF, C. 1920	200	325	375
8 day, exposed balance, 7J, silver, 50mm, HC, C. 1920's . . . . ★	250	425	525
with fancy dial, silver, 55mm, OF, C. 1920's	350	525	675
8 day, exposed balance, 63, silver, 50mm, OF, Day-Date, C 1920 . . .	300	575	675

↶ Note: Some models and grades are not included. Their values can be determined by comparing with similar age, size, metal content, style, models and grades listed.

↶ Watches listed in this book are priced at the collectable fair market value at the Trade Show level, as complete watches having an original case, an original white enamel dial, and with the entire original movement in good working order with no repairs needed, unless otherwise noted.

COMPARISON OF WATCH CASE SIZES	
U.S.A.	EUROPEAN
10-12 SIZE	40—44MM
16 SIZE	45—49MM
18 SIZE	50—55 MM

HUGUENIN & Co.

Swiss

Founded by Adolphe Huguenin and the firm name registered in 1880. Purchased by Hamilton W. Co. in March of 1959. Best known for the 2-Train, 1/4 second jump watch.

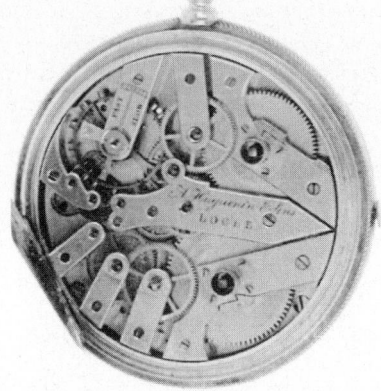

Huguenin & Co. 2-Train 1/4 second jump watch, center sweep hand, enamel dial, 54mm, KW KS, 18K, Ca. 1880.

Huguenin & Co., 2-Train 1/4 second jump watch, 2 main barrels & 2 gear trains, 54mm, KW KS, Ca. 1880.

TYPE — DESCRIPTION	ABP	Ex-Fn	Mint
KW, cylinder, silver, 46- 48mm, OF, C. 1870s	$85	$95	$135
KW, silver, 46- 48mm, HC, C. 1870s	125	150	200
KW, cylinder escapement, **18K**, 48mm, OF, C.1870s	250	400	450
KW, fancy engraved 18K, 47mm, HC, C. 1870s	450	600	800
1/4 Sec. Jump, 2-train, **silver**, 50-54mm	1,000	1,500	2,500
1/4 Sec. Jump, 2-train, **gold**, 50-54mm	2,000	3,000	3,500
Chronograph, gold, 45-52mm, OF	800	1,000	1,200
HC	800	1,200	1,500
1/4 hr. repeater, gold, 46-52mm, OF	1,200	1,600	2,000
HC	1,500	2,000	2,500
Minute repeater, gold, 46-52mm, OF	1,800	3,000	3,500
HC	2,500	3,200	4,500
OF, w/ chrono	2,200	3,500	4,000
OF, w/ split chrono	4,500	7,000	8,000
HC, w/ split chrono	5,000	8,000	11,000
HC, w/ chrono., cal. & rnoonphase	4,500	9,000	13,000
Minute Clock Watch, Gold, OF	5,000	10,000	13,000
HC	7,000	11,000	14,000

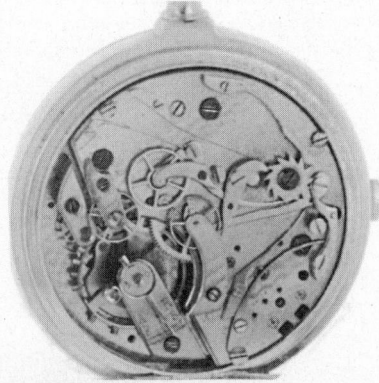

Huguenin & Co., Chronograph, enamel dial, 51mm, 18K, Hunting Case, Ca. 1890.

Huguenin & Co., Chronograph, 3/4 plate movement, 51mm, 18K, Hunting Case, Ca. 1590.

International Watch Co. (Swiss)

The founder of the prestigious Swiss International Watch Co. was an American engineer F. A. Jones from Boston and previously worked for E. Howard Watch & Clock Company. F. A. Jones and C. L. Kidder worked together from about 1869 to 1872 building up a new firm which was the only North-eastern watch factory founded in Switzerland by Americans with machinery made in America. Mr. C. L. Kidder returned to U.S.A. in 1872 and took on a position with Cornell Watch Co. as first Superintendent in the new Newark factory. Mr. Jones stayed to continue building up the factory which was completed in spring of 1875. F. A. Jones in December of 1875 filed for bankruptcy and in 1876 returned to U.S.A. The I. W. Co. factory started by F. A. Jones was short lived and produced about 5,000 watches. In 1877 the production of the factory (now called "Internationale Uhrenfabrik") was delegated to F. F. Seeland of New York. In 1879 Mr. Seeland was removed from his position by managing director Johann Rauschenbach. The company today is still making precision, hand crafted watches.

International W. Co., apertures for jump hr. & mm. disc, 11-15J., enamel dial, Pallweber Caliber, Ca. 1880-90.

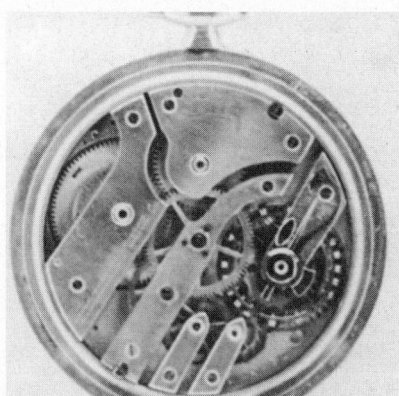

International Watch Co., 54mm, 17 jewels, Adj., serial number 741,073.

TYPE - DESCRIPTION	ABP	Ex-Fn	Mint
Early, KW, Time only, Swiss bar, silver case.	$150	$185	$265
Time only, gold, 40-44mm, OF	400	650	750
HC	625	950	1,150
Time only, gold, 45-50mm, OF	585	850	1,000
HC	850	1,250	1,650
Jones Caliber, 13-16J., grades H, D, S, R, B ★★	675	800	1,200
Jones Caliber, **20J., grade E**, GJS, 3/4, SW ★★★★	1,000	2,000	2,500
Caliber 71-72, 16J., GJS, OF. ★★	625	1,000	1,400
Caliber 72-72, 16J., GJS, HC ★★	725	1,200	1,500
Pallweber, 11-15J., jump hr. & mm. disc, enamel dial, **Niello**, HC	1,500	2,500	3,000
silver, HC.	1,500	2,000	2,500
14K, HC.	2,200	3,000	4,000
Chronograph, gold, 45-50mm, OF.	1,800	2,500	3,000
HC	2,000	3,000	3,500
Split second chronograph, gold, 45-52mm, OF	2,500	4,000	4,500
HC	3,000	5,000	5,500
Minute repeater, gold, 46-52mm, OF.	2,500	4,000	5,000
HC	3,000	5,000	6,500
OF, w/split chrono	5,000	8,000	9,000
HC, w/split chrono.	6,000	9,000	10,500
OF, w/cal. & moonphase	6,000	8,500	10,500
HC, w/chrono., cal. & moonphase	7,000	10,500	12,500
Detent chronometer, gold, 48-52mm, OF	6,000	8,500	9,500
World Time watch, gold, 48-52mm, OF.	8,000	12,500	15,500
Perpetual moonphase calendar, gold, OF	6,000	10,500	12,500

TYPE - DESCRIPTION	ABP	Ex-Fn	Mint
Perpetual moonphase calendar, w/minute repeater, HC	$25,000	$40,000	$60,000
Clock Watch, Gold, 48-52mm, OF.	7,000	10,000	15,000
HC	9,000	12,000	18,000

A new numbering system was started with serial # 01 in **1884**. The old register can not be found and the new uninterrupted serial numbers list started on the 9th of January 1885 with serial number 6,501. The highest known serial number for the "JONES" Caliber is 42,327, & the lowest "SEELAND" Caliber serial number is 26,211, the highest number for "SEELAND" Caliber is 60,014.

PRODUCTION TOTALS

OLD DATE—	SERIAL#	DATE -	SERIAL #	DATE -	SERIAL #	DATE -	SERIAL #
1875 —	7,000	1901-	253,500	1926-	645,000	1951-	1,253,000
1877—	25,000	1902-	276,500	1927-	866,000	1952-	1,291,000
1879—	50,000	1903-	298,500	1928-	890,500	1953-	1,316,000
1881 —	80,000	1904-	321,000	1929-	919,500	1954-	1,335,000
1883 —	100,000	1905 -	349,500	1930 -	929,000	1955 -	1,361,000
NEW		1906 -	377,500	1931 -	937,500	1956 -	1,399,000
DATE —	SERIAL#	1907-	406,000	1932-	938,000	1957-	1,436,000
1884—	6,501	1908-	435,000	1933-	939,000	1958-	1,460,000
1885—	15,500	1909-	463,500	1934-	940,000	1959-	1,513,000
1886—	23,500	1910 -	492,000	1935 -	945,000	1960-	1,553,000
1887—	29,500	1911-	521,000	1936-	955,500	1961-	1,612,000
1888—	37,500	1912-	557,000	1937-	979,000	1962-	1,666,000
1889—	49,000	1913-	594,000	1938-	1,000,000	1963-	1,733,000
1890—	63,000	1914-	620,500	1939-	1,013,000	1964-	1,778,000
1891—	75,500	1915-	635,000	1940-	1,019,000	1965-	1,796,000
1892—	87,500	1916-	657,000	1941-	1,039,000	1966-	1,820,000
1893—	103,000	1917-	684,000	1942-	1,062,000	1967-	1,889,000
1894 —	117,000	1918-	714,000	1943-	1,078,000	1968-	1,905,000
1895—	133,000	1919-	742,000	1944-	1,092,000	1969-	1,970,000
1896—	151,500	1920 -	765,000	1945-	1,106,000	1970-	2,026,000
1897—	170,500	1921-	780,000	1946-	1,131,000	1971 -	2,113,000
1898—	194,000	1922-	783,500	1947-	1,153,000	1972-	2,218,000
1899—	212,000	1923-	793,500	1948-	1,177,000	1973-	2,230,000
1900—	231,000	1924-	807,000	1949-	1,205,000	1974-	2,265,000
		1925 -	827,500	1950-	1,222,000	1975-	2,275,000

The above list is provided for determining the APPROXIMATE age of your watch, Match serial number with date. Watches were not necessarily sold in the exact order of manufactured dale.

OLD STYLE MOVEMENTS

NOTE:**"Jones"** Caliber, had 6 different grades, the highest grade was **E** = 20J, SW, 3/4 plate in nickel, 3 sets of screwed gold settings; next w grade **H** =16-18J, SW, 3/4 plate in nickel; grade **D** =16J, SW, 3/4 plate in nickel; grade **S** = 15J, SW, 3/4 plate in nickel; grade **R** = 15J, 3/4 plate; grade **B** = 13J, 3/4 plate. The **"Jones"** model used a stem-wind & *set,* a long index regulator & exposed winding gears. The *key- wind* models did not have exposed winding gears but used long index regulator. **"SEELAND"** Caliber, usually were full or 3/4 plate, with short index regulator, and lever or pin set.

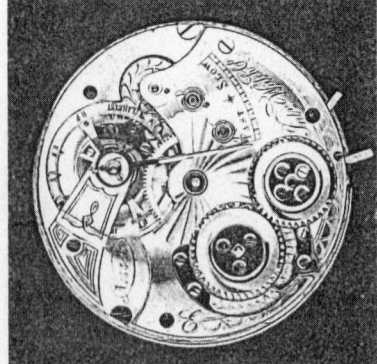

"Jones" Caliber, grade "E", HC, **20J.,** long index regulator, exposed wolf tooth wind gears, gold train, 3 sets of screwed in gold jewel settings, SW, 3/4 plate, overcoil hair-spring, (may have a pat. date on movement of Sept. 15th, 1868) about 16 size 43mm, Ca. 1876.

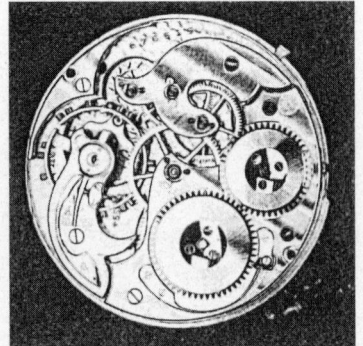

"71" Caliber, 16J., OF. 4 sets of screw style gold jewel settings, 300 made in 1904 & 300 in 1917, also HC Caliber "72", 300 made in 1904 & 300 in 1917, 71 & 72 total=1,200.

Ca.1873

Right: Exact copy and size of small catalog, 23 pages with **16 different** movements & 3 dials. On the Cover: **International Watch Company F. H. Mathez Gen'l Agent F. A. Jones Managing Director. New York, No.5 Maiden Lane.** Note: Patented Feb.2d 1869, also Note: 6 pairs hole jewels, 3 pairs end stones & 2 ruby pallets total=20 jewels.

Illustrated Catalogue of Movements

MANUFACTURED BY THE

International Watch Co.

OF NEW YORK.

GENERAL AGENCY, No. 5, MAIDEN LANE.

Illustrations exact size of movements. 16 Size. 19 Lignes or 43 Millimetres.

Millimetres.

Pattern N.
STEM-WINDER.
Automatic Hand Setting Attachment.
Nickel Movement.

Six pairs genuine Ruby jewels, and three pairs extra-fine Ruby endstones; exposed Ruby pallets; Unique Double Regulator; Elson Attachment; Isochronal Hair Spring; Chronometer Balance (gold rim) accurately adjusted to heat, cold, isochronism and position; named

Schaffhausen.

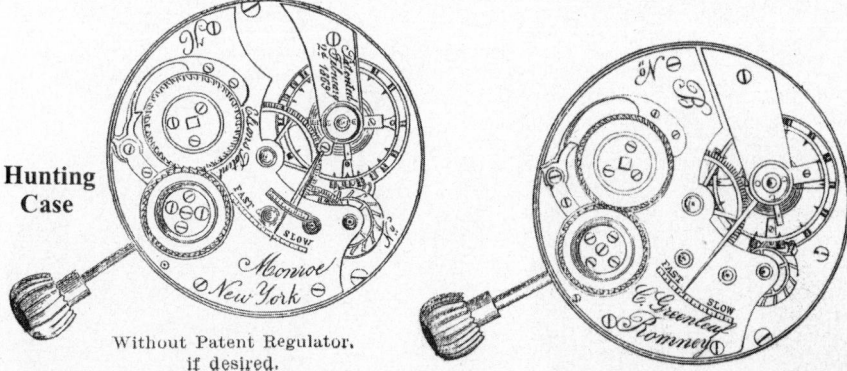

Hunting Case

Without Patent Regulator, if desired.

Pattern H, No.1, stem winder automatic hand setting attachment, nickel movement, six pairs genuine ruby jewels and three pair extra fine ruby end stones, exposed ruby pallets, unique double regulator, Elson attachment, isochronal hairspring, chronometer balance (gold rim), adjusted.

Pattern B, Stem Winder, Nickel movement, Hunting Case, 5 pairs Rubies, and upper center jeweled, with Elson Attachment if desired. Special note: In Preparation an Open Face Stem Winder, will be ready in a few months.

INTERNATIONAL WATCH CO SCHAFFHAUSEN
Fabrique d'Horlogerie de Précision fondée en 1868

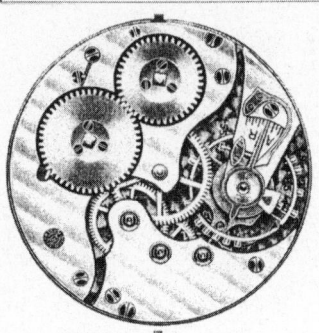

Left, Cal. 57, OF
18 lig., 41mm

Right, Cal. 58, HC
19 lig., 43.15mm

Left, Cal. 52, OF
1st in 1893
18 lig., 41mm
19 lig., 43.15mm

Right, Cal. 53, HC
18 lig., 41mm
19 lig., 43.15mm

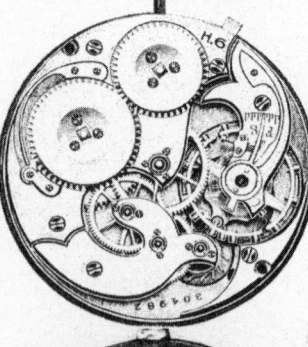

Left, Cal. 71, OF
19 lig., 43.15mm

Right, Cal. 72, HC
19 lig., 43.15mm

Center
Cal., Seeland
19 Lignes
3/4 Plate

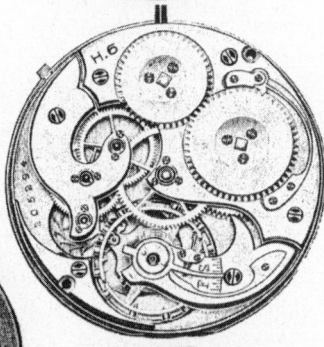

Right: Cal. Pallweber, type III, 19 Lignes,   Left: Cal., Seeland, 18 Lignes, full plate Quality C.
digital time indicator , 1st in 1885.

INTERNATIONAL WATCH CO SCHAFFHAUSEN
Fabrique d'Horlogerie de Précision fondée en 1868

Cal. 65

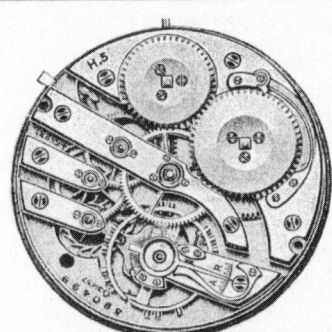

Left, Cal. 65, OF
19 lig., 43.15mm

Right, Cal. 66, HC
19 lig., 43.15mm

Lépine

Left, Cal. 73, OF
17 lig., 38mm

Right, Cal. 74, HC
17 lig., 38mm

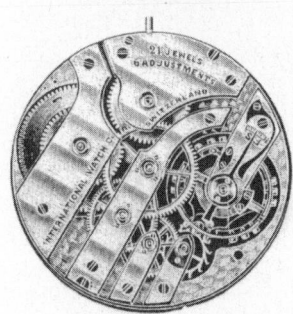

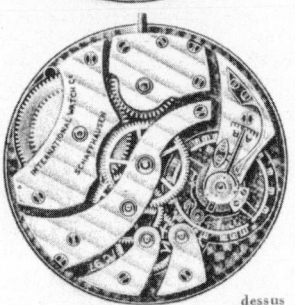

dessus

Left, Cal. 77, OF
17 lig., 38mm

Right, Cal. 95 & 97
HC, 17 lig., 37.8mm

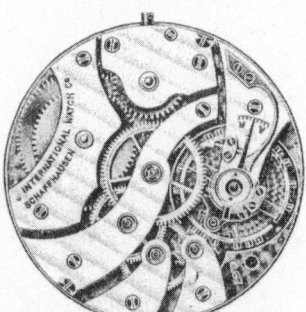

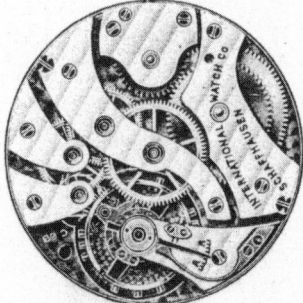

Left, Cal. 67, OF
18 lig., 41mm

Right, Cal. 68, HC
18 lig., 41mm

INVICTA (Swiss)

Founded by R. Picard in 1837. Invicta trade-mark was registered on May 18, 1896 by Files de R. Picard of La Chaux-de-Fonds. Other names used were Seeland Watch Co. and Eno Watch Co.

TYPE - DESCRIPTION	ABP	Ex-Fn	Mint
Time only, gold, 25-38mm, OF	$175	$250	$325
Time only, gold, 40—44mm, 10-12 size, OF.	200	300	350
HC	225	350	400
Time only, gold, 45- 50mm, OF	225	350	450
Gold, HC.	250	375	500
Time only, gold & **enamel**, 45- 50mm, OF	425	700	950
HC	475	800	1,100
1/4 hr. repeater, gun metal , 48mm, OF, C. 1900s	400	500	700
1/4 hr. repeater, silver, 48mm, OF, C. 1900s	450	600	800
1/4 hr. repeater, silver, 50mm, HC, C. 1900s	600	800	975
1/4 hr. repeater, **gold**, 58mm, HC, C. 1900s.	1,000	2,000	2,500
with chronograph	1,500	2,200	2,800
Mm. repeater, gun metal, 52mm, HC, C. 1900s	750	1,000	1,500
silver, HC.	800	1,200	1,700
gold, HC.	1,200	2,500	3,500
W/chronograph, gold, HC	1,500	3,000	3,700

INVICTA, **1/4** hour repeater with chronograph, 18 jewels, Hunting Case about 58MM, Ca. 1895.

JACOT, HENRI (PARIS)

Henri Jacot settled in Paris in 1820 and developed the carriage clock industry. He also invented and improved watchmaking and clock making tools. Henri Jacot died July 31, 1867.

TYPE - DESCRIPTION	ABP	Ex-Fn	Mint
KW, cylinder, silver, 46mm, OF	$85	$100	$125
HC	125	150	195
KW, LADIES, **18K**, 40-44mm, OF	225	300	385
HC	300	350	450
KW, GENTS, **18K**, 48mm, OF.	400	500	700
HC	500	700	900
1/4 hr. repeater, SILVER, 50mm, OF	700	1,000	1,200
1/4 hr. repeater, GOLD, 50mm, OF.	1,400	2,000	2,400

CHARLES E. JACOT

New York & Swiss

In 1837 Charles worked with his uncle, Louis Matthey in New York City. During the 20 year period of working in the U.S.A. he was sold an interest in the firm and the name was changed to Jacot, Courvoisier & Co. Charles E. Jacot had a patent for a star duplex escapement on Apr. 30, 1840 and July 20, 1852. He had about 12 or more watch patents.

In 1857 he returned to Switzerland and formed the company Jacot & Saltzman. In 1876 the name of the firm was Charles E. Jacot. He remained in close contact with his New York connections until his death in 1897. In 1925 the firm Chas. E. Jacot was listed in Le Locle.

TYPE - DESCRIPTION	ABP	Ex-Fn	Mint
Early, KW, Time only, silver case	$165	$225	$300
Early, KW, Time only, gold case, ladies.	200	300	450
Time only, gold, 40-44mm, OF	300	500	600
HC	400	650	800
Time only, gold, 45-50mm, OF	400	650	800
HC	700	900	1,000
Time only, 30J., independent 1/4 seconds, 2 train, gold, OF	1,200	2,700	3,500
HC	1,500	3,200	4,000
3 or 4 star duplex, Patented July 1852, gold case . . . . ★★★★	2,500	4,500	5,500

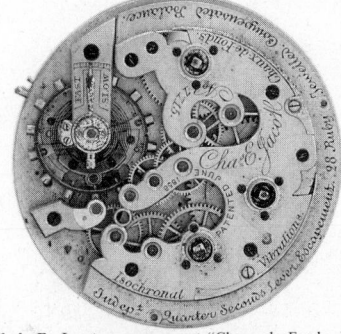

Cha's E. Jacot, Patents, Sept. 64, Nov. 67, Apr. 70;, 50mm, lever escapement, SW, HC, Ca. 1871, S# 8133.

Cha's E. Jacot, on movement "Chaux de Fonda, Indep't Quarter Seconds Lever Escapement 28 Ruby Jewels Compensated Balance. Isochronal Vibrations. Patented June, 1858, S# 7715", 2 train, KW & KS from back.

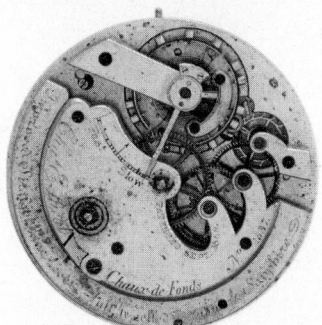

Cha's E. Jacot, on movement "Chaux de Fonds, Improved Straight Line Lever, full jeweled in Ruby & Sapphire, Pat. Sept. 1859, S# 1637", KW & KS.

Cha's E. Jacot, on movement, "Pat, Oct. 1867, N=25338", KW & KS from back, 15 jewels, 40mm.

RIGHT: Cha's E. Jacot's STAR DUPLEX escapement with 3 pointed star, escapement with 4 pointed star Pat. # 1,570 on Apr. 30, 1840 also JULY 20, 1852.

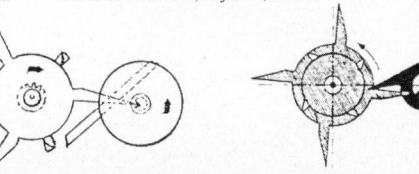

JOSEPH JOHNSON

LIVERPOOL, (1810-1850)

Joseph Johnson of Liverpool started his firm in the early 1800's. It lasted until the mid 1800's. The Johnson firm supplied the U.S. market with low to medium cost key-wind watches.

TYPE - DESCRIPTION	ABP	Ex-Fn	Mint
KW, 7-15J, fusee, silver, 47mm, OF	$125	$275	$325
KW, 7- 15J, fusee, silver, 47mm, HC	150	300	375
KW, 7-15J, swiss, **gilt dial**, fancy case, **18K**, 48mm, OF	275	500	600
KW, lever, fusee, **gold dial**, **Heavy 18K**, 52mm, HC	800	1,200	1,500
KW, **rack lever** escapement, **Silver**, 56mm, OF	300	400	535
HC	400	500	650
KW, **rack lever** escapement, **Gold**, 56mm, OF	700	1,000	1,200
HC	1, 100	1,200	1,500
KW, verge fusee, **multi-color gold dial & THIN case**, 52mm, OF	400	800	1,000
HC	700	1,000	1,200
KW, **15 sec. dial**, detached lever, fusee,			
multi-color gold dial & case, 50mm, OF	800	1,200	1,500

Signed on movement *Josh. Johnson Liverpool Detached Patent*, Key wind Key Set, diamond end stone, Massey style side lever, the escape wheel coverts the second hand to rotate once every 15-seconds rather than the normal 60-seconds. Multi-color gold case and dial with carved decorations on the back of case and outer rim of the case, S #5563, 50mm open face case, Ca. 1850.

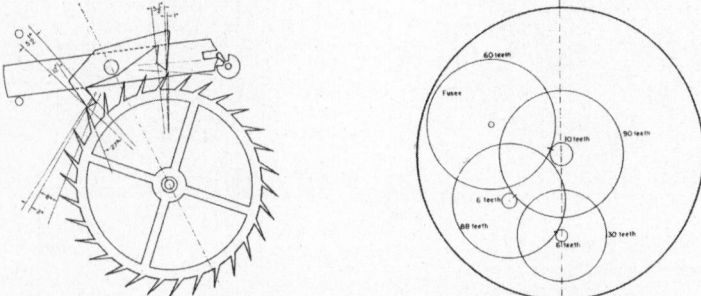

Jos. Johnson Escapement: Right: 30 tooth escape wheel with right angle lever. Left: Layout of movement the fusee has 60 teeth it engages with 10 leaf pinion on center wheel, center wheel has 90 teeth which engages 6 leaves on pinion of third wheel which has 88 teeth it engages with a pinion of 6 leaves on the escape wheel. (slow beat of 3 2/3 seconds)

JULES JURGENSEN (Swiss)

The firm of Jules Jurgensen was an extension of the earlier firm of Urban Jurgensen & Sons, which was located, at various times, in Copenhagen and Le Locle. Jules ultimately established his firm in Le Locle after his father's death in the early 1830's. From that time forward the company produced, generally speaking, very fine watches that were high grade and complicated. It appears that by 1850 the company had already established a strong market in America, offering beautiful heavy 18K gold watches of exemplary quality. Until around 1885, most stem-winding watches exhibited the **bow-setting feature**. After 1885, as the firm started to buy movements from other companies, we begin to see variations in Jurgensen watches. By 1930, Jurgensen watches barely resembled the quality and aesthetics of the early period, and they are not as desirable to the collector.

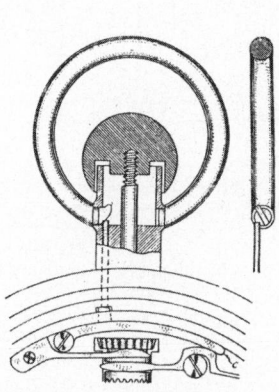

The Jules Jurgensen famous bow-setting feature, wasPatented in 1867.

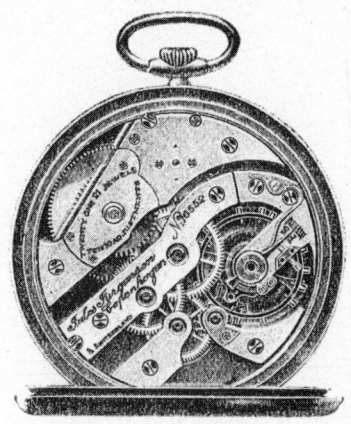

Jules Jurgensen, 1923 MODEL

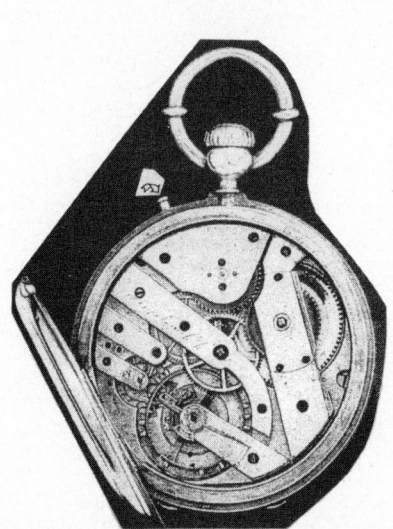

Jules Jurgensen, movement signed on center bridge & case, counter poised lever, 18K hunting case numbered 14709, 20 jewels, wolf tooth winding, early stem wind, uncommon pin set for a J. Jurgensen, 45mm, Ca. 1865.

Jules Jurgensen, movement signed on barrel bridge "*Jules Jurgensen Copenhagen No.6319*". 18K Hunting case, 17 jewels, with gold escape wheel & chron ometer pivoted detent escapement, KWKS, Ca. 1860.

Almost any collectible Jurgensen watch will be fully signed on the dial, movement, and case. Watches not so marked should be examined carefully; and untypical or inelegant stamping should be viewed suspiciously, as there have been some forgeries of these fine watches. Frequently one finds the original box and papers accompanying the watch, which enhances the value.

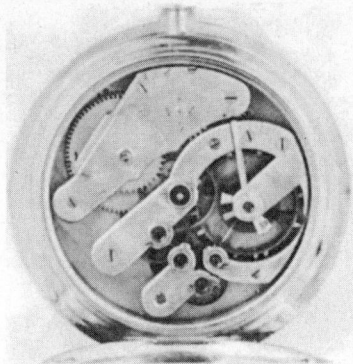

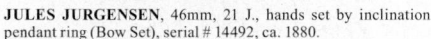

JULES JURGENSEN, 46mm, 21 J., hands set by inclination pendant ring (Bow Set), serial # 14492, ca. 1880.

JULES JURGENSEN, 46-52mm, Minute repeater, 32 jewels, Ca.1890.

TYPE - DESCRIPTION	ABP	Ex-Fn	Mint
Time only, gold, 35- 44mm, Ca. 1930, OF	$600	$750	$1,000
HC	800	1,200	1,500
Time only, gold, 45-55mm, OF	900	1,200	1,700
HC	1,000	2,000	2,500
Time only, gold, 45-55mm, **Pin Set**, OF ★	2,000	3,000	3,500
HC	2,700	3,500	4,000
Time only, gold, 45-55mm, **Bow Set**, OF	2,000	3,000	3,500
HC	2,700	3,500	4,000
Wind Indicator, Enamel dial, 46-52mm, Gold OF ★★★	6,000	12,000	20,000
HC ★★★	7,000	17,000	22,000
Flat digital watch, 18J., gold, 40-44mm, OF, Ca. 1930	4,000	4,500	5,500
1/5 jump sec., with, 27J, 2 main barrels & 2 gear trains, 18K OF	3,500	6,000	7,000
Chronograph, gold, 45-50mm, OF	2,800	4,500	5,500
HC	4,000	5,000	6,500
HC w/register	4,500	6,000	7,500
Split second chronograph, gold, 45-52mm, OF	5,000	7,500	8,500
HC	6,000	8,500	9,500
5 minute repeater, gold, 46-52mm, OF	4,000	6,500	7,500
HC	5,000	7,000	8,000
Minute repeater, gold, 46-52mm, OF	5,000	8,000	9,500
HC	6,000	9,000	11,000
OF, w/ chrono	6,500	8,500	10,000
HC, w/chrono	8,000	10,000	13,000
OF, w/split chrono	10,000	15,000	23,000
HC, w/split chrono	11,000	18,000	28,000
Detent chronometer, gold, 48-52mm, OF	6,500	8,000	10,000
HC	7,000	9,000	12,000
Minute repeater w/detent chronometer esc, gold, 46-52mm,OF ★★★	10,000	15,000	22,000
HC ★★★	12,000	20,000	27,000
Perpetual moonphase calendar, gold, OF	20,000	24,000	30,000
HC	25,000	30,000	35,000
Perp. moonphase cal. w/min. repeater, OF	45,000	60,000	75,000
HC	50,000	70,000	90,000
Tourbillon, Gold, OF/HC ★★★★★	100,000	250,000	350,000
Clock Watch, OF	10,000	16,000	23,000
HC	12,000	22,000	30,000

EDWARD KOEHN

Swiss

Koehn was an innovative watchmaker and a specialist in the design of thin calibre watches. Formerly associated with Patek Phillipe and H. R. Ekegren, he produced watches under his own name from 1891-1930.

TYPE - DESCRIPTION	ABP	Ex-Fn	Mint
Time only, gold, 40- 44mm, OF	$440	$600	$700
HC	600	900	1,200
Time only, gold, 45- 50mm, OF	900	1,200	1,500
HC	1,100	2,000	2,400
Chronograph, gold, 45-50mm, OF	1,300	1,600	2,200
HC	1,500	1,800	2,400
Split second chronograph, gold, 45-52mm, OF	2,000	2,500	3,000
HC	3,000	3,500	4,000
5 minute repeater, gold, 45-52mm, OF	3,000	4,000	4,500
HC	3,300	4,500	5,000
Minute repeater, gold, 46-52mm, OF	2,500	4,000	5,000
HC	3,080	5,000	6,000
OF, w/split chrono	4,000	8,000	10,000
HC, w/split chrono	5,500	9,000	12,000

E. Koehn, of Geneve, 46mm, 18 jewels, note: **free standing barrel**, lever escapement, Ca. 1900.

☞ Note: Some models and grades are not included. Their values can be determined by comparing with similar age, size, metal content, style, models and grades listed.

☞ Watches listed in this book are priced at the collectable fair market value at the trade show level, as complete watches having an original case, an original white enamel dial, and with the entire original movement in good working order with no repairs needed, unless otherwise noted.

COMPARISON OF WATCH CASE SIZES	
U.S.A.	**EUROPEAN**
10-12 SIZE	40—44MM
16 SIZE	45—49MM
18 SIZE	50—55 MM

A. LANGE & SOHNE

A.Lange & Sohne was established with the aid of the German government at Glashutte, Germany in 1845. Lange typically produced 3/4 plate lever watches in gilt finish for the domestic market, and in nickel for the export market. High grade and very practical, these watches had a banking system for the pallet that was later used briefly by E. Howard in America. Lange complicated watches are scarce and very desirable. On May 8, 1945 Russian bombers destroy workshops. All A. Lange & Sohne must be **triple signed** (Dial, Case, Movement) to bring top prices.

PRODUCTION TOTALS

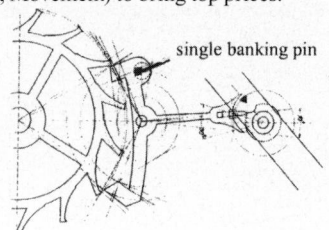

single banking pin

DATE- SERIAL #	DATE- SERIAL #	DATE—SERIAL #
1870— 3,500	1895— 35,000	1920— 75,000
1875— 10,000	1900— 40,000	1925— 80,000
1880— 15,000	1905— 50,000	1930— 85,000
1885— 20,000	1910— 60,000	1935— 90,000
1890— 30,000	1915— 70,000	1940— 100,000

TYPE -DESCRIPTION	ABP	Ex-Fn	Mint
Time only, **A.L.S.** first quality , GJS, **18k gold**, 45- 52mm, OF.	$4,000	$5,500	$8,000
HC	5,500	7,000	9,000
Time only, **D.U.F.** grade, pressed jewels, **14k gold**, 45-52mm, OF	1,500	2,700	3,200
HC	2,000	3,200	3,700
Time only, **O.L.I.W.** grade, pressed jewels, not adjusted	500	700	1,000
World War II model, wind indicator, 52mm, OF (before 1945)	2,000	2,500	3,000
Chronograph gold, 45-50mm, OF	9,000	13,000	20,000
HC	10,000	15,000	22,000
Split second chronograph, gold, 45-52mm, OF	15,000	25,000	30,000
HC	17,000	30,000	35,000
1/4 hr. repeater, gold, 45-52mm, OF	10,000	17,000	22,000
HC	12,000	22,000	27,000
Minute repeater, gold, 45-52mm, OF.	17,000	25,000	30,000
HC	18,000	30,000	40,000
OF, w/split chrono.	20,000	35,000	50,000
HC, w/split chrono	23,000	50,000	60,000
Anker chronometer, gold, 48-52mm, OF.	8,000	10,000	17,000
HC (**Anker** = German for lever escapement)	10,000	15,000	22,000
Detent chronometer, gold, 48-52mm, OF	20,000	30,000	40,000
Karrusel, 14J., 60 min. carriage driven by **center wheel**, 18K . . . . .★★★	50,000	75,000	95,000

Right: To identify a Glashutte movement note balance cock, and single banking pin .

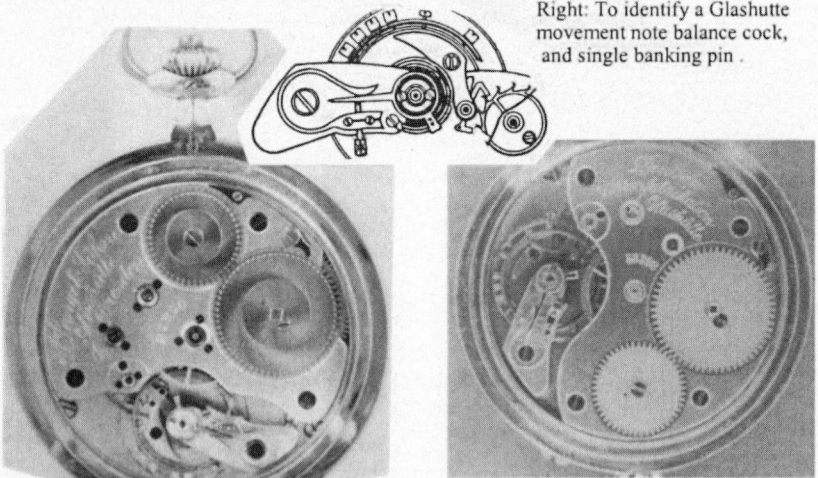

A.LANGE & SOHNE, 52mm, serial number 87250, hunting case. The A.L.S. top grade watches had gold jewel settings & screwed to the plates, diamond end stone, gold lever & gold escape wheel, Adj.to5 positions. Second A.L.S. grade the gold settings are not screwed into plates, and most had no diamond end stone, in 18K cases.

D. U. F. grade by Lange, 50mm, 3/4 plate, engraved on movement "Deutsche Uhren Fabrikation Glashutte," serial number 58,398. The **D. U. F.** grade had pressed jewels, brass & nickel balance, adjusted to 3 positions, t he D.U.F. grades came in 14K cases and introduced in about 1885 with lower production cost to compete with other Co.'s.

TYPE — DESCRIPTION	ABP	Ex-Fn	Mint
Perpetual moonphase calendar, gold, OF	$30,000	$45,000	$60,000
Perp. moonphase cal. w/min. repeater, OF	45,000	80,000	125,000
Perp. moonphase cal. w/min. rep. and chronograph, HC ..... ★★★	100,000	200,000	250,000
Perp. moonphase cal. w/min. rep., leap year indicator, 30 minutes recorder			
2 button split chronograph, 60mm, HC .... ★★★★	185,000	250,000	325,000

A. Lange & Sohne, 60mm Hunter Cased Minute Repeating instantaneous Perpetual calendar with day, date, month and leap year indicator, full split second chronograph operated by two buttons with minute recorder and the phases of the moon. The white enamel dial has Arabic numbers, pierced gold hands, four subsidiary dials indicating day, date and the month is combined with leap year indicator and 30 minutes recorder, and the moon phases is combined constant seconds.

A. Lange & Sohne, the movement made In the typical Glashutte 3/4 plate style with a nickel finish, gold lever escapement with convex entry pallet & concave exit pallet, compensation balance, diamond endstone, gold escape wheel, gold lever, repeating on two gongs. This type of watches have 40 to 60 jewels, 75 wheels, over 300 screws and 24 bridges. The movement was supplied by Audemars Piguet in 1908-1909 & may be one of fourteen with a two button chronograph finished & cased by A. Lange & Sohne. Audemars Piguet supplied about 35 watches of this type to the Glashutte market.

LE COULTRE &CO.

Swiss

Antoine Le Coultre in 1833 formed a company to make ebauches. He created a machine to cut pinions from solid steel as well as other machines for manufacturing clocks and watches. By 1900 they were making flat or thin watches. In 1936 Jaeger & Le Coultre officially merge. The signed watches with Jaeger - Le Coultre logo may fetch more money, but have the same quality grade movement as the signed Le Coultre dial & movement. They make movements & parts for Vacheron & Constantin, P. P. & Co., Omega, Longines & many more.

TYPE - DESCRIPTION	ABP	Ex-Fn	Mint
Early, KW, Time only, Swiss bar, Pre. 1870, silver case	$75	$150	$300
Time only, gold, 40- 44mm, OF	200	325	525
HC	250	450	650
Time only, gold, 45- 52mm, OF	225	400	600
HC	385	550	750
8 day, 15J, wind indicator, 45mm, **18K**, OF	600	1,000	1,400
8 day, 14K, OF	500	900	1,200
8day,S.S.,OF	300	500	700
Roulette wheel style bezel, gold, 40mm, OF	600	1,200	1,500
World time watch, gold, 48-52mm, OF	4,000	5,500	7,000
Chronograph, gold, 45-50mm, OF	700	1,000	1,200
HC	800	1,200	1,500
OF, w/register	750	1,200	1,400
Split second chronograph, gold, 45-52mm, OF	1,000	2,000	2,500
HC	1,400	2,500	3,000

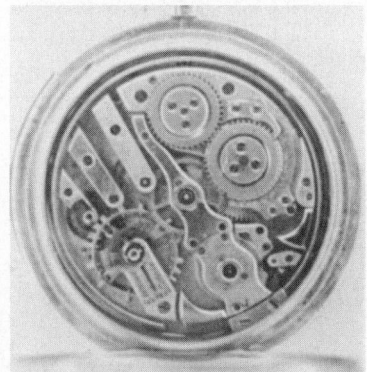 

Le Coultre & Co., 52mm, 32J., minute repeater, exposed winding gears, high grade movement, 14K HC.

Le Coultre & Co., Min. repeater, 17 jewels, note the repeater governor, signed under the repeater hammer "L.C.& Co." Ca. 1930.

TYPE - DESCRIPTION	ABP	Ex-Fn	Mint
1/4 hr. repeater, gold, 46-52mm, OF	$1,000	$1,800	$2,300
HC w/chrono., cal. & moonphase	2,400	5,000	6,000
Minute repeater, gold, 46-52mm, OF	2,000	3,000	3,500
HC	2,300	3,500	4,000
OF, w/chrono. & register	2,400	3,200	3,800
HC, w/chrono. & register	2,600	4,000	4,500
HC, w/split chrono.	3,500	7,000	10,000
HC w/chrono., cal. & moonphase	5,000	8,000	12,000
Perpetual moonphase calendar, gold, OF	7,000	10,000	12,000
HC	7,500	12,000	14,000
Perp. moonphase cal. w/min. repeater, OF	15,000	25,000	30,000
HC	17,000	30,000	35,000
Perpetual moonphase cal. w/ min. rep. & chrono., OF	18,000	27,000	32,000
HC	20,000	32,000	38,000
Clock Watch, gold, 46-52mm, OF	6,000	11,000	13,000
HC	8,000	13,000	16,000

Note: Ebauche movements look under hammers for initials L.C. & Co.(not on all movements)

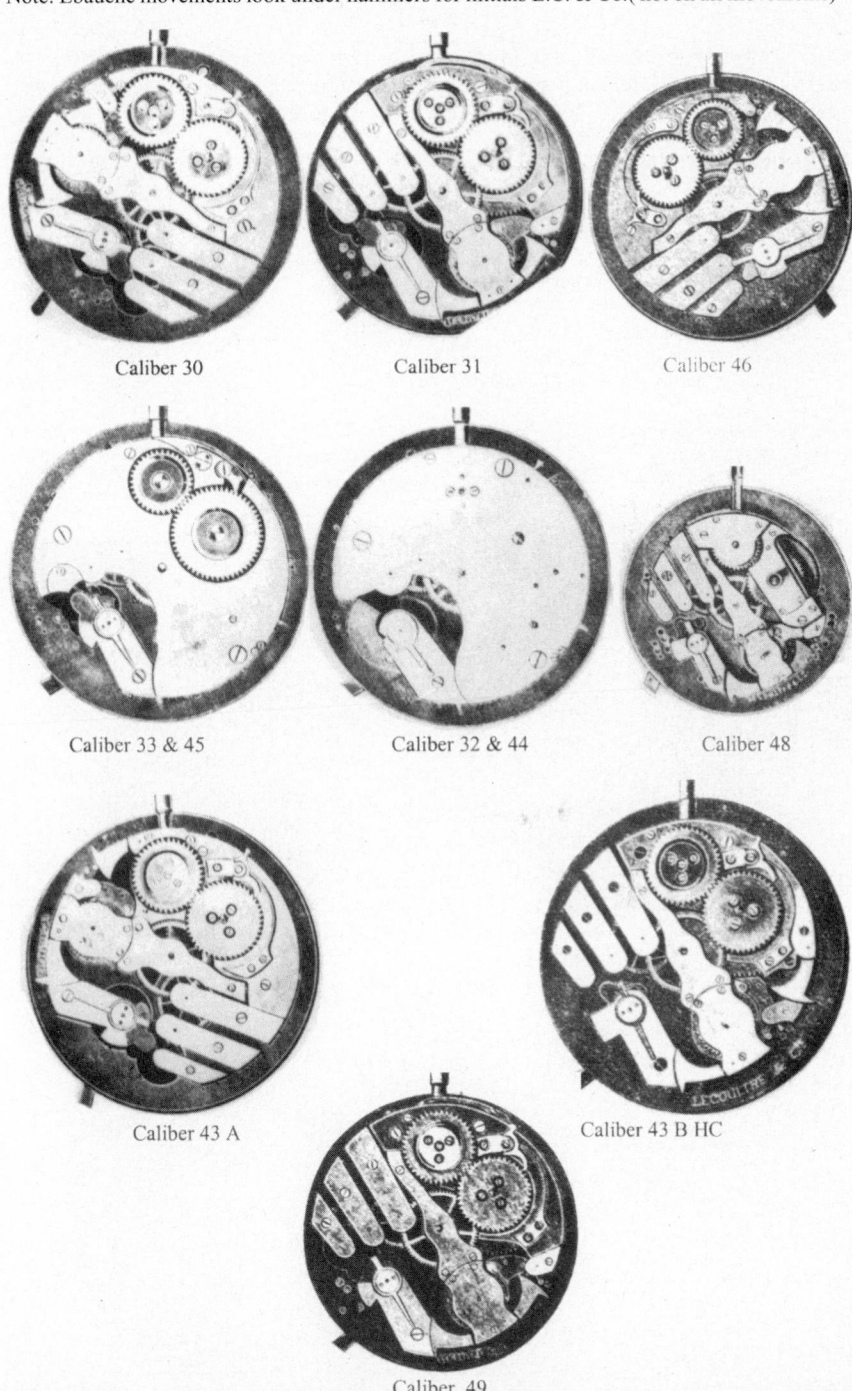

Caliber 30   Caliber 31   Caliber 46

Caliber 33 & 45   Caliber 32 & 44   Caliber 48

Caliber 43 A   Caliber 43 B HC

Caliber 49

LE PHARE

Swiss

Le Phare specialized in the production of repeater ebauches from 1890-1940. They were the first to mass produce or manufacture inexpensive repeaters with interchangeable parts. Le Phare patented a **centrifugal force governor**.

TYPE -DESCRIPTION	ABP	Ex-Fn	Mint
Chronograph, gold, 45-50mm, OF	$600	$800	$1,000
HC	700	900	1,100
Split second chronograph, gold, 45-52mm, OF	1,100	1,300	1,600
HC	1,200	1,500	1,800
1/4 hr. repeater, gold, 46-52mm, OF	900	1,200	1,400
HC	1,000	1,500	1,800
HC w/chrono., cal. & moonphase	2,200	3,000	3,500
Minute repeater, gold, 46-56mm, OF	1,500	2,000	2,500
high grade min. repeater with **helical** balance spring	2,600	4,000	5,000
HC	1,800	2,500	3,000
OF w/chrono. & register	1,800	2,500	3,000
HC w/chrono	1,900	2,800	3,500
HC w/chrono., full cal. & moonphase	2,800	4,000	5,000

Le Phare, 56mm, minute repeater, chronograph and calendar with moon phases, Note the governor at 6 O'clock..-

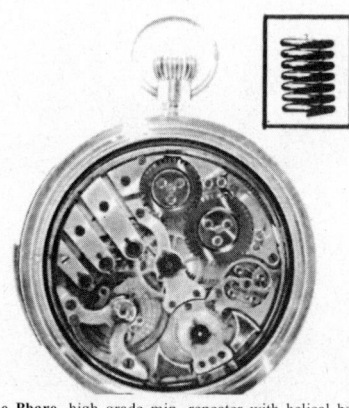

Le Phare, high grade min. repeater with helical balance spring, 5mm, Ca. 1910.

Below: Centrifugal style governor for the repeating mechanism.

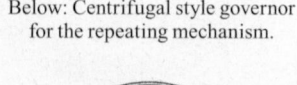

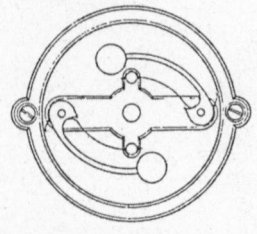

Le Phare, Min. repeater, 54mm, HC, 17J., 3/4 plate, push button, Ca. 1895, Note centrifugal force governor at 6 o'clock.

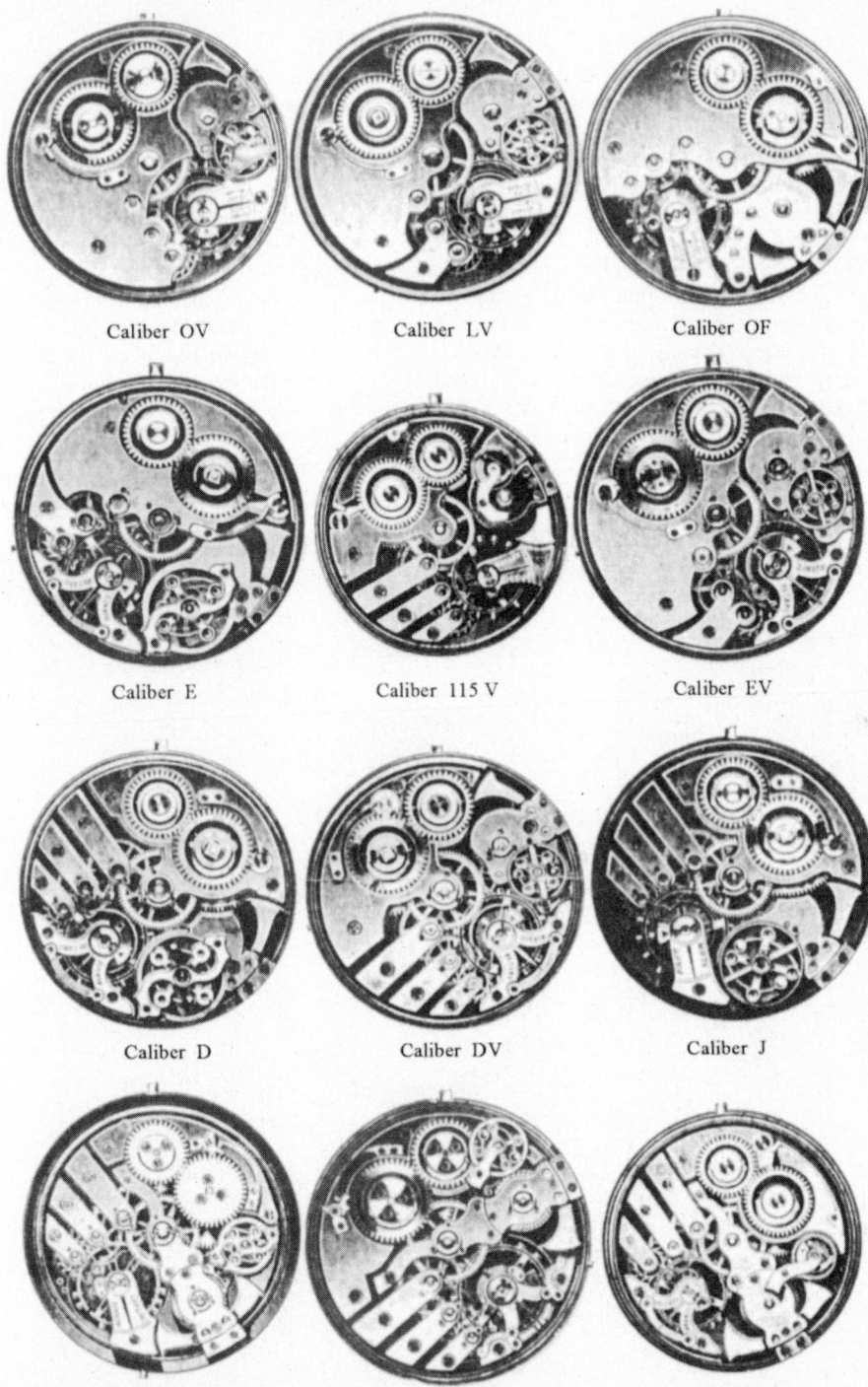

Caliber OV Caliber LV Caliber OF

Caliber E Caliber 115 V Caliber EV

Caliber D Caliber DV Caliber J

Caliber 110 M Caliber ZM Caliber 105

L'Epine or Lepine

Paris France (1720- 1814)

Jean-Antoine L'Epine more than any other one man, revolutionized the form of the watch. He developed and first used the following list of improvements in 1770 to 1790, bar bridges, suspended use of the fusee, free-standing **going** barrel, new style virgule, cylinder and lever escapements, stylized arabic numbers, center seconds, moon style hands, wolf's teeth gearing, gongs for repeaters, much thinner watches about 12-13mm, concealed case hinge, cuvette dust cover, engine turned cases, back wind & back set of the hands, pump or pull wind (1790), and open faced style case which is called L'Epine calibre by the Swiss watch makers. The House of Lepine was sold in 1914.

George Washington was the owner of a L'Epine Gold Watch. Governor Morris was commissioned to acquire for his friend, the President, a reliable watch while on a business trip to Paris, France. On April 23, 1789, Governor Morris selected a Lepine large gold watch with Virgule escapement as the best. Thomas Jefferson was asked to deliver the watch due to the fact the Governor had a delay in Paris. The watch is on exhibit in the Museum of the Historical Society of Pennsylvania located in Pittsburgh, PA.

TYPE – DESCRIPTION	ABP	Ex-Fn	Mint
Time only, **Silver**, KW, verge or cylinder escap., 46-52mm OF.....	$200	$400	$600
Time only, **Silver**, KW, virgule escap., 46-52mm OF............	600	1,000	1,500
Time only, **Gold**, KW, verge or cylinder escap,, plain, 50mm, OF..	500	1,000	1,200
Time only, **Gold**, KW, virgule escap., enamel & scene, 50mm, OF..	2,000	4,000	5,000
Time only, **Gold**, KW, lever with 40 tooth gold escape wheel, Ca. 1778-1790, 50mm, OF........................★★★	2,500	5,000	6,500
1/4 repeater, **Silver**, 52mm, OF.............................	800	1,500	1,800
1/4 repeater, **Gold**, 54mm, OF.............................	1,100	2,000	3,500
Minute Pump Repeater, **Gold**.........................★★★	6,000	12,000	16,500

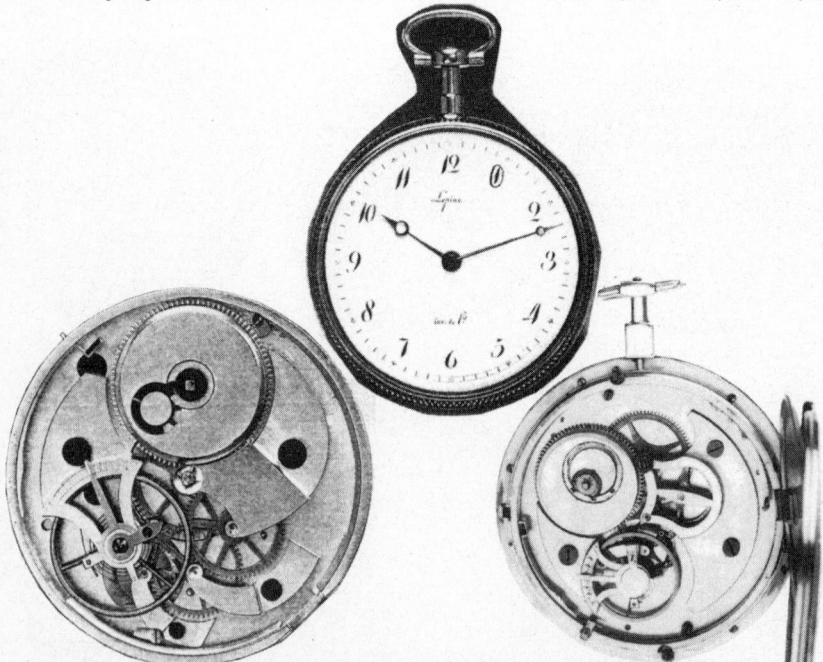

Signed L'pine a Paris on dial , virgule escapement, open face, free standing going barrel, concealed hinged cuvette, KW/KS from back, **number 1 in an oval**, Ca. 1790-95.

Lepine, virgule escapement, note horse-shoe shaped center bridge used for center seconds, free standing going barrel, Ca. 1790-95.

LE ROY ET CIE

Paris

Le Roy et Cie was the final product of a dynasty of great watchmakers, staffing with Julien Le Roy and his son Pierre, whose credits are numerous in the development of horology in the 18th century. There is, however, much confusion and hoopla over "Le Roy" watches. Frequently, you will see watches signed "Le Roy" that have nothing to do with the original family. These watches are unimportant. You have to distinguish between the works of Julien, of Pierre, of Charles, and of their contemporary namesakes. The modem firm, Le Roy et Cie., established in the late 19th century, contracted and finished some very fine and, in some cases, extremely import ant complicated watches, using imported Swiss ebauches.

TYPE—DESCRIPTION	ABP	Ex-Fn	Mint
Verge, KW, paircase, silver, 49-50mm, C. 1775	$325	$400	$600
Verge, fusee, Enamel w/scene, **18K,** 38- 40mm, C. 1760	2,400	5,000	6,000
Miniature, 22mm, diamonds & pearls on enamel, OF	800	1,100	1,500
Time only, gold, 45- 50mm, OF	600	800	1,000
Digital Jump hour, extra thin, gold, Ca. 1930's	650	1,500	2,000
1/4 hr. repeater, gold, 46-52mm, OF	1,200	2,000	2,500
Min. repeater, two train, tandem winding wheels, fully jeweled jump center seconds, gold, 50mm	6,000	12,000	15,000

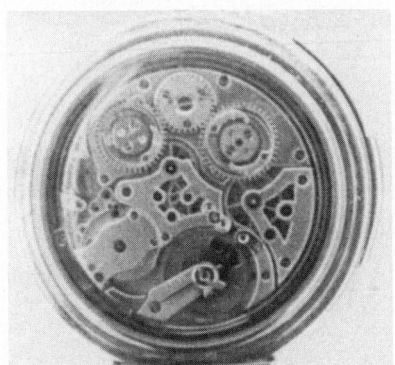

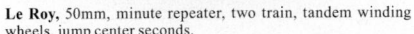

Le Roy, 50mm, minute repeater, two train, tandem winding wheels, jump center seconds.

Le Roy, 22mm, miniature watch with enamel, pearls, with Diamonds on the pin, 18K, OF, ca. 1910.

ᐧᐧ This book endeavours to be a GUIDE or helpful manual and offers a wealth of material to be used as a tool not as a absolute document. Price Guides are like watches the worst may be better than none at all, but at best cannot be expected to be 100% accurate.

ᐧᐧ Characteristics of watches differ for the same age of both case and movement, because these features vary it may not be accurate to date a watch by one single influence. Example: the second hand was not commonly found on watches before 1750, but common about 1800. The first second hand appeared in 1665 and another in 1690. Therefore statements are broad rather than accurate.

ᐧᐧ A collector should expect to pay modestly higher prices at local shops.

LONGINES
Swiss

The beautiful Fabrique des Longines is situated in St. Imier, Switzerland. The company was founded by Ernest Francillon in 1866. They manufactured all grades of watches. Winged hour glass trademark registered in May 1890.

PRODUCTION TOTALS

DATE-	SERIAL #	DATE-	SERIAL #	DATE-	SERIAL #
1867—	1	1911-	2,500,000	1937-	5,500,000
1870—	20,000	1912-	2,750,000	1938-	5,750,000
1875—	100,000	1913—	3,000,000 —Aug.	1940—	6,000,000 —June
1852—	250,000	1915—	3,250,000	1945—	7,000,000 —July
1888—	500,000	1917—	3,500,000	1950—	8,000,000 —May
1893—	750,000	1919—	3,750,000	1953—	9,000,000 —July
1899—	1,000,000 —Feb.	1922—	4,000,000 —Oct.	1956—	10,000,000 —May
1901—	1,250,000	1925—	4,250,000	1959—	11,000,000 —April
1904—	1,500,000	1926—	4,500,000	1962—	12,000,000 —May
1905—	1,750,000	1928—	4,750,000	1966—	13,000,000 —June
1907—	2,000,000 —July	1929—	5,000,000 —Oct.	1967—	14,000,000 —Feb.
1909—	2,250,000	1934—	5,250,000	1969—	15,000,000 —Feb.

Right: Early KW or SW, cal.# L20B, Ca. 1870-85.

LONGINES, 44mm, 21 jewels, U.S. Army AC. adjusted to temp. & 5 positions, World War II model, cal. 2129.

LONGINES, 59mm, 21 Jewels, Railroad Model gold filled open face case, Ca. 1920-1935.

TYPE - DESCRIPTION	ABP	Ex-Fn	Mint
Early KW or SW, cal.# L20B, silver case, Ca. 1870-85	$125	$150	$200
15-17J, silver, 48-50mm, HC, Ca. 1890	100	125	175
KW, for Turkish market, .800 silver, HC, Ca. 1900	100	150	200
15-17J, for Tiffany, Sterling, 45- 50mm OF, Ca. 1905	135	200	250
Time only, **gold**, 40- 44mm, OF	250	375	450
HC	350	450	550
Time only, **gold**, 45- 50mm, OF	300	400	535
HC	450	600	850
15-17J, GF, 40- 52mm, OF, Ca. 1930	60	100	125
21J, GF, 40- 50mm, OF, Ca. 1930	135	200	325
17J, "Express Leader", Adj., LS, **GF**, 48- 50mm, OF	150	200	325
19J, "Express Leader', Adj., LS, **GF**, 48- 50mm, OF	175	250	350
19J, "Express Monarch", Adj., LS, **GF**, 48- 50mm, OF	175	250	350
21J, "Express Monarch", Adj., LS, **GF**, 48- 50mm, OF	225	300	500
23J, "Express Monarch", Adj., LS, **GF**, 48- 50mm, OF	300	500	700
24J, "Express Monarch", Adj., LS, **GF**, 48- 50mm, OF	375	900	1,000
21J, Trans-Continental Express, Adj., LS, **GF**, 48- 50mm, OF	200	300	400
23J, Trans-Continental Express, Adj., LS, **GF**, 48- 50mm, OF	225	400	600
U.S. Army AC, World War II, 21J., silver, 44mm, **WI.,** OF	600	1,000	1,500
U.S. Army, World War II, 17-21J., silver, 44mm, OF	350	500	650

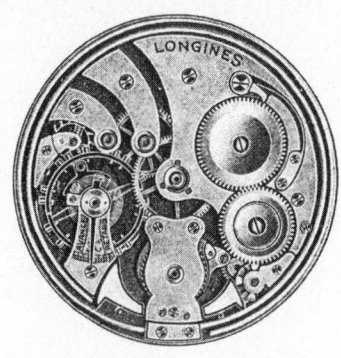

Longines, open face minute repeater movement

Longines, 46mm, Mm. repeater, 24 jewels, 3/4 plate design, open face, Ca. 1915.

TYPE - DESCRIPTION	ABP	Ex-Fn	Mint
World time watch, gold, 48-52mm, OF	$3,000	$4,500	$6,000
8 day watch with wind-indicator, **14K OF**	1,200	2,000	2,500
Chronograph w/register, silver, OF, 48- 50mm, C. 1905	250	500	600
Chronograph, gold, 45-50mm, OF	450	700	900
HC	700	800	1,000
Split second chronograph, gold, 45-52mm, OF	1,000	1,700	2,000
HC	1,200	2,000	2,400
Chronograph, Lugrin's Pat., fly back, silver OF case	375	500	600
1/4 hr. repeater, gold, 46-52mm, OF	1,200	1,800	2,000
HC	1,500	2,000	2,500
HC w/chrono., cal. & moonphase	3,500	4,500	6,000
Minute repeater, gold, 46-52mm, OF	2,000	3,000	3,500
HC	2,500	3,500	4,000
OF w/chrono	2,500	3,300	4,000
HC w/chrono	3,000	3,800	4,500
OF w/split chrono	3,500	6,000	7,500
HC w/split chrono	4,500	7,000	9,000
HC w/cal. & moon- phase	5,000	9,000	12,000
Perpetual moonphase calendar, gold, OF	6,000	10,000	12,000
Perp. moonphase cal. w/min. repeater & chrono., OF	15,000	25,000	30,000
HC	18,000	30,000	35,000
Clock Watch, gold, 46-52mm, OF	6,000	10,000	14,000
HC	8,000	14,000	17,000

Longines, Chronograph, H. A. Lugrin's Pat. June 13, Oct. 3, 1876, Start, Stop, Fly Back.

Longines, 6 day with wind-indicator, Ca. 1930.

MARKWICK, MARKHAM

LONDON (1725-1825)

They enjoyed selling clocks and watches to the Turkish Market. Watches can be found with his name & that of another maker added, Example: Markwick, Markham "Perigal", or "Recordon". Also watches with the names "Story" Ca. 1780, "Borrel" Ca. 1813 and "Perigal" Ca. 1825 are known.

TYPE - DESCRIPTION	ABP	Ex-En	Mint
Pair case, verge, silver plain, 50mm, OF	$300	$500	$600
GOLD	800	1,200	1,500
Pair case, verge, silver w/ **repousee**, 50mm, OF	450	1,200	1,500
GOLD	1,100	2,000	2,500
Triple cased, verge, silver & **Tortoise shell** outer case	850	1,500	2,000
Triple cased, verge, Painted enamel on first & second case, for Turkish Market, 18K gold cases, Ca. 1800	7,500	12,000	15,000
Four cases, verge fusee, Silver Gilt and Tortoise, KW/KS, for Turkish Market, 45mm, Ca. 1820	1,500	2,000	3,000
1/4 hr. repeater, SILVER, 54mm, OF	750	1,100	1,300
GOLD	1,100	2,500	3,000
Pair case, verge, 20K **Gold repousee**, 50mm, OF	4,000	6,000	7,500

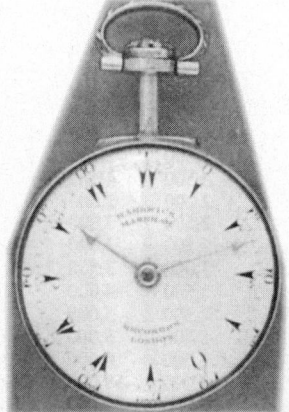

Markwick, Markham, Triple cased, 18K gold cases, Painted enamel on first & second case, made for Turkish Market, Ca. 1800.

Markwick, London, 20K pair case, both case, hand pierced, 1/4 hour repeating on a belt, 55MM, Ca. 1720

MATHEY - TISSOT
Swiss

Firm founded in June 1886 by Edmond Mathey-Tissot. Makers of both complicated and simple watches of good quality.

TYPE - DESCRIPTION	ABP	Ex-Fn	Mint
Early, KW, Time only, Swiss bar, Pre 1870, silver.	$100	$150	$200
Time only, gold, 40- 44mm, OF	285	400	450
HC	425	600	800
Time only, gold, 45- 50mm, OF	435	700	900
HC	600	800	1,100
1/4 hr. repeater, gold, 46-52mm, OF	1,200	1,500	2,000
HC	1,500	2,500	3,000
OF w/chrono., cal. & moonphase	2,000	3,000	4,000
HC w/chrono., cal. & moonphase	2,500	3,500	4,500

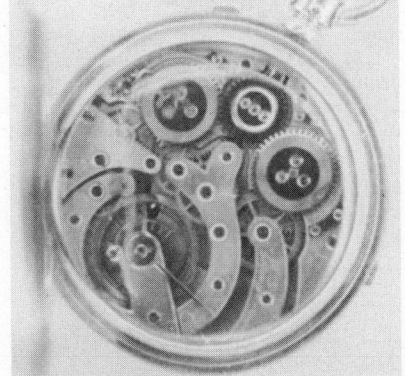

Mathey-Tissot, 52mm, 27 jewels, quarterjump sweep second chronograph, two train, 18k HC.

Mathey-Tissot, mm. repeater with chronograph, day date month & moon phases, HC.

TYPE - DESCRIPTION	ABP	Ex-Fn	Mint
Minute repeater, gold, 46-52mm, OF	$1,500	$2,500	$3,000
HC	2,000	3,000	4,500
OF w/chrono. & register	2,000	2,700	4,000
HC w/chrono.& register	2,200	4,000	5,000
HC w/chrono. & moon ph,. day date month	4,000	8,000	12,000
OF w/split chrono	4,200	7,000	9,000
HC w/split chrono	4,700	9,000	11,000
OF w/cal. & moonphase	3,800	5,000	8,000
HC w/cal. & moonphase	3,500	8,000	12,000
World time watch, gold, 48-52mm, OF	3,500	5,000	6,000
Perpetual moonphase calendar, gold, OF	6,000	10,000	14,000
Perp. moonphase cal. w/min. repeater, OF	15,000	25,000	30,000
HC	20,000	30,000	35,000
Perp. moonphase cal. w/min. rep. and chrono., OF	20,000	30,000	35,000
HC	22,000	35,000	40,000
Clock Watch, Gold, 48-52mm, OF	6,000	12,000	14,000
HC	8,000	14,000	17,000

☞ Note: Some models and grades are not included. Their values can be determined by comparing with similar age, size, metal content, style, models and grades listed.

☞ A collector should expect to pay modestly higher prices at local shops.

☞ Pricing in this Guide are fair market price for complete watches which are reflected from the NAWCC national and regional shows.

McCabe

London

William McCabe of Ireland was a clock & watch-maker who moved to London. This long lived firm has a good reputation for making watches. The son of William, James McCabe became the owner in about 1822. The business was carried on by nephew Robert Jeremy until about 1883.

TYPE -DESCRIPTION	ABP	Ex-Fn	Mint
Time only, Verge escapement, KW, Silver, 58mm, OF	$200	$400	$500
HC	225	450	550
Time only, DUPLEX escapement, KW, Silver, 58mm, OF	225	450	550
HC	250	500	600
Time only, DUPLEX escapement, KW, GOLD, 58mm, OF	700	1,000	1,200
HC	800	1,200	1,500
Enamel, Time only, DUPLEX escap., KW, Silver, 58mm, OF	900	1,200	1,500
HC	1,000	1,400	1,700
Gold &Enamel, Time only, Duplex escap., KW, 55- 58mm, OF	4,000	6,000	8,000
HC	4,500	7,000	9,000
Time only, Lever escapment, gold, 45- 50mm, OF	600	800	1,000
HC	800	1,000	1,200
1/4 hr. repeater, gold, 46-52mm, OF	1,800	2,200	2,500
HC	2,500	3,000	3,500
Detent Chronometer, gold, 48-52mm, OF	4,000	5,500	7,500
HC	5,000	6,500	8,000

Ja. McCabe, "Royal Exchange London", key-wind with fusee, diamond stone, three arm gold balance, right angle lever, Ca. 1835.

∞ A collector should expect to pay modestly higher prices at local shops.

∞ Pricing in this Guide are fair market price for complete watches which are reflected from the NAWCC national and regional shows.

∞ The Complete Price Guide to Watches goal is to stimulate the orderly exchange of watches between buyers and sellers.

MEYLAN WATCH CO. (Swiss)

Meylan Watch Co., founded by C. H. Meylan in 1880, manufactured fine watches, with complications, in Le Brassus, Switzerland.

Right: Minute Repeater

Left: **C.H. Meylan, movement**, 21J, 7Adj., c.1926

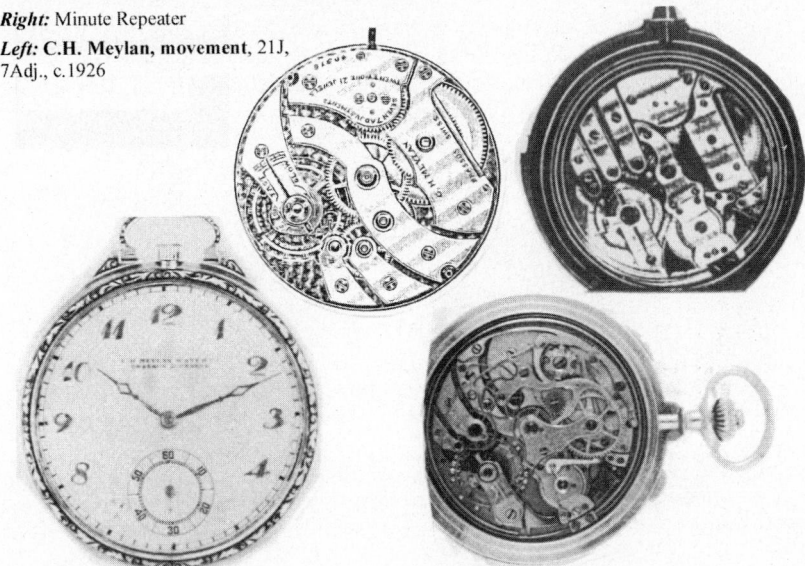

C. H. Meylan, 42mm, 21 jewels, straight tine lever escapement, 18K case with enamel on bezel.

C. H. Meylan, Minute Repeater, split second Chronograph, minute register, 18K gold OF case, Ca. 1895

TYPE - DESCRIPTION	ABP	Ex-Fn	Mint
Time only, gold, 40-44mm, OF	$350	$450	$600
HC	450	575	700
Time only, **platinum**, + diamonds, 40- 44mm, OF	900	2,500	3,200
Time only, gold, 40-44mm, 18K case & **enamel on bezel**, OF	1,000	1,500	1,800
Time only, gold, 45- 50mm, OF	500	600	800
HC	850	1,000	1,200
Chronograph, gold, 45-50mm, OF	600	900	1,200
HC	800	1,000	1,400
Split second chronograph, gold, 45-52mm, OF	1,000	1,800	2,200
HC	1,500	2,000	2,500
5 minute repeater, gold, 46-52mm, OF	1,700	3,000	3,500
HC	1,900	3,500	4,000
Minute repeater, gold, OF	2,400	3,500	4,000
HC	2,600	4,000	4,500
OF w/chrono	2,600	4,000	4,500
HC w/chrono	2,700	4,500	5,000
OF w/split chrono	3,800	5,000	7,000
HC w/split chrono	4,000	6,000	8,000
OF w/cal. & moonphase	4,000	6,000	8,000
HC w/cal. & moonphase	5,000	9,000	12,000
HC w/chrono, cal & moonphase	5,500	10,000	13,000
Tourbillion, gold, 48-55mm, OF	25,000	40,000	50,000
Detent chronometer, gold, 48-52mm, OF	2,500	4,500	5,200
World time watch, gold, 48-52mm, OF	3,700	4,500	5,000
Perpetual moonphase calendar, gold, OF	7,000	9,000	11,000
HC	8,000	10,000	12,000
Perp. moonphase cal. w/min. rep. and chrono., OF	16,000	25,000	30,000
HC	20,000	30,000	35,000
Clock Watch, gold, 48-52mm, OF	6,000	12,000	14,000
HC	8,000	14,000	17,000

MORICAND, CH.

GENEVA

Firm specialized in making verge watches with cases highly decorated with stones and enameled portraits. Associates with brother Benjamin and Francois Colladon from 1752 to 1755, with a firm name of Colladon & Moricand. Later, with Jean Delisle then later in 1780 as Moricand.

Delisle & Moricand, 36MM, 1/4 hour repeater pendant activated, two-footed balance bridge, Ca.1775

Ch. Moricand, 46mm, gilt and enamel with two ladies in a floral garden, KW KS, Ca.1800.

TYPE - DESCRIPTION	ABP	Ex-Fn	Mint
Verge, KW, paircase, **silver**, 50mm, OF	$250	$400	$500
Verge, enamel w/ portrait, **silver/ gilt**, 49-52mm, OF	900	1,700	2,200
Verge, KW, **gold**, 50-54mm, OF	800	1,200	1,500
Verge, KW, **gold** w/ enamel, 52mm, OF	2,000	5,500	7,500
1/4 hr. repeater, **silver**, 54mm, OF	600	1,700	2,000
1/4 hr. repeater, **gold**, 50-54mm, OF	1,000	3,500	4,000
1/4 hr. repeater, **gold** w/ enamel, 54mm, OF	2,500	6,500	8,500

C. MONTANDON

Swiss

This 19th century maker was associated with Perret & Company as well as other Le Locle and Chaux-de-Fonds factories. Montandon specialized in low cost keywind watches for the American market.

TYPE - DESCRIPTION	ABP	Ex-Fn	Mint
KW, cylinder escap., silver, 46mm, OF, C. 1870	$80	$100	$135
KW, silver, 46-48mm, HC, C. 1875	95	125	165
KW, 15J, lady's, **18K**, 40-44mm, OF, C. 1870	150	250	300
HC, C. 1870	200	350	425
KW, 15J, gent's, **18K**, 48mm, OF, C. 1875	275	400	450
Chronograph, gold, 45-50mm, OF	500	900	1,100
HC	700	1,000	1,200
1/4 hr. repeater, gold, 46-52mm, OF	800	1,500	2,000
HC	900	1,800	2,500
Minute repeater, gold, 46-52mm, OF	1,800	2,500	3,500
HC	2,000	3,000	4,000
Minute repeater, w/cal. & moonphase, OF	3,500	6,000	8,000
HC	4,500	8,000	10,000
Minute repeater, w/**chrono.**, cal. & moonphase, HC	5,000	8,500	11,000

MOVADO (Swiss)

L. A. I. Ditesheim & Freres (L. A. I. the initials of the 3 Ditesheim brothers) formed their company in 1881. The name Movado ("always in motion") was adopted in 1905. The Swiss company invented a system of watch making which they called "Polyplan." This was an arrangement of three different angles to the watch movement which produced a curve effect to the case so as to fit the curvature of the arm. Another unusual watch produced by this company in 1926-27 was the "Ermeto." This watch was designed to be protected while inside a purse or pocket and each time the cover was opened to view the time, the watch was partially wound. L., A. & I. Ditesheim (before Movado) used trade names as Ralco, Tanit, Ultra, Apogee, Record, Talma, Noblesse, Salud, Negus, Bonne, Belgravia, Surete and Mintral in about 1895.

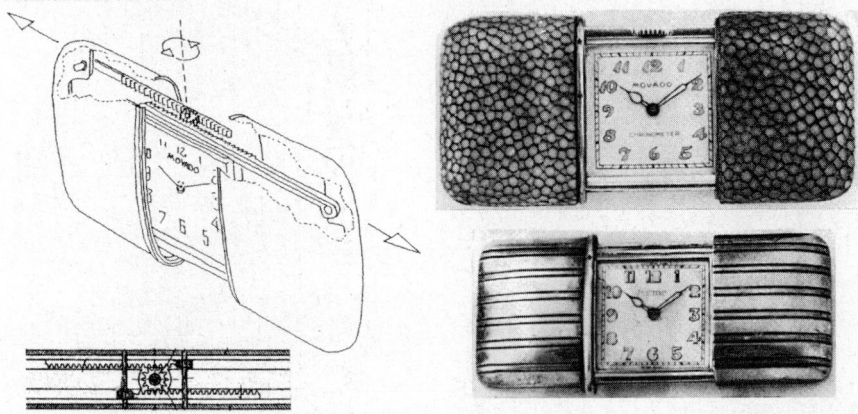

Above: Movado, Automatic RACK-WINDING mechanism, a single opening provides winding for about 4 hours.

Top: Movado, Purse watch, Sting Ray leather, 17 jewels.
Bottom: Movado, Purse watch, silver case, 17 jewels.

TYPE — DESCRIPTION	ABP	Ex-Fn	Mint
SW, 17J, LS, Silver, 43mm, OF, C. 1920	$125	$150	$200
SW, 15J, LS, Silver, 47mm, HC, C. 1920	150	200	250
Time only, gold, 40-44mm, OF	225	275	350
HC	350	425	550
Time only, gold, 45-50mm, OF	425	550	650
HC	625	900	1,100
Purse watch, black leather, 50 x 33mm, C. 1930's	200	300	350
Alarm	275	400	500
silver	250	325	450
Sting Ray leather	265	350	475
18K	800	1,200	1,500
leather, **moonphase & calendar**	800	1,200	1,500
Coin form, 17J, St. Christopher coin, **18K**, closed case, 29mm	600	700	900
Chronograph, gold, 45-50mm, OF	800	1,200	1,500
Minute repeater, gold, 46-52mm, OF	2,200	3,000	3,500
HC	2,500	3,500	4,000
HC w/split chrono. & register	4,000	6,000	7,500

Movado, Purse watch with moonphase & calendar, auto-wind by opening & closing case, leather.

ULYSSE NARDIN

Swiss

Ulysse Nardin was born in 1823. The company he started in 1846 produced many fine timepieces and chronometers, as well as repeaters and more complicated watches. This firm, as did Assmann, found a strong market in South America as well as other countries. Ulysse's son, Paul David Nardin, succeeded him, as did Paul David's sons after him.

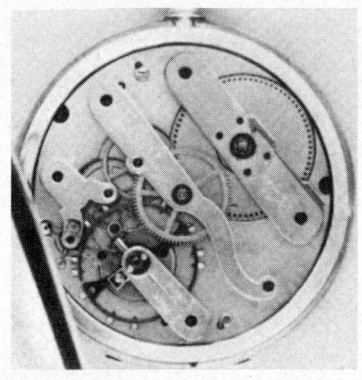

Ulysse Nardin, Keywind, 18 jewels, pivoted detent, bridge movement, 48mm, Ca. 1860.

Ulysse Nardin, pocket chronometer with date 19J. pivoted detent, gold jewel settings, Ca.1890.

TYPE -DESCRIPTION	ABP	Ex-Fn	Mint
Early KW, 18J., **pivoted detent**, bar style mvt., gold, HC, C.1860 ...	$1,200	$2,000	$2,500
Time only, gold, 40-44mm, OF	300	400	525
HC	450	600	700
Time only, gold, 45- 50mm, OF	600	700	750
HC	750	900	1,100
Chronograph, gold, 45-50mm, OF	800	1,100	1,300
HC	1,000	1,500	1,800
Deck chronometer w/box, detent chronometer, C. 1905	1,400	1,800	2,500
Pocket chronometer, lever escape., 21J., GJS, **18K,** HC, C.1910	900	1,500	2,000
Pocket chronometer, **pivoted detent, with date**, gold, 57mm	4,000	4,000	6,000
World time watch, gold, 48-52mm, OF	3,000	4,500	5,000
Karrusel, 52 Min. karrusel, free sprung balance, silver case	3,000	5,000	6,000

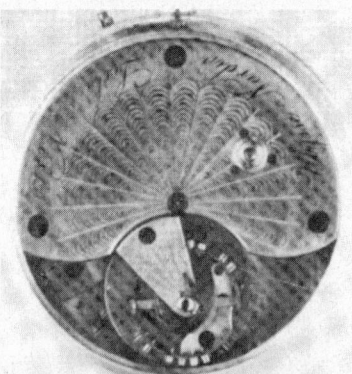

Ulysse Nardin, 53nm, 52 minute karrusel, free sprung balance, ca. 1905.

Ulysse Nardin, pocket chronometer, lever escapement, OF, 21 jewels, gold jewel settings, c. 1910

TYPE - DESCRIPTION	ABP	Ex-Fn	Mint
1/4 hr. repeater, gold, 46-52mm, OF	$1,400	$2,000	$3,000
OF w/chrono., cal. moonphase	2,200	4,000	5,500
HC	1,600	2,500	3,500
HC w/chrono., cal. & moonphase	2,600	4,500	6,000
Minute repeater, gold, 46-52mm, OF	2,800	3,500	4,500
HC	3,000	4,000	5,500
OF w/split chrono	3,800	5,000	7,000
HC w/split chrono	4,200	7,000	9,500
OF w/cal. & moonphase	4,000	7,000	9,500
HC w/cal. & moonphase	5,000	8,000	11,500
HC w/chrono., cal. & moonphase	5,500	9,000	12,500
Perpetual moonphase calendar, gold, OF	8,000	10,000	12,000
HC	10,000	13,000	15,000
Perp. moonphase cal. w/min . repeater, OF	20,000	25,000	30,000
HC	22,000	30,000	35,000
Perp. moonphase cal. w/min. rep. and chrono. , OF	23,000	30,000	40,000
HC	25,000	35,000	45,000
Clock Watch, gold, 46-52mm, OF	6,000	12,000	14,000
HC	8,000	14,000	17,000

NICOLE, NIELSEN & CO.

14 Soho Square, London

Adolphe Nicole in 1840 came to London from Switzerland and joined Henry Capt. By 1858 they had moved to **14 Soho Square**, London. In 1876 Emil Nielsen became a partner in the firm. The company was purchased by S. Smith & Sons in 1904. Tourbillons were made by V. Kullberg and Nicole, Nielsen for the England market. Last watches made Ca. 1933-34. In 1910 the wholesale price for a 1st quality Min. repeater with a chronograph was 95 £, a Min. repeater was 55 £, 1st quality Extra Flat watch was 32 £.

(Made ebauche for Dent, Frodsham, and Smith)

Nicole, Nielsen. 50mm, chronograph, 15 jewels, 3/4 plate, gilded movement, ca. 1890.

Nicole, Nielsen, 64mm, min. repeater, split-second chronograph, tourbillon, free sprung escapement, most were made for Frodsham.

TYPE —DESCRIPTION	ABP	Ex-Fn	Mint
Time only, gold, 45- 50mm, OF	$600	$1,000	$1,200
HC	700	1,200	1,500
Chronograph, gold, 45-50mm, HC	1,200	2,000	2,500
Minute repeater, gold, 46-52mm, OF	2,700	4,000	5,000
HC	3,000	5,000	7,000
OF w/chrono. & register	3,500	5,500	7,500
HC w/chrono. & register	4,000	6,000	8,000

TYPE — DESCRIPTION	ABP	Ex-Fn	Mint
Minute repeater, **tourbillon**, split-second chronograph,			
free sprung escapement, gold, 64mm......................	$80,000	$150,000	$200,000
Tourbillon, gold, 48-55mm, OF	50,000	75,000	100,000
Karrusel, gold, 48-55mm, OF	6,000	12,000	14,000
Perpetual moon phase calendar, gold, OF	12,000	14,500	18,000
HC	14,000	17,000	22,000
Perp. moonphase cal. w/min. rep. and chrono., OF.............	23,000	30,000	35,000
HC...	24,000	35,000	40,000
Clock Watch, gold, 48-55mm, OF	10,000	17,000	22,000
HC	12,000	22,000	27,000

NON-MAGNETIC WATCH CO.

Swiss

(NOT MARKED PAILLARD'S PATENT)

TYPE - DESCRIPTION	ABP	Ex-Fn	Mint
Time only, gold, 45- 50mm, OF...........................	$275	$335	$425
HC...	350	400	525
Chronograph, gold, 45-50mm, OF.........................	500	700	850
HC...	600	800	1,100
Split second chronograph, gold, 45-52mm, OF.................	750	1,000	1,200
HC...	850	1,200	1,500
1/4 hr. repeater gold, 46-52mm, OF.......................	1,000	1,800	2,000
HC...	1,200	2,000	2,500
Minute repeater, gold, 46-52mm, OF.......................	2,000	3,000	4,500
HC...	2,200	4,000	5,000
OF w/split chrono	3,700	5,500	7,500
HC w/split chrono	4,200	6,500	8,500
HC w/chrono., cal. & moonphase	4,500	8,000	12,000

Non-magnetic W.Co., min. repeater, jeweled through the hammers, 50mm.

Omega pocket watch movement, 45-48mm, 15 jewels, serial number 9,888,934.

6⁄ Watches listed in this book are priced at the collectable fair market value at the trade show level, as complete watches having an original case, an original white enamel dial, and with the entire original movement in good working order with no repairs needed, unless otherwise noted.

OMEGA WATCH CO.

Swiss

Omega Watch Co. was founded by Louis Brandt in 1848. They produced watches of different grades. In 1930, they began to produce different lines with Tissot under the name Societe Sussie pour l'Industrie Horlogere. Omega is now part of the SMH (Societe Suisse de Microelectronique et d' Horlogerie).

PRODUCTION TOTALS

DATE-SERIAL#	DATE-SERIAL#	DATE-SERIAL#	DATE-SERIAL#	DATE-SERIAL#	DATE-SERIAL#
1895-1,000,000	1944-10,000,000	1962-19,000,000	1969-30,000,000	1975-39,000,000	1985-48,000,000
1902-2,000,000	1947-11,000,000	1963-20,000,000	1969-31,000,000	1977-40,000,000	1986-49,000,000
1908-3,000,000	1950-12,000,000	1964-21,000,000	1970-32,000,000	1978-41,000,000	1986-50,000,000
1912-4,000,000	1952-13,500,000	1965-22,000,000	1971-33,000,000	1979-42,000,000	1989-51,000,000
1916-5,000,000	1954-14,000,000	1966-23,000,000	1972-34,000,000	1979-43,000,000	not used-52,000,000
1923-6,000,000	1956-15,000,000	1967-25,000,000	1972-35,000,000	1980-44,000,000	1991-53,000,000
1929-7,000,000	1958-16,000,000	1968-26,000,000	1973-36,000,000	1982-45,000,000	1993-54,000,000
1935-8,000,000	1960-17,000,000	1969-28,000,000	1973-37,000,000	1984-46,000,000	1995-55,000,000
1939-9,000,000	1961-18,000,000	1969-29,000,000	1974-38,000,000	1984-47,000,000	1998-56,000,000

The above list is provided for determining the APPROXIMATE age of your watch. Match serial number with date. Watches were not necessarily sold in the exact order of manufactured date.

Note: By 1980 ETA Calibers were being used by Omega.

TYPE - DESCRIPTION	ABP	Ex-Fn	Mint
15J, SW, gilt, silver, 48mm, OF, C.1900.	$90	$150	$175
15J, SW, gilt, silver, 48mm, HC, C.1900	110	225	250
Time only, gold, 45- 48mm, OF.	325	550	775
HC	500	650	1,000
Chronograph, gold, 45-50mm, OF.	770	1,000	1,300
HC	900	1,100	1,650
Pulsation (Doctor Watch), gold HC	1,000	1,300	2,000
Chronograph, gold, 45-50mm, **Double-Dial**, OF	2,200	3,850	5,000
Minute repeater, gold, 46-52mm, OF.	2,000	3,300	3,850
HC	2,200	3,850	5,000
OF w/split chrono	4,200	6,600	7,700
HC w/split chrono	4,400	7,700	11,000
HC w/chrono., cal. & moonphase	5,300	8,800	11,000

Omega, Chronograph, gold, 45-50mm, **Double-Dial**, open face, Multi-color enamel dials.

In 1894 the creation of the Omega **"19"** caliber, remarkable for the perfection of its construction, the ingenuity of certain mechanisms (time-setting) and its modest price, owing to new manufacturing methods. The 19 caliber resulted from the FIRST introduction in Switzerland of the DIVIDED ASSEMBLY SYSTEM based on the interchange-ability of standard parts, a system which would be adopted progressively by the entire Swiss watch industry. This was also the year when Omega chronometers began receiving official rating certificates from the Neuchatel, Geneva and Kew/ Teddington (London) observatories. That year the owners of the company registered the word **Omega** as the new trademark.

The source of information from the book OMEGA The History of a Great Brand.

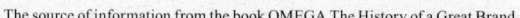

Omega 19 Grade DDR, 23 jewels with 2 diamond end stones, jeweled barrel arbor, **18** screwed gold jewel settings, a swan-neck regulator with graduated snail. Signed *Ls Brandt & frere SA*, grade DDR, 23 jewels, Adjusted to 5 positions and movement serial number is 2584692.

TYPE - DESCRIPTION	ABP	Ex-Fn	Mint
23J, grade **DDR** =RR grade, **18** GJS, 2 diamond end stones, **GF**, OF★	$550	$875	$1,300
19J, grade **DR** =RR grade, **15** GJS, **GF** OF	350	525	775
23J, grade **CCCR** = RR grade, **15** GJS, **GF** OF	375	650	875
19J, grade **CCR** = RR grade, **10** GJS, **GF** OF	325	475	675

Omega 19 Grade CCCR, 16-18 size, 23 jewels, signed Omega Watch Co. Swiss, 15 gold settings, S# 3,658,546.

16 size Movement

Omega 19 caliber, basic MOVEMENT open face 16 size, & 20 caliber = 18 size. (used for official chronometers)

CHARLES OUDIN

PARIS

Oudin was a pupil of Breguet and became a talented maker from 1807-1830. He produced quality timepieces and invented an early 'keyless" watch. He signed some of his Watches "Eleve de Breguet" = Student of Breguet.

Charles Oudin Dial & Movement, 51mm, 32J., Minute repeater with Chronograph, Ca.1910.

TYPE-DESCRIPTION	ABP	Ex-Fn	Mint
Verge, KW silver single case 45mm OF, G. 1865	$330	$500	$650
Early, KW, Time only Swiss bar silver OF	85	95	150
GOLD, OF	330	500	700
Split sec. chrono., 29J, w/ register,**18K**, 51mm, HC, C. 1900	880	1,500	2,000
Minute repeater, gold, 46-52mm, OF	2,200	3,000	3,500
HC	2,400	4,000	5,000
OF w/chrono. & register	2,400	3,500	4,000
HC w/chrono. & register	3,300	5,000	6,000

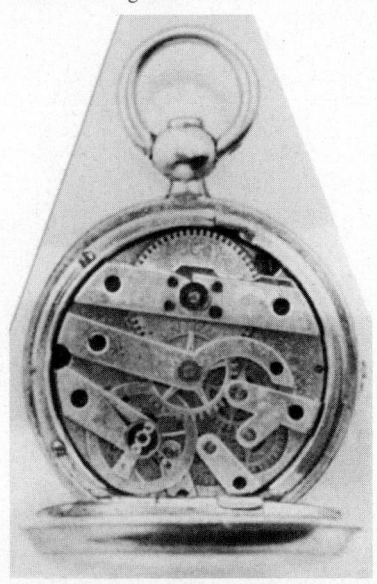

"CHs. OUDIN, Paris," engraved on
movement, Key Wind, cylinder
escapement, Swiss bar, Ca 1865.

PATEK, PHILIPPE & CIE.

Swiss

Patek, Philippe & Cie. has produced some of the world's most desirable factory-made watches. Antoine Norbert de Patek began contracting and selling watches in the late 1830's, later became partners with Francois Czapek and generally produced lovely decorative watches for a high class of clientele. In 1845 Adrien Philippe, inventor of the modern stem-winding system, joined the firm of Patek & Cie., and in 1851, the firm established its present name. Between Philippe's talent as a watchmaker and Patek's talent as a businessman with a taste for the impeccable, the firm rapidly established an international reputation, which lasts to this day. Early Patek, Philippe & Cie. watches are generally signed only on the dust cover, but some are signed on the dial and cuvette. It was not until the 1880's that the practice began of fully signing the dial, movement and case-perhaps in response to some contemporary forgery but more likely a necessity to conform to customs' regulations for their growing international market. Many early and totally original Patek watches have suffered from the misconception that all products of the company are fully signed. Never the less, collectors find such pieces more desirable. It requires more experience, however, to determine the originality of the earlier pieces. As with many Swiss watches they were originally cased in U.S.A., but this may lower their value.

PRODUCTION TOTALS

DATE—	SERIAL#	DATE—	SERIAL #	DATE—	SERIAL #
1840—	100	1950—	700,000	1940—	900,100
1845—	1,200	1955—	725,000	1945—	915,200
1850—	3,000	1960—	750,000	1950—	930,300
1855—	8,000	1965—	775,000	1955—	940,400
1860—	15,000	1970—	795,000	1960—	960,500
1865—	22,000			1965—	975,600
1870—	35,000	DATE—	SERIAL#	1970—	995,700
1875—	45,000	1920—	801,000		
1880—	55,000	1925—	802,000	DATE—	SERIAL#
1885—	70,000	1930—	823,000	1960—	1,100,800
1890—	85,000	1935—	824,000	1965—	1,130,900
1895—	100,000	1940—	835,000	1970—	1,250,000
1900—	110,000	1945—	856,000	1975—	1,350,000
1905—	125,000	1950—	867,000	1980—	1,450,000
1910—	150,000	1955—	878,000	1985—	1,600,000
1915—	175,000	1960—	889,000	1990—	1,850.000
1920—	190,000	1965—	890,000		
1925—	200,200	1970—	895,000		

The above list is provided for determining the APPROXIMATE age of your watch. Match serial number with date. Watches were not necessarily sold in the exact order of manufactured date.

EARLIER KEY WIND

NOTE: Watches signed *PATEK & CIE.* Usually have serial numbers from about 1,129 to 3,729, Ca. 1845 to 1850. Usually signed on cuvette with serial number & Patek & Cie., and not on the movement. **"Patek et Czapek"** found signed on cuvette for earlier KEY WIND watches.

Important note: From about 1880 forward all watches were signed on dial, case & movement.

1854 Tiffany & Co. became a official customer of the Patek firm.

Patented their **Stem Wind** system in **1861.**

Patek, Philippe & Cie., 15-17J., KWKS, gilt movement, lever escapement ("moustache lever"), signed on 18K cuvette, 47mm, Ca. 1865-69..

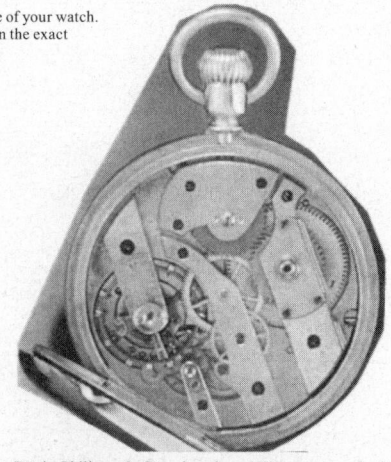

Patek, Philippe & Co., signed on 18K cuvette, early Stem Wind, **moustache lever**, wolf tooth winding, 18J, gilt movement, S#45,483, 49mm, Ca. 1875.

Patek, Philippe & Cie., 18 jewels, engraved gold dial with enamel center, 18K, 43mm, Ca. 1920's.

Patek, Philippe & Cie. 43mm, time only, 18K, open face.

Patek, Philippe & Co., Perpetual calendar, moonphase, min. repeater & split second chronograph, 18K, OF.

P.P.& Co. signed "Chronometro Gondolo", 24 hr. dial, 19-20J, moustache lever, gold train, 55mm, Ca. 1908.

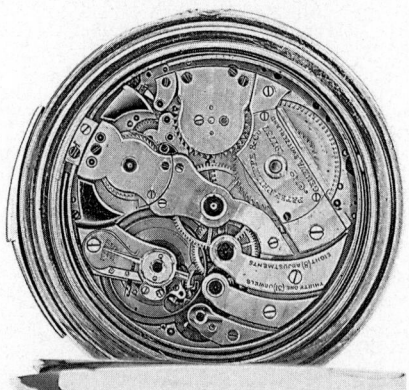

Patek, Philippe & Co., dial & movement, min. repeater, 29J, perpetual calendar, day, date, month, moon-phases, 18K.

TYPE - DESCRIPTION	ABP	Ex-Fn	Mint
EARLY Time only, KWKS, gilt mvt., lever or cylinder escapement pre 1865, signed on gold case, 40-45mm	$1,200	$1,500	$2,200
EARLY Time only, 18J., SW, gilt mvt., moustache lever, Ca 1870-75 wolf tooth winding, signed on gold case, 45-52mm	1,500	2,000	2,700
Time only, gold, 25- 30mm, ladies, OF	700	1,000	1,200
HC	1,000	1,500	2,200
Time only, gold, 32- 44mm, OF	1,800	3,000	3,500
HC	2,500	3,500	4,000
Time only, **Platinum**, 32- 44mm, OF	2,500	5,000	6,500
Time only, **enameled bezel**, gold, 32- 44mm, OF	2,700	4,000	5,500
Time only, gold, 45- 55mm, OF	2,500	3,500	4,000
HC	3,000	4,000	4,500
Time only, with **Wind Indicator**, gold, 45- 50mm, OF	4,000	12,000	15,000
Military, Silver deck Watch with Wind Indicator	6,500	10,000	14,000
Time only, Chronometro **Gondolo**, gold, 38mm, OF	2,000	3,500	4,500
Time only, Chronometro **Gondolo**, gold, 50-55mm, OF	2,500	4,000	5,500
Time only, Chronometro **Gondolo**, gold, **24** Hr. dial, 52mm, OF....★	3,000	10,000	15,000

Patek, Philippe & Co., enameled bezel, 18K OF, 42mm

Patek, Philippe & Co., perpetual calendar & moon phases, signed, 18 jewels, 49mm, Ca. 1949

TYPE – DESCRIPTION	ABP	Ex-Fn	Mint
Chronograph, gold, 45-50mm, OF	$3,200	$4,000	$5,000
HC	4,000	5,000	6,000
OF w/register	3,600	4,500	5,500
HC w/register	4,200	5,500	6,500
Split second chronograph, gold, 45-52mm, OF	5,200	8,000	9,500
HC	6,000	9,000	11,000
OF w/register	6,000	9,000	11,000
HC w/register	7,500	11,000	16,000
1/4 hr. repeater, **Niello** Silver & Gold case, 45-50mm, OF	4,500	9,000	10,000
1/4 hr. repeater, gold, 46-52mm, OF ★	4,500	8,000	9,500
HC ★	6,000	9,000	11,000
5 minute repeater, gold, 46-52mm, OF	3,500	7,000	8,500
HC	4,000	8,000	9,500
OF w/split chrono	8,000	13,000	15,000
HC w/split chrono	9,000	14,000	18,000
Minute repeater, gold, 46-52mm, OF	6,000	9,000	12,000
HC	10,000	15,000	20,000
OF w/chrono	10,000	12,000	16,000
HC w/chrono	12,000	18,000	25,000
OF w/chrono & register	11,000	15,000	20,000
HC w/chrono & register	14,000	20,000	27,000
Minute repeater, 2 **train**, self contained, triple signed, 18K, OF	18,000	32,000	40,000

TYPE - DESCRIPTION	ABP	Ex-Fn	Mint
Minute repeater, w/split chrono., gold, 46-52mm, OF	$15,000	$20,000	$30,000
HC w/split chrono	16,000	25,000	35,000
OF w/split chrono & register.	16,000	26,000	35,000
HC w/split chrono & register	20,000	30,000	40,000
Perpetual moonphase calendar, gold, OF	25,000	40,000	45,000
HC	27,000	50,000	55,000
Perp. moonphase cal. w/min. repeater, OF	50,000	80,000	90,000
HC	60,000	85,000	110,000
Perpetual moonphase cal. w/ min. rep. & chrono. , OF.	60,000	90,000	130,000
HC	75,000	95,000	135,000
Perpetual moonphase cal. w/ min. rep. & split sec. chrono. , OF . .	100,000	175,000	225,000
HC	120,000	200,000	250,000
Clock Watch, gold, 48-52mm, OF	25,000	45,000	60,000
HC	28,000	55,000	75,000

Patek, Philippe & Co. Digital Jump Hour, with minute hand & second hand, 18jewels, 45mm, 18K.

Patek, Philippe & Co., gold coin watch, 100 pesetas, secret push-piece opens lid to disclose dial, 35mm, Ca.1928.

TYPE - DESCRIPTION	ABP	Ex-Fn	Mint
Lady's pendant watch w/ brooch,18K & small diamonds, 27mm . . .	$2,400	$5,000	$7,000
Gold Coin, 100 pesetas 18K, 18J., coin opens to disclose dial	4,000	5,500	7,000
Digital Jump Hour, W/minute hand & sec. hand, 45mm, 18K	30,000	40,000	50,000
Karrusel, gold, 48-55mm, OF	70,000	100,000	150,000
Tourbillon, gold, 48-55mm, OF . . . . ★★★★ 125,000	200,000	275,000
HC . . . . ★★★★ 185,000	250,000	300,000
Detent chronometer, gold, 48-52mm, OF	25,000	40,000	60,000
HC	30,000	45,000	65,000
World time watch, gold, 48-52mm, OF	25,000	35,000	45,000
World time watch, Cloisonne map of America, pink gold case	100,000	200,000	300,000

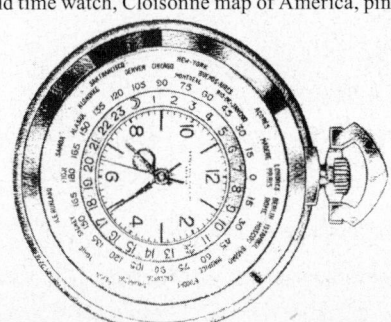

World time watch, gold, 48-52mm, OF

PICARD, JAMES
GENEVA

Watch dealer and finisher in the latter part of the 19th Century. Known for his complicated watches and pocket chronometers of high quality.

TYPE - DESCRIPTION	ABP	Ex-Fn	Mint
Time only, gold, 45- 50mm, OF............................	$450	$600	$725
HC..	600	700	875
Chronograph, gold, 45-50mm, OF.........................	750	1,000	1,200
Split sec. chronograph, 27J., independent jumping 1/5 seconds,			
Tandem wind, 2 gear train, 56mm, 18K , OF	2,200	3,500	4,000
Split second chronograph, gold, 45-52mm, OF.................	1,500	2,500	3,000
HC w/register.......................................	1,800	3,000	4,000
5 minute repeater, gold, 45-52mm, OF	2,800	3,500	4,000
HC..	3,200	4,000	4,500
Minute repeater, gold, 45-52mm, OF.......................	3,300	4,000	5,000
HC..	3,200	4,500	6,000
OF w/split chrono	4,400	6,500	7,500
HC w/split chrono	6,000	8,500	9,500
OF w/cal. & moonphase	7,000	9,500	11,000
HC w/chrono., cal. & moonphase.......................	8,000	10,000	12,000
Tourbillon, gold, 48-55mm, OF	20,000	40,000	45,000
Detent chronometer, gold, 48-52mm , OF....................	3,000	5,500	7,000
HC..	4,000	6,500	7,500
Perp. moonphase cal. w/min. rep. and chrono, OF :...........	15,000	30,000	35,000
HC..	20,000	35,000	45,000
Clock Watch, gold, 48-52mm, OF	7,000	12,000	14,000
HC..	9,000	14,000	17,000

James Picard, 27J, Split sec. chronograph, independent jumping 1/5 seconds, 2 gear train, 56mm, **Tandem wind**, Ca. 1885.

☞ A collector should expect to pay modestly higher prices at local shops.

The Complete Price Guide to Watches goal is to stimulate the orderly exchange of watches between buyers and sellers.

ALBERT H. POTTER & CO.

(Note: For further information on Potter timepieces, see U.S. Watch Section.)

Albert Potter was born in Saratoga county, New York. He started his apprenticeship in 1852 with Wood & Foley Albany (N.Y.). When this was completed he moved to New York to take up watchmaking on his own. He made about 35 watches in USA that sold for $225 to $350. Some were chronometers, some were lever escapements, key wind, gilded and movements, some were fusee driven, both bridge and 3/4 plate. Potter was a contemporary of Charles Fasoldt and John Mulford, both horological inventors from Albany, N. Y. Potter moved to Cuba in 1861 but returned to New York in 1868. In 1872 he worked in Chicago and formed the Potter Brothers Company with his brother William. He moved to Geneva about 1876. His Geneva ultra high grade ebauches timepieces may have been made by the maker Charles Ami LeCoultre of Le Sentier, Le Brassus area. In 1896 the firm failed with about 600 watches being made.

TYPE - DESCRIPTION	ABP	Ex-Fn	Mint
Time only, gold, 45- 48mm, OF	$4,000	$6,500	$8,000
HC	4,500	7,000	8,500
Pocket chronometer, pivoted detent ,free-spring balance, porcelain dial, bridge mvt., 58mm, 18K case, C.1875	12,000	27,000	35,000
Calendar, nickel, offset seconds and days of week dials, SW, 18K, 50mm, OF, C. 1800.	7,000	12,000	17,000
Regulator dial (center minute hand, offset hours, offset seconds), half moon- shaped nickel mvt., 18K, 50mm, OF, C.1880.	10,000	17,000	22,000
Minute repeater, gold, 46-52mm, OF	15,000	20,000	25,000
HC	20,000	25,000	30,000
Detent chronometer, gold, 48-52mm, OF	15,000	27,000	32,000
HC	18,000	32,000	37,000
Perp. moonphase cal. w/min. repeater, HC	25,000	55,000	75,000
Perp. moonphase cal. w/min. rep. & chrono., HC	30,000	80,000	110,000
4 SIZE, 21J., hour repeater, original 18K HC. . . . . ★★	4,000	5,200	7,000

Below trade mark found on some cases.

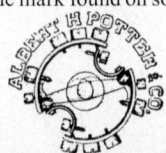

Albert Potter, 22 jewels, hunting case, helical hair spring, Free sprung, detent escapement. Note: The style bridge used for his pocket Chronometer, 58mm, Ca. 1880.

Albert Potter, 21 jewels, Note kidney-form bridge, Serial # 22, Ca. 1880. Note: A. H. Potter used a unique patented style of stem-wind & stem-set for his Geneva watches.

PRIOR, GEORGE & EDWARD PRIOR

LONDON

George Prior born in 1793 and died in 1830. He was a recipient of two prestigious awards and well known for his pieces for the turkish market. He also produced tortoise shell and triple-case watches with the outer case featuring wood with silver inlay. He made gold watches with Oriental chased cases, watches with pierced outer cases and triple-cased enamel engraved and repeaters.

Edward Prior born in 1800 and died in 1868.

TYPE - DESCRIPTION	ABP	Ex-Fn	Mint
Verge, pair case, plain silver, 50mm, OF	$405	$500	$700
Verge, pair case w/ repousee, silver, 50mm, OF	900	1,200	1,500
Verge, **Triple** case w/Shagreen outer case, Gilded case, 57mm	1,080	1,500	2,000
Verge, **Triple** case w/ **tortoise shell**, silver, 56mm, OF	1,350	1,800	2,200
Verge, **Quadruple** cases w/ **tortoise shell**, silver, 56mm, OF	1,800	2,400	3,000
Verge, pair case, GOLD, 48-52mm, OF	1,800	2,300	3,000
Verge, pair case, GOLD & enamel, 48-54mm, OF	2,520	5,000	7,000
1/4 hr. repeater, pair case, GOLD & enamel, 50mm, OF	5,400	7,000	9,000

Left: Edward Prior, 57mm, Triple Shagreen case, white enamel signed dial, verge with fusee, KW KS, Ca. 1820.

Right: George Prior, Quadruple case with third case made of tortoise shell, fourth outer case of embossed silver, the first two cases made of silver, verge escapement, note the stag beetle hour hand and poker minute hand, c. 1810.

ROLEX WATCH CO.

Swiss

Rolex was founded by Hans Wilsdorf in 1905 & in 1908 the trade-mark **"Rolex"** was officially registered. In 1926, they made the first real waterproof wrist watch and called it the **"Oyster."** In 1931, Rolex introduced a self-wind movement which they called **"Perpetual"**. In 1945, they introduced the **"Date-Just"** which showed the day of the month. The **"Submariner"** was introduced in 1953 and in 1954 the **"GMT Master"** model. In 1956, a "Day-Date" model was released which indicates the day of the month (in numbers) and the day of the week (in letters.)

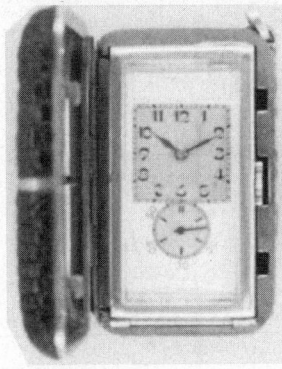

Rolex, SPORTING PRINCE, 17 jewels, Adjusted to six positions, silver & leather case.

Rolex, 42-43mm, 18 jewels, three adjustments, cam regulator, exposed winding gears.

IMPORTANT:

The following is a guide to help determine the age of your Rolex watches. However on *some* Oyster style watches Rolex added *inside* the case a Roman number (I,II,III,IV) to denote first, second, third, or fourth quarter + "53", "54", "55", "56" to denote the year of production. Example outside Oyster case #955454 inside case IV-53 which = last quarter of 1953. Example outside Oyster case #282621 inside case III-55 which = third quarter of 1955. Rolex went back to 100,000 in 1954 on some cases.

ROLEX ESTIMATED PRODUCTION DATES

DATE-SERIAL#	DATE—SERIAL#	DATE-SERIAL#	DATE-SERIAL#	DATE-SERIAL#	DATE-SERIAL#	DATE-SERIAL#	DATE-SERIAL#
1925 - 25,000	1937 - 99,000	1949 - 608,000	1961 - 1,480,000	1973 - 3,741,000	1985 — 8,815,000	1992 1/4 - C000,001
1926 - 28,500	1938 - 118,000	1950 - 673,500	1962 - 1,557,000	1974 - 4,002,000	1986 — 9,292,000	1993 1/4 - S000,001
1927 - 30,500	1939 - 136,000	1951 - 738,500	1963 - 1,635,000	1975 - 4,266,000	1987 — 9,765,000	1995 — W000,001
1928 - 33,000	1940 - 165,000	1952 - 804,000	1964 - 1,713,000	1976 - 4,538,000	1987 1/2 - R996,999	1996 — T000,001
1929 - 35,500	1941 - 194,000	1953 - 950,000	1965 - 1,792,000	1977 - 5,005,000	1987 3/4 - R000,001	1997 1/2 - U000,001
1930 - 38,000	1942 - 224,000	1954 - 999,999	1966 - 1,870,000	1978 - 5,481,000	1988 — R999,999	1999 — A000,001
1931 - 40,000	1943 - 253,000	1955 - 200,000	1967 - 2,164,000	1979 - 5,965,000	1989 — L000,001	2000 1/2- P000,001
1932 - 43,000	1944 - 285,000	1956 - 400,000	1968 - 2,426,000	1980 - 6,432,000	1990 — L999,999	2001 1/2- K000,001
1933 - 47,000	1945 - 341,000	1957 - 600,000	1969 - 2,689,000	1981 - 6,910,000	1990 1/2 - E000,001	2002 3/4- Y000,001
1934 - 55,000	1946 - 413,000	1958 - 800,000	1970 - 2,952,000	1982 - 7,385,000	1991 1/4 - E999,999	2003 3/4- F000,001
1935 - 68,000	1947 - 478,000	1959 - 1,100,000	1971 - 3,215,000	1983 - 7,860,000	1991 1/2 - X000,001	2005 — D000,001
1936 - 81,000	1948 - 543,000	1960 - 1,401,000	1972 - 3,478,000	1984 - 8,338,000	1991 3/4 - N000,001	2006 — Z000,001

The above list Is provided for determining the APPROXIMATE age of your watch. Match serial number with date. Watches were not necessarily sold in the exact order of manufactured date. The above list was furnished with the help of TOM ENGLE.

Hans Wilsdorf started in 1905 with his brother-in-law using the name of Wilsdorf & Davis. They used movement supplier <u>Aegler</u> in Bienne and bought cases in London. In 1919 Wilsdorf started the "Manufacture des Montres Rolex", the movements were manufactured in Bienne but finished in Geneva. 1950 the **Turn-o-graph** was used, the forerunner of the **SUBMARINER**.

ROLEX, split seconds Chronograph, register, S. S. case.

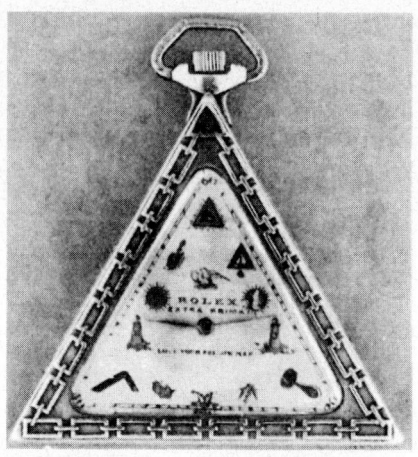

ROLEX, Masonic watch, mother of pearl dial, 15J.

TYPE - DESCRIPTION	ABP	Ex-Fn	Mint
17J, silver, 45mm, OF, C. 1920's.	$450	$775	$875
17J, 3 adj., CAM regulator, **14K**, 43mm, OF, C. 1920	650	1,100	1,325
1/4 Century Club, 17J, **14K**, 41mm, OF, C. 1940.	775	1,200	1,550
Thin line, 17J, **18K**, 42mm, OF, C. 1940	775	1,100	1,325
Time only, gold, 40-44mm, **18K**, OF.	775	1,100	1,325
HC	875	1,325	1,650
Time only, gold, 45-50mm, **18K**, OF	1,100	1,650	2,000
HC	1,325	2,200	2,750
Rolex, **SPORTING PRINCE**, 17J, Adj. 6P ★★	3,325	5,000	6,000
Duo dial, fancy-shaped, 17J, **18K/WG**, OF, 41mm, C. 1930.	2,200	3,300	4,400
$20 dollar coin watch in closed case, triple signed, C.1950	2,750	3,850	4,400
World time watch, gold, 45-52mm.	10,000	13,200	16,500
Chronograph, split seconds, register, S.S. case, 50mm.	3,300	5,000	7,150
Masonic, mother of pearl dial, silver case, Ca.1930s. ★★★	4,400	6,000	7,150

Romilly, Gold , verge, pair case with polychrome enamel & scene, 52mm, OF, Ca.1730.

ROMILLY, JEAN

PARIS

Became a master Watchmaker in 1752 after studying in Geneva and Paris. In 1755, he completed a repeater with beating seconds and a large balance (at one oscillation per second). He also made watches with a 8 day power reserve. Also known for his very ornate paintings on enamel.

TYPE - DESCRIPTION	ABP	Ex-Fn	Mint
Time only, KW, verge, silver, 46-52mm OF	$500	$700	$1,000
Time & Calendar, verge, silver, 50mm, OF	1,200	1,500	2,000
Gold , verge, pair case, plain, 48mm, OF	1,800	2,000	2,500
Gold ,verge, pair case w/ enamel & scene, Ca.1730, 52mm, OF	3,500	6,000	8,000
1/4 repeater, **SILVER**, 52mm, OF	2,000	2,500	3,500
1/4 repeater, **GOLD**, 54mm, OF	3,000	4,000	5,000

ROBERT ROSKELL

Liverpool

Roskell was active from 1798-1830 and worked in both Liverpool and London. He made fine rack lever fusees and gold dial watches. Other family members also produced watches for many years in Liverpool.

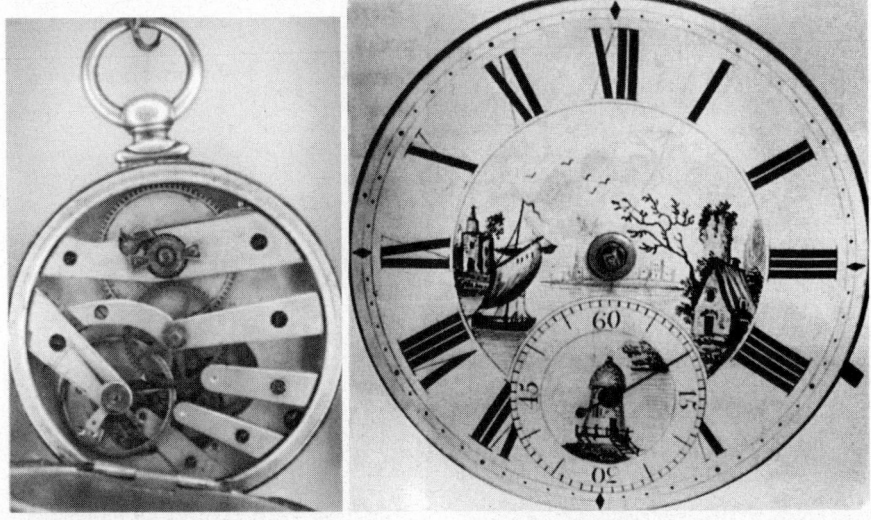

R. Roskell, 47mm, bar style movement, cylinder escapement, Ca. 1850. (Swiss ebauche)

Roskell, Monochrome Scene, Hour & Min. Hand removed to show scene, KW KS, Ca. 1810-20.

TYPE -DESCRIPTION	ABP	Ex-Fn	Mint
KW, (Swiss ebauche) 15J, silver, 48mm, OF, C. 1830-70	$75	$100	$125
KW, (Swiss) 15J, silver, 46-48mm, HC, C. 1830-70	100	125	150
KW, 13J, dust cover, fancy gold dial, **18K**, 47mm, OF, C. 1830-70	275	400	500
KW, Tortoise shell case	525	800	950

Roskell, 48mm, lever escapement, KW KS, Ca.1830.   Roskell, 55mm, Rack & pinion lever fusee, KWKS, Ca. 1825

TYPE - DESCRIPTION	ABP	Ex-Fn	Mint
Rack & pinion lever fusee, porcelain dial, silver, about 1800-25, OF.	$350	$500	$600
Rack & pinion lever fusee, gold dial, Gold, about 1800-25, OF,.....	500	800	1,000
2 day marine chronometer fusee, spring detent escapement, helical hairspring, 54 hr. wind ind., gimbal & box...........	1,500	2,500	3,000
Debaufre escapement, KW KS, silver, 55mm, OF ....★★	2,500	4,000	5,000

Debaufre escapement,
D-shaped & inclined pallet.

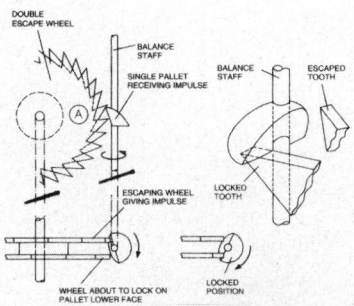

Roskell, 55mm, movement with Debaufre escapement, D-shaped and inclined pallet, KW KS, Ca. 1840.

Robed Roskell, 52mm, London, fusee, spring detent escapement, helical hairspring, 54 hr. wind ind., KW KS.

ROSKOPF (Swiss)

Maker of pin lever, early low cost stem wind watches, often found with fancy dials. A **true** Roskopf watch has only *3 wheels* in its train of gears.

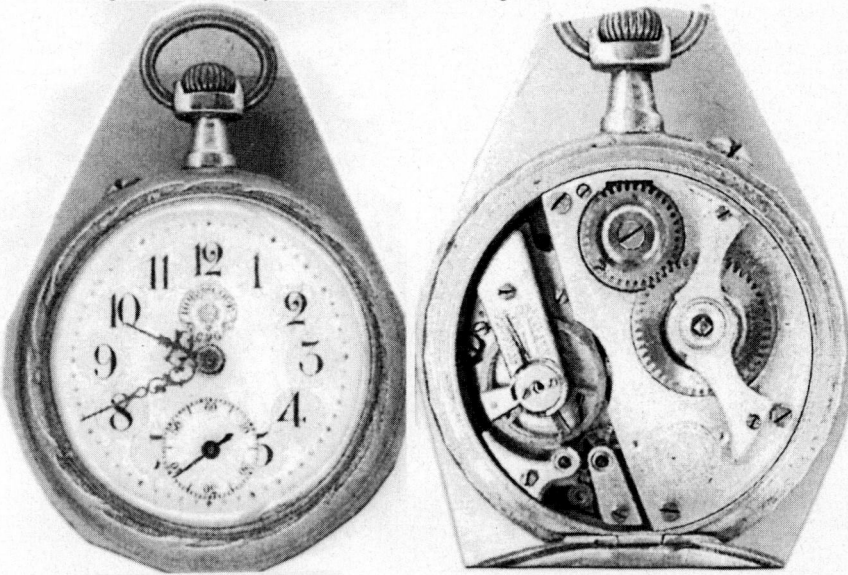

Roskopf, multi-colored blue enamel dial, nail set.　　Roskopf, 45mm, pin lever escapement, 3 wheel train.

TYPE—DESCRIPTION	ABP	Ex-Fn	Mint
4J, pin lever, **3 wheel train**, nail set, base metal, OF, Ca. 1885	$65	$75	$125
Fancy dial, oversize plain case, 55mm, OF, Ca, 1880.	75	150	200
Fancy enamel dial, **fancy enamel case**, 55mm, OF, Ca. 1880	125	200	300

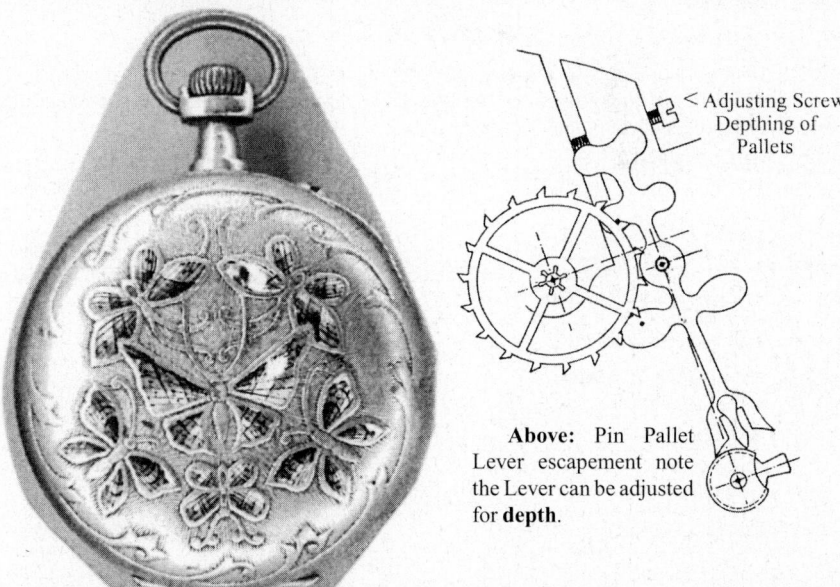

< Adjusting Screw Depthing of Pallets

Above: Pin Pallet Lever escapement note the Lever can be adjusted for **depth**.

Right: Roskopf, multi-colored enamel with blue & purple Butterflies & silver case, nail set.

THOMAS RUSSELL & SONS

London

Thomas Russell & Sons produced quality early keyless watches including Karrusels and chronometers. (Circa 1870-1910)

TYPE - DESCRIPTION	ABP	Ex-Fn	Mint
Time only, gold, 45-48mm, OF	$600	$750	$950
Chronograph, gold, 45-50mm, OF	1,000	1,350	1,600
Split second chronograph, gold, 45-52mm, OF	1,500	3,000	3,500
Minute repeater, gold, 46-52mm, OF	2,200	3,500	4,000
HC	2,800	4,500	5,500
Karrusel. 18K. 51mm. OF, C. 1890	3,700	6,000	7,000

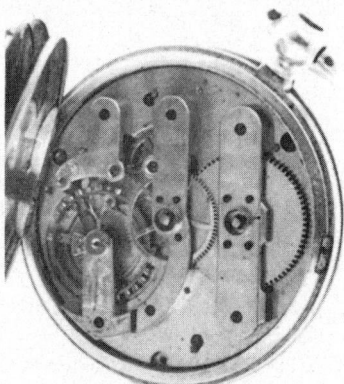

Signed Thomas Russell& Sons Liverpool, KW KS, lever with a club foot escape wheel, Ca. 1905.

Sandoz, 52mm, KW, nickel bridge, gold train, Ca. 1880.

SANDOZ & FILS

SWISS

Large family of watchmakers in the La Chaux-de-Fonds area. Known for repeating watches and pocket chronometers of fine quality.

TYPE —DESCRIPTION	ABP	Ex-En	Mint
Time only, gold, 40- 44mm, OF	$325	$400	$500
HC	400	500	600
Time only, gold, 45- 50mm, OF	500	600	700
HC	600	700	1,000
Chronograph, gold, 45-50mm, OF	700	900	1,000
Split second chronograph, gold, 45-52mm, OF	1,500	2,000	2,500
HC w/register	2,250	3,000	3,500
5 minute repeater, gold, 45-52mm, OF	2,000	2,500	3,000
HC	2,200	3,000	4,000
Minute repeater, gold, 45-52mm, OF	2,000	3,000	3,500
HC	2,500	4,000	5,000
OF w/split chrono	4,000	5,000	7,000
HC w/split chrono	6,000	8,000	10,000
OF w/cal. & moonphase	7,000	9,000	10,000
HC w/chrono., cal. & moonphase	8,000	10,000	12,000
Tourbillion, gold, 48-55mm, OF	20,000	30,000	40,000
Detent chronometer, gold, 48-52mm , OF	4,000	5,000	6,500
HC	5,000	6,000	7,000
World time watch, gold, 48-52mm, OF	5,000	7,000	8,000
Perp. moonphase cal. w/min. rep. and chrono, OF	18,000	25,000	30,000
HC	22,000	30,000	35,000

TAVANNES
Swiss

Created watches in 1895, other names used Dvina, La Tavannes, Obi, Lena Azow, and Kawa.

TYPE - DESCRIPTION	ABP	Ex-Fn	Mint
15J, GF, 35mm, HC, C. 1910	$85	$95	$135
15J, **14K**, 35mm, HC, C. 1910	200	300	350
17J, **14K**, 42mm, OF, C. 1915	225	325	400
21J, **14K**, 45mm, OF, C. 1920	250	350	500
Enamel Bezel & gold, **14K**, 40mm, OF	400	700	800
Enamel Scene & gold, **18K**, 45mm, OF, C. 1925	4,000	8,000	12,000

Non-Magnet Watch Co. occupied the old Tiffany plant in 1889.

TAVANNES, Enamel Scene, 45mm, 18K, OF, C. 1925.   **Tiffany & Co.** 21J., HC, manufactured by Tiffany, Ca. 1875.

TIFFANY & Co.

In 1837 Charles Lewis Tiffany opened a store with John P. Young. They enlarged this operation in 1841, with the help of J. L. Ellis, and imported fine jewelry, watches and clocks from Europe. They incorporated as Tiffany & Co. in 1853. Tiffany made clocks, on special order, in New York around the mid- 1800's. In 1874 Tiffany & Co. started a **watch** factory in Geneva, which lasted about 4 years (low production). Patek, Philippe & Co. assumed the management of their Geneva watch business. The watch machinery was returned to America. Tiffany, Young & Ellis had been a client of Patek, Philippe & Co. since 1849. Tiffany & Co. introduced Patek, Philippe to the American market in 1885. Audemars, Piguet and International Watch Co. also made watches for this esteemed company. Tiffany & Co. sells watches of simple elegance as well as watches with complications such as chronographs, moon phases, repeaters, etc.

Engraved on cuvette "**Tiffany, young & Ellis,** by Jules Jurgensen, fully jeweled, S # 5526, Ca. 1850s.

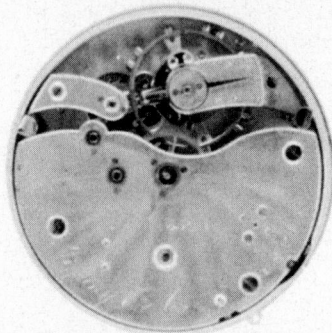 

Tiffany & Co. 21J., *manufactured* by Tiffany, open face, note: the lever has a screw at pallet, S # 13,596.

Tiffany & Co., 21J., *manufactured* by Tiffany, HC, S# 1516, some models engraved on balance cock Wilmot patent.

TYPE - DESCRIPTION	ABP	Ex-Fn	Mint
Tiffany, Young & Ellis, KW KS, gold, 48MM, OF	$1,500	$2,000	$2,500
Tiffany 21J., **manufactured** by Tiffany, gold, 50-55MM, OF ⋯⋯⋯ ★	400	700	1,000
Tiffany 21J., **manufactured** by Tiffany, gold, 50-55MM, HC ⋯⋯⋯ ★	500	1,000	1,200
Time only, gold, 40- 44mm, OF	300	400	600
HC	450	600	800
Time only, gold, 40-44mm, (P.P.Co.), **18K, enamel on bezel**, OF	3,000	4,500	5,500
Time only, gold, 45- 55mm, OF	600	800	1,000
HC	700	1,200	1,500
Chronograph, gold, 45-50mm, OF	1,000	1,500	1,800
HC	1,500	2,000	2,200
OF w/register	1,200	1,800	2,200
Split second chronograph, gold, 45-52mm, OF	2,400	4,000	4,500
HC	2,800	4,500	5,500
5 minute repeater, gold, 46-52mm, OF	2,500	4,100	5,000
HC	3,000	4,500	5,500
OF w/split chrono.	4,000	5,500	7,500
HC w/split chrono	5,000	6,500	8,000
Minute repeater, gold, 46-52mm, OF	2,500	5,000	5,500
HC	3,500	5,500	7,500
by **P. P. & Co.,** flat, 29J., gold, 45mm, OF, C.1912 ,,	8,000	10,000	12,000
OF w/split chrono. & register	6,000	10,000	13,000
HC w/split chrono. & register	7,000	11,000	15,000
HC w/chrono., cal. & moonphase	9,000	13,000	19,000
World time watch, gold, 48-52mm, OF	10,000	12,500	16,000
8 day watch with wind indicator, enamel dial, gold OF	1,500	2,500	3,000
Moonphase, full calendar, gold, OF	3,500	5,000	6,000
Perpetual moonphase calendar, gold, OF	8,000	12,000	15,000
Perp. moonphase cal. w/**min. rep.** and chrono, OF	30,000	40,000	50,000
HC	35,000	50,000	60,000

 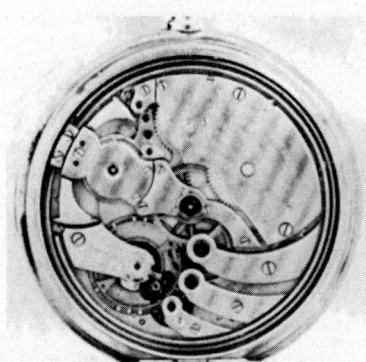

Tiffany & Co., 50mm, **25J.**, split-second chronograph.

Tiffany & Co., flat min. repeater, 29J., signed P. P & Co., ca. 1911.

Geneva

Timing & Repeating W. Co. watches were based on American Waltham model designs and look similar to American Waltham model. They used H. A. Lugrin's patented chronograph mechanism, patented June 12 and October 3, 1876 also July 6 and September 28, 1880. Mr. Lugrin was a foreman for E. Eugene Robert Co. in New York from about 1870 to 1880s. Lugrin used his modular construction and fitted them to American Waltham, Longines and other companies to form a chronograph. E. Eugene Robert Co. in 1890 became A Wittnauer Co. In the mid 1890s the Timing & Repeating W. Co. was formed.

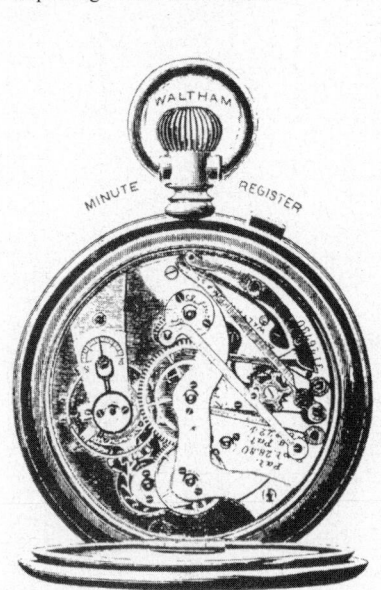 

American Waltham W. Co., Chronograph movement, Min. register, Patented Sept. 28, 1880 - Eng. Pat. #3224.

Timing & Repeating W. Co., Chronograph movement. Min. register, Patented Sept. 28,1880- Eng. Pat. #3224.

TYPE -DESCRIPTION	ABP	Ex-Fn	Mint
Chronograph, 17J, GF, 45mm, OF, C. 1900	$150	$200	$250
Chronograph w/register, 17J, GF, 45mm, OF, C. 1900	185	250	300
Chronograph, 17J, gilt mvt., silver, 45mm, HC, C. 1900	200	300	400
Chronograph w/register & split sec., 17J, GF, 45mm, OF, C. 1900	250	400	500
5 Min. Repeater, 15 jewels. gold jewel settings, **14K** Gold case	2,200	3,000	4,000

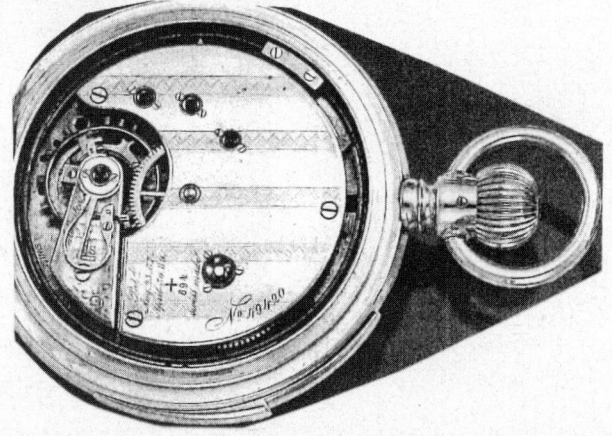

5 Min. Repeater, 15 jewels, gold jewel settings, signed "Patd. Aug.23.87, April 30.89 + 894 Swiss made, S#49420.

TISSOT

Swiss

The firm of Charles Tissot & His was founded in 1853 in Le Locle by Charles Tissot. This skilled watchmaker worked from his home and in 1907, a factory was started. In 1971, the world's first plastic wrist watch was made.

TYPE —DESCRIPTION	ABP	Ex-Fn	Mint
Early, KW, Time only, Swiss bar, Pre. 1870, silver case	$75	$125	$185
Time only, gold, 40- 44mm, OF.	250	400	450
HC.	300	450	500
Time only, gold, 45- 50mm, OF	425	600	700
HC.	500	700	800
2-Train 1/4 second jump watch, silver, 50mm,	650	1,000	1,200
2-Train 1/4 second jump watch, **gold**, 50mm.	1,700	3,000	3,500
Chronograph, gold, 45-50mm, OF.	700	1,000	1,200
Split second chronograph, gold, 45-52mm, OF	1,400	1,500	2,000
HC w/register.	2,000	2,500	3,000
5 minute repeater, gold, 45-52mm, OF	2,000	3,000	3,500
HC	2,200	3,500	4,000
Minute repeater, gold, 45-52mm, OF.	2,300	3,500	4,000
HC	2,500	4,000	5,000
OF w/split chrono	3,500	5,000	6,000
HC w/split chrono	4,000	6,000	7,000
OF w/cal. & **moonphase**.	5,000	8,000	10,000
Tourbillon, gold, 48-55mm, OF	30,000	45,000	55,000
Detent chronometer, gold, 48-52mm , OF	3,000	5,250	7,250
HC	4,000	5,750	7,750
World time watch, gold, 48-52mm, OF	7,000	9,000	12,000
Moonphase, full calendar, gold, OF.	2,000	3,500	4,000
HC	2,500	4,000	4,500
Moonphase, full calendar, **chronoghaph**, gold, OF	4,000	5,000	5,500
HC	4,500	5,500	6,000
Moonphase, full calendar, **min. repeater, chronograph,** gold, OF. .	5,000	9,000	12,000
HC	6,500	10,000	14,000
Perp. moonphase cal. w/min. rep. and chrono, OF	15,000	25,000	35,000
HC	20,000	30,000	40,000
Clock Watch, gold, 48-52mm, OF	5,000	12,000	14,000
HC	7,500	14,000	17,000

Tissot, 2-Train 1/4 second jump watch, center sweep hand, enamel dial, 28J., gold train, 54mm, KWKS, 18K, Ca. 1880.

Tissot, minute repeater, with chronograph, day date month, moonphase, 27 jewels, 18K, HC , Ca. 1910.

M. I. TOBIAS & Co.

The M. I. Tobias firm started in Liverpool, about 1805. The Tobias family did not manufacture watches and specialized in exporting watches to U.S.A. Watches signed *M.J. Tobias* are swiss made. The Tobias family activity extends from about 1805 to 1868. (As with most firms, they had several different grades.)

M. I. Tobias & Co., Lord Street, Liverpool, 2 train independent sec., Pat.21 Feb, 1848, 52mm, right angle lever.

M. I. Tobias, 18K mum-color gold dial & gold case, KW/KS, fusee, diamond end stone, Ca. 1845, 52mm.

TYPE - DESCRIPTION	ABP	Ex-Fn	Mint
KW, 7-15J, 47-52mm, **Swiss**, silver, OF	$75	110	$135
HC	100	150	175
KW, 7-15J, 47-52mm, **English**, silver, OF	100	135	200
HC	125	150	225
KW, 7-15J, lever or verge fusee, fancy **gold** case, 48mm,OF	250	400	500
KW, lever or verge fusee, **gold dial, Heavy 18K**, 52mm, HC	700	1,000	1,200
KW, **2 train** independent sec., **Silver**, 56mm, OF	300	425	500
KW, verge fusee, **multi-color gold dial & case**, 52mm, OF	700	1,000	1,200
HC	800	1,200	1,500
KW, **rack lever** escapement, **Silver**, 56mm, OF	300	425	500
HC	400	500	600
KW, **rack lever** escapement, **Gold**, 56mm, OF	700	900	1,000
HC	900	1,000	1,200
Captain's watch, center sec., sub-sec., gold dial, **18K**, 51mm, OF	1,300	2,250	2,750
18K, 51mm, HC	1,500	2,750	3,250

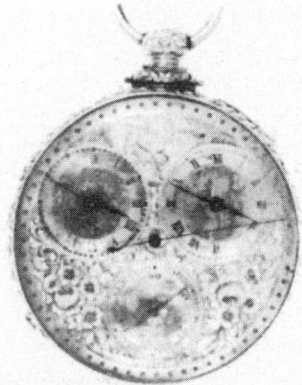

Tobias, (Liverpool), 51mm, 18K, OF, Captain's watch, center & sub-seconds, gold dial.

TOUCHON & Co.

Swiss

Touchon & Co. started using this name as a trade mark in 1907. They manufactured complex and simple watches. In 1921 they associated with the firm of Wittnauer & Co.

Touchon & co., 47mm, 29 jewels, minute repeater, open face, jeweled through hammers.

Touchon & co., 47mm, 29 jewels, split-second chronograph and minute repeater, ca. 1910.

TYPE - DESCRIPTION	ABP	Ex-Fe	Mint
Time only, gold, 45- 50mm, OF	$400	$500	$700
HC	500	700	1,000
1/4 hr. repeater, gold, 46-52mm, OF	800	1,500	2,000
HC	900	2,000	2,500
OF w/chrono	900	2,000	2,200
HC w/chrono	1,100	2,200	2,750
OF w/chrono., cal.& moonphase	2,000	3,000	3,500
HC w/chrono., cal. & moonphase	2,400	3,500	4,000
5 minute repeater, gold, 46-52mm, OF	1,500	2,500	3,000
HC	1,800	2,700	3,500
Minute repeater, gold, 46-52mm, OF.	2,200	3,500	4,000
HC	2,500	4,000	5,000
OF w/chrono. & register	2,700	3,800	4,500
HC w/chrono. & register	2,900	4,200	5,000
OF w/split chrono	4,500	6,500	7,000
HC w/split chrono. & register	4,500	7,500	8,500
HC w/chrono., cal. & moonphase	4,500	8,000	12,000
HC, **Perp**. moonphase cal	18,000	25,000	30,000
HC, **Perp**. moonphase cal. and chrono	20,000	30,000	35,000
World time watch, gold, 48-52mm, OF	4,000	5,000	6,500
Perpetual moonphase calendar, gold, OF	6,500	10,000	12,000
Clock watch, gold, 46-52mm, OF	6,000	12,000	14,000
HC	8,000	14,000	17,000

COMPARISON OF WATCH CASE SIZES	
U.S.A.	**EUROPEAN**
10-12 SIZE	40—44MM
16 SIZE	45—49MM
18 SIZE	50—55 MM

VACHERON & CONSTANTIN

Swiss

The oldest Swiss factory, founded by Jean-Marc Vacheron, in 1775. The firm of Vacheron & the firm of Constantin were in business about the same date 1785, but the association bearing the name today did not come into being until 1819. In these early periods, different grades of watches produced by Vacheron & Constantin bore different names.

The association with Leschot, around 1840, catapulted the firm into its position as a top quality manufacturer. Before that time, their watches were typical of Genevese production. Vacheron & Constantin exported many movements to the United States to firms such as Bigelow, Kennard & Co., which were cased domestically, typically in the period 1900-1935. In its early period the firm produced some lovely ladies' enameled watches, later it produced high grade timepieces and complicated watches, and to this day produces fine watches.

ESTIMATED PRODUCTION DATES

DATE-SERIAL #		DATE-SERIAL #		DATE-SERIAL #	
1830 -	30,000	1880 -	170,000	1925 -	400,000
1835 -	40,000	1885 -	180,000	1930 -	410,000
1840 -	50,000	1890 -	190,000	1935 -	420,000
1845 -	60,000	1895 -	223,000	1940 -	440,000
1850 -	75,000	1900 -	256,000	1945 -	484,000
1855 -	95,000	1905 -	289,000	1950 -	488,000
1860 -	110,000	1910 -	322,000	1955 -	512,000
1865 -	125,000	1915 -	355,000	1960 -	536,000
1870 -	140,000	1920 -	385,000	1965 -	560,000
1875 -	155,000			1970 -	585,000

The above list is provided for determining the approximate age of your watch. Match serial number with date. Watches were not necessarily sold in the exact order of manufactured date.

☞ The date a watch **sold** is not an indication of the date it was **produced.**

Early movements manufactured with the machines invented by George-Auguste Leschot. The machines were built in the Vacheron Constantin factory ca. 1839 to 1840. In about1863 to 1865 V. & C. manufactured a inexpensive watch using the names Abraham Vacheron or Abm. Vacheron also the name of Chossat & Cie.

Vacheron & Constantin, 44mm, 18 jewels, enamel bezel, 18K, Ca. 1930.

Early Vacheron & Constantin's With Different Names

1755 - Jean-Marc Vacheron	1857 - C'esar Vacheron
1785 - Abraham Vacheron	1869 - Charles Vacheron & Cie
1786 - Abraham Vacheron - Girod	1870 - Veuve C'esar Vacheron & Cie
1810 - Vacheron - Chossat & Cie.	1887 - Ancienne Fabrique Vacheron & Constantin SA
1819 - Vacheron & Constantin	1896 - Vacheron & Constantin SA

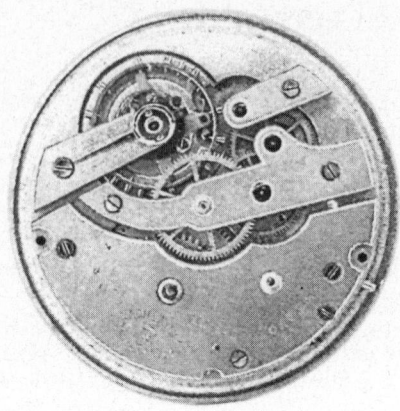

Signed **"VACHERON & CONSTANTIN"**
13-15 Jewels, gilt movement, Ca.1925.

TYPE - DESCRIPTION	ABP	Ex-Fn	Mint
Early bar movement, lever escap., **signed Vacheron & Constantin**			
time only, KW KS, silver case, 30-39mm, OF	$250	$400	$600
(same as above) 40-44mm, OF	250	425	625
(same as above) 45-48mm, OF	275	425	650
(same as above) 45-48mm, **HC**	325	500	700
Early Le-Pine bar movement, duplex escap., GOLD & ENAMEL			
KW KS, **signed Vacheron & Constantin,** 49mm, OF	4,000	7,000	10,000
Time only, 18K gold & **enamel bezel,** 40-44mm, OF	1,200	2,500	3,500

Vacheron & Constantin, 49mm, Early Lepine bar style movement, duplex escapement, GOLD & ENAMEL, KW KS, **signed Vacheron & Constantin**, 49mm, OF, Ca. 1840.

Vacheron & Constantin, Gold coin 50 pesos 900 fine, coin hollowed out to receive watch,
LEFT view shows dial & movement.

TYPE -DESCRIPTION	ABP	Ex-Fn	Mint
Time only, **18K** gold, 40-44mm, OF	$600	$1,000	$1,500
HC	900	1,200	2,000
Time only, gold, 45-50mm, OF	1,000	1,500	2,000
HC	1,600	2,000	2,500
X-thin, 17J., **Aluminum**, weight =20 grains, OF, C. 1940	1,800	2,800	3,800
Deck chronometer, wooden box, 21J., silver, 60mm,OF, C.1943	3,500	5,500	7,500
Gold coin 50 pesos 900 fine, coin hollowed out to receive watch	2,500	4,000	4,500

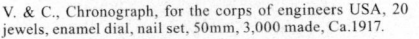

V. & C., Chronograph, for the corps of engineers USA, 20 jewels, enamel dial, nail set, 50mm, 3,000 made, Ca.1917.

V. & C., Astronomic with moon phase, perpetual calendar, minute repeater, split-second chronograph, 1905.

TYPE - DESCRIPTION	ABP	Ex-Fn	Mint
Chronograph, 20J, corps of engineers USA, **Silver**, 45-50mm, OF	$1,200	$1,800	$2,500
Chronograph, gold, 45-50mm, **V & C case**, OF	2,000	3,000	4,000
HC	2,500	3,700	4,500
OF w/register	2,200	3,300	4,500
HC w/register	3,200	4,300	5,000

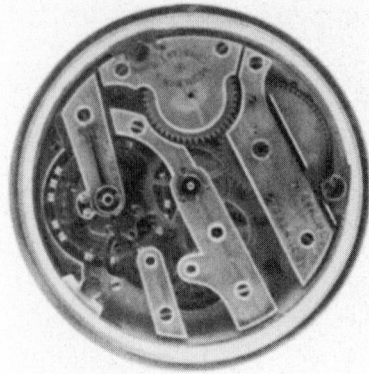

V. & C., 40mm, wolf tooth winding, open face

V. & C., 40mm, 31J., Min. repeater, slide activated, OF.

TYPE -DESCRIPTION	ABP	Ex-Fn	Mint
Split second chronograph, gold, 45-52mm, OF	$4,000	$6,000	$7,500
HC	5,000	7,000	8,500
OF w/register	4,500	6,700	8,000
HC w/register	6,000	8,000	9,500
Minute repeater, gold, 46-52mm, OF	4,500	6,500	9,000
HC	5,000	8,000	12,000
OF w/chrono	6,000	7,500	11,000
HC w/chrono	9,000	11,000	18,000
OF w/chrono. & register	6,000	8,000	12,000
HC w/chrono. & register	10,000	12,000	18,000
OF w/split chrono	7,500	12,000	16,000
HC w/split chrono	10,000	17,000	22,000
OF w/split chrono. & register	8,000	12,000	17,000
HC w/split chrono. & register	12,000	20,000	27,000
OF w/chrono., cal. & moonphase	12,000	22,000	27,000
Tourbillon, gold, 48-55mm, OF	45,000	70,000	110,000
World time watch, gold, 48-52mm, OF	18,000	25,000	35,000
Perp. moonphase cal. w/min. repeater, OF	32,000	55,000	70,000
HC	40,000	60,000	80,000
Perp. moonphase cal. w/min. rep. and split sec. chrono., OF	50,000	75,000	100,000
Perp. moonphase cal. w/min. rep. and split sec. chrono., HC	60,000	85,000	110,000
Clock Watch, gold, 46-52mm, OF	15,000	23,000	28,000
HC	20,000	28,000	33,000

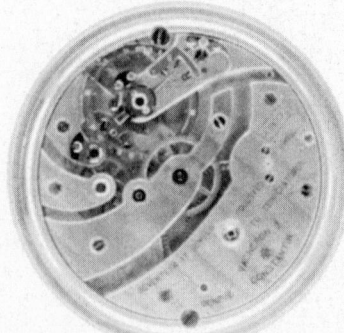

V. & C., extra thin and light weight **Aluminum**, (20 grains), about 12 size, 44mm, OF, 17 jewels, Ca. 1940.

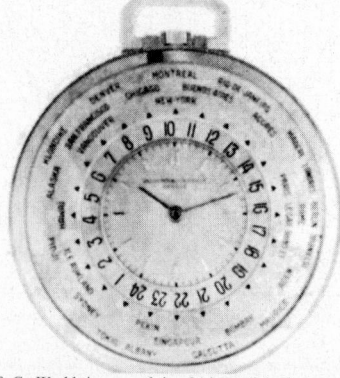

V. & C., World time, revolving 24 hour dial, 31 citys of the world, 18 jewels, 45mm, Ca. 1945

VINER (LONDON)

Charles Viner apprenticed in about 1802 and in records till 1840. The company continued after his death as Viner & Co. Viner also made clocks.

TYPE -DESCRIPTION	ABP	Ex-Fn	Mint
VINER, Verge Fusee / Alarm, 50MM, Silver, OF, Ca.1835	$1,000	$1,400	$2,000
Pull Wind, winds by pulling knob in pendant, 40-50mm, Silver . . .	1,200	2,200	2,700

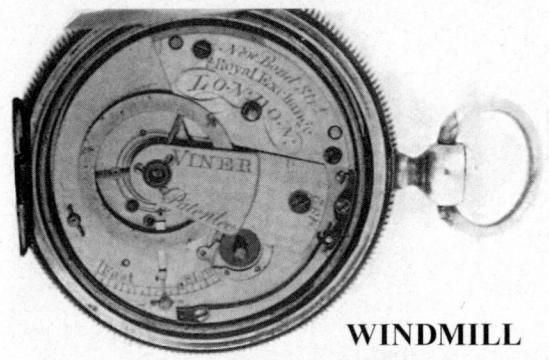

VINER, Verge Fusee with Alarm, marked on cuvette for the two arbors *"wind up"* & the other marked *"warning"*, under sprung hairspring, 50MM, Silver Open Face Case, Ca. 1835.

WINDMILL

LONDON

Joseph and his son Thomas made clocks and watches and at one time employed 10 workers. Started in business in 1671 and lasted till about 1732.

TYPE - DESCRIPTION	ABP	Ex-Fn	Mint
Tho. WINDMILL,1/4 hr. repeater, 55MM, silver, OF, Ca.1675-90 . .	$5,500	$10,000	$15,000
Tho. WINDMILL,1/4 hr. repeater, 55MM, **gold**, OF, Ca.1675-90. ★★	7,000	20,000	25,000

Tho. WINDMILL, 1/4 hour repeater activated by pendant and sounds on inner bell, champleve dial, note D shaped foot on balance bridge, silver Open Face, 55MM, Ca. 1675-90.

ZENITH

Is Lode Swiss

Founded in 1865 by Georges Favre- Jacot. The name Zenith was registered in 1897 & by 1920 they had made 2,000,000

ZENITH, alarm watch, enamel dial, 17J., 50mm, Ca. 1930

ZENITH, Military Deck Watch, 51mm, nickel case, Ca. 1940.

TYPE - DESCRIPTION	ABP	Ex-Fn	Mint
Time only, gold, 40-44mm, OF	$225	$300	$425
HC	375	450	525
Time only, gold, 40-44mm, with **enamel** on bezel, **18K**, OF	600	800	1,000
Time only, gold, 45-52mm, OF	400	500	700
HC	500	800	1,000
RR Extra, 21J., **Grade 56**, (16 size), **Gold Filled** OF	185	300	400
Military Deck Watch, 51mm, nickel case, Ca.1940.	250	400	500
Alarm watch, 17J., nail set, **two barrels**, gold, 50mm, C.1930	1,200	1,600	2,000
Chronograph, gold, 45-50mm, OF	700	900	1,100
HC	800	1,000	1,400
Minute repeater, gold, 46-52mm, OF	2,200	3,000	3,500
HC	2,700	3,500	4,500
OF w/split chrono	4,000	5,500	6,500
HC w/split chrono	4,200	6,500	7,500
OF w/chrono., cal. & moonphase	4,000	6,000	8,000
HC w/chrono., cal. & moonphase	4,500	8,000	10,000
Perp. moonphase cal. w/min. rep. and chrono., OF	18,000	25,000	30,000
HC	20,000	30,000	35,000

ZENITH, 42mm, 18K, enamel on case, open face, 17J., signed ZENITH, Ca. 1930's.

PRE-1850 REPEATERS

Swiss or French 1/4 hr. repeater, verge or cylinder, silver, 55mm, Ca. 1820, OF. Note: Parachute (illo.1)

Swiss or French 1/4 hr. rep., pump, verge or cylinder, 18K, 52mm, OF, Ca.1800s. (illo.2)

TYPE - DESCRIPTION	ABP	Ex-Fn	Mint
Swiss or French 1/4 hr. rep., verge, silver, 55mm, OF (illo.1)	$1,000	$1,500	$2,000
Swiss or French 1/4 hr. rep., cylinder, silver, 55mm, OF (illo.1)	800	1,200	1,500
Swiss 1/4 hr. rep., **pump**, verge, 18K, 52mm, OF, C.1800s (illo.2). . .	2,000	2,500	3,500
Swiss 1/4 hr. rep., **pump**, cylinder,18K, 52mm, OF, C,1800s (illo.2) .	1,500	2,000	3,000
Swiss 1/4 hr., automaton on dial (2 figures), gilt, verge, KW, 55mm, OF, early 1800s.	2,500	3,500	4,000
Swiss 1/4 hr. repeater, 32-35mm, KW KS, **gold**, Ca. 1850 (illo.3) . . .	1,800	2,200	2,800
English, striking device with repetition for hours & 1/4 hour (illo. A)	4,500	6,500	9,000
French 1/4 hr. musical repeater **disc-driven**, KW KS, cylinder,**18K**, 57mm, OF, C. 1825 (illo. B).	3,500	5,500	6,500

Swiss or French 1/4 hr. repeater, cylinder escapement, Swiss bar movement, 32-35mm, KW KS, gold, Ca. 1850, (illo.3)

English gold watch With a Striking device with repetition for hours & 1/4 hour, Verge, gold dial, 48mm Ca. 1730.(illo. A)

French 1/4 hr. musical repeater disc-driven, cylinder, KW KS, 18k, 57mm, OF, C. 1825, (illo.B)

French, 1/4 hr. repeater, gold and enamel superior quality, enameled scene, outer case with pearls, verge, 20K, 52mm, OF, C.1785. (illo.5)

1/4 hr. repeater, Virgule escap., KW, 18K, 46mm, OF, Ca.1840. (illo.6)

TYPE - DESCRIPTION	ABP	Ex-Fn	Mint
Skeletonized 1/4 hr., cylinder, Swiss, 18K, 58mm, OF, C 1810......	$3,000	$5,000	$6,000
French 1/4 hr. repeater, **20K** gold and enamel, verge, enameled scene, superior quality, outer pearls, 52mm, OF, C.1785 (illo.5)	5,000	20,000	35,000
1/4 hr. repeater, Virgule escap., KW, 18K, 46mm, OF (illo.6)	2,200	4,000	5,000
1/4 hr. rep., erotic scene (concealed in cuvette), automated, multi-color gold figures, verge, pump 1/4 hr., 18K, 54mm, OF, C.1800......	4,000	7,500	9,000
French or Swiss pump 1/4 hr. repeater, free standing barrel, **Thin gold** case, cylinder escape., tapered bridges , Ca.1790-1835 (illo.7)	2,000	3,500	4,000
Early 1/4 hr. rep., Paris (Clouzier) gilt dial w/enamel hour cartouches, verge, gilt & shagreen case, 58mm, OF, C.1700.............	5,000	9,000	11,000
1/4 hr. repeater, London, gilt & shagreen paircase, verge, extremely fine, 56mm, OF, C.1700s	5,000	9,000	11,000

French or Swiss pump 1/4 hr. repeater, free standing barrel, cylinder escapement, tapered bridges, **Thin** gold engine turned case, Ca. 1790-1835. (illo.7)

1/4 hour verge repeater, 49mm, 22K gold repousse pair case, repeating on an inner bell, repeat mechanism is activated from the pendant, Ca. 1700-1750, (illo.8)

1/4 hour repeater, musical, 25 musical tines, cylinder, center seconds, KW, 18K, 58mm, OF, Ca.1820, (illo.9)

1/4 hour repeater, verge (London, Dutch), pierced inner case, repousse outer case, gold, 49mm, C.1700, (illo.10)

1/4 Hr. repeating coach watch, with alarm, about 120 MM, verge fusee, silver repousse case, ca. 1700-40. (illo. 11)

TYPE - DESCRIPTION	ABP	Ex-Fn	Mint
1/4 hr. repeater, repousse pair case, verge, **22K**, 49mm (illo.8)	$4,500	$7,500	$9,000
1/4 hr. repeater, musical, **25 musical tines**, cylinder, center seconds, KW, 18K, 58mm,OF, C. 1820 (illo.9)	5,000	6,000	7,000
1/4 hr. rep., verge (London, Dutch), pierced inner case, repousse outer case, gold, 49mm, C.1700 (illo. 10)	5,000	9,000	11,000
1/4 hr. repeating coach watch w/alarm, verge, fusee, silver repousse case, large, C. 1700-40 (illo. 11).	7,000	14,000	16,000
1/4 hr. repeater with automaton dial, verge, Swiss, KW, 3 automated figures on dial and carillon chimes, silver, 52mm, OF, C. 1790	2,000	3,500	4,500
Gold & enamel, 1/4 hr. repeater, London, cylinder, Fusee, paircase, enamel on outer case, 18K, 48mm, C. 1790	3,500	6,000	7,500
Swiss, 1/4 hr. pump repeater, w/ automaton, verge, 18K, 54mm, OF, C. 1800	3,500	5,000	6,000
Virgule escapement, 1/4 hr. repeater, fancy gold & multi-dial, London, KW, 18K, OF, C. 1840	2,200	3,500	4,000

REPEATERS

RIGHT:(illo. A)
1/2 - 1/4 Repeater,
back wind and back
set by folding **button**
system,17J., diamond end
stone,18K HC, Ca.1863.

Watkin's Patent
Ca.Apr.1870 Folding
Button can be attached
to any key watch.

1/4 hour repeater, 17jewels, nail set, gun metal case, 49mm, C. 1910. (illo.12)

1/4 hour repeater with chronograph, gun metal base metal or gold filled, 49-50mm, (illo.13)

TYPE - DESCRIPTION	ABP	Ex-Fn	Mint
1/4 hr. repeater, 17J, gun metal, 49-52mm, C. 1910 (illo.12)	$450	$525	$700
1/4 hr. repeater, 17J, silver, 49-52mm, OF, C. 1910	550	625	750
1/4 hr. repeater, 17J, silver, 49-52mm, HC, C. 1910	600	700	850
1/4 hr. rep. **w/chrono.**,17J, base metal, gun metal or GF, **OF** 49-50mm, C.1910 (illo.13)	650	725	850
1/4 hr. rep. **w/chrono.**,17J, base metal, gun metal or GF, **HC** 49-50mm,C.1910	750	850	1,000
1/2 - 1/4 repeater, back wind & set button, **18K** HC, Ca.1863 (illo. A).	1,500	2,500	3,500

1/4 **hour repeater with Calendar**, 17J, gold filled, 3/4 plate, (illo. 14)

1/4 **hour repeater**, 55mm, 2 Jacquemarts, gill case, Ca.1820. (illo.15)

TYPE – DESCRIPTION	ABP	Ex-Fn	Mint
1/4 hr. repeater with Calendar, 17J, gun metal or gold filled, 3/4 plate, OF, 49-50mm, C. 1910 (illo.14)	$700	$900	$1,200
Swiss 1/4 hr. repeater w/moonphase & calendar, 17J, 18K, 53mm, HC, C. 1900.	3,000	4,000	4,500
55mm, 1/4 repeater, 2 Jacquemarts, gilt case, Ca. 1820 (illo. 15). . . .	2,500	3,500	4,000
Swiss, 1/4 repeater, **musical**, pinned cylinder & comb, 18K, 50-55mm, Ca. 1800. (illo.16)	5,000	7,500	8,500
Swiss 1/4 hr. repeater, **Erotic Scene**, 14K, HC, 50-54mm, ALL ORIGINAL, (note: beware of fakes) (illo.16A).. . . . . ★★	9,000	20,000	25,000
Min. Repeater, 18K, HC.. . . . . ★★★	10,000	25,000	30,000

Swiss 18K, 1/4 repeater, **musical**, pinned cylinder & comb, 50-55 mm, Ca. 1800. (illo.16)

Swiss 1/4 hour repeater, Erotic Scene with automaton action dial, 14K, HC, 50-54mm, (illo.16A)

A bit of musical history in 1796, Antoine Favre of Geneva invented a comb with **vibrating strips.** This innovation lead to the production of the musical pocket watch.

COMPARISON OF WATCH CASE SIZES	
U.S.A.	**EUROPEAN**
10-12 SIZE	40—44MM
16 SIZE	45—49MM
18 SIZE	50—55 MM

Minute Repeater, 48 jewels, 2 train Independent seconds TANDEM wind, 55mm, Ca. 1890,18K HC. (illo. 17)

Swiss minute repeater, 54mm, jeweled through hammers, 14k case. (illo.18)

TYPE - DESCRIPTION	ABP	Ex-En	Mint
Min. rep., 20J, Swiss, gilt mvt., gun metal, 52mm, **OF**, 1910	$700	$900	$1,200
Min. rep., 48 jewels, 2 train Independent seconds **TANDEM** wind, 55mm, Ca. 1890, 18K HC. (illo.19)	5,500	7,000	9,000
Min. rep., 17J, Swiss, gilt, 18K, 52mm, HC, C. 1910	2,500	3,500	4,000
Min. rep., 32 J, Swiss, gilt, 18K, 54mm, HC, C. 1910	2,700	4,000	5,000
Min. rep., 32 J, Swiss, NI, porc. dial, 14K, OF, C. 1905 (illo.18)	2,200	3,000	3,500
Min. rep., 32 J, Swiss, NI, porc. dial, 18K, OF, C. 1905 (illo.19)	2,500	3,500	4,000
Min. repeater, 25J, Self contained, (activated from button on crown) 14K, OF, C. 1915 (illo.17)	3,500	5,000	6,000
Min. repeater, Swiss, ultra thin, 32J, 18K, OF, C. 1930.	4,000	4,500	6,000
Min. repeater, automated, 18K, 54mm, (illo.20).	5,000	12,000	15,000

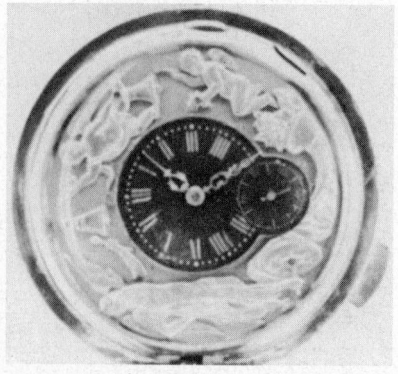

Minute Repeater, 32 jewels., Swiss, enamel dial, wolf tooth winding, 18K, Ca. 1905, (illo.19)

Father& Baby Time, automated min. repeater, 54mm, note father and baby striking bell, 18K. (illo. 20)

Minute repealing **Clock Watch**, 3/4 plate, a on or off strike activated mechanism, three gongs, tandem-winding barrels, 18K, 48-50mm, HC, Ca.1900 (illo.21)

Minute repeater, split second chronograph, Swiss, 18K, 47-50mm, OF, Ca.1900. (illo. 22)

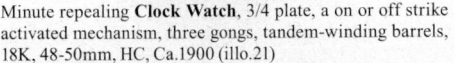

TYPE - DESCRIPTION	ABP	Ex-Fn	Mint
Min. repeating Clock Watch, 18K, 48-50mm, HC, Ca.1900 (illo.21) .	$8,000	$14,000	$17,000
Min. rep. w/ chrono, Swiss ,SW, 18K, large 58mm, OF, C.1900	1,800	3,000	3,500
Min. repeater w/chrono. register, 32J, nickel, very high quality,			
18K, 50mm, OF, C. 1900	3,500	4,500	5,000
Min.rep. w/chrono, 30 mm. register, Swiss, 36J, 18K ,HC, C.1895 . .	3,200	5,000	5,500
Min.rep., split sec. chrono, Swiss, 18K, 47-50mm,			
OF, C.1900 (illo.22)	4,500	8,000	9,000
Min.rep., split sec. chrono, Swiss, 18K, 47-50mm,			
HC,C.1900	5,500	9,000	12,000
Swiss Min. repeater, chrono, moonphase and calendar, 30J or more,			
18K, 60mm, HC, C. 1895	5,000	8,000	10,000
Swiss Min.repeater, moonphase and **perpetual calendar**,			
30J or more, 18K, 60mm, HC, C. 1895 (illo.23) . . . . ★	14,000	25,000	30,000
Swiss mm. rep., **4 hammers & Westminster carillon** on gongs,			
32J, 18K, 53mm, HC, C. 1910 (illo.24) . . . . ★	9,000	30,000	35,000

Swiss minute repeater, moonphase and perpetual calendar, 30J or more, 18K, 60mm, HC, C. 1895. (illo.23)

Swiss min. rep., 4 hammers & Westminster carillon on gongs, 32J, 18K, 53mm, HC, C. 1910. (illo.24)

PRE-1850 ALARMS

TYPE -DESCRIPTION	ABP	Ex-Fn	Mint
Alarm, (**Blois, France**), double silver case pierced and engraved, gilt mvt., cut gut cord fusee, 2 wheel train + verge escape. w/foliot, silver balance cock, 44mm, Ca. 1640 (illo.25)	$13,000	$27,000	$38,000
Alarm, 2 cases pierced, 3 wheel train, Egyptian pierced pillers, verge & foliot, 51mm, Ca. 1665 (illo.26)	10,000	27,000	38,000

ALARM, from BLOIS, FRANCE, double silver case pierced and engraved, silver crown dial with roman numbers, alarm center dial with arabic numbers, gilt movement, cut gut cord fusee, 2 wheel train plus verge escapement with foliot, silver balance cock, 44mm, Ca. 1640. It is believed French watch-making started in the town of **Blois, France.** (illo.25)

 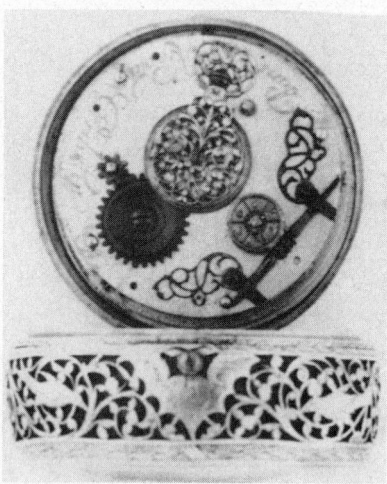

ALARM, 2 cases pierced & engraved, roman outer dial, alarm center dial, blued hands , 3 wheel train, Egyptian pierced pillers, verge & foliot, endless screw adjustment. Paris, 51mm, Ca. 1665. (illo.26)

In 1675 when the adjustable spiral hairspring was invented, the method of regulating a watch changed. Before 1675 a watch was regulated by winding up, or letting down, the mainspring by means of a endless screw driving wheel. The endless screw was fixed to the back-plate. At one end of the endless screw which was squared so take a small key. The power of the mainspring is evened out over a period of time by means of the fusee, however the variation in the strength of the mainspring when regulated would alter the rate of the watch.

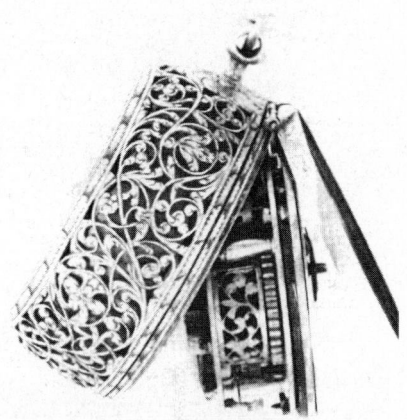

ALARM, strikes on bell, pair cased, verge, C. 1650. (illo.27)

Alarm, pair cased, first case pique nailed skin, second case pierced, 4 wheel train, verge, amphora pillers, 56mm, Ca.1680. (illo.28)

TYPE — DESCRIPTION	ABP	Ex-Fn	Mint
Alarm, strikes on bell, pair cased, verge, C. 1650 (illo.27)	$9,000	$17,000	$22,000
Alarm, pair cased, first case pique nailed skin, 4 wheel train, verge, 56mm, Ca. 1680 (illo.28)	11,000	22,000	27,000
Alarm, Rotterdam, silver pierced case, gilt, tulip pillars, verge, fusee, 48mm, Ca. 1685 (illo.29)	9,000	14,000	20,000
Alarm, Oignon', verge, fusee, large pierced bal. bridge (illo.30)	8,500	11,000	14,000

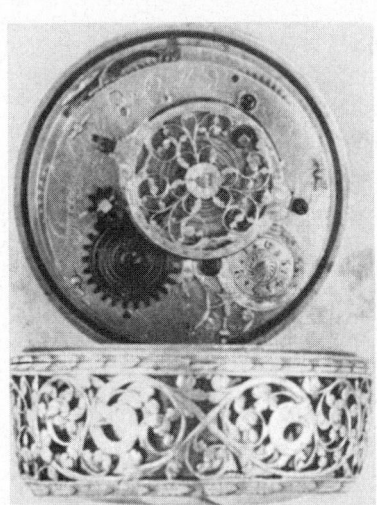

ALARM, Rotterdam, silver pierced case, gilt, tulip pillars, verge, fusee, 48mm, Ca. 1685. (illo.29)

ALARM, "oignon', verge, fusee, large pierced balance bridge, French. Ca. 1675-80. (illo.30)

The term Oignon is the **nickname** of large domed bulb shaped watches, they start to appear after 1675 & having some uniform construction features point to a source of specialized workshops, (ebauches) thus becoming reasonably priced & improved time keeping due to the **Spiral** hair-spring. **French** Oignon watches wind from the front dial side and the balance bridge cock has two screws & usually have domed shaped dials. **English** Oignon watches generally wind from back & the balance cock use a single screw & foot & the dials have a flat appearance. (Ca. 1680 the minute hand starts to appear.)

ALARM, nailed pique shagreen skin, second case pierced silver, balance cock has short feet, 4 wheel train verge, 60mm, London, Ca. 1675-60. (illo.31)

Alarm-Oignon, nailed pique shagreen **Sting-Ray** skin, triple cases, entirely pierced throughout, richly decorated, 4 wheel train, verge, fusee, English, Ca. 1690. (illo.32) **Sting-Ray** skin note the enamel caps arranged in a mosaic pattern.

TYPE - DESCRIPTION	ABP	Ex-Fn	Mint
Alarm, nailed pique shagreen skin, second case pierced silver,			
4 wheel train verge, 60mm, London, Ca. 1670 (illo.31)	$8,500	$11,000	$13,000
Alarm-Oignon, nailed pique shagreen (**Sting-Ray**) skin,			
English-Swiss, verge,fusee, Ca.1690s, (illo.32)	8,500	10,000	12,000
Oignon alarm, verge, French, silver and animal skin cover,			
movement wound from center arbor on dial,			
silver champleve dial, 60mm, OF, C. 1710	8,500	10,000	12,000

OIGNON

The invention of the regulatory spiral hairspring (1675), did for watches what the pendulum did for clocks. The two inventions revolutionized watch and clock making. The precision that was achieved by the introduction of the spiral hairspring had a immediate effect on the shape and larger dimension of the watch. This new hairspring could not be very finely shaped, so the watchmakers had to use larger balances. This led them to make a watch with greater diameter thus the so called "OIGNON." Now that watches were more accurate the watch was soon fitted with a minute hand.

ALARMS

The most common Swiss and German alarms are usually in base metal or gun metal cases. Early makes with porcelain dials are more desirable than later (post 1920's) metal dial alarms.

TYPE - DESCRIPTION	ABP	Ex-Fn	Mint
Swiss alarm sounding on bell,7J, base metal, 49mm,OF, C.1915	$100	$125	$165
Swiss alarm sounding on gongs, 15J, tandem wind,			
gun metal, 50mm, OF, C. 1900	175	200	275
Cricket alarm, w/cricket design, Swiss , SW,			
silver case, 48mm, OF, C.1890	500	700	900

TIMERS & CHRONOGRAPHS

Timer, 1/5 sec., 7J, register, base metal, 48mm, OF.

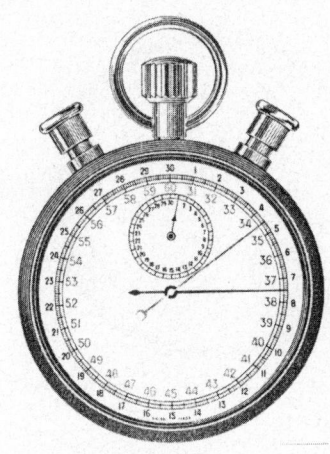

Timer, split second, register, base metal, 56mm, Ca. 1970

TYPE - DESCRIPTION	ABP	Ex-Fn	Mint
Timer, 1/5 sec., register,7J, base metal, 48mm, OF, C. 1940	$35	$60	$70
Timer, 1/5 sec. register, **17J**, base metal, 48mm, OF, C. 1940	40	70	95
Timer, **split sec.**, register, base metal, 46mm, OF, C. 1940	55	100	150
Timer,15-17J, **split sec.**, register, base metal, 56mm, OF, C. 1970	55	100	150
Timer and Watch, **silver**, 48mm, **HC**, 1925	125	175	200
Chronograph, **7J, GF or silver**, 48mm, OF, C. 1905	130	200	250
HC	155	250	300
Chronograph, **15-17J, porcelain** dial, GF or silver, 50mm, OF,	200	300	350
HC	250	350	400
Chronograph, **20J, 18K**, 52mm, OF, C. 1895	500	800	900
HC	750	1,200	1,500

Timer and Watch, sliver, 48mm, HC.

Chronograph, 7-17J, GF. 48mm, OF, C. 1905.

Chronograph, w/register porc. dial, **20J, 14K**, 52mm, HC, a. 1890. (illo.A)

Chronograph, Split Seconds, w/register, porc. dial, **20J, 18K**, 52mm, OF, Ca. 1910. (illo.B)

TYPE - DESCRIPTION	ABP	Ex-Fn	Mint
Chronog. w/register, porc. dial, **15J, silver**, 52mm, OF, C. 1890	$250	$400	$450
HC (illo.A)	300	425	525
Chronog. w/register, porc. dial, **20J, 14K**, 52mm, OF, C. 1890	400	700	800
HC	600	900	1,100
Chronog. w/register, porc. dial, **20J, 18K**, 52mm, OF, C. 1890	600	800	900
HC	800	1,000	1,500
Split sec. chronograph, 15-17J, **.800 silver**, 52mm, OF, C. 1900....	300	700	900
Split sec. chronograph, 19-32J, **18K**, 52mm, OF, C. 1900.........	800	1,700	2,000
HC (illo.B)	1,000	2,000	2,400
Double dial (time on front, chrono. on back), Swiss, 17J, **14K** display case 51mm, OF, Ca. 1885 (illo.C)	800	2,000	2,500
1/4 second jump watch, 26J, two gear train, SW , **18K**, HC, C.1880 (illo.D)	2,200	3,200	3,800

Double dial (time on front, Chronograph on back), Swiss, 17J, 14K display case, 51mm, OF, Ca. 1885. (illo.C)

1/4 second jump watch, 26J, two gear train, two main spring barrels, KW, 18K, 53mm, HC, C.1 680. (illo.D)

POCKET CHRONOMETER

JOHN ARNOLD, chronometer, spring detent, Z balance with adjustable weights, helical hair spring, 18K case, serial #14, upright escape wheel, "INV ET FECT" engraved on movement (made by), his chronometer factory was located in Chigwell (London), #36 pocket chronometers sold for about $500.00 in 1776. (illo.33)

Right: John Arnold spring detent escapement.

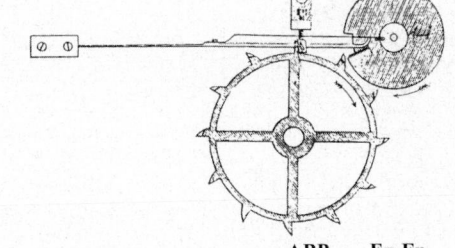

TYPE -DESCRIPTION	ABP	Ex-Fn	Mint
Chronometer, KWKS, spring detent, Z bal., helical hair-spring, "JOHN ARNOLD", 18K case, C. 1776 (illo.33)	$25,000	$50,000	$65,000
French pocket chronometer, gilt bar movement, pivoted detent, 18K, free sprung, KW/KS, 58mm, Ca. 1850 (illo.34).	4,500	7,000	10,000
Chronometer, KW/KS, spring detent, Z bal., helical hair-spring, "J R. ARNOLD", 18K case, C. 1805 (illo.35)	15,000	33,000	45,000

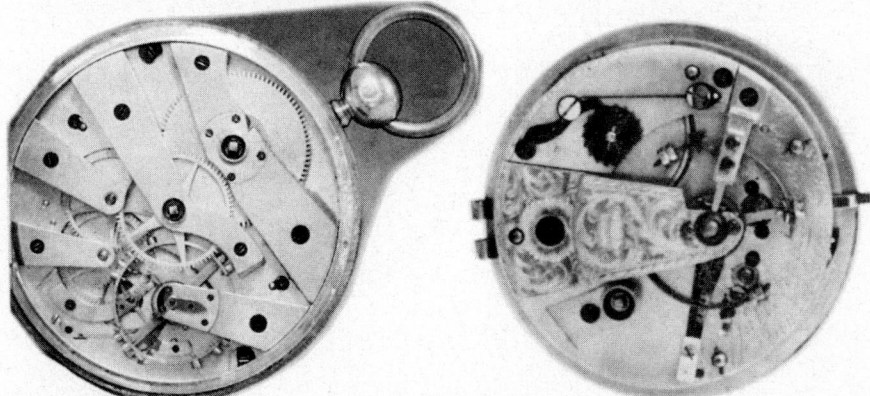

French pocket chronometer, gilt bar movement, pivoted detent escapement, free sprung helical balance spring, KW/KS, 58mm, Ca. 1850. (illo.34)

J. R. ARNOLD, chronometer, KWKS, spring detent, Z balance with screw counterpoise on terminal curves, helical hair-spring, 18K case, 58mm. C. 1805. (illo.35)

JOHANNES KESSELS "ALTON", deck chronometer, KWKS, spring detent, fusee, silver case, C. 1830 . (illo.36)

Detent chronometer, Helical hairspring, Swiss, SW, 18K, wolf teeth winding, 56mm, HC, C. 1900. (illo.37)

TYPE - DESCRIPTION	ABP	Ex-Fn	Mint
Chronometer, KWKS, spring detent, Z bal., helical hair-spring, "KESSELS", silver case, C. 1830 (illo.36)	$4,000	$7,500	$9,500
Chronometer, KW, spring detent, **coin**, OF, C. 1875	600	1,000	1,200
Detent chronometer, Swiss, SW, **18K**, 56mm, HC, Ca.1900 (illo.37).	1,500	3,000	4,000
Detent chronometer, English, w/ wind indicator, **18K**, 48mm, OF . .	3,500	6,200	7,500
Chronometer, pivoted detent, helical hairspring, (French), SW, silver, 56mm, OF (illo.38)	300	1,000	1,200
Pocket chronometer, Swiss, 20 jewel, fancy case, silver and gilt dial, detent, w/ helical spring, **18K**, 49mm, HC, C. 1890 (illo.38A) .	2,600	6,000	8,000

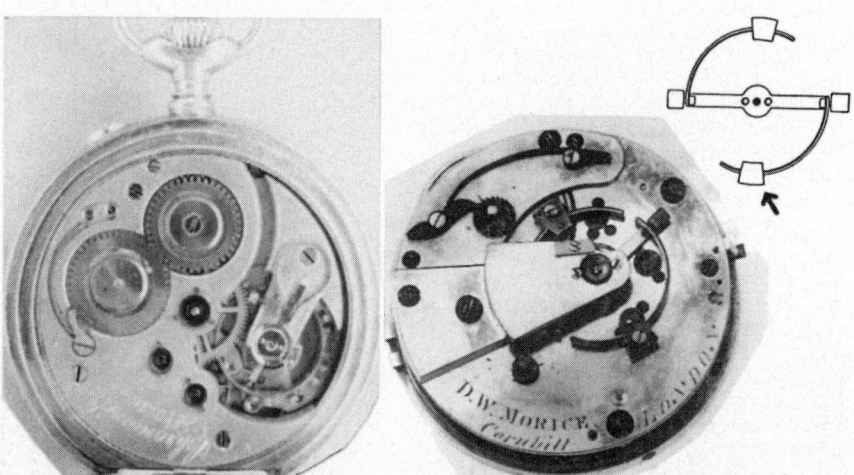

Engraved on movement 'Chronome'tre" (French), 16 jewels, pivoted detent, helical hairspring, stem wind, manufactured by LIP in Besancon France, silver, 56mm, OF, Ca. 1910-30. (illo.38)

Detent chronometer, English, w/ fusee, helical hairspring, note: Trapezoidal weights on balance. (illo.38A)

☞ Note: Some models and grades are not included. Their values can be determined by comparing with similar age, size, metal content, style, models and grades listed,

TOURBILLON, KARRUSEL,
RARE & UNUSUAL MOVEMENTS

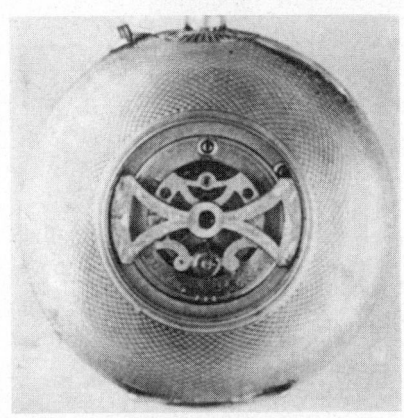

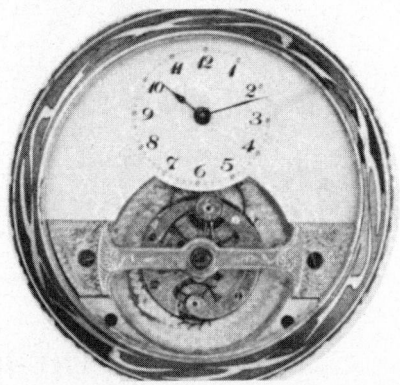

One minute so called "Poor Man's Tourbillon", center seconds silver watch with centered dial & visible Tourbillon carriage from back of watch. Swiss. 54mm. (illo.39)

Signed Mobilis, Visible Tourbillon, 53mm, 13 to 15 jewels, tourbillon carriage is visible from dial side, Pat. No. 30754 (made by Courvoisier Freres), ca. 1905. (illo.40)

TYPE - DESCRIPTION	ABP	Ex-Fn	Mint
Tourbillon, Swiss, center sec., base metal, 54mm, OF (illo.39) ... ★	$1,500	$4,000	$5,000
Tourbillon, 53mm, 13J, **Mobilis**, Ca. 1905 (illo.40) .... ★	2,000	4,000	5,000
Tourbillon, 4 min., 15J, enamel dial, silver, C.1910 (illo.41) ...... ★	2,800	4,500	6,000
Karrusel, **52 min**., English, 3/4, gilt, 16J, SW, silver case, 56mm, OF, C.1885 (illo.42)	2,500	4,000	5,000
18K case, (illo.42)	3,500	8,000	10,000

signed **TOURBILLON**, one complete turn in 4-5 minutes, 15 jewels, enamel dial, silver case, Ca.1930. (illo.41) On dial "BREVET" translation Patented.

52 minute **KARRUSEL**, 57mm, 14J., English, silver case, Ca.1885. (illo.42)

NOTE: The Tourbillon **Mobilis** is signed "Mobilis Pat. no. 30754" the Pat. date was June 11,1904 and was patented by Paul Loichet of Charquemont, France. Tourbillon movement was made by Courvoisier Freres of La Chaux de Fonds Switzerland from 1905 to about 1910.

576

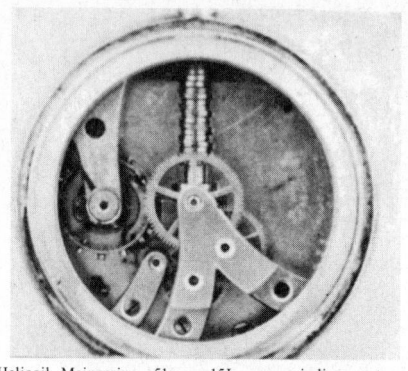

Helicoil Mainspring, 51mm, 15J., rare winding system, cylindrical spring replaces standard mainspring. (illo.43)

Lever with Fusee, KW KS, (Liverpool), hallmarked, silver, undersprung, 46mm, OF, Ca. 1850-70.(illo.44)

EARLY PRE-1850 NON—GOLD

TYPE - DESCRIPTION	ABP	Ex-En	Mint
Helicoil mainspring, Swiss, 15J , cylinder esc.,			
base metal, 51mm, OF, C. 1910 (illo.43)..............★★	$2,000	$4,200	$5,500
Lever, Fusee, (Liverpool), silver, 46mm, OF, Ca. 1850-70 (illo.44) .	135	250	300
Lever or cylinder, BAR, KW KS, silver, 46-52mm, OF (illo.45)	95	125	165
Lever or cylinder, **engraved** BAR, KW KS, silver, 46-52mm,			
OF, Ca. 1840-85 (illo.46)............................	135	175	225
Lever or cylinder, **Le-PINE**, KW KS, silver, 46-52mm (illo.47)	135	150	200
Rack & pinion escap., KW KS, silver, 46-52mm, OF (illo.48)	250	350	475

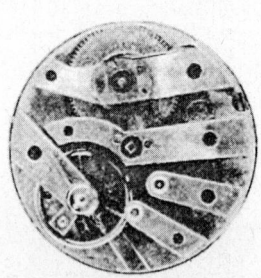

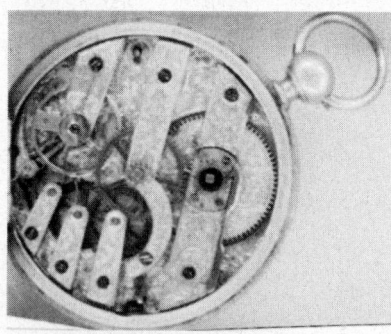

Lever, KW KS, bar style movement, note **curved barrel bridge**, silver, 46-52mm, OF, C. 1830-50. (illo.45)

Lever, **Lepine style bar**, engraved, KW KS, silver, 46-52mm, OF, Ca. 1840-85. (illo.46)

Lever, **Lepine style tapered bar movement**, KW KS, silver, 46-52mm, OF, Ca. 1820-35. (illo.47)

Rack & pinion escapement, KW KS, silver, 46-52mm, Ca. 1830. (illo.48)

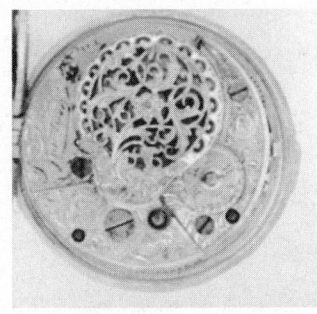

Verge, chain driven fusee, (English) paircase, 52mm, OF, C.1800- 40. (illo.49)

Verge, fusee, (English) paircase, hallmarked, KW, 52mm, OF, Ca. 1780-90. (illo.50)

TYPE -DESCRIPTION	ABP	Ex-Fn	Mint
Verge, Fusee (Swiss), KW, (unmarked) single case,			
silver, 49mm, OF, C. 18 10-40.	$250	$350	$450
Verge (English) paircase, 52mm, OF, C.1800- 40 (illo.49)	250	400	500
Painted "farmer's dial," verge, Swiss / London,			
silver, 52-55m, OF	500	750	950
Cylinder, Fusee, silver, 48-52mm, OF, C. 1830s	250	400	500
Verge, Fusee (Swiss), KW, silver single case, 49mm			
OF, C. 1810-1840	250	375	500
Verge (English) paircase, hallmarked, KW,			
52mm, OF, C. 1780-90 (illo.50).	275	500	600
Miniature, verge, lady's, plain, porcelain dial, hallmarked			
silver, 24mm, OF, C. 1810	700	850	1,100
Gilt & enamel, verge, Swiss or French, 46mm, OF, C. 1800.	800	1,500	2,000
Skeletonized, verge, Swiss, double case, hand-carved movement,			
case silver & horn, 53mm,OF, C. 1800	700	2,000	3,000
Repousse paircase, fancy dial, verge, London,			
hallmarked silver, 49mm, OF, C. 1800 (illo.51)	800	1,500	2,000
Erotic Repousse paircase, Swan & Lady, verge, London (illo.52)	1,000	1,700	2,400

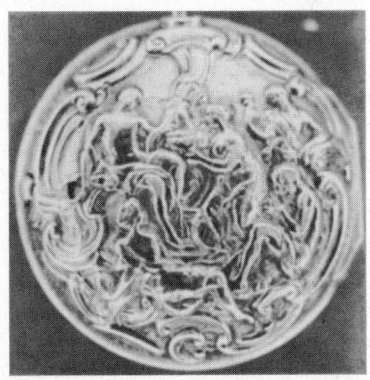

Repousse paircase, fancy dial, verge, English hallmarked silver case, 49mm, OF, C. 1800. (illo.51)

Erotic Repousse silver paircase, Swan & Lady, verge, Fusee, London. (illo.52)

OIGNON watch with mock pendulum. 58mm, Ca. 1700-1720. (illo.53)

Lady & mock pendulum. mock pendulum can be seen at top of Lady's head, 58mm, Ca. 1690 (illo.54)

TYPE - DESCRIPTION	ABP	Ex-Fn	Mint
Oignon watch with mock pendulum, 58mm, ca. 1700-20 (illo.53)...	$2,800	$5,000	$6,000
Lady & mock pendulum, enamel Lady, 58mm, Ca. 1690 (illo.54)...	3,200	6,000	7,000
Verge w/ calendar, repousse paircase, London hallmarked,			
silver, 51mm, OF, C. 1690............................	2,500	5,000	6,000
Dublin, early verge, silver paircase, champleve silver			
dial (signed), 54mm, OF, C. 1720......................	1,800	3,500	4,500
Early verge, large winged cock, signed silver dial, London,			
Egyptian pillars, silver, 55mm, OF, C. 1700 (illo.55).........	2,000	4,000	4,500
Viennese enamel on gilt, verge, fusee, multi-scenes on case,			
KW, 55mm, HC, C. 1780.............................	2,200	4,300	5,500
English, verge w/ calendar, signed champleve dial,			
silver & horn, 54mm OF, C. 1680......................	2,500	5,000	6,000

Early verge, large D shaped foot on the cock, London, signed silver dial, Egyptian pillars, silver, 55mm, OF, C. 1700. (illo.55)

Oignon bulb shaped appearance start to appear after 1675 & having some uniform construction features point to a source of specialized workshops (ebauches) thus becoming reasonable priced & improved tine keeping. **French Oignon** watches wind from the front dial side and the balance bridge cock has two screws & usually have domed shaped dials. **English Oignon** watches generally wind from back & the balance cock use a single screw & foot & the dials have a flat appearance.

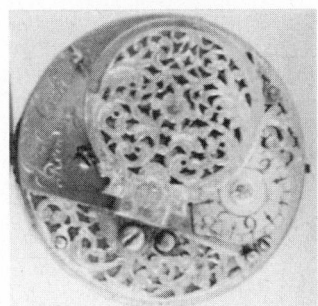

Tortoise shell case, verge with chain driven fusee, calendar, D shaped foot balance cock. C. 1700, (illo.56)

English, verge, hand pierced cock, fusee, silver, note face on balance cock, C. 1720, (illo.57)

TYPE -DESCRIPTION	ABP	Ex-Fn	Mint
Tortoise shell, verge, calendar, Ca. 1700 (illo.56)	$3,000	$5,000	$6,000
English, verge, hand pierced cock, fusee, silver, Ca. 1720, (illo.57). .	2,000	3,000	4,000
Pumpkin Form Case, verge, silver, 40mm, Ca. 1775 (illo.58).	2,500	4,000	5,500
Garooned Case, verge, fusee, 44mm, silver, Ca. 1650 (illo.59)	15,000	30,000	38,000
Painted scene on horn, verge, gilt, 57mm, OF, Ca. 1780 (illo.60). . . .	2,000	4,000	4,500
(Amsterdam) verge fusee, 2 footed cock, 57mm Ca.1685 (illo.60A) .	5,000	7,000	10,000

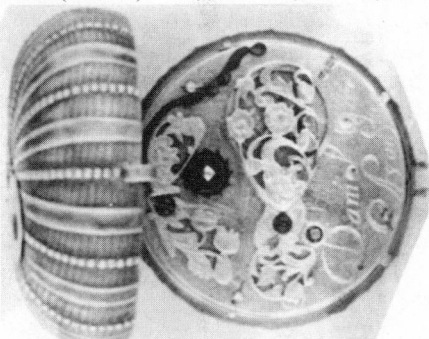

Pumpkin Form Case, verge, silver, Ca. 1775. (illo.58)

Garooned Case, verge, fusee, 44mm, Ca. 1650. (illo.59)

Painted horn (full scene in color) London, verge, gilt, 57mm, OF, C. 1780. (illo.60)

(Amsterdam) verge fusee with mock pendulum, 2 footed cock, 57mm silver & Shagreen pair case, Ca. 1685 (illo.60A)

EARLY NON—GOLD

Early Astronomic watch with day date month calendar, lunar calendar, 57mm, Ca. 1650. (illo.61)

TYPE - DESCRIPTION	ABP	Ex-Fn	Mint
Early Astronomic watch with day date month calendar, lunar calendar, 57mm, Ca. 1680 (illo.61)	$15,000	$38,000	$48,000
Early Astronomic watch with moon phases and triple date, fusee with cut-gut cord, 3 gear train, foliot, Ca.1660 (illo.62).	22,000	50,000	70,000

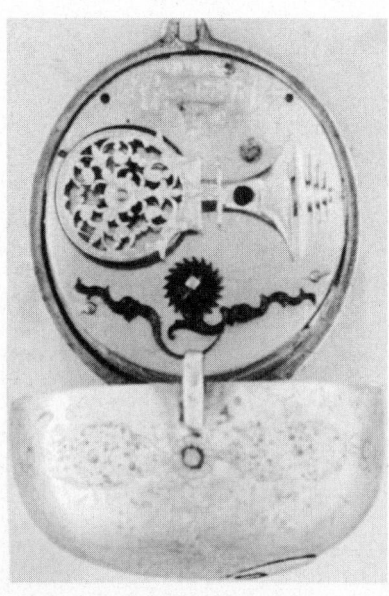

Early Astronomic watch with moon phases and triple date, fusee with
cut-gut cord, 3 gear train, 6 armed folios, Ca.1660. (illo.62)

Early German made silver watch, verge and foliot, silver pierced dial, Hamburg", Ca. 1660. (illo.63)

TYPE - DESCRIPTION	ABP	Ex-Fn	Mint
Early German made silver watch, verge and foliot, silver pierced dial, "Hamburg", Ca. 1660 (illo.63)	$7,000	$20,000	$27,000
Early silver watch, blued steel hand, cut-gut fusee, foliot, rosette for adj., 53mm, Ca.1660 (illo.64)	12,000	28,000	38,000

Early silver watch, silver dial with blued steel hand, cut gut fusee, 3 wheel train, foliot, rosette (endless screw) for adjustment of the motor-spring tension(endless screw), 53mm, Ca1660. (illo. 64)

Pair cased, first case silver covered with nailed skin, verge, cut-gut cord fusee, 3 wheel train, foliot, pierced cock, endless screw adjustment for main spring tension, 45mm, ca. 1660. (illo.65)

Early French watch movement with hour and minute hand, striking bell each hour, hand pierced case & gilt brass movement, cut-gut fusee, c. 1600s. (illo.66)

TYPE - DESCRIPTION	ABP	Ex-Fn	Mint
Pair cased, first case silver & nailed skin, verge, fusee, 3 wheel train, foliot, pierced cock, 45mm, Ca. 1660 (illo.65)	$7,000	$22,000	$27,000
Early Sun and Moon, verge escapement, Ca. 1680-1700.	$4,000	$6,000	$9,000
Early French watch hour and minute hand, striking on bell, cut-gut fusee, c. 1600s (illo.66).	12,000	33,000	40,000
Early Drum Clock, iron plates, 4 wheel train, brass fusee on a steel great wheel, steel contrate wheel with brass teeth, steel verge and foliot balance w/ T-shaped ends, 34mm high (illo.67).	30,000	60,000	78,000

Early Drum style portable time-piece, Clock, iron plates, 4 wheel train, brass fusee on a steel great wheel, steel contrate wheel with brass teeth, steel verge and foliot balance with T-shaped ends . The cylindrical gilt brass case is finely engraved and is about 34mm high, Ca. 1550 - 1560. (illo.67)

𝒶𝓇 Pricing in this Guide are fair market price for complete watches which are reflected from the NAWCC national and regional shows.

PRE-1850 *GOLD*

Lever or verge. Fusee, (Liverpool), 18K, multi-colored gold dial, 52mm, OF, C.1820-75. (illo.68).

Lever or cylinder, BAR style movement, GOLD, 45-52mm,OF, 1840-1865. (illo. 69)

TYPE DESCRIPTION	ABP	Ex-Fn	Mint
Lever, (Liverpool), **18K**, 52mm, OF, C.1820-75 (illo.68)	$300	$400	$600
Verge, (Liverpool), **18K**, 52mm, HC, C. 1820-75	400	800	1,200
Lever or cylinder, **BAR**, GOLD, 45-52mm, OF(illo.69)	250	300	425
(same as above) w/ skeletonized movement,**18K** (illo.70)	375	900	1,200
Lever or cylinder, **Le-Pine** style, GOLD, 45-52mm, OF (illo.71)	250	500	600
Cylinder Fusee, paircase, London, plain case, porcelain dial,**18K**, 48mm, OF, C. 1880	900	1,200	1,500
Verge, multi-color case, Swiss/ French, porcelain dial, **18K**, 42mm,OF, Ca. 1770-1800	1,100	1,700	2,000
Verge, French, gold & enamel patterns on case, KWKS, OF, C. 1805	1,000	1,700	2,200
Verge, (Swiss), **18K**, 52-54mm, plain case, OF, C. 1790-1820	550	1,000	1,200
Verge, Swiss, gold scene, high quality, **18K**, 50mm, OF, C.1790	1,000	1,500	2,000

Lever or cylinder, skeletonized & engraved bar movement, Swiss, 45-52mm, OF,18K. (illo.70)

Lever or cylinder escapement. Lepine style movement, Ca.1820-1835, GOLD, 45-52mm, OF. (illo.71)

Verge, repousse paircase, 20K gold case, 43mm, Open Face, Ca.1720 to 1750, (illo.72)

Early verge, D shaped balance cock, signed dial, London, Egyptian pillars, gold, 55mm, OF, Ca. 1690 to1720. (illo.73)

TYPE -DESCRIPTION	ABP	Ex-Fn	Mint
Verge, repousse paircase, 20K, 43mm, OF, C.1730 (illo.72)	$1,500	$2,500	$3,500
Early verge, large winged cock, signed dial, London, Egyptian pillars, gold, 55mm, OF, C. 1700 (illo.73)	4,000	5,000	6,000
Virgule, Fusee, Swiss or French, **18K**, 50-55mm, OF, C. 1790	1,200	2,500	3,000
Fusee, made in HOLLAND, Ca. 1720-50, silver case (illo.74)	600	1,000	1,500
Skeletonized French, diamonds on bezel, 18k, 39mm, C.1780 (illo.75)	1,800	3,500	4,500
Rack & Pinion lever escapement, **18K**. OF, Ca. 1830 (illo.75A)	600	1,000	1,200

Fusee, movement made in **HOLLAND**, silver case, note the 2 footed bridge style, 55-60mm, OF, Ca. 1720 (illo.74)

Skeletonized French watch, diamonds on bezel, 39mm, 18k, C.1780 (illo.75)

Rack and Pinion Lever Escapement, 18K, OF, Ca. 1830 (illo.75A)

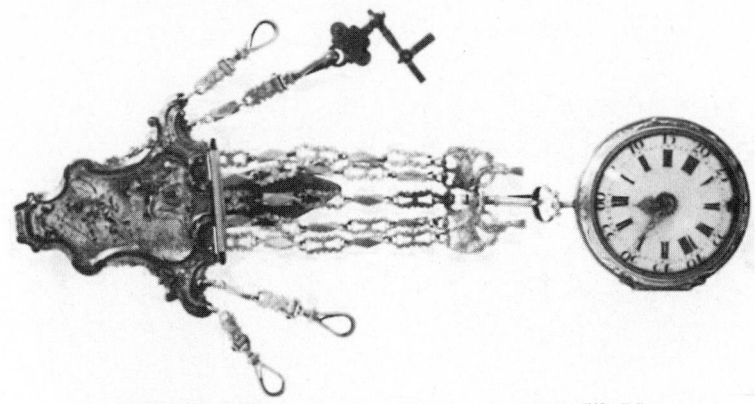

CHATELAINE, verge, fusee, 22k pair case, 45mm, (illo.76)

TYPE -DESCRIPTION	ABP	Ex-Fn	Mint
Chatelaine, verge, fusee, 22k pair case (illo.76)	$3,000	$6,000	$8,000
Early gold & nailed double case watch, c. 1650-60 (illo.77)	20,000	38,000	50,000

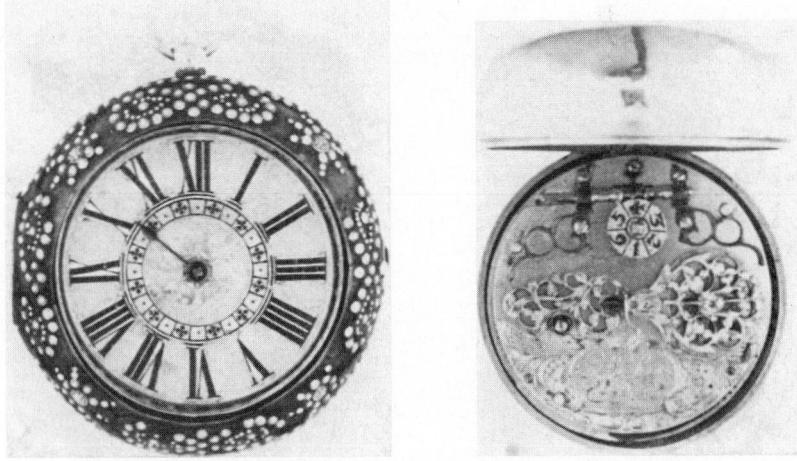

Early gold & nailed double case watch, Champleve gold dial, 3 wheel train, verge, rosette adjustment and endless screw, 50mm, c.1670(illo.77)

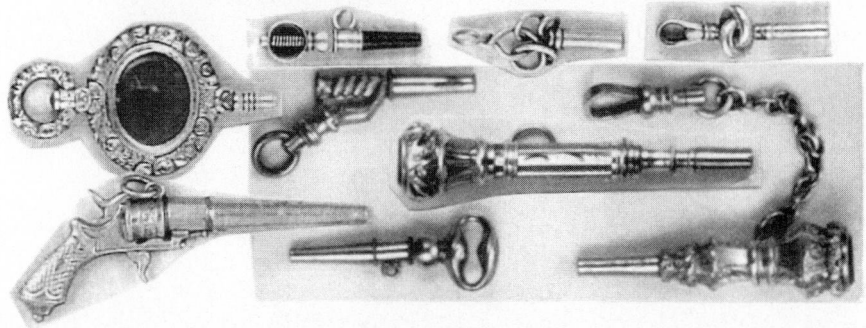

GOLD KEYS, the tops are all gold and the bottom key shaft is base metal, PRICES= $200 to $500 each.

MISC. MEN'S GF / SILVER / BASE METAL

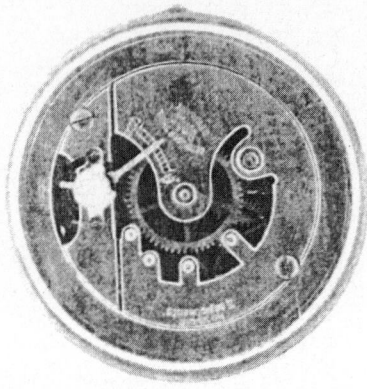

Dollar watch **German**, base metal OF, C.1895. (illo.78)

German, backwind, **waterproof style model,** base metal, OF, C.1885. (illo.79)

TYPE -DESCRIPTION	ABP	Ex-Fn	Mint
Dollar watch **German**, base metal ,OF, C.1895 (illo.78)	$40	$55	$85
German, back wind, **waterproof**, OF, C.1885 (illo.79)	250	450	550
Base metal, 7-17J, SW, 43-48mm, OF, C. 1900-1930	40	55	85
GF or silver, 7-17J, SW, 43-48mm, OF, C. 1895-1940	60	75	110
GF or silver, 7-17J, SW, 43-52mm, **HC**, C. 1895-1940	85	110	165
Swiss Fakes ,73, KW, base metal, OF, 52mm, C. 1870-90	65	85	110
Non-magnetic, pat.# 7546/780, **Moeris**, base metal (illo.80)	95	140	175
Cylinder, (Liverpool), 1/2 plate design (illo.81)	85	110	140

Non-magnetic. pat.#7546-780, **Moeris**, base metal, thumbnail set, SW. OF. (illo.80)

Cylinder escapement, (Liverpool), 1/2 plate design, marked 4 hole jeweled=8 jewels. (illo.81)

COMPARISON OF WATCH CASE SIZES	
U.S.A.	**EUROPEAN**
10-12 SIZE	40—44MM
16 SIZE	45—49MM
18 SIZE	50—55 MM

KW KS, **Chinese Duplex** escapement, 3/4 plate design, note BAT style weights on balance, OF. (illo.82)

KW KS, with a **Compass** on movement, lever escapement, Ca. 1855. (illo.83)

TYPE -DESCRIPTION	ABP	Ex-Fn	Mint
KWKS, **Chinese Duplex**, 3/4 plate design, OF (illo.82).	$250	$440	$550
KWKS, **Compass** on movement, lever escap., (illo.83)	100	330	440
KWKS, 6-15J, silver, 45-52mm, OF, C. 1860-85.	65	110	140
KWKS, 8-17J, silver, 45-52mm, HC, C. 1860-85	75	110	145
Engraved movement, KWKS, 15J, silver, 46mm, HC, C.1870	90	165	220
KWKS, marked railway, pin lever, Swiss (illo.84)	100	165	220
21J, RR type, GF, 48mm, OF, C. 1910-30	80	110	165
25J, Waltham (Swiss made), GF, 48mm, OF, C. 1950	100	220	330
Enamel & **embossed** hunting scene on **base metal** case, enamel dial, 3/4 plate, made in **Beaucourt France**, OF (illo.85)	100	165	220

KWKS, marked railway, pin lever, Swiss, Ca. 1889. (illo.84)

Niello enamel & embossed hunting scene on case, enamel dial, 3/4 plate, made in Beaucourt France, made by Japy Freres at Cie, OF, Ca. 1890. (illo.85)

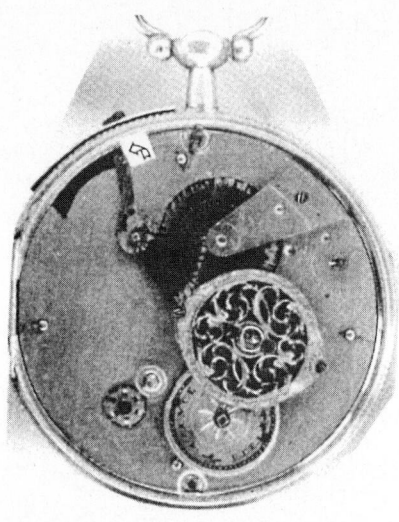

1/4 repeater early rim activated, Swiss or French, silver, OF, Ca.1820. (illo.86)

Automaton, **Adam & Eve**, note snake circles Adam & Eve, hand painted enamel dial, KW KS, OF. (illo. 87)

TYPE -DESCRIPTION	ABP	Ex-Fn	Mint
1/4 repeater early rim activated, silver, OF, Ca.1820 (illo.86)........	$900	$1,200	$1,800
Automaton, **Adam & Eve**, w/ snake, KW KS, OF (illo. 87).........	3,800	6,000	7,500
Spring detent chronometer w/**Tandem** wind, fusee,			
56mm, Ca.1875 (illo.88)	1,000	1,500	2,000
Gamblers playing cards on dial porcelain, Swiss, silver, OF (illo.89) .	300	700	900

Spring Detent chronometer with **Tandem** wind, chain driven fusee, Helical hair spring, 56mm, Ca.1875. (illo.88)

Gamblers playing cards on porcelain dial, Swiss, silver, OF. (illo.89)

Exposed Skeletonized Balance from dial, enamel painted dial, verge, fusee, KW KS, large advance-retard index, Ca. 1790. (illo.90)

TYPE - DESCRIPTION	ABP	Ex-Fn	Mint
Silver Exposed Bal. from dial, enamel painted dial, Ca.1790 (illo.90)	$1,600	$2,500	$3,000
Wandering Digital Jump Hour Hand, 45mm, Ca. 1780 (illo.91)	3,500	8,000	10,000
Jump Digital Hour, W/ Date at 6, sec. hand at 3, Ca. 1820 (illo.92) . .	1,200	2,000	2,500

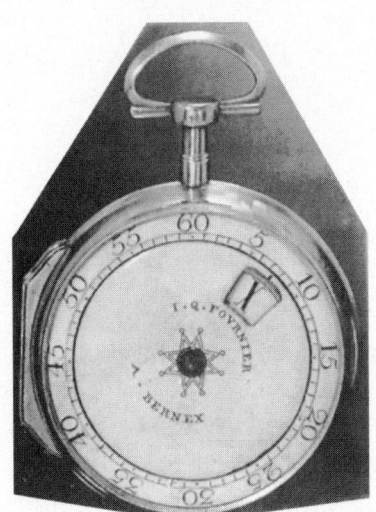

Wandering Digital Jump Hour Hand, Fusee, Cylinder Escapement, 45mm, silver, OF, Ca. 1780, (illo.91)

Jump Digital Hour, W/ Date at 6, sec. hand at 3, sliver, engine turned dial, OF, Ca. 1820 (illo.92)

COMPARISON OF WATCH CASE SIZES	
U.S.A.	EUROPEAN
10-12 SIZE	40—44MM
16 SIZE	45—49MM
18 SIZE	50—55 MM

Day, date, moon phases, Swiss, fancy dial, lever set at rim of case, GF. 46 mm(illo.93)

Day, date, Swiss, fancy dial, **base metal**, 46mm. (illo.94)

TYPE -DESCRIPTION	ABP	Ex-Fn	Mint
Day, date, moon phases, Swiss, fancy dial, **GF**, 46mm (illo.93)	$200	$400	$500
Day, date, moon phases, Swiss, fancy dial, **gun metal**, 46mm	150	350	450
Day, date, Swiss, fancy dial, **base metal**, 46mm (illo.94)	100	250	275
Self winding, (Von Loehr patent), KW, set from back (illo.95)	300	550	700
Mock pendulum (dial side), **all original**, duplex escap. (illo.96)	350	650	750

Self winding, (Von Loehr patent), KW, set from back. (illo.95)

Mock pendulum (seen from face side), duplex escap. Multicolor dial, **FAKES SEEN** (illo.96)

MISC. MEN'S GOLD, PLATINUM

TYPE -DESCRIPTION	ABP	Ex-Fn	Mint
SW, 17J, **14K**, 43-46mm, OF, C. 1910-1940	$200	$250	$300
SW, 17J-19J, **18K**, 43-46mm, OF, C. 1910-1940	250	300	400
SW, 17J, **14K**, 48mm, HC, C. 1910-1940	375	400	525
SW, 17J, **Platinum**, 42mm, OF, C. 1940's	700	1,000	1,200
KWKS, 15J, lever, fancy , gilt dial, **18K**, 45mm, C. 1870	275	400	500
KWKS, 15-20J, lever **18K**, 49-53mm, C. 1870-1885	400	600	700
Lever, Fusee, (Liverpool), 15J, porcelain dial, **18K**, 52mm, C.1860	450	700	850

UNUSUAL NON—GOLD

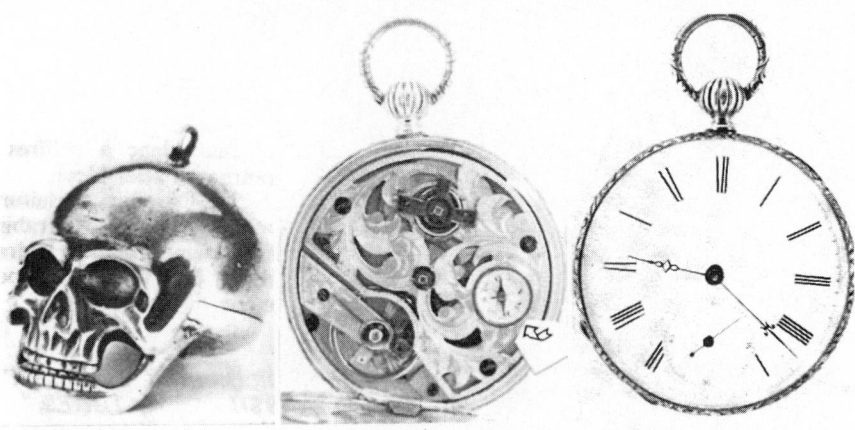

Skull (miniature) form watch, fusee, cylinder escapement, 25mm.

Silver Compass Watch, a small compass set into the movement can be seen through a hole in cuvette, (illo.98)

TYPE -DESCRIPTION	ABP	Ex-Fn	Mint
Skull (miniature) form, fusee, cylinder escape., 25mm, (illo.97)	$1,200	$3,000	$5,000
Silver Compass Watch, a small compass set into the movement can be seen through a hole in cuvette, 43mm, OF (illo.98).........	300	400	500
Blinking Eyes, pin set animated eyes, 46mm, (illo.99)............	200	300	450
8 day, exposed balance, 7J, gun metal, 50mm, C. 1920s (illo.100)....	125	200	300
8 day, exposed balance, 7J, Swiss, **Day & Date,** gun metal, 50mm, C. 1920s............................	250	500	650

Blinking Eyes, pin set animated eyes, 46mm. (illo.99)

8 day, exposed balance, 7J, by Hebdomas but with other name, gun metal, 50mm, C. 1920s. (illo.100)

$\mathcal{GS}$ Note:Some models and grades are not included. Their values can be determined by comparing with similar age, size, metal content, style, models and grades listed.

$\mathcal{GS}$ Note: Watches listed in this book are priced at the collectable trade show level, as complete watches having an original case, an original dial, and with the entire original movement in good working order with no repairs needed.

BAT style weights
on balance

CHINESE DUPLEX
or CRAB LEG DUPLEX

Chinese market, KWKS, duplex esc. silver, 58mm, OF, note BAT style weights on balance, C.1870. (illo.101) OF, C.1870.

Chinese market, KW. duplex esc. silver, 58mm, (illo.102)

TYPE -DESCRIPTION	ABP	Ex-Fn	Mint
For Chinese market, lever esc., 12J, KWKS, silver,			
BAT style weights on balance, 55mm, OF, C. 1880	$175	$400	$500
Chinese market, KW, duplex esc. silver, 58mm, OF, C.1870 (illo 101). .	200	500	600
Chinese market, KW, duplex esc. silver, 58mm, OF, C.1870 (illo.102). .	200	500	600
same as above with a **GOLD CASE**.	500	800	1,000
same as above with a **GOLD CASE** + pearls.	600	1,000	1,500
Chinese market, KW, duplex esc. silver, carved movement,			
58mm, OF, C.1870 (illo103)	250	500	600
Carved movement, lever escap., KWKS, silver, 58mm, OF(illo.104) . .	95	300	400
KW, for Turkish market, 15J, .800 silver, 47mm, HC, C. 1880	125	250	350

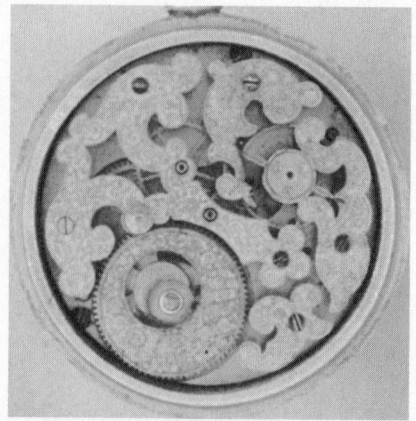

Chinese market, KW, duplex esc. silver, carved movement, 58mm. OF. Ca.1850-70. (illo.103)

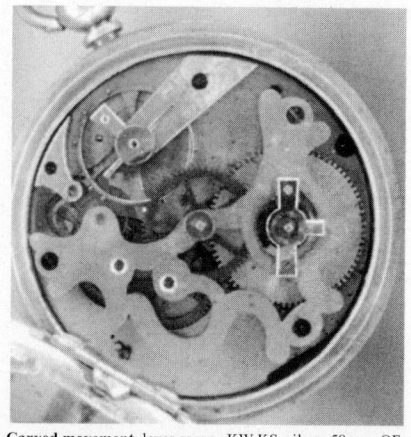

Carved movement, lever escap., KW KS, silver, 58mm, OF, Ca.1850-70. (illo.104)

Oversize, moon phase & calendar, silver, 65-70mm, Ca.1900. (illo.105)

Moonphase triple cal., Swiss, gun metal, 50mm, OF, Ca. 1905. (illo.106)

TYPE - DESCRIPTION	ABP	Ex-Fn	Mint
Oversize PW, 15J, base metal, 65-70mm, C. 1900-1915	$125	$300	$400
Oversize, moon ph. & calendar, silver,65-70mm, Ca.1900 (illo.105) . . .	800	1,500	2,000
Moonphase triple cal., Swiss, gun metal , 50mm, OF, C.1905(illo.106).	300	400	500
Moonphase triple cal., Swiss, silver or GF, 50mm, OF, C.1905	350	500	600
Moonphase triple cal., Swiss, silver, 52-54mm, HC, C. 1905	550	800	1,000
Moonphase calendar, sterling, , oversize 65mm, OF, C. 1895.	700	1,800	2,200
Verge (Swiss) skeletonized KW movement, silver & horn pair-case, 61mm, C. 1800.	650	1,000	1,400
Captain's watch, 2 hour dials, 1 train, KW KS, center second, silver, 50mm, HC, C. 1870 (illo.107).	325	800	1,000
Digital enamel dial, 15J, SW, Swiss, jump hr. & mm. discs, silver, HC, Ca. 1900 (illo.108)	350	700	800
Above with gun metal case	250	450	600

Captain's watch, 2 hour dials, 1 train, KW KS, center second, silver, 50mm, HC, C. 1870. (illo.107)

Digital dial (porcelain), 15J, SW, Swiss, jump hr. & min. discs, silver, HC, C. 1900. (illo.108)

Swiss Pocket Watch with **BAROMETER, Left:** White enamel dial and outer Barometer chapter is signed "Made in France, Watch Barometer Patent", Right: Barometer is attached to movement, 7 jewels, Cylinder escapement, 54MM, Gun Metal, Ca. 18 90. (illo.108A)

TYPE - DESCRIPTION	ABP	Ex-En	Mint
Swiss Pocket Watch with **BAROMETER,** Made in France, 54MM, Gun Metal, Ca. 1890. (illo.108A)	$1,000	$1,500	$2,000
Oversized 1/4 Hour Repeater, 3-1/4" diameter Gun Metal Watch Case, leather box, Ca. 1890. (illo.108B)	600	1,200	1,500

Oversized 1/4 Hour Repeater, 3-1/4 diameter Gun Metal Case, 29 jewels, 3/4 plate gilt movement, large white enamel dial, velvet-lined leather box ,Ca. 1890. (illo.108B)

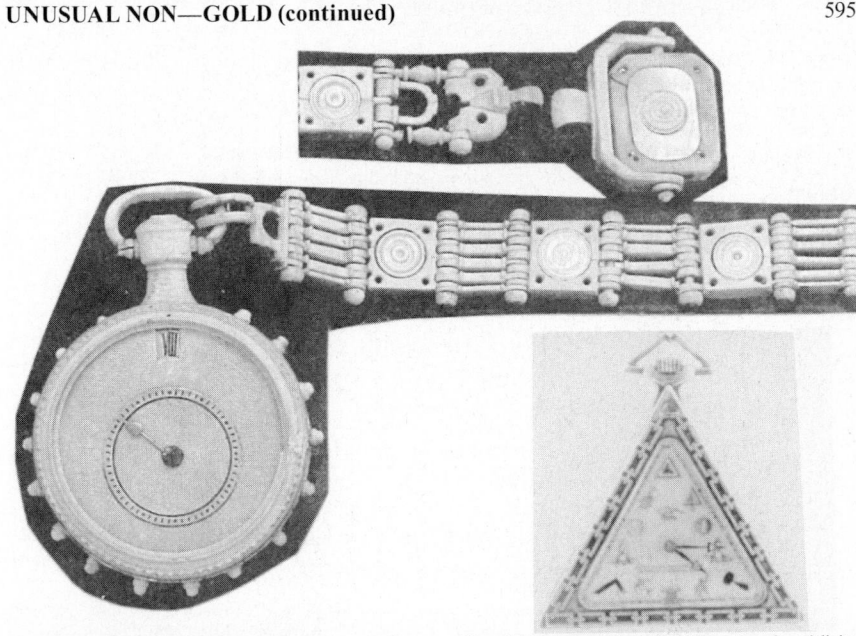

Ivory Case with matching Ivory chain, verge movement, key wind and key set Ca. 1800. (illo.109)

Masonic biangular watch, Swiss , 17J, mother of pearl digital dial, masonic dial, sterling, C. 1920's. (illo.110)

TYPE -DESCRIPTION	ABP	Ex-Fn	Mint
Ivory Case with matching ivory chain, verge movement, digital dial, key wind and key set, Ca. 1800. (illo.109)	$4,500	$9,000	$12,000
Automated w/moving windmill on dial, Swiss, colored scene, exposed balance, 8 day , base metal, OF, C.1910	400	600	800
Masonic triangular watch, Swiss ,17J, **mother of pearl** masonic dial, sterling, C. 1920's (illo.110)	1,100	2,000	2,500
Masonic, as above, with blue stone in crown, 1905	1,500	2,200	3,000
World time w/ 6 zones, Swiss, **Gun Metal**, OF, C. 1900 (illo.111)	700	1,200	2,000
Swiss, **Niello** scene on back of case	900	1,500	2,200
Swiss, **silver**, 52mm, OF, C. 1900	800	1,300	2,000
World time, 24 Cities, w/ coded color rotating dial, **18K GOLD**, 61mm(illo.112)	3,000	7,000	10,000

World time, with 6 zones. Swiss, **GUN METAL**, 52mm, OF, Ca.1900. (illo.111)

World time, 24 Cities, with coded color rotating dial, Ca. 1895, 61mm. (illo.112)

TYPE - DESCRIPTION	ABP	Ex-Fn	Mint
Mysterieuse watch, Swiss, see-through dial, hidden movement			
silver, 52mm, OF, Ca. 1895 (illo.113-114)................	$1,500	$3,000	$3,800
GOLD, 52mm, OF, Ca. 1895 (illo.113-114) ....★★	2,500	5,000	8,000
Wooden works, wooden wheels, wooden case, (illo.115) ......★★	4,000	8,000	12,000
above w/ wooden **chain** and wooden storage style box .. ★★★	6,000	12,000	15,000
Sector watch, fan-shaped, fly back hour & min. hands, 17J,			
"Record Watch Co.," silver, 49x34mm, Ca. 1900 (illo.116)....	1,800	4,000	5,500
Musical, play's 2 tunes, silver, HC, 50mm, Ca. 1900 (illo.117)......	2,400	4,000	4,500

Mysterieuse watch, Swiss, see-through dial, showing dial side of watch, 52mm, OF, Ca. 1895. (illo.113)

Mysterieuse watch, Swiss, see-through dial, showing the hidden movement 52mm, OF, Ca. 1895. (illo.114)

Wooden works, wooden wheels, wooden case, all wooden watch, 50mm, made in **Russia.** C. 1860. (illo.115)

Sector watch, fan-shaped, fly back hour & min. hands, 17J, "Record Watch Co.," silver, 49x34mm, Ca. 1901. (illo.116)

Musical, play's 2 tunes, silver, 30 Tines, HC, 50mm, 1900. (illo.117)

Wandering hour hands, 12 hands appear one at a time and move across minute sector, the 12 hands are on 3 star wheels, pin lever escapement, **gun metal** case, Ca. 1900. (illo.M1)

TYPE -DESCRIPTION		ABP	Ex-Fn	Mint
Wandering hour hands, 12 hands are on 3 star wheel, **gun metal**, pin lever escapement, Ca. 1900. (illo.M1) ....★★		$1,000	$2,000	$3,000
Wandering hour hands and **1/4 repeater**, 12 hands are on 3 star wheel, cylinder escapement, **18K gold**, Ca. 1800. (illo.M2) .... ★★★		6,000	20,000	25,000

Wandering hour hands and **1/4 repeater**, 12 hands appear one at a time and move across minute sector, the 12 hands are on 3 star wheels, cylinder escapement, **18K gold** case. Ca. 1800. (illo.M2)

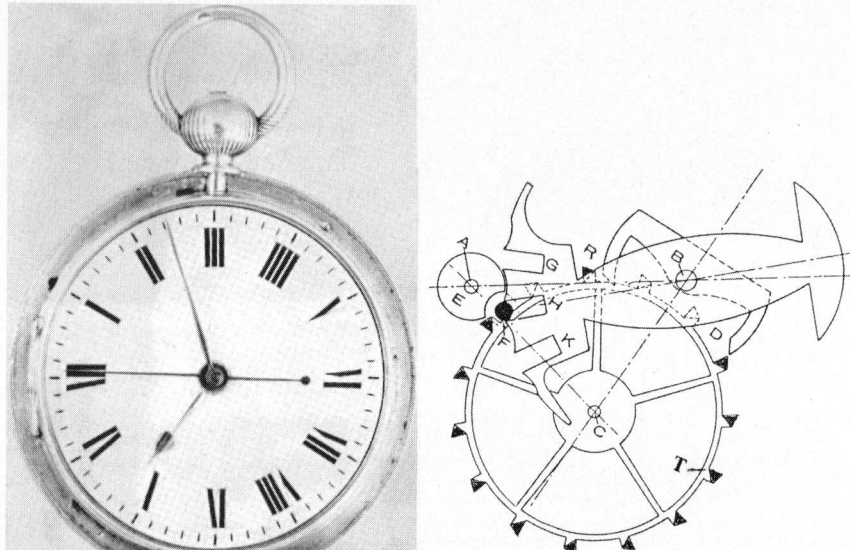

Pouzait style escape wheel, with 15 upright teeth (see "T" on escapement illo.), the center seconds hand jumps (dead seconds), silver 60 MM hunting case, Ca. 1885.(illo. M3)

TYPE - DESCRIPTION

	ABP	Ex-Fn	Mint
Pouzait style escape wheel, with 15 upright teeth, dead seconds, silver, 60 MM, hunting case, Ca. 1885 (illo. M3) ....★	$3,000	$5,000	$7,000
Pouzait, 15 upright teeth on the escape wheel, large 5 arm balance, by Du Bois et Fils, **gold**, 57MM, Ca. 1800 (illo. M4) ......★★	8,000	12,000	15,000

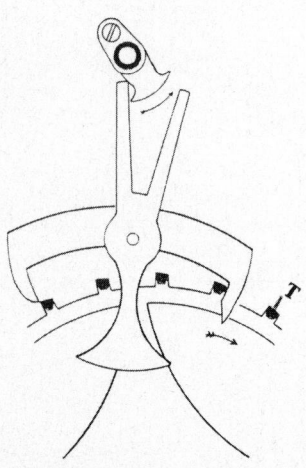

Pouzait style lever with 15 upright teeth on the escape wheel, each swing of the large 5 arm balance is one second, J. M. Pouzait lever escapement was introduced in 1786, the escape wheel with upright teeth are seen in 15 and 30 teeth, escapement seen through plate, many watches of this style were signed and made by Du Bois et Fils, also seen signed Breguet et Fils, Ca. 1800 (illo. M4)

Constant Force escapement, has a system for a force of transmission to the escapement, by a superimposed double wheel maintained in constant force by a calibrated impulse spring. The case is 18K hunter case, enamel dial signed Hess & Metford Geneve Chronometer Constant Force, key wind, 19 jewels, 50mm, Ca. 1850. (illo. E1)

TYPE—DESCRIPTION	ABP	Ex-Fn	Mint
Constant Force escapement, 19J, 55mm, 18K, HC (illo. E1)	$5,000	$7,000	$10,000
Robin detent lever escapement, 20J, 52mm, 18K, HC (illo. E2)	$5,000	$7,000	$10,000

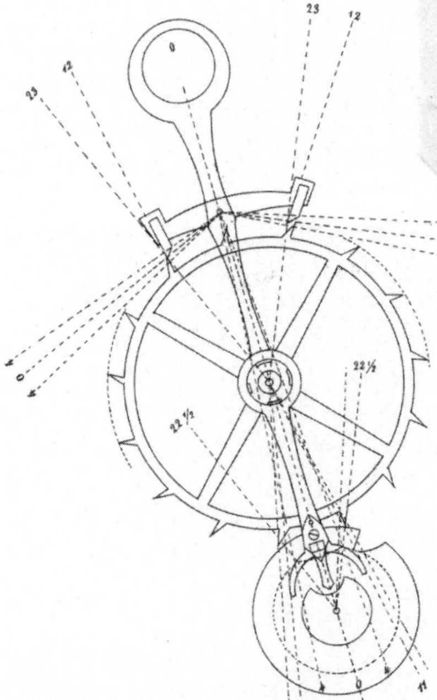

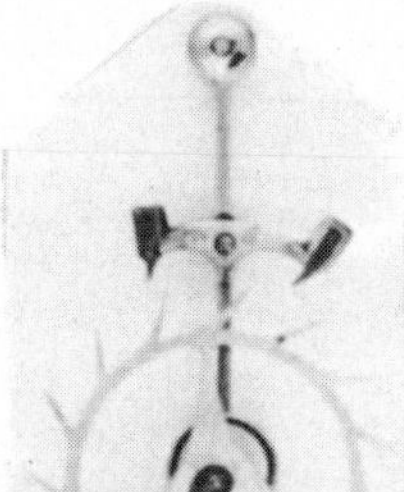

Robin type detent lever escapement, the lever with its two locks, is in straight line with the balance and the escape wheel, but behind the latter. Nickel movement, 20 jewels, in gold screwed settings, 52mm, HC, Ca.1800.(illo.E2)

Thomas Prest patented a devise for winding a watch by the pendant or knob. On October of **1820** he received his UK patent No. 4501. This system had no provision for setting the hands. The first stem-winding and setting of the hands system was invented by Louis Audemars of La Brassus in the Valley de Joux in the year of 1838. In 1842 Jean Adrien Philippe made a watch which could be wound and set by means of the crown. In **1844** Adolphe Nicole took out 2 patent's for winding and setting, one for fusee & chain, one for going barrel, UK patent No. 10348 which looks similar to the Prest with his improvements. In **1845** Philippe receives his patent No. 1317 for his modem winding system. The most successful design by Charles Antoine LeCoultre of Le Sentier in about **1847**.

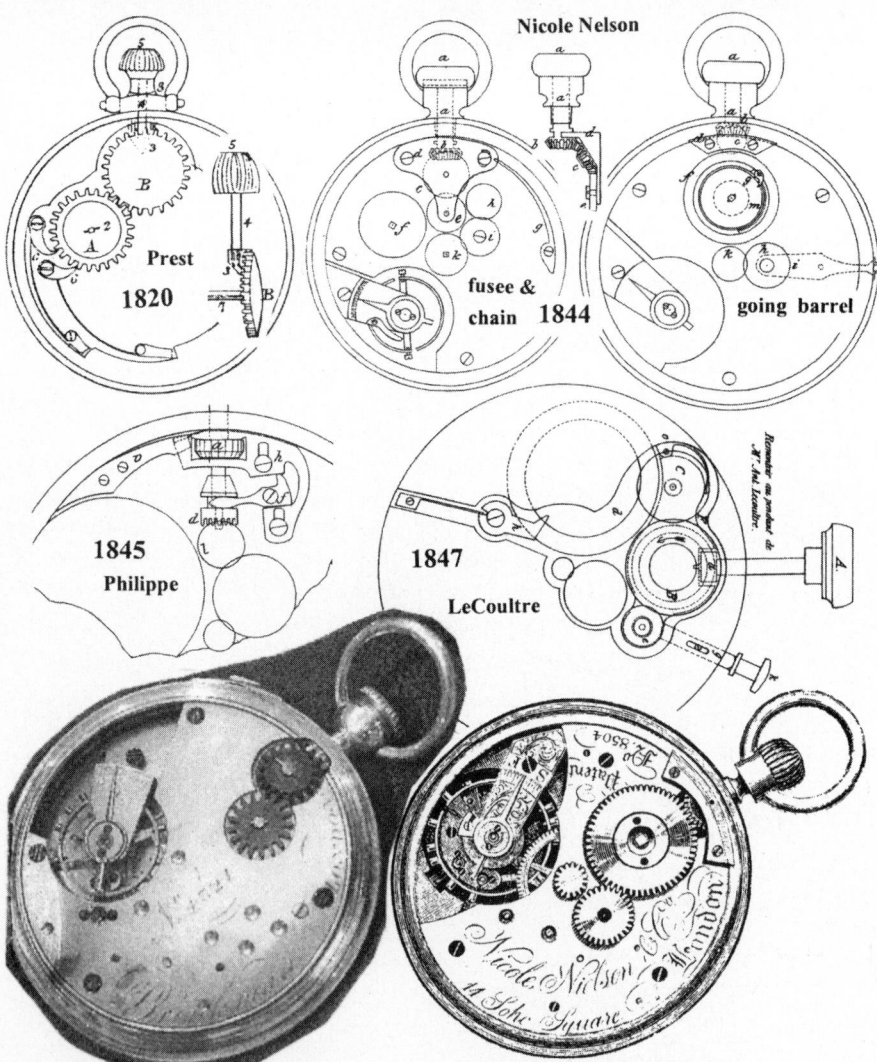

Above: Left, movement signed "Brinkman London No. 4321", (may be Prest design winding system), Ca. 1650.
Right: "Nicole Nilson & co. 14 Soho Square London," Ca. 1657-70s. Also seen signed J. Dent. (See Dent listing)

TYPE - DESCRIPTION	ABP	Ex-En	Mint
Early wind, Ca. 1820-1870, Gold case..........................	$2,000	$3,000	$3,500

Unique winding design (Each time the hunting case style watch is opened to view the time, the mainspring is partially wound) Patented in 1873 by B. Haas. (illo.A)

TYPE -DESCRIPTION	ABP	Ex-Fn	Mint
Unique winding design, 42mm, **gold HC**, (A)	$2,000	$3,000	$4,000
Endless screw winding system, 42mm, **silver HC** (B)	400	800	1,200
Automaton & Musical **Carillon a nest** of 5 bells, 18K,HC (C)	40,000	80,000	125,000

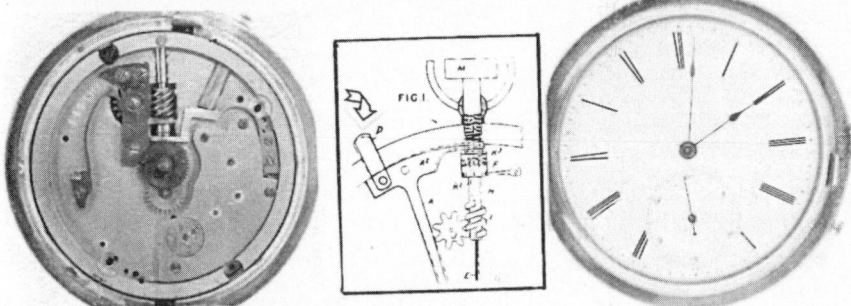

Peculiar Endless screw winding system, stem wind, pin set, 15 jewels, pat. by Lehmann, Pat. #56,683 Ca. 1868, Serial number 85,290. (illo. B)

Musical Carillon with a **nest** of 5 bells & 5 hammers, enamel painted ship scene on back in the manner of Richter, enamel dial with center seconds, Automaton scene, 63mm, Ca 1790. (illo. C)

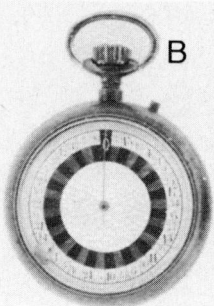

A. Roulette wheel style dial, press a lever & the center pointer spins to a red or black number.
B. Roulette wheel style dial, press a button & the center pointer spins to a red or black number.
C.Horse Race dial, twist the crown & a tiny ball spins & falls into a indentation at one of 9 horses.

TYPE - DESCRIPTION	ABP	Ex-Fn	Mint
A. Roulette wheel style dial, press a lever & the center pointer spins to a red or black number	$220	$400	$500
B. Roulette wheel style dial, press a button & the center pointer spins to a red or black number	220	400	500
C. Horse Race dial, twist the crown & a tiny ball spins & falls into a indentation at one of 9 horses	220	500	675
D. Roulette wheel style dial, press a button & the center pointer spins to a red or black number	220	400	500
E. Horse Race dial, push the crown & 8 horses rotate , the winner appears in an aperture (window).	220	500	675
F. Dice Game, press a lever & the platform spins causing 5 dice to roll and come up randomly	220	400	500
G. Calendar watch key Day, Date & Moon Phase, Ca. 1800-1820	330	550	800

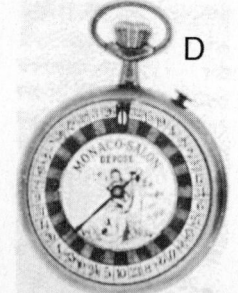
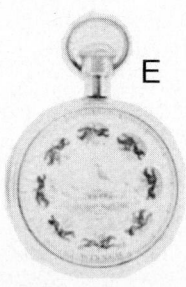
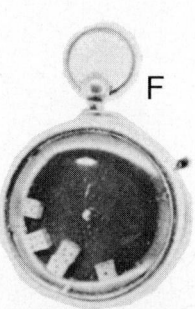

D. Roulette wheel style dial, press a button & the center pointer spins to a red or black number.
E. Horse Race dial, push the crown & 8 horses rotate , the winner appears in an aperture (window).
F. Dice Game, press a lever & the platform spins causing 5 dice to roll and come up randomly.

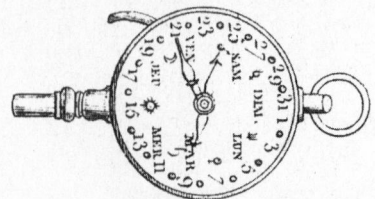
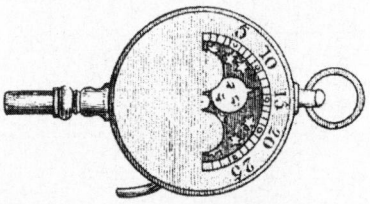

G. Calendar watch key with DAY, DATE & MOON PHASE, Ca. 1800-1820.

NIELLO WATCH CASES

Niello (nye-el-oh) is a black or dark blue composition of lead, silver, copper, sulfur and ammonium chloride. The mixture is fused onto an engraved or cut out metal base by firing the mix in a process similar to **champleve** enameling. Silver was the most often used metal for Niello cases. Rose gold inlay is also seen in combination with Niello. Niello cases appeared in the early 1900s about the same time Art Nouveau and Art Deco was popular. Huegenin Brothers of Le Lode, Favre of Le Lock, Duchene of Geneva, Rene Lalique of Paris and Longines of St. Imier played prominent roles in the design and marketing of Niello cases. Niello cases were never made in quantity by the American case factories.

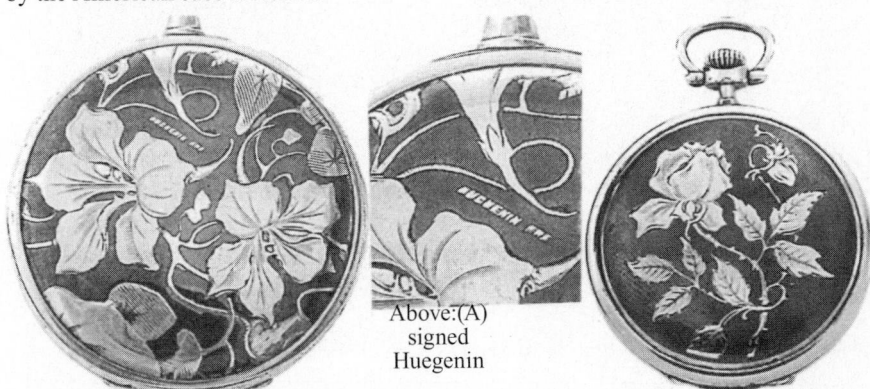

Above:(A)
signed
Huegenin

(A)Niello, silver only, floral motif, signed, 46mm OF, Ca.1905. (B)Niello, silver & rose gold, floral motif, 40mm HC, Ca. 1910

TYPE -DESCRIPTION	ABP	Ex-Fn	· Mint
(A) Niello, silver only, floral motif, signed, 46mm OF	$300	$525	$850
HC	400	625	950
(B) Niello, silver & rose **gold**, floral motif, Ca. 1910,40mm OF	200	335	575
HC	250	425	650
(C) Niello, silver only, Floral motif, signed, 46mm OF	325	575	825
HC	400	625	950
(D) Niello, silver only, Floral motif, **NOT** signed, OF	225	385	700
HC	300	475	800

(C) Niello, silver only, floral motif, signed, 46mm HC.

(D) Niello, silver only, floral motif NOT signed, HC.

(E) Niello, silver only, portrait motif **(Lady Liberty)**, 50mm HC.

(F) Niello, silver & gold, portrait+floral+scene, 47mm HC.

TYPE - DESCRIPTION	ABP	Ex-Fn	Mint
(E) Niello, silver only, portrait Lady Liberty, 50mm OF	$400	$700	$1,200
HC	500	850	1,300
(F) Niello, silver & gold, portrait+floral+scene, 47mm OF	400	685	1,100
HC	500	850	1,300
(G) Niello, silver & gold, with a portrait, (Omega), 47mm OF	400	750	1,200
HC	500	850	1,300
(H) Niello, silver, **equestrian** motif, 47mm OF	325	575	875
HC	400	625	1,000

(G) Niello, silver & gold, portrait motif, (Omega), 47mm HC.

(H) Niello, silver, **equestrian** motif, 47mm HC.

Art Nouveau: A style of art decoration popular from about 1890 to 1910, depicted as curves & flowing intertwining floral designs, Gazelles & female with long hair. Designs by Tiffany & Coco Channel.
Art Deco: Derived from the discovery of King Tut's tomb in 1922. A style of art decoration using Cubism, Egyptian, Aztec & Mayan themes. The angle was in & curves were out.

(J) Niello, silver & rose gold, hunting Motif. 47mm HC.

(K) Niello, silver & gold, hunting motif, 47mm HC.

TYPE -DESCRIPTION	ABP	Ex-Fn	Mint
(J) Niello, silver & **rose** gold, hunting scene, 47 mm OF	$350	$500	$875
HC	400	650	950
(K) Niello, silver & **gold**, hunting scene, 47mm OF	450	700	1,100
HC	550	850	1,300
(L) Niello, silver, **owl**, animal motif, 47mm OF	300	450	800
HC	400	600	950
(M) Niello, silver & **rose** gold, **tiger**, animal motif, 48mm OF	425	725	1,000
HC	500	775	1,100

(L) Niello, silver, owl, animal motif, 47mm HC.

(M) Niello, silver & rose gold, tiger, animal motif 48mm HC.

Art Nouveau: A style of art decoration popular from about 1890 to 1910, depicted as curves & flowing intertwining floral designs, Gazelles & female with long hair. Designs by Tiffany & Coco Channel.

Art Deco: Derived from the discovery of King Tut's tomb in 1922. A style of art decoration using Cubism, Egyptian, Aztec & Mayan themes. The angle was in & curves were out.

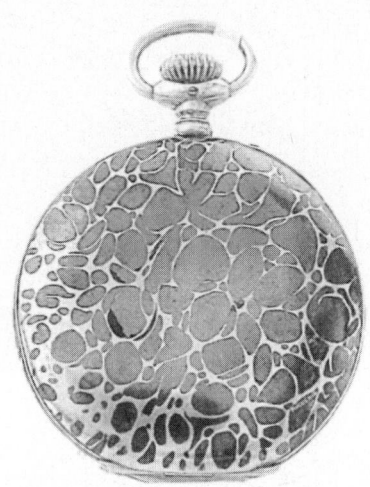

(N) Niello, silver & gold, automobile motif, 47mm HC.   (P) Niello, silver, **signed** pattern motif, 47mm HC.

TYPE - DESCRIPTION	ABP	Ex-Fn	Mint
(N) Niello, silver & gold, automobile motif, 47mm OF	$400	$650	$1,000
HC 500	500	750	1,100
(P) Niello, silver, **signed** pattern motif, 47mm OF	100	285	475
HC 185	185	300	550
(R) 1/4 hour repeater, silver & gold, 50MM, Ca.1905, OF	1,500	1,700	3,000
HC 1,800	1,800	3,000	4,000
(S) **Minute** repeater, silver & rose gold, 54MM, Ca.1900 OF	2,000	4,000	5,500

(R) 1/4 hr. repeater, Niello silver & gold OF, gold crest and with swirling leafs & roses, 50MM, Ca.1905.   (S) Min. slide activated repeater, Niello silver & rose gold,38J., wolfs tooth winding, 54MM, Ca.1900.

Rock crystal & enamel, star shape case, champleve enameled dial, verge, gilt & crystal case, 57x27mm, original French form Ca. 1600-1660, **Shown** Viennese form Ca. 1780-1800. (illo.118)

TYPE —DESCRIPTION	ABP	Ex-Fn	Mint
Rock crystal & enamel, star shape case, champleve dial, **Shown** Viennese verge, gilt & crystal case, 57x27mm, C.1800 (illo.118)	$4,000	$12,000	$17,000
Crucifix form 1/4 hr. repeater & musical, crystal & silver form case, **Shown** Viennese (illo.119)	6,500	17,000	27,000

Crucifix form 1/4 hr. repeater & musical, crystal & silver form case, original French form Ca. 1600-1660, **Shown** Viennese form Ca. 1780-1800. (illo.119)

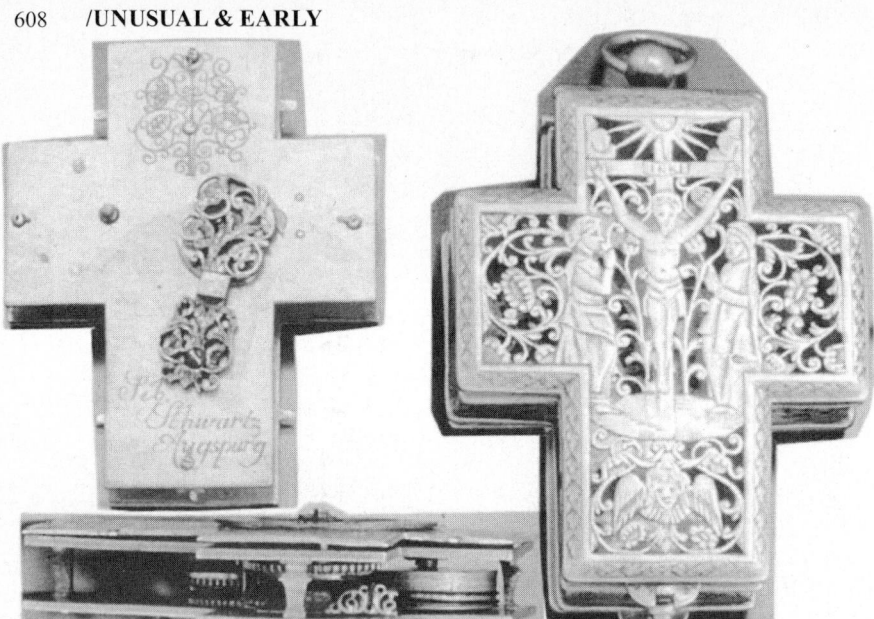

Early Cross Watch, the Cross form pierced silver case depicts the Christ Crucifixion scene. Side view of movement. The Crucifix form fusee movement has a T shaped foliot style balance made of steel and the balance is supported by a hand pierced free form silver cock, a pre-hairspring balance, verge escapement with a gut style fusee, Ca.1640.

TYPE - DESCRIPTION	ABP	Ex-Fn	Mint
Early Cross form Watch	$10,000	$25,000	$30,000
Early Octagon Crystal Watch.	10,000	25,000	30,000

Early Octagon Crystal watch , the movement has a T shaped foliot style balance made of brass and the balance **is** supported by a hand pierced free form silver cock, a pre-hairspring balance, verge escapement with a gut style fusee, Ca.1650.

MEN'S UNUSUAL *"GOLD"*

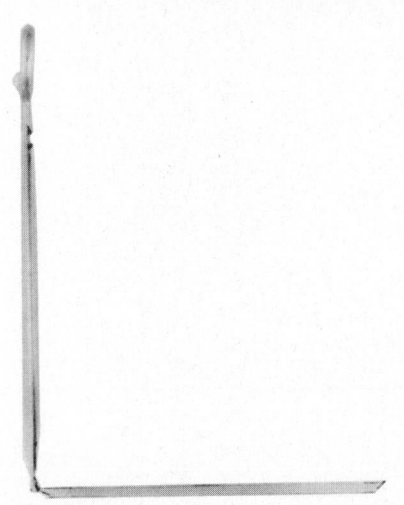

Above note thin watch.
Extra flat watch, **1.5mm thick**, Swiss, 18K, HC, **ACTUAL SIZE**, 5Omm. (illo.120)

TYPE —DESCRIPTION	ABP	Ex-Fn	Mint
Extra flat watch, 1.5mm thick, Swiss, **18K**, HC, 50mm (illo.120) ...	$3,000	$6,000	$12,000
Jump 1/4 seconds, 2 train, 30J, KW, nickel, (Swiss),			
18K, 56mm, HC, C. 1870-90........................	2,000	3,200	3,800
Captain's watch, enameled portraits on case, Maharaja & Queen			
Victoria, KW, lever movement, **18K**, 44mm, HC, C. 1870	4,000	12,000	18,000
Captain's watch, KW, 15J, engraved case & enamel dial, **2 train**,			
18K, 52-58mm, OF, C. 1870 (illo.121)...................	1,000	2,500	3,000
1776-1876 centennial watch, Henry O. Stauffer, bridges in 1776 form,			
17J, **18K**, 53mm, HC, C. 1876 (illo.122)	4,000	7,000	12,000
Above not marked Henry Stauffer, base metal.............	600	2,000	3,000

Captains watch, KW, 15J, engraved case & enamel dial, 2 train,18K, 52-58mm, OF, ca. 1870. (illo.121)

1776-1876 Centennial watch, H. O. Stauffer, bridges in 1776 form, 17J, 18K, 53mm, HC, ca. 1876. Made by Georges Favre-Jacot of le Locle later became *Zenith* (illo.122)

Above: Hour and Minute hands **CONTRACTED.**

Extremely RARE oval watches with hands that **EXPAND** and **CONTRACT.** The hands work much like a pantograph or scissors that follow cams to expand and contract the hands. Eight day going movement , 60 seconds auxiliary dial, also a 1/4 seconds dial. The case has 60 pearls and the watch is thought to be made by **William Anthony** of London, Ca. 1795. William Anthony was famous for his verge watches and watches set in pearls and diamonds, with many of his watches being made for the Chinese market. There is a good example of this type watch and may be seen in Lisbon, Portugal at the Casa Museum "Foundation Medeiros e Almeida.

TYPE –DESCRIPTION

		ABP	Ex-Fn	Mint
Oval watch with hands that **EXPAND** and **CONTRACT**				
eight day, 60 sec. & 1/4 sec. dials, Gold case. . . . . ★★★★★		$90,000	$150,000	$200,000
above with 60 pearls . . . . ★★★★★		95,000	175,000	250,000

Above: Hour and Minute hands **EXPANDED**.

Above: The Expanding and Contracting hour and minute follow an oval or egg shaped lead and follow cam, at the center of the dial. Thus while rotating around the cam, they lengthen & shorten according to the axis of the dial or cam. This system is similar to Pantograph or much like scissors in action.

Moonphase, double dial, calendar, Swiss, 17J, back lid opens to reveal cal. dial, 14K, HC, C.1590. (illo.123)

TYPE -DESCRIPTION	ABP	Ex-Fn	Mint
Captain's watch, KW KS, 15J, ornate case, Swiss, single train, **18K**, 52mm, HC, C. 1870	$800	$2,000	$2,500
Digital dial, hrs. & mm. on digital jump discs, Swiss, 15J, SW, **18K**, 51mm, HC, C. 1905	1,000	2,000	2,500
Moonphase, double dial, full calendar, Swiss, 17J, Moonphase, back lid opens to reveal cal. dial, **14K**, HC, C.1890 (illo.123)	2,300	3,000	3,500
Moonphase, full calendar, gold, OF	2,000	2,600	3,000
Two train, center independent sec.,2 going barrels, lever escap., KW KS, GOLD, 42mm, Ca. 1880, HC (illo. 124)	1,000	1,500	2,000
Art Deco dial, Swiss, 18K, 45mm,OF (illo.125)	1,000	2,000	3,200

Two train, center independent sec.,2 going barrels, lever escap., KW KS, GOLD, 42mm, Ca. 1880, HC. (illo. 124)

Art Deco style with exaggerated numbers on dial, Swiss, 18K, 45mm, OF. (illo.125)

TYPE -DESCRIPTION	ABP	Ex-Fn	Mint
Double dials, world time & moon ph. triple date,**18K** (illo.126)	$5,000	$10,000	$15,000
Perpetual calendar with moonphase and chrono., Swiss , 20J, porcelain dial, 3/4 plate, 18K, 51mm, OF, C.1890-1900	5,500	10,000	12,000
Rare verge, w/ automaton "Serpent, Adam & Eve" on dial with moving serpent, verge, French, 18K, OF, C. 1800	4,500	9,000	12,000
Musical, two train of gears, pin cylinder & 24 blades, one tune, 18K (illo.127)	3,000	6,000	7,000
Waterproof watch w/wind ind. 17J., C.1885 (illo.128)	2,000	3,500	4,500
Cigarette lighter & Swiss watch, Dunhill, Silver, C.1926 (illo.129)	300	500	700
9Kcase	900	1,200	1,400
14K case	1,200	1,500	2,000
$20.00 U.S. gold coin, 17J, mvt. in coin, 35mm, Ca.1920's (illo.130)	1,200	2,000	2,500

Double dials, world time & moon ph. triple date, 18K (illo.126)

Musical, two train of gears, pin cylinder & 24 blades, one tune, 18K. (illo.127)

Waterproof watch w/wind ind. 17J., C.1885. (illo.128)

Cigarette lighter & Swiss watch, Dunhill, Silver, Ca. 1926 (illo.129)

$20.00 U.S. gold coin, 17J, Swiss mvt. in coin, 35mm, Ca.1920s. (illo.130)

Skeletonized Verge & Fusee (French), Multi-color 18K Case & rose cut diamonds, horse-shoe shaped plate, balance end stone is a large Cabochon Ruby, 45MM, KW KS, Ca. 1785.(illo.130A)

TYPE — DESCRIPTION	ABP	Ex-Fn	Mint
Skeletonized Verge & Fusee movement, 45MM, KWKS with Multi-color 18K Case, Ca. 1785 (illo.130A)	$4,000	$7,000	$9,000
Lorgnette Form Watch, 3/8" x 7/8 x 3-1/4", 18K Closed Case, KWKS, Ca. 1850. (illo.130B)	5,000	7,000	9,000

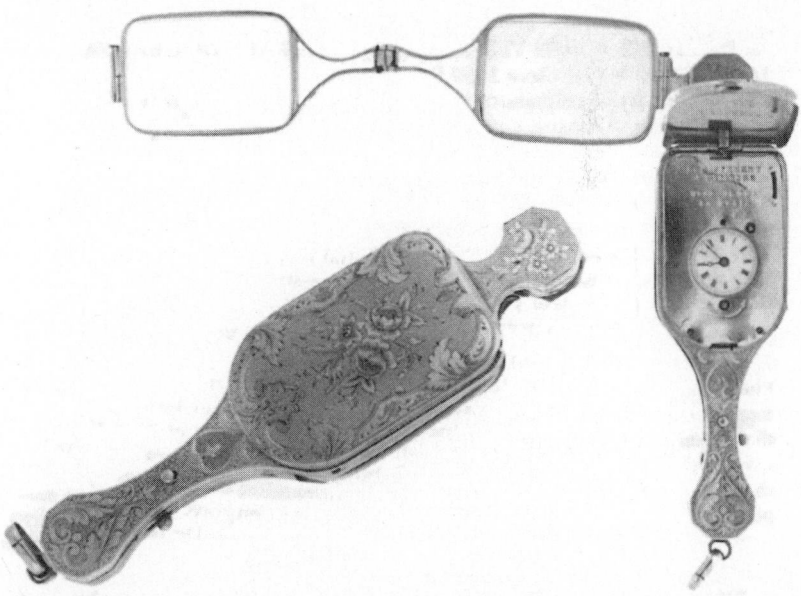

Lorgnette Form Watch, 3/8" x 7/8 x 3-1/4", 18K Closed Case, the case is chased with leaf patterns and arabesque, signed "Echappement a Cylindre Huit Trous en Rubis", the looking frames are rose gold and flip out with a push button, KWKS, Ca. 1850. (illo.130B)

MISC. SWISS LADY'S Ca. 1850- 1950
SILVER or GOLD FILLED

TYPE - DESCRIPTION	ABP	Ex-Fn	Mint
OF or silver, 7-17J, SW, 35mm, OF, C. 1900-1930	$45	$55	$85
OF or silver, 10-15J, SW, 35mm, fancy dial, OF, C. 1910	65	75	125
OF or silver, 7-17J, SW, 35- 40mm, HC, C. 1890-1930	75	100	135
Enamel or silver, cylinder, pinset, 35mm, OF, C. 1910	65	100	200
KWKS, silver, 40- 45mm, OF, C. 1865-1885	75	100	125
KWKS, silver, 37- 45mm, **HC**, C. 1865-1885	100	125	175
Ball shaped, 17J, 35mm, SW, GF or silver with chain	125	165	200

MISC. LADYS Ca. 1850- 1950 *GOLD* (NO ENAMEL)

TYPE -DESCRIPTION	ABP	Ex-Fn	Mint
SW, 7-15J, 14K, 35-40mm, OF, C.1910-1930	$100	$150	$200
SW, 7-15J, 14K, 35-40mm, HC, C.1910-1930	200	300	325
KWKS, 10J, cylinder, 18K, 34- 40mm, OF, C.1865-90	150	250	275
KWKS, 10J, cylinder, 18K, 38-43mm, HC, C. 1865-85	200	325	400
Fusee, lever, fancy dial, 18K, 38- 43mm, OF, C. 1845-75	300	425	500
Fusee, lever, fancy dial, 18K, 38- 43mm, HC, C. 1850s	400	550	600
Ball shaped w/pin, 10J, 14K, 25mm, OF, C. 1890	500	650	700

MISC. LADYS Ca. 1850-1950 ENAMEL ON *GOLD*

TYPE - DESCRIPTION	ABP	Ex-Fn	Mint
KW, enamel (black outlines) 18K, 40- 42mm HC, C. 1860	$250	$400	$500
KW, enamel & dia., Swiss, 10J, 18K, OF, C. 1860	350	650	750
Pattern enamel & demi-hunter, 15J, 18K , 35mm, HC, C.1885	400	600	800
Portrait enamel, KWKS, Swiss, 14K, 34- 42mm, HC, C. 1870	425	900	1,200
Enamel ,with pearls and/ or dia., 10-17J, w/ matching pin, 18K, 23-26mm, OF	800	1,200	1,400
Enamel, w/dia. or pearls, w/ pin, 18K, 26-30mm, HC, C. 1895	1,000	1,500	2,000
Miniature verge, gold & enamel w/ pearls, superior enamel, Swiss, KW, gold case, 27mm, OF, C. 1770	2,500	4,000	5,000
Miniature HC enamel & dia., 17J, Swiss, with orig. pin, 18K,23mm, HC, C. 1890	1,500	2,200	2,800
Ball-shaped (Duchene) Geneva, verge, KW, enamel and gold, 25mm, C. 1800	1,300	2,200	2,600

☞ Note: Some models and grades are not included. Their values can be determined by comparing with similar age, size, metal content, style, models and grades listed.

☞ Note: Watches listed in this book are priced at the collectable Trade Show level, as complete watches having an original case, an original dial, and with the entire original movement in good working order with no repairs needed.

COMPARISON OF WATCH CASE SIZES	
U.S.A.	**EUROPEAN**
10-12 SIZE	40—44MM
16 SIZE	45—49MM
18 SIZE	50—55 MM

LADY'S UNUSUAL *GOLD & ENAMEL*

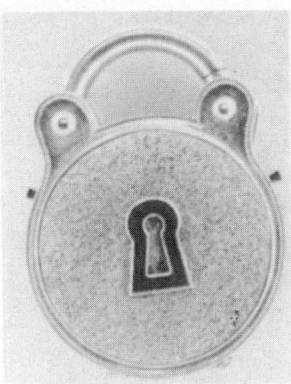

LEFT; Ball-shaped, bezel wind, 18K, enamel & diamonds, Swiss, 16mm, OF, C. 1920. (illo.131) CENTER: Ring watch w/enamel & dia., Swiss, 18K, 18mm, C.1910. (illo.132) RIGHT: Padlock form enamel and gold, Swiss, KW. (illo.133)

TYPE -DESCRIPTION	ABP	Ex-Fn	Mint
Ball-shaped, bezel wind, Swiss, enamel & diamonds on **18K** case, size of a marble, 16mm, OF, C, 1920 (illo.131)	$900	$1,500	$2,000
Above in gold plated case	500	625	800
Ring watch w/enamel & dia,, Swiss, 18K, 18mm, C.1910 (illo.132) . . .	1,000	2,200	3,000
Cherry form enamel & 18K, 17J, closed case, bezel wind, Swiss, 22mm, ...	1,800	4,000	5,000
Flower basket form, enamel and 18K, Swiss, KWKS, with heart form movement, 10J, 18K, 30x24mm, HC, C. 1860	2,500	4,000	6,000
Padlock form enamel and gold, Swiss, KW (illo.133)	900	3,000	4,000
Padlock form enamel and gold (cover over dial,) Swiss-, KW, diamonds on case, heart shaped mvt., 18K, 28x51mm, HC, C.1870	1,200	4,000	5,000
Form watch in shape of leaf, gold & enamel, Bar mvt. (illo, 134)	1,200	3,500	4,000

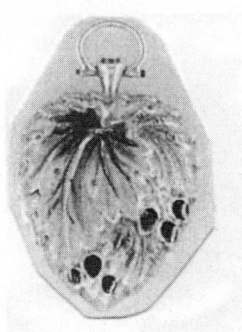
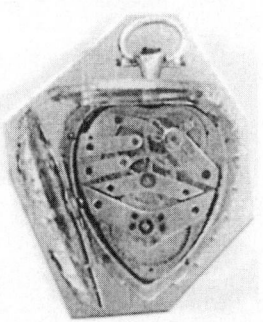

Form watch in shape of **leaf**, gold & enamel, cylinder escapement, Bar movement., KW KS, Ca.1865. (illo.134)

☞ Pricing in this Guide are fair market price for complete watches which are reflected from the NAWCC National and regional shows.

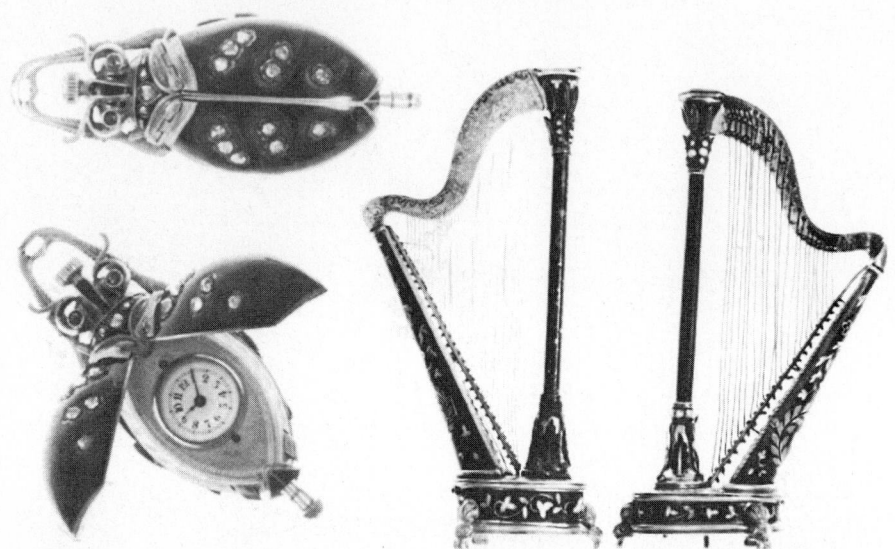

Scarab form gold & enamel, 10J, cylinder, diamonds, closed case w/wings that open, 18K, 54x23mm, C. 1885. (illo.135)

Rare enamel & gold harps, matched pair w/ music, verge, diamonds, lapis and enameled scenes, 3 3/4" high, C. 1830. (illo.136)

TYPE - DESCRIPTION	ABP	Ex-En	Mint
Scarab form gold & enamel, 10J, cylinder, diamonds, closed case w/wings that open, 18K, 54x23mm, C. 1885 (illo. 135)	$4,000	$8,000	$10,000
Lorgnette with enamel & gold, KW, 10J, Swiss, 3 1/4" x 1, cover ornamented w/dia., 18K	6,000	9,000	12,000
Rare enamel & gold harps, matched pair w/ music, verge, diamonds, lapis and enameled scenes, 3 3/4" high, C.1830 (illo.136)	20,000	45,000	60,000
Rock crystal case, silver dial, **Viennese** made, C. 1830 (illo.137)	4,000	15,000	18,000

Rock crystal case, silver dial, Viennese made, C. 1830. (illo.137)

ENAMEL WATCHES

Floral enamel watch. Finely painted floral enamel panel within border of seed pearls. (illo.E-1)

Floral enamel watch. Bouquet of flowers within a champleve border of scrolls enclosing panels of flowers. (illo.E-2)

SIZE AND DESCRIPTION	ABP	Ex-Fn	Mint
55mm, finely painted floral, seed pearls, (Bovet also Ilbery),18K (illo.E-2)	$10,000	$25,000	$30,000
47mm, gold enamel repeater, with chatelaine of pierced gold links & enamel plaques with enamel key & fob seals (illo.E-1)	8,000	18,000	25,000
Enamel & pearls, hunting scene of lion, for China market, silver gilt duplex escapement, 62mm, Ca. 1845 (illo.E-3)	4,000	7,000	9,000
Enamel and 18K case, automated horseman and windmill also fountain, horse drinks water (illo.E-4)	25,000	40,000	55,000
Enamel floral scene, enamel and pearls on gold case, finely painted floral bouquet, 55mm (illo.E-5)	18,000	35,000	50,000
Enamel and 18K case, MINUTE- REPEATER, HC, surrounded with pearls, 55mm, (illo.E-5A)	12,000	20,000	27,000
VIENNESE enamel watch, the front cover shows a lady and gentleman in a scene, the back cover pictures three boys in a scene, 55mm (illo.E-6 & E-6A)	1,500	3,500	5,000
54mm, 29J., 1/4 repeater, pearls & enamel, silver case (illo.E-8)	1,800	3,500	4,000
VIENNESE Lapis Lazuli enamel watch, verge fusee, top and bottom covers are finely cut solid lapis stone, champleve enamel dial, Ca. 1830 (illo.E-9).	2,800	8,000	10,000

&⌒ French watch-making believed to have started in town of Blois, France. French Enamel Watches also believed to have started in Blois, in early 1600's.

Enamel & pearls, hunting scene of lion, for China market, duplex escapement, 82mm, Ca. 1845. (illo.E.3)

Enamel and 18K case, automated horseman and windmill also fountain, horse drinks water. (illo.E.4)

Enamel floral scene, enamel and pearls on gold case, finely painted floral bouquet, 55mm (illo.E-5)

Enamel and 18K case, MINUTE- REPEATER, Hunting Case, surrounded with pearls, 55mm, Ca.1890. (illo.E-5A)

VIENNESE enamel watch, the front cover shows a lady and gentleman in a scene, the back cover pictures three boys in a scene, 55mm. see movement below. (illo.E-6)

VIENNESE enamel watch, same watch as above, two-footed balance bridge, the inner lids are decorated with polychrome enamelled scenes. (illo.E.6A)

54mm, 29J, 1/4 hour repeater, Pearls and enamel on a silver case, ca. 1885. (illo.E-8)

VIENNESE Lapis Lazuli enamel watch, verge fusee, top and bottom covers are finely cut solid lapis stone, champleve enamel dial, Viennese made, Ca. 1830 (illo.E.9)

Floral enamel watch, 57mm, bouquet of flowers within a gold case set with split pearls. (illo.E-10)

Enamel scene watch, 58mm, finely painted scene of ships in harbor. (illo.E-1 1)

SIZE AND DESCRIPTION	ABP	Ex-Fn	Mint
57mm, floral enamel, duplex, (Bovet), pearls, 18K, (illo.E-10)	$8,000	$20,000	$25,000
58mm, harbor scene enamel, duplex, 18k, Ca. 1790 (illo. E-11)	15,000	35,000	40,000
43mm, basket form champleve enamel, 18k, Ca.1800 (illo.E.12). . . .	2,800	7,500	9,500
42mm, champleve border, finely painted flowers, (Le Roy), gold case & chain.	2,500	4,000	5,000
37mm, rose gold guilloche enamel demi-hunter	350	500	600
36mm, gold enamel & champleve enamel, verge, Ca. 1800	1,500	4,000	5,000
35mm, gold champleve enamel, (L'Epine), cylinder	700	1,200	2,000
35mm, gold enamel & seed pearls, rose cut diamonds	300	800	1,000
34mm, gold egg-shaped form enamel, verge, (Austrian)	1,200	5,000	7,000
30mm, gold miniature enamel, verge, seed pearls, Ca. 1800	800	2,500	3,000
27mm, gold enamel lapel brooch with seed pearls & rose cut diamonds, Ca. 1890.	550	900	1,000
27mm, gold fine enamel lapel brooch with cut diamonds by C. H. Meylan (illo.E.13)	1,500	3,000	3,800

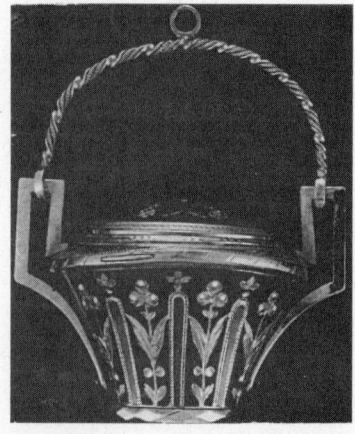

Enamel form tapered oval basket with rising rope handle, enhanced with panels of flowers. 18K case. (illo.E-12)

A chased enamel gold lady's pendant watch. Enamel portrait of a lady. (illo.E-13)

(ILLO. A)   (ILLO. B)   (ILLO. D)

Size and Description	ABP	Ex-Fn	Mint
27mm, Art Noveau design, multi-colored flowers gold & diamond pendant watch & pin, 18K, OF, Ca.1890 (illo. A)	$1,000	$1,500	$1,800
25mm, Enamel & pearls & diamonds, star shaped gold settings, pendant and pen, 18K, OF, Ca. 1890 (illo. B)	900	1,200	1,500
25mm, enamel pendant with pin, golden frame of vines around a scene of a lady, 14K, OF, Ca. 1900	1,000	1,500	2,000
24mm, pearl pendant watch with pin, seed pearls also on classic fleur-de-lis designed pin, 14K OF, Ca.1885 (illo. C)	1,000	1,200	1,500
24mm, enamel and gold pendant watch with a starburst gold and pearl pin, 10 J, cylinder movement, 18K, OF, Ca.1900 (illo. D)	800	1,200	1,500
22mm, ball-shaped enamel & pearl pendant watch, exposed balance, lever escapement can be seen back crystal (illo. E)	1,400	2,000	2,500
20mm, 17J, three-finger bridge miniature movement, Adj.5P, by Ditisheim platinum OF case, Ca. 1930s (illo. F)	1,100	2,000	2,500

(ILLO. C)

(ILLO. E)

(ILLO. F)

Am. Waltham W. Co.

Date	Serial #
1852	50
1853	400
1854	1,000
1855	2,500
1856	4,000
1857	6,000
1858	10,000
1859	15,000
1860	20,000
1861	30,000
1862	45,000
1863	65,000
1864	110,000
1865	180,000
1866	260,000
1867	330,000
1868	410,000
1869	460,000
1870	500,000
1871	540,000
1872	590,000
1873	680,000
1874	730,000
1875	810,000
1876	910,000
1877	1,000,000
1878	1,150,000
1879	1,350,000
1880	1,500,000
1881	1,670,000
1882	1,835,000
1883	2,000,000
1884	2,350,000
1885	2,650,000
1886	3,000,000
1887	3,400,000
1888	3,800,000
1889	4,200,000
1890	4,700,000
1891	5,200,000
1892	5,800,000
1893	6,300,000
1894	6,700,000
1895	7,100,000
1896	7,450,000
1897	8,100,000
1898	8,400,000
1899	9,000,000
1900	9,500,000
1901	10,200,000
1902	11,100,000
1903	12,100,000
1904	13,500,000
1905	14,300,000
1906	14,700,000
1907	15,500,000
1908	16,400,000
1909	17,600,000
1910	17,900,000
1911	18,100,000
1912	18,200,000
1913	18,900,000
1914	19,500,000
1915	20,000,000
1916	20,500,000
1917	20,900,000
1918	21,800,000
1919	22,500,000
1920	23,400,000
1921	23,900,000
1922	24,100,000
1923	24,300,000
1924	24,550,000
1925	24,800,000
1926	25,200,000
1927	26,100,000
1928	26,400,000
1929	26,900,000
1930	27,100,000
1931	27,300,000
1932	27,550,000
1933	27,750,000
1934	28,100,000
1935	28,600,000
1936	29,100,000
1937	29,400,000
1938	29,750,000
1939	30,050,000
1940	30,250,000
1941	30,750,000
1942	31,050,000
1943	31,400,000
1944	31,700,000
1945	32,100,000
1946	32,350,000
1947	32,750,000
1948	33,100,000
1949	33,500,000
1950	33,560,000
1951	33,600,000
1952	33,700,000
1953	33,800,000
1954	34,100,000
1955	34,450,000
1956	34,700,000
1957	35,000,000

AURORA W. Co.

Date	Serial #
1884	10,001
1885	60,000
1886	101,000
1887	160,000
1888	200,000
1889	215,000
1891	230,901

COLUMBUS W. Co.

Date	Serial #
1875	1,000
1876	3,000
1877	6,000
1878	9,000
1879	12,000
1880	15,000
1881	18,000
1882	21,000
1883	25,000
1884	30,000
1885	40,000
1886	53,000
1887	75,000
1888	97,000
1889	119,000
1890	141,000
1891	163,000
1892	185,000
1893	207,000
1894	229,000
1895	251,000
1896	273,000
1897	295,000
1898	317,000
1899	339,000
1900	361,000
1901	383,000

SPECIAL BLOCK OF SERIAL NOS.

Date	Serial #
1894	500,001
1896	501,500
1898	503,000
1900	504,500
1902	506,000

ELGIN WATCH Co.

Date	Serial #
1867	10,000
1868	25,001 Nov,20th
1869	40,001 May, 20th
1870	50,001 Aug. 24th
1871	185,001 Sep. 8th
1872	201,001 Dec. 20th
1873	325,001
1874	400,001 Aug.28th
1875	430,000
1876	480,000
1877	520,000
1878	550,000
1879	625,001 Feb.8th
1880	750,000
1881	900,000
1882	1,000,000 March,9th
1883	1,250,000
1884	1,500,000
1885	1,855,001 May,28th
1886	2,000,000 Aug.4th
1887	2,500,000
1888	3,000,000 June 20th
1889	3,500,000
1890	4,000,000 Aug.16th
1891	4,449,001 Mar.26th
1892	4,600,000
1893	5,000,000 July 1st
1894	5,500,000
1895	6,000,000 Nov.26th
1896	6,500,000
1897	7,000,000 Oct. 28th.
1898	7,494,001 May,14th
1899	8,000,000 Jan.18th
1900	9,000,000 Nov.14th
1901	9,300,000
1902	9,600,000
1903	10,000,000 May 15th
1904	11,000,000 April 4th
1905	12,000,000 Oct.6th
1906	12,500,000
1907	13,000,000 April 4th
1908	13,500,000
1909	14,000,000 Feb.9th
1910	15,000,000 April 2nd
1911	16,000,000 July 11th
1912	17,000,000 Nov.6th
1913	17,339,001 Apr.14th
1914	18,000,000
1915	18,587,001 Feb.11th
1916	19,000,000
1917	20,031,001 June,27th
1918	21,000,000
1919	22,000,000
1920	23,000,000
1921	24,321,001 July,6th
1922	25,100,000
1923	26,050,000
1924	27,000,000
1925	28,421,001 July,14th
1926	29,100,000
1927	30,050,000
1928	31,500,000
1929	32,000,000
1930	32,599,001 July
1931	33,000,000
1932	33,700,000
1933	34,558,001 July,24th
1934	35,000,000
1935	35,650,000
1936	36,200,000
1937	36,978,001 July,24th
1938	37,900,000
1939	38,200,000
1940	39,100,000
1941	40,200,000
1942	41,100,000
1943	42,200,000
1944	42,600,000
1945	43,200,000
1946	44,000,000
1947	45,000,000
1948	46,000,000
1949	47,000,000
1950	48,000,000
1951	50,000,000 Sept. 7th
1952	52,000,000
1953	53,500,000
1954	54,000,000
1955	54,500,000
1956	55,000,000

HAMILTON WATCH Co.

Date	Serial No.
1893	1-2,000
1894	5,000
1895	11,500
1896	16,000
1897	27,000
1898	50,000
1899	74,000
1900	104,000
1901	143,000
1902	196,000
1903	260,000
1904	340,000
1905	435,000
1906	500,000
1907	588,000
1908	680,000
1909	750,000
1910	790,000
1911	860,000
1912	940,000
1913	1,000,000
1914	1,100,000
1915	1,200,000
1916	1,300,000
1917	1,400,000
1918	1,500,000
1919	1,600,000
1920	1,700,000
1921	1,800,000
1922	1,900,000
1923	1,950,000
1924	2,500,000
1925	2,100,000
1926	2,150,000
1927	2,200,000
1928	2,250,000
1929	2,300,000
1930	2,350,000
1931	2,400,000
1932	2,440,000
1933	2,480,000
1934	2,520,000
1935	2,560,000
1936	2,600,000
1937	2,900,000
1938	3,200,000
1939	3,400,000
1940	4,000,000
1941	4,250,000
1942	4,500,000

DATE LETTERS
2B on 950B=1941-43
C on 992B=1940-69
S on 950B=1941-65
4C On 4992B=1941-68
3992B=1943-45

HAMPDEN W. Co.

Date	Serial #
1877	59,000
1878	70,000
1879	100,000
1880	140,000
1881	180,000
1882	215,000
1883	250,000
1884	300,000
1885	350,000
1886	400,000
1887	480,000
1888	560,000
1889	640,000
1890	740,000
1891	805,500
1892	835,000
1893	865,000
1894	900,000
1895	930,000
1896	970,000
1897	1,000,000
1898	1,120,000
1899	1,255,000
1900	1,384,000
1901	1,512,000
1902	1,642,000
1903	1,768,000
1904	1,896,000
1905	2,024,000
1906	2,152,000
1907	2,280,000
1908	2,400,000
1909	2,520,000
1910	2,650,000
1911	2,700,000
1912	2,760,000
1913	2,850,000
1914	2,920,000
1915	3,000,000
1916	3,100,000
1917	3,240,000
1918	3,390,000
1919	3,500,000
1920	3,600,000
1921	3,700,000
1922	3,750,000
1923	3,800,000
1924	3,850,000
1925	3,900,000
1926	3,950,000
1927	3,980,000

E. HOWARD & Co.

Date	Serial #
1858-60)	113-1,800
1860-61)	1,801-3,000
1861)	3,001-3,100
1861)	3,101-3,300
1861)	3,401- 3,500
1861-71)	3,501-28,000
1868-83)	30,001-50,000
1869-99)	50,001-71,500
1869-90)	100,001-105,500
1880-99)	200,001-227,000
1895)	228,001-231,000
1884-99)	300,001-309,000
1895)	309,001-310,000
1890-95)	400,001-405,000
1890-99)	500,001-501,500
1896-1903)	600,001-601,500
1896-1903)	700,001-701,500

HOWARD WATCH Co. (KEYSTONE)

Date	Serial #
1902	850,000
1903	900,000
1909	980,000
1912	1,100,000
1915	1,285,000
1917	1,340,000
1921	1,400,000
1930	1,500,000

ILLINOIS WATCH Co.

Date	Serial #
1872	5,000
1873	20,000
1874	50,000
1875	75,000
1876	100,000
1877	145,000
1878	210,000
1879	250,000
1880	300,000
1881	350,000
1882	400,000
1883	450,000
1884	500,000
1885	550,000
1886	600,000
1887	700,000
1888	800,000
1889	900,000
1890	1,000,000
1891	1,040,000
1892	1,080,000
1893	1,120,000
1894	1,160,000
1895	1,220,000
1896	1,250,000
1897	1,290,000
1898	1,330,000
1899	1,370,000
1900	1,410,000
1901	1,450,000
1902	1,500,000
1903	1,650,000
1904	1,700,000
1905	1,800,000
1906	1,840,000
1907	1,900,000
1908	2,100,000
1909	2,150,000
1910	2,200,000
1911	2,300,000
1912	2,400,000
1913	2,500,000
1914	2,600,000
1915	2,700,000
1916	2,800,000
1917	3,000,000
1918	3,200,000
1919	3,400,000
1920	3,600,000
1921	3,750,000
1922	3,900,000
1923	4,000,000
1924	4,500,000
1925	4,700,000
1926	4,800,000
1927	5,000,000
(Sold to Hamilton)	
1928	5,100,000
1929	5,200,000
1931	5,400,000
1938	5,500,000
1948	5,600,000

ROCKFORD W.Co.

Date	Serial #
1876	1,200
1877	22,600
1878	43,000
1879	64,000
1880	95,000
1881	136,000
1882	167,000
1883	200,000
1884	226,000
1885	247,000
1886	267,000
1887	287,500
1888	308,000
1889	328,500
1890	349,000
1891	369,500
1892	390,000
1893	410,000
1894	430,000
1895	450,000
1896	470,000
1897	490,000
1898	510,000
1899	530,000
1900	550,000
1901	570,000
1902	590,000
1903	610,000
1904	630,000
1905	650,000
1906	670,000
1907	690,000
1908	734,000
1909	790,000
1910	824,000
1911	880,000
1912	936,000
1913	958,000
1914	980,000
1915	1,000,000

SOUTH BEND W. Co.

Date	Serial #
1903	380,501
1904	390,000
1905	405,000
1906	425,000
1907	460,000
1908	500,000
1909	550,000
1910	600,000
1911	660,000
1912	715,000
1913	765,000
1914	800,000
1915	720,000
1916	840,000
1917	860,000
1918	880,000
1919	905,000
1920	935,000
1921	975,000
1922	1,000,000
1923	1,035,000
1924	1,070,000
1925	1,105,000
1926	1,140,000
1927	1,275,000
1928	1,210,000
1929	1,240,000

SETH THOMAS W. Co.

Date	Serial #
1885	5,000
1886	20,000
1887	40,000
1888	80,000
1889	150,000
1890	235,000
1891	330,000
1892	420,000
1893	510,000
1894	600,000
1895	690,000
1896	780,000
1897	870,000
1898	960,000
1899	1,050,000
1900	1,140,000
1901	1,230,000
1902	1,320,000
1903	1,410,000
1904	1,500,000
1905	1,700,000
1906	1,900,000
1907	2,100,000
1908	2,300,000
1909	2,500,000
1910	2,725,000
1911	2,950,000
1912	3,175,000
1913	3,490,000
1914	3,600,000

BALL WATCH Co. (Hamilton)

Date	Serial #
1895	13,000
1897	20,500
1900	42,000
1902	170,000
1905	462,000
1910	600,000
1915	603,000
1920	610,000
1925	620,000
1930	637,000
1935	641,000
1938	647,000
1939	650,000
1940	651,000
1941	652,000
1942	654,000
Ball-(Waltham)	
1900	060,700
1905	202,000
1910	216,000
1915	250,000
1920	260,000
1925	270,000
Ball-(Illinois)	
1929	800,000
1930	801,000
1931	803,000
1932	804,000

Ball- (Elgin) 1904-1906
S # range
11,853,000-12,282,000

Ball- (E. Howard & C0.)
1893-1895
S # range
226,000-308,000

Ball-(Hampden)
1890-1892
S # range
626,750-657,960-759,720

Audemars Piguet

DATE	SERIAL #
1882	2,000
1890	4,000
1895	5,350
1900	6,500
1905	9,500
1910	13,000
1915	17,000
1920	25,000
1925	33,000
1930	40,000
1935	42,000
1940	44,000
1945	48,000
1950	55,000
1955	65,000
1960	75,000
1965	90,000
1970	115,000
1975	160,000
1980	225,000

International W.Co. (Schaffhausen)

DATE	SERIAL #
1884	6,501
1886	23,500
1888	37,500
1890	63,000
1892	87,500
1894	117,000
1896	151,500
1898	194,000
1900	231,000
1902	276,500
1904	321,000
1906	377,500
1908	435,000
1910	492,000
1912	557,000
1914	620,500
1916	657,000
1918	714,000
1920	765,000
1922	783,500
1924	807,000
1926	845,000
1928	890,500
1930	929,000
1932	938,000
1934	940,000
1936	955,500
1938	1,000,000
1940	1,019,000
1942	1,062,000
1944	1,092,000
1946	1,131,000
1948	1,177,000
1950	1,222,000
1952	1,291,000
1954	1,335,000
1956	1,399,000
1958	1,480,000
1960	1,553,000
1962	1,666,000
1964	1,778,000
1966	1,820,000
1968	1,905,000
1970	2,026,000
1972	2,218,000
1974	2,265,000
1975	2,275,000

A. Lange & Sohne

DATE	SERIAL #
1870	3,500
1875	10,000
1880	15,000
1885	20,000
1890	30,000
1895	35,000
1900	40,000
1905	50,000
1910	60,000
1915	70,000
1920	75,000
1925	80,000
1930	85,000
1935	90,000
1940	100,000

LONGINES

DATE	SERIAL #
1867	1
1870	20,000
1875	100,000
1882	250,000
1888	500,000
1893	750,000
1899	1,000,000-Feb.
1901	1,250,000
1904	1,500,000
1905	1,750,000
1907	2,000,000-July
1909	2,250,000
1911	2,500,000
1912	2,750,000
1913	3,000,000-Aug
1915	3,250,000
1917	3,500,000
1919	3,750,000
1922	4,000,000-Oct.
1925	4,250,000
1926	4,500,000
1928	4,750,000
1929	5,000,000-Oct.
1934	5,250,000
1937	5,500,000
1938	5,750,000
1940	6,000,000-July
1945	7,000,000-June
1950	8,000,000-May
1953	9,000,000-July
1956	10,000,000May
1959	11,000,000Apr.
1962	12,000,000May
1966	13,000,000June
1967	14,000,000-Feb
1969	15,000,000-Feb

OMEGA

DATE	SERIAL #
1895	1,000,000
1902	2,000,000
1908	3,000,000
1912	4,000,000
1916	5,000,000
1923	6,000,000
1929	7,000,000
1935	8,000,000
1939	9,000,000
1944	10,000,000
1947	11,000,000
1950	12,000,000
1952	13,000,000
1956	15,000,000
1958	16,000,000
1961	18,000,000
1963	20,000,000
1965	22,000,000
1967	25,000,000
1968	26,000,000
1970	29,000,000

PATEK PHILIPPE &

DATE	SERIAL #
1840	100
1845	1,200
1850	3,000
1855	8,000
1860	15,000
1865	22,000
1870	35,000
1875	45,000
1880	55,000
1885	70,000
1890	85,000
1895	100,000
1900	110,000
1905	125,000
1910	150,000
1915	175,000
1920	190,100
1925	200,200
1950	700,300
1955	725,400
1960	750,500
1965	775,600
1970	795,700
1920	800,800
1925	805,900
1930	820,000
1935	821,000
1940	832,000
1945	853,000
1950	864,000
1955	875,000
1960	886,000
1965	897,000
1970	898,000
1940	909,000
1945	915,000
1950	930,000
1955	940,000
1960	960,000
1965	975,000
1970	995,000
1960	1,100,000
1965	1,130,000
1970	1,250,000
1975	1,350,000
1980	1,450,000
1985	1,600,000
1990	1,850,000

ROLEX (Case S #)

DATE	SERIAL #
1925	25,000
1926	28,500
1927	30,500
1928	33,000
1929	35,500
1930	38,000
1931	40,000
1932	43,000
1933	47,000
1934	55,000
1935	68,000
1936	81,000
1937	99,000
1938	118,000
1939	136,000
1940	165,000
1941	194,000
1942	224,000
1943	253,000
1944	285,000
1945	348,000
1946	413,000
1947	478,000
1948	543,000
1949	608,000
1950	673,500
1951	738,500
1952	804,000
1953	950,000
1954	999,999
1955	*200,000
1956	*400,000
1957	*600,000
1958	*800,000
1959	1,100,000
1960	1,401,000
1961	1,480,000
1962	1,557,000
1963	1,635,000
1964	1,713,000
1965	1,792,000
1966	1,870,000
1967	2,164,000
1968	2,426,000
1969	2,689,000
1970	2,952,000
1971	3,215,000
1972	3,478,000
1973	3,741,000
1974	4,002,000
1975	4,266,000
1976	4,538,000
1977	5,005,000
1978	5,481,000
1979	5,965,000
1980	6,432,000
1981	6,910,000
1982	7,385,000
1983	7,860,000
1984	8,338,000
1985	8,815,000
1986	9,292,000
1987	9,765,000
1987 1/2	9,999,999
1987 3/4	R000,001
1988	R999,999
1989	L000,001
1990	L999,999
1990 1/2	E000,001
1991 1/4	E999,999
1991 1/2	X000,001

VACHERON

DATE	SERIAL #
1830	30,000
1835	40,000
1840	50,000
1845	60,000
1850	75,000
1855	95,000
1860	110,000
1865	125,000
1870	140,000
1875	155,000
1880	170,000
1885	180,000
1890	190,000
1895	223,000
1900	256,000
1905	289,000
1910	322,000
1915	355,000
1920	385,000
1925	400,000
1930	410,000
1935	420,000
1940	440,000
1945	464,000
1950	488,000
1955	512,000
1960	536,000
1965	560,000
1970	585,000

The above list is provided for determining the **approximate** age of your watch. Match serial number with date. Watches were not necessarily sold in the exact order of manufactured date.

A BIT OF WRIST WATCH HISTORY

While no one is sure who invented the first wrist watch or when the first wrist watch was ever worn. Watch-bracelets were created by great makers for ladies of great wealth. Queen Elizabeth I had a small jewel-studded watch that was made to fasten on the arm (about **1575**). David Rosseau made a watch which was about 18mm in diameter (the size of a dime) in the late 1600s. In **1810** Breguet made his first ladies wrist watch & **1868** for Patek Philippe & Co.

 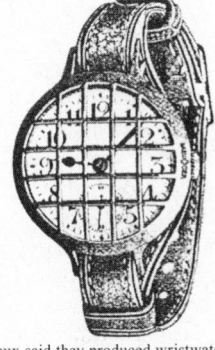

Early BRACELET that holds a small pendant-watch, with a lid that opens on this 18K & enamel case to view the watch, Ca.1840.

Girard-Perregaux said they produced wristwatches which were to be used by officers of the German Navy about 1880. The 1,000 watches used a protective mesh guard.

Wrist watches were at first thought to be too small and delicate to be practical for men to wear. However, during World War I a German officer was said to have strapped a small pocket watch to his wrist with a leather webbed cup. This arrangement freed both hands and proved to be most useful. After the war, the wrist watch gained in popularity. Girard - Perregaux factory said they made wrist watches around **1880** and were designed to be used by officers of the German Navy. In **1892** Omega makes the first minute repeating wrist watch in the world, they used a movement by Audmars Piguet. In **1898** the Omega small Caliber 42.86 was manufactured & by **1902** were being sold as wrist watches. Herman Aegler of Bienne, Switzerland in **1902** manufacture wrist watch movements, the Aegler manufacture became the largest supplier of movements for Rolex. A Omega ad in **1904** states 12 wrist watches being used by military in the Boer War (**1899-1902**). Cartier created the famous Santos wrist watch in **1904**. **1905** the Ditisheim brothers named their Movado, meaning "always in movement". In **1908** Gruen W. Co. are now selling wrist watches and the Rolex trade mark is registered. **1909** Cartier patented the deployment wrist watch buckle. Wrist watch movements were basically derived from the ladies pocket or pendant watch. About **1910-15** American Watch Co. and Elgin Watch Co. were offering wrist watches for sale. **1910** a wrist stop watch was advertised by Fritz Moeri of Saint-Imier of Switzerland. Eterna in **1912** developed the first alarm wrist watch. In **1912** Movado produced the Polyplan movement. (below)

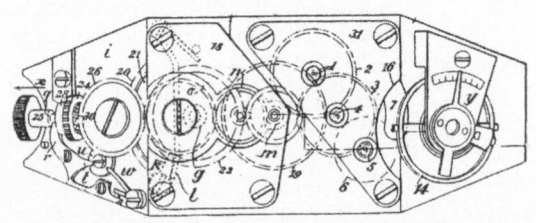

In **1912** Omega in collaboration with Movado and Ulysse Nardin, Omega creates the 18 P CHRO caliber chronograph, specially made for aviation.

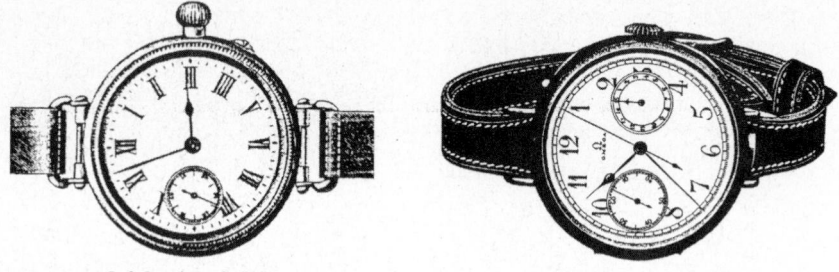

Left: Longines ad, 1909.　　　　　　　　Right: **1913** ad for Omega chronograph.

1913 a 8 day wrist watch by "Hebdomas". In **1918** the American Armed Forces buys 5,000 wrist watches from Omega. In **1919-20** Elinvar, was invented and the Cartier "Tank" wrist watch arrives. These early round wrist watch used enamel dials and for other shapes wrist watches metal dials were preferred. **1920s** Hamilton, Illinois and others begin producing wrist watches.

Miniaturization was a great challenge to many of the famous watch makers including Louis Jaquet, Paul Ditisheim, John Arnold and Henri Capt. The smallest watch in semi-mass production was 12mm by 5mm. In early **1930**, the American Waltham Watch Co. made a 9mm by 20mm Model 400 watch.

Miniaturized wrist watch by Waltham model # 400. Note size comparison to dime.　　Oscillating weight for self winding Wrist Watch.　　HARWOOD self-winding wrist watch, RIM SET, Ca.1928.

By **1920** the round styles were being replaced with square, rectangular and tonneau shapes and decorated with gems. By **1928** wrist watches were outselling pocket watches, and, by **1935**, over 85 percent of the watches being produced were wrist watches.

Self-wind pocket watches were first developed by Abraham Louis Perrelet in **1770** and by Abraham Louis Breguet about **1777**. Louis Recordon made improvements in **1780**, but is was not until **1923-4** that the principle of self-winding was adapted to the wrist watch by John Harwood, an Englishman who setup factories to make his patented self-wind wrist watches in Switzerland, London, France, and the United States. His watches first reached the market about **1929**. The firm A. Schild manufactured about 15,000 watches in Switzerland. Mr. Harwood's watch company removed the traditional stem or crown to wind the mainspring, but in order to set the hands it was necessary to turn the bezel. The Harwood Watch Co. failed around **1931** and the patent expired.

1924 Plexiglas was first used for crystals. **1926** Rolex patented "Oyster" cases. Rolex patented and invented the screw down crown. **1929** Omega makes a superior anti-shock wrist watch "Armure" and the same year Rolex launches the Prince wrist watch RF# 971 which was used for six years. **1929** LeCoultre made a caliber 101, which was the smallest movement in the world and still is. **1930** Lip makes the first wrist watch with a Tourbillon

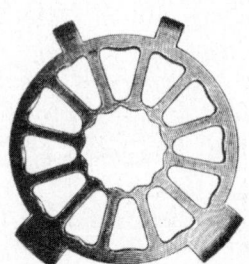

Snap on protector for Wrist Watches, Ca.1920s.　　　Gruen Curvex wrist watch AD 1st appearance in 1935.

In **1931** the Rolex Watch Co. introduced the Rolex Oyster Perpetual, the first waterproof & self winding wrist watch. 1932 LeCoultre creates the Duoplan movement and Longines introduced the Lindbergh type wrist watch. In **1933** the first "Incabloc" shock protection device was used. **1933** the first appearance of the "Nivarox" hairspring. In the mid to late 1930s the wrist watches became more technical advanced with a higher jewel count (21 jewels) and two button chronographs which stop, start and return to zero functions. Split second chronographs, perpetual calendars, world timers and more. Different metals are used stainless steel, platinum, painted dials made of metal and wrist watches were being made thinner. In **1935** the Glucidur (berrylium-bronze) balance made it's first appearance. Gruen produces and patented the Curvex wrist watch in **1935**. By **1940** wrist watches came in all shapes and types including complicated chronographs, calendars, and repeaters. Novelties, digital jump hour and multi-dial were very popular, as well. In **1942** Felsa invented a bi-directional rotor for a self-winding movement. The lugs became part of the case design and the lugs appear in different fancy shapes as tear drops and flared cases.

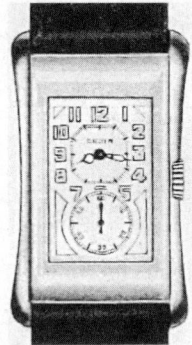

Right: Gruen flared case with Crown-guard, Ca.1931　　　**Rolex** Oyster Perpetual, BUBBLE BACK, Ca. 1940.

1945 Rolex launches the "Date Just", the first automatic water-resistant wrist chronometer with a visible date through a dial aperture. **1947** Vulcain creates the "Cricket" which has a alarm. 1948 Eterna introduced the ball-bearing rotor style watch. 1949 Patek Philippe patents their "Gyromax" balance Wheel.

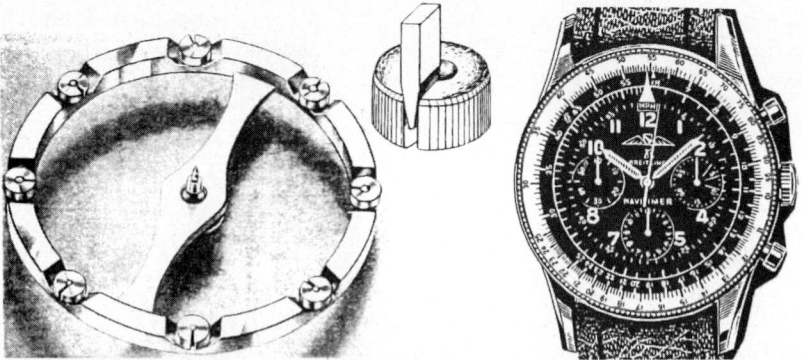

Right: Patek Philippe, "Gyromax" balance wheel.   Breitling launches the "Navitimer", Ca. 1952.

1950 Rolex creates the "turn-o-Graph", RF# 6202. 1950 U. S. Time Corp. introduced the "Timex" watch. **1952** Omega produces the renowned chronometer "Constellation". 1952 Breitling launches the "Navitimer", the wrist watch was designed for pilots. **1953** Rolex produces the first automatic diver's wrist watch water resistant to 100 meters, the "Submariner", RF.# 6204. Professional wrist watches are being made for electrical engineers such as the "Milgaus", the "Submariner", for the swimmers and divers, GMT models for the travelers, the rolex RF.# 6036 called the "Jean-Claude Killy" and the Daytona chronograph RF.# 6034. 1954 Buren introduced the Micro-rotor self wind watch. A dramatic change occurred in **1957** when the Hamilton Watch Co. eliminated the mainspring and replaced it with a small battery that lasted well over one year. In **1960** the balance wheel was removed in the "Accutron" by Bulova and replaced by a tuning fork with miniature pawls.

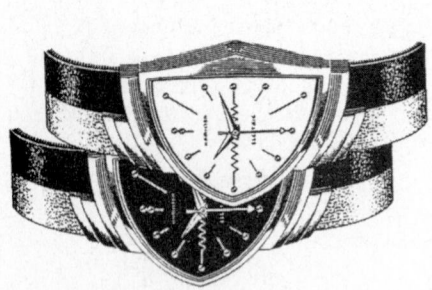

Above: Ventura", by Hamilton W. Co., the "Van Horn" and   Accutron by Bulova, "Alpha" Spaceview, Ca. **1960**.
"Ventura" were both introduced in **1957**.

1960 Movado introduces the "Museum Watch". 1962 Rado makes the first scratch proof wrist watch. **1965** the "Speedmaster Professional" which Omega supplied the wrist watch that was worn on the outside of the space suit the first space walk. The Omega "Speedmaster" was one of the most successful watch in the history of watchmaking. **1965** saw the start of a period of watch manufacturing that is herald as the most difficult crisis ever experienced by the Swiss watch industry. However watch makers continued to produce mechanical marvels and hard times were experienced for the next decade or so.

627

1969 Seiko, with the Quartz Watch, remolds the watch industry with the "Astron" model. In **1970** Tissot had a transparent idea with it's "Idea 2001", the first plastic watch, a synthetic movement and case made of transparent plastic. In **1978** Dr. George Daniels makes a Gold-cased one-minute tourbillon with his co-axial escapement (not requiring oil). In the period **1980-1996** Daniels used Swiss made wrist watches and converted them to his coaxial escapement, he used Omega, Zenith, Rolex and Patek Philippe watches. Overriding all was George Daniels 25 year quest for a lower friction escapement, his success and then the years long battle to gain a reluctant Swiss acceptance culminating in the Omega model. Omega introduced a limited edition of 6,000 watches featuring the co-axial escapement in 1998. They sold for about $6,600.00.

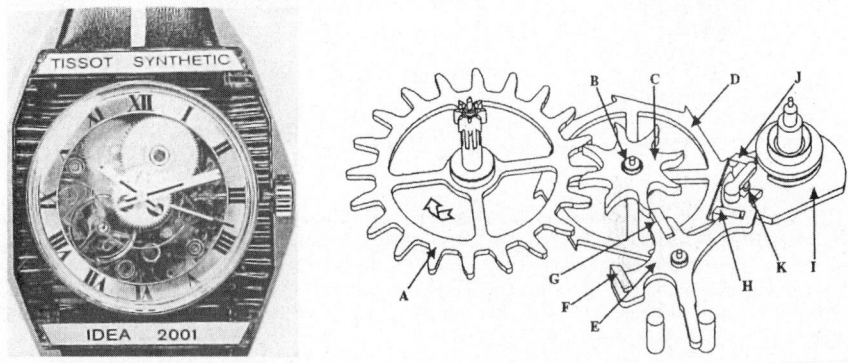

Tissot: idea 2001 Synthetic" 1st watch made of plastic.   Diagram of George Daniels, Co-Axial escapement

1981 Swatch christened their new baby **Swatch**. In August of **1982** ETA supplied 4,000 Swatches in 25 different models, and by March of **1983** launched their campaign to the public. **1986** Citizen is now the number one producer of Quartz type watches replacing Seiko. **1990** Jurghan launches their radio controlled wrist watch which receives a signal from an atomic clock. **2002** a World Time Platinum wrist sold for a record price $4,026,524.00, a RF# 1415 by P. P & Co.

Swatch: Early Design wrist watch by Swatch, Ca. **1982**.

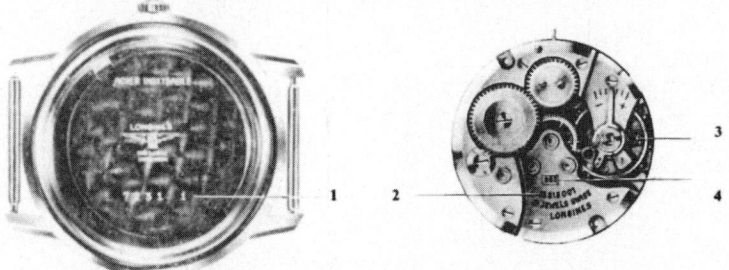

1. Case number.   2. Movement serial number.   3. Caliber number.   4. Caliber number.

NOTE: Some wrist watches have a grade, reference or caliber number engraved on the case, or movement For example, Patek, Phillipe & Co. has a caliber number 27-460Q. The '27' stands for 27mm; the '460Q' is the grade; the 'Q" designates Quantieme (Perpetual calendar and moon phases).

AUTOMATIC WINDING

The self winding watch uses the movements of the body in order to wind up the mainspring slowly and nearly continuously. The first pocket self-winding watches were executed by a watchmaker from Le Locle, Abraham-Louis Perrelet, around 1770.

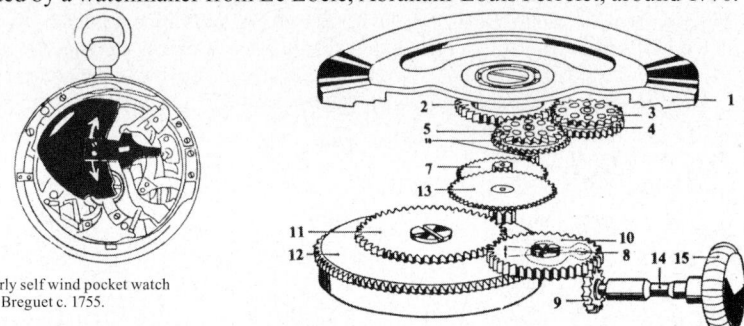

Early self wind pocket watch by Breguet c. 1755.

ETERNA-MATIC automatic winding mechanism with rotor oscillating on *5 ball bearings 1st introduced in 1949.* 1—Oscillating weight. 2.—Oscillating gear. 3.—Upper wheel of auxiliary pawl-wheel. 4.—Lower wheel of auxiliary pawl-wheel. 5. —Pawl-wheel with pinion. 6.—Lower wheel of pawl wheel with pinion. 7.—Transmission-wheel with pinion. 8.—Crown-wheel yoke. 9.—Winding pinion. 10. —Crown-wheel. 11.—Ratchet-wheel. 12. —Barrel. 13. —Driving runner for ratchet-wheel. 14. —winding stem. 15. —Winding button.

They were improved soon after by Abraham-Louis Breguet. In the case of the pocket watch, the movements causing the winding of the watch were essentially the result of walking. This system of winding was never widely adopted. The watch was a fancy model and not a really useful one. Herman von der Heydt was the only maker in America to work with the self winding pocket watch. However, inventors always kept the idea of the self-winding watch in mind.

In 1923, the British firm Harwood took up once again the solution of the problem of automatic winding, for wrist watches. This was the spark which rapidly resulted in research to improve and simplify this type of mechanism. A company was formed in London to manufacture Harwood's watch, and before long over 500 jewelers in the United Kingdom were selling his automatic watch. A second company was formed in France, and a third in the United States. The business flourished about two and one-half years. Then, in 1931, these companies were liquidated.

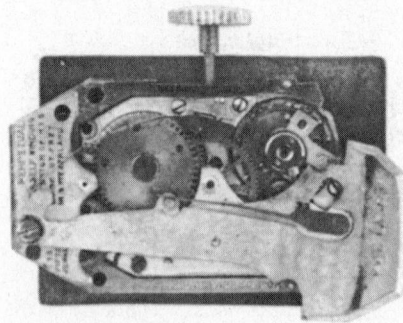

Early self-winding wrist watch by FREY W. Co., Ca. 1930's.
NOTE: The pendulum style weight for self-winding.

Early self-winding wrist watch by AUTORIST W. Co. Ca.1930's. Winding by moving flexible tugs.

CHRONOGRAPH

The term chronograph is derived from the Greek words chronos which means "time" and grapho which means "to write." The first recording of intervals of time was around 1821 by the inventor Rieussec. His chronograph (Time- Writer) made dots of ink on a dial as a measure of time. Around 1862 Adolph Nicole introduced the first chronograph with a hand that returned to zero. The split second chronograph made its appearance around 1879. Today a chronograph can be described as a timepiece that starts at will, stops at will, and can return to zero at will. A mechanical chronograph had a sweep or center second hand that will start, stop, and fly back to zero. The term chronometer should not be confused with chronograph. A chronometer is a timepiece that has superior time keeping qualities at the time it is made. The CHRONOGRAPH **1 button** wrist watch was 1st. advertised in 1910 & a **2 button** CHRONOGRAPH in 1939 by Breitling.

A. Day window. **B.** Split second hand. **C.** Calendar pusher. **D.** Register for seconds. **E.** Calendar pusher. **F.** Date hand. **G.** Register for total hours. **H.** Sweep center second hand. **I.** Month window. **J.** Start/stop pusher. **K.** Register for total minutes. **L.** Return pusher. **M.** Date of month.

TRADE MARK	MANUFACTURER	TRADE MARK	MANUFACTURER
	VALJOUX Now part of the ETA group		LANDERON
	VENUS		FONTAINEMELON

CHRONOGRAPH MECHANISM

NUMBERS & NAMES USED IN THE EBAUCHE BOOK
"TECHNOLOGICAL DICTIONARY OF WATCH PARTS" Ca. 1953

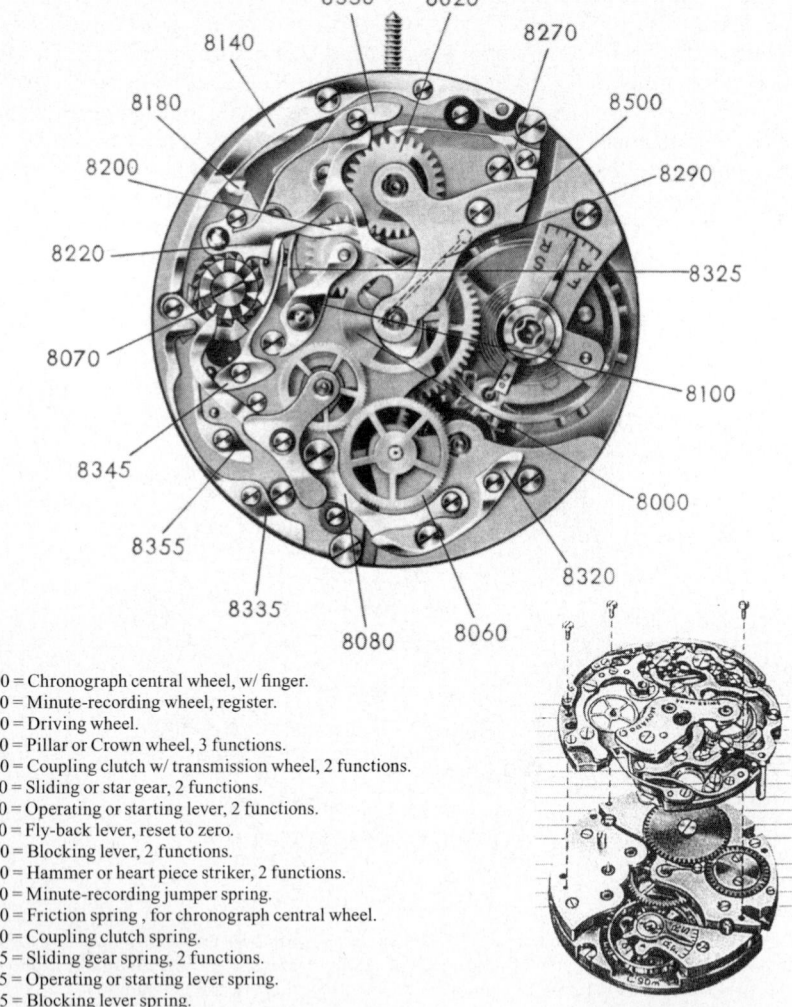

8000 = Chronograph central wheel, w/ finger.
8020 = Minute-recording wheel, register.
8060 = Driving wheel.
8070 = Pillar or Crown wheel, 3 functions.
8080 = Coupling clutch w/ transmission wheel, 2 functions.
8100 = Sliding or star gear, 2 functions.
8140 = Operating or starting lever, 2 functions.
8180 = Fly-back lever, reset to zero.
8200 = Blocking lever, 2 functions.
8220 = Hammer or heart piece striker, 2 functions.
8270 = Minute-recording jumper spring.
8290 = Friction spring , for chronograph central wheel.
8320 = Coupling clutch spring.
8325 = Sliding gear spring, 2 functions.
8335 = Operating or starting lever spring.
8345 = Blocking lever spring.
8350 = Hammer or heartpiece lever spring, 2 functions.
8355 = Pillar or crown wheel jumper or block.
8500 = Chronograph bridge, for center & mm. recording wheels.

ABOVE: Illustration of a
Modular construction or a
chronograph Attachment.

The chronograph is a fitted attachment to a time only watch movement, with a additional function that can be used independently of the time indication. The chronograph ebauche factories who make 80% of the raw chronograph attachments (about 10 ebauche manufacturers), are rarely known by the public. The chronograph modular or attachment are made to be fitted or added to a time only movement. The same is true of repeaters. Companies as Patek Philippe, Audemars Piguet, Rolex and many more are fitted with ebauche chronograph attachments to their <u>own</u> time only movement. Watch Companies as Breitling, Heuer, Eberhard and many more are finished with ebauche chronograph attachments fitted to raw movements made by other wrist-watch ebauche factories.

LEFT: CHRONOGRAPH with 1 push piece & CENTER 2 push pieces. **RIGHT:** CHRONOGRAPH module or attachment

Chronograph with two push pieces:

Action and movement of hands : The pusher No .1 sets the hands in action and second action stops the same hands.

Pusher No. 2 brings the hands back to zero. During their movement this pusher is a fixture, thus preventing the accidental return of the hands to zero. The double pusher chronograph permits an interruption in the reading, the hands are set going again from the position they stopped, thus indispensable for any time lost during a control of any description.

HOW TO READ THE TACHOMETER-TELEMETER DIAL

The **TACHOMETER** may have a spiral scale around center of dial, this indicates miles per hour, based on a trial over one mile. It indicates speeds from 400 to 20 miles per hour on three turns. Each turn of spiral corresponds to one minute (scale for first 8 seconds being omitted), the outer turn from 400 to 60(0 to 1 minute) and the center turn from 30 to 20 miles per hour (2 to 3 minutes).

When passing the first marker of mile zone, start chronograph hand by pressing push piece. When passing following mile marker, press push piece again. The chronograph hand now indicates the speed in miles per hour on the spiral. If a mile has been made in less than one minute the speed will be indicated on outside turn of spiral; from 1 to 2 minutes on middle turn and 2 to 3 minutes on center turn.

EXAMPLE: If a mile has been made in 1 minute and 15 seconds the chronograph hand indicates 48 miles per hour on middle turn of spiral.

The **TELEMETER** scale around margin of dial is based on the speed of sound compared with the speed of light. Each small division is 100 meters. The scale is read in kilometers & hundreds of meters. Approximately 16 divisions equal 1 mile.

To determine the distance of a storm: When you see the flash of lightning press push piece of chronograph. When hearing thunder press again, the chronograph hand will indicate on the Telemeter scale the distance in kilometers and hundreds of meters. One kilometer equals 5/8 of a mile.

NOTE: The chronograph is a fitted attachment to a time only watch movement, with a additional function that can be used independently of the time indication. The chronograph ebauche factories who make 80% of the raw chronograph attachments (about 10 ebauche manufacturers), are rarely known by the public. The chronograph module or attachment are made to be fitted or added to a time only movement. The same is true of repeaters. Companies as Patek Philippe, Rolex, Audemars Piguet and many more are fitted with ebauche chronograph attachments to their <u>own</u> time only movement. Watch Companies as l3reitling, Heuer, Eberhard and many more are finished with ebauche chronograph attachments fitted to raw movements made by other wrist-watch ebauche factories.

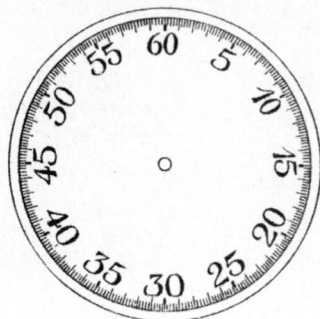

Dial No. 1 is a simple stop watch and chronograph dial. Graduated into fifths of seconds.

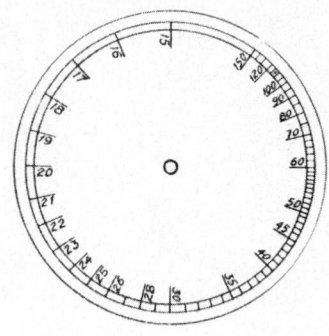

Dial No.2 is used to time a car over a quarter-mile track and read the numbers of miles per hour directly from dial.

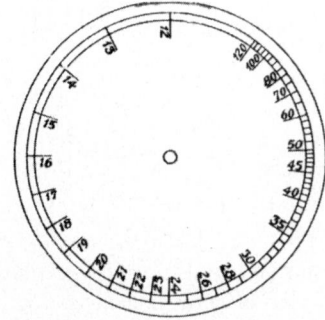

Dial No.3 is used to measure speed in kilometers per hour over a course of one fifth of a kilometer.

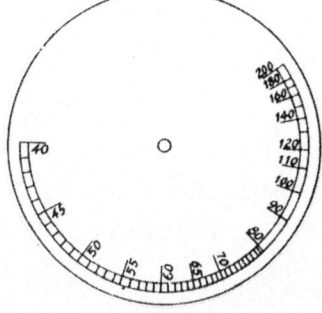

Dial No.4 used by physicians to count the pulse beats of a patient.

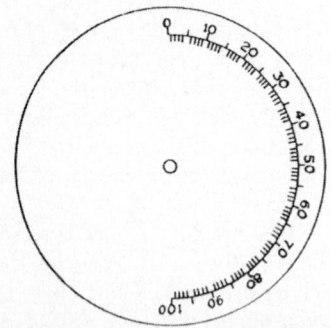

Dial No.5 is used by artillery officers for determining distance by means of sound in kilometers.

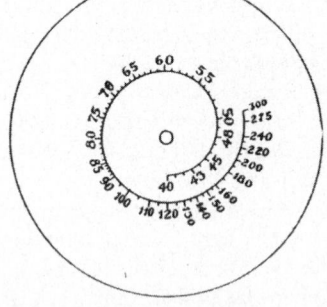

Dial No. 6 shows a tachometer: many watches are made with several scales on the same dial in order to cover a greater range of functions. The figures are sometimes grouped in a spiral form or in several circles, thus the hand may make more than one complete revolution.

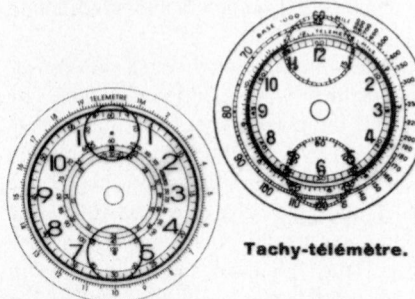

Tachy-télémètre.

Tachy-télémètre.

Tachy-télémètre.

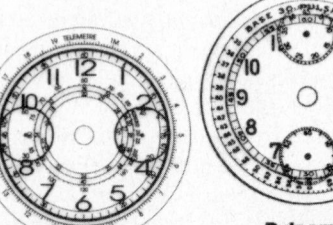

Pulsomètre.

WRIST WATCH CASE AND DIAL STYLES

Barrel

Maxine

Square

Round

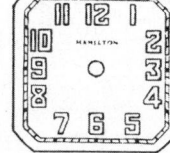

Square Cut Corner

Cushion

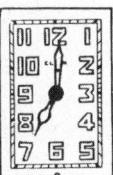

Rectangle

Flared

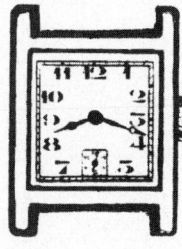

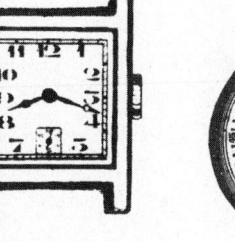

Curved or Curvex

Round
(Ladies style; converts to lapel or wrist)

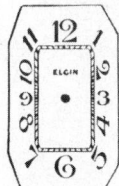

**Rectangle
Cut Corner**

Tonneau

Baguette

Oval

< LEFT
EXAGGERATED
NUMBERS

RIGHT >
ART DECO

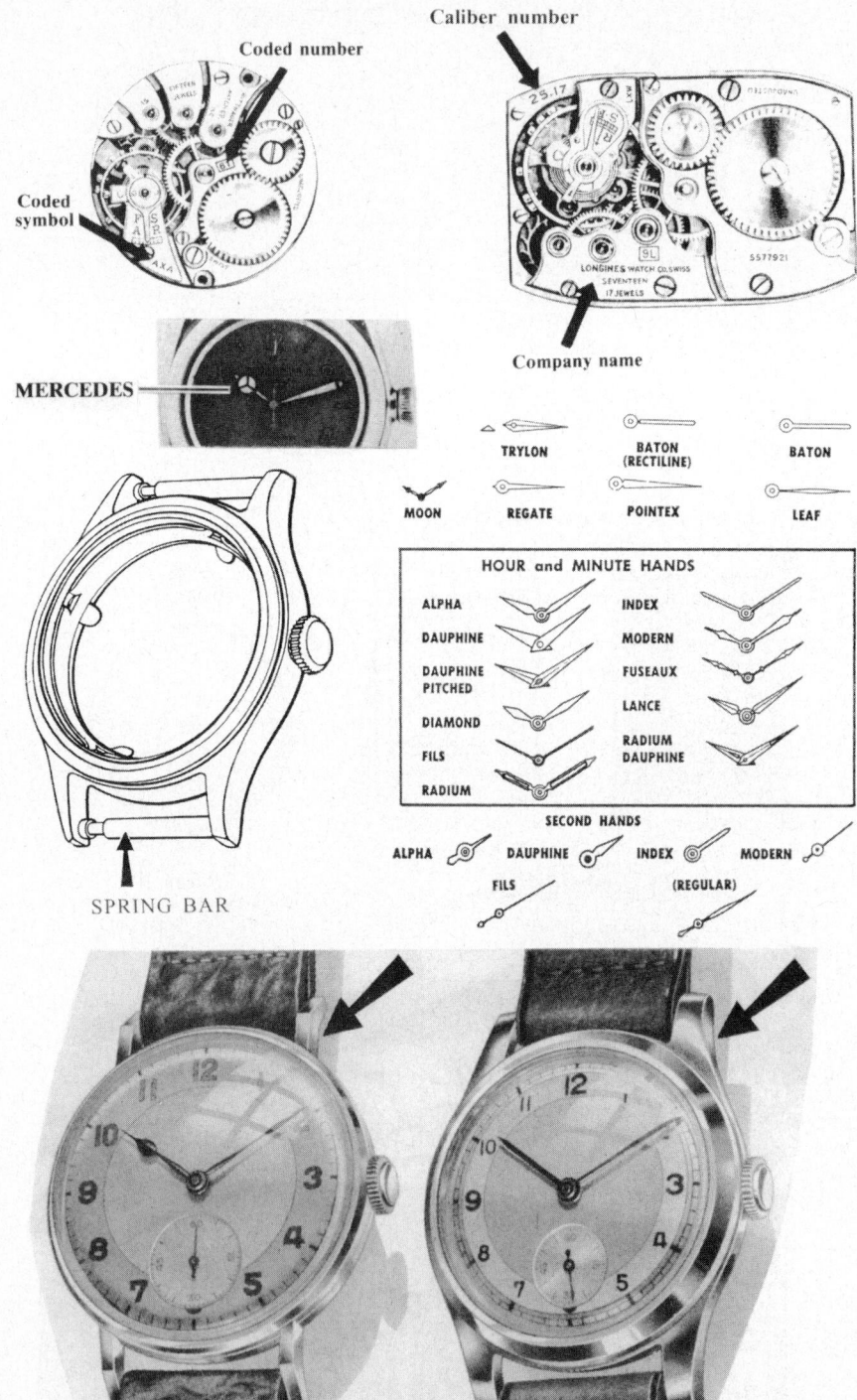

Coded number

Caliber number

Coded symbol

Company name

MERCEDES

TRYLON   BATON (RECTILINE)   BATON

MOON   REGATE   POINTEX   LEAF

HOUR and MINUTE HANDS

ALPHA   INDEX

DAUPHINE   MODERN

DAUPHINE PITCHED   FUSEAUX

DIAMOND   LANCE

FILS   RADIUM DAUPHINE

RADIUM

SECOND HANDS

ALPHA   DAUPHINE   INDEX   MODERN

FILS   (REGULAR)

SPRING BAR

LEFT: Watch has SOLDERED lugs.   **RIGHT:** Watch has SOLID lugs or ONE PIECE lug

SWISS CODE INITIALS

Between the years of 1880 & 1927 over 8,000 trademarks & brand names were registered in Switzerland. Some Swiss watches have three initials on the balance bridge. These initials are not model identification but are for house identification.
Following is a list of import initials with the name of the firm. The Code is found on Balance Cock.

AOC—Roamer
AOG—Ch. Aerni S.A.
AOH—Hamilton
AOL—Adolph Schwarcz & Son
AOX—Alstater W. Co.
AXA—Wittnauer
AXJ—A.R.Je Meylan stopwatch Co.
AXP—Aristo Import Co. Inc.
AXR—Mural W. Co.
AXZ—Benrus
AYP—Audemars Piguet
AZK—Sellita Watch Co.
AZO—AD Allemann & Son Ltd.
BOL—Lemania
BOM—Berman W. Co. Inc.
BOP—Robert Ronnel
BXC—Ball, Avis, Garland
BXD—Leonidas W. Fy.
BXJ—Midland
BXL—Lion
BXN—Benrus
BXP—Imperial, Bayer,
    Pretzfelder & Mills
BXP—Ulysse Nardin
BXU—Eickmann & Co.,
    E.Baumann, Aristo Imports Inc.
BXW—Bulova
BYM—Michael Z. Berger
BZK—Berci Inc.
BZM—J.C.Penny, Towncraft
COC—Crawford
COR—Cornell, Orloff
COW—Croton
COY—Cyma
CXC—Concord
CXD—Cypres
CXH—Avis W. Fy., Clinton
CXJ—Central
CXL—Leonidas W. Fy.
CXM—Clinton, Wolbrook,
    Circle W. Corp.
CXV—Cort
CXW—Central; Benrus
CXY—Croydon
CYW—Chesterfield
CZA—Canoe
DOB—Dreffa W. Co.
DOW—Deauville
DWQ—Langendorf, Lanco
DXO—Minerva
DYR—Den—Ro, Bernard Vuille
EOE—Elrex, Pierpont W. Co.
EOM—EMO W. CO.
EON—Avalon, Calvert
EOP—Harvel, Rensie
EOT—Lavina
EOY—Compass Instrument &
    Optical Co. Inc.
EXA—ETERNA
EXC—Everbrite
EXO—Empire
EXM—Savoy, Milos
EXW—Empire W. Co.
EZR—Enicar
FWR—Amko W. Co.
FXE—Provis
FXF—Fairfax, Rytime
FXN—W. Rouch
FXU—Louis Aisenstein & Bros
    Roamer W. Co..
FXW—Louis
FYG—Eloga W. Co.
FYL—Dreffa W. Co.
GOC—Crawford, Rexton
GOG—Greygor, Hoga
GXC—Gruen, Onsa
GXI—Gotham (Ollendorff)
GXM—Girard—Perregaux
GXR—Crysler, Grant,
    Heyworth W. Co.
GXT—Silvana
GXW—Gothic
GYH—Hilton
GYP—Global W. Co.
GZR—Grensler Lee
HOB—Jackson W.Co. Wakmann
HOM—Homis
HON—A. Hirsch, Tissos,
    Universal Geneve
HOP—Hall
HOR—Lanco; Langendorf
HOU—Oris

HXF—Harman
HXH—Harvel
HXL—Easton
HXM—R. H. Macy & Co.
HXN—Harvel
HXO—Harold K. Oleet
HXL—Easton
HXW—Helbros
HXW—Jos.Boillat fils, Louis
HYL—Hamilton
HYO—Hilton W Co.
HYQ—Hilton
HYW—Harper W.Co.
HZE—Hetega
IXK—Pilgrim Electronic Corp.
JXE—Normandie
JXJ—Alprosa, Jutes Jurgensen
JXL—Sultana W. Co.
JXR—Gallet, Jules Racine Co.
KBH—Endura
KOT—Landau
KXA—Astin W. Co.
KXB—Ernest Borel
KXF—Clebar W,Co. Zodiac
KXJ—Wm. J. Kappel
KXV—Louis
KXZ—Kelton, Benrus, Central
KZX—Rutex,J.Weber, Sellita
LBA—Oilech & Wajs
LOA—Emil Langer, Selza
LOD—Latham
LOE—Delbana, Hydepark,
    Emil Leichter, Packard
LON—Lorna W. Co.
LOT—Lathin
LOV—Levrette, Robbin
LOY—Lathin
LXA—Elbon, Laco, Nassu,
    Tremont, Winton,
LXE—Evkob
LXJ—Jaegar—LeCoultre
LXM—Accro Bond, Accro W.Co.
LXW—Longines
LYE—Aureole
LZF—Joseph Laufer
LZL—Henry Gireaux W. Co.
MOG—Mead & Co.; Boulevard
MOK—Montauk W. Co.
MOU—Buttes W. Co., Delbana,
    Leonidas, Tower
MOV—Marvin
MWS—Lebur Time Co.
MXE—Monarch
MXF—Harman
MXH—Seeland
MXI—Movado
MXT—Mathey—Tissot
MXU—Zimet W. Co.
NGH—Universal Geneve
NJD—Nastrix
NOA—U.Nardin
NOG—Enicar, Kuper W. Co.
NOH—Heyworty, A, Hirsch
NOK—Pilot, Ralco
NOS—Defender, Heritage, Nova
NOU—Louvie W. Co., Vulcain
NXJ—National Jewelers Co.
NXO—Oris
NXS—Popper W. Co.
NYN—Conoseur W. Co.
OWT—Carvelle
OXG—Omega
OXL—Wyler
OXY—Artis
OYM—Cromwell
OYT—Shriro (Sandoz)
POB—General, Helvetia
POF—Alexora, Delaware, Eloga,
    Gorgerat, Grenar, Nuhall,
    Rogers, Rosieres, Sellita
POH—Perfine W. Co.
POX—Lucerne, Wega
PWY—Spera
POY—Camy; Copley
PXA—Pierce
PXP—Patek, Philippe
PXT—Paul Breguette
PXW—Monarch, Parker, Renise
PYC—Pedre
PYS—Langel
PYS—Guyora
QXL—Emerson, Lauret

QXO—Kelbert
QXY—Acme Lyceum
ROC—Raleigh
ROD—Regent
ROH—Calvert
ROL—Ribaux
ROM—Avia,Belvu, Reyco,
    EW. Reynolds Co.
ROP—Rodania
ROP—Zone—x W. Fy.
ROR—Audemars Piguet
ROW—Rolex
RXE—Brenet
RXG—Olympic, Zodiac
RXM—Galmor
RXV—Juvenia
RXW—Parker, Rima
RXY—Liengme
RYW—Ritex
RXZ—Benrus
SOA—Felca
SOE—Semca
SOL—Stuart
SON—Defender
SOW—Seeland, Sussex
SOX—Cortebert
SOX—Orvin, Seas, Serco,
    Seas Roebuck & Co., Tradition
SWU—Alben Semag
SXE—Savoy; Banner
SXK—Cardnial, Rosieres, Royce
SXK—S. Kocher & Co.
SXS—Franco
SXU—Segud W. Co.
TOB—Pronto
TOC—Capt & Co.,E.Schlup—Abrecht
TOH—Banner, Rivera
TXJ—Latham
TXW—Tavannes
TYW—Elgin, Seth Thomas
TYX—Trebex
UOA—Actua
UOB—Aero, Enicar, Heloisa W. Co.
UOR—RADO
UOW—Universal
UWP—Palmer Sales Co.
UXM—Medana, Meyer & Studeli
UXN—Marsh
UXO—Wega
UYW—Stanley W. Co.
VCS—Britix
VOB—Certina
VOS—Eloga, Sheffield Merchandise
VXB—Chase, Hamlin, Louis
VXN—LeCoultre & Co.
VXN—V & C & LeCoultre
VXO—Transit
VXT—Hilton, Kingston
VXX—Libcla
VYE—Benrus
WOA—Tower
WOB—Wyler
WOG—Breitling, Wakmann
WOR—Creston
WXC—Buren, Legant,
    Montgomery Ward
WXE—Welsbro
WXO—Waltham
WXW—Benrus Wadsworth
WXW—Westfield
WYX Continental, Harvester
XOU—Pronto W. Co.
XOV—Alstate, Marcel
XXZ—Kelton
XYG—Westclox
XYH—Alpha
YOA—Perfecta W. Co
YOU—Hallmark
YXD—Crysler, Lucerne
YXV—Hampden
YXY—Elgin
ZBH Mondaine
ZFX—Zenith W.Co.
ZOA—Baylor
ZOB—Belvior, Evans
ZOK—Telda
ZOV—Titus W. Co.
ZXW—Benrus, Watches Inc.
ZYB—Hawthorne W. Co.
ZYV-Hampden (new company)

WATCH CONSOLIDATION

Like many industries consolidation of the major market brands increase vendors market share and higher volume to increase profitability. Many of the famous names of she past are no longer independent, but owned by a larger company. Concentration is bad when boarders between various brands become indistinct; it lessons their unique character. Interesting to note is that Swatch Group owns 90% of movements. Below are some of the conglomerates and a list of the watch brands under their control.

OWNER	BRAND NAME
Artime	Philip Watch Sector No Limits
Audemars, Piguet Bottinelli Families + shareholders	Audemars Piguet Jaeger Le Coultre 40% Renaud, Papi
Chung Nam Group	ISA Roamer
Citizen	Citizen Miyota
Desco	Maurice Lacroix
Diehl family	Junghans
Dixi Paul Castella	Mondia
Egana	Benetton Caravelles Chromachron Dugena 70% Esprit Morellato Pierre Cardin ZenRa
Eterna SA	Eterna Porche Design
Fossil Inc.	Fossil, Diesel, Zodiac DKNY, Relic
Frey family	Minerva
Bvlgari	Bvlgari, Daniel Roth Gerald Genta, Sector
Gerd-R. Lang	Chronoswiss
Sowind SA	Daniel Jean Richard Girard-Perregaux
LVMH (Louis Vuitton, Moet, Hennessy)	Chaumet, Christian Dior Ebel, Fred, Joallier Favre-Leuba Fendi, Givenchy Gucci 20% Tag Heuer Zenith
Maddox AG	Bernini BWC Cerutti
NAWC (North American W. Co.) Renley W. Co.	Concord, Coach Watch ESQ, Movado Le Phare-Jean d' Eve Sultana
Timex Corp.	Humvee, Indigo Ironman, Timex

Poljot Watch Factory of Moscow Russia
Poljot = Flight
ETA (Named after the 7th letter of
the Greek alphabet).

OWNER	BRAND NAME
Richemont Group (Cartier family) Dials by	Alfred Dunhill A. Lange & Sohne Baume & Mercier Cartier IWC (International W. Co.) Jaeger Le Coultre Montblanc, Piaget Officine Panerai Stern Group Vacheron Constantin Van Cleef & Arpels 80% Yves Saint Laurent
SAB (Swiss Army Brands)	St. John Swiss Air Force Swiss Army Watches Victorinox Wenger
Scheufele	Chopard
Schneider Family	Breitling Kelek
Seiko	Alba, Credor Lassale Lorus Pulsar Seiko Spoon
Stern family **P. P. & Co.** **P. P. & Co.**	Patek Philippe Cases by Calame & Cie. Parts by Ergas Sarl
Swatch Group case maker by springs & escapements Hi grade movement watch hands by	Blancpain, Breguet Calvin Kline (CK) Certina, Endura ETA (movements) Favre & Perret Flick Flak Glashutte Original Hamilton, Leon Hatot Jaquet-Droz, Lanco Lemania (movements) Longines, Mido by Nivarox - Far Omega, Pierre Balmain by Frederic Piguet Rado, Record Renata (movements) Swatch Tissot, Union Unitas (movements) Universo Valjoux (movement)
Wilsdorf Foundation	Rolex, Cellini, Tudor

dials by Beyeler & Cie, crowns by Boninchi SA
Bracelets by Gay Freres

BRAND NAME & OWNERS

The table below list the brand name alphabetically and the owner of the company.

Brand Name	Owners
A. Lange & Sohne — Richemont Group	
Alfred Dunhill — Richemont Group (Cartier Family)	
Audemars Piguet — Audemars, Piguet, Bottinelli families, + Shareholders	
Baume & Mercier — Richemont Group (Cartier Family)	
Benetton — Egana	
Bernini — Maddox AG	
Blancpain — Swatch Group	
Bovet — Thierry Oulevay & Roger Guye	
Breguet — Swatch Group	
Breitling — Schneider Family - Kelek	
Bvlgari — Bvlgari Group	
BWC — Maddox AG	
Calvin Kline (CK) — Swatch Group	
Caravelles — Egana	
Cartier — Richemont Group (Cartier Family)	
Certina — Swatch Group	
Cerutti — Maddox AG	
Chaumet — LVMH (Louis Vuitton, Moet, Hennessy)	
Chopard — Scheufele Family	
Christan Dior — LVMH (Louis Vuitton, Moet, Hennessy)	
Chromachron — Egana	
Chronoswiss — Gerd-Rudiger Lang	
Citizen — Miyota	
Concord — NAWC (North American Watch Co.)	
Corum — Jean-Rene Bannwsrt 10% Severin Wundermann 90%	
Daniel Roth — Bvlgari Group	
Dunhill — Richemont Group (Cartier Family)	
Ebel — LVMH (Louis Vuitton, Moet, Hennessy)	
Endura — Swatch Group	
ETA (mvm't) — Swatch Group	
Eterna — Eterna SA	
Favre-Leuba — Benedom SA	
Flik Flak — Swaych Group	
Fortis — Rolf Voght family; Prince Ernst August vas Hannover	
Franck Muller — Franck Muller Group	
Genta — Bvlgari Group	
Girard-Perregaux — Sowind Group SA	
Givenchy — LVMH (Louis Vuitton, Moet, Hennessy)	
Glashutte Original — Swatch Group	
Gucci Watches - Gucci, LVMH, PPR	
Hamilton — Swatch Group	
Hermes — Hermes family	
IWC Schaffhausen — Richemont Group	
Jaeger-LeColture — Richemont Group 60%	
Jaques-Droz — Swatch Group	
Jughans — Diehl family	
Kelek — Schneider family	
Lanco — Swatch Group	
Lassale — Seiko Watch Corp.	
La Phare- Jean d'Eve — Renley Watch Co.	
Lemania (mvm't) — Swatch Group	
Limes — Ickler Gmbh	
Longines — Swatch Group	
Zenta Ra — Egana	

Brand Name	Owners
Lorus — Seiko Watch Corp.	
Marvin — Revue-Thommen	
Maurice Lacroix — Desco von Schulthess, Bodmer family	
Mido — Swatch Group	
Minerva — A. & J.J. Frey	
Miyota — Citizen	
Mondia — Dixi Paul Castella	
Montblanc — Richemont Group (Cartier Family)	
Morellato (49%) — Egana	
Movado — NAWC (North American Watch Co.)	
Muhle Glashutte — Nautische Instrument	
Officine Panerai — Richemont Group (Cartier Family)	
Omega — Swatch Group	
Parmigiani — Parmigiani Fleurier - Sandoz family	
Patek Philippe — Stem family	
Philip Watch — Artime	
Piaget — Richemont Group (Cartier Family)	
Pierre Balmain — Swatch Group	
Pierre Cardin — Egana	
Frederic Piguet (mvm't) — Swatch Group	
Porche Design — Eterna SA	
Pulsar — Seiko Watch Corp.	
Rado — Swatch Group	
Raymond Weil — Seville Watch Corp.	
Renata (mvm't) — Swatch Group	
RGM — Roland Murphy	
Roamer — Chuung Nam Group	
Rolex — Wilsdorf Foundation	
Sector No Limits — Artime	
Speidel — Hitch	
Spoon — Seiko Watch Corp.	
St. John — SAB (Swiss Army Brands)	
Sultana — Renley Watch Co.	
Swatch — Swatch Group	
Swiss Air Force — SAB (Swiss Army Brands)	
Swiss Army Watches — SAB (Swiss Army Brands)	
Tag Heuer — LVMH (Louis Vuitton, Moet, Hennessy)	
Timex — Timex Corp.	
Tissot — Swatch Group	
Tutima — Tutima Uhrenfabik	
Ulysse Nardin — Rolf W. Schnyder	
Union — Swatch Group	
Unitas (mvm't) — Swatch Group	
Universal Geneve — Stelux Holdings	
Vacheron Constantin — Richemont Group (Cartier Family)	
Valjoux (mvm't) — Swatch Group	
Van Cleef & Arpels — Richemont Group 80% (Cartier Family)	
Ventura — Ventura Design on time SA	
Victornox — SAB (Swiss Army Brands)	
Wenger — SAB (Swiss Army Brands)	
Xemex — Xemex Swiss watch	
Yves Saint Laurent — Richemont Group (Cattier Family)	
Zeneth — LVMH (Louis Vuitton Moet, Hennessy)	

Above: October, 1940 AD

WRIST WATCH LISTINGS

COMPLETE WATCHES ONLY

The prices shown in this book are averaged from dealers listings, catalog sales, auction results, trade shows and internet transactions. Each entry is followed by three prices: A, B and C. The three levels represent watches as follows:

A   B   C

A - An approximate dealer buying price, ABP, for a watch which is running and complete.

B - A dealer selling price for a watch, fully restored, good case and dial.

C - A dealer selling price for a mint condition watch, all original.

Variations can take place in the pricing structure due to several factors. The cost of restoration, for example, can be quite high and some lower level watches may not warrant the restoration cost. Also, complicated watches such as repeaters, chronographs, etc., as well as early watches, especially verge and other early escapements, can also be very costly to restore. Therefore, the variations in the A level price and the C level price can vary widely if the restoration costs are excessive. The availability of parts for certain vintage and antique watches is becoming more endangered as every year passes. Some watches are simply not restorable do to this parts dilemma. The ease of sale for certain type of watches will aslo have an effect on pricing at a dealers or wholesale level. Certain watches are simply more in demand and can be sold at a quicker rate to eager collectors. Watches which are slow to sell must be held in inventory; therefore, the A level prices will be lower to offset the inventory holding cost. All watches can bring significantly higher prices when the condition is outstanding. Watches which are in virtually new condition with pristine original dials, original boxes, certificates or bills of sale (especially rare wrist watches) will often bring record price levels above the top indicator listed in this publication.

Many of the watch manufacturers were commissioned to put jewelers' or jobbers' names on their movements in place of their own. Because of this practice, the true manufacturers of these movements are difficult to identify. Between the years 1880 & 1927 over 8,000 trade-mark titles were registered in Switzerland, such as Alpha, Bulova, Camy, Jaeger, Reverso, Submariner, Valjoux, Zodiac, etc. Warning: There are currently fake wrist watches being sold on the worldwide market.

Important Notice. All of the information, including valuations, in this book has been compiled from the most reliable sources, and every effort has been made to eliminate errors and questionable data. Nevertheless, the possibility of error, in a work of such immense scope, always exists. The publisher or authors will not be held responsible for losses which may occur in the purchase, sale, statements of its advertisers, or other transaction of items, because of information contained herein. Readers who feel they have discovered errors are invited to write and inform the publishers, so that they may be corrected in subsequent editions.

᠙᠎ Wrist Watch terminology or communication in this book has evolved over the years, in search of better & more precise language with a effort to improve, purify, adjust itself & make it easier to understand.

DIALS FOR MINT PRICES MUST BE ALL ORIGINAL

ABERCROMBIE & FITCH, 17J., chronog., by valj.,3 reg.
14K $1,100 $1,800 $2,000
s. steel $350 $650 $900

Abercrombie & Fitch, 17J., **Seafarer**, chronog., waterproof
18k. $1,100 $1,800 $2,200
s. steel $400 $750 $1,000

Abercrombie & Fitch, 17J., chronog. by valj.,3 reg., Ca.1950
s. steel $350 $650 $850

ABRA, 17J., step case, c. 1930s
base metal. $40 $80 $115

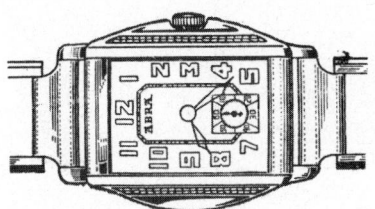

ABRA, 17J., carved ease, c.1930s
base metal. $40 $80 $115

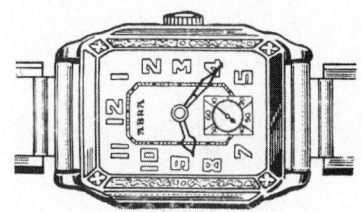

ABRA, 17J., engraved ease
base metal. $40 $80 $115

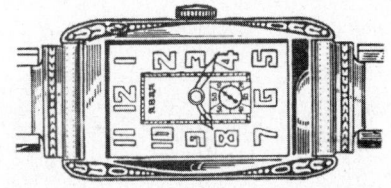

ABRA,15J., curved case, c.1930s
base metal. $50 $95 $130

ABRA, 17J., jump hour
s. steel $150 $350 $400

ACE, 17 jewels, Ca. 1936
gold filled $55 $100 $130

DIALS FOR MINT PRICES MUST BE ALL ORIGINAL

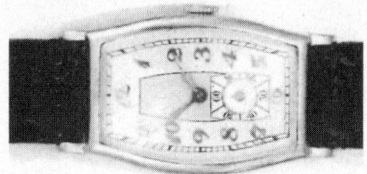

ACRO, W. Co., 17 jewels, **Hinged Back**, Ca. 1930s
18k. $200 $375 $425

ADMES, 17 jewels, self wind, waterproof, center sec.,
14K $125 $225 $325
gold filled $50 $100 $130

AGASSIZ, 17 jewels, **World Time**
18k. . . . . ★$7,000 $13,000 $15,000

AGASSIZ, 17 jewels, fancy bezel,
18k. $400 $700 $850

AGASSIZ, 18 jewels, for Tiffany & Co., 48mm, oversize
18k. $700 $1,300 $1,500

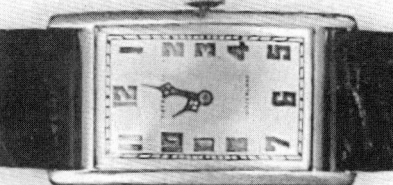

AGASSIZ,173., C. 1940s
18K(W). $375 $750 $900

AGASSIZ, 18 jewels, barrel shaped dial, 40mm,
18k. $250 $475 $600

AGASSIZ, 17 jewels, for Tiffany & Co., 45mm
18k. $700 $1,300 $1,400

ALAVENTE, 7J., "Mystery", **simulated** jewels, ca. 1965
base metal. $75 $150 $200

ALPHA, 17J., chrono. 2 reg., cal.48, c.1950s
14K $400 $750 $900
s. steel $175 $300 $400

ALPINA, 17J, autowind, c. 1950s
18K $150 $265 $350

ALPINA, 17 jewels, automatic, Ca. 1950
18k. $175 $300 $400

ALPINA, 17 jewels, automatic, Ca. 1950
14K $175 $300 $400

ALPINA, 17J., chronograph, ca. 1940
14k. $275 $500 $600

ALPINA, 17 jewels, automatic, water proof, aux. sec.
18k. $200 $375 $500

ALSTA, 17 J, chronograph, **3 reg**.
14k. $350 $625 $750
base metal $150 $300 $500

ALSTA, 17 jewels, wrist alarm
gold filled $150 $200 $250

ALTERNO, 15J., **Reverso**, Ca. 1935
s. steel $500 $900 $1,200

ALTUS, 17 jewels, ref.827
18k. $185 $325 $400

AM. WALTHAM, 21J.,"Adair', ca.1941
gold filled $60 $100 $160

AM. WALTHAM, 21J., "Albright", ca.1940
14k. $125 $250 $325

AM. WALTHAM, 17J., "Allen', ca.1940
gold filled $60 $100 $150

AM. WALTHAM, 21J., "Bonus", sold for $75.00 in 1937
case signed "**Schwob & Wuischpard**" 14K gold
14K $150 $250 $325

AM. WALTHAM, 21J., "Boxford", gold numbers, ca.1941
18k yellow. $200 $400 $450
18Kred $225 $400 $500

AM. WALTHAM, 17J., "Braintree", Side Wrist, ca.1940
gold filled $85 $150 $225

AM. WALTHAM, 21J., "Cadet", sold for $77.50 in 1937
14K $135 $250 $300

AM. WALTHAM, 17J., "Camden", ca.1941
gold plate.. . . . . $70 $125 $200

AM. WALTHAM, 21J , "Campton", note waterproof case,
Bezel, c. 1940, 14k. $225 $450 $550

AM. WALTHAM, 17J., "Canton", gold numbers, ca.1941
gold filled.. . . . . $60 $100 $150

AM. WALTHAM, 10J., "Chandler", sweep sec., ca.1941
gold plate $45 $80 $100

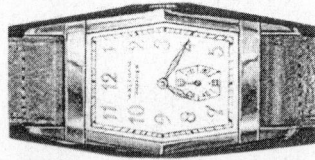

AM. WALTHAM, 17J, "Charlton",ca.1940
gold plate $75 $125 $150

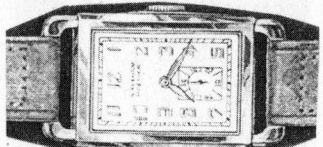

AM. WALTHAM, 9J, "Conway",ca.1941
gold plate $75 $125 $150

AM. WALTHAM, 17J., "Creston", ca.1941
gold filled $80 $150 $200

AM. WALTHAM, 17J., "Cronwell", ca.1940
gold filled $80 $150 $175

AM WALTHAM, 17J, "Danbury", coin edge, ca 1941
gold filled $65 $100 $175

AM. WALTHAM, 17J., "Dighton", thin model, ca.1941
gold filled yellow or red $80 $100 $175

AM. WALTHAM, 9J., "Duxbury",ca.1941
gold plate $50 $100 $140

AM. WALTHAM, 17J., "Escort", sold for $47.50 in1937
gold filled $75 $125 $165

AM. WALTHAM, 17J., "Fairmont", ca.1940
gold filled $80 $150 $200

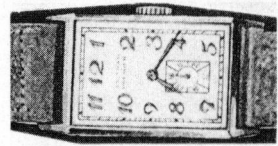

AM. WALTHAM, 17J., "Fremont", gold numbers, ca.1941
14 k $155 $275 $400

AM. WALTHAM, 21J., "Gardner", gold numbers, ca.1940
gold filled $90 $150 $200

AM. WALTHAM, 17J., "Goodwin", ca.1941
gold filled $90 $150 $200

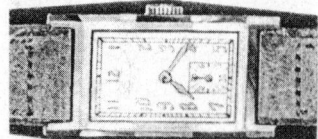

AM. WALTHAM, 17J., "Granby", gold numbers, ca. 1941
14k. $150 $300 $400

AM. WALTHAM 17J., "Heath", ca. 1941
gold filled $90 $150 $200

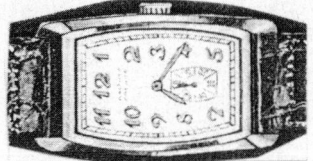

AM. WALTHAM 21J.," "Hingham", gold numbers, ca. 1941
14k. $175 $350 $450

AM. **WALTHAM**, 17J., "Hollis", applied numbers, ca.1941
14k. $150 $350 $400

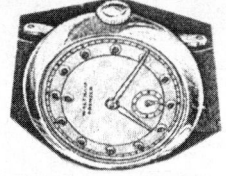

AM. **WALTHAM**, 21J., "Hubbard", 13 rubies
or sapphires set in gold on dial, ca.1941
14k yellow. $175 $300 $450
14k red $200 $350 $500

AM. **WALTHAM**, 17J., "Jeffery", ca.1941
gold filled $100 $175 $225

AM. **WALTHAM, 17J., "Lebanon", ca.1941**
gold filled $100 $175 $225

AM. **WALTHAM**, 17J., "Mendon", ca.1941
gold filled $100 $175 $225

AM. **WALTHAM**, 17J,"Norton", ca.1941
gold filled $100 $175 $225

AM. **WALTHAM**, 17J, "Oberlin", ca 1941
gold filled $80 $150 $200

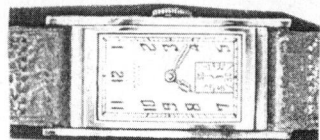

AM. **WALTHAM**, 17J., "Pacer", Sec. hand, ca1941
gold filled $80 $150 $200

AM. **WALTHAM**, 21J., "Pacer", no sec. hand, ca 1937
case signed "**Schwob & Wuischpard**" 14 k gold
14K $150 $275 $350

AM. **WALTHAM**, 21J., "Paddock", sold for $75.00 in 1937
14K $175 $300 $375

AM. **WALTHAM**, 17J., "Patriot", sold for $45 in 1937
gold filled $80 $150 $200

AM. **WALTHAM**, 17J.,"Patten", hidden lugs, ca.1941
14k yellow. $175 $300 $375
14K red $225 $350 $400

AM. **WALTHAM**, 17J.,"Paxton", ca.1941
gold plate $75 $125 $150

AM. WALTHAM, 17J,"Peabody", ca.1941
gold plate $75 $130 $155

AM. WALTHAM, 17J., "Penton", ca.1941
gold filled $80 $150 $200

AM. WALTHAM, 17J., "Preston", ca.1941
gold filled yellow $90 $150 $200
gold filled red $100 $175 $250

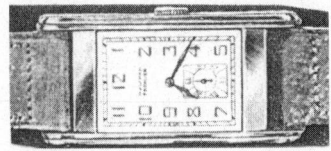

AM. WALTHAM, 17J., "Quincy", ca. 1941
gold filled $80 $150 $200

AM. WALTHAM, 17J., "Reading", ca.1941
gold filled $80 $150 $200

AM. WALTHAM 17J "Regal" ca.1941
gold plate $95 $165 $200

AM. WALTHAM, 17J., "Reward", sold for $70.00 in 1937
14k. $175 $300 $375

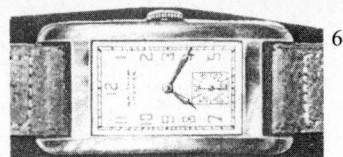

AM. WALTHAM, 17J,"Richford", ca.1941
gold filled $80 $150 $200

AM. WALTHAM, 17J., "Rowe", ca.1941
gold filled $75 $125 $175

AM. WALTHAM,21J.,'Sheraton", ca.1941
14k. $135 $200 $275

AM. WALTHAM, 17J.,"Side-wrist", ca.1941
gold filled.. . . . . $125 $250 $300

AM. WALTHAM, 17J., "Stan Hope", ca.1941
gold filled $80 $150 $200

AM. WALTHAM 9-17J "Submarine" ca.1941
gold filled=17J $65 $130 $165
Chrome=9J. $35 $70 $80

AM. WALTHAM, 17J., "Swagger", sold for $45.00 in 1937
gold filled $65 $110 $160

AM WALTHAM, 17J , "Townsend", ca.1941
gold plate yellow $95 $130 $165
gold plate red $100 $165 $200

AM. WALTHAM, 21J., "Traveler", ca.1941
gold filled $80 $150 $200

AM. WALTHAM, 17J., "Tulane", ca.1941
gold filled $80 $150 $200

AM. WALTHAM, 18J., "Upton", ca.1941
gold filled $80 $150 $200

AM. WALTHAM, 18J., "Upton", **pulse computing dial**
gold filled $125 $225 $275

AM. WALTHAM, 21J.,"Wachusett", gold numbers, ca.1941
gold filled $80 $150 $200

AM. WALTHAM, 17J., "Wesley ", ca.1941
gold plate red $95 $155 $175

AM. WALTHAM, 17J., "Windfield", ca.1941
gold filled $100 $165 $200

AM. WALTHAM, 9J., "Wollaston", ca. 1941
gold plate yellow or red $90 $150 $190

AM. WALTHAM 21J., "Woodland" gold numbers ca. 1941
14k. $200 $325 $375

AM. WALTHAM,17J.,"Wyman",ca.1941
gold filled $90 $150 $200

AM. WALTHAM, 7-15J., "Generic" , ca.1929
gold filled $80 $150 $200

AM. WALTHAM, 7-15J., "Generic", ca.1929
gold filled $80 $150 $200

AM. WALTHAM, 7-15J.,"Generic", ca.1929
gold filled $80 $150 $175

AM. WALTHAM, 7-15J., "Generic", ca.1929
gold filled $65 $150 $190

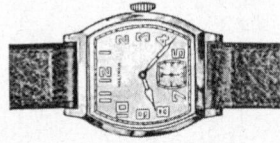

AM. WALTHAM, 7-15J.,"Generic", ca.1929
gold filled $65 $150 $190

AM. WALTHAM, 7-15J.,"Generic", ca.1929
gold filled $65 $100 $160

AM. WALTHAM, 15J.,"Harley-Davidson, c.1935
gold filled $100 $175 $225

AM. WALTHAM, 17J., curved, Ca.1930s
14k. $175 $350 $450

AM. WALTHAM, 17J., Driver style, Ca. 1935
gold filled $95 $150 $175

AM. WALTHAM, 21J., cal.750B, GJS, c.1950s
14k. $175 $300 $375

AM. WALTHAM, 17J., cal.750B, c.1951
gold filled $90 $150 $200

AM. WALTHAM, 15J., "Masonic" model, c.1925
14k(original dial) $200 $450 $600

AM. WALTHAM, 15-17J, solid lugs, c.1920s
sterling silver $175 $225 $300

AM. WALTHAM, 15-17J, 'Ruby' enamel dial, c 1920s
gold filled $125 $250 $300

AM. WALTHAM, 17 J, barrel shaped dial, c. 1920
14k. $175 $300 $350

AM. WALTHAM, 17 J, Premier, diamond dial, Ca 1938
14K (rose) $450 $800 $1,000

AM. WALTHAM, 15J.,enamel dial ,wire lugs, Ca. 1915
silver $150 $300 $350

AM. WALTHAM, 19J, **enamel dial**, C. 1905
silver $175 $325 $375

AM. WALTHAM ,17 jewels, **enamel dial** , wire lugs
14k. $275 $600 $800

AM. WALTHAM, 21J, stepped case, curved back
14k. $175 $350 $425

AM. WALTHAM, 7-15 jewels, **wandering sec.**, C. 1930
gold filled $125 $250 $300

AM WALTHAM, 17 jewels, **wandering sec.**, c. 1930
Gold filled $175 $275 $400

AM. WALTHAM, 17J., **enamel dial**, for Tiffany & Co
14k. $200 $400 $500

AM. WALTHAM, wandering min, **jumping hour.**, c. 1933
gold filled $450 $700 $1,000

AM. WALTHAM, 17J., center sec.
gold filled $45 $80 $150

AM. WALTHAM, 17 jewels, center sec.
gold filled $45 $80 $150

AM. WALTHAM, 15jewels, **winds at 12**, wire lugs, c. 1916
silver & enamel dial $200 $450 $550

AM. WALTHAM, 15 J., case by **Rolland Fischer**
silver $350 $600 $800

AM. WALTHAM, 15J., enamel dial, center lugs, c.1915
silver $175 $350 $500

AM. WALTHAM, 17J., **multi-color enamel dial**, c. 1910s
gold filled $100 $200 $325

AM. WALTHAM, 15J, **multi-color enamel dial**, Ca. 1920
silver $150 $300 $400

AM. WALTHAM, 7-15J., **pulsations**, solid lugs, c.1925
silver $225 $400 $525

AM WALTHAM, 17J.,"Riverside", GJS, c.1918
silver $300 $650 $800

AM. WALTHAM, 15 jewels, c. 1930
gold filled $45 $90 $150

AM. WALTHAM, 7J., **oxidized bezel**, c.1930s
gold filled $100 $175 $225

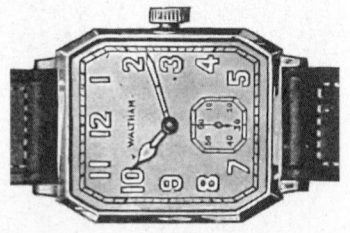

AM. WALTHAM, 7-15J., **cut corner dial**, c.1930s
gold filled $75 $150 $200

AM. WALTHAM, 15 jewels,
gold filled $60 $100 $150

AM. WALTHAM, 15J., **engraved oxidized bezel**, c.1930s
gold filled $60 $150 $200

AM. WALTHAM, 15J.,engraved case
gold filled $60 $150 $200

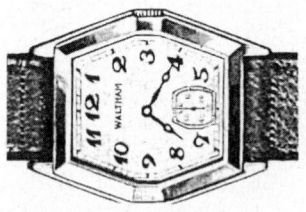

AM. WALTHAM, 17 jewels, 18K applied #s
silver $150 $275 $300

AM. WALTHAM, 7-15 jewels, engraved case
gold filled $60 $150 $200

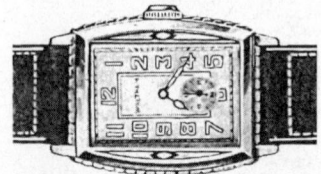

AM. WALTHAM, 7-15jewels,carved case
gold filled $60 $100 $150

AM. WALTHAM, 15 jewels, **curved back**
14k. $175 $350 $400

AM. WALTHAM, 7-15 jewels, engraved case
gold filled $60 $100 $150

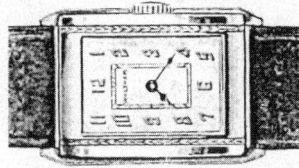

AM. WALTHAM, 17 jewels, **18K applied #s**
14k white $200 $350 $400

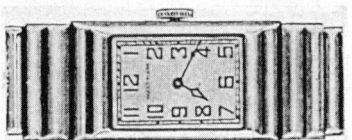

AM. WALTHAM, 15-17 jewels,
gold filled $60 $100 $150

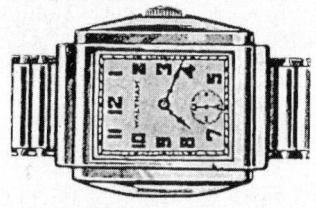

AM. WALTHAM, 7-15 jewels,
gold filled $60 $90 $125

AM. WALTHAM, 15J., case by Rolland Fischer,
silver....................... $400 $700 $950

AM. WALTHAM, 15 jewels, 'Depollier," **early water
proof, (Canteen style),** c. 1917
silver....................... $350 $700 $1,000

AM. WALTHAM, 15 jewels, protective grill, c. 1907
gold filled $200 $350 $435
14k....................... $500 $900 $1,200

AM. WALTHAM, 15 jewels, protective grill, c. 1907
silver....................... $200 $450 $600

AM. WALTHAM, 17 jewels, military with **hack setting**
s. steel....................... $85 $150 $200

AM. WALTHAM, 9J., luminous dial, military, Ca. 1943
s. steel $85 $140 $175

AM. WALTHAM, 17 jewels, WINDS at 12, wire lugs
gold filled $150 $300 $350

AM. WALTHAM, 17 jewels, center lugs
14k..................... $175 $350 $400

AM. WALTHAM, 17   jewels, curvex, 42mm
14k......................... $350 $600 $700

AM. WALTHAM, 17 jewels, curvex, 52mm
14k......................... $600 $1,000 $1,400

AM. WALTHAM, 17 jewels, curvex, 42mm
gold filled $75 $140 $175

AM. WALTHAM, 15 jewels, enamel bezel, Ca. 1927
14K(W)..................... $550 $1,100 $1,400

AM. WALTHAM, 17 jewels, curved, aux. sec.
gold filled $60 $125 $150

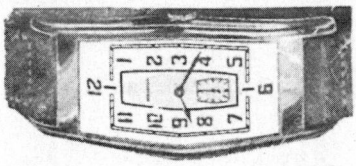

AM WALTHAM, 17 jewels, curved
gold filled $100 $175 $200

AM. WALTHAM, 21 jewels, C.1938
14K $150 $325 $450

AM. WALTHAM, 17 jewels, curved
gold filled $100 $175 $200

AM. WALTHAM, 17 jewels, curved
gold filled $60 $100 $150

AM. WALTHAM, 15J., note bow swings, screw back case,
solid lugs, enamel dial, early water proof, c. 1920s
14K .... ★★★★★$1,000 $2,000 $2,850

AM. WALTHAM, 17 jewels, enamel bezel
14k. $500 $1,000 $1,400
14k(w). $500 $1,000 $1,400
gold filled $225 $400 $550

AM. WALTHAM,21J., enamel bezel, "Ruby" model, c. 1928
14k(w). $350 $600 $800

AM. WALTHAM, 7J., enamel bezel, Ca. 1920
Nickel $125 $250 $350

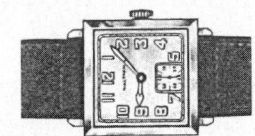

AM. WALTHAM, 15 jewels, square, 1929
gold filled $50 $90 $150

AM. WALTHAM, 7-15jewels, cut corner, ca. 1929
gold filled $100 $175 $250

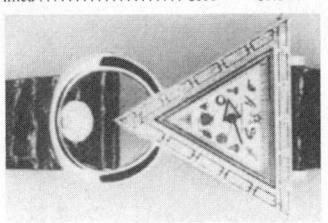

AM. WALTHAM, 17J., triangular, masonic symbols
fancy hands, mother of pearl dial, Ca. 1950
gold filled $600 $1,100 $1,400

AM. WALTHAM, 7-15J., luminous dial, c.1928
base metal. $50 $100 $125

AM. WALTHAM, 7-15J., cushion case, c.1928
gold filled $60 $100 $150

AM WALTHAM, 7-15J., tonneau case, c. 1928
gold filled $60 $100 $150

AM. WALTHAM, 7J., luminous dial, c.1928
base metal. $50 $100 $125

AM. WALTHAM, 7J., **radial**, luminous, c. 1928
gold filled $60 $100 $150

AM. WALTHAM, 17J., luminous dial, c.1929
gold filled $60 $100 $150
14k(w). $150 $300 $375

AM. WALTHAM, 17J., aux. sec., c. 1928
14k(w). $125 $250 $300

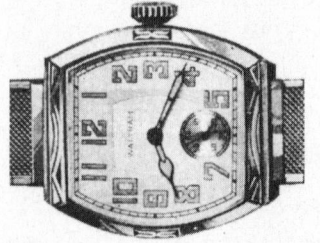

AM. WALTHAM,7-15J., **lugless case**, c.1928
gold filled $60 $100 $150

AM. WALTHAM, 15J., generic, luminous dial, c.1928
14k. $200 $400 $500

AM. WALTHAM,15J., generic style brush finish, c.1928
14k. $200 $400 $450

AM. WALTHAM,7J., luminous dial, c.1928
gold plate $60 $100 $150

AM. WALTHAM,17J.,GJS, ca. 1940
14K $125 $300 $400

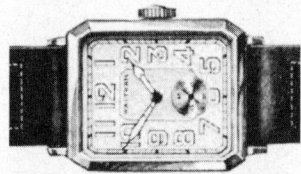

AM. WALTHAM,7-15J., cut corner case, c. 1929
gold filled.. $60 $100 $150

AM. WALTHAM, 15J., **fluted case for men**, GJS, c.1925
14k(w)+enamel. $225 $425 $500

AM. WALTHAM,7-15J., **Butler finish** = (smooth), c.1928
gold filled . . . . $60   . $150 $200

AM. WALTHAM, 7-15J., GJS, Ca. 1927
14K(w) $150 $300 $350

AM. WALTHAM,7-15J., **engraved case, etched dial**, c.1929
14k(w). $50 $100 $125
gold filled $20 $40 $70

AM. WALTHAM, 15J., engraved case, etched dial, c.1928
14K(W) $65 $125 $175
gold filled $20 $40 $65

AM. WALTHAM,7-15J., enamel case, c.1928
14k(w). $100 $175 $200

AM. WALTHAM,15J., enamel case, c.1929
gold filled (w) $75 $100 $125

AM. WALTHAM,15-17J., **enamel bezel**, c.1929
14K (Y). $550 $900 $1,200
14K (W) $500 $900 $1,200

AM. WALTHAM,15-17J., enamel decoration on case, c.1929
14K $70 $125 $150

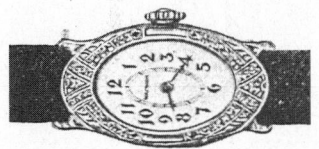

AM. WALTHAM,15-17J., c.1929
14K $60 $125 $150

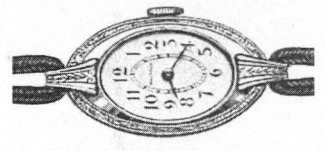

AM. WALTHAM,15-17J., 6 1/2 Ligne, c.1929
14K $60 $125 $150

AM. WALTHAM,15-17J., 6 1/2 Ligne, c.1929
14K $60 $100 $150

AM. WALTHAM,15J., 6 1/2 Ligne, c.1929
gold filled $40 $65 $50

AMERICAN WALTHAM WATCH CO. IDENTIFICATION BY MOVEMENT

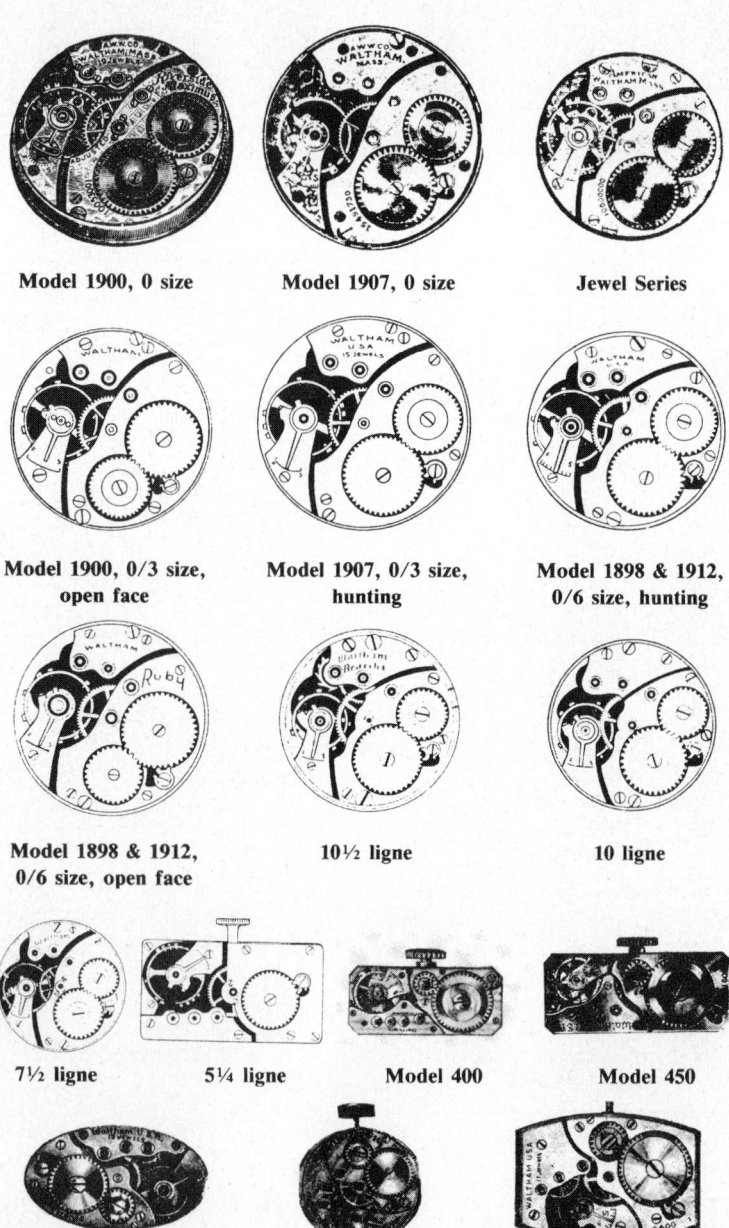

| Model 1900, 0 size | Model 1907, 0 size | Jewel Series |

| Model 1900, 0/3 size, open face | Model 1907, 0/3 size, hunting | Model 1898 & 1912, 0/6 size, hunting |

| Model 1898 & 1912, 0/6 size, open face | 10½ ligne | 10 ligne |

| 7½ ligne | 5¼ ligne | Model 400 | Model 450 |

| Model 650 | Model 675 | Model 750 |

AMERICUS, 17 jewels, **"8 day"** movement, c. 1933

18k.	★★★★ $700	$1,200	$1,500
gold filled	★★ $200	$400	$500
s. steel	★★ $200	$400	$500

ANGELUS, 17J., day, date, moon ph., C. 1949

s. steel	$375	$625	$750

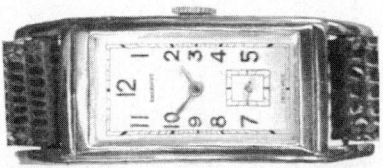

AMERICUS, 7 jewels, curved, c.1935

gold filled	$75	$150	$200

ANGELUS, 17 jewels, chronograph, 2 reg., water proof

14k.	$500	$900	$1,100
18k.	$600	$1,000	$1,400
s. steel	$400	$700	$850

ANGELUS, 17 jewels, chronograph, 2 reg., c. 1943

18k.	$500	$800	$1,200
14k.	$400	$700	$1,100
gold filled	$200	$400	$550

ANGELUS, 17J., **date and alarm**, c.1955

s. steel	$150	$300	$400

ANGELUS, 17J., chronograph, **triple date**, C. 1949

s. steel	$600	$1,000	$1,450
14k.	$900	$1,400	$2,000
18k.	$1,200	$2,000	$2,500

ANGELUS, 27 jewels, **1/4 hour repeater**

s. steel	$1,700	$3,250	$4,000

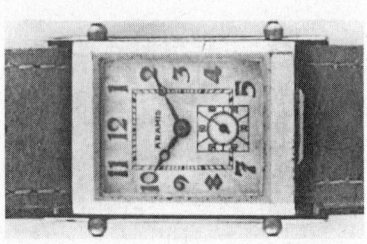

ARAMIS, 15 jewels, early **self wind, lug action winding by back & forth motion of watch case**, c. 1933
s. steel . . . . ★★$400 $800 $1,200

ARBU, 17 jewels, triple date, **moon phase**
18k. $700 $1,350 $1,500
s. steel $250 $475 $600

ARBU, 17 jewels, chronograph, 3 reg., day-date-month
18k. $600 $1,000 $1,200
s. steel $400 $700 $850

ARBU, 17 jewels, **split second chronograph**
18k. $2,500 $4,500 $5,500

ARCTOS, 17J., **"PARAT"**, world map on dial, c.1955
base metal $100 $200 $275

ARDATH, 17J., chronograph, triple date, c.1947
s. steel $300 $550 $600

ARISTO, 17 jewels, chronog., water proof
14k. $300 $600 $750
s. steel $200 $350 $450

ARISTO, 171., chronog., 3 reg., **triple date, moonphase**
14k. $800 $1,600 $2,100
s. steel $400 $750 $1,000

ARISTO, 17 jewels, day-date-month, **moon phase**
s. steel $300 $550 $700

ARSA, 17 jewels, chronog., day-date-month, Ca. 1950
18k. $600 $1,200 $1,600

ARSA, 17 jewels, **day-date-month, moon phase**
18k. $700 $1,250 $1,500
s. steel $275 $425 $550

ARSA, 15 jewels, day-date-month, **moon phase**
18k. $500 $1,000 $1,500
s. steel $250 $450 $550

ASPREY, 16 jewels, curved hinged back
9k $150 $275 $380

ASPREY, 17J., **date**, ca. 1930s
14k. $300 $575 $675
gold filled $175 $300 $350

ASPREY, 15 jewels, **duo dial**
18k. $750 $1,300 $1,700

ASPREY, 17 jewels, **enamel dial, center lugs**
9k $200 $375 $425

AUDAX, 15J., Ca.1938
9k $95 $175 $200

☞ Some grades are not included. Their values can be determined by comparing with similar age, size, metal content, style, grades, or models such as time only, chronograph, repeater etc. listed.

AUDEMARS PIGUET PRODUCTION TOTALS

Date-	Serial #	Date-	Serial #	Date-	Serial #	Date-	Serial #	Date-	Serial #
1882 -	2,000	1905 -	9,500	1925 -	33,000	1945 -	48,000	1965 -	90,000
1890 -	4,000	1910 -	13,000	1930 -	40,000	1950 -	55,000	1970 -	115,000
1895 -	5,350	1915 -	17,000	1935 -	42,000	1955 -	65,000	1975 -	160,000
1900 -	6,500	1920 -	25,000	1940 -	44,000	1960 -	75,000	1980 -	225,000

AUDEMARS PIGUET, 33J., minute repeater, gold train, platinum & 18K with 40 diamond bezel, diamond dial & diamonds on band
18K & platinum $50,000 $95,000 $125,000

AUDEMARS PIGUET, Royal Oak Offshore, auto wind, Chronograph, 10 atmospheres
s. steel $3,250 $6,000 $8,000

AUDEMARS PIGUET, 29 J., **minute repeater**, c. 1917
18k. $40,000 $75,000 $90,000

AUDEMARS PIGUET, 33J., day date, moon ph., c.1989
18k. $1,700 $3,000 $3,500

AUDEMARS PIGUET, 29 J., **minute repeater**, c. 1925
platinum $50,000 $90,000 $120,000

AUDEMARS PIGUET, day dale, moon ph., C. 1980s
18k. $1,500 $2,750 $3,000

AUDEMARS PIGUET, 19 3., **tourbillon**, self-winding tourbillon can be seen from dial side
18k. $8,000 $13,000 $19,000
Platinum $9,000 $15,000 $22,000

AUDEMARS PIGUET, chronograph, triple date, moon ph.,
tear drop lugs, c. 1940s
18k.........................$15,000 $30,000 $25,000

AUDEMARS PIGUET, 18 J., triple date, moonphase
18k.........................$4,000 $8,000 $12,000

AUDEMARS PIGUET, 36 jewels, gold rotor, day-date
month, moon phase, perpetual, c. 1980s
18 k C&B $5,000 $8,000 $10,000

AUDEMARS PIGUET, skeletonized, triple date, moon
phase, perpetual , c. 1980a
platinum $11,000 $18,000 $24,000
18k.........................$9,000 $14,000 $20,000

AUDEMARS PIGUET, 17J., chronog., 3 reg., c. 1945
s. steel $8,000   14,000 $18,000
18k.........................$16,000 $22,500 $30,000

AUDEMARS PIGUET, 18J., "Le Brassus," chronng. Skeletonized
18k C&B...................$7,000 $10,000 $15,000

AUDEMARS PIGUET, 22 jewels, chronog., 2 reg.,
s. steel $4,000 $8,000 $11,000
18k.........................$8,000 $15,000 $18,000

AUDEMARS PIGUET, 18 jewels, skeletonized
18k.........................$2,500 $4,000 $5,500

AUDEMARS PIGUET, **Star Wheel,** showing the pausing of time on Sapphire discs bearing the hours and moving over a concentric circular aperture showing the minutes
18k. $3,000 $6,000 $8,000

AUDEMARS PIGUET, 12 diamond dial c. 1960
platinum $1,500 $2,500 $3,000

AUDEMARS PIGUET, 11 diamond dial
18k. $1,200 $2,500 $3,000

AUDEMARS PIGUET, 36 jewels, skeletonized
18k. $4,000 $7,000 $9,000

AUDEMARS PIGUET, 12 sapphire dial, c.1950
18k. $1,800 $3,000 $3,500

AUDEMARS PIGUET, 17 J., center lugs, skeletonized
18k. $3,000 $6,000 $7,000

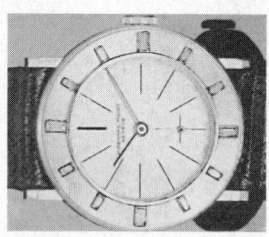

AUDEMARS PIGUET, 17 jewels, 12 diamond bezel
18k (w) $2,000 $3,250 $4,000

AUDEMARS PIGUET, 17J., Dodecagonal, black dial
18k. $1,000 $2,250 $1,700

AUDEMARS PIGUET, 36 jewels, self-winding
18k. $1,500 $2,500 $3,000

AUDEMARS PIGUET, 17J., diamond dial, c. 1970
18k. $1,000 $1,600 $2,000

AUDEMARS PIGUET, 17 jewels, adj. to 5 positions
18k C&B $1,500 $2,500 $3,000

AUDEMARS PIGUET, **fancy shaped**, c.1960s
18k $3,000 $5,000 $6,000

AUDEMARS PIGUET, 17 jewels, rope style bezel
18k C&B $1,500 $2,500 $2,800

AUDEMARS PIGUET, 36 jewels, self-winding
18k $1,000 $1,700 $2,200

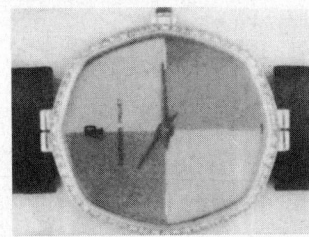

AUDEMARS PIGUET, 17J., diamond bezel, center lugs
18k $1,500 $2,500 $3,000

AUDEMARS PIGUET, 36 jewels, lazuli dial
18k C&B $1,500 $2,500 $3,000

AUDEMARS PIGUET, 20J., rope style bezel, c. 1980s
18k case, 14k band $1,000 $1,500 $1,900

AUDEMARS PIGUET, 17 jewels, thin style
18k C&B $1,600 $2,300 $3,000

AUDEMARS PIGUET, 20J., "Le Brassus", Ca. 1970
18k C&B $1,500 $2,500 $3,000

AUDEMARS PIGUET, 17J RF# 8326, fancy bezel, c. 1950
18k $1,400 $2,800 $3,500

DIALS FOR MINT PRICES MUST BE ALL **ORIGINAL**.

AUDEMARS PIGUET, 17J., "Philosopher", hour hand only
18k. $1,600 $3,000 $3,800

AUDEMARS PIGUET, **painted world time**, fancy lugs
s. steel. $5,000 $8000 $12,000

AUDEMARS PIGUET, 20 jewels, thin model
18k. $800 $1,400 $1,800

AUDEMARS PIGUET, **painted world time** , c. 1940s
14k. $5,000 $9,000 $12,000

AUDEMARS PIGUET, 17J., engraved bezel, c. 1963
18k. $1,000 $1,700 $2,200

AUDEMARS PIGUET, 18 jewels, gold train
18k. $1,750 $3,000 $3,500

AUDEMARS PIGUET, 17J., wide bezel, thin model
14k C&B. $900 $1,800 $2,000

AUDEMARS PIGUET, 18J., **hidden lugs**, Ca. 1950
18k. $1,500 $2,400 $3,000

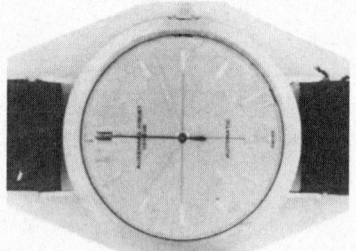

AUDEMARS PIGUET, 21J., auto wind, center sec.
18k. $1,100 $2,000 $2,500

AUDEMARS PIGUET, 18 jewels, aux. sec. c. 1940
18k. $1,500 $2,800 $3,500

AUDEMARS PIGUET, 17 jewels, for Tiffany & Co.
18k C&B $1,700 $2,500 $3,000

AUDEMARS PIGUET, 18 jewels, aux. sec.
18k $2,000 $3,300 $3,800

AUDEMARS PIGUET, 18 jewels, black dial, Ca. 1960
18k(w) $1,200 $1,600 $2,500

AUDEMARS PIGUET, 18 jewels, hooded lugs
18k $1,800 $3,000 $4,000

AUDEMARS PIGUET, 17J., engraved bezel, c. 1966
18k $800 $1,500 $2,000

AUDEMARS PIGUET, 18J., date auto wind, Ca. 1990
18k $1,000 $2,000 $2,500

AUDEMARS PIGUET, 18 jewels, center sec., c. 1950
18k $1,400 $2,200 $3,000

AUDEMARS PIGUET, 18J., straight line lever escape.
18k $1,000 $1,700 $2,200

AUDEMARS PIGUET, 17 jewels, mid-size
18k $800 $1,500 $1,800

AUDEMARS PIGUET, 55J., mid size, flat bezel, Ca. 1969
18k $1,000 $1,800 $2,400

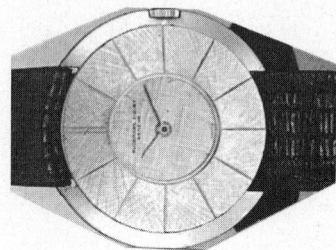

AUDEMARS PIGUET, gold textured dial, c.1960s
18k. $1,000 $1,700 $2,400

AUDEMARS PIGUET, 18J., aux. sec., c.1950s
18k. $1,000 $1,800 $2,500

AUDEMARS PIGUET, 18J., auto wind, waterproof
18k. $2,000 $3,500 $4,000

AUDEMARS PIGUET, 18 jewels, **painted dial**, Ca. 1970
18k. $900 $1,800 $2,500

AUDEMARS PIGUET, 21J., sweep sec., automatic -18k rotor
18k. $2,300 $3,800 $4,500

AUDEMARS PIGUET, 19J., center sec.
18k. $1,500 $2,750 $3,250

AUDEMARS PIGUET, 18J., Manual wind, waterproof
18k. $1,200 $2,000 $2,500

AUDEMARS PIGUET, 17 jewels, gold train
18k. $1,200 $1,600 $2,000

AUDEMARS PIGUET, **triple date, moon ph., dial & mvt.
Signed** "A L 'Emeraude, Lausanne" Cal # GHSM, Ca.1926
18k. $12,000 $22,000   30,000

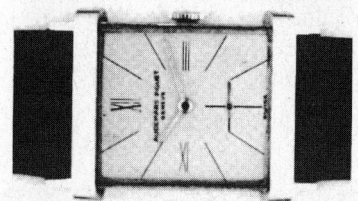

AUDEMARS PIGUET, 18 J., **top hat**, aux. sec., c. 1950
platinum $3,000 $5,500 $7,000

AUDEMARS PIGUET, 17J., gold train,
2 tone case in platinum & gold
18k (w) C&B.............\$2,000   \$3,250   \$4,000

AUDEMARS PIGUET, engraved bezel, c.1950s
18k.....................\$1,500   \$2,250   \$2,800

AUDEMARS PIGUET, 17 jewels, gold train
14k C&B...................\$1,400   \$2,000   \$2,500

AUDEMARS PIGUET, 18 J., textured bezel, c. 1950
18k \$1,000   \$1,800   \$2,200

AUDEMARS PIGUET, 2 tone dial, c. 1930s
18k........................\$2,000   \$3,500   \$4,000

☞ Some grades are not included. Their values can be determined by comparing with similar age, size, metal content, style, grades, or models such as time only, chronograph, repeater etc. listed.

AUDEMARS PIGUET, 18J, curvex, large bezel, c. 1950
18k.......................\$1,000   \$2,000   \$2,500

AUDEMARS PIGUET, 18 jewels, Sq. lugs, c. 1950's
18k.......................\$1,100   \$2,100   \$2,600

AUDEMARS PIGUET, **Royal Oak, date**, auto wind, c.1973
18K & s. steel \$2,000	\$3,000	\$4,000
18K C&B \$4,000	\$6,000	\$7,000
18K C&B, day/date/moonphase..\$5,000	\$7,000	\$8,000
18K C&B, perpetual/moonph. ..\$9,000	\$13,000	\$15,000
s. steel, auto wind \$1,500	\$2,500	\$3,000
s. steel, LARGE, auto wind \$1,600	\$2,600	\$3,200
2-tone, LARGE, auto wind. \$1,800	\$2,800	\$3,400
Ladies, 18K, C&B \$1,800	\$3,000	\$4,000
Ladies 18K C&B, day/date/ auto \$2,200	\$4,000	\$5,500

Note: Add 20% for new style button release clasp.

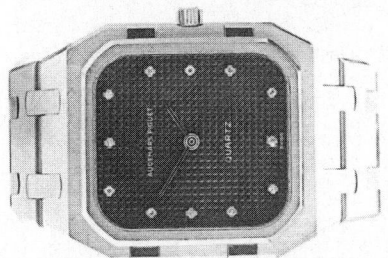

AUDEMARS PIGUET, quartz, 12 diamonds, c. 1981
s. steel......................\$700   \$1,300   \$1,600

AUDEMARS PIGUET, Ladies, 72 small diamonds, C. 1930's
plat. case & band $1,500 $2,500 $3,500

AUDEMARS PIGUET, ladys, 36 diamonds, c.1930s
plat. case...................$1,000 $2,000 $2,800

AUTOMATIQUE, 17J., wind indicator, cal.F699, c. 1955
s. steel......................$100 $165 $225

AUTORIST, 15 jewels, **lug action wind**, enamel dial
s. steel......................$300 $600 $900

AUTORIST, 15 jewels, **lug action wind**, c. 1930
s. steel......................$350 $650 $800

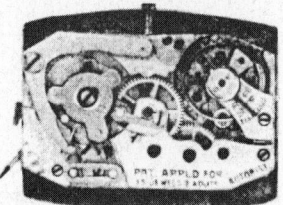

AUTORIST, 15 jewels, lug action wind, movement.

AUTORIST, 15 jewels, **lug action wind**, c. 1930
gold filled...................$300 $600 $900

AUTORIST, 15 jewels, **lug action wind**, (lady's)
s. steel......................$150 $300 $500

AVALON,17J., aux. sec.
gold filled...................$50 $100 $125

AVIA,15J., center see., Ca. 1953
9K rose.....................$100 $150 $200

BALL W. CO., 25 jewels, "Trainmaster", auto wind. adj. to 5 pos.,
ETA.
10k...........................$400 $750 $1,000
gold filled...................$275 $500 $600

BALL W. CO., 25 jewels, "Trainmaster" auto wind, adj. to 5 pos., ETA.
s. steel (auto wind) $250 $450 $600

BAUME & MERCIER, 17J., chronog., 2 reg.,c.1950s
18k. $400 $800 $1,000

BALL W. CO., 21 jewels, "Trainmaster" manual wind, adj. to 5 pos.,
gold filled $200 $400 $500
stainless steel $200 $400 $500

BAUME & MERCIER, 18J., chronog., **3 reg.** & dates
s. steel $350 $600 $1,200

BAUME & MERCIER, 18J., triple date, moon phase
s. steel $400 $650 $800

BAUME & MERCIER, 18J., chronog., 3 reg. & dates
18k. $1,500 $2,500 $3,000

BAUME & MERCIER, 17J., chronog, 2 reg., c.1949
gold filled $250 $500 $650

BAUME & MERCIER, 18 jewels, **tachymeter**, c 1940
s. steel, **original** black dial $500 $800 $1,200

BAUME & MERCIER, 17J., triple date, chronog. moon ph., c.1950s
18k. $1,600 $3,250 $3,500

BAUME & MERCIER, 17J., 2 dials, 2 time zones & 2 movements
18k. $500 $1,000 $1,200

BAUME & MERCIER, 18J., chronog, fancy lugs
18k. $1,800 $3,400 $4,000

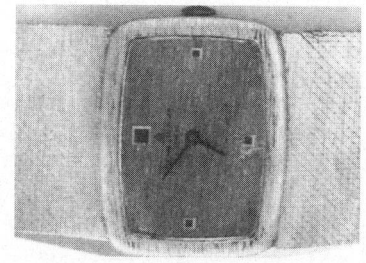

BAUME & MERCIER, 18 jewels, gold dial, date
14k C&B $600 $875 $1000

BAUME & MERCIER, 17J., chronog., triple date
18k. $1,100 $1,900 $2,500

BAUME & MERCIER, 18 jewels, thin model
14k C&B $650 $875 $1,000

BAUME & MERCIER, 18J., triple date, moon phase
18k. $600 $1,200 $1,500

BAUME & MERCIER, 17 jewels, center sec., c. 1956
14k. $200 $350 $400

BAUME & MERCIER, 17J, fancy lugs, aux. sec., c. 1955
14k......................... $225 $350 $400

BAUME & MERCIER,17J., auto-w., Wind ind., Ca.1950a
base metal................... $125 $250 $300

BAUME & MERCIER, 17J., RF#49300, c. 1965
14k..........................$150 $275 $325

BAUME & MERCIER, 17J.,diam. mystery dial, c.1950s
14k(W) $700 $1,200 $1,500

BAUME & MERCIER, 18J., 'Riviera", date, e. 1980s
18k & s. steel................. $300 $500 $600

BAYLOR, 17J., hidden lugs
gold filled $50 $90 $125
14k......................... $120 $200 $275

BAUME & MERCIER, quartz, enamel dial, Ca. 1990a
14k......................... $300 $550 $650

BAYLOR, 17J., diamonds on bezel & dial, c 1948
14k......................... $200 $400 $600

BAUME & MERCIER, 30J., "Baumatic", Ca. 1976
18K(W)..................... $300 $550 $650

BAYLOR, 25J., auto-wind, wind-ind., Ca. 1958
14k......................... $200 $375 $450

BEMONTOIR, 15J., enamel dial, c. 1920
14k. $75 $125 $175

BENRUS,17J., day date
base metal. $30 $60 $80

BENRUS, 18J., **mystery-diamond dial**
18k. $300 $550 $700
gold filled $125 $250 $300

BENRUS, 15 jewels, day, date, c. 1948
s. steel $75 $150 $200

☞ Pricing in this Guide are fair market price for COMPLETE
watches which are reflected from the NAWCC National and
regional shows.

BENRUS, 15 jewels, quick change date
gold filled $75 $150 $200

BENRUS,17J., "Sky Chief", chronog., 3-reg., c.1945
s. steel. $300 $600 $800

BENRUS,17J., "Sky Chief", **triple date**, chronog.,3-reg, c. 1940s
s. steel $400 $750 $900

BENRUS,17J.,Wrist Alarm c.1945
base metal. $75 $150 $250

BENRUS (continued)

BENRUS, 15jewels, jumping hour, wandering min.
gold filled (**Chevron style case**) $150 $300 $500
gold filled $150 $300 $500
s. steel $100 $250 $400

BENRUS, 15 jewels, calendar, auto wind, fancy lugs, c.1950
14k. $150 $300 $350
gold filled $60 $125 $175

BENRUS,17J., Dial-O-Rama, Direct read, c. 1958
gold filled $225 $400 $600

BENRUS, 15J., auto wind, fancy bezel, by ETA, c. 1950
gold filled $40 $100 $125
14k. $150 $200 $350

BENRUS,17J., fancy legs
gold filled $50 $100 $125

BENRUS,17J., auto wind with **wind indicator,** Ca. 1955
gold filled $60 $100 $150

BENRUS,17J., fancy lugs
gold filled $50 $80 $100

BENRUS,17J., dial-0-rama, direct read, c. 1958
Gold Filled $175 $400 $550

BENRUS,21J., Diamond Dial, Ca. 1956
gold filled $150 $300 $400

BENRUS, 15jewels, fancy lugs, c. 1948 .
14k........................ $125 $250 $350
gold filled $70 $125 $200

BENRUS, 15J., auto-wind, **water-proof**
gold filled $50 $80 $100

BENRUS, 15jewels, **fancy bezel**, cal. BB14
14k..........................$150 $300 $450
gold filled $75 $125 $200

BENRUS, 21J., aux. sec., c. 1950s
14k......................... $90 $150 $225

☞ Pricing in this Guide are fair market price for complete watches which are reflected from NAWCC National and regional shows.

☞ Some grades are not included. Their values can be determined by comparing with similar age, size, metal content, style, grades, or models such as time only, chronograph, repeater etc. listed.

BENRUS, 17J., 3 diam. dial, one diam. on each hand, c.1955
14K $125 $250 $350

BENRUS, 21J., aux. sec., **fancy lugs**, c.1950
gold filled $40 $70 $100

BENRUS, 17J., **hidden lugs**
14K $100 $200 $300

BENRUS, 17J., cadillac logo, c.1950s
gold plate $40 $100 $150

BENRUS, 17J., movement by ETA, c. 1955
gold filled $45 $100 $125

BENRUS, 15J., engraved bezel, c.1935
14k............................$150 $300 $350

BENRUS,17J., **flared case**, cal.180, c. 1951
gold filled $60 $100 $150

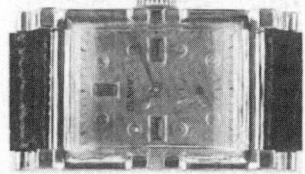

BENRUS, 17J., rhinestone dial, c. 1945
gold filled $60 $125 $150

BENRUS, 7J., rhinestone dial, fancy legs, c. 1948
base metal..................... $35 $65 $100

BENRUS, 17J., date, fancy lugs, c.1950
gold filled $75 $150 $200

BENRUS,17J., rhinestone dial, cal. bb1, c. 1945
gold plate $35 $100 $125

BENRUS, 17J., aux. sec., c.1940
14k......................... $100 $200 $275

BENRUS, 7J., Ford Logo, Ca. 1950
gold filled $45 $125 $150

BENRUS, 15J., aux sec.
gold filled $55 $100 $125

☞ Pricing in this Guide are fair market price for complete watches which are reflected from the NAWCC National and regional shows.

BENRUS, 15J.,fancy legs
14K $150 $350 $400

BENRUS, 17J., hidden lugs, cal. 11 ax, Ca.1951
14k..........................$150 $350 $400

BENRUS,15J.,fancy hooded lugs, cal# ax 11, Ca.1946
14k..........................$175 $300 $400

BENRUS, 15J., **enamel bezel**, c. 1930
14k(w)......................$350 $700 $875

BENRUS, 17 jewels, Flared case, Ca. 1955
14k..........................$200 $400 $550

BENRUS,17J., aux sec., Cs.1935
gold filled $45 $100 $125

BENRUS, 15 jewels, **flip-up case**, c. 1940
gold filled $200 $385 $450

BENRUS,17J., hooded lugs, c.1948
14k..........................$125 $300 $350

BENRUS,17J., hooded lugs, cal. AX11, c. 1950
14k..........................$250 $425 $500

BENRUS, 15 jewels, hooded lugs
gold filled $60 $100 $125

BENRUS, 15 jewels, cal. AX, 3 small diam. dial, c 1950
14k..........................$175 $300 $375

Wrist Watches listed in this section are priced at the collectable fair
market Trade Show level as complete watches having an original
gold-filled case and stainless steel back, also with original dial,
leather watch band, and the entire original movement in good
working order with no repairs needed.

BENRUS, 17 jewels, curved, hooded lugs, Ca. 1950s
14k. $250 $400 $500

BENSON J. W., 15 jewels, curved back, C. 1942
9k $100 $200 $300

BENSON J. W., 15-16J., made in England, aux sec. Ca.1955
9k . . . . ☞$300 $500 $750

BENSON J. W., 15J., of London, Ca.1938
9k $100 $200 $300

BENSON J. W., 15 jewels, enamel dial, London
9k $100 $200 $300

BENSON J. W., 15 jewels, enamel dial, hunter case, Ca. 1920
Silver. $200 $400 $475

BENSON J. W., 15 jewels, enamel dial, 2-tone flared case
9K $200 $375 $425

BLANCPAIN, 17J., **"Aqua Lung"**, auto-wind, date, 1000 Ft.
revolving bezel, 37 mm, Ca.1960
S. S $900 $1,400 $1,900

BLANCPAIN, 23J., day-date-month, perpetual, auto-wind
s. steel - perpetual $1,500 $3,000 $4,000
18K - perpetual. $2,500 $4,500 $5,500

BLANCPAIN, 17J.,hooded lugs, c.1945
14k. $200 $375 $425

BLANCPAIN, 16J., fancy lugs, Ca.1958
14K $175 $300 $350

E. BOREL, 17J., cocktail dial, date, c. 1969
base metal $75 $175 $275

BOILLAT FRERES, 17 jewels, "Blita," waterproof
s. steel $35 $60 $80

E. BOREL, 15J., *"Regulator Dial"*, hour dial, minute dial,
with center sec., c.1940
s. steel $400 $800 $1,100

E. BOREL, 17 jewels, chronometer, aux. sec.
18k. $175 $300 $350
gold filled $45 $85 $100

E. BOREL, 17 jewels, auto wind, date
gold filled $65 $100 $125

E. BOREL, 17J., cocktail style, c. 1960s
gold filled $100 $200 $300
s. steel $100 $200 $300

BOUCHERON, 17J, c 1930s
18k. $250 $500 $650

Some grades are not included. Their values can be determined by comparing with similar age, size, metal content, style, grades, or models such as time only, chronograph, repeater etc. listed.

Wrist Watches listed in this section are priced at the collectable fair market Trade Show **retail** level as **complete** watches having an original gold-filled case and stainless steel back, also with original dial, leather watch band, and the entire original movement in good working order with no repairs needed.

DIALS FOR MINT PRICES MUST BE ALL ORIGINAL.

BOULEVARD, 17J., "STOP", c.1950s
s. steel $75 $110 $200

BREGUET, 17J., chronog., triple date, Ca. 1950
s. steel $5,000 $8,500 $10,000

BOVET, 17 jewels, chronog., 2 reg., c. 1940
s. steel $150 $275 $325

BREGUET, auto-w., triple date, moon ph., perpetual
18k. $12,000 $18,000 $25,000

BOVET, 17 jewels, chronog., triple date & 3 reg.
14k. $700 $1,500 $2,000
gold filled $500 $850 $1,000

BREGUET, jump hour, c. 1980s,
18k. . . . . ★$6,000 $10,000 $14,000
platinum $10,000 $15,000 $19,000

BREGUET, 21 jewels, skeletonized
18k C&B $4,500 $7,500 $9,000

BREGUET,37J., auto-w., date, moon ph.,45 hr. wind ind.
18k. $9,000 $15,000 $18,000

BREGUET, 17 jewels, silver dial, thin model
18k. $1,500 $2,500 $3,000

BREGUET, 17 jewels, curvex
platinum $2,500 $5,000 $6,000

P. BREGUETTE, 17J., gold jewel settings, Ca.1948
14k. $110 $225 $300

P. BREGUETTE, 17J., gold jewel settings, flared case
14k. $175 $300 $400

P. BREGUETTE, 17 jewels, top hat, diamond dial, c. 1940
14k. $450 $800 $1,200

Add up to **50%** over mint for new old stock (N.O.S.)

P. BREGUETTE, 17J., triple date, c. 1960s
gold filled $125 $200 $250
s. steel $125 $150 $225

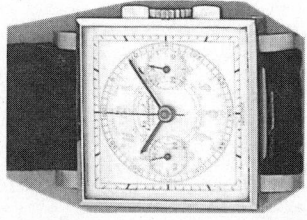

Breitling, 17 J., Precision, red & blue Tacky-rings, Ca. 1940
s. steel $1,200 $2,000 $3,000

Breitling, 17J., "Chronomat," slide rule bezel
18k. $2,000 $2,500 $3,000
gold filled $800 $1,100 $1,700
s. steel $850 $1,200 $1,500

Breitling, 17J., **Navitimer**, date, slide rule bezel, RF 7806
s. steel $1,000 $1,800 $2,000

Add up to **50%** over mint for new old stock (N.O.S.)

BREITLING, 17J., **Chronomat.**, RF 808, c. 1950
gold filled $800 $1,200 $2,000

BREITLING, 18J., date, moon ph., split chronog. Ca. 1950's
18k $4,000 $8,000 $10,000

BREITLING, 17J., chronog., RF#1199, sq. button, c. 1958
s. steel $400 $700 $900

BREITLING, 17J, chronog., "Navitimer," RF 806

18K C&B	$3,500	$6,000	$8,000
18K case only	$3,000	$5,000	$6,000
gold filled	$700	$1,500	$1,900
s. steel	$700	$1,500	$1,900

BREITLING, 17J., chronog., "Cosmonaute", **24 hour**, 3 reg.
18k $3,500 $6,000 $7,000
s. steel $1,000 $1,800 $2,400

BREITLING, 17 J., chronog., "Navitimer," **AOPA logo**, Ca. 1952
s. steel $900 $1,600 $2,000

AOPA logo ☞

A.O.P.A., the initials of Aircraft Owners & Pilots Association,
This logo first appeared in 1952 05 the "Navitimer", a word
derived from <u>Navi</u>gation, **Navi** + the word Timer. The AOPA
logo and other logos are being collected such as Blue Angles
(U.S.Navy), Red Arrow (Royal Air Force), Frecce Tricolori
(Aeronautica Militare Italiana), Patrouille Suisse (Escadre de
Surveillance), Thunderbirds (U.S. Air Farce), Blue Impulse
(Japan Self Defense Force), Team 60 (Swedish Air Force)
Patrouille de France (French Air Force) and others.

BREITLING, 17 jewels, split sec. chronog., 2 reg.
s. steel $3,000 $5,500 $7,000

Add up to **50%** over mint for new old stock (N.O.S.)

BREITLING, 17 J., chronog., "Chronomat," 3 reg.
s. steel $500 $900 $1,200

BREITLING, 17 J., telemeter, 1 button, hinged lugs
s.steel-44mm $800 $1,400 $2,000

BREITLING, 17J., 1 button, Chronograph, Ca 1930
s. steel $700 $1,200 $1,600

BREITLING, 17 jewels, tachymeter, Ca.1930
s. steel $1,000 $1,600 $2,000

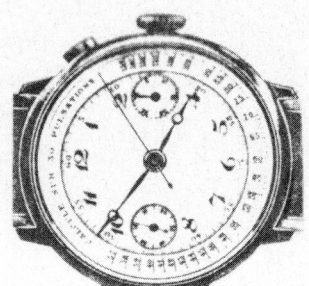

BREITLING, 17 jewels, chronog., pulsations
s. steel $500 $900 $1,200

BREITLING, 17 jewels, chronog., 2 reg.
s. steel $500 $900 $1,500

BREITLING, 17 jewels, tachymeter, center hinged lugs
s. steel - 35mm $500 $900 $1,300

BREITLING, 17J., chronog., RF#765, c. 1960
14k. $1,200 $2,000 $2,500
s. steel $500 $900 $1,200

BREITLING (continued)

683

BREITLING, 17 jewels, chronog., Toptime, 24 HR
s. steel $800 $1,200 $1,000

BREITLING, 17 jewels, chronog., 2 reg. RF#790
18K **refinished dial** $700 $1,200 $1,500
18K original dial $1,400 $2,200 $2,800

BREITLING, 17J., chronog., 2 reg., "Premier", RF#790
18k $1,500 $2,300 $2,950

BREITLING, 17J., chronog., 3 reg., RF#787, c.1942
14k $1,000 $1,400 $2,000
18k yellow $1,400 $1,800 $2,400
18k pink (add $300) $1,700 $2,100 $2,700

Add up to **50%** over mint for new old stock (N.O.S.)

BREITLING, 17 jewels, chronog., "Premier," 3 reg.
s. steel $800 $1,400 $1,800

BREITLING, 17 J., chronog., day-date-month, 3 reg.
18k $2,000 $3,000 $3,800
s. steel $900 $1,600 $2,000

BREITLING, 17 jewels, chronog., 2 reg. RF # 178
s. steel $500 $900 $1,200

BREITLING, 17 jewels, chronog, 2 reg. RF # 769
18k $1,200 $2,000 $2,400
s. steel $450 $800 $950

BREITLING, 17J., **split sec**. chronog., "Duograph", C.1945
18k........................$5,000 $9,000 $12,000
s. steel $3,000 $6,500 $9,000

BREITLING, 17J., **Super Ocean**, RF # 2005, c.1960
s. steel $900 $1,500 $1,800

BREITLING, 17J., chronog., 3 reg., RF#815, c.1968
gold filled $500 $950 $1,200

BREITLING, 17J., chronog., RF#2110, c.1970
s. steel $600 $1,000 $1,500

BREITLING, 17J., **AOPA** logo, Toptime, RF#810, c.1968
s. steel $500 $900 $1,200

BREITLING, 17J., chronog. RF#2009-33, c. 1975
s. steel $300 $550 $700

BREITLING, 17J., **Tour de France**, c. 1945
18K $1,000 $1,700 $1,900

BREITLING, 17J., Co-Pilot, enamel bezel, RF # 765, c. 1960
s. steel....................$1,000 $1,800 $2,500

Add up to 50% over mint for new old stock (N.O.S.)

BREITLING, 17J., **Cosmonaute** II, 24 hr., Ca. 1990
s. steel C&B $700 $1,400 $1,800

BREITLING, 17J., **Old Navitimer II**, gold bezel, Ca. 1990
s. steel & G-Bezel $600 $1,000 $1,200

BREITLING, 17J., **Navitimer 92**, self-wind, Ca.1992
s. steel case $700 $1,300 $1,500
18K case $2,500 $4,000 $4,800

BREITLING, 17J., Chronomat, date, self-wind, Ca.1990
s. steel $600 $1,100 $1,400
18K & s. steel C&B $1,100 $2,000 $2,400

BREITLING, 17J., Chronomat Yachting, date, Ca. 1990
s. steel C&B $700 $1,300 $1,600

BREITLING, 17J., **Chrono Cockpit**, date, Ca.1990
18K & s. steel C&B $800 $1,400 $1,600

BREITLING, 17J., "Blue Angel 92", **total production 1,000**
s. steel & gold bezel $1,200 $2,000 $2,400

BREITLING, 17J., **Corono QP**, day date moon ph., Ca. 1990
18K C&B $4,000 $7,000 $9,000

BREITLING, 17J., **Corono 1461**, day date moon ph., c.1990
s. steel C&B $1,500 $2,300 $2,600

BREITLING, 17J., **Chrono Longitude**, date, Ca.1990
s. steel & gold C&B $900 $1,600 $1,800

BREITLING, 17J., **Navitimer Airborne**, date, Ca.1990
s. steel case $700 $1,200 $1,500

BREITLING, 17J., **Navitimer AVI**, date, Ca.1990
s. steel case $500 $900 $1,000

BREITLING, 'Golden Knights, only 50 made, only 20 **made available to general public**, to bring top price watch should have a factory letter, papers & 2 boxes. (**U.S. Army**)
s. steel $1,400 $2,000 $2,400

BREITLING, "Blue Angels Limited Edition", only 100 made, **only 25 made available to general public**, to bring top price watch should have a factory letter, papers & 2 boxes.
Sonic Minute Repeater (US. Navy)
Titanium $2,000 $3,500 $4,000

BREITLING, "Top Gun", Limited Edition, 1,000 made
s. steel & gold bezel $900 $1,400 $2,000

BREITLING, "Blue Angela Limited Edition 96", Montbrillant
18K $2,500 $4,500 $5,500

UTC (Universal Time Coordinated), small Quartz that is fitted between lugs & used for second time zone = **$300 to $450**

BREITLING, "Team 60", Limited Edition, 1,000 made, Pluton model, Ca. 1995
s. steel $400 $650 $850

BREITLING, 17J., chronog., RF#1450, 3 reg., c.1970
s. steel $300 $500 $700

BUCHERER, 17 jewels, note: **day date in lugs**
18k. $350 $600 $700

BREITLING, 17J., day date month,
18k. $300 $500 $700

BUCHERER, 17 jewels, chronog., 2 reg.
18k. $500 $850 $1,000

BREITLING, 21J., "UNITIME", date, 24 hour, c. 1958
stainless $1,900 $2,700 $3,250

BUCHERER, 17J., chronog., 2 reg., C. 1959
18k. $400 $750 $850
s. steel $250 $400 $600

BREITLING, 21J., auto-wind, rf#2528, c.1959
s. steel $80 $125 $200

BUCHERER, 25J., triple date moon ph., cal.693, c.1950
18k. $800 $1,300 $1,800

BUCHERER, 21J., 3 dates, moon ph., diamond dial
18k. $2,000 $4,000 $5,500

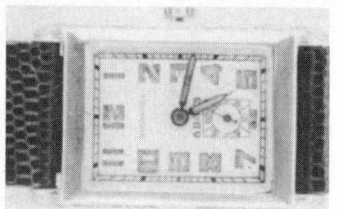

BUCHERER, 15 jewels, **8 day** movement
18k. $600 $1,100 $1,300
gold filled $250 $450 $600

BUECHE-GIROD, 17 J., day-date-month, **moon ph**,
s. steel $225 $400 $500

BUECHE-GIROD, 17J., by Piguet, cal.99, c. 1975
18k. $200 $350 $450

BUECHE-GIROD 17J dual time movements,
18k. $500 $900 $1,200

BUECHE-GIROD, 17J jewels, Sq. lugs
18k. $300 $525 $650

BUECHE-GIROD, 17 jewels
18k C&B. $400 $700 $900

P. BUHRE, 17 jewels, aux. sec.
gold filled $60 $90 $125

P. BUHRE, 17J., alarm, C. 1956
s. steel. $50 $100 $125

☞ Some grades are not included. Their values can be determined by comparing with similar age, size, metal content, style, grades, or models such as time only, chronograph, repeater etc. listed.

BULOVA WATCH CO.

In 1875 Joseph Bulova starts a Wholesale jewelry business. Basically, it was always a Swiss-USA company & in 1930 Bulova sets up to make bridges and plates at Woodside, NY. By 1934 the company manufactured watches by the millions, using ebauches manufactured in its own Swiss plant. The New York Plant by now was making escapements, dials, plates and other parts and also cased and assembled the watches. About 1940 or sooner they were able to make complete watches, By the early 1950s they produced over a million watches a year of which over half were imported movements & the remaining were domestic. The *Accutron* was introduced on October 25, 1960, it was the first electronic watch made, The watch used a tuning fork that vibrated 360 times a second using a transistorized electronic circuit and a battery which would last for about a year. Micro-miniaturization of components was a technical achievement The tuning fork vibrates, a jewel-tipped (pawl spring) index finger advancing the index wheel, The index wheel is only 0.0945 inches in diameter ● (about the size of a pin head) yet it has 320 ratchet teeth, The coil is less than a 1/4 inch long but contains 8,000 turns of wire that is 0.0006 inches in diameter. The original 214 model, (identified by absence of a crown) was produced until about 1966 and about a 2,000,000 were made. The newer 218 model has a crown at the 4 O'clock position. By 1975- 76 the Accutron production ended and about 5,000,000 were sold.

The "Spaceview" so named due to the conventional dial was left off so the tuning fork can be viewed from the top using a transparent crystal. With the conventional dial missing it had to be replaced with a dial spacer. The "Spaceview Alpha", as delivered from factory, used a transparent crystal with dots and a dial spacer only. The "Spaceview H" used a crystal and a dial reflector (chapter ring) not a dial spacer. There are many different original factory combinations of the "Spaceview" crystals with many different styles of hands, Spaceviews came in both 214 & 218 models.

Marks Indicating Age Of Bulova Movements

1924	✳	1929	♉	1934	◯	1939	♉	1944	◯
1925	◯	1930	♉	1935	△	1940	♉	1945	△
1926	△	1931	♉	1936	☐	1941	✳	1946	46
1927	☐	1932	T	1937	→	1942	T	1947	47
1928	☽	1933	✗	1938	☽	1943	✗	1948	48

   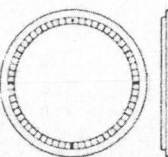

"Spaceview Alpha" with **dots** on crystal & dial space   "Spaceview H" with chapter ring & dial reflector

Different Spaceview transparent dot crystals   Above: Different Hands

Different Hands -   tuning fork (white-red-gold) seconds hands -   also orange second hand

Spaceview "**Alpha**", was the 1st model, Ca 1960
1963 ad **Alpha** model sold for **$200**

BULOVA, Accutron, "**Spaceview Alpha**" Ca 1960
Accutron the first transistorized watch was sold Oct. 25, 1960.
14k. $400 $800 $1,100

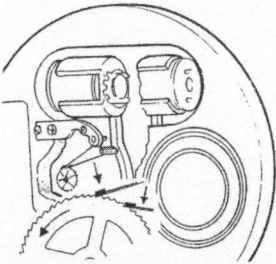

Accutron tuning fork vibration-to-rotary motion conversion the
indexing mechanism. Magnified view of index wheel with 2 jewels,
a ratchet & pawl system advancing the wheel.

BULOVA, Accutron, "Spaceview B", yellow
dots & hands, sold for $150 in 1964.
s. steel $200 $350 $500

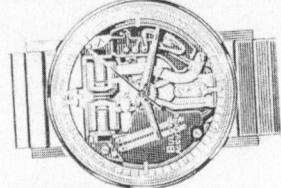

BULOVA, Accutron, "Spaceview H"
gold filled $200 $325 $425

Note: model **214** = back set & model **218** = crown at 4.

BULOVA, Accutron, "**Spaceview T**", clearview dial,
orange second hand, sold for $135.00 in 1967.
s. steel $200 $375 $450

BULOVA, Accutron, RF # 202, RR
approved, sold for $125.00 in 1964.
s. steel $100 $200 $300
gold filled $150 $225 $325

BULOVA, Accutron, RF #210 gold bezel & a steel case
s. steel & 14k. $175 $300 $400

BULOVA, Accutron, RF #213, sold for $125.00 in 1964.
s. steel $75 $175 $250

BULOVA, Accutron, RF #214
s. steel $75 $175 $250

BULOVA, Accutron, RF # 216, sold for $175.00 in 1964.
s. steel $75 $175 $250

BULOVA, Accutron, **RF # 218, bow tie lugs**
s. steel $125 $250 $325

BULOVA, Accutron, **RF # 223**
s. steel $125 $250 $325
14k. $275 $525 $650

BULOVA, Accutron, **RF # 241, bow tie
lugs,** sold for $125.00 in 1967.
s. steel $100 $250 $350

BULOVA, Accutron, **RF # 252**, red second
hand, sold for $110.00 is 1967.
s. steel $100 $175 $250

BULOVA, Accutron, **RF # 254**, red second
hand, sold for $125.00 in 1967.
s. steel $75 $125 $250

BULOVA, Accutron, **RF # 301**, basket
weave band, sold $150.00 in 1967.
gold filled $100 $175 $250

BULOVA, Accutron, **RF # 400**
gold filled $100 $175 $250

BULOVA, Accutron, **RF # 401**, sold for $150.00 in 1964.
s. steel $100 $175 $250

BULOVA, Accutron, **RF # 403**, sold for $175.00 in 1964.
gold filled $100 $175 $250

BULOVA, Accutron, **RF #411**
gold filled $100 $175 $250

BULOVA, Accutron, RF # 412 gold filled bezel & s. steel
gold filled & s. steel case $100 $175 $250

BULOVA, Accutron, RF # 413, GE bezel & s. steel case
gold filled & s. steel case $75 $125 $225

BULOVA, Accutron, RF # 417
gold filled $100 $225 $275

BULOVA, Accutron, RF # 420
gold filled $125 $225 $275

BULOVA, Milady's Accutron, RF # 430, sold for $185.00 in 1967.
gold filled $50 $100 $150

Note: model 214 = back set & model 218 = crown at 4.

BULOVA, Accutron, RF # 500, center
lugs, sold for $300.00 in 1964.
14k. $250 $550 $750

BULOVA, Accutron RF # 505 Ca. 1960
14k yellow or white $300 $575 $750

BULOVA, Accutron RF # 513
14k. $200 $400 $550

BULOVA, Accutron RF # 514 Florentine engraved case
14k. $300 $450 $600

BULOVA, Accutron, RE # D515, 20 diamonds
on case, sold for $750.00 in 1967.
14K(w)C&B $550 $800 $1,000

  NOTE: Some Bulova cases are stamped with a year
date code letter & number. L = 1950s, M = 1960s, N = 1970s,
P = 1980s, T = 1990s.
example: L3=1953, M4=1964, N5=1975, P6=1986, T7=1997.

BULOVA, Accutron RF # 560
14k. $200 $400 $600

BULOVA, Accutron RF # 602
18k. $400 $750 $900

BULOVA, Accutron, RF # AK, Day &
Date, sold for $200.00 in 1967.
gold filled $100 $185 $275

BULOVA, Accutron, RF # AG, Day at 12 &
Date at 6, sold for $185.00 in 1967.
s. steel $100 $185 $275

BULOVA, Accutron, RF # CK, date at 6, sold for $135.00 in 1967.
s. steel $100 $225 $350

Note: A small **predictable** position error can be taken
into consideration in the daily regulation of your Accutron. In the
12 - down **vertical** position the rate is about 5 seconds per day faster
conversely in the 6-down **vertical** position a rate of 5 seconds per
day slower. You can take advantage of this, if slow place it in the 12-
down <u>vertical</u> position at night and it will gain back lost time, if fast
use the 6-down <u>vertical</u> position to slow it down

BULOVA, Accutron, RF # CL, tortoise-toned dial
sold for $250.00 in 1967.
14K $250 $450 $525

BULOVA, Accutron, "Mickey" day & date, **RARE** (218)
s. steel(214). $250 $500 $700
14K C&B(original dial). . . . . ★★★$600 $950 $1,200

BULOVA, Accutron, date, "M 8" on back - Ca. 1968.
14k. $250 $400 $575

BULOVA, Accutron, Ca. 1969-70.
14k. $300 $600 $800
Note Below: Bulova Accutron regulator, to regulate use a
tooth pick and move regulator up or down. (Tuning Fork)

12 O'CLOCK   SLOWER

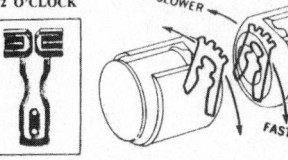
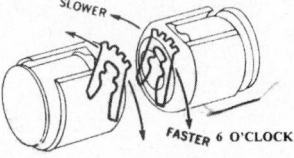

FASTER 6 O'CLOCK

NOTE: Some Bulova cases are stamped with a year date code letter & number . L = 1950s, M = 1960a, N = 1970s P = 1980s, T = 1990s. example: L3=1953, M4=1964, N5=1975, P6=1986, T7=1997.

Note: model **214** = back set & model **218** = crown set at 4.

BULOVA, Accutron, 'Spaceview"
s. steel $175 $300 $450

BULOVA, Accutron, "Spaceview"
s. steel $150 $300 $400

BULOVA, Accutron, "Not Factory", cal. 214, c. 1963
gold filled $75 $150 $200

BULOVA, Accutron, "Spaceview"
18k. $500 $900 $1,200
14k. $300 $600 $750
s. steel $150 $300 $400

BULOVA, Accutron, cal. 214, c. 1963
s. steel $150 $275 $400

BULOVA, Accutron, "Spaceview," Accutron second hand
gold filled $150 $250 $400

BULOVA, Accutron, "Spaceview," c. 1960
18K. $500 $850 $1,200
14k. $300 $650 $850
gold filled $150 $275 $400
s. steel $150 $275 $400

BULOVA, Accutron, "Spaceview," c. 1961
gold filled $150 $250 $350

DIALS FOR MINT PRICES MUST BE ALL ORIGINAL.

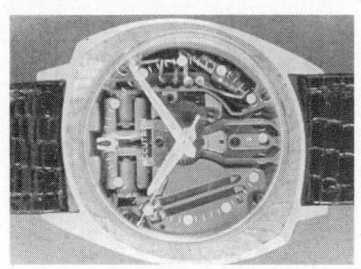

BULOVA, Accutron, "Spaceview," c. 1967
gold filled $150 $275 $425
s. steel $150 $275 $425
14k $250 $500 $675

BULOVA, Accutron, "Spaceview," center lugs
14k C & B $600 $1,200 $1,400

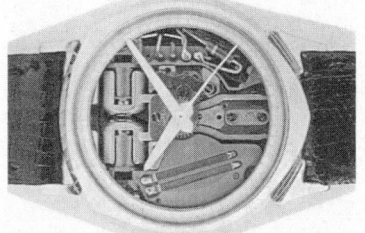

BULOVA, Accutron, **Not Factory**, Alpha, waterproof
14k. $175 $300 $400

BULOVA, Accutron, **Not Factory** dial, date, cal.218
14k 2 tone $200 $400 $600

BULOVA, Accutron, "Spaceview," **Bowtie lugs**
gold filled $175 $350 $450

BULOVA, Accutron, Skeletonized, date, cal.218, Ca.1967
14k. $300 $600 $750

BULOVA, Accutron, center lugs
s. steel $150 $300 $375
gold filled $150 $300 $375

Accutron the **first** electronic watch was sold Oct. 25, 1960.
By 1966 Accutron had sold over 1 1/2 million, and by 1976, 5 million watches.

BULOVA, Accutron, day, date, sold for $135.00 in 1976
gold filled $80 $150 $250

☞ Some grades are not included. Their values can be determined by comparing with similar age, size, metal content, style, grades, or models such as time only, chronograph, repeater etc. listed.

☞ A collector should expect to pay modestly higher prices at local shops.

BULOVA, Accutron, "Spaceview," RED second hand.
s. steel $200 $350 $475

BULOVA, Accutron, "Spaceview," **Not Factory**
s. steel $75 $125 $175

BULOVA, Accutron, 2 tone, Ca. 1967
gold filled $200 $350 $450

BULOVA, Accutron, "Spaceview," gold bezel
14k. $250 $500 $650
gold bezel & s. steel case $175 $325 $425

BULOVA, Accutron, oval,   "Spaceview"   Ca. 1962
18K $400 $700 $950
14K $250 $400 $525
gold filled $150 $250 $325
s. steel $150 $250 $325

BULOVA, Accutron, M# 214, railroad approved, Ca. 1962
gold filled $100 $200 $300
s. steel $100 $200 $300

BULOVA, Accutron, "Spaceview,"
s. steel $150 $250 $350

BULOVA, Accutron, M # 218, RR approved, **red 24 hr.** #s, sold for
$125.00 in 1976.
gold filled $100 $200 $300

BULOVA, Accutron, RR approved
gold filled $100 $200 $300

BULOVA, Accutron, cal. 214," Pulsation", c. 1966
14k. . . . . ★$450 $800 $950

BULOVA, Accutron, RR approved
s. steel $110 $225 $325

BULOVA, Accutron, "Alpha", model 214, 6 diamond dial
14k. $400 $700 $900
18K . . . . ★$650 $1,200 $1,500

BULOVA, Accutron," **Mark IV" / RR approved**, date
Crown at 2 sets the hour hand, Crown at 4 sets Time & Date two
hour hands for two time zones
s. steel $175 $350 $500

BULOVA, Accutron, sweep sec. hand
gold filled $125 $210 $325

BULOVA, Accutron, cal. 214, " Pulsation", c. 1966
gold filled $175 $335 $500
14k. . . . . ★$400 $800 $950

BULOVA, Accutron, masonic dial (all original dial)
NOTE: This dial can be printed for about $35.00.
14k. $250 $400 $500

BULOVA, Accutron, asymmetric
14k......................... $275 $575 $750

BULOVA, Accutron, asymmetric, 2- tone dial, Ca. 1963
14k......................... $325 $650 $750

BULOVA, Accutron, "ASTRONAUT A", 24 hour dial, the a. steel
case & band sold for $175.00 in 1964.
18k C & B $900 $1,600 $2,100
14k......................... $600 $1,000 $1,400
gold filled $275 $475 $700
s. steel $250 $400 $625

BULOVA, Accutron, "ASTRONAUT B", rotating bezel
s. steel $250 $400 $600

BULOVA, Accutron, "ASTRONAUT C", **18k**
case & band, sold for $1,000.00 in 1964.
18k C & B $1,000 $1,600 $2,100
also made with a gold filled case & 14K bezel
GF case & 14K bezel $300 $600 $850

BULOVA, Accutron, "Astronaut Mark II", time zone,
window at six o'clock, date at 12, note: on back N2 = 1972
14k......................... $300 $500 $650
s. steel $225 $265 $400

BULOVA, Accutron, "Astronaut Mark II", time zone, original
sales price was $275.00 in S. Steel.
14k......................... $350 $500 $650
gold filled $175 $325 $450
s. steel $175 $325 $450

BULOVA, Accutron, "ASTRONAUT Mark II", auxiliary
time zone window at 6- o'clock & date at 12-o'clock.
14k......................... $275 $550 $700

BULOVA, Accutron, "Astronaut Mark II", time zone with a
extra red hour hand, date at 3 o'clock, on back M9 1969
gold filled $175 $325 $450

BULOVA, Accutron, "Spaceview"
gold filled $175 $300 $375

BULOVA, Accutron, "Astronaut Mark II E", travel time zone
sold for $185.00 in 1967, orange sec. hand & hour markers
s. steel $175 $300 $400

BULOVA, Accutron, 4 diamond dial, Ca. 1967
gold filled $150 $275 $400

BULOVA, Accutron, Ca. 1966
gold filled $100 $200 $275

BULOVA, Accutron, "spaceview", sold for $180.00 in 1976
gold filled $150 $275 $400

BULOVA, Accutron, **fancy lugs**
gold filled $90 $175 $250

BULOVA, Accutron, date, gold filled bezel
s. steel $75 $150 $200

BULOVA, day, date, sold for $150.00 in 1976
gold filled $75 $135 $225

BULOVA, Accutron, date, **Tiffany & Co.** M7=1967,
note: accutron **tuning fork** second hand.
14K $250 $525 $650

BULOVA, Accutron, day, date, sold for $185.00 in 1976,
gold filled $75 $150 $225

BULOVA, Accutron, date
18K $300 $550 $700
gold filled $100 $175 $250

BULOVA, Accutron, date, Ca.1972
base metal. $50 $100 $150

★Note the design of case (shaped like a Accutron tuning fork).

BULOVA, Accutron, **Spaceview Anniversary**, model 214
gold filled & s. steel $300 $525 $675
s. steel (large case) $300 $525 $675

BULOVA, Accutron, gold filled bezel, day date
gold filled $75 $165 $250

BULOVA, Accutron, red second hand, Ca. 1970
s. steel $175 $325 $450

BULOVA, day date
s. steel $75 $125 $175

BULOVA, Accutron, **wood bezel**, day date
gold filled $100 $200 $300

BULOVA, Accutron, day date
gold filled $75 $150 $200

BULOVA, Accutron, red dial, date
gold filled $125 $175 $225

BULOVA, Accutron, day date, Ca.1972
gold filled $75 $125 $175

BULOVA, Accutron, numbered bezel, day date
14k. $300 $550 $600

BULOVA, Accutron, date
gold plate $75 $125 $175

BULOVA, **Accuquartz**, note band with **accutron symbol**
18k C & B $700 $1,200 $1,400

BULOVA, Accutron, day date, c. 1970
14K $250 $475 $550
s. steel $100 $150 $200

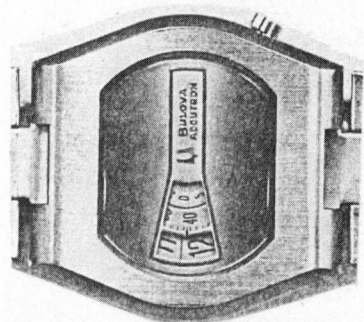

BULOVA, Accutron, model 2186, direct read
gold filled $150 $250 $350

BULOVA, Accutron, **Accutron 14K Gold Band**, Ca.1972
14k C & B $500 $850 $1,000

BULOVA, Accutron, **DEEP SEA**, 666 ft. depth, day date, 12 & 24 hr. dial, crown at 2 rotates outside dial so locate city.
s. steel $250 $450 $600

BULOVA, Accutron, **DEEP SEA "A"**, 666 feet, day date, crown at 2 rotates elapsed for REMAINING time dial, sold for $195.00 in 1967.
SNORKEL model similar to above but in a square case.
s. steel $175 $365 $500

BULOVA, Accutron, **DEEP SEA**, 666 feet, date rotating enamel bezel for REMAINING time.
s. steel $200 $365 $500

DIALS FOR MINT PRICES MUST BE ALL **ORIGINAL**.

BULOVA, Accutron, day date, note Accutron style sec. hand
s. steel $185 $285 $450

BULOVA, Accutron, date, Ca. 1968
gold filled $75 $125 $175

BULOVA, Accutron, day, date, sold for $125.00 in 1976
gold filled $75 $150 $225

BULOVA, Accutron, day, date, sold for $450.00 in 1976
14k $250 $475 $550

BULOVA, Accutron, "Spaceview", Bowtie lugs
18K $500 $1,000 $1,300

BULOVA, Accutron, cal. #221, textured bezel
sterling & 14k $100 $175 $225

BULOVA, Accutron, model "AO", asymmetrical,
Sold for $225.00 in 1971.
gold filled $75 $125 $175

BULOVA, Accutron, day, date, sold for $125.00 in 1976
gold filled $75 $150 $225

☞ NOTE: Some Bulova cases are stamped with a year date
code letter & number. L = 1950s, M = 1960s, N = 1970s
P=1980s,T 1990s.
example: L3=1953, M4=1964, N5=1975, P6=1986, T7=1997.

BULOVA, digital,
s. steel $125 $250 $300

BULOVA, 17J., chronog., "660 feet" dive watch, c.1972
s. steel $200 $375 $450

BULOVA, enamel bezel
s. steel $100 $200 $250

BULOVA, 16 jewels, military style, rotating bezel
s. steel $300 $550 $650

BULOVA, 15J., one button chronog.,1/5 sec.,C.1946
14k. $400 $700 $800
gold filled $150 $300 $400

BULOVA, 17J., Alarm, cal.11 aerc, c.1967
s. steel $100 $200 $275

BULOVA, 17J.,one button chronog.,cal.10BK,c.1947
gold filled $150 $300 $400

BULOVA, self winding, c. 1960
14k. $150 $275 $350
gold filled $50 $100 $200

BULOVA, 17J., fancy lugs, aux. sec., Ca. 1951
gold filled $50 $100 $175

BULOVA, 23 jewels, waterproof
14k. $125 $250 $325

BULOVA, 23 jewels**, date, 6 adj.**, c. 1951
gold filled $80 $160 $225

BULOVA, 17J., cal.11 af, ca.1959
gold filled $40 $85 $150
14K $100 $200 $300

BULOVA, 17 jewels, fancy long lugs, C. 1954
gold filled $65 $125 $165

BULOVA, 17J., center sec., auto wind, Ca.1951
gold filled $50 $100 $165

BULOVA, 21J, fancy lugs, c.1950
gold filled $50 $90 $165

BULOVA, 23 J, Mystery dial, center sec., c. 1959
14k. $150 $275 $325

BULOVA, 15J., military style,c.1940
s. steel $50 $125 $175

BULOVA, cal. 700, **canteen** style, c. 1946
s. steel . . . . ★★★$350 $700 $800

BULOVA, 15J., military style, cat 10 bnch, c.1940
s. steel $75 $125 $165

BULOVA, 17J., U.S.A. military, c.1945
s. steel $75 $125 $165

BULOVA, 17J., 20 diamond dial
14k(w) $185 $325 $400

BULOVA, 23J., 12 diamond dial, c. 1959
14k(w) $200 $400 $600

BULOVA, 30J., diam. dial, cal#10B2AC, C.1960s
14k(w) $200 $400 $600

BULOVA, diamond dial, c. 1939
platinum $600 $1,100 $1,400
14k(w) $400 $800 $900

BULOVA, 21 jewels, hidden lugs, diamond dial, c. 1935
14k. $400 $750 $900

BULOVA, **hidden lugs**, diamond dial, c. 1945
14k. $400 $700 $900

BULOVA, 21 jewels, diamond dial, long lugs, c. 1941
14k(w)..................... $250 $500 $650

BULOVA, 17J., 3 diamond dial, cal.8,ae, c.1949
14k........................ $200 $375 $425

BULOVA, early auto wind movement (see below)

BULOVA, early auto wind, "Champ", c. 1930. Some may be
signed on dial "Aster"
gold filled .... * * * $300 $600 $725

BULOVA, 17 jewels, curved, cal 7AP, c. 1939
14k........................ $300 $550 $700

BULOVA, 17J., drivers watch, c.1935
gold filled $200 $400 $550

BULOVA, 17J., engraved. Ca. 1928
gold filled $85 $165 $185

BULOVA, 17J., 5th ave., cal.6am, engraved bezel, c.1935
gold filled $60 $100 $150

BULOVA, 21J., stepped bezel, curved,
gold filled $75 $150 $200

BULOVA, 21J., plain bezel, curved,
gold filled $75 $150 $200

BULOVA, 17J., cal. 7ap, c.1937
gold filled $75 $150 $200

BULOVA, 17J., curved, cal.7ap, c.1936
gold filled $75 $150 $225

BULOVA, 17J., cal.13al,c.1935
14k. $200 $375 $450

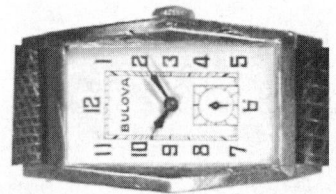

BULOVA, 17 J., cal 9af, c. 1929
s. steel $45 $80 $100

BULOVA, 17J., cal.7ap, c.1934
gold filled $75 $150 $200

BULOVA, 15J., cal 10ac, c1938
gold filled $75 $150 $200

BULOVA, 17 jewels, curved, c. 1939
gold filled $75 $150 $200

BULOVA, 21 jewels, curved, c. 1939
gold filled $100 $200 $250

BULOVA, 21J., cal#6AE,
14k. $200 $400 $450

BULOVA, 17 jewels, duo dial, c. 1935
gold filled(S.S.back) $350 $700 $800
s. steel $300 $600 $700

BULOVA, 17 jewels, **2 tone**, duo dial
gold filled(S.S.back) $400 $750 $850
s. steel $350 $600 $700

BULOVA, 17 jewels, 2 tone dial, **flexible lugs**, fancy bezel
s. steel $75 $150 $200

Wrist Watches listed in this section are priced at the collectable
fair market Trade Show level **as complete** watches having an
original gold-filled case and stainless steel back, also with original
dial, leather watch band, and the entire original movements in
good working order with no repairs needed.

BULOVA, 21J., **President, wandering sec.**, c. 1932
gold filled $150 $300 $400
gold filled (**32 jewels**). $200 $375 $450

BULOVA, 17 jewels, cal. 10GM, fancy lugs, c. 1953
gold filled $75 $150 $175
14k. $175 $350 $450

BULOVA, 15J., fancy lugs, c.1952
gold filled $75 $150 $175

BULOVA, 21J., fancy lugs, c.1952
14k. $200 $400 $600
gold filled $60 $125 $165

BULOVA, 17J., fancy lugs, cal.8an, c. 1951
14k. $300 $600 $800
gold filled $100 $200 $300

BULOVA, 17J., cal.8ad, fancy lugs, c.1939
gold plate $60 $125 $150

BULOVA, 21J., cal. 7ak, c.1945
gold filled $75 $150 $175

BULOVA, 21J., c.1950s
14K $150 $300 $375
gold filled $60 $100 $150

BULOVA, 21J., scalloped case, c.1950s
gold filled $90 $175 $200

BULOVA, 7J., c.1945
gold filled $60 $120 $150

Pricing in this Guide are fair market price for complete watches which are reflected from the "**NAWCC**" National and regional shows.

BULOVA, 17J., fancy lugs, Ca. 1941
14K $175 $275 $350
gold filled $75 $150 $175

BULOVA, 17J., Ca.1953
gold filled $75 $150 $200

BULOVA, 21J., **curved case**, c.1948
14k. $150 $300 $350

BULOVA, 21J., cal.7ak, c.1945
gold filled $75 $150 $175

BULOVA, 17J., cal.8ae, fancy hidden lugs, c.1941
gold filled $75 $125 $200

BULOVA, 21J., c.1945
gold filled $75 $100 $165

BULOVA, 17 jewels, cal. 7AK, c. 1930
gold filled $85 $135 $185

BULOVA, 17 jewels, fancy long lugs, c. 1942
14k. $200 $325 $400

BULOVA, 17 jewels, cal. 10BM, Ca. 1954
gold filled $60 $125 $165

BULOVA, 17J., cal. 8AC, **flip up, photo watch**, c. 1940
gold filled $200 $375 $450
14k. $350 $600 $700

〜 Some grades are not included. Their values can be deter
mined by comparing with **similar** age, size, metal content, style,
models and grades listed.

BULOVA, 15 jewels, wandering hr. mm. sec., c. 1928
s. steel $150 $300 $400

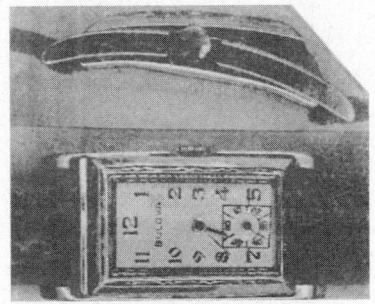

BULOVA, 17J., **right angle case**
gold filled $150 $300 $350

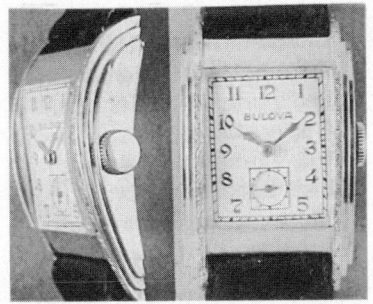

BULOVA, 17J., right angle, cal. 8AZ, c. 1938
gold filled $150 $300 $400
14k. $300 $600 $700

BULOVA, 17J., center sec., cal. 10bac, c.1935
gold filled $65 $125 $200

BULOVA, 17 jewels, aux. sec.
14k. $125 $250 $300

BULOVA, 17J., cal.8ac, fancy lugs, c.1940
gold plate $45 $100 $125

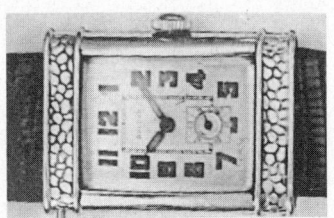

BULOVA, 17 jewels, fancy bezel
gold filled $100 $200 $250

BULOVA, 17J., flared top of case & sides,
gold filled $75 $150 $175

BULOVA, 17 jewels, **bell shaped lugs**
14k. $150 $300 $400

BULOVA, 21J., hidden lugs, c. 1961
gold filled $75 $150 $175

BULOVA, 21J., hidden lugs, c.1950s
14k. $150 $300 $400

BULOVA, 17J., engraved bezel only
base metal. $50 $100 $150

BULOVA, 21J., hidden lugs, c.1945
gold filled $75 $150 $175

BULOVA, 15J., cal.11ac, c 1958
gold filled $50 $100 $175

BULOVA, 17J., BMW- logo, c.1957
gold filled $70 $150 $200

BULOVA, 15J., cal 10ae, c.1935
gold filled $50 $100 $165

BULOVA, 17J., FORD logo, c. 1947
base metal. $40 $125 $175

BULOVA, 7J cal. 10bc, c. 1949
gold filled $60 $120 $150

BULOVA, 17J., engraved lugs & bezel, cal.10an,c.1928
s. steel $45 $100 $125

BULOVA, **Masonic** dial, Ca. 1944
gold filled $100 $200 $250

BULOVA, 15 jewels, **Senator**,
gold filled $75 $150 $175

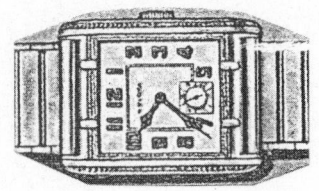

DIARS FOR MINT PRICES MUST BE ALL **ORIGINAL**.
BULOVA, 15 jewels, Ambassador,
gold filled $60 $120 $150

BULOVA, 17 jewels, **Oakley**,
gold filled $60 $120 $150

BULOVA 17jewels **Argyle**,
14K $200 $300 $400

BULOVA, 17 jewels, **LONE EAGLE**, stepped style case
gold filled $75 $150 $175

BULOVA 15 jewels Norman,
gold filled $60 $120 $150

BULOVA, 15 jewels, **LONE EAGLE**, tonneau style ease
gold filled $60 $125 $150

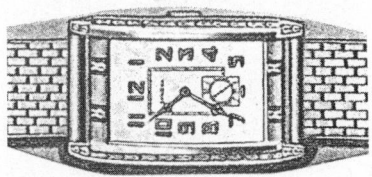

BULOVA, 15 jewels, **Spencer**,
gold filled $60 $120 $150

BULOVA, 17J., **LONE EAGLE**, radium & cut corner dial
gold filled $75 $150 $200

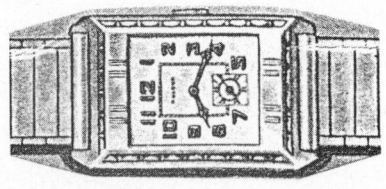

BULOVA, 17 jewels, **Wellington**,
14K $200 $400 $450

DIALS FOR MINT PRICES MUST BE ALL **ORIGINAL**.

BULOVA, 17 jewels, fancy lugs
14k.........................$150 $300 $400

BULOVA, 17 jewels, "The Ambassador"
gold filled $75 $150 $175

BULOVA, 17 jewels, "The Curtis,"
gold filled $95 $150 $175

BULOVA, 15 jewels, "The Athelet"
gold filled $75 $150 $175

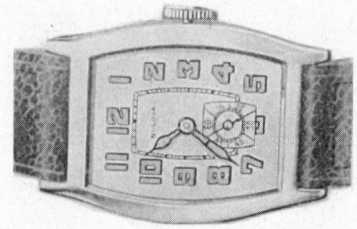

BULOVA, 17 jewels, "The Governor,"
14K.........................$150 $300 $375

BUREN, 17 jewels, day-date-month, moon phase
s. steel $225 $400 $475

BUREN, 17 jewels, long lugs
14k (rose) $135 $250 $300

BUREN, 17 jewels, center lugs, c.1940
9k $100 $200 $250

BUTEX, 17J., triple date, moon ph.
gold filled $200 $400 $500

CARLTON, 15 jewels, "**Rite angle**" case, c. 1939
gold filled $125 $200 $250
14k.........................$250 $500 $550

CARTIER, "**Pasha**", automatic, 300ft, **recent**
18k C & B $4,000 $7,000 $8,000
18k leather $1,600 $3,500 $4,500

CARTIER, "Golf", **Quartz**, 100 ft., **4 counters, recent**
18k C & B $9,000 $14,000 $16,500
18k leather $6,000 $9,000 $12,000

CARTIER, "**Pasha**", automatic, 300 ft., **rotating bezel, recent**
18k C & B $4,000 $7,500 $8,500
18k leather $1,700 $3,600 $4,500

CARTIER, "Diabolo", automatic, 100ft, **tourbillon, recent**
18k leather $25,000 $40,000 $50,000

CARTIER, "**Pasha**", automatic, 300ft, W/grill, **recent**
18k C & B $5,000 $9,000 $11,000
18k leather $2,500 $4,500 $5,500

✍ Pricing in this Guide are fair market price for
COMPLETE watches which are reflected from the "NAWCC"
National and regional shows.

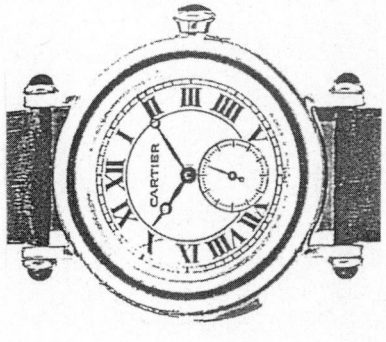

CARTIER, "Diabolo", manual wind, Min, **Repeater, recent**
18k leather $30,000 $50,000 $60,000

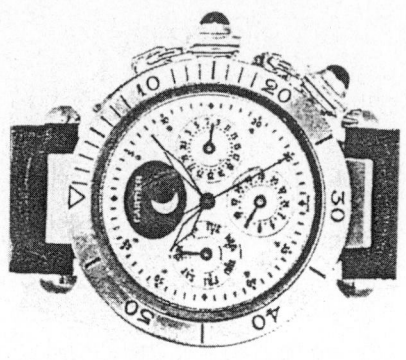

CARTIER, "**Pasha**", automatic, rotating bezel, 100 ft., **recent**
18k C & B $8,000 $13,000 $15,000
18k leather $6,000 $9,500 $11,000

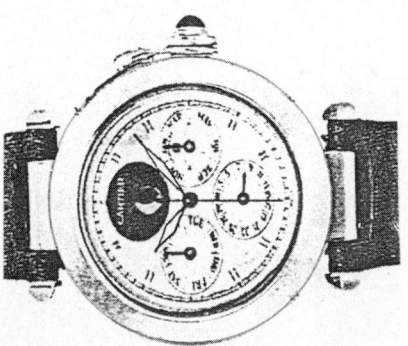

CARTIER, "Pasha", automatic, moon phases, 100 ft., **recent**
18k C & B $8,000 $12,000 $14,000
18k leather $5,000 $8,000 $10,000

CARTIER, "Pasha', **Min. Repeater**, moon phases, **recent**
18k C & B $40,000 $68,000 $75,000
18k leather $35,000 $62,000 $70,000

🖙 Pricing in this Guide are fair market price for COMPLETE watches which are reflected from the NAWCC National and regional shows.

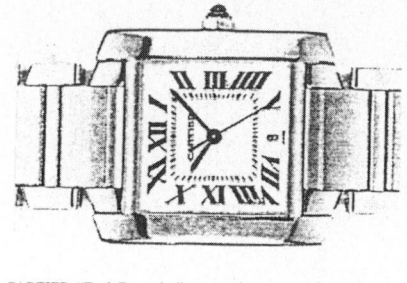

CARTIER, "Tank Francaise", automatic, date, 100 ft., **large**
18k C & B $5,000 $7,500 $9,000
18k leather $1,800 $3,300 $4,000

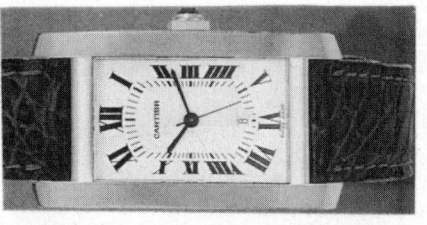

CARTIER, "Tank Americaine", automatic, date, **recent**
18k C & B $4,000 $7,500 $9,000
18k leather $2,500 $3,800 $4,500

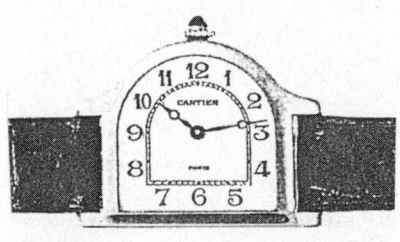

CARTIER, "Cloche", manual wind, **recent**
18k leather $1,800 $3,500 $4,500

CARTIER, "Santos Ronde", automatic, rotating bezel,100 ft., **recent**
18k C & B $2,000 $4,000 $5,500

CARTIER, 18J., **8 day Mvt.,** tank style, by E. W. Co.
18k *$14,000 $24,000 $30,000

CARTIER, 18 J., sapphire crown & bezel, c. 1970
18k $2,500 $4,500 $6,000

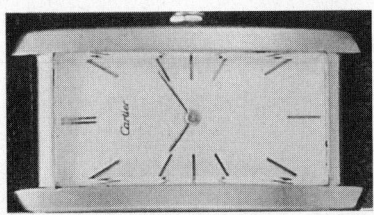

CARTIER, 18 jewels, curved, tank style, Ca.1970,s
18k $4,000 $7,000 $8,000

CARTIER, 18 jewels, curved, signed E. W. Co., c.1930s
18k $4,000 $7,000 $8,000

CARTIER, 18J., tank style, platinum case & band
platinum C&B *$7,000 $13,000 $15,000

NOTE: With original **Cartier 18K** Deployment clasp ADD $400
to $600.

CARTIER, 18 jewels, tank style case, c. 1970s
18k $1,800 $3,500 $4,000

CARTIER, 20 jewels, tank style case, c. 1950
18k $1,800 $3,250 $4,000

CARTIER, Must de, **quartz**, tank style case, c. 1980s
Vermeil =(gold over sterling)
G.P. vermeil $200 $400 $600
SAME STYLE CASE AS ABOVE
CARTIER, Must de, **Mechanical**, tank style case, c.1980s
Vermeil "(gold over sterling)
G.P. vermeil $200 $400 $600

CARTIER, 18 jewels, tank style, European W. Co.
platinum $5,000 $9,000 $14,000

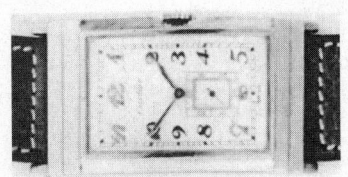

CARTIER, 18 jewels, by Movado
14k $900 $1,500 $1,800

CARTIER, 18 jewels, **duo plan**, European W. Co.
18k C&B $2,000 $3,500 $4,000

CARTIER, 18J., by Le Coultre, long lugs
18k $1,500 $2,800 $3,500

CARTIER, 18 jewels, curved, hidden lugs
18k $3,000 $5,500 $6,500

CARTIER, 18 jewels, by Universal, c 1960
18k $750 $1,400 $1,600

CARTIER, 18 jewels, center lugs, c. 1930
18k $1,800 $3,500 $4,000

CARTIER, 18J., "Cabriolet" reversible, by Le Coultre, C.1930
18k $10,000 $18,000 $24,000

CARTIER, 18 J., **reversible** to view **2nd time zone**
18k $12,000 $20,000 $25,000

CARTIER, 18 jewels, Gents, by European W. Co. c. 1927
18k $3,000 $6,000 $7,500

CARTIER, 18J., early E.W.Co., C. 1928
18k $2,500 $4,500 $5,500

CARTIER, 18J., lady's watch by European W. Co.
18k C&B $1,200 $2,500 $3,000

CARTIER, 18 J., sovonnette (hunter case style), C. 1928
18k $5,000 $9,000 $12,000

CARTIER, 18J., E.W.Co, Tank Normale, Ca. 1925
18k $2,500 $4,500 $5,000

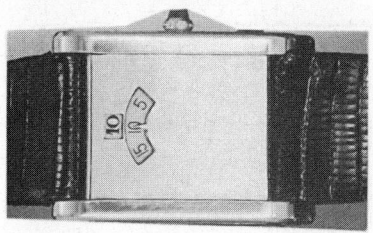

CARTIER, 18 J., guichet tank, jump hr. & min. by E.W.Co.
18k $20,000 $35,000 $45,000

CARTIER, 18 jewels, "Santos", octagonal, date
18k & s. steel C&B............. $700 $1,400 $1,600

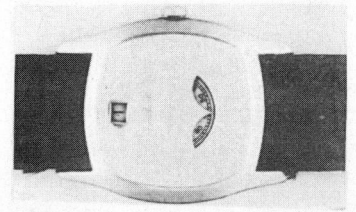

CARTIER, 18 J., jump hr. & mm., E. W. Co. c. 1930
platinum $25,000 $40,000 $50,000

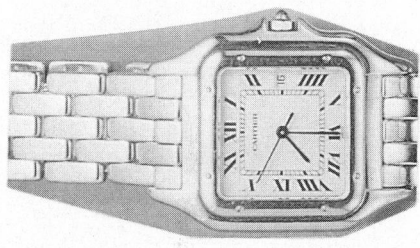

CARTIER, Panthere, date, water resistant, Medium size

s. steel band	$600	$1,100	$1,400
1 stripe of gold, quartz.........	$500	$900	$1,200
2 stripes of gold, quartz........	$600	$1,200	$1,600
3 stripes of gold, quartz........	$1,200	$2,100	$2,600
18k reg. C & B................	$3,000	$5,500	$6,500
18k large C & B..............	$3,500	$6,000	$7,000
lady's, s. steel band	$500	$1,000	$1,300
lady's, 1 stripe of gold	$500	$900	$1,100
lady's, 2 stripe of gold	$700	$1,400	$1,800
lady's, 3 stripe of gold	$700	$1,600	$2,000
lady's, 18k C & B	$3,500	$5,000	$6,000

CARTIER, 18 J., "Santos", mechanical, cal.21
mens 18k.................... $1,800 $3,000 $3,500
ladies 18k $1,800 $2,500 $3,000

CARTIER, 25 jewels, chronog., European W. Co.
18k...................... $40,000 $65,000 $80,000

CARTIER, 18 J., "Santos," 18k & s. steel case, band, **Lady's**
platinum & 18k C&B.......... $3,500 $7,000 $9,000
18k & s. steel C&B............. $700 $1,400 $1,800

CARTIER, 18 jewels, "Santos," date, Gents, Ca. 1980's
18k & s. steel C&B............. $700 $1,200 $1,800

CARTIER, 29 jewels, min. repeater, c. 1925
18k...................... $75,000 $120,000 $150,000

CARTIER, 18 jewels, c. 1925
18k......................$2,000 $3,500 $4,000

CARTIER, 18 jewels, asymmetric, E. W. Co., c. 1928
18k......................$4,000 $7,000 $10,000

CARTIER, 18 J., oval maxi, C. 1968
18k......................$4,000 $7,500 $10,000

CARTIER, 18 jewels, by Le Coultre
18k......................$1,000 $2,500 $3,000

CARTIER, 18 J., bamboo style bezel, Gents, C.1970s
18k......................$1,800 $3,500 $4,500

NOTE: With original **Cartier 18K** Deployment clasp **ADD $400 to $600**.

CARTIER, 18 J., large cut corner bezel, C. 1970s
18k......................$1,800 $3,000 $4,000

CARTIER, 18 J., "Helm", single lug, C. 1950s
18k......................$6,000 $9,000 $12,000
platinum..................$10,000 $18,000 $22,000

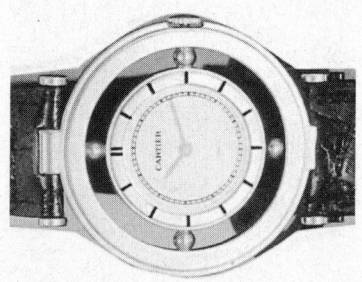

CARTIER, 18 J., by E.W.CO., single lug, C. 1949
18k......................$3,000 $6,000 $8,000

CARTIER, 29 J., **min. repeater, by Le Coultre**, c. 1930
platinum..................$40,000 $75,000 $90,000

CARTIER, 18 J., triple date, moon ph., tear-drop lugs, marked
European Watch & Clock Co., Ca. 1945
s. steel $5,000 $9,000 $12,000
18K $8,000 $12,000 $15,000

CARTIER, 18 J., Ca 1985
18K $1,200 $2,000 $3,000

CARTIER, 18J, day of week & date chapter, by Le Coultre
14k. $800 $1,500 $2,000

CARTIER, Quartz, 296 diamonds on bezel & 18k Band
18k. $10,000 $17,000 $22,000

CARTIER, 18 J., lady's, back wind, E.W.CO., c.1940s
18k. $1,000 $2,000 $2,500

CARTIER, 18J., tonneau, lady's, c. 1920
platinum $3,000 $6,000 $8,000

CARTIER, 18 J., lady's, E.W.Co., C.1949
14k(w) C&B $600 $1,100 $1,400

CERTINA, I 7J., "NEWART", auto-wind, date, c. 1965
14k. $100 $200 $300

CENTRAL, 7J., cal.39, c.1937
gold filled $55 $100 $125

CHEVROLET, 6J., in form of car radiator, C. 1927
silver $750 $1,100 $1,500

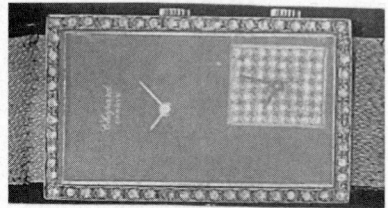

CHOPARD, 18 J., 2 dial , 2 time zones, diam. bezel
18k C&B $1,500 $3,000 $3,500

CLEBAR, 17 jewels, chronog., 2 reg., cal.2248, c.1952
gold filled $150 $300 $400
base metal $125 $275 $325

CHOPARD, 18 J., skeletonized, diamonds on case & hands
18k. $1,500 $3,000 $4,000

CLEBAR, 17 jewels, chronog., 3 reg. c.1950s
gold filled $250 $400 $475
s. steel $250 $400 $475

CHOPARD, 28J., triple date moon ph., cal.900, c.1980
18k. $900 $1,500 $2,000

CLEBAR, 17J., chronog., triple case, moon ph.
gold filled $600 $1,100 $1,300
s. steel $600 $1,100 $1,300

CHOPARD, 20J., RF#2113, c.1978
18k. $300 $550 $650

CHOPARD, 17J., RF#2134, c.1978
18k. $200 $400 $600

CLEBAR, 17 jewels, center lugs, chronog., c. 1938
s. steel $300 $575 $650

CONCORD, 17J., aux. sec., ca. 1947
14k. $175 $275 $375

CONCORD, 17 jewels, center sec.
14k. $200 $375 $450

CONCORD, 17 jewels, chronog. 2 reg., c.1940x
s. steel $175 $300 $400

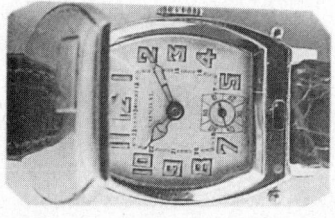

CONDAL, 15J. **hunter style**, flip top, C. 1928
silver $250 $500 $600

CONTINENTAL, 17J., 3 **diamond dial**
14k. $150 $250 $350

CORNAVIN, 17J., day date, c. 1960
gold filled $100 $195 $250

CORNAVIN, 17J., date, auto, RF#1243, C.1963
gold filled $50 $100 $150
s. steel $50 $100 $150

CORONET, 17J., chronog.
s. steel $150 $275 $350

CORTEBERT, 17 jewels, "Chronometre" ,Ca. 1945
18K $200 $350 $450

MILLIMETERS 10   20   30   40   50

CORTEBERT, 17 J., "Sport," triple date, moon phase

18k	$500	$850	$1,000
gold filled	$200	$400	$600

CORTEBERT, 17 jewels, center sec.

s. steel	$30	$60	$75

CORTEBERT, quartz, U.K. military, (CWC)

s. steel	$50	$100	$125

CORTEBERT, (CWC), chronog., by Valjoux, c.1971

s. steel	$250	$450	$550

CORUM, 17 J., twenty dollar gold piece= 22K, coin 18k band.

22k leather band (quartz)	$1,500	$3,000	$4,000
22k, leather band (M. wind)	$1,200	$3,000	$4,500
22k, gold band, (M. wind)	$3,000	$4,000	$5,500

CORUM, 24k gold ingot, 15 Grams, manual wind

24k	$1,000	$1,700	$2,000

CORUM, 17 J., in form of Rolls-Royce car Grill

18k (reg.)	$2,000	$4,000	$5,000
18k (large)	$2,600	$4,500	$5,500

CORUM, 17 jewels, "Golden Bridge", in line train, recent

18k	$2,000	$4,000	$5,000

CORUM, 17 jewels, rope style bezel

18k C&B	$1,100	$2,000	$2,500

CORUM (continued)

725

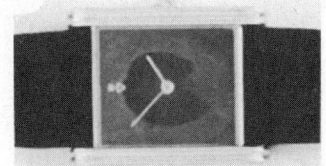

CORUM, 17 jewels, peacock feather dial
18k. $600 $1,000 $1,200

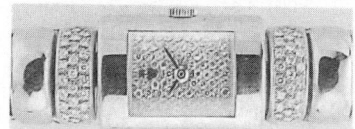

CORUM, 21 jewels, "**Pave**" diamond dial, c.1990
18k C&B. $2,000 $3,000 $3,500

CORUM, 21 jewels, gold dial
18k. $250 $375 $500

CORUM, 17J., "**Graff**", 2 time zones, Ca. 1965
18K $600 $1,100 $1,300

CRAWFORD, 17J., chronog. engraved bezel
base metal. $125 $250 $300

CRAWFORD, 17J., hooded lugs, c. 1940
14k. $100 $200 $300

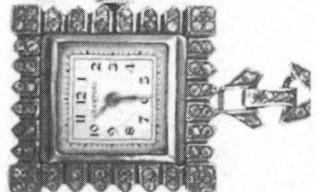

CRAWFORD, 17J., pendant watch, marcasites
base metal. $55 $100 $150

CROTON, 17 jewels, day date
gold filled $40 $75 $100

CROTON, 17 jewels, diamond bezel & dial
14k(w). $200 $400 $500

CROTON, 17 jewels, chronog., c. 1948
s. steel $185 $300 $375

CROTON, 17 jewels, chronog., c. 1946
s. steel $200 $350 $400

CROTON, 17 jewels, cal.630, c.1943
gold filled $65 $100 $150

CROTON, 17 jewels, Ca 1937
14k. $100 $250 $300

CROTON, 17 jewels, fancy lugs
14k. $200 $400 $500

CROTON, 7J., **drivers** style, **winds at 12** o'clock, c.1938
gold filled $100 $165 $250

CROTON, 17 jewels, swinging lugs, cal.f3x, c.1940
14k. $100 $200 $300

CROWN, 7J., luminous dial
base metal. $40 $75 $100

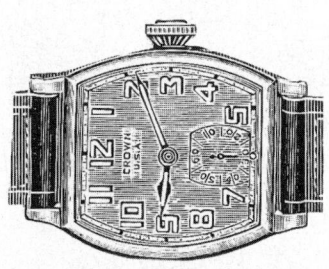

CROWN, 7J., luminous dial
gold filled $50 $100 $125

CYMA, 15J., aux. sec., ca 1935
nickel $40 $100 $150

CYMA,7J.,enamel dial, wire lugs, (signal corp. USA),c.1928
silver. $150 $300 $400

CYMA, 17 jewels, aux. sec.

18k.	$150	$300	$350
14k.	$125	$275	$325
gold filled	$50	$100	$125

CYMA, 15J., Ca. 1930

gold filled	$65	$125	$175

CYMA, 15J., military style, cal.234, Ca.1945

s. steel	$75	$200	$250

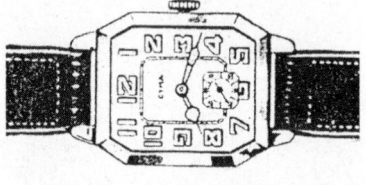

CYMA, 15J.,

base metal	$30	$75	$100

🖝 Some grades are not included. Their values can be determined by comparing with similar age, size, metal content, style, models and grades listed.

🖝 A collector should expect to pay modestly higher prices as local shops

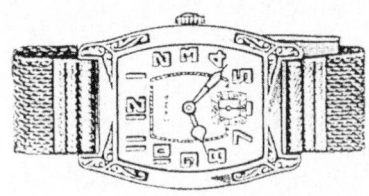

CYMA, 15J. , engraved case

chromium	$40	$100	$125

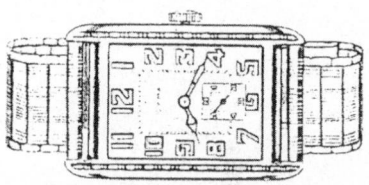

CYMA, 15J., engraved case

chromium	$40	$100	$125

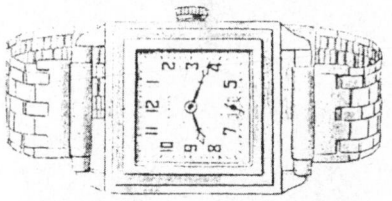

CYMA, 15J., 2-tone case

chromium	$40	$100	$125

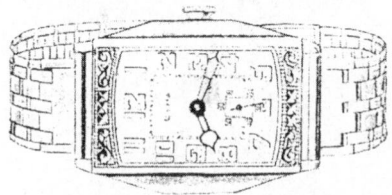

CYMA, 15J., engraved case

chromium	$40	$100	$125

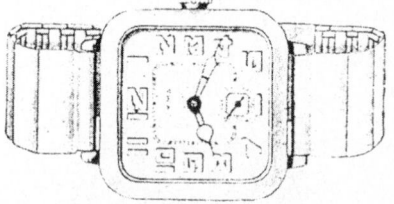

CYMA, 15J.,

chromium	$40	$100	$125

🖝 Pricing in this Guide are fair market price for complete watches which are reflected from the **"NAWCC"** and regional shows.

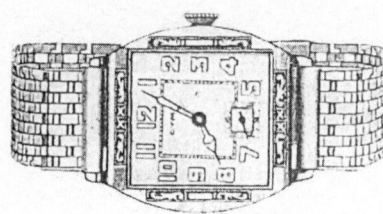

CYMA, 15J., engraved case
chromium $40 $100 $125

DAU, 15J., wire lugs, c.1915
14k. $75 $90 $135

DAYNITE, 7J., **8 day movement by Hebdomas**, Ca. 1920
s. steel $200 $375 $500

DELBANA, 17J., fancy hooded lugs, c.1951
14k. $100 $200 $300

DIDISHEIM, 15J., "Winton", enamel art deco bezel, c.1927
14k (wt) $150 $275 $350

P. DITISHEIM, 16 J., "Solvil," fancy bezel, c. 1935
18k $400 $700 $900

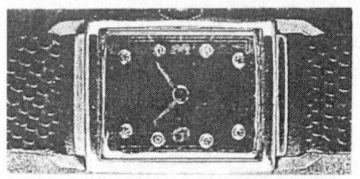

P. DITISHEIM, 17 J., "Solvil," diamond dial, c. 1947
18K $400 $700 $900

P. DITISHEIM, 17 J., "Solvil," diamond dial, c. 1948
platinum $600 $1,200 $1,500

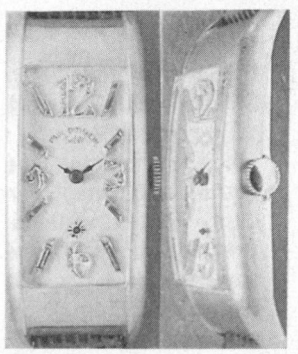

P. DITISHEIM, 17 J., "Solvil," curved, diamond dial
platinum $1,500 $3,000 $3,500

P. DITISHEIM, 17 jewels, diamond dial, curved
platinum $1,200 $2,500 $3,000

P. DITISHEIM, 17 J., baguette diamonds, fancy bezel
platinum $1,200 $2,000 $2,300

P. DITISHEIM, 17 jewels, hinged lugs, enameled bezel
14k. $600 $1,000 $1,500

DOME, 25 jewels, triple dates, moon ph., auto wind
18k. $450 $850 $1,000

DORIC, 17J., **fancy lugs**, two tone case, c. 1935
gold filled $55 $100 $135

DOXA, 17 jewels, aux sec.
gold filled $50 $65 $125

DOXA, 17 jewels, center sec., fancy lugs
14k. $125 $275 $350

DOXA, 17 jewels, chronog., fluted lugs
14k. $350 $600 $700

DOXA, 17J., chronog., date, 3 reg., by Valjoux
gold filled $200 $400 $500
14k. $400 $650 $1,000

DOXA, 17 jewels, chronog., triple dates, **moon phase**
14k. $1,000 $2,000 $2,750

DOXA, 17 jewels, chronog., 2 reg., c. 1942
gold filled $300 $600 $800

DOXA, 17 jewels, chronog., cal. 1220, c. 1940
gold filled $200 $350 $450
s. steel $250 $550 $550

DOXA, 17 jewels, center sec
s. steel $50 $90 $125

DOXA, 17 jewels, center sec., c. 1949
gold filled $50 $100 $125

DOXA, 17J., "Grafic" date,
14k. $100 $200 $300

DOXA, 17J., cal. 1361, c.1948
14k. $175 $300 $400

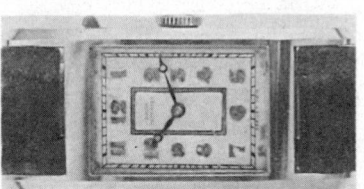

DRIVA, 15 jewels, repeater, repeats on gong, **1/4
repeater** activated by bolt above hand, c. 1930
s. steel $3,000 $6,000 $7,000

DRIVA, 15 jewels, 5 min. **repeater**, activated by bolt
14k. $2,250 $4,000 $5,000

DRIVA, 17 jewels, double teardrop lugs, c.1945
14k. $200 $400 $500

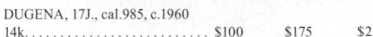

DUGENA, 17J., cal.985, c.1960
14k......................... $100 $175 $250

DUNHILL, 17J., date, auto w., alarm by Le Coultre, c. 1965
s. steel...................... $700 $1,300 $1,600

DUNHILL, 15J., by Bulwark W. Co., engraved bezel, c. 1930
gold filled.................... $45 $75 $100

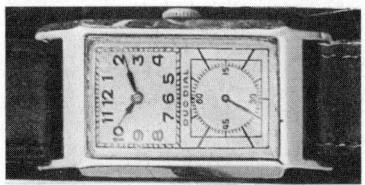

DUODIAL, 15 jewels, c. 1934
9k $525 $1,000 $1,500

EBEL, 21 jewels, chronog., self winding, perpetual cal.
18k.........................$4,000 $7,000 $9,000

EBEL, 18 jewels, Ca.1959
18k......................... $200 $400 $500

EBEL, 18 jewels, applied gold numbers, c. 1950
18k......................... $300 $600 $700

EBEL, 18 jewels, Ca. 1958
14k......................... $200 $400 $500

EBEL, 17 jewels, slide open to wind
leather.........................$150 $250 $325

EBEL, 17 jewels, chronog., 2 reg., enamel dial
s. steel...................... $200 $400 $500

EBEL, 17 jewels, chronog., c. 1955
14k. $350 $700 $900
gold filled $200 $375 $450

EBEL, 17 jewels, chronog, "pulsation", c. 1943
s. steel $300 $575   675

EBEL, 17 jewels, chronog., 3 reg., c. 1941
14k. $500 $900 $1,100
s. steel $200 $400 $500

EBEL, 17J., "Sport", c.1949
gold filled $60 $80 $135

EBEL, 17J., cal.119, auto-wind, c.1950
s. steel $60 $1200 $150

EBEL, 17J., cal.93, auto-wind, center sec., c.1950
18k. $250 $500 $600

EBERHARD, 15 jewels, Protective Guard, Ca 1920
Silver. $300 $550 $650

EBERHARD, 18 jewels, split sec. chronog., 3 reg.
18k. $6,500 $12,000 $15,000

Pricing in this Guide are fair market price for complete watches
which are reflected from the NAWCC Nations and regional shows.

EBERHARD, 17 J., tele-tachymeter, enamel dial, c. 1930
18k........................$1,600 $3,000 $4,000

EBERHARD, 17J., water proof, auto wind, triple date, moon phases
18k rose...................$1,200 $2,200 $2,500

EBERHARD, 17jewels, "Extra Fort", chronog., 2 reg., note:
Button at 4 slides to lock chronograph action.
18k........................$1,500 $2,750 $3,100

EKEGREN, 18jewels, **Jumping hr.,** c. 1920
platinum $4,000 $10,000 $15,000
18k........................$3,000 $8,000 $10,000

EBERHARD, 17 J., chronog., center lugs, 1 button, enamel dial
s. steel $800 $1,500 $2,000

ELECTRA W. Co., 17J, chronog., 1 button, hinged back,
enamel dial
silver.....................$450 $900 $1,100

EBERHARD, 17J., wire lugs, enamel dial, c.1928 **watch fits inside
of early waterproof case**
silver.....................$400 $600 $800

ELECTRA W. Co., 17J, chronog., 1 button, hinged back, wire lugs,
enamel dial
silver.....................$650 $1,100 $1,500

ELGIN, 17J., Fancy hidden lugs, Ca. 1950
gold filled $125 $225 $325

ELGIN, 17J., **hidden logs, 7 diamonds & 8 baguettes**
14K $300 $550 $650

LORD ELGIN, 21J., extended lugs, Ca.1955
14k. $150 $300 $450

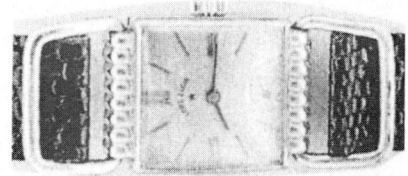

LORD ELGIN, 21J , hinged lugs
gold filled $75 $125 $175

LORD ELGIN, 21J., extended lugs,
gold filled $135 $225 $300

ELGIN, 15-17J., hooded lugs, gold jewel settings, Ca. 1925
gold filled $125 $225 $300
14k(w) $300 $550 $650

LORD ELGIN, 21J., hooded bezel, Ca. 1933
14K $165 $300 $375

LORD ELGIN, 21J., Ca. 1948
14K $100 $250 $300

ELGIN, 19J., fancy bezel, c.1950s
gold filled $175 $275 $350

LORD ELGIN, 21J., **3 diamonds**, cal.626, c.1950
14k(w) $175 $300 $400

ELGIN, 21J., cal.626, 3 diamonds, Ca.1950'a
14k. $150 $300 $400

ELGIN, 17J., stepped hooded lugs, c. 1925
gold filled $75 $125 $185

ELGIN, 17J., stepped case, Ca. 1935
gold filled $75 $125 $175

ELGIN, 17J., side lugs, Ca. 1958
gold filled $100 $200 $300

ELGIN, 15J., cal. 554, Ca. 1950's
gold filled $75 $125 $175

ELGIN, 7-15J., **stepped case**, sold for $25.00 in 1936
gold filled $75 $125 $175

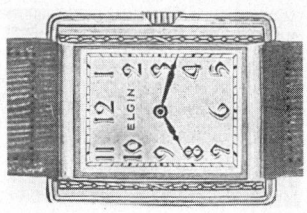

ELGIN, 15J., Sq. lugs, embossed dial, Ca.1929
gold filled $75 $125 $175

ELGIN, 21J., Lord Elgin, Ca. 1945
14k. $150 $300 $400

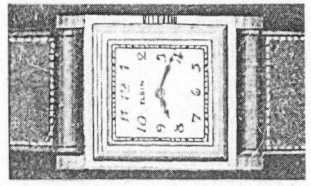

ELGIN, 15J., Crown Guard, Ca.1929
gold filled $75 $125 $175

ELGIN, 17J **Dollar markers** on dial, Ca. 1955
gold filled $75 $110 $175

ELGIN, 19J., cal. 626, Ca. 1946
14k. $175 $325 $450

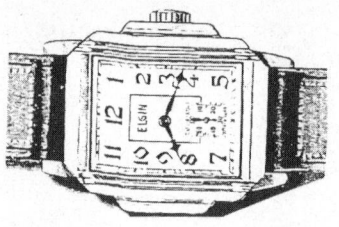

ELGIN, 17J., embossed dial, sold for $35.00 in 1936,
gold filled $75 $125 $175

LORD ELGIN, 21J., **11 diamonds**, Ca. 1946
14K $200 $450 $600

LORD ELGIN, 21J.,
gold filled $75 $125 $175

ELGIN, 15J., Legionnaire. Ca. 1929
gold filled $75 $125 $185

ELGIN, engraved case, Ca. 1924
14k. $125 $250 $350

LORD ELGIN, 21J., cal.625, c. 1950
14k. $150 $300 $400

LORD ELGIN, 21J., cal. 713 GJS, c.1958
14k. $150 $300 $400

ELGIN, 17J., deluxe, Ca. 1955
gold filled $75 $125 $175

LORD ELGIN, 21J., cal.559, c.1942
gold filled $75 $125 $175
Wrist Watches listed in this section are priced at the collectable
fair market Trade Show level as **complete** watches having an
original gold-filled case and stainless steel back, also with original
dial, leather watch band, and the entire original movement in good
working order with no repairs needed.

LORD ELGIN, 21J., GJS, c. 1936
14k. $125 $225 $325

LORD ELGIN, 21J., GJS, cal.626, c.1940
14k. $125 $225 $325

ELGIN, 17J., **Adonis**, engraved, Ca. 1929
gold filled $125 $225 $300

ELGIN, 17J., "Dura Power" mainspring LOGO,
gold plate $70 $100 $125

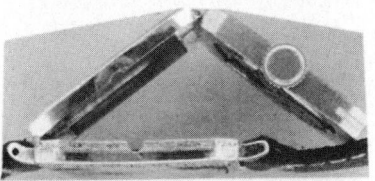

ELGIN, 7J., **hinged case, engraved case,** c. 1920s
gold filled $75 $125 $175

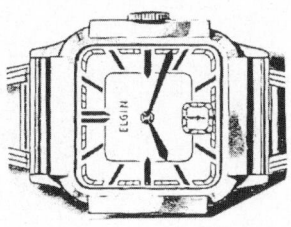

ELGIN,17J., embossed dial, sold for $25.00 in 1936
gold filled $75 $125 $175

ELGIN, 17 jewels, raised numbers
14k. $125 $275 $325

LORD ELGIN, 21 jewels, curved, raised numbers
14k. $125 $275 $350

ELGIN, 17 jewels, **embossed dial**
14k. $125 $275 $350

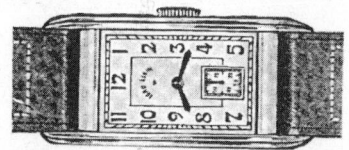

LORD ELGIN, 21 jewels, curved
gold filled $75 $125 $175

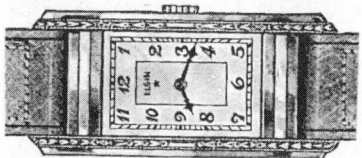

ELGIN, 17 jewels, curved, "Streamlined"
gold filled $75 $125 $175

☞ Some grades are not included. Their values can be determined by comparing with similar age, size, metal content, style, grades, or models such as time only, chronograph, repeater etc. listed.

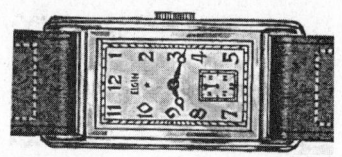

ELGIN, 17 jewels, raised numbers
gold filled $75 $125 $175

ELGIN, 15 jewels, curved, fancy bezel
gold filled $75 $125 $175

LORD ELGIN, 21 jewels, curved
platinum $300 $600 $700

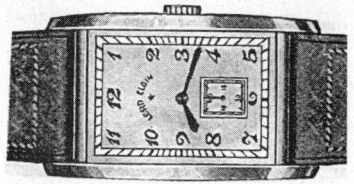

LORD ELGIN, 21 jewels, curved
14k. $175 $350 $450

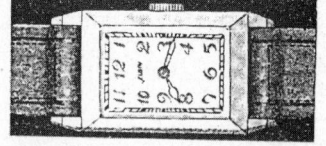

ELGIN, 15 jewels, Ca. 1929
Sterling $100 $150 $225

ELGIN, 17 jewels, curved
gold filled $75 $125 $175

ELGIN, 15 jewels, drivers style, winds at 12 O'clock
gold filled $150 $250 $375

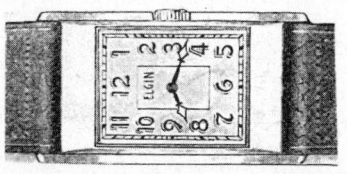

ELGIN, 17 jewels, "Ristflo" winds at 12 O'clock
gold filled $135 $200 $300

ELGIN, 17 jewels, crown guard
gold filled $75 $125 $175

ELGIN, 17 jewels, hidden lugs
gold filled $75 $125 $175

ELGIN, 17 jewels, embossed dial, thin model
gold filled $75 $125 $175

ELGIN, 17 jewels, curved, thin model
gold filled $75 $125 $175

ELGIN, 17 jewels, stepped case
gold filled $65 $125 $125

ELGIN, 17J., center sec., cal.11553, c. 1928
gold filled $100 $175 $225

ELGIN, 15 jewels, "William Osler" recess crown
gold filled $75 $150 $200

ELGIN, 7 jewels, center sec., recess crown
gold filled $75 $150 $200

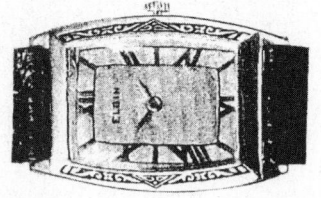

ELGIN, 17J., engraved case, c.1928
gold filled $75 $110 $175

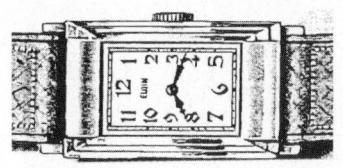

ELGIN, 17J., sold for $47.50 in 1936
gold filled $75 $150 $175

ELGIN, 7-15J., engraved case, c. 1928
14K $150 $300 $400
gold filled $75 $150 $175

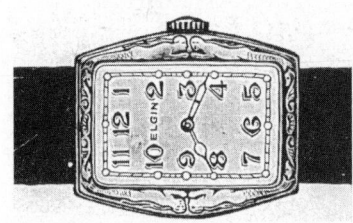

ELGIN, 15J., engraved **Mermaid design case**, c. 1928
gold filled $200 $375 $500

ELGIN, 15J., engraved case, c. 1928
gold filled $75 $150 $200

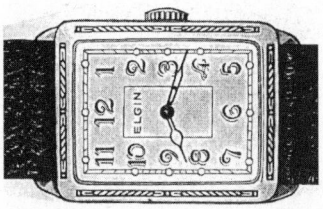

ELGIN, 15J., curved engraved case, c. 1928
gold filled $75 $150 $200

ELGIN, 7J., Ca. 1925
nickel $50 $100 $125

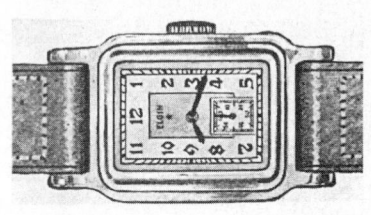

ELGIN, 17 jewels, "Crusade"
gold filled.... . . . . $75 $150 $175

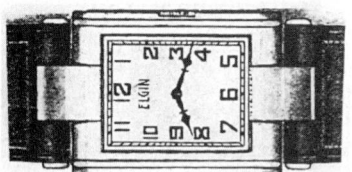

ELGIN, 15 jewels, center lugs
gold filled $75 $150 $185

ELGIN, 7 jewels
gold filled $75 $150 $175

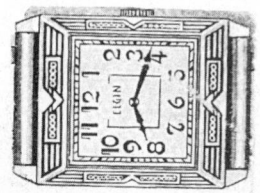

ELGIN, 7 jewels, fancy bezel
nickel $70 $120 $135

ELGIN, 7 jewels, stepped bezel
s. steel $50 $100 $150

ELGIN, 7 jewels, fancy bezel
gold filled $75 $150 $175

ELGIN, 15J., wire lugs, stem at "12", c.1920s
silver $100 $300 $375

ELGIN, 15J., combination lighter and Elgin Watch
Sterling $200 $400 $500

ELGIN, 15J., cut-corner case, Art Deco numbers, Ca. 1925
gold filled $75 $150 $175

ELGIN, 15J., (note the radial), engraved case, c. 1925
gold filled $75 $150 $175

LORD ELGIN, 21J., stepped case, c.1930
gold filled $75 $125 $175

LORD ELGIN, 21J., stepped case, c.1930
gold filled $75 $125 $175

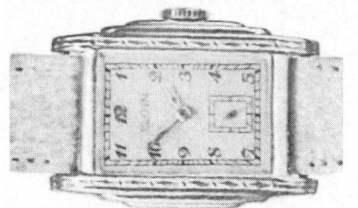

ELGIN, 7J., stepped case, c. 1925
gold filled $75 $125 $175

ELGIN, 17J., **BMW** logo, Ca. 1955
gold filled $75 $150 $200

LORD ELGIN, 21J., GJS, c.1937
14k. $150 $300 $400

ELGIN, 17J., stepped case, c.1930
gold filled $75 $125 $175

ELGIN, 17J., curved, stepped case, c.1927
gold filled $75 $125 $175

ELGIN, 17 jewels, raised numbers
gold filled $75 $125 $175

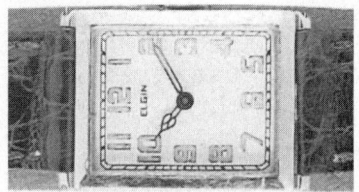

ELGIN, 17 jewels, c.1927
14k. $150 $300 $400

☜ Some grades are not included. Their values can be determined by comparing with **similar** age, size, metal content, style,
models and grades listed.

LORD ELGIN, 21 jewels, diamond dial
14k(w)...................... $200 $425 $500

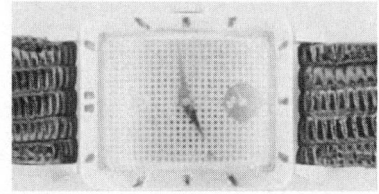

ELGIN, 19 jewels, c. 1947
14k...........................$150 $275 $350
gold filled $85 $125 $185

LORD ELGIN, 21 jewels, diamond dial
14k(w)...................... $200 $425 $550

LORD ELGIN, 21 jewels, aux. sec., fancy lugs
14k......................... $200 $400 $500

LORD ELGIN, 21J., cal.670, c. 1948
gold filled $100 $185 $225
14k........................... $265 $400 $550

Wrist Watches listed in this section are priced at the collectable
fair market **Trade Show** level as **complete watches** having an
original gold-filled case and stainless steel back, also with original
dial, leather watch band, and the entire original movement in good
working order with no repairs needed.

ELGIN, 19 jewels, flared case
14k......................... $200 $425 $550

ELGIN, 19 jewels, flared case , fancy lugs
14k......................... $250 $500 $600

ELGIN, 7-15J., **Star dial**, Military, manual wind
gold filled $100 $200 $250

ELGIN, 7-15J., cushion case,c.1930
chromium.................... $50 $100 $125

ELGIN, 7-15J., **star** dial, solid lugs, Ca 1925
s. steel...................... $100 $175 $225

ELGIN, 15J., **pierced** shield, **star** dial, wire lugs, c.1918
silver $250 $400 $525

ELGIN, 15J., U.S.GOV'T grade II, c.1960s
s. steel $75 $150 $200

ELGIN, 15J., **pierced shield**, c.1918
silver $250 $450 $575

ELGIN, 15J., military style, 24 hr. dial, c.1942
s. steel $125 $200 $250

ELGIN, 15J., **canteen** style case, **star** dial, wire logs, c.1919
nickel . . . . ★★ $400 $700 $775

ELGIN, 15J., military style, cal.539, c.1940
s. steel $75 $150 $200

ELGIN, 15 jewels, "Official Boy Scout" model
s. steel $125 $150 $275

☞ A collector should expect to pay modestly higher prices at local shops

☞ Some grades are not included. Their values can be determined by comparing with similar age, size, metal graph, repeater etc. listed.

ELGIN, 16J., **canteen** style case, U.S.N.234C, c.1930s
s. steel . . . . ★★★ $400 $700 $800

ELGIN, 7 jewels, "Official Boy Scout" model
s. steel $60 $125 $150

ELGIN, 15 jewels, enamel dial, wire lugs, c.1915
Silver. $100 $300 $400

ELGIN, 15jewels, enamel dial, wire logs, c. 1915
silver $175 $300 $400

ELGIN, 15 jewels, center lugs
gold filled $100 $200 $275

ELGIN, 15 jewels, center lugs, c. 1922
silver $125 $250 $350

ELGIN, 15J., case by **Rolland Fischer**, c. 1928
silver $300 $600 $700

ELGIN, 7J., center sec., sold for $27.50 in 1936
gold filled $75 $150 $175

ELGIN, 21 jewels, "Black / Golden Knight"
gold filled $100 $200 $235
14k. $200 $400 $500

ELGIN, 7 jewels, "Avigo" Ca. 1929
base metal. $85 $175 $200

Wrist Watches listed in this section are priced at the collectable fair market Trade Show level as complete watches having an original gold-filled case and stainless steel back, also with original dial, leather watch band , and the entire original movement in good working order with no repairs needed.

ELGIN, 21J., center sec., wire lugs, cal. 680, c. 1952
gold filled $75 $150 $175

ELGIN the **only** American Co. to **manufacture** a self-winding movement. The 760 & 761 also used a Free Sprung Balance.
ELGIN, 27-30J., auto-wind, grade 760-761
gold filled $75 $125 $200

ELGIN, 17 jewels, **Alarm**, Ca 1960
gold filled $100 $200 $275

ELGIN, 19J.,cal.681 , c.1959
gold filled $75 $150 $175

ELGIN, 21J., water-proof, c.1952
s. steel $55 $100 $125

LORD ELGIN, 21J., **enamel bezel**, cal.688, c.1948
gold filled $80 $165 $250

ELGIN, 23 J., "B. W. Raymond," R. R. approved
14k. $385 $700 $800
gold filled $200 $400 $500
s. steel $200 $400 $500

LORD ELGIN, 21I., **shockmaster**, aux. sec., ca 1955
14K $125 $250 $300

☞ Some grades are not included. Their values can be determined by comparing with **similar** age, size, metal content, style, grades, or models such as **time only**, chronograph, repeater etc. listed.

DIALS FOR MINT PRICES MUST BE ALL ORIGINAL .

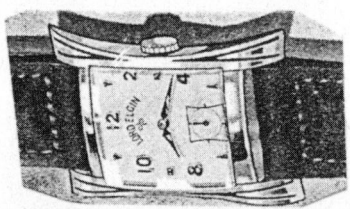

LORD ELGIN, 21J., "Oxford", sold for $100.00 in1954
gold filled $75 $150 $200

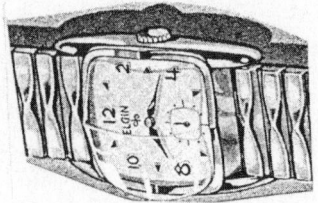

ELGIN, 17J., "Sinclair", sold for $39.75 in1954
gold filled $75 $150 $175

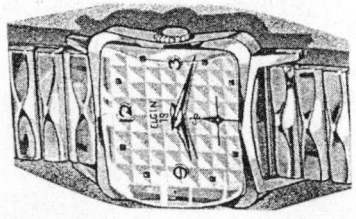

LORD ELGIN, 21J., "Thornton", sold for $71.50 in1954
gold filled $100 $175 $200

ELGIN, 19J., "Gulfport", sold for $69.55 in1954
gold filled $75 $150 $175

ELGIN, 19J., "Garfield", sold for $69.50 in1954
gold filled $75 $150 $200

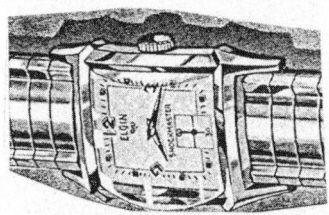

ELGIN, 17J.," Edgewater" sold for $62.55 in1954
gold filled $75 $150 $175

ELGIN, 17J., "Milburn", sold for $59.50 in1954
gold filled $75 $150 $200

ELGIN, 17J .,"Windsor", auto wind, sold for $95.00 in1954
gold filled $75 $150 $185

ELGIN, 17J.," Dante" auto wind sold for $71.50 in1954
s. steel $75 $150 $185

LORD ELGIN, 21J., "Wakefield", sold for $71.50 in1954
gold filled $75 $150 $175

LORD ELGIN, 21J., **diamond on lugs not factory**, c. 1958
14k(w)...................... $300 $600 $800

LORD ELGIN, 21 jewels, mystery dial, c. 1957
14k(w)...................... $200 $400 $500

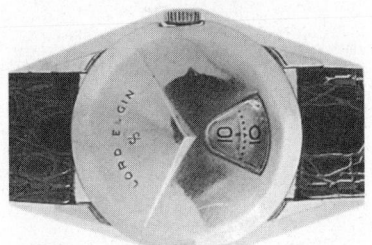

LORD ELGIN, 21J., direct reading, Chevron style, Ca. 1957
gold filled $275 $500 $650

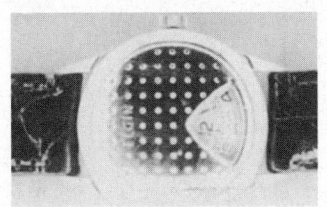

ELGIN, 17 J., in form of golf ball, rotating hr. & min.
gold filled $300 $600 $700

LORD ELGIN, 21 jewels, applied numbers, c. 1946
14k........................ $200 $400 $550

LORD ELGIN, 21 jewels, curved, applied numbers
14k...................... $175 $300 $400

LORD ELGIN, 21 jewels, diamond dial, faceted crystal
14k........................ $175 $300 $400

ELGIN, 17 jewels, hinged back
14k(w)...................... $150 $300 $350

ELGIN, 17 jewels, enamel bezel, Ca. 1930
14k(w)...................... $300 $600 $750

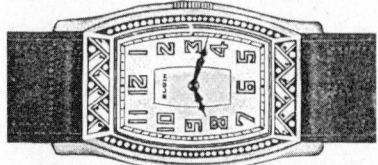

ELGIN, 15 jewels, Art Deco bezel, c. 1935
gold filled $125 $200 $250

☞ A collector should expect to pay modestly higher prices at local shops

☞ Some grades are not included. Their values can be determined by comparing with similar age, size, metal content, style, grades, or models such as time only, chronograph, repeater etc. listed.

ELGIN, 15 jewels, 2 tone case, c. 1930
gold filled 2tone case.... .... $100 $195 $250

ELGIN, 15 jewels, enamel bezel, c.1920
14k(w).................... $300 $600 $800

ELGIN, 17 jewels, raised numbers
gold filled $75 $150 $175

ELGIN, 15-21J., enamel bezel, 2 tone, in 1929 sold for $24.00
14k......................... $350 $700 $900
gold filled $150 $300 $350

ELGIN, 15J., Luminous hands, sold for $27.50 in 1929
gold filled (Y or W)............. $75 $150 $175

ELGIN, 7 jewels, engraved bezel
s. steel....................... $50 $100 $125

ELGIN, 17 jewels, aux. sec., curved
gold filled $75 $150 $175

ELGIN, 17 jewels, curved
gold filled $75 $150 $175

ELGIN, 17 jewels, curved
gold filled $75 $150 $175

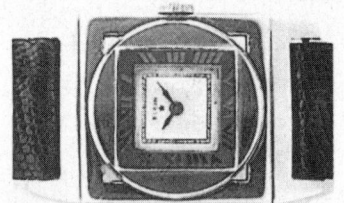

ELGIN, 21 jewels, blue enamel bezel, c. 1920
14k(yellow gold) $800 $2,000 $2,750

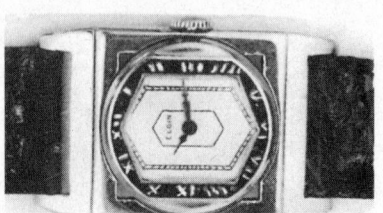

ELGIN, 15 jewels, enamel bezel
14k......................... $800 $2,000 $2,750

LORD ELGIN, 21J, grade 670, large lugs, anniversary of 50 million watches made serial # 50,000,000 to 50,000,999, gold plated movement, Ca. 1951
18k. . . . . ★★★$1,500 $3,000 $3,500

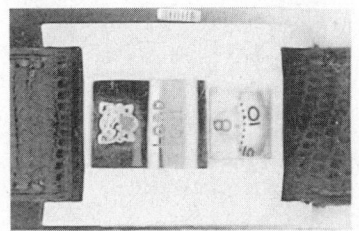

LORD ELGIN, 21J., Jump Hr. & Wandering Min., curved
gold filled $350 $700 $900

ELGIN, 17 jewels, double dial
gold filled $450 $800 $1,000

LORD ELGIN, 21 jewels, hooded lugs, c. 1952
14k. $250 $500 $600

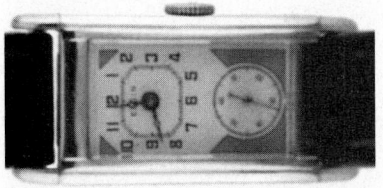

ELGIN, 17J, Doctors Watch, 43mm
gold filled $500 $900 $1,200

LORD ELGIN, 21 jewels, curved, c. 1957
14k. $265 $450 $550

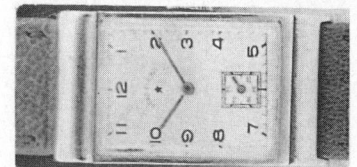

LORD ELGIN, 21 jewels, hooded lugs, c. 1950s
14k. $175 $300 $375

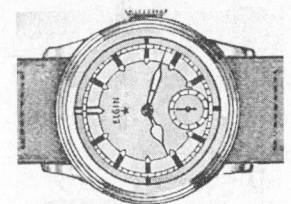

ELGIN, 15 jewels, waterproof
s. steel $40 $80 $100

ELGIN, 15 jewels, center sec.
gold filled $50 $100 $125

ELGIN, 7 jewels, aux. sec.
gold filled $50 $100 $125

LORD ELGIN, 21 jewels, stepped case
18k. $250 $500 $600

LORD ELGIN, 21 jewels, stepped case, curved
14k. $150 $300 $400

ELGIN, 17jewels, stepped case
14k. $150 $300 $400

LORD ELGIN, 21 jewels, curved
gold filled $75 $125 $175

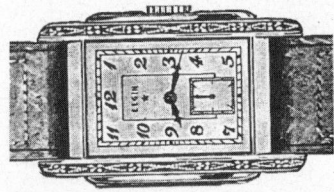

ELGIN, 17 jewels, curved, fancy bezel
gold filled $75 $125 $175

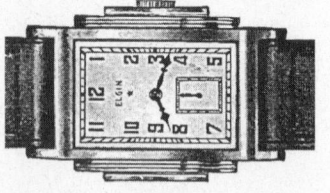

ELGIN, 17 jewels, curved, stepped case
gold filled $75 $125 $175

ELGIN, 17 jewels, curved, stepped case
gold filled $75 $125 $175

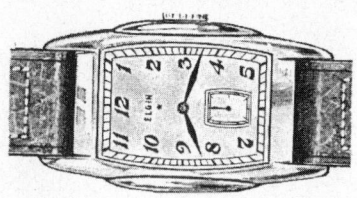

ELGIN, 17 jewels, curved
gold filled $75 $125 $175

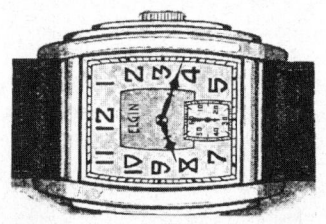

ELGIN, 19 jewels, stepped case
gold filled $75 $125 $175

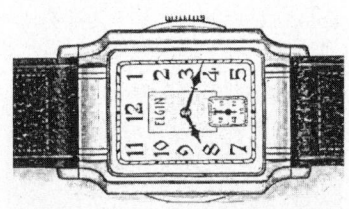

ELGIN, 15 jewels
gold filled $75 $125 $175

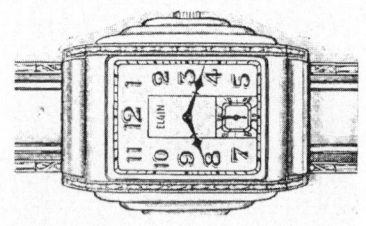

ELGIN, 7 jewels, fancy bezel
base metal. $45 $125 $125

ELGIN, 7 jewels, fancy bezel
gold filled $75 $125 $175

LORD ELGIN, 21 jewels, curved, c. 1938
14k.........................$175 $300 $400

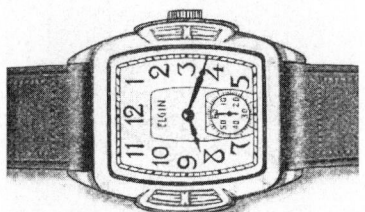

ELGIN, 15 jewels, fancy bezel
gold filled $75 $125 $175

ELGIN, 21 jewels, curved
gold filled $75 $125 $175

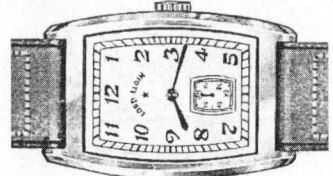

LORD ELGIN, 21 jewels, raised numbers
14k.........................$175 $300 $400

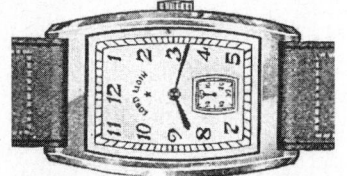

LORD ELGIN, 21 jewels, curved
14k.........................$175 $300 $400

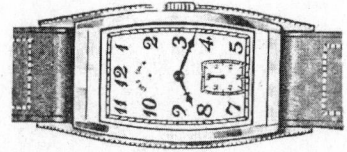

LORD ELGIN, 21 jewels, curved
14k.........................$175 $300 $400

LORD ELGIN, 21 jewels, aux. Sec.
gold filled $75 $125 $175

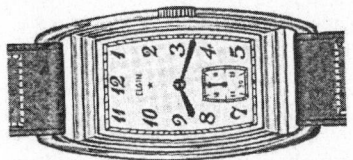

LORD ELGIN, 21 jewels, curved
14k.........................$175 $300 $375

ELGIN, 17 jewels, curved
gold filled $75 $125 $175

ELGIN, 17 Jewels, raised numbers
14k.........................$175 $300 $350

LORD ELGIN, 15 jewels, electric, 6 adj., Ca. 1962, (sold for
$89.50, July of 1962), grade 725, in good running order
gold filled .... ★★ $150 $300 $350

**Elgin pioneering effort in electric watches
started in 1955.**

LORD ELGIN, 15 jewels, **electric**, c. 1962 (back—act)
s. steel . . . . ★★ $150 $265 $350

LORD ELGIN, 15 jewels, **electric**, c. 1962 (grade 725, 6 adj.)
gold filled . . . . ★★ $150 $265 $350

ELGIN,. 17 Jewels, Lady Elgin, flared case, cal. 650, c.1950
14k. $75 $150 $175

ELGIN, 15 Jewels, art deco, c.1925
gold filled $40 $75 $100

ELGIN, 15 Jewels, art deco, c.1928
14k. $90 $125 $200

ELGIN, 17 Jewels, art deco, c. 1928
18k(w). $125 $150 $225

ELGIN, 15J., art deco, Tiger & Lady, rare enamel, Ca. 1929
14K(W). $400 $600 $900

ELGIN, 15 jewels, art deco, Ca. 1928
gold filled $50 $75 $125

ELGIN, 15 jewels, art deco, Ca. 1928
gold filled $30 $50 $75

ELGIN, 15 jewels, art deco, Ca. 1928
gold filled $30 $50 $75

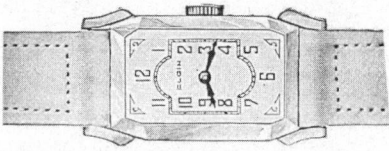

ELGIN, 15 jewels, sports model, Ca. 1928
14k. $75 $100 $150

ELGIN, 17J., 20 diamonds, art deco, Ca. 1928
18k. $225 $275 $365

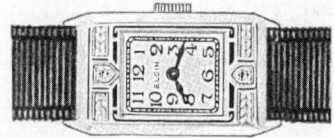

ELGIN, 15 jewels, 2 diamonds, art deco, Ca 1928
gold filled $75 $95 $150

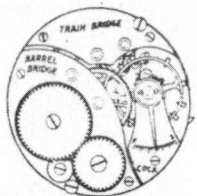 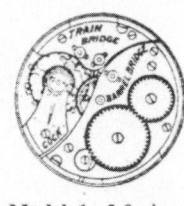 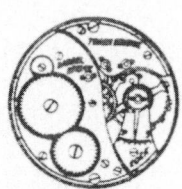 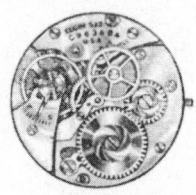

Model 3, 3-0 size, three-quarter plate, open face, pendant set, first serial number 18,179,001, Grade 414, March, 1915.

Model 1, 5-0 size, three-quarter plate, hunting, pendant set, first serial number 14,699,001, Grade 380, Feb., 1910.

Model 2, 5-0 size, three-quarter plate, open face, pendant set, first serial number 17,890,001, Grade 399, Feb., 1914.

Model 2, 8-0 size, Grade 532, 539, sweep second.

Model 7, 8-0 size, Grades 554, 555,

Model 20, 8-0 size, Grades 681, 682.

Model 1, 10-0 size, three-quarter plate, open face

Model 2, 15-0 size, Grades 623, 624, 626.

   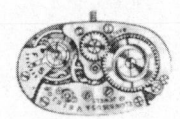

15-0 Size, movement, Grades 670, 672, 673.

15-0 size, movement. Grade 674.

15-0 size, movement, Grades 557, 558, 559.

Model 2, 21-0 size, Grade 541, 533, 535.

Model 3, 21-0 size, Grade 547, sweep second.

Model 4, 21-0 size, Grades 617, 617L, 619, 619L.

Model 9, 21-0 size, Grades 650, 651.

Model 9, 21-0 size, Grades 655, 656.

GRADE 725, 15 jewels,"electric" model movement

"ELECTRIC", case showing back—set

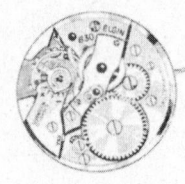
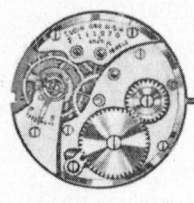

Grade 607, self wind.

Grade 630, sweep second.

Grade 641, 642

Grade 643, self wind.

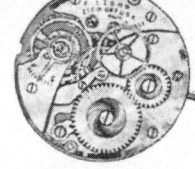

Grades 644, 645, self wind.

Grade 647, sweep second.

Grade 661

Grade 666, sweep second.

Grade 668, sweep second.

Grade 685

Grade 687

Grade 700

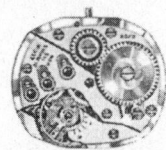
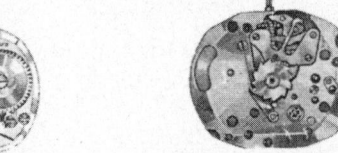
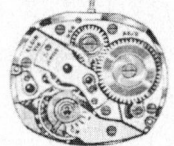

GRADE 710 & 719
719 = DIRECT READ
TRAIN SIDE

719 = DIAL SIDE
OF MOVEMENT

Grade 716

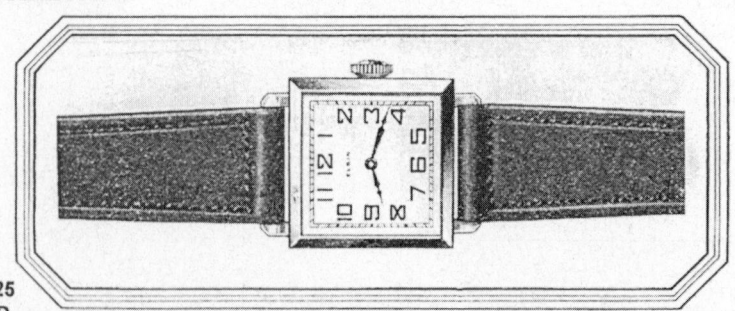

1925 AD

Elgin strap watches for men, in gold and gold-filled cases of yellow, white or green; also silver and nickel. Prices ranging from $20 to $75.

ELOGA, triple calendar,
gold filled bezel $110 $200 $275

EMERSON, 17J., hooded lugs,
gold filled $50 $100 $135

ENICAR, 17 jewels, auto- wind, center sec.
gold filled $40 $80 $135
18k. $175 $300 $350

ENICAR, 17J., chronograph, 2 reg. Ca. 1955
s. steel $175 $300 $400

ENICAR, 17 jewels, censer sec.
s. steel $40 $80 $100

ENICAR, 17 jewels, triple date, moon phase
gold filled $200 $400 $500

ENICAR, 15 jewels, egg shaped with compass, c. 1918
silver $250 $600 $750

ENICAR, 17J., auto-w., date, 24 hour bezel, C. 1970
s. steel $100 $175 $225

ESKA, 17J.,chronog., triple date, moon phase
14k. $1,200 $2,000 $2,500

ESKA, 17 jewels, chronog., 2 reg., C. 1950s
s. steel $150 $300 $400

ESKA, 17 jewels, chronog., 2 reg., c. 1940
s. steel $600 $1,000 $1,400

ESKA, 17 jewels, multi-colored enamel dial
18k $1,200 $2,100 $2,800

ETERNA, quartz, dale, by ETA, cal#954, C. 1975
s. steel $45 $65 $95

Pricing in this Guide are fair market price for complete watches which are reflected from the "**NAWCC**" National and regional shows.

 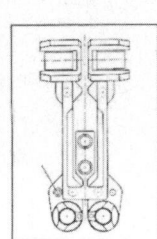

ETERNA, "Sonic," double tuning fork (for position errors), c.1967
s. steel $100 $135 $200

ETERNA, 17 jewels, chronog., triple date, 3 reg.
s. steel $400 $750 $900
18k $700 $1,200 $1,400

ETERNA, 21 jewels, date, auto-w., cal. # 14390, c.1960
"**Eternamatic**" (5 ball-bearing rotor)
18k $175 $325 $400

ETERNA, 19 jewels, c.1944
14k $125 $250 $300

ETERNA, 16 jewels, aux. sec., c.1945
gold filled $55 $110 $150

ETERNA, 19 jewels, c.1938
gold filled $50 $100 $125

ETERNA, 17 jewels, gold jewel settings, c.1935
14k. $135 $250 $300

EVANS, 17 jewels, rhinestones on bezel & dial, c. 1948
gold plate $55 $100 $150

EVANS, 17 jewels, chronog., 2 reg., c. 1940
18k. $300 $500 $600

EXACTUS, 17J., chronog., triple date, moon ph.
s. steel $450 $800 $1,100

EXCELSIOR, 17 jewels, chronog., 2 reg.
14k. $250 $500 $600
gold filled $150 $250 $350

EXCELSIOR, 17 jewels, chronog.
gold filled $150 $300 $375
s. steel $150 $300 $375

EXCELSIOR PARK, 17 jewels, chronog.
s. steel $175 $350 $400

FAIRFAX, 6J, engraved case, c. 1929
base metal. $40 $80 $110

FAIRFAX, 6J, engraved case, c. 1929
base metal. $40 $100 $125

FAIRFAX, 6J, butler finish case, c.1929
base metal. $40 $100 $125

FAITH, 17J, flip top case HC style, by Hyde Park, c.1950
gold filled $140 $235 $300

FAVRE LEUBA,17J., triple date, cal.Valj.89, c.1948
s. steel $100 $175 $200

☞ A collector should expect to pay modestly higher prices at local shops

☞ Some grades are not included. Their values can be determined by comparing with **similar age, size, metal content, style, grades, or models such as time only, chronograph, repeater etc. listed.**

FAVRE LEUBA,17J., "Bivouac", altimeter with aneroid capsule transmitting variations of atmospheric pressure to the barometric mechanism, revolving bezel, Ca. 1968.
s. steel $150 $335 $450

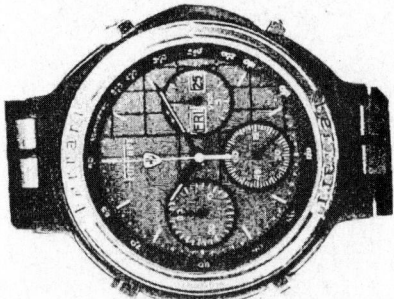

FAVRE LEUBA,17J., "Bathy 50" depth reading to about 165 feet, waterproof to 470 feet, Ca. 1968
s. steel $155 $335 $450

FERRARI, quartz, chronog., c.1988
base metal. $75 $125 $200

FELCA, 17 jewels, auto wind
gold filled $40 $75 $125
14k. $100 $200 $225
18k. $175 $300 $350

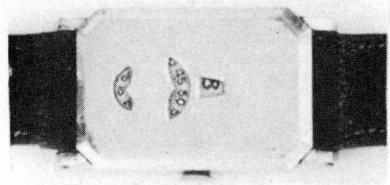

FONTAINEMELON, S. A., 17 J., gold train, digital
14k. $1,000 $2,000 $2,800

FREY, 15J., engraved case, c. 1933
base metal. $40 $100 $125

FRAMONT, 17J, timer, dale, cal. 290, c.1970
s. steel. $75 $150 $185

FREY,15J., engraved stepped case, c. 1933
base metal. $40 $100 $125

FREY, 25J., rotating outside chapter, c. 1970
s. steel. $50 $85 $110

FREY, 15J., engraved case, c. 1933
base metal. $40 $100 $125

FRIEDLI, 17 jewels, auto wind, center sec.
gold filled $50 $75 $125
18k. $175 $300 $350

FREY, 15J., Early auto- wind, with a pendulum type weight,
Ca.1930a
gold filled . . . . ★★$250 $500 $700

FRODSHAM, 17J., Ca. 1935
18k(w). $300 $600 $700

GALLET, 15 jewels, wire lugs, Ca. 1925
silver $75 $150 $200

GALLET, 15 jewels, waterproof, auto wind
s. steel $60 $90 $135

GALLET, 17 jewels, chronog., single button, c. 1950
s. steel $250 $475 $550

GALLET, 17J., chronog., by Racine, US air force, c. 1978
s. steel $275 $450 $600

☞ Pricing in this Guide are fair market price for complete
watches which are reflected from the "**NAWCC**" National and
regional shows

GALLET, 17 jewels, chronog., 3 reg., c. 1945
s. steel $300 $600 $700

GALLET, 17 jewels, chronog., 3 reg., c. 1942
gold filled $300 $600 $700

GALLET, 17J., chronog., 2 reg., single button, C.1925,
silver "small size" $600 $1,100 $1,300

GALLET, 17J., chronog., 3 reg., triple date, moon ph.
18k. $1,500 $2,500 $3,000

GALLET, 17J., chronog., 3 reg., triple date
14k. $850 $1,300 $1,800
s. steel $500 $900 $1,100

GALLET, 17 jewels, chronog., 3 reg., e. 1955
s. steel, waterproof. $335 $600 $800

GALLET, 17 jewels, 2 reg., Ca. 1958
s. steel $200 $400 $500

GALLET, 17 jewels, chronog., 2 reg.
14k. $300 $600 $800
s. steel $175 $300 $400

GALLET, 17 jewels, chronog., mid size, c. 1940
s.steel $300 $600 $800

GALLET, 17-23J., chronog., "Flying Officer", Ca. 1958
s. steel $300 $600 $800

GALLET, 17 jewels, chronog., waterproof
s. steel $200 $400 $500

GALLET, 17 jewels, 2 reg.
s. steel $150 $300 $350

Some grades are not included. Their values can be determined
by comparing with similar age, size, metal content, style,
grades, or models such as time only, chronograph, repeater
etc. listed.

GALLET, 17 jewels, chronog., 2 reg.
s. steel $300 $500 $600

GALLET, 17 jewels, **regulator** dial, chronog.
s. steel $500 $900 $1,200

GALLET, 17 jewels, chronog., 2 reg.
gold filled $200 $350 $500

P. GARNIER, 17 jewels, minu-stop, c. 1965
s. steel $150 $300 $350

GALLET, 17 jewels, chronog., 2 reg.
s. steel $200 $400 $500

P. GARNIER, 17 jewels, world time, c. 1968
s. steel $185 $300 $325

GALLET, 17 jewels, chronog., 2 reg., c. 1939
s. steel $225 $450 $600

GARLAND, 17J., center sec., water-proof.
s. steel $40 $80 $100

Pricing is this Guide are fair market price for complete watches which are reflected from the "**NAWCC**" National and regional shows.

Wrist Watches listed is this section are priced at the collectable fair market Trade Show level as complete watches having an original gold-filled case and stainless steel back, also with leather watch band, and the entire original movement in good working order with no repairs needed.

GENEVE, 15 jewels, doctors watch, c. 1939
s. steel $450 $900 $1,100

GENEVE, 15 jewels, doctors watch, c. 1937
s. steel $450 $900 $1,000

GENEVE, 17 jewels, curly lugs, c.1950
14k. $250 $500 $650

GERMINAL, 17 J., center sec.
s. steel $40 $70 $95
14k. $100 $200 $250

GERMINAL, 15J., **early auto wind, case action**, c. 1933
s. steel . . . . ★★★ $450 $750 $900

GIRARD-PERREGAUX, Tourbillon with golden bridge, a hand is
attached to the one minute tourbillon for seconds, wind indicator at
12, manual wind.(Limited edition)
18K $12,000 $25,000 $35,000

GIRARD-PERREGAUX, 17J., auto wind, C. 1951
s. steel $75 $150 $175

GIRARD-PERREGAUX, 17J., alarm, c.1960
gold filled $125 $250 $300

GIRARD-PERREGAUX, 39J., center sec. automatic, c.1955
14k. $200 $400 $500

☞ Some grades are not included. Their values can
be determined by comparing with similar age, size,
metal content, style, grades, or models such as time only,
chronograph, repeater etc. listed.

GIRARD-PERREGAUX, 17J., auto w., center sec., c.1948
18k. $200 $400 $550

GIRARD-PERREGAUX, 17J., Gyromatic, center sec., c.1960
s. steel $95 $135 $200

GIRARD-PERREGAUX, 17J., Gyromatic, cal.47ae, c.1953
14k. $185 $300 $400

GIRARD-PERREGAUX, 17J., Sea Hawk., c.1960
gold filled $100 $165 $200

GIRARD-PERREGAUX, 17J., aux. sec., c.1958
gold filled $75 $150 $165

GIRARD-PERREGAUX, 17J., "Sea Hawk", aux. sec., c.1950
s. steel $75 $125 $175

GIRARD-PERREGAUX, 17J., Gyromatic, date, c. 1960
gold filled $75 $125 $165

GIRARD-PERREGAUX, 39J., Gyromatic, "HF", date, c. 1960
18k. $275 $550 $600

☞ Some grades are not included. Their values can be determined by comparing with similar age, size, metal content, style, grades, or models such as time only, chronograph, repeater etc. listed.

GIRARD-PERREGAUX, 39J., chronometer "HF", c.1970
s. steel $100 $175 $200

GIRARD-PERREGAUX, 17 jewels, triple date, aux. sec.
s. steel $100 $200 $275

GIRARD-PERREGAUX,17J.,"Gyromatic",date
gold filled $100 $175 $200

GIRARD-PERREGAUX, 17J., chronog., 2 reg., waterproof
s. steel $250 $475 $600

GIRARD-PERREGAUX,17J.,"Gyromatic",date, Ca.1960
18k. $250 $500 $600

GIRARD-PERREGAUX, 17J., by Valjoux cal.72, c.1955
s. steel $350 $600 $750

GIRARD-PERREGAUX, 17J., triple date, autow.
s. steel $150 $300 $350

GIRARD-PERREGAUX, 17J., chronog cal.285, c. 1940
gold filled $350 $600 $700

GIRARD-PERREGAUX, 17J., pulsations, c. 1948
14k. $400 $750 $900

GIRARD-PERREGAUX, 17 J., chronog., 3 reg., c. 1952
s. steel $400 $750 $850

GIRARD-PERREGAUX, 17J, chronog., triple date, **moon phase**
18k. $1,200 $2,200 $3,000

GIRARD-PERREGAUX, 39J., Ca. 1955
14k. $125 $200 $300
18k. $150 $300 $400

GIRARD-PERREGAUX, 17J., hooded lugs, Ca.1900
14k. $175 $300 $400

GIRARD-PERREGAUX, 17J., "gyromatic", cnter sec.
14k. $175 $350 $450

GIRARD-PERREGAUX, 17J., RF#2459, c.1970
14k. $150 $250 $350

GIRARD-PERREGAUX, 17J., cal.a6 3606, GJS, c.1955
14k. $150 $250 $350

GIRARD-PERREGAUX, 17J., recess crown, GJS, c.1954
14k. $175 $400 $500

GIRARD-PERREGAUX, 17J., cal.86, GJS, Ca.1948
14k. $125 $250 $350

GIRARD-PERREGAUX, 17J., cal.86ae, GJS, c.1940
s. steel $60 $120 $150

GIRARD-PERREGAUX, 17J., two tone case, GJS, Ca.1942
14k. $200 $400 $500

GIRARD-PERREGAUX, 17J., GJS, c.1953
14k. $150 $300 $400

GIRARD-PERREGAUX, 17J., cal. 86ae, GJS, c.1942
s. steel $75 $125 $175

Wrist Watches listed in this section are priced at the collectable fair market **Trade Show** level as **complete** watches having an original sold-filled case and stainless steel back, also with original dial, leather watch band, and the entire original movement in good working order with no repairs needed.

GIRARD-PERREGAUX, 17J., recess crown, GJS, c.1947
gold filled $75 $150 $175

GIRARD-PERREGAUX, 17J., "1791", GJS, c.1942
s. steel $75 $150 $200

GIRARD-PERREGAUX, 17J., cal.91ae220, GJS, c.1948
gold filled $75 $150 $200

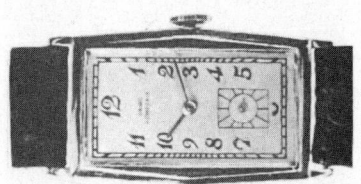

GIRARD-PERREGAUX, 17J., GJS, c.1936
gold filled $75 $150 $250

GIRARD-PERREGAUX, 17J., cal.86ae, GJS, c.1942
14k. $200 $400 $500

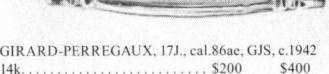

A collector should expect so pay modestly higher prices at local shops

GIRARD-PERREGAUX, 39J, automatic, center sec.
14k.......................... $200 $400 $500

GIRARD-PERREGAUX, 17 jewels, aux. sec.
gold filled $75 $150 $200

GIRARD-PERREGAUX, 17 jewels, Ca. 1948
14k.......................... $200 $400 $475

GIRARD-PERREGAUX, 17J., C. 1948
14k.......................... $200 $400 $450

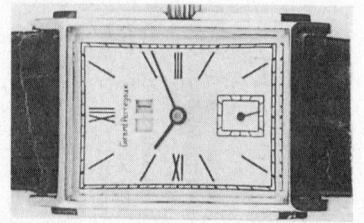

GIRARD-PERREGAUX, 17 J., date, stepped case,
18k.......................... $350 $600 $700
14k.......................... $300 $550 $600

GLASHUTTE, 17J., 2 reg., fluted bezel, c.1942
s. steel $700 $1,500 $1,700

GLASHUTTE, 15J., signed Úhrenfabrik Glashutte, c.1935
18k.......................... $300 $600 $700

GLASHUTTE, 15J., signed "GUB", Ca.1950's
gold filled $200 $375 $425

GLYCINE, 17J., **Airman** auto-wind, 24hr., **date**, c.1970
s. steel $275 $450 $650

GLYCINE, 17J., 15 diamond dial, cal.4645, c.1945
14k.......................... $450 $800 $1,000

GLYCINE the first modular self-winding works patented in 1931 by E. Meylan of La Chaux-de-Fonds.

GLYCINE, 17J., **Airman**, 24 hr. dial, autow, date, C.1960s
s. steel $250 $500 $700

GLYCINE, 17 jewels, **curved**, c. 1938
18k $200 $400 $475

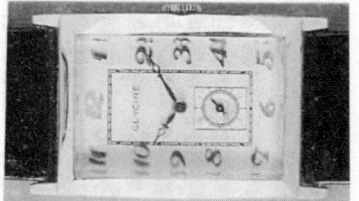

GLYCINE, 17 jewels, aux. sec., c. 1934
14k(w) $200 $300 $475

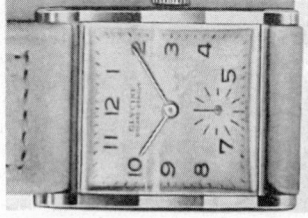

GLYCINE, 18 jewels, faceted crystal & bezel
gold filled $75 $150 $175

GOERING W. Co., jump hr., wandering sec., C. 1935
14k $800 $1,300 $1,500

GOERING W. Co., **jump hr.**, wandering sec., C. 1935
chrome $150 $300 $375

GOERING W. Co., center sec., C.1935
base metal $30 $65 $90

GOERING W. Co., 15J., engraved case, C. 1935.
gold filled $40 $100 $125

GOERING W. Co., 15J., engraved case, C.1935
gold filled $40 $100 $125

GOERING W. Co., 15J., engraved case, C.1935
gold filled $40 $100 $125

DIALS FOR MINT PRICES MUST BE ALL **ORIGINAL**.

GOERING W. Co., 15J., rectangular, C.1935
gold filled $60 $100 $125

GOERING W. Co., 15J., **ladies** engraved case, C.1935
gold filled $30 $55 $85

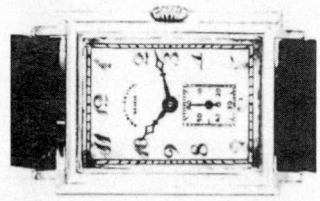

GOLAY, 18 jewels, aux. sec., c. 1928
18k & platinum $1,000 $1,800 $2,250

GOLAY, 32 jewels, **min**. repeater, adj. to 5 positions (pocket watch
movement)
18k $5,000 $10,000 $15,000

GRANA, 16J., **Masonic dial**, original dial, GJS, ca. 1948
14k $200 $400 $500

GRUEN, 17J., curved, precision, cal. 330, Ca. 1937
platinum . . . . ★ $1,600 $3,000 $4,000

GRUEN, 15J., enamel dial, wire lugs, c. 1915
silver $200 $350 $400

GRUEN, 17J., **driver's watch**, winds at 12, cal.400, c.1938
gold filled $200 $400 $550

GRUEN,17J., curved, drivers, cal.401, RF#352, c.1932
gold filled $400 $700 $1,000

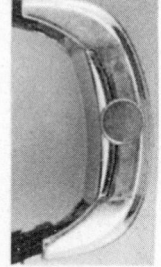

GRUEN, 17J., extremely curved, drivers, c. 1932 , and side view
of watch
gold filled $600 $1,300 $1,800

GRUEN, 17 J., extremely curved, driver's watch
gold filled $600 $1,200 $1,800

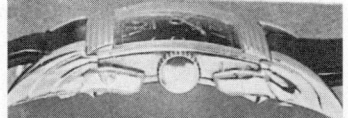

GRUEN, 17 J., driver's watch, flexible long lugs, RF#641
gold filled $650 $1,200 $1,800

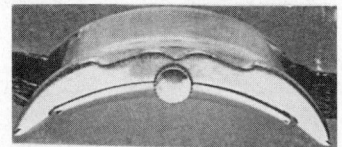

GRUEN, 17 jewels, curvex, c.1949
gold filled $250 $500 $650

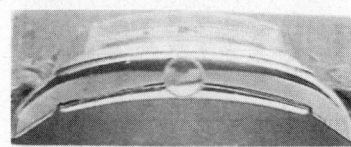

GRUEN, 17 jewels, curvex, 35mm long
gold filled $200 $400 $550

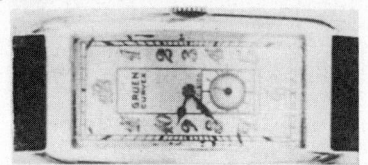

GRUEN, 17J, curvex **Majesty**, 52 mm long. C.1937
gold filled $1,200 $2,000 $2,400
14k. . . . . ★★★ $2,500 $4,500 $5,000

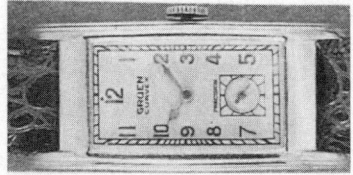

GRUEN, 17J, curvex, precision, C.1936
14k. $450 $850 $1,000

GRUEN, 17 jewels, curvex, c. 1937
gold filled $250 $475 $550

GRUEN, 17 jewels, curvex, RF# 228, c. 1935
gold filled $175 $350 $450

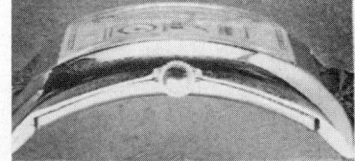

GRUEN, 17 jewels, curvex, 50mm long, c. 1937
gold filled $500 $1,000 $1,500

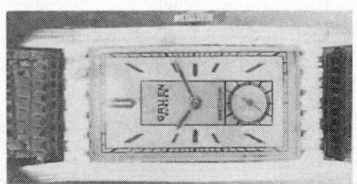

GRUEN, 17 jewels, curvex, c.1937
s. steel $275 $500 $700

GRUEN, 15-17 jewels, curvex, 46mm lug to tug, Ca 1940s.
gold filled $275 $500 $750

GRUEN, 17J., note bezel, curvex, ca.1936
gold filled $275 $400 $550

GRUEN, 17 jewels, curvex, RF#334, Ca.1939
gold filled $200 $400 $550

☞ First CURVEX was introduced on October 26,1935, it was series #311, the 2nd series was #330 in 1939, and in 1940 series # 440 was issued.

GRUEN, 17 jewels, Precision, **2 Tone case**, Ca. 1933
18K **2 tone** $375 $700 $900

GRUEN, 17J., Precision, "Antique" sold for $100 in 1930
14K $200 $400 $600

GRUEN, 17J., Precision, "Antique" & inlaid black enamel
18K(W). $200 $400 $600

GRUEN, 15J., curvex, RF#226, c. 1936
gold filled $185 $300 $400

GRUEN, 15J., curvex, stepped case, RF#278, c. 1936
gold filled $175 $335 $400

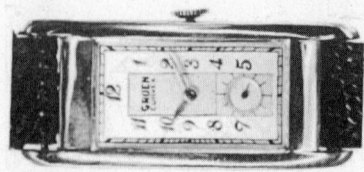

GRUEN, 15J., curvex, RF#255, cal.500, c. 1936
gold filled $185 $300 $375

GRUEN, 17J., curvex, RF#266, cal.165, c. 1935
gold filled $175 $350 $400

GRUEN, 17J., curvex, RF#280, cal.330, c. 1936
gold filled $200 $375 $450

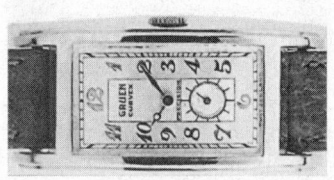

GRUEN, 17J., curvex, stepped case, RF#280, c. 1937
14k. $350 $600 $900
gold filled $200 $400 $550

GRUEN, 17J., curvex, precision, RF#292, cal.330, c. 1937
gold filled $200 $400 $550

GRUEN, 15J., curvex, RF#202, cal.500, c. 1936
gold filled $200 $400 $550

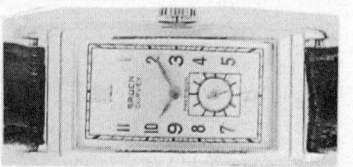

GRUEN, 17J., curvex, RF#308, cal 330, c. 1936
14k. $300 $600 $800
gold filled $200 $325 $400

"Curved to fit the wrist"

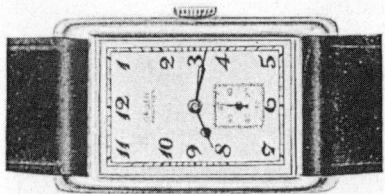

GRUEN, 17J , curved, aux sec., curved crystal, precision, sold for
$135.00 in 1931
14k(w) $250 $475 $650

GRUEN, 17J., curvex, cal#440, hooded lugs, ca.1943
14k $200 $400 $500

GRUEN, 17 jewels, curvex, fancy lugs
14k $200 $400 $500

GRUEN, 17 jewels, curvex, long lugs
14k $225 $400 $500

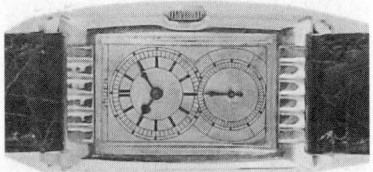

GRUEN, 15-17 jewels, **tu-tone case**, doctors watch, c. 1937
14k W & Y $2,500 $4,650 $5,250

GRUEN, 15-17 jewels, **jumping hr.**, double dial
s. steel $2,500 $5,000 $6,500
14k $3,500 $6,000 $8,000

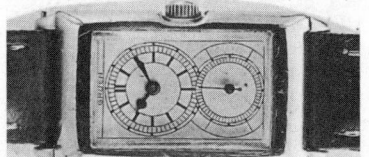

GRUEN, 15-17 jewels, doctors watch
gold filled $900 $1,750 $2,000

GRUEN, 15-17 jewels, curved, c. 1930s
gold filled $250 $400 $500

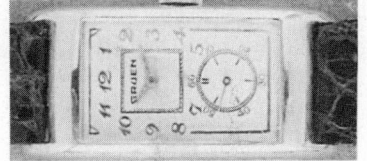

GRUEN, 15-17 jewels, doctors watch, curved, c. 1938
gold filled $700 $1,400 $1,800

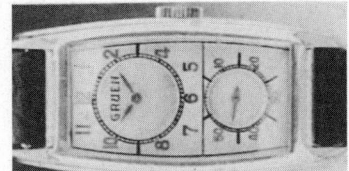

GRUEN, 15-17 jewels, doctors watch
gold filled $700 $1,400 $1,600

GRUEN, 15-17 jewels, doctors watch, c. 1932
gold filled $750 $1,450 $1,700

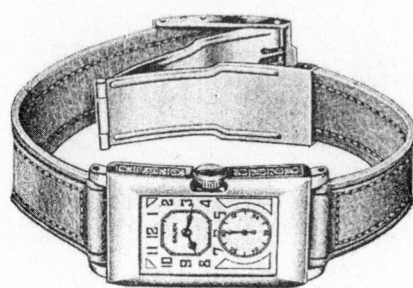

GRUEN, 15-17J, doctors watch, sold for $75.00 in 1931
14K(W)....................$2,500 $4,000 $5,000

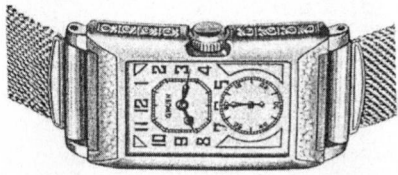

GRUEN, 15-17 jewels, doctors watch, sold for $67.00 in 1929
gold filled $700 $1,400 $1,800

GRUEN, 15-17 jewels, doctors watch, sold for $60 in 1929
gold filled $750 $1,400 $1,800

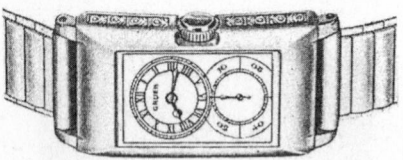

GRUEN, 15-17 jewels, doctors watch, sold for $67.50 in 1929
gold filled $750 $1,400 $1,800

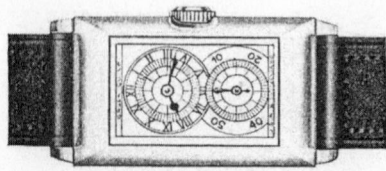

GRUEN, 15-17 jewels, doctors watch, sold for $75.00 in 1931
gold filled $800 $1,400 $1,800
14K $2,000 $3,500 $4,800

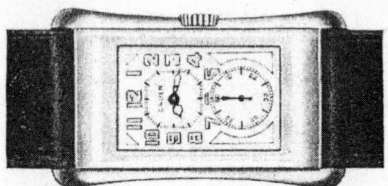

GRUEN, 15-17 jewels, doctors watch, sold for $55.00 in 1931
base metal................... $600 $1,200 $1,400

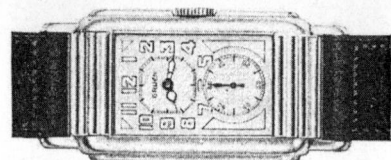

GRUEN, 15-17J., doctors watch, sold for $115.00 in 1931
2 TONE 14K case $3,000 $4,500 $5,000
14K(W or Y)................. $1,650 $3,000 $3,500

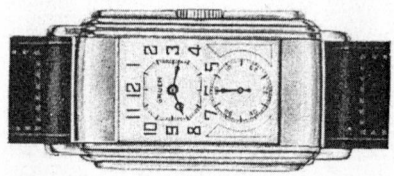

GRUEN, 15-17J., doctors watch, sold for $115.00 in 1931
2 TONE 14K case $3,000 $4,500 $5,000
14K(W or Y)................. $1,600 $2,800 $3,200

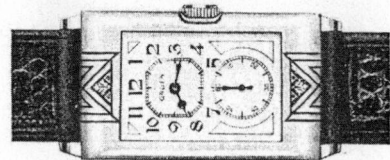

GRUEN, 15-17 jewels, doctors watch, sold for $85.00 in 1931
14K(W)....................$2,500 $4,250 $4,800

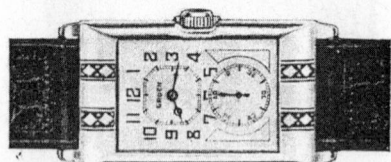

GRUEN, 15-17 jewels, doctors watch, sold for $85.00 in 1931
14k(w).....................$2,500 $4,250 $4,800

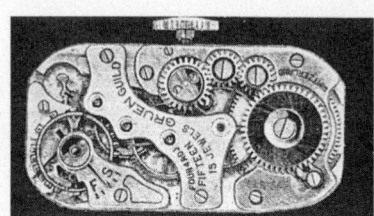

Gruen Doctors watch movement by Aegler (Swiss)

GRUEN. 15 jewels, in form of car radiator, curved
nickel $800 $1,500 $1,800

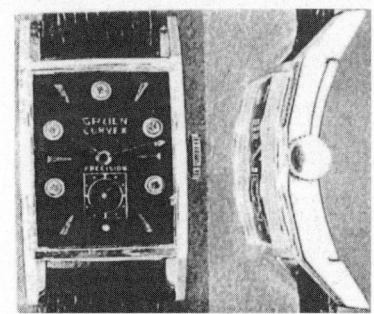

GRUEN, 17J., RF# 615, curvex, diamond dial, faceted crystal
14k. $500 $900 $1,200

GRUEN, 17J., **diamond** dial & bezel, RF # 568, Ca. 1946
14k. $300 $550 $700

GRUEN, 17 jewels, veri-thin model, fancy lugs
14k. $225 $500 $700

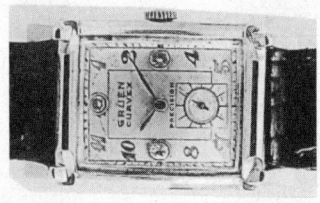

GRUEN, 17J., curvex, 3 diam., RF#568, cal.440, c. 1945
14k(w). $250 $425 $500

GRUEN, 17 jewels, auto wind, cal. 840, c. 1952
18k. $300 $575 $650

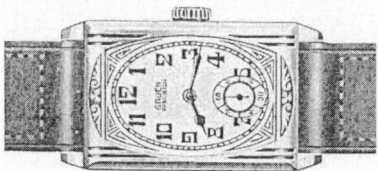

GRUEN, 17J., "Antique", sold for $65 in 1930
gold filled $100 $200 $300

GRUEN, 17 jewels, curvex, fancy lugs
gold filled $110 $200 $250

GRUEN, 17J.. "Antique" & inlaid enamel, large second hand
18K(w) $300 $600 $700

GRUEN, 21J, RF#798, curvex, diamond dial, fancy lugs
14k (w) $350 $650 $800

* Signed on dial **Gruen 21** = 21 Jewels & **American** Made.

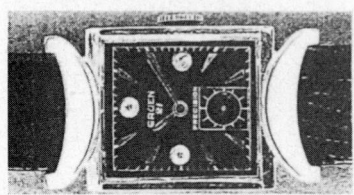

GRUEN, 21 jewels, diamond dial, fancy center lugs, Ca. 1944
14k........................ $300 $600 $700

GRUEN, 21 jewels, fancy lugs, Ca. 1944
14k........................ $275 $475 $550

GRUEN, 17 jewels, curvex, fancy lugs, c. 1943
gold filled $100 $200 $250
14k..........................$185 $325 $400

GRUEN, 17 jewels , diamond dial, Ca. 1947
14k........................ $300 $600 $700

GRUEN, 21J., **flared**, diamond dial, Ca. 1945
14k(w)...................... $400 $750 $950

GRUEN, 21 jewels, Precision, RF# 558, cal.335, Ca. 1944
  Flexible long lugs
gold filled $100 $200 $300

GRUEN, 17 jewels, curvex, diamond dial, c. 1951
14k(w)C&B ...... /............ $750 $1,300 $1,500

GRUEN, 17 jewels, curvex, diamond dial, c. 1950
14k(w)...................... $350 $500 $775

GRUEN, 17J., so called **50th Anniversary, with a engraved**
quadron precision extra **mvt. G# 119**, Adj., also used **G# 123**
14k(w)................... ★★$700 $1,300 $1,800

GRUEN, 17 jewels , curvex, c.1951
14k.......................... $300 $575 $650

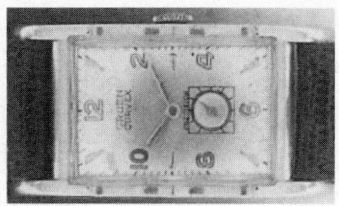

GRUEN, 17 jewels , curvex, "Belmont"
14k. $200 $400 $550

GRUEN, 17J., curvex, large lugs, RF#449, cal.440, c. 1945
gold filled $125 $175 $250

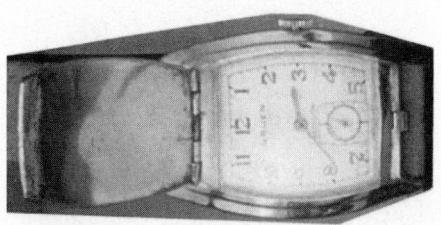

GRUEN, 17J., Hunter style case, "Veri-Thin", Ca. 1940s
gold filled $600 $1,200 $1,500

GRUEN, 17J., curvex. RF#449, cal.440, c. 1943
gold filled $100 $175 $250

GRUEN, 15J., RF#93, cal.179,c. 1925
gold filled $70 $125 $175

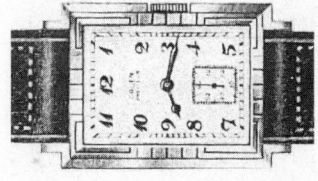

GRUEN, 17J., Precision Quadron, crown guard, Ca. 1931
14K(W). $165 $325 $450

GRUEN, 17J., curvex, stepped lugs, RF#449, cal.440, c.1945
gold filled $70 $125 $200

GRUEN, 17J., curvex, RF#498, cal.440, c. 1945
gold filled $70 $125 $200

GRUEN, 17J., curvex, RF#498, cal.440, c. 1945
gold filled $100 $175 $225

Wrist Watches listed in this section are priced as **complete**
watches having an original sold-filled case and stainless steel
back, also with original dial, leather watch band, and the entire
original movement in good working order with no repairs needed.

GRUEN, 17J., curvex, RF#530, c. 1948
gold filled $70 $125 $175

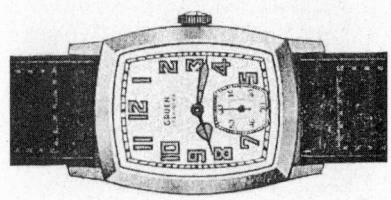

GRUEN, 17J., precision, sold for $125. in 1930
18K(W) $200 $400 $500

GRUEN, 17J., veri-thin, RF#530, cal 430, c. 1945
14k. $150 $300 $350

GRUEN, 17J., curvex, RF#607, "Citadel", c. 1943
gold filled $100 $175 $200

GRUEN, 17J., curvex, RF#544, cal.440, c. 1942
gold filled $100 $200 $275

GRUEN, 17J., fancy lugs, curvex, RF#610, c. 1945
14k. $400 $800 $900

GRUEN, 17J., veri-thin 3 diam., RF#558, c. 1945
14k(w) $150 $300 $350

GRUEN, 17J., curvex, RF#610, cal.370, c. 1945
14k. $350 $700 $900

GRUEN, 17J., curvex, RF#576, cal.440, c. 1942
gold filled $90 $125 $200
14k. $185 $275 $350

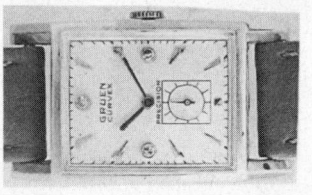

GRUEN, 17J., 3 diam., curvex, RF#615, cal.370, c. 1945
14k. $300 $600 $800

GRUEN (continued)

* Signed on dial **Gruen 21** = 21 Jewels & **American** Made.

GRUEN, 17J., curvex, RF#642, "Marshall", c. 1945
gold filled $100 $200 $250

GRUEN, 17J., curvex, RF#750, cal.370, c. 1940
gold filled $100 $175 $225

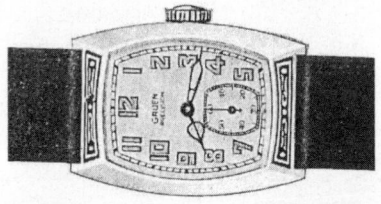

GRUEN, 15J., Precision, Antique finish, sold for $55 in 1930
gold filled(W) $150 $250 $275

GRUEN, 17J., curvex, RF#773, cal.370, c. 1945
gold filled $100 $175 $225

GRUEN, 21J., twisted bezel, RF#657, cal.335, c. 1944
gold filled $125 $200 $300

GRUEN, 17J., curvex, faceted crystal, cal.440, c. 1947
14k. $175 $350 $450

GRUEN, 21J., precision, RF#674, cal.430, c. 1944
gold filled $75 $125 $150

GRUEN, 21J., precision, RF#801, cal. 335., c. 1944
14k. $175 $300 $400

GRUEN, 21J., precision, RF#738, cal.335, c. 1944
14k. $150 $300 $400

GRUEN, 17J., "Collegian", curvex - precision, Ca. 1944
gold filled $100 $250 $300

GRUEN, 17J., RF #578, Curvex Precision Ca.1943
gold filled $75 $150 $175

GRUEN, 17 jewels, RF#650, curvex, c.1950
14k. $200 $400 $600

GRUEN, 17J., RF#755, stepped bezel, **Auto wind**, Ca. 1950
gold filled $125 $200 $275

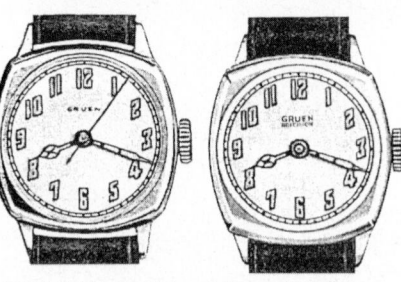

GRUEN, 15-17, Radium dial, center & no sec., Ca. 1925
14k. $150 $275 $325

GRUEN, 19 jewels, precision, c. 1920
14k. $200 $350 $400

GRUEN, 17 jewels, Curvex, RF#610, 3 diam. dial, Ca.1945
14k(w) 6 diam.case. $400 $750 $900
*Signed on dial Gruen 21 = 21 Jewels & **American** Made.

GRUEN, 17 jewels, curvex
14k. $200 $350 $400

GRUEN, 21J., "Precision", RF#709, cal.335, Ca. 1945
gold filled $75 $125 $175

GRUEN, 17J., RF # 575, Curvex Precision, Ca.1945
gold filled $90 $150 $225

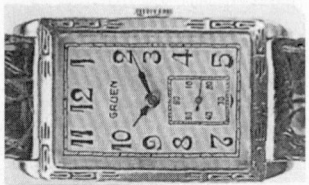

GRUEN, 15 jewels, RF#8w, cal.157, Ca. 1929
gold filled $75 $125 $200

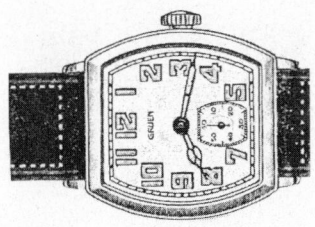

GRUEN, 15 jewels, 3 Adj., sold for $25.00 in 1930
nickel $50 $100 $175

GRUEN, 17J., veri-thin, cal.405, c. 1946
gold filled $65 $100 $175

GRUEN, 17J., curvex, **RF#450**, cal.440, C. 1940
gold filled $150 $300 $400

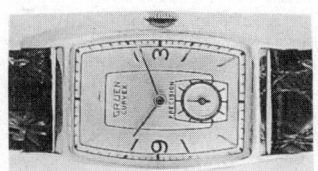

GRUEN, 17J., curvex, **R.F#450**, cal.440, c. 1940
14k. $300 $550 $650

GRUEN, 17J., curvex, **RF#450**, cal.440, c. 1942
14k. . . . . $ 300 $550 $600

GRUEN, 17J., curvex, **RF#364**, cal.440, c. 1940
gold filled $150 $275 $350

GRUEN, 17J., precision, **RF#271**, cal., c. 1936
gold filled $165 $275 $325

Note: Different dial styles were used on same RF# and Caliber.

GRUEN, 17J., curvex, **RF#448**, cal.440, c. 1941
gold filled $100 $200 $250
14K $200 $400 $500

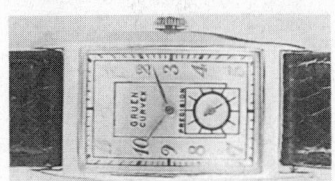

GRUEN, 17J., curvex, **RF#448**, cal.440, c. 1944
gold filled $110 $150 $250
14k. $200 $400 $500

GRUEN, 17J., curvex, **RF#879**, cal.370, c. 1942
14k. $200 $375 $500

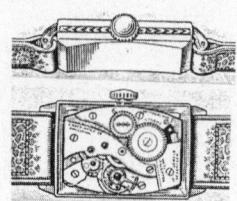

Gruen Quadron rectangular movement

GRUEN, 17J., curvex, **RF#293**, cal.330, c. 1940
gold filled $125 $225 $350

GRUEN, 17J., fluted bezel, **RF#240**, cal.335, c. 1935
14k. $200 $375 $475

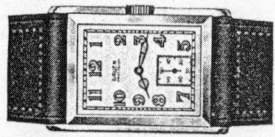

GRUEN, 17J., crown-guard, quadron mvt# 59, Ca. 1927
18K $250 $475 $550

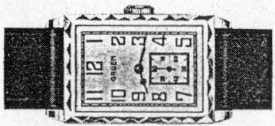

GRUEN, 15-17J., inlaid enamel case, quadron mvt, Ca. 1927
gold filled $70 $125 $200

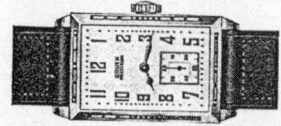

GRUEN, 15-17J., engraved case, quadron mvt# 47, Ca. 1927
gold filled $70 $125 $200

GRUEN advertising campaign in 1908 was the first to introduce
wrist watches in U.S.A.

GRUEN, 17J., crown-guard, quadron mvt, Ca. 1927
14K $200 $400 $500

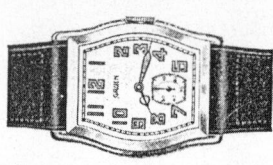

GRUEN, 17J., crown-guard, quadron mvt, Ca. 1927
gold filled $70 $125 $200

GRUEN, 15J., enamel on nickel case, mvt# 158, Ca. 1927
nickel $100 $250 $300

GRUEN, 15-17J., enamel Art Deco, Ca. 1927
gold filled $125 $250 $300

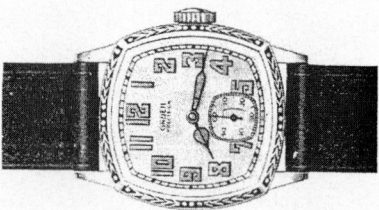

GRUEN, 15J., aux. sec., radium dial, sold for $55. in 1927
14K(W). $200 $400 $500

GRUEN, 15-17J., engraved case, radium dial,, Ca. 1927
nickel $75 $150 $175

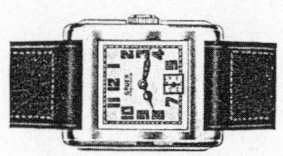

GRUEN, 15-17J., crown-guard, Ca. 1927
14K $150 $300 $400

GRUEN, 15-17J., engraved case, mvt # 13, Ca. 1927
14K $200 $400 $500

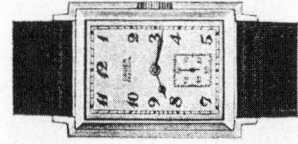

GRUEN, 17J., crown-guard, sold for $135 in 1931
14K(W). $150 $300 $400

GRUEN, 17J., crown-guard, sold for $160 in 1931
14K(W). $150 $300 $400

GRUEN, 17J., "**Centurion**" sold for $85 in 1930
14K(W). $300 $600 $800

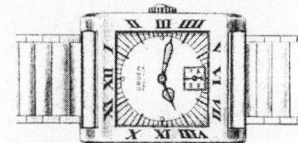

GRUEN, 15J., inlaid green enamel, sold for $47.50 is 1930
gold filled (W) $135 $250 $275

GRUEN, 15J., inlaid red & black enamel, sold for $55 in 1931
gold filled $70 $135 $200

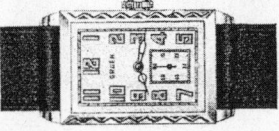

GRUEN, 15J., antique finished, told for $55 in 1930
gold filled $70 $135 $175

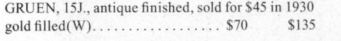

GRUEN, 15J., antique finished, sold for $45 in 1930
gold filled(W). $70 $135 $175

GRUEN, 15J., crown-guard, sold for $45 in 1930
gold filled $70 $135 $175

GRUEN, 15J., antique finished, sold for $35 in 1930
gold filled $70 $135 $175

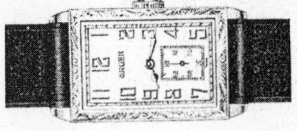

GRUEN, 15J., Quadron movement, sold for $50 in 1931
gold filled $70 $135 $170

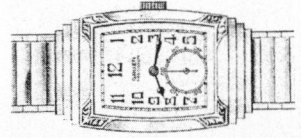

GRUEN, 17J., Precision movement, sold for $100 in 1930
14K $200 $400 $475

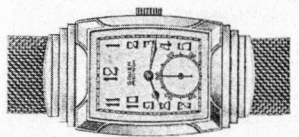

GRUEN, 17J., Precision movement, sold for $100 in 1930
14K $200 $400 $475

GRUEN, 17J., curvex, RF#602, cat.370, c. 1943
14k. $250 $500 $650

GRUEN, 17J., curvex, RF#449, cal.440, c. 1945
14k. $165 $300 $400

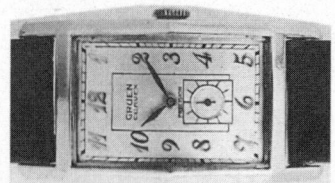

GRUEN, 17J., Curvex Precision, RF # 601, Ca. 1949
gold filled $125 $250 $300

GRUEN, 17 jewels, curvex, RF # 271, c. 1936
gold filled $200 $350 $400

GRUEN, 17 jewels, precision, fancy lugs
14k. $200 $400 $450

🖝 Some grades are not included Their values can
be determined by comparing with similar age, size,
metal content, style, grades, or models such as time only,
chronograph, repeater etc. listed.

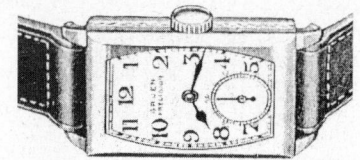

GRUEN, 17 jewels, Precision, Ca. 1928
14k(W) $175 $300 $400

GRUEN, 17J., Curvex Precision, RF #600, Ca.1945
gold filled $125 $250 $300

GRUEN, 17 jewels, curvex, fancy lugs
14k. $200 $400 $500

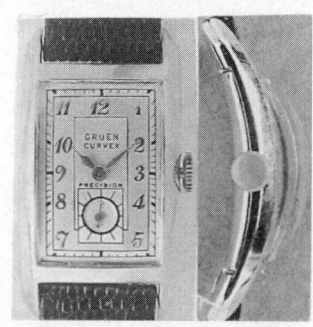

GRUEN, 17 jewels, curvex, c. 1939
14k. $200 $400 $600
gold filled $150 $250 $300

GRUEN, 17 jewels, "Eagle", curvex, fancy lugs, c. 1951
14k. $400 $700 $900

The *Adjutant* features a case and crystal curved to fit the wrist

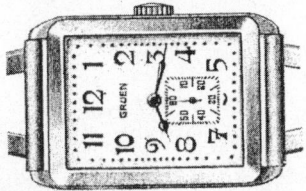

GRUEN, 15J., "Adjutant", curved case, 1931 sold @ $57.50
gold filled $90 $175 $250

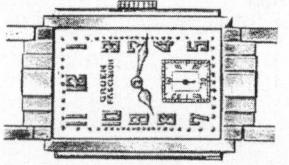

GRUEN, 17J., "Annapolis", Quadron mvt., 1931 @ $90.00
gold filled $90 $175 $225

GRUEN, "Arlington or Fleetwood" cal.325=17J., sold@ $67.50
in 1931 & "Carlton" cal.325, 21J., 1931 sold@ $92.50, all 3 use
Quadron style movement. Note: Quadron mvt. # 325 = **21J.** & has
capped escape wheel + center jeweled & pallet fork" capped also
used a different balance staff & pallet arbor.
gold filled(W) **21J** $100 $175 $225
gold filled(W) 17J. $75 $175 $200

GRUEN, 17J., "Ascot", 1931 sold for $55.00
gold filled $100 $175 $200

GRUEN, 15J., "Aviator", 1931 sold for $42.50
gold filled(W) $135 $175 $225

GRUEN, 15J., "Chief or Courier", 1931 sold for $27.50
nickel $55 $100 $125

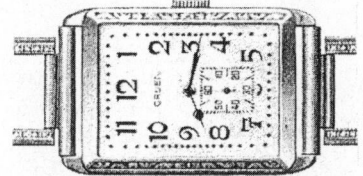

GRUEN, 15J., "Commander", 1931 sold for $50.00
gold filled(W). $75 $125 $150

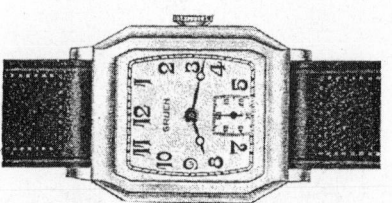

GRUEN, 15J., "Courier or Chief", 1931 sold for $27.50
nickel $55 $125 $150

GRUEN, 15J., "Culver", 1931 sold for $57.50
gold filled $60 $125 $140

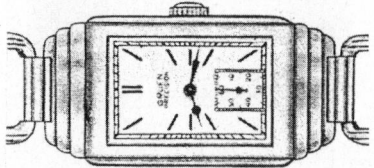

GRUEN, 17J., "Dartmouth", Quadron mvt.,1931@ $85.00
gold filled $75 $150 $175

GRUEN, 17J., "Kensington", 1931 sold for $45.00
gold filled $75 $150 $175

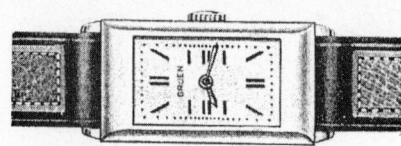

GRUEN, 15J., "Lakehurst", 1931 sold for $47.50
gold filled $60 $100 $125

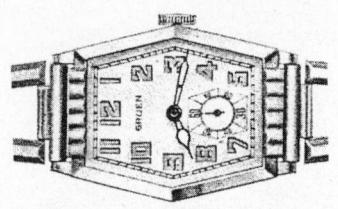

GRUEN, 15J., "Stadium", 1931 sold for $42.50
gold filled(2 tone) $75 $150 $200

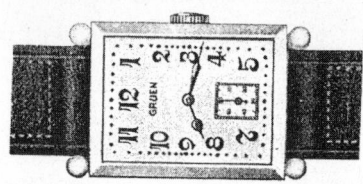

GRUEN, 21J., "Longacre", Quadron mvt., 1931 @ $100.00
Note: Quadron mvt. # 325 = 21 jewels, Ca. 1931.
14K(Y) $185 $375 $500
14K(W) $185 $375 $500

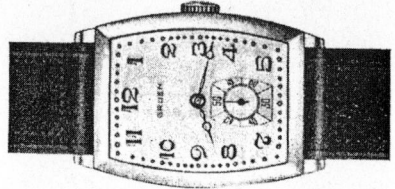

GRUEN, 15J., "Stanford", 1931 sold for $35.00
gold filled $60 $100 $125

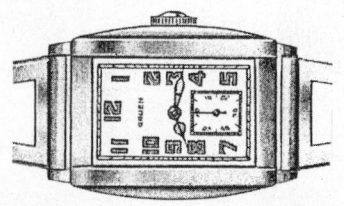

GRUEN, 17J., "Marcus", 1931 sold for $47.50
gold filled $100 $225 $275

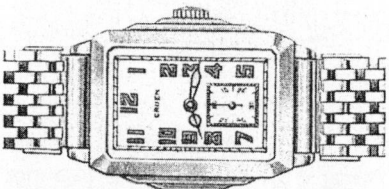

GRUEN, 15-17J., "Varsity", 1931 15J@ $55.00, 17J@$60 00
gold filled $75 $150 $200

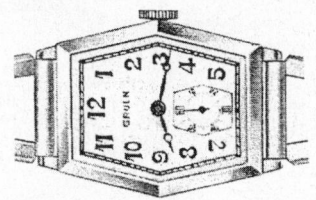

GRUEN, 15J., "Wesleyan", 1931 sold for $37.50
gold filled(W). $75 $125 $150

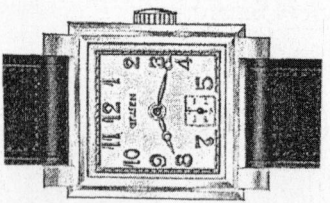

GRUEN, 15J., "Rutgers", 1931 sold for $35.00
gold filled $90 $150 $200

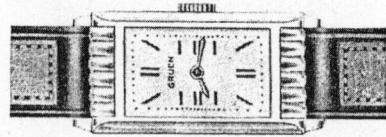

GRUEN, 15J., "West Point", 1931 sold for $52.50
gold filled(2 tone) $85 $150 $175

GRUEN, 15J., "Scout or Trooper", 1931 sold for $25.00
nickel $55 $150 $200

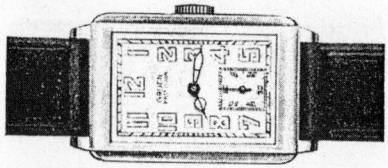

GRUEN, 17J., "Whitehall", Quadron mvt.1931 @ $75.00
gold filled $75 $125 $150

GRUEN, 17J, physicians 1 button chronog., screw back
s. steel $350 $650 $850

GRUEN, 17J., triple date, cal.415, c. 1953
s. steel $100 $250 $325
gold filled $100 $250 $325

GRUEN, 17J, physicians 1 button chronog., screw back
18k. $1,200 $2,000 $2,400

GRUEN, 17 jewels, rope style bezel with diamonds
14k. $250 $475 $550

GRUEN, 17J., jump 24 hour, c. 1970
s. steel $175 $300 $400

GRUEN, 17J., "Day-Night", cal.n150, waterproof, Ca. 1960
The "Day-night" markers have a self-powered illumination system.
base metal. . . . . ★ $125 $250 $300

GRUEN, 17J., alarm, date, c. 1964
s. steel $150 $300 $375

GRUEN, 17J., **"Airflight"**, jumping hours, c. 1960
base metal. $200 $400 $550

GRUEN, 17 jewels, 17 diamonds, RF# 744, Ca. 1955
14k(w)...................... $300 $600 $850

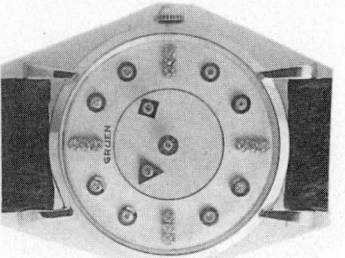

GRUEN, 17J., mystery dial, Ca. 1950
14k(w)...................... $500 $1,000 $1,250

GRUEN, 17jewels, veri-thin model, fancy lugs
14k...........................$175 $325 $375

GRUEN, 15J., sold for $32.50 is 1928
gold filled $90 $135 $225

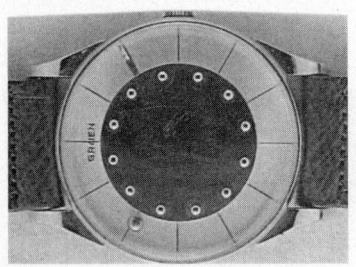

GRUEN, 17J., mystery dial, cal#215, ca.1965
gold filled $135 $250 $350

GRUEN, 15-17J., barrel shaped, Ca 1939
gold filled $75 $125 $150

GRUEN, 17J., veri-thin, fancy bezel, Ca. 1948
gold filled $100 $175 $225

GRUEN, 17J., veri-thin model, fancy lugs, 24 hr. dial
14k........................... $100 $200 $300

GRUEN, 15-17J., **curvex**, RF# 544, Ca. 1949
gold filled $150 $275 $325

GRUEN, 17J., fluted center lugs, cal.343, c. 1936
gold filled $50 $90 $125

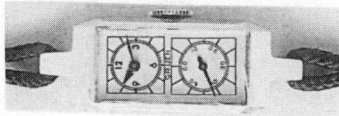

GRUEN, 17J., nurse style double dial, ca.1937
s. steel $175 $350 $500

E. GUBELIN, 17 jewels, chronog. 3 reg., Valj.72, c. 1950
18k(waterproof) $1,000 $1,700 $2,200

E. GUBELIN, 19 jewels, chronog., day-date-month
18k $1,200 $1,800 $2,500

E. GUBELIN, 19J., chronog. by Valjoux, **waterpf**, 3 reg.
18k $1,000 $1,750 $2,200

E. GUBELIN, 29 jewels, min. repeater
18k C&B $20,000 $37,500 $50,000

E. GUBELIN, 25J., ipso-matic, triple date, moon ph.
14k & steel back $1,000 $2,000 $2,500
18k $2,000 $4,000 $4,500

E. GUBELIN, 15J., triple date, c.1945
s. steel $300 $550 $650

E. GUBELIN, 19 jewels, 18k case, 14k band
18k & **14k C&B** $650 $1,100 $1,400

E. GUBELIN, 17J., ca. 1970s
18k. $175 $350 $400

E. GUBELIN,25J., cal#F690, autow., center sec., ca. 1950s
18k. $275 $500 $600
s. steel $125 $200 $275

E. GUBELIN, 17J., autow., ca. 1952
s. steel $125 $250 $300

E. GUBELIN, 25J., ipso-matic, c.1955
14k. $300 $550 $650

E. GUBELIN, 17-25J., alarm, autow., ipso-vox, c.1960
18k. $1,000 $1,800 $2,200

E. GUBELIN, 17-25J., ipso-vox, date, autow., alarm, c.1960
s. steel $400 $800 $950

E. GUBELIN, 17J., carved lugs, center sec., c. 1944
18k. $300 $575 $650

E. GUBELIN, 17J., 3 baguettes, 8 diamonds, autow., c.1948
platinum $900 $1,650 $2,250

E. GUBELIN, 15J., **back wind duoplan**, c.1935
s. steel $200 $375 $450

E. GUBELIN, 15J., Ca. 1935
18k(W) $350 $700 $800

E. GUBELIN, 25J., milled bezel, autow., center sec., c. 1955
18k $300 $550 $750

E. GUBELIN, 19 J., hunter style pop-up lid, c. 1930
18k (w) $2,000 $3,500 $4,000

E. GUBELIN, 19 jewels, fancy hooded lugs
18k $400 $800 $1,000

E. GUBELIN, 17 jewels, jumping hr., c. 1924
14k $3,000 $5,500 $7,000

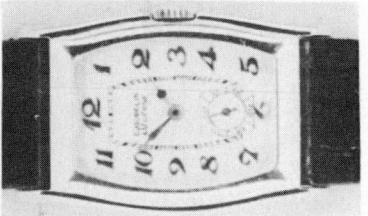

E. GUBELIN, 19 jewels, curvex, 2 tone
18k $500 $900 $1,200

E. GUBELIN, 25J., triple date, moon phase, autow., c. 1950
18k $2,500 $4,000 $5,000

E. GUBELIN, 19J., center sec., flared case, c. 1950
18k $450 $775 $900

E. GUBELIN, triple date & moon ph., by Audemars-Piguet, Ca.
1930
18k $12,000 $22,000 $28,000

E. GUBELIN, 17-21J., milled bezel, center sec., Ca. 1958
18k $200 $400 $500

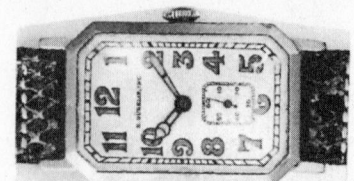

E. GUBELIN, 17 jewels, by Vacheron & Constantin
18k. $1,500 $2,200 $3,200

E. GUBELIN, 18 jewels, curved, stepped case, c. 1940
18k. $400 $750 $1,000

GUINAND, 17J., chronog., day-date-month, 3 reg.
18k. $900 $1,400 $1,800
s. steel $400 $750 $900

GUINAND, 17J., chronog., triple date, moon phase
18k. $1,000 $1,750 $2,300
s. steel $600 $1,100 $1,400

HAFIS, 15J., center sec., cushion style
gold plane $35 $75 $100

HAFIS, 15J., luminous dial
gold plate $35 $75 $100

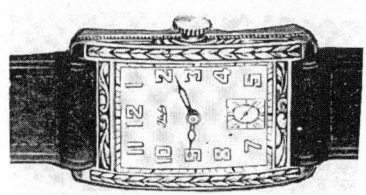

HAFIS, 15J., engraved case
gold plate $40 $100 $125
14k. $125 $175 $225

HAFIS, 15J., engraved case
gold plate $40 $100 $125

HAFIS, 17J., "Queen Druga", 52 diamonds
Platinum $250 $475 $600

HALLMARK, 17 jewels. day-date-month, autowind
gold filled $65 $130 $200

HAMILTON WATCH CO.

Hamilton made their first ladies bracelet watch in 1912. During the Art Deco period they were very successful with the "Coronado", "Piping Rock" and "Spur" model wrist watches using a enamel bezel. A dramatic change occurred for the watch industry in April, 1957 when the Hamilton Watch Co. eliminated the mainspring and replaced it with a small battery that lasted well over one year. The "Ventura" and "Van Horn" model 500 goes on sale and the Hamilton Watch Co. won the race to introduce the worlds' first electric Wrist Watch, also the first watch with no moving parts, the revolutionary "Pulsar" on May 10, 1970.

A very brief review of the 500 series moving coil and contact control system. The coil is fixed on the balance and a electric current flows in the magnetic field, producing a electromagnetic force. At the moment the magnetic field reaches the right and left side of the coil, the contact spring are closed by a small pin on the balance. Thus electric current through the coil will receive an impulse from the electromagnetic force and give the balance one impulse each swing. The basic principle is the same for electric motors.

Below Left: **500** balance & coil.   Center: **501** balance & coil.   Right: **505** balance & coil.

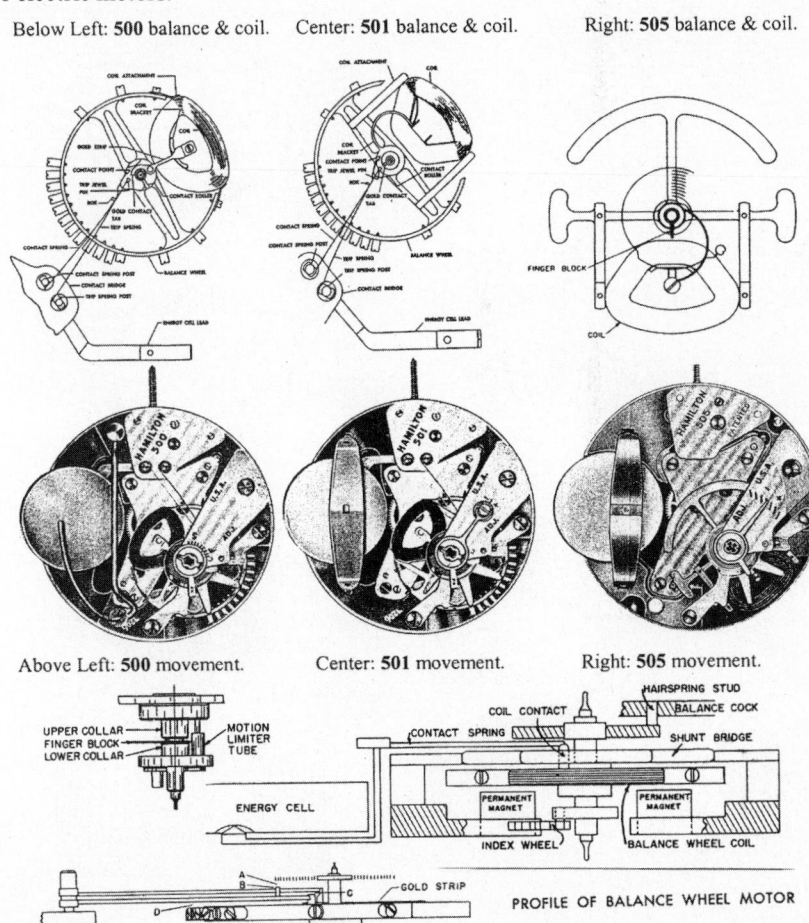

Above Left: **500** movement.   Center: **501** movement.   Right: **505** movement.

PROFILE OF BALANCE WHEEL MOTOR

DIALS FOR MINT PRICES MUST BE ALL ORIGINAL.   Prices for electric watch to be in **good running order**.

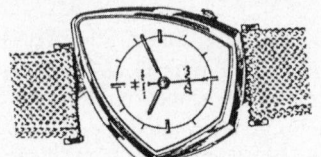

HAMILTON, electric, "Altair", Ca. 1962
gold filled .... ★★ $1,500 $2,750 $3,500

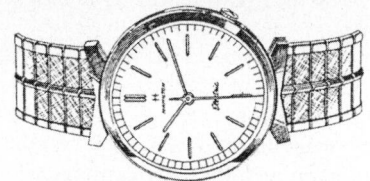

HAMILTON, electric, "Aquatel", Ca. 1961
gold filled $100 $250 $350

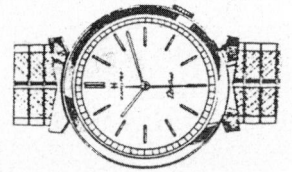

HAMILTON, electric, "Aquatel B", Ca. 1962
gold filled $100 $200 $300

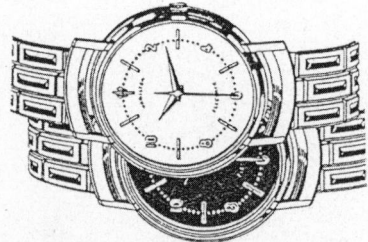

HAMILTON, electric, "Atlantis", Ca. 1958
gold filled $100 $200 $300

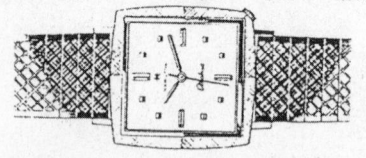

HAMILTON electric, "Centaur", Ca. 1965
gold filled $100 $175 $250

HAMILTON, electric, "Clearview" **display back**, sold for $100.00 in 1965
s. steel case & GF bezel ......★★ $300 $525 $650

HAMILTON, electric, "Converta I", Ca.1958
18k bezel & s. s. case $200 $375 $475

HAMILTON, electric, "Converta II", Ca.1958
14k bezel & s. s. case $125 $200 $350

HAMILTON, electric, "Converta III", Ca.1958
GF bezel & s. s. case. $125 $225 $300

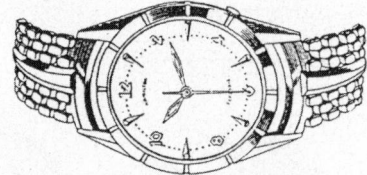

HAMILTON, electric, "Converta IV", Ca.1958
S.S. bezel & case $100 $200 $250

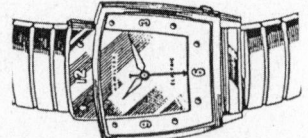

HAMILTON, electric, "Everest", Ca. 1958
gold filled $250 $500 $650

HAMILTON, electric, "Everest II", sold for $99.50 in 1964
gold filled $200 $400 $500

HAMILTON (continued)

Prices for electric watch to be in **good running order**.

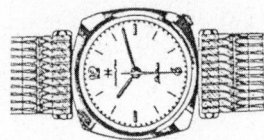

HAMILTON, electric, "Gemini" Ca.1962
gold filled $100 $200 $250

HAMILTON, electric, "Gemini II", sold for $125.00 in 1964
gold filled $100 $200 $250

HAMILTON, electric, "Lord Lancaster E" , Ca.1963
14k, 12 diamonds $400 $700 $850

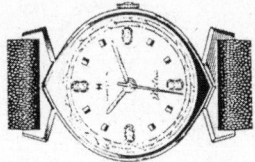

HAMILTON, electric, "Lord Lancaster J" ,Ca.1965
gold filled, 8 diamonds. $275 $450 $600

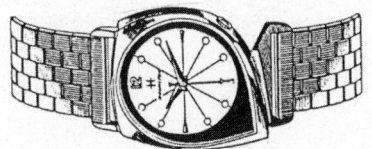

HAMILTON, electric, "Meteor," c. 1960
gold filled . . . . ★$500 $850 $1,000

HAMILTON. electric "Nautilus" 200, single lugs Ca. 1962
14k. $200 $350 $400

HAMILTON, electric, "Nautilus" 201, Ca. in 1964
14k. $150 $275 $400

HAMILTON, electric, "Nautilus" 202, sold for $160.00 in 1964
14k. $150 $275 $400

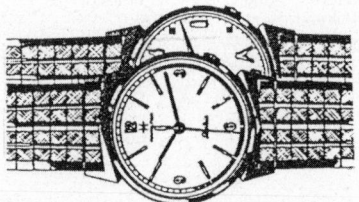

HAMILTON, electric, "Nautilus" 400, Ca.1962
gold filled $100 $200 $250

HAMILTON, electric "Nautilus" 401, Ca.1964
gold filled $100 $200 $250

HAMILTON, electric, "Nautilus" 402, Ca. 1963
gold filled $100 $200 $250

HAMILTON, electric, "Nautilus" 403, pocket watch, Ca.1965
gold filled . . . . ★★$250 $450 $600

DIALS FOR MINT PRICES MUST BE ALL ORIGINAL.

HAMILTON, electric, "Nautilus" 404, Ca.1964
gold filled $110 $200 $225

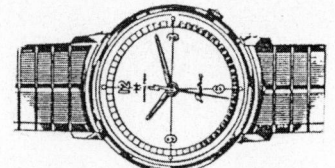

HAMILTON, electric, "Nautilus" 503, Ca.1964
s. steel $110 $200 $250

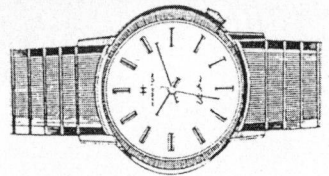

HAMILTON, electric, "Nautilus" 405, Ca.1966
gold filled $110 $200 $225

HAMILTON, electric, "Nautilus" 506, Ca.1965
s. steel $110 $200 $250

HAMILTON electric "Nautilus" 450, Ca.1963
gold filled bezel $110 $200 $225

HAMILTON, electric, "Nautilus" 507, Ca.1966
s. steel $110 $200 $250

HAMILTON, electric, "Nautilus" 500, Ca.1962
s. steel $110 $200 $225

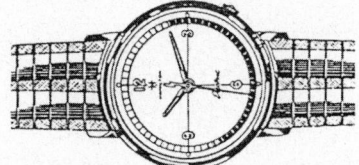

HAMILTON, electric, "Nautilus" 508, Ca.1962
s. steel $110 $200 $250

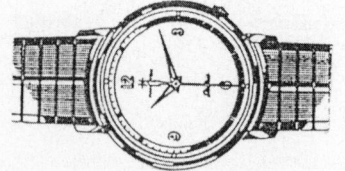

HAMILTON, electric, "Nautilus" 501, Ca. 1962
s. steel $110 $200 $225

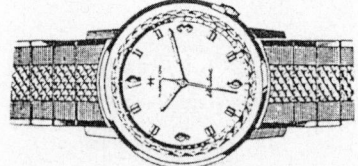

HAMILTON, electric, "Nautilus" 509, Ca. 1966
s. steel $110 $200 $250

HAMILTON, electric, "Nautilus" 502, Ca. 1963
s. steel $125 $200 $225

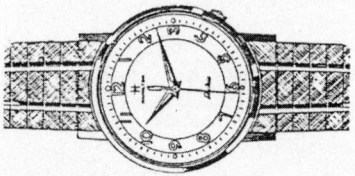

HAMILTON, electric, "Nautilus" 600, Ca. 1963
rolled gold. $100 $200 $250

Prices for electric watch to be in **good running order.**

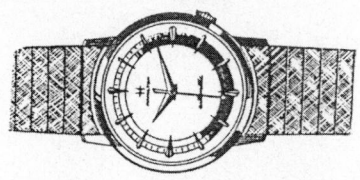

HAMILTON, electric, "Nautilus" 601, Ca. 1963
rolled gold. $100 $200 $250

HAMILTON, electric, "Nautilus" 602, Ca. 1965
rolled gold. $100 $200 $250

HAMILTON, electric, "Nautilus" 604, Ca. 1965
rolled gold. $100 $200 $250

HAMILTON, electric, "Nautilus" 605, Ca. 1965
rolled gold. $100 $200 $250

HAMILTON, electric, "Pacer," 2 tone ,Ca. 1957
14k. . . . . ★★★ $1,500 $2,750 $3,500
gold filled $400 $750 $900
gold filled (black dial) $450 $800 $1,000

Wrist Watches listed in this section are priced at the collectable fair market Trade Show level as complete watches having an original gold-filled case and stainless steel back, also with original dial, leather watch band, and the entire original movement in good working order with no repairs needed.

HAMILTON, electric, "Pegasus", engraved bezel, sold for $125.00 in 1965
gold filled $275 $500 $650

HAMILTON. electric, "Polaris", Ca. 1960
14k Y. $300 $600 $750
14k W $400 $800 $900

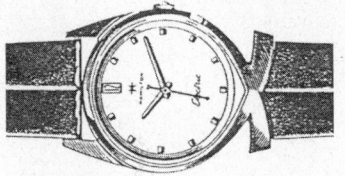

HAMILTON, electric "Polaris II", Ca. 1965
14k. $300 $575 $700

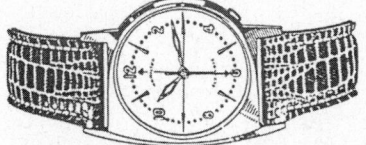

HAMILTON, electric, "Regulus' Ca. 1958
s. steel $500 $900 $1,100

HAMILTON, electric, "Regulus" II, Ca. 1962
s. steel $110 $200 $250

☞ A collector should expect no pay modestly higher prices at local shops

DIALS FOR MINT PRICES MUST BE ALL ORIGINAL.

HAMILTON, electric, "R. R. Special", Ca. 1962
model#52 = all 10k GF $150 $275 $375
model#51 = GF bezel only $150 $275 $375
model#50 = all s. steel $150 $275 $375

HAMILTON, electric, "Sea-Lectric II" Ca. 1962
s. steel $100 $200 $300

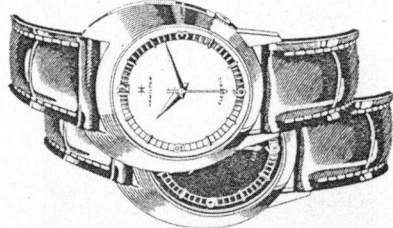

HAMILTON, electric, "Saturn" Ca. 1960
gold filled . . . . ★$400 $775 $875

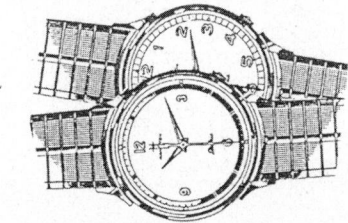

HAMILTON, electric, "Skip Jack" Ca. 1961
s. steel $110 $200 $250

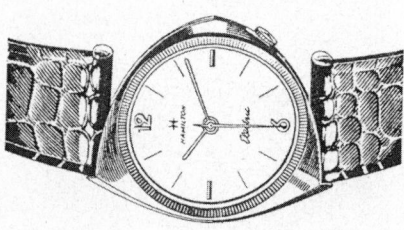

HAMILTON, electric, "Savitar" Ca. 1961
14k. . . . . ★$450 $850 $950

HAMILTON, electric, "Spectra" Ca. 1957
18k Rose gold . . . . ★★★★ $1,000 $2,000 $2,500
18k . . . . ★★★ $700 $1,300 $1,600
14k . . . . ★★ $500 $900 $1,100
gold filled . . . . ★★ $300 $600 $700

HAMILTON, electric, "Savitar 11", Ca.1965
gold filled $250 $500 $600

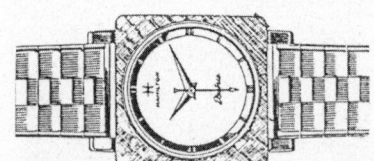

HAMILTON, electric, "Spectra" II, Ca. 1963
gold filled $100 $200 $300

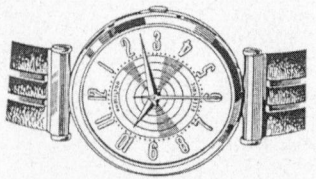

HAMILTON, electric, "Sea-Lectric I", GF bezel, Ca. 1965
s. steel $125 $250 $375

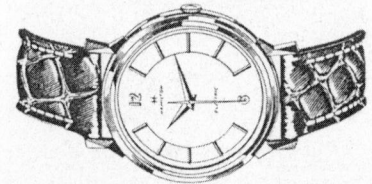

HAMILTON, electric, "Summit" Ca. 1961
14k. $200 $375 $450

Prices for electric watch to be in **good running order**.

HAMILTON, electric, "Summit" II, Ca. 1964
gold filled . . . . ★$200 $350 $400

HAMILTON, electric, "Titan IV-B" Ca. 1966
14k C&B . . . . ★★★★ $600 $1,100 $1,200

HAMILTON, electric, "Taurus" Ca. 1962
gold filled $110 $200 $300

HAMILTON, electric, "Uranus" ,Ca. 1959
gold filled $150 $300 $350

HAMILTON, electric, "Titan", Ca. 1958
gold filled $150 $300 $375

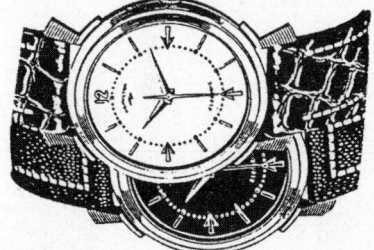

HAMILTON, electric, "Van Horn", Ca.1957
14k. $250 $450 $500
14k +diam. dial. $400 $700 $800

HAMILTON, electric, "Titan II" Ca. 1961
gold filled $235 $400 $500

HAMILTON, electric, Vantage, Ca. 1958
gold filled $185 $350 $425

HAMILTON, electric, "Titan III", Ca. 1964
gold filled $235 $400 $500

HAMILTON, electric, "Vega" ,Ca. 1961
gold filled . . . . ★$675 $1,200 $1,500

DIALS FOR MINT PRICES MUST BE ALL ORIGINAL.

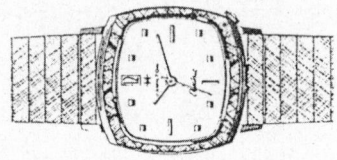

HAMILTON, electric, "Vela" , sold for $115.00 in 1966
gold filled $150 $250 $350

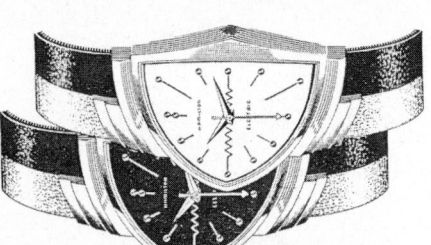

HAMILTON electric, "Ventura",
14k sold for $200.00 in 1957
18k rose. . . . . ★★★★ $2,500 $4,000 $4,250
18k. . . . . ★★★ $1,500 $3,000 $3,500
14k(W) . . . . ★★ $1,700 $3,250 $4,000
14k(Y). $1,000 $1,800 $2,500

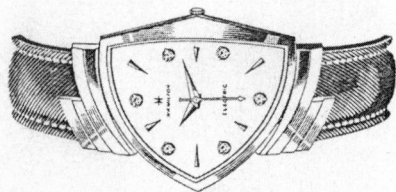

HAMILTON electric, "Ventura", **6 diamond dial**, Ca. 1957
14K $1,100 $2,000 $2,800

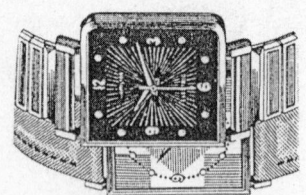

HAMILTON, electric, "Victor", ca.1957
gold filled $225 $450 $550

Hamilton, electric, "Victor II" ,Ca. 1961
14k(y & w) $250 $450 $600

HAMILTON, 19 jewels, "Adrian", ca. 1953
gold filled $100 $200 $250

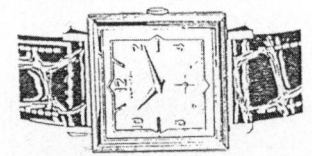

HAMILTON, 17 jewels, "Alan", ca.1942
gold filled $100 $175 $200

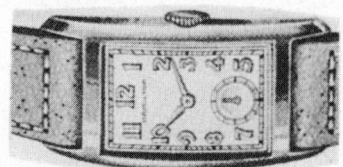

HAMILTON, 22 jewels, "Aldrich", Ca, 1958
14k. $150 $275 $350

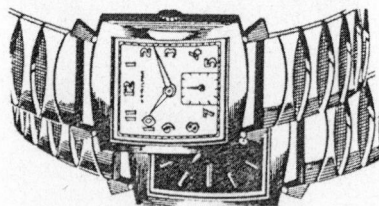

HAMILTON, 19 jewels, "Allison", Ca.1937
14k. $175 $350 $475

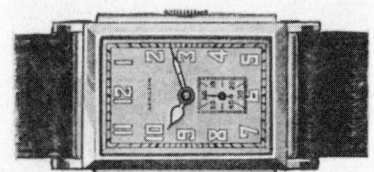

HAMILTON, 17J., "Amherst", 14k markers ,Ca. 1956
gold filled $100 $200 $250

HAMILTON, 19 jewels, "Andrews", ca.1930
gold filled . . . . ★$250 $425 $475

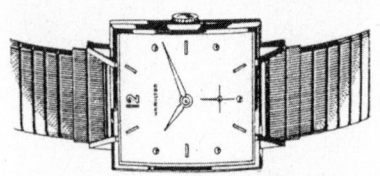

HAMILTON, 22J., "Ansley", 14k markers, Ca. 1960
gold filled $100 $175 $225

HAMILTON, 17J.," Austin ", Ca. 1949
gold filled $100 $175 $225

HAMILTON, 17J., "Aqualine ", 14k markers, Ca. 1957
gold filled $75 $125 $150

HAMILTON, 17J, "Bagley," applied numbers, Ca. 1939
gold filled $100 $175 $275

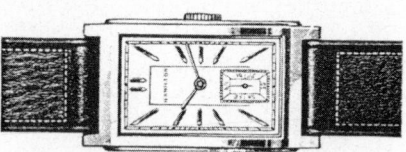

HAMILTON, 19J., "Ardmore", Ca. 1935
14k. $275 $550 $600

HAMILTON, 19J.," Bailey ", c.1949
gold filled $100 $175 $225

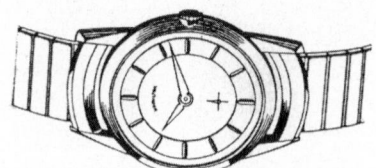

HAMILTON, 17J., " Arnold",Ca. 1957
rolled gold. $50 $100 $125

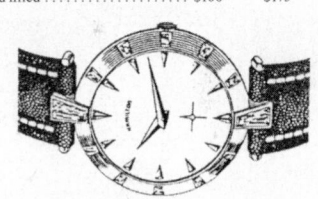

HAMILTON, 22J., "Barbizon", diam. bezel, Ca. 1957
18k(w) . . . . ★★★★★ $2,500 $4,500 $5,500

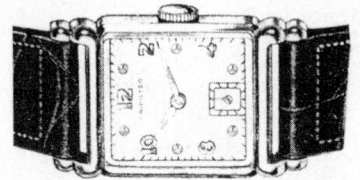

HAMILTON, 19J., "Ashley", grade 982, Ca. 1948
gold filled $100 $175 $225

HAMILTON, 22J., "Baron", 5 diam. dial, BIG lugs, c.1960
14k. $185 $400 $500

HAMILTON, 22J., "Attache", 14k markers, c. 1961
gold filled $175 $235 $335

HAMILTON, 22J., "Baron II", 5 diamond dial, Ca. 1961
14k. $185 $400 $500

HAMILTON, 22J, "Barry", sterling silver dial, ca. 1957
gold filled $100 $175 $200

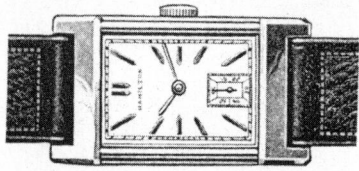

HAMILTON, 17J., Bartley", Ca.1936
gold filled $135 $250 $300

HAMILTON, 19J "Barton", tu tone dial, c 1948
14k. $200 $400 $550

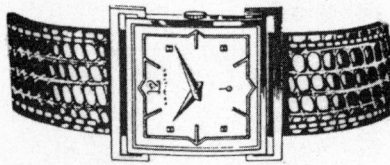

HAMILTON, 22J., Baton", 14k markers, ca. 1958
14k. $175 $400 $500

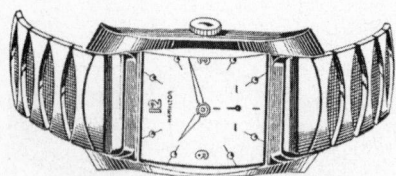

HAMILTON 17J.,"Baxter", sterling silver dial, Ca. 1957
gold filled $100 $200 $275

HAMILTON,17J.,"Beldon", 2 tone dial, sealed case, c.1949
gold filled $100 $175 $225

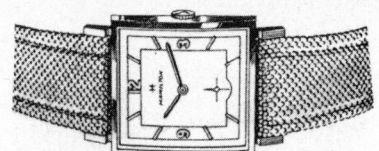

HAMILTON, 22J., "Bentley", 14k markers, ca. 1961
gold filled $100 $175 $200

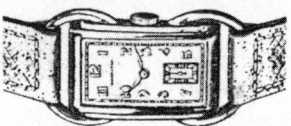

HAMILTON, 19J., "Bentley", 14k markers, Ca. 1937
14k. $450 $850 $1,000

HAMILTON 17-19J.,"Benton" ,14k markers, c. 1952
14k. $250 $500 $700

HAMILTON 17J.,"Berkshire" , 14k markers, Ca. 1953
14k. $200 $500 $600

HAMILTON 22J.,"Blade", asymmetrical, note lugs, Ca.1962
gold filled . . . . ★ $200 $400 $500

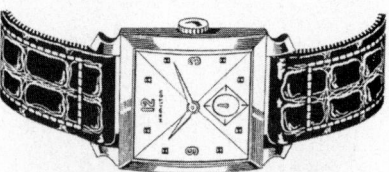

HAMILTON, 22J.," Blair ", sterling silver dial, c.1957
gold filled $100 $175 $200

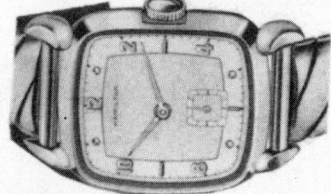

HAMILTON, 17-21J.," Blake", c.1949
gold filled $100 $175 $200

HAMILTON, 17J., "Boatswain", center sec., c. 1958
rolled gold.................... $50 $100 $125

HAMILTON, 17J., "Boatswain II" ,c. 1961
rolled gold.................... $50 $90 $110

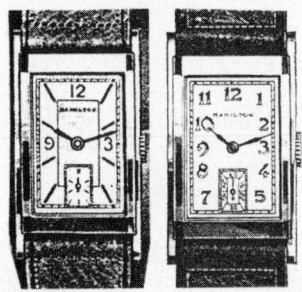

HAMILTON, 17J.," Boone ", Curved, Ca. 1936
gold filled $100 $200 $250

HAMILTON, 19jewels, "Boulton" ,Ca. 1941
gold filled $125 $225 $250

HAMILTON, 22J., "Boulton II", 14k markers, c. 1961
gold filled $100 $175 $250

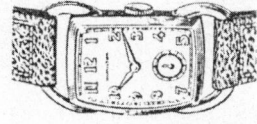

HAMILTON, 17J.,"Bowman", c. 1939
gold filled $175 $250 $300

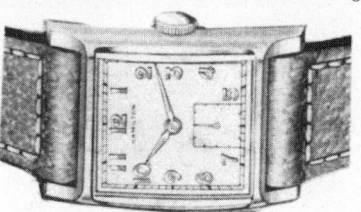

HAMILTON, 17J.,"Boyd", c.1949
gold filled $100 $180 $225

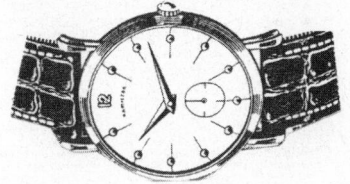

HAMILTON, 22J., "Bradford", 14k markers, c. 1954
14k.........................$150 $275 $350

HAMILTON, 22J., "Bradford B", 11 diam. dial, c. 1954
14k......................... $200 $400 $475

HAMILTON, 17J., "Brandon", swing lugs, ca. 1946
gold filled $100 $200 $250

HAMILTON, 17 jewels Brandon Ca 1948
gold filled $100 $175 $225

HAMILTON, 19J.,"Brent" faceted crystal, c. 1949
gold filled $100 $175 $225

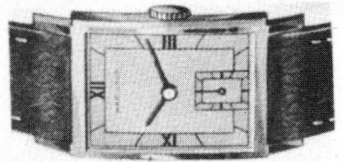

HAMILTON, 22J.," Brewster', sterling silver dial, Ca.1957
gold filled $100 $175 $200

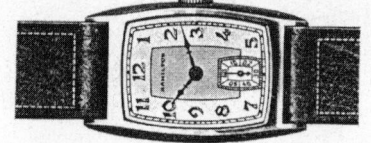

HAMILTON, 17 J, "Cabot" ,cal. 960, Ca.1938
gold filled $100 $200 $250

HAMILTON, 19 jewels, "Brock" ,c. 1939
14k(coral) . . . . ★★★ $300 $550 $650
14k(yellow). $175 $400 $500

HAMILTON, 17J.,"Cabot",luminous Ca. 1957
s. steel $55 $100 $125

HAMILTON, 19 jewels, " Brockton", c. 1952
10k. $100 $250 $325

HAMILTON, 17 J, "Cadet" , Ca.1957
rolled gold. $50 $100 $125

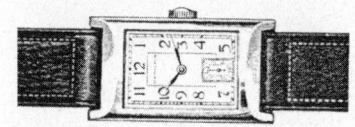

HAMILTON, 17J., "Calvin", applied gold numbers, ca.1936
gold filled $100 $175 $225

HAMILTON, 19J.," Brooke ", Curved, Ca. 1938
gold filled . . . . ★ $400 $700 $800

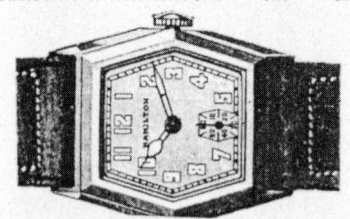

HAMILTON, 17J.,"Cambridge", ca. 1930
14k(w). . . . . ★★★ $800 $1,500 $1,700
14k(y) . . . . ★★★ $800 $1,500 $1,700

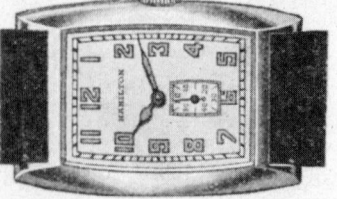

HAMILTON, 19 jewels, "Byrd" ca. 1930
18k. . . . . ★★★★ $2,000 $3,500 $4,000
14k(W). . . . . ★★ $1,200 $2,000 $2,700
14k(Y). . . . . ★★ $1,000 $1,800 $2,200

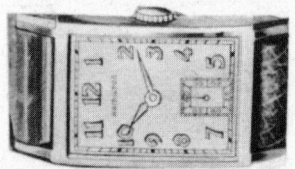

HAMILTON, 19J.," Cambridge ", c.1949
HAMILTON signed case
platinum . . . . ★ $500 $1,000 $1,200

HAMILTON, 19 jewels, "Cameron" ,c. 1937
14k. $200 $400 $550

HAMILTON, 17J.," Carlton ", c.1949
gold filled $100 $175 $200

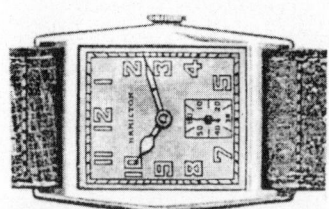

HAMILTON, 17J.,"Captain Rice", Ca. 1930
14k(w or y) . . . . ★★★ $500 $850 $1,000

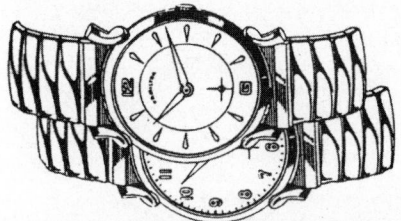

HAMILTON, 17J.,"Carlyle" ,c. 1958
rolled gold. $45 $100 $125

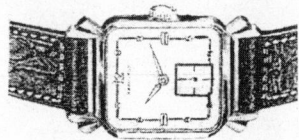

HAMILTON, 17J.," Carl ", Ca. 1953
gold filled $100 $185 $225

HAMILTON, 17J., "Carteret" 14k markers, Ca. 1958
14k. $150 $300 $400

HAMILTON, 17J.," Carlisle ", 44mm, cal. 937, Ca. 1937
gold filled $125 $250 $375

HAMILTON, 17J.,"Casino", 5 diamond, Ca. 1957
14k Y or W $185 $350 $400

HAMILTON, 17J.," Carson , Ca. 1935
gold filled $100 $175 $225

HAMILTON, 19J.," Cedric ", c.1949
gold filled $100 $175 $225

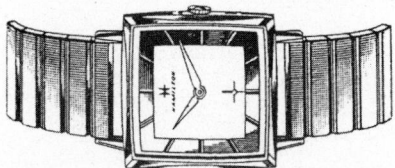

HAMILTON, 17J., "Carson" ,c. 1961
rolled gold. $75 $150 $200

Wrist Watches listed in this section are priced as the collectable
fair market **Trade Show** level as **complete** watches having an
original gold-filled case and stainless steel back, also with original
dial, leather watch band, and the entire original movement in good
working order with no repairs needed.

☞ A collector should expect to pay modestly higher prices at
local shops

HAMILTON, 22J., "Chadwick", 14k markers, c. 1959
14k. $150 $275 $325

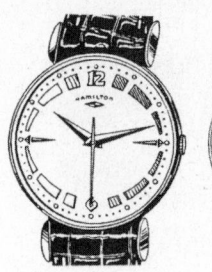

HAMILTON, 18J.,"Clearview",left=1958,right=1961
14k (1958) $165 $300 $350
14k (1961) $135 $250 $300

HAMILTON, 17J.,"Chanticleer", alarm & power reserve, c. 1957
gold filled $200 $375 $450

HAMILTON, 17J.," Clinton ", c.1949
s. steel $60 $100 $125

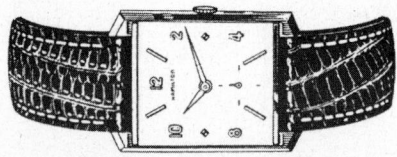

HAMILTON, 22J., 'Chapman', 14k markers, Ca. 1958
gold filled $75 $150 $200

HAMILTON, 17J.," Clyde ", c.1950
gold filled $100 $175 $200

HAMILTON, 17-19J., "Chatham", Ca. 1953
14k. $300 $600 $700

HAMILTON, 17J., 'Clark', Ca. 1936
gold filled $135 $250 $350

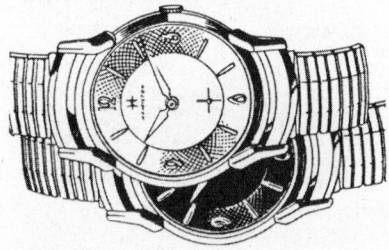

HAMILTON, 17J., "Coburn", c. 1958
rolled gold. $45 $100 $125

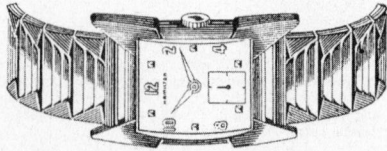

HAMILTON, 17-18J "Clark", sterling silver dial, Ca. 1957
gold filled $125 $250 $350

HAMILTON, 17J., "Colby ", c 1957
rolled gold. $75 $150 $175

HAMILTON, 17J.,"Contour", Drivers, Crown at 12, c. 1938
gold filled $300 $600 $800

HAMILTON, 17J., "Conway", c. 1961
rolled gold. $50 $125 $175

HAMILTON, 17J., " Cordell", Ca. 1961
14k C & B $300 $550 $650

HAMILTON,17J., "Coronado ", black enamel bezel, ca. 1928
14k(w or y) $1,000 $1,800 $2,500

HAMILTON, 22J., "Corvet", 14k markers, c. 1961
gold filled $75 $125 $165

HAMILTON, 17J., "Courtney", 14k markers, c. 1958
14k. $135 $250 $350

HAMILTON, 22J., "Courtney", 6 diamond dial, c. 1958
14k. $200 $400 $500

HAMILTON, 17J.," Craig ", c.1949
gold filled $100 $175 $250

HAMILTON, 19J., "Cranston ", gold markers, c. 1952
gold filled $100 $200 $250

HAMILTON, 22J., "Crispin", sterling silver dial, c. 1957
14k. $135 $200 $250

Wrist Watches listed in this section are priced at the collectable
fair market Trade Show level as complete watches having an
original gold-filled case and stainless steel back, also with original
dial, leather watch band, and the entire original movement in good
working order with no repairs needed.

5 Time Zones, Introduced Jan. 6th, 1956, the G hand = Greenwich
Pacific - Mountain - Central - Eastern

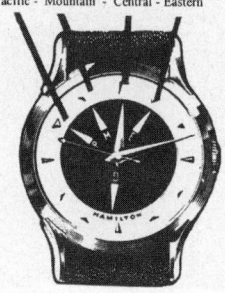

HAMILTON, 17J., "Cross Country", S time zones, ca. 1956
★Marked Illinois W. Co. on movement, (sold for $75.00)
gold filled $250 $475 $650

HAMILTON, 18J.,"Cross Country II", 5 time zones,
sold for $85.00 in 1957
gold filled $250 $400 $550

HAMILTON, 18J., "Croydon", sweep seconds, ca.1953
s. steel $45 $75 $110

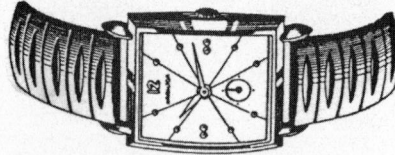

HAMILTON, 22J., "Cullen", 14k markers, c. 1957
gold filled $100 $175 $225

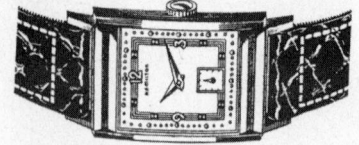

HAMILTON, 22J., "Curtiss", hinged lugs, Ca. 1953
14k. $200 $400 $500

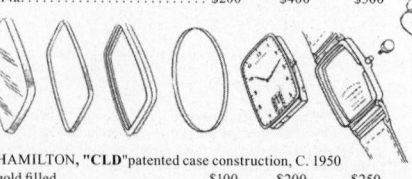

HAMILTON, "CLD"patented case construction, C. 1950
gold filled $100 $200 $250

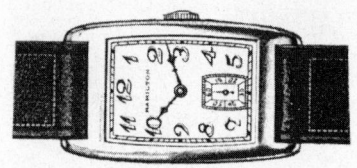

HAMILTON, 19J, "Custer", Ca 1936
14k. $225 $400 $550

HAMILTON, 17J., "Cyril", Ca. 1957
gold filled $100 $200 $250

HAMILTON, 17J., "Darrell", cal#747, c. 1951
gold filled $100 $200 $250

HAMILTON, 17J., "Dawson ",c. 1959
gold filled $100 $175 $200

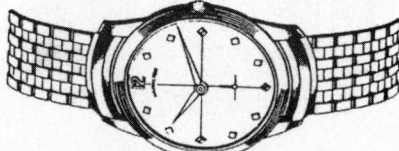

HAMILTON, 17J., "Dean",c. 1957
gold filled $100 $175 $225

HAMILTON, 17J., "Deauville ", c. 1962
rolled gold. $45 $90 $120

HAMILTON, 17J.," Dennis", Ca 1961
14k. $125 $250 $350

HAMILTON, 17J.," Dennis ", Ca 1948
gold filled $125 $225 $275

HAMILTON, 17J.," Dewitt ", c. 1950
gold filled $100 $200 $250

HAMILTON, 17J, "Dexter", c 1959
rolled gold. . . . . $ 50 $100 $175

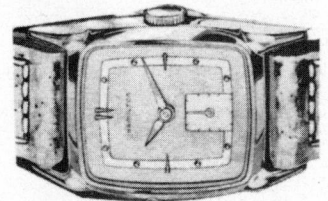

HAMILTON, 17J.," Dexter ", c.1950
gold filled $100 $200 $250

HAMILTON, 17J.," Dickens ", 44MM long, Ca. 1937
Note: Also see **Gilman** = 14k (look-a-like)
gold filled $150 $300 $375

HAMILTON, 17J.,"Dixon' left=Ca 1936, right= Ca. 1953
gold filled= 1936 . . . . $100 $200 $250
gold filled= 1953. . . . . $100 $200 $250

HAMILTON, 17 jewels, "Dodson" ,c. 1939
gold filled $125 $225 $275

HAMILTON, 19J.," Donald ", c.1941 note: Turner 10K (look-a-like)
14k. $200 $400 $550

HAMILTON, 19J,' Donovan ", center lugs, Ca. 1935
14k. $500 $900 $1,100

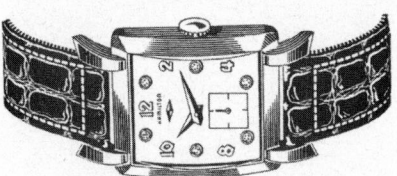

HAMILTON, 22J.,"Donavan II", 6 diamonds, Ca. 1956
14k. $250 $500 $600

HAMILTON, 22J.,"Donavan II", Ca.1955
14k. $200 $400 $550

DIALS FOR MINT PRICES MUST BE ALL ORIGINAL.

HAMILTON, 17J.," Dorsey ", Ca. 1936
14k. $200 $400 $550

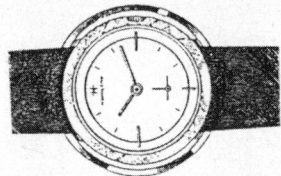

HAMILTON, 17J.," Doublet ", Ca 1962
14k. $165 $275 $350

HAMILTON, 17J.," Drake ", Ca.1951
14k. $175 $350 $500

HAMILTON, 17J.," Drake ", Ca. 1935
gold filled $150 $275 $350

HAMILTON, 17J.,"Drew", Ca.1957
rolled gold. $40 $90 $110

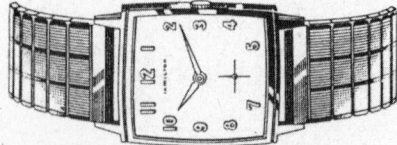

HAMILTON, 17J., "Drummond ", 14k markers, c. 1959
gold filled $75 $150 $175

HAMILTON, 17J.," Dunham ", c.1951
gold filled $75 $150 $200

HAMILTON, 19 jewels, "Dunkirk" ,c. 1937
14k. $275 $500 $600

HAMILTON, 17J., "Dwight", gold numbers, ca. 1948
gold filled $100 $200 $225

HAMILTON, 17 jewels, "Dyson" ,c. 1951
gold filled $100 $175 $200

HAMILTON, 17J.," Eaton ", c.1948
gold filled $100 $200 $250

HAMILTON, 22J.,"Edgemere B", sterling silver dial, c.1957
gold filled $75 $100 $125

DIALS FOR MINT PRICES MUST BE ALL ORIGINAL,

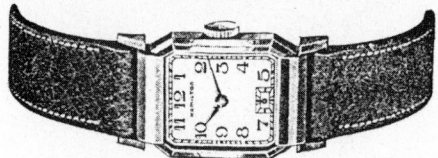

HAMILTON, 17J., "Eliott", Cal.980, Ca. 1936
gold filled $100 $200 $250

HAMILTON, 17J., "Emery", c.1949
gold filled $100 $200 $225

HAMILTON, 17 jewels, "Eric ,c. 1941
gold filled $100 $200 $250

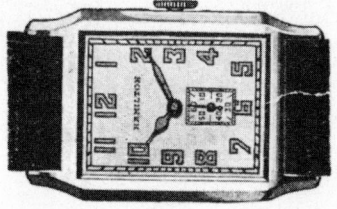

HAMILTON, 17 jewels, "Ericsson" ,Ca. 1930
18k. . . . . ★★★★ $1,100 $2,200 $2,100
14k Y or W . . . . ★★★ $800 $1,500 $1,700

HAMILTON, 17 jewels, "Emerson" ,c. 1941
gold filled $100 $200 $250

Wrist Watches listed in this section are priced at the collectable
fair market **Trade Show** level as **complete** watches having an
original old-filled case and stainless steel back, also with original
dial, leather watch band, and the entire original movement in good
working order with no repairs needed.

✍ A collector should expect to pay modestly higher prices
at local shops.

HAMILTON, 17 jewels, "Endicott" , C. 1941
gold filled yellow $100 $175 $200
gold filled coral. . . . . ★★★★ $400 $800 $1,000

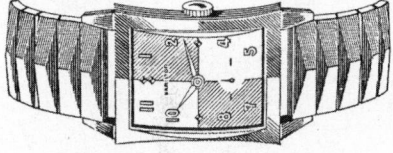

HAMILTON, 17J., "Errol" 2-tone sterling silver dial, c. 1957
gold filled $100 $200 $250

HAMILTON, 17 jewels, "Essex" ,c. 1941
gold filled yellow $100 $200 $250
gold filled coral. . . . . ★ $200 $375 $450

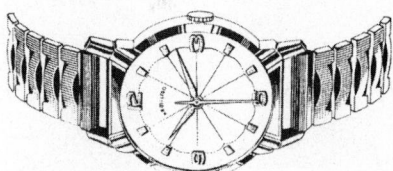

HAMILTON, 17J., "Essex", c.1957
rolled gold. $40 $75 $110

HAMILTON, 17J., "Farrell", 14k #s, c.1959
rolled gold. $40 $75 $110

HAMILTON, 17J, " First Mate", c. 1960
rolled gold. $40 $80 $110

HAMILTON, 17J., "Fleetwood", c.1949
14k. $150 $275 $350

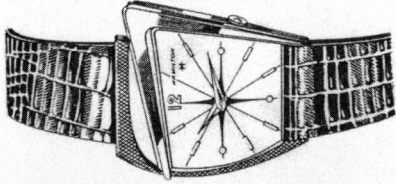

HAMILTON, 22J., "Flight I", 14k **marks** & # 12, ca. 1960
14k case. . . . . ★★ $2,500 $4,250 $5,000

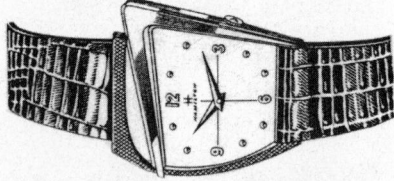

HAMILTON, 22J., "Flight II", 14k **dots** & #s 12,3,6,9, c.1961
gold filled case . . . . : . . ★ $1,200 $2,500 $3,000

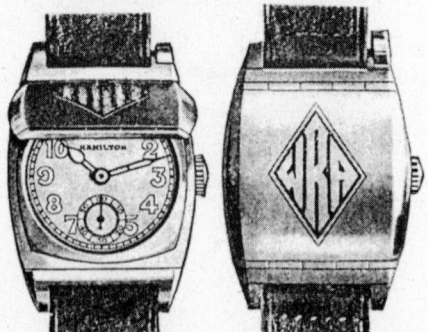

HAMILTON, "Flint Ridge", flip top is lug activated, Grade
917=17J, Grade 979=19J, Ca. 1930
14k (w or y). . . . . ★★ $2,000 $4,000 $4,500

HAMILTON, 19 jewels, "Foster" ,c 1939
14k. $250 $500 $650

HAMILTON, 17J., "Franklin", c.1949
gold filled $100 $200 $275

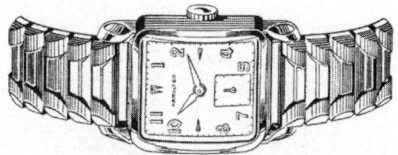

HAMILTON, 17J.," Fulton", sterling silver dial, c. 1957
gold filled $100 $200 $250

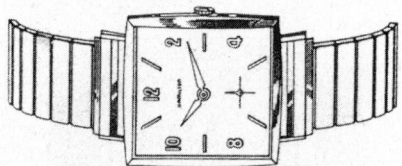

HAMILTON, 17J, " Gardner", c 1961
rolled gold. $50 $125 $175

HAMILTON, 17J.," Gary ", c.1949
gold filled $100 $200 $250

HAMILTON 19J.," Gilbert ", c.1941
14k. $200 $400 $500

HAMILTON, 19 jewels, "Gilman" ,44mm long, c. 1937
Note: Also **see Dickens** = *Gold Filled* (**look-a-like**)
14k. . . . . ★ $300 $600 $750

HAMILTON, 19 jewels, "Glenn Curtis", Ca.1931
14k(Y or W) . . . . ★★ $300 $575 $800

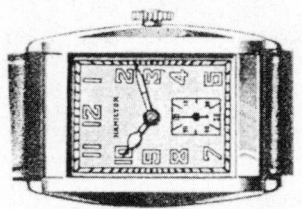

HAMILTON, 17J.,"Gladasone", cal.9g1, c.1931
gold filled W $125 $250 $300
gold filled Y $125 $250 $300

HAMILTON, 11J., "Golden Tempus", c.1957
14k **regular style** dial $300 $600 $700
14k **time zones** dial $450 $850 $1,000

HAMILTON, 19J.," Glendale ", engraved case, Ca. 1928
14k W . . . . ★★★ $1,200 $2,500 $3,500
14K Y . . . . ★★★★ $1,200 $2,500 $3,500

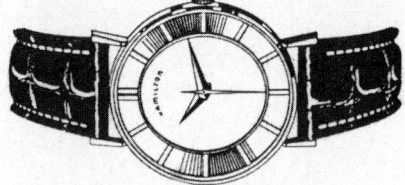

HAMILTON, 18J., "Diamond Tempus", (masterpiece),
NOTE:**Both with 11 diamond dial,** c.1957
14k regular style dial $500 $900 $1,100
14k time zones dial. $600 $1,100 $1,300

HAMILTON, 17J., "Glendon", c. 1961
rolled gold. $40 $80 $110

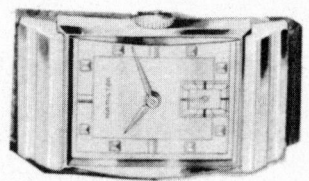

HAMILTON, 18J., "Golden Tempus II", 14k #s, c.1959
gold filled $100 $175 $200

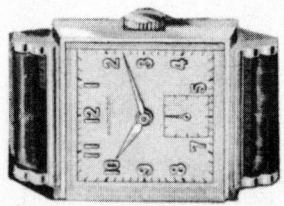

HAMILTON, 17J ," Glenn ", c 1948
14k. $200 $400 $500

HAMILTON, 19J ," Gordon ", c 1941
platinum $1,000 $1,800 $2,200
18k. $350 $700 $800

DIALS FOR MINT PRICES MUST BE ALL ORIGINAL.

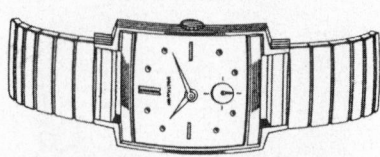

HAMILTON, 22J., "Gramercy", 14k #s, c.1958
gold filled $100 $175 $200

HAMILTON, 17J., "Grover", c.1949
gold filled $100 $200 $250

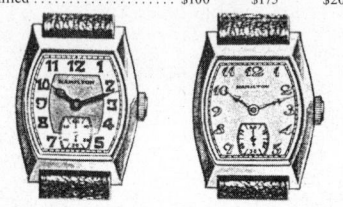

HAMILTON, 17 jewels, "Grant", Ca 1933
sterling $200 $400 $500
gold filled $150 $300 $350

HAMILTON, 18J.,"Guardsman I" ,sterling silver dial, c. 1957
gold filled $75 $150 $175

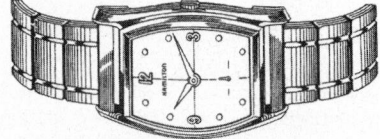

HAMILTON, 17 jewels, "Grant", Ca. 1957
rolled gold. $55 $125 $175

HAMILTON, 17J.,"Guardsman II", c. 1957
gold filled $75 $150 $175

HAMILTON, 17 jewels, "Greenwich" Ca. 1931
gold filled(Y or W). $100 $200 $250

HAMILTON, 17J., "Haddon", sold for $69.50 in 1952
gold filled $75 $150 $200

HAMILTON, 18J.,"Grenadier I" ,sterling silver dial, c. 1957
gold filled $75 $150 $175

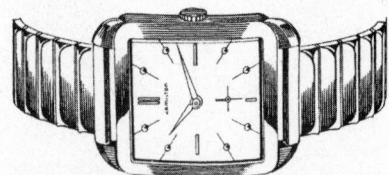

HAMILTON, 17J.,"Halesworth B" ,sterling silver dial, c. 1957
gold filled $75 $150 $200

HAMILTON, 18J.,"Grenadier II", sterling silver dial, c. 1957
gold filled $75 $150 $175

HAMILTON, 17J.," Harris ', Ca. 1937
gold filled $75 $150 $200

HAMILTON, 18J., "Hartman", **hinged lugs**, Ca.1953
18k, sold for $225.00 ...... ★★★ $250 $450 $600
14k, sold for $175.00 ....★★ $200 $400 $500

HAMILTON, 17J.,"Hassings", 14k sold for $75.00 in 1928
14k (Y or W)................. $200 $400 $600
gold filled (Y or W) $100 $200 $250

HAMILTON, 19J.," Hayden ", c 1941
gold filled $100 $200 $250

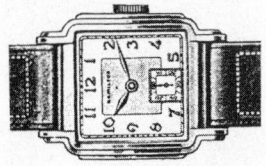

HAMILTON, 17J., "Heyward", sold for $37.50 in 1936
gold filled $100 $200 $250

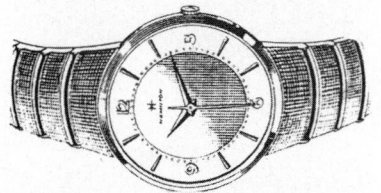

HAMILTON, 18J., "Holden", ca.1961
gold filled $60 $110 $150

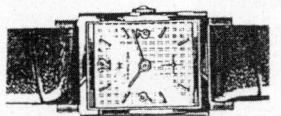

HAMILTON, 17J.," Huntley ", Ca.1961
14k...........................$175 $325 $425

HAMILTON, 17J., "Howard", on dial & movement, c.1946
gold filled ....★★ $200 $400 $500

HAMILTON, 17J "Jason", sold for $55.00 in1957
s. steel $40 $80 $110

HAMILTON, 17J.," Jeffrey ", c.1949
gold filled $125 $250 $300

HAMILTON, 19 jewels, "Judson" Ca. 1935
gold filled $125 $250 $300

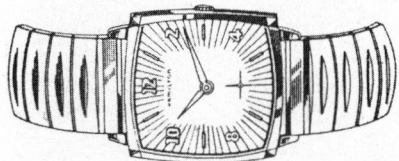

HAMILTON, 17J.," Keane", c.1958
rolled gold. $50 $125 $175

HAMILTON, 19J.," Keith ", c. 1949
14k. $200 $400 $500
18k. $300 $500 $600

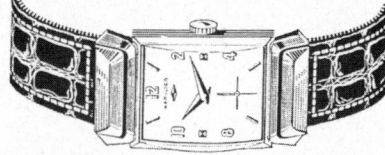

HAMILTON, 22J.,"Kevin", **swivel lugs**, sterling silver dial, 14k
mumbers, Ca. 1954
18k. . . . . ★ $400 $750 $900

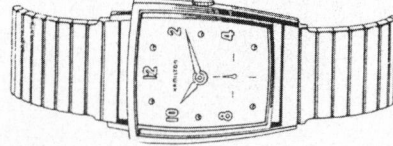

HAMILTON, 17J., " Khyber", 14k #s, c.1959
gold filled $175 $300 $350

HAMILTON, 17J., "Kinematic I", Ca. 1957
rolled gold. $40 $80 $110

HAMILTON, 17J., "Kinematic II", Ca.1960
rolled gold. $40 $80 $110

HAMILTON, 19J.,"Kirby",c.1949
gold filled $100 $200 $250

HAMILTON, 17J.," Kirk ", c. 1949
14k. $150 $250 $350

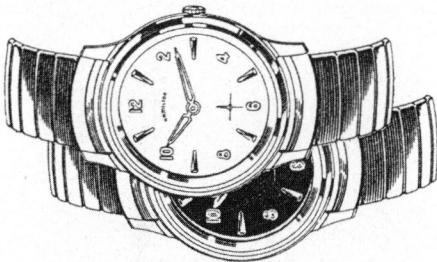

HAMILTON, 17J.," Lakeland", c.1959
s. steel $40 $75 $110

HAMILTON 17J., "Lambert", c. 1950
gold filled $100 $175 $200

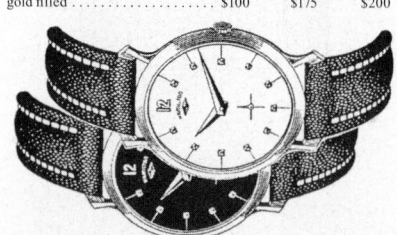

HAMILTON 22J., "Lance I" sterling silver dial, Ca.1957
14k Y or W $100 $175 $225

HAMILTON, 22J.,"Lance II", sterling silver dial, Ca. 1957
14k Y or W $100 $150 $225

HAMILTON, 22J.,"Lance II", (masterpiece), 12 diamonds sterling
silver dial, Ca. 1957
14k W $200 $375 $425

HAMILTON, 22J.,"Landon", Ca. 1957
rolled gold. $50 $125 $175

HAMILTON, 17J, (Lange is =14k) Langdon is = G. filled Ca. 1949
14k. $150 $275 $325
gold filled $50 $90 $125

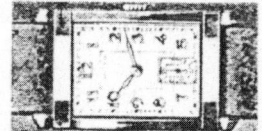

HAMILTON, 17J.," Langford ", Ca.1937
14k. $185 $300 $400

HAMILTON, 17J, "Langley, 14k sold for $100.00 in1933
14k. $300 $600 $700
18k. . . . .★★★★ $700 $1,400 $1,600

Wrist Watches listed in this section are priced at the collectable
fair market Trade Show level as complete watches having an
original gold-filled case and stainless steel back, also with original
dial, leather watch band, and the entire original movement in good
working order with no repairs needed.

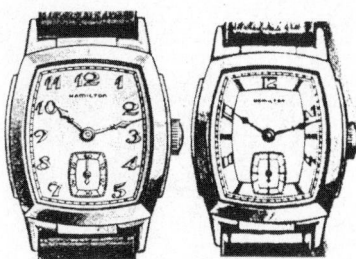

HAMILTON, 17J.," Lawrence", Ca.1936
gold filled $100 $185 $250

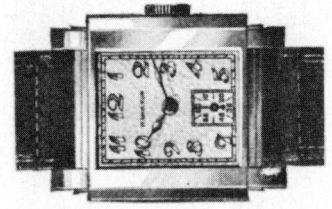

HAMILTON, 17 jewels, "Lee" Ca. 1934
gold filled (w) . . . . ★★★ $300 $500 $600
gold filled (y) $200 $400 $500

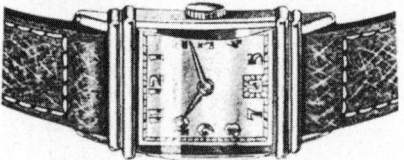

HAMILTON, 19J., "Lester", gold numbers, ca. 1941
gold filled $100 $175 $200

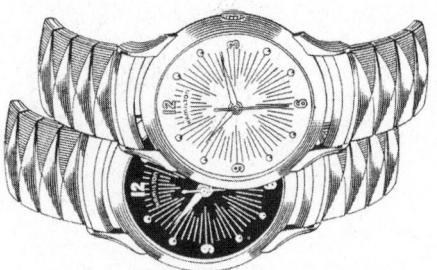

HAMILTON, 18J.,"Lincrest", Ca. 1957
gold filled $50 $100 $150

HAMILTON, 17J., "Lindsay", sold for $65.00 in 1952
gold filled $100 $200 $225

HAMILTON, 17 & 19 jewels, "Linwood" Ca. 1937
gold filled . . . . ★ $175 $375 $425

HAMILTON, 19 jewels, "Livingston", Ca. 1930
gold filled (Y) . . . . ★ $175 $350 $450
gold filled (W) . . . . ★★ $200 $400 $550

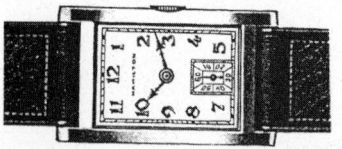

HAMILTON, 19J., " Lowell", Ca 1935
14k. $225 $375 $450

HAMILTON, 17J.," Lowell", Ca.1961
rolled gold. $40 $75 $110

HAMILTON, 18J., "Lyle B", sterling silver dial, Ca. 1957
14k. $200 $400 $600

HAMILTON, 18J., "Lyndon", sold for $71.50 in 1952
gold filled $75 $135 $200

DIALS FOR MINT PRICES MUST BE ALL ORIGINAL.

HAMILTON, 22J., "Malcom", sterling silver dial, Ca.1955
14k. $200 $400 $500

HAMILTON 17 jewels "Martin" Ca. 1941
gold filled coral. . . . . ★ $125 $175 $250
gold filled Y $75 $150 $200

HAMILTON, 17J., "Martin", Ca. 1966
gold plate $50 $90 $125

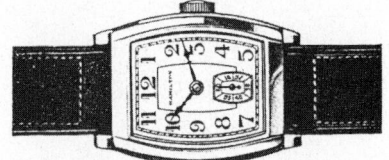

HAMILTON, 17J.,"Mason", sold for $40.00 in 1935
gold filled (w or y) . . . . ★★ $125 $225 $275

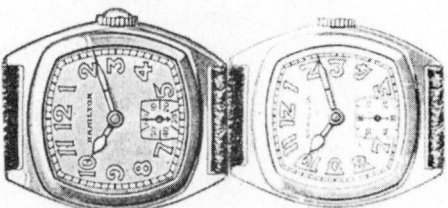

HAMILTON, 19J.,"Meadowbrook", right = radial, Ca. 1927
14k. . . . . ★★★ $250 $400 $500
18k. . . . . ★★★ $450 $875 $1,100
Platinum . . . . ★★★★ $2,000 $3,500 $4,500

HAMILTON, 19J., "Medford" , sold for $71.50 in 1952
gold filled $100 $200 $250

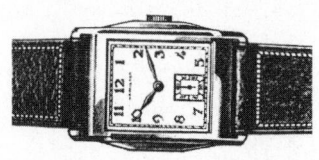

HAMILTON, 17J., " Merritt", Ca.1937
gold filled $75 $150 $225

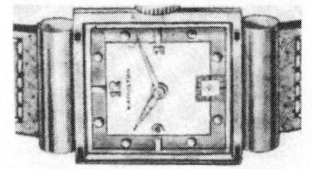

HAMILTON, 19 jewels, "Midas," hidden lugs ,c. 1941
14k yellow. $200 $400 $500
14k (coral). . . . . ★ $225 $450 $550

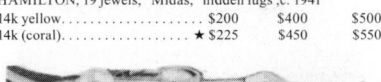

HAMILTON, 19J.," Milton ", c.1948
gold filled $100 $200 $250

HAMILTON, 17J., " Montclair", 14k #s, c.1961
14k. $100 $200 $300

HAMILTON, 17J.," Morley ", c.1936
gold filled $100 $200 $250

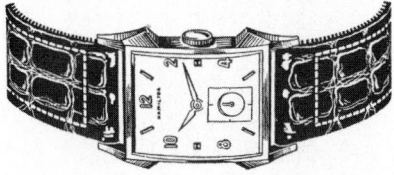

HAMILTON, 22J., "Morton", **sterling silver dial**, c.1957
gold filled $100 $200 $225

HAMILTON, 17J., "Mount Vernon", Ca. 1932
gold filled . . . . ★ $225 $450 $500

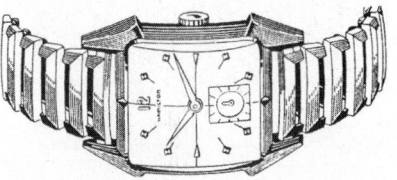

HAMILTON, 17J.,"Murray", sterling silver dial, c. 1957
gold filled $100 $175 $200

HAMILTON, 17J.," Myron ", c.1941
gold filled $100 $175 $225

HAMILTON, 22J., "Newlin", 14k #s, c.1951
gold filled $50 $95 $125

HAMILTON, 17J.," Neil ", c.1941
gold filled $75 $125 $150

DIALS FOR MINT PRICES MUST BE ALL **ORIGINAL**.

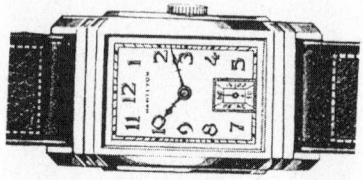

HAMILTON, 17J., "Nelson", Ca.1936
gold filled $100 $195 $250

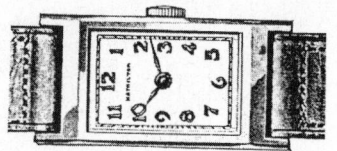

HAMILTON, 17 jewels, "Norfolk", Ca. 1936
gold filled $100 $175 $200

HAMILTON, 17J., "Newton", cal.747, Ca. 1954
gold filled $100 $200 $250

HAMILTON, 22J., "Norton", 14k #s, c.1961
14k. $125 $250 $350

HAMILTON, 17J, Norde is 14k, Nordon, 18J, is gold filled Ca 1949
14k. $125 $225 $275
gold filled $50 $95 $135

HAMILTON, 19 jewels, "Oakmont"
14k (y). . . . . ★ $600 $1,200 $1,400
14k (w) $600 $1,200 $1,400

HAMILTON, 19 jewels, "Norman" ,c. 1949
gold filled $100 $175 $225

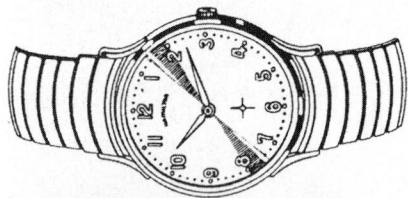

HAMILTON, 17J., "Orson ", c.1961
gold filled $75 $95 $125

HAMILTON, 17J., " Norman", 14k #s, c.1958
gold filled $50 $95 $125

A collector should expect to pay modestly higher prices at local shops.

HAMILTON, 19J., "Otis", reversible, sold for $67.50 in 1938
14k. . . . . ★★★★ $3,500 $6,500 $9,000
gold filled . . . . ★ $800 $1,600 $2,300

HAMILTON,17J., "Pacermatic", **automatic** on dial, cal. 667
swiss movement, **tu-tone case**, Ca. 1961, beware of **FAKES**
gold filled . . . . ★★★ $800 $1,500 $1,700

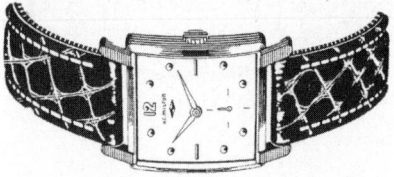

HAMILTON, 19 jewels, "Paige" , c. 1941
gold filled $100 $200 $250

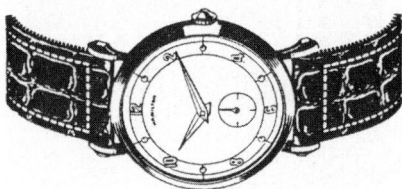

HAMILTON, 22 jewels, "Paige", sterling silver dial, c. 1957
14k. $150 $300 $400

HAMILTON, 22J., " Parker B", 14k #s, **anti-magnetic**, sold for
$95.00 in 1957
10k. $100 $200 $225

HAMILTON, 17 jewels, "Paxton", c. 1957
rolled gold. $40 $75 $110

HAMILTON, 17 jewels, "Perry" ,Ca. 1933
gold filled Y $135 $250 $300
gold filled W . . . . ★★ $175 $300 $400

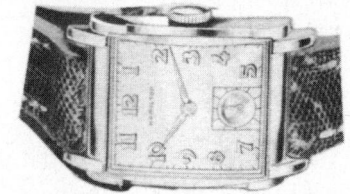

HAMILTON, 19J.," Perry ", c.1948
gold filled $100 $200 $250

HAMILTON, 22J., "Peyton ", c. 1959
gold filled $50 $95 $125

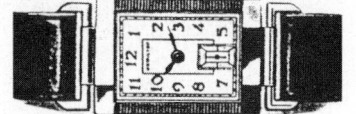

HAMILTON, 19 jewels, "Pierre" , Ca. 1936
14k. $300 $600 $750

HAMILTON, 17J.,"Pinehurst", note **radial**, CA. 1930
14k (y). . . . . ★★★ $1,500 $2,500 $3,000
14k (w) . . . . ★★★ $1,500 $2,500 $3,000

HAMILTON, 19J.,"Piping Rock", enamel bezel, ca. 1928
14k (y). $800 $1,400 $1,600
14k (w) $900 $1,500 $1,800
See Ca. 1948 Piping Rock next page

LIGNES

HAMILTON, 17J., "Piping Rock", grade 747, ca.1948
14k Y $800 $1,400 $1,600
14k W . . . . ★★★ $1,000 $1,500 $1,800

HAMILTON, 17J.,"Powell", ca.1957
gold filled $50 $95 $125

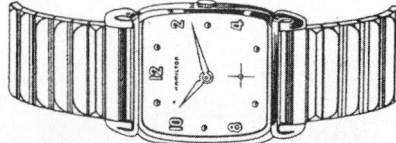

HAMILTON, 17J., " Prentice", c.1959
rolled gold. $70 $125 $175

HAMILTON, 17J., "Prescott ", told for $45.00 in 1936
gold filled $100 $175 $200

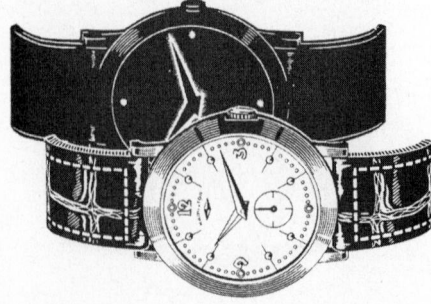

HAMILTON, 22J., "Prescott B", sterling silver dial, Ca. 1957
14k. $125 $225 $275

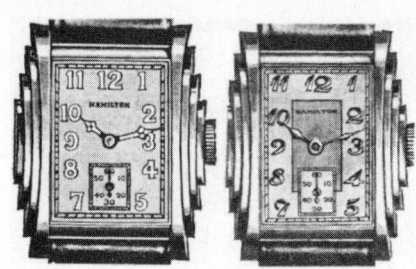

HAMILTON, 17J, "Putnam", sold for $50.00 in 1932
gold filled (w or y) $200 $400 $500

HAMILTON, 22J.,"Radburn", 14k #s, c.1959
14k. $150 $300 $400

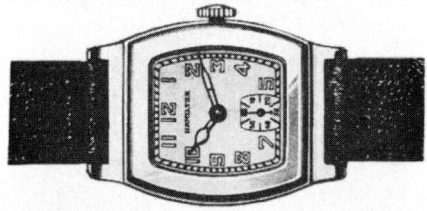

HAMILTON, 17J," Raleigh ", Plain, ca.1931
gold filled Y $175 $250 $350
gold filled W $175 $250 $350

HAMILTON, 17J.,"Raleigh", Engraved, ca.1931
gold filled Y $185 $300 $375
gold filled W $185 $300 $375

HAMILTON 19J.,"Raleigh", gold numbers, ca. 1953
gold filled. $100 $150 $200

HAMILTON, 17J.," Ramsey", c.1961
rolled gold. $40 $75 $110

HAMILTON, 17J., "Randolph" ,c. 1935
14k........................... $125 $200 $250

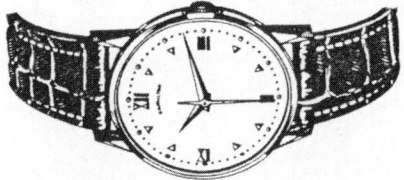

HAMILTON, 18J.," Randolph", 14k #s, c.1958
14k........................... $125 $200 $250

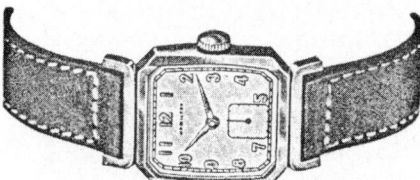

HAMILTON, 17J., "Raymon", ca. 1950
s. steel....................... $75 $125 $175

HAMILTON, 17 jewels, "Reagan" , c. 1937
gold filled................... $100 $175 $200

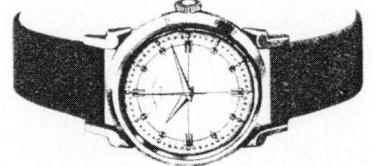

HAMILTON, 17J., "Reardon", ca. 1949
14k...........................$150 $200 $250

HAMILTON, 19J., " Richmond", curved, Ca.1933
18k Y......................... $300 $600 $700
18k W ....★★ $500 $900 $1,100

HAMILTON, 17J., Robert=gents & Roberta= ladies, Ca. 1953
14k gents.................. $300 $600 $700
14k ladies $125 $225 $300

HAMILTON, 18J., " Rodney", 14k #s, Ca.1953
Masonic dial................ $100 $175 $250
gold filled $75 $125 $175

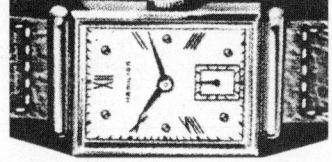

HAMILTON, 19J., "Rodney", ca. 1941
14k coral.................. ★ $300 $500 $700
14k Y....................... $200 $400 $600

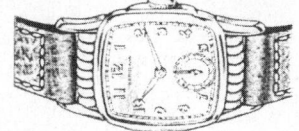

HAMILTON, 17J., "Roland", Ca.1937
gold filled $100 $200 $250

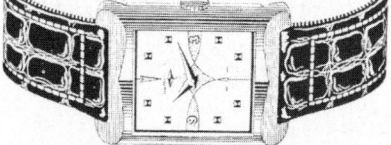

HAMILTON, 17J., "Roland", sterling silver dial, Ca. 1955
14k........................... $350 $700 $800

HAMILTON, 22J.," Romanesque M", c.1960
14k...........................$175 $300 $350

DIALS FOR MINT PRICES MUST BE ALL **ORIGINAL**.

HAMILTON 17J "Romanesque N"c. 1960
gold filled $50 $100 $125

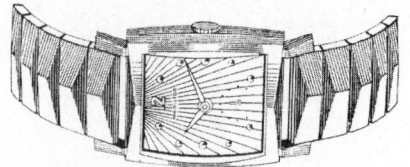

HAMILTON, 17 jewels, "Russell", c. 1957
gold filled $100 $200 $250

HAMILTON, 22J., " Romanesque R", c 1960
gold filled $50 $100 $125

HAMILTON, 19 jewels, "Rutledge" ,c. 1935
platinum $700 $1,300 $1,600

HAMILTON, 22J., "Romanesque S",c.1960
gold filled $75 $150 $200

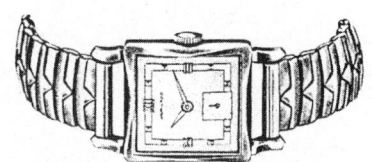

HAMILTON, 17J., "Ryan", sold for $65.00 in 1952
gold filled $75 $150 $200

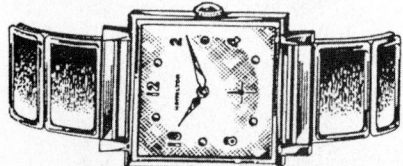

HAMILTON, 17J., "Romanesque T", c. 1960
rolled gold. $50 $125 $175

HAMILTON, 17 jewels, "Samson", c. 1957
gold filled $75 $95 $135

HAMILTON, 19 jewels, 'Ross' ,c. 1939
gold filled yellow $100 $175 $225
gold filled Coral . . . . ★ $150 $275 $325

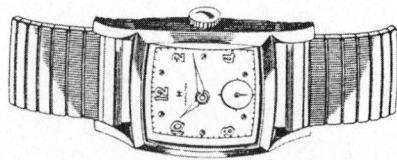

HAMILTON, 17J., "Sawyer", 14k #s, c.1955
gold filled $85 $150 $200

HAMILTON 17 jewels, "Russell", hinged lugs , c. 1941
gold filled $100 $200 $250

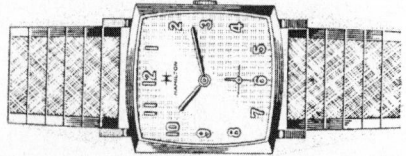

HAMILTON,17J., "Scott", sold for 79.50 is 1966
gold filled $75 $125 $200

HAMILTON (continued)

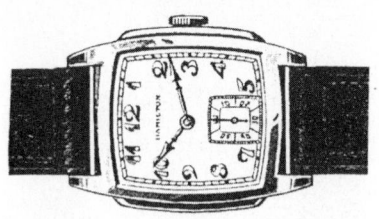

HAMILTON, 17J.," Scott ", GJS, Ca., 1935
gold filled Y $100 $175 $200
gold filled W .... ★ $125 $225 $275

HAMILTON, 19J.," Scott ", GJS,982, Ca.1949
14k......................... $300 $550 $700

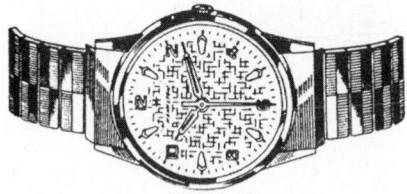

HAMILTON, 17J., " Sea Breeze", c. 1961
rolled gold.................... $35 $75 $110

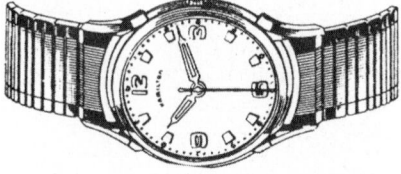

HAMILTON, 17J., " Seabrook", c.1961
rolled gold.................... $35 $75 $100

HAMILTON, 17J., " Sea-cap ", c.1961
rolled gold.................... $35 $75 $100

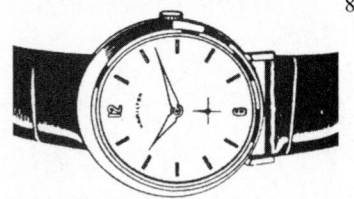

HAMILTON, 22J., " Sea Cliff", 14k #s, c.1961
gold filled $50 $75 $125

HAMILTON, 17J., " Sea - crest", c.1961
s. steel $35 $75 $100

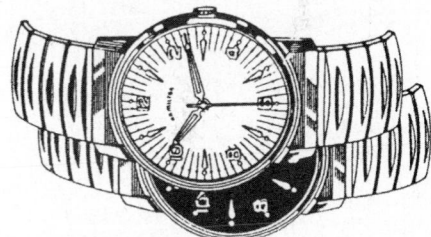

HAMILTON, 17J., " Sea- glo ", c.1961
s. steel $35 $75 $100

HAMILTON, 17J., " Sea - guard", c. 1962
s. steel $35 $75 $100

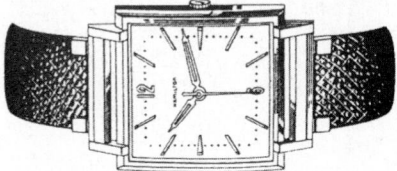

HAMILTON, 17J., " Sea - mate", c.1961
rolled gold.................... $50 $125 $175

HAMILTON, 22J., "Sea Ranger", 14K #a, c. 1961
gold filled $75 $100 $150

DIALS FOR MINT PRICES MUST BE ALL ORIGINAL.

HAMILTON, 17J., "Sea Rover B", c. 1961
s. steel $40 $75 $100

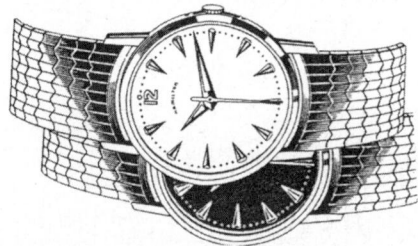

HAMILTON, 17J.," Sea- scape ", c.1961
gold plate $35 $75 $100

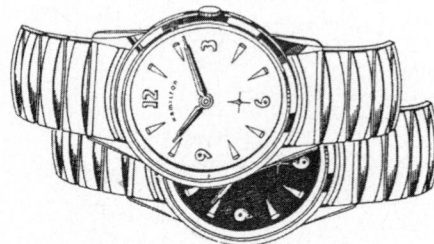

HAMILTON, 17J., " Sea- scout B ", c.1961
s. steel $40 $75 $100

HAMILTON, 17J., " Sea- skip", c.1962
s. steel $35 $75 $100

HAMILTON, 17J., " Seaview" ,14k #s, c.1961
14k. $125 $150 $225

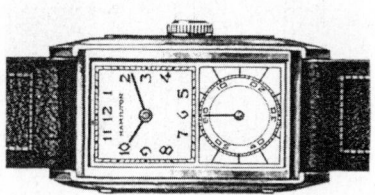

HAMILTON, 17J.,"Seckron", dual dial, grade 980, c.1935
gold filled $750 $1,350 $1,500

HAMILTON, 17J.,"Seckron", grade 980B, dual dial, c.1940
gold filled $750 $1,350 $1,500

HAMILTON, 17J., "Sectometer", sweep sec., ca. 1945
gold filled (hack) $75 $140 $165

HAMILTON, 18J.,"Sectometer B", sweep sec., ca1948
gold filled (hack) $75 $140 $175

HAMILTON, 18J.,"Sectometer C", sweep sec., ca. 1951
14k(hack) $135 $275 $300

Wrist Watches listed in this section are priced at the collectable
fair market Trade Show level as complete watches having an
original gold-filled case and stainless steel back, also with original
dial leather watch band and the entire original movement in good
working order with no repairs needed.

HAMILTON, 18J., " Sedgman", Ca. 1952
14k. $150 $300 $350

HAMILTON, 17 jewels, "Sentinel,", Ca. 1941
gold filled(hack). $75 $150 $165

HAMILTON, 18J., "Seville", c.1958
gold filled $50 $95 $125

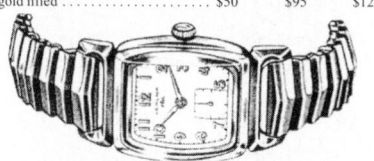

HAMILTON, 19J., "Sheldon", sold for $89.50 in 1953
gold filled $100 $175 $200

HAMILTON, 19J., "Sherwood", (also-Seneca), Ca.1935
14k. $200 $400 $500

HAMILTON, 22J.," Sherwood M", 14k #s, wood dial, **American walnut wood dial**, c.1961
14k. . . . . ★ $700 $1,000 $1,500

HAMILTON, 17J., "Sherwood N'", 14k #s, auto-wind, wood dial, **Mexican Mahogany wood dial**, c.1961
14k. . . . . ★ $500 $900 $1,400

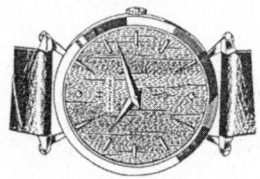

HAMILTON, 22J.," Sherwood R", dial is made of wood, **(dial is American walnut)** c.1961
14k. . . . . ★ $400 $850 $1,300

HAMILTON, 19J.," Sherwood", c. 1949
gold filled $125 $200 $250

HAMILTON, 17J.,"Sheryll", matched styling so the **Sherwood** for men, Sheryll = ladies watch, Ca. 1949
gold filled $50 $95 $125

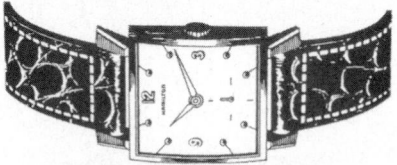

HAMILTON, 22 jewels, "Sinclair" ,c. 1957
14k. $135 $300 $400

HAMILTON, 17 jewels, "Sidney" ,c. 1937
gold filled $125 $225 $275

HAMILTON, 22J., "Sir Echo" , 14K #s, 6 diamond, c.1957
14k(W) $175 $375 $425

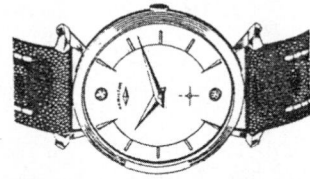

HAMILTON, 22J., " Sir Echo", 2 diamonds, 14K #s, c.1957
14k(W) $150 $275 $325

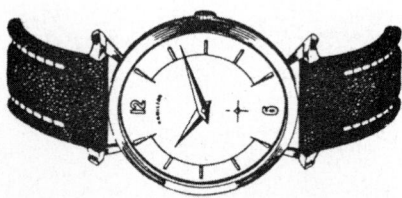

HAMILTON, 22J., " Sir Echo", 14K #s, c.1957
14k(W) $150 $275 $325

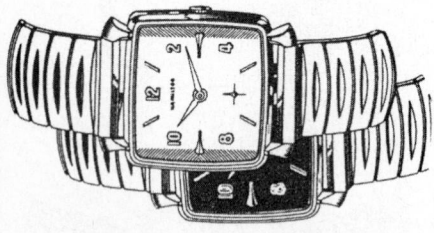

HAMILTON, 17J., "Sloane", c.1959
rolled gold. $45 $125 $175

HAMILTON, 17J.,"Spencer", gold numbers, ca. 1951
10k, With Masonic symbols $150 $300 $400
10k. $100 $200 $300

𝒢𝒮 A collector should expect to pay modestly higher prices at local shops

HAMILTON, 19J., "Spur", enamel bezel, ca. 1928
14k (y). . . . . ★★★ $2,000 $3,250 $3,500
14k(w). . . . . ★★★ $2,000 $3,250 $3,500
14k(w) box & papers. . . ★★★★ $2,500 $4,000 $5,500

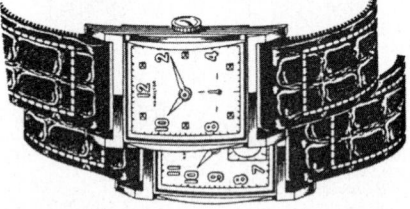

HAMILTON, 22J., "Stafford", 14K #5, c. 1952
14k. $175 $325 $450

HAMILTON, 18 jewels, "Steeldon" ,c. 1949
s. steel $50 $90 $125

HAMILTON, 17 jewels, "Stanford" ,c. 1940
gold filled $100 $175 $200

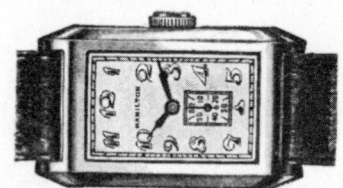

HAMILTON, 19 jewels, "Stanley" Ca. 1930
gold filled $150 $250 $325

HAMILTON (continued)

HAMILTON, 22 jewels, "Staunton", c. 1957
14k.........................$135 $200 $250

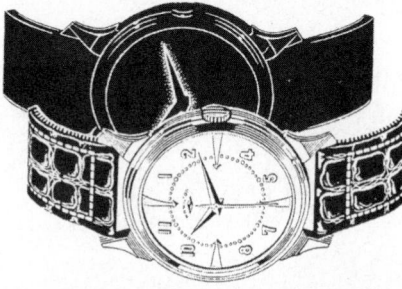

HAMILTON, 18J., "Stormking I", sterling silver dial, c. 1957
18k..........................$200 $400 $550

HAMILTON, 18J., "Stormking II", sterling silver dial, c. 1957
14k.........................$150 $250 $275

HAMILTON, 18J., "Stormking III", sterling silver dial, c.1957
14k.........................$150 $250 $275

HAMILTON, 18J., "Stormking IV", 14k #s, c. 1957
gold filled $75 $100 $150

HAMILTON, 18J., "Stormking IV Military", c. 1957
s. steel 24 hour $150 $265 $350

HAMILTON, 18J., "Stormking V", sterling silver dial, c. 1957
s. steel.........................$50 $100 $135

HAMILTON, 18J., "Stormking VI", c. 1955
gold filled $50 $100 $135

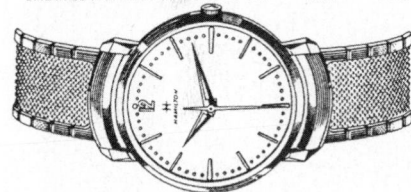

HAMILTON, 18J., " Stormking VII", c.1961
gold filled $50 $100 $135

HAMILTON, 18J., "Stormking VIII", 14k #s, c. 1957
10k.........................$100 $175 $225

HAMILTON, 17J., "Stormking IX", 14K #s, c. 1961
14k.........................$125 $200 $250

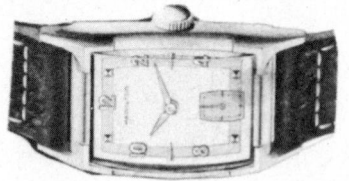

HAMILTON, 19J., "Stuart", c. 1949
gold filled $100 $175 $225

HAMILTON, 17J., "Surf", c. 1957
s. steel $50 $90 $125

HAMILTON, 17-19 jewels, "Sutton" Ca. 1936
gold filled $150 $250 $300

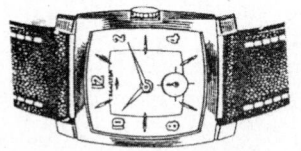

HAMILTON, 22 jewels, "Sutton" ,Ca. 1957
14k $185 $375 $425

HAMILTON, 17J., "Talbot", Ca.1937
gold filled $90 $150 $200

HAMILTON, 17J.," Talbot", c.1961
gold filled $75 $150 $200

HAMILTON, 17J., "Taylor", hinged lugs, Ca.1935
gold filled $125 $225 $265

HAMILTON, 22J., "Thor", 14K #s, c.1959
gold filled $175 $350 $500

HAMILTON, 19J., "Tildon", sold for $225.00 in 1953
14k $350 $650 $700

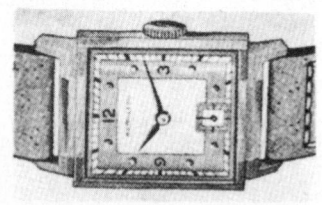

HAMILTON 18J "Todd", c 1951
gold filled $50 $90 $150

HAMILTON, 19 jewels, "Touraine" ,c. 1935
14k $175 $325 $450

HAMILTON, 17J, "Transcontinental A", Time Zone, Ca. 1957
gold filled $200 $375 $450
Transcontinental B next page

HAMILTON, 17J, "Transcontinental B", Time Zone, Ca.1957
14k. $500 $900 $1,200

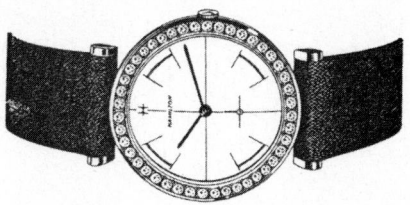

HAMILTON, 22J., " Tuxedo II' 44 diarnonds,14K #s,
Ca. 1961
14k(w). $300 $575 $700

HAMILTON, 22J., " Trent" ,sterling silver dial, c.1955
gold filled $100 $175 $225

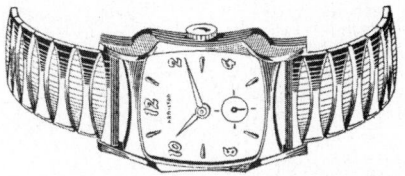

HAMILTON, 17J, "Tyrone, 14k markers, Ca.1957
gold filled $100 $175 $225

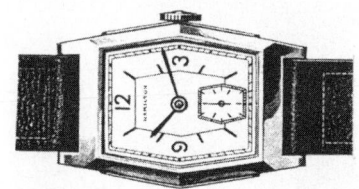

HAMILTON, 17J., "Turner", Ca.1936
gold filled Y $100 $175 $225
gold filled W . . . . ★★ $125 $225 $300

HAMILTON, 17J., "Vardon", sealed. c.1949
s. steel $50 $100 $125

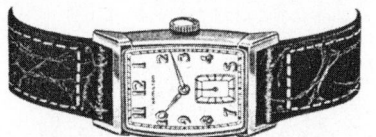

HAMILTON, 19J., "Turner", sold for $100.00 in 1953 (look-a-like)
Donald, 14k
10 k(w or y). $150 $275 $325

HAMILTON, 22J., "Valiant", 14K #s, c.1959
gold filled $175 $325 $450

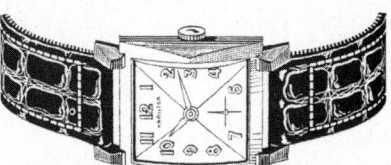

HAMILTON, 17J, "Vernon", sterling silver dial, Ca.1957
10k. $100 $200 $275

HAMILTON, 22J., "Tuxedo B" , 44 diamonds,14K#s, Ca. 1956
14k(w). $250 $475 $650

Wrist Watches listed in this section are priced at the collectable
fair market Trade Show level as complete watches having an
original gold-filled case and stainless steel back, also with original
dial, leather watch band, and the entire original movement in good
working order with no repairs needed.

☞ A collector should expect to pay modestly higher prices
at local shops

DIALS FOR MINT PRICES MUST BE ALL **ORIGINAL**.

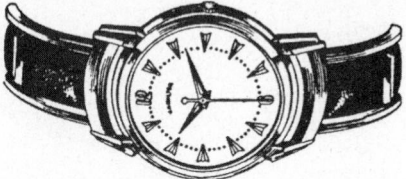

HAMILTON, 17J., "Viking" , c.1961
rolled gold. $50 $90 $125

HAMILTON, 17J., "Viking II", c 1961
rolled gold. $50 $90 $125

HAMILTON, 17 jewels, "Vincent" , c. 1941
gold filled $100 $200 $275

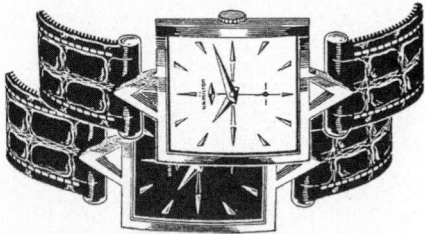

HAMILTON, 22J., "Viscount", sterling silver dial, ca 1955
14k. . . . . ★★ $400 $700 $900

HAMILTON, 17J., "Ward", ca.1957
gold filled $100 $175 $225

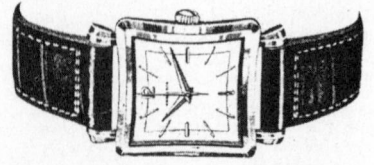

HAMILTON, 18J., "Warwick", sold for $150.00 in 1953
gold filled $100 $175 $225

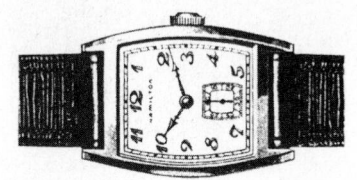

HAMILTON, 17 jewels, "Watson", Ca. 1930
gold filled plain. $100 $175 $225
gold filled engraved . . . . ★★★ $200 $375 $500

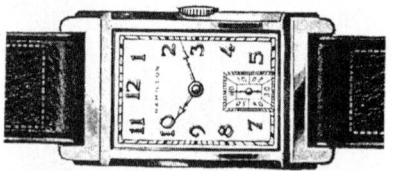

HAMILTON 19 jewels, "Wayne", Ca. 1935
14k. $275 $550 $600

HAMILTON, 17 jewels, "Webster", Ca. 1932
14k W . . . .★★★★ $500 $900 $1,200
gold filled. $100 $200 $300

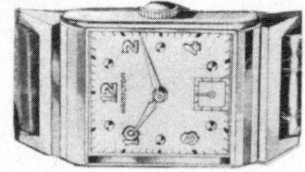

HAMILTON, 19J.,"Wesley", c.1941
14k. $200 $400 $500

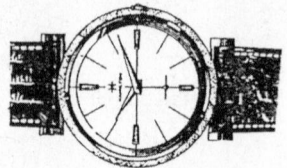

HAMILTON, 17 jewels, "Whitford", Ca. 1960
14k. $125 $225 $300

☞ A collector should expect to pay modestly higher prices at local shops

HAMILTON, 17 jewels, "Whitman" ,c. 1940
gold filled $100 $200 $250

HAMILTON, 17J, "Whitman", sterling silver dial, Ca. 1957
gold filled $50 $100 $150
gold filled Masonic dial $75 $125 $175

HAMILTON, 17 jewels, "Whitney" ,Ca. 1932
gold filled(w or y) . . . . ★★ $200 $400 $500

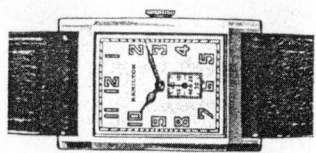

HAMILTON, 19 jewels, "Wilkinson", Ca 1930
14k(w or y) . . . . ★★★★ $1,200 $2,250 $2,600

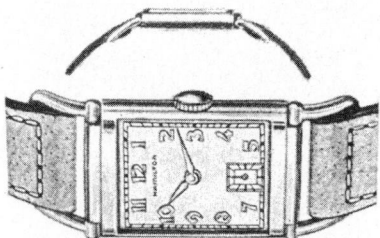

HAMILTON, 19jewels, "Wilshire", hinged lugs, c. 1941
gold filled yellow $175 $250 $300
gold filled coral. . . . . ★ $200 $325 $375

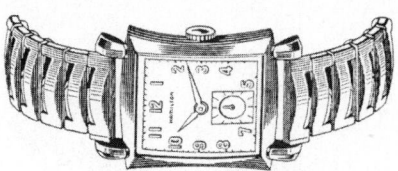

HAMILTON, 17 jewels, "Wilson", **flared**, Ca. 1954
gold filled $100 $175 $225

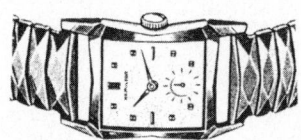

HAMILTON, 19J., "Windsor", sold for $87.50 in1953
gold filled $100 $175 $225

HAMILTON, 18 jewels, "Winfield", Ca. 1957
14k. $150 $275 $325

HAMILTON, 19 jewels, "Winthrop" ,c. 1939
gold filled $100 $200 $225

HAMILTON 17 jewels., "Yorktown" c. 1940
gold filled $125 $250 $300

HAMILTON, 17 jewels, "Yeoman II", Ca. 1965
gold filled $50 $90 $110

DIALS FOR MINT PRICES MUST BE ALL **ORIGINAL**.

HAMILTON, 17 jewels, "Accumatic II" ,c. 1957
rolled gold. $55 $90 $130

HAMILTON, 17 jewels, "Accumatic X"
s.steel $55 $90 $130

HAMILTON, 17 jewels, "Automatic XI"
s. steel $55 $90 $130

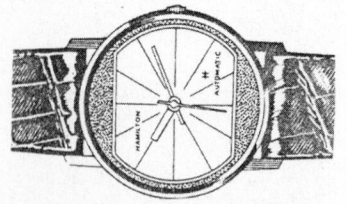

HAMILTON, 17J, "Accumatic A-201", Ca. 1968 shaped like a
early TV screen dial.
14k. $150 $175 $250

HAMILTON, 17 jewels, "Accumatic A-575", date
s. steel $55 $90 $130

HAMILTON, 17 jewels, "Accumatic A-650"
rolled gold. $55 $90 $130

HAMILTON, 17 jewels, "Accumatic A-651"
gold plate $55 $90 $130

HAMILTON, 17 jewels, "Automatic K-203"
14k. $125 $250 $300

HAMILTON, 17 jewels, "Automatic K-303"
10k. $95 $175 $250

HAMILTON, 17 jewels, "Automatic K-304"
10k. $95 $175 $200

Note: Hamilton acquired the Buren Watch Factoryof
Switzerland in 1966 and adapted a ultra thin self-winding
movement for the Thin-o-matic. (Bruen closed in 1972.)

HAMILTON, 17 jewels, "Automatic K-414"
gold filled $60 $100 $150

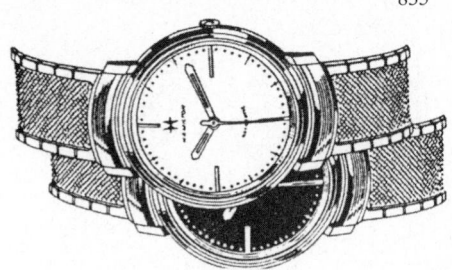

HAMILTON, 17 jewels, "Automatic K-417"
gold filled $60 $100 $150

HAMILTON, 17 jewels, "Accumatic VII"
rolled gold. $50 $80 $130

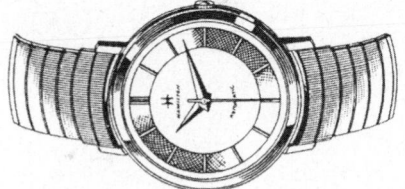

HAMILTON, 17 jewels, "Automatic K-418"
gold filled $70 $100 $150

HAMILTON, 17 jewels, "Automatic K-415"
gold filled $60 $100 $150

HAMILTON, 17 jewels, "Automatic K-419"
gold filled $70 $100 $150

HAMILTON, 17 jewels, "Automatic K-416"
gold filled $60 $100 $150

HAMILTON, 17 jewels, "Automatic K-420"
gold filled $70 $100 $150

HAMILTON, 17 jewels, "Kinematic II"
rolled gold. $50 $75 $130

HAMILTON, 17 jewels, "Automatic K-458"
gold filled $70 $100 $150

🖝 Some grades are not included. Their values can be determined by comparing with similar age, size, metal content, style, grades, or models such as time only, chronograph, repeater etc. listed.

🖝 Pricing in this Guide are fair market price for complete watches which are reflected from the NAWCC National and regional shows.

HAMILTON, 17 jewels, "Automatic K-459"
gold filled $60 $90 $140

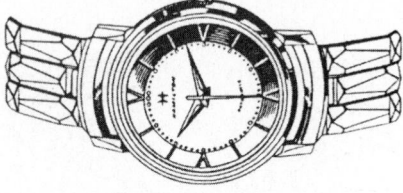

HAMILTON, 17 jewels, "Automatic K-650"
gold plate $65 $95 $125

HAMILTON, 17 jewels, "Automatic K-460"
gold filled $60 $90 $140

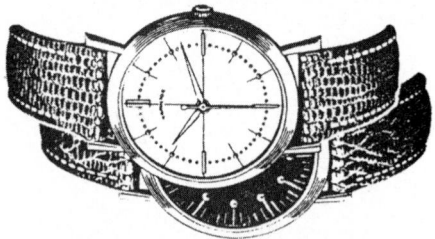

HAMILTON, 18 jewels, "Thincraft II"
gold filled $50 $75 $100

HAMILTON, 17J, "Automatic K-475", with date, *Swiss movement*,
sold for $100.00 is 1960
gold filled . . . . ★★★ $1,200 $2,000 $2,500

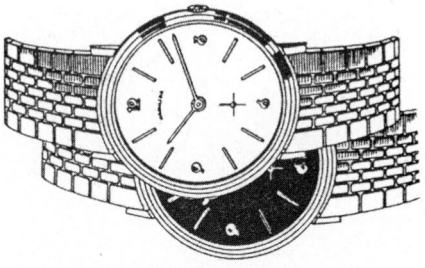

HAMILTON, 17 jewels, "Thinline 2000"
14k $150 $200 $275

HAMILTON, 17 jewels, "Automatic K-503" Ca.1962
s. steel $50 $90 $130

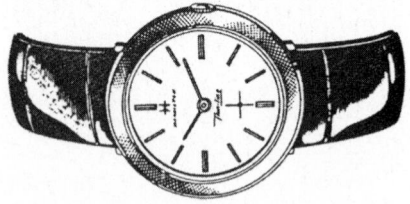

HAMILTON, 17 jewels, "Thinline 2001"
14k $150 $200 $275

HAMILTON, 17 jewels, "Automatic K-507"
s. steel $50 $90 $130

HAMILTON, 17 jewels, "Thinline 3000"
10k $100 $175 $200

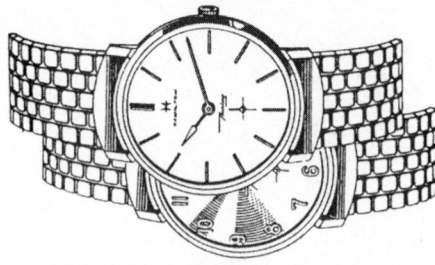

HAMILTON, 17 jewels, "Thinline **4000**"
gold filled $50 $90 $110

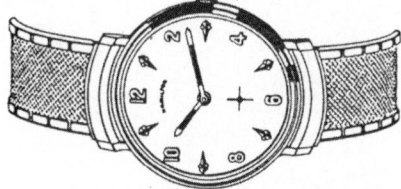

HAMILTON, 17 jewels, "Thinline **4001**"
gold filled $50 $90 $110

HAMILTON, 17 jewels, "Thin-o-matic", **date**
rolled gold. $50 $90 $110

HAMILTON, 17 jewels, "Thin-o-matic", **Masterpiecce**
14k. $100 $200 $250

HAMILTON, 17 jewels, "This-o-matic **T-200**"
14k. $100 $200 $250

HAMILTON, 17 jewels, "Thin-o-matic T-201", **6-diamonds**
14k. $150 $275 $350

HAMILTON, 17 jewels, "Thin-o-matic **T-201**"
14k. $100 $175 $250

HAMILTON, 17 jewels, "Thin-o-matic T-202"
14k. $100 $175 $250

HAMILTON, 17 jewels, "Thin-o-matic **T-300**"
10k. $100 $175 $225

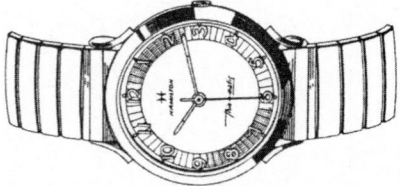

HAMILTON, 17 jewels, "Thin-o-matic T-400"
gold filled $40 $90 $110

HAMILTON, 17 jewels, "Thin-o-matic **T-401**"
gold filled $70 $150 $200

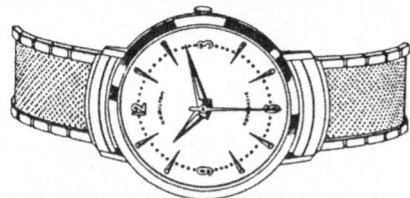

HAMILTON, 17 jewels, "Thin-o-matic **T-402**"
gold filled $60 $100 $130

HAMILTON, 17J, "Thin-o-matic **T-403**', Swiss movement Ca. 1960
rolled gold (with date) . . . . . ★★★ $450 $850 $950
gold filled W . . . . ★★ $400 $700 $850
gold filled Y . . . . ★ $300 $550 $650

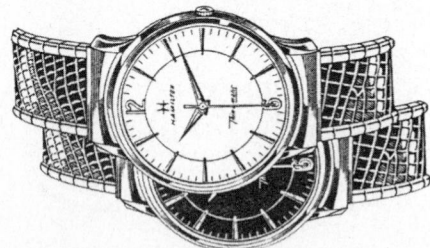

HAMILTON, 17 jewels, "Thin-o-matic **T-404**"
gold filled $60 $100 $130

HAMILTON, 17 jewels, "Thin-o-matic **T-405**"
gold filled $60 $100 $130

HAMILTON, 17 jewels, "Thin-o-matic **T-450**"
gold filled $60 $100 $130

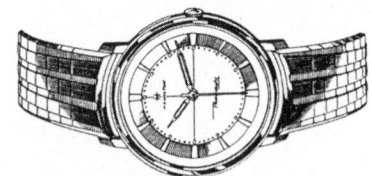

HAMILTON, 17 jewels, "Thin-o-matic **T-451**"
gold filled $60 $100 $130

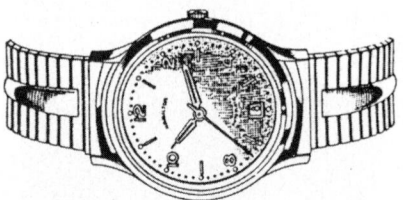

HAMILTON 17 jewels "Thin-o-matic **T-475**"
gold filled $50 $100 $130

HAMILTON, 17 jewels, "Thin-o-matic **T-476**", date
gold filled $50 $100 $130

HAMILTON, 17 jewels, "Thin-o-matic **T-500**"
s. steel $50 $100 $130

☞ Some grades are not included. Their values can be determined by comparing with similar age, size, metal content, style, grades, or models such as time only, chronograph, repeater etc. listed.

HAMILTON, 17 jewels, "Thin-o-matic **T-501**"
s. steel $50 $100 $130

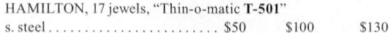

HAMILTON, 17 jewels, "Thin-o-matic **T-502**"
s. steel $50 $100 $130

HAMILTON, 17 jewels, "Thin-o-matic **T-575**" date
s. steel $50 $100 $150

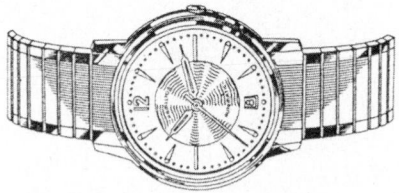

HAMILTON, 17 jewels, "Thin-o-matic **T-650**"
rolled gold. $50 $100 $130

HAMILTON, 17 jewels, **"Thinline 5000"**
s. steel $50 $100 $130

HAMILTON, 17 jewels, "Cushion ",(round), grade 987, ca. 1927
gold filled $75 $150 $200

HAMILTON, 17 jewels, "Cushion", plain, grade 987, ca. 1927
14k. $200 $400 $500
gold filled $75 $150 $200

HAMILTON, 17J.,"Cushion" ,no sec., grade 986, c.1923
gold filled $75 $150 $200

HAMILTON, 17 jewels, "Cushion", engraved, grade 987, note
radial, ca.1927
14k. $200 $400 $500
gold filled $100 $150 $200

HAMILTON, 17 jewels, tonneau engraved
14k. $225 $450 $600
gold filled $100 $200 $250

HAMILTON, 17J., "Tonneau" plain
14k. $200 $400 $550
gold filled $75 $200 $250

HAMILTON, 17J "Square", cut corner, no sec., ca.1927
gold filled $75 $150 $200
14k. $150 $300 $400

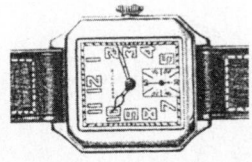

HAMILTON, 17J., "Square B", cut corner, with sec., ca.1927
gold filled $75 $150 $200
14k. $150 $300 $400

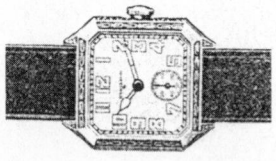

HAMILTON, 17J., "Square", cut corner, enameled, ca.1927
gold filled $85 $150 $200
14k. $150 $300 $400

HAMILTON, 17J., Square cut corner, engraved LUGS
gold filled $75 $150 $200

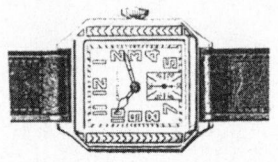

HAMILTON, 17J., "Square B", engraved, ca. 1931
gold filled $75 $150 $200
14k. $150 $350 $500

HAMILTON, 17 jewels, "Raleigh", engraved fancy, Ca. 1930
gold filled $100 $200 $250

HAMILTON, 17J., "Barrel", Plain bezel, ca.1928
gold filled $75 $150 $200
14k. $150 $300 $450

HAMILTON, 17J., "Barrel", engraved, ca.1927
gold filled $75 $150 $200
14k. $150 $300 $450

HAMILTON, 17J., grade 987, w/ gold or Platinum buckle, note
Radial, sold for $485.00 in 1927
Platinum . . . . ★★★ $1,700 $2,500 $3,000

HAMILTON, 17J., cal.987, enamel on case, c.1930
14K $450 $900 $1,200

HAMILTON, 17J, *Hamilton Illinois* on dial, sold by Hamilton &
Illinois marked on case with Illinois mvt. (*crossover*).
gold filled $100 $175 $225

HAMILTON, 19 jewels
platinum C&B $1,650 $2,750 $3,250

HAMILTON, 17 jewels, engraved bezel, hinged back Note **Radial**
14k(w) $600 $950 $1,200

HAMILTON, 17- 19J., "bomb timer", c.1943
gold filled $400 $700 $900

HAMILTON, 17J., "Oval", plain or engraved, grade 987, sold for
in1927 $70.00 Gold Filled & $105.50 14K.
gold filled . . . . ★ $800 $1,300 $1,500
14K(White - Green).. . . . .★★★ $1,500 $2,500 $3,000

HAMILTON, 17-19J., "bomb timer", c.1943
base metal. $250 $500 $600

HAMILTON, 17 jewels, engraved bezel, c. 1920
14k. $150 $300 $400

HAMILTON, 15 J., military frogman style, waterproof
(USN BU SHIPS on dial), canteen style.
base metal. $450 $700 $950

HAMILTON, 17 J., military issue, **hack** setting, c.1960s
base metal. $100 $200 $275

HAMILTON, 17 J., British issue note broad arrow symbol, Grade
649, swiss movement
base metal. $100 $150 $175

HAMILTON, 7 J., military issue, hack setting, note "H3" for
Hydrogen 3 and radioactive symbol, c. 1970s
base metal. $75 $150 $200

HAMILTON, 17J., "Aqua-date", autow, waterproof- 600 feet
elapsed time indicator, sold for $115.00 in 1966
s. steel. $150 $275 $350

HAMILTON, 17J., chronomatic "A", auto wind, Ca.1975
s. steel $300 $550 $600

HAMILTON, 17J., chronomatic "B", auto wind, Ca.1975
s. steel $300 $550 $600

HAMILTON, chronomatic "C", auto wind, Ca.1975
s. steel $150 $300 $400

Hamilton, 17J., Chrono Diver stem wind Ca.1975
s. steel $275 $500 $575

HAMILTON, ELECTRONIC railroad approved, Ca.1975
s. steel $100 $200 $275

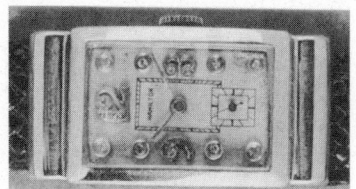

HAMILTON, 17-19 jewels, diamond dial, hooded lugs
14k. $700 $1,300 $1,500

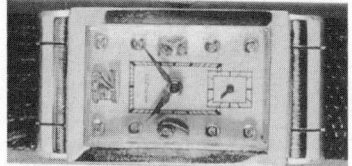

HAMILTON, 17-19 jewels, diamond dial
14k(w). $700 $1,300 $1,500

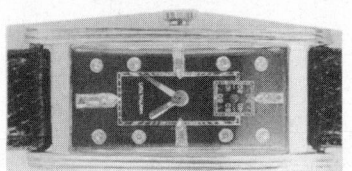

HAMILTON, 17-19 jewels, diamond dial , curved
platinum $900 $1,500 $2,200
14k. $700 $1,200 $1,400

HAMILTON, 17-19J., **Top Hat**, diamond dial, c. 1940
14k. $700 $1,200 $1,400

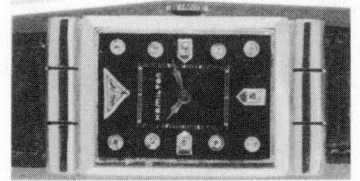

HAMILTON, 17-19 jewels, diamond dial
14k. $700 $1,200 $1,700

HAMILTON, 17-19 jewels, diamond dial, hooded lugs
14k. $700 $1,300 $1,700

HAMILTON, 17-19 jewels, diamond dial
14k. $650 $1,200 $1,600

HAMILTON, 17-19 jewels, diam. dial, c.1941, **TOP HAT**
platinum $1,000 $2,200 $3,200
14k(w). $700 $1,300 $1,500

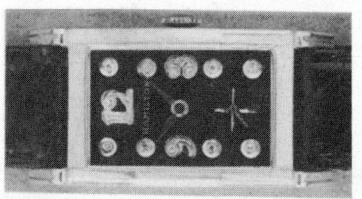

HAMILTON, 17-19 jewels, diamond dial
14k(w). $700 $1,400 $1,600

HAMILTON, 17-19 jewels, diamond dial, hooded lugs
Platinum $1,000 $2,200 $3,200

HAMILTON, 17-19 jewels, diamond dial
platinum $1,000 $2,200 $3,200
14k(w). $800 $1,500 $2,000

HAMILTON, 17-19J., mystery dial with diamonds & **bezel** Swiss made

18k.	$500	$900	$1,200
14k.	$400	$750	$1,000

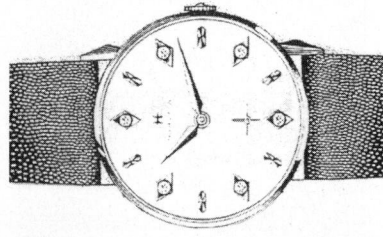

HAMILTON, 17J. "Lord Lancaster B", sold for $89.50 in 1966
gold plate $85 $150 $200

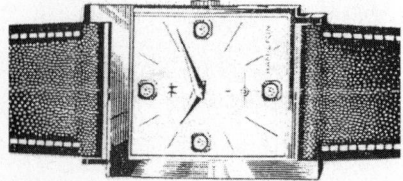

HAMILTON, 17J. "Lord Lancaster C", sold for $125 in 1966
gold filled $150 $250 $300

HAMILTON, 17K. "Lord Lancaster H", sold for $115.00 in 1966
gold plate $85 $150 $200

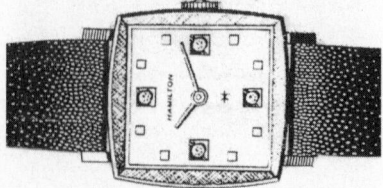

HAMILTON, 17J. "Lord Lancaster K", sold for $89.50 in 1966
gold plate $85 $150 $200

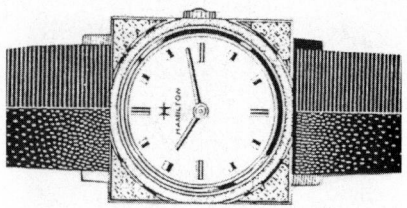

HAMILTON, 17J. "Lord Lancaster L", 24 diamonds, Ca. **1966**
14K(W). $200 $400 $550

HAMILTON, 17J. "Lord Lancaster M", 40 diamonds, Ca. 1966
14K(W). $200 $400 $550

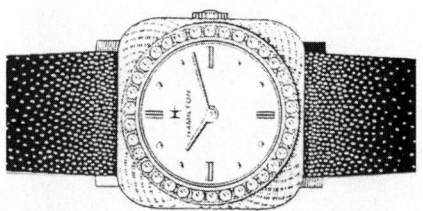

HAMILTON, 17J. "Lord Lancaster N", 36 diamonds, Ca. 1966
14K(W). $250 $450 $550

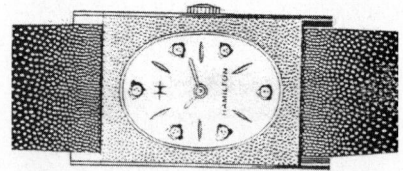

HAMILTON, 17J. "Lord Lancaster R", sold for $210.00 in 1966
14k(w). $175 $275 $350

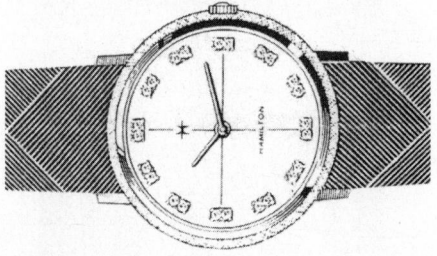

HAMILTON, 17J. "Lord Lancaster T", sold for $275.00 in 1966
14K(W). $175 $300 $400

HAMILTON, 17J.,Chronograph,Valjoux, cal# 7733, Ca.1971
s. steel $200 $400 $550

HAMILTON, 17J., Date, chronog. Valjoux cal#7733,Ca.1971
s. steel $225 $400 $500

HAMILTON 17J., Chronograph, Screw Back
s. steel $175 $300 $400

HAMILTON,17J., 40 diamond bezel, Ca. 1955
18k(w). $300 $550 $650

HAMILTON,17J., "Bianca", diamond & sapphire, c.1933
18k(w). $150 $250 $325

HAMILTON,17J., "Bryn Mawr", c.1933
14k. $60 $100 $125

HAMILTON,17J., "Briarcliffe", c.1933
gold filled $30 $50 $75

HAMILTON,17J., "Caroline", cal.995, c.1933
gold filled $20 $40 $75

HAMILTON,17J., "Cedarcrest ", cal.995, c.1933
14k. $50 $90 $125

HAMILTON,17J., "Chevy Chase A", c.1933
14k(w). $60 $90 $125

HAMILTON,17J., "Chevy Chase B", cal.989 , c.1933
14k.......................... $70 $100 $125

HAMILTON,17J., "Chevy Chase C", cal., c.1933
14k(w)....................... $60 $100 $125

HAMILTON, 17J., "Chevy Chase E", c.1933
14k(w)....................... $70 $100 $125

HAMILTON,17J., "Diane", c.1933
14k.......................... $60 $90 $125

HAMILTON, 17J., "Drexel" , cal.955, c.1933
14k.......................... $70 $75 $100

HAMILTON,17J., "Edgewood", c.1933
gold filled $30 $50 $75

HAMILTON,17J., "Eugenie",44 diamonds, c.1933
platinum $250 $400 $550

HAMILTON, 17J., "Glenwood", cal.955, c.1933
gold filled $30 $50 $75

HAMILTON,17J., "Linden Hall", c.1933
gold filled $30 $50 $75

HAMILTON,17J., "Maritza", 6 diamonds, cal.955, c.1933
18k(w)....................... $80 $100 $125

HAMILTON,17J., "Mayfield", cal.955, c.1933
gold filled $30 $50 $75

HAMILTON,17J., "Newcomb", cal.989, c.1933
gold filled $30 $50 $75

HAMILTON,17J., "Nightingale",40 diamonds, c.1933
18k(w)....................... $200 $300 $500

HAMILTON,17J., "Portia", 8 diamonds, c.1933
18k(w)....................... $200 $300 $500

HAMILTON,17J., "Trudy", c.1948
14k.......................... $50 $75 $100

Grade 986A, 6/0 size
Open face, ¾ plate movt., 17 jewels, double roller

Grade 987, 6/0 size
Hunting, ¾ plate movt., 17 jewels, double roller

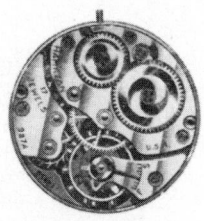

Grade 987A, 6/0 size
Open face, ¾ plate movt., 17 jewels, double roller

Grade 987S, 6/0 size
Hunting, ¾ plate movt., 17 jewels, double roller

Grade 747, 8/0 size
Open face, ¾ plate movt., 17 jewels, double roller

Grade 980, 14/0 size
Open face, ¾ plate movt., 17 jewels, double roller

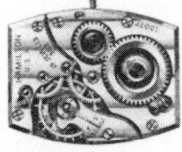

Grade 982, 14/0 size
Open face, ¾ plate movt., 19 jewels, double roller

Grade 982M, 14/0 size
Open face, ¾ plate movt., 19 jewels, double roller

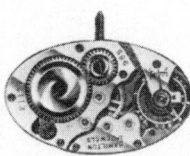

Grade 989, 18/0 size
Open face, ¾ plate movt., 17 jewels, double roller

Grade 997, 20/0 size
Open face, ¾ plate movt., 17 jewels, double roller

Grade 721, 21/0 size
Open face, ¾ plate movt., 17 jewels, double roller

Grade 995, 21/0 size
Open face, ¾ plate movt., 17 jewels, double roller

Grade 911, 22/0 size
Open face, ¾ plate movt., 17 jewels, double roller

Grade 911M, 22/0 size
Open face, ¾ plate movt., 17 jewels, double roller

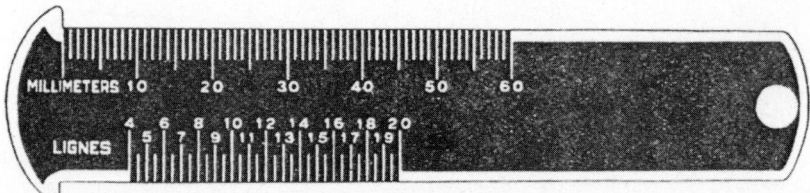

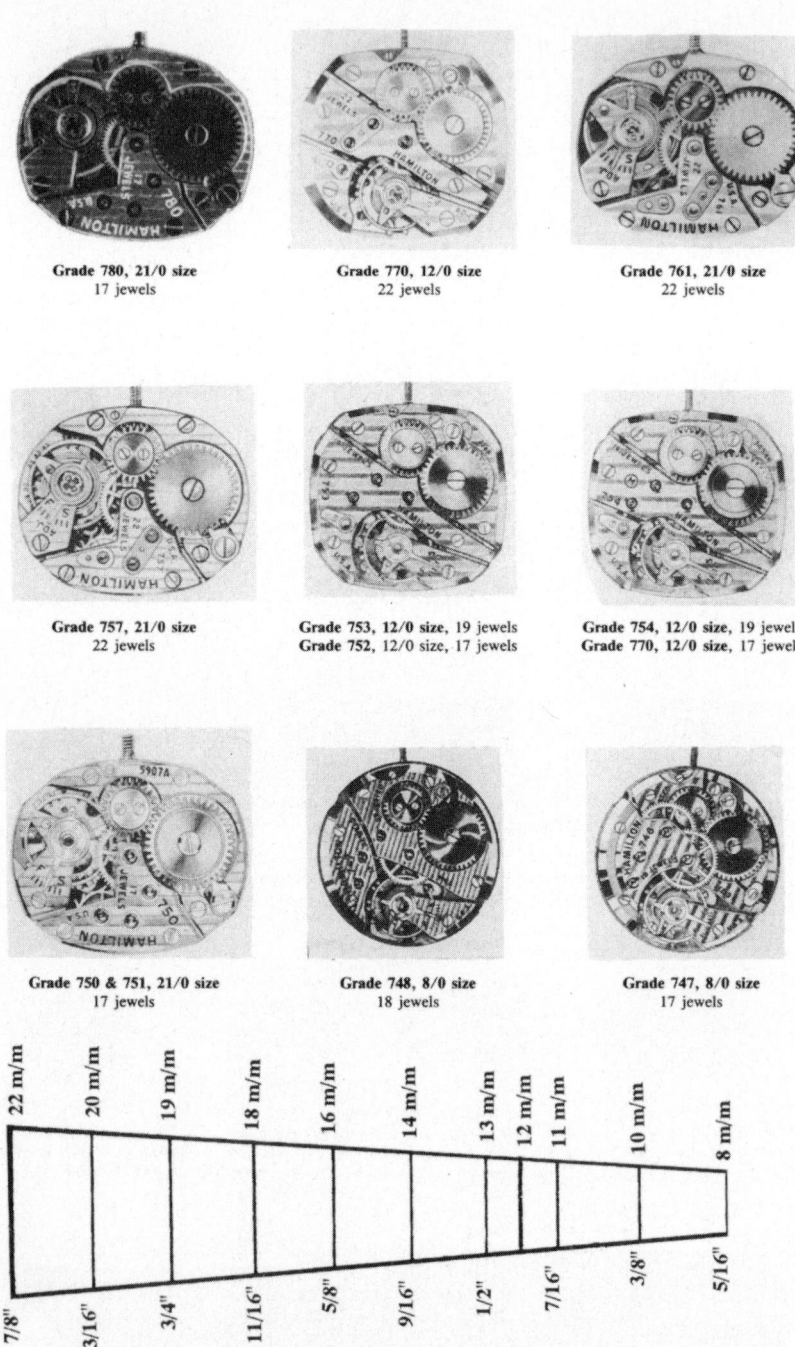

Grade 780, 21/0 size
17 jewels

Grade 770, 12/0 size
22 jewels

Grade 761, 21/0 size
22 jewels

Grade 757, 21/0 size
22 jewels

Grade 753, 12/0 size, 19 jewels
Grade 752, 12/0 size, 17 jewels

Grade 754, 12/0 size, 19 jewels
Grade 770, 12/0 size, 17 jewels

Grade 750 & 751, 21/0 size
17 jewels

Grade 748, 8/0 size
18 jewels

Grade 747, 8/0 size
17 jewels

22 m/m 20 m/m 19 m/m 18 m/m 16 m/m 14 m/m 13 m/m 12 m/m 11 m/m 10 m/m 8 m/m

7/8" 13/16" 3/4" 11/16" 5/8" 9/16" 1/2" 7/16" 3/8" 5/16"

To determine your wrist watch band size use the above gauge and measure between the lugs. The band sizes are listed on each side of the gauge.

Grade 735, 8/0 size
18 jewels

Grade 730, 8/0 size
17 jewels

Grade 679, 17 jewels
Grade 692, 694 - calendar

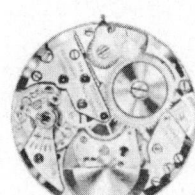

Grade 666 & 663, 17 jewels
Grade 668 - calendar
similiar to 626-629

Grade 658, 661, 667, 17 jewels
Grade 665, 23J, Grade 664, 25J
Grade 662, 690 - calendar, 17J

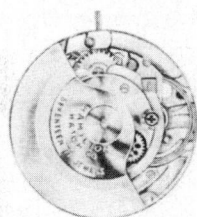

Grade 623 & 624, 17 jewels

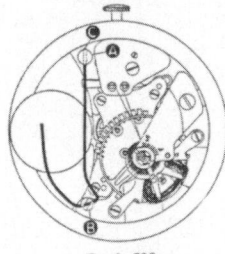

Grade 500
Electric

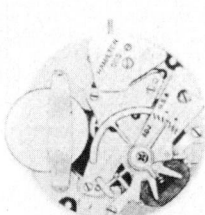

Grade 505, electric, 11 jewels

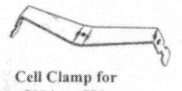

Cell Clamp for
500A or 501

THE SPUR

1930 AD

A Hamilton the true Sportsman will
love. In either 14K yellow or white
gold with numerals of gold in a black
enamel circlet on the outside of the
case—19 jewel movement, $125

HAMPDEN,15J., **old stock, all original**, engraved case, c. 1925
Note the **radial**
gold filled $100 $200 $300

HAMPDEN, 17 jewels., c. 1936
14k. $165 $300 $400

HAMPDEN, 17J., by Lonville W. Co., c. 1936
gold filled $75 $150 $250

HAMPDEN, 17 jewel, regulator dial, c.1938
gold filled $400 $700 $800

HAMPDEN, 15J, **old stock, all original**, c. 1928
14k. $150 $300 $350
gold filled $100 $125 $165

☞ Some grades are not included. Their values can be determined by comparing with similar age, size, metal content, style, grades, or models such as time only, chronograph, repeater etc. Listed.

HAMPDEN, 11=15J., "LEVER SET" ,3/0 size, old stock, all original, c. 1928
silver $125 $200 $300

HAMPDEN, 15J, **old stock, all original**, c. 1928
14k. $150 $300 $375
gold filled $100 $175 $200

HAMPDEN, 11J., Molly Stark, old stock, all original, c. 1928
base metal $40 $75 $100

HAMPDEN, **7J.,** tonneau shaped, old stock, all original, c. 1928
gold filled $75 $125 $135

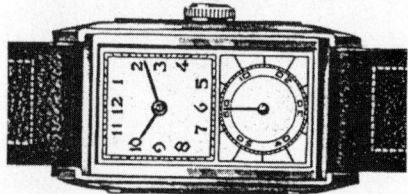

HARMAN,7J.,doctor style doctors watch
gold filled $300 $600 $800

HARMAN,17J., **one button** chronog., mid size, c.1940s
s. steel $200 $350 $400

HARMAN,17J., **two button** chronog., mid size, c.1945
gold filled $150 $275 $375

HARVARD, 17 jewels, chronog., tach-telemeter
s. steel $200 $375 $500

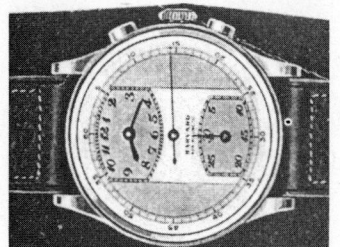

HARVARD, 17 jewels, 1/5 sec. chronog.
s. steel $265 $500 $650

Wrist Watches listed in this section are priced at the collectable
fair market **Trade Show** level as **complete** watches having an
original gold-filled case and stainless steel back, also with original
dial, leather watch band, and the entire original movement in good
working order with no repairs needed.

☞ Pricing in this Guide are fair market price for complete
watches which are reflected from the "**NAWCC**" National and
regional shows.

HARVEL, 17 jewels, date-o-graph
s. steel $125 $250 $325

HARWOOD, 15 jewels, early self winding, c. 1928
18k (w) $1,200 $2,500 $3,000
14k. $900 $1,800 $2,200
gold filled $300 $500 $700
s. steel $200 $350 $550
sterling $300 $600 $800

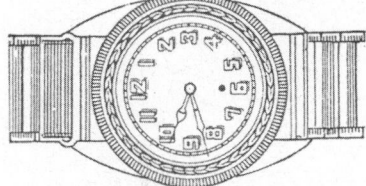

HARWOOD, 15 J., rim set by turning bezel clockwise
9k $600 $1,000 $1,200

HARWOOD, 15 jewels, back set , c.1925
18k. $800 $1,500 $2,000

HASTE, 17J., triple calendar moon ph.
gold filled. $200 $400 $525

HAYDEN, 7J., by Solomax W.Co., hinged case
gold filled $75 $110 $150

HEBDOMAS, 7-15J, visible escapement, 8 day movement
s. steel $500 $900 $1,200

HEBDOMAS, 7-15J, 8 day movement, Ca.1915
s. steel $400 $700 $900

HELBROS, 17 jewels, aux. sec., alarm
gold filled $100 $135 $250

HELBROS. 7 jewels. "Fairfax', Ca 1928
gold filled $50 $100 $150

HELBROS, 17 jewels, aux.sec.
gold filled $40 $75 $100

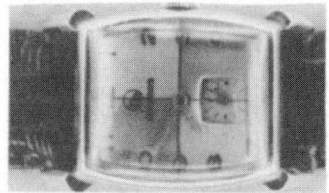

HELBROS, 17 jewels,
14k. $95 $200 $275

HELBROS 7J Federal c 1929
base metal $35 $100 $125

HELBROS,17J., 24 hour dial
base metal $40 $100 $175

HENDA, 15J, direct read, c. 1930
nickel $110 $300 $350

 Pricing in this Guide are fair market price for complete
watches which are reflected from the 'NAWCC' National and
regional shows.

HERMES, 17J., big wire lugs, enamel dial
14k. $125 $225 $300

HELVETIA, 15 jewels, Ca. 1935
9k $100 $200 $250

HELVETIA, 21 jewels, auto wind
gold filled $45 $75 $100

HEUER, 15 jewels, chronog., 2 reg., one button,
14k. $1,000 $2,000 $2,500

☞ Some grades are not included. Their values can be determined by comparing with similar age, size, metal content, style, grades, or models such as time only, chronograph, repeater etc. listed.

☞ Pricing in this Guide are fair market prices for complete watches which are reflected from the "NAWCC" National and regional shows.

HEUER, 17J., chronog., 3 reg., 3 dates, moon phase
18k. $1,800 $3,200 $4,000
s. steel $1,100 $1,900 $2,500

HEUER, 17 J, chronog., 3 reg., "Carrera", c.1960
s. steel $700 $950 $1,300

HEUER, 17 jewels, chronog., 3 dates, 3 reg. c.1948
14k. $700 $1,400 $1,800
s. steel $500 $900 $1,200

HEUER, 17 jewels, "Carrera," chronog., 2 reg., c.1960s
14k. $1,000 $1,900 $2,500
s. steel $800 $1,500 $2,000

HEUER,17J., "Carrera", RF# 2547, day date month, Ca. 1970
14k. $1,200 $2,200 $2,750
s. steel $800 $1,500 $2,000

HEUER,17 J, "Monaco", date, 38 x 40mm, c. 1974
base metal. $1,250 $2,000 $2,500

HEUER,17J., "Camaro", by Valjoux #7730, c. 1965
14k. $600 $1,100 $1,500
s. steel $300 $700 $850

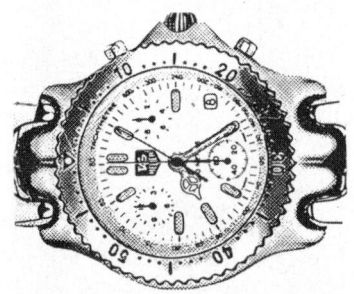

HEUER,17J, **TAG**, split sec., date, 600 ft., gold & s. steel,
sold new for $1,895.00 in Ca.1991
gold tone $150 $250 $350
s. steel & gold tone $150 $250 $350

HEUER, 17 jewels, day-date-month, moon phase
s. steel $400 $700 $900

HEUER,17J., "Autavia", cal.72, micro rotor, c. 1972
s. steel $400 $850 $1,100

Wrist Watches listed in this section are priced at the collectable
fair market **Trade Show** level as **complete** watches having an on
gold-filled case and stainless steel back, also with original dial,
leather watch band, and the entire original movement in good
working order with no repairs needed.

☞ A collector should expect to pay modestly higher prices at
local shops

☞ Some grades are not included. Their values can be
determined by comparing with similar age, size, metal
content, style, grades, or models such as time only,
chronograph, repeater etc. listed.

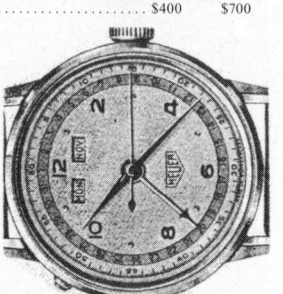

HEUER, 17 jewels, day-date-month
14k. $300 $500 $550
s. steel $150 $225 $365

E. HUGUENIN, 17J, "Black Star", Ca. 1940
14k $200 $400 $500

ILLINOIS, 17J., GJS, 207 on Mvt., model 250 on case
14K . . . . ★★★★★ $1,200 $2,000 $2,400

ILLINOIS, 15-17J., gold center wheel, Ca.1925
silver(Grill protection) $300 $500 $650

ILLINOIS, 17J, **direct read**, Aluminum, case & band, c. 1925
Chrome, case & band $200 $300 $400
Aluminum case & Aluminum band
. . . . ★★★★★ $1,500 $2,300 $3,000

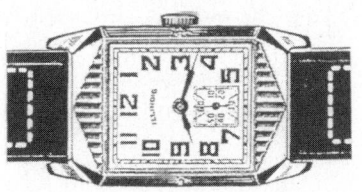

ILLINOIS, 17J., "Art Deco", grade #207, Ca.1925
same case style as Chesterfield
gold filled $300 $450 $550
yellow stripes $700 $800 $950

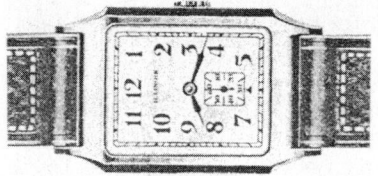

ILLINOIS, 17J., "Andover", Ca. 1929
gold filled $150 $300 $350

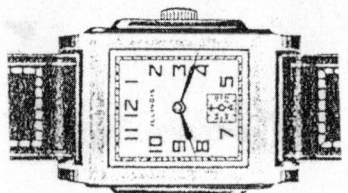

ILLINOIS 15J., "Arlington also Hawthorne", Ca. 1929
gold filled $150 $300 $350

ILLINOIS, 17J., case # 196, "Art Deco", cal.207, c.1925
same case style as Chesterfield
gold filled $200 $300 $400

ILLINOIS, 17J., "Ardsley", Ca. 1929
gold filled $150 $350 $450

ILLINOIS, 17 jewels, "Aviator"
gold filled $200 $400 $500

ILLINOIS, 17-21J.=Beau Monde=14k, Beau Gest =WGF
14k. $400 $700 $800
gold filled W $200 $350 $375

ILLINOIS, 21J., "BARONET", GJS, cal.601, c.1925
14k. $400 $850 $950
gold filled $200 $350 $400

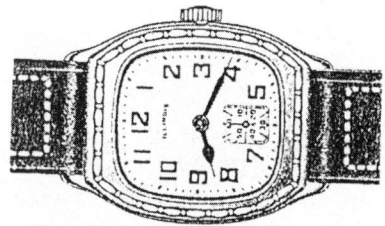

ILLINOIS, 15J "Beau Royal"
gold filled. $200 $375 $400

ILLINOIS, 19J., "Beau Brummel"
14k. $600 $1,000 $1,200

ILLINOIS, 17J., "Blackstone"
gold filled $150 $300 $400

ILLINOIS, 17-19 jewels, "Beau Brummel" 19J sold for $60 & 15J
for $50. in 1929
gold filled $275 $400 $500

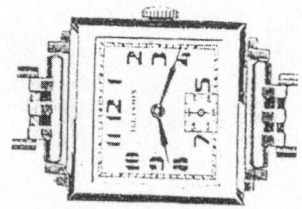

ILLINOIS, 15J., showing as advertised the "Bostonian" with metal
band also look a like "Commodore" came in leather.
gold filled $150 $250 $325

ILLINOIS, 17J, "Beau Brummel", also aux.sec @ 6,Ca.1929
gold filled $275 $400 $500

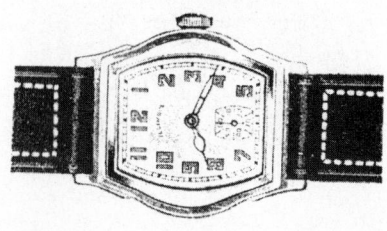

ILLINOIS, 17J., "Cavalier"
gold filled $165 $300 $400

ILLINOIS, 15 jewels, "Champion"
gold filled $150 $250 $300

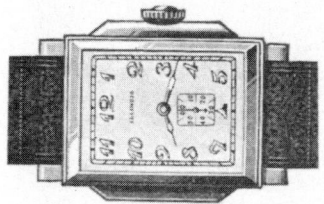

ILLINOIS, 15 jewels, "Chatham"
gold filled $150 $300 $375

ILLINOIS, 17J., "The Chief's", chased bezel, note radial
gold filled (w) $150 $300 $375

ILLINOIS, 15-17J., "Chieftain", 15J. sold for $40. in 1929
gold filled $350 $600 $700

ILLINOIS, 15-17J showing as advertised the "Commodore" with
leather band also look a like Bostonian came in metal.
gold filled $150 $275 $325

ILLINOIS, 19-21 jewels, "Consul"
14k. $600 $1,100 $1,500

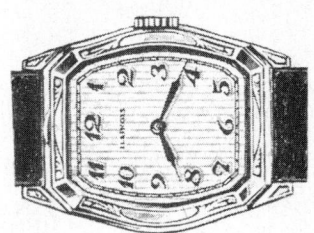

ILLINOIS, 19-21J., "Consul", 21J. sold for $90. in 1929
14k. . . . . ★ $650 $1,100 $1,300
14k engraved bezel. . . . . ★★★ $750 $1,200 $1,400

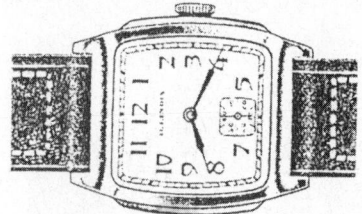

ILLINOIS, 17J., "Derby also Pimlico"
gold filled $150 $300 $375

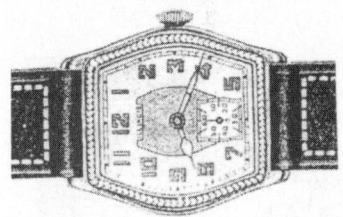

ILLINOIS, 15-17J., "Ensign", aux. Sec. 6, sold for $40. in 1929
gold filled plain bezel. $175 $300 $385
gold filled engraved bezel. $200 $350 $425

ILLINOIS, 15-17J., "Ensign" engraved bezel, aux. sec at 9
gold filled $250 $400 $475

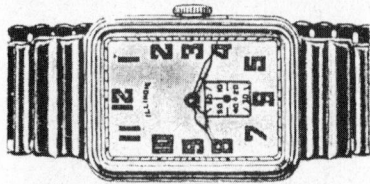

ILLINOIS, 17J., " Frontenac"
gold filled $175 $300 $375

ILLINOIS, 17J., "Finalist also Chesterfield"
gold filled $225 $400 $500

ILLINOIS, 17J., "Futura", rect. mvt., sold for $60. in 1929
gold filled $200 $375 $450

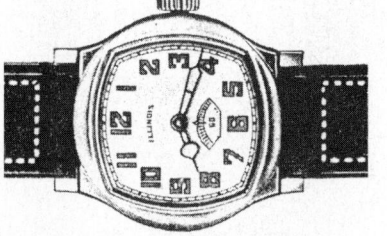

ILLINOIS, 17J., "Guardsman", plain, rotor second dial
gold filled $350 $550 $600

ILLINOIS, 17J., "Guardsman", engraved, cal.307, c.1929
gold filled $350 $575 $650

Note: Many Illinois look the same but with two names old ads show same **style case** but with different bands. Example in 1931 a advertisement for a New Yorker with leather band grade 607, 17J., priced at $50.00 & Manhattan with metal band grade 607,17J., priced at $55.00. The same 1931 ad a New Yorker with leather band grade 601,21J., priced at $75.00 & Manhattan with metal band grade 601, 21J., priced at $85.00. Larchmont leather & Vernon metal, Commodore leather Bostonian metal and others with same **style case** & different bands.

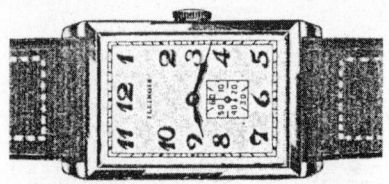

ILLINOIS, 17 jewels, "Hudson"
gold filled $175 $300 $375

ILLINOIS, 17J., "Jolly Roger", engraved bezel, Ca.1929
gold filled (smooth bezel) $350 $600 $850
gold filled (green, engraved). $400 $750 $1,100
gold filled (White, engraved). $275 $500 $650

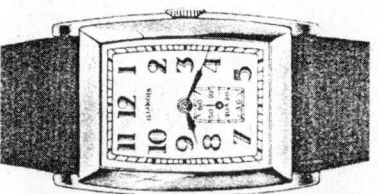

ILLINOIS, 17J., "Kenilworth" also "Gallahad"
gold filled $200 $375 $450

ILLINOIS, 17 jewels, "Larchmont also Vernon",
gold filled $150 $300 $350

ILLINOIS, 17J, "Major", engraved bevel & plain lugs
gold filled plain lugs. $175 $325 $450
gold filled engraved lugs $175 $325 $450
gold filled plain bezel. $175 $325 $450
note right dial=**radial**, & sold for $42.50 in 1929

ILLINOIS,17-21J., "Manhattan or New Yorker", aux. sec. At 9
14k. $385 $600 $800

ILLINOIS, 17-19J., "Marquis", plain,19J.sold for $60 in 1929
gold filled $200 $375 $450

ILLINOIS, 17-21J, "**Yorktown** or New Yorker", with smooth bezel
& aux. sec. at 9, also came with aux. see. at 6
gold filled $200 $350 $475

ILLINOIS, 17J., "Male", engraved, sold for $42.50 in 1929
gold filled $175 $350 $450

ILLINOIS, 17-21J., "Manhattan", aux. sec. at 6, metal band
14k. $300 $600 $800

ILLINOIS, 17J., "Mate" ,plain
gold filled $150 $300 $400

ILLINOIS, 17-21J "New Yorker", aux. sec. at 6, leather band
gold filled $200 $375 $450

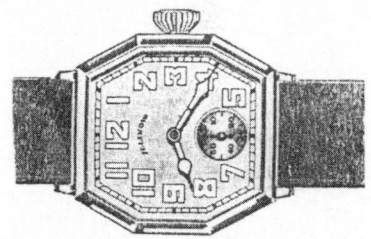

ILLINOIS, 17J., engraved case in "Maxine", plain, ladies
gold filled $150 $350 $400

ILLINOIS, 17-19 jewels, "Marquis", engraved, curved case
gold filled $200 $400 $450

ILLINOIS, 17 jewels, "Maxine", wire lugs, ladies
14k. $175 $300 $375

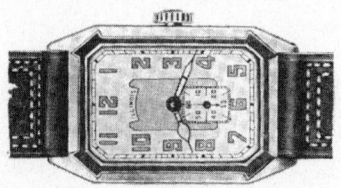

ILLINOIS, 17J., "Medalist also Wembley", rect. mvt, c.1929 sold for $60. in 1929
gold filled $150 $300 $400

ILLINOIS, 17 jewels, "Piccadilly" in white or yellow G.F. came with Luminous or Modern as a option sold for $45. in 1929
gold filled plain............... $800 $1,400 $1,600
gold filled engraved $900 $1,700 $1,900

ILLINOIS, 17 jewels, "Pilot"
gold filled $200 $375 $425

ILLINOIS, 17 jewels, "Prince"
gold filled $200 $375 $425

ILLINOIS, 17J., "Ritz", white bezel & yellow center case also called "Valedictorian"
gold filled $300 $600 $800

ILLINOIS, 15 jewels, "Rockingham also Potomac"
gold filled $200 $400 $500

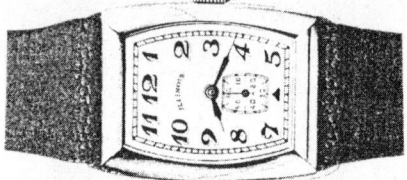

ILLINOIS, 17J.," Rockliffe ", cal 805, c.1925
14k......................... $350 $650 $750

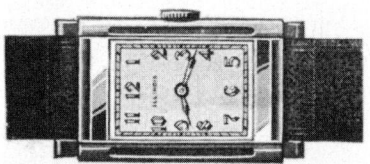

ILLINOIS, 15jewels, "Sangamo"
gold filled $200 $375 $450

ILLINOIS, 17J., "Skyway", engraved case, G#307
gold filled ....★★★ $1,200 $1,800 $2,000

ILLINOIS, 17J., "Special", plain bezel, ca.1929
nickel $200 $325 $450

Note: Auxiliary seconds = (aux. sec.), aux. sec. at 6 o'clock position is a hunting model, aux. sec. at 9 is a open face model.

ILLINOIS, 17J., "Special", engraved bezel, Ca. 1929
nickel $200 $300 $450

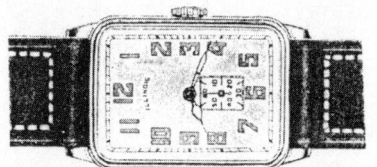

ILLINOIS, 17J., "Trophy also Westchester"
gold filled $125 $275 $350

ILLINOIS, 17J., "Speedway", sold for $42.50 in 1929
gold filled $250 $375 $525

ILLINOIS, 17J., "Tuxedo", 2 tone, sold for $75. in 1929
14k. $450 $850 $1,000

ILLINOIS, 15jewels, "Standish"
gold filled $150 $300 $375

ILLINOIS, 17J., "Viking", sold for $42.50 in 1929
gold filled $225 $375 $475

ILLINOIS, 17J., " Sterling", direct read, c.1929
sterling silver $200 $400 $475

ILLINOIS, 17 jewels, "Off Duty", stars on bezel, Ca. 1927
gold filled .... ★★★ $700 $1,300 $1,600

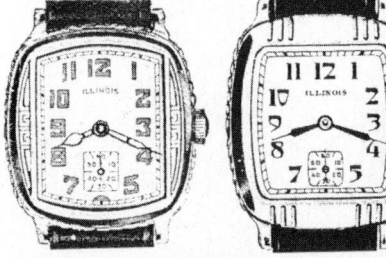

ILLINOIS, 15-17J., left "Townsman" carved Case right
"Metropolitan", 2-tone carved case
gold filled Townsman $250 $375 $450
gold filled Metropolitan ...... ★ $400 $675 $885

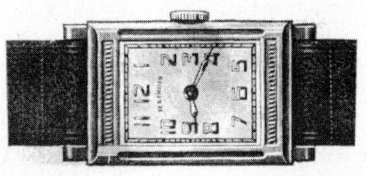

ILLINOIS, 15J., "Urbana",
gold filled $175 $300 $375

Note: Auxiliary seconds = (aux. sec.), aux. sec. at 6 o'clock
position is a hunting model, aux. sec. at 9 is a open face model.

ILLINOIS, 17J., Debonair model "A", ca. 1953
base metal. $100 $200 $250

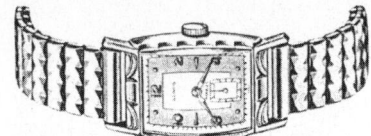

ILLINOIS, 17J., Debonair model "B", ca.1953
base metal. $100 $200 $250

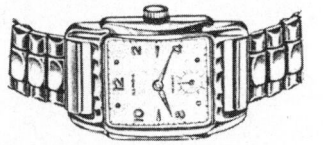

ILLINOIS, 17J., Debonair model "C", ca.1953
base metal. $100 $200 $250

ILLINOIS, 17J., Debonair model "D", ca.1953
base metal. $50 $100 $150

ILLINOIS, 17J., Debonair model "E", ca. 1953
base metal. $50 $100 $150

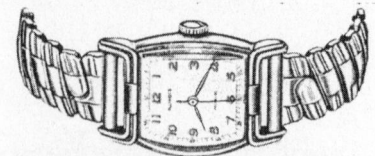

ILLINOIS, 17J., Debonair model "F", ca. 1953
base metal. $100 $200 $250

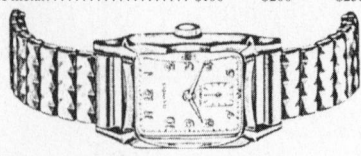

ILLINOIS, 17J., Topper model "A", ca.1953
base metal. $100 $200 $225

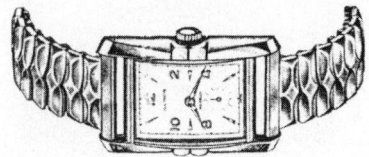

ILLINOIS, 17J., Topper model "B", ca.1953
base metal. $100 $200 $225

ILLINOIS, 17J., Automatic model "A", ca.1953
gold filled $90 $135 $225

ILLINOIS, 17J., Automatic model "B", ca. 1953
base metal. $40 $100 $150

ILLINOIS, 17J., Automatic Signamatic / wind ind., ca. 1953
gold filled $150 $200 $375
base metal. $50 $100 $150

ILLINOIS, 17J., Automatic Nautilus "A", ca.1953
waterproof anti-magnetic
s. steel $50 $100 $150

ILLINOIS, 15-17J., Generic, Telephone Dial, **enamel dial**
14k. $700 $1,200 $1,400

ILLINOIS, 15-17J., Generic, Admiral Evans, enamel dial
sterling $400 $700 $800

ILLINOIS, 15J., Generic, seconds at "9" c.1929
gold filled $175 $375 $475

ILLINOIS, 15-17-19J., Generic, Square cut corner **plain**
gold filled $125 $300 $400

ILLINOIS, 15-17-19J., Generic, Square cut coiner engraved
gold filled $125 $300 $400

ILLINOIS, 17J., Generic Cushion Form, round dial
gold filled $150 $300 $350

ILLINOIS, 19J., Generic Cushion Form, plain, sec. At 6
gold filled $150 $300 $350

ILLINOIS, 19J., Generic Cushion Form, engraved, sec. at 9
gold filled $150 $300 $375

ILLINOIS, 19J., Generic Cushion Form, plain, sec. at 9
gold filled $150 $250 $350
14k (enamel dial) $200 $500 $600

ILLINOIS, 15-17J., Generic, Ca.1926
sterling silver $250 $500 $650

Note: *Generic* period about 1915 to about 1927 is a period
ILLINOIS advertised "Only delivered fitted in cases supplied by
jobbers". July 1st 1924 ad **retail** selling price "Movement only NO.
907, 19 jewels at $35.00, & NO. 903, 15 jewels $26.50". Jewelers
cost "Movement only NO. 907, $20.00 & NO. 903, $14.50". After
about 1934 Illinois wristwatch ads fade away and not seen again
till about 1953, ads state cased & timed by Hamilton. See July 1926
Illinois ad and jobbers ad this book.

ILLINOIS, 17J., Generic, Cushion round, engraved, c.1926
gold filled $150 $300 $350

ILLINOIS, 17J., Generic, Cushion round, plain, c.1926
nickel $100 $275 $300

ILLINOIS, 17J., Barrel & side of case engraved, c.1928 S#
5,091,926, G# 24, 3/0 size, M# 4 HC, gold gilded train
base metal $125 $275 $300

ILLINOIS, 17J., Generic, Barrel engraved, sec at 9, c. 1926
gold filled $125 $325 $400

ILLINOIS, 17 jewels, GENERIC, hand engraved, wire lugs
14k(W) $200 $400 $500

ILLINOIS, 17J , GENERIC, tonneau style, hand engraved,
14k (W) $150 $325 $500

ILLINOIS, 15-19J., GENERIC, square, c. 1925
gold filled $125 $300 $350

ILLINOIS, 17J., black or blue enamel bezel, c. 1929
base metal $200 $375 $450

ILLINOIS, 15J., GENERIC, c.1926
gold filled $100 $300 $350

ILLINOIS, 17J., GENERIC, engraved case
silver $135 $350 $375

ILLINOIS, 15J., GENERIC, engraved bezel, GJS, c.1926
14k(w)...................... $200 $400 $600

ILLINOIS, 15J., GENERIC, winds at 12:00 o'clock
silver...................... $200 $400 $500

ILLINOIS, 17J., Golden Treasure "A", c.1953
14k........................... $65 $100 $150

ILLINOIS, 17J., Golden Treasure "B', c. 1953
14k........................... $65 $100 $150

ILLINOIS, 17J., Kimberly "A", 8 diamonds, c. 1953
gold filled $75 $95 $150

ILLINOIS, 17J., Kimberly 'B'. 2 diamonds, c.1953
gold filled $70 $110 $150

ILLINOIS, 15-17J., lady's watch, black enamel on bezel
14k........................ $100 $175 $225
gold filled $30 $50 $75

BELOW A JULY 1926 AD
By The ILLINOIS WATCH CO.

6-O SIZE OR ELEVEN LIGNE

Only delivered fitted in cases supplied by Jobbers

Illustrations simply indicate some of the different styles of cases, made by
various watch case manufacturers, for these movements.

No. 907, 19 Jewels   No. 903, 15 Jewels
$35.00 *Movements Only* $26.50

19 and 15 ruby and sapphire jewels: compensating balance with timing
screws; double roller escapement; Breguet hairspring; steel escape wheel;
polished winding wheels; recoil click; silvered or gilt metal dials; full or
three-quarter open.

BELOW GENERIC or JOBBERS AD Ca. 1926
ADVERTISING ILLINOIS WATCHES FOR SALE

No. 1045   The Ace $37.30
3/0 Illinois 17 Jewel
White Engraved Stellar Quality Star Case
Silver Dial Luminous Figures and Hands
Established retail price with each

No. 1047   The Whippet $36.20
3/0 Illinois 17 Jewel
Stellar White Plain Barrel Case
Silver Dial Luminous Figures and Hands
Established retail price with each

ILLINOIS, 17J., "Eliza" c.1929
gold filled $65 $100 $125

ILLINOIS, 17J., "Long Beach", c. 1929
gold filled $55 $100 $125

ILLINOIS, 17J., "Lynette", c.1929
gold filled $50 $75 $100

ILLINOIS, 17J., "Mariette ", c.1929
gold filled $50 $60 $80

ILLINOIS, 17J., ' Marionette ", c1929
gold filled $50 $60 $80

ILLINOIS, 17J., "Marlette", c.1929
gold filled $50 $60 $80

ILLINOIS, 16J., "Mary Todd", c.1929
18k(w) $125 $250 $300

ILLINOIS, 16J., "Mary Todd", black enamel bezel, v.1929
18k(w) $150 $250 $300

ILLINOIS, 16J., "Mary Todd", c.1929
18k. $150 $250 $300

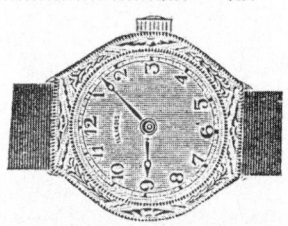

ILLINOIS, 17J., "Mateel", c.1929
14k(w) $70 $150 $200

ILLINOIS, 17J., ' Miami ", c.1929
gold filled $55 $65 $85

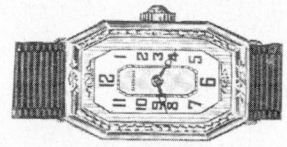

ILLINOIS, 17J., "Narragansett", c. 1929
14k. $85 $150 $200

ILLINOIS, 17J., "Newport ", engraved case, c. 1929
gold filled $55 $65 $85

ILLINOIS, 16J., "Queen Wilhelmina", 22 diamonds and
8 synthetic sapphires
18k(w) $200 $400 $500

ILLINOIS, rectangular, Grade 207, 17 jewels

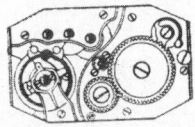

ILLINOIS, rectangular, 1st, 2nd & 3rd model

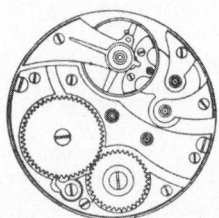

ILLINOIS, Model #4, 3/0 size, bridge, hunting, movement.

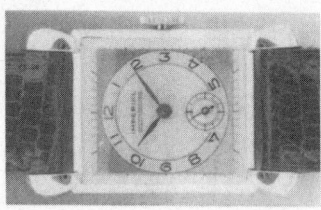

IMPERIAL, 17J., fancy lugs
14k(W) $200 $400 $475

IMPERIAL, 7J., enamel dial, wire lugs, Ca. 1915
silver $100 $200 $350

☞ Some grades are not included. Their values can be determined by comparing with similar age, size, metal content, style, grades, or models such as time only, chronograph, repeater etc. listed

INGERSOLL, 2 J., "Rist-Arch", stepped case
base metal $20 $50 $75

INGERSOLL, "Swagger",
base metal $20 $50 $75

INGERSOLL, 7 jewels
base metal $20 $45 $65

INGERSOLL, 7 jewels, radiolite dial wire lugs
W/ original band $30 $65 $100
base metal $20 $40 $60

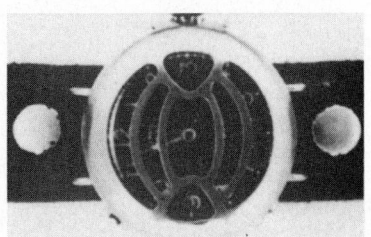

INGERSOLL, 7 J, military style, **protective grill cover wire lugs, all original band and cover.**
base metal $85 $100 $150

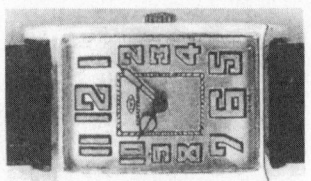

INTERNATIONAL W. CO., 17J., Ca. 1926
18k......................... $650 $1,200 $1,500

INTERNATIONAL W. CO., 17 jewels, c. 1925
18k......................... $500 $900 $1,200

INTERNATIONAL W. CO., 16J., **enamel dial**, c. 1920
silver...................... $450 $800 $1,000

INTERNATIONAL W CO, 17 jewels
14k......................... $400 $700 $800

INTERNATIONAL W. CO., 16J., **enamel dial**, 12 in **red** cal.53,
Ca.1920
18k......................... $500 $800 $1,000

INTERNATIONAL W CO 21 J., **auto-w**, center sec.,
Ca. 1940
18k......................... $700 $1,200 $1,500

INTERNATIONAL W. CO., 17 jewels, c. 1920
18k......................... $500 $800 $1,000

INTERNATIONAL W. CO., 17J., "Art Deco", Ca. 1925
TU-TONE case w/ enamel on bezel
18k.........................$1,500 $3,000 $3,500

INTERNATIONAL W. CO, 17 jewels, **curved**
14k......................... $700 $1,200 $1,500

INTERNATIONAL W. CO. 17 jewels
14k C&B.................... $600 $1,100 $1,300

INTERNATIONAL W. CO., 17 jewels, c. 1940
18k. $400 $700 $900

INTERNATIONAL W. CO., 17J., c. 1945
14k. $400 $650 $800

INTERNATIONAL W. CO., 17J., Tiffany on dial, c. 1942
14k. $400 $800 $1,000

INTERNATIONAL W. CO., 17 jewels, hidden lugs
14k. $400 $750 $950

INTERNATIONAL W. CO., 17J., aux. sec.
14k. $300 $550 $650

Wrist Watches listed in this section are priced at the collectable fair market Trade Show level as complete watches having an original gold-filled case and stainless steel back, also with original dial, leather watch band, and the entire original movement in good working order with no repair needed.

INTERNATIONAL W. CO., 17J., RF # 1160, auto wind, Ca. 1964
18k. $450 $850 $1,100

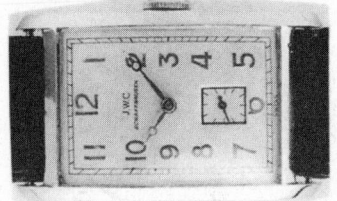

INTERNATIONAL W. CO., 17 jewels, Ca. 1937
18k. $500 $900 $1,200

INTERNATIONAL W. CO., 17J., c. 1926
s. steel $300 $500 $700

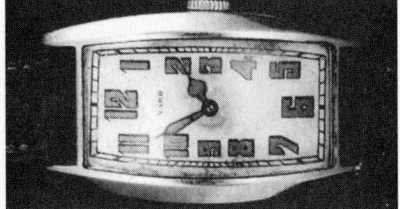

INTERNATIONAL W. CO., 17 J, on dial "Yard"
18k. $700 $1,500 $1,800

INTERNATIONAL W. CO., 17 J., curved, on dial "Yard"
platinum $1,000 $1,900 $2,500

INTERNATIONAL W CO, 17 jewels, **hinged back**
14k........................ $400 $800 $1,100

INTERNATIONAL W. CO., 17 jewels, center sec.
18k........................ $550 $1,000 $1,200

INTERNATIONAL W. CO., 17 jewels, curved
14k........................ $600 $1,100 $1,300

INTERNATIONAL W. CO., 17J., cen. sec., auto-w., date
platinum $1,700 $2,750 $3,500

INTERNATIONAL W. CO., 17J, date, auto-wind, waterproof
18k........................ $900 $1,700 $2,250

INTERNATIONAL W. CO.,17J., RF# 802a, cal.8541, auto wind,
Ca.1960
s. steel $400 $700 $900

INTERNATIONAL W. CO.. 21 jewels, auto wind, date
18k........................ $800 $1,400 $1,750

INTERNATIONAL W. CO., 21J., "Ingeneur", date, c.1976
18k non-magnetic......... ★★ $2,000 $2,800 $3,200
s. steel non-magnetic........ ★ $1,000 $1,600 $2,000

☞ Some grades are not included. Their values can be
determined by comparing with similar age, size, metal, content,
style, grades, or models such as time only, chronograph, repeater
etc. listed.

INTERNATIONAL W. CO., 17 jewels, center sec.
18k........................ $500 $1,000 $1,200

DIALS FOR MINT PRICES MUST BE ALL ORIGINAL.

INTERNATIONAL W. CO., 21J., date, auto wind, c. 1960
18k. $1,000 $1,750 $2,000

INTERNATIONAL W. CO., 17J., center sec.cal.89, c.1957
18k. $500 $1,000 $1,250

INTERNATIONAL W. CO., 21J., cal.853, auto wind, Ca. 1961
18k. $800 $1,600 $1,800

INTERNATIONAL W. CO., 17J., wide lugs, c. 1960
18k. $600 $1,000 $1,400

INTERNATIONAL W. CO.,17J., Bombe' lugs, cat. C89, Ca.1952
18k. $600 $1,200 $1,400

INTERNATIONAL W. CO., 21J., cal.C852, auto wind, Ca. 1952
18k. $600 $1,100 $1,400

INTERNATIONAL W. CO., 21J., cal.853, **auto wind**, Ca. 1951
18k. $500 $1,100 $1,400

INTERNATIONAL W. CO., 17J., cal.89, c. 1962
s. steel $300 $500 $700

INTERNATIONAL W. CO., 17J., ca. 1960s
18k C & B $1,100 $1,900 $2,250

INTERNATIONAL W. CO., 17J., center sec., Bombe' lugs
18k. $500 $1,000 $1,300

INTERNATIONAL W. CO., 17J., fancy lugs, cen. sec.
18k. $600 $1,200 $1,400

INTERNATIONAL W. Co., 18 jewels, center sec.
18k. $650 $1,100 $1,300

GO Pricing in this Guide are fair market price for complete watches which are reflected from the **"NAWCC"** National and regional shows.

INTERNATIONAL W. CO., 17J., auto wind, Ca 1960
18k. $500 $1,000 $1,200

INTERNATIONAL W. CO., 17 jewels, center sec.
18k. $400 $900 $1,100

INTERNATIONAL W. CO., 17 jewels, center sec., cat.402
18k. $400 $800 $1,100

INTERNATIONAL W. CO.,17 jewels, center sec., cat. 89
18k. $400 $900 $1,100

Wrist Watches listed in this section are priced at the collectable fair market Trade Show level as complete watches having an original gold-fitted case and stainless steel back, also with original dial, leather watch band, and the entire original movement in good working order with no repairs needed.

INTERNATIONAL W. CO., 17 jewels, center sec., cal.89
18k.......................... $500 $1,000 $1,100

INTERNATIONAL W. CO., for Royal Navy, ca.1950
s. steel...................... $700 $1,200 $1,500

INTERNATIONAL W. CO., 36J., "Da Vinci," chronog. auto wind,
triple date, moon ph., center lugs
18k C & B $5,000 $8,500 $12,000
18k......................... $3,500 $6,500 $9,500

INTERNATIONAL W. CO., 17J., winds at 12 o'clock
s. steel...................... $600 $1,100 $1,300

INTERNATIONAL W. CO., "Porsche Design", date, autowind,
compass, sapphire mirror, RF#3510-LMW, Ca. 1988
Titanium.................. $1,200 $2,100 $2,800
base metal................. $800 $1,400 $1,600

INTERNATIONAL W. CO., 17 jewels, Autowind, Ca. 1958
s. steel...................... $350 $700 $900

INTERNATIONAL W. CO., 17J., anti-magnet, Ca. 1942
s. steel...................... $250 $450 $650

A collector should expect so pay modestly higher prices at local shops.

INTERNATIONAL W. CO., 17 jewels, c. 1948
18k. $500 $1,000 $1,100

INTERNATIONAL W. CO., 17J., aux sec., cal.83, c.1938
14k. $400 $800 $1,000

INTERNATIONAL W. CO., 17J., aux. sec., c.1948
s. steel $300 $700 $850

INTERNATIONAL W. CO., 17J., cal.461, c.1962
18k. $400 $1,000 $1,100

INTERNATIONAL W. CO., 17J.,date, 30 ATM=1,000 ft.
s. steel $400 $700 $950

INTERNATIONAL W. CO., 17J., Bombe' lugs, Ca. 1952
18k. $500 $1,000 $1,200

INTERNATIONAL W. CO., 15J., cal. 83, ca. 1945
14k. $400 $800 $1,000

INTERNATIONAL W. CO., 17J., mid-size, Ca. 1945
s. steel $200 $400 $600

INTERNATIONAL W CO, 17J, 36 small diamonds
platinum $350 $600 $800

INTERNATIONAL WATCH CO.
MOVEMENT IDENTIFICATION

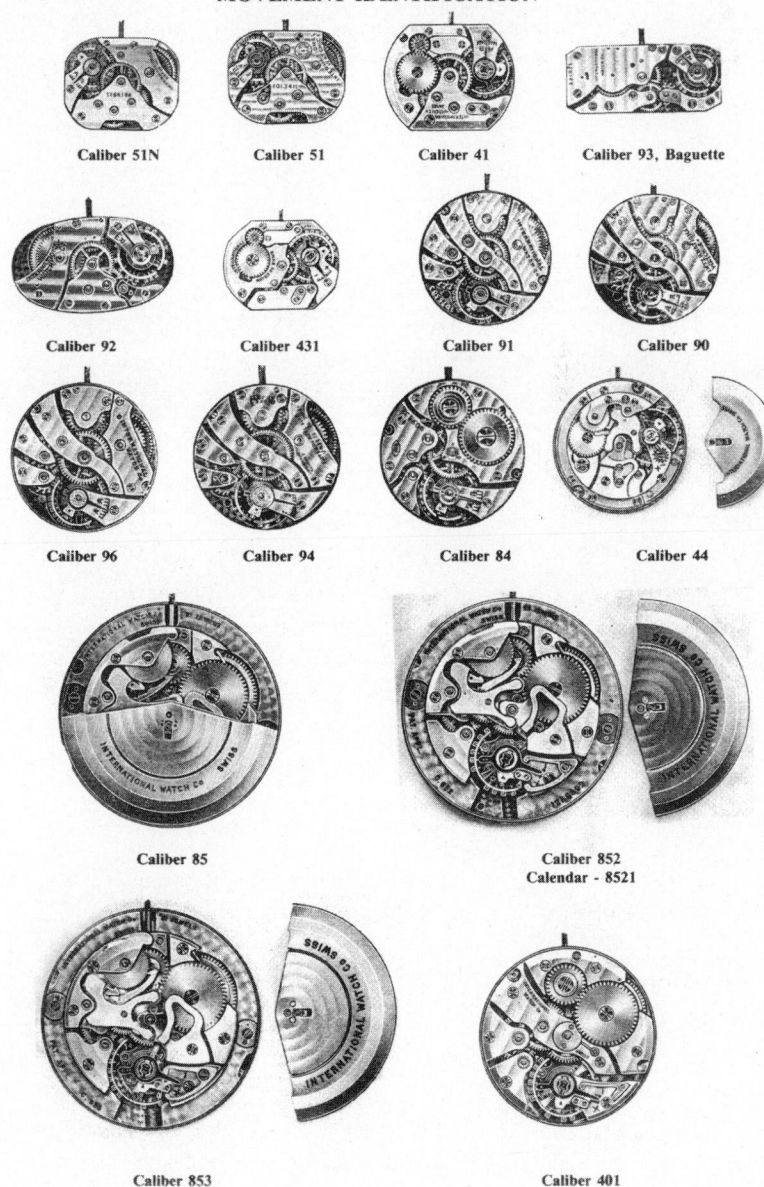

Caliber 51N   Caliber 51   Caliber 41   Caliber 93, Baguette

Caliber 92   Caliber 431   Caliber 91   Caliber 90

Caliber 96   Caliber 94   Caliber 84   Caliber 44

Caliber 85

Caliber 852
Calendar - 8521

Caliber 853
Calendar - 8531

Caliber 401

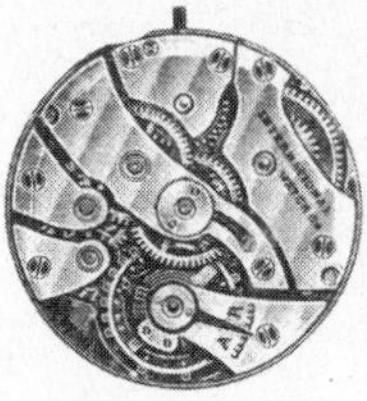

Caliber 60

Caliber 62

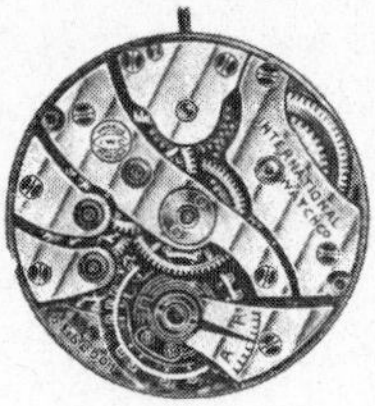

Caliber 61

Caliber 86

Caliber 75 & 76

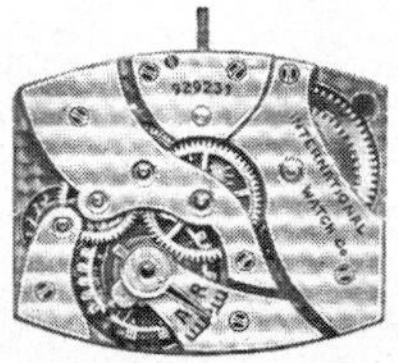

Caliber 87

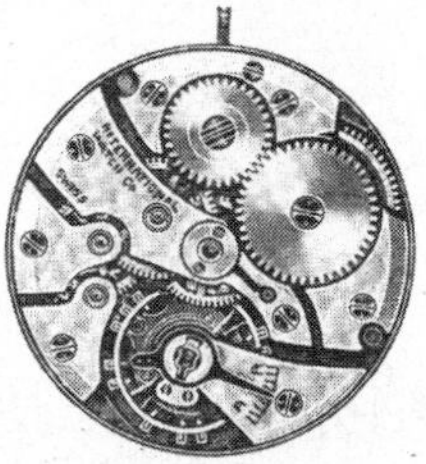

Caliber 89

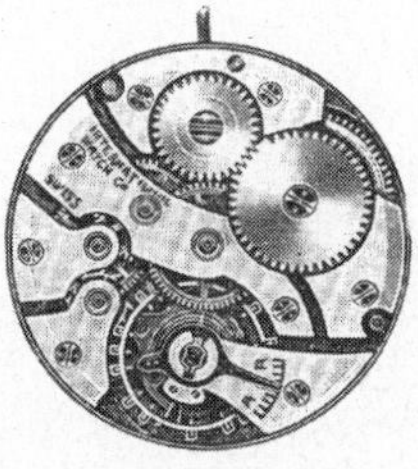

Caliber 88

Caliber 70

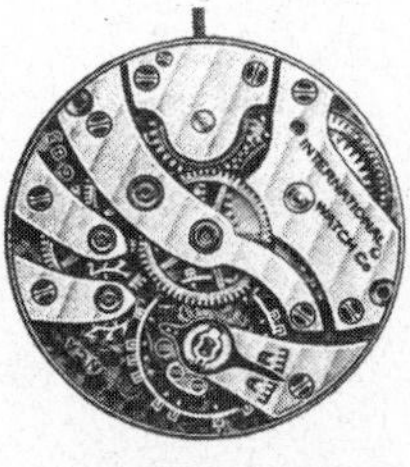

Caliber 83

Caliber 64

Caliber 63

Caliber 64

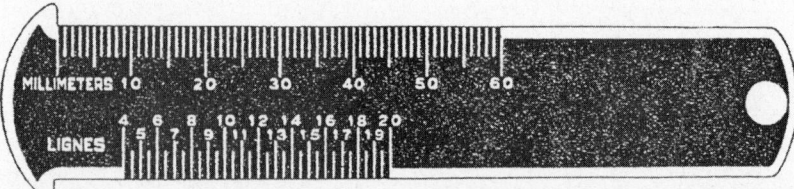

INVICTA, 15 jewels, chronograph, min reg. at 6 o'clock, decimal
aperture for sec. at 12 o'clock
18k.........................$1,500 $3,000 $3,500

INVICTA, 17 jewels, date, center sec.
18k.........................$200 $400 $450
s. steel.........................$65 $100 $150

INVICTA, 17 jewels, day-date, waterproof
18k.........................$150 $300 $400
s. steel.........................$60 $100 $125

INVICTA, 17 jewels, day-date-month
18k.........................$200 $400 $500
s. steel.........................$75 $100 $150

☞ Some grades are not included. Their values can
be determined by comparing with similar age, size,
metal content, style, grades, or models such as time only,
chronograph, repeater etc. listed.

☞ A collector should expect to pay modestly higher prices
at local shops

INVICTA, 17 jewels, day-date-month, moon phase
18k.........................$600 $1,200 $1,500
s. steel.........................$200 $400 $600

INVICTA, 17 jewels, waterproof
18k.........................$125 $250 $300
s. steel.........................$40 $75 $100

INVICTA, 17 jewels, auto wind, waterproof
18k.........................$125 $250 $350
s. steel.........................$50 $85 $125

JAEGER W. CO., 17J., RF#5 184, chronog., Ca.1942
s. steel.........................$200 $375 $450
18k.........................$400 $800 $900

☞ Pricing in this Guide are fair market price for COMPLETE
watches which are reflected from the NAWCC National and
regional shows.

JAEGER W. CO., 15J., **duoplan, backwind**, c.1935
s. steel $250 $425 $550

JARDUR W. CO., 17J.,RF#29840, c.1950
s. steel $250 $400 $500

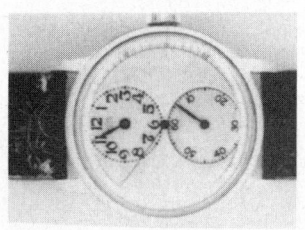

JEAN LOUIS, 17 jewels regulator dial, c. 1930
14k $500 $850 $1,000

J. E. Watch Co., 17J., c.1950
gold plate $40 $80 $100

JEWEL. 15 jewels. dual dial, c. 1938
gold filled $250 $550 $750

JOHNSON-MATTHEY, 15J., 5-10-15 gram ingot 24k gold
24k 5 gram $200 $350 $500
24k 10 gram $400 $650 $700
24k 15 gram $700 $950 $1,100

JUNGHANS, 16J., chronometer, c. 1965
14k $150 $250 $350

JUNGHANS, electronic "Ato Chron" , C.1978
14k $150 $275 $325

JUNGHANS, 17J., cal. J88, c.1980
s. steel $200 $400 $600

Wrist Watches listed in this section are priced at the collectable
fair market Trade Show level as complete watches having an
original gold-filled case and stainless steel back, also with original
dial, leather watch band, and the entire original movement in good
working order with no repairs needed.

DIALS FOR MINT PRICES MUST BE ALL ORIGINAL.

JURGENSEN, 31J, 5 mm. repeater, **recased**, c.1906
18k. $4,000 $8,000 $9,000

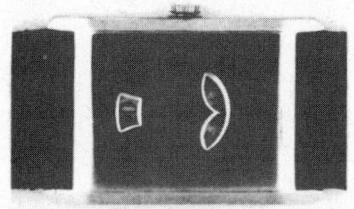

JURGENSEN, 151, jumping hr., revolving min. c.1930s
18k. $2,500 $5,000 $6,000

JURGENSEN,17J., large lugs, recess crown, c.1950
14k. $200 $375 $450

JURGENSEN,17J., long lugs, c.1948
18k. $275 $425 $500

JURGENSEN,17J., recess crown, fancy lugs, c.1952
14k. $200 $400 $450

J. JURGENSEN, 17J., 2 tone, center lugs, c. 1940
14k. $200 $400 $500

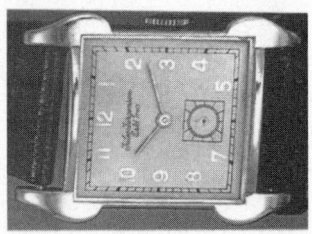

JURGENSEN, 17 jewels, fancy lugs, ca. 1949
14k. $300 $550 $650

JURGENSEN, 17 jewels, fancy lugs
14k. $300 $550 $600

JURGENSEN, 17 jewels, extra fancy lugs, c. 1946
18k. $450 $850 $1,000

JURGENSEN, 17 jewels, c. 1950
18k. $200 $400 $475

☞ Pricing in this Guide are fair market price for COMPLETE
watches which are reflected from the NAWCC National and
regional shows.

J. JURGENSEN, 17 jewels
18k...........................$165 $300 $400

J. JURGENSEN,17J. center sec.. c.1946
14k...........................$150 $300 $375

JURGENSEN,17J., aux. sec., c.1948
14k...........................$150 $300 $375

J. JURGENSEN,17J. aux. sec., c1940
14k...........................$150 $300 $375

J. JURGENSEN, 17J., textured bezel, c 1960
14k...........................$125 $250 $350

J. JURGENSEN,17J., hidden lugs, c.1948
14k...........................$150 $300 $375

J. JURGENSEN,17J. hidden lugs, c1940
14k...........................$150 $325 $375

J. JURGENSEN,17J., top hat style, c.1952
14k........................... $300 $550 $675

J. JURGENSEN, 17J., hidden lugs, c.1950
14k........................... $300 $550 $650

J. JURGENSEN,17J hidden lugs, c.1948
14k...........................$150 $300 $375

J. JURGENSEN, 17J., flared case, Ca. 1954
14k........................... $235 $400 $500

☞ Some grades are not included. Their values can be determined by comparing with similar age, size, metal content, style, grades, or models such as time only, chronograph, repeater etc. listed.

J. JURGENSEN, 17J., by Valjoux, 30mm, cal. 69, c. 1944
14K $500 $900 $1,000
s. steel $300 $450 $600

J. JURGENSEN, 17J., extended bezel, c.1950
14k. $300 $600 $700

J. JURGENSEN, 17J., auto-w., cen. sec., Ca. 1954
14k. $225 $425 $500

J. JURGENSEN, 17J., cal.1139, c.1950
18k. $225 $400 $450

J.JURGENSEN,17J., cal.8273, extended lugs, c.1958
14k. $195 $400 $450

J.JURGENSEN,17J., center sec., date, c.1960
14k. $150 $275 $325

J.JURGENSEN,17J., aux, sec., c.1968
14k. $150 $300 $350

J.JURGENSEN,17J., center sec., mid size, c.1940
14k. $150 $275 $325

Wrist Watches listed in this section are priced at the collectable fair market Trade Show level as complete watches having an original gold-filled case and stainless steel back, also with original dial, leather watch band, and the entire original movement in good working order with no repairs needed.

☜ Some grades are not included. Their values can be determined by comparing with similar age, size, metal content, style, grades, or models such as time only, chronograph, repeater etc. listed.

J. JURGENSEN,17J., 3 diamond dial, date, c.1960
14k(w) $150 $300 $400

J.JURGENSEN,17J., 40 diamond bezel, c.1960
14k(w) $300 $600 $800

J. JURGENSEN, 17 J., 12 diamond dial, ca. 1960s
14k(W) $185 $300 $400

JUVENIA.17J.,3 dates, moon ph., screw on back c. 1950s
18k. $525 $950 $1,200

Wrist Watches listed in this section are priced at the collectable
fair market **Trade Show** level as **complete** watches having an
original gold-filled case and stainless steel back, also with original
dial, leather watch band, and the entire original movement in good
working order with no repairs needed.

JUVENIA, 21 jewels, gold movement
18k. $200 $400 $450

JUVENIA, 17J.,
s. steel $30 $75 $100

JUVENIA, 17J.,
s. steel $30 $75 $100

JUVENIA, 17J.,
s. steel $50 $90 $130

☞ Some grades are not included. Their values can
be determined by comparing with similar age, size,
metal content, style, grades, or models such as time only,
chronograph, repeater etc. listed.

JUVENIA, 17J,
s. steel $65 $125 $175

JUVENIA, 17J.
s.steel $50 $100 $150

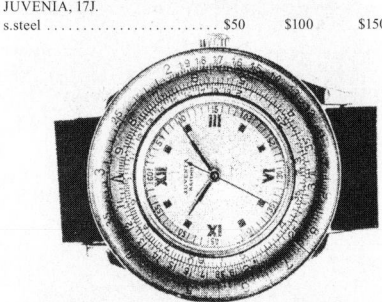

JUVENIA, 17J., "Arithmo",
s steel $100 $225 $300

KELBERT, 17J, triple date, moon ph., ca.1945
gold filled $200 $400 $500
s. steel $250 $375 $500

KELEK,17J., digital, tachymeter, auto-wind, c.1970
s. steel $175 $275 $400

KELTON, 7 jewels, curved, stepped case
gold filled $40 $125 $150

KELTON, 7 jewels, "Drake"
gold filled $40 $100 $150

KENT W. CO.,17J., Continental W. Co.(French), chronog.
s. steel $250 $400 $450

KINGSTON, 17 jewels, day-date-month, moon phase
gold filled $250 $500 $550

KELBERT, 17 jewels, fancy lugs, c. 1949
gold filled $80 $150 $225

DIALS FOR MINT PRICES MUST BE ALL ORIGINAL.

KINGSTON,17J., cal G10, hidden lugs, c.1943
gold filled $50 $100 $150

KORD, day date month, moon ph., auto wind
s. steel $300 $550 $650

KURTH, 17 jewels, "Certina"
gold filled $40 $60 $100

LACO, 17J., center sec., c. 1955
gold plate $30 $50 $75

👓 Some grades are not included. Their values can be determined by comparing with **similar** age, size, metal content, style, grades, or models such as **time only**, chronograph, repeater etc. listed.

👓 Pricing in this Guide are fair market price for complete watches which are reflected from the **NAWCC** National and regional shows.

LANCEL (Paris),17J., one button chronog. by Nicolet, c.1960
gold filled $225 $400 $475

A. LANGE & SOHNE,17J., 55mm., c.1940
s. steel $1,500 $2,500 $3,000

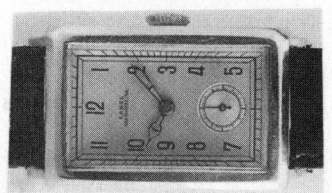

A. LANGE & SOHNE, 17J, (Glashutte), c.1936
14k. $1,000 $1,500 $2,000

LANGE "UHR" (Glashutte),15J., c.1936
14k. $1,000 $1,500 $2,000

LANGE "UHR" (Glashutte),17J., c.1937
s. steel $600 $900 $1,100

LANGE, 17J, (Glashutte), date, auto wind, waterproof
18k. $750 $1,400 $1,600

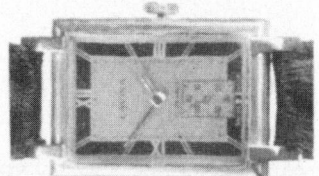

LAVINA, 17J., ca.1937
9K $100 $200 $275

LE COULTRE, 15 jewels, wire lugs, c. 1919
silver $200 $400 $450

LE COULTRE, 18J , skeletonized
18k. $1,200 $2,000 $2,500

LE COULTRE. 19 jewels, alarm
18k. $1,000 $1,900 $2,500
14k. $850 $1,500 $1,700
gold filled $300 $600 $800
s. steel $300 $650 $850

LE COULTRE, 19 jewels, alarm, sold for $99.00 with gold
filled case & $235.00 with 18K case in 1950
18k. $1,000 $1,800 $2,500
14k. $650 $1,200 $1,600
gold filled $400 $700 $800
s. steel $400 $700 $800

LE COULTRE, 17J., auto-wind, alarm, cal 815, c.1960
gold filled $400 $700 $800

LE COULTRE, 17J., ruby dial, alarm, auto wind, c.1960
gold filled $400 $700 $1,000

LE COULTRE, 17J.,cal.814, memovox, alarm, c.1960
14k. $800 $1,300 $1,500
gold filled $400 $700 $800

LE COULTRE, 17J., cal.p815, alarm, c.1960
gold filled $400 $700 $800

LE COULTRE, 17J., RF#3025, wrist-alarm, c.1948
gold filled $400 $700 $800

LE COULTRE, 17J., wrist alarm, Ca.1949
gold filled $450 $750 $900

LE COULTRE, 17J., 'Polaris", memovox, underwater alarm tested
to 600 feet, date, Ca. 1968, s. s. band by Le Coultre.
s. steel $1,500 $2,700 $3,000

LE COULTRE, 17J.,memovox , alarm, auto wind,c.1973
14k & s.s $800 $1,500 $1,600

LE COULTRE, 17J., RF#2676, date, memovox, c.1960
gold filled $400 $700 $800

LE COULTRE 17J., date, auto-w., memovox, c. 1975
s. steel $300 $600 $750

LE COULTRE, 17J., auto wind, date, memovox, c.1976
gold filled $450 $750 $1,200

LE COULTRE, 19 J., date, Memovox, ca. 1959
18k. $1,000 $1,800 $2,500
gold filled $500 $900 $1,000
s. steel $500 $900 $1,100

LE COULTRE, 19J., **alarm, date**, autowind
14k. $800 $1,500 $1,800

LE COULTRE, 19jewels, alarm, date, autowind, ca.1950
18k. $1,200 $2,300 $2,850
gold filled $400 $800 $1,000
s. steel $500 $900 $1,200

LE COULTRE, 17-19J., World Time, Memovox, ca. 1956
s steel $1,000 $1,800 $2,000

LE COULTRE, 17J., Powermatic Nautilus "S" wind-ind., auto-w.,
sold for $85.00 with gold filled case in 1950
gold filled $200 $375 $450

LE COULTRE, 17J., cal. 481, wind-ind., auto-w., c. 1954 the cal.
481,up & down wind-ind. has Differential Gearing
gold filled $200 $300 $425

LE COULTRE, 17J., auto wind, wind indicator, sold for $150.00
with a 14K case in 1951
14k. $400 $750 $1,000

LE COULTRE. 17 jewels, auto wind, screw back
18k. $300 $600 $700

LE COULTRE, 17J., "Master Mariner, auto wind, c.1960
14k. $300 $500 $600

LECOULTRE, 17J.,cal.p478, center sec.c.1947
s .steel $100 $200 $300

LE COULTRE, 17J., "Master Mariner", auto wind, c. 1952
14k. $350 $650 $750

LE COULTRE, 17J .,"Master Mariner", auto-wind, c.1960
s .steel $200 $325 $375

∽ A collector should expect to pay modestly higher prices at
local shops

LE COULTRE, 17J., "Master Mariner", autow., date, Ca.1960
gold filled $125 $225 $275

LE COULTRE, 17J., auto-wind, cal.p812, c.1955
gold filled $125 $200 $250

LE COULTRE, 17J., RF#.480-C-380, autow., Ca.1955
14k. $250 $475 $550

LE COULTRE, 17J., RF#555-149, Ca.1955
14k. $200 $375 $475

Wrist Watches listed in this section are priced at the collectable
fair market trade show level as complete watches having an
original gold-filled case and stainless steel back, also with original
dial, leather watch band, and the entire original movement in good
working order with no repairs needed.

LE COULTRE (continued)

DIALS FOR MINT PRICES MUST BE ALL ORIGINAL.

LE COULTRE, 17J., cal. 812, auto-wind, c.1952
s. steel $175 $325 $375

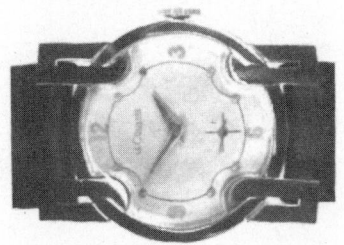

LE COULTRE, 17J.,"Coronet", cal.480cw, c.1951
gold filled $225 $500 $575

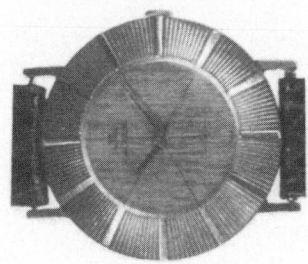

LE COULTRE, 17J., cal.480, wide bezel, c.1958
gold filled $150 $300 $375

LE COULTRE, 17J., cal.480, c.1955
14k. $200 $400 $500

LE COULTRE, 17J., RF#7534, c.1960
14k. $350 $750 $850

LE COULTRE, 17J., 11 diamond dial, RF#197, c.1955
14k(w) $285 $575 $650

LE COULTRE, 17 jewels, center lugs, c. 1960
18k. $400 $750 $850

LE COULTRE, 17 jewels, "Pershing", fancy lugs, c. 1950
14k. $300 $600 $750

⌒ Pricing in this Guide are fair market price for complete watches which are reflected from the **NAWCC** National and regional shows.

⌒ Some grades are not included. Their values can be determined by comparing with similar age, size, metal content, style, grades, or models such as time only, chronograph, repeater etc. listed.

LE COULTRE, 17J., fancy lugs
14k. $300 $600 $700

LE COULTRE, 17J., fancy lugs, ca. 1950s
18k. $350 $650 $900

LE COULTRE, 17 jewels, fancy lugs, c. 1952
14k. $300 $550 $600

LE COULTRE, 17 jewels, fancy bezel & lugs
14k. $700 $1,400 $1,600

LE COULTRE, 17 jewels, fancy bezel & lugs, Ca 1953
14k. $385 $800 $900

LE COULTRE, 17J., fancy bezel, Ca.1952
gold filled $125 $250 $300

LE COULTRE, 17J., auto wind, textured bezel, c. 1950
18k. $250 $500 $600

LE COULTRE, 17 jewels, center sec, c. 1949
18k. $400 $750 $800
s. steel $150 $300 $450

LE COULTRE, 17J., cen. sec., 24 hr dial, c. 1940
s. steel $200 $400 $500

This book endeavours to be a GUIDE or helpful manual and offers a wealth of material to be used as a tool not as an absolute document.

LE COULTRE, 17J., "Quartermaster", 24 hr dial, auto-w., RF#114
s. steel $475 $750 $1,000

LE COULTRE, 17J., alarm, auto-w., date, Ca. 1964
s. steel $400 $800 $900

LECOULTRE, 17J., auto-w., cal. 813, RF#388-870, Ca.1959
gold filled $125 $150 $250

LE COULTRE, 17J., quartz, cal.352, c.1970
gold filled $55 $100 $125

LE COULTRE, 17J., center sec., cal.468/ACa.1940
s. steel $150 $275 $300

LE COULTRE, 17J.,date alarm , auto-w, c.1975
gold filled $300 $600 $750

LE COULTRE, 17J., center sec., Ca. 1930s
silver $175 $300 $375

LE COULTRE, 17 jewels, alarm, date, auto wind
s. steel $350 $600 $750

LE COULTRE, 17J., chronog., 2 reg.
14k. $600 $1,100 $1,400
s. steel $450 $700 $900

LE COULTRE, 17 jewels, chronog., 3 reg.
18k. $1,800 $2,750 $3,250

LE COULTRE, 17J.,chronog.,cal.281,c.1940
s. steel $450 $700 $900

LE COULTRE, 17 jewels, mystery dial, c. 1955
14k yellow. $600 $1,000 $1,200

LE COULTRE, 17J., chronog., FR#2644, blue dial,
s. steel $800 $1,300 $1,500

LE COULTRE, 17J., 15 diamond mystery dial, RF # 182
14k(W) $700 $1,200 $1,600

LE COULTRE, 17J., chronog. 3 reg., ca. 1958
14k. $1,500 $2,800 $3,250
s. steel $850 $1,500 $1,800

LE COULTRE, 17J., 2 diamond mystery dial, RF # 182
14k(W) $500 $1,000 $1,300

LE COULTRE, 17J., 36 diamond mystery dial, waterproof, auto wind, "**Vacheron Galaxy**"
14k(w). $1,500 $2,500 $3,000

LE COULTRE, 17J, diamond dial, textured bezel, c. 1960s
14k(w). $200 $400 $600

LE COULTRE, 17J., **date**, cal 810, c.1952
14k. $250 $500 $600

LE COULTRE, 17J., date, center sec., c.1950
14k. $250 $500 $600

👌 Some grades are not included. Their values can be determined by comparing with similar age, size, metal content, style, grades, or models such as time only, chronograph, repeater etc. listed.

LE COULTRE, 15 jewels, triple-date, c.1945
s. steel $600 $1,200 $1,500
14k. $800 $1,700 $2,000
18k. $1,200 $2,100 $2,500

LE COULTRE, 17J, triple date, moon ph., c. 1940s
18k. $1,300 $2,500 $3,000
gold filled $550 $1,100 $1,500

LE COULTRE, 17J., triple date, moon ph., fancy lugs
14k. $1,000 $2,000 $2,750

LE COULTRE, 17J., auto-w., Memovox, world time, c.1960
Beware of **FAKES**
14k. $1,200 $2,400 $3,000

DIALS FOR MINT PRICES MUST BE ALL ORIGINAL.

LE COULTRE, 17J., weems style, cal.450, c.1942
s. steel $600 $900 $1,200

LE COULTRE, 17J., Memovox, world time, date, c. 1968
14k. $1,200 $2,400 $3,000

LE COULTRE, 17J., "Futurematic", cal.817, c.1952
gold filled $300 $600 $750
14k $500 $1,200 $1,500

LE COULTRE, 17 jewels, "Futurematic" power-reserve
18k. $700 $1,400 $1,800
14k. $500 $1,200 $1,500

LE COULTRE, 17J, "Futurematic", auto- w., W. Ind. sold for
$95.00 with s. steel case in 1950
18k. $700 $1,400 $1,800
gold filled $300 $500 $700
s. steel . . . . ★ $400 $550 $800

LE COULTRE, 23 J., auto-w., date cen. sec.
14k. $150 $300 $400

LE COULTRE, 17J., Master Mariner, auto-w., date
gold filled $100 $150 $225
14k. $150 $300 $400

LE COULTRE, 17J., day date, mid size, ca. 1940s
gold filled $100 $200 $300
Wrist Watches listed in this section are priced at the collectable fair
market Trade Show level as complete watches having an original
gold-filled case and stainless steel back, also with original dial,
leather watch band, and the entire original movement in good
working order with no repair needed.

LE COULTRE, 17J., fancy lugs, aux. sec., ca. 1948
14k...........................$400 $800 $900

LE COULTRE, 17J., auto-w., ca. 1950s
14k...........................$300 $500 $600

LE COULTRE, 17J, fancy lugs
14k...........................$300 $500 $600

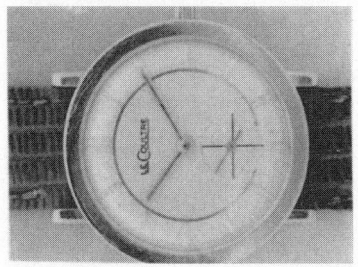

LECOULTRE, 17J., aux. sec. ca.1950a
14k...........................$200 $400 $500

LE COULTRE, 17 jewels, fancy wide bezel, ca1955
14k(W)......................$500 $900 $1,000

LE COULTRE, 17J., alarm, date,
14k...........................$600 $1,100 $1,300

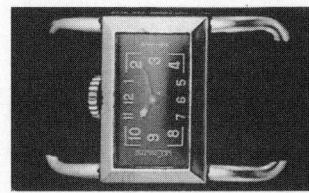

LE COULTRE, 15J., drivers style wind at 12,c. 1960s
s. steel......................$250 $450 $500

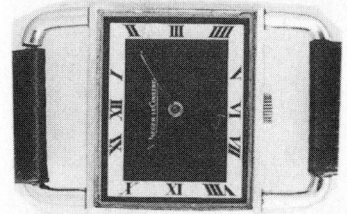

LE COULTRE, 17J.,drivers style crown at 6, RF#9041
s. steel......................$300 $450 $500

LE COULTRE, 17J., RF#9041, cal.818, crown at 6, c.1960s
18k...........................$350 $650 $700

LE COULTRE, 17J, "Reverso," center sec., c. 1930
18k. $3,000 $6,000 $8,000
s. steel $1,250 $2,500 $3,000

LE COULTRE, 17J., "Reverso," c. 1940s
18k. $3,000 $6,000 $7,000
s. steel $1,200 $2,300 $3,000

LE COULTRE, 17 jewels, fancy hooded lugs, c. 1952
14k. $300 $600 $800

LE COULTRE, 17 jewels, fancy lugs
14k. $250 $500 $600

LE COULTRE, 17 jewels, large fancy lugs
14k. $400 $750 $850

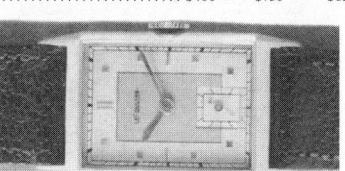

LE COULTRE, 17J., curvex,
14k. $250 $475 $550

LE COULTRE, 17J., curvex, ca. 1940s
14k. $250 $500 $600

LE COULTRE, 17J., stepped lugs, ca. 1944
gold filled $125 $250 $300

LE COULTRE, 17J., aux. sec., ca. 1940s
gold filled $150 $250 $300

LE COULTRE, 17J., square lugs, ca. 1948
14k. $400 $800 $1,000

LE COULTRE, 17J., extended lugs, c. 1938
gold filled $125 $225 $275

LE COULTRE, 17J., aux. sec., c.1940
14k. $200 $400 $500

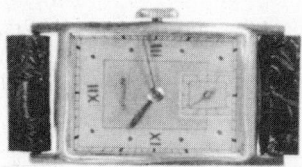

LE COULTRE, 17J., tu tone dial, c.1940
gold filled $150 $250 $300

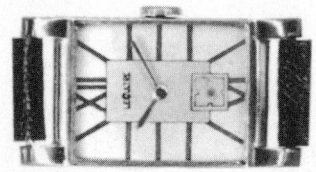

LE COULTRE, 17J., large lugs, c.1938
gold filled $200 $350 $500

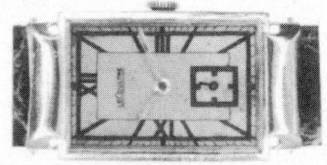

LE COULTRE, 17J.hidden lugs, c.1942
14k. $225 $400 $550
gold filled $150 $275 $300

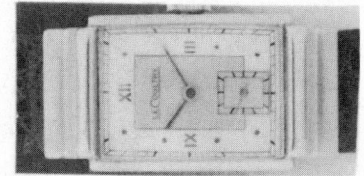

LE COULTRE, 17J., hooded lugs, ca. 1940s
14k. $300 $600 $700

LE COULTRE, 17J, fluted bezel, Ca. 1949
gold filled $150 $300 $350

LE COULTRE, 17J., fancy bezel, ca. 1940s
14k. $400 $750 $1,000

LE COULTRE, 17J, Asymmetric, RF#2406, 15 diamonds,
c. 1957
14k. $500 $900 $1,200

LE COULTRE, 17J., Asymmetric, cal.438, 4cw, c.1957
gold filled $175 $300 $400

LE COULTRE, 17J, Asymmetric, diamond dial, RF#2406,
c. 1960
14k. $400 $800 $1,000

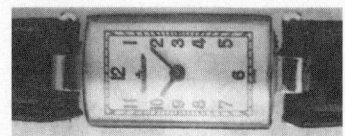

LE COULTRE, 15J., **Duoplan, back-wind**, c. 1930
18k. $600 $1,000 $1,200

LE COULTRE, 17 jewels, **uniplan**, c. 1938
14k(w). $350 $600 $700

LE COULTRE, 15J., **Duoplan, back-wind**, c. 1930
14k(G&S) $800 $1,000 $1,200
18k. $1,100 $2,000 $2,500

LE COULTRE, 17 jewels, fancy lugs, c. 1948
14k. $500 $1,000 $1,200

LE COULTRE, 17J., fancy lugs, cal.438-4cw, c.1951
18k. $800 $1,500 $1,900

LE COULTRE, 17jewels, fancy lugs
14k. $700 $1,400 $1,900

LE COULTRE, 17 jewels, **diamond dial**, fancy lugs
14k. $700 $1,500 $2,000

LE COULTRE, 17J., diamond dial, ca. 1940s
14k. $400 $750 $900

LE COULTRE, 17J., 12 diamond dial, cal.4870cw, c.1958
14k(w). $300 $600 $600

LE COULTRE, 17J., 15 diamond mystery dial ca. 1940s
14k. $1,000 $2,000 $2,500

LE COULTRE, 15J., hinged case, c.1920
14k. $400 $750 $900

✍ Pricing in this Guide are fair market price for complete
watches which are reflected from the NAWCC National and
regional shows.

LE COULTRE, 17J., stepped case & lugs, cal., c.1950
gold filled $150 $250 $350

LE COULTRE, 17J., aux. sec., c.1940
14k. $185 $300 $400

LE COULTRE, 17J., cal.493, auto wind, c.1955
14k. $300 $600 $750

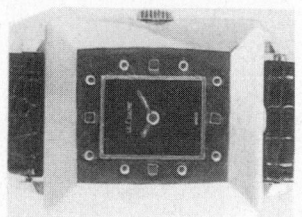

LE COULTRE, 17J., cal.438-4cw, wide bezel, c.1950
14k. $250 $475 $550

LE COULTRE, 17J., textured bezel, c.1952
14k. $250 $475 $550

🖛 Pricing in this Guide are fair market price for complete
watches which are reflected from the NAWCC National and
regional shows.

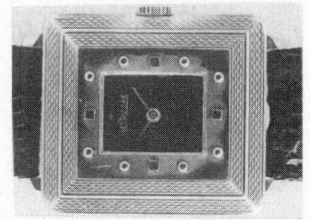

LE COULTRE, 17J., textured bezel, c.1950
14k. $250 $500 $750

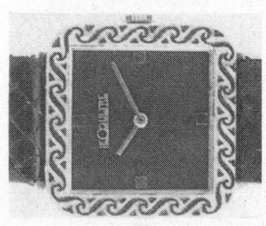

LE COULTRE, 17J., RF#7540,enamel bezel, cal., c. 1960
14k, ... $400 $800 $1,000

LE COULTRE, 17J., auto wind, cal.p812, c.1948
gold filled $150 $300 $325

LE COULTRE, 17 jewels, Ca.1958
18k. $350 $600 $750

LE COULTRE, 17J., textured bezel, cen. sec.
18k. $300 $600 $700

LE COULTRE, 17J, aux.sec. auto wind, ca. 1940s
14k......................... $300 $600 $800

LE COULTRE, 17J, triple date, moon ph., fancy bezel sold for
$99.50 with gold filled case in 1951
18k................... ★★ $3,000 $5,000 $6,000
14k.........................$2,000 $4,000 $5,000
gold filled $1,500 $2,500 $3,500

LE COULTRE, 17 jewels, c. 1945
18k......................... $250 $475 $650

LE COULTRE, 17 jewels, fancy lugs, c. 1948
14k......................... $350 $600 $700

LE COULTRE, 17 jewels, Ca. 1940
14k(rose).................... $250 $500 $700

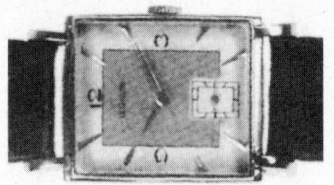

LE COULTRE, 17jewels, center lugs, c. 1945
14k......................... $225 $450 $550

LE COULTRE, 17 jewels, c. 1950s
14k......................... $200 $400 $600

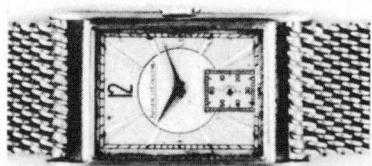

LE COULTRE, 17 jewels, 18k case & band
18k C&B..................... $800 $1,600 $2,000

LE COULTRE, 17 jewels, date cal. 810, c. 1952
14k......................... $350 $675 $800

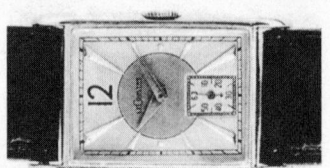

LE COULTRE, 17 jewels, two tone dial
14k......................... $300 $600 $700
18k......................... $350 $700 $800

LE COULTRE, 15 jewels, by Blancpain, c.1925
gold filled $125 $200 $300

LE COULTRE, quartz, date, waterproof, c. 1960s
18k. $200 $375 $475

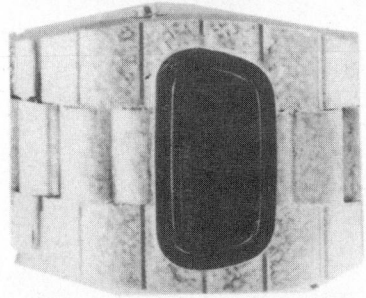

LE COULTRE, electric, digital calendar (good running order)
silver & gold filled $150 $250 $350

LE COULTRE, 17J, "Aristocrat", sold for $71.50 with gold
filled case either Gents or Ladies model in 1951
gold filled $400 $600 $700

LE COULTRE, 17 jewels, small, "Aristocrat", c. 1953
gold filled $250 $475 $550

LE COULTRE, 15J., lady's
14k(W) $95 $150 $200

LE COULTRE, 15J., lady's art deco, by Blancpain, c.1925
silver $250 $400 $550

LE COULTRE, 15J., lady's REVERSO, c.1940
s. steel $500 $800 $1,000

LE COULTRE, 15J., **Duoplsn, back-wind**, c. 1930
silver $300 $600 $700

LE COULTRE, 17J., lady's MYSTERY dial, c.1959
gold filled $100 $175 $250

LE COULTRE, 17J., photo-watch, winds at 12, Ca 1950
14k. $400 $750 $900

LEMANIA, 17 jewels, auto wind
s. steel $50 $75 $125

LEMANIA, 17 jewels, chronog., military, ca.1970s
s. steel $600 $1,200 $1,700

LEMANIA,17J., chronog., 3 reg., c.1946
14k. $600 $900 $1,100
18k. $800 $1,200 $1,650

LEONIDAS,17J., chronog., triple date, c.1945
gold filled $300 $500 $700

LEMANIA, 17 jewels, chronog., 2 reg., auto wind, c. 1950
18k. $500 $800 $1,000

LEONIDAS, 17 jewels, triple date, 3 reg.
18k. $700 $1,000 $1,300
s. steel $400 $600 $800

LEMANIA, 17 jewels, chronog., waterproof
s. steel $400 $650 $800

LEONIDAS, 17 jewels, auto wino, triple date, moon phase
s. steel $300 $500 $700

LEONIDAS, 17 jewels, chronog., 2 reg.
s. steel......................$150 $275 $375

LEVRETTE,17J., chronog., (fly back), center lugs, c.1935
18k(1 button)...............$1,000 $1,500 $2,000

LE PHARE, 17J., chronog., triple date, 3 reg., antimagnetic
14k..........................$500 $900 $1,200

LIBELA,7J., direct read, c. 1952
base metal...................$125 $250 $350

LE PHARE, 17 jewels, chronog.,2 reg., antimagnetic
18k..........................$375 $600 $700
14k..........................$275 $500 $600
s. steel......................$135 $275 $375

LIP, 15J., chronog., tu-tone, center lugs, (French), c.1940
gold filled & s. steel...........$550 $800 $1,000

LE PHARE, 17J., triple date, moon ph., waterproof, autow.
18k..........................$700 $900 $1,200
gold filled $350 $500 $700

LIP, electric, bulbous crown, (French)
s. steel......................$200 $300 $400

Wrist Watches listed in this section are priced as **COMPLETE** watches having an original gold-filled case and stainless steel back, also with original dial, leather watch band, and the entire original movement in good working order with no repairs needed

PRODUCTION TOTALS
LONGINES DATE OF MOVEMENT MANUFACTURE

DATE–SERIAL #	DATE–SERIAL #	DATE–SERIAL #
1867 — 1	1911 - 2,500,000	1937 - 5,500,000
1870 — 20,000	1912 - 2,750,000	1938 - 5,750,000
1875 — 100,000	1913 - 3,000,000 - Aug.	1940 - 6,000,000 - June
1882 — 250,000	1915 - 3,250,000	1945 - 7,000,000 - July
1888 — 500,000	1917 - 3,500,000	1950 - 8,000,000 - May
1893 — 750,000	1919 - 3,750,000	1953 - 9,000,000 - July
1899 - 1,000,000 - Feb.	1922 - 4,000,000 - Oct.	1956-10,000,000 - May
1901 - 1,250,000	1925 - 4,250,000	1959-11,000,000 - April
1904 - 1,500,000	1926 - 4,500,000	1962-12,000,000 - May
1905 - 1,750,000	1928 - 4,750,000	1966-13,000,000 - June
1907 - 2,000,000 - July	1929 - 5,000,000 - Oct.	1967-14,000,000 - Feb.
1909 - 2,250,000	1934 - 5,250,000	1969-15,000,000 - Feb.

LONGINES, 15J., center lugs, enamel dial, ca. 1923
silver $200 $400 $600

LONGINES, 18J ,wire lugs, ca.1928
14k. $300 $500 $550

LONGINES, 15J., enamel dial, exaggerated #'s, Ca 1923
18K $500 $900 $1,200

LONGINES, 15J., wire lugs, enamel dial, c.1927
silver $200 $375 $400

LONGINES,15J., metal dial, GJS, c.1925
14k. $150 $275 $350

LONGINES, 15J., wire lugs, ca.
silver $150 $275 $350

LONGINES,17J., tu-tone, GJS, c. 1936
14k & s. s. $150 $300 $450

LONGINES,17J., double dial, cal.932, c.1937, Doctors Style
s. steel $700 $1,500 $1,850

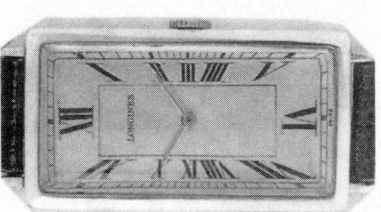

LONGINES,17J., large & curved, GJS, exaggerated numbers
gold filled $250 $500 $600

LONGINES, 15J., GJS, c.1922
silver $200 $400 $600

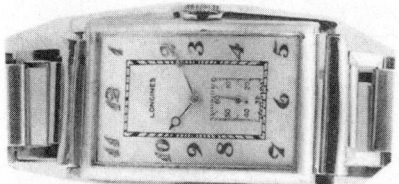

LONGINES, 17J., GJS, cal.940, c.1931
14k. $200 $300 $450

LONGINES, 17J., GJS, cal.1086, c.1928
14k. $300 $500 $700

LONGINES, 15-17J., enamel dial, Ca. 1920s
14k. $550 $1,000 $1,500

LONGINES, 17J., large Lindberg model 47mm., movable center
dial (weem's second netting), Ca. 1930s
18k. . . . . ★★★ $7,000 $14,000 $20,000
silver $3,500 $5,500 $7,500
nickel $3,000 $4,500 $6,000

LONGINES, 17J., small Lindberg model, original retail price for
gold filled $97.50, movable center dial, Ca. 1930s
18k. . . . . ★★ $4,000 $5,000 $7,000
14k. $2,500 $3,500 $5,000
gold filled $700 $1,000 $1,500
s. steel $800 $1,200 $1.800

LONGINES, 17J., Weems U.S. Patent 2008734 on dial

gold filled	$300	$450	$650
s. steel	$450	$575	$750
14k	$650	$850	$1,100

LONGI7NES,17J., 1 button, 2 reg., c.1946

14k	$2,000	$3,000	$3,500

LONGINES, 17J., 'Weems', revolving bezel, Ca. 1940s

gold filled	$250	$400	$600
s. steel	$400	$500	$700

LONGINES, 17J., 1 button, fly back hand, center recording, RF# 5034, Ca. 1940

s. steel	$900	$1,700	$2,000

LONGINES, 17J., "Weems", revolving bezel, Ca. 1940s

gold filled	$350	$500	$950
s. steel	$500	$700	$950

LONGINES, 17J., one button chronog., 2 reg., Ca. 1928

18k	$1,650	$2,500	$3,200

LONGINES,17J., fly back hand, center recording, c.1945

s. steel(1 button)	$700	$1,350	$1,700

LONGINES, 17 jewels, chronog., 1 button, 2 reg., c. 1923

silver	$1,400	$2,000	$2,500

LONGINES, 17J., chronog., one button, instant reset
gold filled $600 $900 $1,400
14k. $1,400 $2,000 $2,800

LONGINES, 17J. chronog., ref. 1333, enamel dial, Ca. 1925
silver(1 button). $1,000 $1,700 $2,300

LONGINES, 17J., chronog. 2 reg., tach.
14k. $2,000 $3,000 $4,500

LONGINES,17J., chronog. c.1942
s. steel. $1,200 $2,000 $3,000

LONGINES,17J., RF#6474, c.1955
s. steel. $1,500 $2,800 $3,500

LONGINES, 17 jewels, chronog., 2 reg., Telemeter Anti Magnetic,
Ca. 1940a
18k. $1,500 $2,800 $4,300

LONGINES, 17 jewels, chronog., 2 reg.
14k. $1,800 $2,800 $4,000
s. steel. $1,500 $2,800 $3,500

LONGINES, 17J., 1 button, chronog., ca. 1945
gold filled $350 $700 $900

LONGINES, 17 jewels, chronog. 1 button
14k. $1,000 $1,500 $2,500

LONGINES,17J., GJS, c.1965
18k. $175 $325 $400

LONGINES,17J., chronog., cal.539, c.1969
s. steel $300 $550 $700

LONGINES, 17J., GJS, cal.23z, c.1958
gold filled $50 $100 $165

LONGINES,17J., Valjoux 726, cal.332, c.1972
s. steel $400 $750 $850

LONGINES, 17J., GJS, cal.194, c.1963
gold filled $50 $100 $165

LONGINES, 16J., military issue, waterpr., ca. 1940s
s. steel $500 $1,000 $1,400

LONGINES,17J., GJS, cal.352, auto wind. c.1960
14k. $150 $300 $400

LONGINES,17J., GJS, cal., c.1960
14k........................ $125 $250 $300

LONGINES, 17J., GJS, cal.23z, c.1955
14k........................$150 $300 $400

LONGINES,17J., aux. seconds, Ca. 1960
gold filled $50 $100 $165

LONGINES, 17J., large lugs, GJS, c.1952
18k........................ $250 $400 $500

LONGINES,17J., Aux. seconds, gold jewel settings, automatic,
Ca. 1957
14k........................$150 $300 $400

LONGINES,17J one lug at 11 & one at 5, GJS, 1955
14k........................ $250 $450 $600

LONGINES,17J., RF#2033p GJS cal c 1958
14k $150 $300 $400

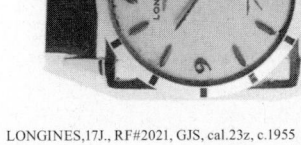

LONGINES,17J., RF#2021, GJS, cal.23z, c.1955
14k........................ $300 $550 $750

LONGINES,17J., large fluted lugs, GJS, c.1940
14k. $300 $600 $750

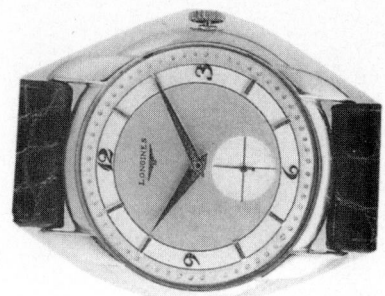

LONGINES,17J.,GJS,cal.23z,c.1954
18k. $275 $400 $600

LONGINES,17J., GJS, cal.18LN, c.1952
14k. $225 $425 $600

LONGINES, 15 jewels, c. 1940s
18k. $225 $350 $500
14k. $175 $300 $450
s. steel $100 $165 $175

LONGINES,17J., GJS, cal.22a, auto-wind, c.1958
14k. $200 $400 $600

LONGINES, 17J., fancy lugs, diamond dial,
14k. $450 $650 $850

LONGINES,17J., GJS, cal.10L, c.1952
14k. $125 $250 $350

LONGINES, 17 jewels, fancy lugs, c. 1954
14k. $300 $550 $750

LONGINES, 17 jewels, fancy lugs, c. 1949
14k. $300 $550 $750

LONGINES, 17J , center sec., GJS, c.1948
14k. $150 $300 $350

LONGINES, 19J.,Conqueat, auto-wind,
14k. $350 $650 $750

LONGINES, 17J., GJS, cal. 19as, autow., c. 1955
gold filled $50 $100 $165

LONGINES, 17J., GJS, cal.221s, c. 1950
14k. $200 $375 $525

LONGINES,17J., "Admiral" GJS, cal.340, autow., c.1960
14k. $150 $300 $400

LONGINES,17J., "Flagship", GJS, cal.340, autow., c.1960
18k. $200 $375 $500

LONGINES,17J., RF#3759, GJS, cal.22as, autow., c.1949
14k. $200 $450 $550

LONGINES, 17J., GJS, center sec., Ca. 1951
gold filled $125 $175 $250

LONGINES, 17J., center sec., GJS, cal., c. 1940
14k. $150 $300 $350

LONGINES,17J., GJS, center sec. c.1943
14k $125 $250 $300

LONGINES, 17J., military, Ca.1942
s. steel. $250 $550 $600

LONGINES, 17J., GJS, "Flagship", date, autow., c.1964
gold filled $75 $125 $200

LONGINES, 17J., 36,000 (beat), auto-wind, "Ultra-Chron"
14k. $200 $300 $400

LONGINES, 17J., Date, GJS," 5 Star Admiral", autowind,
Cal.501, Ca.1968
gold filled $100 $125 $200

LONGINES, 17J., a-wind, "5 star Admiral", date, Ca.1963
gold filled $75 $100 $175

LONGINES,17J., "5 star Admiral", cal.506, autow., c.1965
14k. $150 $275 $350

LONGINES, 17J., high frequency, date, autow., c.1972
s. steel $75 $125 $225

LONGINES, 17 jewels, "Flagship" autowind
14k. $150 $275 $400

LONGINES, 17 jewels, gold jewel settings, Ca. 1950
s. steel $75 $100 $150

LONGINES, 17 jewels, center seconds
14k. $175 $300 $400

LONGINES, 17J aux. Seconds, large lugs
14k. $175 $325 $425

LONGINES, 17J., auto wind
14k. $125 $250 $350

LONGINES, 19J., "Conquest", auto-w., date, ca. 1962
s. steel $200 $400 $500

LONGINES, 17J., "Grand Prize", auto-w., date, Ca. 1950
gold filled $75 $100 $175
14k. $200 $300 $400

LONGINES, 17J., "Conquest", auto-w., date, w.-indicator
s. steel $350 $550 $650

LONGINES, 17J., date, ca. 1940s
14k $300 $500 $600

LONGINES, 17J., mystery dial (special dial), cal.232 c.1960
gold filled $300 $400 $450

LONGINES 17J., mystery dial,
gold filled $200 $300 $500

LONGINES, 17 jewels, mystery hand, ca.1962
gold filled $200 $300 $500

LONGINES, 17 jewels, mystery hand, autowind
14k $300 $700 $900

LONGINES, 17 jewels, mystery hand, 12 diamond dial
14k $450 $800 $1,100

LONGINES, 17J., mystery 39 diamond dial, RF#1017
14k(w) $600 $1,200 $1,700

LONGINES, 17 jewels, diamond dial, center lugs
14k $700 $1,200 $1,500

LONGINES, 17J., "Ultra Chron," diamond dial, autow.
14k......................... $225 $400 $600

LONGINES, 17 jewels, 'Ultra Chron," date, autow., c. 1949
14k.........................$175 $350 $450

LONGINES, 17J., auto-w., aux. sec., special dial
14k......................... $200 $300 $500

LONGINES, 17J., auto-w., aux. sec.
14k......................... $200 $350 $500

LONGINES, 17J., aux sec.
14k......................... $200 $300 $450

LONGINES, 17J., diamond dial
14k(W) $200 $375 $550

LONGINES, 17J.,diamond bezel
gold filled $175 $250 $350

LONGINES, 17J.,3 diamond dial
gold filled $125 $200 $300

LONGINES, 17J., diamond dial,
14k(W) $200 $350 $500

LONGINES, 17 jewels, cocktail style, 36 diamond dial
14k(W) $250 $425 $575

LONGINES, 17J., 12 diamond dial, textured case
14k(w) $200 $350 $500

LONGINES,17J., GJS, 34 diamond dial, date, autow., c.1962
14k $300 $500 $700

LONGINES, 17J., 44 diamond bezel, GJS, cal.22L, c.1952
18k(w) $450 $800 $900

LONGINES,17J., 14 diamonds, GJS, cal.370, c.1960
14k $150 $325 $450

LONGINES,17J., 4 diamonds, cal.194, c.1958
gold filled $100 $200 $300

LONGINES, 17J., 37 diamonds on bezel 24 on dial, c.1958
14k(w) original factory $400 $900 $1,200

LONGINES, 17J., 14 diamond dial, Ca. 1960
14k $200 $400 $500

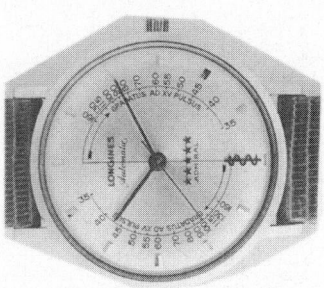

LONGINES, 17J., "Admiral", GJS, auto-wind, doctor's dial,
c. 1960
14k......................... $400 $600 $800

LONGINES, 17J., GJS, Ca. 1935-
14k (rose) $300 $500 $675

LONGINES, 17J., GJS, faceted crystal, Ca.1951
gold filled $75 $125 $200

LONGINES, 17J , GJS, cal.9L, Ca.1939
gold filled $75 $150 $200

LONGINES, 17J., 4 diamonds, GJS, cal.23z, c.1948
14k......................... $250 $400 $550

LONGINES, 17J., 5 diamonds, GJS, cal 8in, c.1940
14k(w) $150 $250 $350

LONGINES, 17J., 8 diamonds, GJS, cal.22L, c.1958
14k......................... $200 $400 $450

LONGINES, 17J.,4 diamonds, textured bezel,cal.194, c.1955
gold filled $75 $125 $175

LONGINES, 17J., 8 diamonds, GJS
14k......................... $125 $250 $300

LONGINES, 17J.,3 diamonds, hidden lugs,GJS,c.1943
gold filled $75 $125 $200

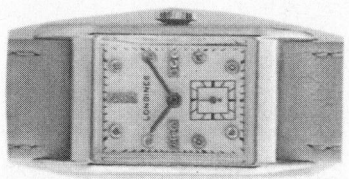

LONGINES, 17J., 17 diamonds, GJS, c.1951
14k.......................... $300 $600 $700

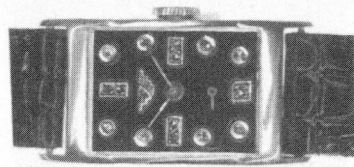

LONGINES, 17J., 15 diamonds, GJS, cal.9L, c.1945
platinum $750 $1,500 $2,000
14k.......................... $300 $650 $850

LONGINES, 17J., 18 diamonds, RF#176, GJS, c.1950
14k(w)..................... $300 $500 $700

LONGINES, 17J., 16 diamonds, cal.9LT, c.1958
14k(w)..................... $250 $500 $650

LONGINES, 17J., 4 diamonds, GJS, cal.L8474, c. 1960
gold filled $75 $125 $200

LONGINES, 17J., 6 diamonds, RF#2763, GJS, c.1955
14k..........................$175 $350 $400

LONGINES, 17J., 8 diamonds, GJS, cal.9LT, c.1958
14k(w)..................... $200 $400 $600

LONGINES, 17J., 5 diamonds, GJS, c. 1945
14k C&B.................... $600 $900 $1,200

LONGINES, 17J., 5 diamonds, GJS, cal.9L, c.1952
14k.......................... $300 $500 $600

LONGINES, 17 jewels, 17 diamond dial, c.1951
14k(w)..................... $350 $675 $800

LONGINES, 17 jewels, diamond dial, hidden lugs, c. 1938
s. steel $125 $250 $350

LONGINES, 17 jewels, fancy hidden lugs, diamond dial
14k(w) $450 $700 $1,000

LONGINES, 17jewels, diamond dial, c. 1944
14k. $350 $650 $850

LONGINES, 17 jewels, 17 diamond dial, c. 1951
14k. $250 $500 $600

LONGINES, 17 jewels, diamond dial, c. 1935
platinum $1,200 $2,000 $2,500
14k. $600 $1,200 $1,500

LONGINES, 17 jewels, 18 diamond dial
14k (w) $150 $275 $375

LONGINES, 17 jewels, flared, 6 diamond dial
14k. $500 $800 $1,200

LONGINES, 17 jewels, 4 diamond dial
14k. $175 $250 $350

LONGINES, 17 jewels, 12 diamond dial
s. steel $150 $200 $300

LONGINES, 17 jewels, stepped case, Ca. 1951
14k. $250 $400 $600

LONGINES, 17 jewels, c. 1923
gold filled $75 $125 $200

LONGINES, 17jewels, flared, c. 1959
14k. $450 $700 $1,000

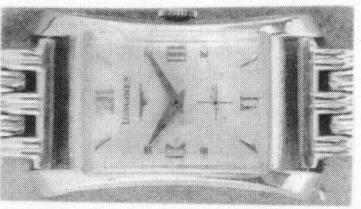

LONGINES, 17 jewels, flared
14k C&B $750 $1,200 $1,600

LONGINES, 17 jewels, fancy lugs, c. 1943
14k......................... $300 $600 $700

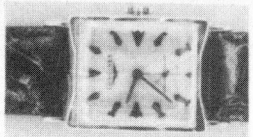

LONGINES, 17 jewels, torpedo shaped numbers
14k.........................$150 $250 $450

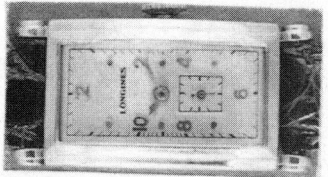

LONGINES, 17 jewels, curved, fancy lugs, c. 1939
14k......................... $300 $500 $700

LONGINES, 17 jewels, center lugs, c. 1955
14k......................... $200 $400 $600

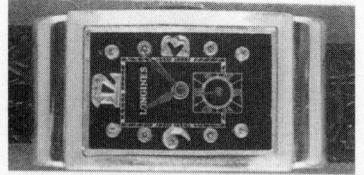

LONGINES, 17 jewels, hooded lugs, diamond dial
14k(w)..................... $600 $1,200 $1,500

LONGINES, 17 jewels, hooded lugs
14k......................... $200 $300 $450

LONGINES, 17 jewels, diamond dial, fancy lugs
14k yellow.................. $450 $800 $1,000

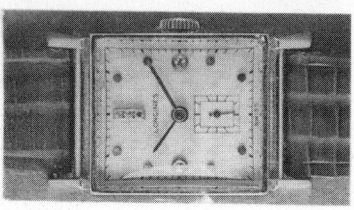

LONGINES, 17 jewels, diamond dial, c. 1944
14k.........................$175 $300 $500

LONGINES, 17 jewels, fancy lugs
14k.........................$175 $325 $400

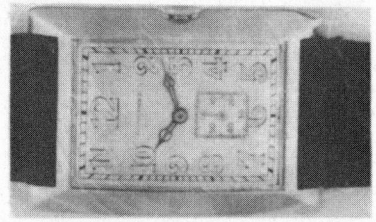

LONGINES, 17 jewels, c.1930
18k......................... $400 $600 $900
14k......................... $300 $500 $800
gold filled $100 $200 $275

LONGINES, 17J., 2 diamonds & 1 baguette, Ca. 1944
14K $600 $1,100   1,500

LONGINES, 17 jewels, diamond dial
14k(W) $300 $500 $600

LONGINES, 17J.,curved,
14k. $200 $350 $450

LONGINES, 17 J., stepped case,
14k. $300 $550 $600

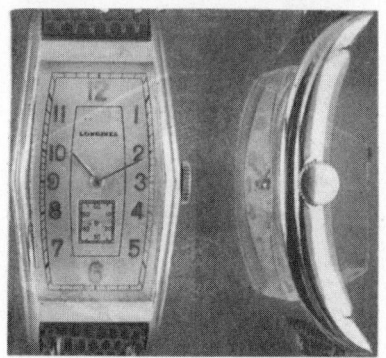

LONGINES, 17J., curvex, 52mm, ca. 1930
gold filled $200 $300 $500

LONGINES, 15J., tonneau, GIS, C. 1925
silver $150 $250 $450

LONGINES, 17J., stepped case, GJS, cal.9L, c.1939
14k. $200 $300 $450

LONGINES, 17J., **extended lugs**, GJS, cal.9L, c.1942
14k. $200 $300 $550

LONGINES, 17J., cut corner, cal.94w, c.1929
gold filled $75 $150 $200

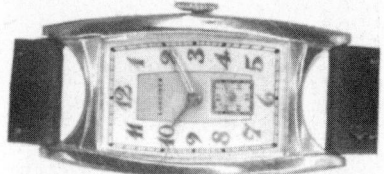

LONGINES, 17J., tonneau, cal.9L, c.1945
gold filled $125 $200 $300

LONGINES, 17J., carved bezel, GJS, cal.9LT, c 1950
gold filled $75 $125 $200

LONGINES, 17J., butler finish, GJS, cal., c.1951
gold filled $75 $125 $200

LONGINES, 17J., beveled bezel, GJS, cal., c.1935
gold filled $75 $125 $200

LONGINES, 17J., aux. sec., GJS, cal.9L, c.1948
gold filled $75 $125 $200

LONGINES, 17J., carved case, GJS, cal.9LT, c.1950s
14k. $175 $350 $500

LONGINES, 17J., butler finish, GJS, cal.9LT, c.1957
14k. $200 $375 $450

LONGINES, 15-17J., butler finish, c.1926
gold filled $75 $125 $200

LONGINES, 17J., stepped case, GJS, cal 9LT, c.1955
14k. $200 $350 $500

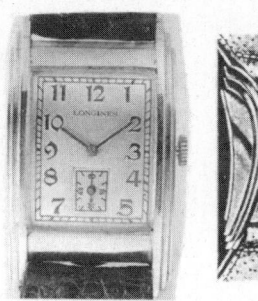

LONGINES, 17J., right angle, GJS, curved, c. 1938
gold filled $175 $300 $400
s. steel $200 $350 $450
14k. $450 $750 $1,100

LONGINES. 17J., fancy lugs, GJS, cal.9LT, c.1957
14k. $175 $300 $375

LONGINES, 17J., fluted lugs, GJS, cal.9L, C.1949
gold filled $100 $175 $300

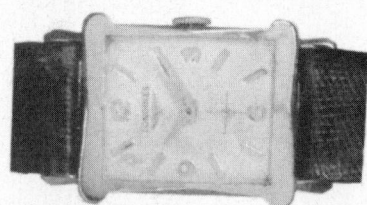

LONGINES, 17J., carved case, GJS, cal.9LT, c.1959
gold filled $100 $175 $300

LONGINES, 17J., spur lugs, GJS, cal., c 1948
gold filled $100 $175 $300

LONGINES, 17J., extended lugs, GJS, cal.9LT, c.1955
14k. $250 $450 $550

LONGINES, 17J., gold jewel settings, Ca. 1951
gold filled $75 $125 $200
14k(w) $175 $350 $400

LONGINES, 17J., fancy bezel, GJS, Ca. 1950
14k. $150 $300 $375

LONGINES, 17J., RF#1475, GJS, cal. 10L, c.1945
14k. $175 $350 $400

LONGINES. 17J., fluted sides, GJS, cal.9LT, c.1950
gold filled $100 $150 $275

LONGINES, 17J., GJS, c.1955
14k. $175 $350 $400

LONGINES, 17J., carved case, GJS, cal.9LT, c.1955
14k. $225 $400 $550

LONGINES, 17J., RF#3327, GJS, cal.10L c.1948
gold filled $75 $125 $250

LONGINES, 17J., flared case, GJS, Ca. 1956
14K $200 $400 $525

LONGINES, 17J., extended lugs, GJS, cal.9LT, c.1951
14k. $200 $400 $500

LONGINES, 17J., aux. sec., GJS, Ca.1951
14k. $175 $300 $400

LONGINES, 17J., butler finish, GJS, cal.9L, c.1955
14k. $175 $350 $400

LONGINES, 17J., aux. sec., GJS, cal.9LT, c.1950
14k. $175 $300 $400

LONGINES, 17J., butler finish, GJS, cal.8LN, c. 1942
14k. $150 $250 $375

LONGINES, 17J., beveled lugs, GJS, cal.8LN, c.1947
14k. $150 $250 $375

LONGINES, 17J., wide bezel, GJS, cal.23z, c.1950
gold filled $75 $125 $200

LONGINES, 17J., GJS, cal.23z, c.1957
14k. $175 $300 $400

LONGINES, 17J., fancy lugs, GJS, cal.10L, c.1951
gold filled $75 $125 $200

LONGINES, 17J., GJS, cal. 23Z, Ca. 1950
gold filled $100 $150 $225

LONGINES, 17J., beveled case, GJS, cal.9LT, c.1955
gold filled $75 $125 $200

DIALS FOR MINT PRICES MUST BE ALL ORIGINAL.

LONGINES, 17J., curly lugs, GJS, cal.23z, c.1950
gold filled $100 $150 $225

LONGINES, 17J., stepped case, GJS, cal.23z., c.1955
14k. $200 $300 $450
gold filled $75 $125 $200

LONGINES, 17J., checked dial, GJS, cal.22L, c.1957
14k. $175 $300 $375

LONGINES, 17J., carved case, GJS,
gold filled $75 $125 $200

LONGINES, 17J., RF#1050, mystery dial, cal.23z, c.1960
14k. $300 $500 $650

LONGINES, 17J., hooded lugs, GJS, cal.8LN, c.1942
gold filled $75 $125 $200

LONGINES, 17J., center seconds, GJS, hidden lugs, Ca.1942
14k (rose) $175 $300 $375

LONGINES, 17J., RF#2255, hidden lugs, GJS, c.1955
14k. $250 $500 $700

LONGINES, 17J., textured bezel, GJS, cal.22L, c.1950
14k. $250 $500 $750

LONGINES, 17J., hidden lugs. assymetrical case
14k (rose) $400 $750 $1,000

LONGINES, 17J., contract case or recent case,
14k. $150 $300 $400

LONGINES, 17 jewels, 42mm
14k(w). $250 $400 $550

LONGINES, 17 jewels, **hinged** lugs
14k. $200 $400 $600

LONGINES, 17 jewels, Ca. 1939
14k. $175 $300 $500

LONGINES, 17 jewels, curvex, slanted lugs
14k(w). $150 $300 $400

LONGINES, 17 jewels, fancy lugs, c. 1942
14k. $250 $500 $700

LONGINES, 17 jewels, fancy U shaped lugs, c. 1947
14k. $250 $475 $600

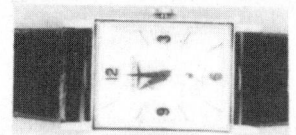

LONGINES, 17 jewels, curved, flared
14k. $150 $225 $300

LONGINES, 15 jewels, chased bezel
14k. $500 $1,000 $1,400

LONGINES, 15 jewels, engraved bezel, c. 1928
14k(w). $600 $1,500 $1,700

LONGINES, 17J., faceted crystal, center seconds
14k. $175 $300 $400

LONGINES, 17J., fancy lugs & diamond bezel
14k(W) $400 $775 $1,000

LONGINES, 17J., curved case, Ca. 1930s
14k. $250 $475 $625

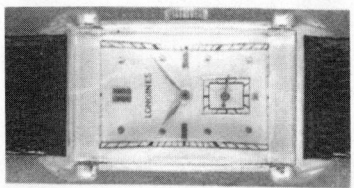

LONGINES, 17J., fancy lugs
14k. $275 $450 $650

LONGINES, 17J., fancy lugs,
14k. $250 $400 $575

LONGINES, 17J., cal#232, ca. 1948
14k. $150 $300 $400

LONGINES, 17J., aux. sec.
14k. $150 $275 $400

LONGINES, 17J., ca. 1952
14k. $200 $300 $500

LONGINES, 17J., cal#10L, center sec.,
14k. $250 $350 $550

LONGINES, 17J., center sec., fancy lugs, ca.1946
14k. $200 $300 $500

LONGINES, 17J., fancy lugs, cal#10L
14k. $200 $300 $500

LONGINES, 17J., aux. sec.
14k. $175 $300 $400

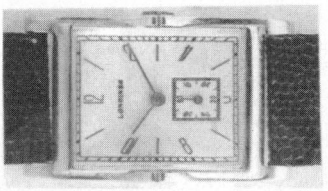

LONGINES, 17J., offset lugs
14k. $250 $500 $650

LONGINES, 17J., fancy lugs, ca. 1951
14k. $200 $375 $425

LONGINES, 17J., fancy bezel
14k. $150 $250 $375

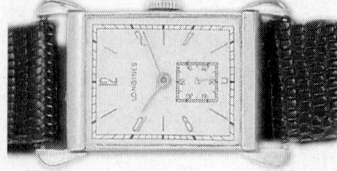

LONGINES, 17J., **flared case**, GJS, c. 1955
gold filled $150 $250 $350

LONGINES, fancy lugs, c. 1945
gold filled $200 $375 $500

LONGINES, 17J., flared case, textured dial
14k $300 $600 $850

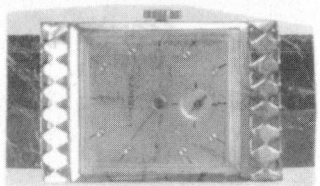

LONGINES, 17J., hidden lugs, Ca. 1940
14k(rose). $300 $400 $700

LONGINES, 17 jewels, **enameled** bezel, c. 1928
14k. $400 $700 $1,000

LONGINES, 17 jewels, formed case
14k. $300 $600 $650

LONGINES, 17J., antimagnetic, military
s. steel $300 $500 $800

LONGINES MOVEMENT IDENTIFICATION

Cal. No. 4.21, Ca.1930

Cal. No. 5.16, Ca.1922

Cal. No. 6.22, Ca.1932

Cal. No. 7.45, Ca.1916

Cal. No. 7.48, Ca.1925

Cal. No. 8.23, Ca.1931

Cal. No. 8.47, Ca.1916

Cal. No. 9.32, Ca.1932

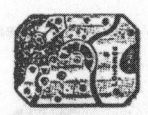
Cal. No. 9.47, Ca.1922

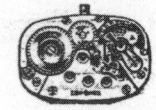
Cal. No. 12.19, Ca.1934

Cal. No. 13.15, Ca.1936

Cal. No. 25.17, Ca.1935

LONGINES date of movement manufacture

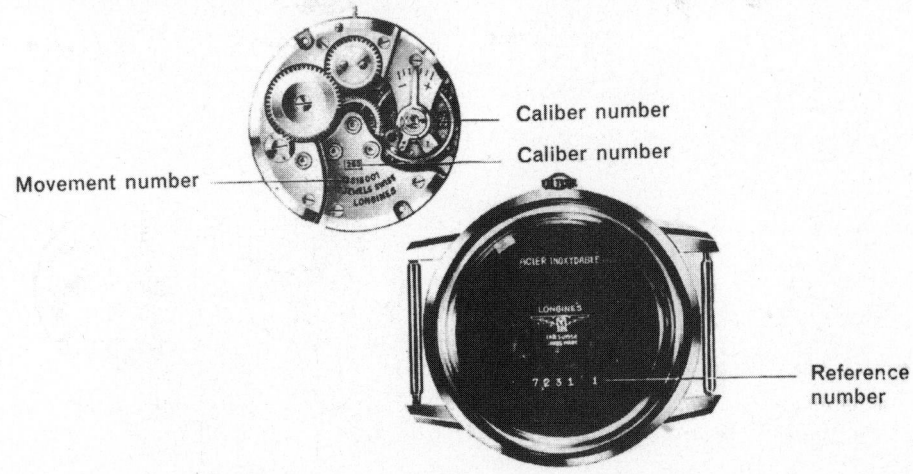

Caliber number

Caliber number

Movement number

Reference number

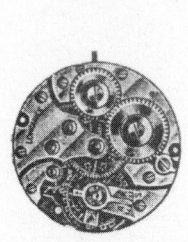
Cal. No. 10.68, Ca.1932

Cal. No. 10.68, Lindburg

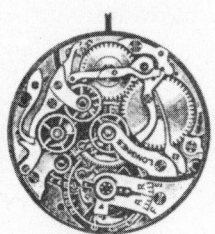
Cal. No. 12.68, Ca.1938

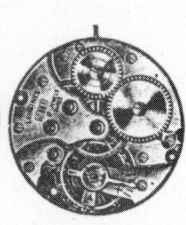
Cal. No. 12.68 Z, Ca.1939

Cal. No. 14.16, Ca.1951

Cal. No. 14.16 S, Ca.1954

Cal. No. 14.17, Ca.1952

Cal. No. 15.18, Ca.1941

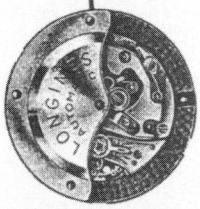
Cal. No. 19 A, Ca.1952

Cal. No. 19.4, Ca.1953

Cal. No. 19.4 S, Ca.1953

Cal. No. 22 A, Ca.1945

Cal. No. 22 L, Ca.1946

Cal. No. 23 Z, Ca.1948

Cal. No. 23 ZD, Ca.1954

Cal. No. 25.17, Ca.1935

Cal. No. RR 280, Ca.1963

Cal. No. 290, Ca.1958

Cal. No. 310

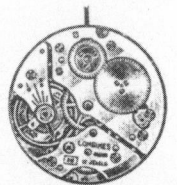
Cal. No. 312

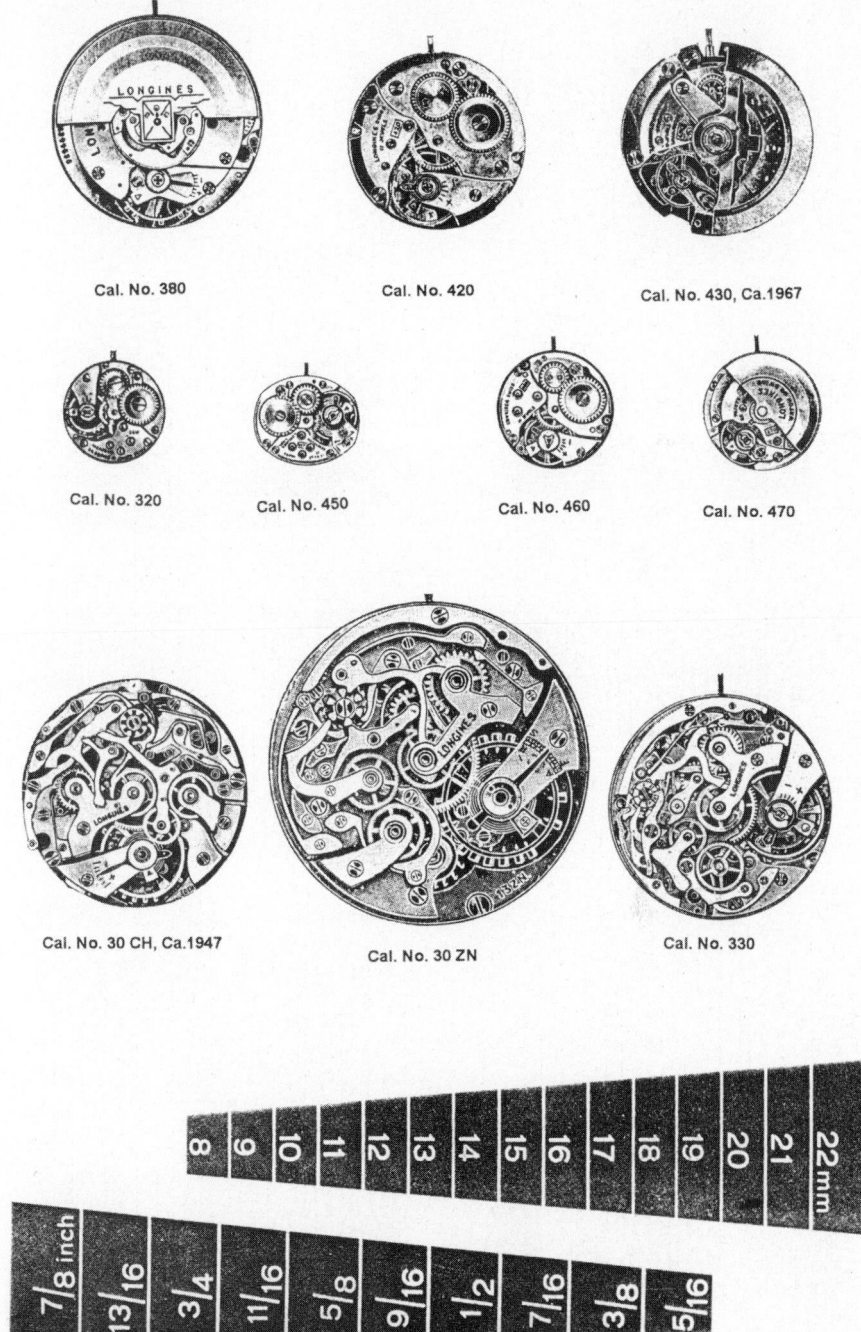

Cal. No. 380

Cal. No. 420

Cal. No. 430, Ca.1967

Cal. No. 320

Cal. No. 450

Cal. No. 460

Cal. No. 470

Cal. No. 30 CH, Ca.1947

Cal. No. 30 ZN

Cal. No. 330

To determine your Wrist watch band size use the above gauge and measure between the lugs.

LONGINES, 17J., "COMET", cal.702, c.1972
s. steel $175 $325 $400

LONGINES, 17J., lady's style, center lugs, c.1948
14k C & B $175 $300 $400

LONGINES, 15J., lady's style,
14k C & B $175 $275 $375

LONGINES, 15-17J., **ring watch** lady's style, Ca. 1949
14k. $175 $300 $350

LORTON, 17 jewels, chronog., c. 1950
s. steel $200 $350 $400

LOUVIC, 17J., mystery dial, long triangular case, c. 1950
base metal. $60 $125 $200

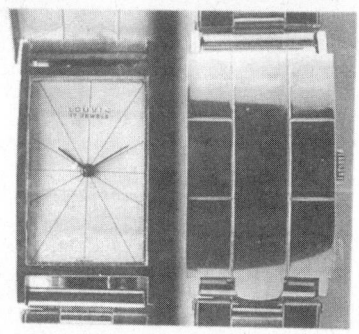

LOUVIC, 17J., hunter style case, Ca. 1965
s. steel $75 $150 $200

LOUVIC, 17J., mystery diamond dial, ca. 1960
s. steel $200 $400 $500

LUCERNE, 17 jewels, 14k case & band, 3 diamonds
14k C & B $200 $350 $450

LUCIEN PICCARD, 17J., movement by Ditisheim
14k ladies $100 $200 $300

LUCIEN PICCARD, 17 jewels, gem set bezel
14k. $200 $400 $600

LUSINA, 17 jewels, aux. sec., fancy lugs
gold filled $60 $100 $150

LUCIEN PICCARD, 17 jewels, "Seahawk," auto wind
18k C & B $600 $950 $1,100

LYCEUM, 17J., beveled case, aux. sec.
14k. $100 $200 $275

LUCIEN PICCARD, 17J., auto wind, wind indicator, c. 1958
s. steel $75 $150 $200

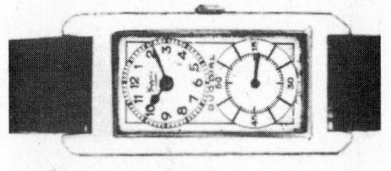

MAPPIN, 15 jewels, duo dial, c. 1930
9k $600 $1,000 $1,200

LUCIEN PICCARD, 17 jewels, skeletonized
18k. $300 $600 $700

MARLYS, 15J., GJS., c.1935
14k. $125 $250 $300

☞ Some grades are not included. Their values can be determined by comparing with **similar** age, size, metal content, style, grades, or models such as **time only**,chronograph, repeater etc. listed.

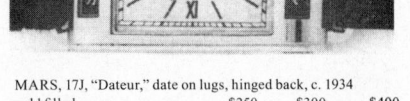

MARS, 17J, "Dateur," date on lugs, hinged back, c. 1934
gold filled $250 $300 $400

MARVIN, 17J., center sec., cal.520s, c. 1943
14k. $100 $200 $275

MARVIN, 17J., non magnetic,
gold filled $50 $65 $100

MARVIN, 17J., c.1943
base metal. $50 $100 $150

MASTER, 17J., tonneau case, c.1943
gold plate $30 $75 $100

MASTER, 17J., stepped case,
gold plate $30 $75 $100

C. H. MEYLAN, 17 jewels, c. 1940s
18k. $200 $400 $600

C. H. MEYLAN, 18 jewels, **jump** hr, c 1920
18k. $3,000 $5,000 $7,000

C. H. MEYLAN, 16 jewels, wire lugs
14k. $225 $475 $600

C. H. MEYLAN, 27J, 1 button chronog., 2 reg., enamel dial
18k. $2,750 $4,250 $5,000

C. H. MEYLAN, 18J., ladies , Octagon case, c.1917
platinum $300 $500 $600

DIALS FOR MINT PRICES MUST BE ALL ORIGINAL.

J. E. MEYLAN, 17J., chronograph, 2 reg., ca. 1937
14k. $600 $1,100 $1,300
s. steel $300 $550 $650

J. E. MEYLAN,17J., stop watch,
s. steel $175 $350 $400

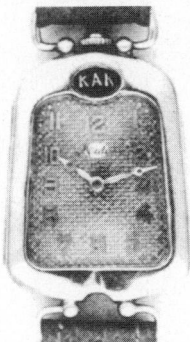

MIDO, 15J., "KAR", in form of car radiator, Ca. 1930s
Note: winds at 12
silver $1,500 $2,500 $3,200

MIDO, 17 jewels, chronog., "Multi-centerchrono", c. 1952
s. steel $350 $500 $700

MIDO, 17 jewels, chronog., "Multi-centerchrono"
s. steel $400 $600 $800
with telemeter dial $500 $700 $900

MIDO, 17J., choronog., Pulsations, cal.1300, c.1954
gold filled $400 $800 $1,000
14k. $600 $1,000 $1,200
18k. $700 $1,200 $1,400

MIDO, 15J., "DIRECT-TIME", Jump hour, Ca. 1932
14k (w) $500 $1,000 $1,500
18k (w) $600 $1,200 $2,000
s. steel $350 $700 $1,000

MIDO, 17J., carved case, cal.2m, c. 1947
14k. $150 $300 $350

DIALS FOR MINT PRICES MUST BE ALL ORIGINAL.

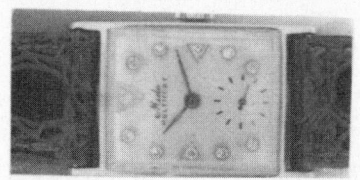

MIDO, 17 jewels, diamond dial
s. steel $100 $150 $200
14k. $175 $300 $400
platinum $300 $600 $800

MIDO, 17J., **"Radiotime"**, to correct time push button on crown advances minutes & seconds hand, Ca. 1939
gold filled . . . . ★★$500 $800 $1,000

MIDO, 17 jewels, fancy lugs, c. 1945
14k. $150 $300 $350

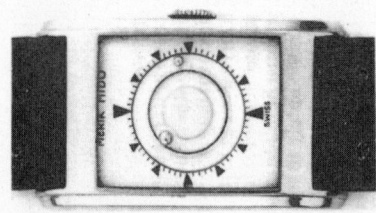

MIDO, 15 jewels, mystery dial, c. 1935
s. steel $500 $800 $1,100

MIDO, 17J., multifort grand luxe, autow., date, ca. 1950s
18k C & B $500 $900 $1,100

MIDO, 17J., RF#7204, cal.d917b, autow., date, c.1958
s. steel $100 $200 $250

MIDO, 17J., RF#228, **mid size** case, autow., c.1943
s. steel $75 $150 $200

MIDO, 17J., autowind, Ca. 1958
s. steel $100 $175 $225

MIDO, 17J., **mid size** case, cal.917r, autow., c.1949
s. steel $75 $150 $200

☞ Some grades are not included. Their values can be determined by comparing with similar age, size, metal content, style, grades, or models such as time only, chronograph, repeater etc. listed.

MIDO, 17J., super auto-wind, muiltfort extra,
14k. $135 $250 $325
s. steel $75 $150 $200

MIDO, 17J., "Power Wind", c.1955
s. steel $75 $150 $200

MIDO, 17J., rotating bezel, autow., c.1960
s. steel $195 $300 $400

MIDO, 17J., multifort grand luxe, extra-flat
s. steel $100 $150 $225

MILDIA, 17 jewels
s. steel $30 $60 $100

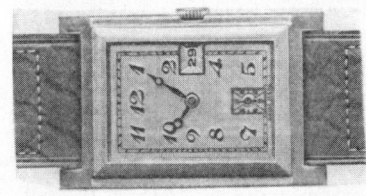

MIMO, 15 jewels, date
gold filled $100 $200 $300

MIMO, 17J., "De Frece", **date**, c.1935
14k(w) $150 $250 $350

MIMO, 17 jewels, Jumping hr., wandering min. & sec.
gold filled $300 $400 $600

MIMO, 17 jewels, 8 day, 6 gear train, c. 1950s
gold filled $400 $550 $750

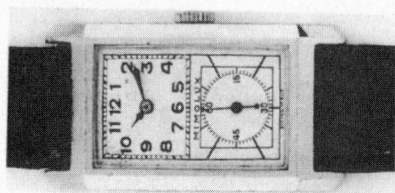

MIMO, 17 jewels, duo dial, doctors watch
s. steel $500 $750 $1,000

MIMO, 15 jewels, engraved bezel
gold filled $35 $75 $100

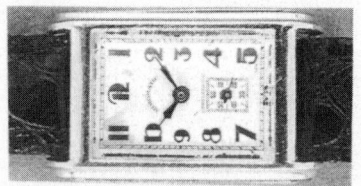

MIMO, 15 jewels, "Mimomatic," c. 1932
s. steel $100 $125 $200

MINERVA, 29J., **min. repeater,** repeats on 2 gongs
18k. $10,000 $14,000 $20,000

MINERVA, 17 jewels, chronog., 2 reg. telemeter km
18k. $700 $1,200 $1,400
s. steel $275 $400 $500

MINERVA, 17 jewels, one button chronog., 2 reg., enamel dial,
Ca. 1920
gold $500 $800 $1,000

MINERVA, 17 jewels, waterproof, chronog., c. 1950s
14k. $400 $700 $900
s. steel $250 $450 $600

MINERVA, 17J., 3 reg. chronog., Valjoux cal.723, c.1955
14k. $750 $1,100 $1,350
s. steel $500 $800 $1,000

MINERVA, 19jewels, chronog., 3 reg.
s. steel $300 $500 $600

Watches listed in this book as "Misc. Swiss" are just a few examples of miscellaneous jobbers, distributors & jewelry firms. Ex: Abc Watch Co., to Zuma Watch Co., etc. with the name xxxx out.

MINERVA, 17 jewels, one button chronog., c. 1942
s. steel $250 $400 $500

MISC. SWISS, 15J., shield cover, enamel dial, ca. 1927
silver $500 $700 $850

MINERVA, 17J., chronog., day-date-month, 3 reg.
18k. $800 $1,300 $1,500

MISC. SWISS,15J., **rim wind, wire lugs**, cal., c.1920
s. steel *$250 $400 $500

MINERVA, 17 jewels, center sec., auto wind
gold filled $40 $75 $100

MISC. SWISS,15J., mother of pearl dial, c.1925
s. steel $100 $200 $275

MISC. SWISS, 15J., **wire lugs, exaggerated** nos, c. 1925
silver $150 $300 $400

☞ Some grades are not included. Their values can be determined by comparing with **similar** age, size, metal content, style, grades, or models such as **time only**, with chronograph, repeater etc. listed.

MISC. SWISS, 15J., hunter style, wire lugs, ca 1926
silver $350 $600 $750

MISC. SWISS, 15J., wire lugs, Ca. 1918
silver $80 $150 $200

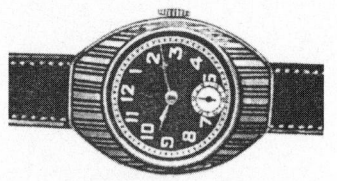

MISC. SWISS, 15J., wire lugs, Ca. 1918
silver $80 $135 $175

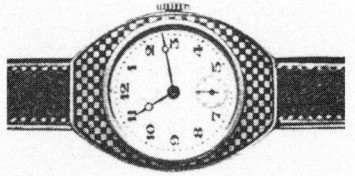

MISC. SWISS, 15J., wire lugs, Ca. 1917
base metal $40 $75 $100

MISC. SWISS, 15J., wire lugs, Ca. 1917
silver $75 $125 $175

MISC. SWISS, 15J., wire lugs, Ca 1917
base metal $40 $75 $100

Watches listed in this book as Misc. Swiss are just a few examples
of miscellaneous jobbers, distributors & jewelry firms. Example
Abc Watch Co., so Zuma Watch Co., etc. with the name xxxx out.

MISC. SWISS, 15J., wire lugs, Ca. 1917
silver $50 $100 $125

MISC. SWISS, 15J., wire lugs, Ca. 1917
silver $75 $125 $165

MISC. SWISS, 15J., wire lugs, Ca. 1917
silver $75 $125 $165

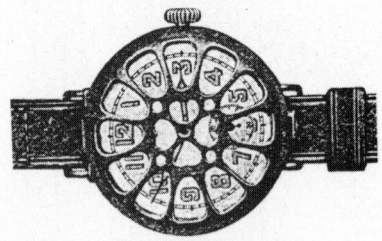

MISC. SWISS, 15J., protective grill, wire lugs, Ca. 1917
silver $175 $300 $400

MISC. SWISS, 15J., wire lugs, Demi Hunter style, Ca. 1919
base metal $40 $75 $100

MISC. SWISS, 15J., wire lugs, Ca. 1917
silver $50 $100 $125

MISC. SWISS, 15J., wire lugs, Ca. 1917
14K $65 $110 $150

MISC. SWISS, 15J., wire lugs, Ca. 1917
14K $70 $150 $200

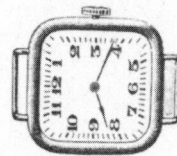

MISC. SWISS, 15J., wire lugs, Ca. 1917
14K $70 $125 $165

MISC. SWISS, 15J., wire lugs, Ca. 1917
14K $70 $125 $165

MISC. SWISS, 15J., wire lugs, Ca. 1917
14K $70 $125 $165

Watches listed in this BOOK as Misc. Swiss are just a few examples of miscellaneous jobbers, distributors & jewelry firms. Example Abc Watch Co., to Zuma Watch Co., etc. with the name xxxx out.

MISC. SWISS, 15J., wire lugs, Ca. 1917
14k. $70 $125 $165

MISC. SWISS, 15J., wire lugs, Ca. 1917
14K $75 $125 $165

MISC. SWISS, 1SJ., horseshoe style, Ca. 1935
base metal $65 $135 $200

MISC. SWISS, 17J., nail set, 31 X 52mm, **exaggerated** nos., ca.1915
18k. $1,200 $2,200 $3,000

MISC. SWISS, 1SJ., exaggerated no.s, 42mm, ca.1916
silver $500 $800 $1,000

MISC. SWISS, 15J., exaggerated no.s, 40mm. Ca.1916
18K $1,100 $2,000 $2,500

MISC. SWISS, 15J., exaggerated no.s, 40mm. Ca. 1916
18K $1,100 $2,200 $3,000

MISC. SWISS, 15J., exaggerated no.s, 35mm. Ca. 1920
14K $500 $1,000 $1,200

MISC. SWISS, 15J., exaggerated no.s, 40mm. Ca. 1916
18K $1,100 $1,500 $2,000

MISC. SWISS, 15J. , exaggerated no.s, wire lugs, Ca 1916
14K $175 $350 $400

Watches listed is this BOOK as Misc. Swiss are just a few examples
of miscellaneous jobbers, distributors & jewelry firms. Example
Abe Watch Co., to Zuma Watch Co., etc. with the same xxxx out.

MISC. SWISS, 15J., exaggerated no.s, 35mm. Ca.1916
18K $450 $800 $1,200

MISC. SWISS, 15J., exaggerated no.s, 40mm. Ca.1916
18K $1,600 $2,500 $3,500

MISC. SWISS, 15J., exaggerated no.s, wire lugs, Ca. 1916
silver $100 $200 $250

MISC. SWISS, 15J., exaggerated no.s, wire lugs, Ca.1916
silver $125 $200 $300

MISC. SWISS, 15J., exaggerated no.s, 28mm. Ca.1916
silver $85 $150 $200

MISC. SWISS, 15J., wire lugs, Ca. 1917
silver $70 $125 $175

MISC. SWISS, 15J., wire lugs, Ca. 1917
silver $135 $200 $225

MISC. SWISS, 15J., wire lugs, Ca.1917
silver $135 $200 $225

MISC. SWISS, 15J., wire lugs, Ca.1917
14k. $150 $300 $400

MISC. SWISS, 15J., Ca. 1925
14K $150 $275 $325

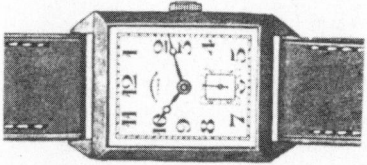

MISC. SWISS, 15J., Ca. 1925
14K $150 $300 $350

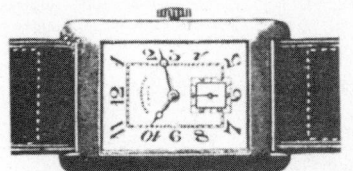

MISC. SWISS, 15J., Ca.1925
14K $150 $300 $350

MISC. SWISS, 15J., Ca. 1925
14K $150 $300 $350

MISC. SWISS, 15J., Ca. 1925
14K $150 $300 $350

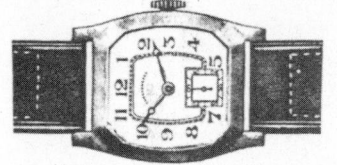

MISC. SWISS, 15J., Ca.1925
14K $150 $300 $350

MISC. SWISS, 15J., Ca.1925
14K $150 $300 $350

☞ A collector should expect to pay modestly higher prices at local shops.

Wrist Watches listed in this section are priced as complete watches having an original gold-filled case and stainless steel back, also with original dial, leather watch band, and the entire original movement in good working order with no repairs needed.

Watches listed in this BOOK as Misc. Swiss are just a few examples of miscellaneous jobbers, distributors & jewelry firms. Example Abe Watch Co., to Zuma Watch Co., etc. with the name xxxx out.

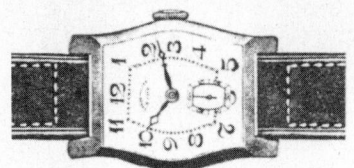

MISC. SWISS, 15J., Ca. 1925
14K $150 $300 $350

MISC. SWISS, 15J., Ca. 1925
14K $135 $250 $300

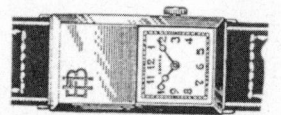

MISC. SWISS, 15J., Ca.1930
14K $200 $325 $400

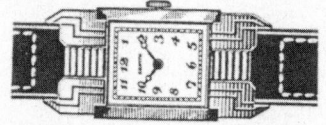

MISC. SWISS, 15J., Ca. 1930
18K $175 $325 $400

MISC. SWISS, 15J., Ca.1930
18K $175 $300 $375

MISC. SWISS, 15J., Ca.1930
18K $175 $325 $400

MISC. SWISS, 15J., Ca.1930
18K $175 $325 $400

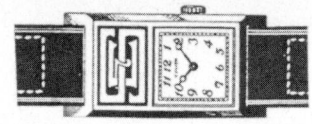

MISC. SWISS, 15J., Ca.1930
14K $150 $275 $300

MISC. SWISS, 15J, Ca 1930
18K $175 $325 $400

MISC. SWISS, 15J., Ca.1930
18K $125 $200 $275

MISC. SWISS, 15J., flex lugs, Ca. 1930
18K $175 $300 $375

MISC. SWISS, 15J., aux. sec., ca. 1930s
gold filled $75 $125 $200

☞ Some grades are not Included. Their values can be determined by comparing with **similar** age, size, metal content, style, grades, or models such as **time only**, chronograph, repeater etc. listed.

MISC. SWISS, 15J., enamel dial, wire lugs, ca. 1925
silver...................... $100 $200 $300
14K $800 $1,400 $1,800

MISC. SWISS, 15J., wire lugs, nail set, ca. 1925
silver........................ $125 $200 $300

MISC. SWISS, 17 jewels, hunter, "Flip up"
gold filled $200 $375 $450

MISC. SWISS, 15 jewels, "Flip open" Ca. 1930
gold filled $200 $350 $450

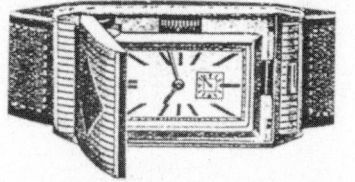

MISC. SWISS, 17J, Flip Top **winds by opening lid**, Ca. 1932
gold filled $400 $800 $900
base metal.................... $300 $600 $700

MISC. SWISS, 17J., case flips up to view photo, c.1950
gold filled $150 $275 $335

MISC. SWISS, 17J., day date month moon phase, Ca. 1955
gold filled $500 $850 $1,000
14k $1,400 $2,000 $2,500

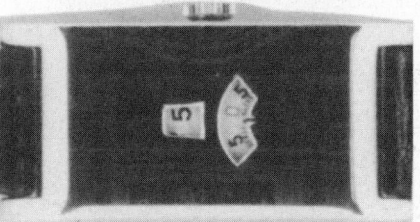

MISC. SWISS, 17J., jump hr., wandering min., c. 1930
9k $350 $700 $900
14k......................... $500 $1,000 $1,200

MISC. SWISS, 17J., wandering min., hr. by red mark
s. steel $150 $300 $350

MISC. SWISS, 17 jewels, fancy bezel
14k........................... $125 $200 $250
18k........................... $175 $250 $300

MISC. SWISS. 17 jewels, masonic symbols, c. 1950s
s. steel & gold filled $900 $1,200 $1,500

MISC. SWISS, 17 jewels, masonic symbols, c. 1975
base metal $500 $850 $1,200

MISC. SWISS, 15 jewels, early auto wind, c. 1930s
s. steel $300 $500 $650

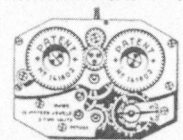

(note tandem wind)
(see watch below for prices)
MISC. SWISS, 15J, 2 barrels, 8 day movement , (8 HOURS)

MISC. SWISS, 15 jewels, **2 barrels, 8 day watch**, Ca. 1935
base metal $150 $250 $350
s. steel $175 $325 $400
silver $300 $550 $650

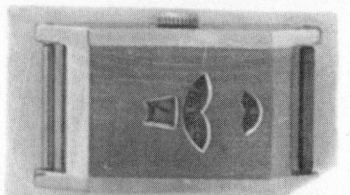

MISC. SWISS, 17 jewels, digital hr., min.& sec.
s. steel $200 $400 $500
gold filled $200 $400 $500
s. steel (8 day) . . . .★$300 $500 $700

MISC. SWISS, 15 jewels, **double dial**, c.1935
9K $375 $600 $900

MISC. SWISS, 15 jewels, Center lugs, c.1936
9K $100 $200 $300

MISC. SWISS, 17J, drivers style winds at 12, Ca. 1930
gold filled $150 $200 $300

MISC. SWISS, 7J, Corvette or Mercedes Benz, c.1970
base metal $100 $175 $275

MISC. SWISS, 29J, repeater, 2 jacquemart, **all original**
18k. $3,000 $5,500 $7,000

Watches listed in this BOOK as Misc. Swiss are just a few examples of miscellaneous jobbers, distributors & jewelry firms. Example Abe Watch Co., to Zuma Watch Co., etc. with the name xxxx out.

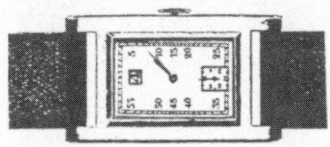

MISC. SWISS, 17J., jump hour at 12:00, Ca. 1930
14k. $700 $1,200 $1,800
18K $900 $1,400 $2,000

MISC. SWISS, 17J., silver coin, Ca. 1960
silver. $100 $300 $450

MISC. SWISS, 15J., one button chronog. wind and sets as 12,
center hinged lugs, enamel dial, c.1920s
silver $1,000 $1,800 $2,400

MISC. SWISS, 17J., world time, date, Ca. 1965
s. steel $75 $150 $200

MISC. SWISS,15J., 1 button chronog., enamel dial, wire lugs,
Ca.1923
silver. $800 $1,200 $1,800

MISC. SWISS, 2J., perpetual calendar, Ca. 1970
base metal. $110 $175 $250

MISC. SWISS, 15-17J., enamel dial, 1 button chronog.
s. steel $700 $900 $1,200

MISC. SWISS, 17J.,early 1 button chronog., ca.1929
18k. $1,000 $1,800 $2,500

MISC. SWISS, 15J., one button chronog., ca. 1925
silver. $650 $1,200 $1,600

MISC. SWISS,15-17J., **enamel dial**, 1 button chronog., 2reg.
s. steel. $600 $1,000 $1,500

MISC. SWISS, 17J., one button, chronog., ca. 1950
gold filled $300 $550 $700

MISC. SWISS, 17J., 2 reg., chronograph
s. steel. $150 $300 $350

MISC. SWISS, 17J, chronog., 2 reg.
gold filled $175 $300 $375

MISC. SWISS,17J., "chronographe" on dial, c.1940
base metal. $150 $300 $375

MISC. SWISS,17J., by Venus
s. steel. $150 $275 $350
14k. $200 $400 $500
18K $300 $500 $600

Watches listed is this BOOK as Misc. Swiss are just a few examples
of miscellaneous jobbers, distributors & jewelry firms. Example
Abc Watch Co., to Zuma Watch Co., etc. with the name xxxx out.

MISC. SWISS, 17J., triple date, chronog., 2 reg., c.1955
s. steel $350 $650 $800

MISC. SWISS, 17J., chronog., triple date, moon ph., c. 1945
14k. $900 $1,300 $1,700
s. steel $500 $900 $1,200

MISC. SWISS, 17 jewels, **split sec**. chronog., 2 reg.
18k. $2,000 $3,500 $5,000
s. steel $2,200 $2,200 $2,600

MISC. SWISS, 18 jewels, **Jaeger, chronog.**, c. 1930s
18k. $400 $800 $1,000

MISC. SWISS, 17J., **triple date, moon ph.**, ca. 1967
gold filled $275 $500 $700

MISC. SWISS, 17 jewels, **early auto wind**, Ca. 1930
14k. $250 $500 $600

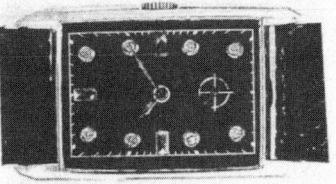

MISC. SWISS, 17J., **diamond dial**, Ca. 1945
14K $300 $600 $700

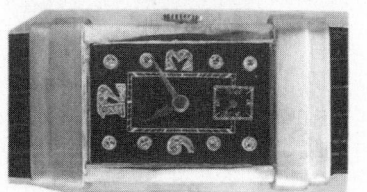

MISC. SWISS, 17J., diamond dial, **top hat**, Ca. 1945
platinum $800 $1,600 $1,800

MISC. SWISS, 17J., **mystery diamond dial**, Ca. 1960
gold filled $150 $300 $400

MISC. SWISS, 17J., Rhinestone dial & bezel, Ca. 1950
gold filled $75 $150 $225

MISC. SWISS, 17J., fancy bezel, Ca. 1938
14K $150 $300 $400

MISC. SWISS, 17J., Rhinestone dial & bezel, Ca. 1950
gold filled $75 $125 $200

MISC. SWISS, 17J., fancy bezel, Ca. 1947
gold filled $85 $125 $165
14K $165 $325 $400

MISC. SWISS, 17J., hidden lugs, Ca. 1934
gold filled $50 $100 $125

MISC. SWISS, 17J., fancy bezel, Ca. 1930
18K(W). $350 $650 $800

MISC. SWISS, 17J., fancy lugs, Ca. 1945
14k. $185 $400 $500
18K $235 $500 $700

MISC. SWISS, 7J., stepped case, Ca. 1935
gold filled $50 $100 $175

MISC. SWISS, 17J., fancy lugs, Ca 1940
gold filled $50 $100 $125

Watches listed in this BOOK as Misc. Swiss are just a few examples
of miscellaneous jobbers, distributors & jewelry firms. Example
Abc Watch Co., to Zuma Watch Co., etc. with the name xxxx out.

MISC. SWISS, 17J., **wandering minute & hour**, Ca. 1938
base metal. $150 $300 $400

MISC. SWISS, 15J., Ca. 1938
14K $200 $400 $475

MISC. SWISS, 15J., Ca. 1925
silver $85 $150 $200

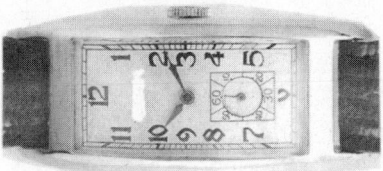

MISC. SWISS, 21J., curved, Ca. 1938
gold filled $125 $250 $300

MISC. SWISS, 17J., Fancy lugs, Chronometer, Ca. 1950
14K $185 $325 $375

MISC. SWISS, 17J., Fancy lugs & bezel, Ca. 1950
gold filled $100 $175 $225

Watches listed in this BOOK as Misc. Swiss are just a few examples of miscellaneous jobbers, distributors & jewelry firms. Example Abc Watch Co., to Zuma Watch Co., etc. with the name xxxx out.

MISC. SWISS, 17J., Fancy lugs, Ca. 1950
gold filled $125 $250 $300

MISC. SWISS, 17J., Fancy lugs, Ca. 1950
14K $185 $325 $400

MISC. SWISS, 21J., Fancy lugs, Ca 1955
18K $225 $400 $450

MISC. SWISS, 17J., Fancy lugs, Ca. 1948
gold filled $75 $150 $175

☞ Some grades are not included. Their values can be determined by comparing with similar age, size, metal content, style, grades, or models such as time only, chronograph, repeater etc. listed.

MISC. SWISS, 17J., enamel & gold bezel, pin set, c.1925
18k $185 $300 $350

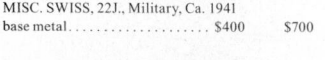

MISC. SWISS, 22J., Military, Ca. 1941
base metal $400 $700 $800

MISC. SWISS, 15J., wire lugs, Ca. 1930
14K rose $75 $150 $175

MISC. SWISS, 15J, Ruby on case, Ca 1950
14K $75 $150 $175

MISC. SWISS, 15J, Military, Ca. 1942
s. steel $75 $150 $175

MISC. SWISS, 15J., Ca. 1930
14K case & band $225 $400 $500

MISC. SWISS, 15J., **Ring watch**, Ca 1955
14K $100 $200 $225

MISC. SWISS, 16J., Military, Ca. 1940
Base metal $75 $150 $175

Watches listed is this BOOK as Misc. Swiss are just a few examples of miscellaneous jobbers, distributors & jewelry firms.
Example Abc Watch Co , so Zuma Watch Co, etc. with the name
xxxx out.

MISC. SWISS, 21J., horseshoe shaped, Ca. 1939
gold filled $125 $250 $300

MONARCH, 7 jewels, stepped case
gold filled $60 $110 $140

MONTE, 16J., "Ancre", ca.1938
14k. $200 $400 $500

MONARCH, 7 jewels,
gold filled $60 $110 $140

MONARCH, 7 jewels, engraved bezel, curved
gold filled $70 $140 $175

MORIVA, 17J., auto-w. with wind indicator,
s. steel $75 $150 $200

MONARCH, 7 jewels , curved
14k. $200 $400 $550
gold filled $100 $200 $250

HY. MOSER & CIE., 14J., "Signal Corps USA", ctr. lugs
silver $375 $650 $900

MONTBRILLANT, 15J., one button chronog. Ca 1915-
20 MONTBRILLANT = early **BREITLING**
18k. $1,200 $2,300 $2,700

HY. MOSER & CIE., 14-18J., one button chronograph, wind
and set at 12, center lugs, 2 reg. Ca. 1920s
silver $1,500 $2,300 $3,000

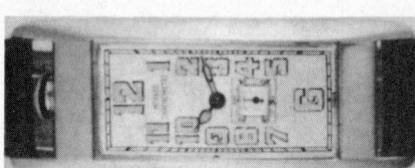

MOVADO, 15J., polyplan winds at 12 o'clock, 46mm, curved, c. 1910
18k.........................$4,500 $8,500 $10,000

MOVADO, 15J., polyplan, winds at 12 o'clock,
14k.........................$4,000 $7,500 $9,000

MOVADO, 15J polyplan, winds at 12 o'clock,
silver.......................$2,200 $3,750 $4,000

Movado, Purse Watches See P.W. section Movado

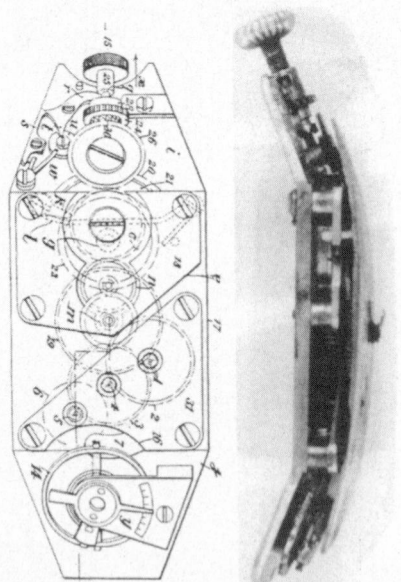

ABOVE: Polyplan
MOVADO, side view of movement with three inclined plans.

MOVADO, 15J., "Chronometre", c.1930
14k.........................$175 $265 $335

MOVADO, 17J., day date month, "Sportsman"
14k......................... $350 $575 $700

MOVADO, 17J., day date month, snap back
18k......................... $800 $1,500 $1,800

MOVADO, 17J., triple date, snap back, "calendomatic"
18k......................... $900 $1,600 $1,900

MOVADO, 28J., date, "kingmatic",c.1959
s. steel..................... $80 $100 $150
14k(w)..................... $225 $375 $425

MOVADO, 17J., month date, ca. 1950s
14k. $300 $550 $650

MOVADO, 17J., 1 button chronog., c.1948
s. steel $400 $675 $800

MOVADO, 17 jewels, .day-date-month,   c.1945
18k. $900 $1,600 $1,900
14k. $700 $1,200 $1,500
s. steel $400 $600 $800

MOVADO, 17J., chronog., 2 reg., c. 1940
14k $900 $1,400 $1,800

MOVADO, 17J, triple date, moon phases, Ca. 1959
Rose GF & s.s. $700 $1,200 $1,500
s. steel $650 $1,100 $1,400
14k. $1,500 $2,750 $3,500

MOVADO, 17J., 3 reg., chronog.
s. steel $900 $1,400 $1,800

MOVADO, 17J., 3 reg . . . . . . .chronog.,
18k. $1,900 $2,600 $3,000
14k. $1,700 $2,200 $2,600
s. steel $900 $1,200 $1,700

MOVADO. 17J., Tempograf, chronog., 2 reg., c. 1935
s. steel $900 $1,500 $1,800

The Movado trademark M over flat V was Registered in 1958.

MOVADO, 17J., 3 reg. chronog., date, auto wind
18k. $800 $1,400 $1,650
s. steel $300 $600 $750

MOVADO, 17J., El Primero date at 5, auto wind, c. 1972
s. steel $400 $700 $850

MOVADO,17J., RF#2652, rotating chapter,cal.352, c.1958
s. steel $400 $750 $850

MOVADO, 17J., center sec., cat 261, c.1948
18k. $175 $300 $400

MOVADO, 17J., cal # 246, Cabochon crown, Ca. 1955
18K $300 $550 $700

MOVADO, 17J., center sec., auto wind, c.1948
14k. $200 $375 $425

MOVADO, 17J., "Cronoplan", Ca. 1940s
s. steel $700 $1,350 $1,500

MOVADO, 15J., aux. sec., cal.75, c.1946
s. steel $100 $150 $175

☞ Some grades are not included. Their values can bedetermined by comparing with **similar** age, size, metal content, style, grades, or models such as **time only**, chronograph, repeater etc. listed.

MOVADO, 17J., aux. sec., cal.135, c.1960
s. steel $100 $175 $200

MOVADO, 17J., auto-wind, cal.8577, c.1957
14k $175 $300 $375

MOVADO, 17J., Tiffany & Co. on dial, center sec.,
14k $250 $475 $525

MOVADO, 15J., 2 colors of gold, tonneau, Ca. 1940
18k $400 $750 $850

The Movado trademark M over flat V was Registered in 1958.

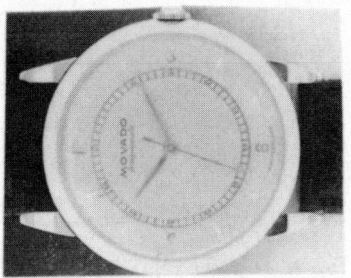

MOVADO, 17J., "Kingmatic", center sec.
14k $235 $400 $475

MOVADO, 17J., center sec.
s. steel $100 $175 $200

MOVADO, 20J., auto-wind,
14k $185 $375 $450

MOVADO, 28J., center sec., Kingmatic,
14k $185 $375 $450

In about 1895, L.A. & I. Ditesheim (before Movado) used trade names for pocket watches such as Ralco, Tanit, Ultra, Apogee, Record, Talma, Noblesse, Salud, Negus, Bonne, Belgravia, Surete and Mintral.

MOVADO, 17J., aux. Sec
18k.............................$175 $375 $400

MOVADO, 17J., auto-w., ca. 1949
14k...........................$200 $375 $400

MOVADO, 17J., nonmagnetic, RF # 11730, Ca. 1940
s. steel.....................$100 $175 $225

MOVADO, 15 jewels, center lugs, c. 1930
18k..........................$250 $475 $550

MOVADO, 17J , textured 18k dial.....
18k..........................$250 $400 $500

MOVADO, 15 jewels, aux. sec.
14k C&B...................$400 $750 $900

MOVADO, 17 jewels, aux. sec., center lugs
14k..........................$200 $375 $400

MOVADO, 17J., cal.7025, GJS, c.1964
18k..........................$200 $375 $450

MOVADO, 17J., hidden lugs, red - 2-tone dial, c. 1960
18k..........................$300 $600 $700

MOVADO, 17 jewels,"Museum" date , at 12 o'clock
14k C&B...................$500 $900 $1,000

MOVADO, 15 jewels, fancy lugs
18k. $250 $450 $550

MOVADO, 17J., wide bezel, c.1958
gold filled $100 $175 $200

MOVADO, 17J., diamond bezel,
18k. $250 $500 $600

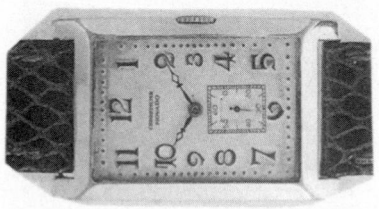

MOVADO, 17J, RF#621,c.1932
gold filled $100 $200 $250

MOVADO, 17J., stepped case, "Curviplan", GJS, c. 1942
14k. $300 $600 $800

MOVADO, 17J., aux. sec., c.1940
14k. $175 $350 $400

MOVADO, 17J., extended lugs, c.1945
14k. $185 $350 $400

MOVADO, 17J., aux. sec., c.1945
14k. $185 $350 $400

MOVADO, 17J., extended lugs, GJS, c.1940
14k. $175 $350 $400

MOVADO, 17J., **tu-tone case**, RF#13906, Ca. 1948
14k tu-tone $200 $400 $500

MOVADO, 17J., *Andy Warhol*, "Times/5", Ca.1988
Note:Total of 5 watches (only 3 watches shown)
Quartz (250 made) . . . . . . ★★★ $3,500 $6,000 $8,000

MOVADO, 15 jewels, curved, chronometre
14k. $400 $750 $850

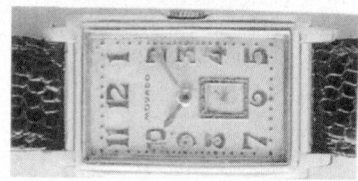

MOVADO, 17J., cal#510, ca.1941
14k. $275 $425 $575

MOVADO, 17J., curviplan,
gold filled $150 $200 $250

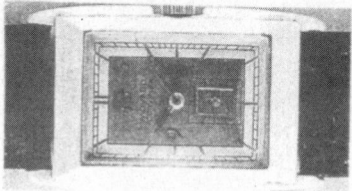

MOVADO, 17J., curviplan, ca.1941
14k. $400 $750 $850

MOVADO, 17J., **RF # 43872**, ca. 1945
14k. $200 $400 $600

Wrist Watches listed in this section are priced at the collectable
fair market Trade Show level as COMPLETE watches having an
original gold-filled case and stainless steel back, also with original
dial, leather watch band, and the entire original movement in good
working order with no repairs needed.

MOVADO, 15 jewels, exaggerated numbers, c. 1929
18k. $300 $600 $750

MOVADO, 17 jewels
14k. $150 $300 $350

MOVADO, 17 jewels, automatic, aux. sec.
18k. $300 $600 $800

MOVADO, 17 jewels, fancy lugs, c. 1947
14k. $200 $400 $500

MOVADO, 17J., Ca. 1940s
14k. $200 $400 $500

☞ Pricing in this Guide are fair market price for COMPLETE
watches which are reflected from the "NAWCC" National and
regional shows.

MOVADO, 17 jewels
18k. $300 $600 $750

MOVADO, 15 jewels, cal. 440, Ca. 1940
18k. $300 $575 $700

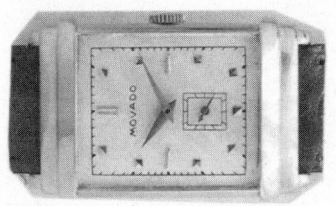

MOVADO, 17 jewels, , Ca.1948
14k. $200 $400 $500
18k. $300 $600 $750

MOVADO, 15 jewels, gold jewel settings, Ca. 1930
18K(W). $300 $575 $700

MOVADO, 17 jewels, Ca. 1940s
18K $300 $600 $800

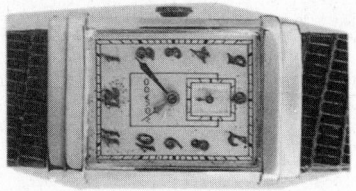

MOVADO, 17 jewels, hidden lugs, Ca. 1940
14k. $250 $500 $600

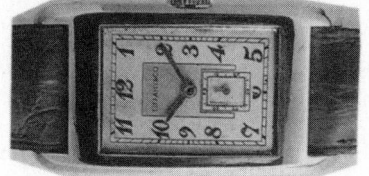

MOVADO, 17 jewels, gold jewel settings, Ca. 1940s
14K $200 $400 $650

MOVADO, 17 jewels, curviplan, , GJS, Ca. 1937
14k. $250 $500 $600

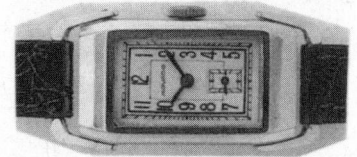

MOVADO, 15J, hinged lugs, gold jewel settings, Ca 1930s'
s. steel. $125 $200 $225

MOVADO, 17 jewels, ladies, alarm, Ca. 1960
18k. $100 $200 $275

MOVADO, 17J., gold jewel settings, cal.510, Ca.1940
14k. $200 $400 $600

MOVADO MOVEMENT IDENTIFICATION

Caliber 35

Caliber 65

Caliber 575

Caliber25, 27-Sweep Second

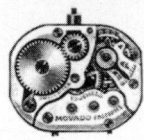

Caliber 28

Caliber 575, Ermeto-Baby

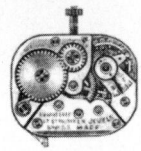

Caliber 578, Ermeto Calendine

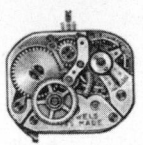

579, Calendoplan Baby

Caliber 5

Caliber 15

Caliber 50SP

Caliber 105, 107-Center Second

Caliber 190

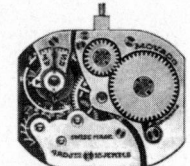

Caliber 375, 377-Center Second

Caliber 440, 443-Center Second

Caliber 510

Caliber 260M, 261

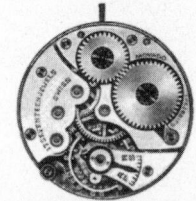

Caliber 150MN, 157-Sweep Second

Polyplan
(first used in 1922)

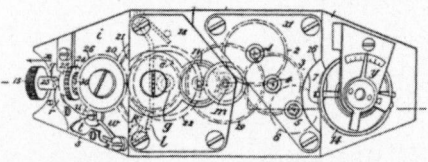

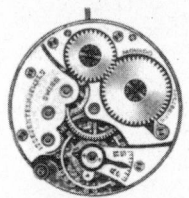

Caliber 155, Calendermeto

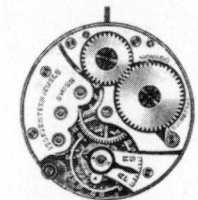

Caliber 470, 477-Center Second

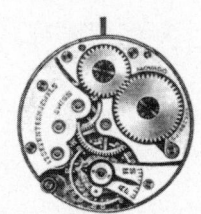

Caliber 473, 473SC-Calendar/Moon phase

Caliber 475, 475SC-Center Second

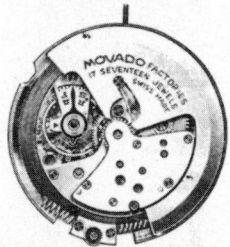

Caliber 225, 255M

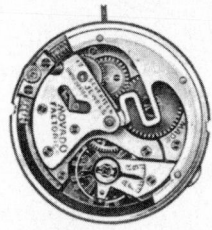

Caliber 115

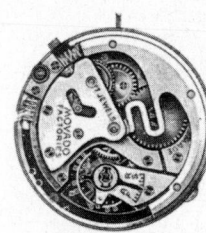

Caliber 118

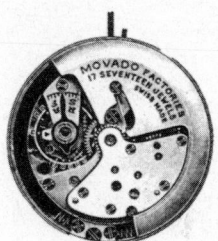

Caliber 220, 220M

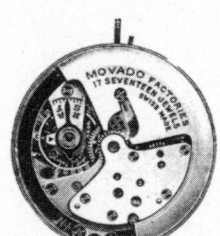

Caliber 221, 226

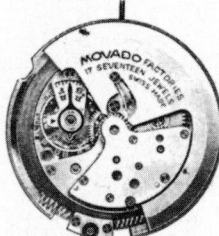

Caliber 223, 228

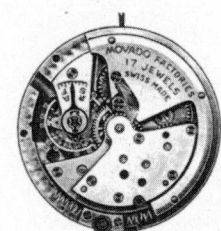

Caliber 224, 224A

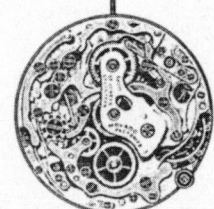

Chronograph
Cal. 90M, 95M
12''' – 26,60 mm

U.NARDIN, 29 J., "Astrolabium," self wind, waterproof, local time, equinoctial time, months, signs of zodiac, elevation & azimuth of sun & moon, aspect in which sun & moon stand to each other. **recent**
18k. $8,000 $12,500 $17,500

U.NARDIN, 17J., one button pulsations, ca.1920
18k. $1,500 $2,800 $3,200

U.NARDIN, 17J., one button, enamel dial, Pulsations, Ca. 1920
18k. $1,500 $2,800 $3,200

☞ Pricing in this Guide are fair market price for COMPLETE watches which are reflected from the NAWCC National and regional shows.

☞ Some grades are not included. Their values can be determined by comparing with similar age, size, metal content, style, grades, or models such as time only, chronograph, repeater etc. listed.

U. Nardin, 17 jewels, chronog., c.1950s
18k. $1,000 $1,800 $2,000

U. NARDIN, 17 jewels, split sec, chronog., c. 1910
silver $3,000 $6,000 $7,000

U. NARDIN, 17 jewels, chronog., 3 reg. c. 1940s
18k. $1,500 $2,800 $3,200

U. NARDIN, 25 jewels, date
14k. $250 $500 $650

U NARDIN, 17 jewels, auto wind, c. 1952
14k. $265 $450 $550

U. NARDIN, 21J.,auto-wind
18k. $300 $550 $600

U. NARDIN, 17J., center sec., chronometer, c.1950
gold filled $75 $150 $200

U. NARDIN, 17J., aux sec.
s. steel $100 $150 $200

U. NARDIN, 17J., center sec., auto-wind, c.1950
14k. $265 $400 $450

U. NARDIN, 17J., aux. sec.
18k. $200 $375 $450

U. NARDIN, 17J., center sec., auto-wind, c.1950
18k. $300 $550 $600

U.NARDIN, 17J., fancy lugs
18k. $250 $475 $525

☞ A collector should expect to pay modestly higher prices as local shops.

☞ Pricing in this Guide are fair market price for **COMPLETE** watches which are reflected from the NAWCC National and regional shows.

U.NARDIN, 17J., aux. Sec., carved lugs, c.1950
18k. $200 $400 $500

U.NARDIN, 17J., aux. sec., chronometer, c.1950
14k. $150 $275 $325

U.NARDIN, 17J., aux. sec., chronometer, c.1947
18k. $200 $400 $500

U.NARDIN, 17J., aux. sec., chronometer, C.1951
14k. $225 $350 $400

Wrist Watches listed in this section are priced as complete watches
having an original gold-filled cane and stainless steel back, also
with original dial, leather watch band, and the entire original movement in good working order with no repairs needed.

☞ Some grades are not included. Their values can
be determined by comparing with similar age, size,
metal content, style, grades, or models such as time only,
chronograph, repeater etc. listed.

U.NARDIN, 17J., aux. sec., chronometer, c.1964
gold plate $65 $100 $125

U.NARDIN, 17J., aux. sec., chronometer, c.1948
gold filled $75 $150 $175

U. NARDIN, 17J., fancy lugs
14k. $225 $400 $500

U.NARDIN, 25J., chronometer, auto-w., date, c.1975
s. steel $200 $400 $500

U. NARDIN, 17J., fluted case, chronometer
14k. $200 $400 $500

U. NARDIN, 17J., aux. sec., chronometer, c.1949
14k. $175 $375 $475

U.NARDIN, 17J., aux. sec., chronometer, c.1950
18k. $200 $400 $500

U.NARDIN, 17J., extended side lugs, chronometer, c.1951
14k. $175 $375 $475

U.NARDIN, 17 jewels, faceted crystal & bezel
s. steel $100 $150 $175

☞ Some grades are not included. Their values can
be determined by comparing with similar age, size,
metal content, style, grades, or models such as time only,
chronograph, repeater etc. listed.

U.NARDIN, 17 jewels, chronometer, c. 1935
18k. $250 $400 $500

U.NARDIN, 17 jewels, WW I military style
s. steel $300 $550 $650

U. NARDIN, 15jewels, c. 1925
gold filled(w) $95 $150 $200

U.NARDIN, 15J., enamel dial, Ca. 1925
silver $200 $400 $500

U.NARDIN, 17J , lady's chronometer, c 1947
14k C&B $375 $500 $600

NATIONAL W. Co., 16 J., 1 button Chronog.,
red & black color enamel dial, Ca. 1925
silver $400 $800 $1,100

NATIONAL W. Co., 15J., day-date-month,
gold filled $75 $150 $200

NEW ENGLAND W. Co., 7J., Addison, Alden, Cavour,
Hale, and other models, Ca. 1915, colored dial add ($25)
14k. $65 $100   125
gold filled $25 $50 $75

NEW HAVEN, 7 jewels, "Gem", engraved bezel
base metal $50 $65 $75

NEW HAVEN, 7 jewels
base metal $50 $65 $75

NEW HAVEN, 2 jewels, "Elf" ladies, etched case
base metal $20 $25 $50

NEW HAVEN, 7 jewels, "Duchess" ladies, etched case
gold plate $20 $25 $45

NEWMARK, 17J., military chronog., c.1979
s. steel $175 $300 $400

NEW YORK STANDARD, 7 jewels, wire lugs
gold filled $35 $60 $75
base metal $20 $40 $50

NICE WATCH Co., 17J., one button chronog., c.1930
base metal $200 $400 $500

NICOLET W. CO., 17)., one button chronog., Ca. 1960
gold filled $200 $375 $450

CHARLES NICOLET, 17J., chronog., ca. 1945
18k. $250 $500 $600

MARC NICOLET, 17J, aux. seconds
14k. $150 $275 $325

NITON, 18J., jump hr., (showing dial and movement)
(also made ebauche for P.P.& CO.)
18k(W) $2,500 $4,000 $5,000

NIVADA, 21J., center sec., c.1960
base metal. $35 $75 $100

NIVADA, 21J., center sec., date, auto-w, c.1965
s. steel $45 $85 $100

NIVADA, 25J., waterproof, triple date, moon ph., c. 1940
14k. $450 $850 $1,000
gold filled $150 $350 $500

Pricing in this guide are fair market price for complete watches
which are reflected from the NAWCC national and regional shows.

NORMANDIE 17 jewels, compass, c. 1945
s. steel $100 $175 $225

NORMANDIE, 17J., gold train, hidden lugs, cal.4873
14k. $100 $250 $350

OCTO, 17J., fluted lugs, signed Octo on movement
Tiffany & Co. on dial
14k. $275 $550 $750

OGIVAL, 17 jewels, auto wind
gold filled $35 $60 $75

OLLENDORFF 17 jewels, fancy lugs
14k. $125 $300 $400

OLLENDORFF, 17 jewels, movement plates made of **gold**
14k. $175 $300 $400

OLLENDORFF, 7J., direct read, stepped case, c. 1930
base metal. $100 $275 $375

OLMA, 17J., **early** auto-wind, by Wyler, c.1928
s. steel $150 $275 $350

OFAIR, 17J., chronog., cal. Valjoux 72c, c.1948
gold filled $250 $400 $500
14k. $450 $800 $1,000
18k. $600 $1,000 $1,200

Wrist Watches listed in this section are priced at the collectable
fair market Trade Show level as COMPLETE watches having an
original gold-filled case and stainless steel back, also with original
dial, leather watch band, and the entire original movement in good
working order with no repairs needed.

☞ Some grades are not included. Their values can
be determined by comparing with similar age, size,
metal content, style, grades, or models such as time only,
chronograph, repeater etc. listed.

OMEGA CODES FOR 7-DIGIT REFERENCE

For Example: Ref. BB.145.xxxx = 18k pink gold gentleman's wa-
ter-resistant, manual winding, chronograph wristwatch. The xxxx,
the last four digits, refer to the case, dial and bracelet types.

1st Digit	2nd Digit	3rd Digit
1 - Gent's Watch	1 - Manual winding without second	1 - Non-water-resistant
2 - Gent's Jewellery Watch	2 - Manual winding small second	2 - Non-water-resistant Calendar
3 - Gent's Bracelet Watch	3 - Manual winding centre second	3 - Non-water-resistant chronometer
4 - Gent's Jewellery Bracelet Watch	4 - Manual winding chronograph	4 - Non-water-resistant chronometer calendar
5 - Lady's Watch	5 - Self-winding without second	5 - Water-resistant
6 - Lady's Jewellery Watch	6 - Self-winding centre second	6 - Water-resistant Calendar
7 - Lady's Bracelet Watch	7 - Self-winding chronograph	7 - Water-resistant chronometer
8 - Lady's Jewellery Bracelet Watch	8 - Electronic chronograph	8 - Water-resistant chronometer calendar
	9 - Electronic	

OMEGA METAL CODES

Code	Description	Code	Description	Code	Description
AB	platinum + yellow gold 18k	DN	2-colored plated 10Y	MR	chromiun-pltd black, bezel 20M yel.
AT	platinum	DP	steel, pink gold 18k	ND	plated 20M yellow on steel
BA	yellow gold 18k	DR	bezel pink gold 18k on steel	OA	plated 40M yellow on steel
BB	pink gold 18k	DS	bezel yellow gold 14k on steel	PA	plated 40M yellow on steel, steelback
BC	white gold 18k	DX	2-colored plated 10M yellow	PE	miniature clock
BD	yellow gold 14k	ED	plated 10M 2N18	RP	silver plated 40M yellow
BF	white gold 14k	EF	plated 10M 1N14 steelback	RS	silver 0.925
BG	yellow gold 9k	EX	plated 10M 1N14	SC	PVD grey
BJ	gold, multi-colored 18k	FD	plated 80M yellow	SE	PVD yellow
BK	gold, bezel steel	FE	plated 80M pink	SI	steel + titanium
BL	pink gold 9k	GD	plated 80M yellow steelback	SO	oxidized steel
BP	pink gold 18k	GF	plated 80M white steelback	SR	chromium-plated black
BR	gold 2-colored 18k yellow-pink	HG	plated 40M yellow	ST	steel
BT	yellow gold 18k + titanium	HH	plated 2-colored 40M	SU	steel, aluminum ring
BU	yellow gold 18k bezel aluminum	JD	plated 40M yellow steelback	TA	titanium + gold case & bracelet
CD	cap yellow gold 14k	JE	plated 40M pink steelback	TB	titanium + pink gold bracelet / titanium + pink gold
CE	cap pink gold 14k	KD	plated 20M back 40M yellow		
DA	steel + yellow gold 18k	KF	plated 20M back 40M white	TD	titanium + plated 20M yellow / titanium + plated 10M bracelet
DB	steel + pink gold 18k	LD	plated 20M 2N18		
DC	bezel white gold 18k on steel	LE	plated 20M pink	TE	titanium + PVD yellow
DD	steel + yellow gold 14k	LX	plated 20M 1N14	TI	titanium
DE	steel + pink gold 18k	MD	plated 20M yellow steelback	TL	titanium/tantalium + pink gold 18k
DF	steel + yellow gold 18k steelback	ME	plated 20M pink steelback	TR	titanium + pink gold titantium bracelet
DG	bezel pink gold 18k on steel	MF	plated 20M white steelback	TT	titanium + palladium titanium bracelet
DH	bezel pink gold 18k on steel	MK	plated 20M back & bezel steel	TZ	titanium + pink gold bracelet, gld logo
DL	2-colored plated 20M yellow	MP	plated 20M 2-colored yellow-pink	UT	chromium plated
DM	2-colored plated 10M 1N14			YA	hard metal yellow
				YR	hard metal black

OMEGA PRODUCTION TOTALS

DATE — SERIAL #	DATE — SERIAL #	DATE — SERIAL #	DATE — SERIAL #	DATE — SERIAL #
1894 - 1,000,000	1952 - 13,000,000	1967 - 25,000,000	1973 - 37,000,000	1986 - 49,000,000
1902 - 2,000,000	1954 - 14,000,000	1968 - 26,000,000	1974 - 38,000,000	1986 - 50,000,000
1906 - 3,000,000	1956 - 15,000,000	1968 - 27,000,000	1975 - 39,000,000	1989 - 51,000,000
1910 - 4,000,000	1958 - 16,000,000	1969 - 28,000,000	1977 - 40,000,000	not used-52,000,000
1915 - 5,000,000	1959 - 17,000,000	1969 - 29,000,000	1978 - 41,000,000	1991 - 53,000,000
1923 - 6,000,000	1961 - 18,000,000	1969 - 30,000,000	1979 - 42,000,000	1993 - 54,000,000
1920 - 7,000,000	1962 - 19,000,000	1969 - 31,000,000	1979 - 43,000,000	1995 - 55,000,000
1934 - 8,000,000	1963 - 20,000,000	1970 - 32,000,000	1980 - 44,000,000	1998 - 56,000,000
1926 - 9,000,000	1964 - 21,000,000	1971 - 33,000,000	1982 - 45,000,000	
1944 - 10,000,000	1965 - 22,000,000	1972 - 34,000,000	1984 - 46,000,000	
1947 - 11,000,000	1966 - 23,000,000	1972 - 35,000,000	1984 - 47,000,000	
1950 - 12,000,000	1966 - 24,000,000	1973 - 36,000,000	1985 - 48,000,000	

Note: By 1980 ETA Calibers were being used by Omega. The above list is provided for determining the aproximate age of your watch. Match serial number with date. Watches were not necessarily sold in the exact order of manufactured date.

OMEGA-DANIELS CO-AXIAL ESCAPEMENT

YEAR - CASE#

1894 - 1,000,000
not used-2,000,000
1902 - 3,000,000
1907 - 4,000,000
1913 - 5,000,000
1918 - 6,000,000
1925 - 7,000,000
1929 - 8,000,000
1935 - 9,000,000
1943 - 10,000,000

Case numbers and earliest production totals

OMEGA, 27J., "DeVille", limited edition, Co-axial, autowind, water resistant to 5 atm, RF# 5921, Ca. 1999 limited to 1,000 each for Yellow, Pink, White & 100 in Platinum
18K (Y-P-W) $2,500 $3,500 $5,000

OMEGA, 27J., Co-axial, auto-wind, GMT, Cal. 2628
s. steel $2,000 $2,700 $3,000

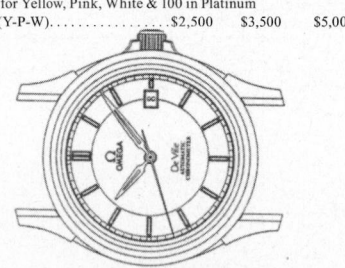

OMEGA, 27J., Co-axial, auto-wind, RF#4832, Cal. 2500
s. steel $2,000 $2,700 $3,000

OMEGA, 15J., wire lug, enamel dial, Ca. 1925
silver $185 $300 $400

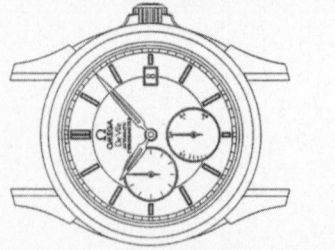

OMEGA, 27J., Co-axial, wind-indicator, auto-wind, RF#4532, cal. 2627
s. steel $2,000 $2,700 $3,000

OMEGA, 15J., center lugs, enamel dial, Ca. 1930
18k $400 $800 $900

OMEGA, 15J., wire lugs, Ca. 1930s
18k.......................... $600 $950 $1,200

OMEGA, 24J., "Constellation", auto-wind, cal.551, c.1962
2 tone ease $225 $400 $600
14k.......................... $450 $800 $900

OMEGA, 15J., wire lugs,
14k.......................... $500 $850 $1,000

OMEGA, 24J., "Constellation," auto-w., date, c. 1959
18k.......................... $600 $900 $1,200

OMEGA, 24J., "Constellation", auto-wind, cal 505, c.1958
18k.......................... $700 $1,100 $1,500

OMEGA, 24J.,date, "Constellation", auto wind, chronometer
18k.......................... $500 $900 $1,200
14k.......................... $300 $600 $800
2 tone case $200 $400 $500

OMEGA, 24J., "Constellation", chronometer, auto-wind
2 tone ease $200 $400 $600
18k.......................... $650 $1,000 $1,200

OMEGA, 24J., "Constellation", auto-wind, c.1960
14k.......................... $600 $900 $1,200
2 tone case $300 $400 $600
s. steel...................... $300 $400 $600

OMEGA, 24J., Constellation', auto-wind, c.1968
gold filled $300 $500 $550

OMEGA, 17-24J., Chronometre, auto-w.,
14k. $400 $750 $900

OMEGA, 24J., "Constellation", auto-wind, c. 1969
s. steel $200 $400 $500

OMEGA, 17J.,"Seamaster', chronometer, auto wind
18k. $400 $750 $900

OMEGA, 24 jewels, "Constellation," auto wind, date, pie pan dial
18k pink c&b . . . . ★★★$2,000 $3,500 $4,000

OMEGA, 17J., "Seamaster", auto-wind
s. steel $125 $250 $350

OMEGA, 7J., "Constellation", **quartz**, cal.1342, c.1970
18k & s. s. $300 $550 $600

OMEGA, 17J., "Seamaster", auto wind, c.1953
gold filled $125 $250 $275

OMEGA, 17J., "Seamaster Deluxe", auto-wind
18k. $350 $700 $800

OMEGA, 24J., "Seamaster", auto-w, date, Ca. 1963
18k (rose) $400 $700 $800

OMEGA, 20J., "Seamaster", auto-wind, cal.501, c. 1957
s. steel $125 $250 $300

OMEGA, 24J., "Seamaster", auto-wind, c. 1962
14k. $300 $500 $575
s. steel $150 $275 $350

OMEGA, 17J., "Seamaster", auto-wind, cat.1570, c.1955
gold filled $125 $250 $275

OMEGA, 24J., "Seamaster", auto-wind, cal.562, c.1962
gold filled $125 $250 $275

OMEGA, 17 jewels, "Seamaster", date, auto-w., waterproof
18k. $350 $650 $750

OMEGA, 17 jewels, "Seamaster," auto wind
14k. $300 $600 $700

OMEGA, 23J.,"Seamaster", auto-wind, cal.1022, c.1978
s. steel $125 $250 $275

OMEGA, 16-18J., gold train, center seconds, auto wind
s. steel $125 $250 $300

OMEGA, 17 jewels, automatic, date at 6
14k. $400 $750 $800

OMEGA, electronic, "F300," c. 1950s
18k C & B $700 $1,300 $1,500

OMEGA, 16J., center sec., c. 1940
s. steel $125 $250 $300

OMEGA, 16J., **U.S. Army**, cal., c.1948
s. steel $200 $400 $500

OMEGA, 16J., center sec., c.1948
s. steel $150 $275 $350

OMEGA, 15J., Military (**England**), c.1946
s. steel $275 $500 $700

OMEGA, 17J., "Seamaster", diamond dial, cal.563, auto wind,
Ca.1955
14K $400 $700 $800
s. steel $200 $400 $450

OMEGA, 17J., "Railmaster", center sec.
s. steel $250 $450 $500

OMEGA, 15-17J., 24 hour marked, Ca 1930
s. steel $200 $400 $500

OMEGA, 17J., aux. sec., cal.266, c.1945
14k $250 $450 $500

OMEGA, 15J., **Military, large**, c.1930
s. steel $350 $700 $900

OMEGA, 17J., auto-wind, c.1949
18k $300 $600 $800

OMEGA, 17J., 12 diamond dial, center sec.
14k(W) $300 $550 $600

OMEGA, 17J., auto-wind, c. 1949
18k $300 $550 $700

OMEGA, 17J., aux. sec., cal.360, c.1950
14k........................$170 $300 $400

OMEGA, 17J., auto-wind, c.1952
18k........................ $300 $600 $800

OMEGA, 17J., auto-wind, cal.342, c.1955
gold filled $100 $200 $250

OMEGA, 17J., aux. sec., cal.266, c.1956
s. steel........................$150 $275 $300

OMEGA, 17J., fancy lugs, ca.1948
14k......................... $300 $550 $700

OMEGA, 17J., cal 620, c. 1960
14k......................... $200 $400 $550

OMEGA, 17 J, wide bezel & lugs, cal.369, auto wind, c.1947
platinum ....★★$2,000 $4,000 $5,000

OMEGA, 17J., RF#347sc, cal.471, auto wind, c.1956
18k......................... $300 $500 $600

OMEGA, 17J., wide bezel, center sec., auto-w., c.1955
14k......................... $250 $400 $600

OMEGA, 17 jewels, curved center lugs, auto wind
14k. $300 $600 $800

OMEGA, 17 jewels, aux. sec.
18k. $250 $500 $550

OMEGA, 17J., fancy lugs, ca. 1948
14k. $200 $450 $500

OMEGA, 17J., 9 diamond dial, ca. 1955
14k(W) $225 $425 $550

OMEGA, 15J., small lugs, c.1935
gold filled $100 $200 $350

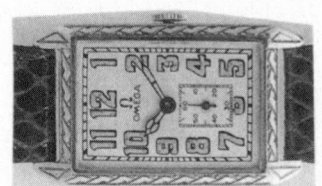

OMEGA, 15J., engraved case, c.1925
14k. $300 $600 $750

OMEGA, 15 jewels, large, c. 1935
14k. $350 $600 $800

OMEGA, 17J., bevelled case, c.1936
s. steel $100 $225 $300

OMEGA, 15J., aux. sec., c.1937
s. steel $150 $250 $300

OMEGA, 17 jewels, c. 1937
s. steel $100 $200 $300

OMEGA, 15J., small lugs, c.1937
s. steel $100 $225 $300

OMEGA, 17J, c. 1938
14k $200 $400 $450

OMEGA, 15J, extended lugs, c. 1939
14k $300 $500 $600
gold filled $125 $200 $300

OMEGA, 17J, aux. sec., cal 302, c. 1948
gold filled $125 $250 $300

OMEGA, 17J., fancy lugs, ca. 1950s
14k $250 $450 $600

OMEGA, 17J, faceted crystal,
14k(W) $200 $400 $500

OMEGA, 17J, aux. sec.
14k C&B $650 $1,000 $1,200

OMEGA, 17J, "De Villie"
18k $275 $500 $600

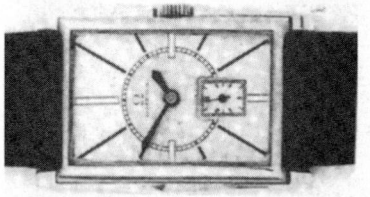

OMEGA, 17J, aux. sec.,
14k $200 $400 $500

OMEGA, 17J, hidden lugs, asymmetric
14k $500 $900 $1,100

OMEGA, 17J., flared & hidden lugs, c.1947
14k $300 $550 $600
18k $400 $700 $800

OMEGA, 17J., flared & sculptured lugs, cal 302, c. 1953
14k $300 $550 $650

OMEGA, 17J., flared & extended lugs, cal.301, c.1948
14k. $300 $550 $650

OMEGA, 17 jewels, c. 1948
14k. $285 $500 $700

OMEGA, 17 jewels, sculptured lugs
14k. $500 $1,000 $1,500

OMEGA, 15J., sliding case, winds at 12, Ca.1930s
"**Marine**" model
18k. $1,500 $2,850 $3,500

OMEGA, 15 jewels, hidden winding stem, c. 1930
"**Marine**" model, wire lugs
14k. $1,000 $1,800 $2,000
s. steel $800 $1,500 $1,700

OMEGA, 17 jewels, one button chronog., c. 1935
18k. $1,750 $3,500 $4,500

OMEGA, 17J., 2 reg. chronog., ca. 1940s
s. steel $400 $700 $800
14k. $700 $1,100 $1,300
18k. $900 $1,500 $2,000

OMEGA, 17J., 2reg., chronog., c. 1958
18k. $1,000 $1,750 $2,200

OMEGA, 17J., "Seamaster", chronog., cat.321, c. 1962
s. steel $500 $800 $1,200
14k. $1,000 $1,800 $2,000
18k. $1,200 $2,000 $2,500

OMEGA, 17 jewels, chronog., "Seamaster," c. 1963
14k......................\$1,200   \$2,000   \$2,500
s. steel......................\$500   \$800   \$1,200

OMEGA, 17J., "Speedmaster Pro. **Mack II**", auto-w, c.1975
s. steel......................\$300   \$550   \$750

OMEGA, 17J., "Speedmaster", chronog., c. 1950
s. steel......................\$800   \$1,400   \$1,800

OMEGA, 22J., "Seamaster", date, 2 reg., auto-wind, c. 1975
s. steel......................\$400   \$700   \$800

OMEGA, 17J., "Speedmaster Pro.", chronog., c. 1969
"the first watch worn on the moon" on back of watch
18k C&B, Cal 861.............\$2,500   \$4,000   \$5,500
s. steel, Cal 861..............\$500   \$900   \$1,200
Add \$300 for Cal 321, 1st model

OMEGA, 17J., Speedmaster, auto-wind, chronog., e. 1975
s. steel......................\$400   \$700   \$800

OMEGA, 17J., Speedmaster Pro. MarkIII, auto-w, c.1978
s. steel $400 $700 $850

OMEGA, 17 jewels, chronog., "Flightmaster", 3 reg., auto-w
18k C & B $2,500 $4,000 $5,000
s. steel $400 $800 $1,000

OMEGA, 17J., "Seamaster", chronog., cal.321, c. 1970
s. steel $300 $600 $800

OMEGA, 17J., "Seamaster", chronostop, c. 1965
s. steel $250 $475 $600

OMEGA, 17 jewels, chronog., "Seamaster", 3 reg., auto-w
14k. $600 $1,200 $1,400

OMEGA, 17J., "Seamaster", chronostop., rotating bezel,
s. steel $300 $600 $800

OMEGA, 19J., alarm, "Memomatic", c.1975
s. steel $300 $600 $700

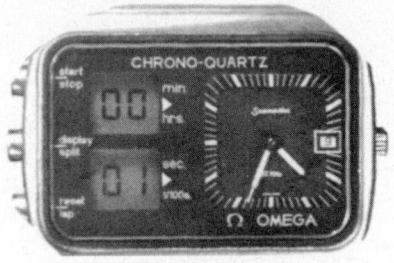

OMEGA, "Chrono-quartz, cal.1611, c.1975
s. steel $275 $500 $700

OMEGA, 17 jewels, day-date-month, moon phase
18k. $900 $1,600 $2,200
14k. $800 $1,400 $2,000

OMEGA, quartz, marine chronometer
s. steel $350 $800 $1,000

OMEGA, 17J., day-date-month, moon phase, c. 1940
s. steel $650 $1,100 $1,400
14k. $800 $1,400 $1,800

OMEGA, 15J., ladies, wire lugs, c.1925
silver $50 $100 $125

OMEGA, 17J., day-date-month, moon phase, c. 1950s
14k. $2,000 $3,750 $4,500
18k. $2,500 $4,500 $6,000

OMEGA, 17J., ladies center sec., c.1938
silver $100 $150 $175

OMEGA, 17J., ladies, sapphire stones on lugs, c.1950
14k C&B.................... $400 $700 $850

OMEGA, 15J, ladies, non-magnetic, c.1945
s. steel...................... $50 $100 $125

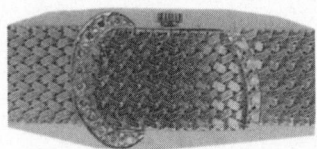

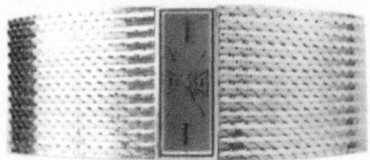

OMEGA, 17J., ladies flip open, 16 diamonds, c.1955
14k C&B.................... $600 $900 $1,200

OMEGA, 17J., ladies, RF#8065, c.1965
18k C&B.................... $400 $500 $750

Cal. No. 711, Ca.1966   Cal. No. 730, Ca.1967   Cal. No. 980, Ca.1969   Cal. No. 1040, Ca. 1971

Cal. No. 320, Chronograph   Cal. No. 321, Chronograph

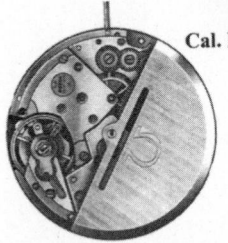

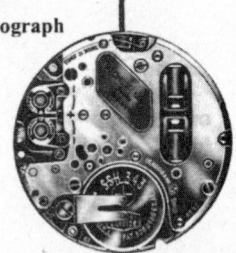

Cal. No. 1010, Ca.1973

Cal. No. 1250-1260,
Ca.1970

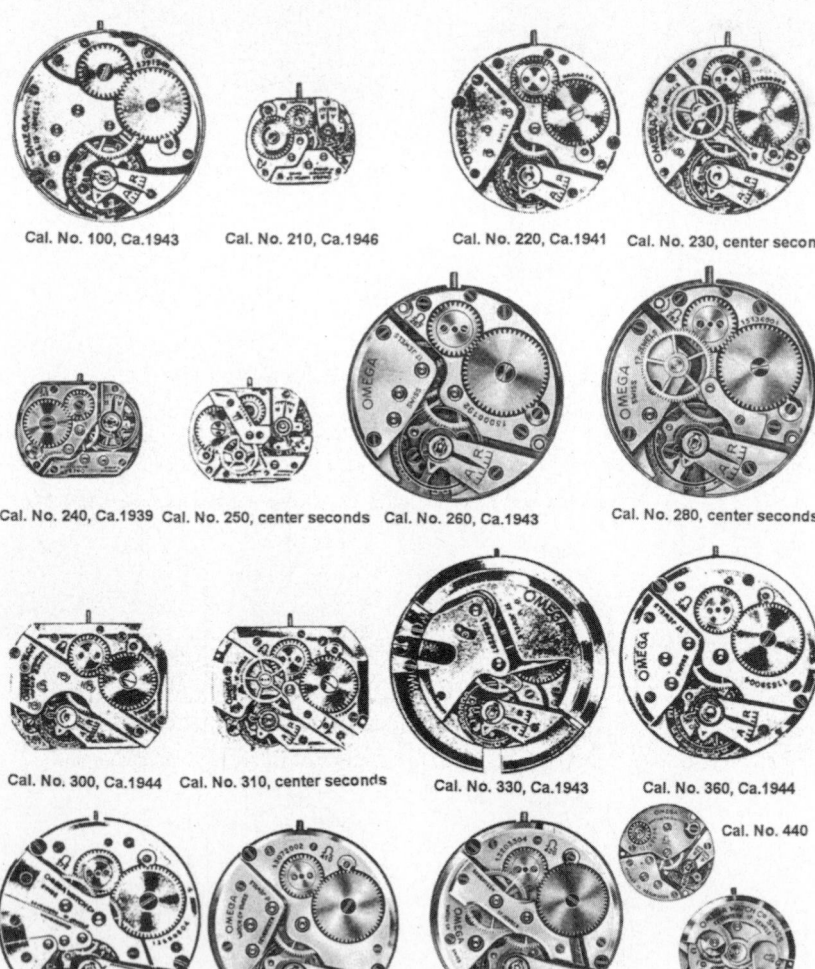

Cal. No. 100, Ca.1943   Cal. No. 210, Ca.1946   Cal. No. 220, Ca.1941   Cal. No. 230, center seconds

Cal. No. 240, Ca.1939   Cal. No. 250, center seconds   Cal. No. 260, Ca.1943   Cal. No. 280, center seconds

Cal. No. 300, Ca.1944   Cal. No. 310, center seconds   Cal. No. 330, Ca.1943   Cal. No. 360, Ca.1944

Cal. No. 440

Cal. No. 372, jumping seconds   Cal. No. 410, Ca.1951   Cal. No. 420, center seconds   Cal. No. 455, Ca.1955

Cal. No. 470, Ca.1955

Cal. No. 480, Ca.1955

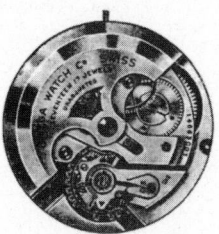
Cal. No. 490, Ca.1956

Cal. No. 500, Ca.1956

Cal. No. 510, Ca.1956

Cal. No. 520, center seconds

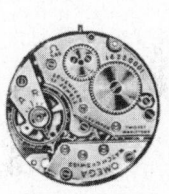
Cal. No. 540, Ca.1957

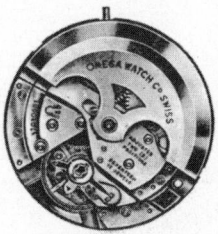
Cal. No. 550, Ca.1959

Cal. No. 570, Ca.1959

Cal. No. 590, Ca.1960

Cal. No. 600, Ca.1960

Cal. No. 620, Ca.1961

Cal. No. 580, Ca. 1959

Cal. No. 660, Ca.1963

Cal. No. 670, Ca.1963

Cal. No. 690, Ca.1962

Cal. No. 700, Ca.1964

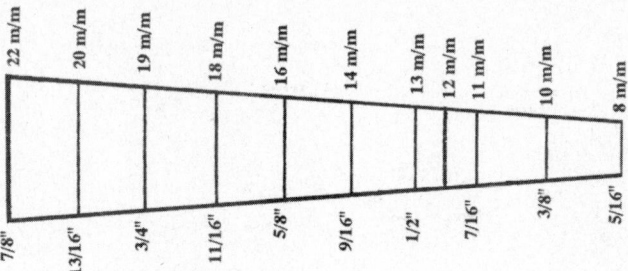

To determine your wrist watch band size use the **ABOVE GAUGE** and measure between the lugs. The band sizes are listed on each side of the gauge.

When performing any underwater activity, the dynamic pressure generated through movement is greater than the static pressure. Below a ranking of water resistance for most watches.

1 **meter** = 3.28 ft., 330 ft. =about 100 **meters**. 33.89 ft. =1 **atmosphere**, 100 ft. = about 3 **atmospheres**.

30M/100Ft/3ATM/3Bar = sweat-resistant
50M/160Ft/5ATM/5Bar = shower only, rain
100M/300Ft/10ATM/10Bar = swimming (**no diving**)
200M/660Ft/20ATM/20Bar = snorkeling, skin diving
1000M =scuba diving -3,300 ft.

ORFINA, 17 jewels, triple date, moon phase, bombe' lugs
gold filled $200 $400 $600

OPEL, 21 jewels, waterproof
gold filled $45 $70 $85

ORFINA, 17 jewels, triple date, moon phase, **carved lugs**
gold filled $200 $400 $600

ORATOR, 17 jewels, auto wind
s. steel $45 $70 $85

ORFINA, 17 jewels, day-date-month
gold filled $75 $150 $200

ORIS, 27J., date, auto wind, Ca. 1996
s. steel $125 $200 $250

PABRO, 17 J, 76 diamond watch, c.1930
Platinum $350 $600 $750

PARKER, 17J., 2 reg.chronog.,ca.1948
s. steel $150 $300 $375

ORVIN, 17 Jewels, day-date, c. 1945
s. steel $45 $100 $125

PATEK, PHILIPPE & CIE.

Swiss

Patek, Philippe & Cie. has produced some of the world's most desirable factory-made watches. Antoine Norbert de Patek began contracting and selling watches in the 1830's, later became partners with Francois Czapek and generally produced lovely decorative watches for a high class of clientele. In 1845 Adrien Philippe, inventor of the modern stem-winding system, joined the firm of Patek & Cie., and in 1851, the firm established its present name. Between Philippe's talent as a watchmaker and Patek's talent as a businessman with a taste for the impeccable, the firm rapidly established an international reputation which lasts to this day. A classic wrist watch the "Calatrava" model 96 was 1st used in 1932. The case and dial was designed at a time of transition from pocket watches to wrist watches. The coin was used as a perfect geometric shape to design a wrist watch case that has harmony and balance. Many variations from the classic model 96 have been used, but to most collectors the classic model 96 is known as the Calatrava model. The original 96 Calatrava model used a flat bezel, 31mm one piece case (lugs are not soldered on), manual wind, white dial, barrette-shaped hour markers, dauphine hands and aux. seconds chapter with a inside and outside circle and long 5 sec. markers. A black dial was added in 1937. The recent classic style Calatrava case is RF # 3796. To date there are many P.P. & Co. wrist watches named Calatrava.

PRODUCTION TOTALS

DATE-SERIAL#	DATE-SERIAL#	DATE-SERIAL#	DATE-SERIAL#	DATE-SERIAL#
1840 - 100	1905 - 125,000	1920 - 800,000	1940 - 900,000	1960 - 1,100,000
1845 - 1,200	1910 - 150,000	1925 - 805,000	1945 - 915,000	1965 - 1,130,000
1850 - 3,000	1915 - 175,000	1930 - 820,000	1950 - 930,000	1970 - 1,250,000
1855 - 8,000	1920 - 190,000	1935 - 824,000	1955 - 940,000	1975 - 1,350,000
1860 - 15,000	1925 - 200,000	1940 - 835,000	1960 - 960,000	1980 - 1,450,000
1865 - 22,000	1950 - 700,000	1945 - 850,000	1965 - 975,000	1985 - 1,600,000
1870 - 35,000	1955 - 725,000	1950 - 860,000	1970 - 995,000	1990 - 1,850,000
1875 - 45,000	1960 - 750,000	1955 - 870,000		
1880 - 55,000	1965 - 775,000	1960 - 880,000		
1885 - 70,000	1970 - 795,000	1965 - 890,000		
1890 - 85,000		1970 - 895,000		
1895 - 100,000				
1900 - 110,000				

The above list is provided for determining the APPROXIMATE age of your watch. Match serial number with date. Watches were not necessarily sold in the exact order of manufactured date.

Patek, Philippe & Cie. REFERENCE # INDEX

Note:Most Stainless Steel Pateks **usually** bring higher prices than 18K due to small production.

All Patek Philippe watches are listed in 18K Yellow gold case unless otherwise specified. A premium should be added if found in 18K Pink or White and especially Platinum. Dealer contact is suggested!

PATEK PHILIPPE,18J, **CLASSIC Calatrava**, RF#96, 33mm, cal 12L 120, c. 1930s

18k.	$3,500	$6,000	$7,000
18k Rose	$4,000	$7,000	$8,000
s. steel	$4,000	$6,000	$7,500
platinum	$10,000	$15,000	$20,000
platinum + diam. dial	$11,500	$16,000	$21,000

The above CLASSIC Calatrava case and dial model 96 was 1st used in 1932. It was designed at a time of transition from pocket watches to wrist watches. The coin was used as a perfect geometric shape so design a wrist watch case that has harmony and balance. Many variations from the classic model 96 have been used, but to most collectors the CLASSIC model 96 is known as the Calatrava model. The original 96 Calatrava model used a flat bezel, 31mm one piece case (lugs are not soldered on), manual wind, white dial, barrette-shaped hour markers, dauphine hands and aux. seconds chapterwith an inside and outside circle and long 5 sec. markers. A black dial was added in 1937. The recent classic style Calatrava case is RF #3796. To date there are many Calatava styles and models.

PATEK PHILIPPE, 18J, aux. sec., RF#96, 33mm, cal 12L 120, c.1937

18K	$4,000	$6,000	$7,000

PATEK PHILIPPE, 18J, diamond dial "Calatrava", RF#96, 31mm, cal 12L 120 or 27AM, c. 1930s-50s

platinum	$14,000	$20,000	$25,000

"PATEK PHILIPPE" watches should be signed on the case, dial & movement to bring the prices listed in this book.
(triple signed P.P.Co.)

PATEK PHILIPPE, 18J, "Calatrava," mid size, diamond dial,
RF# 96, 31mm, cal 12L-120, OR 27-AM
platinum $14,000 $20,000 $25,000

PATEK PHILIPPE, 18J, "Calatrava", enamel dial, Breguet style
numbers, RF#96, 32mm, cal 10L, c. 1940s
Platinum . . . . ★★$15,000 $22,000 $28,000
18k. . . . . ★$10,000 $15,000 $20,000

PATEK PHILIPPE, 18J, Calatrava, triple date note moon phases
at 12, RF#96, 30mm, cal 10-L c.1930
In 1996 a **similar** watch sold for $1.7 million US dollars
18K $500,000 $600,000 $900,000
platinum $600,000 $700,000 $1,000,000

PATEK PHILIPPE, Calatrava, RF#96, retrograde perp. calendar,
moonphases, 30mm, cal 11 c.1937
18K $275,000 $450,000 $600,000

PATEK PHILIPPE, Reverso, 18J, RF#106, 23 x 37mm, cal 9,
c.1930s
18K white $60,000 $100,000 $125,000

PATEK PHILIPPE, 18J, "Reverso", RF#106
18k white gold $40,000 $65,000 $100,000
s. steel . . . . ★★ $40,000 $65,000 $100,000

PATEK PHILIPPE, 26J, chronog., Calatrava, RF#130, 35mm,
cal 13, c. 1940s
18k pink gold $35,000 $50,000 $60,000
18k. $30,000 $45,000 $50,000

PATEK PHILIPPE, 26J, **split sec**. chronog. **one button**, for
Cartier, Sq. button for Rattrapante hand, crown for start stop
functions, 8 adj., **Breguet dial**, RF#130, 33mm, cal 13L, c.1938
18k. $250,000 $350,000 $500,000

DIALS FOR MINT PRICES MUST BE ALL ORIGINAL.

PATEK PHILIPPE, 18J, chronog., **black dial,** RF# 130, 33mm, cal 13L, c. 1940's
18k & s. steel (**case**) $50,000 $70,000 $85,000

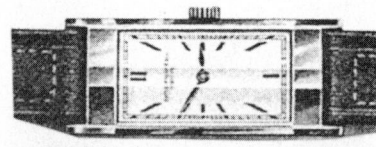

PATEK PHILIPPE, 18 jewels, , curved, RF # 137, 44mm, c. 1931
18k $4,000 $6,000 $7,500

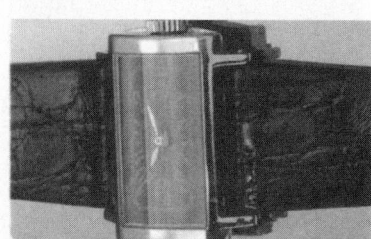

PATEK PHILIPPE, 18J., horizontal case, RF#139 &426, cal-8L, 28x22mm, cal 8L, c. 1937
18K $7,500 $11,000 $13,000

PATEK PHILIPPEE, 15J, large bezel, RF # 244
18k $2,800 $4,500 $6,000

PATEK PHILIPPE, 18J, RF # 404, 20x35mm, cal 9L 90, c. 1938
18k. $4,000 $6,000 $7,500

PATEK PHILIPPE, 18J, curved, RF # 406, 20x37mm, cal 9L 90, c. 1930s
18k. $5,000 $6,500 $7,500

PATEK PHILIPPE, 18J, RF# 409, cal 9L 90, c. 1934
18K $4,000 $5,500 $7,000

PATEK PHILIPPE, 18J, RF# 420, c. 1930s
18k. $3,000 $5,500 $7,000

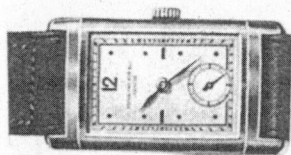

PATEK PHILIPPE, 18J, RF# 422, c. 1950s
18k. $3,000 $5,000 $6,500

PATEK PHILIPPE, 18J, curved, RF # 425, 20x43mm, c. 1935
18k. $5,500 $7,000 $8,000

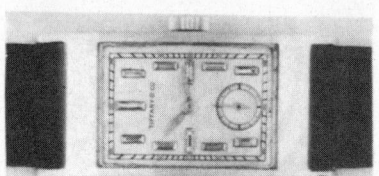

PATEK PHILIPPE, 18J, diamond dial, RF # 425, 20x43mm,c. 1940
platinum (**dial not original**) $7,500 $9,000 $11,000

PATEK PHILIPPE, 18J, Adj. to 8 positions, curved, RF # 425, 20x43mm, c. 1935
18k..........................$4,500 $7,000 $8,500
platinum $7,000 $10,000 $13,000

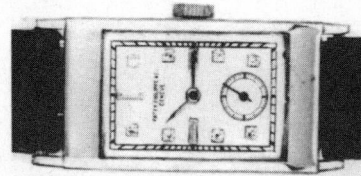

PATEK PHILIPPE, 18J, diamond dial, RF # 425, 20x43mm,c. 1940
platinum $10,500 $14,000 $17,000

PATEK PHILIPPE, 18J, diamond dial, RF # 425, 20x43mm,c. 1940
18K $7,000 $9,000 $11,000
platinum $10,000 $14,000 $18,000

PATEK PHILIPPE, 18J, diamond dial & bezel, RF # 425, 20x43mm, c. 1940
platinum $10,000 $15,000 $20,000

PATEK PHILIPPE, 18J, RF#425, 20x43mm, c. 1940s
18k..........................$4,500 $6,000 $7,500

PATEK PHILIPPE, 18J, RF# 425, 20x43mm, c.1936
18k..........................$4,500 $6,500 $8,000

PATEK PHILIPPE, 18J,"Staybrite," **curved case,** RF # 430
s. steel.....................$8,500 $12,000 $15,000

PATEK PHILIPPE, 18J, stepped case, RF # 433, 24x37mm, cal 9L, c. 1940
18k..........................$5,000 $7,000 $8,000

PATEK PHILIPPE, 18J, "Calatrava" aux. sec., RF#448, 28mm, cal 10L, c. 1930s
18k..........................$3,500 $5,000 $5,500
s. steel.....................$3,000 $4,500 $5,000

PATEK PHILIPPE, 18J., fluted bezel, RF# 462, Ca. 1937
18k..........................$4,000 $6,000 $7,000

PATEK PHILIPPE, 18J, curved, RF # 490, 491, 21x42mm, cal 9L 90, c. 1937
18k..........................$6,000 $9,000 $11,000
s. steel.....................$7,000 $10,000 $12,000

PATEK PHILIPPE, 18J, extended lugs, 2 tone, men's, RF#497, 25x37mm, cal 9L, c. 1940s
18k(y & w) $10,000 $17,000 $23,000

PATEK PHILIPPE, 18J, unusual shape lugs, RF#497, 25x37mm, cal 9L, c. 1940s
18k........................$8,000 $13,000 $15,000

PATEK PHILIPPE, 18J., horizontal case, 2 tone, RF#504, 25x35mm, cal 9L 90, c. 1939
18k........................$9,000 $15,000 $20,000

PATEK PHILIPPE,18J., extended lugs, **two tone case**, RF # 513, 20x33mm, cal 9L 90, c. 1943
18K $7,000 $12,000 $14,000

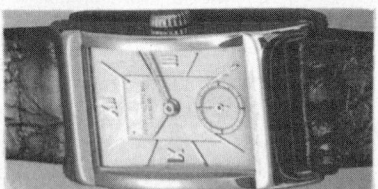

PATEK PHILIPPE, 18J, curved, RF #513-1, 20x33mm, cal 9L 90, c. 1940
18k........................$4,000 $6,000 $7,000

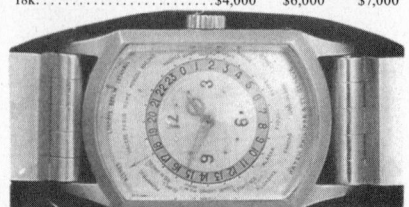

PATEK PHILIPPE, 18J, world time zone, 24 hr. rotating outside chapter, **tu-tone** case and band, RF#515, cal 10L, c. 1930s
18K C&B $400,000 $750,000 $1,000,000
Pateks 1st example of world time wrist watch.

PATEK PHILIPPE, 18J, wedge shaped and stepped "Bombe" WW, RF# 524, 23x39mm, cal 9-90, c. 1938
18k........................$10,000 $18,000 $25,000

PATEK PHILIPPE, 18J, chronog., RF# 530, 37mm, cal 13L, c. 1937
18k........................$40,000 $65,000 $80,000

PATEK PHILIPPE, 18J, stainless hooded lugs., RF# 531, 34mm, cal 12-120, c. 1940s
18k........................$5,000 $10,000 $12,000

PATEK PHILIPPE, 18J, RF#534, c. 1940s
18k(2-tone dial) $3,000 $5,000 $6,000

PATEK PHILIPPE, smallest "World Time" WW in the world, RF# 542, 28mm, cal 10, c. 1938
18k........................$40,000 $50,000 $70,000

PATEK PHILIPPE (continued)

PATEK PHILIPPE, 18J, fluted cylindrical lugs, RF # 556, 21x30mm, cal 8L 85, c. 1939
18k....................... $7,500 $10,000 $12,000

PATEK PHILIPPE, 18J, RF#565, 35mm, cal 12L 120 & 27AM, c. 1940s
18k....................... $5,000 $9,000 $12,000
Stainless Steel $7,000 $11,000 $15,000

PATEK PHILIPPE, 18J, large "Calatrava", aux. sec., RF#570, 35mm, cal 12L 120 or 27AM, c. 1950s
18k....................... $5,000 $9,000 $12,000

PATEK PHILIPPE, 18J, chronog.,2 reg., RF# 591, 34 mm cal 13-CC, c.1938
18k (black dial)............. $50,000 $60,000 $80,000

PATEK PHILIPPE, 18 jewels, RF # 655, 22x30mm, cal 9L 90, c. 1930s
18k....................... $4,500 $6,000 $8,000

PATEK PHILIPPE, 18J, **hooded satin lugs,** RF # 1402, 21x38mm, cal 9L 90, c. 1940s
18k asymmetric $12,000 $17,000 $24,000

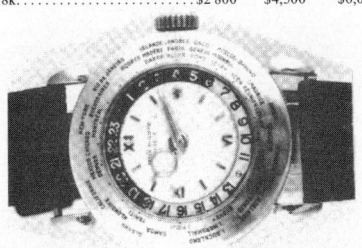

PATEK PHILIPPE, 18J, RF # 1408, 26x37mm, c. 1940s
18k....................... $2 800 $4,500 $6,000

PATEK PHILIPPE, 18J, "World Time," **41 cities**, RF#1415, 31x38mm, cal 12L, c. 1938
At auction sold for over $4,000,000.00, in platinum, in 2002
18K....................... $50,000 $70,000 $100,000
platinum $400,000 $700,000 $1,000,000

PATEK PHILIPPE, 18J, rectangular curved, "Vendome" lugs, RF#1420, 22x40mm, cal 9-90, c. 1930s
18K pink $12,000 $20,000 $30,000

PATEK PHILIPPE, 18J, fancy lugs, RF#1426, 31mm, cal 12L-120 c. 1940s
18k....................... $5,000 $7,500 $9,000

PATEK PHILIPPE, 18J, RF#1431, 26x37mm, cal 10L 200, c. 1940
18K $2,500 $5,000 $6,000

PATEK PHILIPPE, 18J, RF # 1432, 26x37mm, c. 1940s
18k. $3,000 $5,000 $6,000

PATEK PHILIPPE, 18J, RF#1433, 33mm, c.1940s
18K $2,000 $3,750 $4,500

PATEK PHILIPPE, 18J, **split sec**. chronog., RF #1436, 33mm,
cal-13, c.1938
At auction, sold for over $2,000,000.
Platinum $200,000 $300,000 $500,000
18k. $125,000 $200,000 $300,000

PATEK PHILIPPE, 18J, hooded lugs, RF # 1438, 23x34mm,
cal 9L 90, c. 1940s
18k. $3,000 $6,000 $7,000

PATEK PHILIPPE, 18J, RF# 1442, 21x33mm, c. 1940s
18k. $3,500 $6,000 $7,000

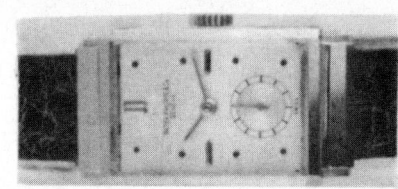

PATEK PHILIPPE, 18J., RF # 1444, 20x33mm, cal 9L 90,
c. 1940s
18k. $5,000 $7,500 $9,000

PATEK PHILIPPE, 18J, top hat style, RF # 1450, 22x38mm,
cal 9L 90, c. 1940s
18k C&B yellow $7,000 $10,000 $12,000
18k C&B pink. $8,000 $11,500 $14,000

PATEK PHILIPPE, 18J, top hat style, RF # 1450, 22x38mm,
cal 9L 90, c. 1940s
18k, yellow $6,000 $8,000 $9,500
18k, pink $9,000 $11,500 $13,000
platinum. $15,000 $20,000 $25,000

PATEK PHILIPPE, 18 jewels, RF#1461, 32mm, cal 10L200, c.1948
18k. $3,300 $5,000 $6,000
18k pink $3,500 $6,000 $7,000

PATEK PHILIPPE (continued)

PATEK PHILIPPE, 18J, aux. sec., RF#1461, 33mm, cal 10L 200, c.1948
18k. $3,300 $5,000 $6,000

PATEK PHILIPPE, 23J, chronog., waterproof, round buttons, 30 min. reg., RF#1463, 35mm, cal 13-CC, c. 1950's
18k. $40,000 $80,000 $100,000

PATEK PHILIPPE, 18J, 2-tone dial, RF #1463, 35mm, cal 13-CC, c.1940s
18k. $50,000 $70,000 $80,000

PATEK PHILIPPE,18J, fancy lugs, RF#1480, 24x40mm, cal 9L 90,
18k. $7,000 $12,000 $15,000

PATEK PHILIPPE, 18J, overhanging lugs, RF # 1481, 24x32mm
18k. $6,000 $9,000 $11,000

PATEK PHILIPPE, 18J, triple lugs, RF#1482, 22x39mm, cal 9L90, c. 1946
18k. $15,000 $20,000 $30,000

PATEK PHILIPPE, 18J, hidden lugs, RF # 1486, 26x36mm, cal 10L 200, c. 1950s
18k. $3,000 $5,500 $7,500

PATEK PHILIPPE, 18J, RF # 1486, 26x36mm, cal 10L 200, c. 1950s
18k C&B $4,000 $6,000 $7,000

PATEK PHILIPPE, 18J, fancy lugs, RF # 1487, 21x37mm, cal 9L 90, c. 1940
18k. $8,000 $12,500 $17,000

PATEK PHILIPPE, 18J, curled lugs, RF#1491, 33mm, cal 12L, c. 1940s
★Add $2,000 for sweep seconds and Breguet dial.
18K Yellow $7,000 $10,000 $12,000
18K Pink $8,000 $13,000 $15,000

PATEK PHILIPPE, 18J, **Curled lugs**, RF#1491, 33mm, cal 12L 120 & 27SC, c. 1940 *Center Seconds and Breguet dial add $2,000.*
18k. $8,000 $9,000 $12,000

PATEK PHILIPPE,18J, twisted lugs, RF#1497, cal 12-SC, c. 1940s
18k pink $8,000 $12,000 $18,000

PATEK PHILIPPE, 18J, RF# 1493, 24x39mm, cal 9L 90, c. 1950s
18k. $4,000 $6,500 $7,500

PATEK PHILIPPE, 18J, Calatrava, manual wind, RF#1505, 32.5mm, c.1941, cal 10-120
18K . . . .★★★★★$600,000 $750,000 $850,000

PATEK PHILIPPE, 18J, RF#1509, 33mm, c. 1940s
18k. $3,000 $5,000 $6,000
18k pink $3,500 $5,500   6,500

PATEK PHILIPPE, 18J, aux. sec., RF#1513, 35mm, cal 27 SC, c. 1943
18K $2,500 $5,000 $6,000

PATEK PHILIPPE, 18J, man. wind, RF#1516, c.1950
18K $3,300 $5,000 $6,000

PATEK PHILIPPE, 18J, aux. sec., RF#1517, 32mm, c. 1940s
18k. $2,800 $5,000 $6,000

PATEK PHILIPPE, 23J, chronog., triple date, moon ph. Perp calendar, Caltrava case, RF#1518, 35mm, cal 13,c. 1940s
18k. . . . .★★$120,000 $160,000 $200,000

PATEK PHILIPPE, 18J, Perpetual, Moon Ph., RF#1526, 35mm, cal 12L, c. 1940
18k. $50,000 $85,000 $110,000

PATEK PHILIPPE, 18J, fancy lugs, RF# 1530, 23x32mm,
cal 9L 90, c. 1940s
18k. $5,500 $8,500 $9,000

PATEK PHILIPPE, 18J, RF#1543, 33mm, c. 1947
18K $3,300 $6,000 $7,000

PATEK PHILIPPE, 18J, fancy lugs, RF# 1531, 23x23mm,
cal 9L 90, c. 1950s
18k. $3,000 $5,500 $7,000

PATEK PHILIPPE, 18J, unusual hooded lugs, RF#1550, 32mm,
cal 10-110
18K $7,000 $10,000 $15,000

PATEK PHILIPPE, 18J, RF # 1532, 23x36mm, cal 9L 90,
c. 1950s
18k. $4,000 $5,500 $7,000
s. steel $3,500 $5,250   6,750

PATEK PHILIPPE, 18J, oval lugs, RF # 1557, 25x34mm,
cal 10L 110, c. 1943
18k. $4,500 $6,000 $7,000

PATEK PHILIPPE, 18J, fancy lugs, RF# 1535, c. 1940s
18k. $3,000 $6,500 $7,500

PATEK PHILIPPE, 18J, hinged back, RF # 1559, 20x33mm,
cal 9L 90, c. 1940s
18k. $4,500 $7,000 $8,000

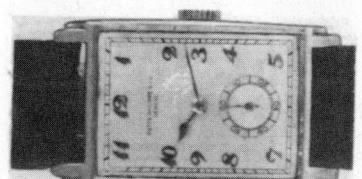

PATEK PHILIPPE, 20J, conical lugs, center sec., RF# 1536,
35mm, cal 12L-SC
18k. $4,500 $7,000 $8,500

PATEK PHILIPPE, 18J, RF # 1559, 20x33mm, cal 9L 90, c. 1943
18k. $5,000 $7,000 $8,500

PATEK PHILIPPE, 18J, RF # 1560, 23x32mm, cal 9L 90, c. 1948
18k. $5,000 $7,000 $8,500

PATEK PHILIPPE, 18J, RF# 1560, 23x32mm, cal 9L 90, c. 1948
18k. $4,000 $6,000 $7,500

PATEK PHILIPPE, screw back, round button, split second
chronograph, RF#1563, 35mm, cal 13, c. 1940s
3 known to exist in yellow gold
18K $250,000 $500,000 $700,000

PATEK PHILlPPE, 15 jewels, RF # 1564, 25x37mm, cal 9L 90,
c. 1950
18k. $3,500 $5,500 $7,500

PATEK PHILIPPE, 18J, RF # 1564, 25x37mm, cal 9L 90, c. 1950
18k. $5,000 $8,000 $10,000

PATEK PHILIPPE, 18J, RF # 1566, 26x34mm, cal 10L 200,
c. 1940s
18k. $4,000 $6,500 $8,000
18k pink $4,500 $7,000   8,500

PATEK PHILIPPE, 18J, RF # 1567, 23x32mm, c. 1940s
18k. $4,000 $7,000 $9,000

PATEK PHILIPPE, 18J, fancy lugs, RF# 1568, 22x34mm, c. 1940s
18k. $3,000 $6,500 $8,000

PATEK PH1LIPPE. 18J, RF # 1570, 26x38mm, cal 9L 90, c. 1940s
18k. $4,500 $6,500 $7,500

PATEK PHILIPPE, 18J, RF#1571, 34mm, c. 1940s
18k. $3,500 $5,000 $6,000

PATEK PHILIPPE, 18J, hidden lugs, RF # 1574, 26x36mm,
cal 10L 200, c. 1945
18k.........................$3,000 $5,000 $6,000

PATEK PHILIPPE, 18J, RF # 1575, 24x33, c. 1940s
18k yellow..................$2,800 $4,000 $5,500
18k pink $3,500 $5,000 $6,500

PATEK PHILIPPE, 18J, center sec., RF# 1578, 35mm, cal 27SC,
c. 1950s
18k.........................$4,000 $6,500 $7,500

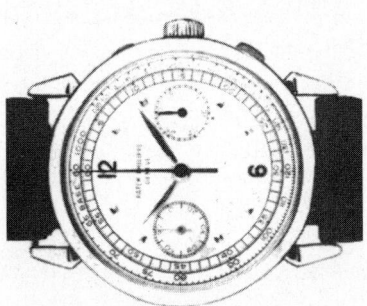

PATEK PHILIPPE, 18J, chronog., fancy lugs, RF#1579, 36mm,
cal 13, c. 1940's
18k.........................$40,000 $55,000 $70,000

PATEK PHILIPPE, 18J, concave lugs, RF # 1580, 21x44mm,
cal 9L 90, c.1950s
18k.........................$7,000 $10,000 $14,000

PATEK PHILIPPE, 18J, **hooded flared lugs**, aux. sec., RF#1584,
34mm, cal 12L 120, c. 1940s
18k.........................$6,000 $8,000 $12,000

PATEK PHILIPPE, 18J, concave & hooded lugs, RF#1585,
34mm, cal 12L 120, c. 1940s
18k.........................$6,000 $10,000 $12,000

PATEK PHILIPPE, 18J, curved, RF# 1588, 23x38mm, cal 9L-90
c. 1940s
18k.........................$5,000 $7,000 $8,500

PATEK PHILIPPE, 18J., beveled crystal, RF # 1588, 23x38mm,
cal 9L 90, c. 1945
18k pink $10,000 $14,000 $17,000
18k yellow.................$8,000 $12,000 $14,000

PATEK PHILIPPE, 18J, RF#1589, 33mm, c. 1955
18K(rose) $3,500 $6,000 $8,000

PATEK PHILIPPE, 18J, RF# 1595, 35mm, cal 12L 120, c. 1949
18K(rose) $3,500 $5,500 $7,000

PATEK PHILIPPE, 18J, RF#1590, 35mm, cal 12L 600AT, c. 1951
18K $3,300 $5,500 $6,500

PATEK PHILIPPE, 18J, moveable lugs, RF # 2066, 24x37mm,
cal 8L 85, c. 1944
18K $7,000 $10,000 $13,000

PATEK PHILIPPE, 18J, hidden lugs, RF # 1592, 22x32mm,
cal 9L 90, c. 1944
18k. $3,000 $5,500 $6,500

PATEK PHILIPPE,18J., RF # 2334, 22x32mm
18K $4,500 $6,500 $7,500

PATEK PHILIPPE, 18 jewels, RF # 1593, 20x41mm, cal 9L 90,
c. 1950s
platinum $18,000 $25,000 $32,000

PATEK PHILIPPE, 18J, lapidated lugs, RF # 2403, 21x30mm,
cal 9L 90, c. 1947
18k. $7,500 $10,500 $13,000

PATEK PHILIPPE, rectangle polychrome "cloisonne" enamel dial,
c. 1950s, RF # 1593, 25x40mm, cal 9-90.
18k. $30,000 $60,000 $75,000

PATEK PHILIPPE, 18J, applied gold numbers, RF # 2404,
21x33mm, cal 9L 90, c. 1948
18K $8,000 $11,000 $14,000

PATEK PHILIPPE, 18J, fancy lugs, RF # 2404, 21x33mm, cal 9L 90, c. 1948
18k. $6,500 $9,000 $12,000

PATEK PHILIPPE, 18J, RF#2424, 31x36mm, c. 1951
18K yellow $4,500 $6,000 $7,500
18K pink $6,000 $8,000 $10,000

PATEK PHILIPPE, 18J, RF#2406, 35mm, cal 12L 400, c. 1950s
18k. $3,500 $5,500 $6,000

PATEK PHILIPPE, 18J, RF#2429, 33mm, cal 10L 200, c. 1950s
18k yellow. $3,300 $5,000 $6,000
18k pink $4,000 $7,000 $9,000

PATEK PHILIPPE, 18J, fancy lugs, so called "Topolino", RF # 2414, 22x42mm, cal 9L 90, c.1949
18k. $7,500 $11,000 $16,000

PATEK PHILIPPE, 18J, curved rectangle, RF # 2415, 24x42mm, cal 9-90
platinum $15,000 $30,000 $50,000

PATEK PHILIPPE, 18J, fancy lugs, twisted, RF#2431, 33mm, cal 12-L120, c. 1948
18k. $15,000 $22,000 $28,000

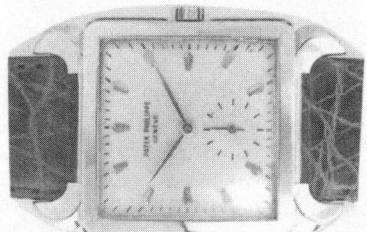

PATEK PHILIPPE, 18J, carved lugs, RF#2423, 31x36mm, c. 1946
18k yellow. $4,500 $6,000 $7,500
18k pink $5,500 $9,000 $11,000

PATEK PHILIPPE, 18J, RF# 2434, 25x38mm, cal 9L 90, c. 1950s
18k. $4,000 $6,500 $7,500

DIALS FOR MINT PRICES MUST BE ALL **ORIGINAL**.

PATEK PHILIPPE,18J., RF # 2437, 30x46mm, cal 10L-200, stepped lugs, c.1940
18K $4,000 $6,000 $7,000

PATEK PHILIPPE, 18J, Eiffel tower, flared caes, RF#2441, 25x41mm, cal 9L 90, c. 1951
18k $30,000 $50,000 $60,000

PATEK PHILIPPE, 18J., triple date, moon ph., RF#2438, 37mm, cal 27SCQ, c. 1962
Sold at auction for $200,000.00, in 2002
18k $75,000 $150,000 $200,000

PATEK PHILIPPE, 18J, banana model, **massive flared case,**
RF # 2442, 27x43mm, cal 9L 90, c. 1948
18k $20,000 $30,000 $35,000
platinum $39,000 $48,000 $60,000

PATEK PHILIPPE, 18J, fluted dropped lugs, RF # 2440, 28x43mm, cal 10L 200, c. 1947
18k $7,000 $11,000 $15,000

PATEK PHILIPPE, 18J, RF # 2445, 26x37mm, cal 9L-90, c. 1940s
18k $5,000 $9,000 $12,000

PATEK PHILIPPE, 18J, Eiffel tower, Pagoda flared case, Roman dial, RF#2441, 29x41mm, cal 9L 90, c. 1940s
18k $33,000 $50,000 $60,000
The Pagoda series was started in 1997. 150 pieces in Platinum, 250 pieces in White Gold, 500 pieces in Pink Gold, 1,100 pieces in Yellow Gold.

PATEK PHILIPPE, 18J, RF # 2447, 27x35mm, c. 1950
18K $2,500 $5,000 $6,500

PATEK PHILIPPE, 18J, "Calatrava", RF# 2451, 31mm, cal 10L 200, screw back, c. 1952

18K	$3,000	$5,000	$7,000
Stainless Steel	$3,000	$5,500	$7,500

PATEK PHILIPPE, 18J, RF#2452, 35mm, cal 12L 400 & 27AM, c. 1950s

18k	$5,000	$7,500	$9,000

PATEK PHILIPPE, 18J, diamond dial, flared, RF # 2456, 21x42mm, cal 9L 90, c. 1950s

18k	$10,000	$15,000	$18,000

PATEK PHILIPPE, 18J, flared case, RF # 2456, 21x42mm, cal 9L 90, c. 1950s

18k	$5,000	$8,000	$10,000

PATEK PHILIPPE, 18J, flared case, RF # 2456, 21x42mm, cal 9L 90, c. 1950s

18k	$5,000	$8,000	$10,000

PATEK PHILIPPE, 18J, center sec., RF#2457, 31mm, cal 27-SC c. 1950s

18k yellow gold	$4,000	$5,500	$6,500
18k pink gold	$5,500	$7,000	$8,500

PATEK PHILIPPE, 18J, RF#2459, 36mm, cal 12L 120, c. 1950s

18k	$3,500	$6,000	$7,000

PATEK PHILIPPE, 18J, center sec., RF#2460, 32mm, cal 27SC, c. 1950s

18k	$3,500	$5,500	$6,500

PATEK PHILIPPE, 18J, RF # 2461, 22x44mm, cal 9L 90,
c. 1950s
18k. $5,000 $7,500 $9,000

PATEK PHILIPPE, 18J, center sec., RF#2466, 32mm, cal 27SC,
c. 1949
18k. $4,200 $6,000 $7,500

PATEK PHILIPPE, 18J, flared case, RF # 2468, 21x39mm,
cal 9L 90, c. 1940s
18k. $10,000 $15,000 $20,000

PATEK PHILIPPE, 18 J, made for E. Gublin, RF # 2469,
26x36mm, cal 9L 90, c. 1950
18k. $5,500 $7,000 $8,500

PATEK PHILIPPE, 18J, triple lugs, RF#2471, 21x39mm,
cal 9L 90, ca.1951
18k. $30,000 $45,000 $60,000

PATEK PHILIPPE, rectangle polychrome "cloisonne" enamel dial,
RF #2471, 21x39mm, cal 9-90, c. 1960s
18k. $25,000 $45,000 $65,000

PATEK PHILIPPE, 18J, ribbed case & fancy lugs, RF # 2472,
27x37mm, cal 10L 200, c. 1950s
18k. $3,500 $6,500 $8,000

PATEK PHILIPPE, 18J, RF #2474, 26x37mm, cal 10L 200,
c. 1950s
18k. $3,500 $5,000 $6,500

PATEK PHILIPPE, 18J, curved, RF# 2476, 27x39mm, cal 9L 90,
c. 1950s
18k. $4,500 $7,000 $8,000

PATEK PHILIPPE, 18J, RF # 2477, 28x37mm, cal 9, c. 1953
18k $5,000 $7,000 $8,500

PATEK PHILIPPE, 18J, guilloche bezel, RF # 2479, 29x39mm,
cal 9L-90
18k. $4,000 $6,000 $8,000

PATEK PHILIPPE, 18J, top hat, diamond dial, RF # 2480,
21x37mm, cal 9L 90, c. 1950s
platinum $16,000 $22,000 $27,500

PATEK PHILIPPE, 18J, center sec., RF # 2481, 37mm, cal 27SC,
c. 1950s
18k. $5,000 $7,500 $10,000

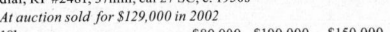

PATEK PHILIPPE, 18J, landscape cloisonne polychrome enamel
dial, RF #2481, 37mm, cal 27 SC, c. 1950s
At auction sold for $129,000 in 2002
18k. $80,000 $100,000 $150,000

PATEK PHILIPPE, 18J, RF#2482, 36mm, cal 27SC, c. 1950s
18k. $4,500 $5,500 $7,000

PATEK PHILIPPE, cen. secs.polychrome "cloisonne" enamel dial,
RF#2481, cal 27-SC, 36mm, c. 1954
18k. $45,000 $70,000 $85,000

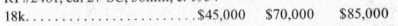

PATEK PHILIPPE, 18J, stylized hooded lugs, RF#2481, cal 9L-90,
22x38mm
18k. $8,000 $12,000 $15,000

PATEK PHILIPPE, 18J, RF#2484, 33mm, cal 10L 200, c. 1950s
18k. $3,300 $5,000 $6,000

PATEK PHILIPPE. 18J, RF # 2486, 31x36mm, cal 10L200, c. 1950s
18k. $3,500 $5,000 $6,000

PATEK PHILIPPE, 18J, RF #2488, 28x33mm, cal 10L 200, c.1940s
18k. $2,800 $5,000 $6,000

PATEK PHILIPPE, 18J, textured bezel, RF # 2496, 26x34mm, cal 10L 200, c. 1940s
18k. $3,000 $4,000 $5,500

PATEK PHILIPPE, 18J, fancy offset lugs, RF# 2491, 25x35mm, cal 10L 200, c. 1950s
18k. $4,000 $6,000 $7,500

PATEK PHILIPPE, 18J, diamond bezel, RF #2496, 26x34mm, cal 10L 200, c. 1950s
platinum $10,000 $16,000 $20,000

PATEK PHILIPPE, 18J, extra long lugs, RF#2494, 33mm, cal 27 AM, c. 1950
18k. $3,100 $5,000 $6,000

PATEK PHILIPPE, 37J, Perpetual, triple date, moon ph, RF #2497, 37mm, cal 27SCQ, c. 1950s
18k. $60,000 $80,000 $125,000

PATEK PHILIPPE, 18J, RF#2493, 29x40mm, cal 10L 200, c. 1953
18K $3,500 $5,000 $6,500

PATEK PHILIPPE, 23J, chronog., triple date, moon ph. perpetual calendar, arabic dial, RF#2499 (1 series) square button, 37mm, cal 13-CC, c. 1950s
At auction with black dial for $ 700,000.00 in 2002
18k. $185,000 $265,000 $350,000

PATEK PHILIPPE, 23J, chronog., triple date, moon ph.
perpetual calendar, RF#2499 (2 series), 37mm, cal 13-CC,
c. 1950s
18K $150,000 $235,000 $300,000

PATEK PHILIPPE, 23J, chronog., triple date, moon ph.perpetual
calendar, sapphire crystal, RF#2499 (4 series), 37mm, cal 13-CC,
c. 1950s
18k $100,000 $180,000 $250,000

PATEK PHILIPPE, 23J, chronog., triple date, moon ph.
perpetual calendar, glass crystal, RF#2499 (3 series), 37mm, cal
13-CC, c. 1950s
18k $125,000 $225,000 $275,000
4 black dials known to exist.

PATEK PHILIPPE, 18J, RF#2500, 32mm, c. 1950s
18k $2,800 $5,000 $6,000

PATEK PHILIPPE, 18J, fancy lugs, RF# 2503, 20x40mm,
cal 9L 90,c. 1950s
18k $14,000 $24,000 $26,500

PATEK PHILIPPE, 23J, chronog., triple date, moon ph.
perpetual calendar, RF#2499 (3 series)only 2 in platinum, 37mm,
cal 13-CC, c. 1950s
platinum $350,000 $500,000 $600,000

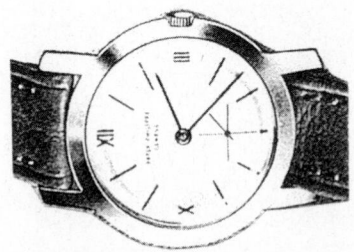

PATEK PHILIPPE, 18J, RF # 2506/1, 30mm, cal 10L 200, c. 1950s
18k $3,000 $5,000 $6,000

PATEK PHILIPPE, 18J, center sec., screw back, RF#2508, 35mm, cal 27SC, c. 1950s
18k.........................$6,000 $10,000 $12,000

PATEK PHILIPPE, 18J, screw back, RF#2509, 35mm, cal 12L 400 & 27AM.c. 1950s
18k....................$4,000 $8,000 $10,000
18k pink $6,000 $10,000 $12,000

PATEK PHILIPPE, "Aviator's", huge square buton, split secs, chrono., RF #2512, 45mm, cal 13, c. 1950
18k.........................$50,000 $100,000 $150,000

PATEK PHILIPPE, 18J, RF #2513, 27x37mm, cal 10L200, c. 1950s
18k.........................$4,000 $6,000 $8,000

PATEK PHILIPPE, 18J, RF # 2514-1, 30x40mm, cal 27SC, c.1940s
18k.........................$3,500 $5,000 $6,500

PATEK PHILIPPE, 18J, RF#2515, 34mm, c.1950s
18k.........................$2,800 $5,000 $6,000

PATEK PHILIPPE, 18J, RF # 2516, 26x34mm, cal 10L 200, c. 1950s
18k.........................$3,000 $5,000 $6,000

PATEK PHILIPPE,18J.. fluted hooded lugs, RF#2517, 26x34mm, cal 9L 90, c. 1953
18k.........................$8,000 $13,000 $18,000

PATEK PHILIPPE, 18J, large lugs, RF # 2518, 26x38mm, cal 9L 90, c. 1960s
18k.........................$6,000 $9,000 $11,000

PATEK PHILIPPE, 18J, extended lugs, RF#2520, 26x41mm, cal 9L 90, c. 1950s
18k C&B $10,000 $14,000 $18,000

PATEK PHILIPPE, 18J, "World Time," cloisonne polychrome enamel map on dial, **41 cities**, RF#2523, 36x43mm, cal 12L, c.1952
18k . . . . ★★★$450,000 $750,000 $1,000,000

PATEK PHILIPPE, 29 jewels, min repeater, RF#2524, 33mm, cal 12L, c. 1956
18k $185,000 $250,000 $325,000

PATEK PHILIPPE, 29 jewels, min. repeater, six watches finished by E. Gublin, ,RF# 2524-1,35mm, c.1950's, 18k case & band, triple signed
18k C&B $250,000 $325,000 $400,000

PATEK PHILIPPE, 18J, RF#2525/1, 33mm, c. 1950s
18k $3,200 $5,000 $6,000

PATEK PHILIPPE, 30J, auto-w, screw back, enamel dial, RF#2526, 35mm, cal 12L 600 AT, c. 1950s

18K pink . . . . ★★★$20,000	$30,000	$40,000
18K yellow . . . . ★★$15,000	$25,000	$35,000
18k white. . . . . ★★★$25,000	$35,000	$45,000
Platinum . . . . ★★★★★$150,000	$300,000	$500,000

Rare black enamel dial, with 100% MINT
10 made. . . . . ★★★★★$70,000 $80,000 $100,000

PATEK PHILIPPE, 18J, RF#2530-1, 27x35mm, cal 10L 200, c. 1956
18k C&B $5,000 $8,000 $10,000

PATEK PHILIPPE, 18J, RF # 2531, 25x37mm, cal 9L 90, c. 1950s
18k $4,000 $5,500 $7,000

DIALS FOR MINT PRICES MUST BE ALL **ORIGINAL**.

"PATEK PHILIPPE" watches should be signed on the case,
dial & movement to bring the prices listed in this book.
(triple signed P.P.CO.)

PATEK PHILIPPE, 18J, screw back, manual wind, RF#2533,
33mm, cal 27SC, c. 1950s
18k........................$4,000 $6,000 $8,000

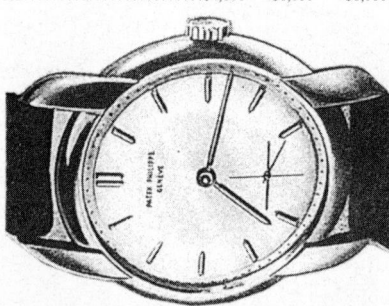

PATEK PHILIPPE, 18J, RF#2536, 32mm, cal 12L 400, c. 1950s
18k........................$4,500 $7,000 $9,000

PATEK PHILIPPE, 18J, aux. sec., RF#2537, 33mm, cal 12L 400,
c. 1950s
18k........................$3,000 $5,000 $6,000

PATEK PHILIPPE, 18J, RF#2540, 31x42mm, cal 12L, c. 1960s
18k........................$4,000 $5,000 $6,000

PATEK PHILIPPE, 18J, RF# 2541, 32mm, c. 1950s
18k........................$4,000 $5,500 $6,500

PATEK PHILIPPE, 18J, waterproof, "Calatrava", RF#2545,
31mm, cal 12L 400, c. 1950s
18k........................$4,500 $6,000 $7,000

PATEK PHILIPPE, 18J, unusual bat ear styled lugs, RF # 2546, cal
10-200, c. 1950s
18k........................$6,000 $10,000 $15,000

PATEK PHILIPPE, 18J, massive lugs, RF # 2548, 33mm, cal 10L
200, c. 1950s
18k........................$7,200 $11,000 $13,000

PATEK PHILIPPE, 18J, RF#2549, 33mm, cal 10L 200, c. 1950s
18k.................... ★★$22,000 $28,000 $37,000

PATEK PHILIPPE, 18J, RF#2550, 33mm, cal 10L 200, c. 1950s
18k........................$12,000 $17,000 $23,000

PATEK PHILIPPE, 18J, RF #2553, 22x38mm, cal 9L 90, c. 1960s
18k........................$4,500 $6,500 $8,000

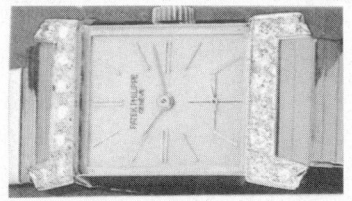

PATEK PHILIPPE, 18J, 16 diamond bezel, RF#2553, cal 9L-90, 22x38mm, c. 1960
18k C & B $8,000 $12,000 $15,000

PATEK PHILIPPE, 18J, RF #2554, 29x35mm, cal 9L 90, c. 1950s
18k white gold $18,000 $22,000 $30,000
18k yellow gold.............$10,000 $15,000 $20,000

PATEK PHILIPPE, 18J, center sec., waterproof, RF# 2555, 32mm-Calatrava, cal 27-SC
18k........................$5,000 $7,500 $9,000

PATEK PHILIPPE, 18J, RF#2557, 30mm, c. 1950s
18k........................$2 800 $5,000 $6,000

PATEK PHILIPPE, 18J, RF#2568-1, 35mm, c. 1957
18K $2,500 $5,000 $6,000

PATEK PHILIPPE, *Amagnetic*, water resistant, RF# 2570-1, 35mm, cal 12-400, c. 1950s
18k pink $7,000 $10,000 $15,000

PATEK PHILIPPE, 18J, *Amagnetic* on dial, RF# 2570, 35mm, cal 27, c. 1960
18k........................$6,000 $10,000 $12,000

PATEK PHILIPPE, 23J, chronog, day-date month, moon phase made for E. Gueblin, RF# 2571, 35mm, c.1951
18k C&B $100,000 $150,000 $180,000

PATEK PHILIPPE, 18J, "Calatrava", RF#2588, 32mm, c. 1940s
18k $3,500 $4,500 $6,000

PATEK PHILIPPE, 18J, RF#2573, 33mm, cal 23 300, c. 1960s
18K $2,500 $4,000 $5,000

PATEK PHILIPPE, 18J, RF # 2589, 33mm, cal23300, c. 1970s
18k $2,800 $4,500 $5,500

PATEK PHILIPPE, 18J, center sec., RF # 2574, 27x34mm, c. 1960s
18k C&B $5,000 $7,000 $9,000

PATEK PHILIPPE, 18J, RF#2592, 33mm, cal 13L 300, c.1956
18K(center lugs) $3,000 $4,500 $5,500

PATEK PHILIPPE, 18J, RF#2577, 35mm, cal 10L 200, c. 1957
18k $3,000 $5,000 $6,000

PATEK PHILIPPE, 18J, **time zone**, hour hand can be stepped forward or backward 1 hour at a time, RF #2597, 35x43mm, cal 27 400 & 27 AM, c. 1960s
18k $45,000 $60,000 $85,000

DIALS FOR MINT PRICES MUST BE ALL ORIGINAL.

PATEK PHILIPPE, 18J, **2 hr. hands 2 time zones**, RF #2597, 35x43mm, cal 27 400 & 27 AM, c. 1960s
18k.........................$45,000 $60,000 $85,000
18k pink $100,000 $145,000 $235,000

PATEK PHILIPPE, 21J, "Calatrava", RF#3025, 30mm, c. 1950s
note: center seconds and Breguet dial
18k.........................$4,000 $6,000 $8,000

PATEK PHILIPPE, 18J, RF #3404, 28x30mm, cal 23L 300, c.1960
18k C&B....................$3,000 $5,000 $6,000

PATEK PHILIPPE, 18J, RF # 3405, 27x34mm, cal 23L300, c. 1959
18k.........................$2,500 $4,000 $5,000

PATEK PHILIPPE, 18J, RF#3410, 35mm, cal 27AM 400, c. 1971
18K C&B....................$4,000 $5,500 $6,500

PATEK PHILIPPE, 18J, center sec., RF#3411, 35mm, cal 27SC, c. 1950s
18K.........................$3,000 $5,500 $6,500

PATEK PHILIPPE, 18J., designed by Gilbert Albert, RF#3412, 31x42mm, cal 23 300, c. 1958
18k.........................$30,000 $60,000 $70,000

PATEK PHILIPPE, 18J., asymmetric case designed by Gilbert Albert, RF#3413, 31x37mm, cal 23 300, c. 1958
18k.........................$25,000 $50,000 $60,000

PATEK PHILIPPE, 18J, RF # 3406, 27x27mm, cal 23 300, c. 1960s
18k.........................$2,500 $3,500 $5,000

DIALS FOR MINT PRICES MUST BE ALL **ORIGINAL**.

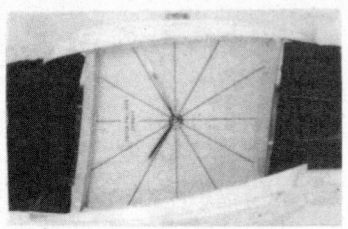

PATEK PHILIPPE, 18J., asymmetric, RF#3424, 27x40mm, cal 8L85, c. 1960
18k yellow gold. $20,000 $30,000 $40,000

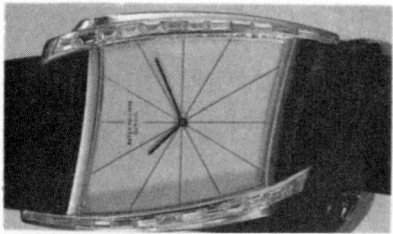

PATEK PHILIPPE, 18J., asymmetric, diamond set on bezel, RF # 3424, 27x40mm, cal 8L85, c. 1960
platinum $30,000 $45,000 $55,000

PATEK PHILIPPE, 37J, auto-wind, RF#3429, 35mm, cal 27 460, c. 1960s
18k. $5,000 $8,000 $12,000
18k white. $6,000 $10,000 $14,000

PATEK PHILIPPE, 37J, date, auto-wind, RF#3445, 34mm, cal 27 460M, c.1961
18K yellow $5,000 $8,000 $10,000
18K white $7,000 $11,000 $14,000

PATEK PHILIPPE, 37J, triple date moon ph, RF#3448, 37mm, cal 27 460Q, c.1968
platinum . . . . ★★★$80,000 $130,000 $150,000
18K $40,000 $80,000 $100,000

PATEK PHILIPPE, 37J, day-date-month, moon phase, waterproof, **perpetual date at 3**, RF#3450, 37mm, cal 27 460Q, c. 1985
18k. $70,000 $125,000 $150,000

PATEK PHILIPPE, 18J, blue sapphire bezel, RF # 3465, 26x38mm, cal 23 300, c. 1971
platinum $10,000 $14,000 $18,000

PATEK PHILIPPE, 18J, textured dial & bezel, RF #3467, 26x36mm, cal 23 300, c. 1960s
18k. $3,000 $5,500 $6,000
18k C&B. $3,500 $6,000 $7,000

PATEK PHILIPPE, 36J, auto-wind, RF# 3473, 33mm, c. 1962
18K $4,000 $7,000 $9,000

PATEK PHILIPPE, 37J, date, auto wind, RF #3514, 33mm,
cal 27 460, c. 1965
platinum $24,000 $26,000 $32,000

PATEK PHILIPPE, 18J, RF#3495, 33mm, cal 27SC, c.1969
18K $2,700 $5,000 $6,000

PATEK PHILIPPE, 37J, Auto-wind, date, RF#3514/1, 33mm,
cal 27 460, c. 1967
18K C&B $5,000 $8,000 $12,000

PATEK PHILIPPE, 18 J., diamond set case, RF#3497, cal 8.78L,
c. 1963
platinum C&B $16,000 $25,000 $30,000

PATEK PHILIPPE, 18J, RF #3519, 25x33mm, c. 1967
18k white. $2,500 $3,500 $5,000

PATEK PHILIPPE, 18J, RF#3509, 34mm, c. 1968
s. steel $2,500 $4,500 $6,000

PATEK PHILIPPE, 37J, auto wind, RF#3541, 36mm, c. 1966
18K $5,000 $7,000 $9,000

PATEK PHILIPPE, 18J, RF # 3555, 27x34mm, c. 1968
18k.....................$2,500 $3,500 $4,500

PATEK PHILIPPE, 37J, auto wind, RF# 3558, 35mm, cal 27460M, c. 1968
18K $3,500 $6,000 $8,000

PATEK PHILIPPE, 18J, auto wind, **back set,** RF#3565, 35mm c. 1970s
18k (fancy bezel) $5,000 $7,000 $8,000

PATEK PHILIPPE, 18J, RF#3574, 33mm, c. 1960s
s. steel.....................$3,000 $4,500 $5,500

PATEK PHILIPPE, 18J, diamond dial & bezel, RF # 3588, 35mm, c. 1970s
18k C&B....................$7,000 $9,500 $11,000

PATEK PHILIPPE, 37J, auto wind, date, RF #3601, 33mm, cal 28 255C, c. 1970s
18k C&B... ....$5,500 $7,500 $9,000

PATEK PHILIPPE, 36J, date, textured dial, automatic, RF#3604, 35x36mm, c. 1977
18K(w) $2,800 $6,000 $7,000

PATEK PHILIPPE, 18J, RF#3606, 32mm, c. 1970s
18k C&B....................$3,000 $4,500 $5,500

PATEK PHILIPPE, 18J, RF #3633, 29x33mm, cal 215, c. 1980s
18k C&B.................. $3,500 $5,000 $6,000

PATEK PHILIPPE, 18J, RF #3745, 32x27mm, c. 1980
18k C&B.................. $3,000 $4,500 $5,500

PATEK PHILIPPE, 36J, "Nautilus", large size, RF # 3700,
41mm, cal 28 225C
s. steel...................... $4,500 $5,000 $6,000
s. steel (RF# 3710) $6,500 $7,000 $8,000

PATEK PHILIPPE, Calatrava, Rose only, RF #3796, 32mm
18k (**Rose**) $4,000 $7,000 $8,000
18k yellow.................. $3,000 $5,500 $6,500

PATEK PHILIPPE, 18J, **Lapis & 54 Diamonds**, RF# 3727,
29x31mm, cal 16 250, c. 1974
18k......................... $6,000 $8,000 $10,000

PATEK PHILIPPE, 30J,"Calatrava", water resistant, auto wind
gold rotor, RF# 3796, 30x37mm, cal 215-S
18k......................... $5,000 $8,500 $11,000

PATEK PHILIPPE 29J, "Nautilus", gold & steel, automatic,
RF#3800, 36mm, cal 335 SC, ***Full Size**
18K $9,000 $9,500 $11,000
18k & s. steel................. $4,500 $5,000 $6,000
s. steel $4500 $5,000 $6,000

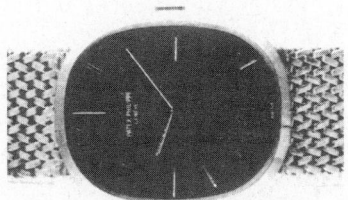

PATEK PHILIPPE, 23J, "Ellipse", RF#3738, 30x35mm, cal 177,
c. 1960s
18k C&B.................. $3,500 $5,000 $6,000

PATEK PHILIPPE, 36J, "Nautilus", diamond bezel, Fullsize, RF# 3800-2, cal 335-SC
18k. $11,000 $12,000 $14,000

PATEK PHILIPPE, 29J, auto wind, date diamonds=.91ct., pave diamonds=63ct., ruby markers, automatic, RF#3800/103, 36mm, cal 335SC
18k C&B. $17,000 $19,000 $23,000

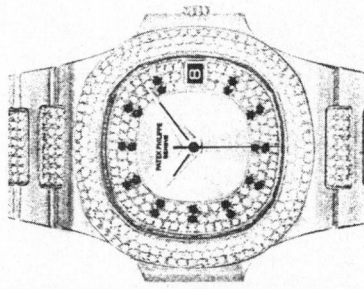

PATEK PHILIPPE, 29J, auto wind, date diamonds=2.40ct, pave diam.=.63ct., ruby markers, automatic, RF#3800/105, 36mm, cal 335SC
18k C&B. $20,000 $22,000 $26,000

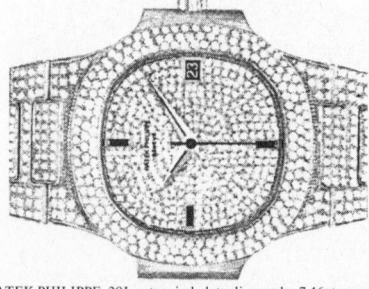

PATEK PHILIPPE, 29J, auto wind, date,diamonds=7.46ct., pave diam.=1.50ct., sapphire markers, automatic, RF#3800/108, 36mm, cal 335SC
18k C&B. $30,000 $33,000 $40,000

PATEK PHILIPPE, 50 sec. tourbillon, 57 hr. power reserve 5 gear train, RF#3834, 28 x 47mm, cal 34T, c. 1960
18k. $225,000 $275,000 $325,000

PATEK PHILIPPE, skel., auto wind, RF#3878, 31x35mm, cal240SQ
18k. $9,000 $15,000 $20,000

PATEK PHILIPPE, 18J, skeleton, diamonds=.85ct., manual wind, RF# 3884, 31x38mm, cal 177SQ
18k. $10,000 $15,000 $20,000

PATEK PHILIPPE, 18J, skeleton, diamonds=.62ct., RF#3885, 31mm, cal 177SQ
18k. $10,000 $15,000 $20,000

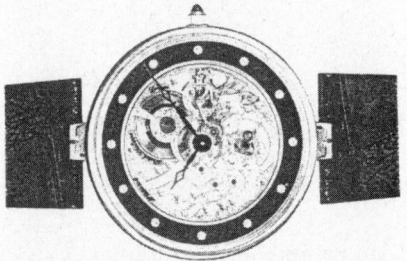

PATEK PHILIPPE, 18J, skeleton, RF#3886, 31x38mm, cal 177SQ
18k. $8,000 $12,000 $16,000

PATEK PHILIPPE, 18J, skeleton, RF#3885, 31mm, cal 177 SQ
18k.........................$8,000 $12,000 $15,000

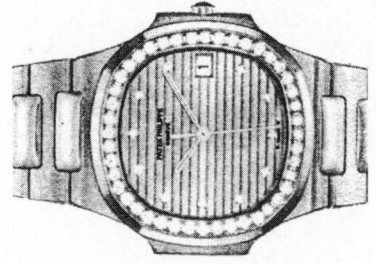

PATEK PHILIPPE, quartz, date. Carran dial diamonds=.68ct.,
RF#3900/3, 31mm, cal E 23SC
platinum $12000 $14000 $17,000

PATEK PHILIPPE, **mid size, QUARTZ**, rf#3900/1, date
s. steel.....................$2,000 $3,000 $4,000

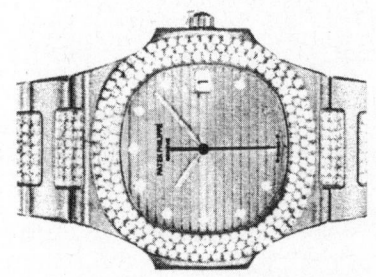

PATEK PHILIPPE, quartz, date, diamonds=2.27ct., RF#3900/5,
31mm, cal E 23SC
18k C&B...................$9,000 $10,000 $13,000

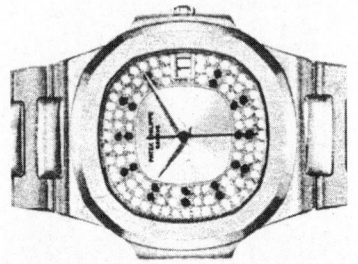

PATEK PHILIPPE, quartz, date, pave diamonds=.50ct, ruby hour
markers, RF#3900/101, 32mm, cal E 23SC
18k.........................$6,000 $7,500 $10,000

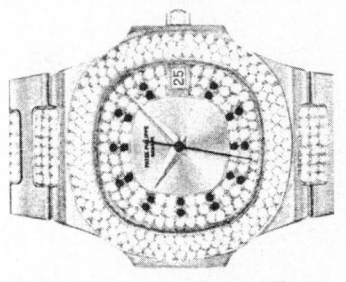

PATEK PHILIPPE, quartz, date, diamonds=2.27ct pave
diamonds=.50, ruby markers, RF#3900/105, 32mm, cal E 23SC
18k C&B...................$10,000 $11,000 $14,000

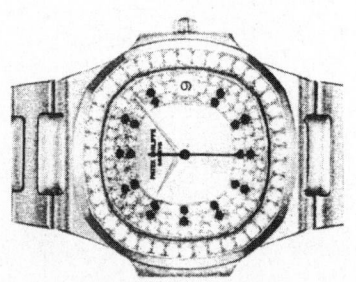

PATEK PHILIPPE, quartz, date diamonds=.68ct, pave
diamonds=.50, ruby markers, RF#3900/103, 32mm, cal E 23SC
18k.........................$7,000 $8,500 $11,000

PATEK PHILIPPE, 18J, "Officier," RF#3960, 33mm, cal9L,
c.1989, *18k 2,200 made, 18k(w) 150 made, platinum 50 made*
18K, 2000 made $14,000 $16,000 $19,000
18k(w), 150 made $16,000 $18,000 $21,000
platinum, 50 made $26,000 $29,000 $33,000

PATEK PHILIPPE, 18J, Jump Hour, RF #3969, 28x37mm, cal 215HG, c. 1989, 150th Anniversary model, 450 in Pink gold and 50 in Platinum.
18k......................$20,000 $35,000 $47,000

PATEK PHILIPPE, 18J, chronog, triple date moon ph 24 hr indicator leap year indicator, round buttons, RF#3970E, 36mm, cal 27-70Q
18k......................$45,000 $65,000 $75,000
platinum $65,000 $90,000 $115,000

PATEK PHILIPPE, 39J., auto-wind, min repeater, perpetual day date month calendars, moon ph., 24 hr. ind., leap year ind., RF#3974, 36mm, cal 27RQ, c. 1989
18K $175,000 $275,000 $400,000

PATEK PHILIPPE, auto-wind, min repeater, RF#3979, 34mm, cal R27 PS, c. 1995
5 exist in platinum $100,000 $175,000 $250,000

PATEK PHILIPPE, 29 jewels, min. repeater, 32x40mm, cal 101-5L, c. 1920
platinum $400,000 $500,000 $800,000

PATEK PHILIPPE, 18J, "Chronometro Gondolo"
18k......................$15,000 $25,000 $30,000

PATEK PHILIPPE, 16J, c. 1923
18k......................$3,500 $7,500 $9,000

PATEK PHILIPPE, 18J, note **radial**, c. 1910
18k......................$3,500 $5,500 $7,000

PATEK PHILIPPE, 18J, c. 1920s
18k......................$5,000 $7,500 $9,000

PATEK PHILIPPE, 18J, c. 1920s
18k........................$3,500 $5,500 $7,000

PATEK PHILIPPE, 18J
18k........................$3,000 $6,000 $7,000

PATEK PHILIPPE, 18J, cal 9, 23x34mm, c. 1910
platinum..................$10,000 $15,000 $20,000

PATEK PHILIPPE, 18J, c. 1930s
18k........................$4,000 $7,000 $8,500

PATEK PHILIPPE, 18J, c. 1930s
18k........................$4,500 $8,000 $9,500

PATEK PHILIPPE, 15J, mid-sized, 2 tone, 28 mm, cal 10-L
Note: winds at 12
18k (y & w)................$7,000 $10,000 $12,000

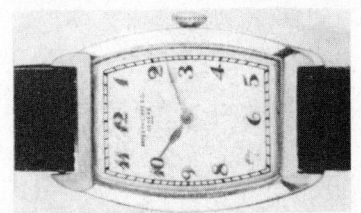

PATEK PHILIPPE, 18J, 26x36mm, cal 9, c. 1925
18k........................$5,500 $8,000 $10,000

PATEK PHILIPPE, 18J, sub secs, 26x38mm, cal 9, c. 1920s
18k........................$6,500 $10,000 $15,000

PATEK PHILIPPE, 15J, for Baily, Banks & Biddle, 30x35mm, cal
12L, 30x35mm, c. 1920
18k........................$4,000 $6,000 $7,000

PATEK PHILIPPE, 18J, hooded lugs, 30x34mm, cal 9-L, c. 1930s
18K........................$5,000 $9,000 $10,000

PATEK PHILIPPE, first "Officier", enamel dial, wire lugs, 31mm, cal 10, c. 1917
18k. $6,500 $10,000 $15,000

PATEK PHILIPPE, 15J, enamel dial, 33mm, cal 12-L, c. 1910
18k. $8,000 $10,000 $12,000

PATEK PHILIPPE, 18J, small "Calatrava", 32mm, c. 1940s
18k. $3,200 $4,500 $6,000

PATEK PHILIPPE, single button chronog., 30 min reg., 39x42mm, cal 13, c. 1920s
white gold. $275,000 $450,000 $600,000

PATEK PHILIPPE, 28J, **split sec**. chronog., 30 min reg., 34x42mm, cal 13L, c. 1930s
18k. $400,000 $600,000 $1,000,000

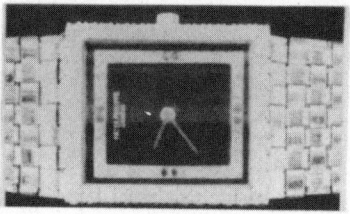

PATEK PHILIPPE Quartz, diamonds on dial & case, RF# 3976, cal E-15
18K C&B $4,000 $6,000 $7,500

PATEK PHILIPPE, 18J, hidden dial, 18k & plat, c. 1930s
"Cabriolet", remade in 2001 & list for $13,900 in 2001
18k & platinum (1930s). $30,000 $45,000 $50,000

PATEK PHILIPPE, 18J, inclined & curved case, 23x38mm, c. 1940s
18k. $22,000 $28,000 $33,000

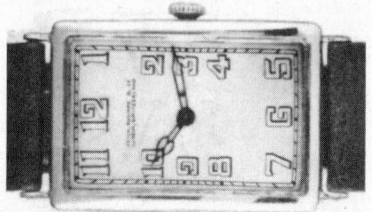

PATEK PHILIPPE, 18J., **hinged back**, 30x47mm, c.1920s
note: **NO seconds**
18k. $9,000 $14,000 $18,000

PATEK PHILIPPE, 29 jewels, min. repeater, 30 X 34mm, cal 12L
18k......................$325,000 $500,000 $700,000

PATEK PHILIPPE, 18 jewels
18k $4,000 $6,500 $8,000

PATEK PHILIPPE, 18 J., **hinged back**, 30x47mm, c. 1920s
note: **auxiliary seconds**
18k........................$10,000 $14,000 $18,000

PATEK PHILIPPE, 18J., decorated enamel case, c. 1920s
18k........................$12,000 $17,000 $22,000

PATEK PHILIPPE, 18J, engraved bezel hinged back, 22x30mm,
c. 1920
18k......................$9,000 $13,000 $17,000

PATEK PHILIPPE, 18 jewels, c.1930s
18k......................$3,000 $6,000 $7,000

PATEK PHILIPPE, 18J, hinged back, stepped case, 24x30mm,
c. 1920's
18k......................$5,000 $6,500 $7,500

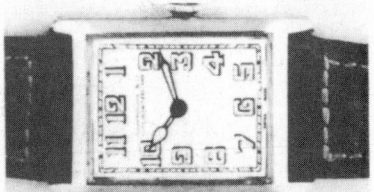

PATEK PHILIPPE, 18J, hinged back, 24x33mm, c. 1920s
18k......................$4,000 $7,000 $9,000

PATEK PHILIPPE, 18J, aux. sec, 24x34mm, cal 9, c. 1940
18k......................$4,000 $6,500 $8,000

PATEK PHILIPPE, 18J, **2 tone**, hooded & stepped lugs, 23x40mm
18k......................$14,000 $18,000 $22,000

PATEK PHILIPPE, 18J, M# 9, curved style, c. 1940's
18k......................$7,000 $8,500 $10,000

PATEK PHILIPPE, 18J, lady's watch, c. 1940s
18k.........................$1,000 $1,800 $2,200

PATEK PHILIPPE, 18J, Hooded Lugs, 21x38mm
s. steel.....................$6,000 $7,500 $9,000

PATEK PHILIPPE, 18J, lady's watch
18k.........................$1,200 $2,000 $2,500

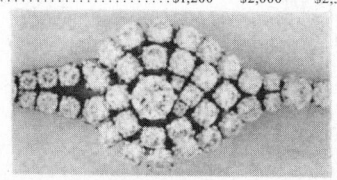

PATEK PHILIPPE, 18J, lady's, hinged lid set in diamonds
18k.........................$8,000 $10,000 $14,000

PATEK PHILIPPE, 18J, lady's watch
18k C&B....................$2,500 $4,000 $4,500

PATEK PHILIPPE, 18J, lady's watch, diamond bezel
platinum $3,000 $4,500 $5,500

PATEK PHILIPPE, 18J, cal 9, c. 1910s
18k C&B....................$4,500 $6,000 $8,000

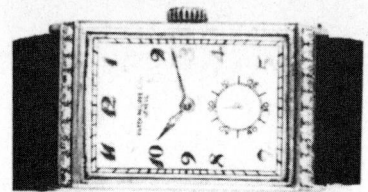

PATEK PHILIPPE, 18J, hinged back, diamond bezel
18k.........................$7,000 $10,000 $13,000

PATEK PHILIPPE, 18J, lady's watch, c. 1940s
18k C&B....................$2,500 $3,000 $4,500

PATEK PHILIPPE, 18J, lady's watch, min. repeater
18k.........................$65,000 $75,000 $100,000

PATEK PHILIPPE, 18J, lady's watch, c. 1950s
18k.........................$1,400 $3,000 $4,000

PATEK PHILIPPE, 18J, lady's watch, c. 1940s
18k.........................$1,400 $3,000 $4,000

PATEK PHILIPPE, 18J, lady's watch, c. 1950s
18k.........................$900 $1,500 $1,800

PATEK PHILIPPE, 18J, lady's watch, c. 1950s
18k.........................$2,500 $4,000 $5,000

PATEK, PHILIPPE
MOVEMENT IDENTIFICATION

Caliber 6¾, no. 60
S.no. 865000-869999
(1940-1955)

Caliber 7, no. 70
S.no. 943300-949999
(1940-1960)
S.no. 940000-949999

Caliber 8, no. 80
S.no. 840000-849999
(1935-1960)

Caliber 8, no. 85
S.no. 850000-859999
(1935-1968)

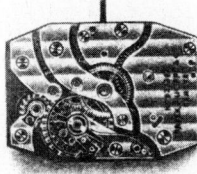

Caliber 9, no. 90
S.no. 833150-839999
S.no. 970000-979999
(1940-1950)

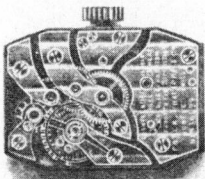

Caliber 9, no. 90a
830000-833149
(1940-1950)

Caliber 10, no. 105
S.no. 900000-909999
(1940-1945)

Caliber 10, no. 110
S.no. 910000-919999
(1940-1950)

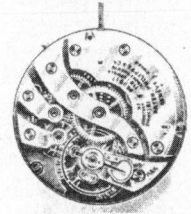

Caliber 10, no. 200
S.no. 740000-759999
(1952-1965)
S.no. 950000-959999
(1945-1955)

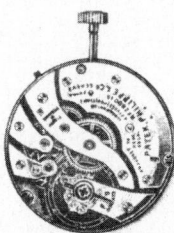

Caliber 23, no. 300
S.no. 780000-799999
(1955-1965)

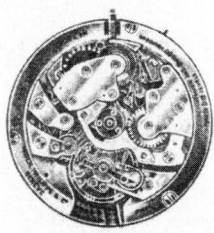

Caliber 12, no. 600AT
S.no. 760000-779999
(1952-1960)

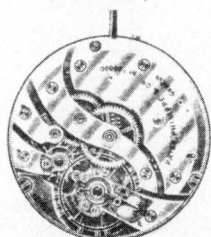

Caliber 12, no. 400
S.no. 720000-739999
(1950-1965)

Caliber 12, no. 120
826900-829999 (1935-1940)

Caliber 12, no. 120A
92000-929999 (1940-1950)
960000-969999 (1946-1952)
938000-939999 (1952-1954)

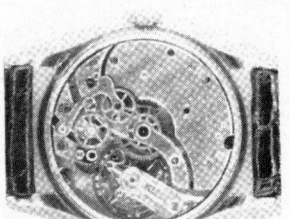

Caliber 12 , center seconds

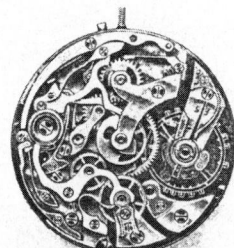

Caliber 13, no. 130A

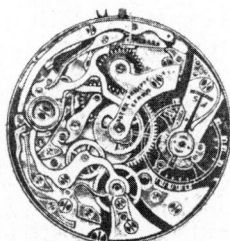

Caliber 13, no. 130B

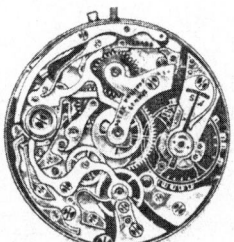

Caliber 13, no. 130C

Chronograph, no. 862000-863995 (1940-1950); no. 867000-869999 (1950-1970)

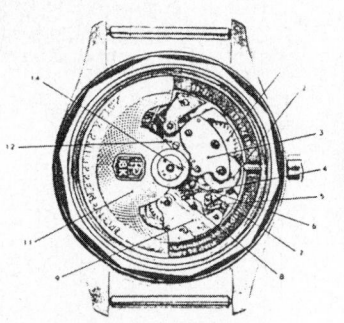
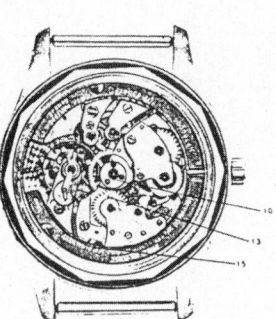

Caliber 12-600 AT, S.no. 760,000-779,999 (1960-1970)

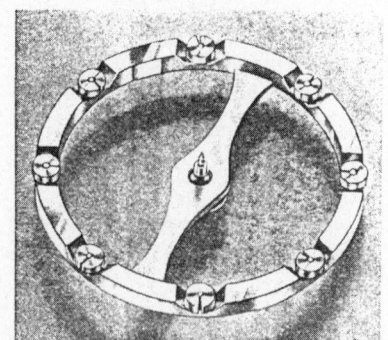

GYROMAX BALANCE WHEEL

DIALS FOR MINT PRICES MUST BE ALL **ORIGINAL**.

PATRIA, 7 jewels, enamel dial, **compass**, Ca. 1920

s. steel	★$250	$450	$550
sterling	$350	$550	$700

PERPETUAL W. CO., 15 jewels, c. 1930s, early auto-wind

14k	$600	$800	$1,100
gold filled	$400	$500	$600

PATRIA, 7 jewels, enamel dial,

silver	$75	$135	$200

PERPETUAL W. CO., 15J., fluted bezel, and sold for $37.50 in 1933, early auto-wind

base metal	$200	$350	$450

PERPETUAL W. CO., 15jewels, fluted bezel, early auto-wind

gold filled	$300	$450	$600

PERFINE, 17 jewels, chronog., 2 reg.

gold filled	$150	$275	$350
s. steel	$100	$200	$300

PERPETUAL W. CO., 15J., diamond bezel, c. 1930s

platinum	$400	$600	$700

PERPETUAL W. CO., 15 jewels, rim wind & set, original retail price in 1933 was $31.50

14k	$600	$800	$1,000
gold filled	$250	$375	$500
s. steel	$200	$300	$375
base metal	$150	$250	$300

PHILLIPE. W. CO., 17J., RF#2501,chronog., c.1950

s. steel	$125	$250	$300

DIALS FOR MINT PRICES MUST BE ALL **ORIGINAL**.

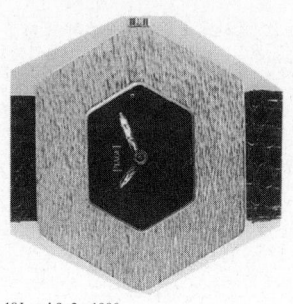

PIAGET, 18J., cal.9p2 c.1980
18k(w) $500 $700 $800

PIAGET, 18 jewels, 2 movements, 2 dials,
18k. $600 $900 $1,100

PIAGET, 18J., center sec., RF#1176, cal.f1560, c.1952
18k. $350 $600 $700

PIAGET, 18 jewels, black dial
18k. $400 $600 $800

PIAGET, 18J., center sec., c. 1950
18k. $400 $600 $700

PIAGET, 18 jewels, center sec., auto wind
18k. $500 $800 $1,000

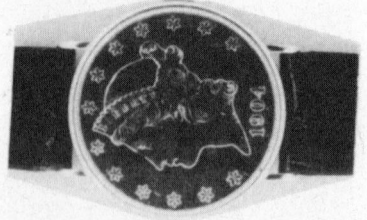

PIAGET, 18 jewels, 1904 $20 dollar gold piece, flip top
22k $800 $1,600 $2,000

Some grades are not included. Their values can be determined by comparing with similar age, size, metal content, style, grades, or models such as time only, chronograph, repeater etc. listed.

PIAGET, 18 jewels, ref. #8177, auto wind
18k. $500 $800 $1,000

PIAGET, 18 jewels
18k. $500 $800 $1,000

PIAGET, 18 jewels, oval style
18k C&B $500 $800 $950

PIAGET, 30 jewels, auto wind, gold rotor
18k. $500 $800 $1,000

PIAGET, 18 jewels, oval style
18k. $250 $500 $700

PIAGET, 18 jewels, 18k case, 14k band
18k &14k C&B $700 $1,000 $1,200

PIAGET, 18 jewels, textured bezel
18k. $600 $900 $1,100

PIAGET, 18J., for Van Cleef, center lugs, thin model
18k. $500 $800 $1,000

PIAGET, 18J, 2 time zones & 2 movements
18k. $700 $1,200 $1,400

PIAGET, 18J., RF#9821 ,c.1975
18k C&B $700 $1,000 $1,200

PIAGET, 30 jewels, auto-wind, textured bezel
18k. $500 $800 $1,100

PIAGET, 18J., RF#9298, c. 1970
18k. $600 $1,000 $1,200

PIAGET, 18 jewels,
18k. $600 $1,000 $1,200

PIAGET, 18 jewels, "Emperor", RF#7131C516
18k plain dial $2,500 $3,500 $4,200
18k pave dial. $3,000 $4,000 $5,000

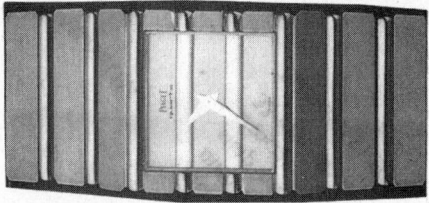

PIAGET, "Polo", RF#7131C701, quartz
18k C&B $3,000 $4,000 $5,000

PIAGET, "Polo", RF#15562C701, quartz
18k. $3,000 $3,500 $4,500

NOTE: PIAGET identification # the first 3 to 5 = case design, a letter as A, B, C, =bracelet design. All models beginning with 7, 8 or 15 may be worn while swimming.

PIAGET, "Polo", RF#15562C701, quartz
18k C&B $2,200 $3,000 $4,000

PIAGET, RF#8065D4
18k C&B $1,200 $1,900 $2,500

PIAGET, 17 jewels, Ca. 1957
18k. $400 $550 $700

PIERCE,7J., Doctors style, Ca. 1930
base metal. $150 $300 $400

Wrist Watches listed in this section are priced at the collectable fair market Trade Show level as complete watches having an original gold-filled case and stainless steel back, also with original dial, leather watch band, and the entire original movement in good working order with no repairs needed.

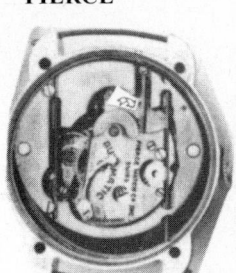
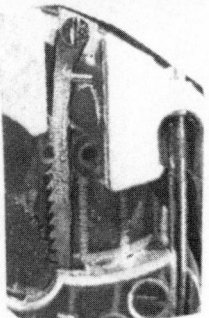

PIERCE, 17J., early auto wind, "**Parashock**," Ca. 1930s
weight moves from 12 to 6 O'clock
s. steel $250 $350 $500
18k . . . . ★★★$1,000 $2,000 $3,000

PIERCE, 17J., triple date, moon ph.
gold filled $250 $450 $600

PIERCE, 21 jewels, "Duofon", **Alarm**, Ca. 1955
s. steel $75 $165 $200

POBEDA, 15J., tonneau, Ca.1930s
14k pink $150 $225 $275

PIERCE, 17 jewels, chronog. one button
s. steel $225 $400 $550

POLJOT, 25J, "Selena", limited, made in Moscow, Moon Ph.
Russian chronograph, date, M-wind, Ca. 2002
s. steel $200 $275 $325

PIERCE, 17 jewels, chronog., c. 1940s
s. steel $150 $300 $400
14k $350 $500 $700
18k $425 $700 $900

PONTIFA, 17 jewels, chronog, day-date-month, 3 reg.
14k $400 $800 $1,000
s. steel $250 $475 $600

PRAESENT, 17J., triple date, moon ph., mid size, c. 1948
gold filled $200 $350 $500

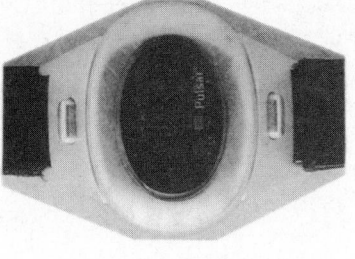

PULSAR, LED. (light emitting diode), **working**, ca.1975
14k. $300 $400 $500
gold filled $75 $150 $250

PROVITA, 17J., cal.1525, c.1973
18k. $150 $200 $250

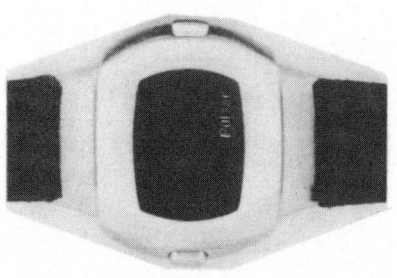

PULSAR, L.E.D. (light emitting diode), working, c.1975
18k. $400 $700 $1,000
14k. $300 $500 $700
gold filled $75 $150 $250
s. steel $75 $150 $250

PRONTO, 17 jewels, triple date, auto wind, waterproof
s. steel $75 $125 $175

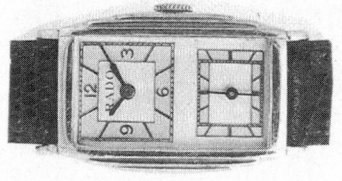

RADO, 7J., doctors style double dial, c.1938
gold filled $200 $400 $500

PULSAR, L.E.D.(light emitting diode), working, Ca.1975
18k. $300 $500 $650
14k. $300 $400 $550
gold filled $75 $150 $250
s. steel $75 $150 $250

RADO, 17J., date, ca.1960
gold plate $30 $50 $75

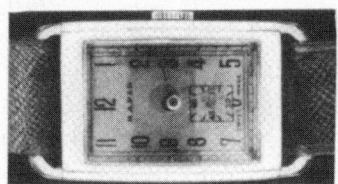

RAPID, 17J., on mvt. PATHE W CO.
gold filled $40 $75 $100

RECORD, 17J., split sec. chronog., date, moon phase
18k. $3,000 $5,500 $7,000

RECORD, 17 jewels, split sec. chronog.
18k. $3,500 $5,500 $7,000
s. steel $1,500 $2,500 $3,500

RECORD, 17 J., triple date, moon ph., auto wind,
2 reg. chronograph.
18k. $1,200 $2,200 $3,000

RECORD, 17 jewels, triple date, moon phase, c. 1940s
18k. $600 $1,100 $1,300

RECORD, 17 jewels, day-date-month, moon phase
s. steel $300 $600 $800

RECORD, 17 J., triple date, moon phase, auto wind
18k. $600 $750 $1,000

REGINA, enamel dial, center lugs, c. 1929
silver $135 $300 $400

☞ Some grades are not included. Their values can be determined by comparing with similar age, size, metal content, style, grades, or models such as time only, chronograph, repeater etc. listed.

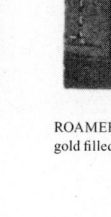

REMBRANT, 17J., chronog., c.1942
18k.	$250	$450	$550
s. steel	$100	$175	$275

ROAMER, 17 jewels, hidden lugs
gold filled $40 $75 $100

REVUE, 17J., beveled case, cal.54, c.1940
nickel $35 $75 $100

ROCKFORD,7J., **enaml dial** with red 5 min., wire lugs,
S#701,960, G#180,0 size, HC, M# 1, Ca.1910
nickel $100 $200 $300

RIMA, 17J., aux. sec.,
14k. $100 $125 $175

ROCKFORD, 15J., "Winona", made in USA, S#761074
gold filled	$200	$325	$475
base metal	$150	$200	$275

ROAMER, 17 jewels, date, auto wind
gold filled $50 $100 $125

ROCKFORD, 17J., "Iroquois", gold train
gold filled $225 $325 $475

ROLEX WATCH CO.

Swiss

Rolex was founded by Hall Hans Wilsdorf in 1905, with his brother-in-law using the name of Wilsdorf & Davis and used movement supplier Aegler of Bienne, Switzerland, and bought cases from London. First wrist chronometer in 1910, In 1908 the trade-mark "Rolex" was officially registered, and by 1919, Wilsdorf started the "Manufacture des Montres Rolex" and the movements were manufactured in Bienne, but finished and cased in Geneva. In 1926, they made the first real waterproof wrist watch and called it the "Oyster". Rolex introduced a self-winding movement they called "Perpetual" in 1931. In 1945, they introduced the "Date-Just," which showed the day of the month. In 1950 the "Turn-o-graph" was used, the forerunner of the Submariner & in 1953 the "Submariner" was introduced and in 1954 the "GMT Master" model. In 1956, a "Day-Date" model was released which indicates the day of the month (in numbers) and the day of the week (in letters).

IMPORTANT:

The following is a guide to help determine the age of your Rolex watches. However on some Oyster style watches Rolex added inside the case a Roman number (I,II,III,IV) to denote first, second, third, or fourth quarter + "53", "54", "55", "56" to denote the year of production. Example outside Oyster case #955454 inside case IV-53 which = last quarter of 1953. Example outside Oyster case #282621 inside case III-55 which = third quarter of 1955. Rolex went back to 100,000 in 1954 on some cases.

ROLEX ESTIMATED PRODUCTION DATES

DATE -SERIALS#	DATE -SERIALS#	DATE -SERIALS#	DATE - SERIAL#	DATE -SERIALS#	DATE - SERIAL #	DATE - SERIAL #
1925 - 25,000	1937 - 99,000	1949 - 608,000	1961 - 1,480,000	1973 - 3,741,000	1985— 8,815,000	1992 1/4 - C000,001
1926 - 28,500	1938 - 118,000	1950 - 673,500	1962 - 1,557,000	1974 -4,002,000	1986— 9,292,000	1993 3/4 - S000,001
1927 - 30,500	1939 - 136,000	1951 - 738,500	1963 - 1,635,000	1975 -4,266,000	1987— 9,765,000	1995— W000,001
1928 - 33,000	1940 - 165,000	1952 - 804,000	1964 - 1,713,000	1976 -4,538,000	1987-1/2 - R999,999	1996— T000,001
1929 - 35,500	1941 - 194,000	1953 - 950,000	1965 - 1,792,000	1977 -5,005,000	1987 -3/4 - R000,001	1997 -3/4 -U000,001
1930 - 38,000	1942 - 224,000	1954 - 999,999	1966 - 1,870,000	1978 -5,481,000	1988— R999,999	1999— A000,001
1931 - 40,000	1943 - 253,000	1955 - 200,000	1967 - 2,164,000	1979 -5,965,000	1989— L000,001	2000 -1/2 -P000,001
1932 - 43,000	1944 - 285,000	1956 - 400,000	1968 - 2,426,000	1980 -6,432,000	1990— L999,999	2001 -1/2 -K000,001
1933 - 47,000	1945 - 348,000	1957 - 600,000	1969 - 2,689,000	1981 - 6,910,000	1990 1/2 - E000,001	2002 -3/4 -Y000,001
1934 - 55,000	1946 - 413,000	1958 - 800000	1970 - 2,952,000	1982 - 7,385,000	1991 1/4 - E999,999	2003 -3/4 -H000,001
1935 - 68,000	1947 - 478,000	1959 - 1,100,000	1971 - 3,215,000	1983 - 7,860,000	1991 1/2 - X000,001	2005— D000,001
1936 - 81,000	1948 - 543,000	1960 - 1,401,000	1972 - 3,478,000	1984 -8,338,000	1991 3/4 - N000,001	2006— Z000,001

The above list is provided for determining the APPROXIMATE age of your watch. Match serial number with date. Watches were not necessarily sold in the exact order of manufactured date. The above list was furnished with the help of Jeffrey P. Hess. Jeff and James M. Dowling authored a book "*The Best of Time*" a unauthorized history of the Rolex Watch Co.

ROLEX MODEL INDEX

ROLEX W. CO. REFERENCE # INDEX

Note: Some Rolex watches will have a double reference number on the case. The backs, bodies and bezels of certain models were interchangeable and it was common practice within the factory to use a body from, for example, a reference #1500 and a back from a reference #1503 which is in the same series.

Original Box & Papers bring higher Prices.

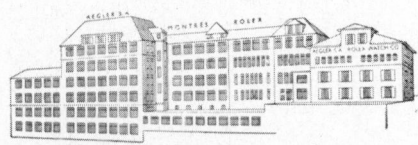

Above: **Aegler, S.A. Montres**. Rolex Watch Co. used the movement supplier **Aegler** of Bienne, Switzerland.

* Below abbreviations used in Rolex section.

BB = bubble back

Chg. or chronog. = Chronograph

Chr = Chronometer

m.wind = manual wind

Pet. = perpetual or automatic winding - self-winding & etc.

Prs. = precision

Oy. = Oyster case (water-proof)

Q. = Quick set for calendar

RF# = reference number or case style

ROLEX, 15 jewels, enamel bezel, Ca 1935
9K $900 $1,400 $2,200

ROLEX, 15J., wire lugs, c.1925
silver $400 $700 $900

ROLEX, 15 jewels, enamel dial, flip top, c.1918
silver $1,100 $1,500 $2,000

ROLEX, 15 jewels, enamel dial, demi- hunter style, Ca.1920
silver $1,100 $1,700 $2,000

ROLEX,17J., RF# 4365, Ca.1920s
s. steel (**redone dial**) $300 $600 $700

ROLEX, 15 jewels, enamel dial, wire lugs, Ca. 1930
9k $750 $1,300 $1,600

ROLEX,15 jewels, enamel dial, ca.1920
Silver $650 $1,000 $1,500

ROLEX,17J., RF # 3665, enamel dial, Ca.1930
s. steel $550 $900 $1,300

ROLEX,17J., "Skyrocket", Ca. 1944
gold filled $400 $700 $900

ROLEX 17J., Pall Mall, manual wind Ca. 1949
s. steel . . . . ★★★$900 $1,500 $2,000
14k. $600 $1,100 $1,300

ROLEX, 18 jewels, Oy., RF # 3039, aux. sec., Ca. 1938
s. steel $600 $1,100 $1,400

ROLEX, 18 jewels, RF # 3716, Oy., Pet., Ca. 1941
18k. $850 $1,400 $1,800
14k. $700 $1,200 $1,600
s. steel $400 $700 $900

ROLEX, 17 jewels, not oyster case, center sec.
18k. $700 $1,200 $1,700
14k. $600 $1,000 $1,400
9k $500 $800 $1,100
s. steel $400 $700 $1,000

ROLEX, 17 jewels, RF# 2416, M.wind, Oy., Ca.1936
s. steel $450 $700 $975

ROLEX, 15j, early waterproof, "Tropical", (case within a case)
18k. $1,700 $3,000 $4,500
silver $1,000 $1,700 $2,400

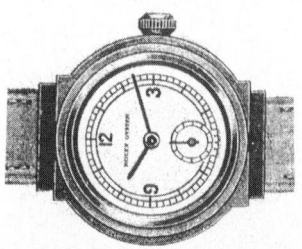

ROLEX, 18 jewels, RF # 2518, Oy., aux. sec., Ca.1938
s. steel $1,200 $2,000 $2,500

ROLEX, 15J., engraved case, c. 1930
s. steel $600 $1,000 $1,200

ROLEX, 17J., "Standard", stepped case, c. 1938
stainless steel $500 $800 $1,200

ROLEX, 17J., 2 tone, center lug "Standard", c.1940
14k & s. s. $800 $1,300 $1,600

ROLEX (Early)

Dials must be original for prices below.

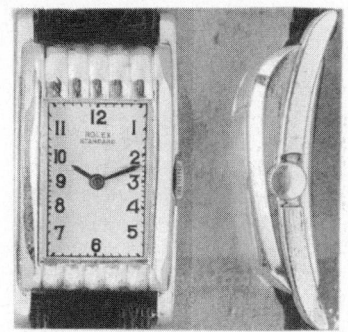

ROLEX, 17 jewels, "Standard," right angle case, c. 1939
gold filled $500 $900 $1,200
14k. $1,500 $2,500 $3,500

ROLEX, 15J., RF # 1878, beveled case, c.1927
s. steel $500 $900 $1,200

ROLEX, 15J., ca. 1937
s. steel $400 $700 $900

ROLEX, 17J., "Standard", c. 1940 (no brass for mint)
gold filled $300 $600 $900

ROLEX, 17J., hidden lugs, center seconds
14k. $1,500 $2,250 $2,750

ROLEX, 15J., stepped case, c. 1938
18k. $900 $1,500 $1,800

ROLEX, 17J., Drivers, Ca. 1935
gold filled $450 $800 $1,000

ROLEX, 17J., Drivers, Ca. 1935
gold filled $1300 $2,000 $2,500

ROLEX, 15J., GJS, c.1935
9K $800 $1,200 $1,500

ROLEX, 18J., hidden lugs, RF # 2537, adj.6 pos. 2 tone, Ca. 1940s
gold & steel. $1,200 $2,000 $3,000

ROLEX, 18J., RF# 4663, **small**, perpetual, chronometer, 24mm case, (auto wind), Ca. 1940s
18K $1,800 $2,500 $3,000

ROLEX, 21 jewels, perpetual, **large**, 34mm, c. 1945
18k. $1,800 $2,600 $3,500

ROLEX, 17J., RF # 619, ROSE gold, c. 1948
18k Pink $900 $1,400 $1,600

ROLEX, 17 jewels, RF # 8126, "Precision", manual wind
18k. $800 $1,300 $1,800

ROLEX, 18J., RF# 4029,
18k. $900 $1,600 $2,000

ROLEX, 18J., Ca. 1940s
s. steel $500 $900 $1,200

ROLEX, 17J., "31 Victories",
18k. $900 $1,600 $2,000

ROLEX, 18J, fluted bezel, RF # 3737
18k. $900 $1,600 $2,500

ROLEX, 17J., RF # 9491, "Precision", Ca. 1958
18k. $1,000 $1,800 $2,400

ROLEX, 17 J., "Precision," faceted bezel
18k. $1,000 $1,800 $2,400

ROLEX, 17 jewels, "Precision," c. 1940s
18k.........................$1,200 $1,800 $2,500
14k......................... $800 $1,200 $2,000

ROLEX, 17 jewels, curved, c. 1940s
gold filled $300 $600 $800

ROLEX, 17 jewels, curvex style
18k C&B $2,500 $3,250 $4,500

ROLEX, 17J., RF # 3893, hidden lugs, Ca. 1943
14k......................... $700 $1,200 $1,500

ROLEX, 18J., RF # 8094, 3 diamond dial , ca. 1940s
18k C&B $1,500 $2,750 $3,250

ROLEX, 17 jewels, "Ultra Prima," gold train
18k.........................$1,000 $1,500 $2,000

ROLEX, 17 jewels, oyster, cushion, 2 tone, c. 1943
14k & s. steel.................$1,000 $1,600 $2,000

ROLEX, 17J., Oyster, RF # 2280, manual wind, c. 1951
s. steel...................... $350 $700 $800

ROLEX, 18J., "Royal", Oyster, mid size, aux. sec.
s. steel...................... $400 $700 $900

ROLEX, 17J., mid size, Oy., Prs, m.wind, RF# 6466, c.1957
s. steel...................... $400 $700 $900

ROLEX, 17 jewels, RF # 678, oyster, enamel dial, c.1934
18k.	$1,800	$3,000	$3,800
14k.	$1,200	$2,000	$3,000
9k	$750	$1,200	$1,500
silver	$500	$900	$1,200
s. steel	$450	$750	$1,300

ROLEX, 17J., Speedking Oyster, Precision, RF # 6021, c.1953
index on bezel
s. steel $350 $600 $700

ROLEX, 18J., "Speed King", Oyster, mid size, center sec.
s. steel $400 $700 $800

ROLEX, 173 , Oy Pet Prs., RF # 6421, "Speedking", Ca. 1960
s. steel $400 $750 $850

ROLEX, 15J., "Aqua",RF#2136,c.1928
s steel $400 $700 $1,000

ROLEX, 17J., RF # 4302, index bezel, 2 tone, Ca. 1944
gold filled & s. steel $400 $750 $900

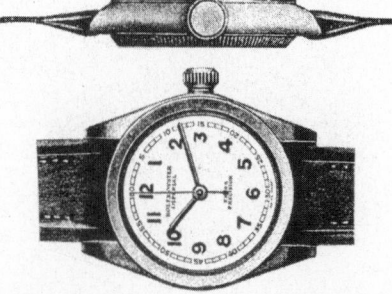

ROLEX, 15J., Oyster, RF # 6071, c.1927
s. steel $500 $850 $1,200

ROLEX, 18J., Oy., Prs., RF# 2595, center sec. Ca.1938
18k. $1,700 $3,000 $3,500

☞ Some grades are not included. Their values can be determined by comparing with similar age, size, metal content, style, grades, or models such as time only, chronograph, repeater etc. listed.

Dials must be original for prices below.

ROLEX, 17J., "Speed King", Oy. Chr. Pet., RF#6056, c.1952
s. steel $350 $650 $800

ROLEX,17J., Oy. Chr., RF # 5020, 2 tone, Ca. 1943
14k & s. steel (**redone dial**) $500 $700 $900

ROLEX,17J., marked "Army", RF # 4647, 2 tone dial, Oyster case, c.1943
s. steel $800 $1,300 $1,700

ROLEX, 17 jewels, index bezel, **Oyster case**, c. 1928
silver $700 $1,100 $1,600

ROLEX, 17J., marked"Army", RF # 4647, c. 1948
s. steel $1,000 $1,600 $1,900

Original Box & Papers bring higher Prices.

ROLEX, 15 jewels, center sec, Ca.1930
9K $1,000 $1,700 $2,700
14K $1,300 $2,400 $3,200

ROLEX, 18J., note dial top half & bottom, RF # 3139
Oyster case,
s. steel $1,000 $1,500 $1,800

ROLEX, 17J., "Royal Observatory" , RF#3121, c.1937
s. steel $400 $750 $1,000

ROLEX, 17 jewels, oyster, RF # 4547
s. steel $400 $800 $900

ROLEX, 15J., RF# 4377, Oy. Chr., **refinished dial**, Ca.1944
s. steel $300 $600 $700
original dial $400 $700 $900

ROLEX, 17J., Oyster Co., "Record", manual wind, c.1940
s. steel $300 $650 $750

ROLEX, 15J., Oy., RF # 2495, "Extra-Prima", Ca.1937
9k enamel dial $400 $800 $1,100
9k $300 $600 $800

ROLEX, 17J., "Neptune", mid-size, manual wind, c. 1939
gold filled $300 $550 $700

ROLEX, 15J., oyster, royal, 2 tone dial, c. 1930s
9k $750 $1,200 $1,700

ROLEX, 17 jewels, oyster, metal dial, c. 1930s
18k. $1,800 $2,500 $3,300
14k. $1,300 $2,000 $2,600

ROLEX, 18J., RF# 3372, OY., Pet., index bezel, Ca. 1940
18k. $2,600 $3,700 $5,500
14k. $2,400 $3,000 $4,200
9k $1,500 $2,200 $2,700
gold filled $800 $1,200 $1,800
s. steel $900 $1,500 $2,200

ROLEX, 18 jewels, RF# 2280, OY., M.wind, Ca. 1938
s. steel $400 $700 $800

ROLEX,17J., Oy. Chr. Pet., RF # 4392, Observatory, Ca.1948
s. steel $800 $1,300 $1,600

ROLEX,17J., "Observatory", Oy., RF #3386, c.1940
gold filled $600 $1,000 $1,400

ROLEX, 15 jewels, oyster, center sec.,enamel dial
18k. $1,800 $2,500 $3,500
14k. $1,200 $1,800 $2,500
9k $800 $1,200 $1,600
silver $500 $900 $1,100
s. steel $400 $700 $800

ROLEX, 15J., RF# 1071, oyster, ca 1930
silver $600 $900 $1,100

ROLEX, 17J., RF# 2940, screw on back is flat & tin can
shaped case, which used a non-magnetic metal (?)
non-magnetic . . . . ★★★★★$1,800 $3,000 $3,500

ROLEX, 18J., 'Viceroy", center sec. Oyster case, ca. 1937
s. steel $500 $850 $1,000

ROLEX, 17 jewels, oyster, extra prima "Viceroy
18k. $1,600 $2,500 $3,000

ROLEX, 26 jewels, "Viceroy", Oy., center sec.
9k (2-tone) $700 $1,300 $1,600

ROLEX, 18J, BB, RF#271, Oy., Pet., Chr., Ca. 1944
s. steel $1,000 $1,700 $2,200

ROLEX,17J., "Viceroy", Oy., RF #3116, c.1942
14k (pink) $1,700 $2,500 $3,500
14k. $1,600 $2,200 $3,300

ROLEX, 18J., B.B., Oy. Pet.Chr., center sec.
s. steel $900 $1,500 $2,000

ROLEX,17J., "Viceroy", Oy., RF# 3359, c.1943
14k (pink) $1,500 $2,200 $3,200
14k & s. steel. $900 $1,500 $2,000

ROLEX, 18J., B.B., Oy., Pet., cal. # 600, aux. sec., ca. 1945
s. steel $900 $1,500 $2,000

ROLEX, 18 jewels, bubble back, RF # 2940, c. 1940s
s. steel (black dial) $900 $1,500 $2,200
s. steel $900 $1,300 $2,200

ROLEX, 25J., Oy. Chr. Pet., RF # 6050, BB, Ca. 1949
s. steel $900 $1,500 $2,000

ROLEX (Bubble Backs)

Dials must be original for prices below.

ROLEX, 18J., BB, RF # 5050, Oy. Chr. Pet., c.1945
9k $1,100 $1,700 $2,200

ROLEX, 18J., Oy., Pet., RF# 3130, BB, aux. sec. Ca.1945
14k. $1,800 $2,800 $3,200

ROLEX, 18J., RF # 3696, B.B., Oy. Pet. Chr., Ca. 1941
9K $1,000 $1,700 $2,200

ROLEX, 18J., B.B., Oy., Pet., chronometer, RF # 3131,
14k. $1,600 $2,800 $3,200
s. steel $900 $1,300 $2,000

ROLEX, 17J., BB, Oy., Pet., RF #3133, **tu-tone**, c.1940
14k & s. steel. $1,100 $1,700 $2,200

ROLEX, 17J., RF # 5015, Oy. Pet., BB, index bezel, c.1949
18k (pink) $2,500 $3,500 $4,500
s. steel $900 $1,300 $2,000

ROLEX, 26 J., Oy., Pet., BB, aux. sec., RF # 3458, Ca. 1940s
18k. $2,400 $3,500 $5,000
14k. $2,200 $2,800 $3,500
9k $1,300 $2,000 $2,500
gold filled $700 $1,100 $1,500
s. steel $900 $1,300 $2,000

ROLEX, 18J., B.B., Oy. Pet., self winding on dial
14k. $2,500 $4,000 $4,600

ROLEX, 18J., B.B., Oy.Chr. Pet., **not** 2 tone, RF # 3131
14k.........................$1,800 $2,500 $3,800

ROLEX, 25J., Oy. Chr. Pet., RF # 2764, B.B., index bezel, 2 tone, c.1945
14k & s. steel.................$1,100 $1,800 $2,500

Bubble-Back was introduced in 1934.

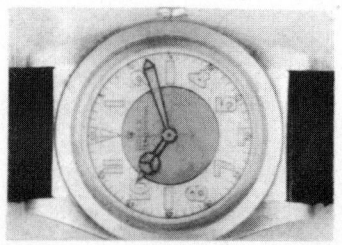

ROLEX, 26 J., Oy., Pet., BB, mercedes hands, c. 1940s 2 tone dial
18k.........................$2,600 $3,700 $5,300
14k.........................$2,400 $3,000 $3,800
9k.........................$1,500 $2,200 $2,800
gold filled $900 $1,200 $1,700
s. steel.....................$1,100 $1,500 $2,200

ROLEX, 18J., Oy. Chr. Pet., RF # 3065, B.B., hooded 2 tone yellow gold
14k Gold & steel.............$3,000 $4,500 $5,750

ROLEX, 17J., BB, Oy. Chr. Pet., RF #6011, c.1948
14k.........................$1,800 $2,800 $3,200

ROLEX, 26J., Oy.Chr.Pet, BB, RF# 2940, center sec., c. 1940s
18k.........................$2,400 $3,500 $5,000
14k.........................$2,200 $2,800 $3,500
9k.........................$1,300 $2,000 $2,500
gold filled $700 $1,100 $1,500
s. steel.....................$900 $1,300 $2,000

ROLEX, 19 jewels, Oy., Pet., BB, center sec., rf#1453
18k.........................$2,400 $3,300 $4,800
14k.........................$2,000 $3,000 $3,500
s. steel.....................$900 $1,400 $2,000

ROLEX, 26J, BB, 2 tone dial, hooded scalloped lugs
s. steel...................★$5,500 $9,000 $11,500
18k & s. steel................$5,000 $8,500 $12,000

Dials must be original for prices below.

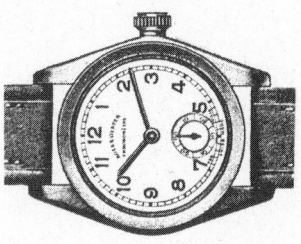

ROLEX, 18J., Oy., Chr., RF# 2574, BB, aux. sec. Ca.1938
18k......................$2,400 $3,500 $4,800

ROLEX, 18J., RF # 2764, Oy. Pet.Chr., B.B., index bezel
18k......................$2,500 $3,800 $5,000

ROLEX, 18J., Oy. Chr. Pet., RF # 2319, B.B., hooded 2 tone **rose gold**
14k Gold & steel $3,000 $4,500 $5,500

DIALS FOR MINT PRICES MUST BE ALL **ORIGINAL**
ROLEX, 26J., bubble back, hooded lugs, RF#3595, Ca. 1942

18k..........................	$5,000	$8,000	$12,000
14k..........................	$3,000	$5,500	$8,000
9k	$1,750	$3,500	$4,500
s. steel & gold...............	$1,500	$3,300	$4,500
s. steel................ ★★★	$7,000	$11,000	$15,000

ROLEX, 17J., center see, cal.1530, c.1955
gold filled $300 $600 $800

ROLEX, 17J., "Precision"
s. steel..................... $350 $600 $900

ROLEX, 17 J .," Precision, fancy lugs,
9k $500 $900 $1,200

ROLEX, 17 jewels, "Precision"
18k....................... $800 $1,400 $1,700

ROLEX, 17J., RF # 2010, Ca. 1960
s. steel $400 $700 $1,000

ROLEX, 15J., RF # 3655, aux. sec. Ca. 1945
s. steel $400 $800 $1,000

ROLEX, 19J.,RF# 8443, c.1965
14k. $500 $900 $1,200

ROLEX,17J., RF # 9083, Precision, Ca.1955
s. steel c&b $600 $1,000 $1,400

ROLEX,17J., center sec., RF#9659, c.1960
14k. $600 $1,000 $1,300

ROLEX, 17 jewels, RF #9659 Ca 1960s
14k C&B $1,200 $2,000 $2,500

ROLEX, 17J., "Chronometer", RF# 4222, Ca.1945
18k. $800 $1,200 $1,700

ROLEX,17J., Pin., RF # 4478, 9 diamonds, Ca.1948
18k. $1,200 $2,000 $2,500

Pricing in this Guide are fair market price for complete watches which are reflected from the "NAWCC" National and regional shows.

ROLEX,18J., RF # 4891, Chronometer, Ca.1957
18k........................$1,200 $2,000 $2,500

ROLEX, 25J., Oy., Pet., Chr., RF#6568, c.1956
s. steel......................$500 $850 $1,000

ROLEX, 18J., Chr., RF# 8952, center sec., Ca. 1950s
14k index bezel..............$1,200 $2,000 $2,500

ROLEX, 17J., RF#6084, Oy., Pet., Chr., Ca.1951
14k..........................$900 $1,500 $1,800

ROLEX, 17 jewels, "Precision," center sec., Roman bezel
18k........................$1,000 $1,800 $2,000

ROLEX, 25J., Oy., Pet., Chr., RF# 6567, center sec., Ca. 1960
14k..........................$800 $1,500 $1,800

ROLEX, 17-18J., index bezel, RF# 4325 or 4327, Ca.1951
18k........................$1,000 $1,800 $2,000
14k..........................$800 $1,400 $1,800

ROLEX, 18J., Oy., Pet., Chr., RF# 8405, c.1950
18k........................$850 $1,500 $2,000

ROLEX, 25J., Oy., Pet., Chr,, RF# 6564, c. 1955
s. steel $500 $850 $1,000

ROLEX, 25J., index bezel, Oy., Pet., Chr., RF# 6581, c. 1954
14k. $1,000 $1,600 $2,200

ROLEX, 25J., Oy., Pet., Chr., RF# 6084, textured dial, c.1953
14k. $1,200 $1,700 $2,200

ROLEX, 25J., Oy., Pet., RF # 6098 ,star dial, c.1956
18k rose. . . . . ★★★$2,800 $3,500 $4,800

ROLEX, 17J., Oy., date, mid size,
s. steel $500 $800 $1,000

ROLEX, 17J., RF #6094 , Oy., Prs., date, Ca.1951
s. steel $500 $800 $1,000

ROLEX, 25J., Oy., Pet., RF #6604 date, c.1958
s. steel $600 $950 $1,200

ROLEX, 26J., Oy., Pet., index bezel, RF # 1501 ,c.1961
s. steel $600 $1,100 $1,500

☞ Some grades are not included. Their values can be determined by comparing with similar age, size, metal content, style, grades, or models such as time only, chronograph, repeater etc. listed.

ROLEX (Oyster)

ROLEX,25J., date, **index gold** bezel, 2 tone case, RF#6305
s. steel/gold bezel $800 $1,500 $1,800

ROLEX, 17J., date, RF #6964, ca.1953
s. steel $500 $800 $1,000

ROLEX, 25J., "**Ovettone**", RF # 6105, auto wind, oyster, note
thin milled bezel, Ovettone = Big Bubble Back, Ca. 1953
14k Pink . . . . ★★$3,000 $4,000 $6,000
14k . . . . ★★$2,500 $3,500 $5,500

ROLEX, 17J., RF # 6694 , m.wind, Oy., date, c.1971
s. steel $600 $900 $1,100

ROLEX, 19J., "**Ovettone**", RF # 6031, 6 positions, Ca. 1953 Note:
Extra section between lugs.
18k. $2,850 $5,000 $6,000

ROLEX, 18J., RF # 6075, 2 tone, index bezel, Ca. 1951
s. steel & 14k $600 $1,000 $1,400

ROLEX, 25J., oyster, perpetual, date, "**Ovettone**", note thin
milled bezel, RF # 4467, Ca. 1950s
18k Pink . . . . ★★$3,500 $5,000 $6,000
18k. ★★$3,000 $4,500 $5,500

ROLEX, 17J., RF #6223, precision oyster, index bezel, Ca. 1954
18k. $900 $1,300 $1,700
14k. $800 $1,200 $1,600
9k $550 $900 $1,200
gold filled $400 $800 $1,000
s. steel $400 $800 $1,000

ROLEX, 19-25J., RF #6634, center sec., gold & s. steel 2 tone case, Ca. 1952
Gold & steel $600 $1,100 $1,400

ROLEX, 16J., Precision Oy., RF # 6082, c.1960
s. steel $400 $700 $900

ROLEX, 17J., RF # 6582, marked bezel "Zephyer" 2 tone, Ca. 1955
similar RF#1008 & 1009, no lugs=RF#9522 aux. see. & RF #9919, no sec.
gold & s. steel $800 $1,500 $1,700

ROLEX, 17J., Oy., Pit., RF # 6424 , Ca.1965
s. steel $500 $850 $1,000

ROLEX, 26J., Oy.330 Ft., Pet., RF # 1002, c.1988
14K $1,000 $1,500 $1,800

ROLEX, 17J., RF#6426, manual wind, c 1961
s. steel $500 $850 $1,000

ROLEX, 17J., RF # 6029, index bezel, rose gold, c.1950s
18k $1,000 $2,000 $2,500

ROLEX, 25J., Oy., RF # 6024 , c.1953
s. steel $500 $850 $1,000

Dials must be original for prices below.

ROLEX, 25J., Oy., Pet., RF # 5502, Ca. 1955
s. steel $500 $850 $1,000

ROLEX, 25J., Oy. Pet., Bombe', 12 diamond dial, RF #1030
s. steel . . . . ★★$1,200 $1,900 $2,500

ROLEX,17J.,Oy.,Chr.,RF#6512,Ca.1961
14k. $700 $1,300 $1,700

ROLEX, 25J., Bombe' lugs, Oy. Pet., RF # 6102, c.1953
14k. $1,200 $1,900 $2,400

ROLEX, 25J., Oy., Pet., Chr., RF # 1025, c.1964
note the triangles on bezel
14k. $1,000 $1,500 $1,850

ROLEX, 26J. Bombe' lugs, Oy., Pet., RF # 6590, c. 1950
14k. $1,000 $1,700 $2,200

Note: **Bombe'** = style of lug which are Convexed.

ROLEX, 17J., Oy. Pet. Chr., RF # 6284 , c.1955
18k. $1,000 $1,700 $2,200

ROLEX, 17J., Oy. Pet., Linz 1877, Bombe' lugs, c. 1950s
18k RF# 5018 . . . . $1,200 $1,800 $2,100

Mint prices are for tight bands in gold & steel
Dials for mint prices must be original

ROLEX,17J., Oy. Prs., RF # 6694, Date, "Honey Comb" textured
dial, Ca.1952
s. steel $400 $800 $1,000

ROLEX, 17J., Oyster precision, RF # 6024 , c.1952
s. steel $400 $700 $900

ROLEX, 26J., Oy., Pet., RF # 1011, Bombe' lugs, Ca. 1960
14k. $1,000 $1,800 $2,200

ROLEX, 17J., Oy., Pet., RF # 6085, index bezel, Ca. 1951
14k. $1,000 $1,600 $2,100

ROLEX, 19 J., Oy., Pet., RF # 6092, Bombe' lugs, c. 1950s

18k.	$1,200	$1,800	$2,500
18k Pink	$1,500	$2,200	$2,800
14k.	$1,100	$1,600	$2,200
14k Pink	$1,400	$2,000	$2,500
9k	$900	$1,200	$1,500
s. steel	$1,200	$1,800	$2,200

ROLEX, 17 jewels, RF# 6466, date, oyster, mid-size, Ca.1961
s. steel C&B $400 $700 $900

ROLEX, 26J., Bombe' lugs, Oy. Pet., RF # 6102, c. 1950
18k. $1,200 $1,800 $2,500

ROLEX, 18 J., RF # 4467, date, *left hand winds at 9 o'clock*
s. steel . . . . ★$2,500 $3,500 $4,500
18k. . . . . ★$3,200 $5,000 $6,500

ROLEX, 26 jewels, RF # 1018, Oyster, Pet., Chr., Ca. 1972
s. steel c&b.................. $500 $900 $1,200

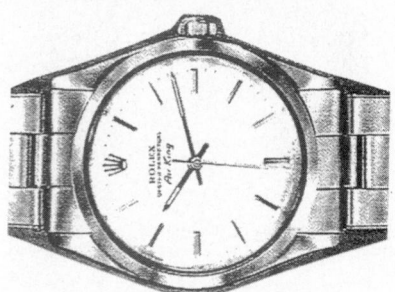

ROLEX, 17-25J., "Air King", Oy., Pet., RF# 5500, Ca.1971
s. steel c&b.................. $600 $900 $1,100

ROLEX,25J., Oy. Chr. Pet., RF # 1550, **rare dial** (crown at 3-6-9), Ca.1960
s. steel .... ★★ $1,200 $1,800 $2,500

ROLEX,28J., RF # 6627, Oy. Chr. Pet., date, mid size, Ca. 1971
18k.......................... $900 $1,600 $2,000

ROLEX, 25J., Oy. Chr. Pet., RF #6585, index on bezel, c.1958
14k.......................... $900 $1,650 $2,000

ROLEX, 25J., "Air King", Oy., Pet., RF # 5501, c.1961
s. steel & gold bezel $700 $1,200 $1,500

ROLEX, 26J., RF # 1007, Chronometer Oyster Perpetual, index on bezel, c. 1965
14k.......................... $900 $1,600 $2,000

ROLEX, 26J., Oy., Pet., Chr., RF # 1005 , c.1961
14k & S. S $800 $1,400 $1,650

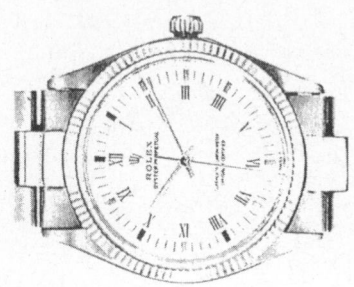

ROLEX, 27J., RF # 1423, Oy., Pet., Chr., Ca.1991
s. steel c&b $700 $1,200 $1,500

ROLEX, 21J., RF # 6309, "Thunderbird", Ca.1965
14k gold bezel, s. steel case $1,000 $1,750 $2,300

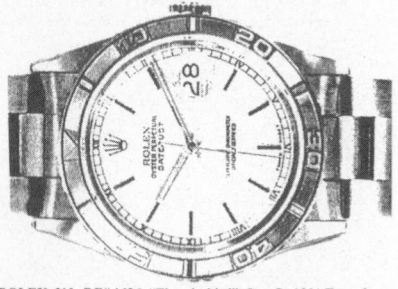

ROLEX, 31J., RF# 1626, "Thunderbird", Oy., Ca.1991 Turn-O-
Graph Bezel, Pet., Chr.
s. steel $1,400 $2,000 $2,500
18K $2,000 $3,000 $4,000

ROLEX, 26-30J., "Thunderbird", Oy., Pet., Chr., RF#1625
18k & s. steel quick set. $2,000 $2,700 $4,000
14k & s. steel C&B non Q $1,100 $1,500 $2,500

ROLEX,17J., Oy. Prs., RF # 6266, Date, Ca.1957
s. steel $400 $700 $900

ROLEX, 25J., Oy., Pet., RF # 6565 , c.1958
s. steel $500 $900 $1,200

ROLEX,25J, RF # 6552, Oyster, Perpetual Ca.1972
s. steel $500 $850 $1 000

ROLEX, 30J., Oy, Pet., Chr., RF # 1500 , date, Ca.1961
s. steel $600 $950 $1,200

Mint prices are for tight bands in gold & steel
Dials for mint prices must be original

Mint prices are for tight bands in gold & steel
Dials for mint prices must be original

ROLEX, 18J., Oy. Prs., RF # 6427, center sec. Ca. 1964
s. steel $450 $800 $1,000

ROLEX,28J., RF # 6800, Oy. Chr. Pet., date-juts, Ca.1982
s. steel $700 $1,300 $1,500

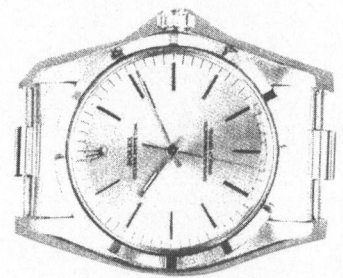

ROLEX, 26J., Oy., Pet., Chr., RF# 1003, index bezel, Ca.1961
18k $1,000 $1,600 $2,000
14k $800 $1,300 $1,700
s. steel $500 $900 $1,200

ROLEX, 26J., quick set, date, Oyster bracelet, c. 1965
14k C&B $2,000 $2,700 $3,500

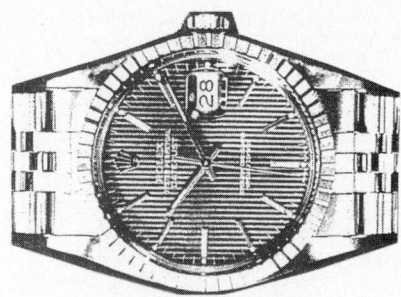

ROLEX, 30J., RF # 1603, Oy. Chr. Pet., Q.date-just, Ca.1987
s. steel $800 $1,200 $1,500

ROLEX, 26 J., **jubilee** band, 10 diamond dial, date just
Later sapphire crystal models add about 25%.
18k C&B quick set $3,800 $4,500 $5,500
14k C&B non quick $2,000 $2,500 $3,200
18K & s. steel C&B quick $1,600 $2,200 $2,800

ROLEX, 31J., RF# 1521, Oy., Pet sapphire crystal, Ca.1991
18k $2,000 $2,500 $2,800
18k & s. steel. $1,200 $1,800 $2,200
s. steel $800 $1,500 $1,800

ROLEX,25J., Oy. Chr. Pet., RF # 6611, day date, Ca 1956
Note: First **President** model **no band**
18k $2,500 $3,500 $4,000

Ladies President models are in Ladies Section

ROLEX, 30J., **Q.date just**, Oy., Pet., Chr., RF# 1601, Ca.1972
s. steel & gold $1,200 $2,000 $2,500

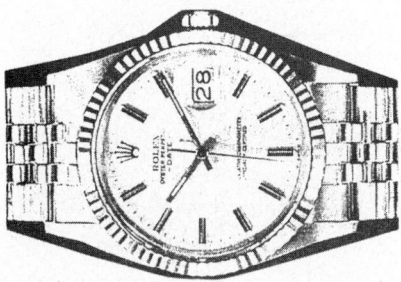

ROLEX, 30J., RF# 1503, Oy., Pet., Chr., , date, Ca. 1973
14k. $2,000 $3,250 $3,850

ROLEX, 21 jewels, date just, center sec., c. 1965
18k non quick set $2,000 $3,000 $3,500

ROLEX, 30J., "Presidential," bark finish, RF # 1807, c.1971
18k C&B(**non quick**) $3,500 $5,000 $6,000

ROLEX first used HACK system in c.1972
ROLEX first used the Quick Set feature c.1977
Sapphire crystals were added in U.S.A. c.1989

ROLEX, 26-30J., "Presidential," day-date, perpetual, non quick,
note textured dial, **Pink gold**, RF#1803 old model
18k C & B . . . . ★★$4,000 $5,500 $6,500

ROLEX, 30 Jewels, "Presidential," day-date, Single Quick set model
RF # 1803, double quick-set
18k C&B double quick-set $6,000 $7,500 $9,000
18k C&B single quick-set $4,500 $6,000 $7,000
18k Single Quick (**head**) $3,000 $4,000 $4,500
18k, new rf# **18238**, Presid. band.$6,000 $8,500 $10,000
18k, new rf# **18238**, Oyster band. $5,000 $8,000 $9,500

ROLEX, 26 jewels, "Presidential," diamond dial, day-date,
perpetual, oyster, RF # 1804, quick set
18k C&B $4,000 $6,500 $7,500

ROLEX, 11J., "Presidential," quartz, RF# 1901 diamond dial &
diamond bezel add $500-$900
18k. $3,000 $5,000 $6,000

ROLEX, 30 jewels, "Presidential," (Tridor), oyster, daydate, diamond dial, perpetual, oyster,

18k (y & w) single quick	$4,000	$6,500	$7,500
18k (y & w) double quick	$5,000	$7,500	$9,000

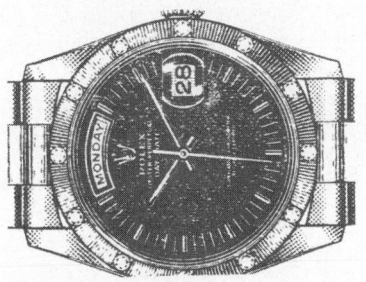

ROLEX, 30 jewels, "Presidential," day-date, perpetual, oyster, diamond bezel, bark finish, RF # 1807

18k C&B(quick set)	$4,000	$6,500	$7,500

ROLEX, 30 jewels, "Presidential," 44 diamonds on dial & bezel, day-date, oyster, perpetual, RF # 1803

18k C & B (non-Quick)	$4,000	$6,000	$7,500

ROLEX, 26 jewels, day-date, 10 diamond dial, **non quick** hidden clasp, RF # 1803

18k C&B	$3,000	$4,000	$5,000
18k C&B (pink) ★★	$3,000	$5,000	$6,000
18k C&B(w)	$4,000	$5,700	$6,800

ROLEX, "Red Sub," c. 1970, 660 ft/200m

s.steel	$4,000	$6,000	$8,000

ROLEX, "Submariner," so called "James Bond," RF # 6205, 38mm, c. 1953

s.steel	$5,500	$8,000	$10,000

ROLEX, 26J., "Submariner", RF # 6536,100m/330 ft, so called "James Bond" c.1958

s. steel (no crown guard) ★★	$4,500	$6,000	$7,000

ROLEX, 25J., early Submariner, RF# 6538, so called "James Bond", 38mm, Large Crown, 200m/660 ft, c. 1957
Note: This style watch worn by 007 Sean Connery

s. steel	$8,000	$15,000	$18,000

ROLEX, "Submariner", RF# 5508, 100m/330 ft, c.1958
s. steel $4,000 $7,000 $9,000

ROLEX, 26J., "Submariner", Oy., Pet., Chr., RF # 5512,
s. steel (chronometer). $1,500 $3,000 $4,500
RF#1680, "Submariner" in red letters. .
s. steel (chronometer). $2,500 $4,000 $5,000

ROLEX, 26J., "Submariner" OY., Pet., Chr., RF # 5513, c. 1970s
s. steel $1,500 $3,000 $3,500

ROLEX, 26 J., "Submariner", perpetual, oyster, date sapphire
crystal, quick set
18k C&B $7,500 $9,000 $11,500
18k & s. steel C&B $2,800 $3,600 $4,500
s. steel $1,800 $3,000 $3,500

ROLEX, 21J., "SEA-DWELLER," up to 4,000 ft., RF # 1666, date,
sapphire crystal, quick set
s. steel $2,200 $3,850 $4,500

ROLEX, 26J., "SEA-DWELLER," RF # 1665,2,000 ft. date all
with Fliplock Band. RF#1660=4,000 & 31J.
s. steel plastic crystal $2,500 $3,500 $4,500
s. steel sapphire crystal $2,800 $3,800 $4,500
s. steel (Seadweller Submariner
 in red letters) $12,000 $16,000 $20,000
Note: Seadweller in red letters is rare, must be original

ROLEX, "Submariner," "comex dial" RF # 16610, c. 1990
s. steel $5,500 $8,000 $10,000

ROLEX, "GMT-Master," RF # 1675, c. 1970s
s. steel $1,850 $2,650 $3,250

ROLEX, "GMT-Master," c. 1980
s. steel $2,000 $3,000 $4,500

ROLEX, 26J., "GMT-Master", RF # 6542, c.1957
s. steel $2,000 $3,500 $4,500

ROLEX, 26J., RF # 1671,"GMT-Master II," date, sapphire crystal,
quick net
18k. $5,000 $7,000 $9,000
s. steel $1,800 $2,800 $3,250

ROLEX, 26 jewels, "GMT-Master," perpetual, oyster, date ruby &
diamond dial, sapphire crystal
18k. $5,000 $7,000 $9,000

ROLEX, 26J., Sea-Dweller, Comex, RF# 1665, date, Ca. 1977
s. steel $5,000 $10,000 $14,000

ROLEX, 17J, **Milgauss** in red, oyster, perpetual, RF#6541
Lighting bolt sec. hand, Milgauss 1st registered in 1954
s. steel $15,000 $27,000 $38,000

ROLEX, 26J., **Milgauss** 1st registered in 1954, RF#1019,
Oy., Pet., Chr., withstands mag. fields to 1,000 Gauss Oersted,
ca.1988
s steel $8,000 $13,000 $20,000

ROLEX, 25J., 'Turn-o-graph", RF # 6202, Ca.1955
14k & s. steel. $2,200 $3,000 $4,000
s. steel $2,700 $3,500 $4,500

Rolex, 26J., **jumping** center sec., RF # 6556, cal #1040, **Tru-beat** on dial, also RF # 6558 & RF #1020, Cal 960
Note: **Jumping center sec. must be working to bring prices listed**.
s. steel . . . . ★$4,000 $7,000 $9,000
14k, ... ★★$6,000 $10,000 $12,000
18K . . . . ★★★★$7,000 $11,000 $16,000

ROLEX, 26J.,"Explorer", RF#1016, Oy., Pet., Chr., Ca.1950
s. steel $1,800 $3,000 $4,000

ROLEX, "Explorer", RF#5500, c.1967
s. steel $1,500 $2,000 $2,500

ROLEX, "Explorer", RF#3310, c.1956
s. steel $2,500 $3,500 $5,000

ROLEX, "Explorer", RF#1610, c.1970
s. steel $1,800 $2,500 $3,000

ROLEX, "Explorer", RF#6350, c.1950s
s. steel $2,500 $4,000 $5,000

ROLEX, 25J.,, "Explorer," RF # 5504, Ca. 1970
s. steel $1,200 $2,250 $3,000

ROLEX, 27J.,"Explorer I", RF#1427, Oy., Pet., Chr., Ca.1991
s. steel $1,700 $2,500 $3,000

ROLEX, "Explorer", Canadian market, c.1960s
s. steel w/ gold bezel. $2,000 $3,000 $4,000

Dials must be original for prices below.

ROLEX, 26 jewels, "Explorer II," RF # 1655, date, so called
"Steve McQueen", c.1961   Note: straight hands.
s. steel $5,000 $10,000 $14,000

ROLEX, "Antimagnetic," 36mm, RF #3695, c.1941
18k $10,000 $15,000 $18,000

ROLEX, 31J., "Explorer II", RF#16550, Oy., Pet., Chr., 24Hr. hand
black dial add $100 to $200 more
s. steel $3,000 $5,000 $7,000

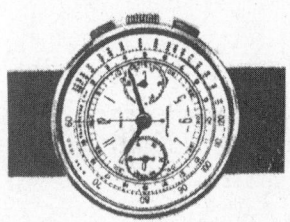

ROLEX, 17 jewels, chronog., 2 reg., RF #3233, Ca.1942
s. steel $3,000 $5,000 $6,000

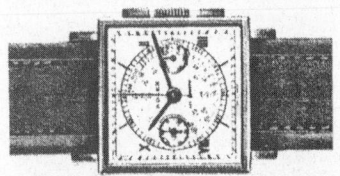

ROLEX, 17 jewels, chronog., 2 reg., RF # 3529, Ca.1942
s. steel $7,000 $11,000 $14,000

ROLEX, 17J., triple-date, moon ph., RF# 8171, 1,000 made
18k . . . . ★★★$25,000 $35,000 $55,000
14k . . . . ★★★$20,000 $30,000 $45,000
s. steel . . . . ★★★$15,000 $20,000 $32,000

ROLEX, 17 jewels, chronog., 2 reg., RF #3284, Ca.1942
s. steel $3,000 $5,000 $6,000

ROLEX,19J., STARS on dial, triple date, RF # 6062, Ca. 1945 also
seen in a very few black dials
18k Pink Gold . . . . ★★★★$40,000 $70,000 $90,000
18k . . . . ★★★★$30,000 $60,000 $80,000

ROLEX, 17 jewels chronog 2 reg. RF #3335, Ca.1942
s. steel $3,000 $5,000 $6,500

ROLEX, 17 J., chronog., center lugs, RF#3233, c. 1940s

18k.	$7,000	$9,000	$12,000
14k.	$5,000	$6,500	$8,000
9k	$3,000	$4,000	$5,000
s. steel	$4,000	$5,000	$7,000

ROLEX, 17J., RF# 3834, one button chronog. 2 reg., Antimagnetic, Ca. 1940's

18k.	★★★★$75,000	$100,000	$125,000

ROLEX, 17 J., chronog., 70-made, flat, tachometer, "Gabus', RF # 8206, c.1940s

18k.	★★★$18,000	$25,000	$37,000

ROLEX,17J., split sec chronog., RF #4113, 15 examples, large 43mm, Valjoux caliber 55 VBR., Ca. 1943

s. steel	★★★★$75,000	$110,000	$150,000

ROLEX,17J., 28mm, small one button chronog., RF # 2303

9k	★★★$8,000	$11,000	$17,000
18k.	$20,000	$30,000	$40,000

ROLEX, 17J., Oy., chronog., 2 reg., RF #3525, Ca.1942

s. steel	$3,500	$5,000	$7,000

ROLEX, 17 jewels, RF #3997, chronog., Ca. 1940

s . steel	$3,000	$5,000	$7,000

ROLEX, 17J., RF # 3055 Antimagnetic, 200 made, 30mm, c. 1956

18k.	$10,000	$16,000	$20,000

ROLEX, 17 jewels, chronog., 3 reg. oyster, RF # 6238, c.1960's

s. steel	$15,000	$22,000	$30,000

ROLEX (Chronograph)

Dials must be original for prices below.

ROLEX, 17J., chronog mid-sized, Antimagnetic, Ca. 1950s
18k.........................$7,000 $10,000 $15,000
14k.........................$6,000 $9,000 $12,000

ROLEX, 17J., RF # 4768, 3 reg., date, tear drop lugs, 1950s
18k.........................$11,000 $19,000 $22,000
14k.........................$10,000 $17,000 $20,000
s. steel.......................$900 $16,000 $19,000

ROLEX, 17J., RF #6238, 3 reg., c. 1950s, rect. markers
s. steel....................$10,000 $20,000 $30,000

ROLEX,17J.,Valjoux cal.23, RF# 4062, Antimagnetic, c.1956
18k.........................$13,000 $18,000 $24,000

ROLEX,17J., Antimagnetic chronog., 3 reg., RF # 6034,
very few produced, Ca.1950s
18k..................★★★$12,000 $15,000 $22,000

ROLEX, 17J., **pulsation**, 3 reg., RF # 6234, Ca. 1960
s. steel, Antimagnetic $8,000 $14,000 $19,000

ROLEX,17J, **triple date**, RF# 5063, c.1948 Antimagnetic, "Jean-
Claude Killey", Beware of **FAKES**
s. steel..................★★$20,000 $55,000 $75,000

ROLEX, 17J., chronog., 6234, Valjoux 72bc
s. steel, Antimagnetic $7,000 $11,000 $15,000
18k, Antimagnetic $10,000 $13,000 $20,000

ROLEX, 17 jewels, chronog., 2 reg., RF #4313, Ca.1950
s. steel $6,000 $9,000 $11,000

ROLEX, chronog., 29mm, RF #3481, c.1939
s. steel $20,000 $30,000 $40,000

ROLEX,17J., Chronograph, triple date & moon-phases, *ALL FAKE,
Valjoux cal. 72C

ROLEX, chronog., "Pre Daytona," RF #6238, c.1964
s. steel $12,000 $18,000 $20,000
18k $25,000 $30,000 $40,000

ROLEX, "Antimagnetic," 36mm, RF #2508, c.1940
18k $11,000 $15,000 $20,000

ROLEX, 17J., chronog., triple-date, gold arrow chapters,
RF # 6036, about 175 made in Y. gold, 144 made pink gold
18k, Antimagnetic $20,000 $28,000 $40,000
14k, Antimagnetic $18,000 $26,000 $35,000
s. steel, Antimagnetic $16,000 $24,000 $32,000

ROLEX, chronog., so called "Monoblocco," RF #4500, c.1946
s. steel $10,000 $15,000 $18,000
18k $20,000 $26,000 $30,000

☞ Pricing in this Guide are fair market price for Complete
watches which are reflected from the NAWCC National and
regional shows.

ROLEX (Daytona)

Dials must be original for prices below.

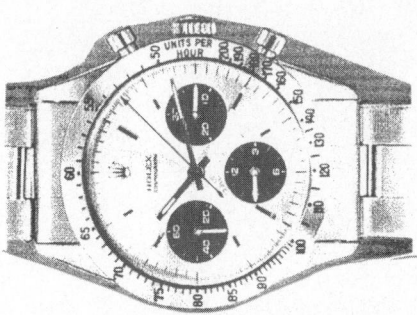

ROLEX, 17 J., tachometer, 3 reg., RF # 6239, c.1960a
18k	$12,000	$20,000	$28,000
14k	$10,000	$15,000	$25,000
s. steel	$10,000	$15,000	$20,000

ROLEX, 17 J., "Daytona", 3 reg., RF # 6241, Ca. 1972
s. steel	$11,000	$16,000	$20,000

ROLEX,17J., exotic dial, RF#6239, Valjoux 727, c.1965
"PAUL NEWMAN", (*beware of reproduction dials*)
18k no band	$20,000	$30,000	$40,000
s. steel	$17,000	$25,000	$35,000

ROLEX, 17J., RF# 6241, Daytona, red outside chapter exotic dial,
"**PAUL NEWMAN**" (Beware of reproduction dials)
s. steel	$18,000	$30,000	$35,000
18k & 18k oyster band	$22,000	$35,000	$45,000

ROLEX,17J., triple-date,3 reg., Antimagnetic, RF# 6036, 2 piece
case, **"Jean Claude Killy"**, c. 1950s.
s. steel	★★★$20,000	$30,000	$45,000
18k	★★★$35,000	$50,000	$60,000

Note: RF#6236 is identical in appearance to the 6036 but is a three
piece case model which can command a price substancially higher.

ROLEX,17J., Oy. screw down pusher 1st used 1976, RF#6265,
s. steel	$10,000	$15,000	$20,000

ROLEX,17J., "Daytona" , Oy., RF # 6263, Ca.1978
s. steel $10,000 $15,000 $20,000
18k. $20,000 $30,000 $40,000

ROLEX, 31 jewels, tachometer, 3 reg., RF # 1652, Oy.330Ft
S.Chr., Pet., triplock crown, screw-down push buttons, Ca.5991
18k. $8,000 $11,000 $15,000

ROLEX, 17 jewels, "Prince," duo dial, RF#1490
18k C&B $6,000 $9,000 $14,000

ROLEX, 17 jewels, RF # 1490, flared, duo dial, c. 1930s
9k $4,500 $6,500 $8,000

ROLEX, 17J., RF # 2245 & RF # 1768, 2 tone case, beware of FAKES
18k. $9,000 $12,000 $18,000

ROLEX, 17 jewels, "Prince," duo dial, stepped case
18k. $7,000 $9,500 $12,000
14k. $6,000 $8,000 $10,000
9k $5,000 $6,500 $8,000
silver $4,000 $5,500 $7,000
s. steel $4,000 $5,000 $7,000
gold filled $2,500 $3,500 $5,000

ROLEX, 17J., RF # 1615, "Observatory", c.1938
gold filled $1,900 $2,800 $3,500

ROLEX, 15J., RF# 3361, "Prince," so called "aerodynamic" cartouche on lower case area, center sec., c. 1940s
18k. $7,000 $9,000 $12,000
18k pink $11,000 $17,000 $20,000

Dials must be original for prices below.

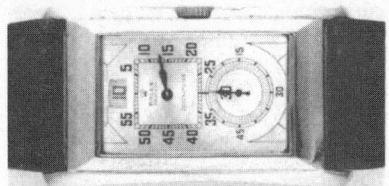

ROLEX, 15J., jumping hr., duo dial, RF # 4402 & RF# 1491, Ca. 1930s

platinum	$15,000	$20,000	$25,000
18k	$13,000	$17,000	$20,000
14k	$10,000	$14,000	$16,000
9k	$7,000	$11,000	$14,000
silver	$6,000	$10,000	$14,000
gold filled	$4,500	$8,000	$10,000
s. steel	$5,500	$9,000	$11,000

ROLEX, 15 jewels, stepped case, RF # 1527

18k	$6,000	$9,000	$11,000

ROLEX, 15 jewels, "Prince," RF # 1343, c. 1935

platinum	$10,000	$14,000	$20,000
18k	$5,000	$7,000	$10,000
14k	$4,000	$5,500	$7,500
gold filled	$2,000	$3,000	$4,000

ROLEX, 15 J., RF # 1527, "Railway," stepped case, 1930s

18k 2 tone	$10,000	$13,000	$15,000
18k	$8,000	$10,000	$12,000
14k 2 tone	$7,000	$10,000	$12,000
14k	$6,000	$8,500	$10,000
9k 2 tone	$6,000	$8,500	$10,000
9k	$4,500	$6,000	$7,000
s. steel	$3,500	$5,000	$6,000

ROLEX, 15 jewels, RF #971, "Prince," duo dial, c. 1930s

s. steel	$4,000	$6,000	$7,000

ROLEX, 15 J., RF # 1862, chronometer, duo dial, c. 1930s

s. steel	$3,500	$5,500	$7,500

ROLEX, 15 jewels, RF #971, flared, duo dial, Adj. to 6 pos.

silver	$3,500	$5,000	$7,000
9k	$4,000	$6,000	$7,000

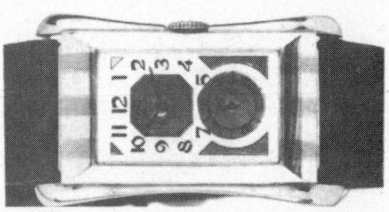

ROLEX, 17J., RF #971,2 tone stripes, Adj. to6 pos.
beware of **FAKES**

18k	$9,000	$12,000	$18,000
14k	$6,500	$9,000	$14,000
9k	$4,500	$7,000	$11,000

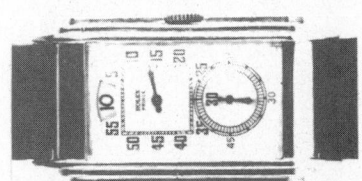

ROLEX,17J., jump hr., duo dial, stepped case, RF# 4376

18k 2 tone	$15,000	$22,000	$25,000
18k	$12,000	$16,000	$18,000
14k	$9,000	$13,000	$15,000
9k	$7,000	$11,000	$12,000
s. steel	$6,000	$9,000	$10,000

ROLEX, 15 jewels, RF #3937, 1/4 century club,

18k	$4,000	$6,500	$8,000

ROLEX, 15 jewels, 1/4 century club,
14k. $4,000 $6,500 $6,500
14k two tone $5,000 $6,500 $8,000

ROLEX, Prince, 1/4 century, c. 1940
18k. $4,000 $6,000 $7,500

ROLEX, 17 jewels,"1/4 Century Club", **BOMBE'**, c. 1960s
18k. $1,300 $1,700 $2,200
14k. $1,100 $1,500 $2,000

ROLEX, "1/4 Century Club," RF #6422, c.1950s
14k. $1,200 $1,700 $2,200

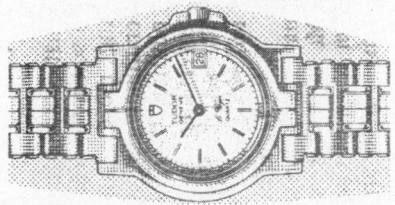

ROLEX, quartz, "Tudor," date, Ca. 1992
s. steel & gold plate $150 $200 $275

ROLEX, 25J., "Tudor", RF # T7809, auto-wind, e. 1978
s. steel $150 $300 $400

ROLEX, 17J., "Tudor", SOLAR, RF # T4463, c.1955
s. steel $200 $350 $450

ROLEX,17J., "Tudor", auto-wind, RF # T7909, c.1955
s. steel $150 $300 $400

ROLEX, 17J., "Tudor", RF # T2765, TURTLE, Zell Bros
Gold filled. $150 $300 $375

Dials must be original for prices below.

ROLEX, 17J., "Tudor", auto-wind, c.1955
18k......................... $500 $900 $1,100

ROLEX, 25J., "Tudor", RF# T7016, submariner, by ETA, c.1970
s. steel...................... $500 $800 $1,100

ROLEX, "Tudor," (Prince)
s. steel...................... $250 $450 $600

ROLEX, 25J., "Tudor", submariner, date, by ETA, RF#T7610, Ca.1985
s. steel...................... $600 $900 $1,200

ROLEX, Quartz, RF # 1563-3, 2 tone, "Tudor", Ca. 1993
18k & s. steel.................. .$150 $300 $400

ROLEX, "Tudor," chronog., date, 165 ft., auto-wind
s. steel...................... $1,000 $1,500 $2,500
Tiger Wood's model............ $900 $1,500 $2,500

ROLEX, 173, RF # T7928, "Tudor", ETA cal. 2438, Ca. 1968
s. steel...................... $600 $1,000 $1,200

ROLEX, "Tudor," chronog., date, RF # T9420, Ca. 1970s
s. steel.................. ★$2,000 $3,000 $4,000

ROLEX, 25J "Tudor," Oyster Ranger II Ca 1973
s. steel $500 $850 $1,100

ROLEX, 17J., "Lurninor Panerai," Italian military diving, RF#
6151-1, Ca. 1940s, Note: Reproductions in 1992
s. steel (1940s) $18,000 $25,000 $30,000

ROLEX, 17J., Panerai, 47 x 47mm, RF# 3646, c.1943
s. steel $25,000 $35,000 $45,000

ROLEX, 15J., lady's, curved, ca.1925
9k $150 $300 $400

ROLEX, 15J., lady's, center lugs, ca.1925
9k enamel dial $300 $500 $650

ROLEX, 18J., lady's,
14k(W) C&B $300 $500 $650

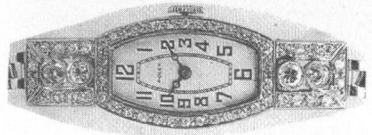

ROLEX, 15J., 54 diamonds, 9K band 18k(w) case, c.1930
9k & 18k $1,200 $2,000 $3,000

ROLEX, 18J., wire lugs, diamond bezel, ca. 1940s
18k(W) $400 $700 $900

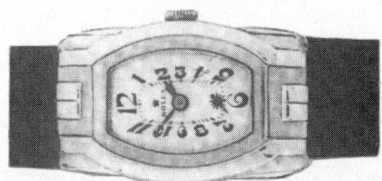

ROLEX, 17 jewels, hooded lugs, 2 tone, **ladies**
Pink & White gold $700 $1,200 $1,600

ROLEX, 15J., lady's, Ca. 1925
18k band $300 $450 $600

ROLEX, 18J., lady's, Ca. 1930s
18k. $300 $525 $650

ROLEX (Ladies)

ROLEX, 17J.,RF # 4554, "Precision", ladies, Ca. 1955
gold filled $100 $200 $250

ROLEX, 17J., ladies, RF #4593, c.1954
s. steel $150 $250 $350

ROLEX, 17J., RF # 1701, ladies, fancy lugs, Ca. 1950
14k. $250 $400 $600

ROLEX, 18J., ladies, Ca. 1948
18k. $200 $375 $450
14k. $150 $275 $400

ROLEX, 18J., ladies
14k. $200 $375 $450

ROLEX, "Precision", ladies, c. 1950
18k. $300 $400 $500

ROLEX, "Precision", ladies, c. 1960s
18k. $500 $700 $1,000

ROLEX,"Precision", ladies, c. 1965
18k. $550 $750 $1,100

ROLEX, 17J., ladies, "Oyster",
14k. $700 $1,200 $1,500

ROLEX, 18J., lady's, bubble back
18k pink $900 $1,400 $1,800
18k. $700 $1,200 $1,600

ROLEX, 17J., BB, ladies, "Oyster", c. 1948
s. steel $350 $600 $900
s. steel & gold $500 $800 $1,200

ROLEX, 17J., Oyster, RF # 5004, plain bezel Ca.1950s Mid size
or ladies
s. steel $400 $650 $700

ROLEX, 17J., Oyster Pet., RF# 5003, index bezel, Ca. 1950s Mid
size or ladies
18k $1,700 $2,400 $3,000

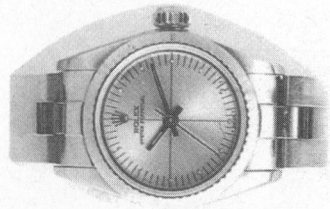

ROLEX, 29J., ladies, "Oyster", RF#6700-3
s. steel &14k,C&B $800 $1,100 $1,500

ROLEX, 17J., ladies, "Oyster", RF#4486, c.1957
14k & s.s. case $400 $500 $700

ROLEX, 17J., ladies, "Oyster", RF # 3492
s. steel $400 $500 $700

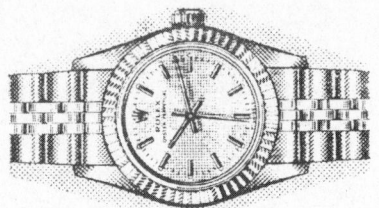

ROLEX, Oyster Perpetual Sapphire Crystal, no date
18k & s. steel no date $1,000 $1,500 $2,000

ROLEX, Oyster Perpetual Datejust, Sapphire Crystal, Quick Set
18k & s. steel. $1,600 $2,800 $3,200

ROLEX, Oyster Perpetual Datejust, Plastic Crystal
18k C&B $3,000 $4,000 $4,500

ROLEX, Oyster Perpetual Datejust, diamond dial &bezel Sapphire
Crystal, Quick Set
18k C&B $6,000 $7,500 $8,500

ROLEX, Oyster Perpetual Datejust, diamond dial, RF# 6917
18k $3,000 $4,000 $5,000

Advertised as accurate timekeeper at a moderate price.
U = unicorn, **M** = Marcoin, **R** = Rolco.
Listed as **U., M., R.**, & 7 to 15 jewels, Ca. 1920s.

Dials must be original for prices below.

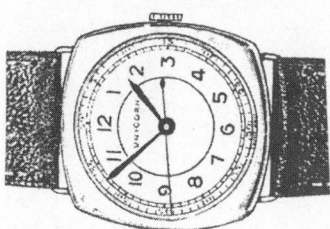

U. M. R., 7-15J., center sec. wire lugs, Ca. 1920s
base metal.................... $250 $450 $600

U M. R., 7-15J., black dial, Ca. 1920s
base metal....................$150 $275 $350
s. steel $300 $600 $700

U. M. R., 7-15J., aux. see., Ca. 1920s
s. steel $150 $350 $400
9K $250 $450 $500

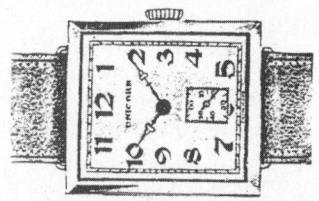

U. M. R., 7-15J., square, Ca. 1920s
s. steel $250 $450 $550
9K $250 $500 $600

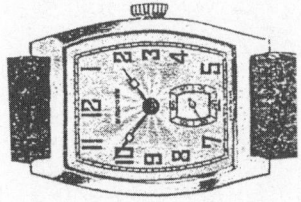

U. M. R., 7-15J., tonneau, very flat, Ca. 1920s
s. steel $250 $400 $500
9K $250 $475 $575

U. M. R., 7-15J., Ladies round wire lugs Ca. 1920s
base metal.................... $50 $100 $150
9K $75 $120 $200

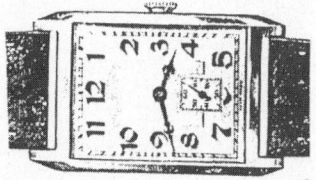

U. M. R., 7-15J., rect., aux. sec, Ca. 1920a
s. steel $300 $550 $650
9K $300 $500 $600

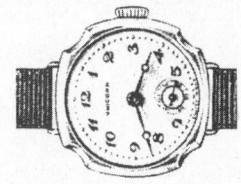

U. M. R., 7-15J., Ladies, wire lugs Ca. 1920s
base metal.................... $50 $100 $150
9K $75 $120 $200

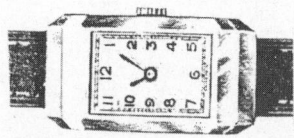

U. M R, 7-15J ,hidden lugs, Ca. 1920s
base metal.................... $125 $250 $325

U. M. R., 7-15J., Ladies, wire lugs, Ca. 1920s
base metal.................... $50 $100 $150
9K $75 $120 $200

6694

Reference number, between the lugs

1705215

Serial number, six or seven figures engraved between the lugs

INSIDE OF BACK
Reference number
in four figures

NON-OYSTER CASE

On recent OYSTER models the number is engraved on the outside of the case between the lugs. Reference number of earlier models will be found engraved on the inside of the back of the case.

OUTSIDE OF BACK
Serial number
in six or seven figures

Reference number for NON-OYSTER models will be found engraved on the inside of the back of the case.

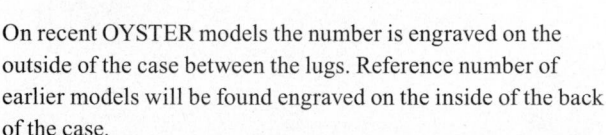

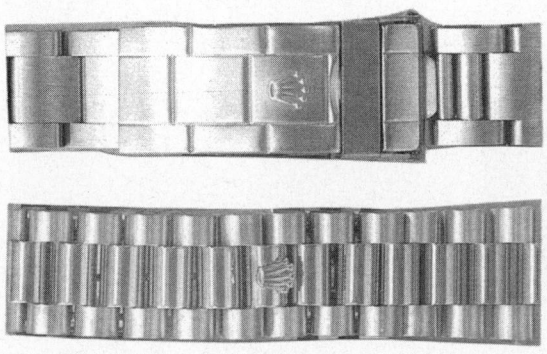

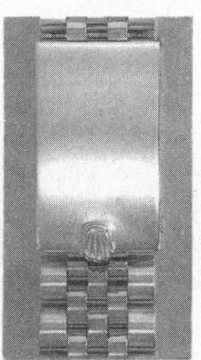

Above: Oyster style bracelet. **Below**: Presidential style band With hidden clasp.
Right: Jubilee style bracelet.

New model Presidential bracelets use 8 screws for adjustment links.
Double quick set Presidential and Jubilee bracelets use 7 screws for adjustment links.
The older models **single quick** Presidential and Jubilee bracelets use 6 screw for adjustment links.

Note: Check Bracelet for stretched links.

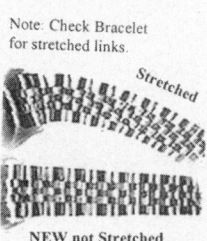

Stretched

NEW not Stretched

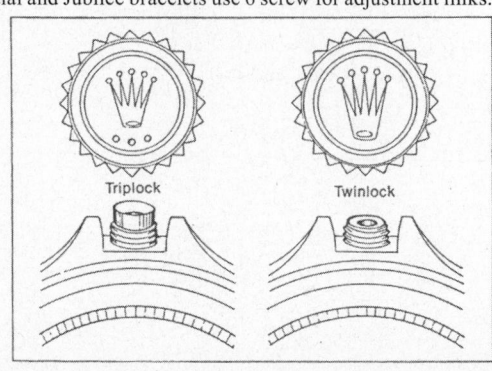

Triplock

Twinlock

ROLEX
MOVEMENT IDENTIFICATION

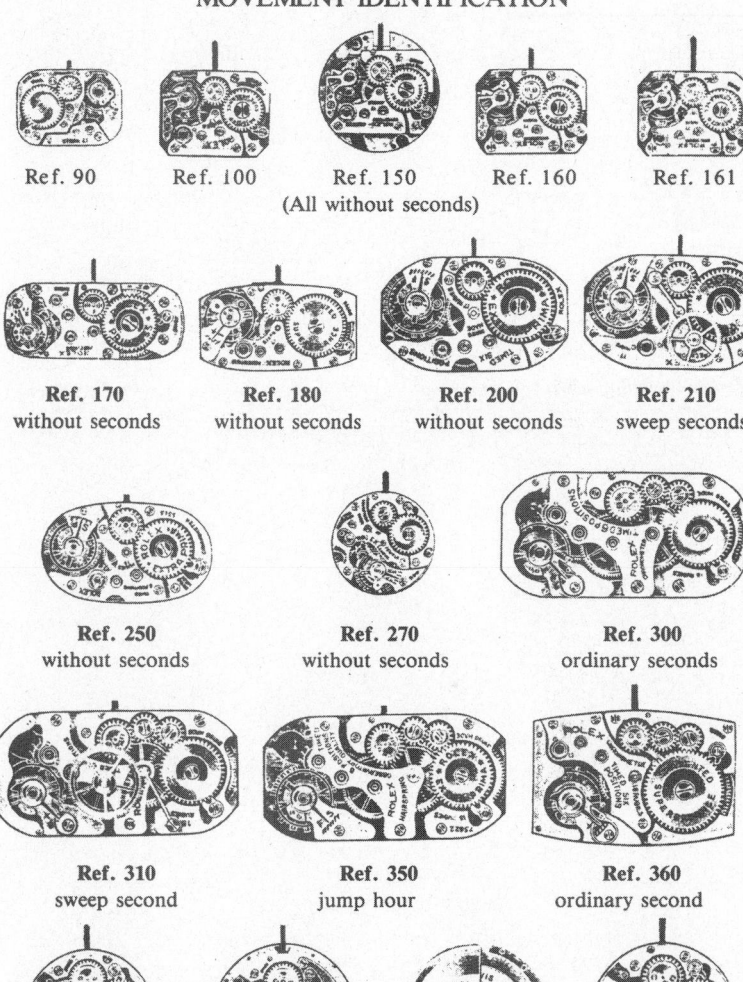

Ref. 90   Ref. 100   Ref. 150   Ref. 160   Ref. 161
(All without seconds)

Ref. 170
without seconds

Ref. 180
without seconds

Ref. 200
without seconds

Ref. 210
sweep seconds

Ref. 250
without seconds

Ref. 270
without seconds

Ref. 300
ordinary seconds

Ref. 310
sweep second

Ref. 350
jump hour

Ref. 360
ordinary second

Ref. 400
ordinary seconds
Ca. 1941

Ref. 420
ordinary seconds
Ca. 1941

Ref. 420
rotor
Ca. 1941

Ref. 500
ordinary seconds
Ca. 1936

When performing any underwater activity, the dynamic pressure generated through movement is greater than the static pressure. Below a ranking of water resistance for most watches.

1 **meter** = 3.28 ft., 330 ft. =about 100 **meters**. 33,89 ft. =1 **atmosphere**, 100 ft. = about 3 **atmospheres**.
30M/100Ft/3ATM/3Bar = sweat-resistant   50M/160Ft/5ATM/5Bar = shower only, rain
100M/300Ft/10ATM/10Bar = swimming (no diving)   200M/660ft/20ATM/20Bar = snorkeling, skin diving
1000M =scuba diving -3,300 ft.

Ref. 510
sweep second
Ca. 1936

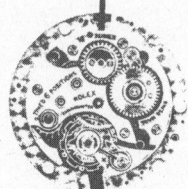
Ref. 520
sweep second
Ca. 1936

Ref. 520
rotor
Ca. 1936

Ref. 530
self wind, sweep sec.
Ca. 1936

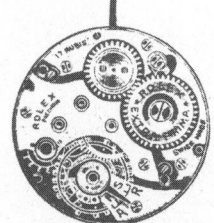
Ref. 600   Ca. 1931
ordinary seconds

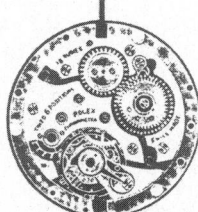
Ref. 620 Ca. 1931
ordinary seconds

Ref. 620 Ca. 1931
rotor

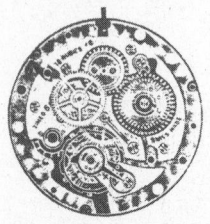
Ref. 630   Ca. 1931
self wind, sweep sec.

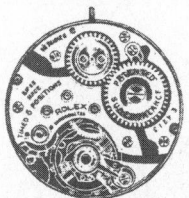
Ref. 700 Ca. 1940
ordinary seconds

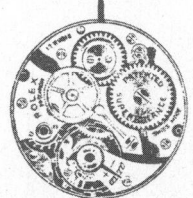
Ref. 710 Ca. 1940
sweep seconds

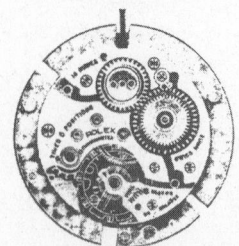
Ref. 720 Ca. 1940
ordinary seconds

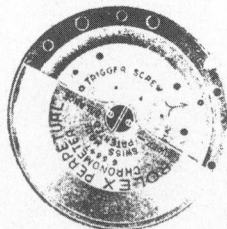
Ref. 720 Ca. 1940
rotor

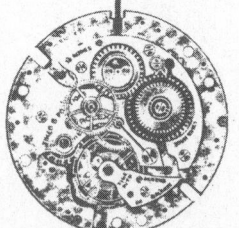
Ref. 730 Ca. 1945
self wind, sweep sec.

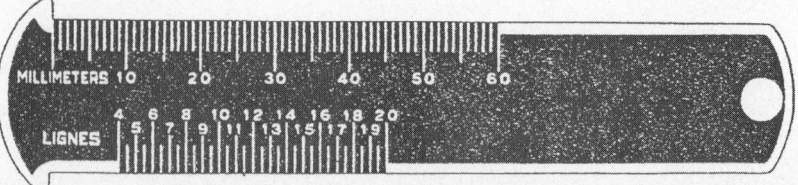

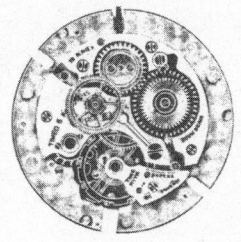

Ref. 740 Ca. 1945
self wind, calendar, sweep sec.

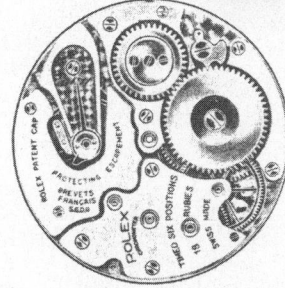

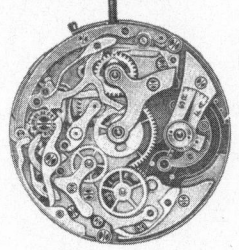

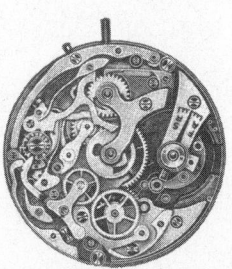

| **Ref. 850** | **Ref. 72** | **Ref. 23** |
| ordinary seconds | chronograph, 3 registers | chronograph, 2 registers |

POSITIONS OF THE WINDING CROWN FOR CALENDAR MODELS

Pos. 1
Crown fully screwed down.
In this position the Rolex Oyster is warranted pressure-proof to a
depth of 330 feet/100 m.
The watch is ready to be worn.

Pos. 2
Crown unscrewed.
When the crown is free of the screw threads, the watch is in position
for handwinding, if necessary.
In quartz models, this is a neutral position.

Pos. 3
Crown pulled out to the first notch.
When turning the crown from three to six o'clock, the date will change rapidly.
This position is used to correct the date when months have less than 31 days.
The timing of the watch will not be altered.

Pos. 4
Crown pulled out to the last notch.
Position for setting the correct time, the date and the day. The watch stops
and enables adjustments to be made, for Day-Date models, when the hands
are turned counter-clockwise, the day of the week changes while the
date remains unchanged. Change the day before correcting the date.

ROLLS, 15J., early auto wind, by Leon Hatot, movement in side case moves back & forth to wind, c. 1920s
s. steel . . . . ★★★$400 $650 $750

ROLLS, 15 jewels, early auto wind, c. 1920s
s. steel $350 $550 $700

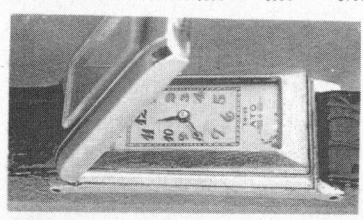

ROLLS, 15 jewels, "ATO," flip top
s. steel $300 $575 $800

ROLLS, 15 jewels, ladies, "ATO," flip top, by Blancpain
18k. $400 $575 $650

ROTARY, 15J., aux. sec., ca.1934
9k $100 $175 $225

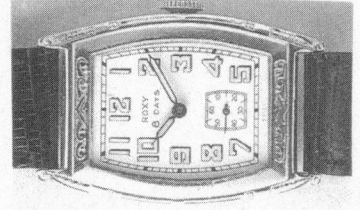

ROXY, 8 day, engraved case, ca. 1930s
s. steel . . . . ★$300 $500 $600

RUSSIAN Military Divers watch, 15J., 60mm, made in Russian factory using Hampden W. Co. parts, signed "Kamhem'.
s. steel $400 $625 $750

SCHILD, 17J., "Aqua lung', tach. chronog., ca.1972
s. steel $150 $300 $500

SCHULTZ, 17J., diamond dial, c. 1930
platinum C & B $1,500 $2,500 $3,000

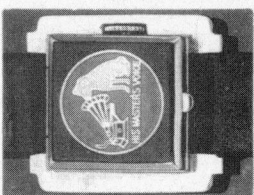

J. SCHULTZ, 17J., enamel hunter style, ca. 1949
18k. $800 $1,300 $2,000

SEELAND, 17J., 'Quadramatic' auto-wind, c.1947
s. steel $35 $75 $100

SEELAND, 17J., manual wind, c.1947
chrome $35 $75 $100

SEIKO, 17J., Chronograph, day date, auto wind, Ca.1974
s. steel $100 $175 $225

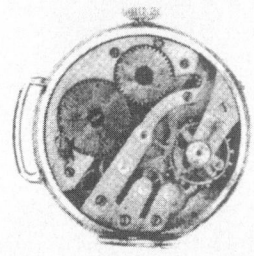

SEIKO, 6J., wire lugs, on dial "LAUREL", ca.1925
Note: Looks like a Swiss Bar Mvt. but was made by the Seiko
Factory.
s. steel . . . . ★$35 $65 $85

Wrist watches listed in this section are priced at the collectable
fair market **Trade Show** level an **complete** watches having an
original gold-filled case and stainless steel back, also with original
dial, leather watch band, and the entire original movement in good
working order with no repairs needed

SEIKO, quartz, rope style bezel
14k. $95 $165 $200

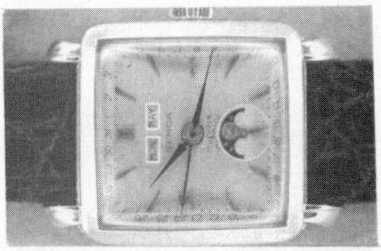

SEMCA, 17J., day-date-month, moon phase, c. 1950s
18k. $800 $1,300 $1,700

SEMCA, 17J., day-date-month, moon phase, c. 1950s
14k. $600 $1,200 $1,500

SETH THOMAS, day date, moon phases, ca 1949
s. steel $175 $350 $475

☞ Some grades are not Included. Their values can be
determined by comparing with **similar** age, size, metal content,
style, grades, or models such as **time only**, chronograph,
repeater etc. listed.

SOUTH BEND,17J., **multi-color dial**, made U.S.A.
base metal................... ★$175 $325 $450

STANDARD,17J., 24 hr. dial, world time, c.1965
s. steel....................... $95 $175 $250

SMITHS, on dial "Everest automatic 25 jewels", marked on movement "Smith Imperial automatic 25 jewels made in England', note
weight is mounted on ball-race, Ca. 1965
9k $300 $550 $700

STOWA, 20-22J., Military watch, Ca. 1942
s. steel...................... $400 $650 $800

SMITHS, 17J., military , Ca.1969
s. steel...................... $95 $125 $175

SPERINA, 7 jewels, **day & date on lugs**
s. steel...................... $65 $110 $135

TAVANNES, 15J., enamel dial, hunter, **flip top**, c.1915
silver....................... $200 $400 $500

TAVANNES, 17J., chronog., c.1940
s. steel $175 $325 $450

TAVANNES, 17J., extended lugs, c.1955
gold filled $65 $100 $125

TAVANNES,17J., 26 x 41mm., **exaggerated** #s, Ca.1920
18k. $300 $800 $1,000

TAVANNES, 17J., GJS, cal.365k, c.1938
14k. $100 $225 $300

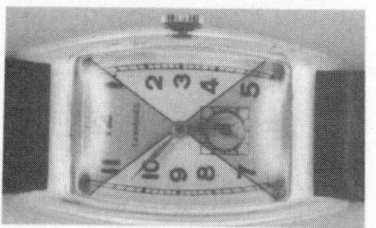

TAVANNES, 17 jewels, hour glass dial, **curved**
14k. $135 $300 $350

TAVANNES, 15 jewels, "334," c. 1939
14k(w) $175 $300 $400

TAVANNES, 17 jewels, aux. sec. ca. 1940s
s. steel $65 $115 $150

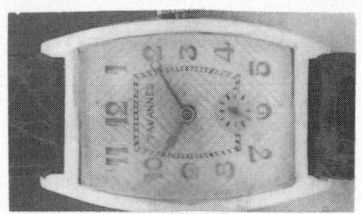

TAVANNES, 17 jewels, aux. sec.
14k. $125 $250 $400

TECHNOS, 17J., "Sky Diver', auto-wind, 500m., c. 1970
s. steel $45 $95 $135

☞ Wrist watches listed in this section are priced at the collectable fair market Trade Show level as complete watches having an original gold-filled case and stainless steel back, also with original dial, leather watch band, and the entire original movement in good working order with no repairs needed.

☞ Some grades are not Included. Their values can be determined by comparing with similar age, size, metal content, style, grades, or models such as time only, chronograph, repeater etc. listed.

TELDA, 17J., chronog., 3 reg. date, moon ph., c. 1980s
s. steel $300 $500 $650

TELDA, 17J., center sec., c. 1948
gold filled $35 $75 $100

NOTE: Examples of Tiffany made up watches are listed but
were not sold by Tiffany & Co.. These off-brand watches will be
listed but not priced as true Tiffany & Co. watches. EXAMPLES:
Kingston?, Emerson?, Banner?, ETC. were not sold by Tiffany. (?)

TIFFANY & CO., 15-17J., enamel dial, Ca. 1905
18k. $300 $600 $800

TIFFANY & CO., 17J., exaggerated numbers, Ca. 1920
silver $500 $800 $1,000

TIFFANY & CO., 18J., by Patek Philippe, exaggerated numbers,
c.1920s
18K $7,000 $15,000 $18,000

TIFFANY & CO., 17J., curved, mvt. by PP & Co., c. 1910
18k. $7,000 $15,000 $18,000

TIFFANY & CO.,17J., Swiss ,c.1926
18k. $300 $600 $700

TIFFANY & CO.,17J., Swiss, c.1930
14k. $200 $400 $500

TIFFANY & CU., 26 Jewels, min. repeater, slide repeat,
automaton, 40mm (conversion)
18k. $2,000 $4,000 $5,000

TIFFANY & CO, 15J., wire lugs, ca. 1928
silver $250 $400 $500

TIFFANY & CO.,17J., by Patek Philippe, wire lugs, c.1915
18k (refinished dial) $3,500 $7,000 $9,000

TIFFANY & CO.,17J., by I.W.C., wire lugs, c.1918
14k. $500 $800 $1,000

TIFFANY & CO., 15J., enamel dial, ca. 1930s
silver. $350 $500 $700

TIFFANY & CO., 17J., Concord W. Co.
14k. $400 $750 $900

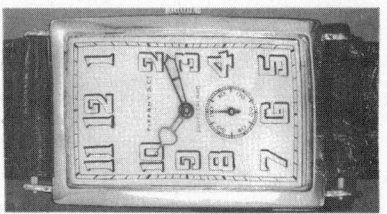

TIFFANY & CO., 18J., by Patek Philippe, Ca 1930a
platinum $14,000 $25,000 $30,000

TIFFANY & CO., 15 jewels, Swiss, Ca. 1926
18k. $500 $900 $1,200

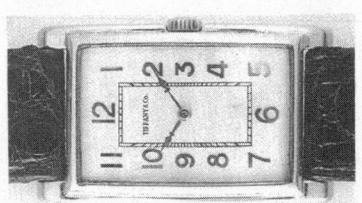

TIFFANY & CO., 17J., by Longines, c.1928
14k. $250 $500 $700

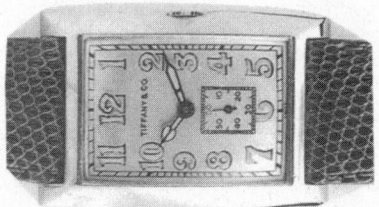

TIFFANY & CO.,17J., aux. sec., Swiss, c.1926
18k(w) $450 $800 $1,000

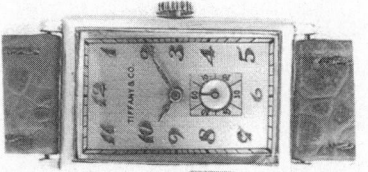

TIFFANY & CO.,17J., Swiss, c.1930
14k. $275 $500 $700

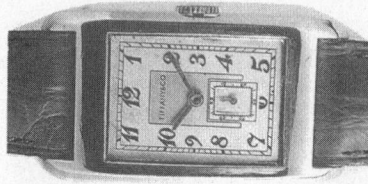

TIFFANY & CO.,17J., GJS, by Movado, c.1940
14k. $300 $600 $800

TIFFANY & CO.,17J., Swiss, hidden lugs, c.1943
14k. $200 $400 $600

TIFFANY & CO.,17J., Swiss, GJS, c.1940
14k. $200 $400 $600

TIFFANY & CO.,17J., by **Hampden** "?", c.1949
14k. $200 $400 $600

TIFFANY & CO.,17J., by I. W. C., c. 1942
14k. $500 $900 $1,000

TIFFANY & CO.,17J., by I.W.C., hidden lugs, c.1942
14k $500 $900 $1,000

TIFFANY & CO., 17J., top hat, by I. W. C.
14K $700 $1,000 $1,500

TIFFANY & CO., 30J., auto-wind, date, Ca.1955
18K $350 $600 $800

TIFFANY & CO.,15J., one button chronog., by Goering, Cal.
69mvt., c.1925
silver $950 $1,700 $2,200

TIFFANY & CO.,17J.,Valjoux cal.72c., c.1948
s. steel $550 $900 $1,100
14k. $1,000 $1,500 $1,800
18k. $1,200 $1,800 $2,200

𝒢𝒮 Some grades are not included. Their values can be
determined by comparing with **similar** age, size, metal content,
style, grades, or models such as **time only**, chronograph,
repeater etc. listed.

TIFFANY & CO.,17J., by Movado, c.1947
14k.......................... $900 $1,700 $2,200

TIFFANY & CO.,17J., by Bovet, c.1940
18k.......................... $800 $1,600 $2,000

TIFFANY & CO.,17J., by Tourneau, Valjoux 72c, c. 1950
s. steel...................... $800 $1,200 $1,500

TIFFANY & CO., 31J., chronog., triple date, moon ph. screw
back, note window for date at 4 & 5
18k........................$2,000 $3,500 $4,500

TIFFANY & CO., 17J., chronog., day-date-month
14k.......................... $900 $1,600 $2,000

TIFFANY & CO., 21J., mvt. by Patek Philippe, c. 1950
18k..........................$3,000 $5,000 $6,500

TIFFANY & CO., 17J., curved , ca. t9Stts
platinum...................$1,200 $2,500 $3,000

TIFFANY & CO.,15J., engraved bezel, c. 1919
18k.......................... $900 $1,500 $2,500

Wrist Watches listed in this section are priced at the collectable fair market **Trade Show** level as **complete** watches having an original gold-filled case and stainless steel back, also with original dial, leather watch band, and the entire original movement in good working order with no repairs needed.

TIFFANY & CO., 15J., ca. 1920s
14k. $300 $550 $650

TIFFANY & CO.,17J., by Zodiac ,c.1942
14k. $200 $400 $500

TIFFANY & CO.,17J., by Hampden "?", c.1945
gold filled $100 $250 $300
14k. $200 $375 $500

TIFFANY & CO.,17J., by Glycine, c.1945
gold filled $100 $200 $250
14k. $200 $400 $500

TIFFANY & CO.,17J., by Ollendorf, c.1945
14k. $200 $400 $600

TIFFANY & CO., 17J., extended bezel, c. 1942
14k. $250 $400 $600

TIFFANY & CO.,17J., Swiss, c.1947
14k. $200 $400 $600

TIFFANY & CO.,17J., by Wyler, c.1950
gold filled $100 $200 $250

TIFFANY & CO.,17J., by Tissot. c.1945
14k. $150 $300 $500

TIFFANY & CO., 17J., fancy lugs & bezel ca. 1950s
14k. $300 $500 $700

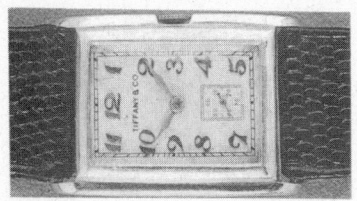

TIFFANY & CO., 17J., applied numbers, Ca. 1950s
14k.......................... $200 $400 $550

TIFFANY & CO., 17J., flared & stepped, ca. 1950s
14k.......................... $300 $400 $600

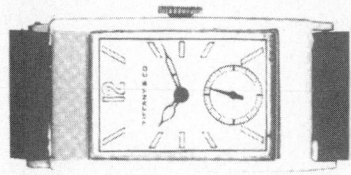

TIFFANY & CO., 17 jewels, Swiss, c. 1935
18k.......................... $350 $500 $700

TIFFANY & CO., 17 jewels, fancy bezel, c. 1942
14k.......................... $300 $500 $700

TIFFANY & CO., 17 jewels, sculptured lugs, c. 1948
14k.......................... $500 $700 $900

TIFFANY & CO., 17J., 3 diamond dial, Swiss,
14k(w)....................... $200 $400 $600

TIFFANY & CO.,15J., rhinestones, c.1948
base metal.................... $100 $200 $250

TIFFANY & CO., 17J., "Movado', triple date, center sec.
s. steel...................... $400 $700 $800

TIFFANY & CO., 17J., by Movado, triple date, c. 1948
gold filled $400 $700 $800
14k & s. s. $500 $800 $900

🖝 A collector should expect to pay modestly higher prices at
local shops

TIFFANY & CO., 17J., by Tissot, triple date moon ph.,
14k. $800 $1,250 $1,750

TIFFANY & CO.,17J. by Helvetia, c.1948
gold filled $100 $200 $250
14k. $150 $250 $400

TIFFANY & CO., 17J., triple date, **moon ph.**
s. steel $400 $700 $800

TIFFANY&CO.,17J., Swiss, c.1940
gold filled $100 $150 $225

TIFFANY & CO.,17J., by Ardath "?", auto-wind, c.1950
14k. $200 $375 $450

TIFFANY & CO.,17J., Swiss, GJS, c.1949
gold filled $100 $150 $225
14k. $150 $200 $350

TIFFANY & CO.,17J., by Nicolet, c.1955
gold filled $100 $200 $250

TIFFANY & CO.,17J., by Zenith, c.1939
14k. $200 $300 $400s

TIFFANY & CO.,17J., c.1948
18k. $550 $800 $1,000

TIFFANY & CO.,17J., curved lugs, c.1950
18k. $250 $400 $550

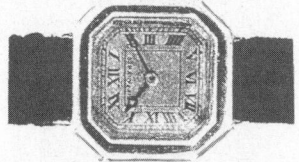

TIFFANY & CO.,17J., ladies, by Longines, c.1920
18k. $200 $275 $325

TIFFANY & CO.,17J., ladies, by I.W.C., c.1948
18k. $100 $200 $300

TIFFANY & CO.,17J., ladies, I.W.C., c.1955
18k. $135 $175 $300

TIFFANY & CO., 15J., 2 tone , ladies, ca. 1939
18k C & B $200 $350 $400

TIFFANY & CO., 15J., early ladies, wire lugs ca.1925
14k. $175 $200 $250

TIFFANY & CO., 17J., ladies, aux. sec., Ca.1940
gold filled $50 $85 $100

TIMECRAFT, 17 jewels, chronog., Ca. 1950
s. steel $100 $200 $275

TIMEX, chronog., slide to start, stop & return to zero
base metal. $50 $75 $125

TIMEX, "Ben Hogan", m/wind, Ca.1961
base metal. $50 $75 $125

TIMEX, engraved bezel, m/wind, Ca. 1970
base metal..................... $5 $10 $35

TIMEX, checkerboard dial, m/wind, Ca. 1968
base metal..................... $5 $10 $40

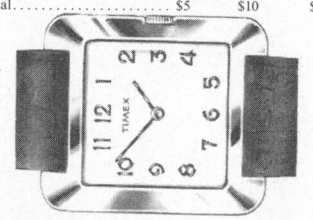

TIMEX, "Monroe', m/wind, wide bezel, Ca. 1961
base metal..................... $5 $10 $35

TIMEX, "Mercury series", m/wind, Ca. 1969
base metal..................... $5 $10 $35

TIMEX, military style, m/wind, Ca.1966
base metal..................... $15 $25 $50

TIMEX, **Electric**, water-resistant, 14k sold for $125 in 1962
14k....................★$75 $125 $250
base metal..................... $5 $10 $35

TIMEX, 'Fun Timer, m/wind, Ca. 1968
base metal..................... $5 $10 $35

TIMEX, 21 jewels, auto-wind, Ca.1962
base metal.....................$15 $20 $45

TIMEX, Electric calendar series, water-resistant, Ca. 1970
base metal.....................$15 $20 $45

TIMEX, Skindiver or Sports series, 600 ft. depth, Ca. 1966
base metal (m/wind) $15 $20 $45

TIMEX, Skindiver or Sports series, 200 ft. depth, Ca. 1968
base metal (m/wind) $15 $20 $45

TISSOT, 17 jewels, 1898 USA 20 dollar gold piece
22K $900 $1,250 $1,500

TISSOT,World Time, auto, 24 hour, 43mm, c. 1968
s. steel $150 $300 $475

TISSOT,17J., one button chronog., Ca.1935
s. steel $300 $500 $600

TISSOT, 21 jewels, world lime, 24 hr. dial, 24 cities, Ca.1950
gold filled $400 $700 $900
s. steel $1,000 $1,500 $1,900
18k. $2,000 $3,250 $4,000

TISSOT,17J., Valjoux cal.726, c.1965
18k. $700 $1,200 $1,500
14k. $600 $1,000 $1,200

TISSOT, 213, world time, 24 hr. dial, 24 cities, mid-size
18k (1950) $2,000 $2,800 $3,600

TISSOT,17J., auto-wind, "Navigator", date, c.1972
s. steel $150 $300 $400

TISSOT, 17J., "Stadium", tachyrneter, c.1960
gold plate $150 $275 $350

TISSOT, 17 jewels, chronog., 3 reg., c. 1956
s. steel $275 $500 $675

TISSOT, 17 jewels, chronog., 3 reg.
gold filled $200 $475 $650
s. steel $200 $400 $650

TISSOT, 17 jewels, chronog., 3 reg.
18k $500 $800 $1,000
s. steel $225 $400 $500

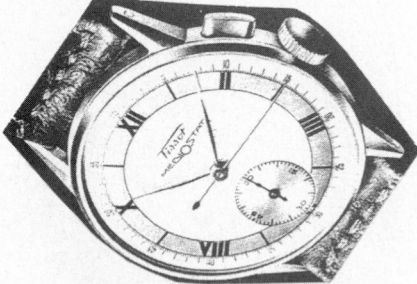

TISSOT, 17J., "Mediostat", stop center second hand, Ca. 1955
s. steel $125 $250 $300

TISSOT, 17J., "Sonorous", Alarm, Cal# 780, Ca. 1960s
s. steel $100 $200 $300

TISSOT, 17 jewels, "Seastar", Cal.782, Date, Ca. 1957
s. steel $90 $150 $200

TISSOT, 17J., "Visodate Camping", Date, Ca. 1955
s. steel $100 $175 $225

TISSOT, *Worlds first transparent plastic watch*, 'Idea 2001', with
model "Synthic, Astrolon & Sytal', cal.2250, Ca. 1971
plastic(working) . . . . ★$250 $500 $700

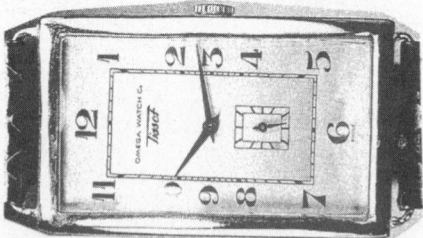

TISSOT, 15J., Omega W. Co. & Tissot signatures, Ca 1938
14k $600 $1,000 $1,800

TISSOT, 15J., 1st Tissot wrist model, "Banana", Ca. 1917
18K $900 $1,500 $2,000

TISSOT (continued)

TISSOT,17J., auto wind, aux. sec., c.1951
18k. $250 $400 $500

TISSOT, 17J., aux. sec., Ca. 1950
14k. $150 $300 $400

TISSOT,17J., aux. sec., c.1942
s. steel $35 $50 $100
14k. $100 $150 $200
18k. $150 $225 $300

TISSOT, 17 jewels, Masonic dial Ca.1955
14k. $150 $400 $600

TISSOT, 17J., censer sec., Ca. 1951
base metal. $45 $75 $125

TISSOT, 15 jewels, wire lugs, aux. sec., Ca. 1915
silver $200 $400 $500

TITUS, 17 jewels, chronog., 2reg.
18k. $250 $400 $500
14k. $175 $300 $400
s. steel $85 $150 $300

TORNEK-RAYVILLE,17J., military, "SEAL", auto-
wind, water-proof, 150M or 490 ft., Ca. 1966
s. steel . . . . ★★$700 $1,200 $1,800

TOUCHON,17J., tonneau case, c.1928
18k(w). $300 $600 $750

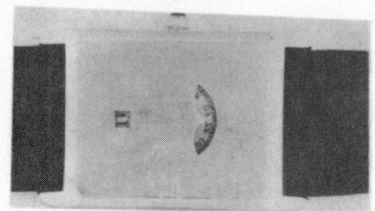

TOUCHON, 17J., jump hr., wandering min., c. 1930s
18k........................$1,650 $2,500 $3,200

TOURNEAU,17J, triple date, 3 reg., moon ph., c. 1952
s. steel $500 $1,000 $1,300

TOURNEAU,17J.,chronog. by Valjoux cal.886, c.1965
18k........................ $700 $1,250 $1,500

TOURNEAU,17J., day date, c.1945
s. steel........................$150 $200 $275

TOURNEAU,17J., beveled lugs, c. 1945
14k........................ $125 $200 $300

TOURIST, 17J., by MEPA, timer, c.1958
s. steel $35 $75 $100

TREBEX, 15 jewels, cut corner dial, c. 1940
gold filled $45 $100 $125

TREBEX, 15 jewels, c. 1940
gold filled $35 $60 $75

TREBEX, 15 jewels, c. 1940s
gold filled $35 $100 $125

TURLER, 15-17J., duo-dial, Ca.1930s
18k. $900 $1,400 $1,800

TURLER, 17 jewels, chronog., triple date, 3 reg.
18k. $800 $1,300 $1,500

UHRENFABRIK GLASHUTTE, 17J., chronog., c. 1940s
s. steel $700 $1,400 $1,600

ULTIMOR, 17J., chronog., cal.51, c.1945
18k. $250 $450 $550

UNITAS, 17 jewels, triple date, moon phase, c. 1948
s. steel $200 $400 $500

URANIA, 15 jewels, military style grill, c. 1915
silver $150 $300 $400

UNVER, 17J., triple date , moon ph., chronog.
s. steel $900 $1,400 $2,100
14k. $1,000 $1,500 $2,250
18k. $1,400 $2,000 $2,500
18k pink $1,500 $2,750 $3,250

UNIVERSAL,17J., "medico compax", c.1949
18k. $1,200 $1,700 $2,000

Wrist Watches listed in this section are priced as complete
watches having an original gold-filled case and stainless steel
back, also with original dial, leather watch band, and the entire
original movement in good working order with no repairs
needed.

UNIVERSAL,17J., uni compax", c.1942
s. steel $450 $800 $1,000

UNIVERSAL,17J., tri-compax, day date moon ph.,c.1955
s. steel $1,200 $2,250 $2,850
14k. $2,800 $4,500 $5,000

UNIVERSAL, 17J., chronog., triple date, moos phase
18k. $1,400 $2,100 $2,600
14k. $1,200 $1,800 $2,200

UNIVERSAL, 17J., chronog., aero compax, diff. meridian, square pushers
14k. $1,600 $2,600 $3,500

UNIVERSAL, 17J. chronog., tri-compax, day date moon ph.
s. steel $1,200 $2,250 $3,250

UNIVERSAL, 17J., chronog., aero compax, duff, meridian, round pushers
18k. $2,000 $3,250 $4,000

UNIVERSAL, 17J., chronog., tri-compax, moon phase
s. steel $1,000 $1,800 $2,700

UNIVERSAL, 17 jewels, chronog., M. #281, c. 1950s
18k. $1,800 $3,000 $4,000

UNIVERSAL, 17J., chronog., compax, massive case
18k.........................$2,200 $3,500 $4,000

UNIVERSAL, 17J., chronog., dato-compax, c. 1950s
14k.........................$1,200 $1,800 $2,500
s. steel.......................$600 $900 $1,200

UNIVERSAL,17J., compax, RF#885107, Valj.cal.72,c.1965
s. steel.......................$500 $900 $1,100

UNIVERSAL, 17J. chronog., 10 ligne size, uni-compax
s. steel.......................$450 $750 $900

☞ Pricing in this Guide are fair market price for complete watches which are reflected from the NAWCC National and regional shows.

UNIVERSAL, day-date-month, moon phase
18k.........................$900 $1,400 $1,700

UNIVERSAL, 17 jewels, day-date-month
s. steel.......................$350 $575 $650
14k.........................$600 $900 $1,200

UNIVERSAL,17J., "Polerouter Sub", date, auto-w., c.1960
14k.........................$300 $600 $700
s. steel.......................$150 $300 $400

UNIVERSAL,28J., "Polerouter Sub", rotating bezel, c. 1980s
s. steel.......................$250 $425 $550

UNIVERSAL, 17 jewels, 'Polerouter", auto wind, day date
18k........................ $400 $800 $950

UNIVERSAL, 23J., auto-wind, date, c. 1965
14k........................$175 $350 $475

UNIVERSAL, 28J., center sec., date, auto-wind, c.1958
18k........................ $250 $450 $550

UNIVERSAL,17J., cal. 138c, date, c.1952
18k........................ $250 $550 $750

UNIVERSAL,17J., cal.52, date, c.1965
18k........................ $200 $400 $600

UNIVERSAL, 17 jewels, Ca. 1952
14k........................ $225 $350 $400

UNIVERSAL,17J., Unisonic chronometer, date, c.1968
s. steel..................... $100 $200 $300

UNIVERSAL,17J., m#264, large lugs, c.1957
gold filled $100 $175 $225

UNIVERSAL,17J., cal.267g, date, center sec. c.1948
18k.........................$275 $550 $700

UNIVERSAL, 16J., cal#230,ca. 1940s
s. steel $100 $175 $300

UNIVERSAL, 17J., fancy lugs, Ca. 1948
14k......................... $225 $375 $450

UNIVERSAL, 17J., fancy lugs
14k......................... $200 $300 $400

UNIVERSAL, 17 jewels, "Cabriolet," reverso, c. 1930s
s. steel $1,500 $2,250 $2,500

UNIVERSAL,17J., center sec., cal.263, c.1950
18k.........................$175 $275 $325

UNIVERSAL,17J., center sec., cal. 138, c. 1950
s. steel $100 $150 $200

UNIVERSAL,17J., center sec., cal.236, c.1955
18k.........................$175 $300 $400

UNIVERSAL,17J., aux. see., Ca.1955
s. steel $100 $225 $300

Wrist Watches listed in this section are priced at the collectable fair
market Trade Show level as complete watches having an original
gold-filled case and stainless steel back, also with original dial,
leather watch band, and the entire original movement in good
working order with no repairs needed.

UNIVERSAL, 17 jewels, auto wind, c. 1955
14k.........................$195 $325 $450
gold filled $100 $175 $225

UNIVERSAL, quartz, day-date, center sec., c. 1960s
18k.........................$150 $275 $300

UNIVERSAL, quartz, ,c. 1981
18k.........................$175 $275 $300

UNIVERSAL, 17 jewels, auto wind
gold filled $100 $150 $175

ᴘ⌒ Some grades are not included. Their values can be determined by comparing with similar age, size, metal contest, style,
models and grades listed.

Wrist Watches listed in this section are priced at the collectable fair
market Trade Show level as complete watches having an original
gold-filled case and stainless steel back, also with original dial,
leather watch band, and the entire original movement in good
working order with no repairs needed.

VACHERON, 36J., skeletonized, triple date, moon phase, leap
year, gold rotor
18k....................... $14,000 $19,000 $22,000

VACHERON, 36J., diamond bezel, triple date, moon ph., leap
year, gold rotor
18k C&B..................$15,000 $22,000 $25,000

VACHERON, 17J., ref. 4764, so called "Yellow Cioccolatone",
triple date, moon phase, c. 1947
18k.......................$45,000 $60,000 $75,000

VACHERON, 17J., triple date, moon phase, c. 1945
18k pink $9,000 $15,000 $18,000

VACHERON, 17J., triple date, moon phase, c. 1950s
18k manual wind $8,000 $16,000 $17,500

VACHERON, 29 jewels, waterproof, auto-w, c. 1960s
18k $2,000 $3,750 $4,250

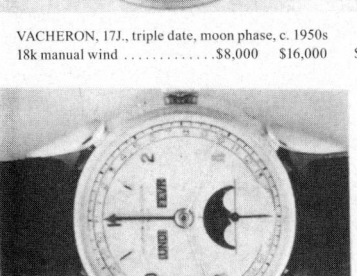

VACHERON,17J., triple date, fancy lugs, moon ph., c. 1940s
18k manual wind $9,000 $15,000 $18,000

VACHERON, 29 jewels, auto., wind, c. 1960s
18k $1,900 $3,300 $4,000

VACHERON, 17J., triple date, fancy lugs, c. 1940s
18k $3,000 $5,000 $6,500

VACHERON, 17 jewels, RF #6094, Ca. 1955
18k $1,200 $2,500 $3,250

VACHERON, 17 jewels, day-date-month, c. 1940s
18k $4,000 $6,000 $7,500

VACHERON, 29J, "Royal Chronometer", center sec., auto wind, date, c.1960s
18k $1,900 $2,500 $4,000

VACHERON, 29 jewels, gold rotor, auto-wind, date
18k. $2,200 $3,500 $4,250

VACHERON, 18J., chronog. 2 reg., ca.1942
s. steel $6,000 $10,000 $15,000

VACHERON, 33J., auto-wind 21k rotor, cal.1124 ,c.1980s
18k & s.s $800 $1,200 $1,600

VACHERON, 17 jewels, chronog., 2 reg. Ca. 1934
18k & 14k band. $20,000 $30,000 $35,000

VACHERON,17J., enamel dial, 1 button chronog., c. 1910s
18k. $25,000 $40,000 $50,000

VACHERON, 19 jewels, chronog., 2 reg., c. 1950s
18k C&B $8,000 $14,000 $18,000

VACHERON, 15J., early chronog., 2 reg., one button, ca. 1921,
large in size
18k. $20,000 $35,000 $45,000

VACHERON, 17 jewels, chronog., 2 reg., c. 1945
18k. $8,000 $14,000 $18,000

VACHERON, 29J., min. repeater, slide repeat, c. 1950
18k.........................$60,000 $95,000 $120,000

VACHERON, 29J., min. slide repeater, diamond dial
platinum...................$80,000 $120,000 $135,000

VACHERON, 29J., min. slide repeater, ca. 1950s
18k.........................$55,000 $80,000 $100,000

VACHERON, 18J., diamond set case, skeletonized
18k(W).....................$4,000 $6,500 $7,500

VACHERON, 18J., skeletonized diamond bezel
18k.........................$4,000 $6,000 $7,000

VACHERON, 17 jewels, skeletonized
18k.........................$2,000 $4,000 $4,500

VACHERON, 17 jewels, skeletonized, c. 1960s
18k.........................$2,000 $4,000 $4,500

VACHERON, 17 jewels, mystery dial with diamonds
18k C&B....................$2,000 $3,500 $4,500

VACHERON, center seconds
18k.........................$1,950 $2,850 $3,500

DIALS FOR MINT PRICES MUST BE ALL **ORIGINAL**

VACHERON, 18 jewels, center sec., c. 1940s
18k..........................$1,500 $2,600 $3,000

VACHERON, 18J., fancy graduated bezel, c. 1950s
18k..........................$5,500 $8,500 $14,000

VACHERON, 18 jewels, **auto wind**, center sec., Ca. 1945
18k..........................$2,400 $4,500 $5,000

VACHERON, 18 jewels, center sec., Ca. 1945
18k..........................$1,200 $3,000 $3,500

VACHERON 18 jewels center sec., Ca. 1945
s. steel......................$800 $1,500 $2,200

VACHERON 18 jewels center sec.
18k C&B...................$1,700 $3,000 $4,000

VACHERON, 18 J., center sec., waterproof, c. 1950s
18k..........................$1,700 $3,000 $4,000

VACHERON, 21J., auto wind, gold rotor, center sec.
18k..........................$2,200 $3,000 $4,000

Pricing in this Guide are fair market price for **complete** watches which are reflected from the "**NAWCC**" Nations and regional shows.

VACHERON, 18J., center sec., ca.1940s
18k. $1,400 $2,500 $3,500

VACHERON,17J., center sec., c.1940
s. steel $700 $2,000 $2,700

VACHERON, 18J., rf#6903, center sec., ca. 1958
18k. $1,400 $2,500 $3,500

VACHERON,17J., center sec., large lugs, c.1949
18k. $2,000 $3,750 $4,500

VACHERON, 18J., center sec., ca.1953
18k. $1,800 $2,500 $3,500

VACHERON,17J., center sec., c.1940
s. steel $700 $2,000 $2,700

VACHERON, 18J., textured dial center sec.
18k. $1,400 $2,500 $3,500

VACHERON,17J., center sec., teardrop lugs, c.1940
18k. $1,000 $2,500 $3,500

VACHERON, 18J., center sec.
s. steel $700 $1,500 $2,200

VACHERON, 18J., fancy large lugs, center sec., ca.1953
18k. $2,000 $3,500 $4,500

VACHERON, 18J., center sec.
18k. $1,200 $2,500 $3,500

VACHERON, 18J., rf#4730, fancy lugs, ca. 1950s
18k. $1,800 $3,500 $4,000

VACHERON, 18J.,textured dial, center sec., ca.1947
18k. $2,200 $3,000 $4,000

VACHERON, 18J.,textured dial, fancy lugs
18k. $2,000 $3,500 $4,000

VACHERON, 18J., rf#4824, ca.1950s
18k(W) $1,100 $2,500 $3,500

VACHERON, 18J., center sec., ca.1944
14k. $900 $3,000 $4,000

VACHERON, 18J., royal chronometer, ca.1950s
18k $1,800 $3,000 $4,000

VACHERON, 17J., center sec. auto-w., ca.1945
18k $2,000 $3,500 $4,000

VACHERON, 29J., center sec., auto wind, c. 1950a
18k $2,000 $3,500 $4,000

VACHERON, 29 jewels, center sec., auto wind, c. 1949
18k $2,000 $3,500 $4,000

VACHERON, 29 jewels, automatic, textured dial, c. 1948
18k $2,000 $3,500 $4,000

VACHERON, 29 jewels, 2 tone dial, center sec.
18k $1,500 $3,000 $4,000

VACHERON, 29 jewels, center sec., center lugs, c. 1950s
18k $1,200 $3,000 $4,000

VACHERON, 29 jewels, center sec.
18k $1,100 $2,800 $3,800

VACHERON,17J., diamond dial, fancy lugs
platinum $4,500 $6,000 $7,500

VACHERON,17J., aux. sec., c.1945
18k. $1,300 $2,400 $3,250

VACHERON, 18J.,aux. sec., fancy lugs, ca. 1944
18k. $1,500 $3,000 $4,000

VACHERON,17J., aux. sec., RF#4073, c.1942
s. steel $800 $1,500 $2,200

VACHERON, 18J., aux. sec.
18k. $1,400 $3,000 $4,000

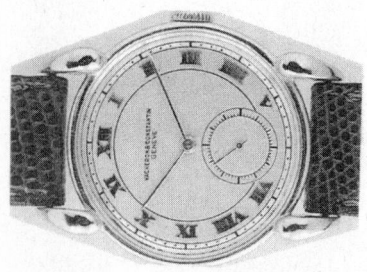

VACHERON,17J., aux. sec., tear drop lugs, c.1945
18k. $1,800 $3,500 $4,000

VACHERON, 18J.,fancy lugs
18k. $1,400 $3,000 $4,000

VACHERON,17J., aux. sec, fluted lugs, e.1950s
18k. $2,200 $3,750 $4,200

☞ Some grades are not included. Their values can be
determined by comparing with similar age, size, metal content,
style, models and grades listed.

VACHERON, 18J., cal#p453/3b,aux.sec.
18k. $1,900 $3,000 $4,000

VACHERON, 18J., aux. sec,
s. steel $700 $1,500 $2,200

VACHERON, 18J., aux. sec., thin model
18k(W) $1,000 $2,500 $3,000

VACHERON, 18J., aux. sec., long lugs, cs.1942
18k. $1,100 $2,500 $3,000

VACHERON, 18J., aux. sec., ca.1951
18k. $1,200 $2,500 $3,000

VACHERON, 18J., winds at 12, ca. 1928
18k. $3,000 $4,500 $5,000

VACHERON, 15J., champagne dial, long lugs, ca.1935
18k. $1,000 $2,500 $3,000

VACHERON, 17 jewels, aux. sec., fancy lugs
18k. $1,600 $2,500 $3,500

VACHERON, 17 jewels, aux. sec., Ca. 1950
18k. $1,200 $2,500 $3,000

VACHERON, 17 jewels, aux. sec., stepped lugs
18k. $2,100 $3,500 $4,000

VACHERON, 17 jewels, 2 tone dial, aux. sec.
18k $1,500 $2,500 $3,000

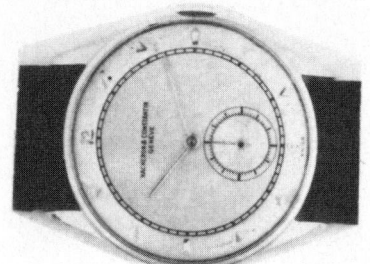

VACHERON, 17 jewels, aux. sec., c. 1940s
18k $1,400 $3,000 $3,500

VACHERON, 17 jewels, aux. sec.
18k $1,600 $2,500 $3,000

VACHERON, 17 jewels, aux. sec., c. 1940s
18k $1,200 $2,500 $3,500

VACHERON, 17 jewels, aux. sec.
s. steel $600 $1,500 $2,200

VACHERON, 17 jewels, aux. sec., large lugs, c. 1950s
18k $2,500 $4,000 $4,500

VACHERON, 17 jewels, aux. sec.
14k C&B $1,400 $2,500 $3,500

VACHERON, 17 jewels, aux. sec.
18k $1,600 $3,000 $4,000

VACHERON, 17 jewels, aux. sec., c. 1940s
18k. $1,200 $3,000 $4,000

VACHERON, 17 jewels, aux. sec.
18k. $1,300 $3,000 $4,000

VACHERON, 17 jewels
18k C&B $2,200 $3,250 $4,000

VACHERON, 17J., RF# 6498, Ca. 1965
18k. $1,200 $2,000 $3,000

VACHERON, 17 jewels
18k. $1,100 $2,500 $2,750

VACHERON, 18J., no sec. hand.
18k. $1,000 $2,500 $3,000

VACHERON, 17J., RF#6099, cal. 1003, c. 1960
18k. $1,000 $2,000 $2,500

VACHERON, 17J., 20 dollar gold piece, RF # 4928
18k. $2,000 $3,750 $4,000

VACHERON, 16J., hidden lugs, Ca. 1945
14k. $1,700 $3,000 $4,000

Wrist Watches listed in this section are priced at the collectable fair market **Trade Shaw** level as **complete** watches having an original gold-filled case and stainless steel back, also with original dial, leather watch band, and the entire original movement in good working order with no repairs needed.

☞ Some grades are not included. Their values can be determined by comparing with similar age, size, metal content, style, models and grades listed.

VACHERON, 16J., wire lugs, silver dial, ca.1917
14k. $2,200 $3,500 $4,700

VACHERON, 18J., tonneau shaped, ca. 1930s
18k. $2,200 $3,500 $4,000

VACHERON, 15J., lady's with wire lugs, ca. 1920
18k(W) $500 $1,200 $1,500

VACHERON, 15 jewels
18k C&B. $1,200 $2,500 $3,000

VACHERON, 17 jewels , 2 tone case yellow & white
18k. $1,200 $2,500 $3,000

VACHERON, 36 jewels, auto wind
18k C&B $2,000 $3,500 $4,500

VACHERON, 21 J., date, auto-w. ca. 1980s
s. steel $800 $1,200 $1,500

VACHERON, 15J., shutters with center slide to view dial, 2 tone
case, ca. 1933
18k. $7,000 $11,000 $15,000

VACHERON, 17J, with shutters, crowns at 3 & 9
18k. $10,000 $15,000 $20,000

☜ Some grades are not included. Their values can be determined by comparing with similar age, size, metal content, style,
models and grades listed.

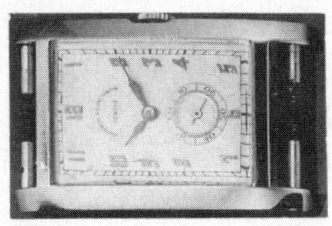

VACHERON, 18J., heavy case, ca. 1930s
18k(W) $3,000 $5,000 $6,000

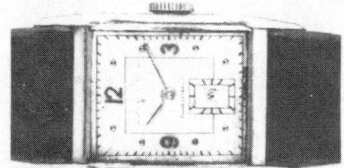

VACHERON, 18J., silver dial, ca. 1941
18k. $2,000 $3,250 $4,250

VACHERON, 18J., applied numbers, ca 1940
18k. $2,000 $3,750 $4,250

VACHERON, 18J., black dial, aux. sec., ca. 1937
18k. $2,300 $4,000 $5,000

VACHERON, 18J., silver dial, ca.1942
18k. $2,000 $4,000 $4,500

Wrist Watches listed in this section are priced at the collectable fair
market Trade Show level as complete watches having an original
gold-filled case and stainless steel back, also with original dial,
leather watch band, and the entire original movement in good
working order with no repairs needed.

VACHERON, 18J., hidden lugs, ca. 1940s
18k. $1,800 $3,000 $3,500

VACHERON, 18J., offset lugs,
18k. $2,200 $3,750 $4,250

VACHERON, 18J., offset Lugs.
18k. $2,000 $3,750 $4,250

VACHERON, 18J., aux .sec.,
s. steel $800 $2,000 $2,500

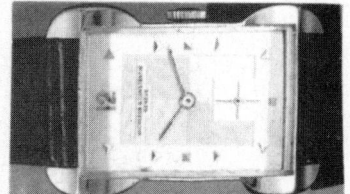

VACHERON, 18J., textured dial, large lugs, ca.1951
18k. $3,500 $5,500 $6,500

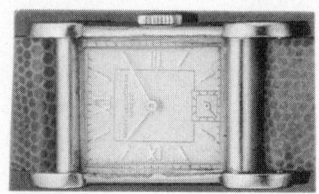

VACHERON, 18J., fancy lugs,ca.1938
18k........................$2,500 $3,650 $4,000

VACHERON, 18J., textured bezel, ca. 1950s
18k........................$2,000 $3,250 $3,500

VACHERON, 18 jewels, aux. sec., c. 1950s
18k........................$1,500 $2,500 $3,000

VACHERON, 18 jewels, aux. sec., c. 1940s
18k........................$1,600 $2,500 $3,000

VACHERON, 17J., applied gold numbers, c. 1940s
18k........................$1,500 $2,500 $3,000

VACHERON, 17 jewels, aux. sec., c. 1945
18k........................$1,100 $2,500 $3,000

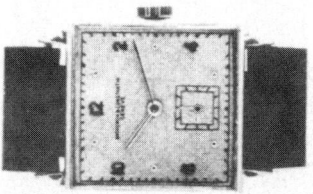

VACHERON, 17 jewels, applied gold numbers
18k........................$1,000 $2,200 $2,800

VACHERON, 17 jewels, fancy lugs
18k........................$1,700 $2,700 $3,500

VACHERON, 17 jewels, c. 1950s
18k........................$1,600 $2,500 $3,000

VACHERON, 17 jewels, fancy Lugs
14k........................$1400 $3,000 $3,500

🖙 A collector should expect to pay modestly higher prices at local shops.

VACHERON, 17 jewels, aux. sec., Ca. 1945
18k. $1,700 $2,650 $3,250

VACHERON, 17 jewels, stepped bezel, fancy lugs, Ca. 1940
18k. $2,500 $3,700 $4,250

VACHERON,17J., hidden barrel shaped lugs, c. 1943
14k. $2,300 $3,500 $4,000

VACHERON,17J., aux. sec., c.1947
18k. $1,500 $2,500 $3,000

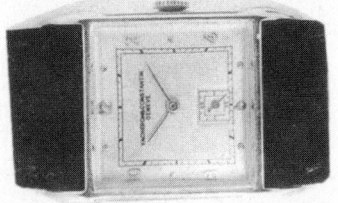

VACHERON,J7J., aux. sec., c. 1942
18k. $1,400 $2,700 $3,250

VACHERON,17J., RF#6249, aux. sec., c.1963
18k. $1,500 $3,000 $3,500

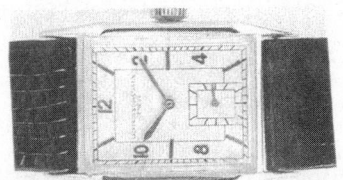

VACHERON,17J., aux. sec., c.1934
18k. $1,600 $3,000 $3,500

VACHERON, 17 jewels, aux. sec., Ca. 1946
18k. $1,600   3,000 $3,500

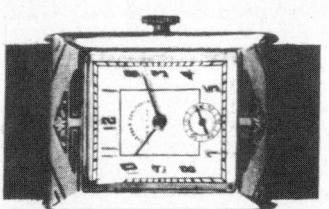

VACHERON, 17 jewels, Art Deco bezel, c. 1925
18k. $4,000 $5,500 $6,500

VACHERON, 15 jewels, exaggerated numbers, Ca. 1917
18k. $2,200 $4,000 $5,000

☞ Pricing in this Guide are fair market price for complete watches which are reflected from the NAWCC National and regional shows.

DIALS FOR MINT PRICES MUST BE ALL **ORIGINAL**.

VACHERON, 17 jewels, aux. sec.,
18k. $2,400 $3,650 $4,250

VACHERON, 15J., hinged back, ca. 1930
18k. $2,200 $3,500 $4,200

VACHERON, 15 jewels, aux. sec.
18k C&B. $2,100 $3,250 $4,000

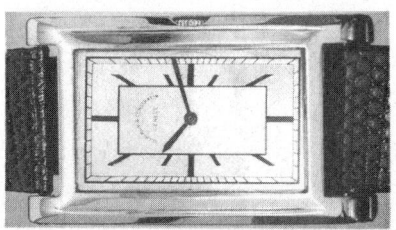

VACHERON, 18J., large 2 tone mans watch, ca.1928
18k. $4,000 $7,000 $8,500

VACHERON, 15 jewels, heavy bezel, c.1925
18K C&B $4,000 $6,000 $7,500

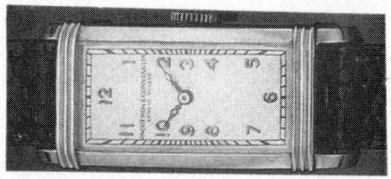

VACHERON, 18J.,long curved case, ca.1929
platinum $4,500 $6,000 $7,000

VACHERON, 17 jewels, fancy long Lugs, Ca. 1940s
18k. $2,000 $3,000 $4,000

VACHERON, 18J., Ca. 1926
18k. $1,800 $3,500 $4,000

VACHERON,15J., curvex, wire lugs,43mm long, ca. 1923
18k. $2,500 $4,000 $5,000

VACHERON, 18J., ca. 1950s
18k. $1,000 $2,500 $3,500

VACHERON, 15J., early movement, ca.1925
18k. $1,300 $2,500 $3,500

VACHERON, 17 jewels, aux. Sec.
14k. $1,000 $2,500 $3,500

VACHERON, 15J,2 tone case, Ca. 1926
18k. $1,100 $2,000 $2,500

VACHERON, 17 jewels, flat & thin model, c. 1960s
18k. $900 $2,000 $2,200

VACHERON, 18J., tank style, ca. 1960s
18k. $1,100 $2,000 $2,500

VACHERON, 17 jewels
18k C&B. $1,500 $2,200 $2,800

VACHERON, 17 jewels, hinged back
18k. $1,000 $2,000 $2,500

VACHERON, 18 jewels, stepped case & beveled lugs
18k. $1,700 $3,500 $4,000

VACHERON, 15J., wire lugs enamel dial, Ca. 1920s
18k. $2,000 $2,500 $3,000

VACHERON, 15 jewels, c. 1920s
18k. $1,200 $2,000 $2,500

VACHERON, 17 jewels, star dial, hidden lugs, c. 1943s
14k......................$1,800 $3,000 $4,000

VACHERON, 17 jewels, 68 diamond bezel
18k......................$2,500 $3,500 $4,500

VACHERON,17J., RF#7252, c.1962
18k......................$1,200 $2,000 $2,500

VACHERON, 17 jewels, flared, curvex, c. 1940s
18k......................$5,000 $7,000 $8,000

VACHERON, 17J., flared,12 diam. dial, aux. sec., c. 1948
platinum..................$6,000 $8,000 $9,000

VACHERON, 17 jewels, flared, c. 1948
18k......................$4,000 $5,500 $6,500

VACHERON, 17 jewels, flared, c. 1940s
18k......................$4,000 $5,500 $6,500

VACHERON, 17 jewels, "Chronoscope," jumping hr., revolving
ruby min. indicator, c. 1930s
18k......................$18,000 $27,000 $35,000

VACHERON, 20 jewels, Adj. to 5 Pos., c. 1970s
18k......................$2,000 $3,500 $4,000

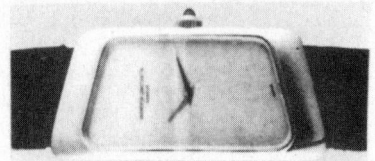

VACHERON, 22 jewels, lady's watch, c. 1970s
18k...................... $800 $1,200 $1,800

☞ Pricing in this Guide are fair market price for complete
watches which are reflected from the NAWCC National and
regional shows.

VACHERON, 17 jewels, aux. sec., ruby dial
18k. $2,000 $3,250 $4,000

VACHERON,16J., black star & forrest, wire lugs, c.1919
18k ladies $300 $600 $800

VACHERON, Ref 4737, so called "Cioccolatone", 21 jewels, center
sec., auto wind, c. 1950s
18k. $8,000 $12,000 $16,000

VACHERON, 17 jewels, heavy bezel
18k ladies $800 $1,400 $1,800

VACHERON,17J., ladies, c.1948
18k ladies $500 $900 $1,100

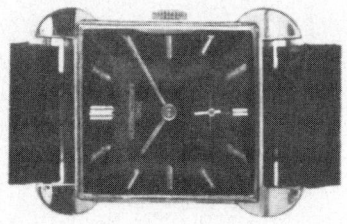

VACHERON, 17 jewels, aux. sec., fancy lugs, c. 1947
18k. $2,800 $4,000 $5,000

VACHERON, 15J., lady's, wire lugs, ca.1919
18k. $300 $500 $700

VACHERON, 17 jewels, lady's watch, c. 1960s
18k C&B $1,000 $1,500 $1,800

VACHERON, 17 jewels , swinging lugs
14k. $1,100 $2,300 $3,000

Wrist Watches listed in this section are priced at the collectable fair
market Trade Show level as complete watches having an original
gold-filled case and stainless steel back, also with original dial,
leather watch band, and the entire original movement in good
working order with no repairs needed.

VACHERON, 17J., cased & timed in U.S.A. by Vacheron &
Constantine , heavy 14k gold bracelet, ladies, Ca.1950s
14k heavy C&B $600 $1,100 $1,500

VAN CLEEF & ARPELS,17J., center lugs, c.1970
18k $250 $400 $500

VULCAIN,17jewels, "Grand Prix", Ca. 1940
s. steel $35 $75 $100

VERNO, 15 jewels, chased bezel
gold filled (w) $45 $100 $125

VULCAIN,17J., "Cricket Alarm", c.1965
base metal $250 $400 $500

VULCAIN, 17 jewels, digital read out
base metal $80 $140 $250

VULCAIN,17J., "Cricket", alarm, c.1948
s. steel $250 $400 $500

VULCAIN, 17 jewels, "Cricket", alarm
14k $400 $700 $850
18k $500 $900 $1,100

VULCAIN,17J., "Cricket Calendar", Ca. 1965
18K $550 $900 $1,100

VULCAIN, 17 jewels, "Cricket," alarm
gold filled $250 $450 $550

WAKMANN, 17J., "Gigandet" Valjoux cal.72, c. 1955
18k $1,100 $1,800 $2,250

VULCAIN, 17 jewels, "Minstop"
s. steel $100 $175 $250

WAKMANN, 17J., chronog., 3 reg., triple date
14k $450 $750 $1,000

WAKMANN,17J., 24 hr. dial, c.1955
s. steel $75 $125 $175

WAKMANN,17J., chronog., 3 reg., triple date, sq. buttons
s. steel $250 $500 $600

WAKMANN, 17 jewels, chronog., 3 reg., c. 1958
s. steel $200 $450 $550

WAKMANN,17J., chronog., Valjoux cal.188, c.1960
s. steel $150 $375 $475

WAKMANN,17J., chronog., Valjoux cal.236, c.1968
s. steel $175 $325 $400

WAKMANN,17J., chronog., c.1955
18k. $450 $750 $850
s. steel $150 $275 $350

WAKMANN,17J., chronog., c.1970s
s. steel $100 $200 $275

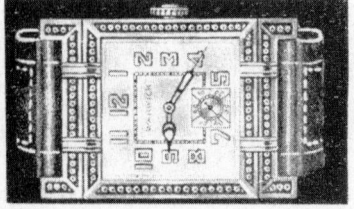

WARWICK, 6J., hinged back, 1930s
gold plate $45 $150 $200

WARWICK, 15J., 1930s
gold plate $45 $100 $125

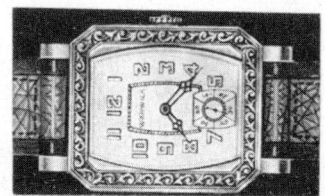

WARWICK, 15J., 1930s
gold plate $45 $100 $125

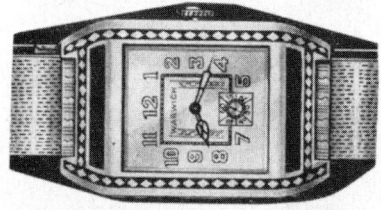

WARWICK, 6-15J., 1930s
gold plate $45 $100 $125

WARWICK, 6-15J., 1930s
gold plate $45 $100 $125

WARWICK, 6-15J., 1930s
gold plate $45 $100 $125

WARWICK, 6-15J., 1930s
gold plate S45 $100 $125

WARWICK, 15J., 1930s
gold plate $45 $100 $125

WARWICK, 15J., 1930s
base metal. $45 $90 $125

WATEX, 7J., fluted case, c.1940
gold filled $100 $200 $275

WELDON,17J., aux. sec., **large lugs** c.1950s
gold filled $75 $150 $175

WELSBRO 17J., single button chronog., c. 1940
s. steel $125 $195 $275

WELTALL W. Co., floral enamel on case, cylinder escp. wire lugs,
Ca. 1910
14k. $100 $200 $300

WEST END, 17J., "**Keepsake**", (by Longines), Ca. 1925
silver $200 $350 $600

WEST END, 17 jewels, center lugs
18k. $150 $275 $325

WESTFIELD, 17J., aux. sec., Ca. 1954
gold filled $40 $75 $125

WITTNAUER. 17 jewels, fancy lugs, Ca. 1955
14k..........................$150 $325 $450

WITTNAUER, 17 jewels, curved case, c.1950
14k.........................$125 $275 $400

WITTNAUER, Asymmetric, 17J., aux. sec., c.1958
gold filled $100 $175 $250

WITTNAUER, 17 jewels, cal.9wn, fancy lugs, c.1954
gold filled $75 $125 $150

WITTNAUER,17J., aux. sec., c.1950
14k. $135 $250 $350

WITTNAUER, 17 jewels, fancy lugs, GJS
14k. $125 $250 $300

WITTNAUER,17J., aux. sec., GJS, c.1948
14k. $135 $250 $350

WITTNAUER,17J., aux. sec., GJS, large lugs, c.1950
14k. $125 $275 $400

WITTNAUER,17J., aux. sec., fancy lugs, c.1955
gold filled $65 $125 $150

WITTNAUER,17J., aux. sec., fancy case, c.1950
gold filled $75 $150 $175

WITTNAUER,17J., chronog., by Valjoux, #72, cal.13w1
s. steel $250 $475 $575

WITTNAUER,7J., mid size ,stopwatch, c.1940
s. steel $125 $250 $300

WITTNAUER, 17J., day date, set year by button
s. steel $100 $200 $300

WITTNAUER,17J., perpetual calendar
base metal $65 $125 $200

WITTNAUER,7J., "Electronic", day date, c.1968
s. steel $40 $75 $125

WITTNAUER,17J., direct read, c.1970
s. steel $45 $125 $200

WITTNAUER,17J., Zircon on dial, direct read, c. 1970
base metal $35 $125 $200

WITTNAUER, 17 jewels, auto wind, sector, date
s. steel $185 $300 $450
gold filled $185 $300 $450

WITTNAUER. 17 jewels, fancy lugs, Ca. 1955
14k. $150 $325 $450

WITTNAUER, 17 jewels, curved case, c.1950
14k. $125 $275 $400

WITTNAUER, Asymmetric, 17J., aux. sec., c.1958
gold filled $100 $175 $250

WITTNAUER, 17 jewels, cal.9wn, fancy lugs, c.1954
gold filled $75 $125 $150

WITTNAUER,17J., aux. sec., c.1950
14k. $135 $250 $350

WITTNAUER, 17 jewels, fancy lugs, GJS
14k. $125 $250 $300

WITTNAUER,17J., aux. sec., GJS, c.1948
14k. $135 $250 $350

WITTNAUER,17J., aux. sec., GJS, large lugs, c.1950
14k. $125 $275 $400

WITTNAUER,17J., aux. sec., fancy lugs, c.1955
gold filled $65 $125 $150

WITTNAUER,17J., aux. sec., fancy case, c.1950
gold filled $75 $150 $175

WARWICK, 6-15J., 1930s
gold plate S45 $100 $125

WARWICK, 15J., 1930s
gold plate $45 $100 $125

WARWICK, 15J., 1930s
base metal. $45 $90 $125

WATEX, 7J., fluted case, c.1940
gold filled $100 $200 $275

WELDON,17J., aux. sec., **large lugs** c.1950s
gold filled $75 $150 $175

WELSBRO 17J., single button chronog., c. 1940
s. steel $125 $195 $275

WELTALL W. Co., floral enamel on case, cylinder escp. wire lugs,
Ca. 1910
14k. $100 $200 $300

WEST END, 17J., **"Keepsake"**, (by Longines), Ca. 1925
silver $200 $350 $600

WEST END, 17 jewels, center lugs
18k. $150 $275 $325

WESTFIELD, 17J., aux. sec., Ca. 1954
gold filled $40 $75 $125

WHITE STAR, 17J., **triple date**, moon phase, c. 1948
s. steel $350 $600 $750

WINTON, 17J., **hooded lugs**
14k. $100 $200 $250

WINTON, 16J., curvex, **hinged back**, c.1930s
silver $125 $250 $350

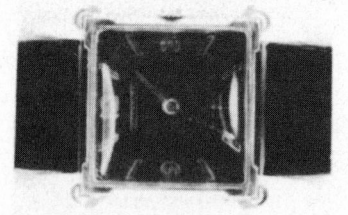

WITTNAUER, 17 jewels, fancy lugs
14k. $100 $200 $300

WITTNAUER, 17 jewels, chronog., day-date-month
s. steel $400 $700 $800

WITTNAUER, 17 jewels, chronog., c. 1948
s. steel $300 $475 $600

WITTNAUER,17J., "Professional", RF#6002, c.1955
18k. $500 $850 $1,000
s. steel $300 $500 $600

WITTNAUER,17J., chronog., waterproof, c.1958
18k. $400 $700 $800
s. steel $200 $400 $500

WITTNAUER,17J., chronog., by Venius, **Time Zone Bezel**, Ca. 1955
s. steel $300 $500 $700

WITTNAUER, 17J., aux. sec., flared case
14k. $125 $275 $375

WITTNAUER, 17J., aux. sec., c. 1950
gold filled $45 $100 $125

WITTNAUER, 17J., aux. Sec.
gold filled $70 $125 $150

WITTNAUER, 15J., aux. sec., tonneau case, c.1945
gold plate $30 $100 $125

WITTNAUER, 17 jewels, fancy lugs, c. 1950s
14k. $150 $300 $400

WITTNAUER, 17J., aux. sec.
gold filled $45 $90 $110

WITTNAUER, 17J., aux. sec., GJS, c. 1955
14k. $125 $250 $325

WITTNAUER, 15J., "Weems", rotating bezel, Ca. 1940
gold filled $300 $550 $700

WITTNAUER, 17J., aux. sec., tu-tone dial, c. 1950
gold filled $65 $125 $150

WITTNAUER, 17J., flared case, Ca.1949
14k. $150 $300 $400

☞ Pricing in this Guide are fair market price for complete watches which are reflected from the NAWCC National and regional shows.

☞ Some grades are not included. Their values can be determined by comparing with similar age, size, metal content, style, models and grades listed.

WITTNAUER,17J., RF#2067, c.1950
gold filled $40 $75 $90

WITTNAUER,17J., auto-wind, c.1960
base metal. $30 $60 $80

WITTNAUER,17J., cal.7630, aux. sec., c.1955
14k. $75 $150 $200

WITTNAUER,17J., 'Alarm", c.1960
gold filled $100 $225 $300

Wrist Watches listed in this section are priced at the collectable fair
market Trade Show level as complete watches having an original
gold filled case and stainless steel back, also with original dial,
leather watch band, and the entire original movement in good
working order with no repairs needed.

WIG WAG, 15 jewels, **early auto wind**, c. 1932
s. steel . . . . ★$400 $650 $800

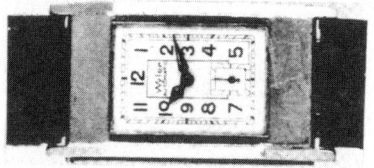

WYLER, 17 jewels, early auto wind, watch winds by
using the muscular movement of the wrist, back set
gold filled . . . . ★ $300 $500 $600

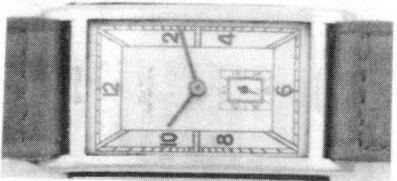

WYLER, 17 jewels, early auto wind, back set
gold filled . . . . ★ $300 $500 $600

WYLER, 17 jewels, center sec., auto-wind
s. steel $55 $100 $125

WYLER, 17 jewels, auto wino, center sec., Ca. 1950
gold filled $50 $100 $125

☞ Some grades are not included. Their values can be
determined by comparing with similar age, size, metal content,
style, models and grades listed.

WYLER, 17 jewels
s. steel $65 $125 $150

WYLER, 17 jewels, diamond dial, c. 1946
s. steel $40 $80 $100

WYLER,17J., center sec., c.1945
s. steel $45 $100 $125

WYLER,17J., center sec., waterproof, ca.1941
s. steel $45 $100 $125

WYLER,17J.,aux.aec.,c.1938
s. steel $45 $100 $125

👉 A collector should expect to pay modestly higher prices at local shops.

Wrist Watches listed in this section are priced at the collectable fair market Trade Show level as complete watches having an original gold-filled case and stainless steel back, also with original dial, leather watch band, and the entire original movement in good working order with no repairs needed.

WYLER,17J., early auto-wind, c.1930
chrome $75 $165 $200

WYLER,17J., **day date month**, c.1946
gold filled $75 $150 $200

WYLER, 17 jewels, chronog., c. 1940s
14k. $350 $600 $700
s. steel $100 $250 $300

YALE, 15 jewels, calendar, c. 1939
14k. $175 $300 $400
gold filled $75 $200 $300

👉 Some grades are not included. Their values can be determined by comparing with similar age, Size, metal content, style, models and grades listed.

👉 Pricing in this Guide are fair market price for Complete watches which are reflected from the NAWCC National and regional shows.

ZENITH, 15 jewels, Engraved bezel, Ca. 1915
gold filled $75 $175 $200

ZENITH, 19 jewels, **chronometer**, 33mm, c. 1950s
gold filled $50 $100 $135

ZENITH,15J., enamel dial, wire lugs, c. 1918
silver $200 $325 $450

ZENITH, 17 jewels, chronog., Ca. 1950
18k. $300 $550 $650

ZENITH,15J., signal corps on enamel dial, center lug, 1918
silver $300 $425 $500

ZENITH, 36 jewels, chronog., auto wind, c. 1969
s. steel $350 $600 $800

ZENITH,17J., single button, Chronog., Ca. 1930
18k. $1,200 $2,000 $2,500

ZENITH, 17J., Chronograph 3 reg., Ca. 1965
14k. $700 $900 $1,100
s. steel $350 $500 $600

ZENITH, 36J., "El Primero", RF#502,auto wind, c. 1970
18k. $600 $1,400 $1,650

ZENITH, 36 jewels, "El Primero", chronog., triple date moon phase, auto wind, c. 1970s
18k. $1,400 $2,600 $3,200

ZENITH,36J., chronog., auto-wind, triple date, moon ph.
s. steel. $600 $1,100 $1,300

ZENITH, 17 jewels, fancy bezel
18k. $175 $300 $375

ZENITH, 17J., auto-wind, date at 5, Ca. 1959
18k. $175 $250 $300

ZENTRA, 24 jewels, ladies, auto wind, c. 1958
14k. $50 $100 $125

ZODIAC, 17J., chronog., 2 reg., fancy lugs, c.1948
gold filled $150 $300 $375
14k. $250 $500 $700
18k. $300 $600 $900

ZODIAC, 17J., chronog., auto-wind, date, c. 1971
s. steel $200 $400 $575

☞ A collector should expect to pay modestly higher prices at local shops

ZODIAC, 17J., center sec., auto-wind, c.1959
s. steel $45 $75 $125

ZODIAC, 17J., day-date-month, moon phase, c. 1957
s. steel $300 $450 $600
14k. $400 $700 $900

ZODIAC, 17 jewels, 24 hour dial
s. steel $50 $100 $150

ZODIAC, 17J., auto-wind, the power reserve has **differential gearing**, c. 1959
14k. $175 $325 $400
gold filled $75 $150 $200
s. steel $75 $150 $200

ZODIAC, 17 jewels, ref. #8088
14k. $100 $175 $225

ZODIAC, 21J., date, "Olympus", date, auto-wind,c.1965
s. steel $90 $175 $275

ZODIAC, 17J., by Valj. cal. 7733, Ca.1965
base metal $125 $225 $350

ZODIAC, 17J., center sec., Ca. 1948
s. steel $55 $100 $125

WATCH TERMINOLOGY

ADJUSTED-Derived from Latin ad justus, meaning just right Adjusted to compensate for temperature, positions and isochronism.

ALARM WATCH-A watch that will give an audible sound at a pre-set time.

ALL or NOTHING PIECE-A repeating Watch mechanism Which ensures that ALL the hour & minutes are struck or sounded or nothing is heard.

ANALOGUE-A term used to denote a watch dial with hands rather than digital display.

ANNEALING-Heating and cooling a metal slowly to relieve internal stress.

ANTI-MAGNETIC-Not affected by magnetic field.

ANTIQUARIAN-Of antiques or dealing in, also the study of old and out-of-date items.

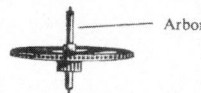
Arbor

ARBOR-The mechanical axle of a moving part; on the balance it is called the staff, on the lever it is called the arbor.

ASSAY-Analyzing a metal for its gold or silver content.

AUTOMATON-Automatic working figures moving in conjunction with the movement mechanism. Striking Jacquemarts or jacks which are figures (may be humans provided with hammers) striking bells to supply the sound for the hour & quarter hours. The hammers take the place of the bells clapper, *Automata* plural of **automaton**.

AUXILIARY COMPENSATION - For middle temperature errors found on marine chronometers.

AUXILIARY DIAL - Any extra dial for information.

AWI - American Watchmakers-Clockmakers Institute, 701 Enterprise Drive Harrison, OH 45030. Tel # **(513) 367-9800**

BAGUETTE-A French term for oblong shape. A watch having it's length at least 3 times it's width. A long narrow diamond.

Balance Cock

BALANCE COCK-The bridge that holds the upper jewels and the balance and secured at one end only.

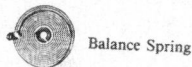
Balance Spring

BALANCE SPRING-Also called the hair spring; the spring governing the balance.

Balance Staff

BALANCE STAFF -The shaft of the balance wheel.

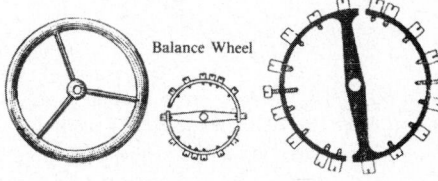
Balance Wheel

BALANCE WHEEL-A device shaped like a wheel that does for a watch what a pendulum does for a clock.

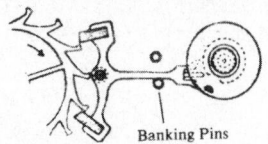

Banking Pins

BANKING PINS- The two pins which limit the angular motion of the pallet.

Bar Movement

BAR MOVEMENT-A type of movement employing about six bridges to hold the train. In use by 1840.

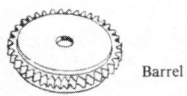

Barrel

BARREL-Drum-shaped container that houses the mainspring.

BEAT-Refers to the tick or sound of a watch; about 1/5 of a second. The sound is produced by the escape wheel striking the pallets.

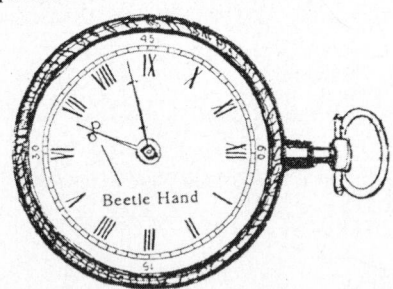

Beetle Hand

BEETLE HAND-Hour hand resembling a stag beetle; usually associated with the poker-type minute hand in 17th and 18th century watches.

BELL METAL-Four parts copper and one part tin used for metal laps to get a high polish on steel.

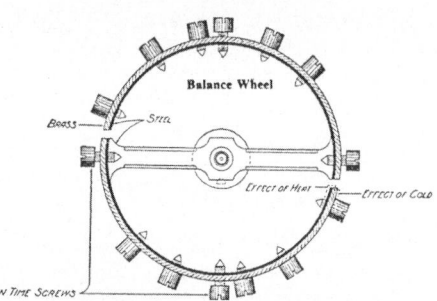

O S. Htg. Bezel,

BEZEL-The rim that covers the dial (face) & retains the crystal. Above snap on bezel.

Balance Wheel

Brass Steel

Effect of Heat — Effect of Cold

Mean Time Screws

BI-METALLIC BALANCE-A balance composed of brass and steel designed to compensate for temperature changes in the hairspring.
BLIND MANS WATCH- A Braille watch; also known as a tact watch.
BLUING or BUING-By heating polished steel to 540 degrees the color will change to blue.
BOMBE - Convex on one side.

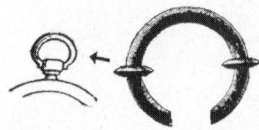

BOW-The ring that is looped at the pendant to which a chain or fob is attached

BOX CHRONOMETER-A marine or other type chronometer in gimbals so the movement remains level at sea.

BOX JOINTED CASE-A heavy hinged decorative case with a simulated joint at the top under the pendant. (BOX CASE)

BREGUET KEY-A ratcheting watch key permitting winding in only one direction.

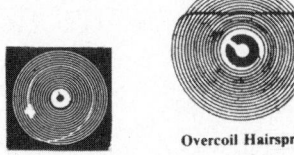

Overcoil Hairspring

BREGUET SPRING-A type of hairspring that improves time keeping also called overcoil hairspring.

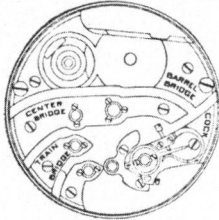

BRIDGE-A metal bar which bear the pivot of wheels and is supported at both ends .(see cock.)

BUBBLE BACK-A Rolex wrist watch which were water proof (Oyster) and auto wind (Perpetual) Ca. 1930 to 1950's.

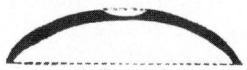

BULL'S EYE CRYSTAL-Used on old type watches; the center of the crystal was polished which achieved a bull's eye effect.

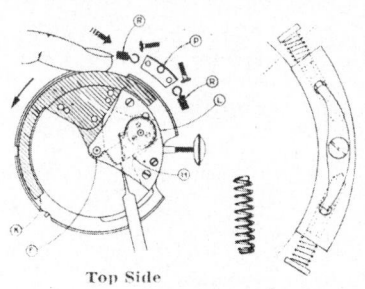

Top Side

BUFFER SPRING - Buffer spring is a stop spring for oscillating weight.

CABOCHON - An unfaceted cut stone of domed form or style. (on some crowns)

CALENDAR WATCH-A watch that shows the date, month and day.

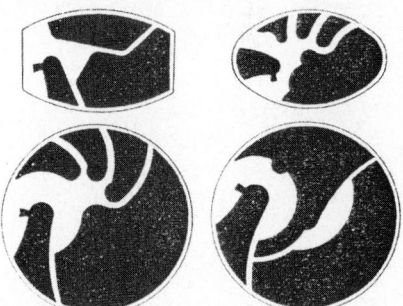

CALIBRE or CALIBER-Size of a watch movement also to describe the model, style or shape of a watch movement.

CAP JEWEL-Also called the end stone, the flat jewel on which the staff rests.

CASE SCREW-A screw with part of the head cut away.

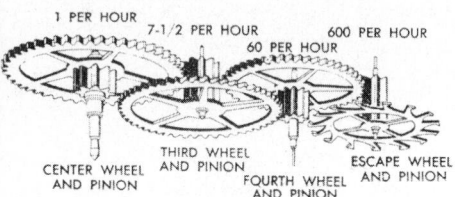

CENTER WHEEL-The second wheel; the arbor for the minute hand; this wheel makes one revolution per hour.

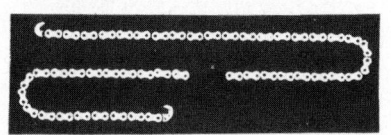

CHAIN (Fusee)-Looks like a miniature bi-cycle chain connecting the barrel and fusee.

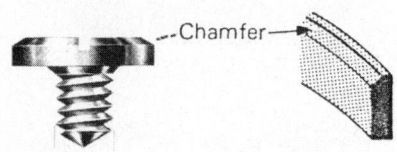

CHAMFER-Sloping or beveled. Removing a sharp edge or edges of holes.

CHAMPLEVE-An area hollowed out and filled with enamel and then baked on.

CHAPTER-The hour, minute & seconds numbers on a dial. The chapter ring is the zone or circle that confines the numbers.

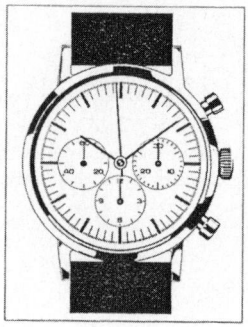

CHRONOGRAPH-A movement that can be started and stopped to measure short time intervals and return to zero. A stopwatch does not keep the time of day.

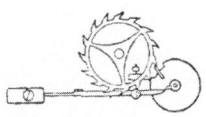

CHRONOMETER ESCAPEMENT - A detent escapement used in marine chronometers.

CIRCA-Approximately. (Ca.)

CLICK-A pawl that ratchets and permits the winding wheel to move in one direction; a clicking sound can be heard as the watch is wound.

CLOCK WATCH-A watch that strikes the hour but not on demand.

CLOISONNE-Enamel set between strips of metal and baked onto the dial.

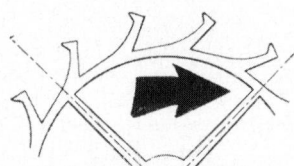

CLUB TOOTH-Some escape wheels have a special design which increases th impulse plane; located at the tipof the tooth of te escapewhel

COARSE TRAIN-16,000 beats per hour.

COCK -The metal bar which carries the bearing for the balance's upper pivot and is supported at one end.

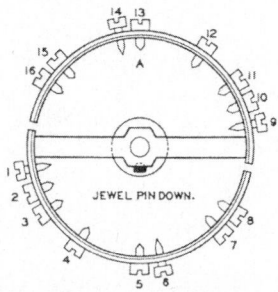

COMPENSATION BALANCE-A balance wheel designed to correct for temperature.

COMPLICATED WATCH-A watch with complicated works; other than just telling time, it may have a perpetual calendar, moon phases, up and down dial, repeater, musical chimes or alarm.

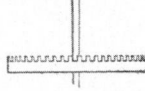

CONTRATE WHEEL-A wheel with its teeth at a right angle to plane of the wheel.

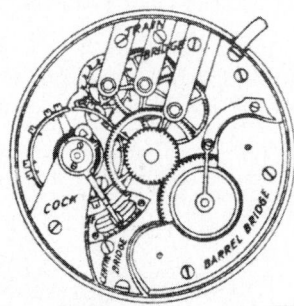

CONVERTIBLE- Movement made by Elgin & other companies; a means of converting from a hunting case to a open-face watch or vice-versa.

CRAZE(crazing)-A minute crack in the glaze of enamel watch dials.

Railroad Style

Round Style   Antique Style
CROWN-A winding button.

Crown Wheel

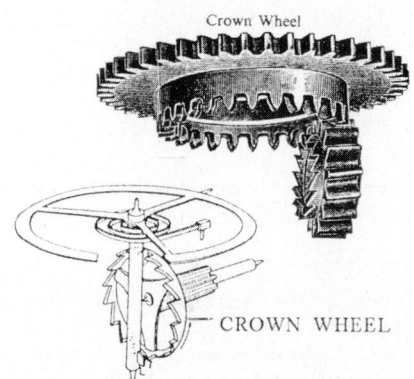

CROWN WHEEL

CROWN WHEEL-The escape wheel of a verge escapement; looks like a crown. Also the lower illustration shows a crown wheel used in a stem winding pocket watch.

Curb Pin

CURB PINS-The two pins that change the rate of a watch; the two pins, in effect, change the length of the hairspring.

CUVETTE

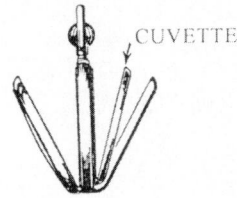

CUVETTE-The inter dust cover of a pocket watch.

CYLINDER ESCAPEMENT- A type of escapement used on some watches.

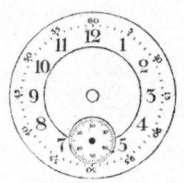

DIAL-The face of a watch. Some are made of enamel.

DAMASKEENING-The art of producing a design, pattern, or wavy appearance on a metal. American idiom or terminology used in <u>all</u> American factory ads. The European terminology was Fausse Cotes or Geneva stripes.

DISCHARGE PALLET JEWEL-The right or 2nd jewel on lever. The 2nd of two pallet jewels with which a tooth of the escape wheel comes into engagement. Also called the **Exit** pallet.

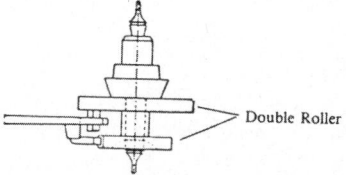

DOUBLE ROLLER-A watch with one impulse roller table and a safety roller, thus two rollers.

DRAW-The angular position of the pallet jewels in the pallet frame which causes those jewels to be drawn deeper into the escape wheel under pressure of the escape wheel's tooth on the locking surface.

DROP-The space between a tooth of the escape wheel and the pallet from which it has just escaped.

DUMB —REPEATER-A repeating watch with hammers that strikes a block instead of bells or gongs.

DEMI-HUNTER-A hunting case with the center designed to allow the position of the hands to be seen without opening the case.

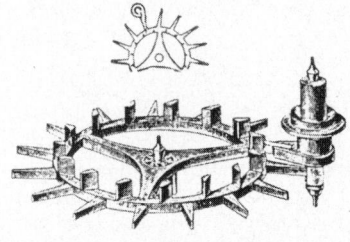

DETENT ESCAPEMENT-A detached escapement. The balance is impulsed in one direction; used on watches to provide greater accuracy. Detent a locking device.

DUPLEX ESCAPEMENT-An escape wheel with two sets of teeth, one for locking and, one for impulse.

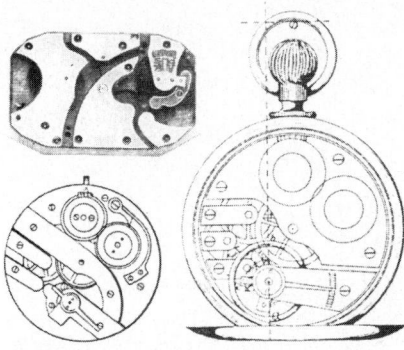

EBAUCHE(ay-boesh)-A movement not **completely** finished or in the rough; not de- tailed; a raw movement; a movement made up of two plates ,train, barrel & did not include a dial, case, or escapement.

ELECTRONIC WATCH-Newer type watch using quartz and electronics to produce a high degree of accuracy.

ELINVAR-A hairspring composed of a special alloy of nickel, steel, chromium, manganese and tungsten that does not vary at different temperatures. Elinvar was derived from the words elasticity invariable.

ECCENTRIC-Not exactly circular, Non-concentric. A cam with a lobe or egg shape.

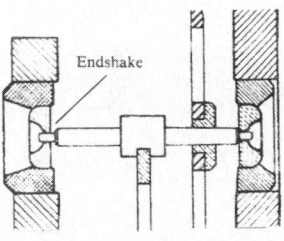

END SHAKE-The up and down play of an arbor between the plates and bridge or between the jewels.

ENGINE TURNING-Engraving a watch case with a repetitive design by a machine.

END STONE-The jewel or cap at the end of the staff.

EPHEMEROUS TIME-The time calculated for the Earth to orbit around the sun.

ESCAPE WHEEL-The last wheel in a going train; works with the fork or lever and escapes one pulse at a time.

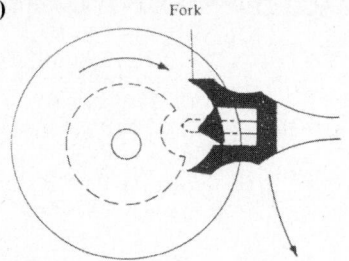

Fork

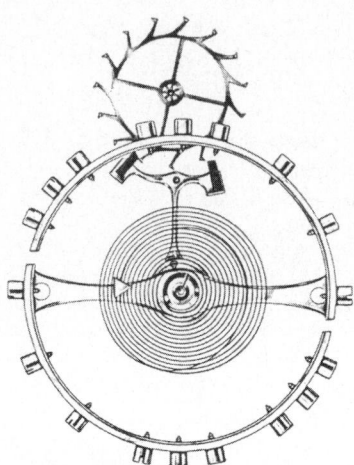

ESCAPEMENT-The device in a watch by which the motion of the train is checked and the energy of the mainspring communicated to the balance. The escapement includes the escape wheel, lever, and balance **complete** with hairspring.

FARMER' S WATCH(OIGNON)-A large pocket watch with a verge escapement and a farm scene on the dial.

FECIT- A Latin word meaning "made by".

FIVE-MINUTE REPEATER-A watch that denotes the time every five minutes, and on the hour and half hour, by operating a push piece.

FLINQUE-Enameling over hand engraving.

FLY BACK-The hand returns back to zero on a timer.

FOB-A decorative short strap or chain.

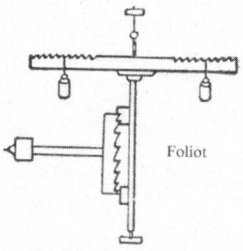

Foliot

FOLIOT-A straight-armed balance with weights on each end used for regulation; found on the earliest clocks and watches.

FORK-The part of the pallet lever that engages with the roller jewel.

FREE SPRUNG-A balance spring free from the influence of a regulator.

FULL PLATE -A plate (or disc) that covers the works and supports the wheels pivots. There is a top plate, a bottom plate, half, and 3/4 plate. The top plate has the balance resting on it.

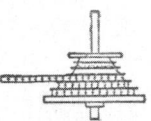

FUSEE-A spiral grooved, truncated cone used in some watches to equalize the power of the mainspring.

GRANDE SONNERIE-(**Grand strike**) a watch or clock that strikes the hour, 1/4 hours and minutes if minute repeater, a Petite Sonnerie strikes hour only.

GENEVA STOP WORK-A system used to stop the works preventing the barrel from being over wound.

GILT (or GILD)-To coat or plating with gold leaf or a gold color.

GOING BARREL-The barrel houses the mainspring; as the spring uncoils, the barrel turns, and the teeth on the outside of the barrel turn the train of gears as opposed to toothless fusee barrel.

GOLD-FILLED-Sandwich-type metal; a layer of gold, a layer of base metal in the middle, another layer of gold-then the layers of metals are soldered to each other to form a sandwich.

GOLD JEWEL SETTINGS-In high-grade watches the jewels were mounted in gold settings.

GREAT WHEEL-The main wheel of a fusee type watch.

GUILLOCHE - A decorative pattern of cross or interlaced lines. (engraving style)

HACK-WATCH-A watch with a balance that can be stopped to allow synchronization with another timepiece.

HAIRSPRING-The spring which vibrates the balance. Above flat style hairsprings. Also called balance spring.

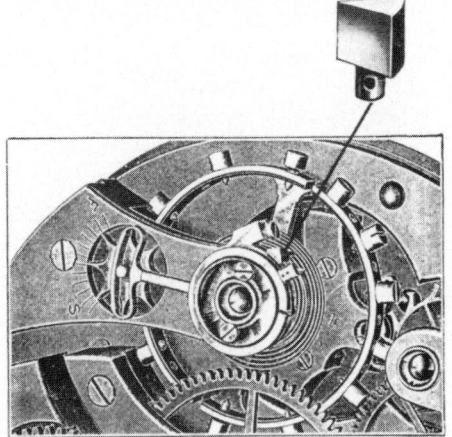

HAIRSPRING STUD-A hairspring stud is -used to connect the hairsping to the balance cock.

HALLMARK-The silver or gold or platinum markings of many countries.

HEART CAM-PIECE-A heart-shaped cam which causes the hand on a chronograph to fly back to zero.

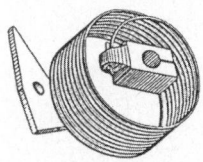

HELICAL HAIRSPRING-A cylindrical spring used in chronometers.

HOROLOGY (haw-rahl-uh-jee)-The study of time keeping.

HUNTER CASE-A pocket watch case with a covered face that must be opened to see the watch dial.

IMPULSE-The force transmitted by the escape wheel to the pallet by gliding over the angular or impulse face of the pallet jewel.

IMPULSE PIN (Ruby pin)(roller jewel)-A pin or jewel on the balance roller table which keeps the balance going.

INCABLOC-A patented shock absorbing device which permits the end stone of the balance to give when the watch is subjected to an impact or jolt. 1st. used in 1933.

INDEX-Another term for the racquet shaped regulator which lengthens or shortens the effective length of the hairspring.

INDEPENDENT SECONDS-A seconds hand driven independently by a separate train but controlled by the time train.

ISOCHRONI5M- "Isos" means equal; chronos means time-occurring at equal intervals of time. The balance and hairspring adjusted will allow the watch to run at the same rate regardless whether the watch fully wound or almost run down.

JEWEL-A bearing made of a ruby or other type jewel; the four types of jewels include; cap jewel, hole jewel, roller jewel or ruby pin, pallet jewel or stone.

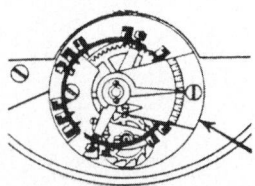

KARRUSEL-An invention of Bonniksen in 1894 which allows the entire escapement to revolve within the watch once in 52 1/2 minutes (in most karrusels), this unit is supported at one end only as opposed to the tourbillon which is supported at both ends and which most often revolves about once a minute.

KEY SET-Older watch that had to be set with a key.

LEAVES-The teeth of the pinion gears.

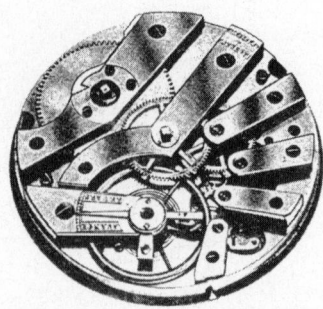

L'Epine' CALIBRE-Introduced by J.A. L'Epine about 1770. Swiss for **open face**.

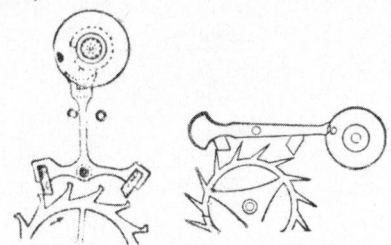

LEVER ESCAPEMENT-Invented by Thomas Mudge in about 1759.

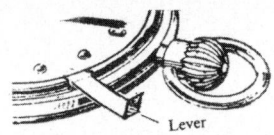

LEVER SETTING-The lever used to set some watches.

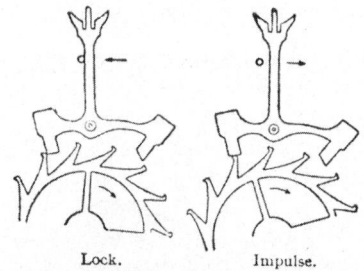

Lock.   Impulse.

LOCKING-Arresting the advance of the escape wheel during the balance's free excursion.

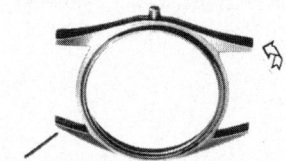

LUGS-The metal extensions of a wrist watch case which the bracelet or band are attached usually with a spring bar.

MAIN SPRING-A flat spring coiled or wound to supply power to the watch. The non-magnetic mainspring, introduced 1947.

MAIN WHEEL-The first driving wheel, part of the barrel.

MALTESE CROSS-The part of the stop works preventing the barrel from being over wound.

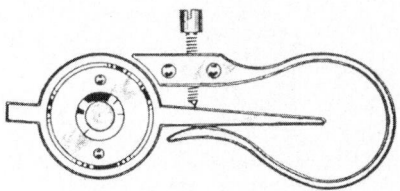

MICROMETRIC REGULATOR-A regulator used on railroad grade watches to adjust for gain or loss in a very precise way.

MICRO-SECOND-A millionth of a second.

MINUTE REPEATER -A watch that strikes or sounds the hours , and minutes on demand.

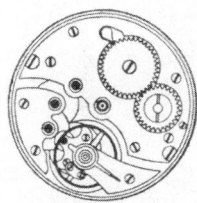

MOVEMENT-The works of a mechanical watch without the case or dial. (quartz watches have modules)

MARINE CHRONOMETER- An accurate timepiece; may have a detent escapement and set in a box with gimbals which keep it in a right position.

MEAN TIME- Also equal hours; average mean solar time; the time shown by watches.

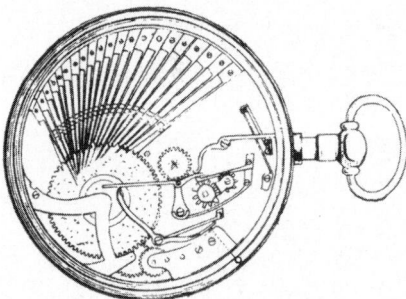

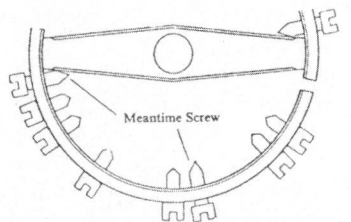

Meantime Screw

MEANTIME SCREWS-Balance screws used for timing,usually longer than other balance screws; when turned away from or toward the balance pin, they cause the balance vibrations to become faster or slower.

MUSICAL WATCH-A watch that plays a tune on demand or on the hour.

MULTI-GOLD-Different colors of gold-red, green, white, blue, pink, yellow and purple.

NANOSECOND-One billionth of a second.

N. A. W. C. C. - National Association of Watch and Clock Collectors 514 Poplar St. Columbia, Pa. 17512.

TEL. 1- 717- 684- 8261

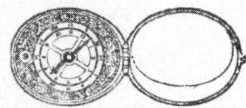

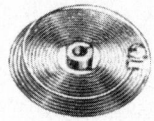

NURENBURG EGG-Nickname for a German watch that was oval-shaped.

OVERCOIL-The raised up portion of the balance hairspring, not flat. Also called Breguet hairspring.

PATINA-Oxidation of any surface & change due to age. A natural staining or discoloration due to aging.

PAIR-CASE WATCH-An extra case around a watch-two cases, hence, a pair of cases. The outer case kept out the dust. The inner case could not be dustproof because it provided the access to the winding and setting keyholes in the watch case.

PALLADIUM-One of six platinum metals, used in watches in place of platinum, because it is harder, lighter and cheaper.

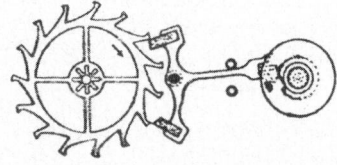

OIGNON-Large older (1675) style watch in the the shape of a onion or in the shape of a bulb.

OIL SINK-A small well around a pivot which retains oil.

PALLET-The part of the lever that works with the escape wheel-jeweled pallet jewels, entry and exit pallets.

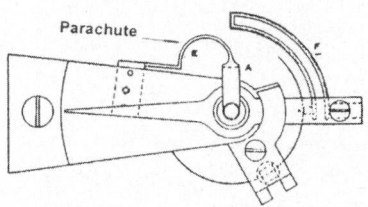

Parachute

OVERBANKED-A lever escapement error; the roller jewel passes to the wrong side of the lever notch, causing one side of the pallet to rest against the banking pin and the roller jewel to rest against the other side, thus locking the escapement and stopping the motion of the balance.

PARACHUTE-An early shock proofing system designed to fit as a spring on the end stone of balance.

PAVE'- A number of jewels or stone set close together. Paved in diamonds.

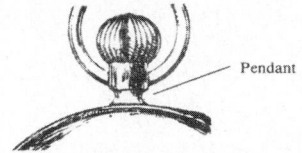

Pendant

PENDANT-The neck of the watch; attached to it is the bow (swing ring) and the crown.

PILLARS-The rods that hold the plates apart. In older watches they were fancy.

PINCHBECK-A metal similar in appearance to gold. Named after the inventor. Alloy of 4 parts copper &3 parts zinc.

PINION-The larger gear is called a wheel.The small solid gear is a pinion. The pinion is made of steel in some watches.

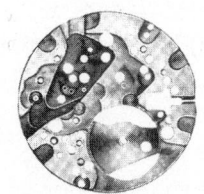

PLATE-A watch has a front and a back plate or top and bottom plate. The works are in between.

POISE-A term meaning in balance to equalize the weight around the balance.

PONTILLAGE (bull's eye crystal)-The grinding of the center of a crystal to form a concave or so called bull's eye crystal.

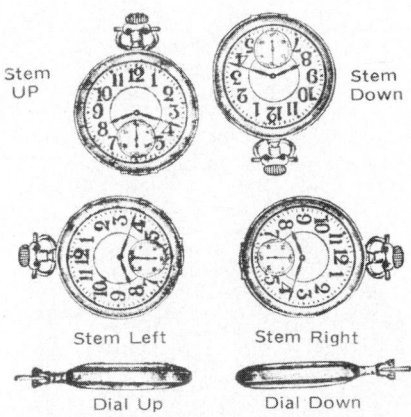

Stem UP   Stem Down

Stem Left   Stem Right

Dial Up   Dial Down

POSITION-As adjusted to five positions; a watch may differ in its time keeping accuracy as it lays in different positions . Due to the lack of poise, changes in the center of gravity, a watch can be adjusted to six positions: dial up, dial down, stem up, stem down, stem left, and stem right. Note: Adj. to 5 positions is also 8 adjustments.

QUICK TRAIN-A watch with five beats or more per second or 18,000 per hour.

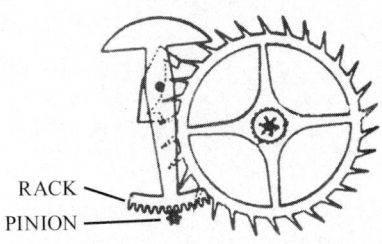

RACK

PINION

RACK & PINION LEVER ESCAPEMENT-Developed by Abbe de Huteville in 1722 and by Peter Litherhead in 1791; does not use a roller table, but a pinion.

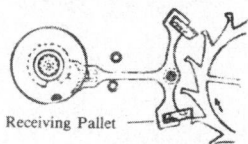

Receiving Pallet

RECEIVING PALLET-Also called left or entrance jewel, the first of two pallet jewels with which a tooth of the escape wheel comes into engagement.

REPEATER WATCH-A complicated watch that repeats the time on demand with a sounding device.

REPOUSSE' -A watch with hammered, raised decoration on the case.

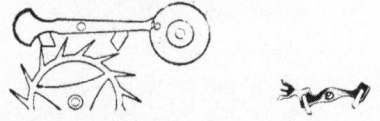

RIGHT ANGLE LEVER ESCAPEMENT Also called English escapement.

ROLLED GOLD- Thin layer of gold soldered to a base metal.

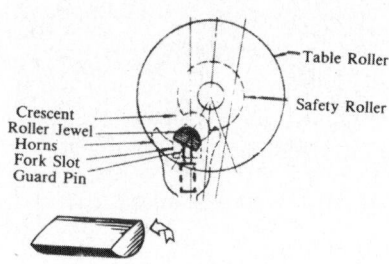

ROLLER JEWEL-The jewel mounted or seated in the roller table, which receives the impulse from the pallet fork.

ROLLER TABLE-The part of the balance in which the roller jewel is seated.

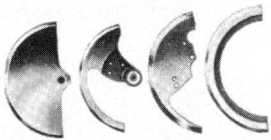

ROTOR-Oscillating weight for self-wind watches.

SAFETY PINION -A pinion in the center wheel designed to unscrew if the mainspring breaks; this protects the train from being stripped by the great force of the mainspring.

SAFETY ROLLER-The smaller of the two rollers in a double roller escapement.

SAPPHIRE CRYSTAL - Scratch resistant glass with a hardness of 9. Mineral glass has a hardness of 5.

SHAGREEN-The skin of a horse, shark, ray fish & other animal usually dyed GREEN or a BLUE GREEN. Then used as ornamental covers for older watch cases.

SIDEREAL DAY-The time of rotation of the Earth as measured from the stars. About 3 minutes 56 seconds shorter than the mean solar day.

SIDE-WINDER-A mismatched case and movement; a term used for a hunting movement that has been placed in an open face case and winds at 3 o'clock position. Open face winds at 12 o'clock.

SILVEROID-A type of case composed of alloys to simulate the appearance of silver.

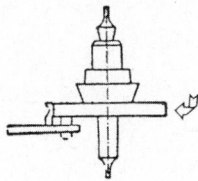

SINGLE ROLLER-The safety roller and the roller jewel are one single table.

SIZE-System used to determine the size of the movement to the case.

SKELETON WATCH-A watch made so the viewer can see the works. Plates are pierced and very decorative.

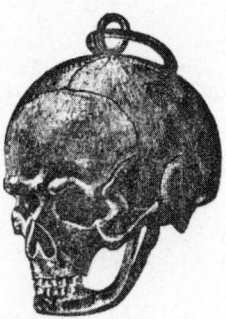

SKULL WATCH-A antique pendant watch that that is hinged at jaw to reveal watch.

SLOW TRAIN-A watch with four beats per second or 14,000 per hour.

SNAIL-A cam shaped much like a snail. The snail determines the # of blows to be struck by a repeater.(A count wheel)

SNAILING-Ornamentation of the surface of metals by means of a circle design; also called damaskeening.

SOLAR YEAR-365 days, 5 hours, 48 minutes, 49.7 seconds.

SOUSCRIPTION- The cheapest Breguet watch which he made with high quality made in batches or group lots in advance to lower the cost.(ebauches)

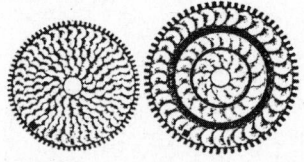

SPOTTING-Decoration used on a watch movement and barrel of movements.

SPRING BAR-The metal keeper that attaches the band to the lugs of a wrist watch & is spring loaded.

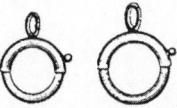

SPRING RING-A circular tube housing a coiled type spring.

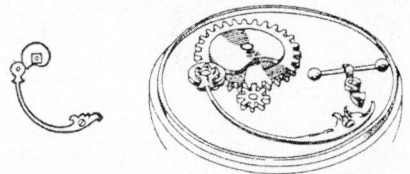

STACKFREED-Curved spring and cam to equalize the uneven force of the mainspring on 16th century German movements.

STAFF-Name for the axle of the balance.

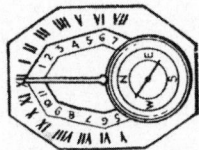

SUN DIAL-A device using a gnomon or style that cast a shadow over a graduated dial as the sun progresses, indicating solar time.

SWIVEL-A hinged spring catch with a loop of metal that may be opened to insert a watch bow.

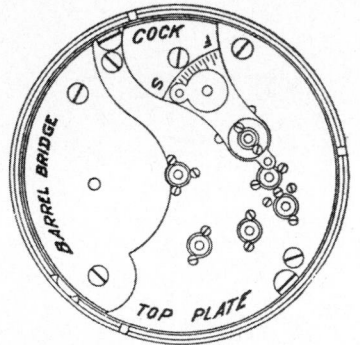

TOP PLATE-The metal plate that usuallycontains the name and serial #.

TORSION-A twisting force.

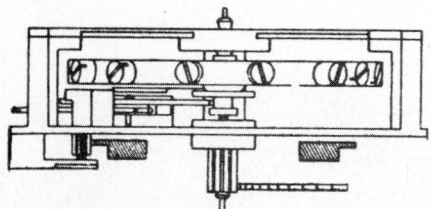

TOURBILLON-(French for whirlwind) A watch that uses a escapement mounted in a carriage and pivoted at both ends and revolves 360 degrees at regular intervals of once a minute. The escape-pinion turns around the fixed fourth wheel. Design to eliminate position errors.

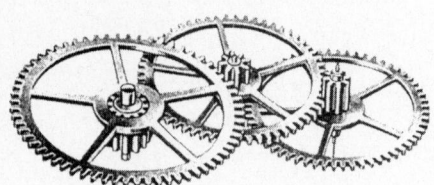

TRAIN-A series of gears that form the works of a watch. The train is used for other functions such as chiming. The time train carries the power to the escapement.

TRANSITION WATCH - Watches sold with both key and stem-winding on same movement.

TRIPLE CASE WATCH-18th and 19th century verge escapement, fusee watches made for the Turkish market. A fourth case sometimes added is called Quadruple case.

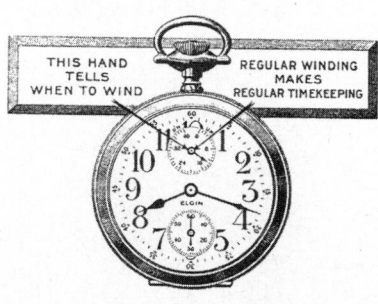

UP AND DOWN DIAL OR INDICATOR- A dial that shows how much of the mainspring is spent and how far up or down the mainspring is.

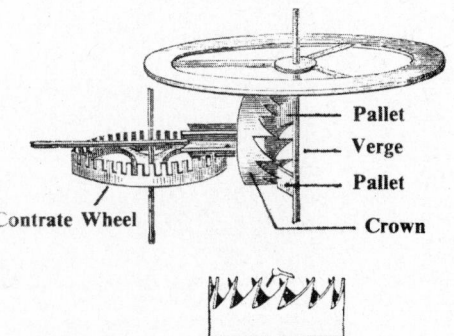

VERGE ESCAPEMENT-Early type of escapement with wheel that is shaped like a crown.

VERMEIL-Gold plated over silver.

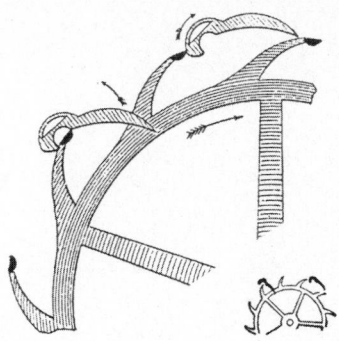

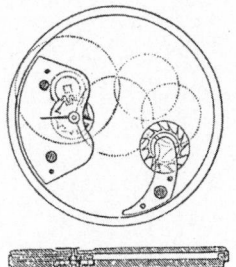

VIRGULE ESCAPEMENT-Early escapement introduced in the mid 1700s.

WIND INDICATOR-A watch that indicates how much of the mainspring is spent. The **illustration** shows a modified Geneva stop works. (see up and down dial)

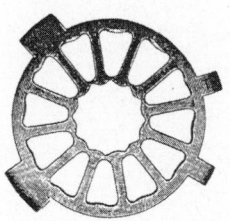

WATCH GLASS PROTECTOR- A snap on metal grill that covers the crystal.

WATCH PAPER-A disc of paper with the name of the watchmaker or repairman printed on it; used as a form of advertising and found in some pair-cased watches.

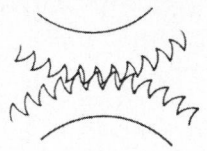

WOLF TEETH-A winding wheel's teeth so named because of their shape.

WORD PRONUNCIATION

Accutron — AC-kew-tron
Agassiz — A-guh-see
Antiquuarian — an-tih-KWAIR-ee-un
Art Nouveau — art new-VO
Astrolabe — AS-trow-<u>labe</u>
Atelier — a-tea-lee-ay
Audemars, Piguet — oh-de-MAHR, p-GAY
Automaton — aw-TAW-muh-tahn
Baguette — bah-get
Bannatyne — BAN-uh-tyne
Basse-Taille — bus-tie
Basacine — bah-seen
Basel — BAH-zuhl
Baume & Mercier — bome-MAY & mair-cyay
Beaucourt— boe-koor
Benrus — BEN-rus
Bergeon — BEAR-juhn
Berne—bairn
Berthoud — bair-Two
Besancon— buh-sahn-son or be-sahn-SON
Bezel — BEZ-EL
Biel — beel
Bienne — bee-en
Blancpain — blahnk-PAn
Blois — blu-wah
Bombe' — boom-bay
Bovet — boe-vay
Bras en L'Air— brah on lair
Breguet et Fils — bre-gay ay fee
Breitling — BRITE-ling
Brevet — bree-VET (or) bree-VTAY
Bucherer — boo-shay-er
Cadrature — kad-drah-TUER
Calibre(er) — KAL-ih-breb or kal-ie-ber
Capt — kapt
Carillon — kah-RIL-yon
Cartier — kar-t-yay
Cartouche — kar-toosh
Champleve — shamp-leh-VAY
Chatelaine — SHAT-e-lane
Chaton — sha-tawn or sha-ton
Chopard — sho-par
Chronograph—Kronn-oh-graff
Chronometer — kroe-NOM-meh-tur
Cie — see
Cloisonne' — kloy-zoe-NAY
Cortebert — cob-teh-ber
Courvoisier — koor-voh-ahs-yeh
Corum — Kore-um
Craze — krayze (or) crazing — krayze-ing
Cuvette — kue-vet
Cyma Travannes — SEE-mah trah-VUNN
Damaskeen — dam-us-KEEN
* damaskeen=A special terminology or American idiom
Detent — dee-TENT
Ditisheim — DEE-tis-heim
Doxa — docks-uh
Droz — droze
Dauphine — dough-feen
Ebauche — AY-boesh or e-bosh
Ebel — AY-ble (sounds like Abel)
Elinvar — EL-in-var
Ermeto — air-MET-oh
Escapement — es-cape-ment
Escutcheon — es-KUHCH-un
et Fils — AY feece
ETA — EE-ta. (Named after the 7th letter of the Greek alphabet).
Fahys — fah-z
Fasoldt — fa-sole-dt
Favre Leuba — fahv-ruh lew-huh
Fecit — FEE-sit =(made by)
Fleur de lis — flur duh lee
Foliot — FOH-lee-oh
Fontainemelon — fone-ten-meh-loh
Francillon — fran-seel-yon
Freid — freed
Frodsham — FRAHD-shum
Fusee — few-ZEE or few-zayh
Gadroon—ga-drewn
Gallet — gah-lay
Girrard Perregaux —jir-ard per-ay-go
Glashutte — glass-huet-te
Glucydur — glu-sch-dor
Glycine — gly-seen
Grande sonnnerie — grawnd shon-uh-ree
Grenchen — GREN-chun
Gublin — goo-blin
Guilloche — gill-low-sha
Gainand — gwee-nahnd
Haute — AUT
Hebdomas — heb-DOM-us
Helical — HEL-ih-kul
Helvetia — hell-VEHT-sia
Henlein — HEN-line

Heuer — hoy-er (the watch co.)
Heuer — oo-air also eu-air (French for time or hour)
Horology — haw-rahl-uh-gee
Huyghes — hi-guhnz
Illinois—ill-ih-NOY
Ingraham — ing-gram
Invar — in-VAR
Isochronism — i-SOCK-roe-nizm
Jacot— zha-koe
Jaeger — YAY-gur
Japy — zja-pee
Jaquet Droz — zha-KAY droze
Jura — yoo-rah (moutains on French & Swiss border)
Jurgensen — YUER-gen-sen
Karrusel — kare-us-sell
Kessels — kahr-rus-SEL
La Chaux de Fonda — lah show duh Fawn
A. Lange & Sohne — ah. lahn gee uhnd soehne
Landeron — lan-der-on
Lapis LAZULI — lah-pis lah-zoon-lee
Lavaliere — la-vahl-yare
Le Coultre — luh-kool-tray
Le Locle — luh LOKEl
Lemania — leh-mahn-yuh
Leonidas — lee-oh-NEE-dus
Le Phare — luh-fahr
Lepine — lay-peen
Le Roy — luh roy
Le Sentier — le san-tyay
Leschot—leh-show
Ligne — line or leen
Longines — long-djeen
Loupe—loop
Lucien Piccard (Amex) — lew-see-en pee-kar (ar-nex)
Lyon — lee-OHn
Mathey — ma-tay
Mido — me-DOE
Mollineaux — MOLE-ih-noe
Montre — MON- tru (Swiss name for WATCH)
Moser, Henri & Cie—awn-ree mow-say eh see
Movado — moe-VAH-doe
Mozart — MOE-tsart
Nardin — nar din
Nivarox — niv-ah-rocks
Neuchatel — noo-sha-TELL
Nicole — nee-kol
Niello — nye-el-oh
Oignon — ohn-yoh
Omega — oh-me-guh
Ormoulu — or-muh-loo
Otav—oh-tay
Oudin—oo-dan as in (soon)
Paillard —pay-lar
Pallet — PAL-let
Parachute — PAR-ah-shoot
Patek, Philippe — Pa-tek fee-leep
Patina—pah-teen-ah
Pave' — pah-vay
Piaget — pee-uh-jaay
Piguet — pee-gay
Pique — pee-kay
Plan-les-Ouates —plan-lay-wat
Quare — kwair
Rado — rah-doe
Remontoire— rem-on-twor
Repousse' — reh-poo-say
Rococo — roe-ko-ko
Roskopf — ROSS-cawf
Sangamo — san-guh-moe
Schaffausen — shaf-HOW-zun
Schild — sheild or shuild
Shugart — sugar with aT, or Shug-gart
Sonnerie — shors-uh-ree
Souscription — sue-skrip-tshown
Stackfreed — stack-freed
St. Imier — sahnt-imm-yay
Tavannes — ta-van
Tempus Fugit — TEM-pus FYOO-jit=(time flies)
Thuret, (Issac) — Tur-ay
Tissot — tee-SOh
Tobias — toe-bye-us
Tompion, Thomas) — Tom-pih-un
Tonneau — tun-noe
Touchon — too-shahn
Tourbillon — toour-bee-yohn
Vacheron & Constantin — VASH-er-on, CON-stan-teen
Vaijoux — vat-zhoo or val-goo
Valle de Joux — valley duh Zhoo
Verse — varj
Veritas — VAIR-ih-tas
Vermeil — vair-may
Vests — ver-too
Virgule — vir-guel
Woerd — verd

European Terminology — U. S. A. Terminology

ACIER . . . . Steel or Gunmetal
AIGUILLES . . . . Hour Hand
ALARUM . . . . Alarm
ANCHOR, ANCRE (Fr.), ANKER (Ger.) . . . . Lever Escapement
ATELIER. . . . . Small Workshop
BAGUETTE . . . . Long & Narrow
BALANCIER . . . . Balance
BOITE-DOUBLE . . . . Pair-case
BOMBE' . . . . Convex or Domed
BRAS EN L'AIR . . . . Arms in the Air
BREVET . . . . Patented
CADRATURE . . . . Attachment (as repeater or chronograph)
CALIBRE . . . . Model or caliber
CHASED . . . . Embossing
CHATON. . . . . Jewel Setting
CHRONOMETRE. . . . . Chronometer
CIE. . . . . Company
COMPENSE . . . . Compensating
CUVETTE or DOME . . . . Inside Hinged Dust Cover
CUIVRE . . . . Copper or Brass
DEPOSE . . . . Registered Trademark
EBAUCHE. . . . . Raw Blank Movement
EMPIERRE . . . . Jewelled
ECHAPPEMENT A' ANCRE . . . . Lever escapement
FAUSSE COTES . . . . Damaskeening
FILS . . . . Sons
FLUTED . . . . Grooved
GENEVE STRIPES . . . . Damaskeening
GUILLOCHE . . . . Engine Turned
HAUTE . . . . High
INVENIT ET FECIT . . . . Invented & Made By
JACQUE-MART. . . . . Figures That Strike Bells
JOURS. . . . . Days As In 8 Days
LEPINE . . . . Open Face
LIGNE . . . . Size
MONTRE (Swiss or French). . . . . Watch
MONTRE A' TACT . . . . Watch by Touch
MARQUE DEPOSE (M.D.) . . . . Registered Trademark
OIGNON or TURNIP . . . . Large Bulbous French Watch
ORMOULU . . . . Gold Gilding
PARACHUTE. . . . . Shock Resisting
PAVE . . . . Cover
PIQUE . . . . Pin Work Decoration
PERPETUELLE . . . . Self-Winding
POLYCHROME . . . . Color
POUSETTE . . . . Push Piece
REPOUSSE . . . . Embossing
RATTRAPANTE . . . . Split Seconds
REFERENCE #. . . . . Case # & Style
REMONTOIRE. . . . . Constant Force also Keyless Winding
RESSORT DE CROCHEMENT . . . . All-or-Nothing
RESSORT SPIRAL. . . . . Hairspring
ROSKOPH. . . . . Dollar Watch
RUBIS . . . . Ruby Jewel
SAVONETTE . . . . Hunting Case
SHAGREEN . . . . Shark or Ray Fish Skins
SPIRAL BREGUET . . . . Overcoil Hairspring
TANGENT SCREW . . . . Endless Screw
TONNEAU . . . . Barrel Shaped
TOUT-OU-RIEN. . . . . All-or-Nothing
UHR. . . . . Timepiece (German)

Vallee de Joux (Swiss - French cradle of watch making)

8 DAYS =8 DIAS, 8 CIOANI, 8 JOURS, 8 TAGE

The following will explain the French days of the week abbreviations, Sunday =**DIM** (Dimanche), Monday = **LUN** (Lundi), Tuesday = **MAR** (Mardi), Wednesday = **MER** (Mercedi), Thursday = **JEU** (Jeudi), Friday = **YEN** (Vendredi), Saturday = **SAM** (Samedi).

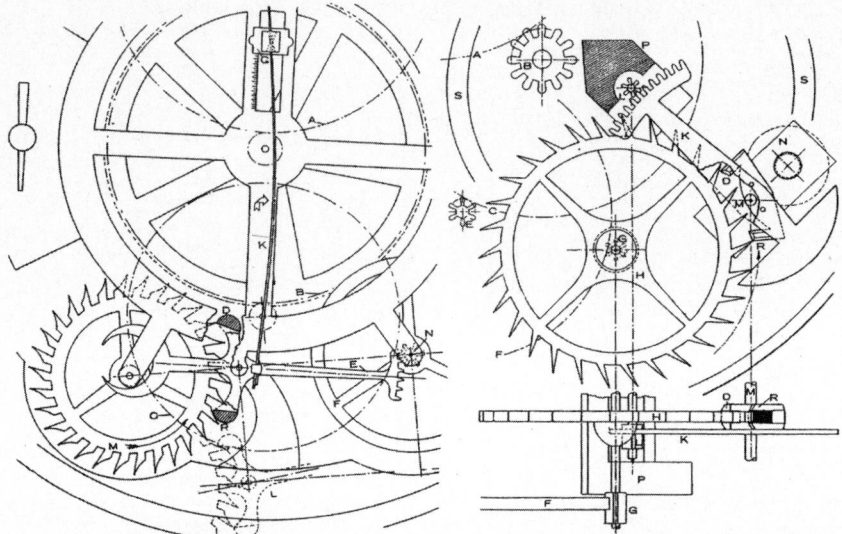

Left: Rack & pinion lever escapement with a STRAIGHT HAIRSPRING **K**, main- wheel A has 30 teeth, center wheel **B** has 96 teeth, 3rd wheel **C** has 96 teeth, 4th wheel **M** is also the escape wheel. In 1722 Abbe' d' Hautefeuille patented this unique rack and pinion lever escapement.

Right: Litherland's type rack & pinion lever escapement, **A** fusee main-wheel drives pinion **B** of center wheel **C**, the third wheel **F** drives pinion **G**, **H** is the 4th or escape wheel. The adjustable sliding block **N** carry the pivot holes for the lever arbor **M** & depth of lever and escape wheel can be varied.

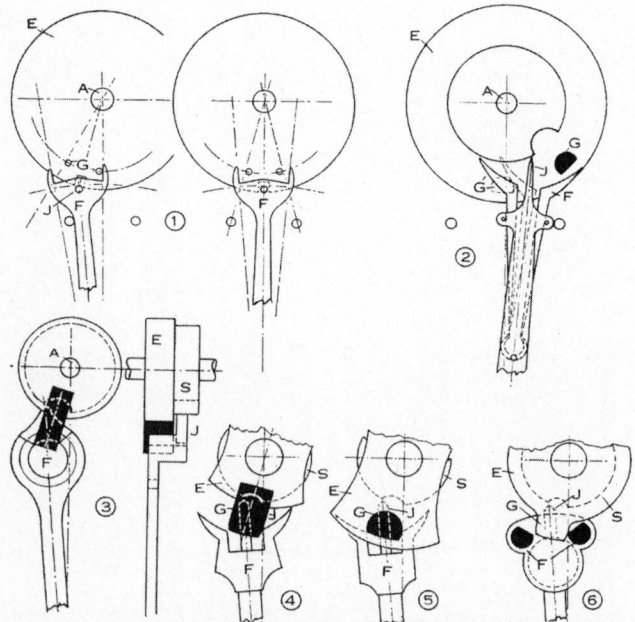

VARIOUS FORK ACTIONS

(1.) Savage 2 pin, **G** is for unlocking, the pin at **F** delivers impulse. (2.) **F** on the spring fork prevents breaking of the impulse jewel **G** when the impulse jewel travels a full circle. (3.) The interior of the fork is cylindrical shell of gold. (4, 5, & 6) Different forms of Louis Huguenin Patents.

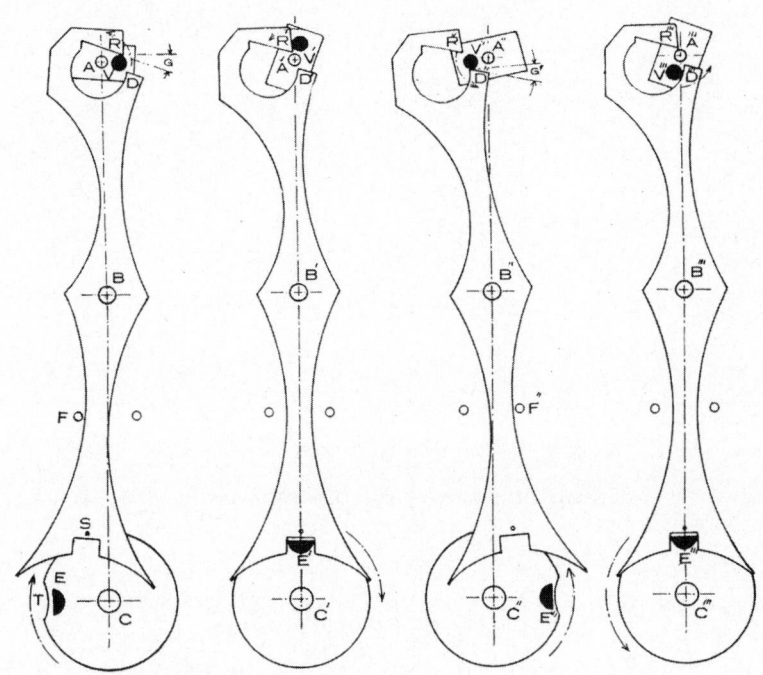

Albert Potter's One Tooth Escape Wheel Lever (Ca. 1887)

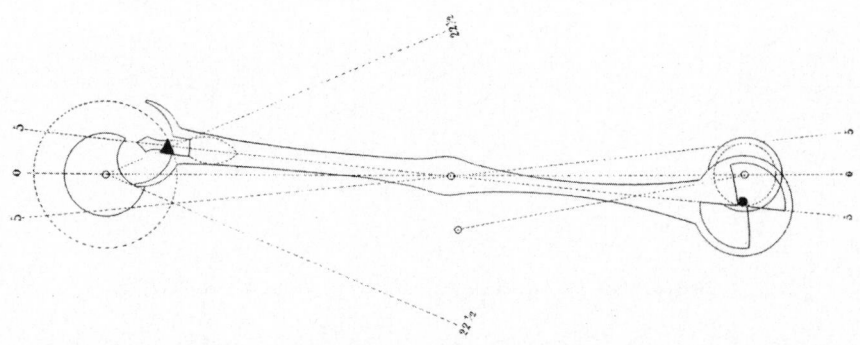

Escapement By MacDowall with one tooth escape Wheel (Ca.1851)

Important Note: Cooksey Shugart acquired the *Major Paul M. Chamberlain* original hand drawn mechanical drawings of escapements used in his BOOK "**Its About Time**".

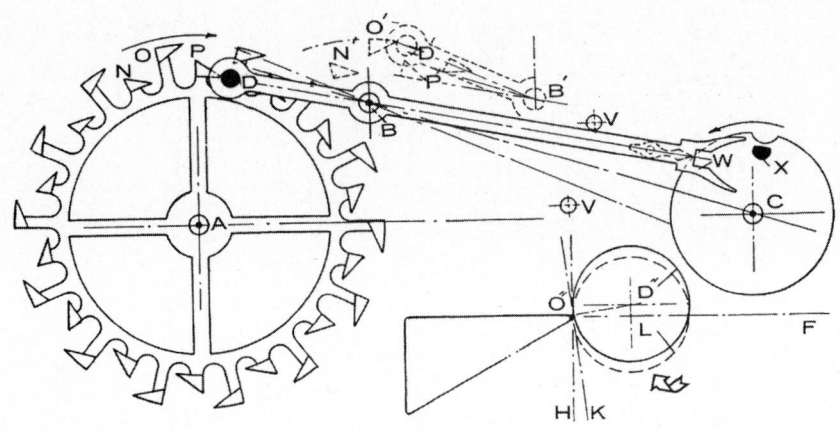

One Jewel Pallet Lever By Edouard Bourquin (Ca. 1875)

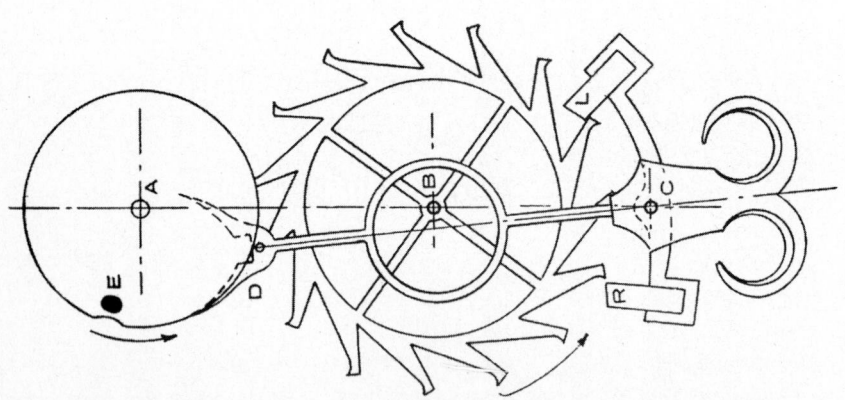

Inverted Lever Escapement By Girard - Perregaux (Ca. 1886)

Note: Escapements may be classified into 2 categories **Frictional & Detached**. (1.) Frictional Rest Escapements example: Verge, Virgule, Duplex and Cylinder. (2.) Detached or Free Escapements example: Lever Escapements, Detent Escapements also combination of lever, Detent and Rotating Escapement as Karrusel and Tourbillon. Frictional Escapements the escape wheel is in contact with the balance staff or a part of it during the **complete** oscillation of the balance. Detached or Free Escapements have an arrangement where the escape teeth wheel are arrested for unlocking & impulse & then made free. Thus the Balance can rotate an arc of an oscillation with **complete** freedom.

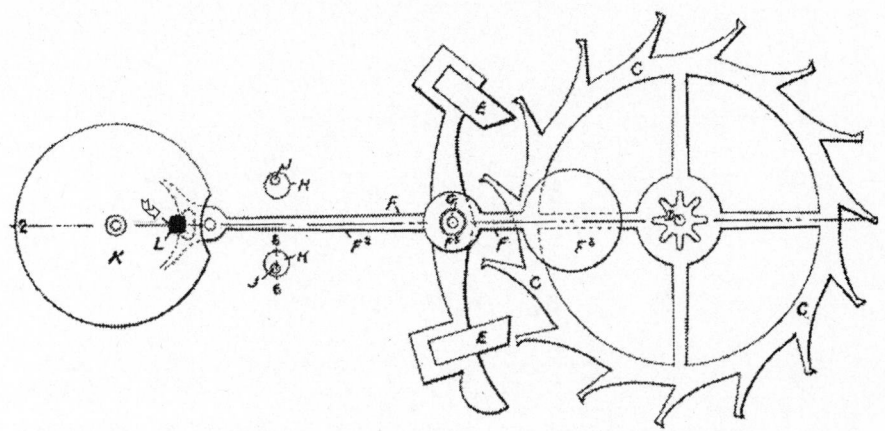

C.V. Woerd patented Escapement. Note: Square Impulse Roller Jewel (L), Pat. in 1887.

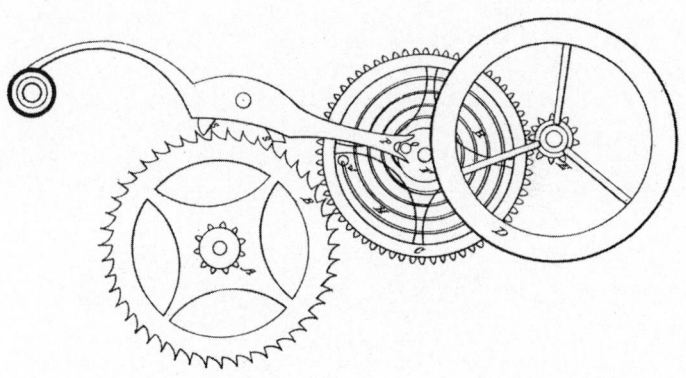

Seconds Beating Watch Escapement by Joseph Jeunet of Pennsylvania, Pat. in 1858. Note: B is the escape wheel with 60 teeth, H is hairspring and D is balance wheel.

Important Note: Cooksey Shugart acquired the *Major Paul M. Chamberlain* original hand drawn mechanical drawings of escapements used in his BOOK 'Its About Time".

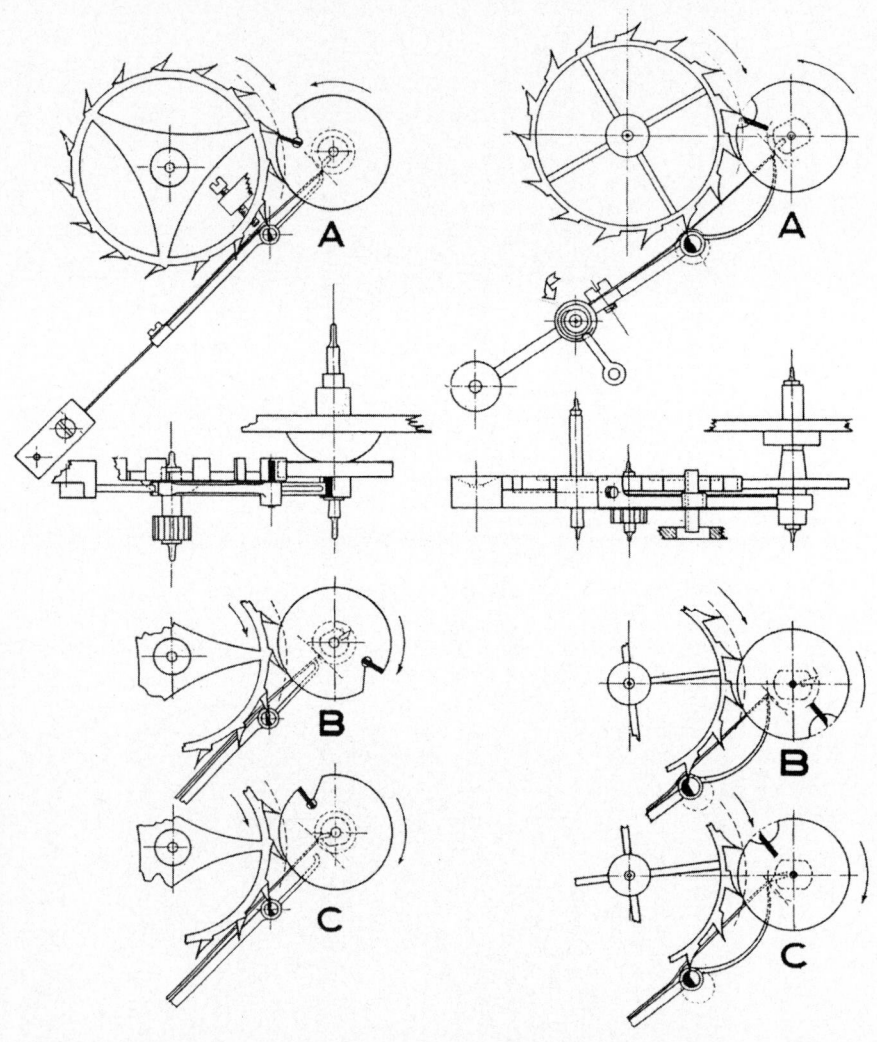

Left is Example of **Detent** Escapement By Arnold, Chas. Frodsham.

Right is Example of a Pivoted or Bascule Escapement by James Nardin.

Note: Escapements may be classified into 2 categories **Frictional & Detached**. (1.) Frictional Rest Escapements example: Verge, Virgule, Duplex and Cylinder. (2.) Detached or Free Escapements example: Lever Escapements, Detent Escapements also combination of lever, Detent and Rotating Escapement as Karrusel and Tourbillon. Frictional Escapements the escape wheel is in contact with the balance staff or a part of it during the **complete** oscillation of the balance. Detached or Free Escapements have an arrangement where the escape teeth wheel are arrested for unlocking & impulse & then made free. Thus the Balance can rotate an arc of an oscillation with **complete** freedom.

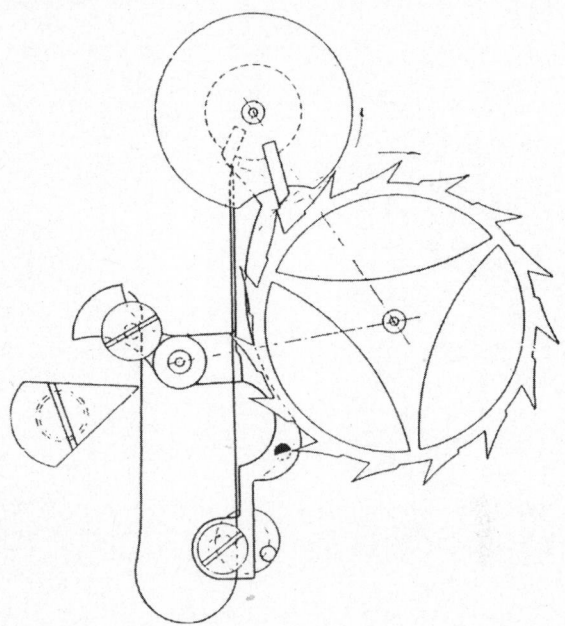

Detent Escapement by George P. Reed Pat. April 1868. Note one spring performs the function of gold spring and locking spring.

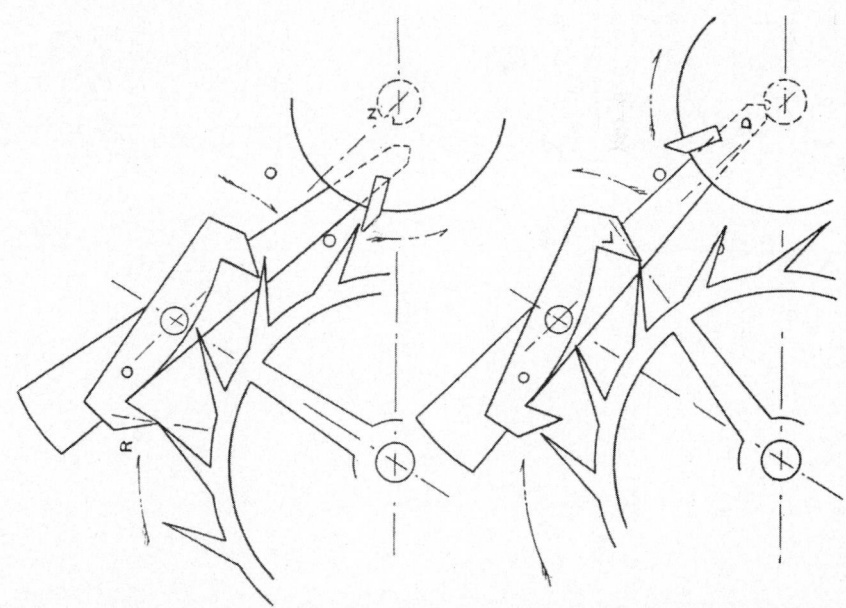

English and engraved on movement "Patent Union Chronometer".

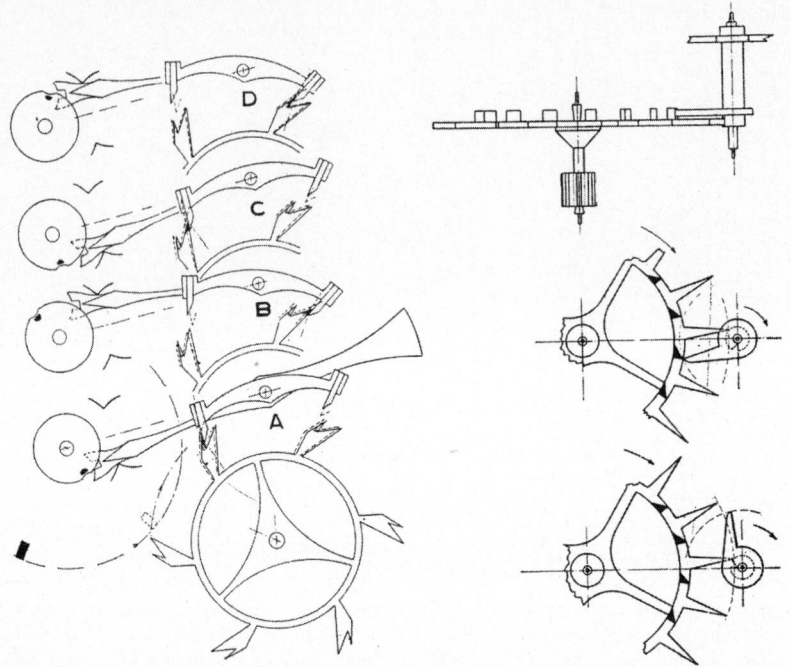

Left: Fleurier style Duplex Escapement.   **Right:** English style Duplex Escapement.
Below: Chinese style Duplex Escapement.

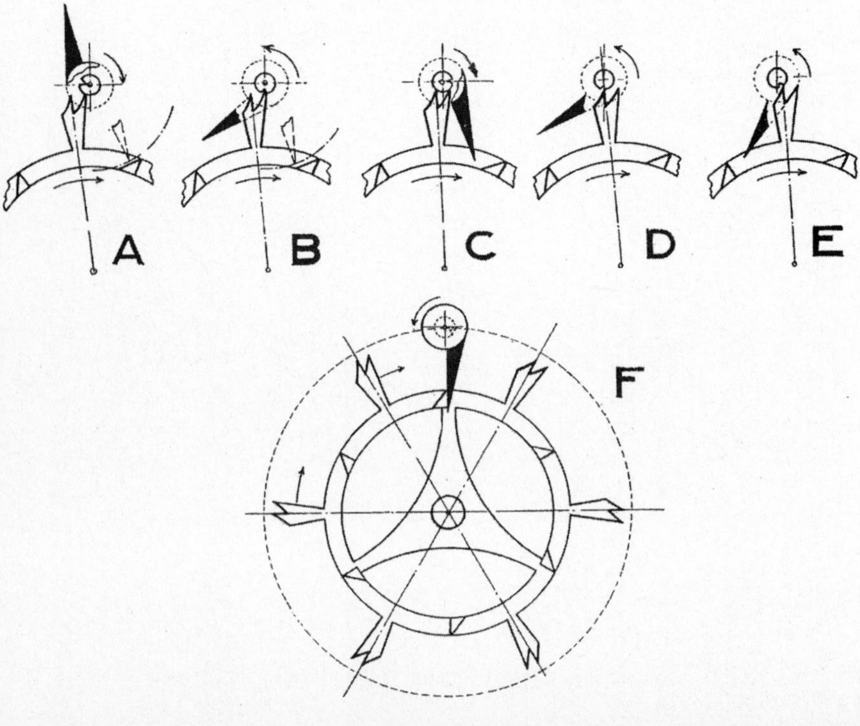

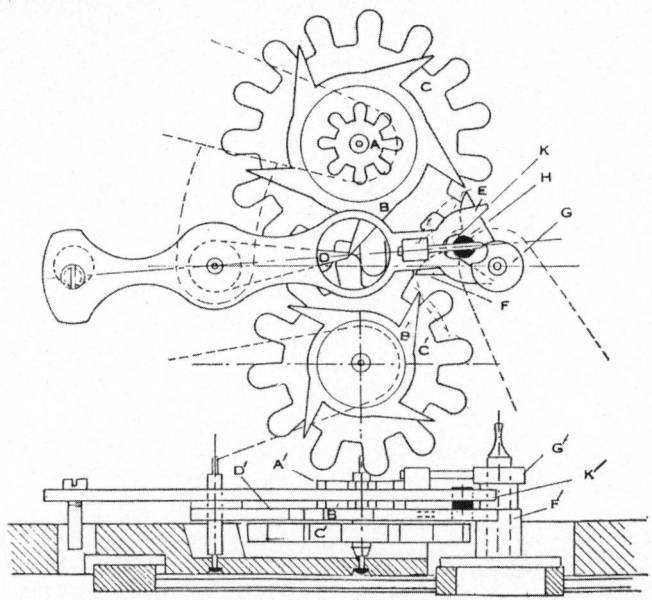

Pinion A drives escape wheels B and B' through gears C and C'. The escape wheel B is locked on D. The locking point D is about to be unlocked by the balance through the ruby pin H and fork K. The tooth following B will deliver impulse to the balance through E, and the tooth B" will lock on D. In the return of the balance, impulse will be delivered in opposite direction through F, acted on by tooth following B".

Above: Breguets Ecsapement he called "**NATUREL**".

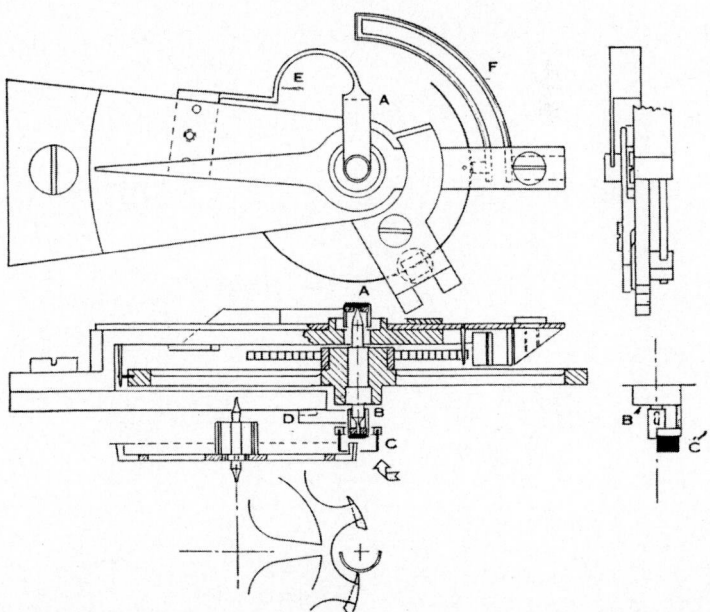

Breguet Hanging Ruby Cylinder (C), Parachute shock absorber (E) and Temperature device (F).

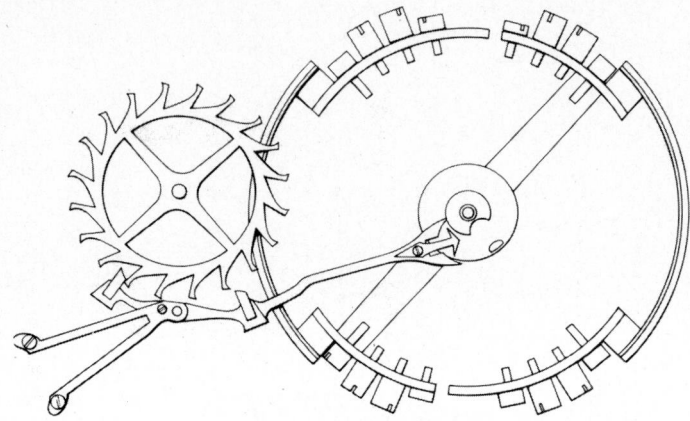

Breguet Lateral Lever Escapement.

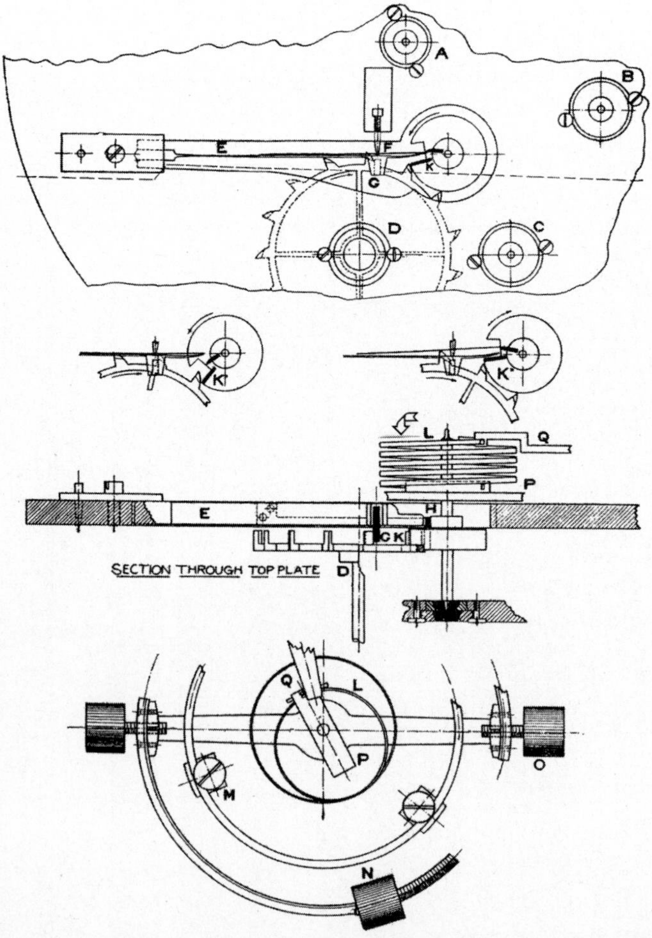

SECTION THROUGH TOP PLATE

Arnold Chronometer Detent Escapement, Pat. in 1782 and Helical balance spring (L), Pat. in 1776.

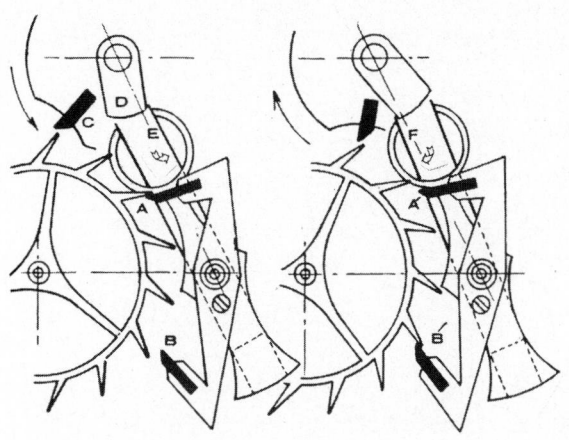

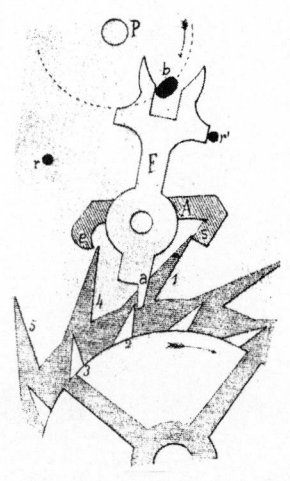

Right: Robin Escapement with Anti-overbanking, note unusual form of fork with two springs E & F.

Left: Robin escapement with Duplex escape wheel.

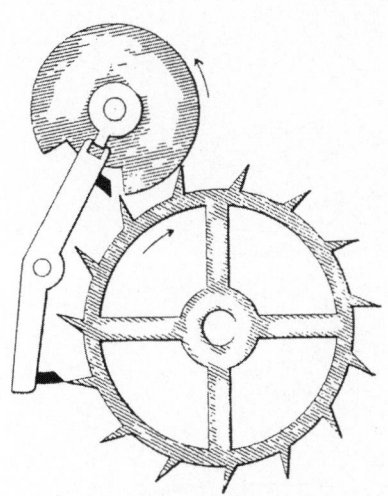

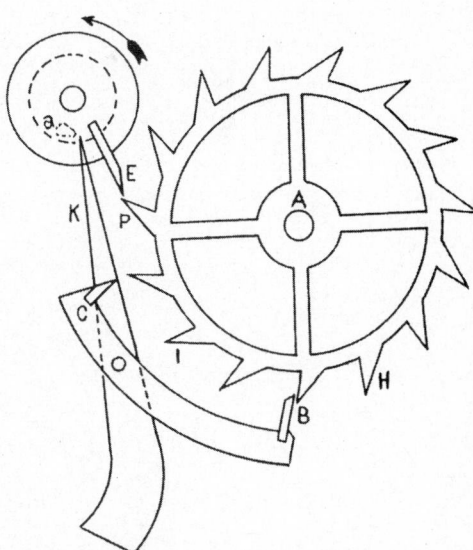

Right: Typical Robin escapement.

Left: Robin escapement, requires over a full turn for locking & unlocking.

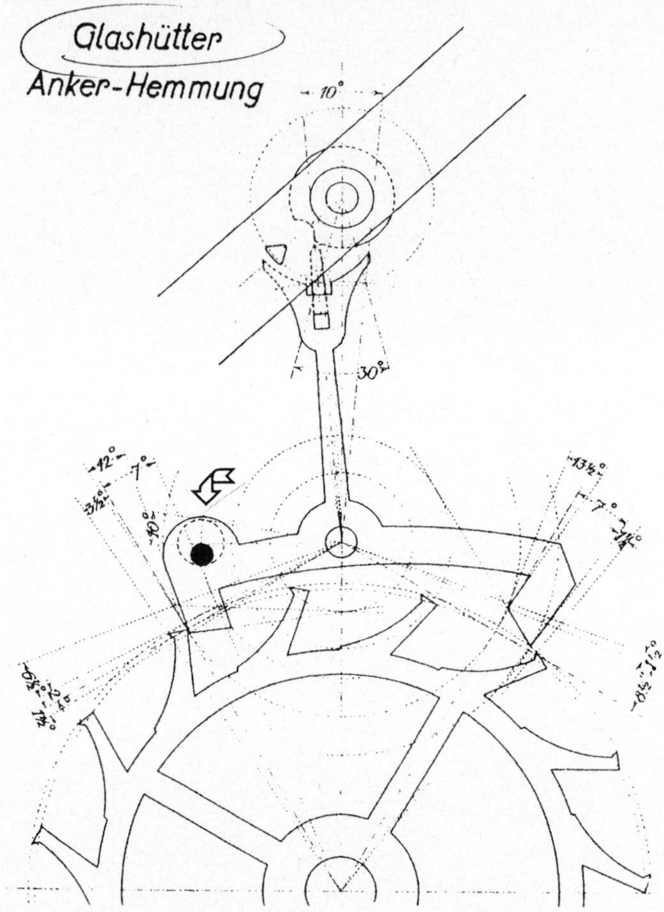

Glashütter
Anker-Hemmung

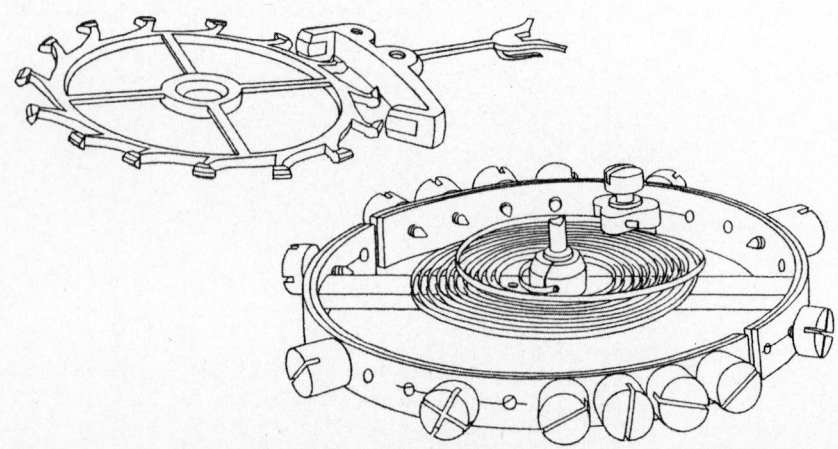

Glashutter = Glashutte, Anker = Pallets and Lever, Hemmung = Escapement.
Note: The One Banking Pin in lever.

Échappement à force constante.

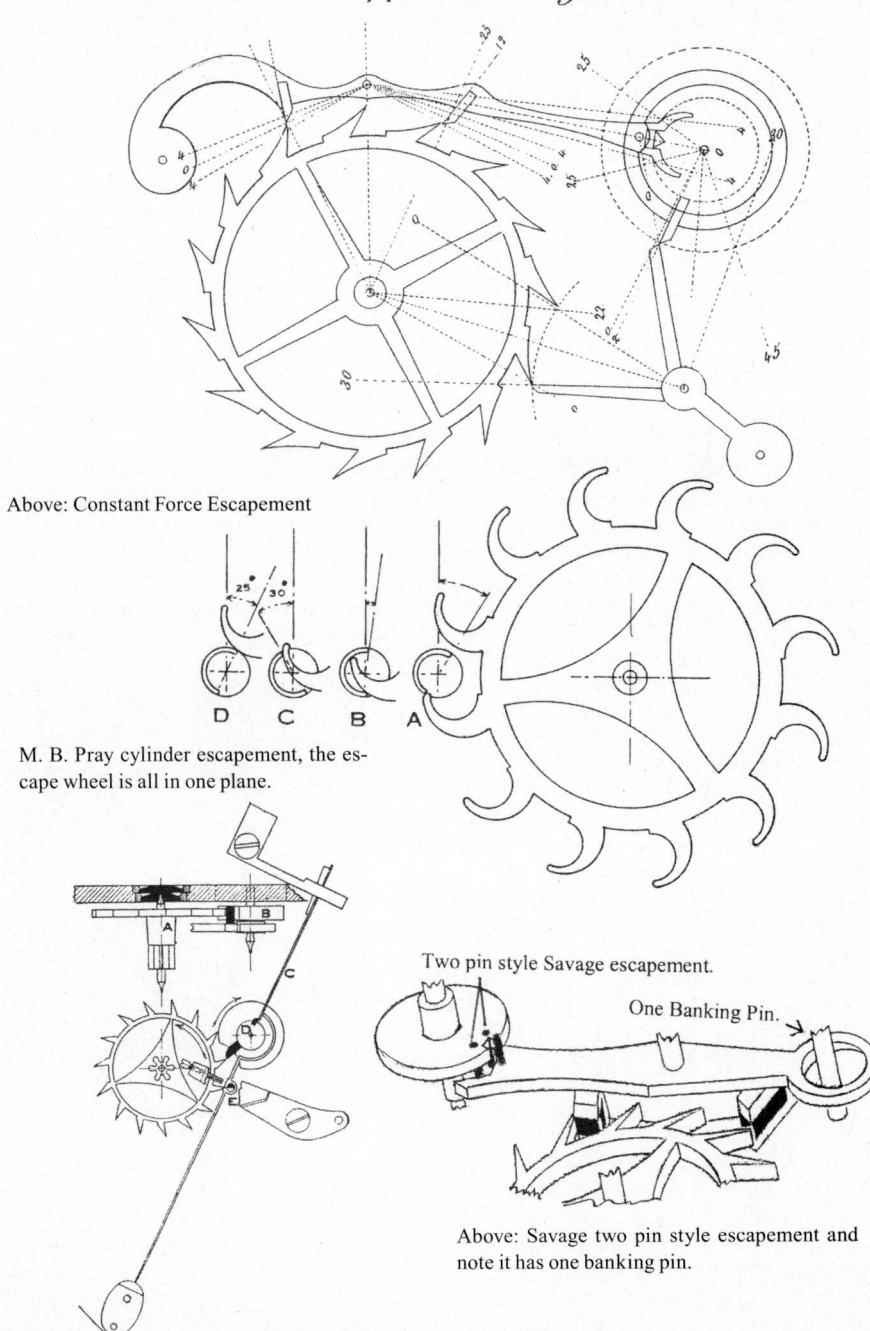

Above: Constant Force Escapement

M. B. Pray cylinder escapement, the escape wheel is all in one plane.

Two pin style Savage escapement.

One Banking Pin.

Above: Savage two pin style escapement and note it has one banking pin.

Peto's Chronometer Escapement, C is similar to a Gold spring and E is similar to passing spring.

THE ART OF MICRO-MECHANICAL MARVELS

There is a breed of self employed independent watchmakers, the Breguet's of today who represent the ultimate in the micro-mechanical watchmaking art. They dare to be different and make watches totally from "scratch". I would ask you to reflect on just what it takes to make, from scratch, a simple watch component, as a screw, each screw has to be turned, the thread cut, the head slit, it must be hardened, tempered and polished. These watches take a wide range of skills and typically 2,000 to 4,000 + hours for one watch to be made. The product of these watchmakers are not widely advertised, they do not have a marketing or distribution organization. Not all of their watches are beyond the range of the true collector and should be the aim of some advanced collector, for good value in todays market as compared to "high end" luxury first tier elite brands. Who are some of these one of a kind watchmakers of today, George Daniels, Derek Pratt, Phillipe Dufour, Christopher Claret, and others. For those watch collectors who may want to focus more on these one of a kind watches, may see some of the watchmakers, who exhibit their watches at the AHI booth (Academy of Independent Horologist) at the Basel Fair each year in Switzerland.

NOTE: With some of the elite brands a ebauche movement is used, for their "limited editions" watches, even though they are highly finished and use high quality materials. These "high end" luxury first tier elite brands, "limited editions" watches do not reflect the cost saving that is usually achieved through manufacturing production.

Dr. George Daniels, the greatest living watchmaker and Abraham-Louis Breguet the greatest watchmaker of all time. George Daniels is really worth meeting, as I did, on May 29th, 1997, at his home on the Isle of Man. A group of us (The Time Trippers) talked with him about watches and visited with Mr. Daniels as we lunched in his garden verandah. He was gracious enough to show his workshop, also his stable of vintage cars and motorcycles. "Making watches came to me as naturally as music did to Mozart", observed George Daniels. At the early age of five he had taken his father's alarm clock apart to see how it worked. By the age of 10, he was repairing watches to earn a little pocket money. He was forced to leave school and earn his keep as a factory worker, he lasted about a week, then started to work as a grocery delivery boy. Pedaling his bicycle gave him such a feeling of freedom, he swore to never work again at something he hated so much. He read every book he could lay his hands on regarding watchmaking while making a living at repairing all types of timepieces and also while in uniform. By the age of 22, he purchased a basic set of tools and set up a shop to repair and restore watches. After World War II, he studied horology in Clerkenwell, London along with related subjects such as math, physics, and geometry. Over the years he worked on a large number of original Breguets giving him a insider's look and knowledge of "The Art of Breguet" which he Authored and Published

George Daniels CO-AXIAL escapement wrist watch with every part individually hand finished and assembled.

into a book. He grew tired of simply restoring old master timepieces so in 1967 he designed a watch and made each component and virtually every part of each first watch himself. How many watches has he made in well over a quarter of a century? Less than 80! In 1978 he makes a Gold-cased one-minute tourbillon with his co-axial escapement (not requiring oil). In the period 1980 to 1996 he used swiss-made wrist watches and converted them to his co-axial escapement, he used Omega, Zenith, Rolex and Patek Philippe watches. Overriding all was Georges Daniels 25 year quest for a lower friction escapement, his success and the years long battle to gain a reluctant Swiss acceptance culminating in the Omega model. Omega introduced a limited edition of 6,000 watches featuring the co-axial escapement in 1998 & sold for $6,600.00.

"The co-axial escapement is the first practical new watch escapement in the 250 years following the invention of the lever escapement by Thomas Mudge in the 18th century. It fulfills all the requirements of a precision watch escapement with the advantage of robust reliability and close precision rate for long term performance. In its present form the co-axial represents the culmination of 20 years of development of the watch escapement. It is intended to sustain the public affection for the mechanical watch during the 21st century". (*George Daniels*)

Dr. Daniels made a small number (about 50) of exquisite co-axial wrist watches at his shop on the Isle of Man with the help of Roger Smith. These wrist watches sold for over $50,000.00. The Time Trippers were again at the Daniels work shop (Aug. 7th, 1999) to see Mr. Smith at work on the co-axial wrist watches. On yet a another trip to London (Apr. 5th, 2000) at the Worshipful Company of Clock Makers we saw two lucky Time Trippers receive their co-axial wrist watch from George Danials. The George Daniels CO-AXIAL escapement wrist watch with every part individually hand finished and assembled. The Omega ebauche is specially prepared and supplied to Mr. Daniels. All other components are made by hand for each watch. The movement is self-winding with gilded plates and blued screws. The watch is fitted with Daniels Co-axail escapement and free sprung balance with adjusting screws. The 18K gold guilloche winding weight keeps the mainspring wound when in use. The dials are sterling silver and finished with three differing guilloche surfaces. The chapter and calendar rings are of 18K gold and hand engraved. The 18K gold hands are saw cut from raw material, filed to shape and hand finished. The case is 18K gold and fitted with a sapphire crystal to front and back. The hand setting crown is machined from 18K gold, as is, the hallmarked buckle.

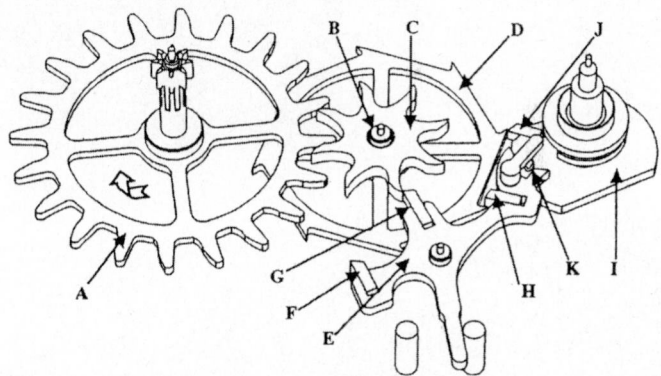

Diagram of the Co-Axial escapement

The escapement is composed of an intermediary wheel A, a double Co-axial wheel B consisting of escapement pinion C and escapement wheel D, pallets E with 3 ruby pallet-stones F,G,H and a roller I carrying a ruby impulse stone J and a ruby impulse pin K. The roller is fitted to the sprung balance. The energy is transmitted to the oscillator in both clockwise and anti-clockwise vibrations. In the Co-axial escapement, the clockwise impulse is delivered to the oscillator directly by the escape wheel engaging the balance roller. The anti-clockwise pulse is delivered to the balance roller via the lever. After each impulse, the escape wheel is locked stationary by the lever locking pallets allowing the balance to **complete** its vibration undisturbed. ("*ALL IN GOOD TIME*" is Dr. George Daniels latest book, a Reflection of a Watchmaker). See George Daniels 8 page WEB site at WWW.DANIELS-LONDON.CO.UK.

Since the inception of wearable timepieces, watchmakers have been faced with the problem of gravity and its effect on the escapement and hence upon the time keeping quality of the watch itself. It must therefore be considered one of the most difficult horological compilation to overcome in watchmaking. A pocket watch was made by Derek Pratt and a wrist watch by Philippe Dufour, using two different approaches to the difficult escapement "error".

Derek Pratt a senior watchmaker of Urban Jurgensen & Sonner **complete**d the pocket watch in 4,300 hours of work between 1981 and 1982. This example of a individual made pocket watch indicating full seconds (jumping seconds) with a carriage-mounted tourbillon incorporating a **one second remontoir** also a twin mainspring barrel and a state of wind indicator. The skeletionized variant of the tourbillon offers maximum visibility of the tourbillon carriage and the twin barrels. Mr. Pratt lives in Switzerland. The Author was privileged to have dinner meetings with Derek Pratt on several occasions.

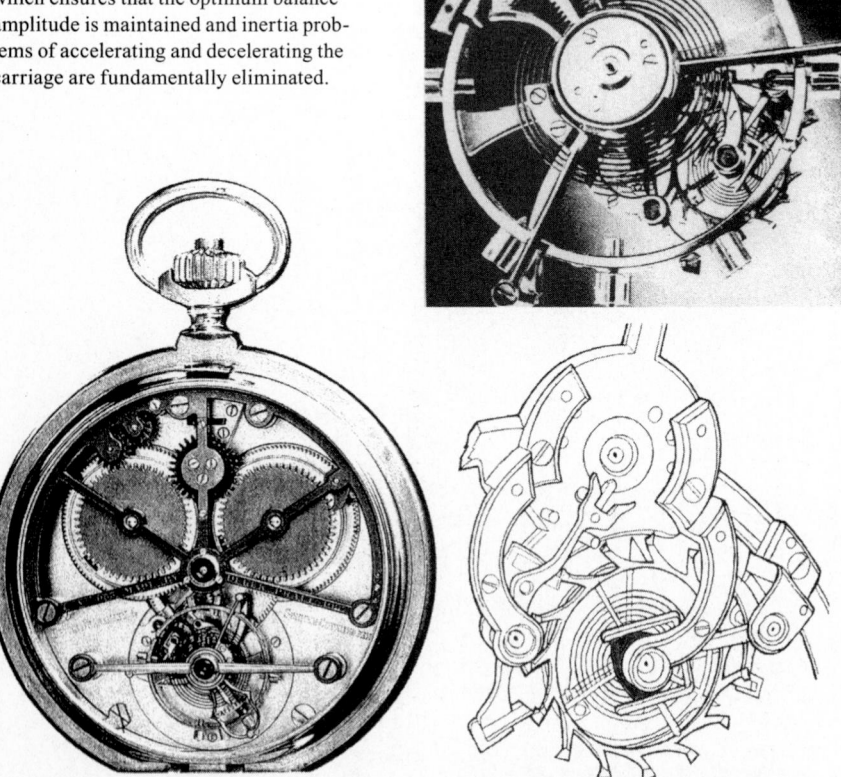

Right: The carriage-mounted tourbillon incorporating **a one second remontoir**, which ensures that the optimum balance amplitude is maintained and inertia problems of accelerating and decelerating the carriage are fundamentally eliminated.

Above left: A view of Derek **Pratt's** one-minute tourbillon with a one-second remontoire mounted in the carriage and twin barrels also a Differential for the wind indication.

Above right: Derek **Pratt's one-second remontoire** incorporated into the one-minute tourbillon escapement, which ensures that the optimum balance amplitude is maintained and inertia problems of accelerating and decelerating the carriage are fundamentally eliminated.

Philippe Dufour's "DUALITY" a wrist watch with a double escapement. The technical aspect double escapement may be deceptive at first glance. A complicated differential system is essential for the operation of the two balances and the mutual compensation of the error, which reduces by half the errors caused by the escapement. The double escapement technical characteristics include 2 levers escapement, 2 Gulucydur balances with timing screws, 2 hairsprings and 40 jewels. Mr. Dufour was awarded a prize in 1992 at the Basel Watch Fair for his "Silence, Grand et Petite Sonnerier Minute Repeater" wrist watch and again with the worlds first double escapement wrist watch. Mr. Dufour is established in La Sentier Switzerland in the *"Vallee de Joux"*.

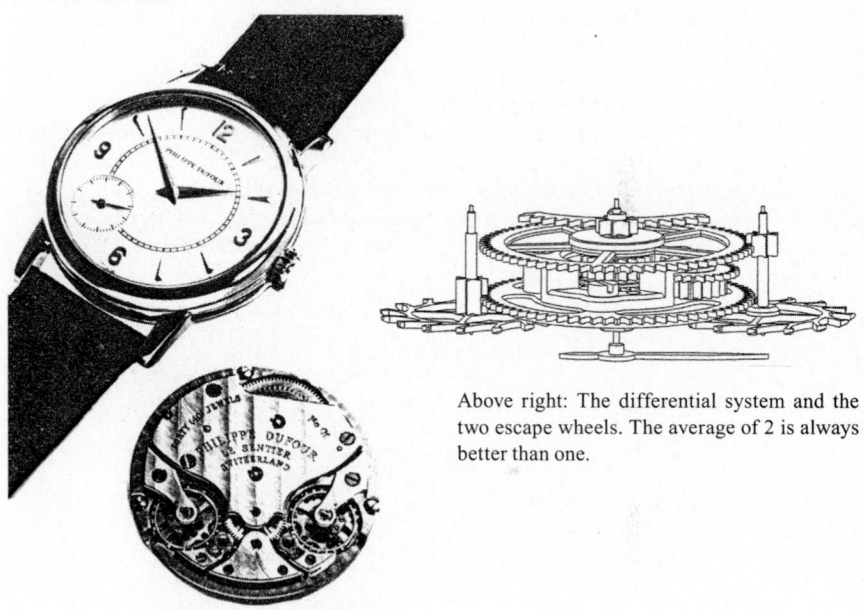

Above right: The differential system and the two escape wheels. The average of 2 is always better than one.

Above: **Philippe Dufour's** *"DUALITY"* wrist watch with a double escapement. The movement has 40 jewels.

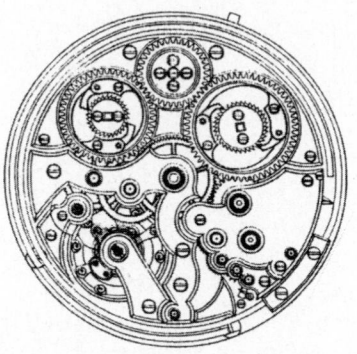

Left: The wrist watch movement, a Silence, Grand et Petite Sonnerier, Minute Repeater of Philippe Dufour (also referred to as a clock watch), about 32MM with 35 jewels. Strike reserve of 24 hours, Time reserve 38 hours.

The author first met **Mr.Christophe Claret** of La Chaux-de-Fonds, Switzerland in 1989. Christophe at the age of 16 embarked upon a 4 year training course at the Geneva watchmaking school. He soon began work with a "cabinotier" watchmaker learning many secrets of complicated watches. Christophe soon set up his own workshop and for six years, bought, restored and resold complicated watches. He went on to create his own company making Minute Repeaters and Tourbillon modules and his own manufacturing sector of high-level machinery which enables the company to produce mechanical parts and movements.

Below Left: Musical wrist watch movement with music on demand or in passing. The technical features of the musical wrist watch, 39-45 jewel, 20 tines or vibrating strips in the comb for the musical tune. The musical drum has about 150 pins which are set by hand. A musical "Power-Reserve" equivalent to **SIX** tunes of 15 seconds each. A detent, which insures each tune is played from beginning to end thus avoiding a tune from stopping in the middle of the piece. The governor is gold and is visible through the dial. A three position selecting slide making it possible to chose between music on the hour, on demand or opting for silence. The movement has two separate going - barrels, one for music and the other for time which has a 50 hour power reserve. The wrist watch has a three position crown, first position the music is rewound, the second the watch is rewound and the third is for setting the hands.

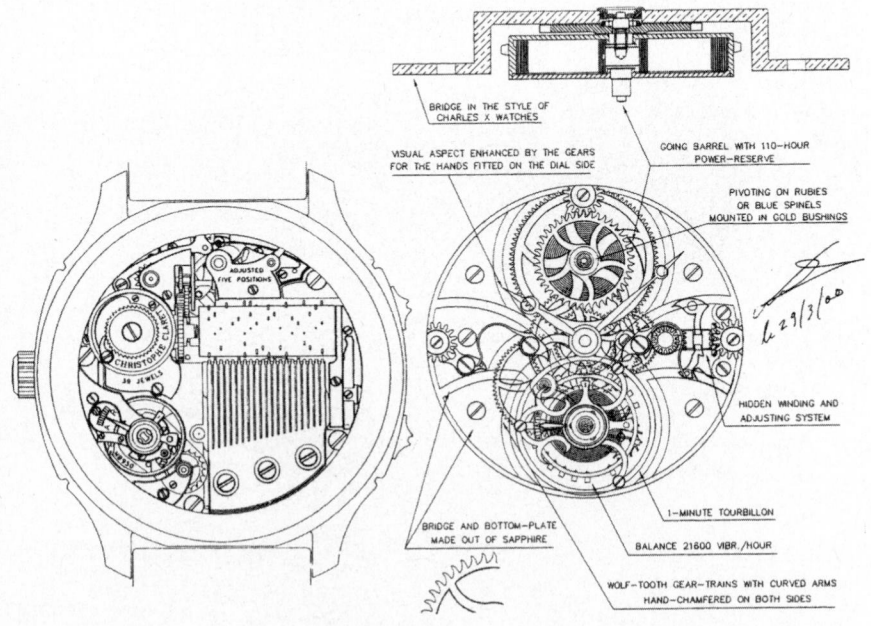

BRIDGE IN THE STYLE OF
CHARLES X WATCHES

VISUAL ASPECT ENHANCED BY THE GEARS
FOR THE HANDS FITTED ON THE DIAL SIDE

GOING BARREL WITH 110-HOUR
POWER-RESERVE

PIVOTING ON RUBIES
OR BLUE SPINELS
MOUNTED IN GOLD BUSHINGS

HIDDEN WINDING AND
ADJUSTING SYSTEM

BRIDGE AND BOTTOM-PLATE
MADE OUT OF SAPPHIRE

1-MINUTE TOURBILLON

BALANCE 21600 VIBR./HOUR

WOLF-TOOTH GEAR-TRAINS WITH CURVED ARMS
HAND-CHAMFERED ON BOTH SIDES

ADJUSTED
FIVE POSITIONS

CHRISTOPHE CLARET SA La Chaux-de-Fonds

Above Right: One minute tourbillon with wolf-tooth gear-trains and curved arms hand-chamfered on both sides. The movement has a going barrel with a 110 hour power reserve. Christophe Claret, a builder of movements and supplier to prestigious brands, has chosen to work in the shadows. He creates and offers high-end complications and aesthetic viewpoints.

Steven Phillips the inventor of a new self-winding system and named it Eternal Winding System. I met with Mr. Phillips at the 2003 Basel Fair and we talked about his remarkable invention that will provide perpetual self-winding of a watch. He said that many people have used a thermostat many times but few have thought about now it works. The heart of a thermostat has a bi-metallic strip, and when the coiled strip is heated, the coil will expand and it tends to unwind. When it is cooled it contracts, and the coil tightens. He took this concept of a bi-metallic coil and created a version that fits in the case of a wrist watch. The coil is attached to a planetary gearing system and transfers rotation from the orbit gear that is driven by the outer end of the bi-metallic coil. The power module is attached to his own movement caliber to achieve the Remontoire effect. Mr. Phillips most challenging task was solving the mechanism to convert both clockwise and counterclockwise motion to wind the mainspring. His planetary gear system solved the transfer of motion that winds the mainspring (he called it a wig-wag system). The name of his company is Budapest Watch Co.in Guilford, Connecticut. He was born in Hungary and came to U.S.A. in 1956.

The invention utilizes a temperature sensitive bi-metallic coil, which is restrained from radial deflection and the free end moves to rotate the shaft in the self-winding mechanism and effects self-winging of the timepiece. The free end of the coil will move with change in temperature. The coil is anchored at its inner end and the other end is thereof, upon movement, will drive a driver member in the form of an orbit gear. The orbit gear will drive a plurality of planet gears, which drive a sun gear mounted to a shaft. The shaft of the sun gear then produces rotation of a cam which drives the bi-directional to uni-directional conversion mechanism.

Left: Planetary gearing system that transfers rotation from the temperature sensitive bi-metallic coil. Right: First experimental prototype of Planetary gearing system.

 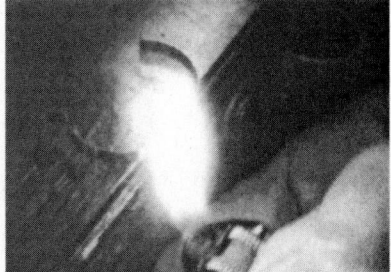

Above: Example of a temperature sensitive bi-metallic coil, left room temperature, right with heat.

INDEX

All individual watch makers are listed alphabetically by last name.
All watch making firms are listed alphsbetically by firm name.

M

N

O

P, Q

T

U

V

W

X,Y,Z

INDEX TO ADVERTISERS

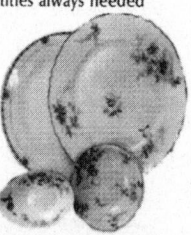

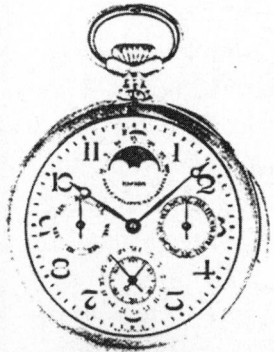

Attention:

Watchmakers, Jewelers, Flea Marketers, Auctioneers, and Repair Shops! Mixed Wholesale Lots Now Available!

WFN Enterprises, Inc. has been liquidating jewelry and gift stores since 1974 and constantly has available both unpicked up repairs and customer reject quartz watches. These are excellent for parts of secondary market sales. Used lots include popular brands such as Pulsar, Seiko, Casio, Timex, Lorus, etc. but with no specific brand guarantee in any given lot. These quartz watches are sold in mixed brand (A-D) lots and are priced as follows:

*Grade A: Like new, minimum wear, watch may or may not be working but 75% of time only needs battery. $5.00 each. Minimum lot size: 20 pieces. Add $10.00 for UPS shipping (USA). $110 Total.

*Grade B: Light to medium used, 50% of time needs only battery. Attractive to consumer eye. $3.00 each. Minimum lot size: 35 pieces. Add $10.00 for UPS shipping (USA) $115 Total.

*Grade C: Heavily worn but servicable. 25% of the time needs only a battery to work but might have heavily scratched crystal or heavy wear on bezel. $2.00 each. Minimum lot size: 50 pieces. Add $10.00 for USA shipping (USA). $110 Total.

*Grade D: Good only for parts. May be analog or digital. May be damaged and some pieces missing. $1.00 each. Minumum lot size: 100 pieces. Add $10.00 for shipping (USA). $110 Total.

---

*Grade A+: Brand new mixed/off brand working quartz watches. Packed bulk, no boxes, no warranties. $8 each. Minimum lot size: 15 pieces. Add $10 for UPS shipping (USA). $130 Total.

---

*On Grades A+, A, B, C and D - Please include second and third choices, as we are sometimes out of some items. Your order will be pro-rated if necessary. Mechanical lots sometimes available. Your inquiry welcome. TERMS: Check, Money Order, in advance, credit to JBT or D&B rated accounts FOB Atlanta, Georgia.UPS, COD available in USA only. We also buy - call for details.

New Premium Brand Closeouts Available

Longines, Jules Jurgensen, Wenger Swiss Army and many other popular brands!
Prices range from $.25 to $.50 on retail dollar for most items. All new with factory warranty. Selection always changing. Call for details.

Contact Mr. Neff • Member: NAWCC
Phone: 770-396-1787 Fax: 770-395-6959 e-mail: wfnsales@mindspring.com
Dept C-2008
WFN Enterprises, Inc.
5579B Chamblee Dunwoody Rd. PMB 215
Dunwoody, GA 30338

Visit my eBay Store: http://store.ebay.com/wfnenterprisesinc.

1195

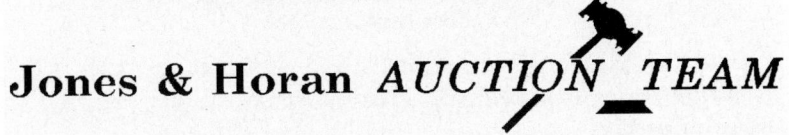

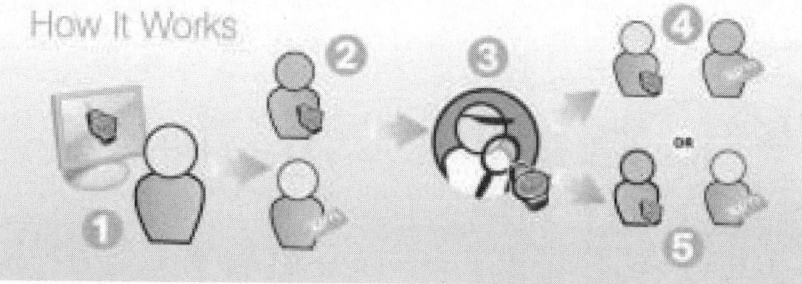

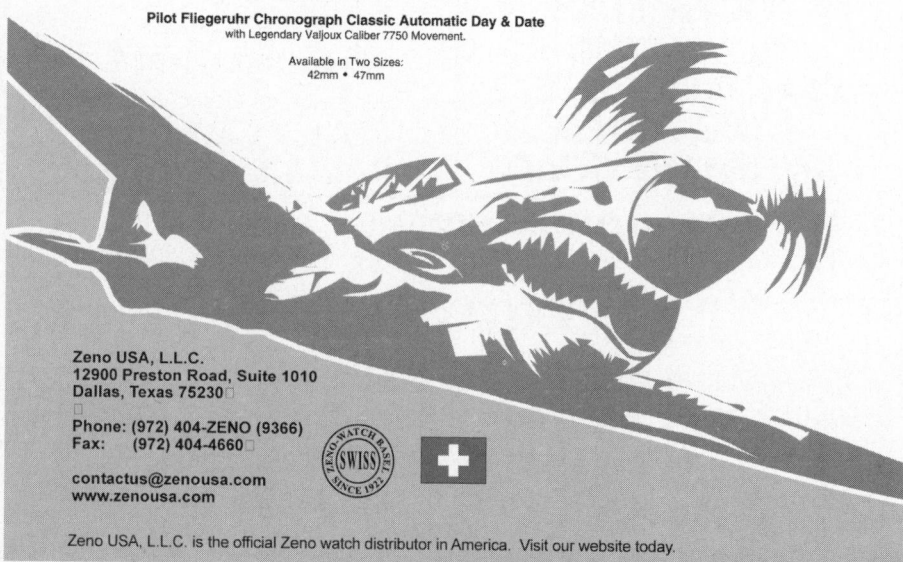

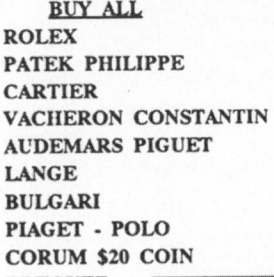

Learn
Watch and Clock Repair

at the School in Columbia

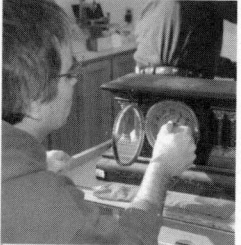

The NAWCC School of Horology offers the "up to the minute" education you need to launch a lucrative, in-demand career.

All students receive
- Eligibility for all applicable VA tuition benefits
- Expert training in horologically specialized classrooms; up-to-date tools, texts, and materials
- Full access to the National Watch and Clock Museum® and the Library and Research Center
- Employment assistance

. . . or from a distance
Field Suitcase Workshop Program

- Training at an affordable cost, within a reasonable distance from home.
- Small class size of 7 – 9 students
- Organized by local chapters with NAWCC certified instructor with years of repair experience.
- Equipment provided - ultrasonic cleaner, lathe, bushing tool, spring winder, depthing tool…
- Students provide personal tools and clock movement, if required.

Contact the
School of Horology
for more information.
514 Poplar Street
Columbia, PA 17512
**Ph: 717-684-8261,
Ext. 218**
www.nawcc.org

The School of
HOROLOGY
OF THE NATIONAL ASSOCIATION OF
WATCH AND CLOCK COLLECTORS

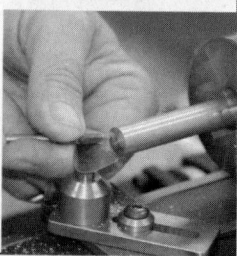

It's the ultimate (time) share.

Founded in 1943, the National Association of Watch and Clock Collectors, Inc. (NAWCC) is a nonprofit scientific organization that serves as a unique educational, cultural, and social resource for its membership and the public at large.

Members include hobbyists, students, educators, casual collectors, and professionals in related retail and manufacturing trades. The one common bond is a fascination with the art and science of timekeeping (horology).

514 Poplar St., Columbia, PA
Ph: 717-684-8261 • www.nawcc.org

The National
ASSOCIATION OF
WATCH & CLOCK
Collectors, Inc.

Don't waste
another minute—
join today!

- -

Mail the Application below and start enjoying your NAWCC Membership benefits today!

Name

Address

City   State/Country   Zip

Phone *home* (   )   *work* (   )

Fax (   )   E-mail

Sponsor **Cooksey Shugart**   Member # **23843**

Are you a former NAWCC member? Yes   No   If yes, #

Charge my   ❏ MasterCard   ❏ VISA   ❏ Discover Card   ❏ American Express

Card No.   Exp. (mo/yr)

Security Code (3 or 4 digit no. on card)

Signature of Card Holder   Amt $

Enclose with remittance and send to:
NAWCC, Inc., 514 Poplar St., Columbia, PA 17512-2130
(717) 684-8261 • Fax: (717) 684-0878 • www.nawcc.org

Annual Dues: U.S. Members—**$65**; Family Members—**$20** (no publication subscriptions); Non-U.S. Members—**$65** (surface mail included).
Payment must be in U.S. funds drawn on a U.S. bank, by international money order, or with VISA, MasterCard, Discover, or American Express.

 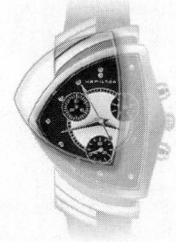 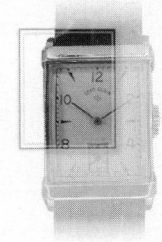

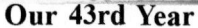

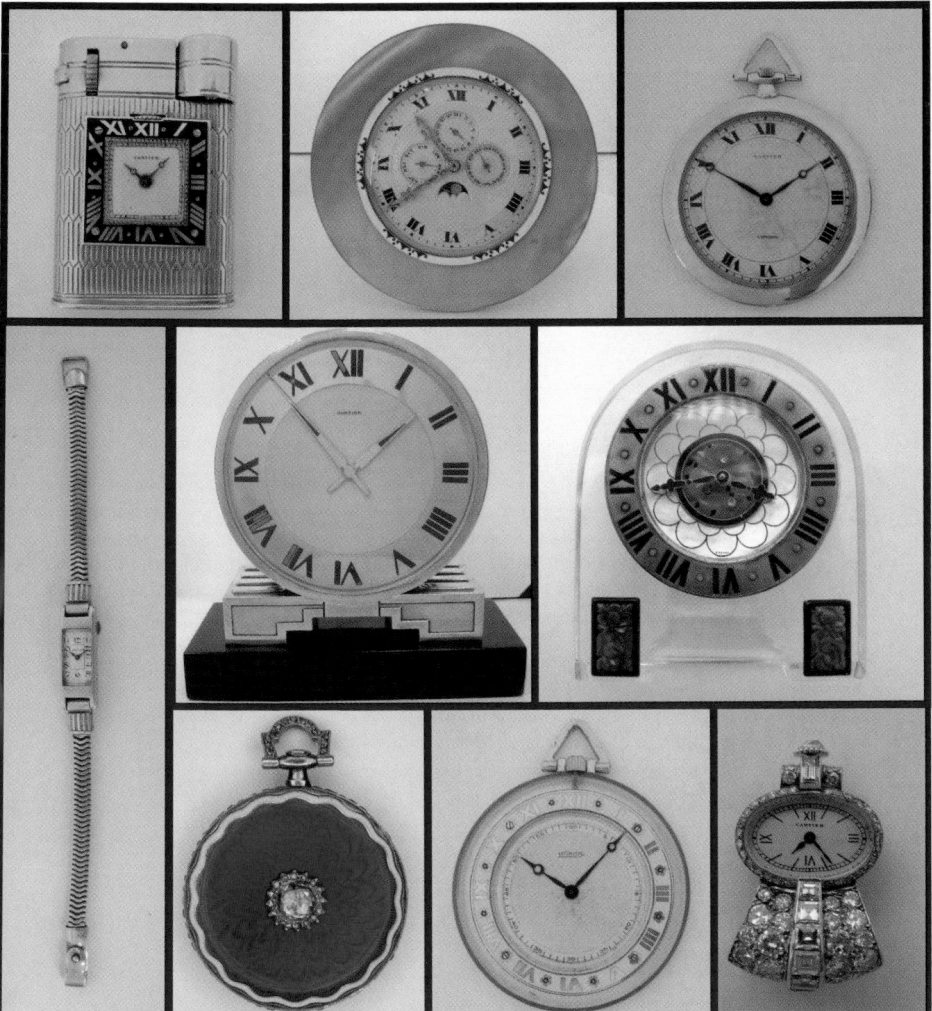